Financing the 1976 Election

Herbert E. Alexander

Professor of Political Science,
University of Southern California

Director, Citizens' Research Foundation

Los Angeles, California

CONGRESSIONAL QUARTERLY PRESS

Library of Congress Cataloging in Publication Data

Alexander, Herbert E

    Financing the 1976 election

    Bibliography: p.
    Includes index
    1. Elections — United States — Campaign
funds. 2. Presidents — United States — Election —
1976. 3. United States — Congress — Elections,
1976. I. Title.
JK1991.A6798   329'.025'0973   79-9099
ISBN 0-87187-180-7

Congressional Quarterly Press
A Division of Congressional Quarterly Inc.
1414 22nd Street, N.W., Washington, D.C. 20037

Preface

This is my fifth quadrennial book on the financing of presidential election campaigns. The 1960, 1964, and 1968 studies were brief and less comprehensive. The 1972 study encountered vast amounts of data regarding political receipts and expenditures, more than in any previous presidential election in American history. New laws, voluntary disclosures, and official and media exposures, particularly about Watergate, produced a new data base. This required a reexamination of research and analytical techniques used previously, and caused us to make considerable modifications to cope with the new data. New laws and court cases affected the 1976 elections in dramatic fashion also. The first experience with presidential public financing led to new ways of dealing with and thinking about the subject.

A new agency, the Federal Election Commission, came into being in 1975, producing immense amounts of data and information, and affecting greatly the contours and analyses of this 1976 study. Some amounts for a given candidacy differ because audit totals of the FEC do not agree with totals in its *Disclosure Series* or with direct or later information the Citizens' Research Foundation received. CRF made certain adjustments that neither the FEC nor Common Cause did. Close-off dates for some CRF analyses differed from FEC or other compilations, thus affecting totals. Some definitions of categories differ, affecting which groups are included or excluded in certain totals. For certain purposes, we included independent expenditures, compliance costs and communications costs, which others have not done. Moreover, the FEC and Common Cause compilations often give totals only for general election candidates, going back to January 1 of the election year or previous year, without separating primary from general election spending, and not accounting for primary loser totals of dollars raised and spent; of course, the FEC disclosure forms are not designed to differentiate accurately primary from general election spending.

Despite the many data compilations, the FEC failed, with a few exceptions, to produce lists of individual contributors. Without comprehensive lists, it was not possible to analyze the contributions or contribution patterns of certain groups. In previous studies, we tested lists of presidential appointees against lists of contributors, and we matched lists of contributors against lists of officers and directors of the top corporations holding government contracts, trade associations, the Business Council, and other such groupings. It is unfortunate that such trend data developed since the 1960s could not be updated or compared, especially in view of the new laws and contribution limits now in effect. The FEC started with 1977 data to computerize contributor lists, which will be available on an ongoing basis in the future.

So many events and facts required description independently by topic that it was difficult to organize the book efficiently; there would have been so many footnotes cross-referencing topics such as fund raising or public financing that for the most part we dispensed with these and, accordingly, the reader should use both the table of contents and the index.

Each successive study is an educational experience for the author and 1976 was notable in the diversity of ways and means found to raise, handle, and spend the large amounts of money used. This study attempts to update and to keep active analyses and categories of data developed over the years by Professors James Pollock, Louise Overacker, and Alexander Heard, and by the Senate Subcommittee on Privileges and Elections (under the chairmanship of Sen. Albert Gore of Tennessee) in 1956.

The data in this study were collected by the Citizens' Research Foundation. Special appreciation is due to many individuals for providing information in personal interviews, through correspondence, and by telephone. Many finance managers and others preferred to remain anonymous. As it would be unfair to name some and not others, I regretfully will not list the many persons in such capacities who graciously cooperated. For example, the tables in Chapter 5 were provided by various anonymity-seeking campaign staffers and hence are not indicated by source in the book.

Four special mentions are in order. The section in this book dealing with the presidential debates of 1976 was published in slightly different form as a separate article by Herbert E. Alexander and Joel Margolis, entitled, "The Making of the Debates" in *The Presidential Debates: Media, Electoral and Policy Perspectives,* edited by George F. Bishop, Robert G. Meadows, and Marilyn Jackson-Beeck, and published by Praeger in 1978.

A senior thesis at Princeton University proved valuable. I gave some guidance and in turn received important information and ideas. Written by Benjamin Engel, the volume is entitled, *Living With Limits: Federal Campaign Law and the 1976 Presidential Election.*

Two related studies were of great value. One, written by Kimball W. Brace, *The 1976 Presidential Primaries: An Analysis of How Many People Participated and How Much Money Was Spent,* was a report compiled for the Democratic National Committee's Commission on Presidential Nomination and Party Structure, dated May 9, 1977. The other, written by Austin Ranney, *Participation in American Presidential Nominations, 1976,* was published by the American Enterprise Institute for Public Policy Research, Washington, D.C., 1977.

This book was written and edited in two places, Princeton and Los Angeles, and so a large number of individuals participated in the preparation of the volume.

I am happy to give special acknowledgment to Joel Margolis, a political scientist who helped write first drafts of substantial portions of the book; to Joseph P. Harkins, who researched and drafted most of Chapter 5 on the presidential prenomination campaigns, among other sections; to Peter C. Roth, who drafted the Carter and Ford general election sections, and labor in politics, among other parts; to Marcia Brubeck, who drafted sections on the media, Korean lobby, and conflict of interest, and who also edited other portions; to Kim Brace for his first draft on the Federal Election Campaign Act and the FEC; to Joseph S. Fichera for analyzing the compliance data; to Todd Zapolski for giving greater appreciation of the grass-roots aspects of campaigning. My appreciation goes to each, although none will recognize his or her handiwork.

Special thanks are due to Caroline D. Jones for her major contribution to analyzing data and writing a draft of Chapter 4. Ms. Jones has been CRF's research associate in Washington, D.C., for 14 years, and she has great talents enabling her to make sense of the mass of figures contained in filings made under federal law.

Linda Sheldon made readable copy out of more scribblings than I care to remember, met every deadline with a smile, and added her sense of language and style to the manuscript. Jean Soete also contributed importantly to the final product.

At the University of Southern California, major analyses and re-drafting were done by three research assistants who are graduate students in the Department of Political Science: Leonard F. Cormier worked the longest period of time, on the FEC *Disclosure Series,* updating other sections, and added a professional touch to all he did; Joseph Peek, a political scientist trained in the law, admirably reworked FEC suits and enforcement sections, among others; and Evan McKenzie worked on portions of the business in politics chapter. Patricia Parker, a graduate student in linguistics, drafted and updated several sections of the book.

Brigitte Huke-Clausing, a graduate student in English, was engaged as editorial assistant, helped write, rewrite, and reorganize, and added a growing command of the files and subject matter to her trained sense of style and clarity.

Two typists in Los Angeles deserve mention: Anna E. Stahnke and Robert Pickett.

Throughout, in both Princeton and Los Angeles, CRF's administrative assistant, Gloria N. Cornette, was a constant source of strength, lightening my administrative responsibilities, providing continuity, minimizing disruptions in moving across the continent, thus enabling me to devote more time to the book.

Patricia Ann O'Connor, the editor for Congressional Quarterly Press, was most understanding and helped to mold the book into its published form. Her associate, John L. Moore, handled final editing and saw the book to completion.

None of those who were so helpful is responsible for errors of omission or commission; for those, as for interpretations, the author bears sole responsibility.

I am happy to acknowledge the encouragement and forbearance of my wife, Nancy, and the good cheers of my children, Michael, Andrew, and Kenneth.

I always appreciate the cooperation and encouragement received from officers and members of the Board of Trustees of the Citizens' Research Foundation, and of my colleagues at the University of Southern California, but the presentation is mine and does not reflect their views.

Without the contributions of numerous supporters of the Citizens' Research Foundation, this study would not have been possible.

Herbert E. Alexander
Los Angeles, June 1979

Table of Contents

APPENDIX

List of Tables

Financing
the
1976
Election

1 Introduction

The 1976 presidential election was unusual in several respects: A southerner, an outsider not attuned to Washington politics, and without access to traditional sources of funds, won the Democratic Party's nomination and subsequently the election; the incumbent had not been on the ballot four years earlier; the two major-party candidates, as well as their running mates, participated in a series of nationally televised debates; for the first time, public funding was provided in different forms by the federal government in both the prenomination and postnomination campaigns; a new law, the Federal Election Campaign Act (FECA), limited the amount of money that could be contributed or spent; and a new agency, the Federal Election Commission (FEC) administered the law and disbursed the public funds.

The new election laws have brought a number of changes, some of which profoundly affect the nature of campaigning. The legislation has led to new political technologies and to the professionalization of politics, creating an environment that has important consequences for voluntarism. Politics in a democracy is properly animated by the voluntary efforts of individuals, political parties, groups, and organizations. As federal election law is increasingly refined, it resembles tax law, with the FEC doing for politics what the Internal Revenue Service does for taxes. This brings two possible effects: one is the need for professionals — accountants, lawyers, and others — to help candidates comply with increasingly complex regulations; the other is the possible chilling of enthusiasm for citizen participation in politics.

The Federal Election Campaign Act and its state equivalents can be compared to the Securities Exchange Act of 1934. That act required public corporations to systematize and publicize their bookkeeping, which led private lawyers and accountants to set standards that in turn brought about a far greater degree of voluntary compliance than the

1

SEC alone would have been able to command. Labor unions felt a similar disciplining effect when the Landrum-Griffin Act was passed. The new election laws and the professionals dealing with them have exerted a comparable influence on politics. But a higher price must be paid for effective governmental regulation of politics because politics is so dependent upon voluntary action. Corporations and labor unions can use money from their treasuries, assigning paid workers to cope with regulations and passing along the cost in higher prices or lower stockholder yields or increased dues. In politics, however, money is a scarce resource. Candidates, parties, and political committees cannot as readily pay salaries to ensure compliance, nor can they pass along the cost. As they allocate financial resources to compliance, their campaigning capability is reduced and financial pressures increase. Moreover, when expenditure limits are in effect, compliance costs may cause candidates to reach spending ceilings — unless, as in the federal case, compliance costs are exempted from the statutory limits on campaign spending. Of course, public funding works to relieve some major financial pressures, while incurring these new ones.

FEC: Regulator and Partner

The combination of government funding with expenditure limits makes the FEC a consulting partner in the operation of campaigns. A constant flow of questions is addressed to the commission, seeking advisory opinions and information; this makes the agency more than a mere regulator, because in responding the FEC must necessarily intrude into campaign strategy, tactics, and planning. Time pressures are real. Unlike other activities subject to regulation, political campaigns have finite schedules. Candidates need quick answers. The pressure of time may not always permit full consideration of all elements in a decision.

Despite the gains in public disclosure of campaign funds, there have been losses as well: The FEC published no contributor lists for 1976, and analyses of contributions from individuals and PAC (political action committee) donors is thus too costly a research for private groups to undertake. Nor have comprehensive data regarding 1976 political broadcasts been compiled by the Federal Communications Commission (FCC).[1] The loss of information about contributions to the 1976 campaigns is a serious omission; still, such data would be less revealing than in 1972 because the strict limits on donations permitted no huge contributions. Some former large contributors were less active in 1976 and the role of fund-raisers changed. The law placed a premium on those who, no longer able to give $50,000 themselves, could attract from among their social contacts, their business associates, and their political acquaintances 50 donors of $1,000 each. Focus is drifting to fund-raisers who can organize and solicit interest groups or tap into existing networks of persons. For example, groups of individuals who had been involved in the McGovern campaign of 1972 used their contacts and fund-raising lists for first one, then another, candidate for presidential nomination in 1976. Focus also has been on the direct-mail experts, the companies with lists and technology to test response to produce needed dollars.

There have always been political dirty tricks, harassment, and charges that attract publicity. The difference now is that the regulation of so many aspects of campaigning provides a wider opportunity to hurt one's opponent — and a full-time commission is available to complain to and to seek advisory opinions from. Since the 1930s the FCC has regulated political broadcasting, where there has been occasional resort to the courts for campaign remedies at the last minute. The creation of a full-time agency such as the FEC, whose whole purpose is the regulation of campaigns, is a similar enactment — a uniquely American answer to a clear problem, but one that will require refinement and revision as more is learned about the operation of such agencies during political campaigns.

Some observers fear that the new election laws invite increasing intervention in the electoral process by the courts and the Congress. Both played dramatic roles in the 1976 elections. In January the Supreme Court decided *Buckley v. Valeo,* among other effects declaring the method of selection of members of the FEC unconstitutional. Congress undertook to reconstitute the commission, got bogged down in enacting the 1976 Amendments, and in the process caused the suspension of the executive functions of the FEC, including the providing of matching funds to candidates then contending for presidential nomination. This suspension was the third major gap in the application of certain federal election laws within a four-year period:

1. from *March 1-April 6, 1972,* when no transition period was provided from the time of the repeal of the Federal Corrupt Practices Act until the FECA of 1971 became effective on April 7, 1972;

2. from *January 1-April 14, 1975,* when the 1974 Amendments became effective on January 1 but there was no functioning FEC to administer and enforce the law until April 14, 1975;

3. from *March 22-May 21, 1976,* when the FEC was unable to carry out certain of its executive responsibilities because it had not been reconstituted as required by the Supreme Court.

This is telling commentary on how carelessly drafted election laws have been, or how lacking in urgency has been the follow-up — or possibly, how cleverly policy makers purposely encourage lapses in the operation of election laws. Moreover, twice — in both 1972 and 1976 — the rules of the game were changed in mid-campaign.

Screening Process

Some had argued that government funding would produce more candidates than usual. While more than 100 candidates filed with the FEC, only 15 qualified for matching grants. Most serious candidates organized their fund raising to achieve early eligibility to receive government funds and, once qualified, all but one accepted them. President Ford, Ronald Reagan, and California Gov. Edmund G. "Jerry" Brown, Jr., considered not taking the money and going the private route, but soon decided to go along with the others. Sen. Robert C. Byrd, D-W.Va., qualified but never submitted requests for funds.

Some observers thought that the candidates with only a regional base, such as Jimmy Carter, would have difficulty qualifying for matching funds; but he, along with other sectional candidates, readily qualified by tying their fund raising into existing organizations or networks of people. Qualifying for the matching grants meant "a kind of license to practice" in the big time, as former Gov. Terry Sanford of North Carolina and a 1976 Democratic hopeful, expressed it.[2] This has become a new threshold, a screening process, for presidential candidates, and certainly will hurt some future candidates.

Of those who received government funds, some campaigns undoubtedly were prolonged as a result of the additional money available, with the candidates hanging on longer than they might have otherwise, in order to get the money. One candidate surprised observers by qualifying easily. That was Ellen McCormack, who ran essentially a single-issue campaign as a Right to Life, antiabortion candidate. McCormack was a political unknown who was able to qualify because the issue she represented was an emotional one that had adherents in sufficient numbers of states, and her campaign to attract attention to her cause rather than to nominate her was well organized to reach them.

Despite government funding, seven candidates — Terry Sanford, Lloyd Bentsen, Birch Bayh, Milton Shapp, Fred Harris, Henry Jackson, and Sargent Shriver — dropped out by mid-primary season when they failed to garner enough votes in several states to be able to continue to contest effectively. However, several of these remained in the contest as a favorite son or to keep their options open for a time, drawing additional funding to the extent they were able to raise more money for matching, although no longer active candidates; matching funds also were used to help pay off debts incurred in the campaign. Then, the 1976 Amendments effectively cut off further funding for them. Candidates who fail to make good showings in the voting in the presidential primaries then find it harder to raise money, thus reducing the matching funds, and so the cycle leading to withdrawal from the race begins.

One clear conclusion is that the combination of contribution limits and government funding increased the costs of fund raising. The effort to outreach successfully is expensive, especially in matchable sums of $250 or under. Accordingly, fund-raising costs were relatively higher than in previous campaigns where contributions could be solicited in larger amounts. Bookkeeping costs also were high, partly to ensure compliance with the disclosure and limitations sections of the law, partly for preparation of claims submitted for matching funds under procedures required by the FEC.

The problems of compliance, particularly related to the 1974 Amendments, became so substantial and costly that changes in the laws were sought early in 1976. The Ford and Carter campaigns petitioned the FEC to exclude compliance costs from the expenditure restrictions. Both organizations argued that compliance should not be considered a normal campaign cost, and both realized that the costs of compliance eventually could inhibit each candidate's election effort unless they were exempted. The FEC refused to allow an exemption, stating that it did not have the authority to do so. In one of the few bipartisan efforts during the campaign, Ford and Carter sought and obtained a legislated exemption of compliance costs that was included in the 1976 Amendments. This provision enabled candidates who were close to the spending limits — Carter, Ford, and Reagan — to isolate compliance costs retroactive to January 1, 1975, and to recalculate their other expenditures. The provision had no effect on candidates whose spending did not approach the limits.

In his March 1977 election reform message, President Carter requested that $500,000 be authorized from checkoff funds to cover compliance costs for presidential candidates in future general election periods. This special subsidy, which was authorized by the Senate but not by the House and consequently died when the 95th Congress adjourned, attests to the real costs of compliance felt by the 1976 campaigners. Candidates for nomination and for election clearly will seek such subventions in the future, as will congressional candidates if congressional public financing is enacted.

Equalizing Effect

The most important effect of the public financing system, symbolized by the success of Jimmy Carter, was the equalized chance it provided to qualified but little-known outsiders to compete effectively.

Lacking access to traditional sources of large Democratic contributions, Carter without public funding probably would have lost out early in the primary season to those candidates, such as Sen. Henry M. Jackson of Washington, who enjoyed such success. But the combination of contribution limits, which lowered the advantage large contributors could provide, and matching funds, which enhanced the value of small contributions, had an equalizing effect. Public funding allowed a Washington outsider, a regional candidate, to break into the field and establish his candidacy.

In terms of the candidate spending limits in the presidential prenomination period, the $10.9 million amount was not sufficient in the hotly contested campaigns for Republican nomination. Both Ford and Reagan cut back spending in the late primaries and over the summer to conserve money for anticipated high spending at the Republican convention. When spending at the convention was unexpectedly low, both candidates had surpluses, but they could have spent more had it been allowed. Reagan, in fact, failed to contest heavily in the Ohio primary to conserve money, and was sorry later. Both candidates could have raised more money and planned to spend it effectively.

If spending limits are provided, they should be generously high to accommodate closely contested races, whether for nomination or for election.

Both major-party nominees, Jimmy Carter and Gerald Ford, accepted public grants of $21.8 million for their general election campaigns and were therefore ineligible to accept additional private money. The national committees of the parties could spend an additional $3.2 million on behalf of the presidential candidates. Although the system worked smoothly, it was apparent that the grants were set at a low level. By way of contrast, the 1972 McGovern and Nixon general election campaigns had spent $30 million and $60 million,[3] respectively, and there was a 33 percent inflation factor between 1972 and 1976. The campaigns responded by channeling a large proportion of their money into mass-media advertising, the most cost-effective way to reach large audiences, and very little into the kinds of field operations and campaign paraphernalia that touch voters directly. The Carter campaign, for example, budgeted $285,000 to be spent in California, exclusive of media, compared with the $1.5 million spent in the state by George McGovern in 1972.

The result of similarly tight budgeting in other states by both candidates was a substantial decrease in campaign activity, lower campaign exposure, and press reports throughout the entire campaign period describing public apathy and predicting record-low voter turnouts, which did occur.

Impact on Parties

The new election laws also affect the party structure. According to one argument, "the only real power that the national parties have is to determine who has access, and the right, to participate in their national conventions and the selection of the presidential candidates. If that power is taken over by the courts and Congress, the effect is likely to be the speedy disintegration of the national parties." [4]

On the other hand, the Supreme Court has decided that the national political parties have a constitutional right of "political association" and that state courts cannot interfere in litigation regarding delegate credentials;[5] otherwise each of the 50 states could establish different qualifications for delegates to the national conventions. This decision seems to lay the groundwork for constitutional protection of stronger national parties.

Some Republican opposition to the principle of public financing of the conventions was in part a response to the party's continuing battle with the Ripon Society, which filed a suit concerning delegate selection. Some feared that public financing could open the door to stricter court interpretations of challenges to party procedures in delegate selection than would be the case if the convention were privately financed. The courts have decided other electoral issues with great impact on the political system — reapportionment, voting rights, extending the franchise to 18-year-olds — and may do as much in regard to election reform.[6]

In addition to the possibility that public financing may increase intervention by the courts and Congress in the operation of the major parties, pre- and postnomination funds may discriminate among parties and candidates. Adamany and Agree addressed the question of inequitable distribution of prenomination monies:

> Is it fair for a party with a heated nomination contest to draw most or all of the matching money? Since all the party's hopefuls are likely to campaign against the opposition party especially against a sitting opposition party president, the nomination grants have general election implications. Yet during the nomination stage, one party's many contenders will claim vastly more of the available public funding than will the uncontested or weakly contested nominees of the other party.[7]

Interestingly, in 1976 the Democrats, with 13 qualifying candidates, drew $14.6 million in matching funds, whereas two qualifying Republican candidates received $9.1 million. If the out-party gains a new advantage over the in-party — an advantage funded through public monies — that gain may help equalize the advantages of incumbency and create more two-party competition. On the other hand, postnomination financing by government may reduce opportunities for minor parties while artificially sustaining one or both of the major parties.

The role and strength of the major parties is, in the opinion of some observers, of possibly greater importance than additional laws or stiffer penalties if future Watergates are to be prevented. Stephen Hess has written:[8]

> Watergate provides a sorrowful reminder of how much we miss by not having a strong two-party system with a professional code of ethics for those who participate in the political process. Running presidential campaigns under the centralized control of the parties' national committees would not produce the millennium. Our parties practice a type of accommodation politics that is not well suited to injecting creativity into public debate. But it is highly unlikely that the Republican National Committee would seriously consider breaking into the Democratic National Committee, or vice versa, if only for the reason stated by David S. Broder in *The Party's Over:* "Our political parties are old, and they expect to be in business a long time. Neither of them has any great temptation to kick down the walls, or to pursue tactics when temporarily in power that will invite revenge from the opposition when it (inevitably) returns to power."
>
> It is doubtful that our political parties could ever regain the central position in our system that they held in the 19th Century.

As Hess concludes, the parties are better positioned to regain control of presidential campaigns than of congressional or state and local campaigns, so presidential politics is a likely arena of contention.

The Price of Reform

Some reformers have failed to recognize a basic truth: democratic reforms mean higher political costs. Power to the people is expensive. It is inconsistent to give voters a choice in the selection of candidates and not expect campaign costs to be substantial. In particular, primary campaigns are expensive, and the impact of money is greatest in the prenomination phase. Similarly, it is unrealistic to give more power to the party grass roots without anticipating that the costs of maintaining the party structure will increase. Should government funding of the parties occur, these facts must be taken into account.

In the last few years pressures for change have been many. Startling patterns of campaign finance are being disclosed under both federal and state laws. The Watergate and Agnew scandals, as well as some state scandals, have exposed almost every corrupt election practice imaginable. The media have closely covered the development of election legislation and generally have editorialized in favor of reform, voicing a notable amount of support for the concept of public funding. Common Cause has continued to lobby and to monitor political fund reports at the federal level and at the state level in some states.

Americans seem increasingly ambivalent about the role of government in their lives. There appears to be a loss of faith leading to a feeling that government seeks to do too much at too high a cost and often does not do well in its endeavors. If the pendulum is swinging in favor of lowered expectations from government, this will affect the gains of the 1970s with respect to election reform. We are on the receding side of election reform, which crested at the height of Watergate in 1974. A counter-reform may be developing, although it is not often articulated. More than lip service is still being paid to reform; many politicians and others have been converted and are faithful to its precepts. Reformers are less strident now, however, and undoubtedly will lose some force by a process of attrition. On the other hand, some reform measures such as the FECA have been institutionalized and will not be repealed. The future of reform will depend in large measure upon the performance of the FEC, which in its formative years has been subjected to extreme pressures from Congress.

As significant as has been the role of the reformers, they could not fashion a major transformation in the American electoral process. Congress acted, Watergate catalyzed, Congress acted again, the FEC struggled to assert its independence, the Supreme Court intervened dramatically, and Congress reasserted itself. By this time, much of the reform momentum had been blunted.

The most enduring changes normally are made by those with a stake in the outcome — by incumbents, by the political parties, by the major interest groups. The reformers and the media set the outer limits of reform, defining it by conditioning the atmosphere. Still, the actual changes are forged in the arena of political pressures, limited by the U.S. Constitution as interpreted by the courts.

Most needed is a philosophy of regulation that is both constitutional and pragmatically designed to keep the election process open and flexible rather than rigid, exclusionary, and fragmented. It is not clear from the efforts made in 1977 and 1978 to extend and revise the FECA that Congress is yet preparing to enact laws reflecting the openness and flexibility a democratic and pluralistic society requires. We do know that the future is increasingly in the hands of power brokers who are more realistic than the reformers and less likely to damage the established fabric of politics. Whether they will skew change toward greater incumbent advantage or lead to fair laws for challengers as well remains to be seen. But an even larger question is whether the restraining and chilling aspects of the legislation will be relaxed and the role of the FEC diminished without damaging the spirit of the law or the goals of reform. Perhaps the chapters that follow will illuminate sufficiently for readers to draw their own conclusions.

Footnotes

[1] *Federal Election Campaign Act of 1973*, appendix A, *Hearings* before the Subcommittee on Commerce, U.S. Senate, 93rd Cong., 1st sess. (1973), Table 11. Hereafter referred to as *FCC, Survey 1972*. See also FCC series: Federal Communications Commission, *Survey of Political Broadcasting: Primary and General Election Campaigns of 1970* (Washington, D.C.: U.S. Government Printing Office, 1971) and similar documents for 1968, 1966, 1964, 1962, and 1960.

[2] Christopher Lydon, "Democratic Hopefuls Live Off the Land," *The New York Times*, July 13, 1975.

[3] Herbert E. Alexander, *Financing the 1972 Election* (Lexington, Mass.: Lexington Books, D.C. Heath and Co., 1976), p. 271.

[4] David S. Broder, "Breaking Up Political Parties," *The Washington Post*, January 30, 1974.

[5] *Wigoda v. Cousins*, 302 N.E. 2d 614.

[6] For a discussion of the judicial impact, see Richard Claude, *The Supreme Court and the Electoral Process* (Baltimore and London: The Johns Hopkins Press, 1970).

[7] David Adamany and George Agree, "Election Campaign Financing: The 1974 Reforms," *Political Science Quarterly*, Vol. 90, No. 2 (Summer, 1975), p. 216.

[8] Stephen Hess in *The Wall Street Journal*, March 25, 1974. See also Stephen Hess, *The Presidential Campaign: The Leadership Selection Process After Watergate* (Washington, D.C.: The Brookings Institution, 1974).

2 Impact of New Laws

In 1971 Congress enacted two pieces of legislation that were major turning points in the history of campaign finance reform: the Federal Election Campaign Act of 1971 (FECA), which replaced the Federal Corrupt Practices Act of 1925, and the Revenue Act of 1971.[1] The latter provided tax credits, or, alternatively, tax deductions for political contributions at all levels, and also a tax checkoff to subsidize presidential campaigns during general elections. The FECA of 1971,[2] which passed in January 1972, a month after the Revenue Act,[3] required fuller disclosure of political funding than ever before — a provision that was to play a key role in the Watergate affair.

Watergate events brought new pressures for still more reform. Nonetheless, it was almost two years before a revised law, called the 1974 Amendments,[4] became fully operative in April 1975. When President Ford signed the bill on October 15, 1974, he expressed doubts about some sections of the law.[5] His doubts were to find reality more than a year later when the Supreme Court declared portions of the law unconstitutional. The law was to take effect on January 1, 1975, and parts of it did, but delays in appointing members of the Federal Election Commission left the law not fully operational until April 14, 1975, when Ford swore in the six commissioners. Less than a year would pass before their method of selection (some by Congress, others by the president) would be declared unconstitutional by the U.S. Supreme Court, in the case of *Buckley v. Valeo.*[6] Along with the creation of the commission, the other major "firsts" in the 1974 Amendments were the establishment of overall limitations on how much could be spent in campaigning, and the extension of public funding to campaigns for the presidential nomination and for the workings of the national conventions.

The *Buckley* decision, which declared parts of the 1974 Amendments unconstitutional, necessitated new legislation by Congress to refine the law according to the Supreme Court guidelines. Accordingly, the 1976 Amendments were enacted.[7] The 1974 and 1976 Amendments, and the *Buckley* case, are described below.

FECA and FEC

Both the 1974 and the 1976 Amendments to the Federal Election Campaign Act changed the ground rules applying to the campaigns of presidential candidates. Both enactments occurred while presidential contenders were in the midst of campaigns, and both left uncertainties in the campaign process.

The 1974 Amendments evolved during the controversial Watergate period, when constant tales of unorthodox campaign practices gained nationwide attention. Allegations of "laundered" campaign funds, illegal corporate contributions, "bought" ambassadorships, and secret monies were constantly before Congress as it deliberated the second major reform of campaign finance laws in three years.

The effect of these events can be seen from a comparison of the Senate Watergate Committee's final report with the 1974 law. Eight of the committee's 11 recommendations on campaign finances were incorporated into the law. In the House of Representatives, debate on the legislation occurred during the final week of the Nixon administration, and the House approved its version of a campaign reform bill just hours before President Nixon announced his resignation on August 8, 1974.

President Ford signed the bill into law on October 15, saying "the times demand this legislation." The 1974 Amendments repealed some provisions of the 1971 law, expanded others, and broke new ground in such areas as public financing and contribution and expenditure limitations. Some observers felt the act restricted the rights of individuals too much. Many of its provisions later were tried in the courts and some were indeed ruled unconstitutional. In the fall of 1974, however, these incidents were far in the future and exerted little influence on the emerging presidential candidates who were chiefly attempting to understand the new campaign regulations. In its final form, the 1974 Amendments to the FECA:

• *Established a Federal Election Commission* (FEC) consisting of six voting members, two of them appointed by the president, four of them designated by congressional leaders, and two nonvoting members, the Clerk of the House and the Secretary of the Senate. All six voting members had to be confirmed by both the House and the Senate. The commission bore the responsibility for formulating rules and policy with respect to the administration of the law, as well as ascertaining that candidates and groups were adhering to the Act, and it was vested with civil enforcement powers.

● *Instituted a multitude of contribution limitations,* including: for individuals, a limit of $1,000 per candidate for each primary, runoff, or general election, and an aggregate contribution of $25,000 to all federal candidates annually; a limit of $5,000 per candidate for each political committee, for each election, but with no aggregate limit; a $50,000 limit for presidential and vice presidential candidates and their families to their own campaign; a limit of $1,000 for independent expenditures on behalf of a candidate; and a prohibition on cash contributions of more than $100 and on all foreign contributions.

● *Established a variety of spending limitations* for federal candidates, including: an overall $10 million total per presidential candidate in the preconvention period (in individual primary states spending was limited to twice the amount a senatorial candidate could spend); $20 million per candidate in the presidential general election; and $2 million for each major political party's presidential nominating convention. These limits were subject to revision according to annual increases in the Consumer Price Index. There were also several "bonuses" included in the bill that supplemented the spending limitations, including a 20 percent overage above the ceiling for candidates' costs in soliciting funds; and, in general elections, a national political party was allowed to spend as much as 2 cents per voting age resident of the United States in support of its presidential candidate.

● *Created a number of disclosure and reporting procedures.* Requirements include: establishment by each candidate of one central campaign committee through which all contributions and expenditures on behalf of that candidate would be reported; reporting names and addresses of contributors of amounts over $10 as well as occupation and place of business of those contributing in excess of $100; identification of recipients of expenditures over $10; filing of full reports of contributions and expenditures with the FEC 10 days before and 30 days after each election, and within 10 days of the close of each quarter. Presidential candidates were not required, however, to file more than 12 reports in any one year.

Perhaps the most imaginative aspect of the new law was the provision instituting public financing of federal elections. The concept had been considered by Congress several times. In 1966 congressional approval had been won for a bill allocating to each major party's national committee about $30 million for the general election period. The law never became operative, but five years later public financing was revived in the Revenue Act of 1971. This act established an alternative tax credit deduction for individuals who contributed to candidates for federal, state, or local political office, and authorized the tax checkoff whereby, beginning in 1973, taxpayers could designate on their tax returns that $1 be paid to a public campaign fund. This revenue would be used to fund presidential general election campaigns.

The Federal Election Campaign Act Amendments of 1974 went further in establishing government funding, providing subsidies for two different stages of presidential campaigns: the primaries and the nominating conventions. The amendments stipulated that if the level of money in the tax checkoff fund was insufficient to finance all three stages of the electoral process, then funds would be disbursed for the general election, conventions, and primaries, in that order.

Prenomination Campaigns

The 1974 Amendments provided that candidates for the presidential nomination could receive up to about $5.5 million in tax-generated funds for preconvention campaign expenses during the primaries and caucuses. To qualify for the money, a candidate had to show the FEC that he or she had raised $5,000 in private contributions of $250 or less in each of 20 states.

In the prenomination period, the government provided limited matching funds based on the fund-raising ability of qualified candidates. In the postnomination period, an outright grant of government funds was provided and no private fund raising by the candidate was allowed. Candidates for the presidential nomination therefore needed to raise private funds for matching on a limited basis. To make this fund raising possible, the 1974 Amendments permitted a 20 percent bonus for fund-raising expenditures, beyond the overall $10 million limit per candidate (adjusted to $10.9 million by indexing). Theoretically, the 1976 prenomination period limited total spending to $13.1 million.

While the law allowed an individual to contribute up to $1,000 per candidate, the government would match only the first $250. To increase the federal funding, a candidate could ask a person willing to contribute $1,000 to split the gift with a spouse or other adult members of the family. Since some private contributions total more than $250, few if any candidates would ever get the total of $5.5 million in matching funds.

National Nominating Conventions

Both major-party national committees were entitled to $2 million (adjusted to $2.2 million by indexing) to pay for the costs of the national nominating conventions. They were not required to use public funds, but the repeal of an IRS rule allowing corporations to deduct advertising in convention booklets as a business expense made private financing more difficult. The 1974 Amendments stipulated that the public funds could not be used to defray any expenses of a candidate or delegate at the convention. The funds could be used only to finance the convention itself or to repay loans made for that purpose.

General Election

A presidential candidate nominated by a major political party could choose to accept $20 million (adjusted to $21.8 million by indexing) in government-supplied funds for the general election campaign. If he did so, he could not raise private funds in addition, although his party could spend up to 2 cents per individual of voting age (roughly another $3.2 million) on his behalf. Spending by the party depended, of course, upon its ability to raise and spend sufficient money to cover the operating expenses.

Since the candidate who accepted government funds could not raise money privately, his campaign would not incur the expense of fund raising. In the case of McGovern's campaign in 1972, such expenses approximated $3.5 million in mail costs for fund-raising purposes, $1 million in newspaper ads, and more in appeals for funds tagged on at the end of paid broadcasts. Hence, with party help within the specified limits and in the absence of fund-raising costs, the available money could be regarded as adequate but certainly not generous.

The Tax Checkoff

The money for all three phases of federal funding was provided by the "tax checkoff." Created by the Revenue Act of 1971, the tax checkoff enabled each individual whose federal tax liability for a year was $1 or more to designate on his federal income tax form that $1 of his tax money be paid to the Presidential Election Campaign Fund. Those filing joint returns could so designate $2 of their tax money.

The 1974 Amendments split political parties into two categories to determine eligibility for public funds. Major parties were defined as those whose presidential candidates received 25 percent or more of the popular vote in the preceding general election, while minor parties were those whose candidates received between 5 and 25 percent of the presidential popular vote. Major-party candidates would be eligible to receive the full amount of public funding in each of the three phases of the campaign. Since only the Republican and Democratic parties received more than 25 percent of the 1972 presidential vote, these two parties alone became eligible to receive public funds before the 1976 election.

Qualified minor parties were eligible for public financing in direct proportion to their share of the vote. For example, if the two major parties received an average of 20 million votes each in the latest election and the minor party received 8 million votes, the minor party would be eligible for 40 percent of the amount in public funds granted to each of the major parties. If a new party emerged that had not been on the ballot four years earlier, or if an older minor party became successful, the candidate of this party would qualify retroactively after the November election; the minor party's candidate would receive his share of the public funds if he obtained 5 percent or more of the presidential vote in the current election.

The public's acceptance of the program started out slowly, but grew as more people became aware of the checkoff on their tax form. Only 3 percent of the taxpayers used the checkoff in 1972. The new provision had been placed on a separate form, however, and many taxpayers had overlooked it. The 1973 tax forms placed the checkoff on the front page and allowed taxpayers to check off funds retroactively if they had missed the provision the year before. This retroactive provision brought in twice the amount of funds checked off in 1972 and the 1973 form again doubled that amount of money. This near doubling of the funds continued in 1974, but the 1975 tax forms, filled out during the heated primary campaign of 1976, attracted only 1.6 percent more people than the previous year's forms.

Despite the slowed increase in the number of people who used the checkoff provisions, $94.1 million was available for the 1976 presidential election year. This sum proved more than enough for the campaign. As of December 31, 1977, the funds had been distributed as follows:

Prenomination matching funds	$23.7 million
National nomination conventions	3.6 million
General election flat grants	43.6 million
Total	$70.9 million

An excess of about $22.4 million was available in case any minor-party candidate qualified (none did). Part of the surplus then reverted to the general Treasury, while the rest was held for the next election. A fund for the 1980 election began with this surplus amount and added $36.6 million from the 1976 tax returns, leaving the Federal Election Campaign Fund with a balance of $61.5 million as of November 1977.

Constitutional Issues

While President Ford signed the Federal Election Campaign Act of 1974 in October, it was not until January 1975 that the law became effective, and it was immediately clouded by a legal suit challenging not only the constitutionality of most of the major provisions of the 1974 Amendments, but also the very existence of the FEC itself. The 1974 Amendments invited legal challenge because Congress had failed to take seriously the warnings of experts that serious constitutional issues were involved; the reformers were so enthusiastic that they pushed to the outer bound of strict regulation. They urged, and Congress agreed to, a tight system of limitations, arguing that so long as private independent expenditures were permitted, limitations could be placed on their amount, as well as on contributions. Overall candidate expenditure limits were thought to be constitutional because they were necessary to an effective system of regulation that would restrain excessive spending, which traditionally had been unfair to candidates lacking personal wealth or access to large contributions. A system of regulation with low and effective limitations was the goal also of some reformers and others who sought to starve electioneering by reducing available money to a point where Congress would enact public funding of senatorial and congressional as well as of presidential campaigns.

Buckley v. Valeo

An unusual FECA provision authorized any eligible voter to start federal court proceedings to contest the constitutionality of any provision of the law. The amendment was designed to speed along any case by permitting questions of constitutionality to be certified directly to the Court of Appeals, which was obliged to expedite the case. A case was brought a few days after the law became effective on January 1, 1975.[8] Plaintiffs covered a broad spectrum of liberals and conservatives, individuals and organizations, including Conservative-Republican Sen. James L. Buckley of New York, former Democratic Sen. Eugene J. McCarthy of Minnesota, Stewart R. Mott (a large contributor), the Conservative Party of the State of New York, the New York Civil Liberties Union, the Mississippi Republican Party, the Libertarian Party, and the Conservative Victory Fund, among others. Defendants included, along with Attorney General Edward H. Levi (the solicitor general actually argued the case in court), the FEC, the Secretary of the Senate (Francis R. Valeo) and the Clerk of the House (W. Pat Jennings), and three reform groups, Common Cause, the Center for Public Financing of Elections, and the League of Women Voters of the United States.

The suit attacked the law's limitation of contributions and expenditures, disclosure provisions, public financing, and limits on independent political activity. In *Buckley v. Valeo,* the courts confronted a difficult judicial task. The problem, in its simplest form, was to balance the First Amendment rights of free speech and free association against the clear power of the legislature to enact laws designed to protect the integrity of the election system. Involved were questions of public discussion and political dialogue, certainly the highest order of meaning of the First Amendment. Basically, the plaintiffs sought to ensure that the reform, however well meant, did not have a chilling effect on free speech or on citizen participation.

The case was argued before the U.S. Court of Appeals for the District of Columbia, which in an August 15, 1975, opinion sustained most of the law's provisions. Appeal was then made to the Supreme Court, the arguments were heard, and on January 30, 1976, a little over a year after the case was initiated, the Supreme Court ruled in a *per curiam* opinion joined in all aspects by three justices, partially by others, with one major dissent and partial dissent by others. The decision was a reversal of many major points that had been considered and upheld by the Court of Appeals. The Supreme Court views have had impact not only on the regulation of federal elections but also on state and local law as well.

Money and Speech. The central question was posed by Justice Potter Stewart during oral arguments: Is money speech and speech money? Or stated differently, is an expenditure for speech substantially the same thing as speech itself because money is necessary to reach large audiences by the purchase of air time or space in the print media. The decision resolved the conflict by asserting the broadest protection to First Amendment rights to assure the unrestrained interchange of ideas for bringing about popular political and social change. Accordingly, the majority concluded that individual expenditure limitations imposed direct and substantial restraints on the quantity of political speech. This applied to limits on both individuals and on candidates in their personal expenditures on their own behalf as well as on spending by or on behalf of a candidate. However, an exception was made with reference to overall candidate expenditure limits, with the Court holding that candidates who accept public funding provided by government also could be obliged to accept campaign expenditure limits as a condition of the granting of the public money. The Court made clear that independent spending by individuals and groups could be considered as a protected form of free speech only if the spending was truly independent and accordingly it could not be coordinated with the candidate or his campaign organization, nor consented to by the candidate or his agent.

On the other hand, the decision upheld the limits on individual and group contributions to campaigns, asserting that these constitute only a marginal restriction on the contributor's ability to engage in free communication. Saying that free expression rests on contributing as a symbolic act to help give a candidate the means to speak out with views congenial to those of the contributor, the quantity of speech does not increase perceptibly with the size of the contribution, and hence limits on contributions are constitutional. The Supreme Court found that there was a real or imagined coercive influence of large contributors on candidates' positions and on their actions if elected, leading to corruption or the appearance of corruption. Therefore contribution limits were acceptable, the Court said, because they serve to mute the voices of affluent persons and groups while also restraining the skyrocketing cost of political campaigns.

The Court 1) sustained all the disclosure requirements of the law, 2) sanctioned the forms of public funding provided by it, and 3) upheld the concept of a bipartisan regulatory commission to administer and enforce the law so long as the agency is within the executive branch of government and its members are appointed by the president. These are the three main directions in which regulation of political finance will proceed, perhaps modified to some extent by efforts to continue contribution limits and by expenditure limits when candidates accept government funding (although their effectiveness is offset by unlimited independent spending by individuals and groups).

Levi's Doubts. In the course of the litigation, the FEC encountered an additional burden when the attorney general announced his doubts about the constitutionality of two portions of the law.[9] It appeared that the Justice Department was abandoning its defense of the new election law when Attorney General Levi said the government would file a friend of the court brief arguing all sides of the matters: 1) dealing with the enforcement powers of the FEC, suggesting that because of its manner of appointment, it could not be considered an executive agency; and 2) dealing with contribution limits, suggesting they were an unconstitutional restraint on free political expression.

It is rare for the attorney general to fail to support fully a law under legal challenge, but the argument was made that the issues were so fundamental that the department felt all sides should be fully aired. The FEC protested to the White House and the Justice Department retreated in part. The FEC was concerned that only partial support by Justice would undermine the defense of the law. While the FEC previously had engaged outside counsel to prepare briefs defending the manner of appointment, the attorney general agreed to defend the law at the Court of Appeals level but not on appeal to the Supreme Court insofar as enforcement powers were concerned. He did agree to defend contribution limits. The impact of this incident upon the Supreme Court cannot be certain, but the Court upheld contribution limits while agreeing that the FEC was improperly constituted.

An Early Case

The constitutional aspects of the law, and the sensitivity of the FEC on the constitutional issue, were pointed up little more than two months after the FEC was organized, while *Buckley v. Valeo* was being litigated. Under the 1974 Amendments the FEC was authorized to initiate, defend, or appeal any civil action for the purpose of enforcing the law. The commission was encouraged to seek compliance informally by means of conference, conciliation, and persuasion, but could take violators to court except in criminal cases. The latter were to be referred to the attorney general for prosecution. On June 23, 1975, an ad was published in *The Washington Post* criticizing President Ford for his Vietnamese and economic policies as well as for his pardon of former President Nixon and his choice of Nelson A. Rockefeller as vice president. The ad, headlined "Would You Elect Ex-Congressman Ford President?," urged Republicans, Democrats and independents to oppose Ford and to convince him to withdraw as a candidate.[10]

It was ascertained that the ad cost $2,368.80, an apparent violation of the $1,000 limit on individual expenditures imposed by the law. The case caused a stir in the FCC, with several commissioners seeking to find a way to interpret the ad as within the limits of the law and thereby avoid a compliance action that could lead to appeals on constitutional grounds. In some urgency, the FEC undertook to establish rules on how to handle complaints and compliance actions. The law prohibits the commission from making public any notice of or investigation into a complaint without the written consent of the person against whom a complaint is made. The issue finally was resolved when the *Buckley* decision made clear that individual expenditures of an independent nature could be made in unlimited amounts, so long as there was no collusion with the candidate or his campaign organization. But the enforcement ambivalence of the FEC in this case was a clear indication of its early uncertainties about how to deal with constitutional issues.

Later, after the 1976 Amendments were enacted, the FEC adopted a policy statement on the subject of independent expenditures. Under the law, no person may contribute more than $5,000 per calendar year to a political committee (excepting a political party committee) making independent expenditures on behalf of federal candidates, and for individuals this amount comes within the total of $25,000 in contributions permitted per calendar year. Contributions to political committees independently supporting only one candidate are limited to $1,000, the same amount as the individual contribution limit per candidate, per election. There is no limit, however, to the making of independent expenditures by an individual so long as they are made directly out of pocket and not by means of contributing to a group; thus an individual can take out a newspaper ad costing $10,000, for example, and pay the newspaper directly for it. Moreover, there is no limit to the amounts an independent group can spend, and the amount is not counted toward the candidate's spending limit. In any case, independent expenditures can be made only if there is no cooperation or consultation with a candidate or his agent.

This effort by Congress and the FEC to limit to $5,000 or $1,000 contributions to committees making independent expenditures may be a troublesome area inviting further litigation on constitutional grounds. During the presidential primaries several organizations, raising money for independent expenditures to be made on behalf of Ronald Reagan, solicited contributions of up to the $25,000 upper contribution limit per individual in a calendar year, as noted below.[11]

Period of Uncertainty

Not only were candidates forced to proceed with their campaigns during 1975 following regulations that might be declared unconstitutional as a result of the *Buckley* suit, but they had to struggle with a law that had become effective but not yet operative. When the law went into effect in January, only two of the six commissioners had been appointed (these two were appointed by the political leaders of the Senate), and candidates were forced to struggle through the law as best they could, without any official interpretations. In essence, the candidates lacked forms, a filing procedure, and guidelines, and no one had determined the expenditure ceilings for each state.

In mid-January political leaders in the House of Representatives finally named their two appointees, but it was not until late February that President Ford proposed two commission members. In late January the U.S. District Court passed the *Buckley* suit up to the U.S. Circuit Court of Appeals because the case raised "substantial constitutional questions." The still-inactive Federal Election Commission, unable to defend itself, relied instead on the Justice Department. At the same time, groups that had pressed for passage of the 1974 Act were suddenly shocked when President Ford recommended for the FEC a budget less than half as large as that originally authorized by Congress. Questions regarding implementation of the Act continued to multiply.

Prenomination Campaigns and the FEC

As March approached and the first presidential primary loomed less than one year away, both chambers of Congress finally began confirmation hearings on the nominated commissioners, since the law specified confirmation by both houses. The House acted fairly quickly, but the Senate did not confirm the commissioners until after the Easter recess in April. On April 14, 1975, the six commissioners were sworn in by Ford.

As the FEC became an official agency, the Circuit Court of Appeals sent the *Buckley* case back to the U.S. District Court for fact-finding and framing of the constitutional issues. Preliminary motions already had taken up three and a half months, and this new referral increased the likelihood of further delays in disposition of the case. The case would certainly not be decided by July 1, 1975, when the political parties would be allowed to seek public financing for their 1976 presidential nominating conventions.

As the political parties and the presidential candidates waited, the new FEC commissioners were faced with immediate difficulties in staffing and budgeting. The newly elected chairman of the commission requested more than two and a half times the amount budgeted by the president. Aware of the need for immediate expertise in the area of campaign finance, the commission soon began hiring people who had lobbied for the legislation, who had been involved in drafting the law, or who had helped implement the 1971 Act. All the while, requests for official interpretations of the Act continued to grow, totaling well over 100 requests just three weeks after the commissioners had been sworn in.

In compliance with the 1974 Act, the law's enforcement authority was shifted from the two Capitol Hill supervisory officers to the full commission 30 days after the commission's general counsel was appointed. Most of this authority pertained to the disposition of various campaign finance reports. Until this time, candidates had continued to file their reports with the state offices, the Secretary of the Senate, and the Clerk of the House. Presidential candidates at last had one central office and prescribed dates on which to file their expenditure and contribution reports.

The FEC and the Nominating Conventions

More than two months after the commissioners had been sworn in, the many questions about the Act from presidential candidates and parties remained unanswered. One week before political parties could begin to seek public funds for their nominating conventions, McCarthy and other plaintiffs in the *Buckley* suit sought an injunction to prevent disbursal of the money until the court had decided the constitutionality of the public financing provisions. The plaintiffs had sought aid and were refused assurances from the FEC and the Treasury Department that no funds would be issued pending the court's decision. Hours before the scheduled court hearing on the injunction, however, commission officials promised that at least seven days' public notice would be given before distribution.

In mid-July, the FEC issued its first "advisory opinion" to clarify the funding of the two political parties' nominating conventions. Republican and Democratic party officials sought guidelines on how much, if any, of the free convention halls, special construction costs, free hotels, and transportation donated by the convention cities, businesses, or associations (which had been common practice in the past) could be accepted in 1976. If these gifts were acceptable, would they count against the $2 million expenditure ceiling?

The commission ruled that certain free services and facilities provided by state or local governments and municipal corporations could be accepted by the two national party committees and would not be charged against the ceiling imposed on each convention. The commission decided, however, that those same services would be prohibited by the 1974 Act if they were donated by a corporation or leased by a corporation to state or local governments or municipal corporations below the fair market value. The commission stipulated that this general corporation prohibition would be suspended for such offers made in the ordinary course of business to nonpolitical conventions of corresponding size and duration.

This first advisory opinion drew sharp criticism from officials of both parties who were responsible for conducting the conventions. The commission's ruling had the effect of prohibiting automobile manufacturers from providing automobiles or buses for the convention, and major national beverage manufacturers from having hospitality suites or other free distribution of their products. The free use of an auditorium or convention center also was prohibited if it was owned by a corporation. When coupled with the $2.2 million expenditure ceiling for convention spending, the ruling caused both parties to cut back on services provided at the convention. The Republicans noted that in 1972, before the ceiling and the prohibition on corporate contributions, spending for their convention had approached $2 million.

Matching Funds for Presidential Candidates

It was not until August, eight months after the law took effect, that the commission gave presidential candidates some guidance regarding the matching of public funds. The commission ruled that, to receive public dollars for every contribution of $250 or less, presidential candidates must submit a photocopy of each check or "written instrument" for which matching federal dollars were sought. These first interim guidelines also required candidates to submit detailed records showing campaign spending and contributions in each state where the candidate claimed he qualified. The commission stipulated that candidates who had failed to keep such records would have to open their accounts and records of contributions to the commission's investigators before the matching funds would be certified.

This requirement for a photostat of a canceled check produced immediate problems for several campaigns. Few of the candidates had imagined that copies of checks might be required and many of the campaigns had not kept such records. Many FEC staff members hoped that candidates would be able to qualify for funds based on their fund-raising abilities after August 11 (the date the guidelines became official). However, it soon became apparent that several candidates could not meet this requirement. In this category were Gov. George C. Wallace, D-Ala., Sen. Henry M. Jackson, D-Wash., and Rep. Morris K. Udall, D-Ariz. The FEC therefore devised a random sampling technique to verify the authenticity of contributions by checking with the reported contributor.

Preliminary discussion over the entire matching-fund concept lead to the first serious split within the commission. The issue was whether the 1974 Act required that public funds match every dollar raised in contributions or only the net amount after deduction of fund-raising expenses. This "gross" vs. "net" controversy pitted the FEC legal staff, which pushed the "gross" proposal, against a number of commissioners, who seemed determined not to allow candidates to be reimbursed for their fund-raising expenditures.

Quite understandably, the presidential candidates and their representatives were upset at commission efforts to deprive them of matching funds they considered rightfully theirs. Up to that point, four presidential candidates had claimed they were qualified for matching funds. A preliminary check with the FEC audit and investigation staff indicated that not one of the candidates qualified for matching funds under the "net" system.

In late August, the legal staff modified its stance, and proposed that a netting requirement be allowed for events such as dinners, cocktail parties, or concerts where "a benefit is conferred upon the contributor." The cost for such events to the candidate would be subtracted from the contribution for matching purposes. Contributions received from solicitations would be matched penny for penny, however, in cases where the contributor received nothing in payment for his contribution. This shifting of positions was enough to break the deadlock that had developed over the issue among the six commissioners.

These new guidelines adopted by the commission greatly affected the fund-raising tactics of all presidential candidates from then on. In essence, they established a dual standard for fund-raising activities. The policy did not ban $100-a-plate dinners, for example, but it discouraged candidates from relying on them because only the net proceeds — perhaps $65 or $75 a person — counted toward qualification for the federal candidate subsidy. On the other hand, the Federal Election Commission's ruling encouraged such activities as direct-mail solicitation of contributions.

Nevertheless, this dual standard for fund raising was modified by the FEC when it attempted to settle the question of whether Governor Wallace could accept royalties from his campaign committee for the sale of items bearing his likeness. While the commission reluctantly approved the monetary transaction, it said the purchase by the campaign committee of an item with "significant intrinsic and enduring value" could not be counted at all for purposes of qualifying for matching public funds. This new language — "intrinsic and enduring value" — made a significant departure from the commission's earlier guideline applying a netting standard when a "private benefit" was conferred upon a contributor.

A month later, in early October, the FEC rewrote the interim guidelines into proposed regulations and scrapped the controversial "net" system. The regulations sent to Congress stated, "contributions eligible for matching are determined without regard to costs incurred by a candidate in raising the contribution." The commission excepted from the rule contributions made for an item of "significant intrinsic and enduring value."

The proposed regulations also required the submission of an alphabetical list of contributors by state containing the address and date of deposit into the candidate's account, the amount of contribution and the amount that is matchable ($250 or less), photocopies of the contributions organized according to the date of deposit, and a copy of the relevant deposit slip and bank statement.

Although the FEC was changing the rules early in the game, presidential candidates temporarily received some good news as the U.S. Court of Appeals on August 15 upheld all but one minor provision of the Federal Election Campaign Act Amendments of 1974. All major principles of campaign reform — contribution and expenditure limits, disclosure, public financing, and the creation of the FEC — were held to be constitutional but, as discussed above, the Supreme Court would soon alter that decision. The one minor provision knocked down by the Court of Appeals was a section of the disclosure law requiring organizations that publicize voting records and similar information to disclose the names of their contributors just as a political committee would have to do.

The FEC and Presidential Candidate Travel

The distinction between campaigning for oneself and campaigning on behalf of one's political party was the next issue to embroil the FEC in controversy as the summer of 1975 drew to a close.

During early 1975 President Ford began making political trips to various parts of the country. The frequency of the trips slowly accelerated, and in late August the press learned that the tab for many of the trips was being picked up by the Republican National Committee rather than the President Ford Committee. This meant the expenses were not being counted toward the expenditure ceiling of the president's campaign committee, and that the contribution of the national committee was not being restricted to $5,000 for a single candidate.

This news outraged many presidential candidates from both parties. Reagan had not been accorded the same privileges as the president by the national committee. Sen. Lloyd Bentsen, D-Texas, charged that the president was circumventing a legal opinion just issued by the FEC. According to this opinion, "once an individual has become a candidate for President, all speeches made before substantial numbers of people are presumably for the purpose of enhancing his candidacy." (The advisory opinion had been issued to Bentsen after he had questioned the commission as to whether corporations could pick up the travel expenses of a presidential candidate when the candidate spoke before the corporation. The FEC said the law prohibited such expenses by corporations.)

The controversy was heightened by the special Senate election in New Hampshire on September 16, just six months before the presidential primary in that state. President Ford planned to campaign in the state on behalf of Republican senatorial candidate Louis Wyman with the RNC again picking up the tab.

Acting upon the recommendation of General Counsel John G. Murphy, Jr., the FEC postponed a decision on the general question of paying for candidate travel and instead granted "one-time exemption" to each presidential candidate. This allowed the candidates to campaign on behalf of senatorial candidates without counting the expenses towards the 1976 primary ceiling. Instead, the expenses incurred by the presidential candidates would be charged against the ceiling of the senatorial candidate. Murphy noted that "while visits by the presidential candidate might have some effect on the presidential campaign, they were likely to have a greater effect on the more immediate election and should therefore be charged to the Senate spending limit."

At the same meeting, however, Murphy expressed general approval of a letter from presidential counsel Philip Buchen outlining White House plans for billing political trips. The letter said that when the president makes a purely political trip, the touring expenses of the president, members of his family, party officials, and White House staff members who perform some political duties would be charged to the "appropriate political committee." Government funds would cover all other White House personnel and Secret Service agents. The "appropriate political committee" never was defined, however, and the RNC continued to pay for the president's political trips.

This arrangement did not receive official approval from the FEC until late November. The commission ruled then that the RNC could pay for President Ford's trips to functions relating to party building until January 1 of the election year. The commission said that trips made after that time would be presumed to be candidate-related and subject to the expenditure limitations of the 1974 Act. The advisory opinion also suggested, but did not require, that the RNC "accord equitable treatment to all of its presidential candidates." The day after the opinion was released the RNC said it had "no intention of paying any of Reagan's campaign expenditures." The national committee had budgeted $500,000 for the president's political travels during 1975.

The FEC's decision was not popular with the Reagan campaign or the Democratic National Committee. Two weeks after the commission announced its ruling, the DNC officially challenged the opinion. The challenge should have required the FEC to review its decision, but nothing happened until after the general election. On December 17, after Carter had been elected president, the DNC officially withdrew the complaint. Nevertheless, the FEC decided to continue its investigation. In late March 1977 the general counsel recommended, and the full commission concurred, that there was "reasonable cause to believe" a violation had occurred with regard to at least one of Ford's trips.

That trip had been made to California, where the president's schedule showed him meeting with the chairman of the President Ford Committee of California and two members of the California state steering committee. The FEC found this activity plainly related to Ford's candidacy. Three months later attorneys for the former president submitted new evidence to rebut the commission's finding. The new information indicated that the meeting lasted no more than 20 minutes, was of a "social-courtesy or handshaking session," and was "entirely incidental to the official California Republican Party activities of that evening and the following day." In late July the commission officially rescinded its earlier finding and closed the case.

Dual Candidacies: A New Problem for the FEC

Since politicians instinctively think about the next election and the next highest office, it seemed only natural in 1975 that the FEC would have to consider the situation of a candidate who ran for two offices at the same time. Senator Bentsen, who campaigned for the presidency and for reelection to the Senate, asked the FEC if he could accept $1,000 from an individual for his senatorial campaign and another $1,000 from the same individual for his presidential campaign. Could he spend the Senate primary limit in Texas and at the same time spend up to twice as much within the state running for president? Could he combine in addition the personal and immediate family expenditure limits of $35,000 for Senate races and $50,000 for presidential elections? Finally, if Bentsen dropped out of the presidential race, would his presidential expenditures count against the Senate limit, and could he transfer remaining funds to his Senate committee?

In mid-September, the commission found answers to some of Bentsen's questions. It ruled that his expenditures in Texas for both campaigns would be limited to the Senate ceiling (half of the presidential ceiling). In the advisory opinion, the commission explained that to allow Bentsen to spend three times as much as his Senate challengers would deny them equal protection under the law as guaranteed by the Fifth Amendment. The FEC noted that the ruling applied only to the Texas primary and would not discriminate against Bentsen in other states. Moreover, since Bentsen is from Texas, he "begins with a significant exposure advantage" over his presidential rivals, the commission said. The FEC also decided that any expenditure made by Bentsen's presidential campaign prior to the issuance of the FEC ruling would not be counted against the Senate ceiling. To make the ruling more palatable to Bentsen, the FEC held that individuals and political committees could contribute the maximum of $1,000 and $5,000 respectively to both the senatorial and presidential campaigns. The commission reasoned that the concern with equal protection under the law "has minimal relevance with regard to limitations on contributions." However, Bentsen family contributions were held to the $35,000 Senate limit for both Texas campaigns. The commission also noted that a dual federal candidate must "establish and maintain two entirely separate campaign organizations," that contributions made with respect to one campaign could not be expended in the other campaign, and that transfers between the two separate campaign committees were not permissible.

Delegate Spending: A Major Loophole

As more and more people read the 1974 Amendments and understanding began, loopholes were found. The loophole most important for the presidential candidates proved to be the discovery that the new law made no mention of delegates to the two parties' nominating conventions. Congress failed to limit the funds raised or spent by an individual who campaigned to be a convention delegate. A presidential candidate could therefore advise supporters to funnel contributions directly to candidacies for delegates who were committed to him, thus shifting much of the cost of local, county, and state-level campaigning to these delegate-candidates and negating the limits imposed on the presidential candidates. Robert Keefe, campaign director for Senator Jackson, characterized the loophole as "big enough to drive a president through." The DNC, acting on behalf of all the Democratic presidential candidates, favored plugging the loophole. At the RNC, however, attorneys questioned whether the FEC had the power to regulate the delegates.

A task force within the FEC drew up several proposals regarding delegates for the commissioners to study. The DNC worked with the major Democratic presidential candidates and established a set of rules by which all candidates agreed they would abide.

This agreement among the candidates is important because it, rather than the FEC staff study, formed the basis for the final FEC ruling on the issue.

The final FEC advisory opinion established three different groups of delegates: authorized, pledged-but-unauthorized, and uncommitted. The authorized delegates were defined as those who received specific authorization from a presidential candidate to raise or spend funds in conjunction with his campaign. There was no specific spending limit for these delegates, but all expenditures by authorized delegates counted toward the presidential candidate's spending limit in the state. Individuals could contribute to the delegates, but each such contribution would count toward the individual's limit for that presidential candidate. All spending over $100 by authorized delegates, excluding cost of travel and subsistence, had to be reported to the presidential candidate. Pledged-but-unauthorized delegates were those who were publicly committed to a specific presidential candidate but had not been authorized by him to raise or spend funds. Spending by these delegates was limited to $1,000 but was not counted against the presidential candidate's ceiling. Contributions to the delegates were also limited to $1,000. These delegates were required to file disclosure reports with the FEC. The uncommitted delegates were those delegates not identified with any presidential candidate. There was no limit to the amount of money these delegate candidates could raise or spend, but the commission warned that it would consider a delegate "who spuriously maintains that he/she is unpledged and who exceeds the $1,000 ceiling to be in violation of the law, determining the existence of sham or collusion upon examination of the facts of an individual case." Again, disclosure reports had to be filed with the commission.

The Election Year

All of these opinions by the FEC greatly affected the course of the 1976 election. Despite the establishment of these rules, however, the candidates were still uncertain about the constitutionality of the Act as a whole. This concern became critically important as 1975 drew to a close and the time for the doling out of public funds approached. In mid-December, Buckley, McCarthy, and others who had challenged the law asked the Supreme Court to block the FEC from distributing federal funds pending the court's ruling on the constitutionality of the public financing provisions of the law. The FEC was ready to ask the Treasury Department to disburse the campaign money to 11 presidential candidates of the two major political parties and for their national nominating conventions.

Despite the fact that the Court was in recess, it refused three days before Christmas to block the payments of political subsidies to the presidential candidates and parties. The Court split 4-4 on the question, and five votes were needed to bar the payments temporarily. The ruling caused concern among lawyers for both sides of the case because of its implications for the constitutionality issue. Some claimed the order showed that some of the justices were deeply troubled about the impact of the sweeping new law on national politics. Others noted that at least four justices were plainly in favor of letting the payments get started. The lawyers conjectured that the justices would not have voted as they did if they had considered the whole subsidy idea unconsitutional.

At any rate, the FEC told the Treasury Department the next day that the following 11 presidential candidates were eligible to receive the initial threshold payment of $100,000: Republicans Ronald Reagan and President Ford, and Democrats Birch Bayh, Lloyd Bentsen, Henry Jackson, George Wallace, Morris Udall, Jimmy Carter, Terry Sanford, Fred Harris, and Sargent Shriver. Three of the 11 candidates were certified to get funds in addition to the threshold amount: Bentsen, Ford, and Sanford. The candidates had to wait until January 2 to receive the $1.9 million, but that afternoon Treasury gave the Republican and Democratic National Committees $710,000 toward the parties' nominating conventions. As the presidential year got into full swing, other candidates soon qualified for public funds. They included Milton Shapp (Jan. 29), Ellen McCormack (Feb. 25), Frank Church (Feb. 26), and Jerry Brown (June 17).

The end of 1975 also brought the presidential candidates a 9.17 percent cost-of-living increase in the expenditure ceilings imposed by the Act. This provision of the 1974 Act raised the expenditure limitations to $10.9 million for prenomination campaigns, $2.2 million for the nominating conventions, and $21.8 million for the general election. The limits in each state were also raised because of the cost-of-living increase.

Buckley v. Valeo *Decision*

Another month passed before the Court decided the constitutionality of the FECA. Finally, on January 30, 1976, after the Act had been in existence for over one year, the Court handed down the massive and complex 137-page *Buckley* decision along with 64 pages of dissenting opinions, upholding three of the four major elements of campaign reform embodied in the federal law — disclosure, public financing, and limits on contributions — but striking down the limits on expenditures. If a candidate accepted public finance, however, the Court allowed spending limits to continue. The Court also struck down separate limits on the amounts a candidate could spend on behalf of his or her own candidacy.

The most important aspect of the decision, however, was the dismantling of the Federal Election Commission — the agency established by Congress to enforce the 1974 Act. The Court said the six commissioners were unconstitutionally appointed because the House and Senate chose four of the commissioners and the House confirmed all six — a violation of Article Two of the Constitution. The Court delayed the effect of its ruling for 30 days to give Congress an opportunity to reestablish the commission within the constitutional boundaries or to arrive at a new formula for enforcement of the 1974 law.

The Court's decision meant that the FEC could not exercise executive functions — it could not, for example, issue advisory opinions or seek civil enforcement of the Act in the courts. Suspension of these powers was of concern to the presidential candidates, however, because the decision also had the effect of cutting off public funds. The FEC interpreted the *Buckley* decision to mean that it could not certify matching fund payments, and although the Court accorded *de facto* validity to the FEC's previous actions, its ruling stated in particular that the commission could make no determinations of candidates' eligibility to receive federal subsidies after the effective date of the opinion. The justices made no mention of the FEC's authority, or lack thereof, to certify additional matching funds for candidates declared eligible by the commission prior to the *Buckley* decision. This omission opened the way for a motion of intervention filed by the candidates who were hampered by the disruption in the flow of matching funds. Over a two-and-one-half week period, lawyers representing seven presidential hopefuls waged a complicated series of battles in the federal courts in an unsuccessful attempt to release federal monies.

Suit to Obtain Matching Funds

The Supreme Court decision in *Buckley v. Valeo* gave Congress 30 days to reconstitute the FEC. When Congress failed to act within that period, the court granted a 20-day stay extending the life of the FEC until March 22, 1976. During this 50-day period the first five presidential primaries occurred in New Hampshire, Massachusetts, Vermont, Florida, and Illinois. With primaries to be held in North Carolina the next day and in New York and Wisconsin a week later, various candidates and groups became immensely concerned about the cutoff in matching funds. A second stay was requested, but the Supreme Court turned it down.

In early April the Democratic National Committee began exploring the potential of a judicial action that could release federal subsidies for eligible candidates. Counsels for the eligible candidates of both parties were invited to discuss the possibility of a lawsuit. To give the suit a bipartisan image, Republicans Ronald Reagan and President Ford were invited, but the president declined because he eventually would have to approve or veto the legislation to reconstitute the FEC. Sheldon S. Cohen, general counsel of the DNC and former internal revenue commissioner, sponsored the initial meeting of counsel in his office on April 15, 1976. Candidates who sent representatives were Democrats Carter, Church, Harris, Jackson, Udall, and Wallace, and Republican Reagan. Jackson's attorney was reluctant to join the suit but cooperated so that his candidate would not appear out of step with the competition.

The Money Squeeze. All of the candidates, most notably Harris and Udall, were feeling the pinch in funds, and at the April 15 meeting each representative stated that his candidate was prepared to litigate the cutoff of federal money. At that time, more than $2 million in matching funds was awaiting FEC certification. For the seven candidates involved in the lawsuit, matching funds constituted approximately one-third of their total receipts. Sheer economic desperation, however, did not provide the only impetus for the suit. The candidates' attorneys believed that the disruption in payments abridged the First Amendment rights of the candidates and of the voters and taxpayers as well.

To coordinate the litigation, officials of the Carter camp recruited attorney Donald D. Eastman of a Washington firm. Eastman and other lawyers in his firm handled the case on a public interest basis and received no fee, although each candidate paid a few hundred dollars to cover expenses incidental to the legal effort. Eastman felt that the presidential candidates could make a serious argument drawing on the First Amendment.

In their legal briefs, Eastman and his colleagues noted that the Supreme Court had recognized the link between adequate funds and effective political speech in its opinion in *Buckley v. Valeo.* The court stated "[V]irtually every means of communicating ideas in today's mass society requires the expenditure of money."[12] The candidates claimed that without federal subsidies they could not maintain suitable communication with the electorate. Each of the seven presidential hopefuls prepared an affidavit that detailed the cutbacks in his campaign necessitated by the lack of federal dollars. In his affidavit, candidate Carter stated that his committee had to reduce by over 50 percent its spending for canvassing, pamphlets, posters, and position papers. Frank Church attested that difficulties with cash flow forced his organization to order printed materials in lots of one thousand instead of 10,000. Fred Harris disclosed that he recalled all field personnel from Pennsylvania and shut down offices in that state, which was holding its primary on April 27. In several states, the Udall '76 Committee had halved its budgets for electronic media. The other candidates reported similar reductions in political activity.

Counsel also claimed that the limitations on contributions that had not been altered by the *Buckley* decision further abridged the candidates' freedom of speech. Congress authorized subsidies for presidential campaigns because it realized that the dialogue between office seekers and voters would be inhibited if there were ceilings on private contributions with no public compensation. Yet Congress's delay in reconstituting the FEC created just the situation that the 1974 Amendments had been written to avoid. The candidates asserted that the unintended result of the *Buckley* decision warranted equitable relief for themselves and the electorate.

In addition, counsel for the candidates contended that the disruption violated certain taxpayers' rights to free expression under the First Amendment. Those taxpayers who had designated one dollar of their tax liability for the Federal Election Campaign Fund intended their money to facilitate primary campaigns. According to Eastman, these taxpayers experienced irreparable injury to their expression as signified by the tax checkoff because their dollars were not being utilized after March 22.

Relief Granted. To present such substantive arguments, the lawyers had to gain access to the proper federal bench by way of a maze of procedural motions. Eastman wanted the Supreme Court to recall and modify its decision in *Buckley v. Valeo,* but because the candidates were not a party to the earlier case, they could not win relief until the Court granted them intervention. On April 22, 1976, Eastman and the other attorneys filed briefs simultaneously with the Supreme Court and the U.S. Court of Appeals for the District of Columbia Circuit, requesting a

leave to intervene out of time in the *Buckley* case. On April 23 the High
Court denied the motion in a brief order. In a concurring opinion,
Justice Lewis F. Powell, Jr., reasoned that the *Buckley* case had been
remanded to the Court of Appeals and therefore "jurisdiction with
respect to relief sought by new parties at this time is vested in that
court."[13] On the same day the Appeals Court granted intervention, and
consequently the candidates asked the lower court to clarify and/or
modify the Supreme Court's *Buckley* opinion in a manner that
permitted the FEC to certify funds to eligible candidates. Eastman felt
that the Appeals Court judges were quite sympathetic to the First
Amendment infringements experienced by the seven candidates. Nonetheless, on April 28, the Court of Appeals ruled that the Buckley opinion
left it "without the power to grant the relief sought by intervenors."[14]

Counsel then filed a notice of appeal from this adverse ruling. The
appeal, which would not come to a hearing until after the May primary
elections, dealt with the lower court's power to interpret a Supreme
Court decision. However, the candidates also moved for relief *pendente
lite* (while a suit is in progress) in the Supreme Court. The Appeals
Court's grant of intervention without a decision on the merits allowed
the candidates to return to the High Court immediately under the
pendente lite procedure. The candidates' team of lawyers requested
either that the justices interpret, modify, or clarify the judgments in
Buckley so as to authorize a resumption of matching payments, or that
they enable the U.S. Court of Appeals to do so.

The Supreme Court formulated a speedy reponse, for on April 30 it
denied the motion for relief *pendente lite.* In effect, the ground rules had
been changed in mid-campaign, but the courts failed to find grounds to
intercede. The pending appeal was mooted when, after President Ford
signed the 1976 Amendments and after the commission had been reconstituted, the FEC renewed certifications of matching funds. However,
damage already had occurred to the fiscally troubled candidates involved in the matching funds suit. Indeed, the candidacies of Fred
Harris, Henry Jackson, and Morris Udall virtually came to a halt after
the crucial Pennsylvania primary.

Reconstituting the FEC

While the various candidates were seeking relief from their short-
ages of funds, Congress slowly began the process of reconstituting the
commission. The proposed revision was complicated, however, when
other controversial changes in the law were suggested. These included
the proposal to extend public funding to senatorial and congressional
campaigns, which was defeated in both houses, and revisions of law

regarding corporate, trade association, and labor PACs, which survived but succeeded in delaying enactment of the law. The Supreme Court originally had given Congress 30 days in which to act, then later had extended the period by another 20 days. The complications caused the reconstitution of the FEC to take 111 days.

Much of the delay occurred because Congress was unable or unwilling to act promptly. President Ford requested a simple reconstitution of the FEC, which he said he would sign promptly, to permit the FEC to continue to operate through the 1976 presidential primaries. He argued that attempts to make other controversial changes would lengthen the delay. Nevertheless, Congress undertook significant revisions dealing with compliance and enforcement procedures, the issuing of advisory opinions, the role of corporate and labor political action committees, and other provisions.

Some observers thought the delay was purposeful, designed by Democratic congressional leaders to help the presidential nomination prospects of Sen. Hubert H. Humphrey, D-Minn. (who was not an active candidate but was thought by many to be a potential candidate if others failed) and to hurt the candidates actively competing in the primaries, and by Republican congressional leaders to improve President Ford's prospects against his challenger, Ronald Reagan. The suspension of matching funds came at crucial times, forcing candidates to rely wholly on private funds and loans during crucial primaries including those in Pennsylvania and Texas.

During the delay, Congress moved slowly toward reconstitution of the FEC. The Senate and the House initially passed substantially different bills but a conference committee finally reached agreement on a substitute bill[15] after intensive lobbying had occurred, with labor and business in conflict on the outcome of House provisions dealing with corporate and labor PACs. But Congress by then was in spring recess and the presidential primary season was in full sway. Key Senate Republicans delayed final approval of the conference committee report until early May; the final vote turned on the PAC provisions, with which Republicans were unhappy, and not on the reconstituting of the commission. Then the focus shifted to the White House, where President Ford took a week to sign the bill while the Nebraska primary passed by. Ford refused to say he would sign the bill, while the other candidates sought his assurances he would sign it to make it easier for them to borrow money against the promise of later-certified matching funds.

The main delay at the White House was caused by the resignation of FEC Chairman Thomas B. Curtis and the difficulties encountered in seeking his replacement. Several of those who were approached expressed unwillingness to take a reduction in income or were uncertain about the future of the commission in view of its stormy relations with Congress. One potential appointee, William D. Ruckelshaus, who had resigned as deputy attorney general during the Watergate "Saturday night massacre" several years before, was reported willing only if he would be elected chairman of the FEC. A White House effort to determine the likelihood of his election brought charges of political pressure. Finally, William L. Springer, like Curtis a former Republican congressman, was nominated. Meanwhile, the Michigan and Maryland presidential primaries had passed.

The Senate promptly reconfirmed the reappointed commissioners, but President Ford argued against swearing them in — on grounds that partisan balance at the FEC should be maintained — until confirmation hearings were held and Springer was confirmed. Since the law requires that decisions be bipartisan, and commissioners occasionally are absent from votes anyway, the argument for partisan balance seemed to entail unnecessary delay, giving candidates less time to use matching money effectively in the Oregon, Idaho, Nevada, Arkansas, Kentucky, Tennessee, and subsequent primaries. On May 21, the Senate Rules Committee held an hour-long hearing and sent the Springer nomination to the Senate floor for quick confirmation. That afternoon the six commissioners were sworn in by the president. Immediately afterward, the renewed FEC certified $3.2 million due for various candidates and $1 million to the major-party national conventions. The FEC staff had continued to process submissions for matching funds while certifications were suspended, so the documentation was ready once the commission's authority was restored.

1976 Amendments

The 1976 Amendments did much more than reconstitute the commission. Through them, Congress sought to rectify some of the problems experienced in the operation of the 1974 Act. President Ford had pondered vetoing the Amendments but reluctantly signed the bill Congress produced.[16] One of his reservations concerned the constitutionality of provisions for a congressional vote of regulations. Accordingly, he instructed the attorney general to test the concept in the courts at his earliest convenience. (Shortly thereafter, former Attorney General Ramsey Clark and Public Citizen Litigation Group, a Ralph Nader organization, filed suit to test this question.)[17]

Other major provisions of the 1976 Act:

● Limited spending by presidential and vice presidential candidates to no more than $50,000 of their own or their family's money on their campaigns if they accepted public financing.

● Exempted from the law's spending limits payments by candidates or the national committees of political parties for legal and accounting services required to comply with the campaign law, but required that such payments be reported.

● Required presidential candidates who received federal matching subsidies and who withdrew from the prenomination election campaign to return leftover federal matching funds.

● Cut off federal campaign subsidies to presidential candidates who won less than 10 percent of the vote in two consecutive presidential primaries in which they ran.

● Established a procedure under which an individual who became ineligible for matching payments could have eligibility restored by a finding of the commission.

● Required that candidates and political committees keep records of contributions of $50 or more. (The 1974 Act required records of contributions of $10 or more.)

● Required that political committees and individuals making independent political expenditures of more than $100 that advocated the defeat or election of a candidate file a report with the election commission. It required the committee and individual to state, under penalty of perjury, that the expenditure was not made in collusion with a candidate.

● Restricted the fund-raising ability of corporate political action committees. Company committees could seek contributions only from stockholders and executive and administrative personnel and their families. Restricted union political action committees to soliciting contributions only from union members and their families. However, twice a year it permitted union and corporate political action committees to seek campaign contributions, by mail alone, from all other employees.

● Strengthened the penalty provisions of the Act and gave the commission greater power to enforce the law.

● Limited an individual to giving no more than $5,000 a year to a political action committee and $20,000 to the national committee of a political party (the 1974 law set a $1,000-per-election limit on individual contributions to a candidate and an aggregate contribution limit for individuals of $25,000 a year).

● Restricted the proliferation of membership organization, corporate, and union political action committees. All political action committees established by a company or an international union would be treated as a single committee for contribution purposes.

The rules were finally set. The commission had given its opinions and interpretations of the laws, the courts had given their mixed blessing, and the candidates had had a chance to iron out their internal problems as they coped with the rules. The enactment of the 1976 Amendments on May 11 gave all contestants and parties a complete set of rules under which they could participate in presidential politics. By this time, however, the prenomination campaigns were nearly past.

The Ford campaign had been relatively healthy financially throughout the period during which matching funds had been withheld, and Reagan charged that President Ford benefited from interest-free credit from the U.S. government, which billed the campaign later while other candidates needed advance money before their charter planes would fly. Ultimately the delays did not especially help Ford, nor did Humphrey become an active candidate. The effect on Ford's campaign was not certain because although Reagan went into debt during this time, he did win primaries in Texas, Indiana, Georgia, and Alabama, while Ford's cash advantage was slowly dissipated. On the Democratic side, the delays did not hurt Carter seriously, although he lost nine of the last 14 primaries in his winning campaign for the nomination; given his momentum, prompt matching funds could have helped him in these later primaries.

In the 1976 experience, the delays, however deliberate, first by Congress, then by the president, affected the candidates unfairly and suggested government manipulation in the operation of a program intended to be neutral. It was not a promising beginning for the first year of government funding. The campaigns of Reagan, Jackson, Udall, Wallace, and others reached crises due to lack of available money because all came to depend on government funding. Carter and Reagan were able to borrow money and their private fund raising continued to be successful. Some of the others found time in their schedules to phone potential donors and reduce staff or other expenses; in some cases, staff members went for weeks without pay. Reductions in spending by some candidates in some primary states certainly influenced the vote, and possibly the presidential nomination as well.

Wayne Hays

Congressman Wayne L. Hays of Ohio had so much power that he was informally dubbed the "Mayor of Capitol Hill." Although chairman of several panels, including the Joint Committee on Printing, the International Operations Subcommittee of the House International Relations Committee, and the Democratic Congressional Campaign Committee, his base of influence was the Committee on House Administration. Before Hays became chairman in 1971, the committee was considered of minor importance, but Hays was a shrewd politician who understood the potential importance of the committee, and he skillfully set about to increase its power and his own. In 1971 he oversaw passage of a resolution permitting the committee to bestow special allowances and benefits on House members without requiring any floor debate or votes. While the Republicans, including minority leader Gerald Ford, opposed the change on the grounds that it was likely to produce a scandal, the Democrats prevailed 233-167. One of the strongest supporters of the measure was Frank Thompson, Jr., D-N.J., later to become chairman of the House Administration Committee, who argued that it would save the House much time and prevent it from getting bogged down in housekeeping details.

The members of the House thus had evaded the necessity of having to vote publicly to increase their perquisites. Hays willingly faced criticism from newspaper reporters and editorialists as well as groups such as Common Cause. He had a safe district and provided excellent constituent services. His compensation lay in his new position of authority: "sooner or later, everyone in the House [had to] come to [him] for a favor."[18]

Hays' actions supported his colleagues. Under his direction the Administration Committee increased the size of House office staffs from 16 to 18, raised the funds for staff hiring by $23,000, increased from 18 to 26 the number of paid annual trips home members could take, and added on six trips a year for each member's staff. The travel allowance was doubled to $2,250 each year. Members could withdraw unused travel allowances in cash, and the committee allowed representatives to use House funds to produce two newsletters a year. Further, the reimbursement rates for auto mileage were raised and a provision for mobile offices (trailers) was approved.[19]

As Hays made possible these benefits for his colleagues, he increased the staff of his panel from 28 to 274 full-time employees, many of whom were affiliated with the House Information System, which oversaw a computer information retrieval system and an electronic voting system.

Opponent of Election Reform

In addition to its internal House responsibilities, the committee oversaw the federal election laws. During his six years as chairman of the committee, Hays was the most outspoken, bitter, diligent, and competent congressional opponent of the FEC and the FECA as well as of public financing of congressional elections.[20] He combined ability, dedication, and a key power base to block, limit, defeat, and alter various federal election proposals. In 1971 he delayed calling up the conference version of the FECA, thus allowing many incumbents additional time to collect campaign funds under the less restrictive law. He favored the 1971 act that required public disclosure but imposed limits only on expenditures for radio and television publicity, and he blamed passage of the 1974 Amendments on the hysteria of Watergate. Nevertheless, it was a law molded and shaped to Hays' satisfaction.

Hays fought bitterly to prevent the creation of the Federal Election Commission. The House version of the 1974 bill provided that the Secretary of the Senate and the Clerk of the House — individuals chosen by the members of Congress — would oversee campaign laws. The Senate version called for an independent commission, and this position prevailed in the conference. During the debate, Hays adamantly attacked public financing of congressional elections. He favored low expenditure limits and appointment by Congress of a majority of members of the FEC. Although the Senate bill included public financing of congressional elections, Hays prevailed in the conference committee and this provision was struck from the final version.

In November 1975 Hays sought to change the procedures under which FEC regulations went into effect. Instead of a congressional veto, Hays wanted to add to a pending postcard registration bill an amendment that would require both houses of Congress to approve affirmatively any commission regulation before it could be implemented. Congressional failure to act within 30 days would automatically kill the regulation. His proposal was not approved. During the same month, Hays won a lengthy battle with the commission concerning the disposition of the original copies of candidate spending and contributions reports. The commission wanted the candidates to file with it first and promised to send copies within two days to the House and Senate. Charging that such a plan violated the Constitution, Hays said that the Clerk and the Secretary should hold the originals. Realizing it could not win, the commission conceded.

During a January 1976 hearing on the commission's request for additional funds, Hays threatened to "cut the guts out of" its budget if it "continued to investigate anonymous complaints of campaign violations by members of Congress that occurred before the Commission was created." [21] Hays' outburst was touched off by reports of a commission investigation of the 1974 expenditures and contributions of Rep. Charlie Rose, D-N.C., a member of the Administration Committee. At the hearing, Rose appeared to be less agitated about the matter than Hays, who threatened to seek a court injunction against such activities if they continued. Hays wanted Thomas Curtis, chairman of the commission, to supply him with the names of the staffers who had undertaken the Rose audit. Curtis protested. Asked why he was so hostile to the commission, the Ohioan remarked:[22]

I'd be hostile to any commission in town if we knew what these commissions were doing. You see, we know what you're doing, because you're doing it to us.

When Hays' attitude changed, it changed suddenly. He recognized public support for the commission and the eagerness of the House Democratic leadership for passage of the bill. Then, too, the AFL-CIO leadership informed him of labor's desire to limit an FEC ruling that granted considerable freedom to corporate political action committees. Hays relented, and in February 1976, after the Supreme Court's ruling in *Buckley v. Valeo,* he announced his support for a bill that would reconstitute the commission with presidentially appointed members; give the commission major responsibility for regulating political campaigns; prohibit the agency from launching investigations based on anonymous complaints; require a majority vote of the full commission for initiation of investigations, civil proceedings, or referrals to the Justice Department; and require the commission to correct violations through a conciliation process.

In addition to his involvement in these and other controversial matters, Hays became a central character in a major shift of power within the House of Representatives when he was nearly ousted as head of the House Administration Committee. The rule of seniority had been nearly inviolate in the selection of House committee chairmen until a change came at the beginning of the 93rd Congress. Although three other committee chairmen were replaced, Hays withstood the assault on his power and retained his position.

Elizabeth Ray Affair

Yet the difficulties of this most powerful foe of the FEC did not end with his narrow victory in retaining his chairmanship. On May 23, 1976, *The Washington Post* printed a front-page story in its Sunday edition claiming that for "nearly two years . . . Wayne L. Hays . . . has kept a woman on his staff who says she is paid $14,000 a year in public money to serve as his mistress." [23] Elizabeth Ray claimed that she had few if any clerical skills, went to her office on Capitol Hill only once or twice a week, and had sexual relations with Hays once or twice a week in her apartment. At first Hays denied the allegations. Then, two days after the story had broken, he reversed himself. In a speech on the floor of the House of Representatives, he said that he had convinced Rep. Mendel J. Davis, D-S.C., a member of the House Administration Committee, to hire Miss Ray after she had returned from an unsuccessful search for work as an actress in Hollywood. Hays subsequently had rehired Ray himself. He admitted having had an affair with her at an earlier time, and claimed that Ray had taken her story to *The Washington Post* as a result of his engagement and subsequent second marriage. She had become hysterical, he said, and had threatened suicide and blackmail. Admitting that he had "committed a grievous error in not presenting all the facts," Hays asked his colleagues for mercy.[24]

Members of the House were taken aback by the Ray allegations and, after numerous investigations into the affair were begun, Hays' colleagues began exerting considerable pressure on him to resign his committee posts.

Ouster and Resignation

On June 3 Hays agreed to give up his campaign committee chairmanship but not his House Administration post. He wanted Thomas E. Morgan of Pennsylvania, chairman of the House International Relations Committee, to replace him as head of the campaign committee, but his request was not honored. On June 9 the campaign committee formally voted to oust Hays as its chairman and replaced him with James C. Corman, a California congressman.

One day later, Hays was found unconscious from an overdose of sleeping pills.[25] Because he was still hospitalized when the Democratic Caucus next met on the 16th, the Democrats voted to postpone for one week a vote on his removal from the chairmanship of the House Administration Committee. Hays resigned as chairman of that committee on June 18. Four days later the Steering Committee nominated Frank Thompson, second-ranking Democrat on the House Administration Committee, as his successor, and the caucus elected Thompson on June 23.

Hays' travail was not yet past. On August 13, he withdrew as the Democratic nominee in his congressional district, claiming harassment of himself and his family by *The Washington Post*. On the first of September, only slightly more than three months after the story's first appearance in the Post he resigned as a member of the House.[26]

In October, the Justice Department attorneys handling the case recommended that the government not seek to prosecute Hays on the grounds that the case would depend largely on Ray's testimony and the lawyers involved did not think she would be a credible witness. On December 8, 1976, the Justice Department formally terminated its investigation of Hays. The department refused to prosecute the former representative, reportedly because of a lack of evidence that Hays had violated any law.

Hays' political demise meant the elimination of the most powerful opponent of the Federal Election Commission and of public financing of congressional elections. Frank Thompson, his successor, supported both, and Common Cause,[27] long a bitter opponent of Hays, found the House Administration Committee somewhat less strongly opposed to some of its ideas.

FECA Impact on 1976 Election

During the 1976 campaigns, there was much discussion about the effects of the 1974 and 1976 Amendments to the FECA. After the election, the FEC commissioned a survey that systematically questioned those directly affected and regulated by the FECA — the candidates who ran for Senate and House offices in 1976 and their campaign operatives. The stated purpose of the study was to determine how the first application of the amended Act had affected participation in the political process.

Data for the study was collected from both in-house materials and outside groups. Internally, the agency determined which questions candidates and their campaign staffs most frequently asked through advisory opinion requests or over the 800 telephone lines. Because the FEC was concerned that the congressional candidate survey be undertaken in a bipartisan manner, both Hart Research Associates, a Democratic polling organization, and Decision Making Information, which polls for Republican candidates, were hired as a team. The cost of the survey was $57,000.

The survey was conducted between January 14, 1977, and February 26, 1977. Altogether 850 individuals were interviewed — 78 percent by mail and the remainder in person. The 850 represented a cross-section, randomly selected, of the 2,150 candidates who filed reports with the FEC and who appeared as primary or general election candidates in 1976 for either the House of Representatives or the Senate.[28]

In April 1977 the commission released the 240-page report that Hart Research Associates and Decision Making Information had prepared. The FEC's accompanying press release announced a "highly professional document . . . [that] provides important data in studying three major areas: (1) the strengths and weaknesses of the campaign finance laws; (2) recommendations for modifying or improving these laws; and (3) judging the performance and shaping the future priorities of the FEC." [29]

Important and useful as the report was, it had noteworthy limitations. The survey was designed to reflect the views only of the congressional candidates who filed with the FEC. It thus omitted the views of party committees, multi-candidate committees, presidential candidates, and the general public. The pollsters made a value judgment in combining into one category ("independents") those candidates who were not affiliated with any party ("true" independents), and minor-party candidates.

These may be two quite distinct groups with views that differ considerably, but this cannot be determined from the data presented. Moreover, for many of the tables, there are no breakdowns by party, house of Congress, incumbency, or winner/loser status.

Most importantly, because the commission sought an accurate sampling of all congressional candidates who filed with it in 1976, the survey largely reflects the views of low-spending nonincumbent candidates who lost either in the primary or in the general election. Fewer than three out of 10 candidates covered by the FECA were elected to federal office. While incumbents and general election winners do not always espouse views different from those of other candidates (and the tables sometimes report differences), it is important to note which candidates answered these questions. The data do not indicate how the members of the Congress feel about the FECA. And while it is indeed true that congressional candidates are the agency's most immediate constituency, the group of individuals sampled does not reflect accurately the most important elements of that constituency, the winners. Nevertheless, the report provides some valuable information about congressional attitudes toward the new laws.

Respondents were asked to select from a list of 20 basic campaign elements the three or four that most helped their campaign. The factor most important for all kinds of campaigns was the personal performance of the candidate, with the use of volunteers the second most often selected. Few respondents noted that elements related to the federal laws had helped their campaigns. From the opposite perspective, none of the 20 items on the list was picked by more than 7 percent of the respondents as being the least helpful. Compliance with federal laws was selected fairly frequently as an element least helpful to campaigns, but within the context of the total campaign, "the FECA did not appear to be a dominant negative factor in the view of most respondents." [30]

When asked what advantages their opponents had, the respondents most frequently checked relations with party organizations and the ability to raise campaign funds. Virtually no respondents indicated that the FECA or reporting requirements had given their opponents an advantage. Despite the fact that many respondents felt that the FECA brought important changes to the campaign process, a greater number found other changes to be more significant. Of the external forces most influencing their campaigns, the candidates thought most important the fact that the " 'voters were turned off to politics due to cynicism toward government.' " [31]

Table 2-1

FEC Survey: Did the 1976 Federal Election Campaign Act improve or hinder the following activities?

	Improved More Than Hindered	Hindered More Than Improved	Did not Affect	Don't Know
	%	%	%	%
Public disclosure	50	15	19	16
Registration drives	10	12	46	32
The role of the political action committees (PACs)	19	30	22	29
Get-out-the-vote drives	9	15	48	28
The role of political parties	15	30	32	23
Volunteer activity	5	16	63	6
The role of minor party candidates	8	30	28	34
The role of independent candidates	7	27	29	37
Getting more candidates to run	6	31	31	32
Getting the campaign's message across to the voters	5	29	48	18
Fund raising	7	52	25	16
Outside independent activity	3	29	36	32

Note: Percentages sum to 100 by rows.

SOURCE: A Study of the Impact of the Federal Election Campaign Act on the 1976 Election, p. 58.

Respondents were presented with a list of 12 campaign activities and were asked how the FECA had affected each (Table 2-1). In general, more respondents felt the FECA hindered these activities than thought it improved them, but for 10 of the 12 activities, a majority either said the FECA did not affect the activity, or declined to state an opinion. For the two activities where a majority felt the FECA had an effect, this effect was viewed in one case as an improvement and in the other as a hindrance. By a 50 percent to 15 percent margin, respondents said that public disclosure had been improved more than hindered by the FECA. And by a 52 percent to 7 percent margin, respondents said that fund raising had been hindered rather than improved by the FECA. A majority or a near majority of almost every subgroup of candidates agreed that the FECA had improved matters of disclosure, except that 51 percent of independents either said it had had no effect or declined to respond. Responses to the fund-raising question reflected a notable partisan split. Forty-six percent of the Democrats said that the FECA hindered more than it improved fund raising, and fully 67 percent of the Republicans agreed. Despite these positions, many Democrats agreed with the Republicans and not all GOP candidates felt that the Act hurt their fund-raising drives. For many of the 12 activities listed, majorities said that the FECA had no effect or that they could not identify an effect. Significant minorities did claim that the roles of political parties and political action committees had been harmed by the law. Nearly one-third of the respondents asserted that the FECA had hindered outside independent activity and reaching the voters.[32]

In general, respondents seemed more likely to perceive the Act's negative effects when the question focused closely on the Act itself than when it referred to exogenous conditions or when the FECA was mentioned in the context of a variety of campaign activities and experiences. The authors conclude that it is impossible to give a single or simple answer to the query: What was the effect of the FECA on congressional campaigns in 1976? Although the Act was sometimes mentioned as a negative factor, other things were mentioned more frequently.

A majority of the respondents said that fund raising had been difficult; only 12 percent said that they had no problems in this area. Central to a candidate's success or failure in fund raising was the perception that he was either a sure winner or a loser, particularly the latter. Economic conditions were also cited. Of the FECA regulations only the limitation on individual contributions was listed as an important factor harming fund raising. Candidates in open-seat contests — rather than incumbents or challengers — were most likely to see contribution limits as creating fund-raising problems. Republicans were more likely than Democrats to see difficulties stemming from federal limitations on campaign financing, with the single exception of limitations on political action committee contributions. While those who raised few funds rarely cited the campaign limitations as a problem, they were the single most important factor for campaigns spending more than $100,000.

Several other considerations relating to the laws that were cited as making fund raising very or fairly difficult included: limitations on political action committee distributions, requirements of public disclosure, limitations on in-kind services, the campaign's concern about the legality of contributions, and the contributors' concern about the legality of contributions (Table 2-2). Although the candidates acknowledged that the FECA had reduced the influence of big contributors, they also felt that their campaigns had to spend too much time raising money, and that the FECA did little to encourage more people to contribute to campaigns.

When the FECA was enacted, some commentators claimed that its disclosure provisions would make the source of funds an issue in some campaigns. To judge from candidates' responses, this did not occur often. Seven percent said that a source of funds for their own campaigns had become a major issue and 11 percent said that it had become a

Table 2-2
FEC Survey: How difficult did each factor below make fund raising for your campaign?

	Very Difficult	Fairly Difficult	Slightly Difficult	No Problem	Not Relevant	No Answer
	%	%	%	%	%	%
The candidate's being considered either a certain loser or a certain winner	34	16	16	16	13	5
People turned off by politics because of scandals	17	22	26	18	11	6
The nation's economic condition	14	24	27	14	13	8
Limitations on individual contributions	15	14	18	32	13	8
Money raised by presidential candidates during primaries	10	10	15	26	30	9
Limitations on political action committee (PAC) contributions (includes any labor, business, or special interest committee)	9	11	16	38	18	8
Requirements of public disclosure	9	8	15	47	14	7
Limitations on in-kind services	8	9	14	42	17	10
Campaign's concern about the legality of contributions	7	10	19	43	13	8
Contributor's concern about the legality of contributions	8	8	20	43	13	8

Note: Percentages sum to 100 by rows.

SOURCE: A Study of the Impact of the Federal Election Campaign Act on the 1976 Election, p. 80.

minor issue. Disclosure was more likely to be an issue in expensive efforts than in inexpensive efforts and candidates were more likely to cite their opponent's source of funds as a campaign issue. In about one-third of the campaigns there was reluctance on the part of at least one individual or group to contribute because of disclosure, and about one-sixth (17 percent) of all campaigns had sufficient problems with these individuals to impair their fund-raising efforts. In both cases, Republicans and those in seriously contested races were most likely to find contributors deterred.[33]

Since there was no direct way of determining how limitations imposed by the FECA on campaign spending altered campaign practices, the authors of the report sought an answer by asking respondents how an additional 20 percent in funds would have affected their campaigns. Thirty percent said that the extra amount would have made much difference, while 23 percent said it would have made no difference at all. The main break occurred between incumbents and nonincumbents: No more than 12 percent of incumbents said an additional 20 percent of funds would have made a great difference, while 36 percent of nonincumbents said that the extra money would have made a great difference. A majority of incumbents, but fewer than one out of six nonincumbents, said that the additional funds would have made no difference at all. If the candidates had had the additional funds, most of the money "would have been spent on media, and within this category, primarily though not entirely on television advertising." [34]

Independent expenditures were an important though little-discussed topic. Ten percent of the respondents said they had learned of independent expenditures made on behalf of their campaigns, 15 percent said they had learned of such expenditures made on behalf of the opposition, and 7 percent said they had learned of independent expenditures made on behalf of both. Two-thirds of the respondents said they had learned of no such expenditures made in their races. The data indicate that Republicans had the benefit of independent expenditures in more cases than Democrats. In general, primary and general election losers stressed the significance of independent expenditures while general election winners rated them less highly.

In-kind contributions were much more common than independent expenditures, the most common form being literature distribution (38 percent of all campaigns). Phone banks, reported by 26 percent of all campaigns, were next in importance and were especially common among Democrats and in seriously contested campaigns. Most campaigns placed volunteers in key positions. Seventy-five percent of the treasurers, 52 percent of the accountants, and 45 percent of the campaign managers volunteered their time to the races covered by this study.

Table 2-3
FEC Survey: The role of the political party was substantially strengthened by the Act.

	Strongly Agree	Partially Agree	Neutral	Partially Disagree	Strongly Disagree	No Answer
	%	%	%	%	%	%
Aggregate	12	15	34	17	17	5
Party affiliation						
Democrat	11	15	41	17	12	3
Republican	9	15	29	19	22	6
Independent	26	11	26	5	23	8
Overall reaction to FECA						
Helped	11	17	40	19	13	1
No difference	11	17	40	14	13	4
Hurt	16	12	27	17	25	3
Outcome of primary						
Winner	5	16	36	20	17	5
Loser	17	14	36	12	15	6
Outcome of general						
Winner	6	16	31	26	15	6
Loser	13	14	34	13	22	4
Office sought						
Senate	13	13	27	25	21	1
House	12	15	36	16	16	5
Campaign spending						
Under $15,000	18	15	35	9	17	7
$15,000-$50,000	11	15	36	18	17	2
$50,000-$100,000	6	13	39	22	17	3
$100,000 plus	8	16	29	26	18	3

SOURCE: A Study of the Impact of the Federal Election Campaign Act on the 1976 Election, p. 111.

When hired staff or paid consultants were used, they were most often campaign managers. The wealthier the campaign, the more likely it was to have a paid campaign manager. A majority of the respondents agreed that the act favored the candidate able to create a large volunteer force.

As Table 2-3 shows, the candidates were divided in their assessments of the Act's impact on political parties. One-third agreed that the Act strengthened parties, one-third disagreed, and one-third were neutral. A majority thought that independent and minor-party candidates labored under a bigger disadvantage in 1976 than in previous elections. Respondents generally felt that the Act favored candidates who could raise money from PACs and other special interest groups.[35]

To determine the effect of the FECA on congressional-presidential campaign relationships, the survey asked respondents whether the Act seemed to create an unnecessary barrier between congressional and presidential campaigns. A plurality gave a neutral response while one-

Table 2-4
FEC Survey: The Act increased the advantage an incumbent already
has in running for re-election.

	Strongly Agree	Partially Agree	Neutral	Partially Disagree	Strongly Disagree	No Answer
	%	%	%	%	%	%
Aggregate	46	26	13	7	5	3
Party affiliation						
Democrat	36	29	15	10	7	3
Republican	55	23	10	5	3	4
Independent	62	21	10	2	3	2
Position in primary						
Incumbent	14	35	16	16	14	5
Challenger	63	15	10	7	5	3
Open seat	52	27	12	5	2	3
Position in general						
Incumbent	15	35	16	17	12	5
Challenger	64	19	8	4	3	2
Open seat	43	33	17	3	2	3
Outcome of primary						
Winner	37	31	11	9	8	4
Loser	55	22	12	4	3	4
Outcome of general						
Winner	19	35	27	13	10	5
Loser	62	20	9	4	3	2
Office sought						
Senate	45	26	6	12	9	2
House	46	26	13	6	5	3
Campaign spending 1976						
Under $15,000	53	23	11	5	4	4
$15,000-$50,000	52	22	15	7	3	2
$50,000-$100,000	32	33	14	10	8	3
$100,000 plus	38	32	12	8	8	3
Times run for federal office						
First time	55	25	11	4	3	3
More than once	33	27	16	11	9	4

SOURCE: A Study of the Impact of the Federal Election Campaign Act on the 1976
Election, p. 119.

third agreed and one-fifth disagreed. There were no partisan differences
in the responses to this issue.[36]

Most of those interviewed — nearly two-thirds of the Democrats
and eight out of 10 independents and Republicans — agreed that the Act
increased the advantages for incumbents. Not only were challengers and
losers more likely than other subgroups to agree strongly with this
statement, a strong majority of the incumbents also concurred. Table 2-
4 describes the candidates' responses in detail. Furthermore, a majority
of candidates rejected the notion that the Act encouraged individuals to
run for office by putting all candidates on a more equal footing. The

respondents clearly did not perceive the FECA as a political equalizer, but rather as a law that benefited incumbent congressmen.

When asked how their campaigns learned about the FECA, 62 percent of those surveyed mentioned the FEC as a source of information. Although a majority of respondents identified two or more sources of information, the commission was identified twice as often as press reports or media (the next most frequently mentioned source). The commission's information received the highest ratings in terms of helpfulness. FEC pamphlets and handbooks were given the highest overall rating, while the campaign representatives also gave the agency's telephone hotline and newsletter high marks. In contrast, the FEC-sponsored seminars were relied on by less than a majority of the respondents. Those who did partake in them gave these meetings a mixed evaluation. Of the non-FEC sources used to keep up with the law, newspaper accounts were most frequently mentioned, but a large majority of those using newspaper accounts thought them of little or no value to the campaign. In general, the candidates indicated that keeping abreast of changes in the law was not an easy task.

Opinions regarding the difficulty of working with the FECA were rather mixed. Two of 10 campaign representatives noted extreme difficulty, while three of 10 mentioned little or no difficulty. In general, the greatest difficulties were experienced by independent and third-party candidates, those whose campaigns were underfinanced, losers, and those generally dissatisfied with their campaigns. Incumbents and candidates with well-financed campaigns said they had few difficulties. When the responses to this question are cross-tabulated with the candidate's overall evaluation of the FECA, the results show that the respondents who felt that the FECA basically helped the campaign process also perceived no difficulty in working with the Act, whereas those who believed the FECA basically hurt the campaign process also perceived great difficulty in working with the Act. Nearly every respondent mentioned at least one specific area of difficulty experienced in connection with the Act, and the keeping of records and filing of reports came highest on the list.

Nearly three out of five of those questioned agreed that the Act had helped reduce illegal campaign activity. Democrats were most likely to agree with this statement and independents most likely to disagree. As could be expected, general attitudes toward the Act correlated positively with reponses to this issue. Most of those who thought the Act had helped the campaign process felt that it had curbed illegal activities, while most of those who felt it had harmed campaigning disagreed.

Nearly all of the campaigns surveyed had contacted the FEC during the campaign, usually by telephone. Calls were most frequently made to

Table 2-5
FEC Survey: In what ways do you feel the 1976 Federal Election
Campaign Act helped to improve the political campaign process? [a]

	First Mention	Second Mention	Total
	%	%	%
Required public disclosure of contributions	13	3	16
Required record of contributions and expenditures	5	2	7
Limited contributions of special interest	7	3	10
Encouraged honesty, made campaigns more open	7	2	9
Limited the amount of individual contributions	4	1	5
Regulated campaign expenditures	1	—	1
Didn't improve the political process	36	1	37
Too much red tape	1	—	1

All other mentions constituted less than a 1 percent mention.

[a] Uncollapsed version: first and second mentions.

Note: Multiple responses allowed. Percentages represent share of total respondents giving each response.

SOURCE: A Study of the Impact of the Federal Election Campaign Act on the 1976 Election, p. 143.

request clarification of reporting procedures and forms. While most campaigns found the reporting and record-keeping requirements difficult to meet, the smaller campaigns of young and first-time candidates apparently required the most assistance in complying with these portions of the Act. The commission's responses to candidates' queries received a mixed rating. One out of three thought the commission had been of great help; one-fifth thought it was of little or no help; and 43 percent said their contact had been of some help. Among all the subgroups, however, the FEC was rated positively for helpfulness.[37]

In general, the FECA was not regarded as a source of particular frustration when it was viewed in the context of the campaign as a whole. It received very mixed ratings, however, when it was related to specific aspects of the campaign. Asked how the Act improved the campaign process, 37 percent felt that it offered no improvement (Table 2-5). Sixteen percent noted disclosure provisions as the single most helpful influence on the political process. Fully one-third of the independents felt that the law had not helped, and Republicans were more likely than Democrats to agree. Not surprisingly, incumbents tended to see more good in the Act than did either their challengers or those candidates running in open seat contests.[38]

Table 2-6

FEC Survey: In what ways do you feel the 1976 Federal Election Campaign Act hurt the political campaign process? [a]

	First Mention	Second Mention	Total
	%	%	%
Too many reports	21	3	24
Fund raising more difficult	9	2	11
Regulations not clear	8	3	11
Gives incumbent an advantage	5	2	7
Favors the wealthy candidate	4	1	5
Discourages potential candidates	4	1	5
Disadvantage to lesser financed candidate	3	2	5
Hampered the campaign effort	3	3	6
Discouraged grass-roots activities	3	2	5
False honesty	2	2	4
Didn't control special interest groups	2	1	3
Contributors didn't want to be identified	2	1	3
Disclosure requirement amount set too low	1	1	2
Opposed to federal financing of campaigns	1	1	2
All other negative responses	5	3	8
General — positive	16	—	16
No answer	11	72	—

[a] Uncollapsed version: first and second mentions.

Note: Percentage base equals 850 interviews.

SOURCE: A Study of the Impact of the Federal Election Campaign Act on the 1976 Election, p. 149.

The campaign managers and the candidates found reporting requirements the most onerous aspect of the Act (Table 2-6). Almost one-fourth of the respondents (24 percent) listed red tape, paperwork, and reports as the aspects of the FECA most damaging to the campaign process.[39] More than one in 10 complained that the Act made fund raising more difficult, while one in 14 declared that it gave incumbents an unfair advantage. As might be expected, senatorial candidates were more sensitive to the Act's restriction of contributions than were House candidates. Candidates challenging incumbents were likely to argue that the Act benefited incumbents. Overall the groups tended to agree that the disclosure provisions, contribution limits, restrictions on special interest groups, and the openness that the Act encouraged were its most helpful aspects. The independents were the most antagonistic group, opposing on the average seven out of 10 aspects of the campaign regulations.[40]

Summary of Evaluation

Below is a brief summary of the evaluation by different groups of various provisions in the law. Public disclosure was viewed favorably by all groups, but most particularly by winners, high-spending candidates, and incumbents. PAC contribution limits were backed more frequently by winners than by losers; independents were hostile. No subgroup strongly supported restriction of in-kind services. Individual contribution limits were opposed most by independents and big campaign spenders. Fund-raising restrictions were opposed most by losing candidates, Republicans, and big spenders. All groups rated the use of volunteers positively. Independents, losers, and candidates challenging incumbents were those least happy with the role of political parties and reporting requirements.

Overall, the verdict on the FECA was mixed: 36 percent said that the Act had basically helped the campaign process, 36 percent felt it had basically hurt the campaign process, 24 percent identified little effect, and 4 percent gave no answer. Among subgroups of respondents, Republicans were inclined to think it basically hurt rather than helped; Democrats, who were not quite so negatively impressed by the FECA, felt the opposite way; and 61 percent of independents — the subgroup responding most negatively — said the Act had hurt the process. Pluralities of incumbents, election winners, and those with campaign budgets exceeding $50,000 said that the Act had basically helped; pluralities of challengers, candidates in open seats, and those with campaign budgets below $15,000 said it had basically hurt. A majority of Senate candidates believed the Act had helped. Incumbents and nonincumbents were significantly divided. By a 42 percent to 25 percent margin incumbents found the FECA basically helpful; challengers found it basically harmful by a 46 percent to 32 percent margin. Candidates in open seats were closely divided, with 40 percent saying the Act basically hurt and 37 percent saying it had helped.

Very few respondents were satisfied with the Act and only 5 percent believed it should be kept in its existing form. About one-third (35 percent) wanted slight modifications, 36 percent wanted major modifications; and 18 percent wanted abolishment of the FECA with a return to the pre-1971 law. Those who had been most positive about the Act overall were most inclined to favor only slight revisions. The most negative group were the independents, 51 percent of whom favored a return to the pre-1971 law and another 26 percent of whom favored major revisions.[41] In sum there was no single consensus about the Act or what should be done about it, although there was general agreement among all but a handful of those regulated by the FECA that changes of some kind should be made in the law.

In assessing the survey's conclusions we should remember that seven of 10 candidates did not win the office they sought, and about six of 10 did not even come close to winning office. Further, many of the respondents were electoral losers who spent relatively little money on their election bids. The candidates who fared best were the incumbents, over 90 percent of whom won reelection; in contrast, more than 90 percent of those who were not incumbents lost.

Although most candidates were satisfied with their campaigns, they did express some concerns about them. Several aspects of the FECA were criticized, particulary its paperwork requirements. Although the law complicated their elections, the candidates on the whole did not consider it a major problem. Public disclosure was the provision in the law they most enthusiastically supported. They felt that the new law harmed their fund-raising efforts, but it was not the major cause of their very real difficulties in this area.

The candidates were sharply divided over the effectiveness of the FECA. Nearly all of them felt that the law should be revised but they could reach no consensus about specific proposals.

The survey is revealing in several general ways. Its data offer a picture of political campaigns considerably at variance with the concern about runaway spending that motivated the 1974 Amendments. Although some serious contenders had large budgets, many of the campaigns described by the report were frugal, homespun operations. It is possible that the FECA's provisions limiting contributions decreased the amount of money spent in congressional campaigns in 1976 as compared with the amount spent in previous election years; the data in the survey do not make it possible to test such a hypothesis, however. The survey does indicate that incumbents have a dramatic advantage over their opponents; and the FECA may well have increased the incumbents' advantages. The respondents — both incumbents and challengers — certainly thought so, and if they are (as the commission argued) the real experts on the FECA and its impact, then perhaps Congress should be concerned about increasing the level of competition for congressional seats rather than passing more laws.

Footnotes

[1] For background and implementation, see Herbert E. Alexander, *Financing the 1972 Election* (Lexington, Mass.: D.C. Heath and Co., 1976), pp. 9-38, 353-365.

[2] Public Law 92-225, 86 stat. 3, 2 U.S.C. 431 *et seq.* See Appendix A, p. 801.

[3] Subtitle H of the Internal Revenue Code of 1954, Public Law 92-178, 85 Stat. 562, 26 U.S.C. Sections 9001 *et seq.* See Appendix B, p. 805.

[4] Public Law 93-443, 88 Stat. 1263 (codified in several titles of U.S.C.). See Appendix C, p. 807.

[5] John Herbers, "Bill to Reform Campaign Funds Signed by Ford Despite Doubts," *The New York Times,* October 16, 1974.

[6] 424 U.S. 1 (1976).

[7] Public Law 94-283, 90 Stat. 475 (codified in several titles of U.S.C.). See Appendix D, p. 811.

[8] *Buckley v. Valeo,* 424 U.S. 1 (1976).

[9] John P. MacKenzie, "U.S. Questions Election Law," *The Washington Post,* May 24, 1975; John P. MacKenzie, "Campaign Act Defense Lack Held a Rarity," *The Washington Post,* May 29, 1975; Simon Lazarus, "A Duty to Defend the Law," *The Washington Post,* July 5, 1975.

[10] *The Washington Post,* June 23, 1975.

[11] See below, Ch. 9, "Independent Expenditures," pp. 515-520.

[12] *Buckley v. Valeo,* 424 U.S. 1 at 19.

[13] *Buckley v. Valeo,* 425 U.S. 946.

[14] *Buckley v. Valeo,* 75-1061 (D.C. Cir., April 28, 1976).

[15] Federal Election Campaign Act Amendments of 1976, *Conference Report,* Report No. 94-1057, U.S. House of Representatives, 94th Cong., 2d Sess.

[16] See Statement by the President, White House Press Release, May 11, 1976.

[17] *Clark v. Valeo, et. al.,* Civil Action No. 76-1227. The suit sought to have the one-house veto provisions of the FECA declared unconstitutional. The U.S. Court of Appeals dismissed the case on the grounds that it did not present a ripe case or controversy within the meaning of that phrase in Article III of the U.S. Constitution. Clark appealed to the U.S. Supreme Court. On April 8, 1977, the commission filed a motion with the Court asking it to dismiss the motion on the following grounds: 1) Clark sought appeal on a matter of jurisdiction whereas the FECA only allows appeals on constitutional questions; 2) there was no record evidence pertaining to a congressional veto of FEC regulations; 3) none of the issues has been reviewed by a lower court; and 4) the issues involved deal with "sensitive questions relating to the separation of legislative and executive powers." On June 6, 1977, the Supreme Court affirmed the Court of Appeals' decision dismissing the suit. The Department of Justice joined the suit at the Court of Appeals stage, urging that the veto be declared unconstitutional. *Clark v. Kimmitt,* No. 76-1105.

[18] Mike Feinsilber, "House Ogre Transformed to Red Robin," *Philadelphia Bulletin,* March 14, 1976.

[19] Hays defended his actions in supporting increases in congressional services. He claimed that the news accounts were distorted. "The average reader is led to believe that a member of Congress has a vast wealth of material assets. Yet, there are members of Congress who are forced to pay communication, travel and office expenses from their own pockets because the allowance system is inadequate for their needs."

"The entire House of Representatives runs on an annual budget that is just slightly more than $233 million . . . it costs a mere $1.25 per man, woman and child in this country to run the House of Representatives for a year." Wayne Hays, "Bearing the Costs of Government," *The Washington Post,* July 19, 1975.

[20] Hays was attacked by Common Cause and others for his conflict of interest as "chairman of the House Administration Committee, which writes the election finance laws, and as chairman of the Democratic Congressional Campaign Committee, which raises and spends the funds to keep Democratic Congressmen in office." David S. Broder, "Hays' Abuse of Power," *The Washington Post,* June 16, 1976. For accounts of Hays' role in the 1971 FECA and the 1974 Amendments, see Herbert E. Alexander, *Money in Politics* (Washington, D.C.: Public Affairs Press, 1972) Chs. 14 & 17; and Alexander, *Financing the 1972 Election* (Lexington, Mass.: D. C. Heath & Co., 1976), pp. 9-22, 591, 596.

[21] Warren Weaver, Jr., "Rep. Hays Chides Election Agency," *The New York Times,* January 28, 1976.

[22] Stephen Isaacs, "Hays Mounts New Attack on Election Commission," *The Washington Post,* January 28, 1976.

[23] Marion Clark and Rudy Maxa, "Closed-Session Romance on the Hill," *The Washington Post,* May 23, 1976.

[24] Lucinda Franks, "Hays, In Reversal, Admits Affair with Staff Member," *The New*

York Times, May 26, 1976; Mary Russell, "Hays to Retire; Cites Health, 'Harassment'," *The Washington Post,* August 14, 1976.

[25] Hays claimed that he mistakenly had taken an overdose of the pills and that he had not attempted suicide.

[26] Between early June, when it began to investigate the Ray allegations, and early September, when Hays resigned from the House, the ethics committee played an important role in bringing about Hays' resignation. During those three months Hays battled with the committee to circumvent his resignation, terminate its investigation, and halt public hearings into his conduct. On August 30, the ethics committee voted 11-1 to hold open public hearings on the charges starting September 16. If Hays did not resign, effective immediately, the committee planned to issue subpoenas for Ray and others involved in the investigation, the hearings to take place as scheduled, whether or not Hays remained a member of Congress. Hays was thus faced with the prospect of a public confrontation with Ray and further humiliation. Richard D. Lyons, "Hays Tried for 2 Months to End Inquiry in House," *The New York Times,* September 3, 1976.

[27] For an account of Hays' relationship with Common Cause, see Alexander, *Financing the 1972 Election,* pp. 596-598.

[28] To ensure statistical reliability, it was necessary to sample about 50 percent of the 2,150 candidates who filed with the FEC and who ran in a congressional election. The universe for this survey was stratified by several factors — Senate/House campaigns, geographic regions, primary/general campaigns, and party affiliation. Overall recovery from the total sample was 64 percent (850 completed interviews) and included 184 personal interviews and 666 completed mail questionnaires. The recovered sample closely paralleled the distribution of the universe along the key stratification factors, and differences between this sample and the universe were found to be minimal.

The target respondent for this study was the person with the most information about the political impact of the FECA on campaign activity — in most cases the campaign manager or the candidate. A letter asked the recipient to respond as promptly as possible and guaranteed anonymity. Two weeks after the initial mailing, a follow-up contact was made if the questionnaire had not yet been returned. Personal interviews were held with major-party candidates for the Senate (64) and randomly selected incumbent representatives (43). In addition, personal interviews were held with people who had not returned their mail questionnaire. Although the nonrespondents differed from the respondents in terms of party affiliation and amount of money spent during the campaign, their responses to the attitudinal questions showed few differences. Federal Election Commission, *A Study of the Impact of the Federal Election Campaign Act on the 1976 Elections* (Washington, D.C., 1977), pp. 31, 168, 169, 170, 171, 172, 174.

[29] Federal Election Commission, "FEC Releases Survey on Impact of Election Law on 1976 Campaign," Press Release, April 28, 1977, pp. 1, 2.

[30] Federal Election Commission, *A Study of the Impact of the Federal Election Campaign Act on the 1976 Elections* (Washington, D.C., 1977), p. 42.

[31] Ibid., p. 55.

[32] Ibid., pp. 57-63.

[33] Ibid., pp. 84-92.

[34] Ibid., p. 92.

[35] Ibid., pp. 94-116.

[36] Ibid., pp. 116, 117.

[37] Ibid., pp. 121-141.

[38] Ibid., p. 146.

[39] Ibid., p. 148. These findings are paralleled by the results of a survey conducted by Sen. Richard Stone, D-Fla., of 740 general election candidates of whom approximately 40 percent responded. Stone quoted from some of the responses:

[We] received several pounds of materials and regulations even though our entire expenses were approximately $30....

Our small party has had to devote considerable resources to record-keeping and filing reports, efforts which certainly could not be matched by newer groupings of citizens just becoming interested in the electoral process....

Even the major-party candidates were not free from worry; one such candidate, who lost a race for a Senate seat, reported spending almost $30,000 to comply with the law.

To help alleviate this problem, Stone submitted an amendment to the FECA that "would authorize the Federal Election Commission to waive the reporting requirements for candidates who certify that they do not anticipate expending or receiving in excess of $1,000 on their election campaign." Richard Stone, "Federal Election Campaign Act Amendments-S. 1344," *Congressional Record,* May 24, 1977, S8536.

[40] Ibid., pp. 152-155.

[41] Ibid., pp. 157-161.

3 The FEC

While recognizing the need for an evenhanded approach at a time of widespread cynicism about the electoral process, the FEC nevertheless has had a stormy beginning. As a result of the *Buckley v. Valeo* decision, the manner of appointment of members of the commission had to be changed. The FEC drew fire within months of its founding from certain members of Congress who were not pleased with the commission's early operations or its initial decisions. The first two regulations the FEC wrote were rejected by Congress.[1]

The congressional attacks on the proposed regulations were evidence of the particular problems built into the structure and functioning of the agency. The original method of appointment of its members, with four appointed by the legislative branch, was designed to ensure congressional dominance. Of the six original appointees, four were former members of the House of Representatives, tending to reinforce the congressional influence. This eased their confirmation by a majority of both houses, in itself an unusual procedure. Following the *Buckley* decision, the procedure was changed by Congress in the 1976 Amendments to conform to the usual practice of presidential nomination and senatorial confirmation.

Because the FEC has the power to regulate congressional campaigns, the potential conflict between the new commissioners' experience and their friendships on Capitol Hill and their need for impartial handling of congressional elections was apparent. To achieve credibility as an independent agency, there was a clear need to establish the FEC's independence from the Congress it was in part established to regulate. Some members of Congress, it turned out, did not want the FEC to be very independent where congressional elections were concerned. The proposed regulations, advisory opinions, and procedures touched the daily lives of members, whether campaigning or not, and some were found objectionable and others considered outside the commission's province.

Another problem was that regulations written by the FEC had to be submitted to Congress along with an explanation and justification. If neither the Senate nor the House disapproved by a formal vote within 30 legislative days the commission could prescribe such regulation, and it would have the force of law.

Both the method of partial congressional appointment and the review of its regulations were unusual and tended to threaten the FEC's independence. Of course, FEC funds are appropriated by Congress, another delicate point. Congress has retaliated or moved against the commission in every imaginable way in its brief history: by real and threatened budget cuts, by restricting its statutory power, by curtailing its discretionary power, by urging certain staff appointments, by threats and by persuasion.

To flesh out and clarify various aspects of the FECA, the commission sent its first proposed regulations to Congress in December 1975 and January 1976. Because the Supreme Court's decision in *Buckley* suspended the commission's rulemaking authority, these proposed regulations could not be implemented. The FEC began redrafting portions of the original regulations to conform to the Court decision, and as the shape of the 1976 Amendments seemed clear, to incorporate them into the regulations.

Congressional Expense Accounts. In its initial proposed regulation, on congressional expense funds, the FEC, whether intentionally or not, served to alert Congress to the power the new agency could claim and to how that power might be perceived by some members to be directed at times against them or against traditional practices they do not want discontinued. This first regulation was submitted to Congress in July 1975 and dealt with the so-called "office slush funds" maintained by some members. It required that they be disclosed at regular intervals and made them subject to the then-new limitations on political contributions and expenditures.

The funds in question, formally known as "constituent service funds," usually come from contributions made outside the campaign framework. They are used to supplement funds provided by the government to pay for day-to-day operations of congressional offices. These "office funds" are used for such items as newsletters, travel back home, and office expenses beyond those authorized by Congress. Not enough money is provided by the government to meet the needs some members perceive, so they pay for them out of their own pockets, if personally able, or by raising special funds. There is a legitimate question whether provisions for so-called representational expenses are sufficient in some cases, and the wave of congressional reform in the 95th Congress has been sweetened by some additional funds and perquisites.

In its proposed regulation, the FEC held that funds raised independently of those authorized "should be viewed as political and not legislative funds,"[2] requiring disclosure in quarterly campaign finance reports. Even more controversial was the requirement that contributions and spending from the accounts be treated as campaign funds under the limitations set by law for the next election of the member maintaining the fund.

Congressional reaction was immediate and included threats to veto the ruling. The Senate subsequently did veto the proposed regulation, by a one-vote margin (48-47), with many senators reluctant to appear to be voting in favor of "slush funds." Apparently some senators voted with the FEC only because they knew their votes were not needed to defeat the measure. None of the 1976 presidential contenders then in the Senate voted against the FEC regulation.

A compromise proposal, which would treat the funds as political only in election years and also would include comparable funds used by congressional challengers as well as by the president and vice president, was then worked out with Senate leaders. It ran into sharp opposition, however, in the House Administration Committee headed by Wayne Hays of Ohio. The Supreme Court ruling that expenditure limits were unconstitutional effectively removed that problem from the proposed regulation and caused its consideration to be suspended until the FEC was reconstituted.

Even after the reconstitution, the fourth draft of the regulation was changed under pressure from some members of Congress. At congressional insistence, the FEC deleted from the proposed regulations a $100 limit on cash contributions. Since the election law set that limit on cash campaign contributions, the change put congressional office funding on a different basis. Similarly, the FEC retreated on its position that office account reports should be filed as attachments to campaign fund reports. Legislators objected that to do so would give the appearance that these funds represented campaign money, and they insisted on maintaining a distinction. The expense account reports were required once each year — on July 31 — but in election years quarterly reports were required.

The proposed regulation was prepared in response to a large number of requests from members of Congress asking whether their office accounts were subject to the limitations in the law. It proved to be an unfortunate tactic for the FEC to seek to regulate a congressional custom before writing basic regulations dealing with disclosure, limitations, and government funding that make up the substance of the law. The effort was bound to cause controversy. Yet the FEC was responding to many requests for advisory opinions on many subjects, some of them marginal, but some from members of Congress who were persistent in seeking quick answers. Basic regulations were given lesser priority.

Point of Entry. Members of Congress also attacked the second proposed FEC regulation, which was more basic to the law than the office fund regulation. The proposed point-of-entry regulation required that originals of all candidate and political committee fund reports be filed first with the FEC; then the FEC would provide microfilm copies of the reports to the Secretary of the Senate and the Clerk of the House within two working days. Such a system would have provided more effective disclosure under efficient procedures, but it was rejected by the House. Under the 1971 law there were three supervisory officers, each independent of the other. The 1974 Amendments failed to specify clearly the role of the Secretary and the Clerk in relation to the FEC, but the law seemed to require an arrangement whereby candidates for the Senate and their committees would continue to file with the Secretary, candidates for the House committees would continue to file with the Clerk, and candidates for president and vice president and their committees as well as multi-candidate (party or special interest or issue) committees would file with the FEC. Clearly, the Secretary and the Clerk had to provide copies of filed reports to the FEC, which was responsible for administering and enforcing the law. The proposed regulation interpreted the law broadly, but it was considered desirable to make it possible for candidates or committees to file all reports at a single address and to reduce costs of photocopying and postage for committees supporting candidates for more than one federal office.

The initial point-of-entry regulation met with the approval of the Senate but not the House. Representative Hays argued that the law as it then stood sufficed and that the Clerk of the House "ought not to have a whole bunch of people handling these papers before they get to him."[3] The presumed prerogative of the House to receive the reports first was argued for two reasons: 1) The U.S. Constitution states that each house is the judge of its own membership, and hence custody of the original reports was essential in case any questions of contested elections or of unethical behavior in fund raising or spending arose; 2) some members checked their disclosure filings with personnel in the Office of the Clerk of the House before filing verified reports, and they were concerned that the FEC would not provide the same service to help them to avoid possible violations of the law. The second reason was more important in the rejection vote because assurances had been made when the House was debating the 1974 Amendments that the leadership would guarantee that the original filings would continue to be with the House Clerk.

Reluctantly the FEC bowed before the opposition and revised its proposal on filing reports — reversing the procedure so that candidates filed first with the Clerk and the Secretary, who then passed on copies to the FEC. However, this proposed regulation also was deferred until after the FEC was reconstituted. The FEC chairman, Thomas B. Curtis, said the change would produce "added cost and confusion."[4]

Clearly, some of the early criticism of the FEC by Congress was unjustified. Some FEC decisions were inevitable and merely implemented a law that was complex and in part badly drafted. The problem for the FEC was to treat Congress at arm's length to ensure its own independence while being responsive to Congress' oversight authority.

The regulations that had been rejected by Congress were rewritten and, along with one on disclosure, had been cleared by Congress but not issued when the Supreme Court released its *Buckley* decision. While Congress rewrote the law to reconstitute the commission, three other proposed regulations that had been prepared were not submitted, and hearings on a fourth were canceled. Thus the FEC was in operation for more than a year without a single regulation in force. The period was extended to two years, as will be shown.

Once the FEC had been reconstituted, the staff presented to the commission its proposals based on the 1976 Amendments. The regulations were published in the *Federal Register* on May 26, 1976, for public comment. The commission then held public hearings, and written comments were received from the public. After the FEC had tentatively approved the regulations, its staff met with the legislators and congressional staffers. These meetings were designed to reduce congressional hostility to the proposals and to inform the commission of congressional desire to get certain changes made in the regulations. The regulations were approved by the FEC in their final form and sent to Congress on August 3, 1976.

Once the regulations were submitted, the question was not whether they were acceptable but whether Congress would remain in session the 30 "legislative" days required for them to go into effect. At this point there was some congressional concern that any tinkering with the proposed regulations prior to the election could endanger the legislative veto power that had been challenged in court by Ramsey Clark and Ralph Nader's public interest law group.[5]

As the Congress neared its early adjournment in time to campaign, commission members made a last-minute appeal to congressional leaders to schedule pro forma sessions so that the regulations could go into effect for the 1976 election. This effort had the support of House Administration Committee Chairman Frank Thompson, Jr., D-N.J., but it failed when Congress adjourned on October 1, two legislative days short of the 30-day requirement. During this period a complication had developed with respect to a provision of the regulations that banned a reverse checkoff to raise political funds, a procedure heavily used by the National Education Association. The NEA engaged in intensive lobbying efforts to delay congressional action on the proposed regulations containing the ban. While there were denials that this was the reason for the postponement in making the regulations effective, it clearly was a contributing factor, illustrating the political maneuvering involved in the relationship between the FEC, Congress, and interest groups. The NEA continued to use the disputed negative checkoff system during the general election period. This left the regulations in limbo, but the commission issued a policy statement on October 5 on the status of the regulations. Among other things the statement declared:[6]

> This announcement provides notice to all affected parties that the Commission intends to administer the Act in a fashion which implements the interpretations set forth in the proposed regulations. All persons subject to the Act should accordingly comply fully with the requirements of the FEC regulations during the 1976 elections. The FEC regulations should be looked upon as interpretative rules under traditional concepts of administrative law and should be taken as an authoritative guide as to how the election laws apply.

On January 11, 1977, the commission resubmitted the regulations with two minor changes. These required more adequate record-keeping of campaign expenditures and allowed corporations and labor organizations to distribute nonpartisan registration or voting information to the general public. March 29 marked the 30th legislative day and in the interim no provision had been vetoed by either house. On April 13, 1977, the commission officially promulgated the regulations. Thus, 16 months after the first version of the regulations had been submitted, 15 months after the Supreme Court had suspended the commission's executive power, 11 months after the agency had been reconstituted and the regulations had been published in the *Federal Register,* and nine months after they had been submitted to Congress in nearly final form, the regulations went into effect. This sequence of events is a telling commentary about the FEC and its relationships with Congress. It took almost two years from the time of the establishment of the FEC to the effective date of its regulations, a period spanning the 1976 elections.

During 1977, while the resubmitted regulations were before Congress, the negative checkoff plan continued to generate much debate. Most of the members of the House Administration Committee favored the NEA payroll-deduction plan but expressed deep concern that any veto of an FEC regulation might bring about a constitutional court test of the one-house legislative veto power. In this spirit, the committee in a meeting on March 17, 1977, passed by a voice vote the following resolution:[7]

> Resolved: that the House Administration Committee by not reporting out a resolution specifically disapproving the proposed FEC regulation 114.5 does not intend that this be interpreted in any way as endorsing or not endorsing any specific enforcement action by the FEC against any specific organization(s) and further that these proposed regulations do not in any way change or modify the applicable law.

This incident demonstrates the tenacity with which Congress seeks to retain the one-house veto and illustrates deference to a strong interest group. In S 926, passed by the Senate in August 1977, the legislative veto period was reduced from 30 to 20 legislative days, but only with respect to the presidential public financing provisions of the law; this bill died when the 95th Congress adjourned.

Also during 1977, each House of Congress adopted Codes of Conduct that include controls over office accounts comparable in stringency to those initially proposed by the FEC. The matter was further clarified by an FEC advisory opinion stating that office expenses paid for by the National Republican Senatorial Committee on behalf of Republican senators would not be considered contributions or expenditures. The payments therefore would not be subject to contribution limitation, although they would have to be disclosed by the NRSC and by the senator involved. But the point-of-entry problem has not been resolved in favor of the FEC.

Advisory Opinions

During 1976 the FEC's authority and function with respect to rendering advisory opinions (AOs), opinions of counsel (OCs), and informal legal informational letters were substantially affected by both the Supreme Court decision in *Buckley v. Valeo* and the 1976 Amendments to the Federal Election Campaign Act.[8]

Prior to the Supreme Court decision, the commission issued binding advisory opinions, and the general counsel also issued opinions of counsel. With the *Buckley* decision, however, the Supreme Court temporarily invalidated many of the commission's powers including the power to issue advisory opinions. The commission then issued only opinions of counsel in areas previously covered by AOs. No new ground was broken and OCs also were stopped after March 22, when Supreme Court stays were terminated. The FEC undertook evaluation of all regulations and AOs following the Supreme Court decision and began to eliminate those dealing with limitations declared unconstitutional by the Court. It also began to revise others dealing with disclosure or public funding and related limits no longer effective. Many of the AOs were criticized by practitioners and scholars for being narrow and legalistic, for inflexibly following the rigidities in the law, and for failing to relax some possibly unconstitutional provisions of the law.

When Congress rewrote the law in 1976, it set new standards for writing advisory opinions, stipulating that the FEC cannot issue rules of general applicability but must apply AOs only to specific facts presented in a request. Any rules of general applicability were required to be incorporated into regulations, which then were subject to congressional disapproval.[9] But the FEC itself was to determine how broadly or narrowly to interpret the law.

The need for advisory opinions continued as new requests were submitted after the enactment of the 1976 Amendments. The commission responded to these requests in two ways. Formal advisory opinions were issued where applicable to factual situations. In other cases, responses to advisory opinion requests (Re:AORs) were given, clearly stating that they were responses based on proposed regulations, not formal advisory opinions. While the advisory opinions carried with them the full protections and immunities granted by the law, the commission's responses to advisory opinion requests, which involved reliance on proposed regulations, did not afford the requesting person, or others in similar situations, the same protection given in connection with an AO. The commission determined early in 1978 that past policy statements should be regarded by the public as having no continuing legal effect, since they were interim pronouncements and regulations had been formulated. It was noted, however, that certain advisory opinions incorporated interpretations embodied in policy statements, and that some of these advisory opinions should be regarded as valid. In addition, policy statements should be regarded as valid insofar as they interpreted the regulations and remained unmodified by the commission.

A Sample Advisory Opinion. In July 1978 the FEC issued an advisory opinion concerning interpretation of the FECA regarding limits on contributions to, and expenditures on behalf of, candidates made by various state and local Republican Party committees in Iowa. The questions asked by the Iowa committees, and the answers supplied by the FEC, illustrate the complexity of the law and the divisions within the commission.[10]

First, the committees asked whether contributions from state and county Republican committees were necessarily subject to one limit, or whether the committees might, under the special circumstances that applied in Iowa, be regarded as separate bodies. In Iowa, state and county committees are statutorily independent from the state committee, which exerts no influence over the county committees' contributions or expenditures. The commissioners commented that the legislative history of the applicable statute was unclear. They concluded, however, that the committees each might be considered subject to a separate limit if they did not receive money from another political committee affiliated with any unit of the party and if the contributions they made in no way reflected the influence of another party unit. The commissioners thus accepted the committees' evidence that county committees in Iowa were fully independent from the state committee.

Second, the Iowa committees asked whether party auxiliary bodies might be regarded as separate from the state committee and whether a separate contribution limit might apply to them. The commissioners decided that the auxiliary groups could not be considered separate, since their political work was carried on in cooperation with the state committee, and that therefore their contributions counted toward the limit that applied to the state committee.

The third question related to reporting requirements. The Iowans wanted to know whether each party unit might contribute as much as $1,000 to candidates for federal office without having to comply with FECA reporting requirements. The commissioners answered that any committee or auxiliary group might contribute as much as $1,000 without having to register with the FEC as a political committee and without having to comply with reporting requirements. If the county or auxiliary unit was a political committee, as defined in the Act, however, and if it was influenced by the state committee, then its contributions would count against the state committee's limits and would be reported accordingly. This interpretation reflected the commissioners' wish to comply with the express desire of Congress to strengthen the role of parties in the electoral process, particularly at the local level.

In their fourth question the Iowa committees expressed confusion about the language of commission regulations in one area. They asked whether, in addition to the broad overall spending limit, other spending limits applied to each party committee at the county level as well as to the auxiliary bodies. The commissioners responded that only one spending limit applied to the entire state party organization; there were no additional spending limits for subordinate committees and other bodies.

The fifth question related to procedures for filing disclosure reports and for delegating responsibility for their filing, and the commissioners answered it with reference to particular forms and commission regulations.

The sixth question asked whether the $1,000 coordinated spending limit for party committees applied to county committees in the 1978 elections as well as in the 1976 elections. The commissioners said that it did not, that the spending limit was intended to apply only to elections for president and vice president.

Finally, the committees requested a broad definition of printed matter that might be considered exempt from spending limits. If slate cards and sample ballots were exempt, which characteristics determined the exemption or nonexemption of brochures and fliers? The commissioners responded that the exemption was intended to be broadly educational and applied to printed matter listing at least three candidates for public office to be elected in that state. They noted that the regulation was not intended to enable party committees to promote specific candidates while evading spending limitations. The inclusion of candidates' pictures on the slate card or sample ballot would not rule out exemption, they said; biographical information other than the candidate's name, his party affiliation, the office he sought, and the like would not be permissible, however, on exempt documents. Finally, they noted that exemption of a document did not mean that it might not be distributed through the mail.

Commissioners Robert O. Tiernan and Thomas E. Harris dissented with the majority interpretation pertaining to the first question. They argued that the majority had incorrectly interpreted the legislative history of the relevant statutes and had incompletely analyzed interpretive regulations developed by the commission. The two commissioners argued that a single contribution limit should be applied to all the organizations in question and that this was the intent of what they termed an "inclusive 'antiproliferation' rule" included by Congress in the 1976 Amendments.[11] In addition, they suggested that the majority opinion overlooked consideration of the possible separate status of each of the Iowa county committees: if limits applied to the state committee were separate from those applied to the county committees, the individual status of the county committees should be considered as well as their collective status.

Annual Report For 1975

The FEC officially began operations on April 14, 1975. Initial concerns centered on questions of staffing and organization and immediate attention was directed toward filling the statutory positions of staff director and general counsel. On April 23, Orlando B. Potter, former assistant to the Secretary of the Senate, was appointed as staff director and on May 1, Professor John G. Murphy, Jr., of Georgetown University became the FEC's first general counsel.[12]

By statute, the staff director is authorized "to appoint and fix the salary of the Commission staff, with the approval of the Commission."[13] Although in certain cases recruitment responsibility was delegated — the general counsel, for example, recruited the legal staff — the staff director played a major role but final power remained with the commission. Recruitment moved rapidly; the staff numbered 55 by the end of June and 124 by the end of the calendar year.

As the legal arm of the FEC, the functions of the general counsel include interpreting the law, representing the agency in compliance and litigation matters, and drafting regulations and proposals for internal operating procedures. The Office of General Counsel was perceived and organized from the start as a separate arm of, and directly responsible to, the commission. While the staff director and general counsel adopted a cooperative relationship, as evidenced by the policy of the legal staff to transmit "draft copies of its opinions and other policy statements through the Office of the Staff Director, thus permitting review and comment by the rest of the Commission staff,"[14] some tensions developed on occasion.

Organization

In addition to recruitment, much of the early time and effort of the staff director was spent in attempting to define the structural organization of the agency. From the outset, the relationship between the staff director and the rest of the staff was kept direct and simple. No provision was made for deputy staff directors and authority flowed directly from the staff director to the heads of the three operational divisions — Disclosure and Compliance, Administration, and Information Services.

The Division of Disclosure and Compliance was further sectioned into the offices of Reports Examining, Public Records, and Audit and Investigation. Reports Examining is responsible for the initial part of the compliance process. In this section, candidate, committee and individual reports are first checked for completeness and accuracy. Follow-up compliance responsibility rests with the Audit and Investigation section, which also determines the eligibility of presidential candidates for matching funds and the amount of public funding received. The Public Records office bears primary responsibility for disclosure. During 1975 this office made public approximately 25,000 pages of documents based on candidate and committee financial reports.

Responsible for personnel, budget management, space and supplies, the Division of Administration represents the housekeeping arm of the agency. In 1975 a large part of the time and effort of this division was spent in the processing of new personnel for the various agency offices. The results of these staffing efforts by the end of the year were as follows:[15]

Commissioners and immediate staff	17
Staff director's office	5
General counsel	26

Information services	20
Disclosure and compliance	44
Administration	12
Total:	124

The Division of Information Services is sectioned into Press Relations, Public Communications, Election Administration, Clearinghouse, and the *FEC Record*. As the titles of these subdivisions indicate, the primary function of this division is the distribution of information to candidates, committees, and the public as to their obligations and responsibilities under federal campaign law. During 1975 these subdivisions of Information Services responded to 5,462 phone and mail inquiries, scheduled regional seminars in 15 major cities and published four separate issues of the commission newsletter (*FEC Record*) which provided summaries "of Commission action on regulations, advisory opinions, report deadlines, and other items of timely and special significance."[16]

Policies, Priorities, and Procedures

At the outset, the FEC articulated two major policy objectives. The first involved what the commission referred to as the "overriding need to establish its credibility at a time of public skepticism and lack of confidence in the political process in general."[17] Toward this end, the agency determined to conduct its affairs in an open manner and to remain as removed as possible from incumbent and partisan interests. With the exception of matters relating to enforcement or personnel it was decided that all deliberations would be open to the press and public. Moreover, on October 30, 1975, the FEC adopted a Code of Ethics "which required that Commissioners and staff alike hold themselves aloof from active participation in political affairs relating to Federal campaigns."[18]

The other self-defined policy objective was voluntary compliance. The presumption, according to the commission, should be "that the participants in the political process [want] to comply with the law and [will] comply if properly advised of their obligations."[19] This presumption, in fact, led directly to the creation of the Division of Information Services with its concomitant emphasis on providing the agency's clients with the basic information needed for meaningful compliance.

The emphasis on voluntary compliance also set the tone for early priorities established by the FEC. Because of the substantial number of inquiries by officeholders and candidates, the FEC soon decided that primary emphasis should be placed on explanation and clarification of the law rather than on investigation of potential wrongdoing. The legal staff, for example, was directed to devote their attention primarily to requests for interpretation or clarification of the law. For much the same reason, the agency decided against a large-scale program of routine audits during 1975. Instead, "the audit and investigation staff was used almost exclusively to implement the public financing program."[20]

Specific procedures established by the FEC also reflected the emphasis on openness and voluntary compliance. Prior to each regularly scheduled meeting, for example, the commission prepared detailed agendas with supplementary material such as draft opinions and proposed regulations, all of which was made available to the public. Perhaps more significantly, in September 1975 the commission decided that prior to submitting any proposed regulations for congressional approval they would have them published in the *Federal Register*, after which a 30-day period would be allowed for the solicitation of public and congressional input.

The latter procedural decision followed almost immediately after substantial congressional disapproval of the FEC's first two proposed regulations, both dealing with disclosure requirements, and points up one of the most troublesome problems faced by the commission in its early months. The agency "found itself in the anomalous position . . . of being in a potentially adversarial position with the very persons who were to review its regulations and provide its funds."[21] Because of this relationship, all sorts of questions arose with respect to the propriety of separate congressional liaison efforts on the part of individual commissioners in lobbying for passage of various FEC proposals. The problem was alleviated to some extent in December 1975 when the decision was made to try to coordinate all congressional liaison activities under the Office of Staff Director.

Implementation

Much of the time and effort of the FEC during 1975 was directed toward initial policy development in the areas of public financing, disclosure, and campaign limitations. Articulation in these areas of broad policy objectives into detailed regulations was accomplished only after a lengthy process characterized by public hearings, congressional briefings, and the issuance of a host of advisory opinions and interim guidelines.

In the area of public financing, the immediate task was to establish appropriate policies to cover the presidential primary matching plans and the convention financing program. Public hearings in this regard began on November 4 and by the following January formal regulations had been drafted and adopted by the commission. Prior to this, however, interim guidelines were issued in August and October of 1975 to inform the candidates and parties as to requirements that had to be met to qualify for funds. The October guideline addressed questions of:[22]

1) whether in-kind contributions could be matched (they could not);

2) whether political committee contributions could be matched (they could not); and

3) whether fund-raising monies could be matched (they could).

The August guideline addressed the much less complicated question of convention financing and "outlined standards for the parties to follow to qualify for financing, procedures for them to apply, and the procedures the FEC would follow in approving and certifying requested payments."[23]

Policy development in the area of disclosure was perhaps the most difficult and time-consuming activity engaged in by the FEC during 1975. The first regulation proposed by the commission was rejected by Congress in early October. Efforts to formulate comprehensive disclosure regulations continued well into the fall of 1975. In addition to briefings for members of Congress, public hearings were held in October. Witnesses included representatives of national and state party committees, counsels for a number of presidential candidates, various members of Congress, and several representatives of business, labor, and public interest groups. A final draft proposal that incorporated many of the suggestions of these witnesses was sent to Congress in December. The 30-day legislative review period had not yet expired when the *Buckley v. Valeo* decision was handed down on January 30.

Initially, the most difficult problem faced in the area of campaign limitations involved the formulation of policy that was coherent and at the same time flexible enough to be applied in a variety of situations. Although the contribution and expenditure limits imposed by the 1974 Act were seemingly clear and straightforward, the commission early on concluded that the complexities of the American political system along with the imaginations of campaign strategists gave rise to circumstances much too problematical to be adequately covered by statute.

Because of this and of the immediacy of the situation, the FEC found it necessary during 1975 to supplement the statute with a series of advisory opinions prior to the promulgation of detailed regulations. Requests for opinions were numerous and involved such matters as:[24]

● the application of the limitations to the federal election activities of state and local political parties;

● whether a loan constitutes a contribution when made to a political party telethon;

● the treatment of current contributions received to pay debts incurred before the effective date of the Act;

- whether an honorarium donated to a charity counts against the limit on honorariums;

- the application of the limits to an unopposed primary candidate;

- whether a contribution to a congressman's office account is to be treated as a political contribution;

- how should contributions by a corporation or a partnership be treated.

Annual Report for 1976

The year 1976 proved to be an eventful first full year of operation for the Federal Election Commission. In January the Supreme Court ruled in *Buckley v. Valeo* that the commission was unconstitutionally constituted since some of its commissioners were appointed by legislative leaders. To keep the FEC functioning until Congress had time to act, the Court ordered two stays totaling 50 days, but the second stay ran out on March 22 while the commission was not reorganized until May 21. During the intervening period, the FEC could not exercise the following powers granted it under the FECA:[25]

1. the promulgation of rules and regulations;
2. the issuance of binding advisory opinions;
3. the initiation of enforcement actions; and
4. the certification of public funds to candidates.

In the midst of this uncertainty, the agency oversaw the first publicly financed presidential election in U.S. history. Moreover, the commission was engaged throughout 1976 in drafting and attempting to promulgate an extensive set of regulations. When it was finally reconstituted, it elected a new chairman and took on responsibility for enforcing the recently enacted 1976 Amendments, which brought significant changes in the law regarding enforcement, limitations and, to some extent, disclosure.

After the Supreme Court in *Buckley* declared the combination of legislative and executive authority for appointment to be unconstitutional, the FEC was reconstituted with six commissioners appointed by the president and confirmed by the Senate. Five of the members had previously served on the commission. The former chairman, Thomas B. Curtis, resigned, and was replaced by William L. Springer. Vernon W. Thomson was selected as the new chairman for a one-year term, while Thomas E. Harris was chosen as vice chairman.

Although the commission normally meets once a week, it met twice a week during the 1976 campaign because of the press of business, or a total of 88 times during the calendar year. Except for meetings dealing with personnel or compliance matters, its sessions are open to the public.[26]

Public Financing

As enacted by Congress in 1974, the program for the public financing of presidential candidates and nominating conventions contained three major elements: 1) a primary matching fund program that offered partial public financing to any candidate who could demonstrate the requisite base of public support; 2) direct grants to the conventions of the two major parties; and 3) full public financing for the candidates of the major parties in the general election. To finance this program Congress used the Presidential Election Campaign Fund, created in 1972, to which taxpayers may allocate one dollar of their taxes. Table 3-1 summarizes the fund's transactions for the year.

Table 3-1
Receipts and Disbursements 1976

Receipts and disbursements presidential election campaign fund, 1976		
Deposits:		$95,838,787.00
Disbursements:		
Primary matching payment (15 candidates)		24,273,401.65
Convention payments		
Democratic	$2,180,869.79	
Republican	$1,963,800.00	4,144,669.79
General election payments		
(Two candidates @ $21,820,000)		43,640,000.00
Total disbursements		72,058,071.44
Balance		$23,780,715.56

SOURCE: Federal Election Commission, *Annual Report 1976,* p. 14. Some amounts later adjusted downward due to refunds to U.S. Treasury.

In its administration of the Presidential Election Campaign Fund, the commission sought to achieve a number of objectives. It sought to be impartial; it tried to be prompt and responsive in handling submissions for payments; and it hoped to offer the public reassurance that public funds were being distributed and used properly.[27]

By January 1 the commission had certified the eligibility of 11 presidential candidates for the primary matching program and had certified initial payments for the two major-party conventions. The agency imposed upon itself a two-week turnaround from submission to verification and in general worked closely with the various presidential candidates to aid them in their record-keeping practices.[28]

Of the 15 presidential candidates who eventually qualified for $24.3 million in matching funds, six accounted for 84 percent of the total, while each of the remaining nine was granted less than $600,000. The average of the contributions submitted for matching was $26.86.[29]

The program, itself entirely new, required both the commission and the candidates to develop new record-keeping and verification procedures, and the FEC operated under extreme time pressures made more acute by the fact of its own creation after fund raising for many primary campaigns had begun. The *Buckley* ruling compounded the FEC's problems, since it suspended the FEC's powers for two months despite the stays granted by the Court. In response to the ruling, the commission worked its staff overtime and accelerated its schedule so that it received requests for payment weekly rather than biweekly. When it became clear that the stay would expire before Congress acted, the commissioners decided to continue accepting and processing submissions, and when the FEC powers were reinstated on May 21 they were able to certify a total of $3.2 million to nine candidates. During the uncertain period four candidates dropped out of the race. The commission acknowledged the adverse effect of the suspension on these four, but claimed to have lessened its impact on those remaining by continuing to process requests.[30]

Throughout the campaign, the FEC was confronted with questions relating to the eligibility of candidates for matching funds. One such question concerned the period of time during which a candidate would remain eligible for additional public funds. The 1976 Amendments changed the criteria. Another question relating to eligibility concerned the period of time during which the commission should continue to approve payments for campaign debts after a candidate had ceased to be active. It became the agency's policy to allow submissions for debts incurred before ineligibility and to recognize as legitimate continuing operating expenses that had been contracted prior to a candidate's ineligibility. The payment period thus extended into early 1977. A third issue centered around the candidate who seemed to some to be spokesman for a cause rather than a seeker of the presidency. In the end, the commission certified Ellen McCormack because she "met all the statutory requirements for eligibility."[31]

The commission both worked with and guided the candidates on submission of their contributions for matching. A field audit, performed by the FEC with the candidates and their committees, assisted the candidates in their record keeping and determined their initial eligibility. The audit enabled the FEC to introduce a degree of standardization into the accounting practices of the candidates. The agency also acted to keep the candidates formally and informally informed of various changes in its verification process.

Verification proved difficult and time-consuming. Initially the commissioners demanded a 100 percent review of all submissions before funds would be matched. This approach proved impractical and to expedite the process, the commission adopted in early January a statistical sampling procedure, and by July concluded that such a system was sufficient for its purposes. In addition, the FEC in June adopted the tactic of withholding from funds requested a set percentage based on the proportion of requests rejected in the four most recent submissions. This procedure was dropped once the volume of submissions diminished enough to give the staff time to review the submissions.

One of the major tasks confronting the agency was determining which contributions were eligible for the matching program.[32] One problem was the lack of a supporting instrument, such as a check, to document the contribution. Another problem involved the aggregation of contributions from a single contributor. The law prohibits matching more than $250 from any one contributor and it proved very difficult both for the commission and the candidate to keep track of contributions that, when aggregated, exceeded this amount.

As might be expected, the candidates' submissions were rejected at varying rates. The factors influencing these rates included: "the number of submissions, the number of contributors on each submission, whether submissions were prepared manually or by computer, [and] the occurrence of specialized methods of fund raising, such as concert tickets, which required independent identification because the identification of the donor was often insufficient."[33] The candidates were permitted to resubmit rejected submissions. While not all did so, those who did found that a substantial portion was eventually certified for payment.

Administration of convention financing in 1976 proved simpler. The statute provided each major party with as much as $2.2 million, paid in quarterly installments, for its nominating convention, with an adjustment for cost-of-living increases. Altogether the Democratic National Committee received $2,016,870, while its Republican counterpart was given $1,581,664.[34]

The FEC formulated several policies with respect to convention financing. It defined acceptable in-kind services as those normally provided to similar conventions. In addition, the commission allowed businesses and unions to donate funds "provided they were used for certain specified purposes, such as promotion or welcoming activities."[35] Both national committees requested that the commission accelerate payments when suspension of its power could be foreseen, but the FEC decided to keep its original schedule.

The final component of the public finance system was the Presidential General Election Campaign Fund, which the FEC found to be simpler in actual operation than the Primary Matching Fund had been. Each of the two major presidential candidates received $21,820,000 from the federal government.

Most of the questions the commission faced during the general election centered around private contributions to the presidential candidates. A definition was needed, for example, of the kinds of activities in which a congressional candidate could engage with his party's presidential nominee. The commission's decision made a distinction between buttons, brochures, and bumper stickers on the one hand, and joint billboards, media events, or other large-scale promotion on the other.

Disclosure

The FEC developed a disclosure system based on a series of reports filed on sets of standard forms. The system requires that, after a candidate and campaign committee registers, they must submit a series of recurring reports detailing expenditures and contributions. The submission must list the names and addresses of contributors of more than $100 and the recipients of the expenditures. Individuals making independent expenditures on behalf of or in opposition to a candidate and labor unions and corporations that spend more than $2,000 in political communications advocating the election or defeat of candidates also must register with the FEC.

As the election draws near, the reporting requirements increase. The reports are issued at intervals, and because each offers a financial picture of the campaign at only one point in time, continuous review and a final report are necessary for a complete picture. By its nature this process, as the commission noted, "places an enormous burden on the press and public."[36]

The FEC placed a very heavy stress on disclosure during the 1976 election. It both aided federal candidates in meeting the reporting requirements and established a Public Records Office so as to provide the public and the press with easy access to the reports. In addition, it began a computerized storage and retrieval program of data taken from the disclosure documents.

As shown in Table 3-2, the commission received disclosure reports in 1976 from 3,022 candidates (230 for the presidency, 415 for the Senate, and 2,377 for the House of Representatives). It also received reports from 5,661 political committees and from 376 individuals and committees who reported having made independent expenditures on behalf of candidates. A total of 9,049 filers, representing 3,390 campaigns, filed a total of 500,000 disclosure documents which represented the $300 million in campaign funds the FEC was charged with monitoring. The commission was quite busy sending as well as receiving documents. In addition to reporting forms, information, and manuals, the agency mailed 150,000 copies of campaign guide pamphlets that explained reporting requirements.

Table 3-2
Campaign Disclosure Documents in FEC Public Records

1975-76: 459,916 pages of documents from:				
	Candidates	**Political Committees**	**Other**	**Campaigns**
House	2,377	2,408		2,671
Senate	415	460		473
Presidential	230	234 (authorized)		246
		166 (unauthorized)		
Party-related		73 (national level)		
		285 (state level)		
		730 (local level)		
Nonparty-related		1,295		
Independent expenditures			139	
Delegate			199	
Communication costs			38	
Totals	3,022	5,651	376	3,390
Total filers	9,049			

1972-74: 806,381 pages of documents previously filed with the Clerk of the House of Representatives, the Secretary of the Senate, or the General Accounting Office.

SOURCE: Federal Election Commission, *Annual Report 1976, p. 131.*

From the beginning the FEC was responsible for the review of presidential, multicandidate, and party-related committee reports. Responsibility for reviewing congressional reports, however, remained by agreement with the Secretary of the Senate and the Clerk of the House until July and September of 1976, respectively, when it was transferred to the agency. Although the transfer had been anticipated from the outset, it proved a sensitive matter.

When reviewing the congressional reports, the commission faced two basic problems: its inability to review all disclosure documents and its "need to establish criteria of 'substantial compliance' with the law." To deal with the former question, the agency adopted the notion of a threshold: Campaigns had to exceed certain limits before they would be reviewed in depth. In August the FEC decided that it would review "only those filers whose aggregate receipts and/or expenditures exceed $10,000. . . . Under this criterion, the FEC would still examine virtually all Senate candidates who were successful in the primary and general elections and the great majority of successful House candidates."[37]

It became necessary to define substantial compliance, because the widely varying experience and sophistication of the candidates and committees were reflected in their submissions. Strict application of the disclosure rules led to a finding that nearly one-third of all reports were "inadequate." To ease the workload on both its staff and those filing, the commission decided to accept reports as complete if, in a given category (such as addresses of contributors), 80 percent of the information was present. The requirement for complete descriptive information was maintained, however, where large contributions or expenditures (generally in excess of $500) were involved.[38]

If the information on a disclosure report was found to be inadequate, the commission sent to the filer a Request for Additional Information form and as many as three further notices, each with a specified time period, before taking formal action. In nearly all cases the filers provided an adequate response after one or two notices.

In 1975 the FEC had decided to microfilm its records to make them available to the public and the Public Records Office continued to make both microfilm and paper copies. In 1976 a computerized retrieval and storage system was begun, but because of the format of the documents, the widely varying ways in which the candidates and committees completed the forms, and the differing versions of the forms that were in circulation, the process was slow and difficult. Nevertheless, the computer system has helped in the preparation of indices and in the implementation of the threshold concept.

There was considerable demand for the FEC products. In 1976 its Public Records Office provided 1.1 million pages of federal campaign finance data for public inspection. Nearly half of these pages related to the 9,000 filers in 1975 and 1976. The number of visitors to the office peaked at several hundred a week during the last month of the election. Besides providing for direct viewing of documents on microfilm, the Public Records Office copied and sold more than 300,000 pages of statements and reports in response to over 3,000 written and phone orders. In addition, the office fielded more than 2,000 information calls about document availability.

The FEC was constantly revising its procedures and forms during 1976. At present the major obstacle to more complete disclosure is the fact that the data are located largely in Washington with only limited amounts at the local level where the contests occur. The FEC is considering ways of transmitting the material to the states in order to permit local analysis of the campaign finance reports.

Campaign Limitations

In the *Buckley* decision, the Supreme Court declared limitations on campaign expenditures and candidate personal spending to be unconstitutional unless the candidate's campaign is publicly financed. Although contribution limits were upheld by the Court, limits on independent expenditures were struck down. In response, Congress in its 1976 Amendments required a notarized statement from individuals making independent expenditures that they had been made "without prior consultation with or at the request or suggestion of the candidate."[39] In addition the law mandated a single $5,000 limit for affiliated multicandidate committees to prevent the proliferation of such committees as a means of evading the contribution limit. In its proposed regulations, the FEC developed a set of criteria to determine which committees were affiliated. It also ruled that state and local political party committees "did not have the right to make their own independent expenditures on behalf of a Presidential candidate." But the regulations that went into effect in April 1977 allow "each local unit of the party (State, county, city, or congressional district), an expenditure of up to $1,000 to further the election of their party's candidate."[40]

Because of the press of time, the FEC decided to focus its monitoring activities on those campaigns having the greatest financial impact on the election, and it concentrated its review on campaigns above a given level of financial activity and on contributions of $500 and more. The computerized system proved helpful in determining which campaigns and contributions exceeded the "threshold" figures that triggered FEC review.

Starting in July, the commission adopted a notification program when it found on disclosure reports apparent surface violations of the limits and restrictions on campaign activity. Up to three letters were sent; if no satisfactory response came after the third letter, the matter was referred for formal compliance action. The program proved successful: The FEC sent 140 initial letters that resulted in the filing of adequately amended reports by 97 percent of the committees involved. Most of these letters dealt with excessive contributions.

In general, most federal candidates and committees, and particularly the presidential ones, complied with the FEC request for additional information or requests that some funds be returned to contributors who had exceeded the lawful limits. Perhaps the commission's major difficulty in this area came in its monitoring of corporate and labor solicitation activities. The agency was forced to rely on complaints to monitor these activities, since disclosure or reporting of them was not required.

Legislative Recommendations

In its administrative role, the commission noted various problems with the FECA. The agency recommended to Congress a number of improvements, most of which focused on "administrative, technical and less controversial policy-oriented amendments."[41] Despite the intention of the legislature, the 1974 and 1976 amendments placed undue strains on candidates and campaign committees in terms of burdensome requirements. The majority of the commission's recommendations called for simplification.

Although a key goal of the law was to provide the public with information on campaign contributions and expenditures, the number of reports required became so excessive as to hinder the press and the public in their efforts to use the data effectively. The FEC noted that the 1974 Amendments forced many candidates to file two sets of reports, one for themselves and one for their principal campaign committee. If one set of these reports was dropped, along with a reduction in reporting dates, the commission estimated that the required number of reports could be reduced from 24 to eight.

The burdens placed on multicandidate committees also seemed excessive and the FEC suggested that Congress grant it the right to waive or exempt committees or candidates from some of the record-keeping, reporting, or organizational requirements of the Act, subject of course to congressional review. Altogether the commission claimed that these changes would reduce the number of reports most candidates and committees have to file from 50 to 90 percent, "while at the same time enhancing the ability of the press and the public to glean from the reports important campaign finance data."[42]

The FEC also proposed changing the contribution limitations from a "per-election" basis to either an "annual" or "election-cycle" basis. This proposal would eliminate the distinction between primary and general election contributions that necessitated dual bookkeeping.

Another recommendation made by the FEC concerned the filing of multiple copies of reports. The Act now requires all candidates and committees to file a copy of each statement with the Secretary of State or other state officer as well as with the commission, and it assigns certain responsibilities to the Secretaries of State. The commission proposed that it be granted the authority to determine when and how reports should be filed with state officers and indicated that microfilmed copies or access to the reports via computer might be made available to the state officials, eliminating the need for duplicate filing. The agency also urged a reduction in how long the state officials were required to preserve the reports, noting that the report-preservation feature had drawn more opposition from Secretaries of State than had any other aspect of their filing responsibilities. The FEC suggested that Congress make the commission the sole point of entry for all disclosure documents filed by federal candidates and committees supporting those candidates. This change would eliminate confusion as to where documents should be filed, would reduce governmental costs and would ease the commission's task of publishing lists of nonfilers and tracing responses to compliance notices.

The FEC suggested that Congress raise the threshold for reporting independent expenditures from $100 to $250 on the grounds that the existing requirement imposed undue reporting burdens, noting that $250 more realistically indicated the point when independent expenditures begin to have an impact on election campaigns. It also urged that, instead of requiring persons making independent contributions to file, persons filing independent expenditure reports be required to report the sources of any contributions in excess of $100 made with the intention of bringing about an independent expenditure.

Presidential Candidates. The handling of the campaign finances of presidential delegates and candidates for such positions left much to be desired. The commission proposed that existing prohibitions on contributions to candidates for office by corporations, labor organizations, government contractors, and foreign nationals be applied to contributions to delegates as well. The agency went on to urge Congress to draw a distinction between those delegates closely tied to a presidential candidate and those individuals who run independently of any presidential candidate; suggesting that contributions to the former be considered contributions to the presidential candidate and that expenditures by such delegates could be charged against the expenditure limitations of the presidential candidate. Unauthorized delegates could be required to report only when they make expenditures or receive contributions in excess of $1,000.

An issue that greatly vexed the FEC during 1976 was the question of the amount of support congressional candidates could legally give their party's presidential ticket. The commission suggested that "occasional, isolated or incidental support" from congressional candidates should not be considered a contribution-in-kind, and that a small sum of money (e.g., $2,500 or one-half-cent times voting age population per district or state) might be allowed to them for supporting, listing, and mentioning the presidential candidate in campaign materials.

A potential difficulty in future presidential years concerns the distribution of public funds when they are insufficient to pay for all primary matching requests, convention financing, and the general election fund. The commission recommended that Congress modify the existing system either to assure candidates full entitlement or at least to eliminate the current discretionary powers of the secretary of the Treasury and the commission in determining the distribution of partial entitlements.

The commission also foresaw and made recommendations concerning candidates who apply for matching funds retroactively. Since spending limitations apply only to candidates who accept public funds, a candidate who had not yet qualified or applied for matching funds could, theoretically, substantially outspend a publicly funded opponent during an early primary, thereby gaining an unfair advantage. To prevent this possible circumvention of the law, the FEC recommended that candidates who exceed state-by-state expenditure ceilings not be eligible for primary matching funds.

Another problem for the FEC during the 1976 campaign was the difficulty of ascertaining the intent of contributors to issue-oriented or cause-oriented candidacies. Determinations had to be made as to whether the contributor was giving to further the nomination of the candidate or merely to further the issue or cause. To help it in future elections, the commission asked Congress for legislation that would require all documents representing contributions that were submitted for matching payments to include the name of the individual whose candidacy they are intended to support.

The FEC also asked Congress to correct an FECA provision that seemed to violate the spirit of legislative intent. The FECA allows a 20 percent fund-raising exemption during the prenomination season, and it clearly makes that exemption applicable to the entire $10.9 million expenditure limit, even though, according to the legislative history, the congressional intent was that the exemption be applied only to the $5.5 million privately raised. Since the 20 percent fund-raising exemption also applies to those presidential nominees who accept public funding for the general election, this provision places candidates who refuse to accept total public funding at a disadvantage. To correct this situation, the commission urged that the fund-raising exemption be dropped and the expenditure limitations be raised accordingly.

Political Parties. There were many complaints about how the FECA affected political parties in 1976. Noting that the role of state and local party committees was severely restricted, the commission suggested permitting state committees of a political party to spend $20,000 or two cents times the voting age population, whichever is greater, on behalf of the presidential candidate of the national party. In addition, the FEC recommended to allow local and subordinate committees of a state committee to distribute pins, bumper stickers, pamphlets, and other similar campaign materials that are usually connected with volunteer activities, and to exempt these activities from the limitations when they are conducted on behalf of the party's presidential candidate. It suggested these activities be subject to disclosure and paid for only with funds not earmarked for a particular candidate.

Despite the intense discussion concerning the desirability of raising or lowering the contribution limits, the FEC made no specific recommendation in this area. It did urge Congress to reconsider the matter, noting the problems of either an overly restrictive or an excessively high limitation. The FEC was more direct with respect to spending limits. It urged that the general election figure be raised to between $25 million and $35 million, that the amount for convention financing be increased, and that the limit for primary campaign spending be raised.

To redress an imbalance, the commission urged Congress to prohibit corporations and labor organizations from bestowing honorariums on federal candidates. On the other hand the FEC felt that the restrictions on corporations and labor unions in the area of nonpartisan registration and get-out-the-vote drives were too restrictive and recommended that these activities be permitted without cosponsoring with a nonpartisan organization.

The commission noted a potential loophole in the law with regard to draft movements. It is not clear whether such movements must report their contributions or expenditures. In addition, since the $1,000/candidate/election limitation on contributions applies only to candidates, an individual presumably could give up to $5,000. Moreover, the existing law permits a multicandidate committee to give two contributions, one to the draft committee and one to the individual after he formally becomes a candidate.

The FEC also urged reinstatement of strict controls on campaign activities conducted for the private profit of either the candidate or the committee, especially when such activities involve converting political funds to personal use. The Act as currently written allows the use of excess campaign funds for any lawful purpose.

Finally, the commission argued for a multiyear "authorization of appropriation" to enable it to improve its long-range planning ability. The present system, according to the commission "drains valuable staff resources each year in attempts to justify an authorization and frustrates intelligent management of the agency."[43]

Performance

In its first year the commission was entering uncharted waters, and some mistakes were inevitable. Despite the difficulties confronting it, however, the agency felt that its first operative year proved that the program could be administered to the satisfaction of the candidates and the public.

The FEC met the deadlines the law imposed and distributed more than $72 million to finance the 1976 presidential election. If the agency made numerous revisions throughout the year in its monitoring and administrative procedures, it was confronted with a massive task — the processing of tens of thousands of documents and the simultaneous distribution of equally large numbers of forms to candidates and political committees, all in the space of only a few months. The various systems had to be "de-bugged." Violators of the Act were notified and most of them complied with the requests. Those who did not were first publicized and if they were still negligent, prosecuted.

The commission adopted a set of policies that relied heavily on good faith efforts by the candidates and their committees. At the local level, voluntary compliance was stressed; in the Washington office a sampling procedure was often adopted. The emphasis was on the major campaigns, the major contributors, and the major expenditures. Given the enormity of the task it confronted and the shortness of time for achieving its goals, the agency may have had no other choices. On the surface, it appears that most federal candidates complied with the Act's provisions. There were relatively few deliberate attempts to violate the law; most of the mistakes resulted from lack of familiarity with the law.[44]

If 1976 provided the agency with learning experiences, it can be expected that the commission's handling of the 1980 election will be much smoother, particularly if some of its recommendations are implemented. There should be a corresponding increase in the understanding of the FECA and the FEC's regulations on the part of political candidates, campaign committees, party organizations and interested private citizens, and this should also prove useful in future elections.[45] It is possible, however, that the commission will have additional tasks thrust upon it that may cause it to encounter further difficulties.

Perhaps the FEC's most basic problem has been its failure to develop and to enunciate a philosophy of campaign regulation. Its ad hoc decisions were sometimes inconsistent and confusing. It seemed to spend an inordinate amount of time on trivial matters, as some of its advisory opinions, information responses to advisory opinion requests, and informational letters attest. The commission admits it needs to develop better relationships with Congress.

Annual Report for 1977

The nonelection year 1977 allowed the FEC a welcome breathing spell. It was the agency's first extended opportunity to reflect upon and evaluate its past experience as a basis for the refinement of procedures and formulation of new policy.[46]

The FEC continued in 1977 to give priority to public disclosure of information based on candidate and committee reports. Disclosure provisions of the FECA require quarterly and year-end reports even during nonelection years. Moreover, pre- and postelection reports were required of candidates and committees involved in special elections. Altogether, the commission reviewed and made public more than 21,500 reports from 6,757 candidates and committees.

Early in 1977 the Disclosure Division was reorganized into five teams, each team bearing responsibility for the review of documents of one of the following categories of filers:[47]

1. Presidential candidates and committees.
2. Senate candidates and committees.
3. House candidates and committees.
4. Party committee filers.
5. Nonparty committee filers.

The "team plan" was designed to encourage the development of expertise with respect to reporting and accounting problems shared by similarly situated candidates and committees. It also allowed candidates and committees an identifiable group of knowledgeable staff members to which specific questions and inquiries could be addressed.

The FEC continued its program of certifying primary matching funds. Eight of 15 candidates who received public funds during the election year continued to receive funds in 1977 for purposes of satisfying campaign debts. Including matching fund submissions pending for the previous year, the commission certified a total of $516,164 during 1977.

Matching Funds Regulation Changed

On February 3, the FEC adopted an amendment to its proposed matching fund regulations. The net effect was to render past-eligibility matching-fund payments conditional upon the availability of privately raised funds. The previous regulations provided for the matching of contributions to the extent of the outstanding debt at the date of ineligibility whether or not private funds were raised after that date.

On May 6, Commissioner Thomas Harris appeared before the Senate Committee on Rules and Administration to discuss S 926, a bill that, among other things, contained a proposal for the public financing of Senate elections. Specifically, Harris provided the committee with information as to:[48]

1. Cost per election year to fund Senate campaigns (estimated between $27.6 million and $38.7 million).
2. Agency cost for staff and equipment to administer and monitor the proposed program (estimated at $1.24 million).
3. Technical suggestions on program implementation and enforcement.

On August 3 the Senate voted to remove the public financing provisions from the bill. Commissioners Harris and Joan D. Aikens testified July 12 before the House Administration Committee on congressional public financing. The testimony did not cover any specific proposed legislation but rather was designed simply to explain to the committee the procedures involved in the 1976 system of presidential public funding and provide tentative cost estimates for congressional public funding. These estimates, based on two hypothetical systems of funding, ranged, when combined with previous estimates for Senate public funding, from $36 million to $62 million.

Budget, Organization, and Operation

For the fiscal year the FEC received an appropriation of $6 million plus an additional $180,000 to compensate for an October 1976 cost-of-living salary increase. For 1978 the commission received an appropriation of $7 million and requested $8,624,000 for 1979.

In January 1977 the FEC created a separate Office of Planning and Management. This office, directly responsible to the staff director, was given overall authority for planning and management. Specifically, the office bears responsibility, in conjunction with the Budget Task Force, for developing the agency budget and evaluating the consistency of programs with commission objectives. Much of the time and effort of Planning and Management during 1977 was spent in attempting to apply the principles of zero-based budgeting to the management of the agency's fiscal affairs.

The Data Systems Office was reorganized early in 1977 to provide broader based computer support. The new division, Data Systems Development (DSDD), expanded its services to provide support not only for the Disclosure Division, as was the case in 1976, but for other divisions as well. By the end of 1977, for example, the DSDD had completed a computer system for personnel and mail control and expected to extend this service in 1978 to include payroll, inventory, budget, and accounting systems.

As a result of the 1976 Amendments that transformed the FEC into an executive branch agency, all staff positions were classified according to civil service standards. The new classification established job descriptions and grade levels for each position. Personnel practices and procedures were further formalized during 1977 through the Office of the Staff Director, which promulgated a comprehensive set of policies on promotions, performance ratings, and grievances.

Legislative Recommendations

The FEC made several recommendations to Congress in 1977, most of which were based on its experience with the audits of presidential campaigns. There were instances in 1976 where candidates accrued interest on public monies prior to the repayment of surplus funds to the Treasury. Because of this, and to ensure the integrity of the public financing program, the commission suggested that all surplus funds be returned to the Treasury at the end of a campaign or, alternatively, any interest earned on public monies be included in the total repayment amount.

The 1976 Amendments allow publicly financed presidential candidates in the general election to use private contributions for the payment of legal and accounting services necessary to ensure compliance with the Act. The commission's own regulations permit a presidential campaign to maintain a separate depository for private funds used exclusively for compliance purposes. To eliminate the need for such private contributions, the commission recommended that the FECA be amended to provide a block grant for legal and accounting services for each candidate and committee receiving public funds.

The FECA does not define exactly what constitutes a bona fide nominating process for purposes of obtaining primary matching funds. Because of this, the FEC has lacked criteria for answering such questions as:[49]

● Can a candidate or political party unilaterally declare that a nomination process has occurred and claim public funding?

● When does a nominating process begin and when does it end?

● Can a minor-party candidate be nominated within a few weeks of a presidential general election, in which case a substantial portion of matching funds might be used to influence the general election?

Because of these and other uncertainties, the commission recommended that Congress amend the law to provide specific guidelines in this area.

A Computer System

The FECA Amendments require the Federal Election Commission to make available to the public the financial disclosure reports filed with the agency by all candidates, committees, and individuals involved in financing campaigns for federal office. This stipulation and the need for efficient means of processing candidates' requests for matching funds, ensuring compliance with the law and executing audits, made it necessary for the commission to secure computer assistance. The approaching 1976 elections demanded development of computer support, and the FEC responded early in 1976 by passing a resolution affirming its desire to use the computer to process information relating to the coming primary and general elections.[50]

Institution of a computer system followed consideration of the needs of the agency, the candidates, and the public, as well as of computer capabilities and the degree to which certain uses of a computer were likely to retain congressional approval for an extended period of time.[51]

The Task Force on Data Processing and Computer Applications, created on October 23, 1975, with Orlando Potter as its chairman, was made responsible for assisting in development of the computer system.

The planned computer support invited speculation regarding possible difficulties in gathering and storing information, and some observers wondered whether a single agency was capable of efficiently processing data that formerly had been collected by three — the General Accounting Office (GAO), the Secretary of the Senate, and the Clerk of the House.[52] Another difficulty involved costs and the limitations of the FEC operating budget. An estimate prepared in February 1976 indicated that the computer system would cost about $550,000 for the first 12 months, including $316,000 for development, programming, processing, and equipment, plus another $185,000 in salaries.[53]

The computer system was designed to improve the commission's efficiency in different areas.[54] When the agency was under considerable pressure to verify submissions from presidential candidates seeking matching funds, the computer made possible a statistical sampling technique whose success led the FEC eventually to drop its requirement for complete review of all submissions. The system also enabled the commission to monitor the total amounts of contributions candidates received at different times from a single source and to identify individual contributions exceeding the legal limit. In addition, the computer permitted the FEC to employ certain thresholds of financial activity in deciding whether to review a campaign. For example, the computer facilitated the agency's decision to review thoroughly only those committees whose aggregate receipts and expenditures totaled $10,000 or more.

Preparation and publication of disclosure documents was executed in 1976 only partially with computer assistance. Some information was compiled manually, since the commission was obliged to meet statutory deadlines for publication. Computer support in preparing these documents came from the Office of Data Systems and Development, which began official operation in August 1976. At the outset it was chiefly concerned with gathering and storing data that had accumulated during the previous months and was continuing to pour into FEC offices. Difficulties with processing this information arose because disclosure forms were not wholly compatible with data entry requirements, different versions of the forms had been circulated at different times, there was variation in the ways candidates completed the forms, and the pressure of time was extreme.[55] Despite various setbacks, the office managed to produce its first two disclosure reports before the election. Establishment of this ongoing publication program enabled the FEC to discharge its responsibility to serve as a disseminator of election statistics for research, analysis, and interpretation by an independent public.

Clearinghouse

The FECA of 1971 provided for a Clearinghouse on Election Administration in the General Accounting Office (GAO). When the 1974 Amendments relieved the comptroller general of his responsibility, the clearinghouse function was vested in the Federal Election Commission. The Clearinghouse has continued to operate, serving as a national center in the neglected field of election administration and as a catalyst in election law research and in the interchange of ideas.

The Clearinghouse conducts independent contract studies of the administration of elections.[56] These studies include, but are not limited to: the method of selection of, and the type of duties assigned to, election board officials and personnel, and practices relating to the registration of voters and voting and counting methods. The products resulting from these research efforts are made available to the general public at cost. The Clearinghouse is involved more with the processes by which elections are managed and conducted, rather than the ways elections are financed.

Early on, the Clearinghouse contracted with the Congressional Research Service of the Library of Congress to publish a monthly *Federal-State Election Law Survey* analyzing federal and state legislation and judicial decisions,[57] and to issue surveys of state election laws.

From its inception at the GAO through its transfer to the FEC, the Clearinghouse has published numerous documents.[58] The *FEC Journal of Election Administration* was initiated by the Clearinghouse in 1977.[59] Generally, its publications have been well received among federal, state, and local election officials, and among students of the electoral process. Speakers are provided at meetings of the Association of Secretaries of State and other such groups. The Clearinghouse also provides advice when sought, and consultation when needed. The Clearinghouse is considered to be an integral part of the FEC operations, but it was not until 1978 that the commission gained congressional approval of complete FEC control of the Clearinghouse budget, which heretofore had been determined by Congress.

In August 1978, FEC General Counsel William C. Oldaker recommended that the agency cease to provide copies of Clearinghouse studies free of charge to anyone except people executing government business directly related to elections. This proposal meant changing the agency's policy of distributing these publications free of charge to state and local officials and charging a fee only to members of the general public who wished to purchase copies.[60]

The FEC rejected Oldaker's proposal on September 21, 1978, accepting the cost increases and contending that the elimination of free distribution would constitute a major change in FEC policy and one that would be unfair to the state and local officials who both administered federal elections and participated in the preparation of Clearinghouse publications.[61]

Audit Authority

One of the Federal Election Commission's most important responsibilities in the 1976 election lay in its audit authority. Part of this authority consists of the power to make periodic audits and field investigations relating to both filed reports and failure to file reports. FEC policy provided for audits of all qualified presidential candidates for nomination as well as those who were on 10 or more state ballots in the general election, all multicandidate committees raising or spending more than $100,000, a random selection of other multicandidate committees and congressional candidates, all the major-party national and congressional committees, and major-party state political committees, as well as other candidates or committees whose reports revealed discrepancies or matters needing clarification.

A major area of audit authority related to the presidential campaigns because public funds were being used. Management review audits were necessary to qualify presidential candidates for matching funds, and audits of publicly financed candidates also were required after the matching period or after the candidate's withdrawal. Funds could be used only for qualified campaign expenses, and these expenses were identified in the course of the audit. Candidates were required by law to return unused public funds.

On August 18, 1975, the commission began audits to determine which presidential candidates would be eligible for federal funds. In the course of a 10-week tour, the auditors sought to learn the nature of accounting problems that candidates encountered with the new law and also to define the procedures that would be used in future audits. Questions to be resolved included whether or not the total amount determining eligibility to receive public funding should include deductions for fund-raising expenses, and whether auditors should attempt to review all contributions or merely a sample for each campaign. Potential auditing problems offered a major reason for trips by auditors to the committees of Jimmy Carter, Lloyd Bentsen, Morris Udall, Henry Jackson, President Ford, and two committees supporting George Wallace. The auditors also announced plans to review the records of Fred Harris, Terry Sanford, and Eugene McCarthy.

When the commission explained its plans to audit these 10 committees, protests were heard almost immediately from the campaign committee of Eugene McCarthy, who at this time was among those challenging the constitutionality of the 1974 election reform law in a suit being appealed to the Supreme Court. McCarthy campaign chairman Ronald Cocome declared that the commission had no legal authority to audit a candidate who was not eligible for matching funds and was suspected of no violations of the campaign laws. Cocome called the planned review "a logical absurdity — and a waste of taxpayers' money." He added, "Rather than encouraging citizens to be active and spirited participants in politics, the thrust of the Commission's activities is to make campaigners an army of clerks and drones and bookkeepers."

In a letter to the commission, Cocome said that McCarthy, unlike the other presidential candidates awaiting audits, had not applied for matching funds and, as an independent candidate, had been declared by the U.S. Court of Appeals in *Buckley v. Valeo* to be ineligible to receive them unless he qualified in the November election. Further, he protested the notion of an "instructional audit," noting that candidates were still required to make disclosures on old reporting forms because the commission had not yet issued the new forms. He announced that the McCarthy committee would not submit to the FEC audit and cited the Bill of Rights as it protected citizens against "unreasonable searches and seizures."[62] FEC Counsel John Murphy responded that the McCarthy committee had misread the law regarding commission auditing authority. Only temporarily halted, the commission voted five to one in favor of rescheduling the audit.

Congressional Audit Policy

Audits of congressional campaigns also aroused controversy. Under a preliminary plan approved September 25, 1975, the commission announced its intention to audit Senate campaigns spending more than $35,000 and House campaigns spending more than $25,000 in the 1976 elections.[63] FEC staff stressed the agency's intention of devoting equal attention to opposing parties and candidates in a given district or state, so that the effects of publicity associated with audits would not be discriminatory. The audits were scheduled to be performed between October 1, 1976, and April 1, 1978. Commissioner Neil O. Staebler attempted to convince his colleagues that the spending threshold was too low, and suggested that only committees spending more than 75 percent of the allowable amount should be audited. His proposal was rejected, and great concern was expressed about the adequacy of the budget for the large number of audits being undertaken since, if the audits applied to the committees of contenders in primary races, 60 or 70 percent of the candidates would be audited.

In November 1976 the commission adopted a cautious approach to the audits of congressional campaigns that was designed to make them possible without unduly alarming incumbent members of the House in particular.[64] The policy provided for audits that would occur, in the case of the average congressman, only once every 20 years. According to the review system, most of the 1,300 congressional campaign committees would be ranked according to the number of anomalies in their reports to the FEC on campaign spending. Anomalies included such oddities as high postage costs without appropriate printing expenses, or heavy fund raising without fund-raising expenses. During 1977 the FEC would audit the first 50 committees on this list plus 134 randomly selected House and Senate committees. Two audit assistants to FEC Staff Director Orlando Potter recommended that the commissioners make one-third of all congressional audits voluntary. The assistants, Gordon A. McKay and Bob Costa, noted that the agency would have difficulty in convincing members of Congress of the value of the audits and particularly in allaying congressional fears regarding the potential for adverse publicity. The two men argued that voluntary audits might make the commission's work seem less threatening. Nevertheless, this suggestion was dropped, as was Commissioner Staebler's proposal that opponents be audited in each case to avoid discriminatory publicity (this would have meant audits of only 20 or 25 of the reports that most provoked curiosity).

The new congressional audit policy was noticeably softer than that applied by the FEC toward other political committees, although it was less lenient than the original proposal set before the commission. It also suffered by comparison with the records of earlier supervisory officers under the 1971 FECA. The GAO had audited 424 committees following the 1972 election, and although the House Clerk had conducted no audits, the Secretary of the Senate had audited every Senate campaign.

In contrast, the FEC planned 271 routine audits for 1977. In defending its selective policy, the commission pointed to budgetary restrictions: Its $6 million budget — more than twice the total of its three predecessors' budgets — financed not only audits but the supervision of the spending of federal funds and start-up costs of various kinds. FEC spokesman David Fiske pointed out that additional special audits could be ordered as part of the investigative process.

As some observers foresaw, the congressional audit policy did not attract support from the House. Frank Thompson, chairman of the House Administration Committee, informed agency officials that audits of the 5 percent random sample of congressional seats up for election in 1976 fell beyond the scope of the FEC's powers.[65] Congressional campaigns could be audited for good cause only, he said. In voicing his objections, Thompson noted: 1) the commission's failure to complete audits of presidential primary campaigns, Republican and Democratic conventions, and the presidential general election campaigns as required by law; 2) the impossibility of making an audit "random" either in fact or in public appearance; 3) the possibility that the audit would be used against the candidate by his opponent; 4) the likelihood that audits would concentrate on the campaigns of less powerful members of the House rather than those of the more powerful members; and 5) the probability that random audits would be unproductive and wasteful of money and resources.

For a time the commission seemed likely to drop the idea of random audits and continue with the plan of auditing campaigns whose reports were distinguished by a high incidence of anomalies. A commission spokesman indicated that the criteria for selection of such campaigns would not be released until the audits had been completed. A preliminary checklist of identifying characteristics included consistent tardiness in filing reports, discrepancies in cash-on-hand totals, failure to respond to commission requests for additional information or clarification, consistent omission of data identifying contributors, and failure to list funds as received despite report of the gift by another committee.[66] Because the commission considered the audit program to be educational, discussion of the proposed audits could not be held in closed sessions without either a determination of "reason to believe" that a violation had occurred[67] or a vote by the commission. The commissioners voted 4-2 in favor of deciding case by case whether to discuss the proposed audits in closed or open session.

Despite Thompson's objections and general resistance in the House, the commission announced that it would conduct a schedule of routine audits of the campaign finance records and reports of candidates who ran in 48 randomly selected Senate and House elections in 1976.[68] In each selected state or district, audits would be performed on all major-party general election candidates; all other general election candidates who received at least 5 percent of the vote or raised or spent at least $10,000; and primary candidates of one party who either received at least 5 percent of the vote or raised or spent more than $10,000 in races where the winning general election candidate was of that party and received more than 75 percent of the vote in the general election but less than that margin in the primary.

First Audits

On October 7, 1976, the FEC released audits of the first of 50 multicandidate committees it had slated for review. As the audits of presidential candidates proceeded, discrepancies occasionally received publicity. Earlier, in September 1976, the commission was reported to have recommended that the Carter campaign be denied $386,000 in federal matching payments because of disclosure problems in reports during the primaries.[69] It was said that this recommendation had been overruled by the agency's legal staff and therefore had not been made public.

Instead of deciding to curtail funds, the commission staff allegedly decided to seek answers to remaining questions during the scheduled audits of all 15 candidates who had collected matching funds. The negative Carter campaign recommendation apparently had been based on omissions of names of endorsers for loans, omission of certain campaign debts, indication of a negative cash balance when a positive one existed, and contributions in excess of the legal limit from several individuals. The auditors objected that the Carter campaign had failed to file the requested amendments correcting misinformation; the commission rejected this conclusion, however, deciding that the Carter campaign substantially had complied with campaign disclosure requirements. Questions raised about the Carter campaign remained unanswered during 1977 because audits were not completed.

One FEC audit disclosed that the presidential campaign of Pennsylvania Governor Milton Shapp had not qualified for federal funding.[70] (The Shapp campaign receives fuller treatment in connection with the prenomination period.) Although no discrepancies in Shapp's reports were discovered by the FEC during its initial check, a postelection audit made public in May 1977 indicated that $5,000 thought to have been raised in small contributions from each of 20 states actually had formed part of larger contributions channeled by Shapp supporters through other individuals. Shapp agreed to repay all of his matching funds, and several of the other individuals involved were fined.

Slow Pace. Despite these and other disclosures stemming from the audits, the commission received much criticism. As much as a year and a half after the conventions, only five out of 15 prenomination audits — those of the Church, Brown, Bentsen, McCormack, and Sanford campaigns — had been made public. The FEC repeatedly was attacked for its slow pace and some commentators asked how long the commission would take to audit a thousand publicly funded congressional election campaigns if 15 presidential campaigns could not be reviewed in 20 months.[71]

Public disclosure, it was pointed out, is not effective or meaningful if it is not timely, and much criticism focused on the commission's policy of auditing the campaigns of candidates who withdrew before undertaking audits of the Ford and Carter campaigns. With no audits of the two principal presidential campaigns available to the public before the general election, the commission acknowledged that illegalities in these two campaigns would be likely to escape its attention. Audits of the Ford campaign were published in March 1978 but audits of the Carter campaign were not released until 1979.

The commission's record in meeting obligations specifically conferred on it by law made it more difficult for the agency to discharge the duties that the law had defined less precisely. Testifying before the House Administration Committee on possible changes in the FECA, the commission encountered opposition to random congressional audits with renewed force in October 1977. Commission staff already had mailed letters to contributors to the 1976 campaigns of 44 incumbent members of the House, and Rep. Lucien N. Nedzi, D-Mich., pointedly remarked, "I hope the commission realizes that kind of inquiry will cut off that source [of campaign money] forevermore."[72] Representative Thompson commented that the FEC's authority to "make from time to time audits and field investigations with respect to reports and statements filed under the provisions [of the law]" would not survive any House-Senate conference on FECA amendments. The FEC nevertheless proceeded and in late December 1977 audits were released for the Democratic Congressional Campaign Committee and the Democratic National Congressional Committee. Audits of congressional candidates began to appear also.

Members of the House did not object only to the FEC's slowness in releasing prenomination audits of presidential candidates and in disposing of complaints and investigations. Other sources of dissatisfaction were that audits consume staff and volunteer time, discourage volunteer finance managers, are expensive for those audited, and can be misleading when constituents and media fail to distinguish between a routine audit and one prompted by suspicion of violations. Congressmen also complained that contributors become nervous when they receive inquiries asking whether they actually have made recorded contributions, and are discouraged from contributing again. Finally, it was charged that audits prove little, since they are not sworn statements. Some congressional resistance to public funding of congressional campaigns in 1977-78 may have derived from knowledge that its enactment would require audits of all candidates accepting the funds. Audited senators did not voice complaints, however, as did their colleagues in the House, and the Senate would be willing to expand FEC power specifically to permit random audits beyond the present provision of authority.

The FEC's slowness not only prompted criticism but delayed repayment by presidential candidates of surplus federal funds.[73] In December 1977 Ronald Reagan, Gerald Ford, Henry Jackson, and George Wallace were reported to owe the government sums totaling more than $600,000 left over from their campaigns, money that they were holding for completion of the FEC audits that would set the exact amount of the refund. Ford and Reagan were reported to have placed the money in a bank; interest on these funds, it was noted, went to the committees rather than to the government.

During 1977 the commission began or completed a total of 154 audits. Of these, 16 pertained to presidential primary candidates, two to general election candidates, four related to conventions or host committees; three audits were made of minor-party presidential candidates, eight were made of Senate candidates, 10 of House candidates, and 11 of party committees. Of multicandidate committees, audits were made of: labor committees (5), corporate committees (1), trade association committees (1), and other unspecified committees (3).[74]

New Audit Policy. In early 1978 the FEC released many congressional audits, which fueled the flame of resistance in the House, and in April the House Administration Committee amended a budget authorization for the FEC, forbidding use of the money to audit randomly selected reports filed by the House and Senate candidates.[75] This action brought adverse publicity, particularly since an FEC investigation was reported to have discovered substantial irregularities in the campaign reports of the chairman of the House Rules Committee. Rep. James J. Delaney, D-N.Y., had filed reports allegedly containing discrepancies in several areas. Some of the questioned disbursements involved "get-out-the-vote" money; one involved payment of $2,000 to individuals manning telephones; still another (and the largest payment questioned) concerned approximately $7,000 paid to the campaign treasurer. Four different reports submitted by Delaney's campaign committee for the months of July and August 1976 disclosed receipts during that period as $18,925, $15,925, $12,925, and $11,522. Ironically, Delaney had been one of those to doubt the wisdom of a procedure whereby Congress authorized expenditure of funds for investigation of its members. As members of Congress sought to terminate the FEC's policy of making random audits, Representative Thompson noted that FEC officials would be told to audit congressmen only when evidence indicated the possibility of civil or criminal violation, and he added that the commission also would be required to notify legislators before their campaigns were audited and allow time for members to make necessary changes before their books came under scrutiny.[76]

The commission approved a new audit policy for 1978 on April 6. The altered policy stated that priority would be given to audits of candidates and committees referred by the Reports Analysis Division or the Office of General Counsel (such referrals indicated the agency's perception that the candidate or committee needed assistance in reporting or record keeping). Second priority was granted to national and state party committees (plans were made to audit three national committees, 13 of their affiliates, nine national party congressional campaign committees, and about 60 state party committees). Third priority was assigned to nonparty and local party committees selected according to volume of contributions or expenditures (all of those receiving or spending at least $500,000 in 1976 or 1977; half of those receiving or spending between $250,000 and $500,000 in 1976 or 1977; 20 committees receiving or spending less than $250,000 in 1976 or 1977; and a group of about 25 committees consisting of those in any category that requested an audit and committees receiving or spending more than $250,000 in 1978).[77]

Program Criticized, Defended

Though the new audit policy showed that the FEC was ready to restrict the number and scope of its audits, controversy over the commission's audit authority continued. A new challenge arose in July when Congress passed an $8.6 million budget for the FEC for fiscal 1979 (an increase over its 1977 budget of $6 million). The Senate, which for years had conducted audits on its own campaigns, passed the bill without opposition; however, the House version carried a restriction that would prohibit money from being used for random audits of congressional campaigns.

Again, Representative Thompson was an outspoken critic of the audit program. Most House members supported Thompson's charges that the audit program, 1) gives the appearance of wrongdoing where none exists, 2) is costly to both the candidates and the FEC, 3) diverts the FEC's attention from more worthwhile programs, and 4) creates endless red tape and paperwork for candidates who comply with record-keeping requirements.[78]

A July 31 report on the random audits conducted on candidates' committees representing 93 general election and 11 primary election candidates revealed that errors permeated the campaign records of congressmen.[79] Nearly 40 percent of those audited did not have the proper records for documentation, did not properly itemize contributions and expenditures, and/or accepted contributions illegally. Yet, despite the large number of errors found, Thompson and other House dissidents reiterated that the huge expense needed to conduct such audits was not justified by the irregularities found, which they judged to be of minor importance. In response to complaints that many errors occurred directly or indirectly due to the inordinate amount of detailed record keeping required by the FEC, Commissioner Harris replied that Congress "is blaming us for what they wrote" into federal law. Harris and other FEC officials still support the audit program, arguing that the original reasons for the program still justify its existence.

A *Washington Post* editorial noted that the minor problems revealed by audits of most presidential candidates were "not a bad record when you consider the complexity of the reporting rules."[80] The editorial concluded, however, that this record does not indicate that public funding could be extended easily to congressional campaigns. Since more than two years would be required to close the books on a few presidential campaigns, the editorial wondered how many years would be needed to audit several hundred publicly funded congressional campaigns.

The pace of the audit process was being monitored by a number of critics who continued to note that the FEC had published no audit of the Carter campaign. One such observer was Republican Party Chairman Bill Brock, who called on Congress in June 1978 to block FEC appropriations until completion of the Carter audit. Brock also requested that Congress delay Carter's nomination of Samuel D. Zagoria as the Republican member of the FEC. Finally, the Republican Party chairman wondered why the remaining presidential candidates for whom audits had not been completed were all Democrats (the FEC was still at work on audits of the Udall, Shriver, Harris, and Bayh campaigns).[81]

Reporter Jerry Landauer emphasized that the FEC's delay in completing the Carter audit was noteworthy, "because the commission's actions will set a precedent for how closely it intends to scrutinize the details of a president's campaign, especially when some of those details may be embarrassing to the White House." His article referred to numerous alleged discrepancies in disclosure of campaign expenditures from public funds. Yet the fact that the FEC had not acted "even in what seem to be clear cases of inadequate compliance with election laws," was due to a number of reasons.[82]

First, in cases of expenditures over $100 aggregate for which candidates and political committees are required to specify the "purpose" of expenditure, a dispute arose within the FEC over what exactly was meant by "purpose." FEC lawyers and auditors had been debating for more than two years how strictly FEC terminology should be interpreted. Ambiguous entries such as "advance," "compensation," and "get out the vote" were inadequate according to FEC auditors, while FEC lawyers judged such entries to be in compliance with the law as it had been written during the campaigns.

In addition to the dispute over statutory language, FEC auditors also questioned certain expenditures as being inadequately documented for public financing purposes, since those candidates who accept public financing must ensure that all campaign expenditures be legally eligible for payment with public tax dollars. Audits of four of the 15 publicly financed presidential candidates in 1976 were delayed on this matter.[83]

Delays in the completion of the Carter audit were further complicated by a series of FEC investigations into numerous possible violations of the campaign law involving in-kind contributions to Carter's publicly financed campaign. In mid-June, FEC Chairman Joan Aikens expressed her hope that the audit would be completed, "by the end of the summer."[84] Accordingly, on August 30, the commission finally resolved its internal dispute over FECA terminology by favoring a lenient interpretation of commonly used entries in campaign documentation. At that time, it appeared that receipt of further information regarding a minor discrepancy was the only item that stood in the way of a finished Carter audit. On October 13 the FEC handed down the third civil penalty that year against the Carter campaign committee for illegally using public funds to cover postelection transition expenses. At that time a commission spokesperson said that it was not known when the audit would be completed.[85]

Suits Filed Against the FEC

Since its establishment in 1975, the FEC has been the object of mixed evaluations. Some observers claim that the complexity and vagueness of the FECA created a broad range of interpretative power for the FEC. In his assessment of the FEC's performance in its first three years, John R. Bolton, one of the counsel for plaintiffs in the *Buckley* case, expressed a serious concern for the future of the American political process under the new electoral regulatory system. Perceiving the FEC as an agency that has often abused the excessive discretion granted it by the statute, Bolton contends that the commission has spent too much time pursuing trivial violations of nonincumbents and too little on greater violations of incumbents, has operated under incomprehensible enforcement procedures, has issued rulings that are inconsistent and contradictory, and has deferred to the will of a self-interested Congress. Fearing that the actions of the FEC may become a deterrent to free political expression, Bolton has concluded that the political process "is simply too complex and too changeable to permit the creation of a stable regulatory framework — much less one that is truly evenhanded or fair."[86]

Of course, not everyone shares Bolton's fears and concerns, and many think them exaggerated. In his rebuttal to Bolton's complaints, John G. Murphy, former general counsel to the FEC, considered Bolton's impressions of the commission's efforts to regulate political campaigning as rather distorted. Although admitting that the FEC sometimes has erred, Murphy argues that the difficulty in applying the FECA does not necessarily demonstrate unconstitutional vagueness, that the FEC has shown no favoritism for incumbents in pursuing nonfilers of preelection reports, and that the commission persistently has applied the law in such a way to lessen the inherent electoral advantages of incumbents. As for Bolton's fearful conclusion about the future of regulating campaign activity, Murphy counters with the contention that "the inadequacies of the law and the FEC since 1974 . . . pale in comparison to the threat of functional oligarchy that faced the nation in the days before."[87]

The arguments of Bolton and Murphy reflect many of the issues with which the FEC has had to deal during its brief existence. Many individuals and organizations, unhappy with the role of the commission, sought relief through the federal courts. Numerous suits have been filed challenging the constitutionality of certain provisions of the Federal Election Campaign Act, the legality of FEC policy decisions, and the inaction of the commission in prosecuting alleged violators of the law.

Ramsey Clark Suit

The FEC, according to the statute that created it, is subject to congressional veto: the right of either House of Congress to disapprove or veto any agency rule or regulation before such rules can become legally effective. Such an attempt by Congress to supervise the actions of an executive agency is not new. Since 1932, when the first legislation incorporating the one-house veto was enacted, Congress steadily has been attaching the veto provision to various measures; in the last 10 years it has been doing it with greater regularity. There are about 300 legislative veto provisions in 200 laws, of which nearly 100 have been enacted since 1968. Critics of the legislative veto perceive it as an unconstitutional infringement of the president's power and a violation of the separation of powers doctrine. Supporters, however, contend that it is simply a way for Congress to exercise some control over the thousands of bureaucratic rules and regulations that have the effect of law.

The Supreme Court in *Buckley v. Valeo* explicitly refused to decide the constitutionality of the congressional veto. In his concurring opinion, however, Justice Byron R. White held the view that statutory provisions subjecting a "properly created independent" agency's regulations to disapproval by either house of Congress do not constitutionally violate the president's veto power:[88]

> . . .I would be much more concerned if Congress purported to usurp the functions of law enforcement, to control the outcome of particular adjudications, or to pre-empt the President's appointment power; but in the light of history and modern reality, the provision for congressional disapproval of agency regulations does not appear to transgress the constitutional design, at least where the President has agreed to legislation establishing the disapproval procedure or the legislation has been passed over his veto.

It seemed only a matter of time before someone decided to challenge the constitutionality of the one-house veto as affirmed in White's concurring opinion.

On July 2, 1976, Ramsey Clark, former U.S. attorney general and a candidate for the New York Democratic senatorial nomination, with the assistance of Ralph Nader's Public Citizen Litigation Group, brought suit to invalidate the one-house veto. The former cabinet member's brief made several arguments. Clark claimed that his constitutional rights were violated by the provision delegating the discretion to disapprove regulations to a single House without giving any standards or criteria to govern the exercise of such discretion and without requiring any statement of reasons. He argued that the veto provisions violated the separation of powers doctrine by giving the legislative branch authority that constitutionally belongs to the executive branch.

Clark further contended that the law gave incumbent members of Congress unfair advantage over their challengers and that the congressional veto violated his "constitutional rights to have the law affecting him enacted by the full legislative process." Moreover, the suit alleged that the provision impaired Clark's "rights to vote, to participate effectively in the political process, and to compete without discrimination in the electoral process." Finally, the brief claimed that while the Supreme Court had refused to rule on the constitutionality of the contested provision, "it is the plaintiff's position that this question is now in a proper posture for resolution and that a speedy disposition of this action is in the interests of all parties and the public at large."[89]

In responding to the suit, the FEC faced a dilemma: whether to defend the law that reduced commission independence, or not to defend it and thereby offend those members of Congress who insisted upon congressional veto power over FEC regulations. The FEC resolved the matter by adhering to procedural questions. The FEC contended that the Clark suit was premature because injury done to the plaintiff was "contingent upon a sequence of hypothetical actions by coordinate branches of government reviewable when and if they occur." The commission futher argued that the suit asked the court "to hypothesize that a congressional resolution disapproving regulations will necessarily be motivated by a wish to protect the incumbency of the members, rather than the public interest."[90] Not satisfied with this argument, both chambers of Congress hired private counsel.

On September 10, 1976, the case was argued before the U.S. Court of Appeals for the District of Columbia. Attorneys for Clark and the Justice Department relied heavily on the Supreme Court's ruling in *Buckley v. Valeo* that, as originally constituted, the commission was an unconstitutional infringement on the powers of the executive branch. They argued that since Congress could not constitutionally appoint members to the commission, it likewise could not, by the one-house veto provision, "designate a single House as a sort of super-executive to oversee and finally determine which regulations should be put into effect."[91] While the plaintiffs argued the case on constitutional merits, the FEC and counsel for the House and Senate confined their remarks to procedural questions.

Failing to find that Clark had a "ripe injury" or "present personal stake" in how rules, regulations, and advisory opinions are reviewed by the legislature, the Court of Appeals, in a 6-2 decision on January 21, 1977, declined to rule on the suit. In addition, Clark's loss in the New York primary cost him standing as an injured party. Finally, the court denied Clark the right to challenge the statute as a voter because his complaints were not directed toward the actual veto or threatened vetoes of specific regulations. In sum, the court declared that Congress would have to exercise its veto power before the provisions could be ripe for review. At the time of the Court of Appeals ruling the newly reformed FEC had not had any of its regulations vetoed. Moreover, because the case was dismissed on ripeness grounds, the court did not decide whether the Justice Department could challenge independently the constitutionality of a federal law.

The Justice Department position was a traditional one for a president to take, objecting to potential congressional veto of executive actions, and President Carter later sent a message to Congress on the subject.[92]

On February 9, 1977, Clark appealed to the U.S. Supreme Court to overturn the lower court ruling. Contending that a number of issues were left undecided in *Buckley,* particularly the issue of the principle of separation of powers and checks and balances, Clark urged the Court not to limit its examination of the lower court ruling on the "ripeness" issue but to resolve as well the constitutional questions surrounding the one-house veto power. In addition, noting that the FEC did not issue any regulations during 1976, the suit claimed that the FEC's difficulty in formulating and issuing regulations was the result of two one-house vetoes of the congressional expense account and point of entry proposals and "the extensive delays resulting from the necessity felt by the Commission to negotiate the substance of any regulations with relevant Congressional committees prior to transmittal to Congress."[93] Without hearing arguments and without issuing an opinion, the Supreme Court, on June 6, 1977, affirmed the Appeals Court's decision.

By simply affirming that Clark was not in a legal position to challenge the statute, the Supreme Court avoided the necessity of determining the constitutional validity of the one-house veto provision. A few months later, however, the Court was given a new opportunity to resolve the issue. A group of federal judges had appealed a decision by the U.S. Court of Claims upholding the congressional veto provision of the Federal Salary Act of 1967. The Claims Court judges, in a 5-4 ruling on May 18, had held that the "necessary and proper" clause of the Constitution gave Congress enough discretion to permit the legislative veto.[94] The Supreme Court, on January 9, 1978, allowed this decision to stand.

League of Women Voters Suit

An FEC policy statement barred corporations and labor unions from contributing to the funding of the 1976 presidential debates sponsored by the League of Women Voters (LWV). The league filed suit and claimed the FEC ruling prevented the organization from raising sufficient funds to pay for the debates. The FEC asked the court to dismiss the LWV complaint on April 12, 1977, on the grounds the "court had no jurisdiction over this matter because the Commission's policy statement is not a final action . . . but represents an attempt . . . to give formal advice in an uncharted area of law."[95] On May 12, 1977, U.S. District Court Judge Howard F. Corcoran rejected the commission's motion to dismiss the suit, and further action was delayed while the commission reconsidered its prohibition on the use of corporate and union contributions to fund the debates.

To reexamine its policy once the debates were aired, the FEC called a hearing for comment. In testimony before the FEC in September 1977, the LWV argued that the ruling had a "chilling effect" on the organization's efforts to raise money to pay for the debates. As a result, the LWV fell $91,000 short of its goal of $350,000 to pay the bill. League President Ruth Clusen argued that organizations would be reluctant to sponsor future debates unless the ruling were overturned. A former staff attorney for the FEC, Benjamin M. Vandegrift, explained the ruling and said the FEC "simply had not had enough experience with the political industry to understand the scope of what we were doing. . . . It seemed better to err on the side of caution." Charles Benton, president of the William Benton Foundation, testified that "public financing imposes a new responsibility and mandate on candidates to make their views public. . . . Sooner or later you will have to tie together public financing and getting information . . . to the public."

Considerable time was spent during the hearing discussing the role of minority candidates in future TV debates. Nicholas Johnson, a former member of the Federal Communications Commission, noted that the Democratic vote might have been split if McCarthy had been allowed to participate in the Ford-Carter debates: "Television is the ballgame in politics. . . . If minor parties are kept off television, they will be weak. If they are given access to it, they will be strong."[96] In December 1977 the FEC finally decided 4-2 in favor of repealing its ban on corporate and union contributions to groups sponsoring candidate debates. The regulation stipulated, however, that such groups must be nonprofit organizations that have a history of neither supporting nor endorsing candidates or political parties.[97] Subsequently, the FEC's motion to dismiss the case was granted, and the case is now closed.

Certification Procedures Challenged

Two 1977 suits related to the U.S. Labor Party's 1976 presidential candidate attacked the FEC's certification procedures. In the first suit, the Committee to Elect Lyndon LaRouche (CTEL) asked the U.S. Court of Appeals to review the commission's actions in two instances: 1) the FEC's refusal on February 10, 1977, to certify matching payments for the party's presidential candidate and 2) the agency's decision to directly contact LaRouche contributors in three states (Delaware, Massachusetts, and Wisconsin) to verify contributions. The second suit was brought by Leroy B. Jones and others as a class action on behalf of all contributors to CTEL and to the U.S. Labor Party residing in Delaware, Massachusetts, and Wisconsin. Filed on April 28, 1977, in the U.S. District Court for the District of Columbia, the complaint charged that the FEC and 10 of its employees, in their efforts to certify contributions to the CTEL, had subjected plaintiffs "to illegal and unconstitutional searches, seizures, threats, harassment, and interferences with the free exercise of constitutionally protected rights of speech, assembly and association."[98] For these alleged unconstitutional acts, the plaintiffs sought a declaratory judgment, a permanent injunction against the FEC, compensatory damages, and punitive relief.

Final action on the first suit is still pending. As for the second complaint, on October 26, 1977, the U.S. District Court (D. C. Circuit) denied the plaintiff's motion for a preliminary injunction and granted the commission's motion for summary judgment. Judge Aubrey E. Robinson, Jr., found that "the FEC's authorization of investigations of claimed contributions to the Presidential election campaign of Lyndon LaRouche and the subsequent actions of the FEC field agents . . . were reasonable and within the statutory authority conferred by [the FECA]."[99]

Chamber of Commerce Litigation

The Chamber of Commerce of the United States announced on March 22, 1977, the creation of the National Chamber Litigation Center (NCLC), a business-oriented, public interest law firm. Supported by membership dues and special contributions, the NCLC opened its membership to U.S. business firms, corporations, trade associations, and individuals. Describing itself as "a voluntary membership organization, seeking to enhance the business point of view before courts and regulatory agencies,"[100] the NCLC filed its first suit against the FEC on behalf of five plaintiffs in the U.S. District Court for the Northern District of Illinois. Bringing the suit were the National Restaurant Association and its political action committee, the Restaurateur's PAC; the National Lumber and Building Material Dealers Association and

LUDPAC, its political action organization; and BreadPAC, the American Bakers Association's PAC.

Certain provisions of the 1976 Amendments to the FECA imposed restrictions on the way trade associations could solicit money. Specifically, a trade association could solicit the shareholders and administrative personnel of a member corporation only after it had obtained the prior written permission of the corporation. Although a corporation might belong to several trade associations, it could permit solicitation by only one association in any calendar year, thus prohibiting other association PACs from fund raising within that company.[101] The purpose of these regulations was to ensure the effectiveness of the contribution ceilings of $5,000 per committee. The NCLC's brief in *Bread Political Action Committee v. FEC* argued that these restrictions denied plaintiffs their First Amendment rights to freedom of speech and association and their Fifth Amendment right to due process of law.

The FEC's motion to dismiss the BreadPAC case was denied, but on October 6, 1977, the court also rejected BreadPAC's motion for a preliminary injunction against enforcement of the solicitation restrictions on trade associations. Judge Prentice H. Marshall conceded that the challenged provisions do infringe on First Amendment rights; but, after considering the history of Supreme Court decisions that upheld such infringements on corporate and union political activities to protect the electoral process, he concluded that "the plaintiff has not shown a strong likelihood or any likelihood . . . of success on the merits as far as the invalidity of this statute is concerned." Moreover, recognizing the corporate nature of trade associations' membership and the "long-standing restrictions that have been imposed upon corporations and unions," Marshall said the limits helped to prevent "circumvention of the basic prohibition against the use of corporate funds." [102]

In a somewhat related case, the political action committee of the U.S. Chamber of Commerce, the National Chamber Alliance for Politics, challenged Section 441b of the FECA, which prohibits PACs from soliciting contributions from other PACs. According to the law, only candidates and their political committees have the right to solicit PAC contributions. Filed July 20, 1978, in the U.S. District Court of the District of Columbia, the Chamber of Commerce suit charged that Section 441b of the FECA abridges the chamber's First Amendment rights to freedom of speech and association, violates the rights of those the chamber is prohibited from soliciting, and denies the chamber's Fifth Amendment right to due process of law by allowing candidates' committees to solicit PACs while denying this right to other PACs.[103] The FEC's motion to dismiss was granted on November 22, 1978. The factors that led to the dismissal were the same as those in the following case of *Martin Tractor v. FEC*.

Martin Tractor v. FEC

One of the 1976 Amendments to the FECA placed limitations on a corporation's right to solicit contributions to its PAC from its employees. Prior to 1976 a corporation could solicit PAC contributions from all its stockholders and employees, provided that such contributions were not "secured by physical force, job discrimination, financial reprisals, or threat of force."[104] Realizing the need for tighter restrictions against potential coercion, Congress adopted Section 201(a) of the 1976 Amendments, dividing a corporation's employees into two classes: Executive and administrative personnel are those employees who are "paid on a salary rather than hourly basis and who have policymaking, managerial, professional, or supervisory responsibilities," while "hourly employees" are those not considered as executive or administrative personnel.[105] Unrestricted solicitation for PAC contributions is allowed only of corporate stockholders and executive or administrative personnel. For hourly employees, a corporation and its PAC is limited to twice yearly solicitations by mail addressed to the employees' homes.

On July 7, 1978, three midwestern companies challenged the constitutionality of the new restrictions on a corporation's right to solicit employee contributions to its PAC. The suit contended that the twice yearly solicitation violated their rights to freedom of speech, assembly, and association, as well as to due process of law. In addition, the failure of the statute to give precise definition of solicitation "creates an impermissible vagueness which prevents ... Plaintiffs from determining the meaning of such term, causes such Plaintiffs to be uncertain as to the extent and application of the prohibition ... , and when combined with the threat of criminal sanctions, restrains one or more of the Plaintiffs in their communications and conduct, and in their administration of PACs, in violation of one or more of such Plaintiffs' rights to due process of law guaranteed by the Fifth Amendment."[106]

The FEC's motion to dismiss the suit was granted on October 18, 1978, by the U.S. District Court for the District of Columbia. In its explanatory memorandum, filed on November 8, the court concluded that neither plaintiffs, nor their political action committees, were entitled to invoke the court's jurisdiction under a provision of the FECA that authorizes certain individuals to sue "for declaratory judgment as may be appropriate to construe the constitutionality of any provision of this act." Use of this provision was limited only to "the Commission, the national committee of any particular party, or any individual eligible to vote in any election for the office of President of the United States." Moreover, even if plaintiffs were qualified to invoke the provision, the court held that no case or controversy sufficiently ripe for declaratory action had been presented.[107]

National Conservative PAC v. FEC

Part of the 1976 Amendments to the FECA recodified the Act's campaign contribution limitations. 2 U.S.C. Section 441(a) limited the amount of contributions to a political committee from individuals to $20,000 in any calendar year and from multicandidate political committees to $15,000 in any calendar year. In 1976, however, the FEC drafted a regulation that provided:[108]

> Contributions made to retire debts resulting from elections held prior to January 1, 1975, are not subject to the limitations of this Part 110 as long as contributions and solicitations to retire these debts are clearly designated and used for that purpose.

This regulation went into effect on April 13, 1977, after Congress failed to disapprove within the required 30-day period.

Desiring to retire certain debts incurred prior to January 1975, the Democratic National Committee requested an advisory opinion from the FEC concerning the legality of DNC's soliciting contributions for that purpose in excess of the $20,000 or $15,000 limitations. The FEC, in response to the request, ruled that statutory limitations on the amount given by an individual or political committee to a political party committee do not apply to "contributions made for the sole purpose of retiring campaign debts resulting from elections before January 1, 1975."[109] On February 15, 1978, the National Conservative PAC, a multiple-candidate political committee, filed suit in the U.S. District Court for the District of Columbia challenging the constitutionality of the regulation, arguing that the advisory opinion was arbitrary and capricious, and contending that the DNC's proposed contribution solicitation violated the law.

Judge Aubrey E. Robinson, Jr., on April 28, 1978, dismissed the suit on grounds that NCPAC had not complied with the procedures of the law, which authorizes a complainant to file suit with the District Court only where the FEC has dismissed a complaint or has failed to act upon a complaint. Since the NCPAC had not filed a complaint with the FEC in connection with the DNC advisory opinion, the judge held that the court had no jurisdiction to entertain a claim of alleged violations of the Act. Robinson also ruled that the NCPAC did not have standing because it was not involved in the advisory opinion request and was not directly affected by the commission's decision. In addition, the court felt that no present justiciable controversy existed: "It is not the advisory opinion which threatens plaintiffs with alleged hardship, but the proposed contribution solicitation by the DNC. There is nothing about AO 1978-1 and its impact upon these plaintiffs which presents to the Court an issue ripe for review."[110]

The NEA Suit

Many organizations that seek to raise money voluntarily from their members for political activities confront the fact that a sizable number of their members may not wish to contribute to such activities. Thus the organizations constantly are seeking methods to overcome this limitation and increase the level of participation among their members. One such method is the negative or reverse checkoff system, designed primarily to increase the amount of money available for political activities. Unlike most voluntary systems, which require the individual to indicate his or her preference before the money is collected, the negative checkoff system automatically deducts funds from a paycheck and forwards the funds to the political unit of the organization. One example of this system is the plan instituted by the 1973 Representative Assembly of the National Education Association (NEA) to fund its political action committee (NEA-PAC). Under the procedure, each NEA member was subject to an automatic deduction of one dollar, in addition to annual dues, from his paycheck to be contributed to NEA-PAC. If any member objected to the political contribution, he had to obtain a special form, fill it out, and mail it to NEA requesting a refund.

With membership of approximately 1.8 million persons employed in public schools and colleges throughout the United States, the NEA political action committee quickly became a formidable and effective organization. The negative checkoff system enabled the NEA to secure the participation of most of its members in states that operate the plan. The system was used in seven states in 1974, 12 in 1975 and 16 in 1976. In 1977 only 16 percent of the memberships requested refunds. The NEA was able to spend $400,000 on behalf of the Carter-Mondale ticket in 1976.[111] Moreover, according to a 1978 Common Cause study, the political committees of NEA and its affiliates contributed a total of $620,556 to the 1974 and 1976 campaigns of 237 current members of the House of Representatives.[112]

The FEC received a series of complaints from individuals and organizations objecting to the NEA negative checkoff system. In fall 1976 both Common Cause and the National Right to Work Committee (NRWC) filed complaints with the FEC charging the NEA with violating not only FEC regulations, but also federal law that prohibits political contributions "by dues, fees or other money required as a condition of membership in a labor organization or as a condition of employment."[113] The NEA maintained that the program was neither illegal nor coercive and gave asssurances that individuals requesting refunds received them and suffered no reprisals from the association.

The FEC agreed with opponents of the negative checkoff plan and banned such plans in regulations submitted to Congress in August 1976 and published in the *Federal Register* in the same month. The NEA engaged in intensive lobbying efforts to delay congressional action on the proposed regulations containing the ban. Congress adjourned on October 1, two days short of the 30 legislative days required to approve the FEC regulations. There were denials that the NEA lobbying was the reason for the postponement of making the regulations effective, but it was certainly a contributing factor. In response, the commission issued a policy statement on October 5 which declared that:[114]

> . . .the Commission intends to administer the Act in a fashion which implements the interpretations set forth in the proposed regulations. All persons subject to the Act should accordingly comply fully with the requirements of the FEC regulations during the 1976 elections. The FEC regulations should be looked upon as interpretative rules under traditional concepts of administrative law and should be taken as an authoritative guide as to how the election laws apply.

The NEA continued to use the disputed checkoff system during the general election period.

In January 1977 the FEC resubmitted the regulations to Congress as required by law. The negative checkoff plan continued to generate much debate during congressional hearings. Most of the House Administration Committee favored the NEA payroll-deduction plan but expressed concern that any veto of an FEC regulation might bring about a constitutional court test of the one-house legislative veto power. In this spirit, the committee in a meeting March 17, 1977, passed by a voice vote the following resolution:[115]

> Resolved: that the House Administration Committee by not reporting out a resolution specifically disapproving the proposed FEC regulation 114.5 does not intend that this be interpreted in any way as endorsing any specific enforcement action by the FEC against any specific organization(s) and further that these proposed regulations do not in any way change or modify the applicable law.

The National Right to Work Committee brought suit in U.S. District Court for the District of Columbia on March 8, 1977, to force the FEC to act on its complaint of October 1976 against the NEA. This was the first suit brought under the FECA provision that allows any party aggrieved by failure of the commission to act on a complaint within 90 days to file a petition with the District Court.

In a related case, two Michigan teachers, Paul and Lore Chamberlain, filed a motion in the same court on March 14 directing the agency to act on a complaint filed with the FEC on October 19, 1976, against the Garden City Education Association, the Michigan Education Association, and the NEA. The original complaint alleged that the associations engaged in the same practices that the National Right to Work Committee's suit claimed were illegal.

Consolidating both the actions, U.S. District Court Judge June L. Green, on August 31, 1977, ordered the FEC to decide within 30 days whether the NEA was violating federal campaign laws.[116] Judge Green interpreted the deadline provision as a requirement on the FEC to make final disposition of all complaints within the 90 days, from preliminary examination to initiation of court action. Considering the number of complaints before the FEC and fearing the effect of the ruling on FEC operations, the commission appealed the decision to the U.S. Court of Appeals in the District of Columbia. Commission Chairman Thomas Harris, in House Administration Committee hearings, requested that Congress modify the 90-day deadline.

The FEC, after failure to achieve a conciliation agreement with NEA, brought action on September 28, 1977, against the NEA and 18 of its state affiliates where the checkoff system was in use. In its suit, the commission asked the court to enjoin the defendants from continuing their use of the negative checkoff system, to prohibit defendants from making further contributions and expenditures from the funds, and to order defendants to return all monies collected.[117] On November 10, 1977, the NEA answered the FEC's suit and filed a counterclaim, charging that a prohibition of their use of the checkoff system to collect political contributions is a violation of NEA members' rights under the First and Fifth Amendments to the U.S. Constitution.

District Court Judge Oliver Gasch, granting on July 20, 1978, the FEC's motion for summary judgment and dismissing NEA's counterclaim, declared the reverse checkoff system for collecting political contributions to be a violation of federal election law. Citing previous Supreme Court decisions requiring "affirmative consent" before a contribution can be considered "voluntary" and permissible under federal law, Judge Gasch rejected NEA's argument that voluntary membership in an organization implies a voluntary choice to support the organization's political activities: "Coincidence of viewpoints between a member and a labor organization's employment objective does not necessarily translate into coincidence of political viewpoints. . . . When a member joins, he likely assumes that he will have to pay his fair share of the cost of the union's normal labor activities. It does not follow that he knows he will also be supporting the union's extracurricular activities in the political arena unless he expressly objects."[118]

The NEA was not prohibited from using a payroll deduction to collect PAC contributions, but the ruling did require that the NEA member "be asked beforehand if he wants a contribution to be deducted along with his dues." Although Gasch refused to order NEA to return all funds or to fine NEA, as requested by FEC, he did order refunds of all PAC contributions that were illegally collected. For more than 200 members of Congress who had received NEA contributions the order created a problem of what to do with their "illegal contributions." The FEC solved the problem by deciding August 31 that candidates for federal office did not have to return contributions made by the NEA, since they had no knowledge of the illegality of the collection procedure.

As instructed by the court, the NEA prepared a plan for returning the money to NEA members who did not wish to contribute to its political committees. The plan involved the publishing of a notice in the NEA newsletter to inform members of the court decision and to direct them to return a preprinted card for the refund. Judge Gasch, on November 2, 1978, rejected the NEA proposal because it continued to place the burden on members who did not wish to contribute. As a solution, the judge ordered the NEA to set up a reverse payback system. According to this plan, the NEA would notify members that refunds will be forthcoming in the mail unless they return cards, printed in the notice, which declared their refusal of the refund and affirmed their wish to contribute.[119]

National Right to Work Committee v. FEC

The FECA allows organizations to solicit political contributions from their members, but not from nonmembers or the general public. On October 20, 1976, the National Committee for an Effective Congress (NCEC), a liberal political action organization, filed a complaint with the FEC, charging the National Right to Work Committee (NRWC) and its political action affiliate, the Employee Rights Campaign Committee (ERCC), with violating this fund-raising restriction.

Incorporated in Virginia shortly after World War II, the NRWC was created to oppose membership in labor unions as a condition of employment. Its political action committee, the ERCC, was formed to support candidates who share its conservative political viewpoint. Virginia law required the NRWC to state whether or not it has members. To prevent possible harassment of persons named on a membership list, the NRWC declared in its articles of incorporation that it would not have members. Claiming that such a declaration was only a technicality, the ERCC, prior to the filing of the complaint by the NCEC, requested an advisory opinion from the FEC as to the legality of its fund-raising campaign during the 1976 election. Shortly thereafter, however, the Supreme Court's decision in *Buckley* prevented the FEC from issuing advisory opinions until after its reconstitution. During this time, the ERCC began its fund-raising campaign. ERCC notified the FEC on August 31, 1976, that it wished to renew its request for an advisory opinion, and on October 4, 1976, the FEC told ERCC that more information on NRWC membership would be required before an opinion could be issued. The additional information was not submitted, and the FEC declined to issue the requested opinion.

Acting on the complaint filed by the NCEC, the FEC investigated the solicitation procedure of NRWC and ERCC and found reasonable cause to believe they had violated the membership restrictions of the FECA. On May 9, 1977, the FEC proposed a conciliation agreement, stipulating that NRWC admit to violating the Act, pay a $5,000 civil penalty, and amend its articles of incorporation to become a membership organization. NRWC agreed to amend its articles but refused to pay the fine. It also requested a clear definition of membership requirements under the Act. The FEC rejected this proposal.

The NRWC and ERCC, on October 20, 1977, filed suit contending that the membership provision of the FECA violated their First Amendment rights of free speech and Fifth Amendment rights of due process and equal protection of the law. Arguing that the FEC has refused to provide a definition of the term "member" and that no standards have been established for compliance, the NRWC asked for a permanent injunction against FEC enforcement of those provisions of the Act. In its motion to dismiss the suit, the FEC pointed out that "since NRWC's Articles of Incorporation forecloses it from being a membership corporation," its solicitation of "supporter" can only be seen as "being directed at the general public, which is exactly what Congress intended to prohibit."[120] The FEC further argued that if NRWC's position is accepted by the court, "any corporation can argue that it must be allowed to solicit any member of the general public it believes to be a supporter of its goals."

Notwithstanding its declaration to the contrary in its articles of incorporation, the NRWC insisted that it did have members, both active and supporting. None in either category, however, had voting rights. The FEC, on December 21, 1977, filed a separate suit against NRWC complaining that NRWC did not qualify as a membership organization under the provisions of the FECA and that its receipt of $76,775 in 1976 contributions by those alleged to be supporters of NRWC was a violation of the Act. The FEC asked the court to enjoin ERCC from further solicitation of this nature and order it to return all past contributions solicited unlawfully. The FEC also argued that NRWC should be forced to disclose the names of its members so that determination could be made as to the nature of their membership. On August 29, 1978, U.S.

District Court Judge Barrington D. Parker denied this last request by FEC, concluding that such disclosure would violate constitutional rights to freedom of association.[121]

Socialist Workers Party Suit

Two sections of the FECA concerning the disclosure of campaign funds have been a major source of dissatisfaction for unpopular minor political parties who perceive them as serious obstacles to party contributions because of potential harassment. One section requires political committees to file periodic reports of receipts and expenditures. Whenever these amounts exceed $100 the report must contain the name, address, occupation, and place of employment of the contributor or recipient. The other section requires that records of contributions and expenditures of $10 be kept but not necessarily reported.

In 1974 the National Campaign Committee of the Socialist Workers Party (SWP) and several of its state and local committees sought a waiver of the FECA disclosure requirements. Since the SWP supported candidates in more than one state, the Clerk of the House, W. Pat Jennings, and the Secretary of the Senate, Francis R. Valeo, ruled that the party and its affiliates did not qualify for a waiver. Subsequently, the Socialist Workers National Campaign Committee, supported by the American Civil Liberties Union, filed suit in U.S. District Court for the District of Columbia to challenge the constitutionality of the FECA's disclosure requirements. The suit charged government agencies with harassment of those associated with the SWP and claimed that disclosure of the identity of those individuals might result in further harassment and possible abridgement of their right to freedom of association. The ACLU argued in its complaint that compliance with the disclosure provisions "will deter and intimidate persons from associating with, contributing to and supporting the plaintiff committees and socialist party candidates."[122]

This suit was one of many brought by the SWP in courts throughout the country, and the party consistently argued that disclosure provisions of election laws were used to harass its members and contributors. In November 1974, the ACLU appealed a California Superior Court decision upholding the constitutionality of California's campaign disclosure laws passed in 1973.[123] SWP and ACLU sought to overturn disclosure provisions in the Texas state law, and they were successful in obtaining a temporary restraining order from the Northern Ohio Federal District Court to prevent Ohio state officials from requiring disclosure reports from SWP in the 1974 elections.[124] The U.S. District Court for the District of Columbia, on October 22, 1975, ordered the D.C. Board of

Elections to grant a disclosure exemption to the 1974 Socialist Workers Municipal Campaign Committee.[125]

The U.S. Supreme Court has long protected controversial political organizations from disclosure when disclosure might discourage their political activity. Relevant decisions in this area have supported the principle that that disclosure was warranted for certain groups only if it was necessitated by the most compelling government interest.[126] Finally, the Supreme Court in *Buckley v. Valeo* recognized the diminished importance of disclosure by minor parties and the threat that disclosure can pose to the foundations of such parties. Although the Court upheld the constitutionality of the FECA's disclosure provisions, it stipulated that case-by-case exemptions from such requirements may be permitted for minor parties if there is a "reasonable probability that the compelled disclosure of a party's contributors' names will subject them to threats, harassment, or reprisals from either government officials or private parties." Sufficient proof for such exemptions may include "specific evidence of past or present harassment of members due to their association ties, ... harassment directed against the organization itself [and/or] pattern of threats or specific manifestations of public hostility."[127]

On January 17, 1977, a three-judge district court, denying the FEC's motion to dismiss, remanded the 1974 SWP case to the FEC and ordered it to develop within six months a full factual record and make specific findings of fact concerning the "present nature and extent of any harassment suffered" by the SWP as a result of the disclosure provisions of the Act.[128] The FEC appealed the decision, but the appeal was dismissed on December 13. Observers noted that documentation sought in the pending District of Columbia action might draw on material released by the FBI in connection with a civil suit brought by the SWP in 1973 in a New York Federal District Court. In this case, as a result of March 1975 orders by Judge Thomas P. Griesa, the FBI was forced to release thousands of pages of internal documents to the SWP. Publicized by the SWP, these papers described 31 years of bureau attention to virtually every officer or official ever named by the party. The activities detailed included a program of systematic harassment encompassing efforts to have members dismissed from their jobs and disclosures to news media of unsavory information about their personal lives. Also described were attempts to encourage police agencies to prosecute on petty charges and general efforts to disrupt the party's internal activities and to pit the group against other organizations in the left and civil rights movements.[129]

It was learned in March 1976 that FBI agents had burglarized the New York City offices of the SWP and its affiliated organizations on at least 92 occasions between 1960 and 1966. The agency claimed that its break-in tactics had been discontinued in 1966 following a directive from J. Edgar Hoover, then director of the bureau. In addition, information eventually reached the press that a second government agency, the CIA, had monitored the party's activities for 23 years.[130]

It was disclosed in August 1976 that FBI investigation of the SWP continued to the present day, and that the bureau had no plans to terminate its inquiry. The court continued to order the FBI to release documents to the SWP, but bureau spokesmen protested, arguing that to furnish the information might jeopardize agents' lives, compromise the bureau's investigative methods, or damage the reputation of innocent individuals. An attempt by government lawyers to have the suit dismissed on technical grounds failed, and the SWP increased its damage claim to $40 million. By September the number of SWP informers known to have been employed by the FBI had increased to 1,000. It was also learned that the bureau still retained 66 informers posing as party members. On September 15, 1976, the Justice Department ordered the FBI to halt its 38-year investigation of the party, noting that the inquiry had failed to produce evidence at any time of wrongdoing by the party or its members.

In October 1976 it was learned that FBI agents had visited the Office of Federal Elections in 1972 to inspect the financial records of the SWP and review lists of donors to the party. The party claimed that 18 of 96 persons whose names were disclosed on 1972 and 1974 lists had been harassed by the FBI.[131]

As the case continued in court, the press reported that the FBI had paid $1.6 million to informers hired to report on the SWP. Concluding that the case could be resolved only by granting SWP counsel access to a representative cross section of the files on the informants, Judge Griesa ruled that the FBI must turn over to the party its files on 18 informers. After Attorney General Griffin B. Bell's refusal to release the files, Judge Griesa, on July 6, 1978, issued an order holding the nation's highest law enforcement officer in contempt. The next day, Bell was given a stay of the contempt order pending the government's appeal of the dispute.

Basing its decision on the evidence of FBI harassment introduced in the New York case, the District of Columbia federal court, in early January 1979, approved a consent decree that exempted the SWP from the disclosure requirements of the FECA, at least through the 1984 election. According to the court's decree, the SWP, to renew its exemption after 1984, again must demonstrate that disclosure of its contributors would continue to violate their constitutional right to freedom of association. The party still was required to keep full financial records of its operations and to submit periodic reports of its income to the FEC.

FEC Enforcement

On February 28, 1974, Elmer B. Staats, comptroller general of the United States, presented a summary of the General Accounting Office's enforcement responsibilities and actions under the 1971 Federal Election Campaign Act.[132] He divided enforcement of campaign finance legislation into two major tasks: obtaining compliance with the words and the spirit of the law, and levying penalties against those who fail to comply. Staats noted that voluntary compliance was more important than compilation of a massive record of prosecutions for failure to comply. The GAO had emphasized compliance with respect to the presidential candidates' reporting requirements.

Staats noted the need for prompt and effective action in cases of violation of the law. Of the 38 cases involving presidential candidates that the GAO had referred to the attorney general, only one civil suit and three criminal actions had been filed so far by the Justice Department. Staats suggested that the creation by statute of a special prosecutor for election and campaign law violations within the Justice Department might produce speedier action and insulate the department from political favoritism in the handling of such matters. Finally, the comptroller general argued that the penalties assessed in such cases must be evenhanded and meaningful. He criticized the small fines levied against large corporations and wealthy individuals in some cases relating to the 1972 presidential election.

The 1974 Amendments consequently sought to consolidate enforcement authority in the Federal Election Commission and gave it responsibility for examining charges of violations of the law and bringing suit where necessary. Observers watched to see whether the combined responsibilities vested in the agency would result in prompt and significant action against violators of campaign laws. An important part of the commission's work consists in fostering compliance,[133] however, and the success of this approach naturally depends to a considerable extent upon the actions of candidates and their advisers.

Given the complexity of the FECA and the mass of paper it generated, the FEC found it necessary to develop a set of regulations for implementing the statute. In June 1976 the commission's legal staff and the Office of Disclosure and Compliance developed a "Memorandum of Understanding on Procedure for Reporting of Violations." The memorandum set forth the procedures for handling matters involving nonfiling, late filing, partial filing, garbled filing, and clerical errors or surface violations.[134] According to the document, the Disclosure Division was responsible for making nonfilers readily identifiable, partly through communications with the Secretaries of State or similar state officials.

The Disclosure Division was to request that the state officials forward to the commission on a regular basis names of persons qualified to go to the state ballot in either a primary or a general election. The goal was to develop a procedure to handle in a similar way the most common technical matters coming to the commission's attention. The basic tool was a progressive set of warning notices sent to the candidates at specified intervals.

In its enforcement actions, the commission follows a well-defined procedure. Enforcement action follows receipt of a signed, sworn, notarized complaint or of information "ascertained in the normal course of . . . supervisory responsibilities," at which time the Office of the General Counsel assigns the case a "Matter Under Review" (MUR) number.

When the possible violation involves candidate failure to meet deadlines and filing requirements, the commission sends two series of letters to the candidates involved. The first such letter indicates that the commission has found "reason to believe" that the Act has been violated; the second states that the agency has "reasonable cause to believe" a violation has occurred.

If the agency determines that there is reason to believe violation has occurred, enforcement proceeds through several stages, all but the first of which can be initiated only by a formal vote of the commissioners.[135] The first stage consists of preliminary review followed by a commission determination of "reason to believe" that a violation might have occurred. A formal investigation in the second stage and notification of the person involved are followed by further deliberation by the FEC. Third, a 30-day period is granted for voluntary compliance or conciliation and, finally, if there is continuing reason to believe that a violation has occurred, civil action proceeds.[136] The case can be closed at any stage if a majority of four commissioners believes that conciliation has been achieved or that evidence of violation is insufficient to warrant further action.

The FEC can issue advisory opinions and regulations, and its audit and investigatory powers help the agency to determine the degree of compliance. The agency also has the power to seek civil court enforcement of court orders and of conciliation agreements. In addition to civil enforcement, the commission has the authority to refer certain serious offenses to the Department of Justice for criminal prosecution. These are "knowing and willful" violations involving the making, receiving, or reporting of any contribution or expenditure having a value in the aggregate of $1,000 or more, or having a lesser value in certain cases.

Publicity, particularly negative publicity, is one technique used by the commission to enforce its mandate. The FECA requires the commission to prepare and publish special reports listing candidates for whom reports were not filed. In accordance with these provisions, the commission periodically publishes the names of candidates who fail to file the required postelection report of their campaign finances. Names are published before as well as after elections. In its press releases, the commission notes that it has the authority to undertake further enforcement action under the statute, including civil court enforcement and imposition of civil fines of not more than $5,000 for any violation and not more than $10,000 for a "knowing and willful violation."

With respect to confidentiality and publicity, the commission treads a thin line. The FECA requires that "any notification or investigation may not be divulged by the commission or by any person without the written consent of the person receiving the notification or the person named as a respondent in the investigation." Violators of this provision are subject to fines of as much as $5,000. The commission also is required to make public the results of all conciliation attempts including conciliation agreements entered into and any finding that no violation of the Act has occurred. The agency responded to this requirement in 1976 by developing a system that would make 45 such cases a matter of public record.[137]

By law, FEC notifications and investigations cannot be made public without the written consent of the person receiving the notification or the person under investigation; yet the Freedom of Information Act gives the public, with certain exceptions, the right to inspect information contained in files of federal agencies. To reconcile the two conflicting directives, Gloria Sulton, a member of the commission's legal staff, prepared a memorandum on public access to materials in compliance actions where the investigation has been completed and a report has been made.[138] Sulton noted that there were nine specific exemptions in the Freedom of Information Act (FOIA) that agencies could cite to prevent disclosure. Analyzing several decisions dealing with the statute, she concluded that while the courts favor liberal disclosure under the Act, they interpret the exemptions strictly (particularly in the D.C. Circuit). She mentioned exemptions as particularly applicable and concluded that the commission could disclose compliance files selectively. Disclosure might, however, require deletion of names or other identifying symbols to avoid an unwarranted invasion of privacy, and selection of cases would require careful consideration in each instance. Regarding disclosure of a case after it had been closed, Sulton noted that an important exemption of the FOIA had been enacted long before passage of the FECA. Implied repeal is a principle of statutory construction, but the courts do not favor repeal of statutes by implication. Still, passage of the 1974 Amendments to the FOIA occurred after passage of the 1974 Amendments to the FECA, and the general rule in law is that if there is an irreconcilable conflict between two acts, the latest legislative expression prevails. Sulton contended, however, that the restrictions in the FECA could be reconciled with the FOIA so that both laws would be effective. She suggested that during the period when a compliance action is under investigation, the commission should not disclose any information about it, but following settlement the provisions of the FOIA would apply to any disclosures. After conclusion of the case, information would not be exempt from disclosure unless the commission could apply one of the nine specific exemptions of the FOIA.

Independent Expenditures

The constitutionality of the amended FECA — and the sensitivity of the commission to the question of constitutionality — became the focus of attention little more than two months after the agency was organized, during litigation of *Buckley v. Valeo.* On June 23, 1975, an advertisement was published in *The Washington Post* criticizing President Ford for his Vietnamese and economic policies as well as for his pardon of former President Nixon and his choice of Nelson Rockefeller as vice president. The ad, headlined "Would You Elect Ex-Congressman Ford President?" urged Republicans, Independents, and Democrats to oppose Ford and to convince him to withdraw as a candidate.

It was ascertained that the ad cost $2,368.80, an apparent violation of the $1,000 limit on individual expenditures imposed by the law. The case caused a stir in the FEC, and several commissioners sought to interpret the ad as constitutional to avoid a compliance action that could lead to appeals on constitutional grounds. The issue was resolved when the Supreme Court decisions made clear that individual expenditures of an independent nature could be made in unlimited amounts, so long as there was no collusion with the candidate or his campaign organization. But the enforcement ambivalence of the FEC in this case was a clear indication of its early uncertainties about how to deal with constitutional issues. Later, after the 1976 Amendments were enacted, the FEC adopted a policy statement on the subject of independent expenditures, as noted elsewhere.

The Buckley Case

The Supreme Court decision in *Buckley* resulted in the commission's temporary loss of its authority to investigate complaints of illegal campaign activity. The court ruling, which after two stays became effective on March 23, 1976, restricted the agency's investigations to obvious discrepancies in reports filed with it by the candidates and the political committees. In addition, the court declared unconstitutional all limits on political spending for or against a candidate when the expenditures were made independent of his official campaign organization. These constraints on the commission's enforcement powers almost immediately resulted in political controversy. Those dissatisfied included the President Ford Committee, which had officially protested the establishment of a "delegates for Reagan" committee in Texas that claimed to be separate from the regular Reagan campaign organization. Officials in the Ford campaign charged that the delegate group used the same advertising as the regular Reagan campaign organization, cooperated in fund raising, and asked delegates for contributions of $1,000 — donations allegedly considered not to be subject to Reagan's expenditure limitations. Commission investigators told the Ford committee that they lacked the authority to look into the matter until Congress passed legislation to reconstitute the commission in compliance with the Supreme Court ruling.

In addition, the Wallace campaign was charged with a potential violation of campaign laws that related to plans to declare Wallace field officers "independent" and thus not subject to spending limits legally imposed on Wallace. In response to this complaint, the commission sent Wallace an informational letter advising him that a field office that operated with his consent would not constitute an independent operation. Again, however, the commission could do no more until Congress acted.

During the period between the U.S. Supreme Court's ruling in *Buckley* and the commission's reconstitution, the agency continued to receive disclosure reports, to make them public, and to check them for errors. Later, when its proposed regulations based on the 1976 Amendments were rewritten, it announced plans to apply to the 1976 presidential and congressional campaigns the regulations it had submitted to Congress, although they did not yet have the status of law. The proposed rules covered the reports that candidates and political committees were required to file, the accounting procedures for contributions and expenditures, and limits on independent campaign spending. To support its position, the FEC cited the decision made by the Supreme Court in 1971 that prescribed respect for the administrative interpretation of the act by the enforcing agency.

Some of the FEC's political difficulties concerning its own investigatory powers stemmed from the commission's failure, at the outset, to adopt a uniform standard with respect to "how much and what type of evidence was necessary before [it] committed staff and resources to a preliminary investigation." For example, despite a detailed series of articles in the *St. Louis Post-Dispatch* concerning efforts by the

Monsanto Corporation to have its executive employees participate in a payroll-deduction plan for making political contributions, the commission dismissed the charges filed against the company. On the other hand, on the basis of a handwritten anonymous letter, the staff closely examined the 1974 campaign records of Rep. Charlie Rose, D-N.C. The investigation found the complaint "without merit." The Rose investigation prompted a storm of protest from Capitol Hill when legislators learned that it was made on the basis of an anonymous complaint.[139] In response to the Rose investigation, the 1976 Amendments reduced FEC powers by constricting the standards the FEC must follow in compliance actions and specifically forbade the commission to undertake any investigation or action on the basis of an anonymous complaint.[140]

After the 1976 Amendments became effective, frivolous complaints diminished and matters requiring extended inquiry increased. The commission reviewed 319 enforcement cases during 1976, 34 of which had been initiated in 1975. About 80 percent resulted from actual complaints and approximately 20 percent were prompted by information confirmed during the course of the commission's supervision. The average number of enforcement matters initiated each month increased to a peak of 70 in October.[141] Two-thirds (210) of the 319 cases were closed after preliminary review, but the commission cautions that these figures can be misleading, since a large portion of the preliminary review closings involved cases filed prior to May 11, 1976, whereas virtually all of the cases that proceeded to inquiry or investigation were filed after May 11, 1976, when the new enforcement amendments went into effect.[142]

During and after the 1976 campaign, the commission also filed a number of civil suits against congressional candidates who had failed to comply with the reporting requirements of the FECA. The FEC asked the District Courts to order each candidate to designate a principal campaign committee; to file the July 10, 1976, quarterly report and subsequent quarterly reports; and to file the report required 10 days before his primary election. The FEC also asked the courts to assess a penalty of not more than $5,000 against each candidate for failing to comply with these requirements of the Act. These suits were filed only after the candidates had failed to respond to many requests from the commission for the required information. By late October 1977 the commission had filed 36 court suits against 1976 congressional candidates who had failed to file campaign reports.

The record of the commission's first 18 months indicates that most of the complaints it handled were dismissed either because the commission lacked jurisdiction over the statute in question or because insufficient evidence of wrongdoing was presented. Some cases were referred to the Justice Department for further scrutiny or were terminated when the candidate agreed to comply with the commission's requests. About 12 percent of the 247 cases available for public inspection resulted from questions raised by the commission staff rather than from complaints filed by opposition candidates or the public.[143]

By November 1976 data indicated that of the 331 complaints presented to the FEC, 285 had been settled with all but 35 dismissed. A large number of cases were dismissed usually because citizens did not have proof, or did not understand the law, and no audits were begun.[144] One case was reconciled through a consent agreement between the FEC and the candidate, 14 were taken directly to court because the candidate filed no reports whatsoever, and some 20 were referred to the Justice Department for possible prosecution. In 1977 the Office of the General Counsel processed 486 enforcement cases. This total included 107 cases pending at the end of 1976, 48 begun in 1977 in response to complaints filed with the agency, and 79 resulting from review within the commission during the year. Two hundred seventy-nine cases were closed in the preliminary review stage during 1977, and 21 were pending at the end of the year. Thirty-five cases were closed during investigation, and 52 were pending at this stage at the end of 1977. Sixteen cases had reached the conciliation stage when they were closed, while another 18 were pending. All 46 cases that had reached the civil action stage were closed; none were pending. During the year the commission sent out 2,500 requests for additional information and 300 letters advising candidates and committees that their reports indicated "surface violations."[145]

After the October 10, 1977, quarterly report, the agency changed its procedures, developing a status report on 346 candidates and committees for which one or more reports had not been filed during the year. Letters and telegrams to these candidates and committees were followed by telephone calls, and 187 subsequently filed the requisite reports. Letters declaring that reasonable cause existed to believe violation had occurred were then sent to the 159 remaining nonfilers, and by the end of December the number had been reduced to 39, or 0.8 percent of the 5,160 candidates and committees required to file during the year. The names of the nonfilers were published by the agency on January 9, 1978; the commission filed 16 suits against nonfilers during 1977.[146]

The commissioners contend that the small number of complaints filed indicates not the agency's ineffectiveness but rather the success of reliance on voluntary compliance. By late November 1976, for example, more than 2,000 written requests and nearly 1,400 phone orders for FEC reports had been received and more than 300,000 pages had been sent out. These figures suggested to one commissioner that the candidates were watching each other with a critical eye. The same individual noted

that of the 3,587 candidate and committee spending reports reviewed by
FEC clerks in October 1976, only 361 resulted in an FEC request for
additional information, only 95 required a second notice, and only three
a third notice. The candidates seemed eager to understand and comply
with the law.[147]

The Justice Department

As the FEC sought to fulfill its roles as judge and jury, administrator, prosecutor, enforcer, and magistrate, controversy grew regarding its
enforcement powers. Although the 1976 Amendments gave the commission "exclusive jurisdiction with respect to . . . civil enforcement" of the
Act, the agency was authorized to refer criminal actions to the attorney
general for action, and no mention was made in the law of possible
independent action by the Justice Department. In a procedural ruling
issued in June 1977, a U.S. District Court judge noted that the Justice
Department has unlimited authority to prosecute criminal violators of
the FECA even if no action has been taken by the commission.[148] The
court also ruled that the commission was not required to give the alleged
violator the opportunity to reach a voluntary conciliation agreement
with the FEC before referring the case to the Justice Department.
Violators of the FECA could thus be prosecuted by either agency.

The Justice Department claimed that its independent prosecutorial
authority extended to cases not investigated by the FEC, cases that the
FEC investigated but declined to prosecute, and violations treated by
the FEC as civil matters. The two agencies subsequently reached an
understanding regarding the general principles under which each would
seek to prosecute violators. It was agreed that the Department of Justice
would pursue "serious and substantial" violations of the Federal Election Campaign Act, while the FEC would concentrate on less serious
non-deliberate violations of the statute. House Administration Committee Chairman Frank Thompson intended to back legislation to prohibit
independent action by the Justice Department, presumably because the
FEC was thought to be more easily influenced by congressional action,
but nothing came of the effort.[149]

Other difficulties have developed with enforcement procedures. For
example, some complaints and actions have been on the books for more
than a year, although many are disposed of in less time. In one case, a
U.S. District Court judge ordered the FEC to decide within 30 days
whether a violation of law had occurred. The judge criticized the FEC
for failing to act within a 90-day period stipulated by the FECA. The
FEC claimed it had taken steps that constituted action, whereas the
judge interpreted the law to demand final action within 90 days.[150]

Complaints

As political opponents checked each other, complaints sometimes resulted, such as that lodged by the Democratic National Committee in October 1976. The Democrats charged the Republican National Committee and its affiliates with violation of the contribution limits. The law provides that each national committee can contribute up to the limit to support each congressional candidate, and that a multicandidate committee (such as the Republican National Congressional Committee) can donate $5,000 more. The Democrats objected to the means by which the RNC gave the additional $5,000 and challenged the status of a third Republican organization that was making a third donation to Republican congressional candidates. In response, an attorney for the RNC stated that the procedure had been cleared in advance with the commission.

Ford. The Republicans were also divided among themselves on some issues. During the primaries, for example, the Reagan campaign charged that President Ford had used White House and other administration aides as campaign speakers at taxpayers' expense and that they should have portions of their salaries charged against the president's spending limits.

During the general election, the FEC investigated two Californians who had established several so-called independent committees to aid President Ford. The president's official campaign organization denied any connection with the groups and turned the matter over to the FEC. The commission discovered that five of the committees shared the same officers, address, and campaign depository. By agreement, four of the five committees were disbanded, and contributions in excess of the legal limit were returned to the donors.[151]

In addition, a fund-raiser for Ford entered into a conciliation agreement with the FEC and was fined $500 for making $22,715 in illegal in-kind contributions. Peter F. Secchia campaigned for Ford until May 10, 1976, when he resigned. He subsequently formed a political committee, Friends of the First Family, which registered with the FEC on June 1 and reported all its disbursements to the agency as independent expenditures. The commission decided that the nature of Secchia's early relationship to the Ford campaign made his expenditures contributions in kind, but in levying the fine it recognized that Secchia had attempted to comply with a law he did not understand.[152]

Carter. The Carter campaign also met with some difficulties. During the primaries, the commission sought to determine if illegal contributions had been made by young children of Carter contributors who already had contributed up to the statutory $1,000 limit. General Counsel Murphy found that contributions from children under seven years of age might not meet standards requiring that contributions be made without direction by others and from the minor's own funds. Accordingly, the money was returned to the children.

In December 1976 the FEC made public reports showing that the Carter campaign committee had failed to list the ultimate recipients of tens of thousands of dollars in get-out-the-vote money passed out during the last four days of the general election campaign. Instead, the reports listed the names of the individuals who had spent the money. The information required by law did exist, according to the controller for Carter's committee, and he indicated that the reports could be amended. In September 1977 the FEC conducted another inquiry to determine whether the Carter campaign had violated the law by failing to report as a contribution the sponsorship by three businessmen of a luncheon for Carter in July 1976. The firms involved were Coca-Cola Co., Ford Motor Co., and the Seagram Company, Ltd., and the expenditures amounted to about $4,500. The contributions would have been illegal, since Carter had accepted public financing of his campaign, and the FEC inquiry centered on Coca-Cola's designation of its share as an independent expenditure. The FEC noted that Carter or his staff presumably had been consulted before the luncheon took place. The FEC was told by a sponsor of the luncheon that it was to be followed by another affair with Ford as speaker. Because of schedule conflicts, however, Ford was unable to accept. According to FEC lawyers, therefore, the event was a "qualified campaign expense," not a nonpartisan affair. The Carter campaign had to return $3,285 to the U.S. Treasury — the value of the in-kind contributions made by the sponsors. [153]

Even after becoming president, Carter became subject to another FEC fine for campaign irregularities. As a candidate, Carter had accepted some campaign transportation in a plane owned by his friend Bert Lance's bank. Only after the rides had been reported in the media did the Carter campaign committee pay for them in August 1977. Although the campaign committee claimed the delay was due to faulty bookkeeping, the FEC decided the delay in repayment amounted to acceptance of illegal aid from a corporation. Carter's campaign committee was fined $1,200.

McCarthy. Eugene McCarthy's campaign also found itself questioned by the commission. The agency charged him with failing to report properly $21,433 in personal contributions; the funds represented honoraria, lecture fees, and travel reimbursements that the FEC claimed McCarthy incorrectly had reported as campaign contributions. Although he acknowledged that this was so, the independent candidate did not amend his reports, and the FEC filed suit. The case had not been resolved by early 1979.

The commission had levied only a few fines[154] in its first two years of operation, including those involving illegal receipt of public financing for Pennsylvania Governor Milton Shapp's 1976 presidential campaign and those on federal candidates who failed to file finance reports.

Congressional Campaigns

Various types of enforcement actions by the FEC also involved congressional campaigns. An FEC suit brought against former Rep. Wendell Wyatt, R-Ore., charged him with aiding and abetting a violation of the 1971 FECA by failure to file required reports. Wyatt pleaded guilty on June 11, 1975, to the charge of failing to report expenditures from a secret $5,000 cash fund he controlled while heading the Oregon reelection efforts of former President Nixon.[155] On July 18, in U.S. District Court in Washington, D.C., Wyatt was fined $750.

In January 1976 Rep. James R. Jones, D-Okla., pleaded guilty in federal court to a misdemeanor charge of failing to report receipt in late 1972 of a cash contribution of between $1,000 and $2,000 from the Gulf Oil Corp. Jones, who announced that he had no plans to resign and intended to run for reelection, was the first sitting congressman to be convicted in connection with the investigation of illegal political contributions made by Gulf Oil. Subject to a fine of up to $1,000 or a jail sentence up to one year, Jones, on March 16, was fined $200 in the case. He has twice since been reelected.

Angelo Gambino, who had been defeated in his bid for the House seat held by Rep. Harold C. Hollenbeck, R-N.J., was fined $1,500 for several violations of the FECA. He admitted to financing his entire campaign with funds from his family's corporation and to failing to register as a candidate or to form and register a principal campaign committee, as well as failing to report all campaign expenditures.[156]

In one case, a commissioner was involved in an apparent violation. FEC Chairman Vernon Thomson's former House campaign committee made transfers of $5,000 and $2,885 from excess Thomson campaign funds to a House candidate, Adolf Gundersen, for his primary and general election campaigns. The Thomson committee also made $25 contributions to four other federal candidates so that it could qualify for the higher $5,000 multicandidate committee contribution limit. After notice that the commission had "found reason to believe" both committees had violated federal law, the Gunderson committee returned $5,885 of the Thomson committee contribution.[157] This led Congress to redefine multicandidate committees in the 1976 Amendments.

In June 1978, the 1976 campaigns of Rep. Fernand J. St Germain, D-R.I., and Sen. Jim Sasser, D-Tenn., attracted attention; St Germain's campaign reportedly had arranged for campaigners to be paid from corporate funds, and Sasser's campaign was fined $865, the amount by which the FEC said the candidate had underpaid several companies for chartering aircraft.

Two congressional candidates were fined by the FEC for accepting "excessive contributions" in the form of loan endorsements by campaign supporters. Loans are defined as contributions for the length of the loan, and even cosigners, guarantors, and endorsers are so considered. The FEC fined a Tennessee congressional candidate, Larry Bater, $300 for using a $30,000 bank loan cosigned by only three members of his campaign finance committee. Robert J. Owens, a Florida congressional candidate, was fined $50 for having a $10,000 bank loan for his campaign cosigned by seven supporters.[158]

An incumbent member of Congress, Rep. Cecil Heftel, D-Hawaii, was charged with violations of the FECA by accepting illegal in-kind contributions from his radio station. Heftel's committee under-reported the value of its use of radio station employees to move the committee headquarters. The committee also had used the station's corporate office space for a few weeks rent free. A conciliation agreement with the FEC stipulated that the Heftel committee and his radio station each pay a fine of $1,330.[159]

The 1976 reelection campaign of one of the most influential members of the House, Rep. James J. Delaney, D-N.Y., became subject to an FEC investigation in 1978. Delaney, a veteran of 32 years in the House, assumed chairmanship of the powerful House Rules Committee after the 1976 election. One of 105 congressmen and candidates picked by computer for a random audit by the FEC, Delaney had spent $50,000 in an election in which he had no opposition. The FEC questioned the disbursement of "walking-around money," sums of cash given to local political workers on election day to produce voters at the polls. Shortly after the initiation of the FEC investigation, Delaney unexpectedly announced his retirement from public office.[160]

The Hansen Case. Possible violation by George Hansen of the law first came to public attention during the 1974 primary campaign. At that time, three Idaho citizens complained to the Clerk of the House of Representatives that Hansen's financial disclosure reports had been filed late and were incomplete. George Hansen, who was challenging incumbent Republican Orval Hansen in Idaho's Second Congressional District, had held the congressional seat from 1965 to 1969. The complaints prompted the House Administration Committee to conduct a preliminary investigation, as a result of which the case was turned over to the Justice Department. Wayne Hays, D-Ohio, who chaired the House committee, indicated in November 1974 that the inquiry had disclosed 30 apparent violations of federal election laws. The allegations included charges that George Hansen had maintained an unreported fund called "Partners in Congress," in which he mixed business and campaign funds; that he accepted about $2,000 in illegal corporate contributions; that his campaign reports failed to disclose the source of a $25,000 loan to his campaign; and that his reports were filed late, contained many inaccuracies, and failed to supply complete information. Hansen expressed his certainty that he would be cleared of the charges. The November election passed while the investigation proceeded, and Hansen won the election despite adverse publicity.

The case lingered in the hands of Justice Department officials, who announced that they had no plans to act on it, and Hays wrote two letters to the department noting the gravity of the allegations. As the possibility emerged that his seating would be contested, Hansen filed amended campaign documents correcting his initial figure of $53,000 for campaign expenditures to more than $100,000. The Idahoan was seated in January, and the Justice Department, unable to find evidence of intentional violation of the FECA, dropped the more serious charges. Eventually the Justice Department and the U.S. Attorney's Office brought suit against Hansen for two misdemeanors. The first count accused him of failing to file a campaign report due on June 10, 1975; the second charged him with failing to file a complete report due on July 22, 15 days before the primary. Hansen pleaded guilty on both counts in U.S. District Court on February 19, 1975. In a prepared statement, he asserted that his errors in reporting campaign expenses resulted from misunderstanding by his staff of bookkeeping procedures. He accused Hays of making "damning and libelous" statements to the press and called the publicity surrounding the case "a vicious smear effort and a political witch hunt." Hansen also complained that his privacy had been invaded by the Pocatello (Idaho) Credit Bureau and Democratic State Treasurer Mel Morgan, whom he sued for illegally obtaining a credit report about him while he was a candidate. [161]

John J. Flynt, Jr., D-Ga., chairman of the House Committee on Standards of Official Conduct, announced that his committee also would investigate; its deliberations produced no findings of unethical conduct, however. In April, Hansen was sentenced to one year in prison for the misdemeanors, with two months to be served in confinement and the balance suspended. The sentence proved controversial, and some Idaho citizens complained that unintentional misdemeanors did not warrant such a severe penalty. They claimed that Hansen had been singled out for unusually harsh treatment, while other politicians who had made the same mistakes were not investigated. On April 25 Hansen stood before United States District Judge George L. Hart, Jr., and pleaded for a reduced sentence. The judge granted the plea, substituting a $2,000 maximum fine for the prison term on the ground that no actual deception had been intended.

A number of Democrats, a few moderate Republicans, and several newspapers called for Hansen's resignation, but the Idaho Republican State Central Committee approved a resolution commending the congressman for years of faithful public service and urging him to continue in office. In September, Rep. Philip M. Crane, R-Ill., read into the *Congressional Record* an article defending Hansen's actions and reproducing part of Hansen's testimony and Judge Hart's remarks.[162] The affair seemed closed, but Hansen now had a large debt that lingered as 1975 came to an end and another election year approached. A letter signed by Sen. Strom Thurmond of South Carolina placed the debt at $81,125 — a figure that apparently did not represent campaign expenses from 1974 alone. This letter was part of a direct-mail effort to raise funds for Hansen. A reporter in Pocatello, Idaho, charged that both Crane's piece in the *Congressional Record* and Thurmond's letter had been written by Hansen himself.[163]

As the primary approached, five candidates in Idaho's Second District began to file disclosure reports. In three reports covering the period October 1, 1975, through June 30, 1976, Hansen listed total contributions of $61,940, $55,305, and $35,423. The FECA provides that contributions of less than $100 do not have to be itemized, and critics of Hansen's campaign pointed out that the unitemized contributions were disproportionately large. The first report, dated January 26, listed $48,257 in unitemized contributions and $13,684 in itemized contributions; the second report, dated April 8, showed $51,380 unitemized and $3,925 itemized contributions; and the unitemized and itemized amounts on the third report, dated July 8, were $31,023 and $4,400. Despite Hansen's advocacy of disclosure in August 1973, a year after he had lost a bid for a Senate seat, he declined to reveal the sources of the unitemized contributions to his 1976 campaign.

In June 1976, as the primaries approached, publicity grew concerning Elizabeth Ray's relations with Wayne Hays, who was said to have used public funds to support his relationship with Miss Ray. Hansen used the issue in his own campaign to cast doubt on Hays' charges during the 1974 investigation of Hansen's campaign finances. By July 1976 Hansen had raised $152,267.47 in campaign contributions, of which $130,258.97 was described as unitemized contributions.[164]

In August 1976 an Idaho woman who had sought unsuccessfully to have Hansen removed from office in 1974 sent a complaint to the FEC requesting that the agency investigate Hansen's campaign records. The complaint called the commission's attention to Hansen's unitemized contributions and also asked whether Hansen could legally employ a member of his congressional staff to act as his reelection committee treasurer. Despite the continued publicity, Hansen won his bid for reelection by a small margin.

In October, just before the election, he appeared in the news in a different context, this time in connection with tardy filing of income tax returns. The IRS announced that it had no record of a tax return from Hansen for 1975, and it appeared that Hansen had been late in filing for 1966 and 1967 — years when he was a sitting congressman — as well as for 1968. The 1966, 1967, and 1968 returns had been filed jointly on May 3, 1969 — a Saturday — by special arrangement with the IRS; the 1969 return was filed on August 29, 1970; returns for 1970 and 1971 were filed jointly on April 14, 1973; and the filing on April 5, 1975, of his return for 1973 was prompted by an investigation to determine delinquency.[165]

Hansen took his seat following the 1976 election, and his financial affairs next came to public attention as a result of an unusual request. Citing the needs of public servants of modest means, Hansen asked the FEC in March 1977 whether a congressman might solicit funds solely for his personal use.[166] The FEC claimed no jurisdiction in the matter, since the funds were not intended to finance a campaign, and announced that such fund raising would not violate federal election laws. The House ethics committee was less encouraging, however, and ruled that a mass-mail appeal for gifts would be a fund-raising event that must, under House rules, be treated as campaign funds, which could not be put to personal use. The committee also ruled that a member's spouse could not make such an appeal on the member's behalf. In October 1977 Hansen's wife was reported to be soliciting funds by mail on her own, and the extent to which her actions violated the ruling was left to the judgment of Hansen's constituency.

The Tonry Case. Although adverse publicity did not prevent Hansen from being reelected, it did prevent reelection of Rep. Richard Tonry, D-La. Tonry received considerable public attention in January 1977 in response to allegations that he had violated a number of election laws. A former Jesuit seminarian who had become a lawyer before entering politics, Tonry was sworn in on January 8, 1977, to replace retiring Congressman F. Edward Hebert from Louisiana's First District. Charges against Tonry initially were brought by James A. Moreau, whom Tonry had defeated by 184 votes in the October primary. Moreau argued that hundreds of votes had been falsified in the primary, that Tonry's seat in the House should be declared vacant, and that Moreau should be declared the winner of the primary.[167] Commentators noted that Moreau's charges might be weakened by the fact that Moreau had not been a candidate in the November general election, when Tonry defeated Republican candidate Robert Livingston, Jr., who did not contest that election's outcome.

Indictments returned by a federal grand jury in December 1976 charged 19 poll commissioners with causing 400 fraudulent votes to be cast in favor of Tonry. Tonry countered the charges, saying that five times as many fraudulent votes were registered in neighboring Plaquemines Parish (which favored Moreau) and that U.S. Attorney General Gerald J. Gallinghouse was conducting his investigation as part of a political vendetta against Tonry and in cooperation with the political machine headed by heirs of the late Judge Leander Perez.

As trials proceeded in Louisiana, the House Administration Committee appointed a three-member unit to conduct its own investigation. Moreau amended his petition to the House, asserting that Tonry had voted several times for himself. In the course of court testimony, 15 poll commissioners admitted stealing 390 votes for Tonry and one admitted stealing between 20 and 25 for Moreau. As Moreau sought to unseat Tonry, Tonry's lawyer argued before the House that conduct of a primary election lay within state rather than federal jurisdiction.

Louisiana state Judge Melvin Shortess upheld Tonry's victory, ruling that the 168 votes demonstrated to have been fraudulent were insufficient to affect the election's outcome. A state circuit court of appeals reversed the decision, identifying 616 questionable votes. The Louisiana Supreme Court upheld the original decision and declared Tonry the winner. Moreau then appealed the decision to the U.S. Supreme Court, which refused to hear the case for "want of a properly presented Federal question."[168]

The court cases and investigations continued, and the poll commissioners who had filed guilty pleas were sentenced to prison terms ranging from one to four months with a three-year period of probation following their release, during which time they were prohibited from participating in the electoral process except as voters.

The investigations produced additional charges against Tonry. Donald J. Zimmer, one of Tonry's key fund-raisers, pleaded guilty to perjury for having denied that $32,000 in bank loans to him and three other men actually were secret cash contributions for Tonry's campaign. An FBI agent testified that Tonry had played an active role in raising and attempting to conceal the illegal contributions. The same FBI witness testified that Tonry had promised a federal appointment to a lawyer who contributed $8,000. Tonry denied having received the $32,000 in contributions and told reporters that he was being framed for resisting one of the nation's most corrupt political machines.[169]

In April 1977 Judge Shortess agreed to hear Moreau's case a second time in light of the poll commissioners' guilty pleas. Judge Shortess ruled that the fraudulent votes were sufficient to nullify Tonry's victory, but that the court was powerless to order a new election because of the congressional investigation then under way. As Moreau considered a possible challenge to the second part of Judge Shortess' ruling, Tonry resigned his seat. Tonry's announcement preempted a meeting of the House Administration subcommittee to decide whether to recommend his removal. Although Tonry declared his intention to run for the seat a second time and emphasized his confidence of victory, news sources reported that he was deeply in debt.[170]

Louisiana Gov. Edwin W. Edwards scheduled an open primary for June, with a runoff in August. As the date for the primary approached, Tonry was indicted on charges brought by U.S. Attorney Gallinghouse of accepting illegal contributions of more than $54,000, offering to trade federal jobs for campaign funds, and obstruction of justice and lying to the grand jury. In the meantime, Moreau announced that he had switched parties and would run in the Republican primary rather than the Democratic one. Major candidates for the June primary included Tonry and state Rep. Ron Faucheux on the Democratic side, and Moreau and Robert Livingston (formerly assistant U.S. attorney under Gallinghouse) on the Republican side. The upcoming race provoked much speculation because Republicans traditionally had been a small group in the district and because a Republican congressional primary never had been held there before.

Winners in the primary were Faucheux and Livingston, and many observers attributed Moreau's and Tonry's defeat to adverse publicity. On July 1, before the scheduled runoff, Tonry pleaded guilty to charges of violating campaign finance laws. He was sentenced to one year in prison and was fined $10,000. Tonry thus became the first congressman to be sent to prison for violating the law that a candidate may not accept an individual campaign contribution exceeding $1,000.[171]

On August 27, Robert Livingston was elected to succeed Tonry, becoming the first Republican to represent Louisiana's First District since Reconstruction. A campaign official estimated that Livingston had spent about $400,000 on his campaign.[172]

Three lawyers representing poll commissioners from Plaquemines Parish charged that false accusations by federal investigators and the media had damaged the commissioners' reputations. The lawyers filed a $3.4 million damage suit naming as defendants individuals who had participated in the investigation.[173]

Tonry was released for good behavior after serving a six-month term in prison. He was said to face possible disbarment by the Louisiana

Supreme Court, campaign debts of more than $120,000, and at least two lawsuits seeking a total of $9.9 million in damages.[174]

Contribution Cases

Various individual and organizational contributors were subject to FEC enforcement actions. The first violation of the $25,000 aggregate limit per individual to come before the FEC involved an elderly Arizona couple who exceeded their legal combined limit of $50,000 by $48,000, giving a total of $98,000 to a variety of Republican and conservative candidates during 1976. Since they had approached the FEC voluntarily, the couple rejected the idea of paying a fine. The FEC finally agreed to count the $48,000 over the legal limit as part of 1977 contributions, thus restricting the couple's contributions in 1977 to $2,000.[175]

In April 1978 the FEC levied its largest fine to date against an individual. J. Carole Keahy, who had been defeated in her bid for a 1976 Alabama congressional seat, shared a $20,000 fine with her father for violating statutory limits on the amounts individuals may contribute to federal candidates. Thomas Keahy had given his daughter access to his business checking account, from which she withdrew $9,672 for primary expenses and $82,831 for general election expenses. She had reported the sums as personal contributions to her own campaign, but the FEC disagreed because she did not have access to the funds at the time she became a candidate.[176]

Organizational Cases. In October 1976 Common Cause filed a complaint charging the American Medical Association's political arm, AMPAC, and some of its state affiliates with violating the $5,000 limit on contributions by political committees by giving more than that amount to 21 congressional candidates. In July, John Murphy, the commission's general counsel, stated that for the purposes of the $5,000 limit the national and state PACs were to be considered a single committee. In case of a violation, the commission could compel recipients of the excess to refund it. If a violation was ruled deliberate rather than inadvertent, the FEC could seek an injunction or refer the case to the Justice Department for possible criminal prosecution. In March 1978 the FEC advised federal candidates that they risked being charged with violation of federal law if they accepted large contributions from both the national and the state committees. FEC regulations state that committees "set up by a membership organization including trade or professional associations . . . and/or by related state and local entities of that organization or group . . . shall be considered made by a single committee with . . . [a] single contribution limit." Rep. Newton R. Steers, R-Md., had accepted a total of $11,100 from AMPAC, the national committee, and MMPAC, the committee formed by the Maryland Medical Association. The commission's letter indicated that Steers would have to return funds and might be found in violation of the law if the two committees were determined to be affiliated.[177]

In May 1978 the commission imposed an $11,000 fine on Gun Owners of America, the largest fine levied to date on a PAC. Gun Owners had devised a plan whereby two affiliated committees (a campaign fund for California elections and a lobbying committee) would jointly raise funds and share costs of administration and direct mail. The group had asked for and received permission from the FEC to receive payments from the California committee for use of national committee facilities and staff and also to request funds for its lobbying organization in a solicitation for political contributions to support the national PAC.

The commission required that payments not exceed those that would be made for services from another source and that the entire cost of the dual-purpose direct mail be borne by the political fund. The national committee advised the commission that direct-mail costs associated with the lobbying organization would be allocated for payment by that organization and, in a letter, FEC special counsel responded that the proposal seemed in compliance with the FEC. Gun Owners then accepted funds from the California group and the lobbying group, but FEC auditors found the amounts to be in excess of the amounts owed. Although the overpayments appeared to be unintentional, the FEC fined Gun Owners $11,000 and noted that the association should rely on commission advice only as stated in an advisory opinion.[178]

TRIM

In its attempt to defend the public's right to know, the FEC occasionally found that its actions were opposed by other public interest groups with similar objectives, this time the American Civil Liberties Union. In one such case, the FEC accused a Long Island group sponsored by the John Birch Society of violating federal law by publishing and distributing by hand 10,000 copies of a brochure containing a candidate's voting record presented in a way that advocated his defeat. The publication in question was a newsletter that cost $135 and urged "lower taxes through less government." The Long Island group (known as Tax Reform Immediately or TRIM) declared in its article that Democratic Rep. Jerome A. Ambro had voted contrary to its views in 21 instances and had not voted in one.

The FEC sought to collect a $100 penalty, and the ACLU opposed the action, contending that TRIM had simply listed votes on major government issues and had urged people to communicate with their representative. According to the ACLU, the brochure did not contain partisan political advocacy and did not mention the candidate's political affiliation or that an election was being held.[179] In addition, on May 4, 1978, the Committee to Re-elect Les AuCoin filed with the FEC a similar complaint against the Oregon TRIM Committee.[180] On June 15, 1978, the FEC filed a similar suit against TRIM's New Jersey affiliate, Northwest Jersey Tax Reform Immediately. This suit charged that NJTRIM had in its newsletter advocated defeat of Democratic Rep. Helen Meyner, and the agency asked the U.S. District Court to fine the group $5,000 for illegally distributing critiques of an incumbent federal officeholder.[181] While each TRIM case seemed *de minimus*, the cumulative effect of several hundred such TRIM committees seemed to be the motivation for the FEC actions.

Party Cases

A suit filed by the FEC in November 1977 was expected to have important implications for informal political clubs operating in many large cities and southern rural areas. This action named six Baltimore Democratic political clubs for failing to register and report as political committees working on behalf of a candidate for political office. The commission's investigation responded to a complaint from independent candidate Bruce R. Bradley, who charged that the Senate campaign of Democratic Rep. Paul S. Sarbanes had paid amounts exceeding $1,000 to 17 clubs, and that the clubs had failed to register as political committees and to report all receipts and expenditures as required by law.

The commission found two committees to have committed no violation of the law. One committee voluntarily complied with the reporting requirements, and eight signed conciliation agreements and subsequently filed the reports. The federal court decision in the case of the remaining six committees will indicate whether such informal political clubs must report any federal election payments of funds given to ward workers to get out the vote on election day.[182]

Labor Cases

Federal election law requires that membership organizations report to the FEC all expenditures directly attributed to any communications that expressly advocate election or defeat of a candidate whenever such expenditures exceed $2,000. In the 1976 general election, the American Federation of State, County, and Municipal Employees (AFSCME) reported having spent approximately $23,858 on behalf of Carter's campaign. Upon investigation, the FEC found reasonable cause to believe that AFSCME had violated the law by not reporting the printing and distributing costs of a poster that presented in caricature Gerald Ford embracing Richard Nixon. On Ford's lapel was a button with the words "Pardon Me" on it. Moreover, the poster was captioned with an excerpt from a speech given by then Vice President Ford on July 25, 1974: "I can say from the bottom of my heart — the President of the U.S. is innocent, and he is right." The cost for printing of the poster was approximately $384, while distribution cost $600. Unable to secure an acceptable conciliation agreement with AFSCME, the FEC asked the U.S. District Court (D.C.) to find the organization guilty of FECA violations and assess a civil penalty of $5,000. The FEC also wished to have AFSCME enjoined from continuing to refuse to file reports on the costs incurred from the communications of material advocating the election or defeat of candidates.[183]

Federal election laws prohibit the use of labor union treasury funds in connection with any election to any political office. Voter registration drives and political donations by unions and their political committees may be funded only through voluntary contributions made by union members, and these funds are at all times to be segregated from the general union treasury. Complaints filed with the FEC by the National Right to Work Committee (NRWC), a conservative organization opposed to compulsory unionism, prompted the commission to bring suit in December 1977 charging the AFL-CIO with persistent violation of federal campaign spending laws. The agency charged the labor federation with a continuing illegal transfer of funds from its Committee on Political Education (COPE) Education Fund, which was a part of the federation's general treasury, to the COPE Political Contributions Committee (COPE-PCC). It was estimated that the transfer involved approximately $392,000 since 1970.

The NRWC had pursued the case in court since May 1977. In addition to complaining of the illegal transfer of funds, the NRWC charged that the AFL-CIO had made illegal in-kind contributions to Carter's campaign, had disregarded federal limitations on campaign contributions, and had illegally solicited contributions to COPE from individuals who were not direct members of the federation. Responding to NRWC complaints of inaction on the part of the FEC, U.S. District Court Judge George L. Hart ordered the commission on November 18 either to sue the AFL-CIO within 30 days or to announce its intention of dropping the case. The FEC had begun negotiations with the union before the court order, but all efforts at conciliation failed.

The FEC lawsuit against the AFL-CIO focused only on the questionable transfer of funds. There was no mention of the broader allegations of illegal contributions and solicitations. The commission asked that the AFL-CIO be enjoined and restrained from transferring monies from the COPE Education Fund to the separate segregated fund of the COPE-PCC, and be assessed a civil penalty in the amount of $10,000. In response to the FEC suit, the AFL-CIO argued that the $392,000 in question represented a partial repayment of funds loaned by the COPE-PCC to the COPE Education Fund under a longstanding practice approved by the General Accounting Office before establishment of the FEC. GAO officials, however, could not recall any such approval.[184]

On June 16, 1978, the U.S. District Court granted the FEC's motion for summary judgment. Concluding that past transfers from the AFL-CIO COPE Education Fund to its political action committee were illegal, Judge Hart enjoined the federation from making any future transfers; he did allow the union to make a last transfer of $312,000 to repay the loan from the political action committee to the education fund.[185]

Unhappy over the number of illegal corporate and union contributions that turned up in candidate reports filed in 1977 and 1978 and in audits of 1976 congressional campaigns, the FEC decided not only to require the return of the illegal contributions but also to fine the candidate as well as the contributor. The FEC advised all candidates "to instruct their staffs to immediately return all contributions which indicate on their face that they are written on corporate or labor union accounts."[186]

Evaluating Effectiveness

Assessments of the effectiveness of the FEC's enforcement activities have been mixed. In answering a complaint about the alleged unfair and unresponsive manner in which the commission treats respondents in compliance matters, John G. Murphy, general counsel for the FEC in 1975-76, presented statistics to show that the agency has effectively regulated political activity without being unduly insensitive or overbearing:[187]

> As of mid-July 1978, the commission had opened a total of 646 formal compliance files, involving over a thousand persons. By the same date, 482 of these files had been closed. Of the 482, only 27 resulted in conciliation agreements, affecting 77 persons. Of these 77 persons, only 47 were required to pay civil penalties (23 of these in a single case). Of these, 33 paid less than $1,000, including ten who paid as little as $50.
>
> If we add the 48 court suits filed (including the 38 against non-filers) to these 27 conciliation agreements, we find the FEC took

action against respondents in 75 out of 646 compliance actions — in less than 12 percent of the cases (and less than 16 percent of the cases closed). This means that somehow, miraculously, a huge percentage of respondents enjoyed findings favorable to them.

Other perspectives, however, have not been so favorable. One criticism of the commission, that of former Sen. Eugene McCarthy, focused squarely on the nature of most of its enforcement activity. McCarthy noted that by July 1, 1977, the commission had brought civil suits against 30 congressional candidates, all of whom had lost either the primary or the general election and most of whom had won only a small percentage of the vote. "If you are waiting for an FEC investigation of the link between campaign contributions and the cargo preference bill, or a check of bank loans to the Carter campaign," McCarthy concluded caustically, "remember that the Commission is burdened with more important work."[188] McCarthy's criticism struck at the discrepancy between principle and practice; although the campaign laws were enacted in response to public concern, their enforcement did not necessarily reflect the national interest in all its aspects to the satisfaction of all observers. The influence of enforcement actions on the public also was open to question, however. Enforcement brought negative publicity whose effects were feared by candidates seeking election. Such publicity may or may not prevent reelection any more than it has in the past, as the case of George Hansen illustrates.

In commenting on the FEC in late 1977, Andrew Mollison remarked, "Federal officeholders appear to be well served by the sleepy, inept operation of a commission that is both dependent on Congress for funds and charged with regulating congressional campaigns."[189] His words formed part of an intensive analysis of the agency's performance, and its findings were highly critical. The commission was charged with frequent failure to meet regulatory deadlines for enforcement actions; failure to enforce some parts of the law; and failure to penalize violators sufficiently. Although its election reports were systematically filed for ready access, the agency accepted no telephone orders for copies of them during the last two months before the general election and answered written requests received during the last two and a half weeks of October only after the election.

The study's findings included more serious charges, however. Of more than 480 complaints submitted to the commission since 1975, all but 54 remained unresolved in November 1977 or had been settled during preliminary stages of investigation. Only 57 percent — slightly more than half — of reports filed with the commission were examined by commission staff, and the agency did not approve guidelines for review conducted by junior staff until after the 1976 election. The commission referred only three criminal cases to the Justice Department during a period of two and a half years. Despite the statutory requirement that the commission act on all complaints within 90 days, a review of 100 complaints received by the agency between July and mid-October 1976 indicated that only 51 had been so handled — and 22 cases remained open one year later. Of another 100 complaints filed between November 1976 and July 1977, 20 had not been completed by November 1977. Following congressional complaints about the commission's first two major investigations of incumbents, both of whom were cleared, no incumbent was penalized for violations of the law until Heftel was. The commission staff, behind schedule in its audits of congressional campaigns, is often threatened by appropriation cutbacks supported by congressmen who fear the infrequent examination of their books. In addition, the published analysis found evidence that the commission lacked a procedure for determining whether any individual had exceeded the annual limit of $25,000 for contributions.

The complexity of commission regulations and the fact that incumbents had readier access to government specialists than did challengers suggested that the commission's operations were discriminatory in some respects. In assessing the commission's handling of the cases on which it had acted, the report concluded that enforcement was characterized by delay, fumbling, insensitivity, and stiff penalties for minor rather than major offenders. The writer attributed the commission's failings in some measure to budgetary restrictions, insufficient professional staff, ill-advised actions in relation to Congress, and the lack of a strong and alert constituency outside the agency.

Information that became available in 1978 suggested, however, that the FEC was becoming more efficient in its operations. As the 1978 elections approached, the agency reported that preelection financial disclosure reports had been made available to the public for 90 percent of all federal primary candidates, and that the documents had been made available before election day. Of 861 candidates on the ballot in 21 states holding primaries from March to June, the FEC study showed that 505 candidates and their committees (about 60 percent) had filed reports within the specified time period; 271 candidates and committees (31 percent) had filed reports late but in time for publication before the election; and 85 candidates and committees (9 percent) had been publicly cited by the FEC as nonfilers. In announcing the figures, FEC Chairman Joan Aikens noted the agency's continuing emphasis on voluntary compliance and said that, under a new program, FEC information aides were now calling candidates to answer questions about federal laws and to remind them of their reporting obligations.[190] One writer, considering the agency's work during the month of May 1978, observed that it was beginning to enforce the law more strictly. He noted that the FEC had imposed fines totaling $31,000 during this period, or nearly three-quarters of the $42,620 in fines levied by the commission since it started operation in April 1975.[191]

Unionizing the FEC

The formation of political action committees by labor unions eventually brought the Federal Election Commission a series of difficulties relating to its own staff, which in September 1978 voted 87-24 in favor of representation by the National Treasury Employees Union (NTEU). NTEU also represented employees of the Internal Revenue Service and the Federal Communications Commission. The six FEC commissioners asked Congress to block the unionization of FEC employees; interestingly, one of the commissioners, Thomas Harris, is a former lawyer for the AFL-CIO. In a letter addressed to key members of the House and Senate, the commissioners requested that the agency be exempted on the ground that representation of FEC staff by a union that maintained a political action committee or endorsed candidates for federal office could pose a conflict of interest in commission operations. The letter was dated one day after receipt by the FEC of a letter from NTEU asking how it should proceed to create a political action committee.[192]

The FEC commissioners' request disturbed some Democrats, who shared concern over possible conflicts of interest within the agency but were reluctant to oppose unionization. The commissioners' action followed an unsuccessful attempt to obtain from the Labor Department exemption of FEC staff from union representation; Francis X. Burckhard, assistant secretary for labor-management relations, disagreed with the commissioners, contending that FEC staff "shared a clear and identifiable community of interest."[193]

On September 13, the House of Representatives rejected, by a 166-217 vote, the FEC plea to prevent commission unionization, and most members of the House Administration Committee, which oversees FEC policies, opposed an amendment endorsed by the FEC to the Civil Service Reform bill. Rep. William D. Ford, D-Mich., voiced his feeling that unionization of the agency did not pose serious potential for conflicts of interest. He maintained that such a possibility could be eliminated by amending the FECA to require the FEC to contract with an independent auditor for any examination of the books of NTEU.[194]

FEC Appointments

Congress' post-Vietnam-Watergate style of seeking to be more influential in policy making has extended itself into the selection of FEC commissioners, despite the *Buckley* decision requiring presidential appointment of all six commissioners.[195] President Carter's first Democratic nominee, John W. McGarry, was suggested by Speaker O'Neill and accepted by the president even though O'Neill already had chosen another commissioner, Robert Tiernan, when the House chose two of the original commissioners. McGarry replaced an original presidential appointee, Neil Staebler, tipping the balance toward more congressional influence over the FEC.

McGarry was chosen only after an earlier White House favorite, Susan King, was dropped following criticism by O'Neill and House Majority Whip John Brademas, D-Ind., that she was a "do-good, Common Cause type." Common Cause sought and played only a small role at the outset, suggesting to the president several names including King, but not persisting in trying to influence the outcome until a belated series of letters was sent opposing the choice of McGarry. One such letter to Carter, and one to Senate Rules Committee Chairman Howard W. Cannon, D-Nev., urged that the executive appointment power not be ceded to the congressional leadership, and warned that McGarry's close relationship with O'Neill and other congressmen would make it difficult for him to act independently on the FEC. A third letter, which was addressed to all members of the Senate Rules Committee, urged outright opposition to McGarry's confirmation since Common Cause had seen "no evidence presented to establish that Mr. McGarry can function as a credible member of the Federal Election Commission."[196] The historical lack of follow-through by reformers was evident; after a masterful job of working for a strict and comprehensive law, Common Cause paid relatively little attention to the operation of the FEC, filing one major complaint against AMPAC but not pursuing a day-to-day watchdog role. Of course, Common Cause has continued to work for congressional public financing, and in that quest needs the help of O'Neill.

Zagoria

The White House action in deferring to Speaker O'Neill in the choice of a Democratic commissioner did not extend to giving similar choice to the Republican congressional leadership in making an appointment of a Republican commissioner. While consideration of the McGarry nomination bogged down in the Senate Rules Committee because of questions about the accuracy of McGarry's financial disclosures, including an anonymous "tax-related complaint," the fate of President Carter's nominee for the Republican vacancy on the FEC seemed doomed from the beginning. According to the Republicans, President Carter promised Senate Minority Leader Howard H. Baker,

Jr., of Tennessee, and House Minority Leader John J. Rhodes of Arizona, that his choice of a GOP nominee would be arrived at only after
"full consultation" with party leaders. According to Sen. Dick Clark, D-
Iowa, the White House later claimed that President Carter did not
remember making any such commitment.

The Republicans submitted two names to Carter, neither of whom
was acceptable to the president, who said that his choice would have to
be a Republican who favored public financing of congressional elections.
Baker and Rhodes complained that public financing was controversial
and that Carter was imposing additional conditions on the nomination.
Carter asked for 10 to 12 new names and the Republicans submitted one,
which was also unacceptable. After long delays, Carter then appointed
Samuel D. Zagoria, a moderate Republican with labor support, which
action Baker and Rhodes called "deeply troubling." Zagoria then disclaimed support for congressional public financing, declaring the White
House never asked his opinion. He charged the press with giving him a
"bum rap" for saying he supported it when he had not taken a position
regarding it and did not intend to compromise himself on future judgments.[197] But that would seem to contradict Carter's statements that he
would only appoint supporters of public funding and the rest of the
election laws.

The proposed combination of three Democratic commissioners,
including McGarry, considered favorable to labor, plus Zagoria, unsettled both the Republican leadership and the corporate community,
who feared the appointments portended undue labor influence in the
work of the FEC. A present commissioner, Thomas Harris, a Democrat,
is a former associate general counsel of the AFL-CIO, which added to
the Republican distrust. When it became known that Harris originally
had suggested Zagoria's name to the White House, Republican opposition reached a new high. Zagoria had a background in labor relations,
having been a Republican member of the National Labor Relations
Board, appointed by President Johnson; moreover, Zagoria had been
administrative assistant to Sen. Clifford P. Case of New Jersey, a liberal
Republican. Of course, congressional Republicans and Democratic presidents traditionally have had arguments over who should decide federal
appointments of opposition members. But the FEC is politically sensitive and requires balance, especially since the commission regulates
corporate and trade association PACs, a rising factor in national politics.
Zagoria would have replaced William L. Springer, whom President Ford
nominated on short notice to reconstitute the FEC.

Whatever Zagoria's stand on public financing, his nomination was
never confirmed because of the manner of his selection. Republicans
insisted that Carter had broken his word to them regarding the consulta-

tion on selection of a nominee and, although there was no dispute about
Zagoria's qualifications for the post, some Republicans vowed to filibuster the motion for confirmation on the floor, should the nomination have
gotten out of committee. On August 12, following negotiations between
the Republican leadership and the White House congressional liaison
staff, Zagoria asked Carter to withdraw his nomination and the administration promised to find another governmental position for Zagoria.

The Zagoria controversy did not enhance the authority or stability
of the FEC. Some Democrats interpreted the Zagoria incident as a
squabble between mainstream and liberal Republicans. Republican
Senators Clifford Case, Charles McC. Mathias, Jr., of Maryland, and
former Senator John Sherman Cooper of Kentucky supported Zagoria at
confirmation hearings, while Republican Congressmen John Rhodes,
Bill Frenzel of Minnesota, and Guy Vander Jagt of Michigan opposed
him. Senator Baker attacked Carter for going back on his word, but left
his options open since he is minority leader of all Senate Republicans,
including Case and Mathias. Some 132 Republican House members
signed a letter criticizing President Carter for appointing Zagoria without the active participation of the Republican Party leadership. Considered in broader perspective, if the FEC is to be effective, it requires good
faith and strong bipartisan support. One way to achieve those is by
Democrats working together with Republicans, not by unilateral
presidental action that affronts the Republican leadership.

McGarry

Although Zagoria, whose integrity had never been questioned, had
been forced to withdraw his nomination, McGarry, whose integrity was
in doubt, was the nominee most persistently backed by the president. In
fact, Zagoria's nomination was withdrawn to expedite confirmation of
McGarry. As part of the agreement to withdraw Zagoria, Senate Republicans promised not to prolong McGarry's hearings unnecessarily. However, as the 95th Congress neared a confirmation vote, the controversy
intensified.

In the September 13 report on McGarry's nomination, Republican
Senators Baker and Robert P. Griffin of Michigan detailed their dissenting views on a number of issues. Of major concern were the views of
Reka Hoff, a tax lawyer of the General Accounting Office. Hoff concluded there were many "improper calculations" in McGarry's tax
returns, including one that had saved him at least $13,000 in income tax
in recent years.[198] Though this audit had been available, it was not
discussed by the Senate Rules Committee before voting 7-2 in
McGarry's favor. McGarry and the White House maintained that

McGarry's tax returns had been audited by the IRS and found satisfactory. Baker and Griffin also charged that the business relationship between McGarry and his law partner, Irving Sheff, was misrepresented in a number of legal documents; House financial disclosure statements regarding the partnership were also questioned. A third issue raised in the nomination report involved numerous instances of McGarry's "lack of candor and forthrightness with the Committee" during their investigation.[199] The Democratic majority on the Rules Committee vindicated McGarry on all counts.

Opposing views were also expressed on September 18, when Common Cause sent a letter to all senators urging them to vote against McGarry. The letter said that McGarry did not meet standards of unquestioned integrity, clear commitment to enforce laws, and firm commitment to the principle of accountability, nor was he affirmatively qualified. Rather, discussion of his confirmation had been couched in terms of a "negative standard — whether Mr. McGarry is clearly disqualified to serve." The letter also drew attention to the fact that McGarry had been employed by the House of Representatives for 15 years, including his current job within the House Administration Committee:[200]

> Mr. McGarry is thus being asked to oversee the campaign finance activities of Members of the House for whom he has directly worked for a number of years, including those individuals who are directly responsible for his obtaining this appointment. We simply do not believe that under the circumstances, Mr. McGarry can carry out his enforcement responsibilities in an independent and credible way.

Meanwhile, the choice of a Republican nominee was unresolved. Not until October 10, 1978, the day the Senate confirmed Zagoria's new appointment to the Consumer Product Safety Commission, did Carter announce that Max Friedersdorf was to replace Zagoria as the Republican nominee to the FEC. Friedersdorf, who had been an aide to both Nixon and Ford, and was currently holding a position as staff director for the Senate Republican Policy Committee, had solid party credentials. This time, the Democrats had hoped to make a deal with the Republicans. That is, they would approve Friedersdorf in return for Republican support for McGarry, even though the FBI's customary check on presidential appointees had not been completed. However, Friedersdorf's nomination came too late for the process of confirmation to begin. A combination of bad timing in Friedersdorf's case and Republican resistance in McGarry's case caused the congressional session to close without confirmation of either nominee.

Recess Appointment

In spite of the fact that McGarry twice failed to receive Senate confirmation, Carter on October 25 made a recess appointment, which is reserved for vacancies occurring while Congress is not in session. McGarry was sworn in for an interim term on the FEC in an unannounced ceremony. The FEC did not learn of Carter's action until the following day, when the action was immediately challenged by Neil Staebler, whom McGarry would replace. Staebler filed suit charging that McGarry's interim appointment violated an FECA mandate that commission nominees win Senate confirmation. Common Cause joined Staebler in the suit; President David Cohen stressed that the "President was making a political payoff to the Speaker. He was playing the shabbiest politics he has played to date on regulatory appointments." [201]

Staebler's lawyer, Common Cause General Counsel Kenneth Guido, noted that McGarry theoretically could serve on the commission until the end of the first session of the 96th Congress even were the Senate to vote him down. He complained that Carter's action threatened to impair the basic right of the public to an electoral system "whose integrity is safeguuaded by an independent, objective and impartial commission." [202]

Ironically, though the search for an independent commissioner was ostensibly a major issue in the controversies over McGarry and Zagoria, Staebler's own impartiality may have been behind Carter's move to replace him. Columnist J. F. terHorst suggested that Carter may have been worried that Staebler would take a close look at last-minute campaign spending by both major parties for the 1978 congressional elections.[203] Others speculated that the administration might be worried about the results of the FEC audit on Carter's 1976 campaign, which were pending publication. Staebler aroused labor opposition by voting in the SunPAC decision to give business equal rights with labor in raising and spending money in support of candidates.

Neil Staebler et al. v. Jimmy Carter et al. specifically requested that the court 1) restrain McGarry from serving on the FEC unless and until the Senate confirmed him, 2) compel the commission to grant Staebler all the rights and privilege of a commissioner until such time, and 3) order the president to withdraw McGarry's "interim" appointment. According to the suit, McGarry was appointed to a vacancy that did not exist.[204] Staebler stressed that the Senate had failed to confirm McGarry's nomination in more than a year, and once Congress adjourned the president filled a vacancy that did not exist until a replacement was confirmed by the Senate. Staebler said he would not vacate his seat on the FEC but would continue to attend all meetings (without voting) until the suit was resolved.

The defendants countered that Staebler's interpretation of the term "vacant" was not what was intended by the FECA, and stressed the need for resolution of statutory ambiguity.[205] Those who support the legality of the appointment cite a Justice Department memorandum in which Assistant Attorney General John M. Harmon pointed out that the courts have upheld an interpretation that gives the president the power to make recess appointments to vacancies that "happen to exist" rather than "happen to occur." Harmon added that Staebler's hold-over service is not inconsistent with the existence of a vacancy; Staebler's term expired April 30, 1977, but without a confirmed replacement, he continued in office. The FEC, which was originally named as one of the defendants, will not participate in the briefing of the court. In explanation of the commission's neutral position in the case, FEC General Counsel William C. Oldaker said that since McGarry had been sworn in and "will henceforth exercise the powers of a duly appointed commissioner, the Commission does not feel that it would be appropriate for it to address any questions regarding the underlying legality of the President's appointment."[206]

In early January 1979, U.S. District Judge Harold H. Greene ruled that Carter had legally appointed McGarry, noting that numerous members of the judicial branch of the federal government had begun their careers "by way of recess appointments." Staebler stated that he would remain in his office until his attorney decided whether to appeal Greene's decision.[207]

Meanwhile, speculation about relationships between the White House, Congress and the FEC continued, focusing especially on the April 1979 expiration of the terms of commissioners Thomas Harris (Democrat) and Vernon Thomson (Republican). Political watchdogs argued that though the possible appointment of former House members may ensure sensitivity to the intent of the law, it may also create a susceptibility to favoritism, especially if public financing is extended to House members.[208]

Commissioner Tiernan

Publicity disclosing questionable conduct by one commissioner proved a source of embarrassment to the Federal Election Commission in 1977, leading the agency to tighten its internal operations. The commissioner was Robert O. Tiernan, who had been appointed to the FEC following loss of his Rhode Island congressional seat in 1974. Although the 1976 Amendments stipulate that each commissioner must serve full time, the conference report hedged the explicit statutory language by permitting certain limited outside activities.[209] This seemed to permit Tiernan to continue his law practice and his work as president and treasurer of the Rhode Island Reds, a professional ice hockey team. Tiernan's multiple interest came to public attention as a result of an article published in *The Wall Street Journal,* which noted that 1,688 long-distance telephone calls had been billed to Tiernan's government credit card during a period of less than two years.[210] The charges — more than $2,750 excluding tax — had been paid by the commission, although many of the calls were traceable to Tiernan's home, his law office, and his beach house, as well as to an owner of the hockey club and to personal business of his son. Following publication of the article, Tiernan instructed his staff to review his telephone charges and announced that he would reimburse the government for calls determined to be personal. Two weeks later he issued a check reimbursing the government for $2,014.02 in telephone expenses. The accompanying press release called for the establishment within the FEC of a procedure for review and verification of telephone billing.[211]

The large number of calls made by Tiernan to his other business concerns prompted Senator Clark of Iowa to ask the Senate Rules Committee to investigate the commissioner's activities. In his letter to Senator Cannon, chairman of the committee, Clark noted the statutory requirement that members of the commission attend to their duties on a full-time basis.[212] The Senate committee asked Tiernan to submit his law office logs voluntarily so that the committee could determine how much time he spent on his Rhode Island practice. Results of a preliminary investigation presented to the committee included the finding that Tiernan's attendance record at FEC meetings was lower than that of the other five commissioners. Tiernan had attended 90.2 percent of meetings in 1975, 77 percent in 1976, and 83.9 percent in 1977.[213] The commissioner disputed the accuracy of these figures.

In December 1977, three months later, news sources disclosed that Tiernan, who voted as a commissioner on regulations and advisory opinions outlining means by which candidates might pay off campaign debts, was himself $5,000 in debt from his unsuccessful 1974 campaign and was being sued by one creditor. Tiernan's campaign debts added to the embarrassment of the FEC, since both available means for settling them could compromise the agency. One method would have involved a fund-raising event, and it would have been difficult if not impossible to ensure that attending donors included no individuals who might have business with the commission. The other means of settlement would have consisted of payments from cash on hand of about 10 cents on the dollar. Such a settlement requires an agreement that must be approved by the FEC, however, and the propriety of a vote by five or six commissioners on a matter of concern to one of them was clearly questionable.

In response to inquiries, Tiernan declared that he would not attempt to settle his debts while he served on the commission[214] whereupon one creditor, the George Town Club, sued for the $1,303 owed it. Earlier, the club had sought to settle but Tiernan refused.

Spotlight, a publication of the right-wing organization Liberty Lobby, devoted considerable space to a series of articles attacking Tiernan.[215] The newsletter contended that the Senate Committee on Rules and Administration had been derelict in its responsibilities to investigate Tiernan when he was appointed and condemned the committee for allowing a House-Senate conference committee to write language in the conference report that would seemingly exempt Tiernan from the requirement that he devote full time to his work as a commissioner. *Spotlight* also criticized Tiernan for failure to resolve his campaign debts. In addition to the $5,000 campaign debt remaining from Tiernan's 1974 campaign, *Spotlight* charged the commissioner with failure to reimburse the Democratic majority printer for the House of Representatives in the amount of $2,000 for printing costs associated with his campaign and hinted at the desirability of investigating Tiernan in conjunction with the probe of Korean intelligence activities connected with Tongsun Park. The FEC also came under fire from the newsletter for failure to respond openly to inquiries about Tiernan's activities and for seeming to protect those whom the agency was charged with regulating.

Thomson — Sasser Case

On January 4, 1977, the FEC voted 5-0, with Commissioner Thomson not participating, to refer to the Justice Department without recommendation a report prepared by its general counsel, John G. Murphy, Jr. This was no ordinary report for it detailed alleged misdeeds by the then chairman of the commission, Vernon Thomson.

The case centered around an alleged breach of confidentiality of one of the commission's investigations. The investigation originated in a complaint filed on August 3, 1976, by Democratic senatorial candidate Henry Sadler, that a Democratic primary opponent, James Sasser, had received illegal bank loans for his campaign from the United American Bank of Nashville, Tennessee, and the First National Bank of Tracy City, Tennessee, and also was making improper use of corporate aircraft. In October, the commission issued subpoenas to both banks and to Gary Blackburn, Sasser's campaign treasurer, to produce — by October 26 and 27 — certain information regarding the allegations.

Just before the deadlines, on October 25, the story of the subpoenas broke in an article in *The Nashville Banner.* On October 27 the commission opened the case with a finding of "reason to believe that an unnamed respondent had violated the confidentiality provisions of [the law]" in connection with its investigations of the Sasser case.[216] The general counsel's report provides a description of events from which the quotations in the following account are drawn.[217]

On the afternoon of October 19, Vernon Thomson spoke with Melvin Laird, a former House colleague, former secretary of Defense, and currently an editor of *Reader's Digest*, at a reception in the University Club. Laird, in an apparently aggressive manner, complained about the lack of speed with which the commission was expediting compliance matters, including complaints of illegal bank loans to candidates in the states of Tennessee, Minnesota, and Maryland. Thomson "vigorously defended the Commission against Laird's challenge that the Commission was not acting effectively." As will be shown, the two men disagreed over Thomson's exact words.

Laird maintains that Thomson was his only source of information concerning the Tennessee case. Three days later, on October 22, Laird asked his secretary, Laurie Hawley, to call Carl Wallace, a former Laird aide and presently vice president of the Purolator Corp., to suggest that he contact the campaign of Republican Sen. Bill Brock of Tennessee concerning information that the FEC "had taken or was about to take action to obtain records from the Sasser campaign."[218] Laird's secretary did reach Wallace, who in turn called Dan Kuykendall, a former Republican congressman from Tennessee.

Kuykendall in turn reached Thomas Bell, Brock's campaign manager, and informed him that the commission "had voted unanimously to issue subpoenas for Sasser's records." The following day, October 23, Bell called Robert Perkins, executive director of the Tennessee Republican Party and a part-time Brock campaign aide. Perkins was "thoroughly familiar with" the FECA. Perkins then phoned Joan Aikens, a member of the FEC, and "said that he had heard that the Commission had voted in open session to subpoena records in the Sasser campaign; Ms. Aikens replied that the Commission had not done so, [and] that she was not at liberty to discuss compliance matters."

The matter did not rest there. Perkins' wife called a commission employee, Victoria Tigwell, who had rented the Perkins' Washington home and had a date that evening with Daniel Reese, executive assistant to the commission's staff director. Tigwell told Reese "she had heard that the Commission had subpoenaed Sasser's records." Reese confirmed this but told her the matter was confidential and should not be discussed. The following day, October 24, Tigwell called Bob Perkins and "confirmed that the Commission had issued subpoenas for Sasser's records." Several hours later, Perkins and Bell spoke by telephone with

Tom Ingram, a reporter for *The Nashville Banner*. They discussed the subpoenas with Ingram. The latter unsuccessfully sought confirmation of the story from Sasser's campaign manager and his campaign treasurer.

Depositions were taken of members of the commission staff who had been present at the commission's October 19 meeting and other employees who might have had knowledge of the actions regarding the Sasser matter. In addition, depositions were taken of Kuykendall, Wallace, Perkins and his wife, and Melvin Laird. The general counsel pressed on. On November 11 he traveled to Nashville to interview individuals involved, whose "responses to close questioning strongly supported the proposition that the breach of confidentiality . . . was not occasioned by careless talk on the part of persons associated with the subpoenaed banks or the Sasser campaign. The fact that the subpoenas had [been] issued was very closely held, on instructions of George Barrett [Mr. Sasser's attorney]."

Thus the trail led back to Washington and a deposition was taken from each of the commissioners. Commissioner Thomson's testimony "completely and unequivocally [denied] that in his conversation with Mr. Laird on October 19, 1976, he did more than defend the commission in general terms, although certain states were mentioned; that he gave Mr. Laird the specifics of any complaint; or that he gave Mr. Laird any information regarding any Commission vote on a compliance matter."

The issue at stake was possible violation of a provision of the FECA, which requires that neither the commission nor any individual "make public" the fact that a notification or investigation of a potential violation of the Act is under way unless given "the written consent of the person receiving such notification or the person with respect to whom such investigation is made." Violation of the section of the statute is punishable by a fine of up to $3,000 and if done "knowingly and willingly" the fine may range up to $5,000.

Until then there had been no interpretation of this section by either the commission or the courts. General Counsel Murphy recommended an interpretation that focused on communication by commission employees to individuals not employed by the commission, of knowledge "that the Commission is conducting an investigation with respect to a specific individual, committee, or other organization or group."

Murphy Conclusions

The general counsel next needed to determine which individuals, if any, had violated the statute under the above interpretation. He concluded that Victoria Tigwell had " 'made public' the Commission's investigation of the Senatorial campaign of James Sasser of Tennessee by specifically communicating to an individual in the private sector, namely Robert Perkins." Tigwell was placed on administrative leave with pay on November 29, 1976, and Murphy recommended that her employment at the commission be terminated.

As for Daniel Reese and William Loughrey, two other commission employees, Murphy concluded that their discussions of the matter were with another commission employee, Tigwell, and thus neither apparently violated the statute. Reese, however, did show a very serious lack of judgment in discussing the matter with Tigwell.

Murphy concluded that Chairman Thomson had failed to disclose to him and to the commission information relevant to the case that included his initial meeting with Melvin Laird on October 19 and his subsequent phone conversations with the former Defense secretary. The general counsel pointed out that determination of Thomson's role in making the investigation public depended in part on certain knowledge of Thomson's words when he spoke with Laird on October 19. While Thomson maintained that he had said nothing specific, Laird recalled the terminology "investigation of the records" and information concerning the commission's intention to pursue the matter.

Murphy also noted that public knowledge concerning the investigation had grown increasingly specific with the passage of time. Laird stated that he had informed Hawley of a rumored investigation of Sasser by the FEC, but Powell — at the end of a chain of informants that had included Wallace, Kuykendall, and Bell — testified that he had been told of a "sure" vote for subpoenas. The increasingly detailed information of each individual indicated to Murphy that Laird's initial transmission to Hawley was even more detailed than either one remembered, and that Laird's memory of the October 19 conversation was probably more accurate than Thomson's. In support of this inference, the general counsel noted that Thomson did not report until December 4 "that he had spoken with Mr. Laird about this investigation and the University Club conversation perhaps as early as November 19th and certainly not later than November 23rd." Murphy concluded:[219]

> ...this record supports a preliminary finding that Mr. Thomson's communication on October 19 directly resulted in knowledge on the part of Mr. Laird that the Commission was conducting an investigation with respect to the Sasser campaign. Accordingly, it is recommended that the Commission find reason to believe that Vernon B. W. Thomson violated . . . the [Federal Election Campaign] Act.

As noted, the commission understandably referred the report regarding a fellow commissioner to the attorney general without making any recommendation. There was interest in and speculation about how the department would rule since the case would set precedents for the treatment of such matters by the commission and the Justice Department.

No Charges

In the end, the department cleared Thomson of the charges. In a letter to the FEC dated May 20, 1977, Assistant Attorney General Benjamin R. Civiletti said that the Justice Department "would not be inclined to invoke criminal [procedures] to redress 'the sort of generalized cocktail party banter in which Mr. Thomson appears to have engaged.' "[220] The commission took no further action following the conclusion of its investigation of James Sasser's campaign finances. FEC investigation of the legality of the bank loans made to Sasser lasted for two years. At the end of that period, in June 1978, the agency dismissed charges against Sasser, thereby clarifying for candidates and bank officials the procedure necessary for reporting bank loans to avoid violation of federal election law. The agency found Sasser's bank loans questionable in some ways, but it decided that the irregularities did not violate the law. It did comment that Sasser had improperly reported the loans, since he had indicated that they were personal funds. No fine was imposed since he agreed to amend his campaign reports.

FEC General Counsel William C. Oldaker, Murphy's successor, prepared a 42-page report on the case that represented the first definitive statement of compliance standards in a key area and one suspected by many observers of widespread abuse. After examining the series of loans Sasser had obtained and partially repaid with campaign contributions, Oldaker concluded, "It would be difficult to prove that the dominant motive was not an acceptable business one but rather was to aid Mr. Sasser's candidacy." Although he determined that the banks had not deliberately favored Sasser's candidacy, Oldaker noted that the actions of a bank official (Charles Turner, a personal friend of Sasser) illustrated the influence one person might exert on a particular candidate's fund raising.[221]

The FEC decision set forth certain guidelines for determination of the legality of bank loans obtained by candidates for federal office. These guidelines required 1) that the loan comply with federal banking regulations, 2) that the amount and terms of the loan be considered, 3) that the loan be processed normally by the bank, 4) that the relationship between the borrower and the authorizing bank official be considered, 5) that evidence exist of the credit worthiness of the borrower, 6) that there be justification for the expectation of repayment, 7) that the amount

and terms of the loan be similar to those offered other individuals, and
8) that relationships between participating banks be considered in
transactions involving more than one bank.[222]

Footnotes

[1] This section is derived from Herbert E. Alexander, *Financing Politics*, pp. 145-148.

[2] Richard D. Lyons, "Congress Leaders Fight Curbs on 'Slush Funds,'" *The New York Times*, September 15, 1975.

[3] Warren Weaver, Jr., "Wayne Hays Today Will Again Tackle Election Board on Rule," *The New York Times*, October 20, 1975.

[4] Warren Weaver, Jr., "Election Panel Revises Campaign Reporting Rule," *The New York Times*, November 26, 1975.

[5] *Clark v. Valeo, et. al.*, U.S. District Court for the District of Columbia, Civil Action No. 76-1227. The suit sought to have the one-house veto provisions of the FECA declared unconstitutional. The U.S. Court of Appeals dismissed the case on the grounds that it did not present a ripe case or controversy within the meaning of that phrase in Article III of the U.S. Constitution. Clark appealed to the Supreme Court. On April 8, 1977, the commission filed a motion with the Court asking it to dismiss the motion on the following grounds: 1) Clark sought appeal on a matter of jurisdiction whereas the FECA only allows appeals on constitutional questions; 2) there was no record evidence pertaining to a congressional veto of FEC regulations; 3) none of the issues has been reviewed by a lower court; and 4) the issues involved deal with "sensitive questions relating to the separation of legislative and executive powers." On June 6, 1977, the Supreme Court affirmed the Court of Appeals' decision dismissing the suit. The Department of Justice joined the suit at the Court of Appeals stage, urging that the veto be declared unconstitutional. *Clark v. Kimmitt*, No. 76-1105.

[6] Federal Election Commission, "Statement of Federal Election Commission: October 5, 1976, press release, October 5, 1976.

[7] "FEC Regulation on Reverse Check-Off Faces Threat of Item Veto in House," *Campaign Practices Reports*, March 21, 1977, p. 4.

[8] This section is derived from Herbert E. Alexander, *Financing Politics*, pp. 156-157.

[9] Advisory opinions (AOs) may be issued only concerning the application of a general rule of law to a specific factual situation involving the requester. A "general rule of law" must be stated in regulations. Opinions cannot be issued for hypothetical questions. AOs issued by the commission may be relied upon by any person involved in the specific transaction dealt with in the request or any person involved in a transaction indistinguishable from the transaction in the request provided in either case that such persons act in good faith and in accordance with the provisions and findings of the AO. Advisory opinions may be requested by holders of federal office, candidates for federal office, political committees, the national committee of a political party, or authorized agents of any of the foregoing persons if the agent discloses the identity of his or her principal. This is a rather narrow list since it seems to exclude state election commissions from seeking AOs concerning the relationships of federal to state law.

[10] Federal Election Commission, Advisory Opinion 1978-9, July 21, 1978, pp. 1-12.

[11] Federal Election Commission, Dissenting Opinion of Commissioner Robert O. Tiernan to Advisory Opinion 1978-9, p. 7.

[12] This informational summary is drawn from the Federal Election Commission's 1975 *Annual Report* (Washington, D.C., 1975).

[13] Ibid., p. 15.

[14] Ibid., p. 16.

[15] Ibid., p. 23.

[16] Ibid., p. 20.

[17] Ibid., p. 29.

[18] Ibid.

[19] Ibid., p. 30.

[20] Ibid., p. 32.

[21] Ibid., p. 33.

[22] Ibid., p. 39.

[23] Ibid.

[24] Ibid., pp. 52, 53.

[25] Federal Election Commission 1976 *Annual Report* (Washington, D.C., 1976), pp. 1, 2.

[26] In 1976 there was an extensive realignment of the commission's organizational structure to improve its efficiency. The commission's staff increased from 162 in 1975 to 197 in 1976; most of the increase was due to the creation of the Office of Data Systems and Development. In addition the commission employed temporary employees during the election cycle. Most of the temporaries had left by March 1977. Ibid., pp. 7-9.

[27] Ibid., p. 15.

[28] The commission certified three candidates on December 18, 1975, eight more on December 23, 1975, another on January 29, 1976, two on February 25 and 26 and the final candidate on June 17, 1976. Ibid., p. 15.

[29] Ibid., pp. 16, 17.

[30] The suspension hurt not only those candidates who already had been certified but also those who were seeking to be. The latter "had to conduct their campaigns without knowing when or if the matching funds might be available." Only one candidate was certified after the commission was reconstituted. Ibid., pp. 2, 18.

[31] In addition the commission adopted a rule that any candidate "who released or instructed his delegates to vote for another candidate was also not actively eligible." Ibid., pp. 19, 20.

[32] On the question of what was a qualified campaign expense, the commission, after some detailed examination, gave up "in recognition that the variety and ingenuity of political campaigners in spending funds for a campaign would simply not lend itself to easy categorization. At the moment the rule which is being followed is simply whether an expenditure is 'ordinary, reasonable, and necessary.' Also expenditures must be documented by other related evidence such as invoices." Ibid., p. 26.

[33] Ibid., pp. 22, 23.

[34] These figures do not include funds initially received by the national committees but later returned, nor the interest earned on those funds while in the committees' possession. Ibid., p. 23.

[35] Ibid.

[36] "Generally, each reporting entity is expected to submit between 12 and 15 documents during an election year including statements, reports, amendments, and miscellaneous correspondence. Thus, the Commission can reasonably be expected to receive from 67,000 to 84,000 documents from committees, plus an additional 10,000 to 15,000 documents to be filed directly by candidates." Ibid., pp. 29, 31.

[37] "A survey of House campaigns in 1972 shows that 92 percent of House candidates who ran in the general election spent in excess of $5,000 while 87 percent spent in excess of $10,000 during the calendar year." The $10,000 threshold "eliminated from the review process about 43 percent of all documents filed. . . . The committees which were eliminated from the review process under the $10,000 threshold were primarily:

    1. House candidates unsuccessful in primary elections.

    2. Local party-related committees.

    3. Small non-party-related multicandidate committees.

    4. Minor presidential-candidate committees."

Ibid., p. 32.

[38] The House and Senate disclosure reports were not included among those examined for adequacy of reporting, since the FEC did not have review responsibility for them at this time. Ibid.

[39] On September 23, 1976, the FEC ruled "that contributions to political committees making independent expenditures would not be subject to the $1,000 limit as long as 'the

contributor does not give to the committee with the knowledge that a substantial portion of the contributor's funds will be . . . expended on behalf of the candidate.' " Ibid., p. 37.

[40] Ibid., p. 38.

[41] Ibid., p. 60.

[42] Ibid., p. 64.

[43] Ibid., p. 77.

[44] It is possible that the candidates, especially those seeking the presidency, were responsive to the commission's dicta because of the outcry over the Watergate scandal. If this was the real reason for the high level of compliance with the FECA, then it is possible that in future elections we may find a greater unwillingness on the part of candidates and campaign committees to be responsive to the commission. Whether we have witnessed a permanent or only a temporary change in the modus operandi of candidates seeking federal office remains to be seen.

[45] The commission's desire to get the relevant data it receives out to the various localities and states may prove helpful in this area. In addition, the FEC should continue its efforts to improve coordination with local and state election officials.

[46] The following informational summary is drawn from the Federal Election Commission's 1977 *Annual Report* (Washington, D.C. 1977).

[47] Ibid., p. 22.

[48] Ibid., p. 37.

[49] Ibid., p. 34.

[50] Commission Chairman Vernon Thomson noted that the FEC's "computer system will for the first time make available extensive summaries and analyses of federal campaign finances prior to the November election. In the past, this kind of data have only been developed long after the elections are over." Federal Election Commission, "FEC Issues Presidential Campaign Finance Summary — Unveils New Computer System," press release, September 21, 1976, p. 1.

[51] Andrew McKay, "Computer Support for Certification Purposes," Memo to Orlando Potter, Federal Election Commission, September 11, 1975, pp. 1-6; Orlando Potter, "Priority List for the Manager, Data Processing Services," Memo to Bob Baker and Jim Pehrkon, Federal Election Commission, October 17, 1975, pp. 1-2.

[52] Bill Loughrey, "Computers and Data Processing," Memo to Commissioner Thomson, December 27, 1975, p. 1.

[53] Federal Election Commission, undated resolution.

[54] The FEC computer system was capable of both on-line data entry and on-line inquiry and included a high-speed printer to handle the great volume of reports. The system was developed by the commission and Interactive Sciences Corporation in Braintree, Massachusetts, where the computer itself was located. Telephone lines transmitted data between Braintree and Washington, D.C. Ten CRT data entry video display units at FEC headquarters were staffed day and night. Federal Election Commission, *FEC Disclosure Series No. 1: Presidential Pre-Nomination Receipts and Expenditures — 1976 Campaign*, (Washington, D.C., 1976) p. 4.

[55] Federal Election Commission, 1976 *Annual Report* (Washington, D.C., 1977), p. 33.

[56] See, for example, the memo from Gary Greenhalgh to the commission, dated September 12, 1978, regarding the kinds of contracts and projects in which the Clearinghouse is currently involved.

[57] July 1, 1973, marked the first publication of the Office of Federal Elections' *Federal-State Election Law Survey: An Analysis of State Legislation, Federal Legislation and Judicial Decisions* (Washington, D.C.: U.S. General Accounting Office, July 1973), which comprises major election legislation, both federal and state, from January 1, 1973, with analyses of relevant Supreme Court, federal and state cases involving election matters. The *Survey* aims primarily "to furnish in the form of a brief analysis the essential provisions of state elections laws and important court decisions in the election law field," and proposed bills in the Congress. The *Survey* was issued as a quarterly starting in 1975, and more recently as a semi-annual published by the Federal Election Commission. Also see *Analysis of Federal and State Campaign Finance Law: Quick Reference Charts* (Washington, D.C.: U.S. General Accounting Office), later published periodically by the FEC.

[58] See *A Study of Election Difficulties in Representative American Jurisdictions: Final Report* (Washington, D.C.: U.S. General Accounting Office, January 1973); *A Study of State and Local Voter Registration Systems: Final Report* (Washington, D.C.: U.S. General Accounting Office, August 1974); *Election Administration Bulletin* (Washington, D.C.: U.S. General Accounting Office, May 1974); *Survey of Election Boards Data Base* (Washington, D.C.: U.S. General Accounting Office, May 1974); *Survey of Election Boards: Final Report* (Washington, D.C.: U.S. General Accounting Office, May 1974); *Survey of Election Boards: Summary of Written Comments* (Washington, D.C.: U.S. General Accounting Office, July 1974); *Describe, Analyze, and Compare the Currently Available Methods of Vote Counting Equipment and to Make Appropriate Recommendation: Final Report,* Prepared for: U.S. General Accounting Office, Office of Federal Elections, Clearinghouse on Election Administration (Vienna, Virginia: Analytic Systems Inc., October 1974); *Experimental Voting System Supplement,* Prepared for: U.S. General Accounting Office, Office of Federal Elections (Vienna, Virginia: Analytic Systems Inc., December 1974); *Election Laws Examination With Respect to Voting Equipment,* Prepared for: U.S. General Accounting Office, Office of Federal Elections (Vienna, Virginia: Analytic Systems Inc., January 1975); Roy G. Saltman, *Effective Use of Computing Technology in Vote Tallying,* Prepared for: Clearinghouse on Election Administration, Office of Federal Elections, General Accounting Office (Washington, D.C.: Information Technology Division, Institute for Computer Sciences and Technology, National Bureau of Standards, March 1975); *Voting Systems: Recommended Procurement Procedures and a Review of Current Equipment,* Vol. 1 (Washington, D.C.: Federal Election Commission, October 1977); *Voting Systems: A Summary of State Voting Equipment Laws,* Vol. 2 (Washington, D.C.: Federal Election Commission, October 1977); *Reducing Voter Waiting Times: How To Allocate Voting Machines to the Polls* (Washington, D.C.: Federal Election Commission, June 1977); *The Training of Election Officials* (Washington, D.C.: Federal Election Commission, September 1974); *State and Local Government Expenditure for Election Administration: Fiscal Years 1970 to 1973* (Washington, D.C.: Federal Election Commission, July 1975); *An Analysis of Laws and Procedures Governing Absentee Registration and Absentee Voting in the United States; Vol. 1; Summary Report* (Washington, D.C.: Federal Election Commission, June 1975); *An Analysis of Laws and Procedures Governing Absentee Registration and Absentee Voting in the United States; Vol. II; Memoranda of State Laws* (Washington, D.C.: Federal Election Commission, June 1975); *Effective Use of Computing Technology in Vote-Tallying* (Washington, D.C.: Federal Election Commission, March 1975); *Handbook of State Election Offices and Functions* (Washington, D.C.: Federal Election Commission, September 1976.)

[59] *FEC Journal of Election Administration* (Washington, D.C.: Federal Election Commission, quarterly starting second quarter, 1977).

[60] "FEC Rejects Counsel's Recommendation to Collect for Clearinghouse Reports," *Election Administration Reports,* September 27, 1978, pp. 1-2.

[61] Ibid., pp. 1-2.

[62] "McCarthy Group Challenges FEC Audit Plan," McCarthy '76 press release, August 22, 1975; "McCarthy Group Refuses to Submit to FEC Audit," McCarthy '76 press release, August 30, 1975.

[63] "FEC 1976 Congressional Audits To Be Based on Spending Ceilings," *Campaign Practices Reports,* October 6, 1975, pp. 5-6.

[64] Andrew Mollison, "Watch," Cox Newspapers Washington Bureau press release, November 12, 1976.

[65] "FEC Advised by Rep. Thompson to Drop Random Audit Plan," *Campaign Practices Reports,* February 7, 1977, pp. 1-2.

[66] "FEC Developing Criteria to Determine Which Candidate Committees to Audit," *Campaign Practices Reports,* April 4, 1977, pp. 7-9.

[67] Under the Government-in-the-Sunshine Act passed by Congress in 1976, the discussion of who is to be audited and why must be in open session unless the commission votes to close the meeting (meaning that disclosure constituting invasion of privacy would occur if discussion took place in open session).

[68] "FEC Commences Routine Audits of Randomly-Selected Congressional Races," Federal Election Commission press release, August 4, 1977.

[69] Joseph Albright, " 'Disclosure Problems' Gave Carter Close Call," *Atlanta Journal*, September 3, 1976. In November 1976 the Carter campaign was reportedly having difficulty in meeting the FEC's requirements concerning receipts. The particular receipts the committee was having difficulty producing included those for travel tickets billed to individuals, stamps bought at the post office, and deposits made to the telephone company.

[70] Andrew Mollison, "Shapp Scheme Could Hurt Funding Bill," *Atlanta Journal*, May 19, 1977.

[71] "Auditing the FEC," *The New Republic*, October 1, 1977.

[72] "In the Midst of Routine Testimony, Up Pops the Question of Campaign 'Audits,' " *Campaign Practices Reports*, pp. 3-4.

[73] Clay F. Richards, "Campaign Debts," UPI press release, December 2, 1977.

[74] Federal Election Commission, 1977 *Annual Report* (Washington, D.C.: 1978), pp. 8f.f.

[75] "House Unit Cuts FEC's Audit Power," Congressional Quarterly *Weekly Report*, April 29, 1978, p. 1056.

[76] Martha Angle and Robert Walters, "In Washington: FEC Investigates Delaney," June 20, 1978; and, "In Washington: House Rails at Random Audits," June 21, 1978.

[77] "FEC Audit Policy," *The FEC Record*, June 1978, pp. 5-6.

[78] "Federal Election Commission Continues in Controversy, Its Random Audit this Time Puzzling All, Even Members," special report, *Campaign Practices Reports*, August 21, 1978, p. 7.

[79] Report on the Random Audits, Memorandum from Bob Costa/Patricia Shering to the Commissioners, July 31, 1978.

[80] "1976: The End of the Campaign," *The Washington Post*, April 6, 1978.

[81] Don McLeod, "Brock Seeks Halt in FEC's Funding," *The Washington Star*, June 4, 1978; Eugene J. McCarthy, "First Things Come Last at Election Board," *The Washington Star*, June 25, 1978.

[82] Jerry Landauer, "Audit Is Still Awaited of Carter's Outlays in the '76 Campaign," *The Wall Street Journal*, June 1, 1978.

[83] "FEC Rules on Carter's 1976 Finances after Pondering Issue Two Years," *Campaign Practices Reports*, October 2, 1978, p. 4.

[84] Martin Tolchin, "Carter Campaign Audit Likely to be Published Soon," *The New York Times*, June 15, 1978.

[85] Grayson Mitchell, "Carter Election Group Fined for Illegal Use of Leftover Funds," *Los Angeles Times*, October 14, 1978.

[86] John R. Bolton, "Government Astride the Political Process," *Regulation*, July/August 1978, pp. 46-55.

[87] John G. Murphy, Jr., "The Federal Election Commission: A Rebuttal," *Regulation*, September/October, 1978, pp. 42-51.

[88] *Buckley v. Valeo*, 424 U.S. 1 at 30 (1978). For a discussion of the legislative veto as this issue figured in *Buckley* and in suits against the FEC, also see John R. Balson, *The Legislative Veto: Unseparating the Powers.*

[89] *Ramsey Clark v. Francis R. Valeo, et. al*, U.S. District Court for the District of Columbia, Civil Action No. 76-1227, Memorandum of Points and Authorities in Support of Plaintiff's 1) motion for certification of constitutional questions to the Court of Appeals; 2) application for three-judge court; and 3) motion to reduce defendant's time to answer complaint, July 1, 1976, pp. 1-7.

[90] "Preliminary Hearing Set on Legal Challenge to Congressional Veto Power Over FEC Rules," *Campaign Practices Reports*, August 23, 1976, p. 9.

[91] "U.S. Appeals Court Dismisses Challenge to Congressional Veto Power over FEC Rules," *Campaign Practices Reports*, January 24, 1977, pp. 2-3.

[92] Ann Cooper, "Congressional Veto Bill Being Pushed in House But Faces Major Hurdles," Congressional Quarterly *Weekly Report*, March 4, 1978, p. 575.

[93] *Ramsey Clark and United States of America v. Francis R. Valeo, et. al.*, Supreme Court of the United States, 76-1105, October term 1976, Jurisdictional Statement on Appeals from, and Petition for Writ of Certiorari to, the U.S. Court of Appeals for the D.C. Circuit and the U.S. District Court for D.C., February 9, 1977, p. 7.

[94] See *C. Clyde Atkins v. U.S.* 556 F.2d 1028 (1977).

[95] *FEC Record,* June 1977, p. 4.

[96] "FEC Chided By Women Voters League for Upsetting TV Debate Payment," *Campaign Practices Reports,* September 19, 1977, p. 3.

[97] "FEC Permits Corporate and Union Contributions to Nonpartisan Groups For Candidate Debates," *FEC Record,* March 1978, p. 1.

[98] *FEC Record,* June 1977, p. 3.

[99] *Campaign Practices Reports,* January 23, 1978, p. 10.

[100] "Federal Election Unit Challenged In Lawsuit," *The New York Times,* March 23, 1977.

[101] See 2 U.S.C. Section 441(b) (4) (D); Sections 114.8 (c), (d), (e), and (f).

[102] *BreadPAC v. FEC,* U.S. District Court, Northern District of Illinois, Civil Action No. 77C947, Transcript of Proceedings, October 6, 1977.

[103] "Chamber of Commerce Suit Hits Curb On Inter-PAC Solicitation of Funds," *Campaign Practices Reports,* July 24, 1978, pp. 4-5.

[104] 18 U.S.C. Section 610.

[105] 2 U.S.C. Section 441b.

[106] *Martin Tractor v. FEC,* U.S. District Court for the District of Columbia, Civil Action No. 78-1259, Complaint filed July 7, 1978.

[107] See *Martin Tractor v. FEC* — F. Supp. — (Civil Action No. 78-1259, November 8, 1978).

[108] 11 CFR 110.1 (g) (1).

[109] "Conservative PAC Loses Lawsuit Against FEC, Democratic Committee," *Campaign Pracices Reports,* May 15, 1978, p. 4.

[110] *NCPAC v. FEC,* U.S. District Court for the District of Columbia, Civil Action No. 78-0270, Complaint filed April 28, 1978.

[111] Michael J. Malbin, "Labor, Business and Money — A Post-Election Analysis," *National Journal,* March 19, 1977, p. 414.

[112] Common Cause news release, September 25, 1978.

[113] See 2 U.S.C. Section 441(b) (3) (A).

[114] FEC, "Statement of FEC: October 5, 1976," press release, October 5, 1976.

[115] "FEC Regulations on Reverse Check-off Faces Threat of Item Veto in House," *Campaign Practices Reports,* March 21, 1977, p. 4.

[116] *National Right to Work Committee v. Thomson,* U.S. District Court for the District of Columbia, Civil Action No. 77-387, Complaint filed August 31, 1977.

[117] *FEC v. NEA,* U.S. District Court for the District of Columbia, Civil Action No. 77-1705, Complaint filed September 28, 1977. The 18 NEA affiliates included California, Connecticut, Idaho, Illinois, Kansas, Kentucky, Massachusetts, Michigan, Nebraska, Nevada, New Hampshire, New Jersey, Pennsylvania, Rhode Island, South Dakota, Vermont, Wisconsin, and Wyoming. New Jersey was dropped from the action when it ended its use of the system in 1977.

[118] "U.S. Judge Rules Against Teachers Union, Says PAC 'Reverse Check-off' Breaks Law," *Campaign Practices Reports,* July 24, 1978, pp. 5-7.

[119] "NEA's Reverse Check-Off Became Reverse Payback In Court Ruling," *Campaign Practices Reports,* November 13, 1978, pp. 7-8.

[120] *NRWC v. FEC, FEC Record,* March 1978.

[121] " 'Right to Work' Names Shielded, *Campaign Practices Reports,* September 18, 1978, p. 2.

[122] *Campaign Practices Reports,* September 23, 1974, pp. 3-4.

[123] *Campaign Practices Reports,* November 4, 1974, p. 8.

[124] *Campaign Practices Reports,* December 16, 1974, p. 9.

[125] *Doe v. Martin,* U.S. District Court for the District of Columbia, Civil Action No. 75-0083, October 22, 1975.

[126] *Talley v. California,* 362 U.S. 60 (1960); *Bater v. Little Rock,* 361 U.S. 516 (1960); *NAACP v. Alabama,* 357 U.S. 499 (1958); and *U.S. v. Rumely* 345 U.S. 41 (1953). Similar decisions relating to controversial organizations engaged in electoral activity included *Pollard v. Roberts,* 393 U.S. 14 (1968), in which the political body involved was the Republican Party of Arkansas.

[127] *Buckley v. Valeo,* 424 U.S. at 68.

[128] *FEC Record,* March 1977, p. 6.

[129] Nicholas M. Hancock, "FBI Harassed A Leftist Party: Documents Show 10-year Campaign of Disruption of Socialist Workers," *The New York Times,* March 19, 1975.

[130] John M. Crewdson, "FBI Burglarized Leftist Offices Here 92 Times in 1960-1966, Official Files Show," *The New York Times,* March 29, 1976.

[131] "FBI Said to Have Inspected Lists of Socialist Workers Contributors," *The New York Times,* October 30, 1976.

[132] Elmer B. Staats, "Enforcing the Campaign Finance Laws," speech before the Citizens' Research Foundation's National Conference on Money and Politics (Washington, D.C., February 28, 1974), pp. 2-8.

[133] The FEC occasionally dismissed charges that might have been construed as violations of the law because the law seemed insufficiently clear and likely to have been misinterpreted by many candidates or their parties. One such case was that of former Sen. John V. Tunney, D-Calif., who had benefited from a fund-raiser held in his honor by singer Helen Reddy. Guests at the event had contributed $3,000 per couple in checks made payable to the Democratic State Central Committee, since the law sets a $1,000 limit on individual contributions but a $5,000 limit on party committee contributions. The state central committee forwarded these funds, together with funds collected at an earlier similar fund-raiser, to Tunney's campaign committee, where they were used to help retire his campaign debt. Tunney argued that the funds had not been specifically earmarked for him, and the Federal Election Commission dismissed the charges against him, apparently deciding to issue new regulations rather than find him in violation, since many candidates and committees might have acted similarly. "Commission Dismisses Charges That Tunney Funding Broke Law," *Campaign Practices Reports,* April 3, 1978, pp. 2-3.

[134] Bill Oldaker, "Memorandum of Understanding on Procedure for Reporting Violations," Federal Election Commission, June 7, 1976, p. 1. Also see William C. Oldaker, "Memorandum on the Handling of Internally Generated Matters," Federal Election Commission, March 17, 1978; Orlando B. Potter, "Memorandum on Proposed Procedures to Assure Security of Commission Compliance Matters," Federal Election Commission, March 20, 1978.

[135] "The Act also provides that any party aggrieved by the failure of the Commission to act on its complaint or by an order of the Commission dismissing a complaint may file a petition with the United States District Court for the District of Columbia. Such petitions shall be filed within 90 days after the filing of the complaint, if a failure to act is alleged; if a dismissal is alleged, the petition must be filed in court within 60 days of the dismissal. . . . To date, one petition has been filed under this provision." Federal Election Commission, 1976 *Annual Report* (Washington, D.C., 1977), p. 50.

[136] "Where the matter involves reports due or complaints filed close to an election the statute allows the conciliation period to be shortened to 'not less than one half the number of days between the date upon which the Commission determines there is reasonable cause to believe such a violation has occurred and the date of the election involved.' " Ibid.

[137] Ibid., p. 51.

[138] Gloria R. Sulton, "Memorandum Re: Public access to materials in 'closed' compliance actions," Federal Election Commission, January 13, 1976, pp. 2, 3, 12-14.

[139] "Of 247 cases investigated, FEC has taken 14 to court," *Campaign Practices Reports,* January 24, 1977, pp. 9, 10.

[140] Alexander, *Financing Politics,* p. 160.

[141] FEC 1976 *Annual Report,* p. 51.

[142] Ibid., p. 52.

[143] "Of 247 cases, . . .," pp. 7-8.

[144] Between January and September 1977, the FEC made public the results of compliance actions in 95 new cases. Of this total, 67 cases were closed following preliminary investigations; four cases resulted in conciliation agreements; and in 24 cases the commission inquiry concluded that the FECA might have been violated and no conciliation agreement was reached. One case of the last-named 24 was referred to the Justice Department for action, 18 resulted in suits filed in District Courts, and no further action was taken on the remaining five.

[145] Federal Election Commission, 1977 *Annual Report* (Washington, D.C., 1978), pp. 15-18.

[146] Ibid.

[147] Andrew Mollison, "Dough," Cox Newspapers Washington Bureau press release dated December 7, 1976.

[148] "Campaign Act Violators Can Be Prosecuted by Both Justice Department and FEC, Judge Rules," *Campaign Practices Report*, August 8, 1977, pp. 8-9.

[149] "Justice Department and FEC Agree on How Each Will Handle Violations," *Campaign Practices Reports*, February 20, 1978, pp. 1-2.

[150] *National Right to Work Committee v. Thomson*, Civil Action No. 77-435, 1977.

[151] "Of 247 cases, . . .," pp. 7-8.

[152] "Ford Fundraiser, Confused by Law, Fined $500 for Illegal Expenditures," *Campaign Practices Reports*, May 1, 1978, pp. 7-8.

[153] "Okay to Hold Political Lunches, FEC Says, But Only If The Guest of Honor Stays Away," *Campaign Practices Reports*, July 24, 1978, pp. 8-9.

[154] "Cabbie Who Ran for President Guilty of False Financing Claim," *Campaign Practices Reports*, March 6, 1978, pp. 7-8.

[155] Timothy S. Robinson, "Ex-Rep. Wyatt Guilty in Funds Case," *The Washington Post*, June 12, 1975.

[156] "Congressional Candidate Fined $1,500," *Campaign Practices Reports*, May 15, 1978, p. 3.

[157] "Of 247 cases, . . .," p. 9.

[158] "Loans With Co-signers Bring Fines As 'Excessive' Political Donation," *Campaign Practices Reports*, November 13, 1978, pp. 6-7.

[159] "First Congress Member Fined By FEC," *Campaign Practices Reports*, November 27, 1978, p. 5.

[160] Myron S. Waldman, "Delaney's Election Costs Challenged," *Newsday*, June 22, 1978.

[161] Jay Shelledy, "Hansen Pleads Guilty to Election Violations," *Lewiston Morning Tribune*, February 20, 1975.

[162] U.S., Congress, House, *Congressional Record*, 94th Congress, 1st Session, September 5, 1975, H8393.

[163] David Morrissey, "The Defense of George Hansen," *Idaho State Journal*, July 18, 1976.

[164] David Morrissey, "Spending Increases," *Idaho Sunday Journal*, July 18, 1976.

[165] Jay Shelledy, "Hansen Chronically Tardy on Tax Returns," *Lewiston Morning Tribune*, October 15, 1976.

[166] William Nye Curry, "Hansen Offers Plan for Officeholder to Seek Funds for Self," *The Washington Post*, March 3, 1977.

[167] "19 Election Officers Indicted in Louisiana for Fraud in Contest to Succeed Hebert," *The New York Times*, January 9, 1977; Bob Livingston, "Louisiana's First District: View of a Continuing Election," *Congress Today!* May 1977, pp. 10-11.

[168] "House Panel Will Take Probe of Tonry Election to New Orleans," *Election Administration Reports*, March 2, 1977, pp. 2-4.

[169] "Illegal Fund Raising Is Laid to Rep. Tonry: New Orleans Court Is Told He Tried to Conceal $32,000," *The New York Times*, April 2, 1977.

[170] John Pope, "Vote Fraud Charge in Tonry Election Goes Back to Court," *The Washington Post*, April 14, 1977; "Tonry Vote Fraud Confirmed in Court; House Still Probing," *The Washington Post*, April 22, 1977; "Rep. Tonry, Figure in Vote Fraud, Resigns But Vows to Run Again," *The New York Times*, May 5, 1977.

[171] "Tonry Pleads Guilty to Campaign Charges," *The New York Times*, July 2, 1977; "Tonry Enters Prison for 'White Collar Types,'" *The Washington Post*, August 16, 1977.

[172] "Republican Elected to House Seat from New Orleans Held by Tonry," *The New York Times*, August 29, 1977.

[173] "Federal Investigators Named Defendants in Case on Behalf of Louisiana Poll Commissioners," *Election Administration Reports*, October 12, 1977, p. 5.

[174] United Press International, "Tonry," press release, February 1, 1978.

[175] "Elderly Arizona Couple Fined $1,000 For Contributing $48,000 Over Limit," *Campaign Practices Reports*, July 10, 1978, pp. 1-2.

[176] "Alabama Candidate and Father to Pay $20,000 in Overspending," *Campaign Practices Reports*, May 1, 1978, pp. 8-9.

[177] Morton Mintz, "Common Cause Accuses AMA Units of Violating Political Donation Limits," *The Washington Post*, October 3, 1978; "National and State Contributions Could Be Trouble for Candidates," *Campaign Practices Reports*, March 20, 1978, p. 10.

[178] "Gun Owners of America Fined Record $11,000 by Election Panel," *Campaign Practices Reports*, May 29, 1978, pp. 1-2.

[179] Peter Kihss, "U.S. Says L. I. Group Broke Election Law, Asserts Political Motives Prompted Publication of Representative's Voting Record in the House," *The New York Times*, Febraury 19, 1978. For a critical article, see David Broder, "Election Commission Is Very Tenacious," *New Brunswick Home News*, February 27, 1978.

[180] "Profile: Tax Reform Immediately (Ad Hoc Committee of the John Birch Society)," *Democratic Congressional Campaign Committee Report*, May 1978, pp. 1-5.

[181] "Court Asked to Fine New Jersey Group for 'Critiques' of Voters in Congress," *Campaign Practices Reports*, June 26, 1978, pp. 1-3.

[182] "Six Baltimore Political Clubs Face Suit for Failure to Register with FEC," *Election Administration Reports*, Volume 7, Number 23, 1977, pp. 1-2.

[183] "FEC Sues Public Employees' Union Over 1976 Cartoon of Nixon, Ford," *Campaign Practices Reports*, November 13, 1978, pp. 5-6.

[184] "Commission Files Suit against AFL-CIO Charging Illegal Transfer of $392,000," *Campaign Practices Reports*, January 9, 1978, pp. 3-4.

[185] *FEC v. AFL-CIO*, U.S. District Court, D.C. Circuit, Civil Action No. 77-2147, June 1978.

[186] "FEC Decides It Will Impose Fines Now On Candidates Who Take Illegal Gifts," *Campaign Practices Reports*, August 21, 1978, pp. 4-5.

[187] John G. Murphy, Jr., "The Federal Election Commission: A Rebuttal," *Regulation*, September/October 1978, p. 45.

[188] Eugene J. McCarthy, "Federal Election Commission," *Citizens for the Republic Newsletter*, November 1, 1977.

[189] Andrew Mollison, "Incumbents Favored, Federal-Election Board Lax on Enforcing Laws," *Atlanta Constitution*, December 11, 1977; "Go Slow, Be Soft Seems Election Panel Strategy," *Atlanta Constitution*, December 18, 1977; "Reform Politics in U.S. 'A Regulated Industry,' " *Atlanta Constitution*, December 25, 1977.

[190] "FEC Releases Statistical Survey on Candidate Filings in Spring Primaries," Federal Election Commission news release dated July 2, 1978, pp. 1-2.

[191] Martha Angle and Robert Walters, "Memoirs Will Keep Archivists Employed: Small Oversight of FEC," *Southtown Economist*, June 4, 1978.

[192] William C. Oldaker, "Response to Advisory Opinion Request from National Treasury Employees Union," Federal Election Commission Memorandum No. 153 to the commission through Orlando B. Potter.

[193] "FEC Fails Again in Last-Ditch Try to Keep Its Staff from Unionizing," *Campaign Practices Reports*, September 18, 1978, pp. 1-3.

[194] "FEC Acts to Keep Union from Its Staff, Arguing PAC Poses Conflict of Interest," *Campaign Practices Reports*, August 7, 1978, pp. 1-2.

[195] This section generally follows *Campaign Practices Reports*, September 28, 1977, pp. 2-3; October 3, 1977, p. 6; October 31, 1977, pp. 4-5; November 14, 1977, pp. 1-3.

[196] Common Cause letter to members of the Senate Rules Committee, signed by President David Cohen and Senior Vice-President Fred Wertheimer, August 14, 1978.

[197] Ron Sarro, "Republican Zagoria Claims 'Bum Rap' on FEC Nomination," *The Washington Star*, November 4, 1977.

[198] Peter Barnes, "Consultant Charges McGarry with Improper Tax Deductions," *The Washington Post*, August 24, 1978.

[199] U.S. Congress, Senate Rules Committee, *Report on the Nomination of John Warren McGarry of Massachusetts to the Federal Election Commission*, Executive Report 95-28, September 13, 1978.

[200] Common Cause letter to all senators, signed by President David Cohen and Senior Vice-President Fred Wertheimer, September 18, 1978.

[201] Congressional Quarterly *Weekly Report*, October 28, 1978, p. 3109.

[202] "FEC Commissioner Suing President Carter to Block Interim Seating of Replacement," *Election Administration Reports*, November 8, 1978, p. 4.

[203] J. F. terHorst, "Our Righteous President Pulls a Fast One," *Los Angeles Times*, October 13, 1978.

[204] *Neil Staebler et al.*, Plaintiffs, *vs. Jimmy Carter, et al.*, Defendants, Memorandum in Support of Plaintiff's Motion for Summary Judgment and in Opposition to Plaintiff's Motion for Summary Judgment. Civil Action No. 78-2028, 1978.

[205] *Neil Staebler, et al., v. Jimmy Carter, et al.*, Memorandum of Points and Authorities in Support of Defendants' Motion for Summary Judgment and in Opposition to Plaintiff's Motion for Summary Judgment. Civil Action No. 78-2028, 1978.

[206] "Finally, McGarry Replaces Staebler — But for How Long? Only Court May Say,"*Campaign Practices Reports*, October 30, 1978, pp. 2-3.

[207] "Election Official Wins Fight to Keep Post," *Los Angeles Times*, January 9, 1979.

[208] Jack W. Germond and Jules Witcover, "Squabbling Over Makeup of FEC to Start All Over Again Next Year," *The Washington Star*, December 31, 1978.

[209] U.S. Congress, House, *Federal Election Campaign Act Amendments for 1976, Conference Report* 94-1057, p. 34.

[210] Jerry Landauer, "How Cheap Is Talk? It Depends on Who Is Doing the Paying: Election-Agency Aide Made Apparently Personal Calls on a Federal Credit Card," *The Wall Street Journal*, August 18, 1977. Less than two weeks later, *The New York Times* reported the embarrassment of public officials in Wisconsin, many of whom were discovered to have made numerous long-distance calls at taxpayers' expense. The calls had been placed to individuals throughout the United States and as far away as Scotland and India, and the bureaucrats who made them included members of the legislature, the governor, and the attorney general. "Wisconsin Shaken by Phone Scandal Involving Officials," *The New York Times*, August 30, 1977.

[211] "Statement of Commissioner Robert O. Tiernan," Federal Election Commission press release, September 2, 1977.

[212] "Rules Committee Asked to Look into Allegations Against FEC Commissioner," press release from the office of Sen. Dick Clark, D-Iowa, August 19, 1977.

[213] "Senate Committee Asks FEC's Tiernan for Data on Time Spent Practicing Law," *Campaign Practices Reports*, September 19, 1977, p. 5.

[214] "Election Aide Hit for Debt," *The Philadelphia Bulletin*, December 26, 1977.

[215] *Spotlight*, December 26, 1977, pp. 11-16.

[216] Federal Election Commission, General Counsel's Report *In Re An Unknown Respondent MUR 298 (76)*, January 4, 1977, pp. 1-3.

[217] Ibid., pp. 3-42.

[218] The report does not discuss why Laird engaged in such an indirect method of communication with the Brock camp; perhaps he was aware of the potential legal problems involved.

[219] Ibid., p. 42.

[220] "Justice Department Clears FEC Commissioner in Alleged Leak of Investigation Data," *Campaign Practices Reports*, May 31, 1977, p. 9.

[221] "Special Reports: FEC Finds There Are Loans And Then There Are Loans As It Rules on Rep. Sasser's Campaign Contributions," *Campaign Practices Reports*, June 26, 1978, pp. 9-12.

[222] Ibid.

4

Spending in the 1976 Elections

The 1976 elections marked another significant leap in reported political spending. There are several reasons for the escalation. Most obvious is the scope of the FECA Amendments, which went into effect on January 1, 1975, requiring that most persons or committees expending significant funds for the purpose of influencing the outcome of a federal election shall file reports with the FEC, and granting to that agency broad oversight and enforcement authority. Political spending was more meticulously reported than in prior years. For the first time, disclosure at the federal level, including senatorial and congressional campaigns, was under the jurisdiction of the Federal Election Commission.

Another element in the escalation was the inflation factor. A 33 percent increase occurred in the Consumer Price Index from 1972 to 1976. Communication costs, especially, skyrocketed. In such areas as media, advertising, and public opinion polling, the increments exceeded 30 percent, and these items are the basic components of political spending.

For the first time, public funds were used to pay some of the necessary costs. The federal funding and the prohibitions on private contributions for the presidential general election freed up considerable private and special interest money, some of which, predictably, was funneled into the congressional campaigns, and some into state and local campaigns. The number of political committees filing at the federal level proliferated — 6,220 compared with 4,744 in 1972.

The hotly contested struggle for the presidential nomination in the Democratic Party was an additional factor; an unprecedented $16 million had been spent by December 31, 1975, and more than $46 million before the struggle was concluded. Moreover, an unusual, highly

Table 4-1
Total Political Spending in Presidential Election Years, 1952-76

1952	$140,000,000
1956	155,000,000
1960	175,000,000
1964	200,000,000
1968	300,000,000
1972	425,000,000
1976	540,000,000

SOURCE: For 1952-72, Herbert E. Alexander, *Financing the 1972 Election* (Lexington, Mass.: Lexington Books, D.C. Heath and Co., 1976), pp. 77-78, derived in part from Alexander Heard, *The Costs of Democracy* (Chapel Hill, N.C.: The University of North Carolina Press, 1960), pp. 7-8.

competitive contest for presidential nomination in the Republican Party occurred, although, combined with the general election period, Ford and Reagan spent less than Nixon alone had in 1972.

Despite the certain components of escalation, there were factors tending to reduce spending: the effective contribution limits, the expenditure limitations applicable in the presidential campaigns, the prohibition of private contributions in the presidential general election, the reduction in financial participation both because public funding was being provided and because Watergate had turned off some previous contributors, and the inhibiting or chilling effects of the FECA and the FEC.

Total Spending

In 1976 candidates and political parties spent well over $100 million more on political activity at all levels than they did in 1972: $540 million, compared with $425 million in 1972. In early 1977 CRF estimated total spending at slightly more than $500 million, but solid evidence later accumulated supports the higher figure. Table 4-1 shows the comparative spending figures from 1952, the first presidential election for which total political costs were calculated, through 1976.

The 1976 spending fell into four major areas (all figures rounded off):

1. $160 million to elect a president, including prenomination campaigns dating from 1973, plus third-party and independent candidates. Spending by the national party and convention committees is included in this category.

2. $140 million to nominate candidates and elect a Congress, including special interest contributions to the candidates, as well as such committees' operating expenditures and other direct spending.[1]

3. $120 million to nominate candidates and elect governors, other statewide officials and state legislators, and to wage campaigns relative to state ballot issues and amendments to state constitutions.

4. $120 million to nominate candidates and elect to office the hundreds of thousands of county and local public officials and to contest local ballot issues.

Table 4-2
Total Presidential Spending,[a] 1968, 1972, 1976

	1968	1972	1976
Republican	$45,000,000	$ 69,300,000	$ 74,500,000
Democratic	37,000,000	67,300,000	83,200,000
Other	9,000,000	1,200,000	2,000,000
	$91,000,000	$137,800,000	$159,700,000

[a] Primary and general election, including spending by the national committees and the convention committees.

SOURCE: For 1952-1972, Herbert E. Alexander, *Financing the 1972 Election*, (Lexington, Mass.: Lexington Books, D.C. Heath and Co., 1976), pp. 77-78.

In the 1976 presidential campaigns, the Democrats outspent the Republicans by nearly $10 million. The general election spending was, of course, roughly equivalent, and the total represented a significant de-

Table 4-3
Ratio of National-level Direct Spending in Presidential Campaigns, Elections, 1956-76

	1956	1960	1964	1968	1972	1976 [a]
Republicans	59	49	63	55 (65)	67	52
Democrats	41	51	37	29 (35)	33	47
Other	--	--	--	16	--	1

[a] Primary and general election, including spending by the national committees and the convention committees.

SOURCE: Derived from Heard, *Costs*, p. 20 and *1956 General Election Campaigns*, Report to the Senate Committee on Rules and Administration, Subcommittee on Privileges and Elections, 85th Cong., 1st sess. (1957), exhibit 4, p. 41. Deficits in 1956 are listed in this report as bills unpaid as of November 30, 1956. Heard's figures for Republicans and Democrats are for the full calendar year 1956, but labor figures are for January 1 - November 30, 1956. Heard's ratio has been revised to include deficits. Figures in parentheses for 1968 are for Republican-Democratic ratio when other (mainly George Wallace) spending is excluded.

Table 4-4
Direct Campaign Expenditures by Presidential and National Party
Committees, General Elections 1912-76

(In millions)					
1912	$ 2.9 [a]	1936	$14.1	1960	$19.9
1916	4.7	1940	6.2	1964	24.8
1920	6.9	1944	5.0	1968	44.2 [a]
1924	5.4 [a]	1948	6.2 [a]	1972	103.7
1928	11.6	1952	11.6	1976	88.7
1932	5.1	1956	12.9		

[a] Totals include significant minor-party spending.

Note· Data for 1912-44 include transfers to states. Total for 1948 includes only the direct expenditures of the national party committees. For 1952-68, data do not include transfers to states, but do include the national senatorial and congressional committees of both parties. For 1972, for comparative purposes, data do not include state and local level information, except for the presidential candidates. The Nixon component includes all spending for his re-election. For 1976, amounts decreased due to public financing and expenditure limitations.

SOURCE: Citizens' Research Foundation

crease from 1972. Primary spending, however, was appreciably higher for the Democrats — more than $46 million, as against $33 million in 1972; on the Republican side, there was nominal spending in 1972, when President Nixon's nomination was assured, contrasted with an expensive $26 million contest between President Ford and Ronald Reagan in 1976. Tables 4-2 and 4-3, with differing data bases, set forth dollar figures and percentages.

Data on the expenditures of national-level committees primarily concerned with the presidential general election are available since 1912.[2] The figures in Table 4-4 include spending by presidential candidates and national party committees. Although there were some unusual years, presidential spending has tended to follow an exponential curve from 1912 on, with 1928 and 1972 occupying the unique position of escalating by over 100 percent. The lid imposed by federal funding notwithstanding, 1976 fits into the historical pattern.

Presidential Spending

More than 50 presidential candidates filed reports of spending for the 1976 nomination or election, but fewer than half were serious candidates. Thirty avowed Democratic candidates spent less than $15,000 each. Eight minor-party or independent candidates were on the general election ballot in 10 or more states. The only serious Republican contenders were Ford and Reagan, with two other Republicans filing in 1975. All of the rest were Democrats. Four — Bentsen, Byrd, Mondale, and Sanford — made exploratory forays but were not in serious contention in the heat of the prenomination campaign. The rest of the Democratic field encompassed 11 contenders: Bayh, Brown, Carter, Church, Harris, Jackson, McCormack, Shapp, Shriver, Udall, and Wallace.

Democratic Primaries

To win the Democratic presidential nomination, Jimmy Carter spent $12.4 million. Other Democratic contenders, (at least 30 at some

Table 4-5
Democratic Presidential Primary Expenditures, 1973-76

| | *(Adjusted totals, principal campaign committee only)* | | | |
	1973	1974	1975	1976
Qualifying for matching fund				
Birch Bayh			$ 290,828	$ 890,015
Lloyd Bentsen	$ 66,502	$ 368,864	1,554,376	711,845
Jerry Brown				1,730,356
Jimmy Carter		24,832	967,834	10,430,275
Frank Church			13,538	1,460,309
Fred Harris			278,960	766,632
Henry Jackson		204,142	2,170,837	3,992,371
Ellen McCormack			28,266	494,302
Terry Sanford		33,911	335,910	247,547
Milton Shapp			280,197	549,685
Sargent Shriver			372,224	496,407
Morris Udall		12,510	859,691	2,576,804
George Wallace	986,199	1,636,979	2,908,941	4,973,824
Other candidates				
Stanley Arnold			13,461	21,696
Philip V. Baker			6,272	10,099
Arthur Blessitt			8,472	9,837
Robert C. Byrd				148,264
Norman Cousins			10,614	18,341
Hubert Humphrey				58,801
Walter Mondale		103,600	18,313	15,225
Adlai Stevenson III				9,040
(all other)				96,086
Totals	$1,052,701	$2,384,838	$10,118,734	$29,707,761

SOURCE: Kimball W. Brace, *The 1976 Presidential Primaries,* A Report Compiled for the Commission on Presidential Nomination and Party Structure, unpublished ms., May 9, 1977. Figures differ from others in this volume, but used for certain breakdowns not otherwise available.

time during the 1973-76 period) spent a combined total of more than $32.2 million. Of the 13 Democratic candidates qualifying for matching funds from the U.S. Treasury, three of them — McCormack, Sanford, and Shapp — spent less than one million dollars each; Bayh, Bentsen, Brown, Church, Harris, and Shriver, less than $3 million each; Jackson, Udall, and Wallace together accounted for more than $21 million.

By late spring there were still five viable contenders for the presidential nomination: Carter, Brown, Church, Jackson, and Udall. The latter four, in their combined spending, accounted for only marginally more than Carter alone. Carter's financial support mounted steadily as the year progressed; only Brown, starting from a zero base in early spring, demonstrated a greater momentum at the end.

Although the emphasis here is on spending, not income, the two sides of the equation usually are in near parallel; Table 4-5 closely mirrors the spending patterns within the framework of the crucial primary time period, January to June 1976, and provides data for other years directed at the 1976 nominations.

Carter. The Committee for Jimmy Carter benefited from a remarkably steady inflow of money, building up in an unbroken pattern from the earliest days in 1974. The orderly development of the three-year campaign permitted its finance chairman to put in place an effective system of cost control that was one of the strengths of the Carter campaign. During the March 25-May 23 period, when federal funds were withheld from all candidates, loans were required to finance the final, crucial primary effort in a number of key states.

For general election spending, the Carter campaign held one important advantage over its Republican opponent; with the nomination virtually assured some weeks before the Democratic National Convention, which preceded its Republican counterpart by one month, the Carter for President Committee had ample lead time to lay orderly plans for the fall campaign. A 17-page Carter financial synopsis of both the primary and general election campaigns within two weeks of the November election, noted elsewhere, pointed up the obvious: The Carter campaign made maximum use of both the private and the federal funds made available to it. Table 4-6 covers the Carter and other Democratic presidential campaigns.

Republican Primaries

The nearly identical primary spending totals of Ford and Reagan — $13.6 million versus $13.1 million (including independent expenditures)[3] — do not reflect the wide disparities in the financial aspects of the two campaigns.

Table 4-6
Democratic Spending in 1976 Presidential Campaigns

Carter			
Primary		$12,400,000	
General election			
by candidate committee	$21,800,000		
by national committee (DNC)	2,800,000		
		$24,600,000	
Independent expenditures and communication			
costs - primary and general election		1,200,000	
Total, Carter		$38,200,000	
Other Democratic candidates			
Primary			
by candidate committees	$33,700,000 [a]		
Independent expenditures and communication costs	200,000		
Total, other candidates		$33,900,000	
Total, Democratic primary			$46,300,000
Total, Democratic general election			24,600,000
Independent expenditures (Carter) not allocated between primary and general election			1,200,000
Democratic National Committee and affiliates [b]			9,700,000
Democratic National Convention committees			2,300,000
Democratic total			$84,100,000

[a] Includes $3.6 million spent (by Bentsen, Jackson, Wallace, et al.) in 1973 and 1974, and $600,000 in spending by a number of other Democratic candidates not included in FEC Disclosure Series No. 7.

[b] Direct expenditures only, not including the authorized party spending on behalf of Carter noted above.

SOURCE: Citizens' Research Foundation

There was, first, the contrast in timing. In midsummer 1975 it was the Reagan challenge that got off to an impressively fast start before the Re-elect the President Committee (RPC) was firmly launched. In early fall, the Ford campaign committee appeared to be in disarray with the dual resignations of Chairman Howard H. "Bo" Callaway and Finance Chairman David Packard. The new team, James Baker and Robert Moot, confronting an unanticipated shortage of seed money from major contributors, initiated a massive direct-mail appeal. Almost immediately their strategy began to pay off. By the end of 1975 the Ford committee had slightly outpaced the Reagan campaign in total contributions, $1.5 million versus $1.4 million, and the Ford campaign was

Table 4-7
Republican Spending in 1976 Presidential Campaigns

Ford		
Primaries		$13,600,000
General Election		
by candidate committee	$21,786,641	
by national committee (RNC)	1,400,000	
		$23,186,641
Independent expenditures and communication costs — primary and general election		200,000
Total Ford [a]		$37,000,000
Reagan		
Primaries		
by candidate committee	$12,600,000	
independent expenditures and communication costs [b]	500,000	
Total Reagan		$13,100,000

Total, Republication primaries	$26,700,000
Total, Republican general election [a]	23,200,000
Independent expenditures (Ford) not allocated between primary and general election	200,000
Republican National Committee and affiliates [c]	22,800,000
Republican National Convention committees	1,600,000
Republican total	$74,500,000

[a] Rounded figure.
[b] $300,000 by individuals and unauthorized delegates, $200,000 by political committees.
[c] Authorized party spending on behalf of Ford noted above not included here.

SOURCE: Citizens' Research Foundation

never seriously constrained for lack of funds. The New Hampshire defeat, however, sharply reversed the financial prospects of the Reagan campaign; the narrow victory in North Carolina saved him financially as well as politically, and money began to pour in. Republican presidential totals, shown in Table 4-7, include independent expenditures, communication costs, and RNC operations.

Reagan. The Reagan for President Committee, formally organized in June 1975, quietly amassed the seed money needed to launch a credible challenge to the president. The most noteworthy aspect of Reagan's campaign financing later was the high level of small contributions. At the conclusion of the primary contest he had submitted about

240,000 contributions for matching, more than twice the number for Ford. At the other end of the spectrum, $500-and-over contributions accounted for 17 percent of Reagan's total from individuals, as against 40 percent for Carter and 49 percent for Ford.

During the tight-money period, April to June, when matching funds were withheld from all candidates until the FEC was reconstituted, the Reagan campaign was in a state of crisis, but private money was sought vigorously when government funds were not available. As the last critical primaries were held, Reagan's contributions exceeded those of President Ford, not including $500,000 in independent expenditures by individuals and groups. This "unauthorized spending" helped to keep Reagan afloat in the later primaries.

Ford. For the general election, tight headquarters control and strict budgeting marked a departure from most previous presidential campaigns with the exception of Nixon's four years earlier. State units were allotted minimal discretionary funds; payroll, telephone, rent, and other operations were budgeted by headquarters. The D.C. office decided when a local headquarters could open, when it must close down. The RPC finance team relied on the Republican National Committee for implementing its cost control system, utilizing the computer facilities in place at the RNC. The coding format proved too sophisticated to be an effective campaign management tool, but the RNC operation smoothly handled the function it was essentially designed for: grinding out the massive campaign finance reports required to be filed with the FEC. This was in marked contrast to a number of other presidential campaigns, in this and previous years, which struggled with reporting revisions that outlived the campaign effort. Some $200,000 in independent expenditures on behalf of Ford could not be separated for primary or general election.

Matching Funds

The U.S. Treasury contributed $23,734,885 to the 1976 presidential primary campaigns of 15 candidates (13 Democrats and two Republicans), and $43,640,000 to the general election campaigns of Carter and Ford, for a total of $67,375,000.

Federal funding thus accounted for 35 percent primary, 95 percent general election.[4] Of the combined money spent in relation to the 1976 presidential election, including third-party and independent candidates, national party committee and convention committee spending, independent expenditures, communication costs and pre-1975 spending, federal funds accounted for more than 50 percent of the total.

Party Assistance

In August 1976 the Federal Election Commission sent to Congress regulations permitting state, county, congressional district, and city committees to raise $1,000 each and spend it in support of their presidential ticket for specified purposes. Since each of the two major parties could include as many as 9,000 such committees, including county and municipal party committees, the change was welcome. After raising $1,000 apiece, the committees were permitted to coordinate expenditure of the funds if they did not pool the money for a single media campaign. The commission stated that certain types of expenditures could be made and that the committee was required to name no minimum number of candidates in advertising so long as the presidential candidate was named. The regulation initially had been designed to help the committees pay for the traditional campaign leaflets, buttons, bumper stickers, and radio commercials linking the presidential candidate with lesser candidates on the same ticket. The new interpretation, expressed in response to a query from Carter's legal counsel, was greeted with enthusiasm by Republicans and Democrats alike. There is little evidence, however, that many party committees actually took advantage of the provision to spend much money on the presidential campaigns,[5] and no compilation of such spending was made by the FEC.

Independent and Third-Party Candidates

Besides the major-party nominees, eight other candidates appeared on the ballot in 10 or more states, one as an independent and seven as third-party nominees. Ideologically, they ranged from extreme right to extreme left: American, American Independent, Communist, Libertarian, Socialist Labor, Socialist Workers, and U.S. Labor parties; plus independent candidate Eugene J. McCarthy.

The American Party nominee, party chairman Thomas J. Anderson of Tennessee, running with Rufus Shackleford, a Florida millionaire tomato grower, expended $188,000 on the campaign.

The American Independent Party, a coalition put together by rightwing fund-raiser Richard Viguerie and publisher William A. Rusher, nominated ex-Gov. Lester Maddox and William E. Dyke, one-time mayor of Madison, Wisconsin. The AIP ticket managed to be on the ballot in almost half of the states, expending only $44,000.

The Communists, nominating perennial candidate Gus Hall and New York state party chairman Jarvis Tyner, had the distinction of being the best financed of the third-party campaigns; their expenditures totaled more than $500,000.

Table 4-8
Third-Party/Independent Candidates, 1976

Name of Candidate	Expenditures Adjusted
Thomas J. Anderson (American Party)	$ 187,815
Peter Camejo (Socialist Workers Party)	151,648
Gus Hall (Communist Party)	504,710
Lyndon H. LaRouche (U.S. Labor Party)	180,653
Jules Levin (Socialist Labor Party)	59,820
Roger MacBride (Libertarian Party)	387,429
Lester G. Maddox (American Independent Party)	44,488
Eugene J. McCarthy (independent candidate)	442,491
Totals	$1,959,054

SOURCE: Federal Election Commission, *FEC Disclosure Series No. 7: 1976 Presidential Campaign Receipts and Expenditures* (Washington, D.C., 1977), p. 28.

The Libertarian Party, under the leadership of Roger MacBride, a television producer, waged a vigorous campaign within the strictures of an under-$400,000 budget.

The Socialist Labor Party, led by Jules Levin, made a slight ripple with $60,000 in its campaign kitty.

The nominee of the Socialist Workers Party, Peter Camejo, was on the ballot in 28 states; he waged a militant 16-month campaign, protesting discriminatory federal funding laws and FEC reporting requirements. Total spending: $152,000.

The U.S. Labor Party, under labor activist Lyndon LaRouche, perhaps spent more money on lawsuits than on campaigning, the cost of the latter being approximately $180,000.

Finally, former Senator McCarthy, running as an independent and possibly hoping to make an impact on the election as he had eight years earlier, found himself unable to command much media attention on a budget of less than $500,000.

Altogether, the third-party/independent campaigns, as shown in Table 4-8, expended approximately two million dollars, only 1.3 percent of the total presidential spending.

Congressional Spending

The Federal Election Campaign Act of 1971 became effective on April 7, 1972. The 1972 congressional totals mainly reflected reported spending from that date forward until December 31, 1972, a period of less than nine months. By contrast, the 1972 presidential totals included most of the pre-April 7 data, picked up through voluntary and court-ordered disclosure. Few congressional candidates made voluntary disclosures. In contrast, the 1976 statistics cover the entire election period from January 1, 1975, to December 31, 1976.[6] This change in the data base provides comprehensive information for 1976. Tightened requirements and stricter enforcement by the FEC, as well as prosecution of earlier campaign finance violations, also broadened disclosure of previously unreported activity. Communication costs are a wholly new element in the 1976 totals. Independent expenditures are a new concept. Notwithstanding, spending at the congressional level made a disproportionate increase in 1976.

Table 4-9
1975-76 Senate Expenditures

By candidates		
Democratic — general election candidates [a]	$18,800,000	
Republican — general election candidates [a]	18,500,000	
Other: independent incumbent, primary losers and third-party candidates [b]	6,700,000	
Total, candidate spending		$44,000,000
By party senatorial committees [c]		
Democratic Senatorial Campaign Committee	370,000	
National Republican Senatorial Committee	1,460,000	
Total, senatorial committees		1,830,000
Independent expenditures and communication costs in behalf of senatorial candidates [d]		490,000
Total, senatorial spending		$46,320,000

[a] Total spending, including primary, for candidates in the general election; separated primary spending not available.
[b] Breaks down as follows: Senator Byrd, Ind.-Va.: $807,000; 100+ primary losers: +$5,000,000; 103 third-party candidates: +$1,000,000. Amounts not available by Democratic and Republican losers; hence major party subtotals are not given.
[c] Direct spending only, transfers to candidates not included.
[d] Independent expenditures by individuals only, those by political committees reportable by candidate. Communication costs by unions, corporations, and membership organizations, not their political action committees, which costs are included in the section on special interests.

SOURCE: Federal Election Commission, *FEC Disclosure Series No. 6: 1976 Senatorial Campaigns Receipts and Expenditures,* (Washington, D.C., 1977), p. 6, and FEC filings.

Table 4-10
1975-76 House Expenditures

By candidates		
Democratic — general election candidates [a]	$32,400,000	
Republican — general election candidates [a]	28,100,000	
Other: Primary losers and third party candidates [b]	11,000,000	
Total, candidate spending		$71,500,000
By party congressional committees [c]		
Democratic Congressional Campaign Committee	4,000	
Democratic Congressional Finance Committee	73,000	
Democratic National Congressional Committee	292,000	
Other party-identified congressional committees [d]	259,000	
	628,000	
National Republican Congressional Committee	6,756,000	
Total, congressional committees		7,384,000
Independent expenditures and communication costs in behalf of congressional candidates [e]		387,000
Total, House spending in excess of		$79,200,000

[a] Total spending, including primary, for candidates in the general election; separated primary spending not available.

[b] Breaks down as follows: primary losers: $10,000,000; third-party candidates: $1,000,000. Amounts not available by Republican and Democratic losers; hence, major party subtotals are not given.

[c] Direct spending only, transfers to candidates not included.

[d] DSG Campaign Fund, Committee for the Reelection of the Class of '74, Thomas P. O'Neill Congress Fund. See Table 4-11.

[e] Independent expenditures by individuals only, those by political committees reportable by candidate. Communication costs by unions, corporations, and membership organizatons, not their political action committees, which costs are included in the section on special interests.

SOURCE: Federal Election Commission, *FEC Disclosure Series No. 9: 1976 House of Representatives Campaigns Receipts and Expenditures* (Washington, D.C., September 1977), p. 11, and FEC filings.

Senate. Senatorial candidates — Republicans and Democrats, including primary losers, plus 103 third-party and independent candidates — spent, or had spent in their behalf, a total of more than $46 million on the 33 senatorial races in 1976. This includes, in addition to the spending by the campaign committees of the contenders, the direct expenditures of the Democratic and Republican Senatorial Campaign Committees (DSCC and RNSC). Direct expenditures consist of fixed costs for headquarters, salaries, and other costs not contributed to specific candidates.

Democratic and Republican spending, as shown in Table 4-9, was nearly equal; the significant disparity is that incumbents outspent their opponents by 50 percent.

Of the $6.7 million "other" figure, we estimated $5.5 million spent by more than 100 primary losers. While this amount is not definitive, it is borne out by historical projection and random-sample research. The 1972 data for the Senate[7] indicates expenditures of $4.7 million by primary losers in that year. Adjustment for transfers between candidate and committee would, to some undetermined extent, reduce the gross figure.

In 1976 there were hotly contested primaries in the media-expensive states of New York, California, Pennsylvania, and Ohio that, together with expensive contests in Arizona and certain southern states, accounted for most of the primary loser total.

There were 102 minor-party and independent candidates for Senate in 1976 reporting to the FEC. This number, three times the 1972 total, is partly attributable to court decisions that make it easier to get on state ballots. In 1972 the 33 such candidates reported spending more than $500,000. In 1976 the independent Byrd campaign in Virginia alone cost in excess of $800,000. Hence, the $1.2 million estimate for 1976 must be considered conservatively low.

House. The sharpest increase in reported political spending between 1972 and 1976 involved the House of Representatives; 1976 figures are shown in Table 4-10. The ratio of House/Senate spending widened. In 1972 that ratio was about three to two; in 1976 the House campaigns outspent the Senate by approximately seven to four. Also, the differential between presidential/congressional spending was cut nearly in half.

In 1972 business and professional, labor and ideological political action committees contributed substantially to the presidential campaigns; in 1976 the special interest money was directed mainly to Congress. Congressional candidates, especially incumbents, also received more money in contributions from individuals. By every test, political money in 1976 found a new focus: the Congress, and especially the House of Representatives.

Of the $11 million in Table 4-10, $10 million reflects expenditures by a roughly calculated 590 House primary losers in 1976; these amounts are based on a CRF study that included both random sampling and a spot check of targeted districts. Because the derived total exceeded informed estimates, a comparison was made with 1972 data,[8] which, including correction for frequent duplicate reporting by candidate and candidate committee, yielded an adjusted expenditure total of more than $9.2 million.

The additional $1 million estimate concerning third-party candidates is conservative. According to data compiled by the Clerk of the House of Representatives in 1972, the spending of independent and

Table 4-11
Direct Spending by Miscellaneous Partisan-identified Congressional Committees

Democratic		
Committee for the Reelection of the Class of '74	$111,000	
Democratic Congressional Dinner Committee	437,000	
DSG Campaign Fund	126,000	
Thomas P. O'Neill Congress Fund	22,000	
Democratic joint Senate/House		$437,000
Democratic total		$696,000
Republican		
Republican Congressional Boosters Club	$ 86,000	
Republican Senate-House Dinner '76	0	
RSG Campaign Fund	29,000	
National Federation of Republican Women [a]	338,000	
Republican joint Senate/House		$453,000
Republican total		$453,000

[a] NFRW spending is loosely related to presidential/congressional/state/local; however, the impact on each of the other categories would be marginal, even if it were possible to allocate.

SOURCE: Citizens' Research Foundation

third-party candidates in the elections that year totaled $1,002,227, but because of unusual circumstances in 1972 that figure, plus an inflation factor, cannot be projected to the 1976 elections. There were well over 200 third-party and independent candidates filing reports for 1976 with the FEC, but many of them reported only token spending. Since no definitive research was undertaken to establish a firm figure, we are deliberately understating third-party spending at $1 million.

Combined Totals. Table 4-11 combines Senate and House direct spending by Democrats and Republicans after contributions to candidates have been subtracted. The candidate contributions made by these committees are subsumed under Senate and House candidate spending, and hence are not added in here. Direct spending consists of fixed costs, for headquarters maintenance, salaries and other costs not contributed to specific candidates.

Table 4-12 summarizes 1976 Senate-and-House-related spending, including elements indicated in Tables 4-9 through 4-11; the components include candidate spending by party, other partisan-identified spending, independent expenditures and spending by third-party and

Table 4-12
Senate- and House-Related Spending in 1976: A Summary

Democratic		
Senate		
Candidate (general election) [a]	$18,800,000	
Democratic Senatorial Campaign Committee	370,000	
		$ 19,170,000
House		
Candidate (general election) [a]	$32,400,000	
Democratic Congressional Campaign Committee, and others	630,000	
		$ 33,030,000
Joint Senate/House		437,000
Total, Democratic congressional, general election candidates		$ 52,637,000
Republican		
Senate		
Candidate (general election) [a]	$18,500,000	
National Republican Senatorial Committee	1,460,000	
		$ 19,960,000
House		
Candidate (general election) [a]	$28,100,000	
National Republican Congressional Committee	6,760,000	
		$ 34,860,000
Joint Senate/House		453,000
Total, Republican congressional, general election candidates		$ 55,273,000
Independent expenditures/congressional		
Senate	$ 490,000	
House	387,000	
Total, independent expenditures		$ 877,000
Other candidates: independents, primary losers, and third-party candidates		
Senate	$ 6,700,000	
House	11,000,000	
Total, other candidates		$ 17,700,000
Special interest and ideological committees, adjusted direct spending		15,100,000
Total, congressional-related spending . . . . in excess of		$141,470,000

[a] Primary losers dealt with as a unit, without computation by party.

SOURCE: Citizens' Research Foundation

independent candidates, primary losers, and finally, direct spending by special interest and ideological committees.

Spending by Special Interests

In the so-called special interest category are included the political action committees of both corporations and labor unions and of a variety of membership organizations relating to business and professions, the health field, and dairy and agricultural interests. Ideological committees also are part of this broad nonparty group, which numbered 1,295 committees reporting to the FEC some time during 1975-76. To put that figure in perspective, on December 31, 1974, there were 608 such committees.[9]

Labor. Since all of the national unions have long had political action committees, the number of union groups reporting to the FEC has risen only marginally over the past two years, to a total of 224 as of December 31, 1976; 73 of these represent national unions, the remainder are state and local affiliates. The spending by labor, however, increased substantially, a continuation of the trend throughout the 1960s and 1970s. Labor money, more than three-fourths of it from AFL-CIO unions, was focused sharply on the Senate and the House.

Perhaps the most significant change in the labor picture is the upsurge of the education interests, represented by such major PACs as the American Federation of Teachers COPE, United Federation of Teachers COPE, Voice of Teachers for Education COPE, National Education Association PAC, the Association for Better Citizenship (ABC) and others.

The AFL-CIO COPE, UAW-VCAP, and NEA-PAC were the three top contributors to federal candidates, their combined total being almost $2.5 million. Altogether, labor PACs contributed to or made expenditures on behalf of federal candidates in the amount of $17.5 million, of which $8.6 million was given to candidates and $2 million or more was spent in communication costs by the parent unions, for an identifiable labor total of $10.8 million, not counting direct expenditures or contributions to party committees, some of which in turn was spent for or contributed to federal candidates.

Corporations. As of January 1, 1975, there were 89 corporate-related political committees; as of December 31, 1976, there were 433. Of this total, however, 60 committees reported no activity whatsoever, while another 193 had only token activity (under $10,000). Only 30 had receipts and/or expenditures in excess of $50,000. Thus, while corporate entities in every sector of business were beginning to establish political action committees, the 1975-76 newcomers to the field were, for the most part, mainly testing the waters. The long-established committees accounted for most of the political activity.

Contrary to the public perception of the funding of the corporate PACs, more than two-thirds of their receipts were in contributions in the $0-$100 range, less than 10 percent in the $500-and-over category. In sum, they had gross receipts of $6,782,322, expenditures of $5,803,415. As did the labor unions, they contributed mostly to candidates for the Senate and the House.

Associations. Unlike the corporate PACs, the political committees of the major trade associations were well in place long before the 1976 elections. More than 100 committees of business and professional associations were registered in 1972. Although business association PACs have greatly increased in number, many of the newcomers are small in membership. Disregarding the numerical breakdown, which can be misleading, and focusing instead on their actual impact, business association PACs are predominantly in the fields of manufacturing, finance, construction and real estate. Together with corporate PACs business-related committees gave more than $7 million to congressional candidates in the 1976 elections.

Membership associations were also active in 1976. In the health field, the American Medical Association's AMPAC was preeminent. Congressional giving by health-related committees, according to Common Cause, was nearly $2.4 million. According to the same source, the agriculture/dairy committees expended nearly $1.4 million in support of congressional candidates. Together with ideological organizations, these nonlabor and nonbusiness committees contributed more than $5 million.

All studies, under whatever sponsorship, support this aggregate. However, component subtotals, as computed by various organizations, can differ markedly because the definition of campaign expenditures varies. Common Cause assigns some committees to categories differing from the FEC and/or CRF. A few illustrations: The Democratic Study Group Campaign Fund is treated as ideological in the Common Cause publication, but as Democratic-partisan herein. The ACRE committees (co-op utilities) are not included in the business category but in membership groups. The Common Cause miscellaneous group includes the big-ticket gun lobby committees, herein treated as ideological. In CRF's study all nonparty committees are assigned to one of five categories: labor/business/health/agriculture and dairy/ideological. Thus it can be seen that many judgmental factors affect the statistical results.

Ideological Committees. Committees in the ideological spectrum range from extreme right-wing to liberal left and include issue-oriented

Table 4-13
Ideological Spending in 1975-76

	Total Spending Adjusted[a]	Contributions to Candidates and Committees
American Conservative Union (ACU)	$ 1,116,016	$ 175,060
Americans for Constitutional Action	245,723	36,994
Americans for Democratic Action/ADA Campaign Committee	41,157	*
Committee for Responsible Youth Politics	97,615	26,128
Committee for the Survival of a Free Congress	2,249,451	315,019
Conservative Victory Fund (ACU)	211,145	99,745
Council for a Livable World	412,510	114,661
Employee Rights Campaign Committee	73,356	57,100
Environmental Action's Dirty Dozen Campaign Fund	194,249	32,729 b
Gun Owners of America Campaign Committee	2,094,821	125,419
League of Conservation Voters	72,077	66,150
National Committee for an Effective Congress	1,298,986	311,950
National Conservative Political Action Committee	2,878,490	424,876
National Women's Political Caucus	86,418	*
NRA Political Victory Fund	58,024	36,595
Right to Keep and Bear Arms	95,411	18,810
United Congressional Appeal	42,688	18,025
Women For:	120,951	*
Women's Campaign Fund	201,612	52,870
Young America's Campaign Committee (also known as Fund for a Conservative Majority)	461,093	54,944
*committees,' plus nonnational committees	——	98,475
Totals	$12,051,793	$2,065,550 d

Total Direct Spending $9,986,243

a Adjusted for loan repayments, refunds, intra-ideological transfers, etc.
b Includes "in opposition to" as well as "on behalf of" federal candidates.
c These committees* made minimal contributions to federal candidates.
d Roughly 90 percent to congressional candidates. The only major presidential item is ACU's $174,000 in independent expenditures for Reagan. A broad mix of state and local candidates, party committees and unregistered committees received approximately $35,000.

SOURCE: Citizens' Research Foundation

groups such as the gun interests, environmentalists and women's committees. Twenty committees are herein treated as ideological, as seen in Table 4-13. An explosion of spending occurred in this category — the most dramatic increase of all nonparty spending. By comparison, no

Table 4-14
Special Interest Contributions to/Expenditures on Behalf of Federal Candidates, Including Primary Losers and Special Election Candidates

Agriculture and dairy [a]		$ 1,530,000
Business, corporate and associations		
Business PACs	$7,090,000	
Communications costs	30,000	
		$ 7,120,000
Professional		
Health [b]	$2,690,000	
Legal	240,000	
		$ 2,930,000
Labor		
Union PACs [c]	$8,950,000	
Communications costs	2,010,000	
		$10,960,000
Ideological		
PACs	$2,100,000	
Communications costs	100,000	
		$ 2,200,000
Total, special interest		$24,740,000

[a] Dairy groups are the major component.
[b] AMPAC (American Medical Political Action Committee) is the major component.
[c] Includes National Education Association.

SOURCE: Citizens' Research Foundation

ideological committee approached $1 million in expenditures in 1972; only the National Committee for an Effective Congress was in excess of $500,000 in that year. The total adjusted ideological spending in 1972 was $2,650,000; total contributions to candidates were less than $1 million. The 1972 figures, however, were for one year only, whereas Table 4-13 includes 1975-76. That fact notwithstanding, the $10 million adjusted direct spending during the 1976 election period shows an enormous increase.

Newcomers to the group account for much of the additional spending. Chief among these are two conservative units: the Committee for the Survival of a Free Congress and the National Conservative Political Action Committee; three gun-lobby-related: Gun Owners of America Political Action Committee, NRA Political Action Committee, and Right to Keep and Bear Arms; and women's committees: National Women's Political Caucus, Women For:, and Women's Campaign Fund.

Throughout the ideological groups, the relation of direct spending/transfers to candidates is disproportionately high when compared with other nonparty committees. This is due to high fund-raising costs, mostly mail campaigns, although some groups provide field staff and pay their expenses, rather than contribute money to candidates.

Since, as previously noted, the spending of the special interest committees is directed primarily toward congressional elections, the direct expenditures of this category are allocated to that quadrant of the four-part equation: presidential/congressional/state/local. Special interest involvement in the presidential race was minimal. A few committees reported contributions to state and, rarely, local candidates, but it is impracticable to break out a proportionate distribution of direct spending between congressional, state, and local.

Table 4-14 combines for all special interest groups estimates of both direct contributions to, and expenditures on behalf of, candidates for federal office. The table covers both primaries and general elections and includes primary losers and special election candidates.

Direct Spending by Special Interest and Ideological Committees. In compiling aggregates of political spending, only direct expenditures of the special interest committees are relevant, since the funds contributed or transferred to candidates and national committees already have been accounted for in those categories. The total raised and expended by all these special interests — approximately $40 million — has been treated earlier.

The direct spending of all special interest groups amounts to about $15 million, derived as follows:

Labor (locals not included)	$3,900,000
Agriculture and dairy/business/professional (includes all corporate, but local membership associations not included)	1,300,000
Ideological	9,900,000
Total direct spending	$15,100,000

It would be unrealistic to include reported direct expenditures of many local groups as federal election spending. The given totals represent minimums because small portions of local direct spending may relate to federal candidates.

Corporate and union PACs are not required to report their administrative costs, hence total spending relating to political activity is actually greater than stated.

Labor PAC spending includes at least some of the costs of a telecast by AFL-CIO President George Meany, delegate expense to the Democratic National Convention, and certain identified mass mailings to membership.

Ideological groups allocate a higher proportion of their funds to direct political spending, as against contributions to candidates. Also, their direct spending includes high fund-raising costs. In the case of one committee, for example (Environmental Action's Dirty Dozen Campaign Committee), fund raising represented more than 80 percent of direct, 70 percent of all, expenditures.

This total, $15.1 million, does not, however, reflect all costs. The FECA encouraged labor union and corporate PACs to establish separate segregated funds for political purposes and to pay their PACs' administrative and overhead costs, as well as fund-raising expenses, from treasury funds. In November 1975 the FEC[10] elaborated the legitimate costs that labor unions and corporations could defray in soliciting PAC contributions.

In 1976 there was no requirement for a labor union or corporation to disclose the amounts spent in administration and fund raising; both of these items were occasionally reported in prior years. Thus the data base keeps shifting, with the effects of revisions in laws and rulings affecting total spending, though we have made no estimate of such costs.

New Categories

FECA Amendments of 1974 established certain new categories of political spending, defined as follows:

—*Independent expenditures:* expenditures made in behalf of or opposing a clearly defined candidate, not made "in cooperation, consultation, or concert with" the candidate or any authorized committee. Total reported: $454,128.

—*Unauthorized delegates:* referring to national party conventions, those delegates receiving no financial or written support from the presidential candidate, their expenditures not be counted against the spending limits. Total reported: $415,968.

—*Communication costs:* partisan communications by corporations, labor and membership organizations to their respective stockholders, personnel or members, the costs of which are to be reported to the FEC when they exceed $2,000 per election. Total reported: $2,147,000.

—*Exempt spending:* Legal or accounting services, in-house, rendered to political committee or candidate to ensure FECA compliance, the value of such services, however, not exempt from reporting requirements. Total reported: see below (Table 4-15). Also for labor union and corporate PACs, administrative costs and fund-raising expenses, to be paid out of their treasury funds, the same totally exempt from reporting requirements. Total costs: see below (Table 4-15).

Table 4-15
Independent Expenditures, Unauthorized Delegates, Communication Costs, and Exempt Spending

Pulling together all the data that can be assembled on these new categories of political spending, the following picture emerges:

Presidential		
In behalf of Carter	$1,200,000	
In behalf of other Democratic presidential candidates	200,000	
In behalf of Ford	200,000	
In behalf of Reagan	500,000	
Total presidential		$2,100,000
Congressional		
In behalf of Senate candidates	$ 490,000+	
In behalf of House candidates	390,000+	
Total congressional		$ 900,000
Total, independent expenditures, unauthorized delegates, and communication costs		$ 3,000,000
Exempt spending (compliance costs, labor and corporate fund-raising and administrative costs)		$+5,000,000 (mostly reported and included in totals, some not reported)
Approximate total		$10,100,000

SOURCE: Citizens' Research Foundation

It is impossible to arrive at a meaningful estimate of two major components of exempt spending. First, although candidates and committees were required to report their exempt spending for legal and accounting services, the reporting methodology varied widely, making an informed estimate virtually impossible; only FEC audits could establish even broad parameters. Whatever the discrete figure, it has been reported and included in appropriate totals. Second, labor and corporate PAC exempt spending is a totally unknown factor, since it is exempt even from reporting requirements. On the basis of what little is known, and taking into consideration historical patterns, total exempt spending in these two categories surely exceeded $10 million.

State and Local Spending

In 1976 state and local candidates were the unintended beneficiaries of government funding of the presidential campaigns and of changing political attitudes. The FECA-mandated concentration of authority in the presidential "principal campaign committee" reduced local involvement in the presidential race, as did the lack of political passion for many of the presidential candidates. There was no galvanizing issue to produce grass-roots activism.

The disenchantment with Washington was counterbalanced to some extent by a mounting concern about local school, tax, and state ballot issues. Although federal spending has been a fairly constant proportion of GNP over the past four years, state and local government spending has ballooned. Consequently, some political money was redirected by political activists to the intrastate arena, for state and local candidates. This sharply increased spending at the nonnational level in 1976 reflected shifting concerns. Special interest spending accounted for some of the congressional increment; private contributions and local interests accounted for the upsurge in state and local spending.

Party Committees

A vast number of party committees, operating at the state and local level, filed reports with the FEC. As the new regulations allow, most state central committees filed only federal-election-segregated account reports. In 1972 62 state central committees, plus other district and county committees, reported gross expenditures of approximately $20 million.

Since there is no comparable data base, no compilation has been made for the 1976 elections, but surely more state and local party committees raised and spent more money in 1976.

The involvement of district, county, and municipal committees in federal campaigns is difficult to assess and impossible to separate between presidential/senatorial/congressional. Hence there is no rationale by which to establish presidential and congressional components, but it should be noted that some small but unknown party factor has not been included in this study of federal campaign costs.

Democratic and Republican Political Committee Receipts and Expenditures

In April 1977 the Federal Election Commission released its index of *National Party Political Committee Receipts and Expenditures* for the 1976 campaign. The index is based on reports filed with the commission for the period of January 1, 1975, through December 31, 1976, and received by March 20, 1977. Although 1,088 party-related political committees filed reports with the FEC, only 35 committees — 18 Democratic and 17 Republican — are analyzed in the index. These 35 committees, however, received and spent a significant portion of the party-related money in the 1976 presidential and congressional campaigns.[11]

The index divides the committees into five categories according to their function within the party and the type of candidates they generally support:[12]

—*National party committee:* six committees generally considered to be the standing political committees of each major party.

—*National party committee affiliates:* subgroup of 11 party political committees representing particular constituencies, or formed for special events.

—*National party convention committees:* four committees established for the sole purpose of administering the national party conventions. These committees received most of their money from public funds, as noted elsewhere.

—*National party congressional committees:* nine political committees that assisted in the election of party candidates for the Senate and the House of Representatives.

—*Party-identified committees:* five political committees, not a part of the party organization, but serving a partisan educational function in addition to assisting in the election of federal candidates.

The index shows, by party and by type of committee, the figures for total receipts and expenditures as reported (gross) and as adjusted (net). The report distinguishes between various types and amounts of receipts and expenditures and gives a dollar breakdown of contributions and the number of contributions where available. Also provided are figures for cash on hand, outstanding debts and final balances as of December 31, 1976.

Those compiling the report stress the importance of examining both the gross and the net figures. The gross figures represent the total amounts reported by each of the committees. The net figures were derived by subtracting from these totals any repaid loans, refunded contributions, rebated expenditures, and redeemed Treasury notes and certificates of deposit. Also subtracted were transfers received from related committees and earmarked contributions that would be reported as a receipt by another committee or candidate.[13] Large amounts of money passed from party committee to party committee in the form of loans, transfers, and in-kind contributions, and the difference between the reported and adjusted totals is substantial. The purpose of adjusting the figures to derive net amounts is to avoid double-counting.

Table 4-16
Summary of National Party Political Committees' Receipts and Expenditures, 1976 Campaign

Democratic

	Receipts as Reported	Receipts Adjusted	Expenditures as Reported	Expenditures Adjusted
National party committees	$25,237,311	$14,625,707	$25,176,374	$14,317,786
National party committee affiliates	552,889	209,013	552,908	333,580
National party convention committees	3,598,803	2,457,171	2,402,541	2,260,909
National party congressional committees	3,278,245	1,949,571	3,319,729	1,982,716
Party-identified committees	568,812	498,389	538,963	468,186
Total	$32,236,060	$19,739,851	$31,990,515	$19,363,177

Republican

	Receipts as Reported	Receipts Adjusted	Expenditures as Reported	Expenditures Adjusted
National party committees	$59,177,902	$29,118,930	$57,924,073	$26,679,143
National party committee affiliates	448,217	112,950	465,945	156,932
National party convention committees	2,381,637	2,067,270	1,933,122	1,619,222
National party congressional committees	15,230,333	13,981,868	12,364,404	11,253,824
Party-identified committees	431,455	424,868	373,531	367,066
Total	$77,669,544	$45,705,886	$73,061,075	$40,076,187

SOURCE: Federal Election Commission, *FEC Disclosure Series No. 4: National Party Political Committee Receipts and Expenditures — Democratic and Republican 1976 Campaign* (Washington, D.C., 1977), pp. 5, 6.

From the adjusted totals, net income and the actual costs involved in the campaign activities of the various party committees can be identified. For the period covered, the net figures show that together the Republican committees received $45,705,886 and spent $40,076,187, more than twice the $19,739,851 received and $19,363,177 spent by the Democratic committees. The comparable gross figures are about $32 million higher for the Republicans and about $13 million higher for the Democrats (Table 4-16).

When the figures are broken down by type of committee some similarities between the two parties are evident. The national party committees, generally representing the presidential wing of the parties, were responsible for the largest proportion of each party's receipts and expenditures. On the Democratic side, the national party committees accounted for 74.1 percent of net receipts and 73.9 percent of net expenditures. Comparable percentages for the Republican national party committees were 63.8 percent and 66.6 percent, respectively. Similarly, the national committee affiliates of both parties were responsible for the smallest proportion of total receipts and expenditures. The Democratic national party committee affiliates accounted for only 1.1 percent of receipts and 1.7 percent of expenditures. The comparable figures for the Republican affiliates were only .2 percent and .4 percent, respectively.

There are noteworthy differences between the two parties with respect to amounts received and spent by the different types of committees. The Democratic national party committees received and spent a higher proportion of their party's total adjusted receipts and expenditures than did their Republican counterparts. In contrast, in the congressional wings of the parties, the Democratic national congressional committees spent and received an average of 10 percent of the adjusted total receipts and expenditures while the Republican congressional committees raised and spent nearly 30 percent of their party's adjusted funds. In dollar amounts, the Democratic congressional committees raised and spent less than $2 million, while their Republican counterparts raised nearly $14 million and spent in excess of $11 million.[14]

The Republican committees raised more money among major contributors than did the Democrats. While 262 Republican donors gave more than $3 million in contributions of $10,000 or more, there were only 34 Democratic donors who were as generous and their total came to only $507,700. The Republicans also did better than the Democrats among individuals giving less than $100. Republican committees received $26.6 million, 58 percent of their total, from these small contributors. The Democratic committees received only $7.3 million in comparable gifts, or 37 percent of their total. In fact for each contribution level — less than $100; $100-$499; $500-$9,999; and $10,000 and above — the Republicans received more than did the Democrats. Still, the bulk of the funds for both parties came in contributions of less than $100.

The Democratic national committees did better than the Republicans in contributions from other political committees. From state and local party committees, for example, the Democratic national committees received $136,333 while the Republican national committees received $80,789. Other nonparty-related committees contributed $1,890,403 to the Democratic national committees and only $818,748 to the Republicans. Taken together, however, these figures represent a comparatively small proportion of each party's total net receipts.[15]

Expenditures by the national committees went primarily to cover internal operating costs. Together, the Democratic committees used

$15,929,623 or 81 percent of their receipts for operating expenses. The Republican committees spent $33,798,272 or 74 percent of their receipts for such expenses. A much smaller proportion of the receipts for both parties went to federal candidates; either to the candidates themselves or directly to vendors on behalf of the candidates. The Democratic committees contributed $3,433,554 or 17 percent of their receipts to federal candidates. Comparable contributions by the Republican committees amounted to $6,287,098 and accounted for 14 percent of that party's receipts.

Here again, there are some noteworthy variations when the figures are broken down by types of committees. Whereas the national party committees of both parties contributed only 16 percent of their funds to federal candidates, the Democratic and Republican congressional committees contributed 41 percent and 21 percent respectively to such sources. The Democratic Party-identified committees also spent a substantial portion (43 percent) of their receipts on the election of federal candidates. The bulk of these funds ($111,750) came from the Thomas P. O'Neill Congress Fund. Contributions to federal candidates from the other committees were either nonexistent or negligible.

As of December 31, 1976, the cash-on-hand balance of the national Democratic committees was $439,520, as compared with $5,499,720 for the national Republican Party committees. When these figures are adjusted for outstanding debts and credits the Democratic committees were left with a deficit of $2,888,193 and the Republican committees with a surplus of $5,422,105. All of the Republican committees enjoyed relatively large balances; the largest reported was by the Republican congressional committees which reported a net surplus of $3,378,459. The chief contributors to the overall Democratic deficit were the national party committees, which reported a deficit balance of $3,209,716.[16]

1976 Aftermath

In September 1978 the FEC released an updated report on the 1977-78 finance activity of political committees. The report covers the period from January 1, 1977, through the end of June 1978. During this period the national Democratic and Republican committees together reported raising $63.9 million and spending $55.9 million. Of this amount $1.6 million was contributed to federal candidates. When adjusted for outstanding debts and credits, the national party committees ended up with cash on hand of $9.2 million.[17]

The national Republican committees continued their financial advantage during this period. Adjusted receipts and expenditures for the

Republican committees were $49.6 million and $42.8 million respectively. Comparable figures for the national Democratic committees were $14.4 million and $13.8 million. The national Republican committees contributed $1.6 million to federal candidates while the national Democratic committees spent only $61,449 for this purpose. Of the total contributions to federal candidates by the national Republican committees, $1.3 million or 80 percent went to House candidates with the remaining $304,168 going to Senate candidates. All of the money contributed by the national Democratic committees went to House candidates. The national Republican committees also retained their advantage in surplus funds. When adjusted for outstanding debts and credits, the cash-on-hand figure for the national Republican committees was $9.3 million as compared with a $126,971 deficit for their Democratic counterparts.[18]

1976 Senatorial Campaigns Receipts and Expenditures

In May 1977 the Federal Election Commission released the sixth index in its *Disclosure Series*. The report describes the financial activity of the 64 candidates (33 Democrats, 30 Republicans, and one independent) for the Senate who appeared on the 1976 general election ballot.[19]

The data in the index were derived from reports filed by the individual candidates, their principal campaign committees, and all other authorized committees. The report covers all campaign finance activity during the period January 1, 1975, through December 31, 1976. It thus combines both the primary and general election stages of the campaigns, and does not separate out either. Receipts and expenditures in the report were adjusted to exclude such items as refunds, loan repayments, and transfers between a candidate and the candidate's authorized committees. More detailed information on individual campaigns can be found in the actual disclosure reports filed with the agency.

The total adjusted receipts for the 1976 senatorial campaigns were $39,129,660 while total adjusted expenditures came to $38,104,745. Individuals, other than the candidates themselves, contributed just less than $27 million, accounting for almost 69 percent of total receipts. Of this amount, in excess of $11 million represented individual contributions of $100 or less. Individual contributions falling between $101 and $499 came to $5.2 million and contributions of $500 and above came to $10.6 million. Party-related political committees contributed about $1.4 million while nonparty or special interest committees contributed almost $6 million. The candidates contributed $891,942 to their own campaigns and made or endorsed loans to their campaigns of $3,660,260 as of December 31, 1976 (Table 4-17).

Table 4-17
Summary of Adjusted Receipts and Expenditures, 1976 Senate Campaigns

Cash on hand 1/1/75		$349,436
Total receipts adjusted		$39,129,660
Contributions $0-$100		$11,088,150
Contributions $101-$499		$5,228,970
Contributions $500 and over		$10,592,867
(Number of contributions- 14,175)		
Candidate contributions		$891,942
Party committees		$1,399,329
Nonparty committees		$5,798,251
Candidates loans, aggregate		$4,275,952
($3,660,260 outstanding as of 12/31/76)		
Other loans, aggregate		$286,713
($100,772 outstanding as of 12/31/76)		
Other income		$364,119
Total expenditures adjusted		$38,104,745
Cash on hand 12/31/76		$1,274,814
Surplus/deficit	For those with surpluses, the leftover funds total	$801,786
	For those with deficits, the debts total	$4,441,309

SOURCE: Federal Election Commission, *FEC Disclosure Series No. 6: 1976 Senatorial Campaigns Receipts and Expenditures* (Washington, D.C., 1977).

Democratic and Republican candidates received approximately equal portions of the total receipts. Together, the Democrats received $19,479,884 or 50 percent of the receipts. The Republicans received $18,840,430 or 48 percent. Sen. Harry F. Byrd, Jr., of Virginia, the lone independent, received $807,346 or approximately 2 percent of the total receipts. On a per-candidate basis, the average Democrat received $590,300 while the average Republican received $628,014.

There were, of course, large variations in amounts received and spent in individual campaigns. At the one extreme, incumbent Democrat William Proxmire of Wisconsin found it necessary to raise only $25 and to spend less than $700 to protect his Senate seat from Republican challenger Stanley Work, who raised and spent more than $60,000. The lowest Republican spender was George Brown from Washington, who raised and spent $10,841. Brown lost to incumbent Democrat Henry Jackson. By far the biggest spender was Republican John Heinz, who spent more than $3 million to win an open seat contest in Pennsylvania. The Democrat spending the most was incumbent John Tunney of

California, who raised and spent almost $2 million only to lose to Republican challenger S. I. Hayakawa.[20]

Republicans received more funds from small individual contributors, while Democrats did better among the larger donors. Republican candidates contributed more than twice as much to their own campaigns as did their Democratic counterparts. Republicans also made more than twice as much in personal loans to their own campaigns; a comparison that is distorted, however, by the large loans Republican John Heinz made to his own campaign, amounting to $2,465,500. Republicans received more ($930,034) than did the Democrats ($468,795) from party-related political committees. The Democrats, however, did much better from nonparty-related political committees. The Democrats were given a total of $3,727,006 while the Republicans received only $1,977,977 from such sources.[21]

Forty-two percent of all funds ($16,254,674) went to incumbent candidates. Challengers were able to raise only $10,571,058 or 27 percent of the total receipts. More than $12 million — 31 percent of total receipts — went to candidates competing for contests in which there was no incumbent. On a per-candidate basis, the average incumbent raised $677,278, the average challenger raised $440,461 and the average open seat contestant raised $768,995.

Incumbents did better than challengers at each level — $0-$100, $101-$499, and $500 and above — of individual contributions. Moreover, incumbents contributed only $19,771 of their own money (0.001 percent) to their personal campaigns, while challengers used nearly 34 times that amount ($666,207) to help finance their electoral efforts. Challengers also had outstanding slightly more in personal loans to their own campaigns than did incumbents.

Challengers received more ($607,562) from political party committees than did incumbents ($349,762). Incumbents, however, did much better from nonparty political committees. Incumbents received $2,875,988 from nonparty or special interest political committees while challengers received less than half that amount from such sources.[22]

Fifty-four percent of all funds ($21,052,900) went to winning candidates. Losing candidates received $18,076,760. On a per-candidate basis, the average winning candidate raised $637,967 and the average losing candidate raised $583,121. Losers received slightly more funds from small individual contributors while winners did better among the larger individual donors. Losers contributed $731,695 to their own campaigns while winners contributed only $160,244. Winners, however, had outstanding almost $3 million in loans to their own campaigns while the comparable figure for losers was less than $1 million — again a comparison distorted by the large loans that John Heinz made to his own campaign. Winning and losing candidates received approximately equal amounts from party-related political committees but winners did significantly better than losers from nonparty-related political committees, receiving \$3,137,479 or 54 percent of the funds from such sources.[23]

In summary, large individual contributions tended to favor Democrats and winners, while smaller donations favored Republicans and losers. All levels of individual contributions favored incumbents over challengers, largely because they are perceived as winners. Republicans and challengers contributed and lent more to their own campaigns than did Democrats and incumbents. Losing candidates contributed more but winning candidates lent more to their own campaigns. Contributions from party-related committees favored Republicans and challengers but were almost equally divided between losers and winners. Contributions from nonparty-related or special interest committees favored Democrats over Republicans, incumbents over challengers and winners over losers.

1978 Elections

On November 3, 1978, the FEC released a report on the finance activity of congressional candidates for the 1978 elections. The report covers the period from January 1, 1977, through October 10, 1978, and, unlike the 1976 *Disclosure Series,* includes summary data on all certified candidates participating in 1977 or 1978 primary, runoff, convention/census, or general elections.[24]

During this period 257 Senate candidates raised \$63.6 million and spent \$61.8 million. Individual contributions of \$100 or more accounted for \$16 million or 25 percent of total receipts. Contributions to and expenditures on behalf of candidates from party- and nonparty-related political committees amounted to \$1.4 million and \$4.6 million respectively. The candidates contributed \$1.7 million and loaned \$5 million to their own campaigns.

Democratic candidates for the Senate (131), Republicans (79), and independent and minority-party candidates (47) raised \$33.6, \$29.7, and \$.3 million respectively. Individual contributions of \$100 or more accounted for 30 percent of Democratic receipts and 20 percent of Republican receipts. As in the 1976 election cycle, Republicans did better (\$1 million) than Democrats (\$.4 million) from party-related committees. Similarly, Democrats did slightly better (\$2.4 million) than Republicans (\$2.2 million) from nonparty-related or special interest committees. Democrats contributed \$1.6 million and lent \$3.9 million to their own campaigns while the comparable figures for Republicans were only \$.1 million and \$1.1 million respectively.

1976 House Campaigns Receipts and Expenditures

In September 1977 the Federal Election Commission released the ninth index in its *Disclosure Series*. The report describes the campaign finance activity of 860 general election candidates for the House of Representatives, including 433 Democrats, 390 Republicans, and 37 independent and minor-party candidates. Not included in the report were candidates who received less than 5 percent of the vote in the general election.[25]

The data in the index were derived from reports filed by the individual candidates, their principal campaign committees, and all other authorized committees. The report covers all campaign finance activity during the period January 1, 1975, through December 31, 1976. It thus includes all primary, runoff, and special elections in this period as well as the general election. Receipts and expenditures in the report were adjusted to exclude such items as refunds, loan repayments, and transfers between a candidate and the candidate's authorized committees. More detailed information on individual campaigns can be found in the actual disclosure reports filed with the agency.

The total receipts adjusted for the 1976 House campaigns were $65,740,937 while total expenditures adjusted came to $60,907,960. Individuals, other than the candidates themselves, contributed just under $38.5 million, accounting for almost 59 percent of total receipts. Of this amount, $23.7 million represented individual contributions of $100 or less. Individual contributions falling between $101 and $499 and between $500 and $1,000 came to $7.5 million and $7.3 million, respectively. Party-related political committees contributed about $5.1 million while nonparty or special interest committees contributed just over $14.7 million. The candidates donated nearly $2.4 million to their own campaigns and had personal loans outstanding of just over $4 million as of December 31, 1976 (Table 4-18).

Together, the Democratic candidates raised $35,058,032 or 53.3 percent of the total receipts, while the Republicans raised $30,201,691 or 46 percent. The remaining 0.7 percent — less than $500,000 — went to minor-party and independent candidates. Democrats also did better than Republicans on a per-candidate basis. The average amount received by Democratic candidates was $80,965 compared with $77,440 for Republicans. The average amount received by independent and minor-party candidates was only $13,006.

These averages, however, conceal sizable differences across individual campaigns. Eighteen candidates, for example, (one Democrat, 11 Republicans, four independents, one People's Party, and one Conservative) raised and spent no money; all of these individuals lost in the

Table 4-18
Summary of Adjusted Receipts and Expenditures, 1976 House Campaigns

Cash on hand 1/1/75	$2,755,317
Total receipts adjusted	$65,740,937
Contributions $0-$100	$23,680,016
Contributions $101-$499	$7,537,932
Contributions $500-$1,000	$7,270,785
(Number of contributions — 10,806)	
Candidate contributions	$2,397,702
Party contributions	$5,125,774
Nonparty contributions	$14,745,341
Candidate loans, aggregate	$5,270,222
($4,054,661 outstanding as of 12/31/76)	
Other loans, aggregate	$1,137,133
Other receipts*	$312,605
Total expenditures adjusted	$60,907,960
Cash on hand 12/31/76	$6,508,466
Total for those with surpluses	$6,209,813
Total for those with deficits	$5,679,914

* "Other receipts" include interest and other miscellaneous receipts.

SOURCE: Federal Election Commission, *FEC Disclosure Series No. 9: 1976 House of Representatives Campaigns Receipts and Expenditures* (Washington, D.C., 1977), p. 4.

general election. At the other extreme, a number of candidates raised and spent upwards of $500,000. The biggest spender was Democrat Gary Familian, who raised $637,800 and spent $637,080 only to lose in a very hotly contested open seat race in California. The largest Republican spender was incumbent Ron Paul of Texas, who raised and spent just over $500,000 but also lost to a Democratic challenger who raised and spent about half that amount.[26]

Republicans received slightly more funds from small contributors, while Democrats did somewhat better among the larger donors. Democratic candidates contributed more than twice as much to their own campaigns as did their Republican counterparts. They also had more than twice the amount of loans outstanding. Republicans received more ($3,658,310) than did the Democrats ($1,465,629) from party-related political committees. The Democrats, however, did much better from nonparty-related political committees. The Democrats were given a total of $9,406,732 or 26.8 percent of their total receipts, while the Republicans received only $5,312,969 or 17.6 percent of their receipts from such sources.[27]

Incumbents and Challengers

Just over 53 percent of all funds ($35,071,334) went to incumbent candidates. Challengers were able to raise only $18,352,022 or 27.9 percent of total receipts. Almost 19 percent of total receipts — more than $12 million — went to candidates competing for contests in which there was no incumbent. On a per-candidate basis, the average incumbent raised $91,094, the average challenger raised $49,600 and the average open seat contestant raised $117,310.

Incumbents did better than challengers at each level — $0-$100, $101-$499, and $500-$1,000 — of individual contributions. Moreover, incumbents contributed only $90,321 of their own money (0.3 percent of their receipts) to their personal campaigns, while challengers used nearly 20 times that amount ($1,700,519) to finance their electoral efforts. Correspondingly, challengers had outstanding more than six times as much in personal loans as did incumbents.

Incumbents and challengers received nearly the same amount of money — just in excess of $2 million — from political party committees. Incumbents, however, did much better from nonparty or special interest political committees, while challengers received only $2,808,106 from such sources.[28]

Almost two-thirds of all funds ($42,490,774) went to winning House candidates. Losers were able to raise only $23,250,163. Winners did better than losers at each level of individual contributions. Losing candidates contributed more than $2 million to their own campaigns and had personal loans outstanding of $2,116,784, while winning candidates spent only $369,844 of their own money and had loans outstanding of $1,937,877. Losing candidates did slightly better than winners from party-related political committees but winners raised almost three times as much from nonparty committees. Winners received almost $11 million while losers received only $3,810,598 from such sources.[29]

Summary

In summary, large individual contributions tended to favor the Democrats, while the smaller donations favored the Republicans. All levels of individual contributions favored incumbents over challengers and winners over losers. Democrats, challengers, and losers spent more of their own money and had more in outstanding loans. Contributions from party-related committees tended to favor Republicans and losers but were almost equally distributed between incumbents and challengers. Nonparty-related committees gave significantly more to Democrats, incumbents, and winners. These special interest committees managed to spend almost three-quarters of their funds on successful candidates — a ratio that can be explained in part by the fact that two-thirds of their contributions went to incumbents.

Recent figures for the 1977-78 election cycle indicate that through October 10, 1978, 1,662 House candidates raised $85.9 million and spent $76.4 million.[30] Individual contributions of $100 or more accounted for $16.9 million or 20 percent of total receipts. Contributions to and expenditures on behalf of candidates from party and nonparty political committees amounted to $3.4 million and $13.3 million respectively. The candidates contributed $3 million and lent $7.2 million to their own campaigns.

Democrats (866), Republicans (614), and independent and minority-party candidates (182) raised $49.5 million, $35.8 million, and $.6 million respectively. Individual contributions of $100 or more accounted for 22 percent of Democratic receipts and 17 percent of Republican receipts. Republicans did better ($2.6 million) than Democrats ($.8 million) from party-related committees but Democrats did better ($8.6 million) than Republicans ($4.7 million) from nonparty-related committees. Democrats contributed ($1.9 million) and lent ($4.8 million) more than twice as much to their own campaigns than did Republicans.

Footnotes

1. Does not include the direct spending by hundreds of non-Washington-based local PACs (union, business, and other), since these committees have a presumption of focus on state and local candidates and issues; however, their contributions to federal candidates would be reflected in reported federal candidate spending.

2. For an historical account of presidential campaign financing, see Herbert E. Alexander, "Financing Presidential Campaigns," in Arthur M. Schlesinger, Jr., ed., *History of American Presidential Elections, 1789-1968* (New York: Chelsea House Publishing in association with McGraw Hill, 1971), Vol. IV, pp. 3869-97.

3. An adjusted $12.6 million reported by the Reagan committee, plus $500,000 in independent expenditures by individuals and political committees.

4. Refers only to money spent by principal campaign committees.

5. Warren Weaver, Jr., "Ruling Allows an Increase in Spending by Candidates," *The New York Times,* September 2, 1976.

6. Expenditures relating to debts from previous campaigns are not included in the 1976 spending total.

7. *The Annual Statistical Report of Receipts and Expenditures Made in Connection with Elections for the U.S. Senate in 1972,* prepared under the direction of Francis R. Valeo, Secretary of the Senate, Supervisory Officer for Senate Elections (Washington, D.C.: U.S. Government Printing Office, October 1974).

8. *The Annual Statistical Report of Contributions and Expenditures Made During the 1972 Election Campaigns for the U.S. House of Representatives,* parts I and II, by W. Pat Jennings, as Clerk of the House of Representatives and Supervisory Officer (Washington, D.C.: U.S. Government Printing Office, April/June 1974).

9. Compiled by the National Information Center on Political Finance, March 31, 1975.

10. Federal Election Commission Advisory Opinion, AO75-23.

11. Federal Election Commission, *FEC Disclosure Series No. 4: National Party Political Committee Receipts and Expenditures: Democratic and Republican — 1976 Campaign,* (Washington, D.C., 1977), pp. 1, 2.

12. Ibid., p. 1.

13. Ibid., p. 2.

14. Ibid., pp. 5,6.

15. Ibid., pp. 11-30.

16. Ibid., pp. 31-40.

17. Federal Election Election Commission, *FEC Reports on Financial Activity 1977-1978 Interim Report No. 2, Party and Non-Party Political Committee, Volume I,* (Washington, D.C., September 1978), pp. 29-73.

18. Ibid.

19. Federal Election Commission, *FEC Disclosure Series No. 6: 1976 Senatorial Campaigns Receipts and Expenditures* (Washington, D.C., 1977), p. 1.

20. Ibid., pp. 9-16.

21. Ibid., p. 5.

22. Ibid., pp. 5, 9-16.

23. Ibid.

24. Federal Election Commission, "FEC Releases Summaries of 1977-78 U.S. Senate and House Campaigns' Financial Activity" Press Release, November 3, 1978.

25. Federal Election Commission, *FEC Disclosure Series No. 9: 1976 House of Representatives Campaigns Receipts and Expenditures* (Washington, D.C., 1977), p. 1.

26. Ibid., pp. 5, 23-99.

27. Ibid., p. 6.

28. Ibid., pp. 7, 8.

29. Ibid., p. 9.

30. Federal Election Commission, "FEC Releases Summaries of 1977-78 U.S. Senate and House Campaigns' Financial Activity" Press Release, November 3, 1978. This is the same report mentioned at the end of the preceding section on the Senate. Unlike the 1976 *Disclosure Series,* which includes data only on general election candidates, this report summarizes the financial activity of all certified candidates participating in 1977 or 1978 primary, runoff, convention/caucus, or general elections.

5 The Prenomination Campaigns

The 1974 Amendments to the Federal Election Campaign Act (FECA) established new rules for presidential prenomination campaigns and caused the 1976 experience to depart significantly from the past. The advent of public financing brought to the competition new faces as well as novel fund-raising methods, and bookkeeping practices hitherto unknown in politics. A rise in the number of state primaries and changes in election rules continued a process, begun after 1968, through which the national party organizations found their control over the choice of their nominees significantly reduced. Thus, the reforms that took effect in 1976, both financial and electoral, set the stage for the most open and competitive nominating procedure in U.S. history.

As they governed the prenomination period, the 1974 Amendments stipulated a $10.9 million spending limit for each candidate for presidential nomination and permitted a 20 percent overage for fund-raising expenses, making the total ceiling $13.1 million. To qualify for the matching funds available under the 1974 Amendments, a candidate had to demonstrate to the satisfaction of the Federal Election Commission that he had raised $5,000 in private contributions of $250 or less in each of 20 states. For a qualified candidate, the federal government matched each contribution up to $250, although total federal subsidies could not exceed half of the $10.9 million limit. In accordance with its mandate, the FEC required detailed documentation to determine candidates' eligibility for public monies, and the law specified that the commission could not certify matching funds until January 1, 1976. As a result, candidates received matching funds later and in smaller amounts than they would have preferred.

The major financial problem facing candidates in the primaries, however, was the cutoff of matching funds brought on by the *Buckley* decision. Candidates already had been forced to proceed with their campaigns following regulations that were being tested in the courts; the Supreme Court decision upheld most of the law but dismantled the FEC, thereby leaving it unable to supply the candidates with matching funds. This hurt many of the prenomination campaigns and the candidates wasted no time in filing suit to renew the flow of matching funds. As noted earlier, the course of the suit followed a series of complicated legal maneuvers, none of which resulted in a resumption of payments.

Although the more than $2 million in funds pending FEC certification provided impetus for the suit, the attorneys believed that the disruption in payments abridged the First Amendment rights of candidates, voters, and taxpayers. The lawyers sought to take advantage of the Court's earlier recognition in *Buckley* of the link between adequate funds and effective political speech. On May 21, when the FEC finally had been reconstituted and the six commissioners sworn in, the renewed FEC immediately certified $3.2 million due for various candidates and $1 million to the major-party national conventions.

By the time matching funds were released, irreparable damage had occurred to some candidates involved in the suit. For instance, Senator Church detailed in court substantial cutbacks in his orders of campaign materials, due to the lack of funds. Fred Harris revealed that he had been forced to halt all campaign activity toward the April 27 Pennsylvania primary. The suspension of matching funds forced some candidates to rely wholly on private funds and loans during crucial primaries, and caused others to miss opportunities which they might otherwise have utilized.

While many candidates blamed their financial problems on the lack of public funds, some had more basic problems. According to Michael J. Malbin,[1] the campaign activities of Jackson, Udall, and Wallace were significantly limited by a shortage of contributions. Democrats, excepting Carter, who had spent freely early in 1976 in anticipation of the release of funds, had difficulties in raising funds by April when Carter seemed a likely winner. On the other hand, Republican candidates were generally well endowed; both Reagan and Ford were finding that they needed to watch the spending limits by the time public funds were released.

As with any reform, public financing brought about both intended and unintended political results. Among the intended results was a new emphasis on money management and accountability on the part of each campaign; gone were the days of secret contributions and undue influence disguised by purposely sloppy bookkeeping. Moreover, federal subsidization greatly improved access to the presidential contest by supplementing the treasuries of candidates who attained a modest degree of private funding. Public funding also helped free each candidate's personal organization from the party hierarchy, which lost control of the primary process, thereby making the nomination more responsive to the electorate at large, at least in theory. Evidence of the wide-open nature of the competition is found in the victorious campaign of little-known Jimmy Carter and the nearly successful insurgency of Ronald Reagan.

Fragmentation

The chief unintended result of campaign finance reform in 1976 was a fragmented field of candidates on the Democratic side. Campaigns that experienced financial trouble from the outset undoubtedly were prolonged by federal subsidies and this may have affected certain outcomes at the polls. In a few states, the votes for floundering liberal candidates, if they had gone to Morris Udall, for example, would have given Udall an edge over Carter. Yet despite government funding, by midprimary season seven candidates — Sanford, Bentsen, Bayh, Shapp, Shriver, Harris, and Jackson — had dropped out.

Several of these candidates formally remained in the race as long as they did because they were in debt and needed to raise matchable contributions and draw additional public funds. To constrain such a practice, the 1976 Amendments cut off matching funds 30 days after a candidate obtains less than 10 percent of the votes in two consecutive primaries. This provision applied to only one 1976 candidate, Ellen McCormack, but in the future it may do more to prevent fragmentation.

The general consequences of public financing tended to be reinforced by electoral and party reforms adopted for 1976. Thirty states held presidential primary elections in 1976, seven more than had conducted primaries in 1972. The typical delegate selected was bound to a certain presidential aspirant, unlike in years past. With nearly three-fourths of all convention delegates chosen directly by the voters in 1976, the traditional power of party leaders waned. In addition to presumed responsiveness to the voter, more primaries meant increased points of access for the lesser known candidates. Not surprisingly, candidates placed the bulk of their spending in the primary states where the potential gains were greatest; however, the proliferation of state primaries also encouraged disunity by making it harder for any one candidate to reach a majority of delegate votes. Even the Carter bandwagon slowed because the Georgian could not win every primary.

Further enhancing the openness of the 1976 prenomination contest were the rules of the two major parties. The Democrats eliminated winner-take-all primaries by instituting proportional representation.

This guaranteed each candidate who received more than 15 percent of a state primary vote a proportional share of that state's delegates. The new system gave a fairer reflection of voter preferences and restrained the brokering power of large-state delegations which, in the past, could deny the nomination to an outsider like Carter. The Republicans, meanwhile, maintained their bonus system whereby states that went Republican in previous elections were rewarded with extra delegate votes. In 1976 this Republican rule assisted Reagan because the core of the challenger's support came from the South and Far West, areas recently strengthened by the bonus formula.

For the most part, primary elections overshadowed the less dramatic caucus process, but party caucuses and conventions did provide some significant highlights and key delegate votes. The earliest state caucuses, especially in Iowa, attracted much media attention and considerable candidate spending. In the Republican Party, the final caucus meetings became a bitter and costly battleground between Ford and Reagan. Party rules in effect for primaries applied as well to caucus states, and caucus meetings at the precinct level were open to all party members. Local caucuses elected representatives who were either pledged to the various candidates or were uncommitted, and these representatives attended gatherings for larger jurisdictions. The process culminated in state conventions which selected delegates to the national party conventions.

Since more than one-fourth of convention delegates were selected by this method in 1976, the caucus system cannot be ignored, but the future of the method is uncertain because it has not achieved the level of participation that the primary system has. Recent federal, state, and party reforms have sought nomination contests that are responsive to the electorate and that make efficient use of campaign funds; but caucuses tend rather to strengthen political parties, or at least certain factions, thus introducing other values that, while legitimate, were not necessarily intended.

In the 1976 election voter turnout in caucus states amounted to less than one-tenth of the turnout in primary states. Because participation rates are so low in caucuses, it does not pay for candidates to spend heavily in them, although psychological advantages are gained by winning. Even though increased expenditures in caucuses might raise popular participation, the primaries, although expensive, seem to offer candidates more for their money. Indeed, one study of the 1976 presidential primaries has shown that primary turnout was significantly higher in states that attracted heavy spending.[2]

As public financing and other reforms altered the basic structure of American electoral politics, the day-to-day functions of campaigning changed as well. With its emphasis on smaller contributions, the new campaign finance law prompted a revision of traditional fund-raising techniques. In the past, candidates had devoted substantial amounts of time to wooing the "fat cat" contributors, but under the amended FECA this approach could yield at most a $1,000 contribution. The 1976 campaigns, therefore, relied on more broad-based fund-raising methods, such as direct-mail campaigns, telethons, televised appeals, benefit concerts, telephone solicitations, and expanded, low-priced versions of the traditional banquet or cocktail party. These changes increased the importance of professional fund-raisers. Most campaigns found that direct appeals by the candidate, whether on television or to crowds of supporters, worked best while direct mail proved only moderately profitable. As a rule, a fund-raising strategy employing several of these techniques was sufficient to qualify the candidate for matching funds.

Several of the candidates' campaign managers felt that by making it more difficult to raise money, the FECA forced them to curtail traditional forms of grass-roots campaigning. They also felt that the law required them to spend too much time and resources on fund raising, bookkeeping, and budgeting. Several managers thought they could have campaigned more effectively if the contribution limit had been higher.[3]

The majority of the 15 candidates who became eligible for federal subsidies had no elaborate system for raising $5,000 in each of 20 states in contributions of $250 or less. Rather, most candidates qualified quickly because their organizations simply raised as much money as possible and they used personal networks of contacts to meet the threshold where necessary. Eligibility was made even easier because, under the law, a donor could split a large contribution among members of his immediate adult family in amounts of $250 or less. Many 1976 campaigns quietly encouraged this practice both to facilitate qualification and to maximize matching funds once qualified.

Another innovation in campaigning was the effort made to comply with the new law and pursuant regulations. The campaigns displayed varying degrees of workable compliance systems, with an essential element being standardized records for contribution and contributor information. In addition, most organizations drew up form letters that were sent to contributors who failed to supply the proper data, and most top finance officials personally inspected all contribution checks in an effort to detect any illegal donations. The more flush campaigns even utilized computer services to store information and balance the financial books, while the less prosperous committees kept their books manually. Manual bookkeeping expended immense amounts of paper and labor, but computerized systems also required work by hand in editing printouts. As a matter of fact, a number of committees discovered that volunteer campaign workers were not skilled enough to make computerization worthwhile, and dropped the system after starting it.

With the need for new clerical and administrative capabilities generated by the FECA, a breed of legal and accounting advisers specializing in campaign finance emerged. Some campaigns hired lawyers and accountants before campaign managers, and these professionals became an integral part of the campaign apparatus, participating in the planning and decision-making process in order to ensure compliance. Other campaigns paid fees for outside services from firms such as Arthur Andersen & Co., which cultivated a good trade among presidential hopefuls with a comprehensive compliance program. Whether internal or external, professional advice captured a respectable portion of campaign receipts, for no candidate could afford a major violation in the post-Watergate era.

Reporting Requirements

Despite the assistance of qualified lawyers and accountants, almost all of the presidential campaigns found the reporting requirements of the FEC burdensome. Periodic reports to the commission demanded the time of campaign officers, and the detail expected in short time spans swamped more than a few presidential operations. As a result, many campaigns filed incomplete reports until after the heat of battle when amendments supplied the accuracy stipulated by the commission and the law. Complaints about the workload notwithstanding, most campaign officials praised the FEC and its staff for handling an arduous task in a reasonable and flexible manner. Moreover, the detailed documentation was instrumental in uncovering the major scandal of the 1976 race, which involved fund-raising irregularities in the campaign of Pennsylvania Gov. Milton J. Shapp. The commission's audit resulted in a return to the government of the matching funds previously granted to Shapp.

There was little incentive for most candidates to report highly accurate state-by-state figures because only a few candidates had sufficient funds to approach the limits in most states. For example, in New York, where the spending limit was $2,231,000, Jimmy Carter spent less than $500,000. If a candidate did come close to a limit and the FEC questioned him, the candidate could amend the filing to lower the figure. In one case, the FEC inquired into Ronald Reagan's campaign when it reported surpassing the New Hampshire limit by $11,640.94. In an amendment, the Reagan officials claimed that the amount had actually been spent in Florida. Later, Reagan was required to return more than $30,000 in matching funds that included repayment for excess monies spent in New Hampshire.

The lack of definitive and operable interpretations of FEC regulations further contributed to inaccuracy. The many small expenses that must be totaled to obtain each state allocation made it virtually impossible to pinpoint a total for each campaign committee. For instance, mailings sent out from a national headquarters in Washington, D.C., to another state should be allocated to that state, while interstate travel is not attributable to any state. This regulation certainly omits some large expenses. Costs "directly relating" to the national headquarters may be eliminated from the state limitations as well. The FEC set standards, but since campaign workers could decide which costs related to national or state efforts, there was only small possibility that an excess of expenditures would be attributed to a given state. According to the FEC, expenditures for print and electronic media disseminated in more than one state, "shall be attributed to each State based on the voting age population in each State which can reasonably be expected to be

Table 5-1
Total Expenditures, Compliance Costs and Matching Funds Received of 15 Candidates Who Qualified for Matching Funds

Candidate	Total Expenditures[a]	Estimated Compliance Costs	Matching Funds
Gerald Ford	$13,576,000	$ 581,000	$ 4,657,008
Ronald Reagan	12,635,326	550,000	4,477,769
Total Republican	$26,211,326	$1,131,000	$ 9,134,777
Jimmy Carter	$12,431,300	$ 348,900	$ 3,600,007
George Wallace	10,500,000		3,291,309
Henry Jackson	6,237,000		1,962,951
Morris Udall	4,750,000		2,020,258
Lloyd Bentsen	2,700,000		511,023
Jerry Brown	1,890,240		599,898
Fred Harris	1,605,000		639,013
Frank Church	1,540,100		640,669
Birch Bayh	1,374,081		545,710
Sargent Shriver	1,020,000		295,712
Milton Shapp	892,092		-0- [b]
Terry Sanford	637,936		246,340
Ellen McCormack	532,848		247,220
Total Democratic	$46,110,597	$ 348,900	$14,600,110
Grand Total	$72,321,923		$23,734,887 [c]

[a] Includes compliance costs and matching funds.
[b] Governor Shapp refunded the full amount he received, $299,066, after discovery of illegalities in his committee's claim of eligibility for matching funds.
[c] A few refunds made in 1978 reduced this figure to $23,594,764 by October 1978.

SOURCE: FEC *Annual Report 1977*, Appendix 5, p. 66.

influenced by such expenditures." Such regulations encouraged loose accounting, and more importantly, provided ready alibis for accusations of overspending.

FEC regulations governing compliance as well as new forms of fund raising substantially increased the cost of campaigning in 1976. Fundraising costs were proportionately higher than in previous campaigns when contributions could be solicited in larger amounts. Bookkeeping costs also rose, partly to ensure compliance with the disclosure and limitations sections of the law and partly to prepare submissions for matching funds. The magnitude of the compliance costs incurred during the prenomination period can be seen in data made available by the three most expensive campaigns, those of Ford, Reagan, and Carter. As shown in Table 5-1, Jimmy Carter spent $348,900 on compliance, which was 2.8 percent of his total expenditures; Ronald Reagan's compliance expenses came to about $550,000 or 4.4 percent of total costs; and President Ford spent $581,000 or 4.3 percent of his budget.

Of course, the costs of abiding by the law must be balanced against the tangible benefits of the FECA — the matching funds. Table 5-1 also

Table 5-2
Summary of Primary Matching Fund Activity, as of December 31, 1976

Candi-date	Number of Sub-missions	Number of Contri-butions Submitted	Average Amount Submitted	Total Amount Submitted	Percentage of Total Request Matched	Total Amount Certified
Bayh	17	6,988	$ 68.02	$ 475,335.94	98.70	$ 469,199.54
Bentsen	3	6,767	84.98	575,052.94	88.86	511,022.61
Brown	9	20,089	34.55	694,174.87	83.64	580,629.65
Carter	21	94,419	41.09	3,880,118.84	89.31	3,465,584.89
Church	18	18,812	33.50	630,151.01	98.82	622,747.04
Ford	21	114,661	43.06	4,937,232.99	94.32	4,657,007.82
Harris	13	56,021	11.74	657,813.91	96.24	633,099.05
Jackson	7	58,372	35.45	2,069,042.97	95.72	1,980,554.95
McCor-mack	8	14,161	18.08	256,093.60	95.32	244,125.40
Reagan	19	238,266	23.11	5,507,153.24	92.40	5,088,910.66
Sanford	3	1,960	126.07	247,100.32	99.71	246,388.32
Shapp	11	4,416	69.61	307,403.71	97.28	299,066.21
Shriver	8	2,745	104.12	285,822.19	99.73	285,069.74
Udall	22	97,764	21.84	2,135,263.72	88.92	1,898,686.96
Wallace	6	240,052	14.75	3,539,579.86	92.89	3,291,308.81
Subtotals	186	975,493	$26.86	$26,197,340.11	92.65%	$24,273,401.65[a]

[a]A few refunds made in 1978 reduced this figure to $23,594,764 by October 1978.

SOURCE: FEC *Annual Report* for 1976, p. 16.

reports the amount of matching funds received by each of the 15 candidates who qualified for federal subsidies. The table shows that the candidates received a total of $23,734,887, excluding refunds made from postcampaign surpluses. Gerald Ford drew the largest amount, $4,657,008, while Ronald Reagan received $4,477,769, the second-largest subsidy. Of the Democrats, Jimmy Carter led in matching funds with $3,600,007, followed by George Wallace with $3,291,309. Obviously, few of the candidates approached the optimal point at which matching funds constituted 50 percent of income, a situation that would occur only if a candidate received all of his private funds in matchable contributions of $250 or less. Further, Table 5-2 illustrates that of those contributions submitted few came close to the $250 limit for matching. The average amount submitted for matching was at most $126.07, submitted by Sanford, and the least, $11.74, submitted by Harris. When the number of campaign contributions was relatively high, the average

Table 5-3
Total Expenditures, Total Votes Cast in Primary States, and Cost Per Primary Vote for 15 Candidates Who Qualified for Matching Funds

Candidate	Total Expenditures	Total Votes Cast in Primary States[b]	Cost Per Primary Vote
Gerald Ford	$13,576,000	$ 5,698,955	$2.38
Ronald Reagan	12,635,326	5,186,534	2.44
Total Republican	$26,211,326	$10,885,489	$2.41
Jimmy Carter	$12,431,300	$ 7,118,936	$1.75
George Wallace	10,500,000	2,558,501	4.10
Henry Jackson	6,237,000	1,134,375	5.50
Morris Udall	4,750,000	1,672,093	2.84
Lloyd Bentsen	2,700,000	346,968	7.78
Jerry Brown	1,890,240	2,449,747	.77
Fred Harris	1,605,000	265,434	6.05
Frank Church	1,540,100	831,035	1.85
Birch Bayh	1,374,081	86,438	15.90
Sargent Shriver	1,020,000	338,473	3.01
Milton Shapp	892,092	88,254	10.11
Terry Sanford	637,936	— [a]	—
Ellen McCormack	532,848	243,316	2.19
Total Democratic	$46,100,597	$17,133,570	$2.69
Grand total	$72,321,923	$28,019,059	$2.58

a
  Sanford withdrew from the race before the primaries began.

b
  SOURCE: Kimball W. Brace, "The 1976 Presidential Primaries: An Analysis of How Many People Participated and How Much Money Was Spent," A Report Compiled for the Commission on Presidential Nomination and Party Structure, May 9, 1977.

matched amounts were low. For example, Wallace submitted the largest number of contributions, 240,052, with an average amount of only $14.75. Average amounts for 10 of the 15 candidates were less than $50.

Matching funds, totaling $23.7 million, comprised 30.5 percent of all candidate expenditures, which amounted to $72.3 million in combined public and private monies since 1973-74 when some of the campaigns started. The private money factor reflects the candidates' needs to accept the largest allowable contributions early in the campaign, before matching funds are disbursed, to gain the necessary "seed" money for large scale fund raising, as well as the difference between the amount of larger contributions of which only $250 was matchable. The private money proportion of total funding also included nonindividual contributions that were not matchable, and other contributions submitted for matching but rejected. Broken down by party, as shown in Table 5-3, Democratic candidates spent $46.1 million, whereas the Republican contenders spent $26.2 million.

If the Democratic candidates are considered separately, the $46.1 million in 1976 compares with the $33 million spent by Democratic candidates for the presidential nomination in 1972. Given the infusion of public money in the matching incentive program ($14.6 million to Democratic candidates), slightly less private money ($31.5 million) was raised in 1976 than in 1972. The excess spending in 1976, then, consisted mainly of government funds. Indeed, several campaign officials complained that the $1,000 limit on individual contributions was too low because it hampered spending for start-up functions.

All fund raising is for the purpose of later spending money to get votes, but the effectiveness of the dollars spent by individual candidates varies considerably. Table 5-3 shows the expenditures made by 15 candidates, the total votes cast in primary states for each and the cost per primary vote for the candidates. This calculation includes funds spent in caucus states, but does not include votes cast in those states and therefore does not give the cost for all votes. Nevertheless, the table provides a rough estimation of the relationship between expenditures and electoral success in the 1976 prenomination campaigns.

Among all the candidates, the ones with high vote tallies had relatively low costs per vote, although the incumbent, Ford, spent $2.38 per primary vote, while the Democratic winner, Carter, only $1.75. This disparity results partly from Carter's early emergence as the front-runner and partly from the lower registration levels of Republican voters. The high costs per vote recorded by candidates such as Wallace ($4.10) and Jackson ($5.50) indicate a highly organized, major campaign effort, begun early, by candidates who were considered serious contenders but who met with severe setbacks later at the polls.

Only three contenders neared the $13.1 million spending limit, suggesting that few candidates remain serious contenders for the duration of the campaign. The campaign with the lowest cost per vote ($.77) belonged to California Governor Jerry Brown, who spent a comparatively small sum and who ran a campaign that had very little lead time, yet met with considerable success in the primaries, especially in his home state.

Another way of comparing spending and voting data is to relate total votes as a function of total expenditures for each candidate. Candidates who spent heavily, such as Carter, Reagan, and Ford, received the most votes, while those who spent the least (McCormack, Sanford, Shapp, Shriver, Bayh) received the fewest votes. Several factors must be borne in mind concerning this result. One denotes a reciprocal rather than a cause-and-effect relationship; i.e., spending money can help a candidate win votes while at the same time success at the polls helps the candidate to raise funds. Jimmy Carter, for example, was most successful in fund raising late in the campaign after he had established himself as the front-runner, while Lloyd Bentsen's fund raising dropped sharply after his early electoral defeats. Another problem is that the relationships shown between dollars spent and votes received is not perfectly linear. Jackson, for example, spent considerably more than Udall, who in turn considerably outspent Brown. The voting results, however, showed an inverse relationship: Brown received the most votes and Jackson the fewest.

Another method of analyzing the effectiveness of campaign spending is to relate spending levels to voting results in each primary state. Spending figures provided by the candidates to the FEC, however, lack uniformity since each candidate used different allocation formulas with different degrees of accuracy. George Wallace, for example, divided his spending fairly evenly among the 50 states, with the result that he was the highest spender in some states that he did not even contest seriously. Jimmy Carter opened a second national headquarters in Washington and allocated all the money spent there to the District of Columbia even though it was not directed specifically at the District's primary. Even so, these figures give a general idea of spending levels in the various states.

In 25 Republican primaries between Ford and Reagan, the higher spender was victorious in 15, indicating a slight advantage from higher spending.[4] On the Democratic side, the biggest spender won only six of 25 primaries; however, if Wallace's totals are excluded, since his reported state-by-state allocations were the most questionable, then the big spender won 19 of the 25. In actuality, the figure is probably about 16 since in a number of states, such as Florida, Illinois, and North Carolina, Wallace probably did spend the most money and yet failed to win

Table 5-4
Candidate Expenditures Per Primary State Related to
Voting Turnout and Costs Per Eligible Voter

State	Amount Spent	Persons Eligible to Vote	Costs Per Eligible Voter	Turnout
Ala.	$ 523,631	1,820,109	$0.29	36.3%
Ark.	37,956	1,020,533	.04	52.4
Calif.	4,086,955	8,204,627	.50	71.6
D.C.	255,864	210,947	1.21	11.1
Fla.	3,854,730	3,381,750	1.14	56.5
Ga.	505,538	2,301,575	.22	30.0
Idaho	197,852	457,965	.43	36.0
Ill.	2,061,646	5,753,155	.36	36.3
Ind.	744,314	2,910,086	.26	42.8
Ky.	440,889	1,545,915	.29	28.4
Md.	854,938	1,679,126	.51	45.1
Mass.	3,122,387	2,872,483	1.09	32.2
Mich.	961,650	4,575,336	.21	38.7
Mont.	243,043	411,090	.59	47.8
Neb.	490,585	736,567	.67	52.1
Nev.	322,419	198,073	1.63	62.1
N.H.	1,614,947	443,583	3.64	43.7
N.J.	852,868	3,490,660	.24	17.3
N.C.	1,496,379	2,265,248	.66	35.3
Ohio	1,719,974	7,397,000	.23	28.0
Ore.	799,432	1,214,400	.66	60.2
Pa.	1,702,203	5,023,278	.34	43.4
R.I.	365,425	527,541	.69	14.2
S.D.	231,850	366,856	.63	38.9
Tenn.	464,983	1,911,583	.24	30.2
Texas	2,374,346	5,329,779	.45	37.1
Vt.	177,164	284,294	.62	25.4
W.Va.	181,151	1,042,502	.17	50.7
Wis.	1,802,215	3,176,000	.57	42.0
Total	$32,487,334	· 70,552,061	$ .46	41.2%

SOURCE: Kimball W. Brace, "The 1976 Presidential Primaries: An Analysis of How Many People Participated and How Much Money Was Spent," A Report Compiled for the Commission on Presidential Nomination and Party Structure, May 9, 1977.

the primary. In 36 percent of the Democratic and 40 percent of the Republican contests, then, the highest-spending candidate did not win the primary. In some cases, such as Jackson in Pennsylvania and Reagan in Ohio, the perceived need to conserve funds rather than to spend adequately may have cost a candidate a potential victory. As a rule, spending adequate money is an essential but not a sufficient precondition for electoral success.

It is also interesting to measure the effect of campaign spending on citizen interest and participation; i.e., to determine whether increased spending by the candidates induces greater numbers of voters to go to the polls. Table 5-4 compares total expenditures on behalf of candidates per eligible voter with voter turnout in each state. (Spending per eligible voter is a more accurate measure of the level of campaign activities than is total spending, since total spending is a reflection of the size of the state.) Turnout tends to rise with increased spending, although the relationship is far from certain. In the seven states where less than 25 cents was spent for each eligible voter, total turnout was 31.2 percent. In the eight with spending of 26 to 50 cents, turnout was 47.1 percent (this figure is slightly inflated since it contains California with its extraordinarily high turnout); in nine states where spending was between 50 cents and a dollar per eligible voter, turnout was 42.1 percent. In five states more than a dollar was spent per eligible voter and the total turnout was 44.7 percent. These figures are not absolute indicators, of course, as evidenced by Arkansas and West Virginia, the two states with the lowest spending levels, where turnouts were higher than in New Hampshire, which had the highest spending level.

The Democrats

Presidential hopefuls in the Democratic Party began preparing for the 1976 nomination as early as 1973, when the unfolding Watergate affair increased the possibility that the party would soon return to the White House. At the 1974 mini-convention in Kansas City, a number of prospective candidates ran hospitality operations. In September 1974, the Democratic presidential race suddenly became wide open when Sen. Edward M. Kennedy of Massachusetts announced that under no circumstances would he be a candidate.

During 1974 several candidates had formed campaign committees that were not subject to the 1974 Amendments until January 1, 1975. Although they were not bound legally by any individual contribution limit, three candidates voluntarily imposed one. Senators Jackson and Bentsen set a $3,000 maximum on contributions to their committees because this figure appeared in an early version of the FECA Amendments. Also observing a $3,000 ceiling was then Senator Walter Mondale of Minnesota, who scrapped his presidential bid later in 1974.

As the 1976 contest unfolded, the well-funded candidates (Wallace, Bentsen, Jackson) tended to be weak at the polls, while the financially strapped, dark-horse candidates (Carter, Church, Brown) showed more popularity with the voters. In addition to the 13 Democrats who qualified for matching funds, Senator Robert Byrd ran a notable favorite-son campaign in West Virginia, and the late Senator Hubert Humphrey almost entered the race. Out of the crowded field, Jimmy Carter soon emerged to foster a surprising degree of unity for the "out-party."

Bayh

Birch Bayh of Indiana commenced his second campaign for the presidency too late to raise the funds needed to overcome other liberal Democrats. In 1972 Senator Bayh had abandoned the nominating contest when his wife, Marvella, underwent major surgery, and for the 1976 campaign, Mrs. Bayh advised her husband not to run. Perhaps this and other personal factors caused the senator to hesitate until October 21, 1975, when he officially announced as the ninth contender for the party nod. The Committee for Birch Bayh in '76 had begun raising funds in August, but met with less success than anticipated. Senator Bayh sought to put together the old Roosevelt coalition and he won many endorsements from mid-level party officials and diverse interest groups. There were doubts about his electability, however, and they were amplified by Bayh's losses in Iowa, New Hampshire, and Massachusetts. The Bayh committee could not afford a comeback attempt in New York, so the Indiana senator effectively ended his candidacy in early March. At that time, the committee showed debts of more than $100,000 after spending almost $1.4 million.

Compliance. Although the Bayh committee encountered no major compliance problems, staff members complained that efforts needed to abide by the law severely drained money and manpower from more important campaign work. At the outset, the committee considered contracting with Arthur Andersen & Co. for an accounting and reporting system, but decided the fee was too high. Instead, the campaign initially relied on its own controller, then later hired full-time an assistant controller and two clerical workers. These employees screened contribution checks and recorded contributor and financial information on computer. In legal matters, the committee counted on its finance chairman, Myer Feldman, who had served as an assistant to both Presidents Kennedy and Johnson, and a few attorneys in Feldman's firm who volunteered their services. After trying to give campaign officers in the primary states a high degree of autonomy, the committee found that the burden of reporting requirements could not be spread to field workers. Eventually a more centralized financial system was developed under which state offices sent all contributions to the Washington, D.C., headquarters, which then supplied the state offices with funds for each week's expenditures.

In spite of his electoral misfortune, Senator Bayh deftly remained eligible for matching funds after his bid, practically speaking, had ended in March. Rather than withdrawing completely, Bayh was careful to "suspend" his candidacy. He explained the difference by saying, "I don't know what the future holds, and I want to keep my options open."[5]

This stance left Bayh eligible for matching funds for expenses incurred until May 11, 1976, when the FEC declared him ineligible. The two-month grace period helped reduce the debt by covering close-down functions, but no new campaign activity occurred.

On June 16, 1978, the FEC released a report of a compliance audit on the Committee for Birch Bayh in '76. The audit covered the period from August 5, 1975, through May 31, 1977. The committee was criticized in the report for failure to disclose: 1) some of the repositories for campaign funds; 2) circumstances and conditions under which some debts and obligations were extinguished; 3) occupation and principal place of business of some contributors; and 4) acceptable documentation of a number of campaign expenditures. In each case, however, the report noted that during the course of the audit the committee did its best to rectify the situation and thereby achieved substantial compliance. The audit also determined that no matching fund payments in excess of eligibility were received by the committee.[6]

Fund Raising. The downfall of the Bayh candidacy can be attributed largely to inadequate fund raising caused by the senator's late start. Encouraged by the ready funding for his 1974 Senate campaign, Bayh counted on his liberal reputation to attract substantial contributions for his presidential bid. When Bayh got into the race, however, candidates Udall, Shriver, Harris, Church, and Carter already were exhausting the liberal money supply. Personal solications, fund-raising events and some direct mail let the Bayh committee survive, but these methods failed to provide enough up-front cash for the televised fund appeals that had been planned originally.

Senator Bayh owed what financial success there was to the skill of Myer Feldman, who had served as a McGovern fund-raiser in 1972. Feldman's solicitation of friends and past Democratic contributors was the foremost means of qualifying Bayh for matching funds. Although the eligibility process proved tougher than expected, Feldman helped raise at least $5,000 in each of 20 states when the candidate officially announced in the fall of 1975. Beyond that point, staff solicitations became less and less fruitful, even though the committee maintained one professional fund-raiser in Massachusetts and another in New York. The burden of catch-up fund raising created among campaign staffers the hope that the Supreme Court would overturn the individual contribution limit in the *Buckley* case. As Feldman complained, "It's that $1,000 limit that has caused the problem."[7]

The disappointing results of personal solicitations limited use of direct mail. In 1975 the campaign sent a mailing to Massachusetts and New York residents on the 1972 McGovern list, but this direct-mail program, formulated in-house, attracted meager contributions. A more productive appeal went to mailing lists from women's activist groups, which favored Bayh because he guided the Equal Rights Amendment through Congress. In general though, returns from direct mail could neither justify nor finance further mailings, and the committee was forced to rely on fund-raising events for the remainder of the primary season.

Events got off to an inauspicious start, for the committee held its first affair as late as December. At first, the staff overly conserved the senator's time, but fund-raisers soon learned that a candidate appearance raised the most money. During the height of the primary elections, Bayh was scheduled for at least one fund-raising event a day. Another error later corrected was to ask for donations at a fund-raiser, instead of before, leaving people unprepared to make large contributions. In general, the campaign sponsored smaller parties in the early primary states, and larger, more profitable affairs elsewhere. For example, one dinner in Bayh's home state charged $100 a plate, and a series of dinners in New York netted $100,000.

All fund-raising techniques collected about $330,000 by the end of 1975, up from only $125,000 at the time of Bayh's October 21 announcement. At the close of the campaign, individual contributions totaled nearly $700,000, with contributions fairly equally divided between the three categories of $100 or less, $101 to $499, and $500 or more. In addition, the Bayh committee received $50,572 from various PACs and $1,350 from other party committees. To retire some $160,000 in debts, the committee continued raising funds for more than a year after Bayh's withdrawal.

In the postcampaign period, informal soliciting in Indiana proved somewhat successful, but dinners and a rock concert were more lucrative. The Bayh committee held about 10 dinners in Washington, D.C., and even more in Indiana, New York, and Massachusetts. In December 1976 the committee sponsored a benefit concert by the popular band Fleetwood Mac in Indianapolis, and the show raised approximately $50,000 exclusive of matching funds. In a less glamorous approach to debt reduction, the committee settled accounts with its creditors for less than the full amount owed. The FEC approved this scheme because the campaign claimed that, while it had exhausted all fund-raising possibilities, it could make at least 75 percent payment on outstanding bills. The arrangement satisfied the vendors involved because they had anticipated writing off the debts and were pleased to receive partial payments.

The committee's efforts erased the debt by the fall of 1977, bringing total receipts to slightly more than $1.37 million. Federal matching funds constituted $545,710, or almost 40 percent, of the total.

Costs. The Birch Bayh in '76 Committee spent nearly half of its budget in four caucus and primary states, while remaining expenditures went toward operation of the national headquarters and to costly set-up functions such as salaries and fund raising.

The Iowa caucuses offered Bayh an opportunity to prove his claim of electability and hasten the flow of contributions. The Bayh forces had planned to battle Morris Udall for the liberal vote, but with the Udall camp in disarray, the Iowa contest narrowed to Bayh and Jimmy Carter, who had spent more time and had organized better in the state than had any of his opponents. Bayh's expenditure of $62,600 hardly compensated for either his late start or attacks from antiabortion groups. Because the senator chaired the Judiciary Subcommittee on the Constitution, which had shelved constitutional amendments restricting abortion, he became the prime target of right-to-life organizations in 1976. Carter, on the other hand, had expressed favor for a "national statute" limiting abortions and won the support of Iowans opposed to abortion. This combination of factors forced the Indiana senator to settle for a distant second place in the Iowa caucus, with 13 percent of the vote, compared with 27 percent for Carter.

In need of a comeback, Bayh looked to the February 24 New Hampshire primary. According to plan, Bayh won endorsements from some state labor leaders, legislators, and mayors, and kept a dawn-to-midnight pace of personal appearances. As a counterattack on Carter's anti-Washington theme, Bayh stressed the need for experience in government, and he aired television and radio commercials in which he declared proudly, "I am a politician."[8] On the weekend before the New Hampshire voting, the Bayh committee imported Indianans who canvassed for their senator. All of the toil and total expenditures of $138,600 brought Bayh 16.2 percent of the ballots cast for a disappointing third place, more than 7 percent behind Representative Udall.

Bayh's weak showing in New Hampshire enhanced the importance of the Massachusetts primary a week later. Once again, the candidate gained backing from certain labor officials and party leaders, including Lt. Gov. Thomas P. O'Neill III. After surveys revealed a negative impact from Bayh's pro-Washington advertising, the campaign discontinued the commercials a few days before the Massachusetts election. Nonetheless, the Bayh media campaign cost an estimated $100,000 in both New Hampshire and Massachusetts. The latter state presented the first test of Bayh's ability to amalgamate the diverse groups in a northern industrial state, and he failed. At the polls, the senator placed seventh with 4.8 percent of the vote. Two days later, on March 4, Bayh suspended his candidacy, reflecting that he had "made a mistake by emphasizing political organizing instead of fund raising."[9]

By closing shop, Senator Bayh abandoned considerable work already devoted to the New York primary. The Bayh organization had lined up delegate candidates in 38 of New York's 39 congressional districts and the candidate had fought hard to place first in a poll of the New Democratic Coalition, the state's reform group. The Bayh committee reported spending $252,000 in New York, but the only practical outcome of the effort was that many Bayh delegate candidates transferred their allegiance to Udall, who emerged as the front-running liberal with Bayh on the sidelines.

The Bayh committee released a functional breakdown of its expenditures which shows that five categories of spending captured over three-fourths of the entire budget. Table 5-5 reports that the highest category comprised payroll expenses, which totaled $356,391. Travel was the next costly function at $256,670, and campaign promotional material followed at $171,958. Office rental plus telephone service cost $175,200, and the campaign spent $113,818 on media. Seven other functions each cost less than $75,000, as shown in the table. All expenditures from mid-1975 through fund raising and close-out in 1977 totaled $1,374,081.

Bentsen

Lloyd Bentsen, the millionaire senator from Texas, conducted a campaign impressive for its initial financial soundness but deficient in later political appeal. Although he officially announced as a candidate for the Democratic nomination on February 17, 1975, Bentsen actually had been running since late in 1973. Fund raising, under the auspices of the Bentsen in '76 Committee, centered on conservative Democrats and the business community, and at least half of Bentsen's monetary support came from the Lone Star State.

Although not well known outside of his home state, Bentsen believed that his performance as a successful businessman and middle-of-the-road politician would suit the national mood. As public opinion polls and contribution patterns disproved this belief, the senator became more and more of a regional candidate, but even his South-Southwestern candidacy proved fruitless when he finished second to last in both the Mississippi and Oklahoma caucus elections. On February 10, 1976, Bentsen reduced himself to a favorite-son candidate, but this plan failed too, for Jimmy Carter swept the Texas primary on May 1. With its several strategies, the Bentsen campaign spent about $2.7 million in two and a half years.

Compliance. The Bentsen in '76 Committee maintained its financial operation in Austin, Texas, under the supervision of some of Senator Bentsen's closest advisers. George Bristol, former administrative assistant in the senator's Texas office, served as finance director, and Robert Thomson, who had been counsel to the Senate Democratic Campaign Committee when Bentsen chaired the body, acted as campaign counsel. The latter received legal fees of about $4,000 a month during 1975.

Bristol and a salaried comptroller devised at the outset of the campaign a computerized financial system that involved a minimum of manual preparation and checking. The system provided updated analyses of income and expenditures, screened illegal contributions and alerted staff members as contributors approached their limits. A few individuals unknowingly exceeded the contribution limit, and they received appropriate refunds. The Bentsen computer system greatly facilitated reporting and worked so well that the FEC adopted a similar format for the compilation of campaign reports. The campaign generally relied on headquarters officials for legal and accounting advice, but it also benefited from the volunteer services of lawyers in some states. One high official commented that the Bentsen committee was so wary of the new campaign rules that political operatives made no major decisions without first getting legal and accounting advice. The committee's compliance effort probably cost more than $150,000, according to an aide, since legal and accounting costs equalled $75,000 in the first half of 1975 alone.[10]

Fund Raising. Before Bentsen's freshman term in the Senate was half over, he was testing the presidential waters. At a Houston dinner party in November 1973, Bentsen raised $375,000 after expenses of more than $65,000. With this seed money, Bentsen toured the country the following year, raising more money and trying to boost his name recognition. The chairmanship of the 1974 Democratic Senatorial Campaign Committee gave Bentsen an additional opportunity to meet labor and party leaders. The presidential campaign manager reported that the Bentsen organization paid for many of the senator's expenses which could have been charged to the Senatorial Campaign Committee.

In a show of fair play, Bentsen voluntarily limited contributions to $3,000 before the 1974 Amendments, and its $1,000 limit took effect. He chose this figure because he had sponsored a $3,000 ceiling in a Senate version of the campaign bill. Bentsen took some criticism, notably from Jimmy Carter, for not setting a more stringent limit, but a spokesman responded that the higher ceiling still demonstrated the senator's "commitment to the spirit of the campaign reform movement."[11] Nevertheless, the extra margin was a great advantage, considering that Bentsen was on friendly terms with many people to whom $3,000 was not a sacrifice.

Throughout 1974 Bentsen unabashedly sought the support of well-to-do business-people. While Bentsen's contributors included many individuals he knew through his highly successful insurance business, the senator also had supporters in the business establishment outside Texas. For example, in mid-December 1974 he attended a luncheon in Los Angeles sponsored by three past followers of Ronald Reagan — Holmes Tuttle, an automobile dealer, Justin Dart of Dart Industries, and Jack Wrather, oil producer and television magnate. Although contributions were not solicited at the affair, it clearly served to introduce Bentsen to California big business. The hosts also may well have been sending an early warning to the White House about the precarious loyalty of Reagan-style Republicans. This event, coupled with the backing of the right wing of the Texas Democratic Party (formerly John Connally's stronghold), branded Bentsen as a conservative. At first this image did not hurt, for in 1974 the Bentsen committee raised more than $600,000, which combined with 1973 income to bring total gross receipts to $1,036,523.

The committee proceeded on the assumption that this war chest would act as a catalyst for the more broad-based financing encouraged by the FECA after January 1, 1975. The Texan did everything that is supposed to shift a fund drive into high gear; he expanded the staff, initiated a direct-mail program, and traveled extensively, visiting 40 states in the first six months of 1975; but the campaign apparently had exhausted the supply of wealthy conservative Democrats. A concert in Missouri lost money. Nationwide mailings helped make Bentsen eligible for matching funds but disappointed expectations. Receipts for the first half of 1975 were $496,606, and in the third quarter of the year Bentsen in '76 spent more funds than it brought in. Another indication of fiscal need came in December when Mr. and Mrs. Lloyd Bentsen contributed $22,000 to the campaign. By year's end the committee showed about $1 million in 1975 contributions.

The advent of federal matching funds slightly alleviated Bentsen's position. In 1976, while spending heavily in the opening caucuses, the senator received $511,023 from the U.S. Treasury. The subsidy constitutes less than one-fifth of total receipts of about $2.65 million, although more than $1 million raised in 1973 and 1974 was not eligible for matching. Bentsen would not accept matching funds after he had dropped out of the race, thereby denying himself some $77,000 due for expenses incurred before his withdrawal. Ironically, the Bentsen committee ran into debt by about the amount in public funds that Bentsen declined.

The committee borrowed $75,500 from Senator Bentsen to pay outstanding bills, and it planned to repay him slowly. In early 1977 the campaign debt stood at $62,000, having been reduced by repeat gifts and conversions of contributions to Bentsen's 1976 Senate campaign.

Costs. Bentsen's spending reflected the committee's belief that income would increase for the duration of the campaign. When this did not come about, the committee found that it had devoted most of its resources to groundwork functions, but was short of cash for the last-minute needs of particular primaries.

Although the Bentsen in '76 Committee would not release breakdowns of expenditures, certain costs can be estimated. In 1973 and 1974 the campaign spent $435,366, the largest portion of which probably went toward travel, while lesser amounts covered costs of fund-raising events and staff. In addition to other methods of fund raising, direct mail cost slightly more than $100,000 according to a campaign official. It may be assumed that Bentsen's overhead costs were quite high, since he staffed two headquarters. The Washington office rented for $900 a month, and in an effort to control spiraling costs, Bentsen reduced the national campaign staff in September 1975. The categories of headquarters, staff, travel, and fund raising most likely accounted for the bulk of 1975 spending, which totaled $1,554,376. This is some $500,000 more than the campaign's income during the year.

The ominous financial situation prompted a change in strategy that resulted in internal strife during fall 1975. At that time, the senator came to believe that the Democratic convention in New York would be deadlocked, and therefore a candidate need not be popular nationally so long as he held a regional base. To build such a base, Bentsen felt that he should diminish his all-out effort and concentrate on the first caucus in Mississippi, Oklahoma, and South Carolina, and the primary in his home state of Texas. Essentially, this "low-risk" strategy was necessitated by the failure of the nationwide spending to spark enthusiastic support. Although polls in mid-1975 gave Bentsen a 33 percent recognition factor, only 1 percent of Democratic respondents favored him for the nomination. The shift to a regional strategy reportedly caused Bentsen's campaign manager, Benjamin L. Palumbo, to resign. Palumbo urged the candidate to test his strength in the northern primaries instead of trying to win a modest number of delegates. As if in reply to this thinking, Bentsen said, "If I had the money, if I were permitted by the law to raise it and if I were permitted to spend it, I'd go into the big industrial states and buy massive TV. I don't, so I think it's smarter to husband my resources and stay the course."[12]

As it turned out, Bentsen did not husband his resources, but spent frantically, especially in the early caucus states. The campaign spent $68,631 in Mississippi in an attempt to win the January 24 caucuses. With 1.6 percent of the vote, Bentsen trailed behind Wallace, an uncommitted bloc of delegates, Carter and Shriver. The defeat made Oklahoma's February 7 voting a make-or-break situation and it broke the senator from neighboring Texas. Bentsen won the backing of many of the state's old guard, but he finished fourth with 13 percent of the vote. The committee reported spending $153,870 in Oklahoma, with TV commercials taking about half of the budget. Bentsen made a partial withdrawal after Oklahoma, stating that he intended to lead "a united delegation from Texas to the Democratic convention."[13] Bentsen campaigned halfheartedly for the presidency in Texas, as he concentrated on reelection to the Senate. Nonetheless, the presidential campaign expended $132,733 in the state, while delegate candidates committed to Bentsen spent a total of $65,140 on their own. In the May delegate-selection primary, Carter destroyed Texas' favorite son by picking up 122 delegates, compared with eight for Bentsen.

In other states, the committee spent heavily for organizing and fund raising before Bentsen's withdrawal. According to FEC reports, the Bentsen in '76 Committee expended $114,738 in California, and $69,849 in New York. Pennsylvania and Virginia followed in the order of spending with $65,070 and $38,418, respectively.

In 1976, expenditures equaled $711,845, bringing aggregate spending for the lengthy campaign to $2,701,587.

Brown

A seemingly offhand comment to reporters in mid-March of 1976 launched the presidential campaign of Edmund G. "Jerry" Brown, Jr., the 38-year-old governor of California. Governor Brown explained his late entrance by remarking, "No one has captured the enthusiasm and the imagination of the Democratic party. I'm offering myself as an alternative."[14]

Although Brown had speculated on a bid in 1975, his campaign got off to a slow start, beginning as a "native son" effort to dominate the California delegation and expanding to a national candidacy. Brown had delayed announcing beyond the time his staff recommended for a successful campaign, and by the time he announced it was too late to qualify for the ballot in some significant primary states. Brown created considerable excitement among the electorate and scored an upset over Carter in the May 18 Maryland primary. Subsequent victories in Nevada, Rhode Island, New Jersey, and California demonstrated Brown's popularity, but could not halt Jimmy Carter's slow but sure progress toward the nomination. At the Democratic convention, where Brown pledged his support of Carter, the Georgian attested to Brown's strength with the quip, "I'd hate to think what would have happened to my campaign if he had unleashed in New Hampshire instead of Maryland."[15]

For a last-minute campaign, the Brown forces raised and spent substantial funds, and even went into debt. The Brown for President Committee spent $1.9 million in the four months from mid-March until the convention in mid-July, plus $300,000 through June 1977.

Compliance. The Brown for President Committee, formed in March with headquarters in Los Angeles, faced difficult legal and accounting problems because of its lack of lead time. Several lawyers organized a crash compliance program. A full-time volunteer inspected all contribution checks and rejected those not meeting legal requirements. The campaign policy was to automatically return all corporate and lobbyist checks. Staff members suspected some of the corporate checks may have been attempts to trap or embarrass the Brown committee. An unusual development was the intervention of the California Fair Political Practices Commission inquiring whether the Brown campaign was accepting contributions from California-based lobbyists. California law prohibits lobbyists from contributing to political candidates, but the applicability of a state law in a federal campaign was at issue; federal law is supreme and normally preempts state law. The policy of the Brown campaign not to accept contributions from lobbyists was undertaken to avoid any embarrassment to the candidate, who had been an advocate of election reform and whose staff, while he was California's secretary of state, had helped to draft the California law. The FPPC ceased pursuing the inquiry when it was made clear that campaign policy was not to accept contributions from lobbyists.

For its first matching funds submission, the committee paid 20 University of Southern California students to alphabetize the contributor lists by state, to sort copies of cancelled contributor checks, and to sort concert cards. The students literally worked around the clock for three days prior to the first submission. The campaign computerized its financial books to ensure accuracy and minimize labor. A highly centralized financial operation was deemed necessary from the start to make the most efficient use of funds and to comply with federal law. Accordingly, field workers received stern instructions to send all contributions to headquarters and to clear all expenditures with the controller. Nonetheless, the committee encountered a problem in meeting disclosure dates for receipts and expenditures of some state committees. In fact, the national treasurer refused to sign some FEC filings because she did not want to be held responsible until amendments could be made to the incomplete reports. For legal representation before the FEC, the Brown committee was billed $8,860 in costs by the Washington law firm of Sargent Shriver in late 1977.

In two instances, the committee attracted the scrutiny of the FEC. After the primaries, Governor Brown made a trip to Plains, Georgia, following up with a televised postscript on the campaign. The FEC monitored these actions to see if Brown in effect was withdrawing from the race. The trip to Plains coincided with the first FEC certification audit undertaken after the 1976 Amendments were enacted and the FEC was cautious in interpreting the new provisions applying to *pro forma* candidates seeking continuing qualification for matching funds. The governor's guarded statements on his status allowed him to remain a candidate so that his debt-ridden campaign could receive matching funds for expenses incurred until the convention.

The Brown forces had less luck gaining matching funds for contributions received in the spring through three rock concerts. Before approving matching payments for concert tickets, FEC auditors required detailed documentation of each sale to ensure that purchasers understood that they had made a political contribution. The campaign had concert-goers sign a statement verifying their contributions, but many filled out the cards improperly (such as one signed by Donald Duck). Furthermore, tickets purchased with cash or by check payable to a retail ticket dealer were declared ineligible for matching, and eligible purchases were matched only for an amount above the "fair market value"[16] of the ticket. These reductions in expected concert profits angered Brown staffers, and they complained that the commission examined their concert receipts more closely than those of other campaigns.

The FEC in its audit found that the committee had paid from matching funds $306 in parking fines issued at a rally in Multnomah County, Oregon. Since the FEC held that these expenditures were not a "qualified campaign expense," the committee refunded the money to the U.S. Treasury.[17]

Fund Raising. The lateness of Brown's announcement shaped fund raising as well as compliance. For a while, the governor considered declining matching funds, as he had done with Secret Service protection, to symbolize his fiscal conservatism, but Brown decided that the lack of time required acceptance of public monies. Direct mail was tested but the response rate was not high enough to warrant further mailings. The Brown committee raised most of its funds by personal solicitations, events, and rock concerts.

Brown qualified for matching funds in one month, largely through the personal efforts of friends and committee members and the help of networks of past supporters, most notably the American Federation of Teachers and Cesar Chavez' United Farm Workers. Fund-raisers found the threshold amount easily obtainable in eight states but more demanding in the others, although in its initial submission the committee was qualified in 22 states.

At a variety of fund-raising events across California and the nation, Brown proved to be an engaging speaker. Brown's drawing power raised money quickly by way of a series of $1,000-a-plate dinners. The campaign also held less formal and expensive affairs, such as a $25-per-person party hosted by Hugh Hefner at the *Playboy* entrepreneur's Los Angeles estate.

Rock concerts offered a unique method of collecting large sums rapidly, and the youngest presidential aspirant was successful with them. Aided by the persuasiveness of Jeff Wald, husband and manager of Helen Reddy, and Ted Ashley, chairman of Warner Brothers Inc., the Brown campaign secured volunteer concerts by rock artists Linda Ronstadt, Jackson Browne, and The Eagles. These acts performed a total of four concerts, three during the prenomination campaign and one after. The Capital Centre in Landover, Maryland, housed one show that grossed about $165,000. A performance in Anaheim, California, brought in $50,000, and a Fresno concert cosponsored with Sen. John V. Tunney, D-Calif., yielded $25,000 for the Brown committee. The fourth concert, held in November 1976 at Hartford, Connecticut, raised $80,000 to help erase debts. The gross concert receipts of $320,000 represented more than one-fourth of all contributions. However, expenses for the four shows totaled approximately $135,000, leaving net receipts of about $185,000. High costs of auditorium rental and related expenses and the low matching for concert tickets reduced the expected value of the Brown benefit performances.

In general, the Brown staff considered raising funds to be most encouraging following the governor's announcement, difficult after Carter's win in Pennsylvania and easy again after Brown's dramatic victory in Maryland. The cutoff of matching funds left Brown unscathed because his committee was not prepared to make submissions until the FEC was reconstituted in late May. At that time, the Brown forces had raised approximately $600,000. Fund raising continued for over a year, and by mid-1977 Brown for President had collected an additional $570,000. Of the first $1,170,000 raised in private funds, 37 percent came in contributions of $500 or more, reflecting the importance of big money in a last-minute campaign. Yet Brown relied heavily on small contributors, with 43 percent of contributions (including concerts) received in sums of $100 or less. The committee estimated that more than 80 percent of contributions came from California.

Other sources of income played a vital role in launching and maintaining the Brown drive. Matching funds of $600,204 constituted more than one-third of total receipts. Also, the committee secured bank loans with anticipated matching funds and concert receipts as collateral. Three loans yielding a gross total of $375,000 were repaid by 1977.

Still outstanding were debts totaling more than $140,000. These debts were reduced by payments when new money came in, and by settlements with several creditors. New income was produced in 1978 when fund-raising events were held in private homes in Los Angeles and San Francisco. About $9,000 was contributed by labor political committees, bringing 1978 income to about $75,000. One large debt of $120,804, owed to the accounting firm of Laventhol and Horwath, was settled for $78,000 pending FEC approval that the work done was for compliance purposes and thus exempt from consideration as a contribution; the accounting firm took the reduction when persuaded that time taken to educate personnel to new laws and procedures should not be billed as services rendered. Another bill for about $34,000, owed to Barry E. Wagman, a political accountant, was settled for about $25,000, also pending FEC approval.

Costs. The crash nature of the Brown campaign led to heavy expenditures of $1.9 million despite the brevity of the effort. Outlays for media and fund raising were high, as were expenditures in the states where Brown actively competed. California, Maryland, Oregon, and New York attracted the largest expenditures.

The May 18 Maryland primary offered Governor Brown's first test at the polls. Maryland's secretary of state had placed Brown's name on the ballot and the campaign did not act to remove it; neither did the committee file a slate of delegate candidates committed to Brown. The candidate first visited the state in late April and the enthusiasm he engendered prompted comparisons with John Kennedy's charisma. The Democratic organization of Gov. Marvin Mandel capitalized on Brown's attractiveness in an attempt to slow the Carter momentum. Mandel and his followers lavishly praised the Californian, while party regulars persuaded some uncommitted delegates to come out for Brown. Carter accused Brown, the apostle of new leadership, of hypocrisy for accepting the Maryland machine's support. Brown strategists deflected the criticism with television and radio advertisements stressing the governor's progressive accomplishments in California. The heavy media drive began three weeks before the primary date and cost at least $90,000 of the total Maryland expenditures of $267,000. The combination of Brown-mania and organizational strength brought the newcomer a popular vote triumph of 48.3 percent to 36.9 over Carter. The come-from-behind win catapulted Brown into prominence for the remaining elections.

Next, Brown shifted his attention to Oregon where his committee was feverishly organizing a write-in campaign for the May 25 voting. Brown spent almost a week in California's northern neighbor, while more than 500 volunteers prepared and disseminated leaflets and direct-mail advertisements concerning write-in procedures. The campaign tried to place write-in information in every Democratic home in the state with printed material and television and newspaper ads. As a reminder, Brown workers had intended to hand each voter a pencil at the polls, but the committee learned such a practice violated state law. The massive education process in Oregon cost $170,000, but failed to deliver the hoped-for miracle. Brown finished third behind Church and Carter with a not unimpressive 23.3 percent vote. Brown fared better on the same day in Nevada where he spent $29,000 to capture 53 percent of the ballots cast.

The following week, in an impulsive decision, Governor Brown canceled three days of work in his home state and flew to Rhode Island to stump for the uncommitted slate. The Brown committee purchased a media blitz worth at least $25,000 to support the uncommitted delegate candidates who had endorsed Brown. Total spending in the tiny state came to $65,000 and helped the slate upset Carter's delegates by 1.5 percentage points.

Before the final primaries, Brown followers in New York initiated a behind-the-scenes program to win the backing of the state's uncommitted delegates and committed delegates whose candidates had dropped out of the race. Brown for President expended some $114,000 in New York, although delegate-hunting took a small portion of the total compared to fund raising and convention expenses. Other inexpensive delegate searches took place in Colorado and Utah.

In New Jersey, Brown once again relied on uncommitted delegates, though this time the slate endorsed Brown and Senator Humphrey jointly. Brown made appearances in the state from mid-May until the June 8 voting, and in the last week of the drive, the candidate's father, former California Governor "Pat" Brown, stumped across New Jersey. The Brown committee maximized news coverage of the candidate to keep down media costs. The committee's total expenditure of $20,000 was surpassed by the estimated $100,000 spent by the Democratic organization on behalf of its delegate slate. The dual allegiance of the "uncommitted" bloc notwithstanding, Brown claimed victory in New Jersey as his side won 82 delegates compared to Carter's 25.

His successful forays outside of California virtually guaranteed Brown a large majority of votes at home. Spending in California reached $668,000, although about half of this amount went into the state campaign and the remainder covered operation of the national headquarters. In the final primary, Brown won 59 percent of the vote for 204 delegates and a base of power at the convention.

The Brown for President Committee did not release a functional breakdown of expenditures, but certain costs can be estimated. FEC filings showed fund-raising costs of $315,000 with concert expenses accounting for nearly half of this figure. The brevity of the campaign necessitated large outlays for media in the states. In addition, Governor Brown made a half-hour appearance on network television on June 25 to conclude his quest for the nomination. The candidate used the opportunity, not to concede Carter's triumph, but to reiterate the Brown mixture of liberalism and conservatism, thus seeking to solidify his position in the party. The Brown committee paid $125,000 for the broadcast — $85,000 to NBC for air time, $25,000 for production, and $15,000 for promotion of the program. Some campaign operatives have said this broadcast was the cause of Brown's deficit and they could not understand why he undertook it. This one expense combined with advertising in the states placed the media budget close to $400,000. A paid staff numbering 32 and other workers who were reimbursed for expenses probably put the total payroll at more than $100,000. Accounting and compliance costs were approximately $180,000, including some staff expenses. Travel and office expenses most likely captured the lion's share of remaining funds. One notable outlay is the Brown committee's payment of transportation and expenses to the Democratic convention for 10 California delegates of limited personal means.

As of May 1977 the Brown for President Committee reported expenditures of $1,746,924, exclusive of $143,316 in debts, bringing total spending to $1,890,240.[18] Later filings showed spending reached $2.2 million.

Byrd

Senator Robert Byrd of West Virginia officially entered the Democratic presidential race on January 9, 1976. Just a few days before, the Senate majority whip had authorized the Robert C. Byrd for President Committee to raise and spend funds in his behalf. Byrd's entrance followed months of hinting that he would accept a place on the party ticket if, as the senator anticipated, a deadlocked convention were in need of a compromise candidate. To gain a power base, Byrd sought control of West Virginia's 33 delegates, leading most observers to label him as a favorite-son candidate. However, Byrd considered entering primaries other than that of his home state on May 11 and, when announcing, he declared, "I'm a national candidate for the national ticket."[19] Lending credibility to this claim, the Byrd committee from its Washington headquarters raised at least $5,000 in each of 20 states and thereby qualified for matching funds. Nonetheless, Senator Byrd chose not to apply for federal subsidies because his spending projections diminished as Carter emerged as the likely nominee.

The enigma of Byrd's presidential candidacy did not reduce his popularity at home. While also running for renomination to his Senate seat, Byrd polled 89 percent of the preference vote in West Virginia, compared with 11 percent for George Wallace. The senator's name also appeared on the ballot in Florida and Georgia, but in these states he made no effort and won less than 1 percent of the ballots cast. The Byrd for President Committee spent quite freely and total costs for the limited operation came to $148,264 with no debts.

Of course, a brokered convention never materialized and Senator Byrd's West Virginia delegation went into Jimmy Carter's column. Yet, assisted by his venture into the national spotlight, Byrd did rise to the position of Senate majority leader in the 1977 session.

Carter

In two years' time, a former naval officer, peanut farmer, and governor of Georgia propelled himself from obscurity to the presidency of the United States. Jimmy Carter commenced a quiet campaign to gain national recognition shortly after the 1972 election, and the Committee for Jimmy Carter began raising funds in 1974. Governor Carter officially announced his candidacy on December 12, 1974, and 17 primary victories and $12.4 million later, the man from Plains claimed the Democratic presidential nomination.

Unlike his competitors, Carter presumed that a first-ballot nomination was possible and, accordingly, he ran in all but one primary and most of the caucus states as well. His pluralities in the Iowa caucuses and the New Hampshire primary established Carter as the front-runner. Later defeats in Massachusetts and New York were offset by key triumphs over George Wallace in Florida and Henry Jackson in Pennsylvania. In May and June, Carter entered a slump, suffering eight losses to newcomers Frank Church and Jerry Brown. However, the "run everywhere" strategy reaped a fair number of delegates for the Georgian even when he lost. With an impressive win in Ohio on June 8, Carter held about 1,100 delegates and consequent endorsements from Wallace, Jackson, and Chicago Mayor Richard J. Daley ensured his nomination.

The Carter financial drive, while always sound, had been unspectacular until the candidate demonstrated his popularity at the polls. After Carter's early victories, both fund raising and spending accelerated rapidly. In spite of the multifront strategy, the Carter committee targeted the most important primary states for the heaviest spending. Like the political aspect of Carter's bid, the financial operation, under the direction of Treasurer Robert J. Lipshutz, displayed an extraordinary degree of foresight and daring. Although the campaign went deep into debt during the period when matching funds were not available, the committee closed its books with a surplus and transferred

$300,000 to the 1976 Democratic Presidential Campaign Committee's compliance fund.

A vital part of the Carter success story is the FECA. Without stringent contribution limits, better-known candidates who had connections with wealthy contributors could have swamped Carter; and without federal subsidies, Carter would have lacked the money to consolidate his initial lead. Fortunately, the Carter committee made public a most comprehensive financial summary of its winning campaign.

Compliance. The compliance operation of the Committee for Jimmy Carter started small and burgeoned as the candidate triumphed at the polls. At the outset of the campaign, the committee rented office space from the law firm of Treasurer Robert Lipshutz, and the national headquarters grew to occupy offices in three buildings near the original site.

Early in 1975 the committee contracted with Arthur Andersen & Co. for the design of a system based on FEC reporting requirements that ensured cash control. During 1975 a volunteer CPA, assisted by two clerical workers, managed the bookkeeping system and the contribution records on a manual basis. Late in that year, the committee decided to computerize the finances, and it hired two former Andersen accountants to automate the contributor list and other data. Another accountant came aboard to supervise spending by state organizations.

To ensure the legality of contributions, paid clerks and volunteers screened checks, edited computer printouts, and mailed form letters to contributors if additional information was needed. At the close of the campaign, the compliance staff had returned $105,600 in contributions for actual or potential legal violations. Some of the contributions were returned because checks were drawn from questionable sources, but most were rejected because the contributor already had reached the $1,000 maximum. In addition, the campaign returned checks totaling $52,500 because certain contributors stopped payment and others lacked sufficient funds in their accounts.

In legal matters, the campaign could depend on two members of the nonsalaried executive committee — Lipshutz and Charles Kirbo, Carter's mentor and confidante. Several lawyers from Lipshutz' firm volunteered their services when needed, and the campaign paid one attorney to oversee the delegate selection process and another to deal with the FEC.

The national compliance staff had trouble properly recording expenditures made by the state and local organizations, which did not report directly to the FEC. Well after Carter won the nomination, his committee was amending its reports because of newly discovered spending by field groups. Most discrepancies had been cleared up by the fall of

1976, and none of them warranted legal penalties. A more serious difficulty arose when the headquarters found that about 10 field organizations had opened unauthorized checking accounts. Campaign officials ordered that the accounts be closed and determined that funding of and spending from the accounts was within the law.

One of the campaign's innovative approaches to fund raising attracted the scrutiny of the FEC. The Carter committee proposed to have farmers donate cotton and poultry that the campaign would sell to businesses. The FEC permitted this practice by ruling that the sellers of goods were the contributors. The commission calculated the amount of a contribution at the current market price of the commodity, and ensured that no individual contributed more than $1,000 worth of a good. Not wishing to press its luck, the campaign decided against applying for a match of the commodities contributed.

The FEC also acted favorably upon a request to extend the time in which the committee could accept contributions. The campaign feared that a candidate could accept no contributions or matching funds after he achieved nomination, even for expenses incurred before the party convention. Stressing that the Republican convention followed that of the Democrats by one month, Carter lawyers asked the commission to interpret the law in a manner that would allow income to flow until all debts were removed. The commission did so, but the interpretation proved superfluous because "smart money" flooded the campaign well before the convention. In fact, private contributions more than covered debts and the committee agreed to decline more than $700,000 in deserved matching funds. In turn, the commissioners approved the transfer of $300,000 from the Committee for Jimmy Carter to the compliance fund for the general election, the 1976 Democratic Presidential Campaign Committee Inc.

At the height of the contest, in May 1976, the compliance operation had become a major undertaking. The campaign maintained 80 bank accounts in the field and six in Atlanta. Compliance and administrative personnel numbered about 60. Excluding salaries and overhead, compliance cost at least $348,900. A more inclusive calculation of compliance expenditures would double this figure.

(The Carter general election section in this book, Chapter 7, discusses FEC audits of the Carter campaigns.)

Fund Raising. A comparatively small base of contributions financed Carter's early political success. Indeed, many observers discounted Carter's chances for the nomination largely because he trailed candidates such as Jackson and Bentsen in receipts. Yet each victory at the polls increased contributions which then facilitated later electoral triumphs.

Fund-raising efforts in 1974 collected $46,723, most of the money coming from friends and past supporters at a pool party hosted by Atlanta real estate man Bill Schwartz. Carter placed a voluntary limit of $1,000 on contributions received before the FECA Amendments compelled such a limitation starting January 1, 1975. The governor castigated opponents Jackson and Bentsen for their $3,000 maximum. This attack was somewhat unfair since the two senators had begun campaigning at a time when the Senate had set the $3,000 amount in an election bill, before both houses jointly set the lower limit. Also in 1974, Carter cultivated a group of potential monetary supporters when he served as chairman of the Democratic Campaign Committee. The position introduced the unannounced presidential candidate to party leaders as he stumped for congressional candidates in 32 states. The governor's aides meticulously copied names and addresses of the party faithful who later would receive pleas for funds. In December, Carter mailed contribution requests to about 30,000 Georgians and 500,000 other Americans whose names were taken from lists of Carter contacts, McGovern 1972 backers and contributors to the Democratic National Committee.

In 1975, with his gubernatorial term completed and his younger brother minding the family peanut business, Carter could campaign full time. He traveled more than 250 days in the year, making appeals for funds and trying to improve a name recognition factor of 2 percent. In the first six months of the year, Carter raised $331,605. To supplement candidate appearances, "Project 20" was launched, a program concentrating mailings and personal solicitations in the southern and early-primary states so that Carter would qualify for matching funds. He attained eligibility for federal monies in August. From January through December of 1975, the campaign raised approximately $850,000.

After November, the Carter organization began to utilize a few fund-raising techniques that offered public relations value as well as immediate monetary gain. A "Cotton for Carter" drive involved a truck driving from California to Atlanta, stopping en route to pick up private contributions of cotton bales. This cotton caravan brought in about $100,000. Other similar programs sought poultry and beef as donations. The campaign also sold Carter-related items, such as gold peanuts and the candidate's autobiography, *Why Not the Best?*, for cash contributions. In late November a series of concerts featuring southern rock musicians opened. The Marshall Tucker, Charlie Daniels, and Allman Brothers bands staged four shows that grossed $138,200 but only netted $33,900 exclusive of later matching grants. Another concert in July 1976 ran a deficit of $13,100. The estimated match for all five concerts was $142,700, making the rock series moderately profitable. In February 1976

Carter participated in a "Georgia Loves Jimmy" telethon carried by TV stations in his native state. The four-hour program combined speeches by the candidate and reports from campaign officials with appearances by singers Gregg Allman and James Brown, baseball stars Hank Aaron and Phil Niekro, and comedian and one-time presidential candidate Pat Paulsen. The telethon, which cost about $100,000, raised about $328,000 with matching funds.

The fund drive got a sorely needed lift late in 1975 when Morris Dees, wizard of McGovern direct mail in 1972, became national finance chairman.[20] Dees chose not to make direct mail the cornerstone of Carter fund raising because he felt that direct mail would not be so productive for a centrist candidate like Carter as it had been for an ideological and issue-oriented candidate such as Senator McGovern. Nonetheless, Dees and his staff formulated several profitable mailings, concentrating on individuals who already had given, although some "prospecting" of nondonors occurred. One innovative appeal to contributors of $100 or more asked them to "double up" and match their previous gifts. The letter, mailed to about 1,900 individuals, brought in an estimated $300,000 and cost only $3,500. Similar requests for repeat gifts from smaller contributors continued throughout the spring of 1976. By May some 40,000 people had given by direct mail, and Dees calculated that about one-third of all private contributions, or more than $2.5 million, came in via direct mail. The campaign did not isolate the postage involved in direct mail, but calculated that mailing lists rental, computer time, and labels cost $163,400.

Dees made the foundation of the fund-raising effort a network of finance committees in "every city of significant size," members raising money through personal contacts and events. The new contribution limits created an emphasis on events with low set-up costs, especially cocktail parties and breakfasts, as opposed to expensive dinners. For example, a breakfast in New York sponsored by Cyrus R. Vance, Henry Luce III, and C. Douglas Dillon raised $75,000 at a cost of $5,000. The finance committees scheduled many $50 and $100 gatherings at which Carter appeared. In a three-week period in April, Carter attended 10 such events. The five cocktail parties, three dinners, and two breakfasts grossed approximately $190,000.

Moreover, Carter came to command contributions above $100 from wealthy backers. For instance, Max Palevsky hosted a $1,000-a-couple dinner in his Malibu mansion that raised $25,000, and in Princeton, New Jersey, Blair Clark, editor of *The Nation,* and his sister, state Sen. Anne Martindell, held a $250-per-person party to raise $20,000 for media use in the state. Reportedly, businessman Michael A. Taylor gathered some $150,000 from Wall Street executives late in the campaign.

Table 5-5
Breakdown of Expenditures, 'Birch Bayh in 1976' Committee

Payroll	$ 356,391
Travel	256,670
Promotional material	171,958
Rent and telephone	175,200
Media	113,818
Postage and mailing	73,051
Professional fees	69,500
Office supplies	50,675
Data processing	43,847
Equipment rental	39,017
Insurance, taxes, licenses, etc.	3,989
Miscellaneous	19,965
Total	$1,374.081

Before Carter took a firm lead in the Democratic scramble, much of the monetary support came from Georgia, generally in smaller contributions. In 1975, nearly half of individual contribution receipts came from Georgians. By March 31, 1976, Georgians were still the major factor in the fund drive, with 37 percent of a contribution total of $2,047,500 coming from Carter's home state. The average contribution from Georgia was $50.71; by contrast, money that arrived later from the traditionally big-money states of New York and California made for average contributions of $108.72 and $82.26, respectively. When Carter desperately needed money for the Pennsylvania primary, Georgians responded with $270,000 of contributions in April.

Indeed, the citizens and institutions of Georgia treated their favorite son well, most notably between March 22 and May 23 when the FEC could not certify matching funds. In that time, when 32 primaries, caucuses, and state conventions were held, the Carter organization weathered the financial storm better than the opposing campaigns, aided by a number of revolving loans from commercial banks. In March and April the Carter committee borrowed a total of $175,000 from the Citizens and Southern Bank of Atlanta, with security of receivables from the press and Secret Service for transportation charges. Based on Carter's personal wealth, a $100,000 loan was secured in April from the Fulton National Bank of Atlanta.

In May the campaign borrowed another $500,000 from Fulton National, using pending matching funds as collateral. The banks checked the committee's records before lending and approved the loans under normal receivable arrangements. The campaign repaid a total of $1,569,700 in June and July for all bank loans. Carter also benefited from loans secured from individuals. The committee secured 192 loans from individuals that totaled $144,400, and by campaign's end $114,300 was repaid and $30,100 was converted to contributions. Officials also delayed paying bills to friendly vendors when necessary. Several Georgia businesses, notably two printing companies, had supplied services to Carter's gubernatorial bids and were willing to extend some credit until payment of matching funds resumed. Carter's media firm, Gerald Rafshoon Advertising, allegedly was owed more than $645,000 at one point in the spring. In spite of regular partial remuneration from the committee, the agency had to obtain its own outside financing to handle the credit arrangement.

Primary and caucus victories shortly before and during the matching funds cutoff generated a steady increase in contributions to Carter. In the first month of 1976, Carter showed receipts of about $125,000 and in February, contributions totaled $400,000. The monthly figure for March rose to $612,000, while in April, individuals gave $732,000. May's receipts topped $1 million. Not surprisingly, more money was raked in between April 1 and June 8, 1976, than from January 1, 1975, through March 31, 1976 ($3,839,100 compared with $2,047,500).

Increasing contributions and the resumption of federal payments only partially compensated for vigorous spending. On June 1, 1976, the campaign owed more than $1 million. To erase debts, the committee planned a string of fund-raisers between the last June 8 primaries and the Democratic convention. Across the country, Carter attended 16 events, including ones in Dallas, Washington, Miami, and New Orleans. In Chicago, Mayor Daley hosted a dinner attended by 4,000 people, and at a luncheon in Houston, Carter spoke before 130 oil business people who together gave about $50,000. Two fund-raisers in Boston brought Carter another $75,000. In the Democrats' convention city of New York, the nominee-to-be attended a $1,000-per-person reception and a $100-per-person cocktail party, and then accepted nearly $12,000 from a group of Puerto Rican supporters. After the June 8 primaries, the campaign received from private sources $3,053,100 or 38.4 percent of all individual contributions.

Prior to June 8 the campaign received little money from political action committees. In the first four months of 1976 the Carter camp took in $20,500 from such committees, and in May it collected $36,800 from PACs. However, after Carter's Ohio triumph, political action committees donated $210,000. Among the corporate committees contributing to Carter were groups affiliated with Lockheed Aircraft, Kennecott Copper, the Southern Railway, and General Electric. Carter received the maximum contribution of $5,000 from the PAC of the Mid-America Dairymen and that of the Associated Milk Producers. Union political funds that assisted Carter were those of the United Automobile Workers, the

American Federation of State, County, and Municipal Employees, the Communications Workers of America, the National Association of Letter Carriers, and the United Transportation Workers. The Amalgamated Clothing Workers' fund gave the $5,000 limit. Late giving by these groups may have reflected their desire to contribute to a proven winner. The PAC total to Carter of $310,600 constitutes only 3.7 percent of all contribution receipts.

Total receipts of the Committee for Jimmy Carter as of October 31, 1976, can be summarized as follows:

Contributions	
Individuals	$ 7,939,700
Political action committees	310,600
Total	$ 8,250,300
Loans	
Individuals	$ 114,400
Banks	1,569,700
Total	$ 1,684,100
Matching funds	$ 3,465,585
Miscellaneous refunds received	$ 203,000
Total	$13,602,985

These figures do not account for a cash balance of $150,000 on March 31, 1977. The campaign kept this reserve for several disputed bills; after settlement of all accounts, the campaign would return the remainder to the U.S. Treasury.

Of the matching funds total, $1,078,500 was received before the March 22 cutoff date, and $2,387,585 was accepted after May 24 when the FEC renewed payments. Federal subsidies comprised slightly less than 30 percent of all income. The portion of public money could have been higher, but the committee declined matching funds of $738,100.

In private funds, the campaign received 145,200 contributions from 112,300 individuals. Some 2,200 people donated the maximum of $1,000, and 139,200 contributions were in denominations of less than $250. The average contribution was $54.68, while the average contributor gave about $70.70.[21] Table 5-6, which lists the 15 states whose residents gave the most to Carter, shows Georgia, New York, California, Florida, and Texas leading in contributions. Georgia's $1,577,200 constitutes almost 20 percent of all individual contributions and exceeds the sum of the New York and California figures. The campaign calculated that fund raising, exclusive of pertinent salaries, cost about $1,234,000 or about 10 percent of all expenditures. Table 5-7, which reports a breakdown of fund-raising costs, shows that events and postage were the largest expenses in the fund drive.

Costs. In his announcement speech, Jimmy Carter predicted that his presidential bid would display "a minimum of expenditures and a maximum of contact with voters."[22] Following this dictum, the Carter committee spent cautiously until early 1976 when it went for broke to win the nomination for its candidate. By the end of 1975 the committee had spent less than $1 million, but in 1976 it expended nearly $12 million.

Table 5-6
Receipts by State to the Committee for Jimmy Carter

	Receipts
California	$ 641,600
District of Columbia	236,500
Florida	534,700
Georgia	1,577,200
Illinois	318,900
Maryland	141,100
Massachusetts	167,600
Michigan	128,300
New Hampshire	14,800
New Jersey	269,500
New York	804,500
Ohio	255,000
Pennsylvania	234,100
Texas	394,400
Wisconsin	52,700
All other states	2,168,800
Total	$7,939,700

Table 5-7
Fund-Raising Expenses of the Committee for Jimmy Carter

	Amount	Percentage
Printing costs	$ 171,400	13.9
Postage and delivery	186,500	15.1
Meetings, fund-raising events, concert expenses	543,200	44.0
Mailing list costs	99,700	8.1
Mailing costs (labels and computer time)	63,700	5.2
Sale items: T-shirts, buttons, pins, bumper stickers	56,700	4.6
Telethon costs	100,000	8.1
Other	12,800	1.0
Total fund-raising expenses	$1,234,000	100.0

In 1974, while still an unofficial candidate, Carter gained free publicity as chairman of the Democratic Campaign Commitee. When on the hustings for House candidates, and indirectly advancing his own interests, Carter and his aides charged expenses totaling $8,000 to the DNC.

From its inception in the fall of 1974 until October 1975, the Committee for Jimmy Carter spent $536,800. The bulk of early spending went toward fund raising and travel for Carter and staff. In July 1975 the committee had only $8,600 on hand and in November it showed a balance of $15,000. To ease cash flow, several top officials went off salary for a few months until matching funds became available in 1976. At the end of 1975 the committee reported expenditures to date of $978,016.

The arrival of Morris Dees and federal subsidies permitted the campaign to spend more freely. In the first three months of 1976 about $2 million was spent, with large and successful investments in the New Hampshire and Florida primaries. When the FEC suspended subsidies, the Carter operation showed a net deficit of $567,800, cutting media and state budgets, deferring hiring, but nevertheless boldly running up debts. The Carter forces borrowed heavily and counted on Carter's rising popularity to eventually attract enough money to cover expenditures. In April the net deficit nearly topped $1 million, and the financial staff simply "sat on" most bills, as one administrator said. At the end of May accounts payable stood at $1.3 million, and the deficit reached its height of $1,684,800. The resumption of matching payments and a deluge of contributions in May, June, and July vindicated the deficit spending. In fact, the committee had a surplus of almost $450,000 in July.

The best understanding of Carter's spending and electoral success lies in the fight in the states. National headquarters officials, in conjunction with Gerald Rafshoon and state coordinators, set flexible budgets for media and other expenditures in the important states. At the close of the campaign the Carter committee had allocated $6,112,400, almost half of all expenditures, to the effort in the states.

In Iowa, the first test of the 1976 hopefuls, Carter relied on a very efficient organization and a myriad of personal appearances to appeal to caucus voters. Shortly before the January 19 voting, media advisers discovered the low local broadcast rates and produced four five-minute TV commercials and several 60-second radio spots at an estimated broadcast cost of $11,000, almost one-third of total expenditures of about $35,000. Carter augmented the grass-roots and media approaches when he hedged on the abortion issue by telling a Catholic newspaper that he would support some sort of "national statute" restricting abortion. Although this statement seemingly contradicted Carter's opposition to an antiabortion amendment to the Constitution, he won much of the Catholic vote. Some 45,000 Democrats turned out for the Iowa caucuses and 37 percent of them voted uncommitted, yet Jimmy Carter grabbed national attention and front-runner status with 27.6 percent of the ballots cast.

The powerful combination of personal contact and media concentration next came to New Hampshire. In January 90 Georgians flew to the state to spend a week vouching for the achievements of their former governor. Members of this "Peanut Brigade" paid their own way, and after returning home they sent 6,000 personal letters to the New Hampshire voters they had met. Of the folksy operation, Campaign Manager Hamilton Jordan stated, "Those Georgians gave Jimmy a lead in New Hampshire that was never lost."[23] In addition the campaign spent $70,400 for media, with radio taking not quite half of the figure. Telephone canvassing cost $20,800 and polling $4,500. All other expenses came to $113,000 for a total of $208,700 in New Hampshire expenditures. In spite of pointed attacks by the other candidates, Carter refused to criticize his opponents by name. His soft-spoken manner helped Carter poll 29.4 percent of the vote, leading Udall by 4,301 ballots.

One week later, on March 2, Carter's momentum slowed in Massachusetts, where for the first time he faced sizable conservative opposition from both George Wallace and Henry Jackson. Originally, campaign strategists had decided to make little effort in the Bay State, and the candidate himself spent but 90 hours there. Encouraged by the New Hampshire results, however, Carter's subordinates made a last-minute media blitz costing $60,200. Jackson, Udall, and Bayh attacked Carter for proposing to eliminate the tax deduction on home mortgages as part of an overall tax reform program. The misunderstanding that developed over tax reform, Carter's late start, and an election day snow storm, all contributed to a crushing defeat for the Georgian. He placed fourth, behind Jackson, Udall, and Wallace, with only 14.2 percent of the vote. The results in neighboring Vermont consoled the campaign somewhat. There, Carter won handily over Sargent Shriver after spending more than $25,000.

After the loss in Massachusetts, Carter desperately needed to beat Wallace in Florida, the first southern primary. Carter had been working the state for months in his gracious, personable style. Relatives and perhaps 1,000 volunteers from Georgia had crossed the border to politick in Florida. Just before the March 9 voting, Carter took off the gloves, openly disparaging Wallace and Jackson. Once again, the grass-roots approach was combined with the hard sell, including $276,900 worth of radio and television, and $40,200 for telephone canvassing. Total expenditures in Florida, which reached $567,800, showed results, for Carter took 34.3 percent of the vote, leaving Wallace and Jackson well behind.

The following week in Illinois, Carter made a significant dent in the favorite-son candidacy of Sen. Adlai E. Stevenson III. While not running delegates in Chicago, where Mayor Daley's slate backed Stevenson, Carter campaigned hard in the rest of the state and spent $127,300. Over one-third of expenditures, $49,900, went to the media. In the "beauty contest" vote, Carter took 48 percent, beating Wallace almost 2-to-1; but more important, the Georgian picked up a surprising 55 delegates, while Senator Stevenson won 30.

On March 23 in North Carolina, Carter virtually ended the White House hopes of George Wallace. The Carter committee poured more than $100,000 into the primary after former North Carolina Gov. Terry Sanford withdrew from the presidential race. Carter won 53.6 percent of the vote compared with 34.7 percent for the Alabaman.

The formidable Carter machine then turned to the primaries in New York and Wisconsin on April 6. In both states, Carter started from behind and barely escaped disaster. At first, the Carter camp tried to downplay the importance of the New York primary because delegates' names appeared on the ballot without indicating the candidate to whom they were committed. This system prompted a rash of challenges to Carter delegate petitions, especially from Jackson who hoped to minimize the competition to his slates. In February a group of Carter supporters challenged New York's ballot format in federal court, but the case became moot three weeks before election day when the state legislature changed the law and placed candidates' names with their delegates on the ballot. This change did not alter the Carter strategy, which concentrated on upstate New York and essentially conceded New York City to Jackson, who had campaigned there the longest. The Carter organization spent $463,900 in New York, with $92,400 going to media; about half of the media budget was spent upstate. The spending failed to improve Carter's position, for he finished fourth with 13 percent of the delegates. Jackson, however, fell well short of the majority that he had predicted and thereby appeared to be less of a challenge to Carter.

The Carter strategy envisioned Wisconsin as the final blow for Morris Udall. To ensure victory, Carter spent $197,500. Of the total, media captured $53,600, telephone canvassing cost $25,500, and polling expenses came to $13,900. Yet Udall took the lead in early balloting and much of the press projected the Arizona congressman as the winner until late returns from rural areas gave Carter a 1 percent edge. The narrow margin left Udall in the race but, fortunately for Carter, the drama it created overshadowed the New York defeat.

Unlike candidates Jackson and Udall, Carter tried to conserve funds in New York and Wisconsin. Treasurer Lipshutz purposely kept a lid on spending to leave enough money for Pennsylvania on April 27, the keystone of the nomination drive. The loans that the Carter committee secured purchased 10 days of unchallenged media in the state. In addition, Finance Chairman Dees pressed his field committees and gathered about $300,000 for other needs in Pennsylvania. The sound financial position might have gone for naught when the candidate made his most serious blunder of the prenomination period. In an interview in early April, Carter stated that he opposed federal efforts to destroy the "ethnic purity" of neighborhoods. Strong reaction from black leaders and white liberals caused Carter to apologize for his choice of offensive language and to clarify his position on public housing. By the Pennsylvania election, voters seemed to have forgiven the gaffe, as Carter carried the state with 37.2 percent. Carter's expenditure of $464,700 far outdistanced the spending of his rivals. The committee spent $140,100 of the total on media, $121,300 for telephone canvassing, and $9,700 for polling. Over half of the media budget went to 30- and 60-second television commercials that attempted to refute the charge that Carter was "fuzzy" on the issues. To counter Jackson's party organization and labor endorsements, the campaign employed 100 phone banks to foster support in both Philadelphia and Pittsburgh.

After Pennsylvania, Carter continued his winning ways in two states that had produced one-time opponents. In Texas, Sen. Lloyd Bentsen ran a rather listless favorite-son campaign and took only eight delegates. Carter grabbed 122 after spending $199,500. In Indiana, former presidential candidate Sen. Birch Bayh endorsed Carter shortly before the state primary. The Carter committee reported expenditures of $75,700 in Indiana, where the Georgian won 68 percent of the vote.

Then the campaign entered a downswing beginning on May 11 in Nebraska. Carter spent one day in Nebraska and expended only $50,000, paying little attention to newly announced candidate Sen. Frank Church of Idaho. Church, however, stumped long and hard in the state and went on to win by fewer than 2,000 votes with 39 percent. Church's win opened the way for the other newcomer, California Governor Jerry Brown, to deal the next blow to Carter in Maryland. Trying earnestly to regain his momentum in the May 18 Maryland voting, Carter attacked Brown and the state organization supporting him, scheduled more appearances and shifted massive funds into media. Expenditures came to $211,700, with media making up over half of the total. Nonetheless, Brown devastated Carter by 48.3 percent to 36.9 in the popular vote. Results on the same day in Michigan hardly compensated. There Carter won his third narrow victory over Mo Udall, by 43.5 to 43.2 percent, at a total cost of $169,100.

The next important primary took place in Oregon in May 25. Although not favored to win, Carter fought hard to make a respectable showing, and he spent more than $94,000, mostly close to election day. Church and Brown, who was running a write-in campaign, imported substantial troops of volunteers from their respective neighboring states, yet Carter took a solid second to Church and beat the Brown write-in by 3 percentage points. In spite of the shortage of first-place finishes, Carter gradually was increasing the number of delegates committed to him. After Oregon, he held nearly 1,000 delegates, about two-thirds of the number needed to win the nomination.

Remaining was the final crucial primary day — June 8, the so-called Super Bowl with 540 delegates at stake in New Jersey, California, and Ohio. In New Jersey, Carter faced the challenge of a supposedly uncommitted slate of delegates that actually ran under the dual banner of Hubert Humphrey and Jerry Brown. Organized by state Democratic Chairman James P. Dugan, the "uncommitted" slate was the only practical outcome of several attempts at an "Anybody But Carter" movement. Carter attacked Dugan's strange ploy, and in an effort to win as many delegates as possible spent $431,300. Of the New Jersey total, $200,700 went to media, mostly for time on Philadelphia and New York television stations. The spending brought Carter 25 delegates, while the Humphrey-Brown forces captured 82.

Before Jerry Brown announced for the presidential nomination, the Carter campaign had expected to carry California and it spent heavily trying to build an organization. After the popular governor entered the race, the Carter camp began to cut back spending and diverted the candidate's travels to Ohio. As national officials minimized the California effort, internal strife struck the leadership of the state organization. In the end, Carter had spent a total of $653,800 in California with $262,800 devoted to media. Against Brown, Carter won 20.5 percent of the vote and a respectable 67 delegates.

Carter stated that he considered Ohio the true contest of June 8, and he lavished much personal and financial attention on the state. Carter started making personal appearances several weeks before the primary and also abruptly canceled a California trip to do some last-minute politicking in Ohio. He won endorsements from labor in southern Ohio, although Udall gained backing from northern union leaders. Carter received some free favorable publicity near voting day when a Udall delegate came out for him in reaction to Udall's negative advertising. Carter media costs reached $304,000 and total expenditures equaled $533,200. The strenuous effort culminated the prenomination campaign as Carter came away with 52.2 percent of the Ohio vote and 119 delegates. The better-than-expected win in Ohio brought endorsements from Wallace, Jackson, and Mayor Daley, which gave Carter a virtual majority of Democratic delegates.

Table 5-8
Expenditures in 15 States by the Committee for Jimmy Carter[a]

	Media Costs	Polling Costs	Telephone Canvassing	All Other	Total
California	$ 262,800	$ 39,000	$ —	$ 352,000	$ 653,800
Florida	276,900	11,000	40,200	239,700	567,800
Ohio	304,000	17,400	—	211,800	533,200
Pennsylvania	140,100	9,700	121,300	193,600	464,700
New York	92,400	9,800	—	361,700	463,900
New Jersey	200,700	13,900	22,800	193,900	431,300
Maryland	132,700	6,700	47,300	25,000	211,700
New Hampshire	70,400	4,500	20,800	113,000	208,700
Texas	63,000	9,300	—	127,200	199,500
Wisconsin	53,600	13,900	35,500	94,500	197,500
Michigan	78,300	10,000	—	80,800	169,100
Massachusetts	60,200	3,900	—	93,200	157,300
District of Columbia	16,200	—	—	119,000	135,200
Illinois	49,900	6,000	—	71,400	127,300
Georgia	15,600	2,500	—	98,700	116,800
All other states	554,500	90,300	2,800	827,000	1,474,600
Total expenditures allocated	$2,371,300	$247,900	$290,700	$3,202,500	$6,112,400

[a] These figures exclude fund-raising expenses.

Summarizing spending in most of the important states, Table 5-8 shows total expenditures and breakdowns for media, telephone canvassing, and polling in the 15 states that received the largest expenditures. The 15 states captured $4,637,800 in expenses or more than one-third of total spending. The remaining states were allocated a total of $1,474,600. Six states were targeted for intensive telephone canvassing — Ohio, Pennsylvania, New Hampshire, Florida, New Jersey, and Maryland.

Because the Carter effort succeeded, late-in-the-campaign expenses became quite high in comparison with those for the most basic functions. Table 5-9, which reports a breakdown of all spending by the Carter committee, shows that fund raising and compliance were in the end only a small portion of the budget. Direct fund-raising costs reached $1,234,000, while direct compliance costs came to only $348,900. For these functions, overhead and staff expenses are counted in the breakdown of political spending. "Political spending" comprised more than three quarters of the budget at $10,690,300. All media constituted the largest category at a cost of $2,767,900. Travel plus lodging for the candidate and staff equaled $2,117,400, with chartered transport costs totaling $896,500. The campaign actually paid only $302,100 for charter

Table 5-9
Functional Breakdown of Expenditures by the Committee for Jimmy
Carter

Political spending	
Media	$2,767,900
Personal services and related costs	1,642,800
Staff travel, lodging, and other reimbursed expenses	1,220,900
Telephone expense	1,064,600 [a]
Office expenses	865,900
Charter transportation costs	896,500 [b]
Promotional items (buttons, bumper stickers, posters, literature, etc.)	577,400
Convention expenses	509,000
Polling expense	314,900
Telephone canvassing	290,700
Organizational meetings and get-out-the-vote expense	201,700
All other	338,000
Total political spending	10,690,300
Fund-raising costs	1,234,000
Direct compliance costs (excluding personal services and overhead)	348,900
Loans and contributions refunded	
Contributions returned	105,600
Contributor checks returned NSF/stop payment	52,500
Total expenditures	$12,431,300

[a] Includes $153,800 in telephone deposits later returned.
[b] Includes $594,400 later paid to the campaign for the travel of the press and Secret Service.

services because the press and Secret Service reimbursed $594,400 for their travel. The next most expensive function was personnel services, which cost $1,642,800. The committee paid relatively low salaries to its workers; the campaign manager and press secretary were paid less than $17,000 a year, while members of the fund-raising staff received $150 a week plus expenses. Disbursements for all telephone service totaled $1,355,300, although $153,800 of this figure was for returned phone deposits. The campaign paid $290,700 to the NTA Company of New York for telephone canvassing and spent $1,064,600 for inhouse telephone use. The campaign paid $865,900 for office expenses and promotional items, probably mostly printed material, costing $577,400. Pollster Patrick Caddell's firm of Cambridge Survey Research received $314,900 for its services. Organizational meetings and get-out-the-vote expenses totaled $201,700. Finally, the committee also had to cover its expenses at the Democratic National Convention, and it reported spending $509,000 at the New York City gala, which voted a unity platform and featured endorsements from all of Carter's one-time opponents.

Church

"It's never too late — nor are the odds ever too great — to try."[24] So declared Frank Church on March 18, 1976, when the senior senator from Idaho announced his candidacy for the Democratic nomination. Although the Church for President Committee had formed in December with his blessing, Church delayed active campaigning until he completed work as chairman of the Senate Select Committee on Intelligence Gathering Activities. The Idahoan's "late, late strategy" envisioned electoral triumphs in the May primaries of the West leading to further success in Ohio, New Jersey, and California on June 8. Then, if all went according to plan, Church would command enough delegates to be a contender after the first ballot. However, the Church strategy went awry because it failed to predict the rise of Jimmy Carter, the demise of Henry Jackson, the endurance of Morris Udall, or the entrance of Jerry Brown. Nonetheless, Church performed well, winning four out of nine primaries entered. In fund raising, the Church committee suffered from the earlier start of other liberal candidates, but had little time to spend more than was available. Only in the last primaries did the committee spend inadequate sums. One week after a third-place finish in Ohio, Church ended his $1.7 million effort by endorsing Jimmy Carter.

Compliance. In the administration of the Church bid, few difficulties arose thanks to the vast experience of the committee's three officers. The chairman and campaign manager, Carl Burke, had managed all of Church's previous campaigns, while the deputy campaign chairman and finance chairman, Henry L. Kimelman, had served as McGovern's finance chairman in 1972. A New York accountant, William Landau, acted as treasurer and directed the compliance operation. Landau worked at the national headquarters in Washington until the campaign ended, when he moved the records to his Manhattan office. The campaign reimbursed the accounting firm in which Landau is a partner for direct payroll costs and incidental expenses incurred in closing out financial operations. The committee had a staff lawyer on the payroll, who was retained as counsel after headquarters were closed to deal with audits and further legal questions, receiving $5,000 for his postcampaign services.

To assist the volunteer officers, the lawyer served as supervisor of the compliance process. A minimum of three people worked on accounting and reporting matters, with additional volunteers handling the paperwork at busy times. Compliance workers screened checks to eliminate questionable and excess contributions; the campaign returned less than $1,000 in contributions drawn on corporate funds and refunded under $500 to individuals who topped the $1,000 contribution limit. The committee had to forfeit the matching funds to some 500 contributions because contributors never replied to form letters requesting additional information.

The Church organization paid approximately $15,000 to a computer service for automation of the books, the contributor list and FEC reports. However, after the FEC twice rejected Church filings, the campaign switched to a manual system for bookkeeping and reporting, and left only alphabetizing of the contributor list on computer. The manual system comprised about 40 looseleaf binders filled with data on contributions and expenditures.

In its audit of the Church campaign, the FEC found a number of minor violations that subsequently were amended. Irregularities included inadequate disclosure of contributions and contributor information, neglecting to itemize certain receipts, and failure to report fundraising events or a loan from the Idaho for Church Committee, a 1974 senatorial campaign group.

Fund Raising. Church's Senate responsibilities for the Intelligence Committee's hearings and its report hurt fund raising by preventing the senator from campaigning extensively. The delay kept Church out of the primary in Massachusetts, where he had intended to make a dramatic showing that would generate contributions. After Church's announcement, income rose to a satisfactory level although funds were never plentiful.

The Church for President Committee benefited greatly from the contacts made by Kimelman in the McGovern effort four years before. His familiarity with liberal Democratic contributors facilitated Church's achievement of eligibility for matching funds. By mid-February, personal solicitations by Kimelman and his state finance chairpeople, and a few small fund-raising events, had given Church the threshold amount in 10 states. In the following five weeks, the campaign made a concerted drive in 13 other states to qualify before the FEC lost its authority to certify matching funds. By the day of the candidate's official announcement, Church fund-raisers had solicited contributions totaling approximately $250,000.

As did some competing campaigns, the Church organization rented the 1972 McGovern contributor list of about 500,000 names for its direct mail. While not endorsing Church, Senator McGovern signed a Mailgram in which he praised his Senate colleague. This Church mailing to past McGovern contributors disappointed expectations as it was only moderately profitable even with matching funds. Direct mailing to other liberal groups continued throughout the spring, with the campaign formulating some appeals in-house and contracting for others. For each method the fund-raising staff considered the returns low and the price high. The committee procured mailing services from an associate of Rapp-Collins, the firm that had conducted McGovern's 1972 mail drive. In addressing the envelopes, the contractor failed to perform to the campaign's liking and a dispute over payment resulted with each party trying to sue the other. In an out-of-court settlement, the Church committee paid less than the contract figure. Even so, direct mail cost the campaign $114,000 exclusive of postage for in-house mailings.

The form of fund raising that proved most profitable was a series of network television broadcasts. As a bargaining tool, Church at first sought to buy a half-hour of program time from the TV networks. When the networks refused as expected, the committee threatened legal action, but settled for the sale of five-minute segments at the end of popular shows. Church taped three spots in which he addressed the issues for 4-1/2 minutes and appealed for donations in the final 30 seconds. In a fourth tape, Finance Chairman Kimelman made the closing pitch for contributions. All three networks carried the four spots in April and May, for a total of eight broadcasts. Each tape cost about $1,500 to produce, and air time and editing charges came to an average of $17,000 a broadcast. Church officials estimated that the televised pleas attracted contributions of at least $350,000, or almost one-third of all private funds.

Television solicitations compensated for fund-raising events that were discouraging in the time before Church withdrew from the race. Although the senator generated enthusiasm among crowds with a combination of polished oratory and western folksiness, the most successful affairs collected only about $10,000 each. Also, Church's late start forced him to concentrate on political, rather than fund-raising, appearances. However, events became an important source of income after the primaries when the committee showed a net deficit of $60,000. Three fund-raising events, supplemented by contacts of past contributors, erased the deficit. During the Democratic National Convention, Jerry Stern, who served as the New York City finance chairman, hosted a $100-a-person cocktail party. Senator Church addressed the guests who together donated about $10,000 exclusive of matching funds. In December 1976, Vice President-elect Walter Mondale was the main attraction at a Church fund-raiser held in Washington, which brought in about $15,000. Another event in San Francisco raised some $5,000. The latter two events garnered approximately $10,000 in matching grants. In early 1977 all fund-raising efforts had left nearly $10,000 on hand for disputed bills and costs of a financial wrap-up.

In a little over a year's time, the Church fund drive had raised nearly $1.1 million in private contributions. Of the total, approximately 63 percent came in denominations of $100 or less, about 24 percent came

in contributions of between $101 and $499, and some 13 percent came in
contributions of $500 or more. Private monies qualified the campaign for
$640,669 in matching funds, bringing total receipts to $1,743,776. Although federal subsidies constituted a large portion of income, the
matching funds cutoff did little harm to the Church bid. Because the
campaign spent lightly until May, private funds and credit sustained it
until the FEC could again certify funds. Loans secured during the
reconstitution of the commission came to a gross total of $136,245.
Church for President was able to borrow up to $100,000 from a Wash-
ington, D.C., bank and $15,000 from Church's 1974 Senate campaign
committee, which still carried a surplus. These loans were repaid at full
value.

Costs. The lateness of the Church candidacy necessitated large
outlays for media and preelection activity in primary states, as opposed
to more basic functions covered by the national headquarters. Church
for President spent more than half of its budget in 13 states. The Church
committee expended $13,538 in 1975 and $1,732,095 in 1976 and 1977,
with expenditures totaling $1,718,557. In addition, $24,213 in independent expenditures were reported made on behalf of Church.

The first test of the late-starting candidate was in the Nebraska
election on May 11. Strategists hoped to make an impressive opening,
and organizing concentrated on two of the state's three congressional
districts. The candidate stayed in Nebraska 10 days, three of them on a
bus tour of rural areas, and his son, the Rev. Forrest Church, spent 25
days there. In contrast, Carter spent only one day in the state. On the
hustings, Church stressed his experience in the nation's capital, while
claiming independence of the Washington establishment. He noted
Carter's vague positions and asserted that the White House was no place
for "on-the-job training."[25] A heavy media campaign started two weeks
before election day, culminating in a televised question-and-answer
program on election eve. Media advertising cost the campaign approximately $55,000 of total expenditures of $155,000. Church's well-planned
attack stunned the Carter camp, as the senator took 39 percent of the
vote to beat Carter by 1 percent.

Looking next to continuing winning ways in Oregon on May 25,
Church campaigned vigorously for five days in the state. In personal
appearances, Church employed the question-and-answer format to
exemplify his belief in "substance over style,"[26] an oblique criticism of
opponents Carter and Brown. The senator from neighboring Idaho reinforced his high name recognition in Oregon with a small media campaign costing approximately $25,000. Total expenditures reached
$140,000. Coming from behind in the polls, Church won 34.6 percent of
the vote, compared with 27.4 percent for Carter and 23.3 for Brown in a

Table 5-10
Expenditures in 13 States by the Church for President Committee

California	$180,000
Nebraska	155,000
Ohio	147,000
Oregon	140,000
Colorado	57,000
Rhode Island	50,000
Montana	36,000
Idaho	35,000
Nevada	15,000
Utah	6,000
Connecticut	3,000
Iowa	2,000
New Jersey	1,000
Total	$827,000

write-in effort. On the same day in his home state of Idaho, Church breezed to victory with 80 percent of the ballots cast, after spending some $35,000.

To give his presidential bid national stature, Church journeyed to Rhode Island for a June 1 primary. Church toured the tiny state for four days, accompanied by Sen. Claiborne Pell and Rep. Edward P. Beard. The candidate won endorsements from local labor leaders and got another assist from Udall, who abandoned his Rhode Island hopes in an effort to give Church an undivided liberal vote. Expenditures for Church totaled $50,000. Yet Church failed to top an uncommitted slate of delegates (for which Brown campaigned) or Jimmy Carter. Results in Montana, however, also on June 1, cushioned the Rhode Island setback, for Church handily beat Carter 60 percent to 25 percent while spending $36,000.

Church was unable to build on his success because he had nowhere to take his momentum on June 8. Plans to run in New Jersey had to be abandoned because of a crowded field consisting of Carter, Udall, and an uncommitted slate that supported both Brown and Hubert Humphrey. Despite urgings from his staff to actively challenge Brown in California, Church decided to limit his effort there several weeks before the primary. Church had first visited California in March when organizing already was under way. Before Brown threatened the Church bid with his surprise entrance, the senator had traveled widely and his committee spent relatively heavily. Media accounted for $55,000 of total expenditures which reached $180,000. The curtailed attempt, however, brought Church only 7.4 percent of the vote, a distant third worth only seven delegates.

Table 5-11

A Functional Breakdown of Expenditures by the National Headquarters
of the Church for President Committee

Payroll		$157,000
Fund raising:		
Events	$ 20,000	
Direct mail	114,000	
		134,000
Media:		
Film production	49,000	
Use (not allocated by state)	56,000	
		105,000
Office:		
General	84,000	
Computer	15,000	
		99,000
Telephone		60,000
Travel		48,000
Promotional items		36,000
Equipment		19,000
Rent		15,000
Postage		12,000
Convention		11,000
Legal		5,000
Other		12,100
Total		$713,100

NOTE: The amounts in Tables 5-10 and 5-11 total $1,540,100 and do not include some
$178,457 not categorized by the committee. Adding this sum brings total spending to
$1,718,557 for the Church for President Committee in a campaign that started too late for
victory.

Without an alternative contest, Church entered the Ohio primary
despite Morris Udall's request for a clear shot at Carter. Rumors arose to
the effect that Church ran in Ohio to guarantee a Carter victory and to
place himself in a favorable light for the vice presidential nomination.
Although the senator denied any ulterior motive, Church did indicate
that he would accept the second spot on the Democratic ticket. Later,
Carter seriously considered Frank Church as a possible running mate.
Speculation notwithstanding, Church defended running in Ohio by
saying that Udall "just hasn't been able to win in states he should have
carried."[27]

The Church bandwagon arrived in Ohio in mid-May and the campaign opened six headquarters across the state. Media outlays of $72,000
attempted to offset insufficient spending for other functions, making
total expenditures about $147,000. In the final week of the primary
campaign, two unfortunate occurrences doomed Church's prospects.
First, a throat and ear infection sidelined the senator for two days, and

second, a break in the Teton River Dam brought him back to Idaho to inspect damage and help to arrange relief measures. On election day in Ohio, Church finished third, winning 14 percent, while Carter captured 52 percent of the votes. The majority for the Georgian made insignificant the question of Church's splitting the Udall vote.

To summarize spending in the states, Table 5-10 reports total expenditures, including fund-raising costs, in 13 states where the Church committee mounted major efforts. Highest expenditures occurred in California, Nebraska, Ohio, and Oregon, four states attracting more than three-fourths of all state spending. Campaigns in the other states cost moderate to minor sums. Spending in the 13 states totaled $827,000, and of this figure some $300,000 went toward media.

The Church committee attributed $713,100 to spending by its Washington headquarters, and Table 5-11 reports a functional breakdown. The most expensive function comprised salaries and expenses for personnel totaling $157,000. Media was the second-highest category of spending, with production costs of $49,000, and air time charges not included in state figures of $56,000. The next-largest expense was $134,000 for fund raising, of which direct mail took $114,000, and events, $20,000. Additional costs for in-house mailings are included in the category of postage. Office expenses reached $99,000, although $15,000 of this amount went for computer services. In addition, most of the $12,100 labeled "other" was spent on office costs involved in closing the campaign books. Telephone service took $60,000 of the budget and travel expenses, including those for a chartered aircraft, came to $48,000. The seven categories of less than $40,000 each produce a sum of $110,100.

Harris

Fred R. Harris ran for president on the platform of "New Populism," calling for a drastic redistribution of wealth and power. Under this banner, Harris aimed to combine the Democratic Party's liberal and labor blocs. Harris eschewed the stylish, rapid spending of his abortive 1972 presidential bid, reasoning that "if you're going to be a citizen President, you ought to be a citizen candidate."[28]

The former U.S. senator from Oklahoma opened headquarters in the basement of his McLean, Virginia, home in 1974 and officially announced on January 11, 1975. The Harris for President Committee encouraged small donations and calculated an average contribution of $14.73. The fund-raising drive relied heavily on the candidate's extensive travels and the work of local organizations. The campaign decentralized its own wealth and power to some 31 state and local committees.

With total costs of about $1.6 million, the campaign turned out to be even more low-budget than Harris intended. He finished well behind the competition in the New Hampshire and Massachusetts primaries but hoped for a comeback in Pennsylvania on April 27. Lack of funds forced Harris to abandon this plan, however, and on April 8, the Oklahoman ceased active campaigning.

Compliance. The national Harris committee kept its books manually until late in the race when it computerized financial and contributor information. Two or three people worked full time to ensure the legality of receipts and disbursements. These workers determined the acceptability of checks and, when necessary, sent form letters to obtain additional information. The screening process revealed no contributions in excess of $1,000 and no contributions needed to be returned. Non-CPAs designed and operated the financial system, while the committee received legal advice from a volunteer counsel. In both legal and accounting matters, the campaign relied heavily on the advice of the FEC staff. Although the national headquarters instructed the numerous field committees on their compliance obligations, some committees did not conform to recommended procedures and this created auditing problems for the national officials but did not warrant government action. One staff member reasoned that the cost of compliance was not very high because the persons doing the work were unpaid.

One compliance problem that did arise for the Harris committee involved campaign activities on behalf of Harris by Rep. John Conyers, Jr., D-Mich. Conyers had, at the request of the Harris committee, campaigned for Harris in New Hampshire and Massachusetts. His expenditures totaled $16,171, which neither Conyers nor the committee reported to the FEC. In February 1977 Conyers filed a complaint with the FEC alleging that the committee's failure to report his expenditures was a violation of the law. Conyers contended that his expenditures were authorized by the committee and therefore were its responsibility. The committee, in turn, argued that Conyers' expenditures were not authorized and, instead, were independent expenditures made by Conyers on Harris's behalf. In April 1978 the FEC ruled that the committee had not authorized Conyers to make all of the expenditures he claimed it had, but that it had shown "a willingness to assist and cooperate" with his efforts. Because of the "numerous contacts and communications" between Conyers and the committee, therefore, his expenditures could not be regarded as independent expenditures. The Harris committee then agreed to amend its reports to disclose the disputed expenditures.[29]

Fund Raising. Harris's populist theme inspired some of the most novel, though not the most lucrative, fund-raising techniques in the nomination contest. In the summer of 1975 the candidate and his family toured the country in a camper, stopping along the way to make stump speeches and pleas for funds. The caravan logged 6,300 miles to attend 55 formal events at a total cost of $9,000, of which $1,800 went for camper rental. On the trip, and throughout the campaign, Harris enthusiastically addressed even the smallest gatherings often held in the homes of supporters. To collect contributions from small groups, an empty ice cream bucket would be passed around after the senator's speeches. Some appearances before large audiences drew honoraria that Harris turned over to the committee treasury; in 1975, he reported spending $9,590 of his own money in the campaign. Other events required contributions at the door, but admission was purposely set low. For example, the campaign held $4.76-a-plate buffets and, at the highest-priced fund-raisers, charged $25 to meet the candidate. In addition, the field committees organized their own neighborhood events, such as cake sales and lawn cuttings, and participated in a nationwide garage sale.

The emphasis on small donations from every part of the United States brought Harris close to the qualifications for matching funds. Subsequently, telephoned appeals for repeat gifts broke the $5,000 threshold in several states, and Harris achieved eligibility for federal subsidies in October 1975.

As the state elections drew near, the Harris for President Committee had to adopt large-scale fund-raising activities. In early fall, the committee contracted for a direct-mail service. The sample mailing went to contributors to the 1972 McGovern campaign and subscribers to several liberal magazines. Initial results prompted the campaign to expand the mailing list, which eventually contained one million names. A member of the fund-raising staff recalled that direct mail "kept us alive day to day." In November 1975 the campaign sponsored fund-raisers in living rooms across the nation at which the major attraction was a Harris radio broadcast carried by the CBS network and other stations. Also, folk singer Arlo Guthrie made a national concert tour, with other artists joining him in some cities. The tour raised about $200,000, but without matching funds it would have been only slightly profitable.

Although Harris did not receive the blessing of many established liberal contributors, he won endorsements from a few influential and famous people. George Hardy, president of the Service Employees International Union, became the first union leader to come out for any candidate when the union's political fund gave $2,000 to the Harris committee. Stanley Sheinbaum, a wealthy free-lance economist and former McGovern fund-raiser, also endorsed Harris. Carroll O'Connor and Norman Lear of "All in the Family" fame were hosts for a Harris fund-raising party in Los Angeles.

At no point in the candidacy did the national, state, and local committees bring in large sums of money. Harris closed 1974 with contributions of only $2,552. In the period before January 1, 1975, no contributions approached $1,000 and Harris and campaign manager James Hightower each lent the campaign $750. The candidate also lent the campaign $30,000 in the next year. During 1975 the national committee raised about $425,000, and in 1976 it collected approximately $275,000 from private sources. The grass-roots fund drive had been designed to maximize federal subsidies and it did so. With $633,099 in matching funds, the Harris for President Committee came close to a 1:1 ratio of private to public funds. However, the figures above do not include about $190,000 raised and spent by the field committees.

When the former senator ended active candidacy in April 1976, he did not completely withdraw so as to be eligible for further matching funds. Harris stated that he would continue to seek the backing of uncommitted delegates and that he hoped to influence the party platform, if not the selection of the nominee. The Harris committee accepted federal funds for expenses incurred through May 11, 1976. At that time, the national committee was in debt by about $40,000 and the state and local committees showed debts of approximately $35,000. Among the creditors was Fred Harris, who was owed $750. To liquidate outstanding obligations, the Harris staff sought to cooperate with other indebted candidates and the Democratic National Committee in jointly sponsored fund-raisers during 1977, but the venture was not implemented.

Costs. Although the Harris campaign shunned frills, its spending more than kept pace with income. In the beginning, the national committee tried to spend on a cash-available basis, but this became impossible. The scarcity of funds forced a reduction in the autonomy of the state and local committees so that spending could be made as efficient as possible. The Harris for President Committee spent approximately $1,380,000, while the field committees expended a total of about $225,000.

The national committee did not compute an exact functional breakdown of its spending, but estimated the magnitude of the larger expenditures. Fund-raising expenses totaled about $400,000, which means that the committee devoted nearly 35 percent of the budget to amassing its income. The Arlo Guthrie concerts cost at least $100,000 and the network radio broadcast was priced at $6,300 for 30 minutes of air time. Direct mail probably accounted for over half of the cost of fund raising. Operation of the national headquarters, including printing, telephone service, rent, equipment, and supplies, cost the campaign about one-fourth of expenditures or some $350,000. Another $350,000 or so went to travel and expenses, and the remainder, about $300,000, was spent on media, salary, and other costs. The campaign certainly was frugal in the area of personnel. In fall 1975 only two members of a national staff numbering 20 were paid. Field staff received reimbursements for expenses, but were encouraged to spend as little as possible. At the height of the campaign, the committee covered rent for several houses in Washington, Boston, and New Hampshire to accommodate nonresident volunteers.

As Harris tried to pull out of the pack of liberals early in the race, his committees concentrated state spending on Iowa, New Hampshire, and Massachusetts. Iowa, the first caucus state, attracted expenditures of perhaps $60,000, but Harris placed fourth with 10 percent of the balloting. Spending little and relying on low-level organization in the Mississippi caucuses, Harris failed to cut into the Wallace vote and took only 1.1 percent of the delegates. In his home state of Oklahoma, Harris trailed behind an uncommitted slate of delegates and Jimmy Carter. The disappointing results of the early caucuses led the Harris staff to use more expensive approaches in the primaries. Heavy media attacks in New Hampshire and Massachusetts brought spending in each state to about $100,000, but were of little consequence. Harris finished fourth with 11 percent of the vote in New Hampshire and fifth with 8 percent in Massachusetts.

Money expended in other states was spent inefficiently because of the FEC's inability to certify matching funds. The campaign opened headquarters in Wisconsin and New York but later cut back efforts for lack of matching funds. For the April 6 primary in New York, Harris originally had delegate slates in 29 of 39 congressional districts. When the candidate announced that financial woes were forcing him to severely limit spending in New York, many delegates switched to other candidates, and by election day Harris had fewer than half of all delegate spots covered. Another significant blow came when the telephone company disconnected the phones in the New York headquarters because the campaign had failed to pay a $10,000 deposit. Harris reduced spending in New York and Wisconsin to conserve funds for the Pennsylvania primary, but the continued suspension of matching payments forced the campaign to fold well before the Pennsylvania voting. In other states Harris incurred organizational expenses before he dropped out. For instance, the California Harris Committee invested $30,000 for a race that the candidate never made.

The chronic financial difficulties of the Harris campaign illustrate two paradoxes of the 1976 prenomination season. First, Harris planned to get much positive press coverage because he was waging a grass-roots campaign embodying the spirit of the new campaign finance law, yet the press labeled him a dark horse largely because he had little money. Second, the bitter irony of the matching funds cutoff was that it especially penalized a candidate such as Harris who had raised the vast majority of his money in small contributions and, therefore, was quite dependent on federal monies.

Humphrey

Unlike the four previous presidential elections, the 1976 campaign did not (officially) include Hubert H. Humphrey, the Democratic nominee for president in 1968. In 1975 the senator from Minnesota stated that he would not run in the primaries, but that he would accept the nomination if a deadlocked Democratic convention turned to him. As the leading Democrat among party leaders and in several Gallup Polls, Humphrey came under tremendous pressure from supporters to change his mind, and he nearly entered the fray several times. In the end, though, only independent expenditures, unauthorized by the senator, composed the Humphrey "campaign." Such expenditures totaled $59,955.

For the New Hampshire primary, a committee led by Rep. Paul Simon, D-Ill., tried to organize a Humphrey write-in drive. The FEC had warned the group that the maximum independent expenditure allowed by the 1974 Amendments was $1,000, but this provision was made inoperative by the *Buckley* decision in January of 1976. By the voting in New Hampshire, the Draft Senator Humphrey for President Committee had spent $11,146.

As the primary elections progressed, many Democrats viewed Humphrey as the only man who could stop former Governor Carter. Lending credence to rumors that he would enter some of the later primaries, Humphrey and the Georgian traded criticisms of one another in March and April. In New York, more than 40 delegate candidates who ran "uncommitted" actually favored Humphrey, and in Wisconsin, known Humphrey backers encouraged voters to support Udall in order to slow Carter. At the height of the campaign in Pennsylvania, the Minnesotan appeared before a number of enthusiastic audiences, and state labor leaders, outwardly endorsing Jackson, let it be known that they preferred Humphrey. Yet after the Pennsylvania primary, Humphrey announced in an emotional speech that he would still sit out the primaries.

Even so, Humphrey remained a threat throughout the primary season. Another unauthorized group formed in May under the leadership of Congressman Simon and Joseph F. Crangle, a former New York

State Democratic chairman. The Humphrey for President Committee voluntarily imposed a $1,000 ceiling on contributions, though the committee was subject to no legal limit since it was independent of a candidate. The committee opened an office in Washington and endeavored to win support from delegates already elected. This low-visibility operation cost $44,448. Other independent and delegate expenditures made on behalf of Humphrey came to a total of $4,361. In addition, a majority of the delegates on the uncommitted slate in New Jersey openly endorsed Humphrey.

As late as June 5, Senator Humphrey was speculating about a postprimary candidacy, but the underground Humphrey drive finally ceased after other Democratic contenders swung to Jimmy Carter. On June 9 Humphrey conceded that Carter "is virtually certain to be our party's nominee."[30]

Jackson

Henry M. Jackson waged a lengthy, expensive, and unsuccessful presidential campaign. The junior senator from Washington announced his candidacy on February 6, 1975, in a five-minute, paid broadcast carried on the CBS network. The announcement speech, which cost $45,000 for air time and production, reflected the abundance of funds in the early stages of the Jackson campaign. Cash on hand topped $1 million during most of 1975, but in 1976 high expenditures in four major primaries rapidly diminished Jackson's war chest. In spite of victories in two of these primaries (Massachusetts and New York), the campaign ended well before the Democratic convention. Jackson had expected, at the very least, to be a contender after an inconclusive first ballot at the July convention. Yet on May 1, 1976, Senator Jackson ceased "active pursuit"[31] of the Democratic nomination. By that time, the Jackson for President Committee had spent more than $6 million.

Compliance. The Jackson committee systematized its financial operations to ensure compliance with the law and Federal Election Commission regulations. Keeping records of contributors and determining the legality of contributions presented a challenge to the staff. Clerical personnel, with the assistance of a direct-mail firm, put contributor information on computer. The computer automatically rejected the contributions of individuals who inadvertently exceeded the $1,000 limit. About $5,000 was returned to contributors for this reason. The campaign established a painstaking, labor-intensive process to confirm the acceptability of contributions. The campaign treasurer personally inspected every check and held in abeyance any suspected of illegality. For example, if a check might have come from the account of an incorporated enterprise, the treasurer sent a letter to the donor asking the source of the contribution. Volunteer workers initiated correspondence to resolve more technical violations, such as a contributor's omission of occupation, business address, or spouse's signature on a check from a joint account.

Among the executive staff were Walter T. Skallerup, Jr., an attorney who served as treasurer, and Martin Katz, a certified public accountant who held the position of controller. Skallerup had worked in the same capacity for Jackson in 1972 and Katz had assisted the McGovern campaign four years before, so each had prior experience with the Federal Election Campaign Act. These men and another volunteer accountant developed and directed the compliance procedures, thus reducing outside consultation. Jackson officials consulted Arthur Andersen & Co., an accounting firm, about the District of Columbia personal property tax and its effect on the campaign headquarters, but the fee amounted to less than $500. The campaign did rely heavily on the advice of the FEC's lawyers and auditors. According to Jackson's staff, the campaign was in daily contact with the FEC after October 1975. Although no exact figures on the cost of compliance are available, a rough but conservative estimate can be made. Two full-time staff members supervised the compliance process for nearly two years at a cost of approximately $25,000 in salaries. Computer time came to $15,000. Clerical salaries and postage and copying costs cannot be isolated, but they place the total cost of compliance above $60,000.

An FEC compliance audit, covering the period January 1, 1975, through June 30, 1977, essentially gave the Jackson committee a clean bill of health, with only two relatively minor criticisms. First, it was noted that the Jackson committee had waited several months before depositing certain contributions, an apparent violation of FEC regulations requiring all contributions be deposited in an appropriate checking account within 10 days of receipt. The committee treasurer's response was that when a check was held it was for the purpose of obtaining additional information as to whether the contribution came from a prohibited source. Secondly, the audit report noted that the occupation and principal place of business was either omitted or insufficient for approximately 25 percent of the contributions. Here committee officials responded that they felt that they made every reasonable effort, such as follow-up letters and phone calls, to obtain the necessary information. In both instances the audit report found substantial compliance on the part of the committee and recommended no action by the FEC. The Jackson committee ended the campaign with a net surplus of $57,118. Of this amount, the audit recommended a matching fund repayment of $17,604 which the committee treasurer subsequently paid.[32]

Fund Raising. The Jackson Planning Committee was formed on July 8, 1974, with the senator's consent and a $5,000 loan from the campaign treasurer. With a staff of three in Washington, the committee proceeded to assess the prospects of a presidential bid and to solicit contributions. Early fund-raising efforts focused on wealthy contributors because there were no limits on money contributed in 1974 since the 1974 Amendments did not take effect until January 1, 1975.

Jackson and fellow Sen. Lloyd Bentsen voluntarily imposed ceilings of $3,000 per individual and $6,000 per couple on 1974 contributions. Under the 1974 Amendments as finally enacted, the limit on contributions became $1,000 per individual for a candidate for federal office. The senators defended their use of the higher ceiling by noting that, prior to enactment, a Senate version of the campaign bill set a $3,000 limit, and the two campaigns were engaged in fund raising before Congress agreed upon the $1,000 figure. Nonetheless, Georgia Gov. Jimmy Carter disparaged this justification, stating that the senators' action violated the spirit of the law and was "equivalent to the same thing President Nixon did back in April 1972, when he rapidly accumulated large sums of money to finance his campaign without revealing the identities of the contributors."[33] However, the law required disclosure of all contributors during 1974 and Jackson and Bentsen fully complied.

Donations of $3,000 comprised a majority of Jackson's 1974 contributions. The Jackson fund drive raised $1,138,000 in 1974, and $615,000 of that amount came from 205 individuals contributing $3,000 each. Several prominent names appeared on the 1974 contributor list. For example, Joseph B. Danzansky, president of Giant Food Inc. of Washington, and N. M. Cohen, Giant's board chairman, each contributed the maximum amount. Three relatives of Cohen, including two Giant vice-presidents, gave a total of $9,000. Other $3,000 contributors were Joseph Robbie, owner of the Miami Dolphins, Daniel K. Ludwig, billionaire shipping magnate, and S. Harrison Dogole, board chairman of Globe Securities Systems Inc. The wives of Robbie and Dogole also gave $3,000. In addition, Felix Rohatyn, a director of International Telephone and Telegraph who played a part in a controversy involving ITT-related campaign contributions, contributed $2,500, and Paul H. Nitze, former deputy secretary of Defense, donated $500.

The Jackson committee did not, however, depend solely on large contributions before January 1, 1975. Personal appearances by the candidate and solicitations by mail, including letters to 1972 backers, broadened the base of financial support. By the end of 1974, 1,166 individuals had contributed. This means that 961 people provided $523,000 in contributions of less than $3,000. The average contribution below the voluntary ceiling was therefore $544.

In any case, the sources of funds were not the major concern of the Jackson campaign. Rather, the initial financial strategy encompassed three goals: 1) to amass enough money for later direct-mail drives, 2) to enable the candidate to concentrate on political matters, and 3) to minimize the availability of funds for other candidates of the Democratic center. Under the direction of Richard Kline, a fund-raiser for Edmund Muskie in 1972, the Jackson strategy achieved the first two goals, though not the third.

The money raised in 1974 proved to be sufficient for the direct mail that the campaign used. Several small mailings went out in the fall of 1974, but the major drive occurred in February 1975. Morris Dees, the architect of McGovern's 1972 direct-mail bonanza, offered free consultation to all Democratic candidates except Governor Wallace, and Jackson accepted. Dees wrote a six-page, single-spaced letter that was sent to 400,000 homes at a cost of $77,462. Returns from this mailing did not warrant any sizable expansion for future mailings, according to staff members. Generally, direct mail is lucrative for candidates who appeal to strong emotions in the voters, and less successful for low-key, centrist politicians. Unlike McGovern in 1972 and Wallace in 1976, Jackson did not arouse widespread passions in the electorate. One exception to the rule was the Jewish segment of the population which, because of Senator Jackson's ardent defense of Israel, gave solid monetary support to the Jackson campaign. In fact, the fund-raising staff rented some mailing lists from synagogues.

Another worthwhile outgrowth of the direct-mail drive was the "Jackson for President Club," which consisted of some 9,000 donors who contributed through the initial mailing. The Jackson committee requested that club members contribute monthly for the remainder of the campaign. The club provided a steady flow of income and "a considerable aggregate amount," in the words of one Jackson aide. Other early contributors received requests for repeat gifts. By letter, telephone, and telegram, the campaign contacted donors who had not yet given up to the $1,000 limit. In these ways, Jackson achieved maximum income from a relatively small mailing list.

Nevertheless, the bulwark of the financial strategy proved to be personal appearances, and Jackson employed two types of fund-raising events. The first involved small gatherings of wealthy guests who were invited to hear the senator speak and were charged $1,000 (or more) for the privilege. Large, open dinners and breakfasts costing $125 a plate comprised the second type. These affairs permitted Jackson to address the political issues, while only indirectly involving the candidate in the less lofty activity of fund raising. One of Jackson's most rewarding appearances was in Los Angeles on January 26, 1975, at the Century

Plaza Hotel where a $250-a-plate roast beef dinner organized by Hershey Gold and other members of the Jewish community grossed about $300,000. The Jackson campaign preferred such events to direct mail because dinners require little "up-front" investment, and cost only about 20 percent of the gross.

Mailing and appearances combined to make Jackson's fund raising efficient and nationally based. The senator announced that he had qualified for federal matching funds on April 26, 1975. He was the second presidential candidate to raise $5,000 in each of 20 states in contributions of $250 or less. The committee used an informal method to reach the threshold in the 20 states. Staff members paid attention to totals in the states, and, where necessary, phoned known sympathizers to drum up more funds. According to the campaign treasurer, requirements for federal subsidies did not represent an "unfair burden," because mailings and Senator Jackson's travels obviated the need for an elaborate fund-raising system in the states.

Although Jackson was not able to preempt Jimmy Carter from the political or financial contest, the senator's fund-raising effort was certainly impressive. In 1975 the campaign collected $2,139,000 in private contributions. This money, together with $49,000 in interest and the $1,138,000 raised in 1974, enabled Jackson to open 1976 with a total income of $3,326,000 and nearly $1 million on hand. During the first five months of 1976 the campaign took in $1,133,000 of contributions and $1,876,000 in matching funds. Public and private funding put Jackson at the $5 million mark in total receipts by March of 1976. By the end of the campaign, total receipts stood at $6,346,000. About 51,000 contributors provided $4,410,000 of the total, yielding an average contribution of $86.50. The Jackson staff estimated that fund raising cost $1,340,000, or 21 percent of all receipts.

Yet the overall soundness of the fund-raising operation does not tell the complete story. In 1976 the campaign expended funds almost as they arrived. To avoid going into debt, Jackson insisted that his organization spend funds strictly on a cash-available basis. One week before the April 27 Pennsylvania primary, the campaign showed a balance of only $100,000. Jackson could have alleviated this shortage by borrowing against some $250,000 due when the FEC could again certify funds. However, Jackson feared that President Ford might veto the FECA Amendments, and thus he considered loans too risky. In the final analysis, the Jackson presidential bid demonstrated that financial success cannot guarantee electoral triumph.

Costs. The Jackson campaign staff estimated that the total cost of the senator's bid reached $6,237,000. What the staff termed "political operations" represented the largest category of expenditure and in-

Table 5-12
Cost Breakdown of Political Operations of the Jackson for President Committee, 1975 through May 1976

	1975	January-May 1976	Total
Media (including printed matter, buttons, etc.)	$ 46,000	$ 936,000	$ 982,000
Salaries	297,000	175,000	472,000
Staff travel	89,000	111,000	200,000
Candidate travel	66,000	65,000	131,000
Advance work expenses	48,000	26,000	74,000
Announcement speech	45,000	—	45,000
Polling	19,000	16,000	35,000
Development	30,000	2,000	32,000
Other	18,000	12,000	30,000
Total	$658,000	$1,343,000	$2,001,000

cluded spending for activities that furthered the campaign as a whole, as opposed to localized operations within the campaign. Such activities cost $68,000 in 1974. Table 5-12, which gives breakdowns within the political operations category, shows that $658,000 was spent in 1975 and $1,343,000 in the first five months of 1976. The data on Table 5-12, provided by the Jackson campaign, indicate that media, salaries, and travel constituted the bulk of spending for political operations. All types of media captured 47 percent of general political spending at $982,000 in 1975 and 1976. Salaries totaled $472,000 in the two years or 23 percent of the category. Travel for the candidate and staff came to $331,000 or 16 percent of all political operations.

Operation of the national headquarters in Washington, D.C., from July 1974 through May 1976 cost $842,000. In 1974 the campaign charged $62,000 to the headquarters. Table 5-13 lists the specified costs within the headquarters category for 1975 through May 1976. Notable expenditures are $307,000 for telephone service, $129,000 for salaries and consultant fees, $62,000 for rent and utilities, and $15,000 for computer services.

Campaign spending specifically attributable to state operations was calculated at $148,000 in 1975 and $1,838,000 in 1976, for a total of $1,986,000 (Table 5-14). In accordance with Jackson's so-called "big state" strategy, heavy expenditures occurred in Massachusetts, Florida, New York, and Pennsylvania.

The Jackson campaign decided not to contest seriously in New Hampshire and conducted only a minor write-in drive. As an alter-

Table 5-13
Cost Breakdown of National Headquarters Operation of Jackson for
President Committee, 1975 through May 1976

	1975	January-May 1976	Total
Telephone (including deposits)	$138,000	$169,000	$307,000
Payroll taxes, Blue Cross, etc.	33,000	48,000	81,000
Salaries and consultant fees	70,000	59,000	129,000
Rent and utilities	43,000	19,000	62,000
Office supplies	33,000	10,000	43,000
Xerox and equipment rental	21,000	12,000	33,000
Income taxes	—	26,000	26,000
Equipment and furniture	23,000	1,000	24,000
Postage	8,000	12,000	20,000
Computer	3,000	12,000	15,000
Service and improvements	14,000	—	14,000
Petty cash	7,000	4,000	11,000
Other	11,000	4,000	15,000
Total	$404,000	$376,000	$780,000

native, the Jackson forces staked their hopes on the March 2 Massachusetts primary. The traditionally liberal state provided an excellent opportunity for a Jackson victory because five other Democrats would splinter the left-of-center vote. Also, busing was a key issue due to the Boston school desegregation controversy. Jackson maneuvered into an antibusing, prointegration position which appealed to moderate Democrats. He advocated a law to put desegregation cases in the hands of three-judge panels, rather than single District Court judges. For conservative Democrats, this stance made Jackson a respectable alternative to George Wallace.

Jackson reached his targeted voters through a $280,000 media campaign. This figure represents 42 percent of the $669,000 poured into the Massachusetts race. Jackson did capture enough votes to win a plurality with 22.2 percent of all ballots cast. The senator's high spending and clever positioning in the field of Democrats paid off, for Massachusetts established Jackson as a front-runner.

The results of the Florida primary seriously threatened that front-runner status, however. One week after Massachusetts, Jackson again employed an expensive media blitz at the price of $241,000. Total expenditures were $523,000. Although Jackson held a lead in the southern Florida voting, he came in third statewide. Essentially, Jackson could not break into the crucial battle between southerners Carter and Wallace. The Washington senator's 24 percent vote, while respectable, slowed his momentum. Contrary to the predictions of Jackson planners, Wallace failed to eliminate Carter. As a result, Jackson faced a considerable challenge to his centrist following.

While Carter chalked up popular vote and delegate victories in Illinois and North Carolina, Jackson focused his energy on the April 6 New York primary. The Jackson team envisioned a win in the Empire State that would prompt similar results in the later primaries of Pennsylvania, New Jersey, Ohio, and California. To start this chain of events, the campaign invested $864,000 in New York. Comparatively little money, $43,000, went toward media because polls indicated that New York City residents already favored the senator. Upstate New York consumed at least $31,000 for radio and television costs, while the traditional campaign media of pamphlets, buttons, and telephone canvassing attracted the remainder of the budget. New York's complicated delegate selection process necessitated extensive use of printed materials. Telephone canvassing cost as much as $117,000 by one month before election day.

Although Jackson placed first, the 39 percent plurality of delegates selected was hardly the "landslide" the senator had predicted.[34] Indeed, the win became a symbolic loss. Many observers felt that Jackson should have done better after high expenditures in a state with a large labor and Jewish vote.

After the unimpressive win in New York, the campaign encountered a number of difficulties. Reportedly, the staff experienced internal strife and money became scarce. Hershey Gold and Senator Jackson himself had to make telephone pleas for funds. Large outlays in the early primaries and the cutoff of federal subsidies before the FEC was reconstituted hindered the fight in Pennsylvania. Spending in the state did not quite reach $200,000, although an early budget projected twice that amount. Media expenses came to a scant $33,000.

Interestingly, one Jackson aide noted that money was not the major problem in Pennsylvania, for politically "the ship was taking on water." Hubert Humphrey addressed a labor group at the start of the Pennsylvania race and the speech encouraged expectations of the Minnesota senator's entry into the presidential contest. Although various labor committees mailed 150,000 pieces of Jackson literature, several union leaders expressed the hope that Humphrey would run. In a television interview on April 11, Jackson conceded that some of his backers preferred Humphrey. In these circumstances, Jackson appeared to some to be a stalking horse for Hubert Humphrey.

In the end, endorsements of Jackson from labor and Mayor Frank Rizzo of Philadelphia could not stop Jimmy Carter. Jackson's weak 25 percent showing trailed Carter by 12 percent and nearly finished the

Table 5-14
Jackson's Operating and Media Costs in the States

States	Operating Costs	Media Costs	Total
Iowa	$ 20,000	$ 0	$ 20,000
New Hampshire	22,000	23,000	45,000
Massachusetts	389,000	280,000	669,000
Florida	282,000	241,000	523,000
North Carolina	33,000	0	33,000
New York	821,000	43,000	864,000
Pennsylvania	163,000	33,000	196,000
Wisconsin	55,000	0	55,000
California	27,000	0	27,000
Washington	41,000	0	41,000
Missouri	23,000	0	23,000
Ohio	19,000	2,000	21,000
Michigan	9,000	0	9,000
Connecticut	27,000	0	27,000
Maryland	11,000	0	11,000
Others	44,000	0	44,000
Total	$1,986,000	622,000	$2,608,000

candidacy. Although Senator Jackson continued making appearances in later primary states such as Connecticut and Maryland, he was reduced to delegate hunting rather than campaigning. In mid-May, with federal subsidies still not forthcoming, Jackson explained, "We're out of money and we can't put on a campaign. I'm here [Maryland] to show that I'm still a candidate."[35] The official closing came after Carter's June 8 Ohio triumph when Jackson appeared before the press, noting somewhat cheerlessly, "We can all add." The former contender urged his 248 delegates to vote for Carter at the convention to unify the party.[36]

Spending in states other than Massachusetts, Florida, New York, and Pennsylvania totaled $331,000. The four major state primaries accounted for 83 percent of expenditures for state operations. Table 5-14, which reports both operating and media costs, shows expenditures in 15 states. Media costs in the states are derived from figures for all media listed in table 5-12.

The financial status of the Jackson for President Committee improved in May once the FEC could again certify funds. The reduction of campaigning allowed the committee to waive $80,000 in matching funds, although the FEC reported certifying a total of $1,980,555 for Jackson through December 1976. As of May 31, 1976, the campaign held a balance of $109,000, although bills were being paid throughout the rest of the year.

McCormack

Ellen McCormack, a housewife from Long Island, sought the Democratic nomination to rally forces seeking to ban abortions under all circumstances. While at times espousing other, generally conservative, stands, McCormack essentially ran her campaign on this one issue. McCormack's principal campaign group, the Pro-Life Action Committee, spent $532,848 in the one-and-a-half year effort that captured 22 delegate votes.

With an emotional issue such as abortion, McCormack supporters found it fairly easy to collect small contributions from many individuals and thereby qualify for matching funds. However, opponents of McCormack, especially the Abortion Rights Action League, challenged her submissions for federal subsidies. Charges arose that the Pro-Life Action Committee failed to make explicit that its solicitations were for a presidential campaign rather than a general antiabortion drive. The staff of the FEC investigated the committee's fund-raising techniques and found that it had sufficiently linked the committee name with McCormack's candidacy. In late February 1976 four commissioners voted in favor of the staff's conclusion that the candidate was eligible for matching funds, while Commissioner Staebler voted against on grounds that there was no certainty that all contributors understood the nature of their contribution.

With the help of right-to-life and church groups, the McCormack committee raised $285,671 in individual contributions, of which some 80 percent came in denominations of $100 or less. These private funds generated $247,220 in matching funds. In addition, the committee borrowed $3,500, including $3,000 in loans from two individuals that put the lenders over the $1,000 contribution/loan limit. This apparent violation surfaced during a routine FEC audit, but the commission took no action because the campaign had repaid both loans promptly.

In the course of the campaign, McCormack traveled widely, and spent heavily on a series of five-minute television commercials; most though not all of the ads dealt with the abortion issue. Her most vigorous campaigns were in the Massachusetts, Illinois, Maryland, and California primaries, although the highest state expenditures reached only $58,000 in Massachusetts. One section of the 1976 Amendments affected McCormack in particular; it provided that eligibility for matching funds cease 30 days after a candidate fails to receive 10 percent or more of the vote in two consecutive state primaries. Thus, McCormack's poor showings in the May primaries made her contributions after June 24, 1976, ineligible for matching fund payments. Nonetheless, the foe of abortion stayed in the Democratic race through the July convention.

In spite of its electoral weakness and limited spending, the Mc-
Cormack campaign demonstrated a problem for public financing in
future elections. The threshold for matching funds eligibility proved to
be fairly low for a candidate who could tie a campaign into a network of
already existent organizational support, thereby easily achieving eligibility in each of 20 states. A large number of such one-issue candidates
could drain the Presidential Election Campaign Fund and confuse the
primary contest. Although the ready availability of public monies may
promote a lively discussion of issues, it also can cause a proliferation of
candidates who are not viable contenders for a presidential nomination.
If public financing was intended to assist candidates, the McCormack
campaign in effect was designed to promote consideration of an issue.
But then numerous presidential candidates in the past have sought to
dramatize issues without serious intent to gain nomination or election.

Mondale

When he was the senior senator from Minnesota, Vice President
Walter F. Mondale explored the possibilities of a presidential bid. In
1973 and 1974, Senator Mondale traveled across the nation, taking
soundings from voters and party leaders. In January 1974 friends from
the senator's home state formed The Mondale Committee to raise funds
and to facilitate Mondale's decision on a presidential candidacy. In less
than a year's time, Mondale chose not to run. The aborted effort cost
The Mondale Committee $137,138 for travel, staff, fund raising, cam-
paign literature, and office expenses.

At the start of his exploration, Mondale struck the note of post-
Watergate reform by hiring Arthur Andersen & Co. as accounting
consultants and by instructing his committee to decline contributions
larger than $3,000 and cash contributions in excess of $50. He adopted
the $3,000 limit from the campaign finance bill that had passed the
Senate in 1973. In its brief life, the committee received only about six
contributions of more than $1,000. In the first nine months of 1974, The
Mondale Committee raised approximately $60,000, most of the total
coming from Minnesota. Mondale's standing with party liberals improved in late September when Senator Edward Kennedy announced
that he would not be a candidate. Indeed, nearly $40,000 rolled into the
Mondale treasury in the week following Kennedy's announcement.

In the fall of 1974, although his name recognition was low in public
opinion polls, Mondale appeared encouraged by his travels and his
success as a speaker on behalf of Democratic congressional candidates.
The senator publicly stated he intended to enter the first 1976 primary
in New Hampshire.

However, the senator was having doubts, and in spite of the campaign's momentum, Mondale withdrew from the Democratic race in a surprise announcement on November 21, 1974. Mondale cited personal rather than political reasons for his action. He explained, "I found I did not have the overwhelming desire to be President which is essential to the kind of campaign that is required. . . . I admire people who have the drive and ambition, but it means being on the road 18 hours a day and away from my family, the Senate and my state."[37] Ironically, Mondale later accepted the rigors of the general election campaign as the running mate of Jimmy Carter, who had displayed the requisite drive and ambition for the primaries.

Although the Mondale campaign spent relatively little money during its brief tenure, it also failed to raise much money and therefore closed its books in the red. After Mondale received the vice presidential nomination, his staff took advantage of the FEC ruling that allowed private contributions to otherwise totally public-funded general election candidates if those contributions were earmarked for debts incurred prior to nomination. A financial drive to erase Mondale's political debts raised about $40,000 from individuals in Minnesota, including contributions of $1,000 each from Jeno Paulucci, Duluth food products executive; four members of the Minneapolis-based Dayton retailing family; and two officers of the Dayton-Hudson Corp. There were numerous other donors who gave the maximum $1,000 allowed, including many Republicans, some of whom had contributed to Mondale campaigns in the past.[38]

Sanford

James Terry Sanford, Duke University president and former governor of North Carolina, became the sixth candidate for the Democratic nomination with an announcement on May 29, 1975. The Citizens' Committee to Nominate Terry Sanford had begun preliminary organizing and fund raising with Sanford's consent in June 1974. This body changed its name to the Sanford for President Committee in 1975. Throughout the campaign, the committee found fund raising a burden, partly because the general public was unfamiliar with Sanford, while party regulars recalled his unsuccessful presidential race in 1972 and his flawed attempts at the vice presidential nomination in 1968 and 1972. While campaigning vigorously in Massachusetts, Sanford suffered chest pains and was hospitalized in mid-January 1976. Although the illness was no more serious than the flu, the attendant publicity and lost campaign time hurt the candidate's chances in the New England primaries. Sanford removed himself from the race on January 23, a full month before any voters would have passed judgment on him. In his withdrawal statement, Sanford stressed political and financial problems, not health, as the cause of his decision. The aborted campaign cost nearly $640,000.

Compliance. The national Sanford committee used no outside professional help to keep financial records in order, even though the 1972 campaign experienced compliance problems with amateur bookkeepers. The forerunner of the Sanford for President Committee maintained headquarters in North Carolina until February 1975, when a national office was opened in Washington, D.C. In the capital, compliance with the law attracted high-level attention. The director of national headquarters spent much of her time preparing FEC filings, while a lawyer and an accountant supervised bookkeeping. When necessary, volunteers performed clerical duties.

Instead of computerizing information on contributors, the campaign employed a manual system based on Rolodex cards. The cards were arranged alphabetically and by state, and listed amounts contributed and background material for each donor. Generally, the compliance staff mailed a form letter to contributors who failed to supply adequate information, but sometimes workers phoned such individuals in an attempt to speed the filing process. The card system revealed about six individuals who went over the $1,000 contribution limit, and the campaign returned checks for the overage to each of them.

Although a manual bookkeeping system saves money and is manageable, it necessitates much volunteer effort. One member of the Sanford executive committee contended that the campaign law and FEC regulations are too complicated for most clerical helpers to deal with. Sanford staffers also complained that the finance requirements diverted the time and energy of persons who were supposed to be organizing and handling political matters; thus, some workers thought the compliance process prevented Sanford's small campaign from getting off the ground.

Fund Raising. In a moment of early campaign hubris, Terry Sanford declared, "I don't see how any serious candidate can fail to raise $4 million."[39] Yet as time passed, Sanford became less of a serious contender precisely because of difficulties in raising money. In 1974 the first Sanford committee raised only $45,861, mostly from past Sanford supporters. None of these contributions exceeded a voluntary limit of $1,000, although about three-fourths of the 1974 funds came in denominations of $250 and above.

The following year, the campaign strove to qualify for matching funds, and to do so it relied on friendly contacts in the states who made personal and telephoned pleas for donations. Although Sanford collected the requisite $5,000 in 20 states by October 1975, the achievement did not come easily and involved much persistence. A more profitable tactic was the personal appearance by the candidate, who put his experience with Duke University fund raising to good use. Sanford spoke before dinners and cocktail parties in his home state, the wealthy states of New York, California, and Texas, and the New England states that were to hold the first primaries. Unfortunately, Sanford could not campaign full time until January 1976, when he began a sabbatical leave from Duke.

Late in 1975 the fund drive started to flag. The campaign already had exhausted much of its financial base, as evidenced by a drop in contributions from the third to the fourth quarter of the year. During the third quarter of 1975, Sanford carried a debt of $78,000, although he would be due more than $100,000 in matching funds when they became available in January 1976. To ease cash flow, the committee borrowed a total of $13,950 from several Washington banks. One bright spot was a solicitation the organization sent to predominantly liberal groups, including contributors to George McGovern's 1974 senatorial campaign and supporters of the Southern Poverty Law Center. This mailing brought an encouraging reponse, but another one, aimed at teachers and educators, drew poorly. Reportedly, the latter mailing prompted Sanford to consider dropping out of the presidential contest. The Sanford committee closed 1975 having raised $310,000, with contributions of less than $250 comprising almost one-third of the total.

After Sanford's withdrawal, the campaign stopped seeking funds and took in only about $6,000 in January 1976. In that month, however, the committee received $246,388 in federal subsidies for expenses incurred before the pull-out. A final audit put total private contributions at $360,597. Of the total, $73,470 came in amounts under $100; $38,479 was in denominations greater than $100 but less than $250; and $248,647 was in contributions of $250 or more. Public and private funds plus refunds, loans, transfers, and sales brought total receipts to $637,602. This income slightly surpassed spending and the campaign returned $48.04 to the U.S. Treasury and donated $78.93 to the United Fund of Durham. The committee treasurer calculated that fund raising cost $39,763, a figure that mainly represents the set-up costs for fund-raising events, however, and excludes costs of some mailings and of all salaries for personnel who worked on the fund drive. A more inclusive estimate of the price of fund raising would approach $100,000.

The candidate's image problem contributed to the fund-raising difficulties of the Sanford campaign and the reverse held true as well. Sanford expressed his predicament this way: "You need enthusiasm to stir up money and you need money to stir up enthusiasm."[40] When bowing out, Sanford partially blamed his failure on the handicap of a nonpolitical office, but also charged that the press gave too much attention to the financial aspect of the 1976 race, and too little to the issues and the candidates' positions on them. Sanford believed that funds would have been more obtainable if only the electorate knew more about his political views.

Costs. Even without the expensive contracted services of accounting consultants, direct-mail houses, and computer time, the Sanford campaign spent its income rapidly. The pattern of spending reflects Sanford's ambitious strategy for becoming the leading liberal candidate. He hoped to gain national recognition and the grateful backing of moderate and liberal Democrats by eliminating George Wallace. Sanford planned to accomplish this feat by beating his fellow southerner in the North Carolina primary, where Wallace had trounced Sanford in 1972. To facilitate an early knock-out of Wallace, state politicians and a group of Sanford supporters in the legislature had worked to move North Carolina's primary from May 4 to March 23. Sanford intended to maintain the drive with entrances in about 20 primaries and organizations in the caucus states.

The Sanford committee began laying the groundwork for the strategy in 1974, spending $33,911 mostly for travel, salaries, and mailings. In the following year, spending increased gradually, and for the last quarter of 1975 expenditures were $105,075. Total 1975 spending stood at

Table 5-15
Sanford for President Campaign, Functional Breakdown of Expenditures

Travel and expenses	$162,421
Consultants[a]	95,985
Salaries	93,461
Office rent, supplies, and services	62,750
Printing and postage	57,994
Telephone	49,969
Fund-raising events	39,763
Taxes	32,916
Hotel [b]	13,140
Media and advertising	12,222
Other [c]	17,315
Total	$637,936 [d]

[a] The campaign's top management personnel were paid as consultants, rather than as salaried workers.
[b] This expense includes non-fund-raising rentals and some bills for sleeping quarters not counted in travel and expenses.
[c] The category includes repayments of loans, a refund to the U.S. Treasury, and a donation, as mentioned above.
[d] This figure includes an estimate of in-kind contributions of $334.

Table 5-16
Sanford for President Campaign, Expenditures in the States and by the
National Headquarters

National headquarters	$480,669 [a]
North Carolina	75,919
Massachusetts	30,440
New Hampshire	16,799
California	9,741
New York	6,136
South Carolina	5,322
Texas	4,058
Iowa	2,300
New Mexico	1,689
Louisiana	1,401
Arizona	1,101
Kentucky	775
Maine	475
Georgia	311
Wisconsin	259
New Jersey	222
Nebraska	155
Pennsylvania	100
Wyoming	50
Florida	14
Total	$637,936

[a] Approximately $120,000 of this amount, though paid by the headquarters, is attributable to the several states.

$336,252, and during 1976 the campaign paid bills totaling $267,773, though most of this money was for debts incurred in 1975.

Table 5-15, which reports the functional categories of spending for the campaign, shows that the largest expenditures were for up-front or fixed costs. The most costly category is travel and expenses at $162,421. Candidate travel probably was above average because Sanford did much commuting from Durham in 1975. The next largest expenditure is for "consultants," who were actually the top management personnel of the campaign and were not paid on a salary basis; costs for salaried workers came to $93,461. The two personnel categories equal $189,446, or over one-fourth of total expenditures. The overhead costs of office rent, supplies, and services total $62,750. These are the types of expenses needed to establish a candidacy regardless of the later fortunes of the office seeker. Since the Sanford campaign never reached the heat of a primary fight, costs for functions closely linked with electioneering are lower. For example, printing and postage come to only $57,994, while telephone services cost $49,969; media expenses were only $12,222. The other smaller categories yield a sum of $108,202. The committee reported total expenditures of $637,936, but included in this calculation a nonmonetary liability of $334 for in-kind contributions. Actual monetary expenditures (including loan repayments, the refund to the federal government, and the donation to close the books) totaled $637,602.

Expenditures broken down by state and the national headquarters also illustrate that Sanford laid the foundation for a national campaign, but never got the chance to build on it. According to Table 5-16, which reports that expenses covered by the national headquarters came to $480,669, only about one-fourth of all income was spent in the states. However, spending of $157,267 in 20 states does not include some $120,000 in expenditures attributable to the various states but paid out of the headquarters. Of all state spending, North Carolina captured the largest share with $75,919, in accordance with Sanford's strategy and the early base of operations there. Massachusetts and New Hampshire, states with early primaries, attracted $30,440 and $16,799, respectively. The committee spent smaller amounts in states that usually give a good return on fund-raising activities, California and New York. Expenditures in the former were $9,741 and $6,136 in the latter. Next in order is Sanford's neighboring state of South Carolina, which took $5,322 worth of expenses. All other states were attributed amounts less than $5,000.

Although Sanford was not able to test his voting strength, his spending came to fruition in that Jimmy Carter adopted his view of the Democratic race. In North Carolina, Carter appealed to Sanford's projected constituency and went on to defeat Governor Wallace.

Shapp

The ill-starred candidacy of Milton J. Shapp began on September 25, 1975, when the Pennsylvania governor announced his candidacy for the Democratic nomination. The Shapp for President Committee, headquartered in Harrisburg, had formed in June to raise funds and publicize the candidate, who barely figured in national opinion polls. His dark-horse bid generated speculation that Governor Shapp was really seeking solid control of the Pennsylvania delegation, the vice presidency, or a cabinet post in a Democratic administration. Shapp insisted, however, that he was pursuing the presidential nomination, and his committee accordingly planned an ambitious financial drive and primary fights in the large states. These intentions came to naught when extremely poor showings in Massachusetts and Florida led the governor to withdraw after spending almost $900,000.

Shapp for President operated under the cloud of recently exposed corruption in Pennsylvania government and a grand jury probe of a $20,000 unreported contribution to Shapp's 1970 gubernatorial campaign. More than a year after Shapp withdrew from the contest, the presidential campaign was implicated in a scandal when the Federal Election Commission unearthed fraud in the Shapp committee's 1976 submission for matching funds. The FEC's 1977 audit revealed that the Shapp committee had met the requirements of raising $5,000 in 20 states improperly by including contributions made by certain persons in the names of others. The FEC ruled that the elimination of such illegal contributions put Shapp under the threshold in five of the states. The commissioners therefore ordered Shapp to repay nearly $300,000 in matching funds that his campaign had received. The governor, who had become a millionaire in the electronics industry before entering politics, promptly agreed to return the sum from his own funds, but denied any knowledge of wrongdoing by members of his campaign staff. In late 1977 the FEC was investigating certain staff members of the Shapp committee to determine if civil or criminal charges should be pressed.

The Campaign. Although Governor Shapp attended many small fund-raising events, the committee primarily raised funds through solicitations made by the staff, which included several professional fund-raisers. Originally, the committee had aimed to qualify for matching funds by October 1975 to demonstrate to the media and the public that Shapp was a serious contender. This goal was proclaimed by the candidate and became an embarrassment when eligibility was still unattained at the end of 1975; it undoubtedly contributed to the pressure that led some fund-raisers astray. In a September press conference, Shapp acknowledged that the threshold had been reached only in his home state, and by mid-December only six more states had surpassed $5,000 in contributions of $250 or less. Later evidence would show that Shapp had met the threshold requirement in 15 states in January 1976, when he erroneously claimed eligibility for public monies.

The fund drive nevertheless achieved some success. In June 1975, before soliciting began, contributions arrived at the rate of $1,000 a day, according to the campaign manager. By the end of September, $121,700 had been raised, with more than 80 percent of the contributions coming from Pennsylvania. At the end of 1975 Shapp had approximately $250,000 in private funds, and efforts during the first month of 1976 brought in an additional $80,000 or more. At the end of the campaign, contributions totaled $367,429. Of this amount, about 30 percent came in contributions of $100 or less, and 28 percent came in denominations of $500 or more.

Not included in the above contribution total are substantial funds provided by Shapp and his wife Muriel. The Supreme Court's ruling in *Buckley* suspended the limit on contributions by candidates to their own campaigns, and shortly after the decision Shapp announced that he would supplement $30,000 contributed by his wife in 1975. By the close of the campaign, Shapp and his immediate family had contributed a total of $141,000. The governor also lent the campaign $98,961, which was outstanding in May of 1977. Shapp's repayment of the $299,066 in matching funds made him no longer subject to the contribution limit reimposed by the 1976 Amendments, which applied only if a candidate accepted matching funds. As a result, the loan will likely be converted to a contribution. The sum of the family contributions, the matching funds reimbursement, and the personal loan is $539,027. This total would be the largest candidate contribution of the 1976 presidential contest and would represent some 60 percent of the Shapp committee's total receipts. It should be noted that such a contribution is less than the millions of personal dollars that Shapp spent in his gubernatorial campaigns.

The Shapp campaign did not disclose a functional breakdown of expenditures, but it may be assumed that expenses for basic functions such as fund raising, travel, salaries, and office operation constituted a large proportion of total spending because only two primary states attracted high expenditures. In Massachusetts the Shapp forces made moderate use of media and spent a total of $159,000, hoping to finish near the top in the March 2 primary. Voters paid little attention to Shapp's efforts and gave him 3 percent of the vote — last place in a field of nine. The governor looked for improvement a week later in Florida where, because he was Jewish, he hoped to do well among the state's large Jewish population. Still, a heavy media campaign and expenditures of $223,500 did not put Shapp in the running. He received 2.5 percent of the ballots cast — an amount insufficient to top the vote for "no preference."

These losses did not diminish general expectations that Shapp would carry Pennsylvania, for he had won the state's governorship by landslides. Moreover, the governor secured his hold on the Pennsylvania delegation when he obtained the support of his bitter adversary, Mayor Frank Rizzo of Philadelphia. Despite the cause for optimism, Shapp withdrew from the presidential race on March 12, 1976, after spending $367,000 in his home state. Most of the money spent in Pennsylvania went toward operation of the national headquarters rather than the primary campaign.

Overall, the Shapp for President Committee spent $280,197 in 1975 and $549,685 in 1976, yielding expenditures of $829,882. A supporting committee in Florida spent another $62,210 to bring total Shapp expenditures to $892,092. In addition, delegate and independent expenditures made on behalf of Shapp came to $632. By mid-1977 the Shapp committee showed outstanding debts of $18,374, which may be paid by the candidate.

The Aftermath. On May 12, 1977, the FEC made public the results of a three-month investigation into the fund-raising practices of the Shapp for President Committee.[41] In the course of a routine audit, FEC staff members discovered that Shapp's initial submission for matching funds, filed January 21, 1976, included contributions made by persons in the names of others, contributions from corporate funds, individual contributions in excess of $1,000, and errors in reporting the state of residence of contributors. In its presentation, the FEC named 40 persons who allegedly made such illegal contributions and three individuals who solicited them. The contributions involved came from five states and included numerous violations.

In Alabama six employees of the Winfield Manufacturing Co. purported to make $250 contributions to the Shapp for President Committee but were actually reimbursed by the company. The company's plant manager, Hugh Walker, and his wife claimed a $500 donation to Shapp, the money for which came from Winfield funds. Seven other Alabamians signed letters stating that they had each made $100 contributions although Eleanor Elias provided the funds; Elias, a $500-a-week Shapp fund-raiser, was named in depositions as an instigator of several fraudulent funding schemes.

In Georgia, Stanley Siegel, an executive of Norstan Industries of Atlanta, provided a total of $1,250 to eight relatives, friends, and Norstan workers who split the sum into contributions of $100 and $250. At a later date, Elias partially reimbursed Siegel. In Texas, an insurance salesman from El Paso, Charles Luciano, divided $1,300 between eight relatives and employees and then made contributions of varying amounts to Shapp. In North Carolina, Gus Nicholas, a Pittsburgh resident with a summer home in the state, funneled $500 to two other men who each reported $250 contributions to Shapp for President. In Nevada, five casino employees signed ticket stubs for contributions at a Shapp fund-raising event, but never gave the $100 apiece attributed to them in Shapp records.

When deducted, the total of $6,770 in improper contributions put Shapp below the $5,000 threshold in each of the five states, which in turn placed the Pennsylvanian short of the 20-state requirement. Therefore, the commission by a 5-0 vote ordered that Shapp repay all of the $299,066.21 in matching funds that his campaign had received. The FEC noted two clues in Shapp's initial submission that gave rise to the investigation. In the five states disqualified as well as a few others, contribution totals were just at or only slightly above the $5,000 threshold, leaving little room for error. Another clue was a pattern of gifts from employees of the same firms, as revealed by the requirement that occupation and employer be disclosed for givers of more than $100.

Governor Shapp's reaction to the FEC's ruling was swift. On the following day, May 13, Shapp stated that he was "appalled" by the commission's findings and he agreed to repay the U.S. Treasury.[42] The former candidate claimed ignorance of any illegal fund-raising methods employed by his subordinates. This move laid to rest speculation by the counsel to the Shapp committee that the governor might challenge the practice of holding a candidate financially responsible for the transgressions of campaign workers.

The FEC took other action against the individuals implicated in the case. At the time of the repayment order, FEC investigators had reached conciliation agreements with 22 persons who signed affidavits admitting their guilt, provided information, and promised further testimony when needed. Of the 22, 16 individuals were subjected to fines ranging from $25 to $500, and one participant was fined $750. Furthermore, the FEC made clear that its investigation would continue and that civil or criminal proceedings might result. The commission referred some aspects of the case to the Justice Department, and attention to the matter led some observers to speculate on the damage it might have done to prospects for public funding of congressional campaigns.[43]

In June 1977 the U.S. Attorney for the Middle District of Pennsylvania announced that his office was in the preliminary stages of an inquiry into Shapp fund raising. In September, however, the Justice Department attracted notice by refusing a request to subpoena Shapp and a top aide to appear before a federal grand jury in Harrisburg. In addition, news sources disclosed that the Justice Department reportedly had turned down a proposal to combine in the investigation the resources of all three federal prosecutors' offices in Pennsylvania. (It was noted that the Middle District office had a small staff and was less experienced in handling complex cases of political corruption.)[44]

In June 1978 the FEC filed suit against Eleanor Elias, charging her with misrepresenting campaign contributions to enable Shapp's committee to qualify for federal funds.[45] The following October, Elias and her husband Samuel were indicted by a federal grand jury "for allegedly having individuals contribute a total of $3,950 in the names of other persons in Alabama, Texas, Connecticut and Georgia."[46] On August 24, 1978, Christopher Passodelis, a Pittsburgh restaurateur, was also indicted by a federal grand jury on charges that he laundered $4,250 in contributions to the Shapp campaign. The 20-count indictment charged that Passodelis had 18 persons in four states contribute his money to the campaign.[47]

Passodelis was convicted in December 1978. In early January 1979 the Eliases pleaded guilty to certain federal election law violations and agreed to cooperate in a further investigation of the Shapp campaign. In return, more serious felony charges concerning willful conspiracy to defraud the government were dropped.[48]

The violations with which Shapp's campaign was charged hold two implications for enforcement of the FECA. First, as commendable as the commission's thorough and forceful action was, detection of abuse came almost a year after the primary campaign had ended. The sheer bulk of documents required by the current public financing system makes unlikely the discovery of irregularities while a campaign is in progress. Later audits are more thorough, but it is not clear how enforcement would proceed if a successful candidate were in office when authorities discovered irregularities in his campaign. Would repayment suffice, or could an incumbent lose the office he had gained, at least partially, by illegal means? Second, a repayment order would be difficult to enforce against a candidate who, unlike Shapp, lacked a personal fortune. Outside funds would be difficult if not impossible to raise for a tainted campaign, especially a losing one. Special circumstances in the Shapp case let the authorities and the public avoid such dilemmas in 1977, but the example points up the potential for difficulties in the future.

Shriver

The Democrats' 1972 vice presidential candidate, R. Sargent Shriver, announced his candidacy for the 1976 presidential nomination on September 20, 1975. The Shriver for President Committee, which had formed in mid-July, was engaged in planning and fund raising at the time of the official announcement. Throughout the early months, Shriver grappled with a problem of image caused by the candidate's relation by marriage to the Kennedys, which fostered uncertainties among the press and the electorate. Some observers suspected that Shriver was holding the door open for brother-in-law Edward Kennedy, in case the Massachusetts senator reversed himself and ran for president. Kennedy's conspicuous neutrality in the Democratic contest reinforced this suspicion. Even without Ted Kennedy in the race, many voters viewed Shriver as nothing more than a pretender to Camelot. Though he lacked experience in elective office, he had proven administrative abilities as director of the Peace Corps and the Office of Economic Opportunity (OEO), ambassador to France, and president of the Chicago School Board.

The unfortunate image and weak organization handicapped the campaign during the opening primaries. Fifth place finishes in the New Hampshire and Massachusetts elections, and a distant third in Illinois, caused Shriver to withdraw on March 22. The brief presidential bid cost $1,020,000, including incurred debts of $261,940 as of May 11, 1976.

Compliance. In July 1975 the Shriver for President Committee initiated consultations with accountants of Arthur Andersen & Co. to establish an efficient system for processing contributions and meeting legal requirements. The campaign employed the firm through October and then decided not to use the system because it was too expensive. Fees for the consultations totaled only about $2,500. Salaried campaign staff provided the actual accounting and clerical work. Compliance cost an estimated $20,000 in clerical salaries and materials; however, much of the work performed to comply with the law would have taken place regardless of the FECA. For instance, the mailing of thank you notes and repeat requests to contributors requires the compilation of dollar amounts and background information of each financial supporter. Two individuals exceeded the $1,000 contribution limit and $65 had to be returned. National staff scrutinized contribution checks and returned some money drawn from incorporated accounts that state and local committees had received. Less than $1,000 came from such sources.

For legal advice, the campaign relied on volunteer counsel, including attorneys from Shriver's large Washington law firm, Fried, Frank, Harris, Shriver, and Kampelman. The committee paid for legal expenses totaling $4,700. In addition, the Shriver staff often sought the opinion of the FEC counsel, feeling that his advice was the most reliable, as well as free.

Fund Raising. To establish their candidate as a serious contender for the Democratic nod, the Shriver organization made eligibility for matching funds the first priority. To attain the threshold of $5,000 in each of 20 states, the staff identified one person in each of the 50 states who could be depended on to head fund raising. Many of those chosen responded eagerly but the results showed such optimism to be "happy talk"; the campaign treasurer then reduced the effort to 22 states thought most likely to be deliverable. Shriver reached the threshold in 20 states in September 1975, an achievement of two months' work. At this time the campaign had raised $186,352 from 920 contributors, for an average contribution of $202.56.

In October 1975 the committee launched a direct mailing with the assistance of Rapp, Collins, Stone, and Adler of New York, the firm that helped make McGovern mailings a success in 1972. The company received $55,500 for its services, of which approximately $17,000 went toward postage and mailing. This mailing was only slightly profitable, since contributions and matching funds combined barely topped the cost. In the winter the campaign formulated its own less expensive mailings. One such mailing, based on rented lists, aimed to reach retired people and white ethnics, two groups responding favorably to the first mailing. Another appeal, mailed in January 1976, sought donations from former OEO and VISTA personnel. The cost of in-house mailings was put at $12,500. In addition, the Shriver forces tried to utilize Kennedy connections with the celebrity world to book benefit performances. A campaign official would not disclose the names of the performers approached, but did state that the celebrities, at the urging of their agents, refused to raise funds for Shriver.

With other avenues unsuccessful, candidate appearances became the mainstay of the fund-raising effort. Shriver traveled tirelessly to attend small cocktail parties organized by local committees. In November alone, he appeared at 23 fund-raisers. Shriver also spoke before larger dinner gatherings of Democrats, which brought in between $15,000 and $20,000. Dinners were held in such centers of wealth as Cape Cod and West Palm Beach. Shriver and his wife sponsored one dinner in Chicago and another lavish gala took place in December on the St. Regis Hotel roof in New York.

Appearances and mailings together attracted approximately $470,000 in private contributions from about 4,800 individuals. Not included in these figures are contributions made after the spring primaries and one generous gift from the candidate.

The biggest financial backer was Sargent Shriver himself, who lent $182,000. After the *Buckley* decision, a candidate could give an unlimited amount to his own campaign. Although the 1976 FECA Amendments reinstated a limit, Shriver lent the money in the time between the Court decision and the signing of the Amendments. Without this personal donation, Shriver's debt could not have been reduced very easily.

Even so, fund-raising activities to retire the debt continued well past the primary campaign. All original contributors received a letter that set the deficit at $85,000 (not counting Shriver's "loan") and requested additional contributions. This mailing brought in about $15,000 with matching funds included. Staff members made personal telephone calls to sympathetic givers in an attempt to generate large gifts. In an innovative step, the campaign sponsored tours of Timberlawn, the Shriver estate, and the homes of Edward Kennedy and Ethel Kennedy, the widow of Sen. Robert F. Kennedy, D-N.Y. Admission to the tours cost $16, while the tours plus "Fun and Games" at Timberlawn went for $25. The October events collected an estimated $25,000 with federal matching.

The Shriver committee closed 1976 with $285,070 in matching funds and slightly under $505,000 in private contributions. These receipts together with the candidate's $182,000 left the campaign some $50,000 short of its $1.02 million expenditures.

Costs. In January 1976, Shriver opened the search for delegates to the July convention. Precinct caucuses in Iowa yielded 3.3 percent of the vote after $23,000 had been spent. Shriver fared better in Mississippi on January 24 with 12.3 percent of the precinct-level ballots. Yet, after expenditures of $24,500, Shriver trailed George Wallace, an uncommitted slate of delegates, and Jimmy Carter.

Shriver entered the February 24 New Hampshire primary, but started well behind the other contenders. According to the candidate, poor organization caused by a lack of "money and time" hurt the effort in the first primary.[49] Fifteen veteran Shriver workers arrived from Washington in early February to fortify the campaign. Nevertheless, Shriver placed a disappointing fifth with 8.2 percent of the vote. Total spending, excluding radio and TV "spillover" from Massachusetts stations, came to $64,000.

Results in Massachusetts a week later were even more disappointing, since the campaign considered the Kennedy connection and a large Catholic vote helpful in the state. Another fifth place, with 7.2 percent of the ballots cast, and total costs of $183,500, spelled the beginning of the end. The Shriver forces pegged Massachusetts as a state where media concentration would be effective. Given the returns, the $155,000 spent on media disproves that strategy. A stronger showing of second place in the Vermont primary could not offset the loss in neighboring Massachusetts. The Vermont election, which was not binding on delegates, gave Shriver 27.6 percent at a cost of $34,500.

Many staffers saw Massachusetts as the make-or-break state and after the March 2 voting rumors that Shriver would pull out abounded. However, the candidate surprised the pessimists by vowing to continue the fight in Illinois on March 16. The Illinois primary brought Shriver's bid to an end, for he ran a poor third behind Carter and Wallace. Previous campaigning drained the treasury so much that Shriver took all staff off salary one week before the Illinois vote. Total expenditures in the state came to $21,500, an inadequate sum for such a large state.

A state-by-state breakdown shows that at least $366,000 was spent on efforts in eight states, not including states where expenditures were below $5,000:

Illinois	$ 21,500
Iowa	23,000
Maryland	8,500
Massachusetts	183,500
Mississippi	24,500
New Hampshire	64,000
Texas	6,500
Vermont	34,500

Table 5-17 shows the 10 major categories of spending, as calculated by the Shriver staff. Operation of the Washington headquarters cost

Table 5-17
Categorical Costs of the Shriver Campaign

National headquarters	$295,000
(includes salaries)	
Telephone	82,000
Radio and TV	155,000
Printed material and postage	88,000
Direct mail	
Mailing house	55,500
In-house	12,500
Fund-raising events	25,000
Travel	95,000
Salaries and living expenses	135,000
(nonheadquarters)	
Rent and supplies	57,000
(nonheadquarters)	
Research	20,000
Total	$1,020,000

$295,000, representing an average of $40,000 a month. Of this, $2,600 a month went toward rent and $18,000 each month was spent for salaries. The second largest expenditure, $155,000 for television and radio advertising in Massachusetts, constitutes the only media cost. Salaries for some national staff members and living expenses for field personnel came to a total of $135,000. Another major expense of $95,000 covered travel for Shriver and staff. The figure is high for a short campaign because some headquarters personnel had to travel to augment state organizations. The next largest category is printed matter and postage, which cost $88,000, with postage being under $20,000. The campaign spent a large proportion of its budget on fund raising. All direct mail added up to $68,000, while fund-raising efforts cost $25,000. Approximately $35,000 in salaries compensated people engaged in the financial drive.

These figures yield a total of $128,000 for fund-raising costs and constitute 12.5 percent of all expenses.

Udall

Morris K. Udall became the first candidate in the 1976 presidential contest on November 23, 1974. Before the official announcement, the lanky Arizona congressman had undertaken an exploratory effort at the urging of some of his colleagues in the House. Udall's travels around the country encouraged him and the Udall '76 Committee formed in August 1974. Ironically, Udall cosponsored the $1,000 contribution limit in the

1974 Amendments that helped to create the chronic shortage of funds for his presidential bid. Despite weak finances and low name recognition, Udall emerged as the most serious liberal challenger to Jimmy Carter; yet strife within the Udall campaign made spending inefficient and victory became impossible. Without a first place in any state primary, Udall never gained the publicity, monetary support, and electoral strength that might have stopped Carter. The candidate dubbed himself "Ol' Seond Place Mo" after recording strong seconds in New Hampshire, Massachusetts, New York, Wisconsin, and Michigan. A week following a valiant but unfruitful fight in Ohio, Udall virtually conceded the Democratic nomination to Carter. The frustrated efforts of the national Udall committee and 29 affiliated committees cost more than $4.7 million.

Compliance. As one of the authors of the new campaign law, Mo Udall insisted on having a meticulous compliance operation. In January 1975 he appointed a long-time friend, Stanley Kurz, to be treasurer. Kurz volunteered his personal services, while his accounting firm of Kurz and Kurz received about $35,000 from the Udall campaign for reporting and auditing work performed over a two-year period. Up to four full-time, paid campaign workers assisted the firm in compliance tasks. Compliance workers had to overcome difficulties in organizing the finances of the 29 state and local committees. For example, the financial staff had trouble persuading some affiliated committees, which maintained their own bank accounts, to send money raised locally into national headquarters. Also, inadequate recording of expenditures by the field committees necessitated a series of amendments to the campaign's FEC reports, a not unusual occurrence for other candidates as well. Early on, Udall '76 computerized its finances and contributor list with the help of PSC Inc. of Washington, D.C. The computer system discovered about $15,000 in contributions that had to be returned because individuals had exceeded the $1,000 limit. For computer services and consultants, the Udall committee spent $192,000, most of which went toward compliance.

In legal matters, the campaign benefited from the expertise of several lawyers on the executive committee and a volunteer counsel whose incidental expenses came to about $2,000. In addition, members of Udall's congressional staff provided interpretations of the FECA and pursuant regulations. An FEC regulation that required copies of all contributor checks caught the campaign off guard. The regulation was retroactive to August 1975 and it forced the Udall organization to request copies of canceled checks from the past year's donors. About 90 percent of the contributors contacted cooperated. The cost of all compliance, including salaries and overhead, was estimated at $300,000.

Fund Raising. Initially, Udall's lack of a national reputation hampered fund raising, but even when he became better known, the fund drive would not take off because Udall failed to win a single primary. The campaign raised $2.7 million in contributions through a costly effort, and only federal matching grants made possible Udall's protracted struggle.

The Arizonan started raising funds in February 1974, and a few events that year garnered a total of $20,975, with the majority of the money coming from Udall's home state. Adhering to the spirit of the 1974 Amendments, Udall voluntarily imposed a $1,000 ceiling on contributions made before January 1, 1975. To generate funds in 1975, the Udall committee employed a four-part strategy consisting of personal solicitations, fund-raising events, televised appeals, and direct mail.

Personal solicitation was the primary method used to attain eligibility for matching funds. Contrary to the expectations of Udall officials, the threshold amounts proved hard to reach. The committee held many meetings to encourage workers in the most promising states to step up face-to-face and telephone contacts with past and potential contributors. By July 1975 the Udall forces had raised $5,000 in 20 states in contributions of $250 or less, and total contributions for the first six months of the year equalled $301,306. Personal solicitations continued throughout the rest of the campaign and increased during financial crises. The candidate himself tried to set aside one hour each day to make telephoned pleas for funds. In 1976 friends of Udall launched a "Lean Cats" program, which tried to produce a large quantity of small contributions.

Many fund-raising events disappointed the hopes of the Udall organization, although, by necessity, it arranged as many of them as possible. In 1975 the campaign tried to book benefit rock concerts, but the musicians approached declined because they were unsure how Udall would fare at the polls. Other people also held this wait-and-see attitude and, accordingly, Udall chose a low-key approach to wealthy possible contributors. He explained, "These kinds of people want to meet you and size you up first; then you go back a second time and try to get some money out of them."[50] The fund-raising staff learned to avoid events that required large investments, such as dinners. The most lucrative dinner, held in Washington, raised only about $15,000. Low-cost cocktail parties, which charged between $25 and $50 for admission, were more profitable. Udall's folksy style worked best at small gatherings of white suburban liberals, a group that became his most solid constituency once he had broken away from the pack of liberal Democrats. For instance, at the height of the Michigan contest, Udall flew to Newton, Massachusetts, outside of Boston, to attend a $25-a-person cocktail party filled with people who had voted for him in the Massachusetts primary. Other successful events highlighted former Watergate Special Prosecutor Archibald Cox, who was a faithful Udall backer. In fact, Cox's first major speaking engagement after the "Saturday Night Massacre" was a testimonial dinner for Udall in Arizona. Cox also made endorsements in newspaper and television advertisements. A desperate financial situation forced the campaign to hold more and more events during the spring primaries, so that the candidate's schedule included frequent daily fund-raisers.

In late April and early May, Udall purchased time on each television network to appeal for donations. The three five-minute broadcasts, modeled after those of Ronald Reagan, came at a time when most observers no longer viewed Udall as a contender. Nonetheless, the programs replenished the coffers enough for Udall to continue until matching payments resumed at the end of May. The Udall committee reported that the cost of TV appeals, fund-raising events, and personal solicitations reached $669,000.

Direct mail, however, was the most expensive additional mode of fund raising, and was the "heart and soul" of Udall finances, according to one of Udall's several campaign managers. The first mailing went out in April of 1975 under the direction of Craver and Co. of suburban Washington. The firm bought several mailing lists of liberal and environmental groups and expanded the Udall list from them. Environmentalists were especially loyal to Udall because of his tough stance for conservation. A later mailing, formulated by Boston media adviser John Martilla and sent to 22,000 individuals, brought in $50,000 in nine days. Eventually, about 62,000 people gave to Udall via direct mail; of these, some 7,000 could be counted on for repeat gifts. However, the high cost of direct mail diminished its return significantly. Udall '76 expended $652,000, or nearly 14 percent of total receipts, for direct mail, in addition to the $699,000 in other fund-raising costs.

The four-part fund drive raised only about $750,000 in 1975, but later support from anti-Carter Democrats increased contributions to approximately $1.6 million in the first half of 1976. The Udall committee estimated that the average contribution in the prenomination period was $32. When Udall's active candidacy ceased in June, his campaign showed a debt of over $700,000, which was to be partially offset by at least $200,000 due in matching funds from the FEC. A much publicized portion of the campaign debt was $123,170 owed to the American Express Co. for lodging and travel charged on Udall's personal credit card. In July 1976 the company filed suit in federal court to receive payment, but the campaign settled the account when matching funds arrived.

To eliminate other debts Udall '76 sponsored a series of fund-raisers beginning with one at the Democratic National Convention. On September 13, 1976, nominee Carter addressed a dinner in Phoenix, Arizona, raising about $50,000, exclusive of matching funds, for Udall. The affair cost about $20,000. On September 22, Senator Edward Kennedy spoke before a Washington cocktail party on behalf of Udall and raised about $14,000 without matching funds. In November the campaign sent a plea to past direct-mail givers and received about $85,000 not counting the match. This mailing got an unexpected boost from sympathy engendered by a household accident in which Udall broke both of his arms. Other events and personal solicitations brought the campaign out of debt in early 1977.

All types of fund raising cost $1,351,000 or just over 28 percent of total expenditures. This sum produced total private contributions of $2,729,742 and matching grants of $2,020,258, for total receipts of $4,750,000. Thus, Udall established one of the highest public-to-private funds ratios of any of the 1976 candidates. Almost three-fourths of the private funds came in denominations of $100 or less. The campaign received approximately 100,000 contributions; but only 2,000 of them were between $101 and $499, and fewer than 500 contributions were of $500 or more.

In 1977 the Udall committee repaid all loans it had secured from individuals near the end of 1975, during the reconstitution of the FEC, and after the nominating convention. Loans borrowed at any time yielded a gross total of $218,045, including $70,000 borrowed from the candidate. Udall and his immediate family made no monetary contributions.

Costs. The Udall campaign might have gone further into debt had not the candidate and his brother Stewart, the campaign chairman, urged a cautious approach to spending. In addition to caution, insufficient funds and internal feuds caused the campaign to spend inadequately in a number of key primaries.

Considering the duration of its effort, the Udall organization spent fairly little. Expenditures in 1974 came to a scant $12,500, though the high initial costs of direct mail accelerated outlays to about $50,000 a month by mid-1975. Spending in 1975 came to approximately $1 million, and the committee owed more than $100,000 at the close of that year. Federal subsidies at first eased the financial situation, but the two-month lapse in matching payments severely damaged Udall's bid. The cutoff inhibited spending in the primaries in New York and Wisconsin where Udall had planned to establish himself as the leading candidate. By early May, Udall was due about $380,000 from the FEC and, without this money, he was forced to forgo important expenditures in later primaries. After Congress had reconstituted the FEC, Udall accused President Ford of stalling in reappointing the commissioners. He asserted, "While Mr. Ford is trying to kill off Reagan, he is shooting me also as an innocent bystander."[51] Expenditures in 1976 came to approximately $3.7 million, including an estimated $150,000 spent after the spring primaries for overhead, salaries, and fund raising. Total campaign expenditures equaled $4,750,000, of which the 29 affiliated committees spent about $1,250,000 and the national committee spent $3,500,000. Expenses reported by delegates committed to Udall totaled $11,661 and independent expenditures made on Udall's behalf came to $2,052.

The proper expenditure of funds in the states became a continuing issue within the national Udall committee. Internal troubles began in Iowa where the financial staff had hoped to limit spending to conserve resources for the New England primaries. Financial officials had set the original Iowa budget at $25,000, but the political staff ran up expenditures to three times that figure, a large portion of which went for television commercials that were generally considered ineffective. The state organization, which spent about $41,500, developed rifts, too. The free spending resulted in only a fifth place with an embarrassing 5 percent of the Iowa caucus vote.

The Iowa money would have been better spent in New Hampshire. There, Udall started early and had a dedicated state organization working out of 14 local headquarters. The congressman campaigned hard in New Hampshire and, toward the end of the drive, estimated that he was picking up 1,000 votes each day that he spent in the state. Perhaps the candidate should have spent more time, for Udall placed second to Carter, trailing by only 4,301 votes. In the effort, the national committee spent $210,000 and the state body expended $190,000. The close second could not attract the publicity and money that Udall so desperately needed. Udall later reflected on the inordinate amount of attention Carter gained from his New Hampshire victory: "We all said we weren't going to let New Hampshire do it to us again, and New Hampshire did do it."[52]

Udall benefited more from a second place to Henry Jackson in Massachusetts' March 2 primary. Udall's 18 percent of the vote reinforced his position as the leading liberal. Heavy media advertising coordinated by John Martilla brought expenditures by Udall '76 to $453,000. Two state committees spent a total of $156,000. After the better-than-expected showing in Massachusetts, Udall moved Jack Quinn out of the campaign manager slot and promoted Martilla to it.

During the rest of March, the campaign husbanded its funds in the hope of making New York or Wisconsin the turning point of the 1976 race. A month before the April 6 voting in New York and Wisconsin, Udall officials decided to give first priority to the latter contest, yet the campaign could not bring itself to abandon New York altogether. Even without using media, the national headquarters spent $174,000, while the state organization expended $107,000. Helped by endorsements from the Americans for Democratic Action and former supporters of Birch Bayh, Udall finished surprisingly well with 25.2 percent of the delegates, for his third second place. However, the money spent in New York might have brought more significant results if spent in Wisconsin.

Campaign strategists looked to Wisconsin for Udall's first first-place finish, and the candidate campaigned extensively in the state, spending many more days than Carter spent there. In the state where the Progressive Party was founded, Udall began labeling himself a progressive rather than a liberal. Nevertheless, the Udall camp had not given Wisconsin top priority soon enough, and the attack got off to a slow start. Jimmy Carter came to the primary with unanticipated momentum from victories in Florida and North Carolina. A private poll conducted three weeks before the voting put Udall in third place behind Carter and Jackson, and the discouraged financial staff responded by keeping a lid on spending. To save $25,000, Stewart Udall took TV ads off the air the weekend before election day. To keep another $20,000, he canceled a mailing to 100,000 rural Wisconsin voters. Yet a poll taken one week before April 6 warranted increased spending, for Udall then trailed Carter by only 4 percentage points. National treasurer Stan Kurz explained that if the political operatives had been encouraging earlier, the financial personnel would have gone for broke. In the end, the national and state committees spent a total of $725,000 in Wisconsin, but a few more dollars might have made the crucial difference. On the night of the balloting, Udall was the apparent victor until 2 a.m., when late returns gave Carter a 1 percent edge of fewer than 5,000 votes. The loss was especially heartbreaking because the votes for either of fellow-liberals Harris or Shriver would have given Udall the victory. Stewart Udall's actions in Wisconsin infuriated John Martilla and the two bickered for two weeks. Shortly before the Pennsylvania primary, Mo Udall fired Martilla, and appointed John Gabusi to manage the campaign for the remainder of the spring.

Although most observers wrote off Udall after Wisconsin, the congressman fought on. He entered Pennsylvania, not expecting to win, but hoping to place second again. Feeling the crunch from the cessation of matching payments, the national headquarters spent $217,000, which included $80,000 worth of media, and the Pennsylvania organization supplemented this with expenditures of $98,000. Election results were even more disheartening; Udall placed third with only 19 percent.

The Arizonan's next bit of bad luck came in Indiana, where he never made the race. The state found that Udall petitions lacked 15 signatures in one congressional district, and it therefore refused to place Udall's name on the ballot. Campaign lawyers filed suit in federal court against the requirement of a certain number of signatures, but a three-judge panel upheld Indiana's law. The U.S. Supreme Court declined to intervene.

The defeat in court left Udall trying for a comeback in Michigan on May 18. Again, the early polls discouraged subordinates, but the candidate campaigned effectively, spending 12 days in the state. Campaign workers carefully staged media events that permitted Udall to speak on the issues, free of charge, on TV news programs in all of the state's major markets. In addition, the campaign spent about $10,000 on radio spots, $54,000 for two 30-second television spots, $4,000 on a five-minute TV program, and $7,000 for telethons. Total expenditures were reported at $215,470. In commercials and on the stump, Udall ridiculed Carter for duplicity on the issues, using direct quotes from Carter statements. This hard-hitting strategy apparently worked, although, once more, Udall could have gained from a little more time and money. He took 43.2 percent of the ballots cast, just over 1,000 votes behind Carter. The near-upset in Michigan slowed Carter's drive and augmented Udall's stamina.

The Ohio primary provided the final showdown in which Udall hoped finally to gain a victory that would deadlock the Democratic convention. The Udall forces concentrated their efforts on the Cleveland metropolitan area and won endorsements from local labor leaders. The national staff designed a barrage of media ads that pointed out contradictions in Carter's positions. Matching funds allowed the national committee to spend $257,000, while the state committee expended $76,000. All the effort failed to stop Carter, who took 52.2 percent of the vote compared with Udall's 21 percent.

The hapless Udall finished the 1976 race with the second-highest amount of delegates. After conferring with Carter, Udall announced on June 14, 1976, that his delegates could vote for the Georgian on the first ballot if they so chose. Thus ended a classic case of what-might-have-been, although Udall stopped short of a complete withdrawal so as to have some influence over the party platform and to maintain eligibility for matching funds.

Together, the national and field committees for Udall spent $4,750,000, and Table 5-18 reports a functional breakdown of these expenditures. The largest category of spending was media, which captured over one-fourth of the budget at $1,205,000. Travel expenses totaling $820,000 constituted the second-largest category. Fund raising,

Table 5-18
Udall Campaign Expenditures, August 1, 1974 to April 30, 1977

Salaries	$ 522,000
Travel	820,000
Media	1,205,000
Consultants and computer services	192,000
Postage	197,000
Telephones	254,000
Rent	44,000
Research	51,000
Fund raising	699,000
Direct mail	652,000
Other	
(includes utilities, petty cash,	
office expenses, and supplies)	114,000
Total expenditures	$4,750,000

exclusive of direct mail, was the next-highest function at $699,000, while direct mail cost $652,000. Salaries were $522,000 and telephone services came to $254,000. Other functions each cost less than $200,000 and totaled $598,000.

Wallace

As soon as debts from his 1972 campaign were settled, Gov. George C. Wallace of Alabama commenced his fourth try for the presidency. In 1973 the Wallace Campaign Inc. changed its Montgomery address to P.O. Box 1976, and began raising funds and organizing supporters. Wallace stayed in the headlines with his recovery from a 1972 assassination attempt, indications of 1976 primary support in several southern states, and a tour of Europe to strengthen his knowledge of foreign affairs. In an attempt to fluster other Democrats, Wallace delayed announcement of his candidacy until November 1975, and kept alive the possibility of a third-party run. His campaign officials maintained contacts with a number of minor parties and conservative coalition groups.

Of all the Wallace campaigns, the 1976 version was the most sophisticated and professionalized. Aggressive fund raising and formidable spending brought total expenditures to $10.5 million. Yet Wallace proved weak at the polls, for time had passed the Alabamian by. Decisive defeats at the hands of fellow-southerner Jimmy Carter in Florida, Illinois, and North Carolina extinguished the governor's long dream of capturing the White House. In late March, Wallace ruled out a third-party candidacy and thereafter his efforts were diminished in the remaining primaries for lack of funds. The last-hurrah campaign officially ended on June 9, 1976, when Wallace turned over his 168 delegates to Carter.

Compliance. Although the compliance operation of the Wallace campaign conformed to the letter of the law, the candidate and his top officials were less assiduous than were some of those in competing campaigns.

To ensure the legality of all contributions, six workers in the national headquarters screened checks and recorded contributor information. A computer stored data and rejected contributions in excess of the $1,000 limit. In spite of this process, the campaign had difficulty proving Wallace's eligibility for matching funds, because it had not kept copies of contribution checks before August 1975 when the FEC required all campaigns to do so. Federal auditors could not verify Wallace's attainment of eligibility until the campaign provided new documentation early in 1976.

In a more serious matter, the campaign reported paying "royalties" to George Wallace for the use of his likeness on medallions and wristwatches sold for contributions. The sale items cost the campaign approximately $100,000, and of this amount the self-proclaimed champion of the common man received $43,999 in personal fees from 1973 through 1975. Wallace claimed the royalty payments went into a special account for care of his paraplegic condition. In September 1975, the Federal Election Commission reluctantly ruled that the payments were legal. The governor also kept friends and relatives on the campaign payroll, including his brother Gerald, who received $6,000 for "legal services" in 1973 and 1974. In addition, the top officers of the Wallace bid were paid, unlike their counterparts in most presidential campaigns. The candidate's brother-in-law, F. Alton Dauphin, Jr., served as finance director, receiving a $25,000 annual salary, and the campaign manager, Charles S. Snider, received a higher salary. The daughters of both Dauphin and Snider also were on the payroll.

Other more novel and uncertain interpretations of campaign law prompted further scrutiny by the FEC. In mid-1975 the commission looked into a credit arrangement between the campaign and the direct-mail firm of Richard A. Viguerie. The mailing magnate had performed services in advance of payment to launch the direct-mail drive in 1973. Later, Viguerie allowed the campaign to stay $200,000 to $300,000 behind in paying bills. Some FEC members felt that the credit constituted a corporate contribution or a loan in excess of the $1,000 limit. However, the commission took no action against the campaign or the direct-mail company. In April 1976 Wallace officials closed field offices, but encouraged supporters to reopen them with their own money plus supplies from the national headquarters. The campaign had hoped the supplies so used would be "independent expenditures" under the *Buckley* decision and therefore need not be credited against spending limitations. FEC Counsel John Murphy cautioned the Wallace Campaign that use of supplies in such a manner did not constitute an "independent expenditure" within the meaning of the *Buckley* decision.

The FEC completed a preliminary audit of the Wallace campaign in July 1976. At that time it questioned the legitimacy of $877,000 worth of expenditures. That figure was reduced through negotiations until the FEC released its final audit in April 1978 and ordered Wallace to repay $96,670 in matching funds used for unqualified campaign expenditures.

The largest item in question was $63,000 in advances given to Wallace campaign workers that were not accounted for. The audit also said the campaign spent more than $28,000 from bank accounts in eight states that was never accounted for. The rest of the money involved apparent personal misuse of campaign funds, much of it by Wallace's campaign chairman, Charles Snider, the FEC said.

After the release of the audit Wallace appeared personally before the FEC, the first presidential candidate ever to do so, and asked for an extension of the deadline by which he had to repay the $96,000. He told the FEC that the missing funds involved "only a question of proper receipts" and noted that many of his campaign expenditures were recorded only on the checks his campaign committee used. He said the committee needed extra time to acquire the checks that would prove the money was used for legitimate campaign expenses. The commission granted him an extension of several weeks.[53]

Fund Raising. At the outset, the Wallace campaign had intended to raise $10 million in contributions and to decline federal subsidies. While symbolizing Wallace's opposition to big government, this plan would have permitted him to chide opponents for politicking at the taxpayers' expense. When the fund-raising goal appeared impossible to reach, the governor compromised his principles. Nonetheless, Wallace led all other Democrats except Carter (who surged ahead only in June 1976) in private contributions.

The Wallace fund drive followed the candidate's particular strengths and weaknesses. Governor Wallace's confinement to a wheelchair limited the number of personal appearances and reduced the value of fund-raising events. The campaign arranged some rallies in 1976, but not nearly the quantity of them held in previous campaigns. As before, the typical 1976 program included a warm-up show by country singer Billy Grammer, a collection among the audience, and a speech by the governor. The Wallace fund-raising appeal had always been directed at the "little man" and, as a result, no program for soliciting wealthy potential contributors existed. The sale of promotional items brought in several hundred thousand dollars, but direct mail provided the bulk of private money for Wallace. As with McGovern in 1972, Wallace's position near an ideological extreme was conducive to an elaborate mail campaign.

In 1973 the Wallace campaign contracted with the Richard A. Viguerie Co. of Falls Church, Va., and in August the direct-mail firm sent letters designed to expand the Wallace mailing list. In the first year of the direct-mail program, Viguerie mailed more than six million pieces to potential contributors and more than 750,000 to established Wallace backers. By August 1974 direct mail had cost an estimated $1.4 million and had yet to bring in equivalent contributions. The prospecting phase of the drive continued until mid-1975 at which time the Wallace house list contained 400,000 names. Finance director Dauphin calculated that letters to individuals new to a Wallace appeal brought in about $208,000 less than expenses for list rental, printing, and mailing. Appeals to past Wallace contributors showed better results and made the direct-mail drive break even in early 1975. By fall of 1975 the Viguerie Co. had been paid a total of $2,344,000.

In late 1975 and into 1976 the campaign made monthly mailings to a hard core of nearly 200,000 contributors. The various letters included opinion polls on red, white, and blue paper, advertisements for promotional items, and autographed pictures of the governor. Repeat appeals suffered according to the law of diminishing returns, and Wallace's electoral disappointments inhibited donations. A mailing in April 1976 collected only $150,000 from a list that previously had brought in up to $700,000. Federal subsidies compensated for lagging contributions and direct mail must be credited with qualifying Wallace for matching funds. Although contributions were concentrated in 10 southern states, direct mail gave Wallace nationwide support based on many small contributions.

The chronology of the campaign's total receipts bears witness to the overall success of direct mail. Income of approximately $267,000 in 1973 combined with 1974 contributions of about $1,759,000 to bring total receipts to $2,026,000 in less than two years of fund raising. In the first six months of 1975 contributions accelerated and the campaign collected $1,671,660. Income declined slightly during the second half of the year, as total 1975 receipts came to more than $3.1 million. Through most of 1975 the campaign held cash balances of about $500,000, a sign that contributions were outpacing expenditures. Mailings and rallies put 1976 contributions at approximately $1.6 million, making total private funds $6.8 million. Raising the money was costly, however, and the Viguerie firm received at least $2.6 million for its services over a three-year period.

In public funds, Wallace received $3,291,309 to match contributions
made after January 1, 1975. This amount represents nearly one-third of
total receipts and about 40 percent of all funds received under the 1974
Amendments. Another sign of the egalitarian nature of Wallace fund
raising is the average contribution, calculated by the FEC at $14.75.
Also, the commission estimated that 89 percent of private funds raised
from 1975 on came in contributions of $100 or less.

Costs. Abundant receipts enabled the Wallace campaign to spend
freely for fund raising, organization, media, and travel. High expenditures in early primaries led to a serious financial crisis, and the
campaign cut back drastically later in the spring.

In 1973 and 1974 the campaign expended nearly all receipts for
further fund raising. Total expenditures in 1973 came to about $986,200
and spending in 1974 reached $1,636,980. At the close of the first year,
the campaign ran in the red, and at the start of 1975 it had only $198,000
on hand. Spending increased sharply in 1975 to $2.9 million, though a
much better balance was achieved. In 1976 spending outstripped both
public and private income for the same period at $4,974,000. Cash on
hand dwindled to $250,000 in March, forcing Wallace officials to econo-
mize. In April the national headquarters stopped funding for 40 of 50
state offices, dismissed 100 employees to reduce paid staff to only 30,
and grounded the campaign's chartered aircraft. Recalling the 1972
deficit, Governor Wallace implored subordinates to avoid going into
debt, but the Wallace Campaign Inc. was trying to pay debts of more
than $30,000 as late as 1977. Expenditures for the three-year campaign
totaled $10,575,944, exclusive of $8,416 in independent expenditures and
money spent by supporting committees and committed delegates.

Although the Wallace campaign would not release a functional
breakdown of its expenditures, certain costs can be estimated. Fund
raising, primarily the expensive direct-mail drive, must have cost close
to $3 million or more than one-fourth of the budget. Salaries, travel, and
media were likely the next most expensive functions. The campaign
paid many people well, over a long period of time. Some 130 individuals
were on the payroll at the height of the presidential race, and top
officials drew salaries in the neighborhood of $20,000 while field organiz-
ers received $12,000 a year. An educated guess would place the total cost
of salaries at approximately $2 million. With so many workers, travel
expenses also had to be high, especially since the governor and his
entourage traveled for several months on a chartered jet that cost
$100,000 a month to operate. To minimize the rigors of traveling,
Wallace decided to utilize a broad media campaign. Early on, field
organizers were equipped with video players that brought the candidate's encouragement to grass-roots workers. In the initial primaries, a

large number of spot announcements and a half-hour program were aired in some areas. Wallace tried to meet the issue of his health head-on with TV ads that showed him tossing a football. In a last-minute search for votes on June 5, 1976, Governor Wallace appeared on a five-minute network television broadcast that cost about $30,000. Travel and media each probably cost between $1 million and $2 million.

Difficulty arises in reporting Wallace spending in the states because the campaign did not have to allocate pre-1975 expenditures. Therefore, the figures given for the states below should be considered conservative estimates.

Wallace planners chose to bypass Iowa and New Hampshire in a successful effort to win first in precinct caucuses in the more friendly territory of Mississippi. Although Wallace publicly discounted his ability to carry a caucus state because his voters would not be interested in the lengthy process, the campaign organization did an impressive job in Mississippi. Letters went out to some 8,000 supporters in the state and White Citizens' Councils assisted in the get-out-the-vote effort. Advertisements urged the Wallace constituency to "stop the liberal grab."[54] In addition, three past governors, all segregationists, endorsed the Alabamian. The campaign reported spending $152,600 in Mississippi to win the 43 percent of the precinct-level voting. However, some observers believed that Wallace should have done better in the state that he carried by 65 percent in 1968.

The Wallace forces aimed to repeat the Mississippi performance in South Carolina on February 28. Offices opened in the state three weeks before the caucus voting, and about 16,000 residents on the Wallace mailing list received campaign literature. Wallace himself visited South Carolina five times and his organization spent $30,000 for media, almost twice the Carter media budget. Total expenditures came to $201,000. With 28 percent of the vote, Wallace led Carter by four percentage points, but an uncommitted slate of delegates took 47 percent. The uncommitted bloc had the backing of many blacks and liberals, and its strength greatly qualified Wallace's victory, in spite of claims to the contrary.

Massachusetts on March 2 provided the first primary test of the Wallace bid. Wallace entered the only state that had voted for George McGovern in 1972 because he intended to prove his strength in a northern industrial state, to benefit from a divided liberal field, and to take advantage of the Boston busing controversy. Six offices across the state supervised workers and coordinated the organizational help of several antibusing groups. The state was saturated with leaflets and a media blitz that cost an estimated $200,000. The candidate canceled appearances in other states to spend a total of three weeks in Massachusetts. In his first visits, Wallace avoided inflammatory remarks on the busing issue, but just before election day he stepped up attacks on court-ordered busing. The massive effort cost $442,000, but did not pay off, for Wallace finished third with 17 percent. That their man carried the city of Boston cheered the Wallace forces, but that was the last heartening event of 1976.

In the Florida primary, it became evident that Wallace had not grasped the significance of changing times. Many of the other can-didates were addressing perennial Wallace complaints in different tones while offering solutions. More important, Jimmy Carter was wooing Wallace's southern backers. Feeling confident of a repeat of his 1972 victory, Wallace diverted his time away from Florida. His effort in the state was poorly organized, and the small size of early crowds worried officials so that massive advertising preceded later rallies. An extensive media drive cost $200,000 out of total expenditures of $745,000. Yet a more dignified Wallace failed to generate the enthusiasm he had stirred four years before and he finished with 30.6 percent to Carter's 34.3.

Next, Wallace returned to the North for the Illinois primary on March 16. Responding to polls that showed voters to be concerned with the state of his health, Wallace escalated assurances about his fitness. In one Illinois town, he quipped, "You don't have to be an acrobat to be president."[55] Six days and $448,000 spent in Illinois brought Wallace a mere three delegates after he had predicted winning 30.

The loss in Illinois dispirited the Wallace forces working for a much-needed victory in North Carolina. In the week prior to the March 23 primary, the state organization began to crumble; one worker com-plained, "It's like nobody is at the helm of this campaign at times."[56] The candidate himself lost his mild manners when speaking personally of opponent Carter. In Raleigh, Wallace called Carter a "warmed over McGovern" and a "liar."[57] The North Carolina media drive cost at least $125,000, with $25,000 going toward one 30-minute special. Total spend-ing in North Carolina reached $358,000, but was not enough to stop Carter. Wallace took only 35 percent of the vote compared with 53 percent for Carter.

For all practical purposes, the defeat in North Carolina eliminated Wallace from the Democratic nomination contest. After shunning a third-party candidacy, Wallace could only hope to gather enough dele-gates to influence the platform and the selection of the candidate at the convention. To conserve money and personal effort, the campaign started to retrench in late March. Officials decided to halt organizing for the Virginia caucuses and to replace rallies with a media effort in Wisconsin. Although Wallace kept his vow to remain in the primaries, the number of appearances made and the amount of money spent indicated that he was simply going through the motions. One exception was Wallace's home state of Alabama where he campaigned energetically to fend off Carter.

The Republicans

Prior to the resignation of President Richard Nixon, the Republican nomination appeared to be an open contest. The most active potential candidate was Sen. Charles H. Percy of Illinois, who struck a note of reform by accepting no individual contributions greater than $5,000 during 1973 and 1974. However, the presidential opportunities narrowed when Gerald Ford became president. Yet Ford soon found that as the nation's first unelected president he commanded few of the usual advantages of incumbency. By 1976 Ronald Reagan's challenge had grown into a major threat, deadlocking the nominating contest of the "in-party." As a result, rumblings, but not serious candidacies, emanated from the camps of John B. Connally of Texas and Sen. James L. Buckley of New York. Only at the Republican convention did President Ford gain a certain hold on the nomination.

One of many ironies of the Republicans' nominating process in 1976 was that the party philosophically opposed public financing, yet their two prospective standard-bearers received the most money in federal subsidies.

Buckley

About 10 days before the Republican convention, a group of conservative Republicans approached Senator Buckley, Conservative-Republican of New York, about the possibility of submitting his name for the Republican presidential nomination. These party members were concerned because they feared that a candidate selected in a "closed convention" by delegates committed to a particular candidate in earlier primaries would result in a divided party; polls had shown that some Ford supporters would not back Reagan if he were the nominee, and some Reagan supporters would not back Ford. These Republicans believed the submission of Buckley's name might serve to carry the convention through the initial ballots, in which delegates from primary states were bound by law to vote for a particular candidate. Thus the nominee ultimately selected, whether Ford, Reagan, or someone else, would be perceived as the informed choice of the Republican Party in an open convention.

At the group's request, the senator agreed to keep an open mind on the matter while the proposal was tested in what he was assured would be private soundings. But the strategy soon became public. Five days before the convention, Buckley acknowledged that he had been approached by individuals interested in placing his name in nomination, and that he had agreed to suspend judgment until they had had a chance to test out the idea.

Despite the senator's assertion that he viewed the proposal as neither pro-Reagan nor anti-Ford, the move was viewed by some as an attempt to deny Ford a first-ballot victory, thus encouraging switches to Reagan on the second ballot. Buckley's actions drew criticisms from the Ford camp and leaders of Buckley's home-state delegation, which favored Ford over Reagan.

After meeting with representatives of the group in Kansas City, Buckley declared on August 16, the day the convention opened, that he would not permit his name to be placed in nomination, and requested that no delegate vote for him. During this period, Senator Buckley neither formed a campaign committee nor reported any spending to the Federal Election Commission.

Connally

Former Democratic Governor of Texas John Connally, who served as secretary of the Treasury under Richard Nixon in 1971 and 1972 and became a Republican in 1973, unsuccessfully played the role of candidate-in-waiting for the 1976 Republican presidential and vice presidential nominations. Although Connally never formed a campaign committee or declared a candidacy for either office, from late 1975 until the summer of 1976 he appeared to be eager for the right opportunity to enter the Republican fray.

In August 1975 Connally raised between $300,000 and $400,000 at a Houston dinner billed as a nonpartisan tribute to the Texan. As personal income, this money funded Connally's travels across the country, enabling him to speak out on the issues and keep his name alive during the primary season. Connally also became the most successful money-raiser of 1976 for the Republican Party, speaking at scores of state and national party functions. Connally hoped that these activities would position him as a compromise candidate if either Ford or Reagan were eliminated. Yet the Ford-Reagan battle remained indecisive for so long that there was no room for the self-styled pragmatic conservative.

The only overt campaigning for Connally occurred when conservative direct-mail wizard Richard Viguerie spent $35,000 of his own money for a Connally write-in drive in the New Hampshire primary.[58] With this independent expenditure, Viguerie sent out letters urging the state's Democrats to write in Connally's name on their party's ballot. Viguerie ran Connally as a Democrat because there were no other conservative Democrats in the New Hampshire race, but the effort netted Connally only 24 votes.

Once Gerald Ford emerged as the likely Republican presidential nominee, speculation developed that the president might choose John Connally for the second spot on the ticket; Connally did nothing to discourage such a possibility. Yet, possibly because of Connally's close association with the Nixon administration and the Watergate and dairy lobby scandals, [59] Ford bypassed the Texan. Connally's 1976 activities however, certainly left him in contention for the 1980 race.

Ford

As the first unelected president, Gerald R. Ford sought the Republican nomination without many of the usual advantages of incumbency. Ford failed to appear unchallengeable despite his extensive campaigning for Republican congressional candidates, successful fund raising for Republican organizations, and an early lead in opinion polls. When behind-the-scenes efforts could not dissuade Ronald Reagan from running, the president was woefully unprepared for a long campaign. Organizational work finally began in June 1975 with formation of the President Ford Committee (PFC), and the chief executive formally announced his candidacy on July 6, pledging "an open and above-board campaign."[60]

From the outset, the PFC experienced factional strife that was hardly mitigated by the eventual resignation of two committee officers — treasurer David Packard, a former deputy secretary of Defense, and campaign manager Howard H. "Bo" Callaway, who had served as Ford's secretary of the Army. Although the Ford committee overcame initial fund-raising difficulties, it never developed a consistent political strategy. Ford vacillated between demonstrating his presidential qualities, by working visibly in Washington, and going out on the stump to attack opponent Reagan.

The disorganized campaign won narrow victories in early primaries, but was incapable of crushing the Reagan challenge, which started anew after Ford's unexpected loss in the North Carolina primary on March 23. Though President Ford controlled most of the delegates from Wisconsin, New York, and Pennsylvania elected in April, he suffered a series of defeats in the Sunbelt states during May. After winning primaries in New Jersey and Ohio, Ford gained the stability needed to pick up delegates elected by state convention and to persuade uncommitted delegates to his cause. At the Republican National Convention in Kansas City, President Ford captured the nomination by a margin of 117 votes. His triumph cost $13.6 million, the most expensive of all 1976 campaigns. Yet Ford's nomination proved to be a Pyrrhic victory, for the battle with Reagan had tarnished the president's image and weakened the party, paving the way for defeat in November.

Compliance. The Ford compliance program strove to demonstrate a break with the 1972 Republican presidential campaign. Indeed, President Ford had wished to run under the auspices of the Republican National Committee to avoid the mistakes of the infamous Committee to Reelect the President, but the Reagan challenge and the new campaign law required an independent organization. As such, the President Ford Committee went all out to abide by the law, spending nearly $600,000 for a comprehensive legal and accounting system.

Unlike other campaigns, the Ford committee had its bank perform many clerical and payroll functions. The Ford committee neither paid for these services, nor were the amounts charged against expenditure limits; the bank received income from compensating balances. Contribution checks went directly from the post office to the Riggs National Bank for deposit; the bank then photocopied checks and kept contributor information so the PFC could handle discrepancies and refunds later. Special computer runs weeded out some $85,000 in contributions from individuals exceeding the $1,000 contribution limit. The Riggs Bank administered the campaign payroll with the help of a computer.

The committee had staff members specialize in certain areas of compliance; one group performed certification and application for matching funds, another oversaw the computerized finances. Other headquarters personnel controlled spending in the states for media and telephone canvassing, while keeping an eye on other expenditures made by the Ford organizations in all 50 states. State committees received advances from the Washington headquarters, but had to account for one payment before getting additional funds. As an incentive, disbursements to the state committees were tied to their fund-raising performance. To guard against unnecessary spending, every state operation ceased shortly after the primary or caucus. It would have been more efficient to keep some offices open for the general election, but the prenomination expenditure limits eliminated such an option.

Despite its meticulous compliance system, the Ford committee became embroiled in a number of controversies involving the president's incumbency. Late in 1975 Ford and the Republican National Committee came under fire because the RNC was paying for the president's travels to speak before Republican groups and the FEC was asked to rule on whether funds spent for the president's travel to build up the Republican Party should be charged against Ford's spending limit for the nomination. The President Ford Committee contended the trips were made in the president's role as titular head of the party and that the test of expenses should be based on the intent and purpose of the trip. The RNC had budgeted $500,000 for party-building efforts in 1975 and by September had spent $309,000.

The Democratic National Committee charged that the trips directly furthered the president's candidacy. For the FEC to rule otherwise, the DNC said, would allow future presidential candidates to be designated as party leader and thus gain electoral advantage. The Citizens for Reagan supported the Democrats' position and also challenged Ford's position as party leader. The Reagan forces claimed their candidate also could be called the party leader since he had raised millions of dollars for the Republican Party in 1975. To fail to count the Ford trips as campaign expenses, they argued, would harm challenges to incumbents from within their own parties.

On November 20, 1975, in a 5-1 vote, the FEC ruled that the Ford trips did not have to be counted as part of his campaign costs until January 1, 1976, after which any presidential appearances primarily would foster Ford's nomination and therefore would count against his spending limit. The president's efforts on behalf of the party did partially benefit his own candidacy, of course, and saved his campaign the $500,000 the RNC had budgeted for Ford's travel.

A similar dispute arose over a social event with political overtones. While spending the 1975 Christmas holidays on a working vacation in Vail, Colorado, President Ford attended a large dinner held by a friend, Sheika Gramshammer. Contrary to PFC instructions, the hostess had mailed dinner invitations and contribution solicitations at the same time, and to many of the same local residents, thus making the social gathering appear to be a fund-raising affair, although the Ford committee disclaimed any such connection. In the end, the federal government picked up the tab for Ford's journey to the resort town, even though Gramshammer had raised at least $10,000 for the campaign under questionable circumstances.

The PFC weathered further criticism concerning the proper accounting of the campaign activities of government personnel. In January 1976 Ford transferred Secretary of Commerce Rogers C. B. Morton to a White House position as domestic and economic adviser and liaison to the PFC. The press and then FEC Chairman Thomas Curtis questioned the move because the taxpayers would be paying for Morton's campaign duties. Under pressure, the White House downplayed Morton's political role, and the controversy ended in late March when Morton became campaign manager. As the primary campaign intensified, other Ford appointees took to the campaign trail and often scheduled partisan and official appearances in the same trip, thereby sparing the PFC high costs. On March 30, 1976, for example, Treasury Secretary

William E. Simon journeyed to New York on government business and, while there, attended a Ford committee reception; his department covered $645 in travel and expenses, but the campaign paid only $29 for its portion of the secretary's time.[61] Believing that these accounting methods sidestepped the spirit of the law, the FEC proposed a regulation for future elections that would make the political committee pay full expenses for administration officials' trips that include campaigning.

The Ford committee encountered other accounting problems during the Republican National Convention. Staff members who worked the convention each received a small gavel as an appreciation gift, but FEC auditors disallowed the $713 expenditure as a qualified campaign expense. Auditors also disqualified $292 in parking fines and $3,467 in staff expenses that were insufficiently accounted for.

Although the compliance difficulties of the President Ford Committee resulted in no legal penalties, they do illustrate the peculiar position of an incumbent president as well as certain inadequacies of the campaign act. On the other hand, the PFC went on the offensive to find possible abuses committed by the opposition. The Ford committee accused Reagan officials of assisting unauthorized delegates in the Texas primary who were supposed to run independently of the candidate's organization. The Ford campaign filed a complaint with the FEC requesting that the delegates' spending be counted against the Reagan expenditure limit because Reagan workers were directing the campaigns of some unauthorized Texas delegate candidates. Additionally, Ford lawyers claimed that independent expenditures made by the American Conservative Union on Reagan's behalf actually were planned in concert with the Reagan committee. As with the accusation against Ford, the FEC took no action on the allegations.

Fund Raising. Ford fund raising began poorly because officials concentrated on attracting large contributions, but when they switched to a more broad-based approach, receipts accelerated. Early financial difficulties embarrassed the incumbent's campaign, while not significantly hampering the electoral effort.

Under the direction of California millionaire David Packard, the fund drive relied almost exclusively on personal solicitations during much of 1975. Initially, financial officers had wanted to raise more than $10 million privately and do without matching funds, but low income ruled out this option. Alternatively, Packard planned to raise $5 million in fully matchable funds in 1975 so that fund raising would be completed when federal subsidies arrived in 1976. Actually, Packard's program raised little more than seed money, with only $707,000 raised by October 1, 1975. One month later, receipts stood at $956,600, but more than 60 percent of the total was in contributions greater than $250.

These results are explained by Packard's use of traditional Republican fund-raising devices made obsolete by the 1974 FECA.

The finance chairman himself contacted many "fat cats" of old, and finance committees in major cities augmented his work with the aid of telephone banks. This national network of solicitors experienced some notable disappointments. Gustave L. Levy, who co-chaired Ford's New York finance committee, later reported having "a lot of trouble" raising money from past Republican givers because of the president's opposition to federal aid for New York City.[62] Contributions came in sluggishly in other key states as well, and by the end of 1975 the campaign had received 20 percent or less of its financial goals from wealthy states such as California, Texas, Florida, and Illinois.

In spite of such difficulties, the Ford contributor list eventually contained large donations from many prominent and prosperous Americans. Among contributors of the $1,000 maximum were Vincent Astor, C. Douglas Dillon, Henry Ford II, Henry Clay Frick, J. Paul Getty, E. Roland Harriman, C. V. Whitney, and five members of the Rockefeller family. Moreover, presidential appointees gave generously to the Ford committee after the Justice Department ruled them exempt from statutory prohibition of contributions from federal employees. The vice president and six cabinet members each contributed $1,000 to their boss' campaign, and Labor Secretary William J. Usery, Jr., donated $500. Additional contributions came from White House staffers, ambassadors and heads of independent agencies. In all, the PFC recorded $62,527 in contributions from 106 government employees, including $1,000 contributions from 36 high federal officials.

Within the PFC grew discontent with Packard's emphasis on large contributions, but the chairman opposed massive direct mail. At the end of October, Packard resigned over the issue, and his successor, Robert Mosbacher, a Houston businessman, broadened the appeal of Ford fund raising. Mosbacher greatly expanded the direct-mail program from the one appeal sent out under Packard's tenure and averted financial ruin. The new finance chairman recruited Robert P. Odell of National Direct Mail Services Inc., who took a leave of absence from his Washington firm to take charge of Ford mailings.

The prospecting drive opened with a mailing to 60,000 New Hampshire voters and another appeal to 400,000 Republican households in Florida, seeking political as well as fund-raising appeal. Additional early mailings went to likely Ford supporters, such as executives listed in *Standard and Poor's*, subscribers to *Golf Digest*, owners of swimming pools, and various conservative political organizations. These mailings yielded a more profitable list of contributors, who received repeat solicitations as many as four times. An early Mailgram to 10,000 prospects brought in several hundred thousand dollars. The Ford committee had less luck than expected with letters signed by its officers or other prominent Ford backers at a time when the National Republican Congressional Committee (NRCC) was raising $1.2 million with a missive signed by the president. As a result, the PFC put out later messages over Ford's signature. In addition, Odell's staff formulated mailings to past contributors to the NRCC and the Republican National Committee. The latter body at first refused release of its contributor list to avoid giving unfair advantage to the incumbent, but the national committee eventually decided to rent the list to both the Ford and Reagan campaigns. The NRCC and RNC lists proved quite lucrative, together bringing in more than $1.3 million. By the close of the campaign, direct mail had raised $2,550,000, through nearly 2.6 million pieces of literature.

Supplementing personal solicitations and direct mail were a large number of fund-raising events, some of which charged an admission as low as $10 per person. The more typical event, however, was high priced and surrounded an appearance by the candidate, GOP congressmen, or other administration officials. For instance, in January 1976 Vice President Rockefeller held a $1,000-a-person reception in his Manhattan apartment, and in March President Ford journeyed to California for a $1,000-a-plate dinner and a $500-a-plate lunch. Most cabinet members also took on fund-raising tasks, although the secretaries of State and Defense and the attorney general did not, to maintain the nonpartisan nature of their positions. Secretary of Housing and Urban Development Carla A. Hills declined a request to raise funds, claiming possible conflicts of interest. The fund-raising affairs proved fairly successful, although in several places tickets had to be given away to fill speaking halls; the affairs also helped to involve local community leadership and the cost factor was low even though four staff people were engaged in arranging events.

All types of fund raising collected only $1.7 million by the end of 1975, and less than half this amount was in fully matchable contributions of $250 or less; however, 1976 receipts improved both in the aggregate and in the size of contributions. In January 1976 the PFC received slightly more than $700,000 in contributions, and in February monthly receipts shot up to $1.5 million. Contributions peaked in March when the monthly total reached nearly $1.6 million. Then private receipts started to drop as Ford lost primaries, and during April and May the committee took in a total of $2.5 million. By the close of the campaign, the PFC had raised $9.3 million from 131,000 individuals in little more than a year. Of the total, 37 percent came in contributions of $100 or less, and 14 percent came in denominations between $101 and $499. Contributions of $500 or more composed 49 percent of total individual contributions; this last category, totaling $4,544,195 from some 5,750 individuals, is both the largest amount and percentage of contributions greater than $499 received by any 1976 campaign. Ten states provided almost half of all individual contributions, as shown below by the amounts collected from each state as of August 4, 1976:

California	$1,171,542
Texas	832,849
New York	749,475
Illinois	620,100
Florida	514,540
Michigan	498,698
Ohio	460,408
Pennsylvania	325,380
New Jersey	255,589
Massachusetts	218,250
Total	$4,645,831

The Ford Committee collected additional funds from political action committees. PACs connected with business and the professions donated a total of $153,000 to Ford, well above the comparable figure contributed to Reagan. Among the committees that contributed to Ford were the political fund of the Union Oil Co., which contributed the maximum $5,000, and the California Medical Association, which gave $2,000. PACs donating $1,000 each were affiliated with LTV Corp. (a major defense contractor), Standard Oil of California, and the Olin Corp., as well as the Association of Builders and Contractors of Michigan. Party-related committees contributed an additional $1,600 to the PFC and interest on deposits brought in $9,541.

The belated but substantial influx of private money in 1976 permitted the Ford campaign to emerge unscathed from the period of FEC reconstitution. While other campaigns went heavily into debt during the matching funds cutoff, the PFC maintained balances of several hundred thousand dollars, obviating any loans. The president's credit with the federal government also eliminated cash-flow problems common to other campaigns; as challenger Reagan continually pointed out, the PFC had little cash tied up in deposits because it charged Ford's travel expenses to the government and reimbursed at a later, more convenient time. Of course, matching funds when available further eased the situation and, in all, the Ford committee received federal subsidies of $4,657,008. This amount, second only to Reagan's matching-funds subsidy, constitutes slightly more than one-third of total PFC receipts of $14 million.

The committee closed its books with a surplus of more than $300,000, after having declined some matching funds to which it was entitled. Of the surplus, $150,000 was transferred to the General Election Committee for compliance purposes and the remainder was to be returned to the U.S. Treasury. The PFC calculated that all fund raising cost nearly $2,174,000 or 16 percent of total campaign expenditures.

Costs. The initial Ford strategy called for early elimination of Ronald Reagan and, accordingly, expenditures were high at the start of the primary season but had to be lowered later. Although the Ford committee in total spent more than any other presidential campaign, in many cases President Ford fared better at the polls in states where the committee spent less.

Despite aggregate expenditures of almost $13.6 million, the PFC started as a low-budget operation. The national headquarters opened with three paid staff members, one of whom noted the stringent budget controls by commenting, "I even pay my own parking."[63] By November 1, 1975, the committee had spent only about $500,000, although the last two months of the year saw increasing outlays for direct mail and media, putting total 1975 spending above $1.4 million. Before receipts from direct mail offset expenses, the PFC was disbursing money faster than it came in. For instance, during one week in November 1975 the committee collected $69,000 in contributions, but spent $134,000. Indeed, campaign officials at one point worried that spending for early primaries might have to be curtailed; however, matching funds and rising contributions arrived just in time for the opening primaries. Preparation for these contests brought expenditures to $1.8 million in February alone and, through May, monthly spending stayed near this level. Consequently, the PFC faced a new problem of spending too much too soon, for as of May 1, 1976, expenditures had reached $8.5 million — almost two-thirds of the legal limit — with half of the primaries and the convention still ahead. Drastic cutbacks resulted, including payless Fridays in April and a 25 percent reduction of staff in May, and in July the monthly expenditure figure was down to $950,000. After the Republican convention, the President Ford Committee reported spending $13 million on expenses subject to the $13.1 million limitation and an additional $581,000 for exempt compliance costs.

The long road to victory at Kansas City started in the Iowa caucuses, where a volunteer working out of his basement apartment headed the Ford drive. To go on to win a majority of Iowa's delegates, the PFC expended a mere $50,000. In contrast, the committee spent heavily in New Hampshire's February 24 primary.

In many visits to New Hampshire, Gerald Ford emphasized his incumbency, holding question-and-answer sessions more than delivering prepared speeches to communicate his presidential abilities. Meanwhile, liberal Republicans such as Commerce Secretary Elliot L. Richardson, and Reps. Paul N. McCloskey, Jr., of California and William S. Cohen of Maine, led the attack on Reagan's conservatism. The PFC also criticized Reagan for vacillating on Social Security issues in a press release that drew an angry response from the former California governor. To an extent, Ford's incumbency turned into a liability when Richard Nixon traveled to China just four days before the New Hampshire voting, because the much-publicized trip reminded voters of the pardon given Nixon by President Ford. The Ford forces tried to counter the effect of the untimely journey with massive telephone canvassing to get out the vote. A heavy turnout and total expenditures of $199,000 brought victory for the president, although his 51 percent win was hardly a vindication.

One week later, President Ford ran in the Massachusetts and Vermont primaries with little opposition from Reagan. Without making an appearance in either state, Ford spent $163,500 in Massachusetts and $2,652 in Vermont, and won by wide margins in both. The next true contest came in Florida on March 9.

The Ford effort in Florida began discouragingly as the state and national organizations fought each other, and the Florida manager, Rep. Louis Frey, Jr., admitted that he preferred Reagan but considered Ford more electable. To put the campaign in more enthusiastic hands, several top-level national officials arrived, bringing the paid staff in Florida to 40 persons. The president himself made two swings through the state and each time drew large crowds and took full advantage of his office. Ford announced construction of a new veterans' hospital and awards of a mass transit grant for Miami and a missile contract for an Orlando company. He also claimed credit for bringing the 1978 International Chamber of Commerce Convention to Orlando. This unabashed use of the federal dole prompted attacks by Reagan, but the president had made the intended impression as an accomplished administrator. As internal tensions eased, the Ford organization established 15 telephone banks and recruited platoons of door-to-door canvassers. The late-starting bid cost $844,000 and delivered 53 percent of the vote to Ford.

The campaign next moved to Illinois where it won assistance from the state Republican organization and popular Senator Percy. The president also gained free television coverage when he gave a lengthy interview to four Chicago anchormen, purposely held one week before the Illinois voting. In Illinois, the PFC spent more than $795,000, which encouraged Reagan to concede the state even before the primary. Ford's triumph with 59 percent of the vote led his committee to send out feelers for a withdrawal by Reagan.

North Carolina's March 23 primary, however, showed such confidence to be unwarranted. The general tone of the Ford bid became inconsistent, for the president made one showcase appearance before 4,000 teenagers at the Charlotte convention of Future Homemakers of America, while at other forums he icily answered Reagan's critique of his administration. During Ford's first trip to North Carolina the above-the-battle image was further tarnished when campaign manager Bo Callaway temporarily resigned in the midst of charges that as secretary of the Army he had used his influence for personal gain. As a Senate investigation dragged on, Callaway's resignation became permanent and, though no criminal proceedings ensued, the potential scandal gave Ronald Reagan a new political lease on life. The Ford committee expended $321,000 in what was to be its knock-out punch, but the president met his first defeat by polling only 46 percent of North Carolina's ballots in a low turnout that worked to his disadvantage.

The PFC had ample time to recover from the loss in North Carolina because Ford ran uncontested in New York and Pennsylvania, which cost the committee $32,000 and $35,000, respectively. These modest investments put more than 200 friendly, though officially uncommitted, delegates in the Ford column. Moreover, the president won all of Wisconsin's 45 convention delegates on April 6 after spending $381,000. In spite of the fact that Reagan had ceased active campaigning two weeks before the voting, Ford declared the Wisconsin results an approval of his foreign policy. This statement set up the president for embarrassment in Texas, where his conduct of foreign affairs and his secretary of State, Henry A. Kissinger, were unpopular among Republicans.

With little excitement or momentum generated by his April successes, President Ford campaigned for the May 1 Texas primary curiously on the defensive. The media program, which cost at least $200,000, featured Sen. John G. Tower rebutting Reagan's claim that the United States had fallen behind the Soviet Union militarily. This represented a shift from previous advertisements that stressed Ford's steady competence and prestigious demeanor, exemplified by film clips from his State of the Union messages. Although the president drew crowds larger than those of his opponent during five days in the state, he simply could not outdo Reagan's hard-hitting style. Another important setback arose when Ford failed to win an endorsement from former Governor Connally. The Ford camp did hold an organizational edge, with phone banks in 26 counties where Republicans were concentrated, but, other than the media approach, the PFC lacked a method to minimize expected losses from Democratic crossover voting. After spending more than $1 million, Ford failed to gain any Texas delegates.

Three days after the stunning Texas results, the president suffered three more losses in Alabama, Georgia, and Indiana. The Ford committee spent only $50,000 in Alabama and $90,000 in Georgia, states where it had anticipated defeat, but in Indiana the president had been favored. There, Ford campaigned vigorously for several days with the backing of the state organization and an elaborate get-out-the-vote drive pushed spending to $236,000. Once again the crossover vote hurt, and the president lost Indiana with 49 percent of the ballots cast.

For Nebraska's May 11 primary, the PFC reverted to the "presidential" approach. In only two days of campaigning in his native state, Ford kept to the high road by speaking of his accomplishments and avoiding question-and-answer sessions, which tended to bring up Reagan criticisms. A heavy media campaign substituted for personal appearances, and in commercials aired by 45 radio stations Sen. Barry Goldwater, R-Ariz., defended Ford's Panama Canal negotiations. Nevertheless, the comeback attempt remained vulnerable to a different Reagan barb — the 1975 embargo on grain sales to the Soviet Union, a topic of anger among Nebraska farmers. Expenditures of $106,500 failed to avert Ford's fifth loss, as he polled 45 percent in Nebraska's noncrossover primary. Cushioning this loss, Ford won handily in West Virginia on the same day with 57 percent of the vote and only $23,000 in expenses.

Defeats in the first half of May made crucial the Michigan primary on May 18, for if Ford had lost in his home state he may well have forfeited the nomination. To ensure victory, the PFC made an immense last-minute effort that escalated total spending to $222,000. The president doubled his previously scheduled time so as to include a whistle-stop tour through the heart of Michigan. Along the way, he openly appealed for independent and Democratic crossover votes. Gov. William G. Milliken and Sen. Robert P. Griffin had the Michigan GOP augment the Ford organizational drive, which included 11 telephone centers and 77 local committees. At the polls, a slim majority of Democrats crossed over for Reagan, but most Republicans and independents went for their favorite son. The man from Grand Rapids took 65 percent of the vote for 55 delegates, and thereby rejuvenated his nomination bid. On the same day, Ford won an uncontested race in Maryland, which brought 43 more delegates in the wake of $62,000 in expenditures.

Next, the campaign transferred its new-found momentum to the May 25 primaries of Tennessee, Kentucky, and Oregon. In the two border states, Ford came from behind by dint of extensive phone canvassing, the hard campaigning of local congressmen, and Ronald Reagan's negative comments about the Tennessee Valley Authority. The Ford committee expended $87,000 in Tennessee and $77,000 in Kentucky to win by a few percentage points in each state. The president won a similarly close race in Oregon with the assistance of the state's liberal Republican Party, large mailings, and heavy telephone and personal canvassing. The PFC spent $163,000 in a victory that captured 16 Oregon delegates.

After winning elections in Rhode Island and South Dakota at a cost of less than $25,000 each, the Ford forces faced the three final primaries on June 8. In New Jersey, running unopposed, Ford won all 67 delegates following committee expenditures of a mere $33,400. Ohio presented more of a contest, although Reagan had filed delegate slates in only three-fourths of the state's congressional districts.

As in other states, the party regulars in Ohio worked for the president, while the national headquarters provided extensive telephoning and a crew of administration advocates. Ford himself traveled the length of the state in an 11-hour motorcade on the day before the Ohio voting. In his visits, the president sowed doubts about the electability of his opponent and reused the technique of the federal purse, promising expansion of a nuclear fuel plant and an Air Force base in southern Ohio. Since expenditures were approaching the cost ceiling, the PFC concentrated media in the two days before the voting. Additionally, a group calling itself "Friends of the First Family" produced and broadcast a five-minute TV commercial as an independent expenditure. Regular committee spending totaled $220,000 and captured 88 delegates with 55 percent of the vote.

The PFC spent considerably more in California, not so much to win, but to keep Reagan tied down in a state he had to carry. Ford workers entered California early to establish committees in all of the major counties; later, they maintained some 20 phone banks throughout the state. On two tours of California, the president touted his record of "peace, prosperity, and trust," while his subordinates questioned Reagan's performance as governor. The California media program was especially costly because it underwent a number of changes. First, the president decided to try slice-of-life dramatizations in which professional actors lauded his achievements. This switch from the stately documentary-style commercials used elsewhere caused PFC ad man Peter Dailey to resign. Yet the production spots, formulated by James Jordan, president of the Batten, Barton, Durstine and Osborne agency of New York, did not help the candidate. Three days before June 8, the new advertisements were scrapped. The campaign replaced them with commercials assailing Reagan for his considering a troop commitment to Rhodesia. In the newest ads, an announcer declared, "Governor Ronald Reagan couldn't start a war. President Ronald Reagan could."[64] The Reagan camp asked both the PFC and broadcasting stations to discontinue this message, but Ford himself defended his aggressive commercials. The bitter struggle in California cost the Ford committee almost $912,000, but the president gained no delegates in the state's winner-take-all election.

After the June 8 primaries, the president stood some 170 delegate votes short of the required majority of 1,130, which increased the significance of 10 states still to choose delegates. Since the PFC had anticipated victory during the primary period, Ford activity in the caucus states was not well organized compared with previous efforts. The president partially overcame this deficiency by visiting some of the state conventions. One exception was Iowa (in the last round of its caucus process), where Ford canceled a scheduled appearance so that he could oversee the evacuation of Americans from Lebanon. Despite his absence, the president captured a slim majority of Iowa delegates. In Connecticut he had better luck, sweeping all 35 delegates after a personal appearance. Of the 10 nonprimary states that made final delegate choices after June 8, Ford won majorities in five. These states are listed below, along with PFC expenditures in each:

Iowa	$ 50,000
Delaware	5,600
Minnesota	32,500
North Dakota	6,250
Connecticut	55,000
Total	$149,350

After the last state convention, 100 or so uncommitted delegates held the key to the Republican nomination. In spite of personnel shuffles and bickering with the White House, the PFC managed to woo undecided delegates fairly effectively. Again, Ford added the personal touch, actively exploiting his incumbency. The president hosted many state delegations at the White House for cocktails, individual photographs and a pep talk, and invited uncommitted delegates to state dinners. Uncommitteds not met personally received a telephone call from the president of the United States and, in some cases, families of delegates got to chat with the chief executive. Ford even checked into mundane local matters at the request of an uncommitted delegate. Although the campaign committee picked up the tab for such political activities, the aura of the presidency was clearly priceless. Ford's persuasiveness brought him even closer to his goal, and on July 21, *The New York Times* calculated that the president was only 18 votes shy of nomination.

Perhaps more than the perquisites of office, a daring move by Ronald Reagan put President Ford over the magic number of 1,130 delegate votes. The challenger's selection of liberal Republican Sen.

Table 5-19
Expenditures of the President Ford Committee

National and state	
headquarters operation	$3,650,000
Media	3,115,000 [a]
Fund raising	(2,174,000)
Payroll and travel	2,000,000
Printing and mailing	1,680,000
Telephone	1,015,000
Legal and accounting	581,000 [b]
Convention	500,000
Polling	305,000
Consultants	210,000
Campaign materials	170,000
Miscellaneous	350,000
Total	$13,576,000

[a] Fund-raising costs are distributed throughout the other figures in the table.
[b] Legal and accounting costs are exempt from the spending limit and bring the President Ford Committee below the $13.1 million ceiling on qualified campaign expenses.

Richard S. Schweiker of Pennsylvania as his running mate pushed sufficient delegates once leaning toward Reagan into the president's column. Erosion of Reagan support in various delegations, most notably West Virginia and Mississippi, brought President Ford the nomination with 1,187 votes. The president's hard-fought victory, however, left Ford and his running mate, Robert Dole of Kansas, in a weak position to face the Democrats in the fall.

The President Ford Committee could not provide a functional breakdown of its expenditures because of computer failure, but Citizens' Research Foundation was able to calculate breakdowns by manual compilation of Ford FEC filings. PFC officials consider the estimates that follow to be reasonably accurate. Table 5-19 summarizes the CRF findings and shows that the costliest category of spending for the Ford committee was operation of national and state headquarters at $3,650,000. The next highest expenses — $3,115,000 — went toward media. Together, payroll and travel formed the third most expensive category at about $2 million. Printing and mailing worth $1,680,000 and telephone services totaling $1,015,000 followed in the order of expense. Six other functions, each of which cost less than $600,000, totaled $2,116,000 as shown in Table 5-19.

Callaway and Morton. During the 1976 presidential campaign, two of Ford's campaign managers, Howard "Bo" Callaway and Rogers C. B. Morton, were criticized on grounds that their activities were violations of either political statutes or the new "Watergate morality."

In 1973 Callaway was appointed secretary of the Army by President Nixon and he served in that position for a little more than two years. One notable action during his tenure was to reduce to 10 years, from 20, the sentence of Lt. William Calley, who had been court martialed for his role in the My Lai massacre in Vietnam. In June 1975 Callaway was named to head President Ford's election campaign and he took over in early July. Although without experience in running a national political campaign, the expectation was that Callaway would be able to shore up the president's flank among conservative southerners against a likely challenge from Ronald Reagan. He sought to accomplish this through overt and covert hints that Nelson Rockefeller would not be chosen by Gerald Ford as his running mate in 1976. Callaway went so far as to say that the former New York governor was Ford's "number one problem." Despite such efforts, Callaway never was able to get a significant number of southern conservative Republicans to back the president, and there was considerable criticism of his handling of the Ford campaign.

On March 12, 1976, NBC News and the *Denver Post* each reported that, prior to leaving his post as secretary of the Army, Callaway had sought to pressure the Forest Service and its parent agency, the Department of Agriculture, to allow the Crested Butte Development Corp. — a Callaway-family-owned corporation — to lease 2,000 acres of federal lands for ski runs on Mount Snodgrass in Colorado.[65] The charges came in the midst of the hotly contested Republican presidential primaries in North Carolina and Illinois. The following day, Callaway took a temporary leave of absence [66] and Stuart Spencer, deputy chairman of the Ford team, replaced him. Despite Callaway's efforts to stay on and to quickly resolve the issue, he resigned on March 30[67] and was replaced on April 2 by Rogers Morton, counselor to the president and an old friend of Gerald Ford.

Morton himself was no stranger to controversy concerning the question of how public officials should act with respect to political matters. In mid-January 1976 the White House had announced that Morton, former secretary of the departments of Interior and Commerce, would assume the title of counselor to the president on February 1. In addition to providing the president with advice about domestic and economic policy matters, Morton's duties were to include speechmaking and coordinating actions between the White House, the President Ford Committee, and the Republican National Committee.

Although Ron Nessen, presidential press secretary, tried to downplay the political aspects of Morton's new job, questions immediately were raised about the legality and propriety of such a post. Thomas Curtis, chairman of the FEC, declared: "I want to alert Morton that they are running into very dangerous waters." [68] While admitting that the FEC had no authority to prevent such an appointment, he declared that in his view federal officeholders could not use "staff members paid with public money for purely political matters," and that this prohibition should apply to members of Congress as well as to presidents. Curtis said that as far as he was concerned the FECA required that those portions of Morton's salary devoted to political matters and travel expenses should be listed as campaign expenses and included under the $10 million limit, which applied to all presidential candidates during the preconvention period.[69]

Morton, as might be expected, disagreed with Curtis. A former chairman of the Republican National Committee and member of the House of Representatives, he argued that "[y]ou can't separate government from politics." He stated that presidential aides should be able to give presidents "political advice from time to time."[70] Morton said that he "would be uncomfortable in an advisory role in the White House being paid by external funds. I think that it would be a very bad precedent to set."[71]

But the door had been opened and the Democrats came charging through with their complaints. Robert S. Strauss, chairman of the Democratic National Committee, attacked Morton's position. Two presidential candidates, Sargent Shriver and Fred Harris, each issued statements on the appointment, Harris filing a complaint with the FEC.

Common Cause joined the attack, challenging the appointment itself as being a violation of a section of the United States Code, which requires "that all appropriations 'in the public service shall be applied solely to the objects for which they are respectively made, and for no other.' " Fred Wertheimer, vice-president of the organization, declared that the "funds appropriated for the staffing of the office of the President were in no way intended to be used to finance partisan political campaigns."[72]

The Ford administration, stung by the criticism, sought to end the controversy quickly. White House Counsel Philip W. Buchen met with Curtis and they agreed on a compromise solution: Morton would work 40 hours a week as a presidential adviser on domestic matters and then undertake his political work as a volunteer in his off-hours; this would eliminate the need for such activities to be counted under the law. The fact that the White House reacted as speedily as it did indicates Watergate's lingering impact on the 1976 campaigns.[73]

Percy

Charles H. Percy of Illinois sought the Republican nomination for president from the summer of 1973 until August 1974, while Nixon was still president. Percy supporters formed the Exploratory Committee to raise funds, finance the senator's travels and begin planning for a 1976 bid. The committee and its successor spent about $212,000 in the process.

Percy traveled the country, speaking to Republican groups and raising funds. As he traveled, he assessed the chances of a moderate gaining the Republican nomination. In early speculation regarding 1976, the senator faced potential opposition from Governor Rockefeller of New York, Governor Reagan of California, and former Treasury Secretary John Connally. Undaunted by the competition, Percy started early and met with success in fund raising. The committee reported receiving $33,404 before September 1, 1973, and another $69,065 during the last four months of the year, bringing the 1973 total to $102,469, more than had been projected. Most of the initial donors were Illinois businessmen who gave between $150 and $2,000.[74] In addition, Percy received $5,000 contributions from William Graham, an executive of Baxter Laboratories of Chicago, and A. C. Nielsen of the television rating company, and the candidate's daughter Sharon, wife of John D. "Jay" Rockefeller IV, contributed $3,500.[75] The committee also sought smaller contributions in a mailing to 9,700 persons who received letters endorsing Percy from Milton S. Eisenhower, brother of the late president.[76] In 1974 the Exploratory Committee changed its name to the Percy Committee. Combined, the two committees spent about $212,000.

Besides travel, office, and fund-raising expenses, the major expenditures went to the Washington consulting firm of Bailey & Deardourff. The firm set up a detailed plan, contained in six loose-leaf binders, for Percy's road to the White House. The plan called for Percy to forgo the early primaries, begin impressively in the 1976 Illinois primary, and then gather momentum in later contests. The entire effort was estimated to cost between $11 million and $12 million. In the spring of 1974 the consultants were presenting a slide show of their strategy to potential supporters, some of whom expressed surprise at the elaborate strategy at such an early date. Meanwhile, the candidate stepped up appearances, making it nearly certain that his explorations had encouraged him to run.[77]

Once Gerald Ford ascended to the presidency, the assumption that the nomination was up for grabs became unlikely. On August 14, four days after Nixon resigned, Senator Percy withdrew from the race, noting (not prophetically) that if President Ford "continues to say and do the right things, he'll be nominated by acclamation."[78]

Probably about half of the total Percy budget went to the Bailey & Deardourff firm, which received $48,556 in 1973.[79] After Percy withdrew, some $2,024 was returned to those who requested a refund, and the remainder, about $7,000, went toward Percy's 1978 senatorial campaign.[80]

Reagan

Former Governor of California Ronald Reagan challenged incumbent President Ford for the Republican nomination, but fell short of victory by 117 convention votes. The Reagan candidacy originated in the growing disappointment with Gerald Ford's moderate policies by the party's right wing. While deciding whether to lead an insurgent attack, Reagan disseminated his conservative ideology by way of the after-dinner circuit, a syndicated newspaper column, and a radio commentary program. These lucrative endeavors functioned as a testing ground for his presidential bid, and the former governor took the first affirmative step in mid-July of 1975 when he authorized the formation of the Citizens for Reagan Committee. Chaired by Sen. Paul Laxalt of Nevada, the committee had fund raising and strategy planning well under way when Reagan officially declared his candidacy on November 20. Immediately after his announcement in Washington, the one-time film and television actor headed for five primary states in a two-day media event.

Reagan intended to knock the president out of the race in the early primaries, but he failed to score a win until the North Carolina election on March 23. Unprepared for a campaign of attrition, the Reagan campaign experienced financial woes, intensified by the cutoff of matching funds. The candidate's adept use of television brought enough funds for survival until the primaries of the South and West, where Reagan demonstrated formidable electoral strength. The damage, however, already was done, for the funding squeeze had prevented effective drives in key northeastern and midwestern states. To no avail, the challenger bitterly fought the incumbent down to the last few uncommitted delegates at the Kansas City convention. Reagan's narrow loss cost $12.6 million.

Compliance. The immense task of administering a long campaign caught the Citizens for Reagan Committee off guard. Based in the Washington headquarters, the staff found FEC requirements, such as allocation of expenditures by state and detailed documentation of contributions, to be demanding and time-consuming. With only a small staff at the outset, the campaign manager, counsel, and other officers pitched in to help. Despite the aid of a computer, storing contributor information and editing the alphabetized contributor list entailed much manual labor. For certain functions, the computer system was later abandoned as too cumbersome. Staff members complained that at times reporting requirements excessively delayed matching funds, claiming that they needed two weeks to process a given set of contributions and the FEC took another two weeks to approve matching money. On the other hand, the vast number of small Reagan contributions, many of them too late to be useful, might have overwhelmed any compliance system.

Preoccupied by receipts, the Reagan committee was able to maintain only minimal control of expenditures. In one FEC filing, the committee reported exceeding the legal spending limit in New Hampshire, but later amendments justified bringing the state's allocation just below the ceiling. By the spring of 1976, the campaign's bookkeeping was in such disarray that it sought a new financial controller to restructure the finances. The second person took weeks to restore order. It was later estimated that compliance activities cost $500,000 to $600,000.

Reagan committee lawyers also were occupied dealing with two regulatory bodies and the Republican National Committee. First, the Federal Communications Commission ruled that old Ronald Reagan movies shown on TV would be subject to equal-time demands by Republican opponents. President Ford, however, eventually waived his right to equal time in regard to Reagan reruns. More seriously, Reagan officials asked the RNC in the fall of 1975 to pay for the candidate's trips to address party organizations, as it was doing for President Ford. The RNC refused, contending that the president, as leader of the party, was merely helping GOP groups across the country and therefore deserved reimbursement from the National Committee. Because such appearances also benefited Ford's renomination bid, Reagan attorneys appealed to the FEC. In late November, the FEC approved the committee's practice in a 5-1 ruling which stated that a president's party chores before January 1 of an election year "are not inherently intended to influence the candidate's nomination."[81]

The Reagan campaign repeated complaints about unfair advantages of Ford's incumbency throughout the prenomination period. Reagan officers pointed out that they had to pay large deposits for travel (as much as $800,000 for a chartered jet), while the President Ford Committee could charge travel expenses to the federal government and repay when billed weeks later. The Ford committee reimbursed the government for campaign-related travel by White House staffers, but Reagan officials asserted that the relevant part of their salaries should have been reimbursed as well. Finally, the Reagan committee objected to preferential treatment given Ford at the national convention in hotel accommodations and gallery passes. Although the committee's legal staff failed to convince the FEC to take action on any of these matters, the Reagan charges reveal a variety of distinct incumbency advantages and raise important questions of equity for future campaigns.

On April 13, 1978, the FEC released its report of a compliance audit of the Citizens for Reagan Committee (CFR) and its postelection successor, Citizens for the Republic (CFTR). Covering the period from July 15, 1975, through March 31, 1977, the audit reported unadjusted receipts of $18.9 million and expenditures of $17.2 million for both committees and noted that almost $10 million of this amount was subject to statutory expenditure limitations.

The report noted the failure of the committee to disclose eight depositories of campaign funds in three states. During the course of the audit the committee rectified this situation and no further action was recommended by the auditors. It was also noted that the committee exceeded the primary election expenditure limit for the State of New Hampshire by $30,285. This sum, according to the recommendations of the auditors, constituted nonqualified campaign expenses and was therefore repayable in full to the United States Treasury. The auditors also recommended that of the $1,616,461 in surplus funds with which the Citizens for Reagan Committee ended the campaign, $580,857 represented matching funds that were also repayable to the Treasury. On August 19, 1977, the FEC approved both of these recommendations and on November 28, 1977, the Reagan committee repaid a total amount of $611,142.[82]

The most significant finding of the audit was the alleged failure of the Reagan committee to secure information concerning the occupation and principal place of business for approximately 40 percent of reported contributors. The FEC requires only that a candidate's committee use its "best efforts" to obtain the required information. The Citizens for Reagan Committee felt this criteria had been satisfied by sending additional contribution solicitations to those persons who previously had contributed to the campaign. The follow-up solicitations, like the original ones, contained a request for the contributor's occupation and principal place of business. The auditors noted, however, that no separate effort specifically requesting the information was undertaken. Citizens for the Republic in late 1977 made another attempt to get contributor information. This still did not satisfy the FEC apparently because CFTR refused to admit that CFR had not used its best efforts earlier. On June 22, 1978, after apparent failure to reach agreement through informal attempts at conciliation, the FEC filed suit in United States District Court.[83] The suit charged that the Citizens for Reagan Committee did not use its "best efforts" to make proper identification of its contributors and asked the court to grant a permanent injunction, assess a civil penalty of $5,000, and award the commission its costs in the action. At the date of this writing no decision had been handed down by the court.

Fund Raising. In dollars raised, the Reagan fund drive was extremely successful, but the bulk of contributions arrived too late to ease the most severe financial problems. Although the campaign employed some traditional fund-raising techniques, direct-mail and television appeals became the mainstay of Reagan's fund raising.

Efforts began in the summer of 1975 with emphasis on personal solicitation as a low-key way to qualify Reagan for matching funds. Although the candidate opposed public financing on philosophical grounds, he decided that the low contribution limits left him no realistic choice but to accept federal subsidies. The committee staff and past Reagan supporters, including Los Angeles millionaire Jack Courtemanche, headed the solicitation program. Their work raised $396,462 by October 1, 1975, and although California residents provided a large portion of this amount, Reagan was able to qualify for public funds well before his official announcement in November.

Also in 1975, the Reagan committee initiated a direct-mail campaign based on several small mailing lists of conservative groups and the list of contributors to the Republican National Committee. This undertaking, however, began too late to confer the full advantages of direct mail. The committee calculated that initial mailings cost 80 percent of the contributions they brought in; included in this estimate is the price of three million pieces of literature that were never mailed for lack of funds and were soon outdated. Prospecting appeals later yielded a more profitable list of proven contributors, and mailings to them for repeat gifts were later the only form of direct mail, bringing in $8 for each dollar spent. In all, the campaign mailed more than seven million contribution requests, placing the cost of direct mail at a minimum of $2.5 million. The Reagan committee paid the large outlays needed for mailings only with great difficulty, and at one point, its direct-mail firm threatened to sue to collect some $700,000 in arrears. By reducing use of direct mail and doing in-house mailings, the campaign treasurer avoided a threatened court battle.

Together, direct mail, solicitations, and fund-raising events could not keep pace with Reagan's rapid spending. Consequently, in March 1976 the campaign turned to televised fund appeals. The Reagan committee applied to the three networks to purchase a half-hour of prime time so that the candidate could address the American people and make a plea for funds at the end of the broadcast. At first, all three networks refused, but then Reagan sent a personal telegram to each network board chairman, and NBC agreed to sell one half-hour on March 31. In his speech, Reagan stressed foreign policy and criticized Secretary of State Henry Kissinger and detente. At an estimated cost of $90,000 for air time and $24,000 for production, the program met with spectacular success, reaching an audience of 15 million people and generating close to $1.3 million in contributions. Without this financial comeback, Reagan's challenge might not have lasted through April.

On July 6 the ABC network aired a second 30-minute presentation in which Reagan attacked Democratic nominee-to-be Jimmy Carter. This broadcast cost about $60,000 for air time plus $25,000 for production and collected approximately $300,000 in donations. The TV appeals, along with direct mail, brought in so much money at once that processing of contributions backed up, forcing the campaign to secure at one point a three-day loan, using as collateral sample returns based on the weight of unopened mail sacks.

Indeed, loans played a crucial role in easing cash flow problems and bringing the campaign through the period until the FEC was reconstituted. In February the committee had borrowed $1 million from the National Bank of Washington, and during the matching funds cutoff, borrowing increased. Loans were rolled over, but in all aggregated $3,346,226. All loans were repaid by summer 1976.

Loans might have been unnecessary had the fund drive caught fire sooner. In the five and a half months of 1975 it was in existence, the committee raised slightly less than $2 million, with about three-fourths of the contributions in denominations of $250 or less. The pace quickened in the first two months of 1976 when $1,471,000 was raised. During March alone, the campaign collected $1,150,000, reflecting new hope after Reagan's upset victory in North Carolina. Aided by later electoral triumphs, Reagan received more than $4.5 million in additional funds by the August convention. This money brought total individual contributions to $9,189,264, some of which could not be used for campaign purposes because such spending would exceed legal limits. Surplus private funds were transferred to the Citizens for the Republic Political Action Committee, a group set up by Reagan to promote his conservative cause. Of the individual contributions total, gifts of $100 or less constituted about 67 percent and those between $101 and $499 presented 16 percent. This means that only 17 percent of all individual contributions came in amounts of $500 or more. The committee estimated that 170,000 individuals gave to Reagan, yielding an average contribution of about $76.60. The campaign also collected more than $30,000 from various party and political action committees, as well as some $24,000 in interest and other income.

Reagan's late-blooming ability at fund raising created a belated influx of matching funds. This totaled $5,088,910 in federal subsidies, not only the highest amount certified to any campaign, but was also more than was needed. The Reagan committee closed the campaign with a $1.6 million surplus, a sign of the late timing of income.

Costs. The pace of fund raising largely determined the Reagan committee's pattern of spending, necessitating cutbacks at important junctures. The early financial squeeze combined with continual controversies over the candidate's political positions to seal the fate of the Reagan challenge.

Almost from its inception, the Citizens for Reagan Committee ran a chronic deficit. From July to October of 1975 the committee spent $295,000 as it concentrated on fund raising, and closed the period $90,000 in debt. By the end of 1975 total expenditures stood at $1.5 million, and in the first month of 1976 the debt rose above $550,000. The advent of matching funds could not wholly offset heavy spending in the opening primaries, for in January and February alone, Reagan spent $3 million. In April, with the debt nearing $1 million and matching funds cut off, the campaign tried to reduce expenditures drastically. Accordingly, the Reagan entourage gave up its Boeing 727 chartered jet, which cost $50,000 a week to operate, most high officials went off salary, and lower staff members received expense reimbursements late.

By May the committee had some $2 million in matching money pending FEC approval, but when disbursments were suspended the campaign became desperate. Reagan accused President Ford of being deliberately vague as to his intentions concerning the campaign finance legislation designed to meet the Supreme Court's specifications. The Reagan committee attained credit from mailing and polling firms simply by withholding immediate payment of bills and scheduling longer repayments.

When matching funds again became available, the financial situation eased, allowing the committee to go into the black in June. During the summer, contributions continued to arrive even though, with the primaries over, outlays for media and travel were shrinking. In July the committee spent about $1.2 million, and expenses for the August convention were lower still, because the campaign economized in order to stay below the $13 million spending limit.

Financial health came too late to affect the political outcome, though. As the campaign deputy manager, Darrel Trent, commented ruefully, "If money had been available (in April and May), it almost certainly would have changed our thinking in Ohio and New Jersey."[84] On the other hand, Reagan strategists' thinking originally downplayed the latter primaries because they expected a swift victory in the early primary states. In turn, losses in these states despite high expenditures laid the foundation for the Reagan committee's later financial crisis.

Even before the first primary in New Hampshire, Reagan forces tried to embarrass President Ford in Iowa's January precinct caucuses. Instead, a last-minute organizational drive and expenditures of $62,000 revealed Reagan's weakness, since a narrow majority of Iowa delegates eventually chosen went to Ford.

As a result, New Hampshire became all-important, and Reagan redoubled his efforts for the February 24 primary. Organizing had begun as early as October 1975 and Reagan made six trips to the state in the time after his official announcement. The campaign initiated Citizens' Press Conferences during which Reagan fielded questions from the audience, a favorable format for the adroit public speaker. These conferences provided material for a series of 60-second radio and television commercials aired throughout the state at a cost of at least $100,000. One upset early in the New Hampshire campaign was Reagan's proposal to transfer $90 billion worth of federal programs to state and local governments. The press and the Ford campaign zeroed in on the proposal. To make matters worse, Gov. Meldrim Thomson, Jr., of New Hampshire, an avid Reagan supporter, rashly predicted a victory for the Californian, thereby inflating general expectations. After spending $219,855, Reagan trailed President Ford by only 1,317 votes. A close second, however, was not the upset that Reagan workers had anticipated, and their disappointment showed. Moreover, the New Hampshire results seemed to refute the Reagan camp's claim that people did not view the president as a real incumbent under the circumstances of his ascent to the White House.

For another chance at an early triumph, Reagan looked to Florida, although he downgraded the importance of the March 9 race to cushion a possible second loss. Reagan expenditures in Florida came to a hefty $791,000, with a large share of the total funding another heavy media campaign. The effort also included a voter-registration drive that aimed to bring conservative Democrats into the Republican fold. Yet Reagan fell short again with 47 percent of the vote, although this time he asserted, "For a challenger, what I have done cannot be called a defeat."[85]

Before the March 19 Illinois primary, Reagan's assault on Ford intensified. His warnings about the need for military preparedness and the "give away" of the Panama Canal revitalized the campaign and helped to increase contributions. Reagan's criticism of U.S. foreign policy was so sharp that it drew an angry and detailed reply from Secretary of State Kissinger in a speech in Boston. In response, Reagan lawyers unsuccessfully urged the FEC to charge part of Kissinger's salary to Ford's spending limit. In addition, the Reagan camp accused Ford of using "pork-barrel politics" because the president had pledged during the Florida primary to provide a mass-transit grant for Miami, and during the New Hampshire contest to keep open the Portsmouth Navy Yard, among other promises of federal aid.[86] The verbal onslaught proved to be a poor match for Ford's organizational strength in Illinois, and the Reagan committee's expenditure of $571,000 brought its candidate a disappointing 40 percent of the ballots cast.

Disheartened, the Reagan forces entered North Carolina expecting their fourth consecutive primary defeat. The campaign opened on an unpropitious note when North Carolina Gov. James E. Holshouser, along with eight other GOP governors, asked Reagan to terminate his presidential bid. This request steeled Ronald Reagan's resolve to stay in the race, although his campaign manager, John Sears, contacted the President Ford Committee to see if it would cover part of the Reagan debt in the event the Californian withdrew after the North Carolina voting.[87] This maneuver remained secret, but Reagan experienced public embarrassment when he had to order some North Carolina supporters to cease circulation of leaflets containing a racist insinuation that Gerald Ford favored Sen. Edward W. Brooke, a black from Massachusetts, for the vice presidential nomination. However, Reagan turned the tide once his North Carolina campaign management edited a month-old videotape of a speech on foreign policy, and aired it on 15 of North Carolina's 17 television stations. The 30-minute address was broadcast during prime time at a cost of approximately $10,000. The positive reaction this telecast engendered disproved the notion that the candidate's ability in a studio would undermine his seriousness and inspired later network broadcasts that saved the campaign. The TV program, coupled with total spending of $560,000, overcame Reagan's initial setbacks, as he carried North Carolina by 52 percent in a victory that surprised everyone, including the victor.

Rather than taking his momentum to the Wisconsin primary on April 6, Reagan chose to prepare for his network television broadcast on March 31. The Reagan committee could not afford polling in Wisconsin, and the cancellation of the candidate's appearances further conserved scarce funds, although nearly $149,000 already had been spent in the state. The money would have been better spent elsewhere, for Reagan won no delegates from Wisconsin.

After his nationwide TV message, Reagan stayed out of the limelight until the May 1 Texas primary because his lieutenants had avoided the elections in New York and Pennsylvania. Reagan strategists reasoned that the campaign could not afford the necessarily large outlays for media in these northeastern contests, and that Ford backers controlled the state organizations. So, Reagan energetically seized the opportunity in Texas, hammering away at Ford-Kissinger foreign policy in conservative territory. Reagan's wife Nancy joined in by spending six days in the state and appearing on radio and television. The Reagan media pitch openly appealed for Democratic crossover votes; one ad featured a former Wallace supporter who explained why, in 1976, conservatives would do better to vote for Reagan instead of the Alabama Democrat. Among oilmen, the candidate curried favor by criticizing the president's failure to veto the 1975 Energy Act. Reagan also won support from some local party chairmen and his delegate candidates spent heavily in their own races. Citizens for Reagan expended $471,000 (less than half the Ford Committee's budget), in a most effective investment that captured all 100 Texas delegates. This sudden surge gave Reagan a cumulative total of 183 delegates only 49 behind Ford.

Following Texas, Reagan won primaries in smaller states in quick succession, beginning on May 4. In Georgia the committee spent $125,000, and in Alabama expenditures nearly reached $100,000. Between the two states, Reagan picked up 85 delegates, putting him ahead in the delegate count for the first time. He also won a tougher battle in Indiana the same day. A media blitz attempted to broaden Reagan's base and adapt to Indiana's diversity. The candidate spent the four days before the election in the state, and his committee spent a total of $237,000. At the polls Reagan took 45 of Indiana's 54 delegates, with the help of independent and Democratic crossover votes which, by one estimate, constituted one-third of the "Republican" vote.

On May 11 the momentum carried into Nebraska, where Reagan spent only a few days and a comparatively low $91,500, but won with a startling 55 percent. One week later, however, Ford's home state of Michigan interrupted Reagan's winning streak. Reagan's spending in Michigan came to almost $156,000, including some $80,000 for general media and mailings to opponents of gun control and abortion. More appeals to Wallace Democrats failed to counteract the votes of moderate Democrats who crossed over to the Republican contest in order to help native son Jerry Ford. As a result, Reagan polled only 34 percent.

Of the six primaries held on May 25, Reagan won three, carrying Nevada, Idaho, and Arkansas by more than 60 percent of the vote in each. Of the three states, the Reagan committee spent the most — $63,000 — in Nevada. Reagan was not so fortunate in Tennessee and Kentucky, two southern states generally thought to be leaning toward him. Partially because he criticized the Tennessee Valley Authority for competing with private enterprise, Reagan went down to defeat in both states' popular vote, although he edged Ford by one delegate in the Tennessee congressional districts. Reagan forces expended $144,500 in Tennessee, while Kentucky cost $110,300.

The only June 8 primary that the Reagan organization fully prepared for was the one in California. Campaign strategists had elected to bypass New Jersey and to make a limited attempt in Ohio, where the committee ran delegate slates in 15 out of 25 congressional districts. In his home state, Reagan campaigned for eight days, spending $1,065,000. The massive effort brought Reagan 66 percent of the ballots cast and 167 delegates from California's winner-take-all primary. After Reagan lost the nomination, staff members and the former governor himself expressed regret at not channeling some of the California resources into Ohio. Still, the Reagan committee did spend $284,700 in Ohio and the candidate made a series of last-minute appearances.

Throughout the primary season, Ronald Reagan attracted more independent expenditures than any other candidate. More than half of all independent expenditures made in behalf of Reagan were spent by the American Conservative Union (ACU). The ACU expended a total of $172,870 to influence primary elections in 13 states. Other noteworthy independent contributions were $32,671 spent by brewing magnate Joseph Coors for newspaper advertising in Florida and Texas, and $63,000 reported by Henry Grover during the Texas primary. Independent expenditures for Reagan totaled $303,614. Reagan's delegate candidates also spent freely for their standard-bearer. Total delegate expenditures came to $179,045, with by far the biggest share of this money spent in the Texas delegate-selection primary.

The primary period, by most reckonings, left Reagan about 270 delegates short of the required majority of 1,130, while Ford needed some 170 delegates more for a first-ballot victory. This tally includes the results of state caucuses that had chosen their delegates by June 8. These 11 states gave Reagan 178 delegates compared with 114 for Ford and 64 uncommitted, according to a *New York Times* survey.

Thus, the nonprimary states choosing delegations after June 8 presented a new battleground, and both camps marshaled their remaining resources for trench warfare in 10 generally small states. Reagan workers took the lead in organizing in the late caucuses, and the candidate built on this base by meeting small groups of Republican electors in his hotel suite at the various state conventions. Of the 10 post-June 8 caucuses, Reagan won a majority of delegates in five states. Total Reagan expenditures in each of these states follow:

Missouri	$ 84,000
Washington	63,000
New Mexico	15,500
Montana	13,500
Utah	23,000
Total	$199,000

The spending figures give a sense of the importance of handfuls of delegates in a close nomination contest. These five victories plus pledges of support from previously uncommitted delegates placed Reagan closer to Ford in the cumulative total, but he remained far from a majority of delegates. At the end of the delegate-selection process, *The New York Times* calculated that Reagan held 1,063 delegates, while President Ford had 1,102, only 28 delegates shy of nomination.

In the month before the August convention, the two opponents vied fiercely to win support from the 94 delegates still uncommitted. In this war of persuasion, the Reagan committee did less lavish wining and dining of delegates than did the Ford organization, because it feared topping the overall expenditure limit. Of course, Reagan lacked the grandeur of the White House, which Ford used to the utmost in cajoling undecided delegates. In any case, because of cutbacks, the Reagan camp spent only about half of the $1 million originally budgeted for the convention. In the end, the financial squeeze hurt Reagan's prospects, as did his selection of moderate Senator Richard Schweiker of Pennsylvania as his running mate. Announcing the candidate's vice presidential choice before the convention was designed to garner votes for Reagan among northeastern delegates, most of whom favored Ford. Failing in this, the bold tactic may have eroded the support of some of Reagan's possible followers who felt betrayed by the selection of a running mate from the opposite side of the political spectrum. On the night of the roll call, President Ford won nomination by a vote of 1,187 to 1,070 for Reagan.

Although Citizens for Reagan did not release an exact breakdown of its expenditures, committee officials did provide approximate costs of certain functions and other expenses can be estimated. Reagan staffers claimed that media costs totaled some $2 million, and the compliance cost as much as $600,000. In addition, the committee spent about $500,000 at the Republican National Convention, and polling for the campaign came to $300,000. The extensive Reagan fund raising cost as much as $2.5 million. Travel expenses for candidate and staff probably topped $2 million, while the categories of payroll and office costs likely were each about $2 million. In 1975, the Reagan committee reported total expenditures of $1,378,982, and 1976 spending totaled $11,214,032. In both years, supporting committees expended $42,312, putting the grand total of Reagan spending at $12,635,326.

Citizens for the Republic

In January 1977 Citizens for the Republic was formed to support the election of conservative Republican candidates. The group replaced Citizens for Reagan, and its officers included Reagan (who served as chairman), Sen. Paul Laxalt (chairman of the Steering Committee), Franklyn C. Nofziger (executive vice-chairman), Jack Courtemanche (treasurer), and Loren A. Smith (secretary). It promised that it would extend support only to Republicans and not to conservative Democrats.

Citizens for the Republic was founded with a starting balance in excess of $1 million, which Citizens for Reagan had raised from private sources for the 1976 campaign and had received in matching funds. By late 1978 Citizens for the Republic had spent $4.5 million. The group maintained a full-time staff and executed most of its fund raising through direct mail.

In February 1977 CFTR began to publish a bimonthly newsletter whose circulation, nearly 40,000 in December 1978, included contributors and the media. Feature articles written by Reagan focused on a variety of conservative issues. CFTR's other activities included regional seminars, including political workshops, and speaking tours for Reagan. The organization contributed to five Republican candidates in special elections for the House in 1977. By the end of 1978 more than $600,000 had been distributed to federal, state and local candidates and to party committees; of that total, $359,041 went to 234 candidates for the House and $75,859 to 25 Senate candidates.

Other candidates for the Republican presidential nomination in 1980 later developed PACs, but the Reagan CFTR was the first candidate's PAC to be established and to contribute money to other candidates at federal, state and local levels. Candidate PACs are being used as a means of gaining support from state and local political activists.

Officials of the CFTR have disagreed with officials of the Republican National Committee regarding the role of the new group and its relation to the Republican organization. Additional friction was created when Reagan and other CFTR officers launched a campaign to oppose the Panama Canal treaties. The Republican National Committee, the National Republican Congressional Committee, and Citizens for the Republic all mailed virtually identical letters over Reagan's signature that raised $700,000 for the RNC. When the RNC refused a request for funds to support partially a campaign focused against the Panama Canal treaties, however, Nofziger telegraphed both the RNC and the RNCC advising them to cease further mailings of the letter. The CFTR proceeded without RNC funding to finance a congressional tour against ratification of the treaties by soliciting funds from individuals and various conservative organizations. Senator Laxalt commented, "If we are going to be effective conservatives, it will have to be outside the RNC. It's obvious they're not sympathetic to our goals."[88]

Presidential Prenomination Receipts and Expenditures

The first report in the FEC's disclosure series was issued in September 1976.[89] It details financial activity reported for the period January 1,

Table 5-20
Total Receipts and Expenditures of 26 Democratic Presidential Candidates and Their Principal Campaign Committees in the 1976 Campaign[a]

(Figures Unadjusted)

Candidate	Receipts Primary	Receipts General	Expenditures Primary	Expenditures General
Ahern, Frank	$ 2,250	—	—	—
Arnold, Stanley	38,795	—	$ 33,876	—
Baker, Philip Vernon	—	—	10,096	—
Blessitt, Arthur Owen	35,441	—	32,909	—
Bona, Frank I.	5,822	—	—	—
Bond, Horace Julian	11,915	—	10,195	—
Brewster, Robert L.	1,042	—	1,512	—
Byrd, Robert C.	229,602	—	173,529	—
Eisenman, Abram	28	—	620	—
Evert, Martha M.	60	—	60	—
Falke, Lee Charles	500	—	447	—
Freeman, Carl Floyd	—	$53	—	—
Gonas, John S.	—	—	254	—
Hays, Wayne	1,764	—	1,763	—
Jackson, Donald L.[b]	110,931	—	111,640	—
Kelleher, Robert L.	38,787	—	37,261	—
Lomento, Frank M.	—	—	63	—
McCabe, John Henry	51	—	2,319	—
O'Cummings, Grady	379	—	2,319	—
Patton, Pat	—	—	1,666	—
Roden, George B.	6,785	—	4,698	—
Roosevelt, Robert	—	—	2,874	—
Ryan, Joseph A.	5,038	—	4,991	—
Schechter, Bernard	—	—	3,072	—
Stokes, Louis	1,992	—	1,992	—
Towers, Reginald S. V.	—	—	$ 224	$15

[a] Receipts and expenditures are provided elsewhere for Democratic presidential candidates who qualified for federal matching funds. The figures given here show the total money received and spent by the candidate and his or her principal campaign committee from January 1, 1975, through August 30, 1976, as reported to the FEC by September 15, 1976. These totals exclude receipts and expenditures by all other committees and by individuals making independent expenditures on behalf of the candidates.
[b] In September 1976 Donald Jackson was indicted by a federal grand jury in Buffalo, New York, for falsely claiming an estimated $110,000 in federal matching funds; this was the first criminal charge brought under the antifraud provisions of the Presidential Primary Matching Fund Account Act.

SOURCE: Federal Election Commission, *FEC Disclosure Series No. 1: Presidential Prenomination Receipts and Expenditures — 1976 Campaign* (Washington, D.C., 1976)

1975-August 31,1976, by presidential and vice presidential candidates, their principal campaign committees, other authorized committees, and individuals who made independent expenditures on their behalf, as well as political committees registering support of a candidate and the microfilm location of each document.

Table 5-21
Total Receipts and Expenditures of Three Republican Presidential Candidates and Their Principal Campaign Committees in the 1976 Campaign[a]

| | (Figures Unadjusted) | | | |
| | Receipts | | Expenditures | |
Candidate	Primary	General	Primary	General
Gordon, J. John	—	—	$1,476	—
Persons, Robert L.	—	—	65	—
Williams, Mary E. Humphrey	—	—	440	—

[a] Receipts and expenditures are provided elsewhere for Republican presidential candidates who qualified for federal matching funds. The figures given here show the total money received and spent by the candidate and his or her principal campaign committee from January 1, 1975, through August 30, 1976, as reported to the FEC by September 15, 1976. These totals exclude receipts and expenditures by all other committees and by individuals making independent expenditures on behalf of the candidates.

SOURCE: Federal Election Commission, *FEC Disclosure Series No. 1: Presidential Prenomination Receipts and Expenditures — 1976 Campaign* (Washington, D.C. 1976)

Several charts and graphs show the total receipts and expenditures, as well as the amounts spent by Democratic, Republican, minor-party, and independent presidential candidates. Expenditures by candidates of unknown party affiliation also are given. Tables 5-20 through 5-25 present data for presidential candidates; only Table 5-25 includes data for vice presidential candidates, and none of the tables includes candidates who spent no money. While the document supplies analyses of financial data supplied by presidential candidates who qualified for matching funds during the primaries, most of the report simply sets forth the statistics stored in the computer. These figures differ from those presented in the introduction to this chapter, partly because the data base differs, partly because these figures are not as refined as are the others.

According to the FEC, a total of $77,875,647 was reported in campaign expenditures by 207 filing presidential and vice presidential candidates. Democratic candidates and their campaign committees received more than $42.4 million and spent approximately $400,000 more than that. Republican candidates and their committees reported receipts approaching $32.5 million and expenditures of almost $30 million. Other candidates received $660,632 and spent $772,288 during the 20 months covered by the report.

The figures provided are those shown in this first disclosure report but the commission itself doubts their accuracy.[90] They are significantly

Table 5-22
Total Receipts and Expenditures of Minor-Party Presidential Candidates and Their Principal Campaign Committees in the 1976 Campaign [a]

	Receipts		Expenditures	
(Figures Unadjusted)				
Candidate and Party	Primary	General	Primary	General
Camejo, Peter (Socialist Workers)	—	$127,141	—	$119,992
Evans, Ronald Wayne (U.S. Labor)	—	550	—	537
Hall, Gus (Communist)	—	51,074	—	50,614
LaRouche, Lyndon H. (U.S. Labor)	—	12,394	—	11,424
Levin, Julius (Socialist Labor)	—	56,239	—	25,222
MacBride, Roger Lea (Libertarian)	—	150,494	—	290,028
Miller, Ernest (Restoration)	—	40,615	—	41,103
Morrow, Conrad Flourney (Symbiotic Union)	—	10	—	10
Wright, Margaret (People's)	—	12,340	—	12,163
Zeidler, Frank P. (Socialist, USA)	—	5,763	—	5,645

[a] The figures given here show the total money received and spent by the candidate and his or her principal campaign committee from January 1, 1975, through August 30, 1976, as reported to the FEC by September 15, 1976. These totals exclude receipts and expenditures by all other committees and by the individuals making independent expenditures on behalf of the candidates.

SOURCE: Federal Election Commission, *FEC Disclosure Series No. 1: Presidential Prenomination Receipts and Expenditures — 1976 Campaign* (Washington, D.C., 1976)

inflated because no adjustments have been made for transfers between candidates and committees, transfers among committees, loans and repayments of loans, unsettled campaign debts, and discrepancies revealed by FEC audits. For this reason, these statistics should be viewed as indicating the flow of money during a campaign rather than as net campaign receipts or expenditures for the period.

The commission's figures indicate that almost one-third of the funds reportedly received by the candidates came from the Presidential Primary Matching Fund Program. A total of 207 candidates filed statements with the commission. Three — Jimmy Carter, Gerald Ford, and Ronald Reagan — spent more than $10 million each. Eight candidates (Birch Bayh, Lloyd Bentsen, Edmund Brown Jr., Frank Church, Fred Harris, Henry Jackson, Morris Udall, and George Wallace) spent more

Table 5-23
Total Receipts and Expenditures of Independent Presidential Candidates and Their Principal Campaign Committees in the 1976 Campaign[a]

| | (Figures Unadjusted) | | | |
| | Receipts | | Expenditures | |
Candidate	Primary	General	Primary	General
Collins, Richard C.	—	$ 224	—	$ 289
Gabor, Patrick W.	—	600	—	500
Liebman, Monte Harris	—	94	—	61
McCarthy, Eugene	—	20,400	—	20,200
Stone, Keith K.	—	605	—	484
Wharton, Gordon H.	—	1,976	—	1,975
Williams, Thomas O.	—	23	—	22

[a]The figures given here show the total money received and spent by the candidate and his principal campaign committee from January 1, 1975, through August 30, 1976, as reported by the FEC by September 15, 1976. These totals exclude receipts and expenditures by all other committees and by individuals making independent expenditures on behalf of the candidates.

SOURCE: Federal Election Commission, *FEC Disclosure Series No. 1: Presidential Prenomination Receipts and Expenditures — 1976 Campaign* (Washington, D.C., 1976)

Table 5-24
Total Receipts and Expenditures of 'Unknown Party' Presidential Candidates and Their Principal Campaign Committees in the 1976 Campaign[a]

| | (Figures Unadjusted) | | | |
| | Receipts | | Expenditures | |
Candidate	Primary	General	Primary	General
Deshon, Charles Wesley	—	$1,724	—	$1,254
Dumont, Don	—	500	—	469
Englefield, Richard H.	—	1,029	—	1,029
Evans, James Leroy	—	—	—	300
George, Malcombe	—	190	—	190
Hemple, Evylin	—	443	—	443
Hoenig, Peggy	—	4,453	—	442
Rodgers, Lucky Buck	—	—	—	1,087
Sell, Danny P.	—	—	—	100
Templeton, Dean	—	896	—	931
Waggoner, Ira B.	—	—	—	61

[a] The figures here show the total money received and spent by the candidate and his or her principal campaign committee from January 1, 1975, through August 30, 1976, as reported to the FEC by September 15, 1976. These totals exclude receipts and expenditures by all other committees and by individuals making independent expenditures on behalf of the candidates.

SOURCE: Federal Election Commission, *FEC Disclosure Series No. 1: Presidential Prenomination Receipts and Expenditures — 1976 Campaign* (Washington, D.C., 1976)

Table 5-25
Level of Expenditures[a] in 1976[b] Presidential and Vice Presidential
Prenomination Campaigns by Political Party

(Figures Unadjusted)

Amount of Campaign Expenditures	Democrats	Republicans	Minor Parties	Independent Candidates	Unknown Parties	Totals
More than $10,000,000	1[c]	2[d]				3
$1,000,000-$10,000,000	8[e]					8
$100,000-$1,000,000	5[f]		3[g]	1[h]		9
$10,000-$100,000	7		6			13
$1-$10,000	19[i]	3	4	6	11	41
No money spent	31	12	9	19	60	131
Totals	71	17	22	26	71	207[j]

[a] Includes expenditures by the candidate and his principal campaign committee; does not include expenditures by other committees or by independent individuals.
[b] Covers the period from January 1, 1975, through August 30, 1976.
[c] Jimmy Carter.
[d] Ronald Reagan, Gerald R. Ford.
[e] George C. Wallace, Henry M. Jackson, Morris K. Udall, Lloyd Bentsen, Edmund G. Brown Jr., Fred Harris, Frank Church, Birch Bayh.
[f] Milton J. Shapp, Terry Sanford, Sargent Shriver, Ellen McCormack, Robert C. Byrd.
[g] Roger MacBride, Peter Camejo, Willie Mae Reid (vice presidential candidate).
[h] Eugene J. McCarthy.
[i] Donald L. Jackson, listed in the FEC's records as having spent more than $111,000, is credited with having spent between $1 and $10,000.
[j] Includes 11 individuals who sought the vice presidential nomination.

SOURCE: Federal Election Commission, *FEC Disclosure Series No. 1: Presidential Prenomination Receipts and Expenditures — 1976 Campaign* (Washington, D.C., 1976)

than $1 million each. Nine other candidates — including Independent Eugene McCarthy and three minor-party candidates — had campaign budgets ranging from $100,000 to $1,000,000. Thirteen candidates spent between $10,000 and $100,000; 41 others reported expenditures of $10,000 or less. One hundred and thirty-one individuals, nearly two-thirds of the total number, did not spend a cent on their campaigns.

The 1971 FECA required the General Accounting Office, the Secretary of the Senate, and the Clerk of the House to make certain compilations of the data they received from political candidates and committees. The 1974 and 1976 Amendments to the FECA do not mandate that the FEC do likewise, except that the commission must produce several indexes and make them available to the public.[91]

Footnotes

1. Michael J. Malbin, "When It Comes to Campaign Finance, Is It Better Red than Dead?" *National Journal,* May 15, 1976, pp. 650 ff.

2. See Austin Ranney, "Participation in American Presidential Nominations, 1976," Washington, D.C.: American Enterprise Institute for Public Policy Research, 1977, pp. 30-33.

3. Jonathan Moore and Janet Fraser, ed., *Campaign for President: The Managers Look at '76* (Cambridge, Mass.: Ballinger Publishing Co., 1977), pp. 151-154.

4. Joel H. Goldstein, "The Influence of Money on the Pre-Nomination Stage of the Presidential Selection Process: The Case of the 1976 Election," Paper Presented at the 1977 National Endowment for the Humanities Summer Seminar: "Presidential Power and Democratic Constraints;" published in slightly revised form in *Presidential Studies Quarterly,* Spring 1978, pp. 164-179.

5. William Claiborne, "Bayh Ends Quest for Nomination," *The Washington Post,* March 5, 1976.

6. Federal Election Commission, *Report of the Audit Division on the Committee For Birch Bayh In '76* (Washington, D.C., June 16, 1978).

7. "On the Track of Lean Cats," *Time,* February 9, 1976, p. 14.

8. Charles Mohr, "How the Bayh Race Deteriorated," *The New York Times,* March 4, 1976.

9. Frank Lynn, "Bayh 'Suspends' Nomination Race," *The New York Times,* March 5, 1976.

10. Barry E. Wagman, "Political Campaign Accounting — New Opportunities for the CPA," Journal of Accountancy, March 1976, p. 41, citing Bruce F. Freed, "This Time Everybody's Got a CREEP," *The Washington Monthly,* November 1975, p. 35.

11. Lou Cannon, "Jackson, Bentsen Defend Raising of Campaign Funds," *The Washington Post,* December 17, 1974.

12. "Bentsen: Trials of an Unrecognized Candidate," Congressional Quarterly *Weekly Report,* November 1, 1975, p. 2326.

13. "Oklahoma Defeat Reduces Bentsen to Favorite Son," Congressional Quarterly *Weekly Report,* February 14, 1976, p. 322.

14. Ken Bode, "Jerry Brown to the Rescue?" *The New Republic,* May 15, 1976, p. 7.

15. "End of the Road," *Newsweek,* July 26, 1976, p. 46.

16. Federal Election Commission, *Proposed Regulations,* May 1976, sec. 130.9 (i)(1).

17. Federal Election Commission, *Report of the Audit Division on Brown for President Committee,* October 1977.

18. Federal Election Commission, *FEC Disclosure Series No. 7: 1976 Presidential Campaign* (Washington, D.C., 1977), p. 16.

19. Spencer Rich, "Byrd Will Seek '76 Nomination," *The Washington Post,* January 10, 1976.

20. For a personal account of Dees' involvement, see Morris Dees, "Fundraising for the Jimmy Carter Presidential Primary Campaign," unpublished manuscript.

21. These figures differ from FEC ones because many contributions were not submitted for matching.

22. "Carter: Entering the Lists," *Time,* Dec. 23, 1974, p. 11.

23. Martin Schram, *Running for President: A Journal of the Carter Campaign,* (New York: Pocket Books, 1976), p. 27.

24. Linda Charlton, "Senator Church Joins Presidential Race," *The New York Times,* March 19, 1976.

25. Sandra Salmans, "Miracle Worker?" *Newsweek,* May 24, 1976, p. 21.

26. Les Ledbetter, "Church's Race Takes the Tortoise's Cue," *The New York Times,* May 23, 1976.

27. Linda Charlton, "Rhode Island Gain Sensed by Church," *The New York Times,* May 31, 1976.

28. "Harris: Again, A Thundering 'New Populism,' " Congressional Quarterly *Weekly Report,* October 11, 1975, p. 2191.

29. "Rep. John Conyers' complaint against the Harris for President Committee," *Campaign Practices Reports*, April 17, 1978, p. 6.

30. Jules Witcover, "Happy Warrior Humphrey Bows Out for Last Time," *The Washington Post*, June 10, 1976.

31. Douglas E. Kneeland, "Jackson Gives Up 'Active Pursuit' of Nomination," *The New York Times*, May 2, 1976.

32. Federal Election Commission, *Report of the Audit Division on the Jackson for President Committee* (Washington, D.C., 1977).

33. Lou Cannon, "Jackson, Bentsen Defend Raising of Campaign Funds," *The Washington Post*, December 17, 1974.

34. "Jackson Achieves a Critical Mass," *Time*, March 15, 1976, p. 13.

35. Elizabeth Becker, "Jackson: Last-Ditch Maryland Effort," *The Washington Post*, May 13, 1976.

36. "Nominee-in-Waiting," *Newsweek*, June 21, 1976, p. 17.

37. James R. Dickenson, "Democratic Field Reduced by One," *Washington Star-News*, November 22, 1974.

38. "Executives Aid Mondale In Paying Political Debts," *The Washington Post*, January 21, 1977.

39. "Sanford Declares Candidacy," *The Washington Post*, May 30, 1975.

40. Wayne King, "Sanford Is Planning to Enter 20 Presidential Primaries," *The New York Times*, September 14, 1975.

41. Federal Election Commission, *Statement of Reasons for Determination of Repayment From Milton Shapp* (Washington D.C., May 12, 1977).

42. James F. Clarity, "Shapp Denies Blame, But Will Repay Fund," *The New York Times*, May 14, 1977.

43. Andrew Mollison, "Shapp Scheme Could Hurt Funding Bill," *Atlanta Journal*, May 19, 1977.

44. William Ecenbarger and Aaron Epstein, "Justice Department Blocks Subpoena of Shapp," *The Philadelphia Inquirer*, September 18, 1977.

45. Jan Schaffer, "Shapp '76 Fund-Raiser Is Accused of Misstating Gifts to Campaign," *The Philadelphia Inquirer*, June 10, 1978.

46. "Two are indicted in 1976 Shapp aid," *The Philadelphia Inquirer*, October 19, 1978.

47. Thomas Ferrick, Jr., " '76 Shapp donor indicted," *The Philadelphia Inquirer*, August 25, 1978.

48. "Friends of Gov. Shapp Plead Guilty to Election Violations," *Los Angeles Times*, January 6, 1979.

49. Lucinda Franks, "Shriver, Stumping for Votes in New Hampshire, Encounters Problems of Organization," *The New York Times*, February 9, 1976.

50. Frank Lynn, "Udall Stumping for Money Here," *The New York Times*, February 4, 1975.

51. Don Prial, "Cash-Strapped Udall Denounces President For Blocking Funds," *The Evening Bulletin* (Philadelphia), May 21, 1976.

52. Lou Cannon, " 'Orgy of Publicity' Benefits Carter Drive, Udall Complains," *The Washington Post*, April 17, 1976.

53. "Wallace Gains Time In Bid to Account For Campaign Fund," *The New York Times*, April 4, 1978.

54. "Wallace in Mississippi: We Thrashed Them," *Congressional Quarterly Weekly Report*, January 31, 1976, p. 243.

55. Agis Salpukas, "Wallace Presses Health Issue," *The New York Times*, March 13, 1976.

56. B. Drummond Ayres, "Wallace Drive in Disarray; Aides Decide to Retrench," *The New York Times*, March 18, 1976.

57. George Lardner, "Wallace Lashes Out in N.C., As Carter, Confident, Leaves," *The Washington Post*, March 21, 1976.

58. "Summary of 1976 New Hampshire Democratic Primary Write In Effort for John Connally," Federal Election Commission document.

59. Herbert E. Alexander, *Financing the 1972 Election* (Lexington, Mass.: D. C. Heath and Co., 1976), pp. 498-500.

60. James M. Naughton, "Ford Announces Candidacy for '76 'To Finish the Job,' " *The New York Times,* July 9, 1975.

61. Rowland Evans and Robert Novak, "The President's Cost-Free Advocates," *The Washington Post,* July 8, 1976.

62. Michael C. Jensen, "Financiers Here Shy Off From Aiding Ford," *The New York Times,* November 9, 1975.

63. Patricia Camp, "Volunteers, Three Staffers Work for Ford," *The Washington Post,* July 10, 1975.

64. Jon Nordheimer, "Ford, in Ad Shift, Describes Reagan as Peace Threat," *The New York Times,* June 6, 1976.

65. "In national forest areas, the government owns the land on the mountain slopes while the land at the base is privately owned. The Forest Service determines which developers receive permits to construct ski facilities on the slopes." William Chapman, "Callaway Debate Scares Crested Butte," *The Washington Post,* April 11, 1976.

66. Callaway, despite his efforts to prove his innocence and regain his campaign post, apparently realized it was a lost hope from the beginning. "From the time NBC went on the air with these charges it was as certain as a Greek tragedy that I would have to leave the campaign." Edward Walsh, "Callaway Quits Ford Campaign; Morton Named," *The Washington Post,* March 31, 1976.

67. Ford, upon accepting Callaway's resignation, reiterated his faith in the Georgian's innocence.

68. William Chapman, "Morton Gets Warning on Political Job," *The Washington Post,* January 15, 1976.

69. Under the Federal Election Campaign law "the salaries of all employees of the President Ford Committee and White House aides on political assignment [were] chargeable against the $10 million spending limit imposed on each Presidential candidate for the preconvention period." Warren Weaver, Jr., "Post For Morton Draws Criticism," *The New York Times,* January 15, 1976.

70. William Chapman, "Morton Named Ford Aide," *The Washington Post,* January 14, 1976.

71. William Chapman, "Meeting On Morton Is Canceled," *The Washington Post,* January 16, 1976.

72. Warren Weaver, Jr., "Strauss Wants Pay Of Morton Labeled A Political Expense," *The New York Times,* January 23, 1976.

73. Curtis himself argued that " 'I think that now we need to lean on the other side of the coin because we've just had Watergate." Chapman, "Morton Gets Warning on Political Job.' "

74. Robert Walters, "Percy Raised $100,000," *The Washington Star,* February 3, 1974. The individual contribution limit of $1,000 per candidate per election did not go into effect until January 1, 1975.

75. "$135,000 Is Raised by Percy," *The Washington Post,* March 22, 1974.

76. "Percy Tests Reaction to Presidential Bid," *The Sunday Bulletin* (Philadelphia), December 16, 1973.

77. Robert Walters, "Percy Maps '76 Bid," *The Washington Star,* April 18, 1974.

78. R. W. Apple, Jr., "Percy Shelves Campaign For White House in 1976," *The New York Times,* August 15, 1974.

79. Walters, "Percy Raised $100,000."

80. Henry Hanson, "Percy Group Keeps $7,000 of Donations," *Chicago Daily News,* December 13, 1974.

81. Lyle Denniston, "GOP Rejects Trip Payments for Reagan," *The Washington Star,* November 21, 1975.

82. Federal Election Commission, *Report of the Audit Division on the Citizens for Reagan* (Washington, D.C., April 13, 1978).

83. *Federal Election Commission v. Citizens for Reagan,* U.S. District Court, D.C. Circuit No. 78-1160.

84. Jon Nordheimer, "Reagan Campaign, in Debt in April, Now Reports Surplus of $1.2 Million," *The New York Times,* September 13, 1976.

85. "Ford Bandwagon Rolls," *Time,* March 22, 1976, p. 7.

86. David S. Broder, "Reagan Blasts Ford," *The Washington Post,* March 13, 1976.

87. Jules Witcover, *Marathon: The Pursuit of the Presidency, 1972-1976* (New York: Viking Press, 1977), p. 413.

88. Democratic Congressional Campaign Committee Report, Volume 1, No. 2, January 1978, pp. 1-4.

89. Federal Election Commission, *FEC Disclosure Series No. 1: Presidential Pre-Nomination Receipts and Expenditures — 1976 Campaign* (Washington, D.C., 1976).

90. Ibid., p. 3.

91. On October 18, 1976, the commission made available the *Index of Communications by Corporations and Membership Organizations* covering the period May 1-October 1, 1976. This was published in updated form in April 1977. It also published in the *Federal Register* a list of multicandidate committees; the purpose of the latter document was to enable the committees to fulfill their compliance responsibilities under the law.

The commission and several private research groups also sought to determine which kinds of statistical information would be most useful to the public in the future; the agency planned to use the conclusions of this analysis in the development of computer programs for the 1978 elections. Federal Election Commission, *Annual Report 1976,* p. 36.

6 Financing the Conventions

The 1974 Amendments to the Federal Election Campaign Act established for the first time an option for public financing of party conventions. Federal subsidies for the 1976 Democratic and Republican national conventions and relative regulations formulated by the Federal Election Commission wrought important changes on the institution of nominating conventions. Yet the new law and the commission left partially intact the traditional role of private and municipal funds in the financing of party gatherings, still necessary since the $2.2 million in public monies for each convention did not cover all of the costs related to the quadrennial meetings.

The Democrats held their convention during July in New York City to validate Jimmy Carter's electoral triumph, and one month later the Republicans met in Kansas City to confer their nomination, by a narrow margin, on President Gerald Ford. Both parties also settled some questions on rules and procedures for future conventions. On other matters, the two conventions set in motion decision-making processes on methods of delegate and candidate selection for 1980 and beyond.

The FECA and FEC Regulations

After much controversy, the 94th Congress enacted government funding of conventions on an optional basis as part of the 1974 Amendments. The Amendments also eliminated any income tax deduction for advertising in convention program books, a major source of funding for past party conventions. Under the law, parties receive convention money from the presidential checkoff fund, and the two major parties are entitled to $2 million plus a cost-of-living supplement. In 1976 the amount receivable by the Democratic and Republican conventions was $2,182,000 each. A minor party is eligible for a partial convention

subsidy if the candidate of such a party received more than 5 percent of
the vote in the previous presidential election; in accordance with the
1972 presidential election results, no minor party qualified for public
funds in 1976. During 1975 the RNC was opposed in principle to public
financing of their convention, adopting a resolution against accepting
the money while seeking alternative private means of financing. Not
readily finding an alternative, however, and not wanting to give any
advantage to their opposition, the Republicans reluctantly did accept
federal funds for their 1976 convention.

Ostensibly, public funding replaced the traditional mode of financing whereby the parties covered convention costs largely by literally
selling their conventions. Formerly, host cities and local businesses
furnished cash and services to the party conventions and national
corporations bought advertising space at considerable cost in program
books. Such outright donations by corporations were not only legal, but
even enjoyed tax status as legitimate business expenses. In 1972 the
Democratic and Republican convention programs had grossed $1 million
and $1.6 million, respectively, from advertising. In contrast, neither
1976 program book contained paid ads. Also absent in 1976 were the
contributions in kind provided in the past, such as free cars from the
auto makers, liquor donated by distilling companies, and the familiar
delegates' lounges run by the airlines. Nevertheless, private and host-
city money still played a role in the 1976 conventions, albeit a limited
and newly regulated one.

Because of time considerations, one of the first tasks the FEC faced
after it began operations was the promulgating of regulations for conventions pursuant to the broad outlines of the campaign law. In June 1975
the commission issued an advisory opinion that permitted certain types
of contributions and expenditures outside the realm of federal subsidies.
Prompted by complaints from the Republican and Democratic National
Committees that a narrowly defined $2.2 million limitation would be
unrealistically low, the FEC ruled that state and local governments
could provide certain services and facilities such as convention halls,
transportation, and security assistance, the cost of which would not
count against the parties' expenditure limits. Those same services, the
commission decided, would be prohibited by the FECA if donated or
leased by a corporation to state or local governments below the fair
market value.

The FEC also made two exceptions to the general prohibition on
corporate contributions and free services. One of these allowed the
parties to accept such items as free hotel rooms and conference facilities
in return for booking a certain number of room reservations, so long as
other conventions of similar size and duration received similar benefits.

A second exception concerned contributions to host committees and civic associations working to attract or assist the political conventions. In years past bipartisan host-city citizens' committees had collected contributions from businesses, particularly those that profit most from convention crowds, to supplement the parties' income. For 1976 the commission placed tight restrictions on this practice, stipulating that host committees be nonprofit and subject to FEC reporting requirements and audit. Additionally, only corporations based in the convention city could contribute to host committees, and their donations had to be made "in the reasonable expectation of a commensurate commercial return during the life of the convention."[1] After the parties and their host committees protested that purely local businesses could not provide sufficient funds, the FEC broadened its contribution regulation to include national corporations with local operations if profits went primarily to the local outlet.

The commissioners were less sympathetic to the parties' cash-flow problems. The FEC had established an installment plan for paying each party its $2.2 million subsidy because the law called for "payments, which in the aggregate, shall not exceed" the legal maximum. Under this plan, each party received an initial payment of not more than 30 percent of the full entitlement, with subsequent grants based on projected expenses and drawn on a quarterly schedule. Both the Democratic and Republican parties disliked the arrangement and requested that lump-sum payments be made. Party officials argued that installments were an unnecessary safeguard since by law the conventions had to return any excess funds to the government and the FEC would audit convention books. The parties pointed out that their spending was made inefficient by the quarterly schedule and that convention officials were spending an inordinate amount of time soothing creditors, because money was not available to pay bills as needed. Despite these protests, the commission maintained its system of partial payments, which proved especially burdensome in the wake of the Supreme Court's *Buckley* ruling when the FEC could not certify payments. When the commission stopped distributing funds on March 22, 1976, the Democrats had received about $800,000, while the Republicans had taken approximately $750,000. The parties did manage to make do until the FEC resumed certification and, in the end, both parties spent well under their entitlements.

The Role of Host Cities and Committees

By sanctioning certain spending in addition to federal grants, the FEC facilitated a partial return to traditional convention finance. As in previous years, the parties engaged in complex site-selection processes and a type of competitive bidding with potential convention cities.

Before choosing their convention locations, the Democrats and Republicans had formed site-selection committees that traveled to prospective cities to inspect facilities and gather information. In the process, committee members obtained lavish treatment from local officials and celebrities at the expense of various business and civic groups trying to attract a convention. For example one two-day excursion by the Democratic site-selection committee cost the Association for a Better New York and the Convention and Visitors Bureau about $10,000. While assessing Los Angeles, committee members were entertained by various Hollywood figures including Gene Kelly, Warren Beatty, and Robert Wagner and his wife Natalie Wood.

As the two prime contenders for the Democratic National Convention, Los Angeles and New York made lucrative proposals. Los Angeles offered the Democrats free use of its municipally owned convention center as well as police services and bus transportation for delegates, a package worth $1.7 million. The California city was rejected, however, partly because of limited hotel space and a less-than-enthusiastic invitation from Governor Brown. In contrast, New York featured abundant and convenient housing, and the fiscally troubled city developed an enthusiastic public relations effort for party leaders. Also, New York City pledged to lease privately owned Madison Square Garden for $1.9 million and turn it over free to the Democrats, and promised to deliver $1.6 million in other services such as parking, transportation, and construction within the Garden.

Similar competition between Kansas City, Miami Beach, Cleveland, New Orleans, Los Angeles, and San Francisco preceded the Republican National Convention. Cleveland offered to make up for its lack of hotel accommodations by moving mobile homes to a downtown parking lot, and leasing, at a cost of $800,000, three cruise ships to be docked on Lake Erie. Yet Kansas City won the vote of the RNC in September 1975, with a pledge of $500,000 in goods and services. If the new system of convention financing ended the undue influence of private interests, it has enhanced the role of municipal interests.

Having settled on their convention locations almost a year in advance, the two parties started an immense amount of planning and spending. The Democrats oversaw extensive construction in Madison Square Garden to convert the facility from a sports arena to a convention hall. The City of New York's $1.9 million lease ran for two months because that much time was needed for necessary improvements including special seating, platforms and booths for the media, a false floor, and a bullet-proof podium. The total construction bill cost the city $1.4

million, including a $250,000 payment to Office Design Associates of New York for planning the alterations. In addition, New York appropriated about $210,000 for insurance, $30,000 to rent a parking lot for convention VIPs, and some $90,000 for buses that transported delegates to and from their hotels. Thus, direct subsidies from New York City to the Democratic National Convention totaled $3,630,000.

Indirect subsidization consisted of special sanitation details and vice squads to police areas near the Garden and delegate hotels as part of the city's overall public relations campaign. At the federal level, the Law Enforcement Assistance Administration (LEAA) provided $2.6 million to the New York police for overtime and other special security costs incurred during the four-day convention, including an estimated $35,000 for a film instructing the police in techniques of crowd control. The Democrats' host committee, the Citizens' Committee for the Democratic National Convention, spent $343,610 to accommodate convention officials, arrange special hotel and restaurant prices, assist visitors, decorate convention facilities, and carry on a promotional campaign of "The Big Apple."

For their convention, the Republicans incurred similar, though lower, costs. Much of the $500,000 pledged by Kansas City went toward air conditioning and construction in the Kemper Arena (also a sports facility, but better suited than Madison Square Garden to a convention). The city's subsidy also purchased a chain-link security fence erected around the arena for $50,000, as well as transportation services for delegates. Unlike New York, Kansas City tried to recoup part of its spending; the shuttle bus service cost each delegate $10 for the week and the city levied a hotel tax of $1 per night per room occupied by those attending the convention.

Another LEAA gant of $2.4 million funded activities of the Kansas City police force related to the Republican gathering. Finally, the Kansas City host committee spent about $60,000 to enliven the stay of convention visitors.

A tabulation of the costs mentioned above shows that, for the Democratic and Republican conventions, New York and Kansas City provided direct subsidies totaling approximately $4,130,000, the two host committees together expended about $403,610, and the Law Enforcement Assistance Administration spent $5 million, for a grand total of $9,533,610 in financing from sources other than the presidential checkoff fund. Despite its size, this figure may be viewed as a worthwhile investment given the free spending of delegates and observers, which boosts the economies of convention cities. Estimates of the amount spent by convention goers approached $10 million in each city in 1976.

The Democratic Convention

The 1976 Democratic National Convention took place in an atmosphere of unity, a departure from the party's two previous conventions. The assembled delegates confirmed the conclusion that former Gov. Jimmy Carter of Georgia would receive the presidential nomination and approved Carter's choice of Minnesota Sen. Walter F. Mondale as his running mate. Moreover, Democrats smoothly handled credentials matters, settled on a party platform, and formulated rules for future prenomination campaigns and conventions.

In sharp contrast to the 1968 and 1972 Democratic gatherings, no credentials challenges reached the floor of the 1976 convention. In 1976 the party's national committee had settled on credentials procedures designed to eliminate disruptive challenges. The rules adopted provided that any credentials challenges would have to cite specific violations of a state's delegate-selection format, since each state's system already would have been approved by the Compliance Review Commission to ensure basic fairness. Further, challenges could be filed only by delegate candidates "personally injured" in the selection process and only within 10 days of an alleged violation.

In June 1976, a month before the convention, the Credentials Committee resolved the few disputes that did arise. Among these, the committee reached compromises in seating the Pennsylvania delegation and rival factions of the Democratic Party of Puerto Rico, and settled a challenge to the New York delegation by increasing the number of women and young people in the state's at-large section. The credentials panel also upheld the principle that a presidential candidate must approve delegates running under his name. This decision permitted the Carter organization to reward certain followers with a delegate seat even though different delegate candidates had received more votes, as happened with eight positions in the Florida delegation. In a similar case, an Indiana delegate who had been elected and then, with Carter's approval, replaced by a labor-backed challenger, received a seat as an alternate plus $200 for his convention expenses from the Georgian's campaign. [2]

The proceedings of the Platform Committee proved as harmonious as those of its credentials counterpart. During spring 1976 panels of the 153-member committee held four regional hearings and listened to more than 100 hours of testimony; then the full committee met to draw up a platform document. The committee's draft largely reflected the thinking of Carter and only one minority plank went on to a floor vote at the convention. This amendment won the delegates' approval by calling for revision of the Hatch Act to "extend to federal workers the same political rights enjoyed by other Americans."

The most excitement of the convention surrounded controversies over the continuation of party-reform rules. In June the Rules Committee had refused to guarantee women an equal share of delegates to the party's 1980 convention. Instead, the committee passed a resolution committing the party to "promote an equal division" of the sexes at future conventions. This more moderate stand dissatisfied the party's Women's Caucus, but the issue never came to a floor fight because the women reached a compromise with Carter. He endorsed a rule still only encouraging equal representation, but wanted it to apply to the 1978 midterm conference as well as the 1980 convention. Also added to the resolution was language committing the national committee to assist state parties in approaching equal division. Carter also promised to establish a women's division within the party but independent of the national chairman.

Another major battle ensued over retention of delegate-selection primaries, but this time the Carter position lost. Known pejoratively as the "loophole" primary, this form of election allows a candidate to win all of the delegates within congressional districts he carries. Opponents claimed that the system violated the 1972 resolution prohibiting winner-take-all primaries. In 1976, 13 states, including six of the largest, employed the delegate-selection format. A slim majority of the Rules Committee had voted to outlaw the delegate-selection system for 1980, but Carter and DNC Chairman Robert S. Strauss pressed for a minority report that would have postponed elimination of the loophole by transferring the question to a study group. By a voice vote, the convention sided with the Rules Committee majority and adopted the ban.

In another rules matter, the convention rejected a resolution that would have reduced the number of signatures needed in the future to move minority reports from convention committees to the floor. In 1976, 25 percent of committee dissenters had to sign a petition to place a minority report before the full convention, instead of the 10 percent needed in 1972, which had contributed to the disorganization of that gathering. In 1976 some liberal delegates proposed a 15 percent requirement for later conventions, claiming that the existing rule stifled debate. On the floor, the revision lost by a vote of 1,354-1/2 to 1,249.

To conduct its business, the Democratic National Convention spent $2,016,870. Receipts for the convention were as follows:

Received from U.S. Treasury	$2,180,869.79
Returned to U.S. Treasury	− 165,133.12
Actual U.S. Treasury funds	2,015,736.67
Earned interest	+ 1,133.58
Total receipts	$2,016,870.25

Initially, the DNC had drawn $2,180,869.79 from the U.S. Treasury, but later refunded $165,133.12 in unused funds, making the final federal subsidy $2,015,736.67. The party also earned $1,133.58 in interest on government funds, but had to pay $494.50 in federal taxes on these earnings.

Table 6-1
A Functional Breakdown of Expenditures for the 1976 Democratic National Convention Committee Inc.

Personnel		$ 399,215.52	
Convention operations:			
District of Columbia office	$ 34,075.76		
New York office	112,848.86		
Printing — preconvention	152,346.76		
Printing — postconvention	12,131.70		
Telephone	231,459.71		
Convention hall expenses	270,418.55		
Tickets and credentials	42,060.69		
Transportation	12,992.60		
Security	157,033.45		
Communications	19,824.22		
Reporting services	5,253.00		
Housing office	36,809.56		
Travel	260,829.23		
Miscellaneous	45,878.41	1,393,962.50	
Convention Standing and Advisory Committee		103,742.23	
Compliance Review Committee		107,206.50	2,004,126.75
Closeout operation			12,245.90
Federal income taxes applicable to interest income			494.50
Total expenditures			$2,016,867.15

Table 6-1, which reports a functional breakdown of Democratic convention expenditures, shows that personnel was the largest category of spending at $399,216. Staffing for the event took such a large portion of the budget because the party carried as many as 38 people on its preconvention payroll, and top officials served for more than a year. Convention Director Andrew J. Shea received a salary of $90,000 as well as expenses, among which was a $1,150-a-month apartment in New York. [3] Convention hall expenses not covered by New York City came to $270,419 and constituted the second costliest function. Travel costs and telephone service followed at $260,829 and $231,460, respectively. Printing before and after the convention totaled $164,478 and security services cost $157,033.

To ensure the security of their convention, the Democrats took a number of extraordinary steps, including contracting for ushers and guards to back up units of city police and federal agents. Within the Garden, the DNC also deployed 25 ushers who worked voluntarily for savings of some $80,000. In addition, the party spent $42,061 for tickets and credentials, which consisted of a three-layer card made of retro-reflective paper for verification by ultra-violet light. To further reduce the possibility of counterfeiting, officials under police escort distributed credentials each day of the convention.

Other notable expenses included a 16-minute film extolling the virtues of the party and a 14-minute film on Jimmy Carter. Host for the former was TV actor Edward Asner who portrayed the character Mr. Dooley, a philosophical Chicago barkeeper created by Finley Peter Dunne at the turn of the century. Under the heading of communications, these presentations and other functions cost $19,824. Moreover, the DNC's two standing committees incurred combined expenses of $210,949. Activities of the Compliance Review Commission, charged with approving state delegate-selection procedures, cost $107,207. The Convention Standing and Advisory Committee expended an additional $103,742. Other functions and costs are shown in Table 6-1.

The Republican Convention

The Republican National Convention officially opened on August 16, as Kansas City became the final battleground in Ronald Reagan's challenge to President Ford. Not surprisingly, the proceedings of the convention invariably carried overtones of the Ford-Reagan contest.

In the week before the convention, the Platform Committee hammered out a draft document praising the Ford administration, but Reagan backers filed a minority report proposing a plank entitled "Morality in Foreign Policy." This report implicitly criticized the policy of detente followed by Ford and Secretary of State Henry A. Kissinger. On the convention floor, the president's strategists chose to sidestep a conservative reaction and swallowed the Reagan foreign policy plank. Earlier, the Reagan command had decided not to press other minority planks that opposed the Equal Rights Amendment and the Panama Canal negotiations, even though such positions might have sparked an emotional stampede toward Reagan. The chance of a last-minute Reagan surge had been minimized further when the Rules Committee abandoned an old Republican provision that permitted any delegate to offer a platform amendment from the floor; in 1976, 25 percent of the 106-member Platform Committee had to approve a minority plank for floor debate to occur.

With the platform a less explosive area, the crucial encounters between Ford and Reagan arose in the Rules Committee, which had made preliminary decisions in the week prior to the convention. In committee, Reagan supporters failed in an attempt to raise to two-thirds the number of delegate votes needed to cut off convention debate. Reaganites lost another committee vote, which would have had the convention conducted by Robert's Rules of Order rather than the Rules of the House of Representatives, the latter being more confusing for political newcomers such as many Reagan delegates.

Ford supporters on the Rules Committee also prevailed on the two most important procedural questions of the convention. On the eve of the first convention session, the committee rejected 59-44 a Reagan-backed proposal that Ford be required to disclose his choice of a running mate, as Reagan had done. This rules change was designed to force Ford to pick a vice presidential choice who would erode some of the president's delegate support. After losing the committee vote on this issue, the Reagan supporters decided not to fight a Ford-backed rule requiring the convention to enforce state primary laws. Ford leaders feared that some of their delegates might vote for Reagan in defiance of state laws binding them to Ford. Since the courts normally will not enforce state laws in a convention situation, reinforcement by party rule helped freeze any faltering Ford delegates.

In spite of the loss in the Rules Committee, the proposed vice presidential selection rule went to the convention floor. There, it was the keystone of the strategy, designed by Reagan campaign manager John Sears, to break Ford's thin lead in the delegate count. Despite Sears' claims of the reform nature of the proposal, most observers saw the running-mate disclosure rule as a desperate ploy initiated because Reagan's choice of Senator Schweiker had hurt the Californian. The convened delegates rejected the rules change by a vote of 1,180 to 1,069. However, the idea of advanced disclosure of running mates gained some popularity and still survives as a potential reform.

Nonetheless, the defeat of the first effort by a national party to regulate a presidential candidate's choice of running mate foreshadowed the end of the Reagan insurgency. The following night, the roll call gave President Ford the party nomination. Yet Reagan did have an important influence in that Ford chose Sen. Robert Dole of Kansas — one of the most conservative of the president's possible running mates — to complete the Republican ticket.

The Republican convention cost $1,581,757. The party's original convention receipts came to $1,963,892.50, of which the U.S. Treasury provided $1,963,800 and bank interest on deposits added $92.50. In 1977 the RNC returned $382,135.52 of the public money it had drawn. This brought the federal subsidy down to $1,581,664.48, as shown in the following table:

Received from U.S. Treasury	$1,963,800.00
Returned to U.S. Treasury	− 382,135.52
Actual U.S. Treasury funds	1,581,664.48
Earned interest	+ 92.50
Total receipts	$1,581,756.98

A functional breakdown of Republican Convention expenditures, reported in Table 6-2, shows that professional fees totaling $210,776 constituted the costliest category. Food and lodging for convention officials followed, at $201,488. Security service was the next most expensive function at $187,465, followed by telephone and postage charges of $128,613 and personnel costs of almost $124,000. Other notable expenses included $76,567 for construction inside the Kemper Arena as well as $88,950 worth of technical services and $26,848 for special lighting and utilities within the hall. As did the Democrats, the Republicans spent heavily ($65,692) on credentials and tickets. All categories of expenditure are shown in Table 6-2.

Table 6-2
A Functional Breakdown of Expenditures for the 1976 Republican National Convention

Salaries and payroll taxes for office personnel in the Washington, D.C., office, at the Republican National Committee headquarters, for office personnel in Kansas City (convention coordinator and staff, convention manager's staff, housing committee staff and those handling news media operations on a long-term basis and numerous other staff on a short-term basis)	$ 123,999.62
Professional fees (artists, architect, technical advisers, computer service, writers, issue experts, legal services)	210,776.46
Agency charges (professional program consultant, computer programing, personnel agency, services required in development of platform)	26,123.14
Transportation (staff, officers of convention, officers and chairmen and vice chairmen of subcommittees of Committee on Arrangements)	90,185.26
Subsistence (food and lodging for staff, officers of convention, officers and chairmen and vice chairmen of subcommittees of Committee on Arrangements)	201,488.33
Office furniture and equipment	90,167.95
Office supplies and services (Washington, D.C., Kansas City and for officers and chairmen and vice chairmen of subcommittees of Committee on Arrangements)	21,472.90
Telephone, telegraph, postage, and routine express charges (major amount for telephone system in convention hall and convention headquarters in Kansas City)	128,612.84

Technical services (electronic installations, staging, prompting device and operation, sound system reinforcement and operation)	88,950.00
Reporting services (all formal and official meetings related to planning and preparation of convention, actual convention sessions and meetings of convention committees)	13,307.83
Meetings and conferences (hotel services, receptions and meals related to convention meetings and conferences)	31,955.08
Construction (press seats, speaker's platform, camera stands)	76,567.48
Music/films (orchestra, director of music arrangements, slide film production)	13,340.74
Convention supplies (gavels, blouses for pages, special housing forms, materials for Platform Committee, etc.)	4,558.36
Security services/ushers	187,464.93
Printing of official documents of convention (call of convention, forms for the certification of delegates, apportionment of delegates, platform, rules, temporary and permanent rolls, order of business, tally sheets, certificate of nomination, seating charts, etc.)	69,846.05
Manufacture of convention badges	24,575.45
Printing of convention tickets	41,116.88
Special lighting and routine utilities	26,848.19
Signs (state standards and all other signs for direction and identification)	10,295.36
Convention hall decorations	27,715.37
Miscellaneous	12,647.33
Insurance	7,132.45
Reimbursement to the Republican National Committee for various office services	15,721.49
Publication of the proceedings of the 1976 Republican National Convention	36,887.49
Total expenditures	$1,581,756.98

Other Costs

Any nominating convention entails a host of costs besides the expenditures of the parties, host cities, and host committees.

As noted previously, each of the major candidates, Ford, Reagan, and even Carter with virtually no opposition, spent several hundred thousand dollars at and in preparation for his party's convention. Elaborate communications and living arrangements facilitated the candidates' convention efforts. For instance, the cost of the Ford telephone and radio communications system was estimated at $100,000 and Carter's hotel suite cost $750 a day. Secret Service protection for the candidates is another hidden cost, which probably approached $100,000 at each convention. [4]

Moreover, the media, both electronic and writing press, staged operations more massive than those of the political parties. In 1976 the three commercial television networks alone spent upwards of $12 million on the Democratic convention, and a similar sum for the Republican one; expenses for the rest of the media ran into the millions.

Indeed, the high cost of covering the Democratic convention in New York raised objections from the press and caused some news organizations to decrease their coverage of the event. Inflated contractors' prices and mandatory union delivery charges had made the rental of office equipment exorbitant. A month before the convention, a chair rented for $37.50, a filing cabinet went for $140 and wastebasket rental reached $10 apiece. The New York Telephone Co. charged three to four times its normal rates so that it could cover any unpaid convention bills. Complaints from the media led DNC Chairman Strauss to confer with New York unions and companies, and in doing so, he achieved more reasonable prices and kept a high level of press coverage for the party convention. [5]

Delegate Costs

The above items do not include the immense out-of-pocket monies spent by the thousands of delegates and alternates, their families, press correspondents, and convention visitors. The total transportation, hotel, and restaurant bill for these people is in the tens of millions and certainly dwarfs the direct costs of the conventions.

Exact figures on delegate expenditures are not available since disclosure of delegate costs for travel, room, and board was not required by law, and the FEC exempted these unless they were paid for by others which were reporting entities. Campaign costs of those in the delegate election or selection process also were not covered by the FECA, although fragmentary information is available. The FEC issued guidelines covering these areas, and while they were neither implemented nor enforced, some disclosure did occur. The 1976 Amendments failed to clarify the disclosure status or enact the FEC guidelines. However, in the FECA revisions considered during 1977 and 1978, such delegate campaign and other expenditures were affirmatively excluded from disclosure. Moreover, the Senate-passed bill said that the following would not be considered contributions or expenditures: funds contributed to a delegate or a delegate candidate for a national or state political convention; unreimbursed payments for travel or subsistence made by a delegate or delegate candidate; or payments of expenses by a state or local political party for sponsoring a party meeting, caucus, or convention held to select delegates to a national convention. Thus such items would be exemptions from individual contribution limits and from candidate expenditure limits.

Party Reform

During the 1970s the Democratic and Republican parties have been reforming their delegate and candidate selection processes. The 1976 nominating conventions were both the product of past reforms and the origin of changes for future conventions and elections.

Democrats. For the Democrats, the two previous reforms that most affected the 1976 convention were the requirement of proportional representation for candidates and the abandonment of a quota system for women, minority, and youth delegates. Although the widespread use of delegate-selection primaries limited the effects of proportional representation in 1976, the convention's closing of the loophole will complete reform in this area in time for 1980.

Replacing the strict quotas used in 1972, the DNC had adopted an affirmative action program in March 1974 at the suggestion of the Mikulski Commission on Delegate Selection and Party Structure. This move effected a reduction of selected groups at the 1976 convention from the levels of 1972. In 1976, 36 percent of delegates were women, compared with 39.7 percent in 1972; 11 percent of 1976 delegates were black or other minority, as opposed to 15.2 percent in 1972; and 15 percent of delegates in New York were 30 years old or younger, down from the 21.4 percent young people four years before.[6] These decreases brought pressure from the black and women's caucuses at the convention, but the Carter camp held the line for retention of affirmative action rather than strict quota systems. The Carter supporters continue to do so.

Another reform called for in 1972 that did not withstand the test of time was a provision directing the DNC to set aside a trust fund of 8 percent of its annual income for financial assistance to needy delegates to the 1976 convention. The 1974 Amendments stated that public funds for conventions could not be used "to defray the expenses of any candidate or delegate." The FEC interpreted this clause to mean that any party payments for delegate expenses would be deducted from the public subsidy and counted against the convention spending limit. Consequently, DNC Chairman Strauss announced that he would not comply with the 1972 8 percent rule, although he did encourage state parties to assist delegates of limited means and also raised some money privately and informally for hardship cases.[7]

The 1976 convention laid the groundwork for further Democratic reforms, although the evolving changes already are being tempered by President Carter's preferences. In September 1977 the party's Commission on Presidential Nomination and Party Structure met in Detroit to draft a preliminary report on rules changes for 1980. Chaired by Morley Winograd, Michigan Democratic chairman, the commission explored reforms that some thought tended to protect President Carter from a credible renomination challenge in 1980.

Before the Winograd commission, representatives of the White House proposed increasing from 15 percent to 25 percent the threshold of primary votes that a candidate must receive to get a share of a state's delegates. For 1980, the raised threshold obviously would inhibit a challenge to Carter, although in later years such a mechanism was designed to build a consensus faster, thus preventing fragmentation of delegate votes that could lead to brokered conventions. A version of this reform more popular with the commission was an escalating threshold, whereby a candidate would need only 15 percent of a state vote to win delegates in the first month of the primary process, but he would need 20 percent in the second month and 25 percent in the final month of primaries.

On June 9, 1978, a DNC rules ratification meeting was held in Washington, D.C. Generally, the DNC adopted the report of the Winograd commission, including the highly controversial proportional representation formula. Though party activists lost their battle to retain the 15 percent threshold used in 1976, they did win some concession that made acceptance of the White House backed proposal easier. [8]

The Winograd commission's original proposal had been substituted by one proposed on behalf of Carter. The new plan dropped the time element from the original and established a flexible threshold — to be set by the state party — which was to be no lower than 15 percent and no higher than 20 percent. The plan was further amended by a restriction that limited application to the last level of the delegate-selection process. This would allow caucus states to use lower thresholds at precinct and county conventions.

Additionally, the DNC approved without debate several other proposals that made significant alterations in the delegate-selection process. These new rules included a shorter period (decreased from six to three months) in which delegates may be selected in every state, raising the question of whether some of the early elections, most notably the New Hampshire primary, can be moved forward by state legislatures to comply with this schedule. Other changes included a requirement that primary states set candidate filing deadlines 30 to 90 days before the election, and an increase in the size of state delegations by 10 percent to accommodate state party and elected officials. The DNC also adopted a limitation on participation in the delegate selection process to Democrats only. This was directed primarily toward Wisconsin, where voters previously had been able to participate in the Democratic election without designating their party affiliation.

A major issue that remained to be decided was the equal sexual division of delegations. At a May executive committee meeting, party leaders had postponed discussion of the issue in anticipation of a Judicial Council ruling on its legality. On June 8 the council ruled that it did not violate the DNC charter's "no quota" language, yet at the June 9 meeting action on this issue was again postponed until discussion of the call to the 1980 convention. Also postponed was the decision on the creation of single-member districts. Although there were some complaints that these issues were being avoided, consensus among party leaders was that these two issues belonged in the call rather than in the rules.

Other matters considered included a proposal that would expand affirmative action programs to include as delegates elderly citizens, blue-collar workers, and individuals with no college education, while maintaining efforts to increase the representation of women, minorities, and young people. Concern also existed over the abuse of a presidential candidate's right to approve delegates committed to him; in 1976 some loyal delegates were elected but replaced by others to satisfy affirmative action rules or to forge political alliances. The problem might be solved by having candidates name in advance twice as many delegate candidates as there are delegate positions.

Republicans. In general, the Republican Party has been substantially less reform-minded than have the Democrats. From 1973 through 1975, the Rule 29 Committee drafted proposals for increasing the participation of women, youth, and minorities in the party, but in 1976 the standing rules committee and the national committee rejected these recommendations. Conservatives opposed the changes on the grounds that the affirmative action proposals resembled the Democratic system.

Another reform was nearly forced upon the party by the Ripon Society, a progressive Republican group. In court, the society challenged the party's "victory bonus" delegate formula, which gives states, regardless of size, extra convention votes if they went Republican in the previous presidential, congressional, or gubernatorial elections. The society contended that this system unfairly favored small states and violated the Supreme Court's one-person, one-vote decisions. Early in 1974 the federal District Court in Washington ruled in favor of Ripon, but the Circuit Court of Appeals overturned this decision. In 1976 the Supreme Court refused to hear the society's appeal and the "victory bonus" remains in effect. For the 1980 convention, though, some of the large northern states will be better represented than in the past because they delivered majorities for Gerald Ford, while southern states that went for President Carter will lose the delegate gains made recently. The western states will be the net winners for 1980 under the bonus system.

At the 1976 convention, the moderate wing of the party and other activists lost an important battle when the delegates refused to establish another independent rules-review panel like the Rule 29 Committee. Instead, the party limited membership of the new Rules Review Committee to members of the national committee, a group whose outlook tends to be fairly traditional. Since the convention, this committee has been considering some minor rules changes, but its chairman, Perry Hooper, a Montgomery, Alabama, judge, predicted, "I don't see any hot issues or bomb-shells." [9] The only major possibility for change concerns the vice presidential selection process, an issue raised by Reagan at the 1976 convention and gaining support in some quarters. The Western State Republican Chairmen's Association has backed a proposal to require each presidential candidate to submit a list of prospective running mates to the RNC 60 days before any convention. Any reforms that might emerge from the Rules Review Committee face an arduous path before enactment; approval would have to be granted by the regular rules committee, the entire national committee, the rules committee of the convention and finally the full convention. Unlike the Democratic Party, only the Republican convention can change rules affecting presidential candidates.

1978 Democratic Conference

As they did in 1974 at Kansas City, the Democrats held a midterm conference in 1978. The 1976 convention passed a resolution calling for a midterm conference, but had left open the size and scope of the mini-convention. In 1977 the party's executive committee approved a plan for a conference consisting of 1,625 delegates, some 400 fewer than attended the Kansas City session. The Carter administration had proposed an even smaller conference to facilitate presidential control, but party activists insisted on a larger size. A majority of the 1978 delegates were to be chosen two from each congressional district; state parties were to select 278 more delegates, and 363 DNC members and 94 elected officials received seats. Each state's district delegates were to be equally divided between men and women. [10]

In December 1977 a party site-selection committee chose Memphis as the host city for the midterm conference. The City of Memphis had lured the conference with $75,000 in cash to defray costs and an additional $75,000 worth of services. Other cities not selected were Seattle, which offered a $106,000 subsidy, Denver, which proffered $147,500, and Honolulu, which presented a package worth $800,000. The Memphis meeting was scheduled for December 10, 1978, and was expected to bring up to $4 million in business to the city. [11]

Footnotes

[1] Federal Election Commission, AOR 1975-1, Convention Financing, June 24, 1975; *Federal Register,* July 15, 1975, p. 26660.

[2] Richard Reeves, *Convention,* (New York: Harcourt, Brace, Jovanovich, 1977), p. 5.

[3] Ibid., p. 62.

[4] Joseph Albright, Cox Newspapers story, July 11, 1976.

[5] "Bite of the Apple," *Time,* June 28, 1976, pp. 48-49.

[6] "Winograd Commission: Democratic Changes May Aid Carter in 1980," Congressional Quarterly *Weekly Report,* September 24, 1977, p. 2041.

[7] "Funds for Needy Delegates Being Raised by Strauss," *The New York Times,* July 15, 1976, p. 28.

[8] Rhodes Cook, "Democrats Adopt New Rules for Picking Nominee in 1980," Congressional Quarterly *Weekly Report,* June 17, 1978, p. 1571.

[9] "The Parties Prepare for 1980: Republicans," *Practical Politics,* October-November, 1977, p. 14.

[10] Helen Dewar, "Democratic Committee Agrees to Hold a Mini-Convention," *The Washington Post,* June 11, 1977.

[11] "Democratic Unit Picks Memphis As Site of '78 Miniconvention," *The Washington Post,* December 10, 1977.

7 General Election Campaigns

For the first time in American history, the general election of 1976 was paid for almost entirely from public funds. The Federal Election Campaign Act, as amended in 1974, provided for a grant of $21.8 million to each of the major-party candidates. Acceptance of these funds was optional, but if a candidate did accept them — as both Ford and Carter did — then he was not permitted to accept any private contributions for his campaign.

Contributions that were received by the Carter campaign after the convention were returned at campaign expense, accompanied by a polite note requesting that the money be donated to the Democratic National Committee.

The candidates also were prohibited from accepting contributions in kind. All typewriters, offices, cars, and all other campaign tools had to be paid for at a reasonable commercial rate to ensure that no hidden contributions were being made. Individuals were free to volunteer their personal services without compensation, so long as their campaign work was done on their own time and they were not reimbursed for it by an employer or benefactor.

Carter

Following the primaries, but before he was nominated, Jimmy Carter asked the Federal Election Commission to extend beyond the conventions the period for accepting contributions and receiving matching payments — to permit him and other candidates to pay off loans and close the books on their prenomination campaigns.

Carter also pointed out that the Republicans would have an extra month to claim matching funds since their August convention was a month later than that of the Democrats. This request for an extension was rejected by the FEC.

Sources of Funds: Public Funding

Several exceptions did exist to the prohibition against private contributions and to the spending limit. The national committees of the major parties were permitted to accept private contributions and to spend up to $3.2 million each on the presidential campaign. The candidates themselves could raise private money to cover the legal and accounting expenses entailed by compliance with the campaign laws, or could use surplus private funds from the prenomination period. The 1976 Amendments provided that compliance costs were exempted from the candidates' expenditure limits.

Furthermore, independent individuals and committees were free to spend unlimited amounts on behalf of the candidate, provided they had no contact with the official campaign. Membership associations, such as labor unions, also could spend unlimited amounts in communications costs but this spending was limited to political appeals directed solely to their members and their families, and not to the general public; certain activities considered to be nonpartisan in nature, such as voter registration drives carried out by labor unions, were another exception.

These exceptions, however, do not obscure the basic impact of the law, which was to restrict direct campaign spending to a low level. By way of contrast, Democratic candidate George McGovern had spent more than $30 million in the 1972 postconvention period, and Richard Nixon twice that amount over the course of pre- and postnomination campaigns; since Nixon's primary opposition was negligible, most of the early spending was directed at the November election. Inflationary factors made McGovern's 1972 spending equivalent to $40 million in 1976 dollars, so even if the DNC had contributed the full $3.2 million allowed by law, which it did not, the Carter forces still would have been held to less than two-thirds the amount spent by his 1972 counterpart in 1972 dollar values.

The low level of funds, however, was partially offset by certain advantages that public financing provided the candidates. It eliminated the need for fund raising, which had cost previous campaigns time, energy, and money. The McGovern campaign, for example, had spent about $3.5 million in mail costs, $1 million in newspaper ads, and more in appeals for funds tagged on at the end of paid broadcasts,[1] and the Carter prenomination campaign, according to treasurer Robert Lipshutz, who welcomed the transition to complete public funding after the convention, had "spent about 20 percent of our personal time" plus "some of the candidate's time" on fund raising.[2]

A second advantage of the public funding system was that it eased the candidates' cash-flow problems. Previous campaigns had to worry not only about the amount of money raised, but also about when it would come in; spending ability was often limited by fluctuations in income. This problem was virtually eliminated in the 1976 general election, when $21.8 million in credit was made available to the major-party nominees shortly after the nominating conventions. The campaigns still had to borrow some money to cover travel expenses for the press and Secret Service and deposits for telephones and furniture, which subsequently were refunded, but the main effect of the grant was to free the candidates to plan and spend the money according to their own timetables.

A third advantage claimed by Carter staffers was that the low limit forced the campaign into more effective and efficient practices. This is a point reformers have used in the past in arguing that unlimited spending leads to excessive spending or abuses or, at least, to campaign inefficiencies.

Democratic National Committee

Although the FECA barred private contributions to presidential campaigns, it did allow for several additional sources of campaign spending above the $21.8 million limit. The national committees of the political parties were permitted to spend two cents for each member of the voting-age population, or $3.2 million, on the presidential election. The parties themselves were permitted to raise this money from private sources, with a limit of $20,000 on individual contributors. (Party contributions are included in the $25,000 aggregate contribution limit for individuals to all federal campaigns in a single calendar year. An individual who already had given $6,000 to congressional and presidential-primary candidates, for example, could then contribute only $19,000 to a political party.)

At the Democratic convention in July, Finance Chairman S. Lee Kling announced that the national committee had committed itself to raising $10 million between the convention and election day. From this sum, the full $3.2 million allowed by law would be spent directly on behalf of the presidential and vice presidential candidates, with lesser amounts earmarked for voter registration, get-out-the-vote programs, congressional and statewide candidates, polling, and fund raising.[3]

In fact, the DNC fell short of its goal. For the entire year of 1976, it raised $7.5 million after spending $1.5 million on fund raising, for a net revenue of $6 million[4] (Table 7-1). Direct-mail solicitation raised a net of $2.5 million, bringing in $3.3 million after spending $800,000. One particularly productive item was the "Demo-gram," printed in "Carter green" and resembling a mailed telegram.[5] Another $3.3 million net was

Table 7-1

DNC and Affiliated Organizations, Revenues and Expenses, 1976

Revenues:		
Contributions		
Direct mail	$3,365,626	
Major contributors and fund-raising events	3,966,516	
Telethon, net of transfers to state		
committees of $639,896		$ 7,332,142
Less: Fund-raising expenses		
Direct mail	825,634	
Major contributors and fund-raising events	639,306	
Telethon	—	−1,464,940
		5,867,202
Other revenues		149,228
Total revenues		$ 6,016,430
Expenses:		
Presidential election		
General	1,870,479	
"Carter Radio"	179,193	
"Get Out the Vote"	543,067	2,592,739
Campaign (Nonpresidential)		
Voter registration	1,177,232	
Surveys	388,610	
"Target 76" costs	340,823	
"Whistlestop"	71,352	
Transfers to other Democratic organizations	69,297	2,047,314
General and administrative		
Payroll and related expenses	1,045,548	
Rent	155,079	
Telephone and telegraph	151,682	
Travel	108,579	
Professional services	85,909	
Printing and office supplies	74,094	
Postage	48,944	
Interest	36,537	
Depreciation	12,394	
Repairs and maintenance	9,914	
Other insurance and taxes	9,474	
Gifts	8,588	
Pension	6,560	1,753,302
Special meetings and projects		
General	165,455	
Campaign training schools	104,311	
Transition	52,815	
Radio program	48,495	
Election services	16,162	387,238
Other expenses		51,383
Total expenses		$ 6,831,976
Expenses in excess of revenues after		
provision for income taxes ($50)		$ (815,596)

SOURCE: Democratic National Committee

realized from major contributors, who were solicited on a more personal basis than was the case with the direct-mail campaigns, and by fund-raising events, such as dinners and concerts. These two categories together grossed $3.9 million after spending $600,000. A small amount was raised from other sources, including a "Democratic General Store" in Georgetown, a fashionable section of the District of Columbia, where one could purchase such delicacies as peanuts, peanut cookies, peanut soup, and peanut pudding. It was revealed that the peanuts came not from Georgia but from Virginia.[6]

Contributions to the DNC generally came in rather small amounts. In the two-year period 1975-76, the party received $11,187,619 in contributions. Of this total, $7,058,407 came in amounts of less than $100, and another $766,990 in amounts of $100 to $499. In the $500 to $9,999 range, 2,341 individuals contributed a total of $2,864,522. Only 33 contributors gave $10,000 or more, for a total of $497,700 in that category. By contrast, the Republican National Committee received 255 contributions, totaling $3,009,205, in the $10,000-and-above category.[7]

The DNC devoted $2.6 million from these revenues to the presidential campaign. Of this, $180,000 was spent on the "Carter Radio" program, by which the campaign maintained a phone hook-up with radio stations to supply them with campaign news and quotes. More than $500,000 was spent on get-out-the-vote drives. Although these drives benefited the entire party slate, the fact that they were listed under "Presidential Election" in the DNC's annual audit indicates that they were designed by the party primarily to benefit Carter and Mondale.

In addition, the DNC obtained a ruling from the FEC allowing it to authorize state or local party committees to assume a portion of the DNC's $3.2 million presidential campaign expenditure limit. Under such authorizations, which were known as "agency agreements" since the state and local committees were acting as agents of the national committee, $228,157 was spent.[8] If this is added to the $2.6 million spent directly by the DNC, then the DNC's contribution to the Carter-Mondale campaign can be figured at $2.8 million, about $400,000 short of the permissible limit.

The DNC's failure to raise its expected $10 million elicited several explanations. Kling pointed to the new campaign laws and the resulting uncertainties among potential contributors, saying, "Our biggest problem was education. People who were used to giving directly to the candidates in the past kept asking us why the national committee suddenly needed money. Then people who had been limited to giving $1,000 during the primaries had to be taught that they could give $20,000 to the national committees." [9]

In any event, the fund-raising failure seems to have caused some friction between the Carter staff and the DNC, as each group sought to blame the other for the poor results. DNC officials attributed the problem to Carter's unwillingness to sacrifice his own campaign time to appear as a drawing-card at party fund-raising events. Party Chairman Robert S. Strauss stated, "Governor Carter doesn't like fund-raising particularly. He's not giving as much time to fund-raising as our fund-raiser would like." [10] Another source close to the Democratic treasury mentioned Carter's public identification with consumer advocate Ralph Nader, saying, "When Carter embraced Nader all the business money dried up." [11]

The Carter camp, in turn, blamed the DNC for its financial failings. Morris Dees, who had managed Carter's prenomination money drive and then served as general counsel for the Carter campaign after the convention, declared Carter "the most cooperative candidate in fund-raising I've ever known" and said, "With a popular candidate this year, and all the party pros getting involved, I felt the DNC could raise $20 million this fall." [12]

Dees claimed that he had made several fund-raising suggestions to the committee in July, all of which were vetoed by Strauss. They included retaining Joel McCleary, Dee's deputy during the spring, to revive the decentralized Carter fund-raising committees for the fall campaign; enlisting Louisville fast-food entrepreneur John Y. Brown to run a national fund-raising telethon of the sort that he had been developing for four years and that had worked well for Carter in Georgia in February; and putting a direct-mail professional in charge of expanding the national committee's contributor list. Dees, for example, would have targeted a mailing at the nearly 10 million subscribers to fundamentalist Christian causes and periodicals.[13] Strauss also was faulted for failing to invite such important Carter supporters as Los Angeles Mayor Tom Bradley and Los Angeles millionaires Max Palevsky and Harold Willens to a West Coast fund-raising reception.[14]

The $20,000 limit on contributions to the party national committees permitted the partial resurgence, although on a far smaller scale than in previous years, of "big money" in politics. Only a few contributions to the DNC seemed questionable. One was for $10,000 from Irvin Kovens, a Baltimore millionaire who, along with Maryland Gov. Marvin Mandel and four others, had been indicted on charges of fraud and corruption in 1975. Kovens had been excused from trial because of ill health, but at the time the contribution was received, five days before the election, the trial of Mandel and the other defendants was under way.[15]

The DNC also received a total of $17,000 from Robert W. Chambers of Atlanta, board chairman of the Cox newspaper chain and his wife, Anne Cox Chambers, publisher of the *Atlanta Constitution.* Anne Chambers later was appointed by President Carter as ambassador to Belgium, one of five such choices declared "unqualified for their ambassadorial assignments" by the American Foreign Service Association,[16] whose standards of judgment, however, favor career foreign service appointees.

Independent Expenditures

A potentially important source of campaign spending, although not in 1976, were independent expenditures. Included in this category were such groups as Health Volunteers for Carter-Mondale, Farmers for Carter-Mondale Volunteers, Southern Farmers for Carter-Mondale, Illinois Consumers for Carter-Mondale, Michigan Citizens for Carter-Mondale, and farm groups in Texas, Indiana, and Minnesota.[17] It also included individuals such as Pennsylvania Gov. Milton J. Shapp, who personally paid for some Carter-Mondale newspaper advertisements.[18]

Independent expenditures came about as follows: The 1974 Amendments had set a $1,000 limit on expenditures by "independent, unauthorized" committees on behalf of a political candidate. The Supreme Court, however, in the *Buckley v. Valeo* decision, struck down this restriction as an unconstitutional restraint of free speech, opening the way for apparently limitless spending.

In his dissent from this portion of the decision, Justice Byron R. White warned that it would result in "transparent and widespread evasion of the contribution limits." [19] Many political observers shared this concern, and predicted that a host of pseudo-independent committees would spring up and make a mockery of the campaign spending limits. Experience proved, however, that at least in 1976 this fear was not well-grounded. Independent spending for Carter by 26 individuals and 24 committees amounted to only $74,298, not a very significant sum.[20] Only eight committees and four individuals made expenditures of more than $1,000 with two of the former and one of the latter exceeding $5,000 (Table 7-2). An expenditure by the United Auto Workers' Voluntary Community Action Program (V-CAP) for $27,074 was the only one greater than $10,000.

The reason for this low level of activity lies primarily in the strictness in defining that a committee, in order to be considered truly independent and thus exempt from the spending limits, must have had absolutely no contact, formal or informal, with the official campaign. Dean Coston, treasurer of Health Volunteers for Carter-Mondale, lamented, "The laws are so strict about being independent, that you can't — even in your mind — commit an affair with anybody who's working with Carter." [21]

In the post-Watergate climate of 1976, most potential contributors preferred to remain uninvolved than to risk breaking the law. For those

Table 7-2
Independent Expenditures for Carter

UAW Voluntary Action Program (V-CAP)	$27,074
Railway Clerks' Political League	8,125
Sidney and Frances Lewis	5,300
Charles Litton	3,252
Committee for Good Government	3,240
Citizens for Carter	1,682
Daniel E. Becnel, Jr.	1,500
Farmers for Carter-Mondale Volunteers	1,370
Health Volunteers for Carter-Mondale	1,241
Mid-Peninsula Environmentalists for Carter	1,103
Carter Slate Committee	1,035

SOURCES: Federal Election Commission, *FEC Disclosure Series, No. 3: Index of Independent Expenditures by Individuals and Receipts and Expenditures by Unauthorized Delegates, 1976 Campaign*, March 1977, pp. 105-107; and Federal Election Commission, *Independent Expenditures by Individuals, Groups, and Political Committees — 1976 Election, January 1, 1975-October 24, 1976*, p. 8.

who were involved, the strictness of the law created enormous difficulties in administration as the committees had to go to great lengths to preserve their independence. Coston spoke of the "Kafka-like situation" in which he could not even use Carter's speeches in his literature, and said, "I don't know what the Carter campaign is doing in the health area and I'm scared to find out." Robert Nelson, chairman of Farmers for Carter-Mondale Volunteers, also considered it "ridiculous" that "we can't seek the advice of the candidates and they can't stop us from doing something they don't want done." [22]

Contrary to the fears of Justice White and others who felt that the candidates would actively exploit the independent committees as a subterfuge to exceed their own expenditure limits, the Carter campaign actually discouraged such efforts. Again citing the difficulties in adhering to the FEC's stringent definition of independence, a Carter staff memorandum maintained that "the dangers inherent in independent expenditures are so great that the policy of the Carter-Mondale campaign is actively to discourage them. The risks are political, financial, and legal. If a wealthy individual decides that he wants to spend $1 million for Carter in television ads in Texas, that million will be charged against our $21.8 million if there is *any* coordination between him and our campaign officials, even if we merely suggested that it would be a good idea to run some ads. We cannot risk the possibility that, in effect, someone else will be spending our budget." [23] The campaign devised a standard reply to inquiries from supporters contemplating independent expenditures, in which it cited "the complexities of the law in this area and the dangers of violation," stated "the policy of the Carter-Mondale campaign to discourage all independent expenditures," referred the correspondent to the FEC for further information, and requested that "you consider helping us as a volunteer — which is perfectly legal — rather than by attempting to make an independent expenditure." [24]

Finally, potential independent spenders faced another obstacle besides discouragement from the official campaign organization. This was the policy of many broadcasting stations that, perhaps out of their own fear of overstepping the bounds of the law, refused to sell air time to independent committees or individuals. Since the stations were not obligated to sell time for political purposes other than to candidates, having the means and the desire to broadcast a message did not always guarantee independent expenditors the opportunity to do so.

Labor

Another important source of spending for the Democratic candidate was organized labor. Unions, as well as corporations, were prohibited from contributing directly to political campaigns or from distributing political appeals to the general population. But they were free to establish political action committees and to spend unlimited amounts on political communications directed toward their own members and their families. Unions took advantage of this latter provision in 1976.

Jimmy Carter had not been the first choice of most labor leaders, but once the Democratic convention made its choice, the labor movement was virtually unanimous in its support of the nominee and the party's platform, which they saw as a repudiation of four years of Republican-inspired stagnation and unemployment. The AFL-CIO Executive Council met shortly after the close of the Democratic convention and unanimously pledged the federation's "all-out support" for the Democratic ticket. President George Meany praised Carter as "a very warm human being" whose "overall purpose is our overall purpose: to put America back to work." [25] Other unions, some from within the AFL-CIO and others outside, also supported Carter. United Auto Workers President Leonard Woodcock was one of the first labor leaders to endorse Carter during the primaries, and a high degree of personal enthusiasm for Carter was reported in that 1.4 million-member union. The National Education Association, representing 1.8 million teachers, took a stand on a national election for the first time by endorsing Carter and Mondale. [26]

Carter's standing in the labor movement was enhanced by his selection of Walter Mondale as his running mate. Mondale, unlike Carter, was a familiar face to union members and in his 12 years in the

Senate had earned a reputation as a staunch friend of labor in the Democratic-New Deal tradition. This connection was very productive during the campaign. After an address by Mondale, for instance, the 300,000-member Plumber and Pipefitters Union, which had supported Nixon in 1972, endorsed the Democratic nominees. Mondale was also assigned to address conventions of the United Auto Workers, the American Federation of Teachers, and other labor organizations on behalf of the Democratic ticket.[27]

Labor organizations reported spending $2,014,326 on political communications to their members and their families in 1976. As long as this spending was directed solely toward union members and their families, it was classified as "internal communications" and did not count against Carter's spending limit. Since it was not considered as independent expenditures, labor leaders were free to consult with campaign officials and to coordinate their efforts to best benefit the campaign. Most of this communication was done by direct mail, which accounted for 87.1 percent of the expenditures. Much smaller amounts were spent on brochures, leaflets, and flyers (6.2 percent), phone banks (2.7 percent), posters and banners (2 percent), and miscellaneous methods of communication, including the distribution of peanuts, tie tacs, car stickers, buttons, lapel pins, and emblems (1.9 percent).[28]

Carter and Mondale were the beneficiaries of $1,160,584 of the reported union communications expenditures, with virtually all of the rest going to Democratic House and Senate candidates.[29] The greatest communications efforts on behalf of the presidential ticket were made by the AFL-CIO, through its Committee on Political Education (COPE), which spent $316,000, and the United Auto Workers, which spent $306,000 (Table 7-3). They were followed by the Communications Workers of America, with $107,000, and the Retail Clerks International Union, with $68,000.

The reported figures do not tell the whole story of labor spending for Carter. Unions that spent less than $2,000 on political communications during the campaign were not required to file with the FEC, and many unions probably tailored their spending to fit this limit. Furthermore, reportable spending included only communications whose main purpose was to advocate directly the election or defeat of a specific candidate. More general admonitions to "vote Democratic" were not reported. Nor were appeals for the election or defeat of a specific candidate if they were part of a communication whose basic purpose was not political, such as a regularly published union newsletter. According to one survey, "virtually every [union] newsletter mailed to members in September and October included material praising Carter or criticizing Ford, usually with a picture of Carter on the cover. Almost none of this was reported to the FEC."[30]

Table 7-3
Reported Labor Political Communications Expenditures for Carter, Primary and General Elections

AFL-CIO COPE	$ 315,981
United Auto Workers	306,013
Communications Workers of America	106,796
Active Ballot Club, Retail Clerks International Union	67,874
Ohio AFL-CIO	38,326
National Education Association	27,903
New Jersey State AFL-CIO COPE	26,858
Building and Construction Trades Department, AFL-CIO	25,668
American Federation of State, County, and Municipal Employees, AFL-CIO	24,169
United Mine Workers of America	20,571
United Steelworkers of America	15,678
International Association of Bridge, Structural, and Ornamental Iron Workers	13,494
District Council 37, American Federation of State, County, and Municipal Employees, AFL-CIO	13,456
California Labor Federation, AFL-CIO Standing Committee on Political Education	11,902
Louisiana AFL-CIO	10,081
Tennessee State Labor Council	9,462
Pennsylvania AFL-CIO	9,430
South Dakota Voter Registration Committee, AFL-CIO	9,176
South Carolina Labor Council, AFL-CIO	8,304
Machinists' Non-Partisan Political League	8,207
Cleveland AFL-CIO Federation of Labor	7,695
Rhode Island AFL-CIO	7,124
Buffalo AFL-CIO Council	6,412
International Ladies' Garment Workers' Union	5,342
Service Employees International Union, PEA	4,711
Kentucky State AFL-CIO COPE	4,704
United Farm Workers of America COPE Committee	4,404
Council 13, American Federation of State, County, and Municipal Employees, AFL-CIO	4,319
Virginia State AFL-CIO	4,225
Indiana State AFL-CIO	4,044
International Brotherhood of Painters and Allied Trades	3,930
Montana State AFL-CIO	3,301
Maryland State and DC, AFL-CIO	3,281
Los Angeles County Federation of Labor, AFL-CIO	3,046
Local 91, International Ladies' Garment Workers' Union	2,494
Toledo Area AFL-CIO Council	2,215
New Hampshire Labor Council, AFL-CIO	2,153
Idaho State AFL-CIO	2,145
Mississippi AFL-CIO	2,099
Others	13,591
Total	$1,160,584

SOURCE: Federal Election Commission, *FEC Disclosure Series, No. 5: Index of Communication Costs By Corporations, Labor Organizations, Membership Organizations, Trade Associations: 1976 Campaign,* (Washington, D.C., April 1977), pp. 19-42.

Also not reported were union expenditures on registration drives and get-out-the-vote drives, which were financially more important than internal communications. These drives were nominally of a nonpartisan nature, but by focusing on areas that had large numbers of union members, high ratios of registered Democrats, and relatively low voting turnouts in the past, labor was able to increase the Democratic majority simply by increasing the voter turnout.[31] Sources from COPE and from the UAW indicated that their unions spent about $3 million each on these drives.[32]

The actual extent of labor's effort for Carter includes unreported internal communications as well as registration and get-out-the-vote drives, in addition to the more than a million dollars in reported communications. According to Michael J. Malbin, a "conservative estimate" would be $11 million, or more than half of what Carter spent on his own campaign,[33] if all three categories of labor outlays are totaled.

Compliance Costs

The one area in which the major-party presidential campaigns were free to accept private contributions and to exceed the $21.8 million spending limit was that of legal and accounting costs related to compliance with the FECA. Until the FEC clarified this provision in October, however, the Carter campaign had assumed that all private contributions were illegal and had returned them. After the FEC ruling, the 1976 Democratic Presidential Campaign Committee (as the Carter campaign was officially called) contacted donors and explained that it would be glad to accept contributions that were earmarked for the special compliance fund.

These contributions were subject to the same $1,000 limit as contributions to individual candidates. By the end of the year $93,000 was raised in this manner, and the total reached $125,000 by the end of March 1977. In addition, two transfers of $150,000 each were received from the Committee for Jimmy Carter, the candidate's prenomination organization. (This committee had surplus private funds because a large amount of money had poured in after Carter's June 8 victory in the Ohio primary, when there were few expenses to be met.) The first transfer was made before the November election and was listed as a loan until after the FEC's ruling on compliance funding, when it was made a grant. The second was made in January 1977.

The compliance effort also received in-kind contributions in the form of professional services provided by volunteer lawyers and accountants. Although these were not technically a form of revenue, since no money changed hands, the campaign calculated their value at $138,000.[34]

The total cash income of the compliance fund, including private contributions and transfers from the Committee for Jimmy Carter, was about $425,000. Compliance costs came to $503,000 as of December 31, 1976, and went even higher as the Campaign Committee continued its close-out operation, including FEC audits and later adjustments in amended reports. The excess of expenditures over receipts, therefore, had to be paid out of the $21.8 million public campaign subsidy.

Expenditures

The 1976 Democratic Presidential Campaign Committee (DPCC) fashioned its financial system with two goals in mind. First, the system had to facilitate reporting to the FEC, and second, the system had to give the national staff in Atlanta tight control over the spending of limited funds. The Carter staff people hoped to have a system that was more efficient than the one used in the prenomination period. The 1976 Presidential Campaign Committee was incorporated on July 15, 1976, and began spending for the general election at that time. The budget director of the committee, Richard Harden, and the controller, Robert Andrews, developed a computerized bookkeeping system with the advice of Arthur Andersen & Co. The Andersen accountants supplied the overall and theoretical design while Harden and Andrews worked out the clerical aspects of the system.

The campaign established a budget committee consisting of Harden, treasurer Robert J. Lipshutz and director Hamilton Jordan. Although this committee presented its plan to Jimmy Carter, the candidate did little work on the details of the budget. Staff members emphasized that the close relationship between Carter and Lipshutz gave the budget and finance staff a good deal of clout vis-á-vis political operatives. The committee's original budget was revised eight times between Labor Day and election day. As situations and assumptions changed in the heat of the campaign, the budget was changed to shift funds to areas where more spending was needed. To change the budget, a responsibility center director had to file a budget amendment which the three-man committee passed on. Two volunteer CPAs, James Libby and Michael Thomas, assisted in the budget revision process by interviewing responsibility center directors and running the new figures through the computer. The two accountants are partners in the Atlanta firm of Bickman, Libby, Thomas, and Braxton.

As noted previously, a network of volunteer accountants was used during the campaign to help with compliance with the FECA. The American Institute of Certified Public Accountants had offered to recruit such volunteers for both candidates but only the Carter campaign took advantage of the offer. Serving as national coordinator of the volunteers was Barry E. Wagman, an accountant experienced in political bookkeeping and the author of *Campaign Treasurer's Handbook,* a Democratic Party publication.

After election day, the Andersen firm returned to audit the campaign. Although the FEC also audited the books, the campaign felt that the subject of campaign finance was so sensitive in 1976 that an independent audit would be valuable.

Lines of authority within the financial system extended from the budget committee to the finance and budget center to the responsibility center directors. There were 39 responsibility centers charged with various functions and contacts with interest groups (Table 7-4). Some of these centers were based in Washington, D.C., but most had offices in Atlanta. The national headquarters consisted of three floors of offices in a fiscally troubled office complex in midtown Atlanta. The other centers were in each of the 50 states. The director of a center was assigned a budget figure, but given a fair amount of discretion on spending within the total figure. The budget and finance staff visited the centers across the country to instruct local workers on the procedures required by law. The staff stressed that financial matters were more important than ever before, not least because collective and individual legal penalties were possible. The need to stay within budgets and to document expenditures was emphasized by several practical controls built into the system.

One such control was that each center was allowed only $100 in petty cash, and receipts had to be presented quickly for Atlanta to replenish a petty cash fund. No bank accounts were permitted in the field except for election day get-out-the-vote money. Also, Atlanta controlled the payroll. The most important financial control was that the campaign paid for goods and services with drafts rather than checks. If the Atlanta office felt an expense was unwarranted or unqualified, it could withhold payment on a draft within 24 hours of receiving notice of the expenditure.

The draft system caused problems because some merchants were either unfamiliar with or suspicious of this form of payment, but banks generally cooperated with draft payments. The campaign felt any inconveniences were worthwhile since personnel knew that even very small expenses would be reviewed and could be canceled by the controllers in Atlanta. Each center would be given books of drafts as they needed money; the drafts were precoded so that when the draft came in, Atlanta would know immediately which center had spent funds. The centers had to describe the expenditure so that the controllers could approve and then enter the amount in one of the functional categories programmed in the computer (Table 7-5). Only the subcategories listed in the consolidated statement could be used, so that all expenses went into the

Table 7-4
1976 Democratic Presidential Campaign Committee Inc., Summary of Expenditures by Responsibility Centers

Jimmy Carter support	$ 36,351
Rosalynn Carter support	163,278
Carter children support	85,709
VP candidate support	185,300
VP wife support	9,180
VP scheduling and advance	389,587
Press	195,551
Issues	239,571
Transportation and advance	328,384
Charter	1,816,438
Treasurer	22,754
Legal services	15,761
Administration	1,176,266
Deposits recoverable	1,475,801
Media	10,612,745
Survey	438,567
Finance and budget	233,069
Postelection expenses	11,548
Transition planning	115,255
Campaign director's office	161,604
Telephone canvassing	527,121
Georgians for Carter	240,933
Special projects	31,766
Congressional relations	69,121
DNC victory party	15,094
Minority affairs	103,108
Labor	11,787
51.3% Committee	18,927
DNC liaison	10,045
Political relations	11,487
Conservationists	10,735
Jews	17,720
Elderly citizens	6,814
Urban ethnic	19,667
Rural	11,697
Urban	10,384
Speakers bureau	29,394
Diplomatic volunteer coordination	50,000
Field director's office	305,017
Subtotal	$19,213,536
51 State responsibility centers	4,135,936
Total expenditures	$23,349,472

computer. Although Atlanta did not reject any field expenditures, it utilized the threat quite often to keep the field personnel in line. The campaign stopped payment on some drafts because services were not rendered. The idea of using drafts rather than checks and large amounts of cash originated with Harden. He felt that this process gave respon-

Table 7-5
1976 Democratic Presidential Campaign Committee Inc., Consolidated Statement of Disbursements July 15, 1976-January 31, 1977

Media production	
TV	$ 464,055
Radio	19,767
Newspaper	11,497
Magazine	3,456
Outdoor facilities	13,624
Other	20,260
Total	$ 532,659
Media use	
TV time	$ 7,819,091
Radio time	1,262,230
Newspaper space	348,909
Magazine space	192,140
Outdoor facilities space	105,212
Other	48,153
Total	$ 9,775,735
Personal services	
Staff payroll/related costs	$ 2,630,899
Consultant/professional fees	54,754
Expense advances made	97,562
Less: Expenses reported for advances	−34,186
Less: Expense advances repaid	−29,039
Net total	$ 2,719,990
Travel	
Commercial airline	$ 469,100
Charter air	2,748,169
Less: charter expenses recovered	−1,548,038
Travel deposits	90,425
Meals and lodging	1,314,110
Ground transportation	140,027
Net total	$ 3,213,793
Other vote getting	
Polling	$ 438,952
Telephone canvassing	253,741
Direct mail	48,427
Campaign material	1,296,921
Meetings	176,273
Voter registration	6,946
Get-out-the-vote	626,805
Other	223
Total	$ 2,848,288
Office	
Occupancy	$ 247,388
Telephone	1,300,542
Postage and delivery	403,324
Equipment and furniture	249,616
Office materials and supplies	167,569
Deposits	1,500,398
Other	333,146
Data processing	67,598
Total	$ 4,269,581
Total disbursements	$23,360,046

sibility centers access to money while leaving ultimate control with the national financial staff.

The committee realized that one of the greatest problems posed by public financing was maximizing spending while not exceeding the expenditure limit. Through the summer and fall the committee budgeted a reserve fund. This fund started at about $2.5 million and dwindled to $1 million in October. The reserve was held until the last week or two of the campaign. The DNC also held some money in reserve that it could spend on behalf of Carter-Mondale. If the committee neared its ceiling too soon, the DNC would take over some campaign activities.

The controllers, with the help of the computer, kept close track of money that would be refunded, such as telephone and office equipment deposits, travel deposits, and travel outlays for the press and Secret Service. These expenditures drove the campaign's gross disbursements above the $21.8 million mark, although the eventual refund of deposits and reimbursement of travel expenses would bring net expenditures below the legal limit. In the meantime, however, while these expenses were outstanding, it was necessary for the campaign to borrow money to cover those expenses in excess of the federal grant. Loans were taken out from the Citizens and Southern Bank of Atlanta, with the campaign committee's deposits used as collateral.

Media

Television. The strict limitations on campaign spending greatly enhanced the importance of broadcast advertising, particularly television, which was considered to be the most efficient method of reaching large numbers of voters at the lowest possible cost. Democratic expenditures for television time actually increased more than 50 percent since 1972, from $4.8 million to $7.6 million, in spite of the overall decline in campaign spending.[35] The increase in the importance of television is seen most dramatically when viewed as a percentage of total campaign expenditures: from less than 16 percent in 1972 to more than 34 percent in 1976.

Carter's advertising was handled by the Atlanta agency of Gerald Rafshoon, who served as media adviser to the campaign. He first worked for Jimmy Carter during the unsuccessful 1966 gubernatorial race, and never had worked for another politician. In 1976 he said that he had been working on this presidential campaign for 10 years.[36]

This degree of loyalty and long association may have been a factor in Carter's successful nomination campaign. The Rafshoon agency allegedly extended considerable credit to the Carter campaign, especially during this critical period of matching fund cutoffs, possibly allowing

Carter access to media that his opponents could not afford. Reportedly, the Rafshoon agency may even have advanced cash for purchase of television broadcast time, in possible violation of the FECA, although this was denied by a spokesman for the agency.[37]

During the prenomination drive, Rafshoon employed a semidocumentary style of advertisement, often showing Carter in informal settings in Plains or on the campaign trail. For the general election, he hoped to combat the Republican charge of inexperience by presenting Carter "in competent settings," such as discussing issues in an office or addressing the Georgia state legislature. At the same time, he did "not abandon or lose completely good-guy Jimmy Carter," and continued to show him in an open work-shirt in the peanut fields.[38] Rafshoon ruled out ads directly attacking the opposition, saying, "Let's face it, the candidate of love and compassion can't do negative stuff." [39]

During the last three weeks of the campaign, Rafshoon had the Carter television spots produced in the New York studio of Tony Schwartz. Schwartz is the author of The Responsive Chord, a theoretical work on television and advertising, and a veteran of every Democratic presidential campaign since 1964. He was best known for his hard-hitting "negative" commercials, such as an anti-Goldwater spot in which the voice of a young girl counting petals on a daisy faded into a countdown to a nuclear explosion. Some observers interpreted the employment of Schwartz as a tacit acknowledgment of the failure of the Rafshoon advertising campaign. Carter had been declining rapidly in the polls at the time Schwartz was brought on, and many advisers felt the campaign needed to be strengthened by an emphasis on traditional Democratic pocketbook issues. One Democratic political consultant, who had had no part in the Carter campaign, commented at the time, "For Southern Democrats the campaign is over once you win the primaries. They never really had a strategy for the fall campaign. It has been the most expensive on-the-job training in the history of politics."

Rafshoon denied this interpretation, insisting that he had turned to Schwartz because of his superior facilities, that Schwartz was working under his close supervision, and that no negative spots would be used against Ford. Nevertheless, the Schwartz commercials signaled a new approach to presenting the candidate. The semidocumentary style and informal dress were abandoned in favor of Carter in a suit and tie, looking directly into the camera, which concentrated on his face. And instead of either speaking in general terms about leadership and trust, or proposing specific solutions to various problems, as Rafshoon had had him do, Carter in the new commercials spoke of the problems themselves and tried to display his concern about them. On inflation or on the plight of senior citizens, Carter sought to speak with compassion.[40]

Rafshoon's favorite advertising vehicle was the five-minute commercial. "There's more depth to it," he explained. "...It takes [Carter] a minute and a half, at least, to answer one good question on an issue. When you go beyond a minute commercial, you might as well go to five minutes. I would rather have Jimmy on two or three issues, with also some flavor of his character and personality, than just one spot where you don't adequately cover any particular subject." [41]

Another advantage Rafshoon found for the five-minute commercial was that it was frequently perceived by viewers to be a news special rather than a paid advertisement, particularly if it was broadcast immediately following a news report.[42] There was also a great financial advantage to the five-minute spots. Broadcasters sold five-minute blocks at their programming rate, while 60-second blocks were sold at the much higher advertising rate. The Carter campaign spent $2,134,743 for 56 60-second spots on the three television networks, an average of $38,120 each. For 71 five-minute advertisements, the campaign paid the networks only $847,599, or $11,938 each. This figure includes $62,698 in editing costs, which were charged to the campaign when the networks had to shorten regular programs to fit the five-minute advertisement in at the end (Table 7-6).

The Carter campaign also spent a total of $295,357 to show a final 30-minute program three times on the evening before election day. Each network broadcast the Carter program, followed by one of the same length by Ford, during a different hour of prime time. Both campaigns hoped thereby to reach each of the evening's television viewers once with its final message. Carter's program, called "Ask Jimmy Carter," featured on-the-street interviews with ordinary citizens in various parts of the country. Each person stated the question he would wish to ask of Carter, then the film cut away to the candidate giving his answer.[43]

The total amount spent by the Carter campaign for network broadcasts of its 60-second, five-minute, and 30-minute commercials was $3,277,699, or about 43 percent of the total television budget. Another $12,000 was spent to broadcast messages aimed primarily at black voters on a "nonwired" network of 14 stations that carried football games between primarily black colleges. The remaining $4,263,466 went to local stations. This includes $71,258 spent on Spanish-language broadcasts, primarily in New York, Illinois, Florida, and five southwestern states (Appendix E).

Radio. The Carter campaign spent $1,086,728 on radio advertising. This was a substantial decrease from the $1.4 million spent by McGovern in 1972, although it consumed a slightly higher percentage of the budget. To a much greater extent than television, radio was used to reach specific demographic audiences. Almost a quarter of the radio budget was directed at three target groups, with $162,129 spent on appeals to black voters, $75,943 on Spanish-speaking voters, and $13,388 on "ethnic" (East European, Italian, and Greek) voters.

The figures budgeted under television time and radio time ($7,553,166 and $1,086,728, respectively) represent the amounts paid out by the campaign, including the Rafshoon agency's commission of 15 percent of the air time. The agency, therefore, received 13 percent of the gross amounts reported here, and the networks and stations 87 percent.

The figures for television and radio use provided by Rafshoon (Appendix E) do not exactly equal those provided by the Democratic Presidential Campaign Committee in Table 7-5. Among the reasons are: First, each set of data represents the books at different times, so that bills and credits included in one set may not have been accounted in the other. Second, some of Rafshoon's invoices for media use may have been punched into the committee's computer as media production. The

Table 7-6
1976 Democratic Presidential Campaign Committee Inc., Network Television Expenditures

		60-Second Advertisements		
Network	**Quantity**	**Cost**	**Average**	**Median**
NBC	13	$ 404,200	$ 31,092	$35,350
CBS	20	741,007	37,050	33,501
ABC	23	989,536	43,023	54,253
Total	56	$2,134,743		

		5-Minute Programs			
Network	**Quantity**	**Time Cost**	**Editing Cost**	**Total Cost**	**Average Median**
NBC	21	$234,587	$ 5,292	$239,879	$11,423 $ 8,108
CBS	27	353,081	27,177	380,258	14,095 14,302
ABC	23	197,233	30,229	227,462	9,890 7,778
Total	71	$784,901	$62,698	$847,599	

Each network carried one half-hour program on the night of November 1, 1976, and the costs are as follows:

NBC	$113,250
CBS	118,182
ABC	63,925
	$295,357

Grand Total:	60-second	$2,134,743
	5-minute	847,599
	30-minute	295,357
		$3,277,699 for 130 network broadcasts.

greatest discrepancy is in the category of television use and this is largely due to duplicate contracts that Rafshoon sent to the committee by mistake, causing the committee's figure in Table 7-5 to be artificially high. The actual total may come down even lower than that indicated in Appendix E as a result of rebates received from networks and stations which for a variety of technical reasons did not run contracted ads or did not run them properly. Incomplete figures included a rebate of $37,000 received from CBS and one of $18,000 from NBC.

Production Costs. Mass-media expenditures involved, in addition to the purchase of air time, the costs of producing the material to be aired. Measured as a percentage of time costs, television and radio production costs were extraordinarily low. Television production cost $464,055, about 6 percent of the time costs, and radio production only $19,767, less than 2 percent. For the McGovern campaign, by contrast, television and radio production costs were more than 16 percent of the time charges.[44] Even that amount was considered low, with many campaigns spending 20 to 50 percent production charges.

Print Media. The role of newspaper and magazine advertising, measured either in comparison to electronic media advertising or in comparison to amounts spent in previous campaigns, was very limited. The Carter campaign spent $348,909 for newspaper space and $190,604 for magazine space, plus production costs of $11,497 and $3,456, respectively. Four years earlier, $962,273 had been spent for newspaper space by national-level McGovern committees.[45] Spending by local committees during that relatively decentralized campaign raised this figure even higher.

More than two-thirds of the newspaper advertising was directed at special audiences. To reach suburban voters, the campaign bought $91,470 worth of advertising in 30 weekly newspapers in major metropolitan areas. Advertisements in black newspapers accounted for $69,554, while appeals to "ethnics" cost $40,463, to Catholics, $23,817, and to Jews, $21,710.

Most of the magazine advertising, by contrast, was directed at the general public. Three-quarters of the budget ($142,590) was spent on spreads in the national news weeklies. Of the remainder, $23,284 was spent on farm publications, $18,454 on black periodicals, $3,657 on Jaycee publications, and $2,620 on retirees' journals. In addition, the campaign spent $66,980 for outdoor billboards, and $35,682 for posters in New York City subway trains.

Drawing together the broadcast, print media, and production spending, Table 7-5 totals $10.3 million, but a later campaign memo documents $10,475,000 as paid to the Rafshoon agency and indicates at

that time some $25,000 additional funds owed, bringing the total to
$10.5 million for media costs.

Travel

The Carter campaign spent $4,761,831 on transportation costs,
including $2,748,169 for the use of chartered aircraft. This represents the
gross amount paid out by the campaign; the DPCC subsequently was
reimbursed $1,548,038 for transportation it provided to journalists cover-
ing the campaign and Secret Service agents protecting the candidate,
making the net campaign expenditure considerably lower.

Regulations adopted by the FEC prohibited indirect subsidization
of campaigns through excessive reimbursement by the Secret Service
and press. At the same time, the campaign wished to avoid having to
absorb the cost of providing transportation for those passengers. DPCC
treasurer Lipshutz, therefore, devised an FEC-approved system by
which the press was charged 150 percent and the Secret Service 100
percent of the commercial first-class air fare for each leg of the trip. By
Lipshutz's estimation, the DPCC would still pay $400,000 more than its
share under this plan.

Lipshutz explained to the FEC that his calculations were based on
consideration of four variables. The first was the method by which the
campaign was charged for use of the aircraft, which involved a fixed
charge per day aircraft is in use, a fixed charge per day aircraft is not in
use, number of landings, number of miles, and hours in service. The
others were the number of empty seats, the cost of providing ground
transportation for the press, and the cost of equipping the planes to
provide proper support for the press.[46] Appendix F shows a copy of the
campaign's Escrow Agreement with United Air Lines for the use of a
chartered aircraft.

States

The Carter campaign employed an unusual innovation in the management of its state campaigns, appointing political outsiders as coordinators in each state. Tim Kraft, the campaign's field operations
director, explained that "anyone who has gained any significant political experience in one state is no longer 'faction pure.' You try to send
people to a place where they don't have any entangling alliances, no
antagonisms." [47] The coordinator for Michigan, for example, was Don
O'Brien, a native Iowan who had run the 1968 Nebraska primary for
Robert Kennedy and then worked in California and Texas for George
McGovern in 1972.[48]

Because of the legal spending limit and the high priority given to media expenditures, the state campaigns were run on extremely tight budgets. Total spending by the 51 responsibility centers (including the District of Columbia) equaled $4,135,936 as of January 31, 1977 (Table 7-7). California had the largest budget, $476,000, but still experienced a severe cutback from the $1.5 million spent in that state by McGovern in 1972.[49] Similarly, Carter spent $190,000 in Michigan after McGovern had spent $900,000, and Pennsylvania coordinator Joe Timilty said his $311,000 budget was "30 to 40 percent of what John Kennedy spent here 16 years ago."[50]

One result of the state budget restrictions, ironic in the face of the limited ability to hire paid campaign workers, was the damper they put on volunteer activity. Robert Handy, head of the Carter-Mondale campaign in Santa Barbara, California, observed two weeks before the election, "What's happening now is that people want to get involved and feel part of the process again, but we're so strapped for funds that we can't give them anything to do. It might be good for a volunteer to go door to door on behalf of a candidate, but unless he can drop off a piece of campaign literature it's a waste of time."[51]

Noreen Walsh, a state volunteer coordinator in New York, also said, "There are a lot of people sitting back waiting who would like to be out there working." The problem, she said, was that the state campaign had not received any Carter literature until the final fortnight, and that Carter headquarters were so short of space that phone work, when there were phones available, and envelope-stuffing, when there were envelopes, had been severely restricted.[52]

Another victim of tight budgeting was what columnist Tom Wicker called "the most 'grass roots' kind of politics — advertising your own preference on your lapel or windshield."[53] The original Carter budget completely eliminated buttons and bumper stickers as unnecessary frills. Richard Harden, director of budgeting and finance for the campaign, said, "Somebody told us that for every 20 bumper stickers you print, only one gets on the back of a car, making it cost $4 to get a sticker on a car bumper. And there's some question as to how much value you get from a bumper sticker."[54]

Eventually, however, the DPCC gave in to pressure from its buttonless campaign workers. By October "we decided it wasn't worth it to have the complaints," according to media adviser Rafshoon, and 200,000 buttons and 200,000 stickers were ordered.[55] The button shortage was further relieved by the decision of many state and local Democratic Party committees to raise funds by designing and selling their own Carter buttons. One study found that at least 1,000 and perhaps as many as 2,000 different buttons were produced for actual campaign use.[56]

Table 7-7
Spending by Carter's State Responsibility Centers

Alabama	$ 33,202
Alaska	20,824
Arizona	18,711
Arkansas	25,205
California	475,584
Colorado	49,280
Connecticut	72,905
Delaware	18,045
District of Columbia	28,363
Florida	133,395
Georgia	23,277
Hawaii	19,050
Idaho	18,068
Illinois	289,336
Indiana	112,736
Iowa	38,656
Kansas	33,002
Kentucky	27,357
Louisiana	67,950
Maine	27,527
Maryland	85,682
Massachusetts	72,941
Michigan	189,957
Minnesota	29,042
Mississippi	29,782
Missouri	107,243
Montana	21,649
Nebraska	19,922
Nevada	27,241
New Hampshire	13,698
New Jersey	110,461
New Mexico	25,900
New York	373,243
North Carolina	32,517
North Dakota	27,352
Ohio	318,506
Oklahoma	64,469
Oregon	38,034
Pennsylvania	311,138
Rhode Island	22,543
South Carolina	28,428
South Dakota	39,356
Tennessee	34,912
Texas	246,467
Utah	14,770
Vermont	11,757
Virginia	120,215
Washington	69,320
West Virginia	19,593
Wisconsin	81,783
Wyoming	15,542
Total	$4,135,936

The shortage of funds for Carter's state campaigns made it necessary for them to coordinate and unify their efforts with those of local candidates and party committees. This was often difficult, as Carter had run in the primaries as the antiestablishment, antiboss outsider, and therefore had to mend fences with the establishment and the bosses. In general, however, the unification worked smoothly. In New York, for example, state coordinator Gerard F. Doherty acknowledged that the campaign finance law "compels you to work more closely with local organizations." [57] The result was that the presidential campaign in that state, for the first time since 1964, operated through the state's Democratic county organizations rather than by setting up parallel "citizens" organizations.[58] Midge Costanza, who had served as cochairman of Carter's primary campaign in New York and remained active in the general election effort, observed a symbiotic relationship between the national and local campaigns: "We have to have a lot of trust in the county organizations. If Carter and Mondale fall short of the mark, what do you think that portends for their local races? It seems to me right now that we need each other." [59]

In California, where party organizations were weak, Carter tried to use the organizational skills of the United Farm Workers instead. He endorsed Proposition 14, a state ballot initiative aimed at ensuring fair labor practices for farm workers, and campaigned with UFW organizer Cesar Chavez and Governor Jerry Brown. The Carter campaign hoped, in turn, not only to gain support among California's Chicanos, blacks, liberals, and labor, but also to directly benefit from the well-organized UFW's extensive registration and get-out-the-vote drives.[60]

Carter also sought to ensure local cooperation by helping to raise funds for Democratic congressional candidates. Since his acceptance of public funds for his own campaign precluded his acceptance of private contributions, he was free to devote all the fund-raising potential inherent in being a major-party nominee to helping other candidates. "The big difference," said campaign treasurer Robert Lipshutz, "is that we're not competing with any of them anymore for money;" and Frank Moore, Carter's congressional liaison director, added, "It's a whole new ball game in fund raising this year and it's going to be easy for us to help a lot of candidates." [61] It was hoped that the congressional candidates would then not only help with the Carter campaign effort but would in the future also cooperate with presidential initiatives if Carter won the election.

The limited state budgets necessitated a greater amount of centralization than has been customary in past campaigns. Through the draft system, national campaign headquarters in Atlanta was able to control all spending. All advertising was designed, directed, and placed out of Atlanta; one Northeast coordinator complained in October that "they're still showing spots of Jimmy Carter shaking his goddamn peanut trees." [62] The candidate's scheduling was controlled from Atlanta, as were most campaign materials.

The nine largest state responsibility centers (California, New York, Ohio, Pennsylvania, Illinois, Texas, Michigan, Florida, and Virginia) spent a total of $2,408,897 as of December 31, 1976. (These figures are slightly less complete than those in the table of state responsibility centers, which includes expenditures as of January 31, 1977.) Media use accounted for $94,332, most of which was spent for radio time ($48,045) and newspaper space ($37,991). Another $4,960 was spent on media production. Other vote-getting activities cost $656,641; this category includes polling, telephone canvassing, direct mail, campaign materials, meetings, voter registration, and get-out-the-vote. Office expenses were the largest expenditure category, totaling $770,687. Personal services, primarily staff payrolls and consultant and professional fees, cost $620,341, and travel, $261,936.

Other Expenditures

As shown in Table 7-8, the Carter campaign spent $706,000 for polls during the general election period. The polls were done by Cambridge Survey Research, headed by Patrick Caddell. In some cases, the surveys were bought by the DNC and then allocated between Carter/Mondale, statewide candidates, and the party itself under a formula devised by the FEC. The figures in Table 7-8 represent only the amount allocated to Carter/Mondale.

Table 7-8
Carter Campaign Costs for Postconvention Polls

National	$120,836
Statewide [a]	540,065
Special projects	20,000
Consulting [b]	25,000
Total	$705,901

[a] Special projects include focus groups.
[b] Consulting includes: consulting, Atlanta staff, and associated expenses.

At its peak, the DPCC had 1,500 people on its payroll. It paid out $2,630,899 in salaries and another $54,754 in consultant and professional fees during the course of the campaign. In New York, the campaign had a staff of about 50 at salaries ranging from $50 to $300 a week. The Ford campaign in that state employed about half that number, at salaries ranging up to $650 a week.[63]

Table 7-5 contains a figure of $1,500,398 under deposits in the office category. This refers mostly to telephone deposits that eventually were to be returned to the campaign committee. Along with travel rebates, media refunds, and exempt compliance costs, this helped reduce the gross campaign expenditures of $23.3 million indicated in Tables 7-4 and 7-5 to below the legal limit of $21.8 million.

One unusual type of expenditure was that made by Carter in an effort to ensure that he would appear on the ballot in all 50 states as "Jimmy" rather than as "James E." or "James Earl" Carter. By mid-October, Carter had won his battle. Only Maine and South Carolina had failed to honor the certification from the Democratic National Committee. In those two states, Carter attorneys filed suit to halt the printing of ballots temporarily. The court agreed in both states with Carter's counsel, who argued that common law recognizes a person's right to adopt a name through custom and usage that is wholly different from the name given him at birth.[64]

Possible Violations

Following the election, a number of allegations were raised concerning possible violations of the election laws by the Carter organization during both the primary and general election campaigns. The following examples of alleged Carter violations of the law or problems with compliance were publicized in part because, as president, he was more vulnerable and his filings were scrutinized more closely by the media and by others than were those of defeated candidates. The examples illustrate the problems of compliance and the possibilities of overlooking certain details, even given the best intentions of a candidate and campaign staff whose commitment to election reform was steadfast.

1. On July 22, 1976, one week after Carter was nominated by the Democratic convention, a luncheon was held in his honor at the 21 Club in New York. The luncheon, attended by 52 businessmen, was sponsored by J. Paul Austin, chairman of the Coca-Cola Co., Henry Ford II, chairman of the Ford Motor Co., and Edgar M. Bronfman, chairman of the Seagram Co., Ltd. Ford and Bronfman each personally paid $1,510 while Austin's share, $1,775, was picked up by a Coca-Cola Co. political action committee.

The FEC investigated the financing of this affair to determine whether the laws prohibiting the campaign from accepting private contributions in the postconvention period had been violated; the FEC considered sponsorship of the event as possibly a contribution to the campaign.[65]

Coca-Cola's political action committee reported its portion of the expense as an independent expenditure. The FEC was skeptical of this designation, assuming that Carter or his staff must have been consulted since Carter had accepted an invitation to address the group. Henry Ford, on the other hand, had, according to a spokesman, become concerned about the legality of his contribution and was reimbursed by the DNC in October 1976, before the FEC began its inquiry.

In July 1978 the FEC decided it was "improper" for private parties to pay for the luncheon, "even though these same sponsors had billed the event as nonpartisan, had invited President Gerald R. Ford, Mr. Carter's opponent, to a similar event and had endorsed neither candidate." The FEC ordered President Carter's campaign committee to pay the U.S. Treasury $3,285.14, the exact amount that had been paid by Bronfman and the Coca-Cola committee to defray costs for the affair. Bronfman and Coca-Cola were fined $500 each, while admitting no wrongdoing in their "conciliation agreements" with the commission. Henry Ford II was not fined, having been foresighted in requiring reimbursement by the DNC. Thus, the FEC took a narrow view of what constitutes a nonpolitical event during campaigns for federal office.[66]

2. The investigation into the banking practices and personal finances of Management and Budget Director Bert Lance in August 1977 brought to light the fact that Carter had taken five unpaid trips on an airplane owned by the National Bank of Georgia in 1975 and 1976. Lance was president of NBG at that time.

Press secretary Jody Powell said the failure to pay for the trips represented "an oversight in campaign bookkeeping." He said the bank would be reimbursed fully by the Carter campaign committee for political trips and by Carter himself for personal trips. For trips on August 30, October 17, and December 29, 1975, the bank was to be reimbursed $766 by the campaign and $370 by Carter. Two other trips, taken on June 13 and 19, 1976, cost $658. White House Counsel Robert Lipshutz asked the FEC to rule whether these flights should be considered a personal or campaign expense.

Some observers considered the unpaid plane trips that were classified as political to be a campaign contribution by NBG. The election law makes it illegal for a corporation to make such a contribution, or for a candidate knowingly to accept it. Jody Powell denied that the law had been violated in this case. The failure to pay for the flights had been "unintentional," he said, and the campaign had "made and will continue to make a good faith effort to deal with the oversights when they come up." [67]

Eventually, the Carter campaign committee and the bank both paid fines in connection with the flights. A report by the FEC's counsel, which was adopted by the commission, stated: "In view of the fact that there were five flights involving Carter and that the committee has not paid for any of them, the general counsel recommends that the commission not consider this to be merely a reporting error." [68] The Carter campaign committee made a payment of $1,100 in August 1977 to cover the cost of the flights. However, "the bank refunded about $300 after recalculating the expenses." In the agreement formally announced on June 26, 1978, the FEC stated that "the failure of the (Carter) committee to pay for the use of the . . . aircraft until August 1977 constituted its receipt of in-kind contributions, in violation" of the FECA. The FEC agreement also stated that the bank's failure to bill the committee until that date constituted an unlawful contribution.[69] In separate "conciliation agreements" with the FEC, the campaign committee and the bank agreed to pay civil penalties of $1,200 and $5,000, respectively. Neither was required to admit to any wrongdoing.

3. Shortly after these flights were revealed, it was disclosed that the campaign had failed to pay for five other flights during a three-day campaign trip to North and South Carolina in April 1975. Two of these had been paid for by an individual, R. R. Allen of Fayetteville, North Carolina, who had previously contributed the legal limit of $1,000 to the Carter campaign; two by a corporation, the Diamond Supply Co. of Charlotte, North Carolina; and one by the state of South Carolina, for a flight on a state-owned plane on which Carter was accompanied by Lt. Gov. W. Brantley Harvey.

One of the flights paid for by Diamond was a round-trip on a company-owned plane to Salisbury, North Carolina. Carter there addressed a Pfeiffer College audience on the subject of political ethics, asking, "Why should a Congressman let an oil company's plane carry him home on the weekend? Whether either party admitted it, it's a bribe, and the Congressman can't get off a jet airplane in his hometown without feeling obligated to the oil company to listen to them a little more the following week. There is no reason for a President or a Governor or a Congressman or a Senator to take a gift from anybody." [70]

White House lawyer Doug Huron said the Carter campaign would reimburse Allen $271, Diamond Supply $569, and South Carolina $200. He said the failure to pay for the flights had been unintentional, and that the campaign previously had paid $151,332 for small charter planes. "It's not like we had a practice of not paying for those plane trips," he said.[71]

4. Another outgrowth of the Lance affair was a charge that Carter, like Lance, had used unsecured bank loans for political purposes. A

November 1977 article in *The New Republic* by Richard Reeves and Barry M. Hager asserted that, during the two-month cutoff of federal matching funds in spring 1976, Carter's campaign was kept afloat by 14 loans totaling $1,525,000 from two Atlanta banks, the Citizens and Southern, and the Fulton; $1,270,000 in credit from suppliers willing to accept delayed payments; and $82,000 in loans from smaller banks and individuals. At the same time, Carter's opponents were unable to obtain such credit; Henry Jackson could borrow only $42,700 and Morris Udall, $70,000. Both of these campaigns suffered serious financial difficulties during this period.

The Carter campaign's net indebtedness, according to this article, reached $556,000 by the end of March, $960,000 at the end of April, and $1,898,000 at the end of May. Its tangible assets at that time were accounts receivable of $300,000, primarily in transportation costs billed to the Secret Service and the press; and matching fund claims submitted to the FEC, but not approved, totaling $650,000. Only $100,000 of the loan money was guaranteed by Jimmy Carter's personal assets; FEC records listed as "guarantor" of the other loans: "None." Six of the loans were made during the time when there was some doubt whether the FEC would be reconstituted by Congress, making anticipated FEC payments an unreliable source of collateral. In other words, according to this article, more than a million dollars in unsecured loan money by southern banks and suppliers represented an investment in Carter's campaign and a gamble on his success.

These charges were fueled by comparisons between the original campaign reports filed by the Carter organization and the 4,800 pages of amended reports filed three days after Carter's election. The original reports showed the campaign to be far healthier than did the amended reports, at one point by more than $1 million. (The discrepancies are covered in greater detail in the section on the Carter primary audit, under item 13 below.)

In a rebuttal to the article, which he termed "a shamefully misleading and disgracefully inaccurate story," press secretary Powell concentrated on the six loans made before the FEC was reconstituted. None of these loans were secured by anticipated FEC funds, he said; all except for $100,000 secured by Jimmy Carter personally were secured by transportation accounts receivable. He also maintained that the soundness of the loans was strengthened by "the fact that contributions for us and accounts receivable for transportation were growing while they were fading for other candidates."

Reeves and Hager responded, however, that by concentrating on six of the 14 loans taken out by the campaign, Powell avoided the issue of relating the campaign's total debts to its total assets to secure those debts. Those assets, the authors maintain, were not sufficient. They also point out that by taking growing contributions into account as a factor in the soundness of the loans, Powell was conceding that the lenders were gambling on the success of the Carter campaign.[72]

5. A similar charge, made by *Newsweek,* was that the Carter committee frequently overdrew its accounts at the Fulton National Bank during the primary period.[73] Such overdrafts would be illegal if they are interpreted as being interest-free loans. *Newsweek* reported overdrafts of $88,092 in March 1976 and $121,645 in May. Campaign treasurer Lipshutz contended that the overdrafts were in fact much smaller, explaining that checks were regularly written and entered on the campaign books as large overdrafts, but were not issued until there was more money in the account.

6. Both Carter's primary and general election campaigns were charged with discrepancies in their use of last-minute get-out-the-vote money. Commonly referred to as "street money" or "walking-around money," these funds are used to compensate election-day workers for their loss of a workday at their regular jobs. The *Los Angeles Times* reported in August 1976 that, because expenditures for "street money" had not been sufficiently documented, the Carter campaign would have to return $150,000 in matching funds to the Treasury. The *Times* also reported that four black ministers in Oakland had received $5,000 for their endorsements in the California primary. One minister, the Rev. J. L. Richard, was quoted as saying, "When a preacher stands up in his church and talks about Jimmy Carter, he's working for Jimmy Carter as far as I'm concerned, and he should get paid for it."

Carter, when informed of the allegations, said, "Obviously I don't know anything about it myself and we have tried to minimize this kind of campaign abuse in every way possible." He directed Robert Lipshutz to investigate any wrongdoing on the part of the campaign staff members. Carter said the use of street money was not illegal but that "we suffer from it" because under the law the candidate would lose matching funds for all expenditures not accounted for by receipts. Carter said that no more than 4 or 5 percent, or $450,000, of his $9 million in preconvention expenditures were undocumented. Lipshutz, however, said undocumented expenses were more likely to be "almost infinitesimal."

Two of the black religious organizations, the Baptist Minister's Union of Oakland and the Mount Zion Missionary District Association, subsequently returned the money they had received from the campaign. Each group had been given $1,000. The Rev. J. L. Richard, who headed both groups, said, "We assumed that this was to be expense money disbursed through the black clergy for workers in the campaign. The questionable implications currently being suggested becloud our original good intentions." Richard denied the report that the organizations had received the money in return for endorsing Carter.[74]

7. The Carter campaign apparently failed to provide sufficient documentation of its disbursement of "street money" and other expenditures during the general election period as well. In an apparent violation of FEC directives, the expenditures were listed in the names of the campaign workers who spent the money, rather than in the names of the ultimate recipients. Some of the individuals and committees listed had been given more than $10,000 to spend.

The FEC had sent a letter to all federal candidates in September 1976, warning them that reporting expenditures under such general categories as "advance to field man" or "travel" was "not sufficient to meet the statutory requirements," and that "the actual use to which the advance is put must be itemized." An analysis of Carter's reports by Jerry Landauer of *The Wall Street Journal,* however, revealed that they included almost $500,000 for otherwise unspecified "get-out-the-vote" activities and $279,000 for "miscellaneous office expenses." Another $603,000 was not described in any way, on the ground that it had all been spent in sums of less than $100. Robert C. Andrews, Carter controller, said DPCC had detailed receipts in its files showing who eventually had received all its expenditures, but had chosen not to include the information in its public reports. He said the reports could be amended to show the real recipients "to the extent required by FEC regulation." [75]

8. The DPCC also was charged by the FEC with inadequately documenting the repayment of its loans after the election. In its quarterly report filed April 10, 1977, the DPCC indicated that more than 200 debts totaling more than $300,000 had been repaid since the end of 1976, but failed to submit the necessary documentation to show that the repayments had been made.

The largest debt in question was $91,140 owed to Citizens and Southern National Bank in Atlanta at the end of 1976, the residue of the $1,155,000 the bank had lent Carter in that year. The April 10, 1977, report listed the Citizens and Southern loans as having been reduced to zero, but did not provide any details of the repayments.

White House aides Lipshutz and Harden said the report to the FEC had been incomplete because of the way the Citizens and Southern loans had been repaid. "We might be inaccurate but we're not dishonest," said Lipshutz. He and Harden explained that the campaign had used accounts receivable money — primarily transportation bills sent to the press and the Secret Service — as collateral for the loans. As these payments came in, the checks were not cashed but automatically were forwarded to Citizens and Southern, thus reducing the loan totals.

Harden had a different explanation for the 201 other debts where repayment had not been sufficiently documented to the FEC. He said that because of a programming error, the campaign's computers had changed these debts from "itemized expenditures" to "unitemized" as they were repaid. "Evidently computers do what you tell them to do even when we tell them to do something wrong," said Harden. He added that the checks were being tracked down one by one to satisfy the FEC.[76]

9. After Carter had been nominated by the Democratic convention but was still owed $387,000 in matching funds, auditors at the FEC recommended that the funds be withheld because of "disclosure problems" in the campaign's financial reports. The recommendation followed two months of correspondence, meetings, and telephone calls between Carter bookkeepers and FEC auditors. Finally, Al Keema, the head of the commission's reports analysis unit, wrote a memo to the legal staff recommending that Carter "not be certified" for a pending matching payment because of "numerous questions" that his campaign had not answered. The memo stated:

> Specifically, Reports Analysis has repeatedly requested certain information which was either omitted from the Carter committee's reports, or which was not fully disclosed on the face of reports submitted.
>
> This information includes not only minor omissions, such as occupation and principal place of business, but also more important omissions of endorsers for loans, outstanding debts, negative cash balances which did not in reality exist, excessive contributions, etc.

After noting that the FEC staff had met "repeatedly" with Carter representatives, the memo concluded: "Reports Analysis believes that failure to file the requested amendments to correct erroneous information or to provide adequate disclosure is, in fact, failure to comply fully with the act." The commission's legal staff, however, rejected this view and, in a one-paragraph memo to the commission, concluded that the Carter campaign had "substantially" complied with the disclosure requirements. The members of the commission then approved the $386,915 matching payment, which was used to pay off outstanding primary campaign debts.[77]

10. In June 1978 it was revealed that the FEC had noted "reasonable cause" to believe that the Carter campaign had violated the election laws, and the White House acknowledged that the president's lawyers were negotiating with the commission for an out-of-court settlement of any such violations. Robert Lipshutz, the president's counsel, contended that the commission's audit had revealed only minor discrepancies amounting to a few thousand dollars. FEC Chairman Joan D.

Aikens said at the time that the commission was "waiting for further documentation from the campaign committee" and hoped to have the audit completed and published by the end of the summer.[78]

On Friday the 13th of October, 1978, "reasonable cause" became belief when the FEC announced that it was fining Carter's 1976 election campaign committee $1,000 and ordering it to refund $17,025 in illegally used public campaign funds.[79] These funds had been used to pay the salaries and travel expenses of 20 campaign aides after Carter won the election but before he was inaugurated. The FEC ruled unanimously that the payment of salaries "for workers during the transition of administrations did not represent 'qualified campaign expenses' and therefore violated federal law. The funds involved came from federal tax revenues."[80] The FEC action had been prompted by a *Los Angeles Times* investigation into the $2 million transition operation, which was publicly financed.

11. On August 8, 1976, a *Los Angeles Times* report spurred the FEC to investigate the possibility that Carter had failed to disclose properly the "purpose" of payments made in connection with his presidential primary campaign. Expenditures totaling $212,275 were reported as "advances" to campaign staff members and/or community leaders or groups.

Three months later, then FEC General Counsel John G. Murphy, Jr., recommended that the commission dismiss the case, stating that "ambiguous entries such as 'compensation' and 'advance' are common in reports filed by" other campaign committees. Murphy pointed out that the Carter reports had been filed prior to the FEC's September 1976 announcement that more specific characterizations would be required to describe the purpose of an expenditure.

On October 19, 1976, the FEC overruled Murphy, yet the investigation soon became ensnared in the FEC's audit of Carter's primary and general election campaign. Many of the expenditures already being investigated were also questioned by FEC auditors as inadequately documented for public financing purposes.

The delay in releasing the Carter audit was primarily due to a dispute between commission lawyers and auditors over what constitutes adequate documentation. Although the FECA requires candidates and political committees to report the purpose of all expenditures over $100 aggregate, the statute does not define what is meant by "purpose." FEC auditors were advocating a much stricter standard than were FEC lawyers. FEC Counsel William G. Oldaker described the dispute:

> The commission auditors do not believe that "get-out-the-vote" is a specific enough purpose or that receipts from payees are detailed enough if they do not include an itemization of how the money was

spent. It is our opinion that the information provided is sufficient to meet the requirements . . . at least as it read during the period in which these expenditures were made.

The FEC voted on February 15, 1978, to accept Oldaker's more lenient standard regarding statutory requirements for reporting. On August 30 the FEC unanimously decided to resolve the issue of the last remaining expenditure in the audit report pending receipt of further information from the Carter campaign.[81]

12. The Carter campaign also was fined $1,950 for an FECA violation involving the commingling of personal and campaign funds by Carter campaign workers in Florida, Kansas, North Carolina, and Oklahoma. The funds in question were payments to advance personnel in the field, who deposited the funds in personal bank accounts; federal law prohibits commingling campaign money with personal funds. FEC found that the funds were in no way misused, however, since the money was promptly disursed to pay legitimate campaign expenses.

The $1,950 fine brought the total fines paid by Carter's 1976 election campaign for violations of the FECA to $11,435.[82]

13. Another primary-related question about Carter's campaign surfaced during the grand jury and Securities and Exchange Commission investigation into the financial activities of Bert Lance and the National Bank of Georgia. The possibility was raised that money loaned by the NBG to the Carter family enterprises may have found its way into the campaign. According to documents provided by Charles Kirbo, trustee of the president's holdings, the NBG's loans to the Carter family peanut business during 1975 and 1976 allowed Carter and his relatives to increase substantially their profits and personal access to cash during those years.[83] Speculation arose that some of the NBG money might have been part of the $50,000 in loans and contributions that the Carter family gave to the campaign, but there was no evidence to support these speculations and no action was taken on the allegations.

The Carter primary audit[84] was released on April 2, 1979, 29 months after Carter was elected president. The audit's main conclusion was that there had been some sloppy record keeping and reporting, but no serious violations of the Federal Election Campaign Act.

The audit covered the period January 1, 1975 (the effective date of the FECA) through June 30, 1978. The Carter committee reported opening cash of $16,376.57, total receipts of $14,635,161.66, total expenditures of $14,648,080.72, and closing cash of $3,456.72. ($10,033,856.50 was the total expenditure amount subject to limitation.)

The FEC auditors sampled expenditures at random and found certain groups of expenditures where the purpose and/or amount seemed inconsistent with the reported payee; for example, "personal expense reimbursements" paid to business entities. The main dispute between the FEC and the Carter committee was over the disclosure of expenditures such as "get-out-the-vote," as noted above. The auditors felt that such labels were insufficient, especially in light of the guidelines on that subject issued by the FEC during the campaign; the audit acknowledges, however, that the guidelines were not issued until September 29, 1976, long after most of the expenditures in question had been made and reported. The FEC found that 21 inadequately documented expenditures totaling $6,072.60 were unqualified campaign expenses and were therefore repayable in full to the U.S. Treasury. This figure subsequently was revised downward to $5,872.60 and a check for that amount was issued by the Carter committee on January 4, 1979.

As a result of the audit, the Carter committee also was fined by the FEC for improper use of depositories, as noted in item 12 above. The auditors determined that expenditures in support of the candidate had been made from at least five undisclosed bank accounts. The accounts belonged to individuals working for the campaign who had desposited the money upon receipt from the Carter committee, before disbursing the funds for campaign purposes. Some of the individuals had commingled the campaign money with personal funds. In a conciliation agreement with the FEC, the Carter committee agreed to a $1,950 fine, a check for which was issued on January 4, 1979.

The audit also disclosed that the FEC had taken issue with the Carter committee's method of disclosing proceeds from the sale of contributed items. The method of disclosure was deemed incorrect by the auditors and the FEC directed the Carter committee to amend its reports accordingly; the committee complied.

There was some criticism of the audit by several persons who had participated in it.[85] They maintained that the audit as conducted had such a narrow focus that it was highly unlikely that it could have uncovered any sophisticated mishandling of funds. The critics, who wished to remain anonymous, did not know of any mishandling of funds but said that the audit staff had not done enough work to find out. The sources said that the auditors did not investigate the circumstances of bank loans, did not compare the campaign's records with those of third parties, and did not analyze the differences between two sets of campaign reports submitted by the Carter campaign.

The double set of reports was the item of greatest concern for those critical of the Carter audit. The Carter campaign had submitted 4,800 pages of amended campaign reports three days after Carter was elected. The amended reports showed large discrepancies in the financial situation of the Carter campaign at various points. For example, for the month of April, in the middle of the cutoff of matching funds when the campaign needed loans to continue operation, the campaign originally reported a surplus of $185,795 when in fact, according to the amended reports, it had a deficit of $970,045, a discrepancy of $1,155,839.

Additional criticism of the audit came in connection with research by some reporters into the deficit.[86] The reporters found that the advertising agency of Gerald Rafshoon apparently extended large amounts of credit to the Carter campaign, in possible violation of the FECA regulations that prohibit corporations from extending credit to candidates unless it occurs in the normal course of business. It was also alleged that the agency advanced cash for television time for the Carter campaign at a time when the agency was having serious financial problems of its own. There was substantial disagreement about the facts surrounding the matter between Robert Lipshutz, under whose direction campaign documents were prepared, and William J. Stack, Jr., trustee of the Rafshoon agency, who insisted that the agency had never advanced cash on behalf of the campaign. Rafshoon's records were obtained by the federal grand jury in Atlanta and were given for investigation to Paul J. Curran, the special counsel appointed by the Department of Justice to investigate whether funds from bank loans to the Carter family peanut business were diverted to Carter's campaign.[87]

14. On June 4, 1979, the FEC finally released the Carter-Mondale general election campaign audit.[88] The 110-page audit with accompanying documentation not only was the FEC's longest audit but inadvertantly was distributed with some audit working papers that were controversial, drawing comment from Jody Powell, the president's press secretary.

Powell minimized references in the work papers to an apparent failure by the Carter campaign to disclose a $134,000 debt to the Rafshoon agency.[89] The FEC referred the auditors' findings to the agency's general counsel for further study, but Carter campaign officials denied that the $134,000 actually constituted a debt. The campaign did disclose about $16,000 of the Rafshoon debt two years after the election in an amended report, but after the debt had been whittled down to the $16,000 amount by agreement that the Rafshoon agency would retain any funds from television and radio stations for spot announcements never run. It was explained that rather than keep the campaign books open, Rafshoon would apply the refunds to the amount owed his agency, so the debt's full size was not disclosed as federal law seemingly would require, until the remaining $16,000 balance was belatedly disclosed.

The FEC audit required the Carter campaign to repay $50,202 to the U.S. Treasury for other reporting violations. One such violation was failure to document about $15,000 in get-out-the-vote money disbursed for election day expenses in various states. Another was for other undocumented expenditures. Some $27,000 was sought for repayment because that amount had been earned by the Carter committee as interest on telephone deposits made with federal funds. FEC Democratic commissioners blocked an effort by commission auditors to require repayment of some $32,000 more than the $50,202 actually called for in the audit. Carter campaign officials indicated they were inclined to repay the amounts rather than contest the audit findings, because it probably would cost more to get the necessary documentation two and a half years after the election than it would to repay the demanded amount.

Other Incidents. Two additional incidents were publicized and are recorded here. Although related to the Carter campaign, they both occurred outside the central campaign, which was not responsible for either incident.

1. The campaign committee of Representative (now Ambassador) Andrew Young paid the bills for the extensive traveling done by Young to promote Carter's candidacy. These expenses possibly could represent an illegal contribution by the Young committee to the Carter campaign.

The situation came to light in October 1977 when a list of contributors filed by the Young committee with the FEC indicated that $9,400 had been raised since January 31, 1977, to pay old campaign debts, in spite of the fact that a report filed by the committee in January had indicated that it had no remaining debts. "When debts suddenly surface that were not disclosed in the postelection report, we flag that situation immediately," an FEC spokesman explained.

Stoney Cooks, Young's campaign treasurer, said he had never been informed that the law required a listing of unpaid bills at the close of a campaign. "I've always assumed," he said, "that you only had to list a debt if you had no means of paying it." Cooke said Young spent "in excess of $10,000" in 1976 in travels around the country on behalf of Carter and Democratic congressional candidates. Young's airline tickets and car rentals were billed to credit cards belonging to Young, Cooks, and one other staff member. By October 1977, $7,183 of the travel bills had been repaid, leaving a debt of approximately $3,000 owed to credit card companies for political travel. Cooks maintained that Young's travel expenses represented a legitimate independent expenditure for Carter, since his itinerary was not coordinated with Carter's presidential campaign even though Young was a prominent Carter adviser. "We purposely orchestrated it that way," said Cooks.[90]

2. In July 1978 it was announced that the FEC had fined an attorney for making illegal campaign contributions to the Carter campaign out of funds taken from Detroit Mayor Coleman Young's cam-

paign committee. The lawyer, Louis R. Lee, allegedly withdrew $38,800 from the account of the People for Detroit Committee, of which he was treasurer. Using the names of 10 other persons, he funneled $9,200 of these funds to the Carter campaign. Mayor Young apparently discovered the withdrawals while preparing an annual report for his committee.[91]

Although Lee was charged with embezzling funds from the Young committee as well as from a private trust he administered, investigators believed that no more than $11,300 was used in connection with a federal campaign.

Democratic Telethons

The Democratic National Committee sponsored four telethons from 1972 through 1975. The telethons were held to achieve five goals: 1) to raise money, 2) to make the process more democratic by relying on large numbers of small donations, 3) to help unify the party, 4) to broaden the contributor base and increase participation from "average citizens," and 5) to project a positive image of the party to the public.[92]

The telethons were seen by many people and raised large sums of money (Table 7-9). The 1972 telethon contributed to the divisions among Democrats, particularly over how the funds raised should be distributed.[93] However, the telethons of 1973, 1974, and 1975 concentrated on raising money, avoided discussion of any particular issue or candidate, and sought to aid party unity. Profits from the programs were

Table 7-9
Net Receipts, Production Costs, and Net Income of the Four Democratic National Telethons[a]

Telethon	Net Receipts	Production Costs	Net Income	Benefit-Cost Ratio [b]
1972	$3,800,000 [c]	$1,900,000 [c]	$1,900,000 [c]	2.0 - 1
1973	4,215,215	2,273,237	1,941,978	1.9 - 1
1974	5,403,672	2,555,839	2,847,833	2.1 - 1
1975	3,661,107	2,751,336	909,771	1.3 - 1

a Data from statement of income and expenses, 1973, 1974, and 1975 telethons; Democratic National Committee.
b This is the ratio of net receipts/production costs.
c Data for 1972 telethon is estimated from newspaper accounts as the statement of income and expenses is not available.

SOURCE: John W. Ellwood and Robert J. Spitzer, "The Democratic National Telethons: Their Successes & Failures," *Journal of Politics* 41, no. 2 (August 1979), in press.

divided between the DNC and the state party organizations. Each subsequent telethon generated increased participation by state and local Democratic Party affiliates.

John W. Ellwood and Robert J. Spitzer conducted a mail survey of contributors to the telethons of 1973 and 1974. Their research was done in cooperation with the Democratic National Committee but their conclusions reflect their own views and not those of the DNC. Ellwood and Spitzer were interested in studying what types of people contributed to the telethons and in assessing how successful the DNC had been in meeting its goals for the programs.

According to the authors, the telethons were successful in attracting new givers to the party. Nearly two-thirds of the 1973 and 1974 contributors had not given to a prior telethon. Almost one-half (48.1 percent) of the 1973 givers had not contributed to any campaign during 1972.[94] The Democrats raised money from a large number of small givers who contributed less than $15 each.

However, the new contributors were not representative of the rank and file of the Democratic Party. The survey showed that the telethons raised money from liberal, urban, affluent, well-educated, and relatively young voters who were generally favorable to the Democratic Party.[95] In other words, the telethons reached activist, liberal Democrats who were highly unrepresentative of the voting age population and quite similar in type to those who dominated the 1972 presidential caucuses and the Democratic convention. The Democratic Party did broaden its contributor base but from an elite group of party activists.

The 1975 telethon was much less successful than its three predecessors in raising money and in commanding a large audience. The decline

Table 7-10
Total Receipts, Number of Contributors, and Mean Contribution for the Telethons [a]

Telethon	Net Receipts	Number of Contributors	Mean Contribution
1972	$3,800,000 [b]	323,282	$11.13
1973	4,215,215	260,888	14.71
1974	5,403,672	389,679	10.91
1975	3,661,107	209,344	12.23

[a] Data obtained from the Democratic National Committee.
[b] Total net receipts for the 1972 telethon are estimated from newspaper accounts and interviews with telethon staff. Profit and loss statement for that year is not available.

SOURCE: John W. Ellwood and Robert J. Spitzer, "The Democratic National Telethons: Their Successes & Failures," *Journal of Politics* 41, no. 2 (August 1979), in press.

in telethon profits was associated with a drop in the number of contributors rather than the size of the contributions. Fewer people watched the 1975 telethon than any of the previous programs.[96]

In the past, the DNC relied on a few individuals to personally guarantee the large bank loans required to cover production costs. The high production cost per receipt and the large sums of money required for start-up costs argued against repeating the programs. More important, the 1974 Amendments put an aggregate limit of $25,000 for the total of any individual's contributions to all federal candidates in any given year. The Federal Election Commission ruled that guarantees such as utilized by the DNC would be counted against the overall limit.[97] This clearly ruled out past loan practices.

The Federal Communications Commission's equal-time provisions limit the use of telethons, since public officials who are formal candidates for reelection cannot appear on such programs without their opponents being given equal time.

Ford

President Ford's general election campaign stressed his incumbency. At an early informal meeting of campaign advisers in June, it was concluded that Ford would be best off with a so-called "no-campaign campaign." They suggested that, after securing the nomination, the president ought to announce at the convention that he would not campaign actively, but stick to his job and let the people vote on the basis of his performance. He would reject the $21.8 million in public funds available to him and offer to debate Carter on a series of substantive issues.[98]

Ford did not in fact go this far; he accepted the subsidy to finance his campaign. But he nevertheless tried to maintain, until the final weeks before the election, what one campaign official called "a low political profile and a high Presidential profile." [99] This entailed remaining in the White House and creating televised public ceremonies out of normally routine bill-signings and messages to Congress, thereby dramatizing the fact of Ford's incumbency and projecting the image of a purposeful, hard-working chief executive.

Early in the campaign, for example, the president created a televised ceremony in the Rose Garden out of his signing of a bill setting standards for day-care centers, and he used the occasion to defend his veto of an earlier version of the bill. "Without this constitutional check and balance," he said, "the original bill might now be law and making day-care services more costly to the taxpayer and increasing federal intrusion into family life." That veto, he said, as well as the 54 others he had made since assuming the presidency, had been made "with one concern in mind — to protect the American people from unrealistic responses to their very real needs, to see that the federal government does not merely serve the people but serves them well." [100] It was an effective — and free — campaign speech.

By giving the president valuable publicity, the Rose Garden Strategy, as it came to be called, saved the Ford campaign considerable money. It also precluded Ford from making a major mistake, or simply appearing dull or clumsy, on the campaign trail. The president's campaign staff bluntly warned him, "Your national approval rating declined when you were perceived as partisan, particularly when we campaign." [101] At one press conference, Ford was asked if he felt he might be "abusing" his office and exploiting the press by using the Rose Garden as a campaign prop. The president smiled and said, "I apologize if I am using the American press," but added that he was merely trying to "convey important information to the American people." [102]

Coverage of the Rose Garden campaign created ethical dilemmas for the media, torn between responsibility to provide full coverage of presidential news and reluctance to provide unfair political exposure to one candidate. Most correspondents solved the problem by identifying staged Rose Garden events as political events, usually referring to "the Ford campaign at the White House" or some variation thereof. Ford aide Michael Duval expressed the theory behind the Ford strategy, however, saying, "We didn't mind the network correspondents saying he was using the White House. People aren't going to remember the voice-over; they're going to remember the visual." [103]

Similar considerations came into play on decisions with respect to the question of how much coverage to provide presidential press conferences. Throughout most of the campaign the networks' standard procedure was to broadcast the conferences live and in their entirety while covering Carter's in excerpt form for brief summaries in evening and morning newscasts. Although some of Carter's aides indicated that they felt cheated by the discrepancy, the networks defended it in terms of potential news value. William J. Small, vice-president of CBS News, explained the reasoning that was evidently employed by all three networks: "When you think purely in terms of news judgment, something big might come out of a session with the President and reporters. You don't expect anything like that to come out of a news conference with someone running for the office who doesn't hold the office." [104]

Toward the close of the campaign, the networks, feeling that Ford's activities were now more political than presidential, curtailed their coverage of his press conferences. All three networks covered his October 20 conference only in the excerpt form similar to that which they provided Carter. They had carried Ford's October 14 conference in full in prime time, and Robert Mulholland, executive vice-president of NBC

News, said that his network had decided that "no new issues concerning the President had arisen in the six days between the two news conferences." Small of CBS added, "We are getting very close to the election and have to put the nearness of it in the equation." [105]

The New York Times also cut back late in the campaign on the extra space it provided Ford. The Times customarily publishes a full transcript of every presidential news conference, but printed no transcript of the October 14 conference and only excerpts of the October 20 session. News executives at the Times considered both conferences largely political and concluded that printing full transcripts would provide Ford an extra element of exposure, since Carter's news conferences were not accompanied by textual material. Political as well as journalistic standards influence press coverage of presidential/political news. During the last week of the campaign, for example, the administration announced the granting of almost $90 million in federal transit subsidies to New York City. The *New York Daily News,* which had endorsed Ford, gave the story a front-page banner headline: "WE GET $90M IN TRANSIT AID." *The New York Times,* which had endorsed Carter, consigned it to relative obscurity on an inside page in its second section.[106]

The Ford campaign derived more direct benefits from its incumbency in the White House, using such presidential perquisites as Air Force One and White House staff aides for political purposes. In some instances it was charged that campaign laws were violated. Michael Duval, for example, continued to draw his salary as a White House assistant counsel while representing Ford in negotiating ground rules for the presidential debates and advising Ford on his appearances. Duval did not drop off the payroll for the period in which he was engaged in political activity. The campaign's explanation was that Duval was a "volunteer" giving part-time help that did not interfere with his official duties. One campaign insider was quoted as saying, in reference to this explanation, "That's ridiculous. Mike has been working on the debates full time." The campaign failed to report Duval's campaign-related expenses as expenditures chargeable against the expenditure limit.[107]

The Ford report filed with the FEC for the month of September identified about 20 White House employees who received about $15,000 in travel fees and other expenses and another $15,000 as consultants to the Ford campaign. According to Rayston C. Hughes, treasurer of the President Ford Committee, these employees conducted all their political activity outside their normal working hours. In addition, according to Hughes, about half the corps of 10 White House advance men were transferred full time to the payroll of the campaign committee.[108] The Ford committee failed to specify in its September report how much money it had spent for the political travels of members of the cabinet, such as Secretary of Agriculture Earl L. Butz and Secretary of Commerce Elliot L. Richardson, who campaigned extensively for the president while he remained in the White House. Nor did it indicate how much it was reimbursing the Air Force for the transportation it provided Ford for his two campaign trips that month.

The Democratic National Committee considered filing a complaint with the FEC based on the apparent failure of the Ford campaign to acknowledge as accountable political spending the salaries of at least a portion of the White House personnel who had been heavily involved in the campaign. One Carter campaign aide complained, "Everything even remotely connected with Carter's campaign must be paid for out of that $21 million, while anything less than total involvement in the Ford campaign gets paid for by the government and is not counted against his $21 million." The Republicans countered that the aides doing campaign work were either on vacation or working voluntarily during evening or weekend hours, and that as long as the aides spent "a substantial majority" of their time on government business no payment by the Ford campaign committee was required.[109]

At an October meeting, the Democratic Steering Committee, however, decided not to press the complaint. One party source was quoted as saying that the members were afraid of appearing "petty," and also cited the difficulty of proving that White House aides were not performing their political duties during their off hours, days off, or accumulated leave. In any event, the Democrats were aware that the secrecy and length of FEC investigation and enforcement procedures would have made any sort of resolution and public reaction to their complaint before the election highly unlikely.[110]

The FEC already had dismissed two similar complaints lodged against the Ford campaign during the contest with Ronald Reagan for the Republican nomination. One concerned Ford campaign manager Rogers C. B. Morton, who served concurrently as a White House counselor, and the other concerned Secretary of State Henry Kissinger, whose expenses for political speeches were paid by the government. FEC Vice-Chairman Thomas Harris, in a statement issued on the Morton case, said, "There is nothing in the language or the legislative history that even hints that Congress meant to deal with Federal employee political activity via the Election Campaign Act. It is inconceivable to me that Congress intended, without mentioning it, to confer on this commission responsibilty for monitoring political activity by government employees." According to Harris, such activities could not constitute a campaign "contribution" because the government would then be the "contributor" subject to the $1,000 limit on individual contributions, a result he termed "absurd"; if judged a contribution-in-kind, then the FEC "as presently staffed and budgeted could not conceivably handle" the administrative burden of examining each case of alleged abuse.[111]

The only dissent to that view came from Commissioner Neil Staebler, who contended that the commission had jurisdiction in cases such as Morton's because the "literal language of the definition of a contribution and expenditure under the act includes 'anything of value used to influence the nomination of a candidate for Federal office.' Regardless of the capacity of the government to be a contributor within the meaning of the act, the value of government resources used by the president for political purposes should be treated as a campaign expenditure." [112]

For a sitting president seeking another term, however, the line between "presidential" and "political" actions is far from clear. Ford was able to take advantage of the power of his incumbency to make policy decisions whose political ramifications would boost his political prospects. The day before he was to meet with Jewish leaders in Brooklyn, for example, the president announced in the White House that he had agreed to provide Israel with sophisticated electronic military equipment previously denied that country. White House press secretary Ron Nessen said questions suggesting political motivation for the decision were "unworthy of an answer." [113] Similarly, the president issued a long-awaited political statement on nuclear energy in Cincinnati in late October. The statement included plans to expand the government's uranium enrichment plant in Portsmouth, Ohio, creating "6,000 new jobs for southern Ohio." Again, administration spokesmen insisted that neither the substance nor the timing of the announcement was politically motivated.[114]

Republican National Committee

The Republican National Committee was determined to play an active role in the 1976 presidential campaign. The Republicans had learned a bitter lesson from Watergate, which they attributed in part to the complete independence from party supervision of the campaign waged by Richard Nixon's Committee to Reelect the President. The 1976 National Convention therefore adopted a new rule directing the chairman of the RNC to appoint a seven-member Select Committee on Presidential Campaign Affairs to "coordinate closely" with the nominee on his or her "full plan of financial expenditures" and to "review and monitor" such campaign spending.[115]

Without mentioning Watergate, Richard Nixon, or CRP by name, the RNC's Rules Committee had recommended the creation of such a committee "to insure that no candidate's personal campaign shall conduct itself in a manner not in the best interest of the Republican Party" and "to insure that all expenditures are in full accordance not only with the law, but with established ethical practices for political campaigns." [116] As the RNC's official publication, *First Monday,* delicately explained, "It wasn't that the Convention didn't trust the president or any other potential nominee. It was just felt that the party should be more accountable for the presidential campaign than it has sometimes been in the past." [117]

Besides consulting with the candidate, the RNC planned to spend the full $3.2 million allowed by law on the presidential campaign. To accomplish this, it hoped to raise $23 million in 1976,[118] later revising the goal to $18 million.[119] In fact, the committee exceeded this target by raising more than $20 million, as is shown in Table 7-11. Yet, in spite of its attempts at coordination, an apparent failure of communication between the RNC and the Ford committee prevented the national committee from playing a full role in the presidential campaign.

The RNC spent only $1,186,724 on the presidential campaign, a more accurate figure than the $1,481,099 indicated in Table 7-11. The categories of expenditures are indicated in Table 7-12. The Campaign Task Force, which spent $161,977, refers to a group including representatives from the Ford and Reagan campaigns that worked in advance of the convention to write a campaign plan for the eventual nominee, whoever he might be. The Task Force total includes $50,000 spent on a project supervised by Richard Thaxton, director of the Political/Research Division of the RNC, to distribute anti-Carter materials to newspaper editors. Consisting of reprints of articles, editorials, and columns, the materials were sent out in four packets in July and August 1976. They included critiques of Carter's 1970 gubernatorial campaign, his subsequent record as governor of Georgia, his positions in the 1976 campaign, and the Senate record of Walter Mondale.

The RNC's Select Committee on the Presidential Campaign, which was responsible for ensuring that there were no violations of the law by the Ford campaign, met but had no expenses that were not distributed elsewhere in the categories in Table 7-12.

After the election, the RNC deposited an additional $1 million in a trust fund to liquidate any unpaid liabilities incurred by the President Ford Committee. This money was returned to the RNC in full on December 1, 1977. In addition, the RNC spent $427,300 on special projects and ballot security and $158,700 on legal fees. These disbursements are distributed among other expenditure categories in Table 7-11.

After the election, finance chairman Jeremiah Milbank said that the RNC had informed the Ford campaign at the time of the national

Table 7-11
Republican National Committee, Statement of Cash Receipts and
Disbursements for Year Ended December 31, 1976

Cash balance, January 1, 1976	$1,004,056
Cash receipts:	
Sustainer program	10,112,078
Campaigner program	666,575
Major Contributors	3,974,800
Dinners	4,286,789
Total income from individual contributions	19,040,242
Miscellaneous	1,493,232
Total cash receipts	$20,533,474
Cash disbursements:	
Fund raising	6,309,164
Party development	3,556,722
Candidate support	2,574,151
Presidential support [a]	2,481,099
Political operations	1,166,092
Affiliated groups	508,453
Administration	985,514
Executive	527,434
Research	414,905
Graphic services	307,320
Communications	273,375
Computer services	202,095
Other	825,700
Total cash disbursements	$20,132,024
Excess of cash receipts over cash disbursements	401,450
Cash and temporary cash investment balance, December 31, 1976	$1,405,506

[a] Includes $1,000,000 trust fund

SOURCE: Republican National Committee

convention that it had raised and was making available the full $3.2 million. The fact that this money was not fully utilized, Milbank told the RNC, was "hard to comprehend in view of the closeness of the election and the fact that it was also expected to be close well before it took place." [120]

Of the $20.5 million raised by the RNC, more than half came from direct-mail solicitations, including mailgrams over President Ford's signature.[121] Most of the mail receipts, $10.1 million, were part of the Republican Sustainer Program of contributors of up to $99. Another $667,000 was raised through the Campaign Program of $100-$499 contributions. The Major Contributor category indicated in Table 7-11 includes three contributor programs: Victory Associates, $500 to $999;

Republican National Associates, $1,000 to $9,999; and Republican Eagles, $10,000 and above. A series of "Salute to the President" dinners, held simultaneously on October 7 in more than 20 cities linked by closed-circuit television, raised $4,287,000. (The party, however, had hoped to raise $7 million to $8 million from the $1,000-a-plate affairs).[122] The RNC incurred expenses of $790,000 in connection with these dinners. In addition, $1,030,000 of the receipts were distributed to various state Republican committees. These disbursements are included under fund-raising costs in Table 7-11.

Other fund-raising events included a $100-a-plate dinner featuring vice presidential nominee Robert Dole in Birmingham, Alabama, which raised $80,000, and a televised fund-raising appeal by unsuccessful candidate Ronald Reagan.[123] Telephone solicitations raised $726,500, which is distributed among the categories in Table 7-11 depending on the size of the contribution.

During 1975-76, the RNC received $28,592,344 in contributions, with greater receipts than its Democratic counterpart at every contribution level. At the less-than-$100 level, the RNC raised $16,303,387, more

Table 7-12
RNC Presidential Allocation 1976

Campaign Task Force	$ 161,977
Carter Chase Team	10,341
Reagan film (15 percent)	77,362
Dane advertising and postage (15 percent)	360,750
Heritage allocation	13,751
Transportation	29,904
Postage	6,179
New releases	7,421
Mailings	17,875
Surveys and telephone	65,970
Miscellaneous costs	7,194
Election night dinner	25,000
Printing and reproduction	147,340
Salaries	3,208
Taxes and benefits	462
Trust fund	1,000,000
Phone bank allocation	234,255
As of Feb. 28, 1977	$2,168,989
Souvenirs	7,679
Legal services	10,056
Total	$2,186,724
Less: Refund from trust fund	1,000,000
Allocation as of December 31, 1977	$1,186,724

SOURCE: Republican National Committee

than twice the Democratic receipts in that category. These small contributions accounted for 57 percent of the RNC's income, slightly less than the 63 percent they brought to the DNC but still a surprisingly high figure. Another $1,844,882 was raised in contributions of $100-$499, and $7,434,870 came from 6,374 contributors of $500-$9,999. In the highest contribution category, those of $10,000 and above, the RNC had almost eight times as many contributors as the DNC. Two-hundred and fifty-five individuals contributed a total of $3,009,205 in this category.[124]

In a few instances, improprieties were alleged concerning RNC fund-raising activities. One incident involved a letter sent to Spanish-American federal employees and contractors by Ben Fernandez, chairman of the Republican Hispanic Assembly. The "Dear Amigos" letter urged attendance at a testimonial dinner for Spanish Americans in the Ford administration and asked for a minimum contribution of $30. To columnists Jack Anderson and Les Whitten, the letter appeared to carry an implied threat of reprisal against employees and contractors who failed to make the contribution.[125]

Anderson and Whitten also exposed alleged illegalities in an "agency agreement" between the RNC and the National Republican Congressional Committee. The RNC had authorized the NRCC to act as its agent in disbursing funds to congressional candidates. The congressional committee, which had extra funds, thus was able to contribute the national committee's legal limit in addition to its own legal limit to Republican candidates in 33 closely contested congressional races. Anderson and Whitten contended that the agreements were illegal unless accompanied by an actual transfer of funds from the RNC to the NRCC, and counted 66 violations of the law. They quoted FEC General Counsel John Murphy, however, as saying that the procedure was legal and that party officials had kept the commission fully informed, although the commission had not officially ruled on the issue.[126]

Another incident involved not the RNC, but an offer made by a private company to Republican state and local committees urging them to exceed their legal spending limits. Regulations adopted by the FEC allowed state and local political party committees to spend up to $1,000 each on behalf of the presidential nominee. Richard Rovsek and Associates, a New York sales promotion firm, sent catalogues of Ford-Dole campaign materials to Republican committees throughout the country. The last page of the catalogue stated, in capital letters, "You are being sent information clearly stating that the $1,000 limit on campaign materials for each state and local headquarters do not apply to the items in this catalogue. You may spend as much on these materials as you feel is necessary to elect the Ford-Dole team. If you have any questions on this call: The President Ford Committee in Washington."

The Ford committee in fact denied any connection with the catalogue. General counsel Robert Visser, who called it "an invitation to people to break the law," wrote a letter to the FEC informing it of the catalogue's existence and stating that the Ford committee was not responsible for it. Rovsek President David C. Esty then conceded that "what we said was completely erroneous. It was a dumb mistake." He said that no order of more than $1,000 had been received, although he characterized sales as good, and that all orders were being acknowledged with a statement correcting the catalogue and informing the party committees that their purchases must be charged against their $1,000 expenditure limit.[127]

Internal Communications

Probably the most significant difference in spending between the two major parties was in the area of internal communications by unions, corporations, and membership associations. While Jimmy Carter was the beneficiary of more than $1.1 million in reported expenditures and perhaps $11 million in total expenditures by labor unions, four corporations and one membership association spent only $44,249 on internal communications favoring President Ford.[128]

The membership association was the National Rifle Association, an active opponent of gun-control legislation, which spent $13,204 urging its members to vote for Ford. Another $88,324 was spent by the NRA for 11 Senate and 126 House candidates, mostly Republicans.

The highest spender of the four corporations was Libbey-Owens-Ford Co., which spent $13,096 on a letter from President Robert C. Wingerter to all of the company's stockholders and executives stating that "an Administration headed by President Ford will make far more common sense . . . than one led by Jimmy Carter." [129] The $8,385 spent by Dresser Industries Inc., a manufacturer of oil industry equipment, included a letter from Chairman of the Board John V. James to the company's 26,000 shareholders stating that "Mr. Ford and his party . . . believe that government should seek to ensure an environment in which business can, with a minimum of interference, achieve its full productive and profitable potential," and that the management of Dresser "strongly recommends that you vote for the election of President Ford." [130] Cooper Industries Inc. spent $5,079 and Pepsico Inc. $4,485 on similar communications.

No corporations sent out internal communications on behalf of congressional candidates; the $31,045 spent by the four companies for Ford represents the total corporate spending for all federal offices. This contrasts greatly with the amounts spent by labor unions: more than a million dollars for Carter and close to another million for congressional candidates, almost all of whom were Democrats. As R. Heath Larry, vice-chairman of the United States Steel Corp., who became chairman of the National Association of Manufacturers after the election, admitted, "We were quite outclassed." [131]

The low level of business involvement was a disappointment for Robert A. Mosbacher, chairman of American Business Volunteers for Ford. Mosbacher, who had been national finance chairman of the Ford primary campaign, wrote to the presidents of the 1,000 largest corporations in the country in early September, urging them to send appeals on behalf of the president to all their executives and stockholders.[132] It was equally disappointing to the Republican vice presidential candidate, Senator Dole, who had exhorted corporations to become involved in politics. Chiding a group of Lexington, Kentucky, businessmen for their lack of activism, he told them, "You're always so nonpartisan, you're going to let George Meany take over the country." [133]

The United States Chamber of Commerce also encouraged businessmen to become involved in the election. In September, the chamber sent a pamphlet to 20,000 of its members informing them that, "for the first time," the new campaign laws permitted business "to enter the election competition — on an equal footing" with labor. The pamphlet described in detail relevant provisions of the campaign laws, provided sample letters to stockholders and executives, and "most emphatically" urged business leaders to "grasp these political rights and utilize them to the fullest." [134]

The response to these exhortations, according to Mosbacher, was "pitifully small . . . appalling." He placed the blame on the post-Watergate climate and the concomitant fear of scandals, declaring that "a few well-publicized excesses have influenced most [corporations] to adopt the ostrich approach." [135] Fred Quigley, vice-president of Dow Chemical Co. and chairman of the National Association of Manufacturers' Public Affairs Committee, offered essentially the same assessment. He said businessmen were "afraid of a bad press. They're afraid they will be accused of being illegal, or of having undue influence. They're gun-shy." [136] Other analysts saw deeper reasons relating to the lack of a single "business" point of view on major public issues. Michael J. Malbin concluded that "it may be impossible, structurally, for business ever to muster the unity of purpose" that labor and other groups possess.[137]

Independent Expenditures

The Ford campaign took a completely neutral attitude toward independent expenditures, which, under the *Buckley* decision, could not be restricted so long as they were completely uncoordinated with the regular campaign. Roy Hughes, treasurer of the President Ford Committee, said the committee's policy was: "We are prohibited from encouraging it. The only thing we can do is advise people about the Supreme Court decision. There can be no overt encouragement." [138]

A total of $216,715 worth of independent expenditures by 87 individuals and committees was reported to the FEC to have been made on behalf of Ford.[139] The FEC report did not differentiate preconvention and postconvention expenditures, making it impossible to determine what portion of this amount was spent on the general election. In any event the amount spent, although much larger than the amounts spent on behalf of Carter, still was not a particularly significant aspect of the campaign. Most potential spenders were either confused by the new election laws or afraid of overstepping, or appearing to overstep, the requirements for complete independence from the official campaign. The prevalent attitude was expressed by Peter Secchia, a Grand Rapids businessman and founder of Friends of the First Family, which raised and spent $33,000 for pro-Ford advertisements during the Ohio primary but decided against continuing in the fall campaign. "We just want to wrap up our books and get out," said Secchia. "Why give the President headaches?" [140]

The FEC was called upon several times to draw the fine line defining independence and thus making independent expenditures legitimate. In one case, the FEC told Ralph Goettler of Columbus, Ohio, that his political consulting firm, Goettler Associates Inc., could contract with a Ford supporter to make independent expenditures on Ford's behalf. Goettler sought advice from the FEC because he was also the sole shareholder and chairman of the board of National Direct Mail Services Inc. The latter firm did campaign work for Ford during the presidential primaries under the direction of Robert Odell, the executive director of finances of Ford's primary campaign committee. Odell was on a leave of absence from his position as president of National Direct Mail Services Inc.

Although the tie to the Ford campaign prohibited National Direct Mail Services Inc. from contracting with an individual or committee wishing to make independent expenditures on behalf of Ford, the FEC decided, it would not necessarily prohibit Goettler's other firm from doing so. Goettler Associates Inc. could enter into such a contract, FEC Associate Counsel N. Bradley Litchfield wrote Goettler, "if, as you represented in [your] letter, you 'have not been involved in operation of' National Direct Mail Services, Inc. In reaching this conclusion, I assume that your noninvolvement means that neither Mr. Odell nor any other person connected with the operations of your Washington company has communicated to you or any other person representing Goettler Associates, Inc. any information concerning the plans, projects or needs of President Ford's Campaign." [141]

In spite of the favorable FEC ruling, Goettler eventually decided against becoming involved with independent expenditures. "It's got too many headaches in it," he said. "Today it isn't whether you're guilty or not, it's whether it could be inferred that you're guilty." But he nevertheless lamented the effect of the new campaign laws in reducing the amount of campaign activity, saying, "The average voter can't learn this year from a neighbor, or a pamphlet stuffed in his door, what is going on in the Presidential race. All he has is a couple of dumb debates." [142]

In a similar case, however, the FEC rejected a draft opinion by its general counsel, John Murphy, that would have permitted independent expenditures by a former Ford volunteer. The commission decided by a 4-2 vote that John H. Wetenhall, Jr., a Ford volunteer throughout the Republican primaries but not connected with the general election campaign, could not join others in forming a political committee organized to solicit contributions in order to make independent expenditures on Ford's behalf. Although not authorized to raise or expend funds and unpaid by the Ford committee for his work, Wetenhall did receive $2,500 in "minor traveling expenses" incurred in his field activities with the Ford committee. [143]

A further damper was placed on independent expenditures in late September when the FEC announced limitations on independent contributions. Independent contributions are contributions to a committee that is making independent expenditures. Although the Supreme Court ruled in *Buckley* that the latter could not be restricted, the former could. Individuals could contribute no more than $1,000 to a committee making expenditures on behalf of one candidate for federal office, and no more than $5,000 to a committee making expenditures on behalf of more than one candidate. Political committees could contribute up to $5,000 to either type of committee. [144] The effect of these contribution limits on at least one committee was expressed by James M. Day, treasurer of the Kansas City-based Vote for Ford Committee. "The day they announced that, our committee was disbanded," he said. "The fund-raiser said you'll never be able to make it work without big chunks of seed money." [145]

An effort to circumvent the independent contribution limit brought to the FEC's attention two Californians who had set up six independent committees. The committees were Businessmen for President Ford, Students for President Ford, Democrats for President Ford, Senior Citizens for President Ford, Independent Voters for President Ford, and the Anybody but Carter Committee. The registration papers of all six committees listed Charles F. Reade, Jr., as national chairman and William F. Morrison as treasurer, and the committee's address in Los Angeles. In an appeal to potential contributors on the Businessmen for President Ford letterhead, Reade asserted that although "private contributions can no longer be accepted" by Ford, "the federal law does authorize you to still independently assist his campaign through contributions up to $5,000 for each" of the six committees. Robert Visser, counsel for the official President Ford Committee, said that when he learned of the existence of the six committees in mid-September he "turned the matter over to the FEC, and they're reviewing it to see who this guy [Reade] is." [146]

The FEC investigated the committees and determined that they "appear to be affiliated" and to support only a single candidate, thus imposing a joint $1,000 limit on contributions to all six committees. The commission notified Reade that it had "reason to believe" that he was in violation of federal law. Three weeks later Reade advised the commission that all but one of the committees had been "terminated" and that contributions in excess of the legal limit had been returned to donors. In accordance with its statutory directive to seek voluntary compliance as an alternative to prosecution, the FEC then dropped the case.[147]

Another independent expenditure aroused controversy not over compliance but because of its allegedly misleading text. At issue was an advertisement for which Herbert Hafif paid $8,500 to have placed in the *Los Angeles Times* on October 27. It carried a heading in large letters asking, "Can a man no longer trusted by the co-chairman of his national steering committee be trusted by you?" In smaller letters it proclaimed "A personal warning about Jimmy Carter by Herbert Hafif." In the text of the ad, Hafif characterized Carter as "a mean, vindictive man" possessing neither "the knowledge nor the background to run a broad-based, responsible presidency."

Robert S. Strauss, chairman of the Democratic National Committee, disputed Hafif's claim to being cochairman of Carter's national steering committee. "I'm on the National Carter Steering Committee. He's not a member of it and never has been," Strauss said of Hafif. "Now at one time he may have been a member of some Carter committee out in California because he had something to do with the campaign early in the primary, and they fired him." A spokeswoman for the Carter campaign also asserted that Hafif had been fired from the campaign before the California primary, and termed his ad "political sour grapes." The independent ad nevertheless caught the fancy of the President Ford Committee, which paid to have it reprinted in a number of newspapers across the country on the day before the election, bringing a Democratic charge of a last-ditch effort at deceptive advertising.[148]

Ford Media

Following a strategy-planning conference of high-level Ford campaign officials held in Vail, Colorado, shortly after the Republican National Convention, newly selected campaign manager James A. Baker III announced that the campaign was budgeting $10 million for advertising. This allocation of almost half of the total campaign budget was justified because mass-media advertising would "reach the largest number of people in the most efficient way." [149]

The advertising budget was revised upward later in the campaign. The actual amount spent reached $11,495,000, or 53 percent of the total campaign budget, illustrating one of the principle effects of the spending limits in effect in 1976 and the resulting reliance on "cost-effective" campaign techniques. (See Table 7-13)

Table 7-13
Ford Media Expenditures, General Election

Network	$2,500,000	
Spot TV	3,885,000	
Radio	1,490,000	
Print	1,290,000	
Subtotal	$9,165,000	
Media		$ 9,165,000
Production		1,655,000
Campaign materials		675,000
Total		$11,495,000

SOURCE: Bailey, Deardourff, and Eyre Inc.

The most expensive media component was television time, for which $2,500,000 was paid to the networks and $3,885,000 to local stations. Another $1,490,000 was spent for radio time, of which all but about $150,000 was for local stations. Table 7-14 shows the amounts budgeted for local television and radio broadcasting in each of the states. The total amount actually spent on local television, as shown in Table 7-13, is almost exactly equal to the budgeted amount. The actual amount spent on local radio, however, was approximately $1,340,000, or 75 percent more than the budgeted total of $764,400. Newspaper space cost the campaign $1,290,000. No money was spent for magazine advertising or for rental of space for outdoor advertising.

These costs reflect only the amount paid for time and space. An additional $1,655,000 was spent on the production costs for television, radio, and print advertising. This figure includes the costs of preparing and shipping the film and tape to the various stations and newspapers.

Campaign materials entailed an additional expenditure of $675,000. These included buttons, brochures, bumper stickers, lawn signs, and banners, as well as the shipping costs to the various states. This brought the total spending to $11,495,000.

The Ford general election advertising campaign was run by the team of Doug Bailey and John Deardourff. Bailey and Deardourff had achieved a widespread reputation as a Republican advertising team with their success in the 1974 gubernatorial campaigns of William Milliken in Michigan and James Rhodes in Ohio, and were called in to revitalize the Ford campaign shortly after the convention.[150]

Table 7-14
Ford Broadcasting Expenditures by State, General Election

	TV	Radio		TV	Radio
Ala.	$ 48,100	$12,200	Mo.	$130,400	$ 28,800
Alaska	—	4,000	Mont.	4,000	3,600
Ariz.	2,300	—	Neb.	—	—
Ark.	—	—	Nev.	14,900	3,100
Calif.	544,500	87,700	N.H.	—	—
Colo.	—	—	N.J.	—	6,600
Conn.	54,000	17,100	N.M.	11,300	3,000
Del.	—	900	N.Y.	612,700	95,000
D.C.	144,800	10,800	N.C.	50,000	15,900
Fla.	135,900	27,400	N.D.	9,600	3,200
Ga.	—	200	Ohio	259,700	58,400
Hawaii	9,300	5,400	Okla.	32,600	6,200
Idaho	—	—	Ore.	61,500	17,100
Ill.	278,000	48,700	Pa.	329,900	58,700
Ind.	66,700	19,900	R.I.	36,400	7,200
Iowa	—	—	S.C.	44,800	8,000
Kan.	—	—	S.D.	6,800	5,300
Ky.	26,500	5,700	Tenn.	53,900	15,500
La.	55,500	12,000	Texas	220,700	55,900
Maine	—	—	Utah	—	—
Md.	67,500	15,300	Vt.	—	—
Mass.	—	2,200	Va.	55,200	22,600
Mich.	344,000	36,100	Wash.	83,200	22,800
Minn.	—	—	W.Va.	—	—
Miss.	21,600	3,200	Wis.	67,500	18,700
			Wyo.	—	—
			Total	$3,883,800	$764,400

Note: State figures indicate the amounts budgeted by the President Ford Committee, not amounts actually spent.

SOURCE: *Broadcasting*, February 21, 1977, p. 70.

The advertisements were produced by an agency, Campaign '76, set up especially for the campaign. Malcolm D. MacDougall, creative director of Campaign '76, explained the advantages of using such an in-house agency: "The savings are enormous and the speed probably can't be matched by any regular agency. There's very little wheel spinning." Campaign '76 produced 60-second commercials and five-minute commercials for less than $10,000 each according to MacDougall, while the average cost to an advertising agency for the production of a 30-second product commercial is $25,000.[151] MacDougall found, in spite of the record sum being spent on advertising, that money was scarce. He believed that the necessity to be budget conscious, however, was actually beneficial in terms of campaign efficiency. "All peripheral campaigns have gone by the boards," he noted. "Nothing aimed at the young, nothing aimed at the old. It's the best thing that could happen — we concentrate on what we're doing and there's less wasted effort." [152]

The new team's first set of television commercials, in a reversal of the approach taken by the primary-campaign advertising directors, sought to portray Gerald Ford the man rather than the institution of the presidency. One five-minute commercial took as its theme the idea that "sometimes a man's family can say a lot about the man." It featured Ford's three sons speaking about their father interspersed with paternal comments by the president, followed by a hug for the president from his daughter and a voice-over pronouncing the Fords "a close, loving American family." [153] Other commercials showed the president in his shirtsleeves with his tie loosened, talking to workers in a print shop, or leaning on a thresher as he chatter with farmers.[154]

The Ford campaign also made use of "negative" advertising. A series of commercials that were released in mid-October each showed a single voter saying something positive about the president, followed by six or eight criticizing Carter. The commercials' credibility was enhanced by the nonecstatic nature of the praise given Ford (he is characterized as "stable" and "not erratic"), and the most effective anti-Carter comments were considered to be those elicited from residents of Georgia: for example, a woman who said, "It would be good to have a president from Georgia — but not Carter," and a man who claimed that neither he nor any of his friends could remember anything Carter had done as governor.[155]

These "negative" commercials were all done with reasonably good taste, and there were never any charges of improprieties or dirty politics. Even Tony Schwartz, who took over some of Carter's advertising late in the campaign, said he found "nothing wrong" with the opposition's tactics. He added that the Republicans' commercials were "far superior to their candidate." [156]

The last 10 days of the Ford campaign were characterized by the most intensive media effort in presidential campaign history — a nationwide "saturation" of television and radio at a cost of $4 million. The mainstay of the campaign was a series of 30-minute television commercials starring former baseball player Joe Garagiola that were shown in the key states of Pennsylvania, California, Illinois, Ohio, and New York in coordination with campaign trips to those states. Designed to simulate news broadcasts, the commercials featured Garagiola narrating film clips of the president's activities of the day and then conducting an interview, which the media dubbed "softball": "How many leaders have you dealt with, Mr. President?" "One hundred and twenty-four leaders of countries around the world, Joe." Each program cost about $75,000 — $30,000 for time, $30,000 for production, and about $15,000 for promotion and other expenses. The "Joe and Jerry Show" was considered a success by Ford strategists. Campaign manager Stuart K. Spencer said the program provided "the most intelligent use of the man's abilities and a maximum restraint on his liabilities," and John Deardourff, who developed the idea for the programs, said that they "get us out of the almost impossible-to-control situation of the stump speech, which inevitably leads to the kind of student anti-Carter stuff we don't want, and into a relaxed, informal, positive atmosphere that works well." [157]

The television programs were augmented by a series of eight five-minute radio addresses on such issues as national defense, tax policy, crime, and inflation. The addresses were broadcast over some 400 to 500 stations on the Mutual Network, at a cost of $47,000.[158]

Newspaper advertising, although it entailed a much smaller budget than electronic media, actually generated more controversy. One ad, which was run in 21 black weeklies, carried the headline "President Ford is quietly getting the job done" over a photograph of the president with Vernon Jordan, executive director of the National Urban League, the Rev. Jesse Jackson, director of People United to Save Humanity, and Stanley Scott, director for Africa of the United States Agency for International Development. Jordan, in a wire to Ford, protested against the "unauthorized use" of the photograph "that implies my endorsement of your candidacy." He noted that the Urban League was a tax-exempt agency that did not endorse political candidates, and requested that "the use of the picture be discontinued at once and that the President Ford Committee make a prompt and public apology for the deceptive action it has taken." [159]

The Ford committee withdrew the picture from its advertisements, but refused to acknowledge any wrongdoing. Peter Teeley, the President Ford Committee's press secretary, said the picture was a "public picture" and that "there is no reference that the individuals pictured with the President are endorsing the President." Teeley nevertheless conceded that, in view of the controversy generated by the picture, its continued use "doesn't make any sense" and that a different picture would be used with the advertisement.[160]

Another controversial Ford advertisement, shown in 350 small-town newspapers in 22 states, reproduced a *Newsweek* cover with President Ford's picture on it and the cover of the *Playboy* with the infamous Carter interview. The advertisement suggested that "one good way to decide this election" was to read the two magazines. When asked if he really hoped that the voters would read the Carter interview, however, an official at the Ford campaign admitted that "in the market where that ad is running they don't get *Playboy.*" Carter objected to the ad, calling it "highly misleading" and accusing the president of trying "to insinuate that I'm a special case and have low morals simply because I granted an interview with *Playboy.*" *Newsweek* also objected to the advertisement, charging that the Ford committee had not sought its permission to reproduce the *Newsweek* cover. Ford defended the use of the advertisement, however, and added that he had refused to be interviewed by *Playboy* because "I don't think the President of the United States ought to have an interview in a magazine featuring photographs of unclad women." [161]

States

Because of the strict spending limitation imposed by law, and the unprecedentedly large amount budgeted for media, relatively little money could be reserved for other forms of campaign activity. Ford treasurer Hughes complained early in the campaign, "We're operating with only a third of the funds available for the 1972 election. It's going to be very hard to make our campaign look like Republican campaigns of the past, and appearance is vital to building political momentum." [162]

A total of $3 million was budgeted to local campaign activities in the 50 states, and $2.8 million actually spent, as shown in Table 7-15. More than 60 percent of this amount was allocated to 10 major industrial states that Ford strategists considered crucial for building a majority in the electoral college and which September polls showed to be within the President's grasp: New York, New Jersey, Pennsylvania, Ohio, Illinois, Michigan, Wisconsin, Texas, California, and Florida.[163]

Even in these key states, however, the amounts of money available were not high. The situation in New York was typical. The Ford campaign had only $232,000 to spend in that state, compared with $3 million spent on behalf of Richard Nixon in 1972. Phillip H. Weinberg, New

York State coordinator for Ford-Dole, observed, "Everybody here says they don't see a campaign taking place, but what they're used to costs a lot of money. We can't afford things like sound tracks and bunting and a lot of brass bands at rallies."

Weinberg said the Ford-Dole campaign in New York had the services of one car, one station wagon, and a truck rented day-to-day for upstate deliveries. "And I wouldn't have done that if there wasn't a United Parcel strike," he said. "In 1972, we didn't even think of that, much less worry. You just had it done." [164]

Thomas H. Kean, director of the campaign in New Jersey, also lamented the austerity budget with which he had to work, and added, "People from local political organizations don't seem to understand this

Table 7-15
President Ford Committee, Budget and Performance Summary —
General Election

Chairman	$ 75,302
Communications	196,721
Administration	1,079,908
Voter groups	1,154,342
Vice presidential campaign	1,508,363
Polling and research	516,605
Political	1,138,275
Campaign '76	12,355,000
Volunteers	17,777
Advocates	263,912
Citizens for Ford	35,470
States	2,834,941
Presidential travel	1,338,061
Legal and accounting	401,738
June/July 1977 expenses not allocated to cost centers	35,542
Accounts payable and closeout	24,784
Federal funds budget plan	$22,976,741
Less:	
Underruns	
Rebates: Press	(1,156,741)
Furniture	
Telephone escrow reserve	
Federal funds total	$21,820,000
Republican National Committee (RNC) Fund:	
Budgeted	1,186,167
Reserve	—
Total RNC fund	1,186,167
Total	$23,006,167
Exempt compliance fund	63,559

SOURCE: President Ford Committee, prepared June 6, 1977.

when they come to our headquarters asking for bumper stickers, literature and buttons. These are the trimmings of a campaign that fuel local enthusiasm, and when somebody wants to go door to door with literature and can't get it, the situation certainly doesn't help our image at all." [165]

Another traditional part of the political landscape, the special committees aimed at specific ethnic and occupational groups, was diminished in 1976. Each group organized under the umbrella of "People for Ford" was given a $100,000 operating budget, although many of them had asked for $500,000. [166]

State and local Republican Party organizations in some areas tried to take up some of the slack left by the campaign's underfinanced effort, but they too were hindered by a spending limit of $1,000 for each committee. In an interview, for example, Ray Hutchinson, chairman of the Texas Republican Party, asked, "You want to see our entire contribution to the president's campaign? There it is on the shelf over there: 5,000 buttons and 75,000 stickers. The law says we can spend no more than $1,000 and we spent $1,020, so the last $20 is probably a felony." [167]

In Virginia, city and county Republican committees throughout the state paid for phone banks with which to poll voters on their preferences and then to encourage registration by those thought to favor Ford. A spokesman for the state Republican committee said that the FEC had ruled that the phone banks did not have to be charged against the spending limits if the callers did not directly advocate the election of the president. [168]

Other Expenditures

Polling for the President Ford Committee was done by Bob Teeter of Market Opinion Research Inc. Table 7-16 shows $521,537 spent on polls during the general election period, a slight discrepancy from the $516,605 reported by the Ford committee under "Polling and Research" in Table 7-15. The Ford campaign spent $263,912 on its advocates program, under which 25 surrogates for the president campaigned on his behalf. The program included every cabinet officer except the secretaries of State and Defense and the attorney general. The most sought-after, albeit hard-to-get advocate, was defeated presidential rival Reagan, who did not campaign until October and then spoke more of the Republicans' conservative platform than of the presidential nominee. [169]

The vice presidential campaign cost $1.5 million, slightly more than the $1.3 million spent on presidential travel, indicative of the fact that Senator Dole had taken on the brunt of the campaign burden while President Ford was pursuing the Rose Garden Strategy.

The President Ford Committee paid $64,000 in legal and accounting costs associated with complying with FECA requirements. These costs were paid from privately raised funds and were exempt from the $21.8 million expenditure limit.

Table 7-16
President Ford Committee, Polling Costs

Postconvention Studies	
U.S. nationals	$ 57,750
Statewide studies	429,700
Special projects [a]	11,987
Consulting	22,100
Total	$521,537

[a] Special projects included such activities as focus groups and advertising tests.

SOURCE: Market Opinion Research Inc.

Ford's Congressional Ethics

During the presidential campaign a number of charges were raised concerning the propriety of Ford's actions when he was a member of Congress. The allegations centered on his use of campaign contributions for personal expenses, his role during Watergate in 1972, and his golfing vacations paid for by corporations.

An informant supplied the FBI with information alleging that Gerald Ford used campaign contributions from the Seafarers International Union and the Marine Engineers Beneficial Association for personal expenses while serving as a congressman from Michigan.[170] On July 13, 1976, the FBI sent a memorandum to Attorney General Edward Levi informing him of the allegation. Levi met with FBI Director Clarence M. Kelley before sending a letter to Special Prosecutor Charles Ruff informing him of the charges.[171] On August 19, 1976, one day after Ford had received the Republican nomination, Ruff issued subpoenas for the records of two Republican committees in Kent County, Michigan, from 1964 to 1974.[172] At the same time, subpoenas were issued for the records of the Marine Engineers Beneficial Association.[173] The White House learned of the investigation in mid-September and on September 21, 1976, *The Wall Street Journal* broke the story.

Within a week, the charges became a campaign issue. Walter Mondale, the Democratic vice presidential candidate, charged that the president had failed to learn the lessons of Watergate. Senator Dole, Mondale's opponent, referred to the investigation as "nothing but election year politics." [174] By the end of the month both Carter and Mondale called on the president to respond to the allegations, which he did at a press conference on September 30, 1976. Ford contended that he had been given a clean bill of health during his confirmation process for vice president in 1974. He noted that his tax returns and records had been thoroughly investigated then by the Justice Department and the FBI. The president said that he had asked his staff not to contact the Justice Department and the special prosecutor because any inquiry " 'would undoubtedly be misconstrued, and I don't want any such allegations being made by anybody.' " [175]

After Ford's news conference, Jimmy Carter issued a statement saying he accepted the president's remarks, and that as far as he was concerned the matter was settled. It was conjectured by some that the Georgian may have taken this position because news reporters had discovered that while governor he and his family had been guests of the Brunswick Pulp and Paper Co. at its plantation.

An IRS audit of Ford was leaked to the press. [176] It showed that in 1972 Ford paid most of his daily living expenses from honorarium funds. The IRS disallowed clothing and plane ticket expenses paid for by campaign funds. The IRS took the position that Ford could not use campaign funds for personal expenses. Ford reimbursed his campaign committee for approximately $1,167 for plane expenses and paid an additional $436 in taxes as a result of the audit.

Special Prosecutor Ruff announced his findings on October 14, 1976. Ruff declared that the "evidence developed during the investigation was not corroborative of the allegation on which it was predicated. Nor did evidence disclosed during the inquiry into that allegation give reason to believe that any other violation of law had occurred. Accordingly, the matter has now been closed." [177]

During this time newspaper stories reported that the president had been the guest of William G. Whyte, the Washington representative for United States Steel, at several golf outings between 1964 and 1973. Whyte was a close personal friend of Ford. The White House disclosed on September 28, 1976, that the president also had been the guest of Bethlehem Steel Co., Firestone Tire & Rubber Co., and the Aluminum Co. of America before becoming vice president.

Several commentators noted that the code of ethics adopted by the House of Representatives in 1968 barred members and their staff assistants from accepting any "gift of substantial value from any person, organization or corporation that have a direct interest in legislation before Congress." [178] Ford said he did not believe he had violated this regulation, since he did not feel the golf outings were gifts of substantial value.

John Dean, former White House counsel, in his book *Blind Ambition,* charged that Ford while a congressman at the request of the White House had sought to prevent an investigation by the House Banking and Currency Committee of Watergate-related material. Dean claimed that Richard K. Cook, then a White House liaison aide, met with Ford and urged him to defeat a motion by Wright Patman, D-Texas, chairman of the Banking Committee.[179] The motion would have given Patman the right to subpoena witnesses and records relating to the financing of the Watergate break-in at DNC headquarters. The motion was defeated on a 21-15 vote with six Democrats joining with the Republicans. Ford denied meeting with Cook on this matter. At his vice presidential confirmation hearings Ford stated that he had sought to block the investigation on his own.

Special Prosecutor Ruff stated in a letter to Rep. John Conyers, Jr., D-Mich., that he would not investigate charges that Ford attempted to block Patman's efforts to launch an investigation of the Watergate matter, since there were no indications of criminal intent. Conyers and two House Democrats, Elizabeth Holtzman of New York and Henry S. Reuss of Wisconsin, had sought such an investigation as a result of the Dean allegation.

Clearly, the Ford campaign was harmed by the allegations. One observer wrote, "In a way, the President was . . . victimized by a post-Watergate zealotry for total exposure of the affairs of public servants and by the public's seeming insistence that they live up to standards that few other men meet." [180] Others questioned the timing of the investigation by the office of the special prosecutor during the campaign. Former Special Prosecutor Leon Jaworski was quoted as saying, "I wouldn't conduct an investigation of this kind at this time myself . . . but would rather let the investigation be conducted after the election." [181] Two syndicated columnists, Evans and Novak, claimed that while the "Special Prosecution Force was a skeleton staff with only two full-time lawyers plus Ruff . . . its name still evokes public memories of its glory days under Archibald Cox and Jaworski. Thus, new accounts of a Special Prosecutor's investigation were far more lethal than of any inquiry through regular Justice Department channels." [182]

Elizabeth Dole

Charges of conflict of interest during the campaign were brought against Mary Elizabeth Hanford Dole, wife of Republican vice presidential nominee Senator Dole and a member of the Federal Trade Commission. After Senator Dole was nominated by the Republican convention on August 19, Elizabeth Dole campaigned almost constantly for him and

President Ford. On September 4 she announced that, in order "to assist [Senator Dole] and at the same time to avoid any possible question of conflict of interest," she would take a leave of absence from the FTC from August 19 through Election Day. She said she would return her salary for that period to the Treasury.[183]

Rep. John E. Moss, D-Calif., chairman of the House Commerce Subcommittee on Oversight and Investigations, charged that the leave of absence was insufficient. In a letter to FTC Chairman Calvin J. Collier, Moss wrote that "the partisan political activities of Mrs. Dole are absolutely inconsistent with the quasi-judicial nature of her responsibilities as a commissioner" and would make it "utterly impossible" for her to return as a sitting commissioner after the election and appear "independent and non-partisan." [184] A study conducted by the Library of Congress at Moss's request, however, concluded that a leave of absence was sufficient to comply with federal laws and rules of ethics.[185]

Audit

An audit completed by the FEC in March 1978 showed that the President Ford Committee had spent $21,811,590.40 on the general election campaign.[186] This was only $8,409.60 below the legal limit of $21,820,000 that had been provided in public funds.

In addition, the Ford committee earned $22,062.77 in interest on a portion of the federal grant that was deposited in the bank. As required by law, the interest was returned to the U.S. Treasury along with the rest of the surplus, for a total refund of $30,472.37.

Aside from a few minor bookkeeping errors, the only problem the FEC found with the President Ford Committee's books was that $700 of its $21,820,000 grant had been spent "in payment of parking violation fines levied against PFC employees and/or volunteers while performing campaign-related duties." The auditors recommended that "the payment of parking violation fines be viewed as an unqualified campaign expense and the value be repaid in full to the U.S. Treasury." The Ford committee subsequently repaid the money.

Common Cause and Its Reform Efforts

During the 1976 election Common Cause launched major efforts to reform the presidential campaign process and aspects of the congressional process as well. In the winter of 1975-76, Common Cause began an ambitious project to change the nature of the presidential campaign. The goal of the organization, according to its chairman, John Gardner, was to make it possible for the public to know where the candidates stood on the issues. Gardner noted that a Louis Harris survey showed that the overwhelming majority of those polled agreed with the statement, "the trouble with most leaders is that they treat the public as though it has a 12-year-old mentality." [187] Common Cause hoped to persuade candidates to offer specific solutions for the crucial issues of the day.

In numerous press conferences, speeches, and articles, Gardner detailed what he and his organization thought was wrong with the current system of presidential campaigns and the federal executive branch. For example, Gardner noted:[188]

> Under the hand of the modern political manager the presidential campaigns are becoming enormously skilled exercises in image manipulation and issue evasion. Too many citizens doubt that their concerns will be answered by any candidate and as a result turn away from politics and voting. The candidates, who should be engaged in robust debate with one another, and lively dialogue with the voters, all too often dodge the crucial issues.

Gardner deplored what he called "the unholy trinity" — the alliance of an executive agency with its clientele groups and their congressional supporters. He suggested, "That's why all old programs never die — or even fade away. . . . Both liberals and conservatives have played the game." [189] Common Cause also claimed that government officials did not respond effectively to legitimate citizen grievances and that most Americans felt that their government was not open and honest.

Common Cause suggested that these inadequacies could be corrected by smoking out the candidates. Gardner stressed his central point: "At every opportunity citizens and the press should deliver a clear message to the candidates: Level with us. Don't appeal to our fears. Tell us the hard choices to be made. Propose solutions." [190]

Initially, Common Cause had focused on Congress in its goal "to make Government work." In 1975 this aim was extended to include the White House and the executive branch.[191]

1976 Campaign Efforts

At a news conference held on November 5, 1975, Gardner and David Cohen, president of Common Cause, listed a number of projects their organization would undertake during the 1976 campaign. These included: creating a citizens' network in each primary and caucus state, issuing candidate profiles, monitoring campaign standards, pressing support for key executive branch reforms, and holding congressional and state candidates to the same standards.[192]

Gardner announced that all presidential candidates had been asked to adhere to campaign standards developed by Common Cause. Gardner urged citizens to measure candidates' performance against such standards as public forums, issue discussion, press conferences, political advertising, campaign responsibility, candidate polls, finance disclosure, and officeholder advantages.

The response from the candidates was quick and positive. Eleven of them — Birch Bayh, Lloyd Bentsen, Jimmy Carter, Gerald Ford, Fred Harris, Henry Jackson, Terry Sanford, Milton Shapp, Sargent Shriver, Morris Udall, and George Wallace — agreed to conduct their 1976 campaigns under standards proposed by Common Cause.[193] Only Eugene McCarthy and Ronald Reagan gave negative replies.

McCarthy's letter, signed by Ronald Cocome, his campaign manager, was an example of bluntness rarely found in politics:[194]

> I find the communication insulting. I don't mind telling you that if any citizen controls are needed, they are controls over arrogance. I don't know who the blazes you think you are . . . in short you can take the enclosed standards and stuff them in your ear!

Gardner responded by claiming: "The public will want to know whether these two candidates disagree with the standards or cannot live with them politically." He urged the public and the media to question McCarthy and Reagan "at every possible opportunity." [195]

Why did so many candidates accept the Common Cause standards? Some claimed that they always had supported such standards; others hoped to gain support among the members of Common Cause; and others may have concluded they had nothing to lose. Once they had agreed to the standards, penalties for noncompliance did not exist.

Some commentators were not enthusiastic over these developments, however. James J. Kilpatrick called Gardner "El Supremo," applauded McCarthy's words, and commented, "If John Gardner is hipped on reports, disclosures and standards, let him inspect his own. . . . It is high time . . . that a few men and women in public life stood up to the arrogant demands of the new inquisitors." [196]

Common Cause sought to reduce the tendency of presidential candidates to promise too much. The organization tried to accomplish this task by asking the candidates to state their budget priorities and taxing proposals. On January 15, 1976, Common Cause "called upon all presidential candidates to make public their proposed national budget priorities for 1977." [197] In a pamphlet entitled, "But Mr. Candidate, How Would You Spend Our Tax Dollars?", the organization listed a number of questions to help citizens and the media quiz the candidates.

At a press conference on April 22, 1976, David Cohen "criticized the Democratic presidential candidates for failing to indicate in a candid way their priorities for federal spending, and for failing to let voters know whether the programs they advocate will require higher taxes." [198] Cohen complained that Henry Jackson and Morris Udall had "failed to indicate even in general terms what total impact the programs they advocate would have on the federal budget. . . . Governors Carter and Wallace . . . reveal nothing about the dollar impact of their programs." [199] Cohen expressed similar complaints about Senators Humphrey and Church and Governor Jerry Brown.

Ross Baker, a political scientist, criticized Common Cause's questionnaire, noting that conservative presidential candidates could only have benefited from the attention given to budgetary questions by the liberal candidates who were more eager for Common Cause approval. Baker commented, "Saddling a candidate with specific budget commitments is the biggest substantive liability a campaign can suffer, yet this is what the questionnaire demanded as the price for a Common Cause *imprimatur*." [200]

Common Cause also sought to alter the ways in which the media covered the campaign. Gardner wanted newspapers to produce an issue page, at least once a week, detailing the candidates' stands on given subjects. He urged the television networks to devote prime time to political analysis during the eight weeks before the election.

On August 23, 1976, Common Cause released issue profiles of the two major-party presidential nominees. This was the culmination of a project designed to determine where the candidates "stood on the issues." The "issue profiles" of Ford and Carter were compiled from speeches, national newspapers, newsmagazines, network interviews, forums, wire service stories, local campaign literature, and material released by the candidates. [201] Some of the topics included: jobs and unemployment; taxes; energy and environment; poverty and income support; discrimination; crime, justice, and personal liberties; and international problems and national security.

Common Cause's attempts to alter the style and substance of the 1976 presidential election appeared to have had a limited impact on the voters. The organization's endeavors in the area of budget priorities, by its own admission, were a failure. The issue profiles provided a handy reference source but were probably filed and forgotten by many. Although Common Cause made candidate debates and forums a central part of its platform, it had no role in the debates — the major innovation during the campaign.

Congressional Reform Efforts

In 1976 Common Cause developed an Open Up the System (OUTS) program designed to determine where congressional candidates stood on reforms favored by the organization. Three hundred and eighty representatives and senators elected to the 95th Congress responded to the Common Cause questionnaire. Large majorities from both parties favored the following: new conflict of interest regulations in the executive branch and Congress, creation of a single House oversight committee for intelligence activities, legislation calling for broadcasting of congressional floor proceedings, and support for the principle of "sunset" legislation.[202]

Not all of the proposals fared so well. While the majority of congressmen promised to support public financing for congressional campaigns in general election contests, they expressed opposition to funding primary races.[203] Common Cause had urged both houses to adopt a rule requiring members to "abstain from voting in committee on any matter that would provide a significant financial benefit to them." [204] It found that large majorities of both houses favored proposals "to end the game of musical chairs between private interests and government agencies with which they have substantial dealings." [205]

In contrast, a proposal to limit the number of terms that a member of Congress could serve on major committees received only lukewarm support. "Committee rotation faces two major obstacles on Capitol Hill: opposition from senior committee members who want to protect their power, and from special interests who want to protect their cozy relationships with those same long-time committee members." [206]

The organization had several uses for the responses received from the questionnaire. It noted that the responses were "always most effective in the hands of . . . members in a congressman's district or a senator's home state." [207] It urged its members to keep tabs on their legislators. In addition, Common Cause hoped to use the responses to create momentum for bills stalled in committees and to gather support from the House and Senate for crucial votes on issues.

The actual impact of the OUTS questionnaire is difficult to determine, but it may have had some effect. The House has begun a limited test of the feasibility and desirability of televised coverage. The House and the Senate both enacted a revised and strengthened code of ethics. The president has established a new set of conflict of interest regulations for key policy-makers in the executive branch.

Of course, Common Cause alone cannot claim credit for all, or perhaps any, of these activities. Nevertheless, it is clear that the thrust of the reforms being made in the American political system is in the direction the organization favors. In summary, the efforts made by Common Cause, if not unique, were probably more intensive and extensive than anything previously attempted in these areas — a reflection of the organization's strength and the growth of an affluent, well-educated middle class interested in and seeking to affect political reforms. The actual results of the organization's campaigns are mixed. Its greatest triumphs may have been among its own members.

As one observer noted,[208] the organization's effort to create a campaign oriented toward the issues might have been expected to fail because it was unprecedented, but pondering the questions it raised may help to clarify expectations. Common Cause's focus on "issues" may lead to consideration of exactly what those issues are, how useful candidates' precise responses to the queries would actually be, and the extent to which full answers from some candidates might penalize others who did not meet the same standards.

Minor Parties

Much third-party activity in the 1976 election was directly traceable to discontent among conservative Republicans with the liberal policies of the Ford administration. By November 1975 those considering themselves Republicans accounted for about 20 percent of the electorate and were outnumbered by self-identified Democrats and by independents.[209] A conservative conference in February 1975 led to the formation of a 13-member "Committee on Conservative Alternatives" headed by Sen. Jesse Helms, R-N.C. Its members discussed the possibility of a conservative breakaway from the GOP to form a third party that would attract Democrats and independents as well as right-wing Republicans. A meeting of the American Conservative Union and Young Americans for Freedom brought forth resolutions that included: endorsement of a constitutional amendment prohibiting abortion; support for a congressional investigation of the propriety of spending federal funds to lobby for the ERA amendment before state legislatures; and opposition to laws allocating tax monies to support political campaigns.[210] Still, Sen. Barry Goldwater, R-Ariz., former Governor Ronald Reagan, and Democratic Governor George Wallace argued that a third party would undermine the Republican Party, and they urged disaffected conservatives to work for their principles within the existing parties.

Despite the lack of enthusiasm from prominent conservatives, right-wing Republicans continued to explore the formation of a third party, predicting that a Reagan-Wallace ticket would provide leadership and attract a winning majority. Some observers were quick to identify obstacles confronting a third party, however. Speaking at the 1975 Conservative Political Action Conference in Washington, Karl Rove, chairman of the College Republican National Committee, commented on the difficulties associated with getting a candidate on the ballot in many states; the adverse effects of the $20 million limitation on spending for presidential campaigns; the resources required to gather lists for fund raising; and the ineligibility of a third party for federal funds until after the election.[211] In March 1975 President Ford announced his intention to run for office in 1976, and interest in Reagan as a third-party candidate grew. Senator James Buckley called a two-day strategy meeting of conservative leaders.

In New Hampshire, a third party began forming around Gov. Meldrim Thomson Jr. Howard Phillips, a conservative third-party advocate and director of the so-called Conservative Caucus, encouraged Thomson, noting that caucus fund-raising efforts had brought in $200,000 since January 1975. Added support came from conservative Richard Viguerie, whose direct-mail fund-raising effort had collected $20 million annually for mostly conservative political clients. A Gallup Poll taken in March indicated that Goldwater and Reagan were among the top three choices of Republicans for the party presidential nomination, and an April poll suggested that a third party more conservative than the GOP might draw support from as much as 25 percent of the voting population (approximately 24 percent of both major parties).[212]

In June the Committee on Conservative Alternatives formed a subcommittee to determine how a third-party presidential candidate could be placed on state ballots. The members of this group included William A. Rusher (publisher of *National Review*), M. Stanton Evans (head of the American Conservative Union), Rep. Robert E. Bauman, R-Md., and Governor Thomson of New Hampshire. Favoring creation of an "Independence Party" and identifying support from Wallace as critical, Rusher endorsed Reagan as a presidential candidate but noted with concern Reagan's interest in the Republican nomination. In August, Reagan made explicit his support for strengthening the GOP and rejected the possibility of a third-party ticket that he would share with Wallace. The need for a potential presidential candidate to select a party before the primary reflected election laws in California, Indiana, Maryland, Michigan, Nebraska, Oregon, and South Dakota that prohibited a candidate from running in the primary of one party and under the auspices of another in the general election. These states represented 20 percent of the electorate.[213]

As talk of a third party continued among right-wing Republicans, Charles A. McManus, founder of Americans for Constitutional Action, quit the conservative political fund-raising organization. McManus objected to the intensive fund-raising activity of Viguerie's firm and claimed that contributors to conservative causes were being exhausted by intensive direct mail.[214] In October, Rusher formed a conservative group called "The Committee for the New Majority," an organization clearly intended to offer Reagan or Wallace the option of a third-party candidacy. In filing with the Federal Election Commission, the committee reported three contributions of $1,000, one of which had come from Viguerie.

Dissent within party ranks brought a concerned response from President Ford, and his reaction in turn provoked distress among liberal Republicans. Sen. Charles McC. Mathias, a liberal Republican from Maryland, considered forming a third party with himself as presidential candidate. (Mathias earlier had considered seeking the Republican presidential nomination.) Although he was approached by McCarthy, Mathias turned down an alliance with the liberal independent contender. As an insurgent and a late-starting candidate, Mathias would need large contributions of seed money. He decided not to run in March 1976 and noted that the Supreme Court decision supporting the $1,000 limit on donors but upholding federal subsidies to major candidates made mounting an independent campaign very difficult.[215] Although he remained a Republican, Mathias continued to be critical of Ford and Reagan, and later was denied a seat on the platform committee at the Republican National Convention.

American Independent Party

In the end, the remnants of the third party that had supported Wallace in 1968 split for the 1976 election between the American Party and the American Independent Party.[216] The National American Party offered its presidential nomination to Thomas J. Anderson of Tennessee, who had been party chairman for four years. The vice presidential nominee was Rufus Shackleford, a millionaire tomato-grower from Florida. This choice reflected the party's failure to enlist Meldrim Thomson or Jesse Helms, both of whom backed Reagan for the nomination. By October 1976 Anderson was on the ballot in 18 states with supporters arguing in court to place him on the ballot in seven others. His campaign spent $187,815.[217]

The American Independent Party merged with the American Independence Party in July 1976. By that time it had qualified for ballot position in 29 states. Party members expressed concern about the appeal Carter might have for voters as a religious southerner whose candidacy had been endorsed by Wallace. Rusher and Helms waited for the Republican nominating convention before selecting the party's candidate; their interest in launching a third party depended on the nomination of Ford. Both Viguerie and Helms identified strong third-party fundraising potential: although the new party would not qualify easily for federal funds in 1976, if its candidate received at least 5 percent of the popular vote the party would be reimbursed in later election years on a basis proportional to the amount given each of the two major parties. Viguerie noted that he owned mailing lists used for Wallace's campaign, and that he had raised between $6 million and $7 million for Wallace, compiling more than 400,000 names and addresses in the process. The American Independent Party split over the question of whom to nominate. Rusher's Committee for the New Majority focused on Jesse Helms. William K. Shearer, party chairman, favored Lester Maddox, the former governor of Georgia, to beat Carter. In August, Viguerie announced his opposition to Maddox and expressed his own interest in the presidential nomination. Maddox became the party's candidate, but opposition from Rusher, Viguerie, and others defeated hopes that the American Independent Party would eventually emerge as the main right-wing focus. The vice presidential candidate was William E. Dyke, one-time mayor of Madison, Wisconsin, and 1974 Republican nominee for governor of Wisconsin.

TABLE 7-17
Adjusted Receipts and Expenditures: Eight Third-Party and Independent Candidates

Thousands of dollars

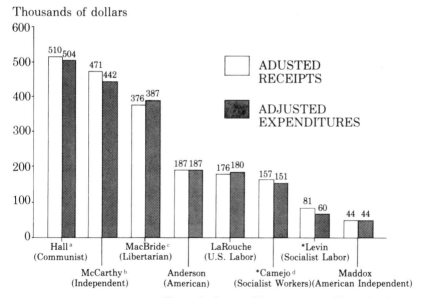

*Figures for these candidates were reported by national party committees, which were designated by the candidates as their principal campaign committees. Therefore, totals may include party-related financial activity that was not clearly separated from campaign activity on disclosure documents.

[a] Cash on hand 1/1/75 was $845.
[b] Cash on hand 1/1/75 was $24,588.
[c] Cash on hand 1/1/75 was - $4,242.
[d] Cash on hand 1/1/75 was $4,552.

SOURCE: *FEC Disclosure Series No. 7: 1976 Presidential Campaign Receipts and Expenditures* (Washington: Federal Election Commission, 1977), p. 26.

The unsuccessful Reagan candidacy for nomination was blamed by some observers with having absorbed all the political money available within the conservative movement, thus making it difficult for either Howard Phillips (in the Conservative Caucus) or Richard Viguerie (in the Committee for the New Majority) to qualify in enough states. Phillips noted that the budget had been as low as $1,000-$2,000 a month and remarked, "You can't raise very much money for an ill-defined contingency." [218] The party's effort now, he explained, would focus on influencing the congressional races. By the end of October 1976 Maddox's name was on the ballot in fewer than half the states. His best support came from Alabama, where 3 percent of the voters queried said they would pick him. The Maddox campaign spent $44,488.[219]

Socialist Workers' Party

The first third-party candidate to be chosen was Peter Camejo of the Socialist Workers' Party, whose nomination was announced in April 1975. Camejo addressed small groups in various cities during this campaign; for example, speaking in Philadelphia in April 1976, he denounced capitalism to 75 people and collected $1,500 in pledges. His 16-month campaign raised more than $300,000. His remarks included the objection that U.S. citizens are taxed a certain percentage for federal funds to finance political campaigns, but that most Americans do not realize that this percentage cannot support a candidate who is neither a Democrat nor a Republican. His party claimed harassment by the FBI and filed a $27 million lawsuit against the agency. By October 1976, Camejo was on the ballot in 28 states. He spent a total of $151,648 on his campaign.[220] The Socialist Workers' Party filed several thousand documents with the FEC in May 1977, claiming that it should be exempted from FECA reporting provisions because its contributors would be subjected to harassment. The request responded to legal indications that political groups could be exempted on such grounds.[221]

U.S. Labor Party

The U.S. Labor Party, political arm of the militant National Caucus of Labor Committees, was viewed by some as the most highly organized and visible radical political operation in the United States, and 1976 was the first general election in which it competed. Appealing chiefly to urban blue-color union members and blacks from organized labor, the party claimed that its presidential nominee, Lyndon H. LaRouche (chairman of the National Caucus of Labor Committees), would be on the ballot in 21 to 28 states. His campaign spent an average of $5,000 a week to finance the lawsuits needed to qualify him for ballot position. Although the NCLC never completely disclosed its income and expenditures, a lawyer in a suit brought against the NCLC by the United Auto Workers stated that the organization had an annual budget of $1.5 million. These funds were said to have come from party dues, small contributions, and the sale of publications. The LaRouche campaign reported expenditures of $180,653.[222]

In the wake of the election, the U.S. Labor Party charged massive voter irregularities in New York State and sought to join the Republicans of four states in lawsuits charging fraud in the election. It mounted a national fund-raising campaign as well, approaching Republicans and prominent conservatives to finance the court challenges in Wisconsin, Ohio, Pennsylvania, and New York. The suits alleged various forms of vote fraud and illegal registration by individuals who voted for Carter. In Wisconsin and Pennsylvania, the U.S. Labor Party also sought to invalidate new laws facilitating voter registration.

Both the Republican National Committee and the President Ford Committee reportedly rejected requests for funds from the Labor Party, and the Labor Party's solicitations, which in some cases implied an alliance with the Republican organizations, irritated some Republicans and other conservatives. Stephen Pepper, a member of the Labor Party's National Committee, said that while the party did not support Ford, it was concerned to oppose widespread abuses of the election.[223]

Communist Party

Another minor party, the Communist Party, nominated as its presidential candidate Gus Hall, a party member since 1927, and as its vice presidential candidate Jarvis Tyner, chairman of the New York State party. The party spent $504,710 on the presidential campaign, funds raised mostly by direct-mail solicitation and collections at rallies, although some unsolicited contributions were reported.[224] The money was spent chiefly for radio and television spots and for candidates' travel. The party, which concentrated on industrial workers and especially the unemployed and those disenchanted with mainstream politics, claimed to have 18,000-20,000 full members and about 3,000 youth members. Like other third-party candidates, Gus Hall complained about the exclusivity of the debates sponsored by the League of Women Voters.

Libertarian Party

The Libertarian Party, whose platform challenged the "cult of the omnipotent state," nominated Roger Lea MacBride, a lawyer and television producer, as its presidential candidate. MacBride, considered by some to be the most active of third-party candidates apart from Eugene McCarthy, opposed federal matching funds for presidential contenders, arguing that in this respect as in others the state played too large a role in the life of its citizens. In August, MacBride estimated that he would be on the ballot in about 35 states and that he would receive one million to 10 million votes. He identified candidates Reagan and Udall as more significant threats to his candidacy than Ford or Carter because they were more "sharply defined" on issues. As will be noted, MacBride spent more than any other minor-party candidate.

Socialist Party

Frank P. Zeidler, former mayor of Milwaukee, became the Socialist Party's first candidate for president in 20 years. His running mate was Quinn Brisben, a Chicago teacher. The Socialist Party, which at one time had backed Norman Thomas and Eugene Debs, estimated in 1976 that it had about 500 current members.

Others

In addition to the parties named above, a number of third parties were less visible. The National Black Political Assembly offered its nomination to Julian Bond and to Rep. Ronald V. Dellums, D-Calif. Both turned down the invitation, and the party finally nominated Rev. Fred D. Kirkpatrick for president. The People's Party nominated Margaret Wright, a black civil rights activist from Los Angeles, to be president, and Maggie Kuhn, the leader of a Philadelphia-based group opposing age discrimination, to be vice president. The Socialist Labor Party listed its candidate, Jules Levin, on the ballot in New Jersey and nine other states. The SLP spent $59,820 on Levin's campaign, collecting the money through fund-raisers, rallies, and sales of stamps.[225] The Prohibition Party, which favord Benjmain Bubar's candidacy, changed its name to the National Statesman Party a year after the election.

As the 1976 election year began, the FEC reported that 62 persons had notified the agency of their intention to run for the White House. Although hundreds of third-party candidates have run in elections since 1832, only nine have succeeded in carrying more than one state, and Theodore Roosevelt, the Bull Moose candidate, was the only one to demonstrate more than regional appeal. In 1976 no minor-party or independent candidate won any electoral votes or as much as 1 percent of the popular vote. Nevertheless, both the efforts of the minor parties in 1976 and the constraints to which they were subject hold significance for the history and financing of U.S. elections.

Several forces gave new life to the notion of a successful third party. First, there were indications of a decline in the importance of party ties. A Gallup Poll in 1976 identified 32 percent of Americans as independents. Voter turnout had declined and some interpreted this trend as revealing a disenchantment with the major political candidates and a feeling of alienation from the political system. Third parties viewed these indicators as encouraging, but many felt that media limitations and financial restrictions prevented their exploitation in 1976.

Third parties were generally bitter about the new campaign financing law, which in their view institutionalized the disparity between major and minor parties. Democrats and Republicans each received $21.8 million in federal funds for general election campaigns; third parties were compelled to rely on private contributions not exceeding $1,000 each. None of the third parties expected to raise more than $1 million. Then, too, the minor parties faced expenses that the major parties did not confront. Third parties were obliged to win ballot positions, circulating filing petitions and complying with complex and varied state laws. Shortages of time and resources made it difficult for third parties to gain ballot positions in more than half the states. An added drain on third parties' limited budgets came in the form of the complex reporting requirements of the FEC. In the words of Stan Karp of the Socialist Labor Party, "What killed us this year was all the liberal reform provisions and the tons of paperwork that came with them." [226] To some, the complicated regulations seemed especially ironic in view of the minor parties' ineligibility for public financing.

Of the third-party efforts, only the campaign of Roger MacBride came close to being well-financed, significantly through MacBride's personal funds. The Libertarian Party's income and expenditures approached $1 million for local and national candidates, of which $387,429 was spent on the presidential campaign.[227] The Socialist Workers' Party estimated that its two-year campaign for Peter Camejo cost about $400,000, much of it spent on seeking access to state ballots. The Camejo campaign spent more than $20,000 in the effort to achieve ballot status in California alone. McCarthy initiated legal challenges in 27 states, the Libertarians went into court in seven, and the Socialist Workers' Party did so in several others. By October 15, the Libertarian Party had achieved ballot status in 30 states, more than any other minor party. At the end of the list of the 11 most prominent minor parties came the People's Party on the ballot in only six states.[228] Only McCarthy and MacBride were on the ballot in enough large states to have a theoretical chance of a majority in the electoral college.

The nationally televised debates of Ford and Carter also were identified by minor parties as discriminatory. Some observers asked

whether MacBride, Camejo, or McCarthy might have won the support
of more voters if each had had $21.8 million to spend or had obtained 15
minutes each night on network television. Maddox, the American Independent Party nominee, cooperated with McCarthy through ex-
changes of information, pleadings, and advance notice in protesting
certain minor candidates' exclusion from the debates. The grounds for
legal action included: 1) a challenge under the equal-time provision of
the Federal Communications Act, 2) questioning the FEC ruling that
sponsorship of the debates by the League of Women Voters did not
constitute an illicit campaign contribution to the two major candidates,
3) contesting the tax-exempt status of the league because of its exclusion
of other major candidates, 4) challenging the status of the debates as
legitimate news events according to the FCC's definition in its ruling,
and 5) charging violation of the "fairness doctrine." [229] Socialist Workers' Party candidate Peter Camejo also cooperated with McCarthy and
Maddox, and in June 1976 attorneys for the three candidates argued
that the debates were not a news event but a production staged for
television, and that the networks should therefore be required to give
equal time to other candidates. The FCC ruled against the plea.

In a related action, Peter Camejo succeeded in winning from the
FCC time on NBC's "Tomorrow" show after Gus Hall, the Communist
candidate, was given time on the program. The FCC agreed with
Camejo that the "Tomorrow" show was not exempt from the equal-time
provision because it was not a bona fide news program. Similarly, the
FCC required NBC to sell a half hour of prime time to Labor Party
candidate LaRouche. The FCC ruling in this instance cited the "reasonable access" provision of a 1971 law, and LaRouche hailed the decision
as the first to force a network to grant more than a couple of minutes to a
third party. NBC responded that it had not originally complied with the
Labor Party request because it had been made at the last minute.[230]
These successes of minor-party candidates were the exception, however.

Third-party claims that the FECA favors major-party candidates at
the expense of minor-party and independent contenders could lead to
further court challenges of the law's constitutionality.

McCarthy

Eugene J. McCarthy, former senator, former Democratic presidential candidate, and current vocal critic of election reform, conducted a
tortured and losing independent campaign for the presidency. However,
the 1 percent of the popular vote that McCarthy received belies the
significance of his campaign. The two-year battle, which cost a remarkably low $500,000, raised a number of questions about the provisions of
the Federal Election Campaign Act with respect to minor-party and
independent candidates.

Although McCarthy ran for his own unorthodox cures for America's ills, he ran more vehemently against recent abuses of presidential power, the two-party system, and legal barriers to independent candidacies. McCarthy never had a realistic chance to beat President Ford or Jimmy Carter, but he did threaten to throw the election to Ford by cutting into Carter's support. Uniquely, McCarthy publicized serious issues facing our electoral democracy. As one McCarthy fund-raiser said, "The country needs a conscience and he provides it. Winning is not always the most important thing." [231]

Committee for a Constitutional Presidency

Before McCarthy was officially a candidate, the campaign commenced under the auspices of the Committee for a Constitutional Presidency. The committee opened offices in Washington, D.C., in August 1974, with the expressed purpose of stimulating "public discussion of basic questions about the constitutional powers and responsibilities of the President which have been dramatized by recent events." [232] The committee intended to nominate candidates for the nation's two highest offices and place their names on the ballot in all 50 states. McCarthy served as honorary chairman of the body and the committee members, largely McCarthy followers from the 1968 and 1972 campaigns, pointed the committee toward McCarthy's third race for the White House.

The committee set about raising funds and established a ceiling on contributions of $15,000 a year from any individual (prior to the $1,000 contribution limit under the 1974 Amendments). Early financial backers included William Clay Ford of the automobile family, Karl Gruhm, president of Tonka Mills in Minnesota, Patrick F. Crowley, a now-deceased Chicago attorney, and Suzannah B. Hatt of New Hampshire. Screen stars Paul Newman and Joanne Woodward contributed $2,500 to the committee in 1974. Comedian Steve Allen and General Motors heir Stewart R. Mott each donated $100 in that year. In all, about $40,000 was raised in 1974.

Part of this seed money covered expenditures for a convention of sorts held in Chicago in August 1974. McCarthy delivered the keynote address to the 300 delegates, who paid for their own food, lodging, and transportation costs. The committee absorbed costs for rental of the meeting room and air-fare and hotel rooms for committee members and McCarthy.

As the spokesman of the Committee for a Constitutional Presidency, McCarthy lectured the public on the unconstitutional and extra-constitutional activities of recent presidents. The Vietnam involvement provided a clear example of such activity, "with Kennedy and Eisenhower bending the Constitution, Johnson circumventing the Constitution with the Gulf of Tonkin resolution and then Nixon violating the Constitution by invading Cambodia." The former senator from Minnesota pulled no punches during President Ford's honeymoon period, stating that Ford "shows no signs in his past record of restoring the presidency to its constitutionally mandated status. In fact, he has supported Presidents Johnson and Nixon as they eroded the Constitution." [233]

In January 1975, when McCarthy announced as an independent, the committee appended "McCarthy '76" to its title.

Criticism of Two-Party System and FECA

McCarthy's attacks on the dominance of the Republican and Democratic parties carried him away from the political mainstream. In McCarthy's view, the two-party system reinforces the drift away from a constitutional presidency. Dependence on the major parties engenders loyalty that works against constitutional, enlightened policies. In this regard, McCarthy criticized Democrats for remaining loyal to LBJ's Vietnam policy and for courting George Wallace in the 1976 race. The Republicans performed equally poorly in the constitutional crisis of Watergate because many could not bring themselves to part with their leader, Richard Nixon. Moreover, McCarthy explained, the two parties cooperated in bipartisan evasion of the Constitution through policies of the CIA and FBI. The violations of law perpetrated by these agencies cannot be blamed solely on a fallen Republican president, he said, because for 25 years the Democratic Congress failed to properly monitor intelligence and investigative operations. To McCarthy, these recent events proved the wisdom of the Founding Fathers who purposely left political parties out of the Constitution.

According to McCarthy, today's two-party system not only weakens a constitutional presidency but produces mediocre leaders and fails to represent significant segments of the body politic. Under Gerald Ford's leadership, the former senator said, the public "is starved for even the appearance of decisiveness at any governmental level." [234] The dearth of capable leaders is exemplified by the Republican's nomination of Nixon and the Democrats' inability to defeat him. The bankruptcy of leadership coupled with the absence of alternative parties alienates voters and inhibits freedom of choice. As McCarthy asserted, "In '68, Humphrey and Nixon surely gave no choice for persons against the war. And in '72, there was no realistic choice or Nixon wouldn't have won by such a landslide." [235]

McCarthy hoped that his campaign would attract adherents among the ranks of independent and disaffected voters. With independent registrants increasing their numbers, and with low voter turnout, McCarthy theoretically had a formidable base of support. Ironically, McCarthy was not a realistic alternative to the Democratic and Republican nominees, partly because the two-party system severely restricted his access to the voters.

The FECA put McCarthy at a disadvantage in relation to the candidates of the major parties. The campaign law provides subsidies for the major parties and their candidates; though it also allows for the possibility of grants for other parties and candidates, the particular provisions virtually exclude minor parties from public money. For example, the Act made available $2.2 million for each major party's convention, but authorized a small subsidy for a minor party only if that party received 5 percent of the votes in the previous presidential election. Given this requirement, the authorization was not used in 1976 nor will it be in 1980.

In 1948 the Dixiecrats and Progressives conducted national campaigns and their combined votes did not equal 5 percent. George Wallace would have qualified the American Independent Party following the 1968 election, since he received some 12 percent of the vote, but his performance was unique in recent political experience. The FECA also states that if a new party's candidate tops the 5 percent mark, the federal government will pay for debts outstanding at the time of the November election. However, this is small comfort to a minor-party nominee or an independent such as McCarthy.

During the primary season, the government matches private contributions to Democrats and Republicans, but does not subsidize other candidates' efforts to gain ballot and media access. The new finance system gives private contributors no incentive to donate to minor candidates because a contribution is not likely to trigger an equal amount of public funds, and can do so only after the general election. During the fall campaign, minor-party and independent candidates must devote time to fund raising while the major party candidates may rely solely on U.S. Treasury funds.

Because the FECA sanctions different conditions and time sequences for major- and minor-party candidates, the law assists only the Democratic and Republican parties. This consequence, McCarthy believes, infringes on the basic rights of the voters. McCarthy declared, "It's like telling people we're going to give you freedom of religion and then saying you have two choices, Episcopal or Anglican." [236] By bolstering the two major parties, Congress severely limits the possibility of change in the electoral system. Without the chance of third parties developing, Americans can govern themselves but only "within the framework of Republican and Democratic politics," [237] to use McCarthy's words.

Besides the specifics of the law, McCarthy criticized the basic concepts of public financing and disclosure of contributors. He warned of the potential for repression inherent in a system that involves a governmental body in the electoral process. To emphasize the point, McCarthy recalled the circumstances of 1776: "The American Revolution was not financed with matching funds from the Crown. King George did not say, 'You raise $100,000 and we will match it. And you can proceed to have a revolution.' " [238] As for the disclosure provisions of the law, McCarthy contended that they violate privacy and set too low a threshold for disclosure of name and address of contributor. The Act requires that contributions in excess of $100 be disclosed; McCarthy responded: "The suggestion that a candidate will sell out for $101 is an insult to his integrity." [239]

McCarthy challenged the constitutionality of the FECA along with Senator James Buckley, the Conservative Party of New York, the New York Civil Liberties Union, Stewart Mott, and other plaintiffs in the *Buckley v. Valeo* suit. A team of lawyers from the Washington firm of Covington and Burling, the American Civil Liberties Union, and other interested attorneys including Ralph Winter, a Yale University professor of law, represented the plaintiffs. Although at least one attorney worked full time on the suit, no legal fees were paid. The 12 plaintiffs agreed to split the task of raising funds for office and incidental expenses that topped $20,000. The American Conservative Union paid the largest share, and the Committee for a Constitutional Presidency still owed part of its share after the 1976 general election.

Placement on State Ballots

While federal law restrained the McCarthy bid, some state laws threatened to extinguish the campaign altogether. The McCarthy '76 Committee faced a tremendous task in placing the ex-senator's name on ballots across the nation. In 1975, 16 states prevented independents from running for president. In the other states, the number of signatures required for placement on the ballot varied widely, ranging from 35 in Tennessee to 150,000 in North Carolina. The McCarthy committee estimated that two million signatures were needed to get on the ballot in all 50 states. The committee began the arduous process in late 1974 when volunteers requested ballot information from the states, and researched and summarized the data. In a few states, the committee initiated legal action before the signature gathering began.

John Armor, a Baltimore attorney, headed the fight against restrictive election laws. Armor recruited volunteer lawyers to represent McCarthy in the state and federal courts, with local chapters of the

American Civil Liberties Union providing much assistance. In some states, McCarthy filed as a coplaintiff with independent voters and candidates and third parties. This practice allowed the attorneys to raise several issues in their challenges. In Vermont, where McCarthy joined forces with the Libertarian Party, the legal costs were split. In other cases where McCarthy collaborated with third parties, the local ACLU chapter usually bore the costs. In a few states where McCarthy was the sole plaintiff he was responsible for the entire legal bill.

States that prohibited independent candidacies were Alaska, Delaware, Florida, Idaho, Illinois, Kansas, Michigan, Missouri, Nebraska, Nevada, New Mexico, Oklahoma, Texas, Utah, and Washington plus the District of Columbia. Officials of the District of Columbia, Alaska, and Washington interpreted their laws in a manner permitting McCarthy to run. Kansas and Illinois reached consent settlements after McCarthy filed suit and Idaho did so after the election. In nine states, courts struck down the laws challenged. In Nevada alone the law was not challenged, due to McCarthy's inability to recruit a volunteer attorney in that state.

Other states, while not preventing independent candidacies, made it difficult for an independent to run. McCarthy successfully challenged deadlines for filing of petitions that were unduly early in Louisiana, Missouri, Rhode Island, and Vermont. Challenge to other procedures succeeded in Iowa, Massachusetts, and Tennessee, but failed in California, the District of Columbia, and New York.

By Election Day 1976 the McCarthy forces had prompted courts to strike down portions of 15 state laws and McCarthy's name appeared on the ballot in 29 states. Three additional cases were won after the election. No judge or court, including the U.S. Supreme Court, denied the McCarthy counsel's argument that the Constitution prevents states from discriminating against independent candidates. However, the committee had to give up petition drives in states that promised complicated and lengthy struggles. Two of the most controversial and harmful failures came in California and New York.

In California, delays in sending petition materials to the campaign lost 10 days for signature gathering. By the filing deadline, McCarthy forces were 18,000 signatures short of the number needed, and they blamed the shortage on the delay. A state court granted a temporary stay but denied permanent relief, refusing both to place McCarthy's name on the ballot and to allow an extra 10 days for petitioning.

In New York, the law requires that candidacy petitions contain at least 20,000 signatures with 100 coming from each of 20 different congressional districts. The petitions must be segregated by congressional district and county within a district. McCarthy workers concentrated the petition drive in shopping centers, where large numbers of signers are available. However, shoppers often do not live in the voting districts where a center is located, and this hampered the arrangement of signatures. Although McCarthy officials filed 28,236 signatures, they did not separate all the petitions by the districts of signers and, worse yet, many signers did not list their voting district.

In the opening blow of the New York State Democratic Committee's no-holds-barred fight to keep McCarthy off the ballot, Gordon Contessa and Irving Schlein challenged the McCarthy petitions. These two Democratic Party regulars were represented by the counsel of the state committee, and party workers provided the tedious research for the line-by-line challenge. The staff of the state Board of Elections reviewed the McCarthy petitions and the Democrats' objections, finding 21,944 valid signatures. The board, composed of two Democrats and two Republicans, split along party lines, with the Democrats rejecting the staff report and the McCarthy petitions. The tie vote permitted McCarthy's name to be placed on the ballot, but the Democratic organization appealed to the state courts.

The trial court ordered McCarthy off the ballot; then the intermediate appeals court reversed the decision and put McCarthy back on the ballot. McCarthy lawyers tried to justify signatures line by line and claimed that the arrangement of the petitions and the large number of signatures indicated substantial compliance with the law. Finally, the state Court of Appeals, New York's highest judicial body, found that the McCarthy workers had not even attempted to record and segregate signatures as the law required. The court stated, "The failure to comply with the provision rendered it impossible for election officials or potential objectors to verify the presence of the requisite number of signatures from the various congressional districts." [240] The case was taken to the U.S. Supreme Court and was considered by the justices but relief was denied.

Of McCarthy's many court battles in the states, New York was the most expensive, reaching more than $20,000. The campaign did not gain ACLU assistance. The lack of volunteer counsel and the complexity and length of the case escalated the costs. The McCarthy staff estimated that the New York Democratic Committee spent more than $50,000 attacking the petitions. This expense is understandable since preelection polls put the former senator's voting strength at 5 percent. If that proportion of the 6.4 million votes cast were subtracted from Carter's total, President Ford would have captured New York's 41 electoral votes, and McCarthy would have given Ford an Electoral College victory with 282 votes to Carter's 256.

Considering all the effort involved and the services rendered, the McCarthy forces spent very little to get on the state ballots. John

Armor, who worked almost full time for McCarthy, was paid approximately one-fourth of his normal fees. In many cases, the local ACLU absorbed costs for legal support such as typing, travel, and telephone. In other cases, the campaign covered legal support costs. For example, the campaign paid slightly less than $100 for expenses in Kansas and approximately $1,024 in Texas. Some individuals who directed the circulation of petitions were paid by the campaign, but this operation also relied heavily on volunteers.

Other Legal Action

McCarthy filed another suit so that he might be included in the televised presidential debates sponsored by the League of Women Voters. McCarthy and Lester Maddox, the candidate of the American Independent Party, first requested that the League of Women Voters allow them to appear along with Ford and Carter. The league turned down this request. Maddox then asked the Federal Communications Commission to rule that the exclusion violated the fairness doctrine and McCarthy sought relief from the U.S. District Court. After adverse rulings from both the FCC and the court, McCarthy and Maddox turned to the U.S. Court of Appeals for the District of Columbia.

McCarthy alone then went to the Supreme Court. One time, the Supreme Court refused to intervene in the case, and a second time, it would not overrule the Appeals Court's denial of relief. The FCC and the courts considered the debates a news event and, as such, the sponsor could invite whomever it desired. When technical difficulties interrupted the first debate for 27 minutes, the networks seemed to control the event, but the debate resumed only when a loudspeaker system for the live audience and television were jointly restored. Nonetheless, the Supreme Court would not compel the appearance of Maddox and McCarthy in later debates, holding that they had "reasonable opportunities to have their views presented in contexts outside of the debates." [241]

Again McCarthy '76 paid a small fee to attorney John Armor for his work on the case. Expenses connected with the debate case brought the total cost to a little more than $2,000. Additional lawyers volunteered their services for the debate cases.

Other legal imbroglios involved the FEC. In the early stages of the campaign when the FEC audited other candidates to certify matching funds, the commission attempted to audit the books of McCarthy '76. The McCarthy forces objected, contending that the FEC had no right to audit a campaign that received no federal funds. Then the commission tried to justify the proposed audit on technical grounds and McCarthy responded by instructing his staff to refuse admission for the auditors.

To avoid yet another court battle, the commission quietly backed down and performed an audit after the November election.

The campaign's troubles continued when the Committee for a Constitutional Presidency requested that the FEC judge the committee to be the equivalent of a national party. If the commissioners granted the request, the committee could have received individual contributions up to $20,000. Without such a ruling, the committee would receive maximum individual contributions of $1,000 as a presidential campaign committee. In October 1976, after a delay that inconvenienced the campaign, the commission denied the request in a 3-3 tie. The FEC's three Democratic members voted against McCarthy. The committee claimed that the voting along party lines was a deliberate attempt to stymie McCarthy's effort. McCarthy asserted that the existing alignment of the commission invites partisanship and that the FEC should have members who are registered as independents.

This incident, the audit controversy, and the FEC's sanction of the exclusive debates led the McCarthy staff to feel that the events reflected hostility on the part of some commissioners.

The General Election

Despite the myriad lawsuits, Eugene McCarthy did not confine his campaign to the courts. He toured the country speaking on the need for reduced military spending and innovative approaches to economic recovery, and also took unprecedented steps in the areas of presidential appointments and vice presidential selection. The former senator attracted more attention as a potential spoiler of Jimmy Carter's race.

On October 9, 1976, McCarthy announced whom he would appoint to a revamped cabinet, if he were elected. The candidate made the announcement in Madison, Wisconsin, before a mini-convention of electors designated as his representatives to the electoral college. He hoped the advance release of the names of officials in a McCarthy administration would increase his support. McCarthy proposed a reduction of the executive departments from 10 to five. Heading a combined Defense and State Department, McCarthy would have appointed Terry Sanford, former governor of North Carolina and 1976 presidential aspirant. Mayor Kevin White of Boston would have served as attorney general. The Agriculture and Interior departments were to merge under Secretary of Resources Walter J. Hickel, a former secretary of the Interior. Howard Stein, president of the Dreyfus Fund and a 1968 McCarthy financial backer, was to oversee the Treasury. McCarthy suggested placing the existing Labor and Transportation departments under Commerce, with Sam Shoen, founder of U-Haul Inc., as secretary.

Other high officials in a McCarthy administration would have been Carla Hills and William Coleman of the Ford cabinet, former Senators J. William Fulbright and Harold Hughes, and C. Dolores Tucker, the secretary of the Commonwealth of Pennsylvania. McCarthy stated that the people mentioned did not necessarily support him, but all had indicated that they would accept a position if McCarthy won.

The purpose of the announcement was to "depersonalize the presidency" and to underline the connection between the quality of advisers and a president's ability. To stress the evil wrought by postelection appointments, McCarthy opined, "If the American people had known that John Mitchell was going to become Attorney General two weeks before the 1968 election, Richard Nixon would have lost." [242]

McCarthy's penchant for preelection candor did not bring him to announce a preference for his vice president. Instead, McCarthy wanted to have the Electoral College name the vice president in the unlikely event that he won. McCarthy quipped, "Vice presidential candidates just clutter up the campaign." [243] As a stand-in candidate for the second spot on the ticket, the Committee for a Constitutional Presidency selected William Clay Ford, a vice president of the Ford Motor Co. and owner of the Detroit Lions. However, Ford's candidacy lasted but a week; the campaign explained that "legal counsel advised us that in several key states, a stand-in candidate must be a resident of those states." [244] So that McCarthy's candidacy would not be invalidated in those states, Ford withdrew from the ticket.

Although it is difficult to classify McCarthy's stand on the issues as either "liberal" or "conservative," his reputation among the public gained during the 1968 campaign was decidedly liberal. Several polls predicted that McCarthy would get 5 percent of the ballots cast, and that most of his votes would be drawn from Carter. Fearful that the Minnesotan might spoil Carter's bid in a close election, many Democrats urged party members not to vote for the liberal standard-bearer of 1968. The most pointed attack came from a group of former McCarthy supporters. Fifty-three 1968 campaign workers signed an advertisement that ran in the late October issues of *The New Republic* and *The Nation*. The signers praised McCarthy's 1968 effort and his 1976 ideas, but asserted that "he knows he will not be elected President." They stated that it would be "tragic" if liberals threw away the chance to elect a Democrat. The ad stated:[245]

McCarthy says he doesn't care if his votes help re-elect Ford. We do. We are not cynical enough to believe both candidates and the group they represent are alike.

Sam Brown, the senator's youth coordinator in 1968, organized this anti-

McCarthy effort, while the Carter-Mondale campaign paid about $2,000 for the two full-page ads.

In reality, McCarthy had less of an impact on the Ford-Carter race than expected. The 650,000 votes recorded for McCarthy did not ruin Carter's lead, though in four states that Carter lost McCarthy's votes could have given the Georgian an edge over Ford. In Maine, where Ford beat Carter by slightly over 3,000 votes, McCarthy polled 11,000. McCarthy captured 14,000 votes in Oklahoma while Carter lost to Ford by 11,000 ballots. In Iowa, Ford led Carter by 11,000 votes while McCarthy received 18,000. A mere 200 votes separated the major-party candidates in Oregon, where McCarthy took almost 40,000 votes. McCarthy drew his highest absolute total in Massachusetts where he received 64,000 votes. After the election, McCarthy explained the significance of his tally this way, "I think the country knows now a third party can have an effect." [246]

Fund Raising and Costs

The McCarthy presidential bid certainly was not well financed. The Committee for a Constitutional Presidency raised a little more than $40,000 in 1974. In the first six months of 1975, the campaign raised an additional $34,000, approximately $15,000 of which represents honoraria for appearances by McCarthy. At the end of 1975, campaign officials reported total contributions of $98,000 and expenditures of $74,000, leaving a balance of $24,000. One half year later, in July 1976, expenditures had risen to $135,000. Contributions also increased, totaling $300,000 by October 1976, but spending at least kept pace. By election day, a minimum of $500,000 had been spent and a debt in the neighborhood of $200,000 remained.

Because the campaign possibly would have received federal subsidies for debts if McCarthy carried 5 percent of the popular vote, a financial statement was filed with the FEC in October 1976. The statement included as "debts" many of the volunteer services rendered during the campaign. For instance, lawyers and other staff members were listed for a total of $100,000 in salaries. A McCarthy aide explained, "These were people who worked hard the whole campaign. If we had gotten to 5 percent, it would have been nice if they could be paid." According to the statement, McCarthy himself was the foremost creditor at $55,000. The aide said this debt was "not phony," for McCarthy had been spending his own money since April 1976.[247] Other actual debts included about $24,000 in legal expenses and $40,000 in loans from individuals that can be converted to contributions. Since the former senator did not reach the 5 percent mark, the campaign had to repay debts with private funds. In 1977 the committee sponsored mailings to all participants in the campaign and fund-raising receptions featuring personal appearances by McCarthy in an attempt to erase the debt.

Tables 7-18 and 7-19 show the expenditure categories of the Committee for a Constitutional Presidency and the McCarthy '76 Committee. The two committees spent a total of $432,804 on the McCarthy campaign. This does not include spending by local committees, which was estimated at $57,000, nor does it include outstanding debts as of June 30, 1977.

Table 7-18
Committee for a Constitutional Presidency

Salaries	$ 41,286.72
Postage	13,081.62
Office supplies and expenses	10,883.22
Telephone	28,735.64
Rent	20,784.06
Travel	70,250.81
Printing and duplicating	10,303.07
Campaign materials	14,399.75
Fund raising	107,504.03
Press	862.12
Transfers to affiliated committees	49,266.10
Legal costs and fees	24,366.97
Miscellaneous	28,348.18
Total	$420,072.29

Note: This covers direct spending by the national Committee for a Constitutional Presidency through June 30, 1977. It does not include local committees' spending, nor does it include spending-in-kind. Both of those items are covered in FEC reports. Also, see FEC reports for debts not paid by June 30, 1977.

Table 7-19
McCarthy '76

Postage	$ 1,623.73
Office supplies and expenses	96.60
Telephone	571.21
Travel	2,183.39
Printing and duplicating	2,253.56
Fund raising	701.67
Consultant fees	2,875.00
Miscellaneous	2,426.55
Total	$12,731.71

Note: This covers direct spending by the McCarthy '76 national committee through June 30, 1977. It does not include local committees' spending, nor does it include spending-in-kind. Both of those items are covered in FEC reports.
Debts are not covered in this sheet unless they were paid by June 30, 1977. See FEC reports.

The campaign would have spent more money, and perhaps gone further into debt, if it were possible. After losing the television debates case, McCarthy attempted to purchase time from the networks so that he could bring his message to the public. The staff negotiated with all three networks in the hope of buying a half hour on the Monday night after the last Ford-Carter debate. All the networks rejected the request, CBS fearing that McCarthy's speech would generate other requests to preempt regular programming for candidate appearances. Although McCarthy did not have the requisite $100,000 on hand, the staff believed an affirmative response from a network would have attracted the funds. The campaign was able to air eight five-minute spot advertisements. All three networks accepted the ads, which were broadcast in late August and late October. Each of the eight spots cost about $15,800 for production and air time, for a total expenditure of $126,000. This figure is not shown on the committee's table of disbursements. Most of it was assigned to the fund-raising category, since the television broadcasts were used for that purpose, and some was covered by debts or spending-in-kind and so does not appear on the table at all. The spots more than paid their way.

The McCarthy expenditures hardly compared with the spending of Carter and Ford, who complained that their $21.8 million was inadequate. From August 1974 until the summer of 1976, the campaign committee paid just four to six full-time staff members and the highest annual salary was $7,000. In the 10 months of the 1976 campaign, $4,800 was the top salary. The campaign manager, Jerry Eller, worked on an entirely volunteer basis, and some 10 field personnel received only expense reimbursements. McCarthy covered some personal expenses with income from his congressional pension, royalties, and honoraria.

In fact, the honoraria, which totaled approximately $25,000, created a controversy as to how the money should be categorized. By law, universities and other organizations that provided honoraria cannot contribute to a campaign, yet the McCarthy committee used speaking fees for campaign expenses. The FEC insisted that the honoraria be counted as a part of McCarthy's personal contribution to his campaign. Unfortunately for him, the fees then became subject to income tax. After an investigation and much bickering, the candidate reported the speaking fees as contributions from personal income, even though some of the appearances were educational lectures on the presidency and not stump speeches.

In spite of the fiscal troubles, McCarthy vowed to keep fighting "for the cause of open politics." [248] A few of the cases concerning ballot access were still pending after the general election, and McCarthy helped to form the Committee for Fair Ballot Access, which aids any candidates, not only independent candidates. The committee is provisionally recognized as a legal charity, and is located in Baltimore.

_____

Footnotes

[1] Herbert E. Alexander, "Public Funding of Campaign Finances," *Vital Issues*, Vol. XXV, No. 9, May 1976, p. 2.

[2] Walter Pincus, "Strict Grip on Outlays is Vowed," *The Washington Post*, July 13, 1976.

[3] Text of speech by Kling to the Democratic convention, pp. 6-7.

[4] Democratic National Committee and Affiliated Organizations, "Statement of Combined Revenues and Expenses for the Years Ended December 31, 1976 and 1975."

[5] Warren Weaver, Jr., "Democratic Chiefs Raising $5.5 Million," *The New York Times*, October 24, 1976.

[6] "Democrats Open a 'General Store,'" *The New York Times*, September 22, 1976.

[7] Federal Election Commission, *FEC Disclosure Series, No. 4: National Party Political Committee Receipts and Expenditures* (Washington, D.C., April 1977).

[8] Democratic National Committee and Affiliated Organizations, "Notes to Financial Statements, December 31, 1976 and 1975," p. 5.

[9] Weaver, "Democratic Chiefs."

[10] Christopher Lydon, "Fund-Raising Image of Strauss Strained by Party's Shortage," *The New York Times*, September 20, 1976.

[11] Christopher Lydon, "Reagan Is Too Busy to Aid Ford in 5 States," *The New York Times*, September 20, 1976.

[12] Lydon, "Fund-Raising Image."

[13] Ibid.

[14] Ibid.

[15] Walter Pincus, "Democratic Unit Got $10,000 from Kovens at Last Minute," *The Washington Post*, December 3, 1976.

[16] Ibid.

Bernard Gwertzman, "Carter Ambassadors — Competence Before Politics," *The New York Times*, June 19, 1977.

[17] Walter Pincus, "Independent Committees Aid Carter," *The Washington Post*, October 15, 1976.

[18] "The only thing stopping us, is us!" advertisement, *The New York Times*, October 15, 1976.

[19] *Buckley v. Valeo*, 424 U.S. 1 at 262.

[20] Federal Election Commission, *FEC Disclosure Series, No. 3: Index of Independent Expenditures by Individuals and Receipts and Expenditures by Unauthorized Delegates, 1976 Campaign* (Washington, D.C., March 1977), pp. 105-107.

Federal Election Commission, *Independent Expenditures by Individuals, Groups, and Political Committees — 1976 Election, January 1, 1975 — October 24, 1976*, p. 8.

[21] Cox news release, October 18, 1976, p. 1.

[22] Pincus, "Independent Committees."

[23] Memo, "To: Staff; From: Bob Lipshutz, Morris Dees, Doug Huron; Re: Federal Election Law and the Campaign," pp. 4-5.

[24] Ibid., Attachment 2.

[25] Lee Dembart, "A.F.L.-C.I.O. Pledges Support to Carter," *The New York Times*, July 20, 1976.

[26] Warren Weaver, Jr., "Labor's Drive for Carter Is the Biggest it Has Made in a Presidential Race," *The New York Times*, October 26, 1976.

[27] Mary Russell, "Mondale's Role: An Old Friend to Labor," *The Washington Post*, August 23, 1976.

[28] Federal Election Commission, *FEC Disclosure Series, No. 5: Index of Communication Costs by Corporations, Labor Organizations, Membership Organizations, Trade Associations — 1976 Campaign* (Washington, D.C., April 1977), pp. 19-41.

[29] Ibid.

[30] Michael J. Malbin, "Labor, Business and Money — A Post-Election Analysis," *National Journal,* March 19, 1977, p. 415.

[31] Weaver, "Labor's Drive."

[32] Malbin, "Labor, Business, and Money," p. 414.

[33] Ibid.

[34] 1976 Democratic Presidential Campaign Committee Inc., "Report of Receipts and Expenditures for a Candidate or Committee Supporting Any Candidate(s) for Nomination or Election to Federal Office," FEC Form 3, January 31, 1977.

[35] Herbert E. Alexander, *Financing the 1972 Election* (Lexington, Mass.: Lexington Books, D. C. Heath and Co., 1976), p. 325.

[36] Philip H. Dougherty, "Atlanta Agency's Busiest Year," *The New York Times,* July 19, 1976; Deirdre Carmody, "Ad Aides See Presidential Candidates as the Issue," *The New York Times,* October 15, 1976.

[37] Jo Thomas, "Campaign Reporting for Carter Queried," *The New York Times,* April 29, 1979.

[38] Jules Witcover, "Carter's Political Unknowns to Keep Reins for Fall Drive," *The Washington Post,* July 4, 1976.

[39] "Big Blitz," *Newsweek,* November 8, 1976, p. 19.

[40] Joseph Lelyveld, "Carter Turns to New York Studio to Tape His Remaining TV Spots," *The New York Times,* October 20, 1976.

[41] Sander Vanocur, "Selling Jimmy Carter in 5-Minute Packages," *The Washington Post,* August 4, 1976.

[42] Ibid.

[43] Les Brown, "Ford and Carter Buy TV Time on Election Eve for Final Efforts," *The New York Times,* October 30, 1976.

[44] Alexander, *Financing the 1972 Election,* pp. 316-318.

[45] Ibid.

[46] Robert J. Lipshutz, letter to Vernon W. Thomson, August 20, 1976. N. Bradley Litchfield, letter to Lipshutz, September 27, 1976.

[47] B. Drummond Ayres, Jr., "Carter Campaign Is Still Led by Little-Known Democrats," *The New York Times,* September 29, 1976.

[48] Ken Bode, "Carter's Cadres," *The New Republic,* October 30, 1976, p. 7.

[49] R. W. Apple, Jr., "California Typifies Lack of Interest Shown Across Nation in Campaign," *The New York Times,* September 19, 1976.

[50] Bode, "Carter's Cadres."

[51] Jon Nordheimer, "Fund Shortage Cools Interest in Race for President," *The New York Times,* October 25, 1976.

[52] Ibid.

[53] Tom Wicker, "The Bland and the Bored," *The New York Times,* September 28, 1976.

[54] Dick Pettys, "Carter Running on Tight Budget," *The Atlanta Constitution,* September 16, 1976.

[55] Stephen Isaacs, "Outlay Limit Unbuttons Campaigners," *The Washington Post,* October 8, 1976.

[56] Irwin S. Stoolmacher, "The Greening of America," *Practical Politics,* March/April 1978, pp. 28-29.

[57] Ken Auletta, "Baby-Sitting for Jimmy in New York," *New York,* October 4, 1976, p. 13.

[58] Frank Lynn, "Democratic Presidential Drive in New York Is Closely Knit to the State Party for the First Time Since 1964," *The New York Times,* September 21, 1976.

[59] Auletta, "Baby-Sitting for Jimmy."

[60] Tom Wicker, "Will a Piggyback on Proposition 14 Help the Carter Candidacy,?" *The New York Times,* October 3, 1976.

[61] Stephen Isaacs, "Carter Campaign Working to Stockpile Hill IOUs," *The Washington Post,* September 14, 1976.

[62] Bode, "Carter's Cadres."

[63] Frank Lynn, "Democratic Presidential Drive in New York Is Closely Knit to the State Party for the First Time Since 1964," *The New York Times,* September 21, 1976; Lynn, "Carter's Forces, in Effort to Recoup In New York, Stress City's Problems," *The New York Times,* October 19, 1976.

[64] "Carter Wins Battle to be Listed as 'Jimmy' on Election-Day Ballots in All 50 States," *Election Administration Reports,* October 13, 1976, pp. 2-3.

[65] "FEC Probing if '76 Carter Luncheon Violated Election Contribution Law," *The Washington Post,* September 13, 1977.

[66] "Carter Campaign Unit to Pay U.S. Treasury $3,285," *The New York Times,* Friday, July 14, 1978.

[67] "Carter to Pay for Flights," *Evening Bulletin* (Philadelphia), August 23, 1977.

[68] Martin Tolchin, "Bank and Carter Committee Fined $6,200 for Campaign Planes Use," *The New York Times,* June 27, 1978.

[69] "Carter, Bank Agree to Pay Penalties in Plane Use Case," *The Washington Post,* June 27, 1978.

[70] *The Baron Report,* September 13, 1977, p. 2.

[71] "Aide Says Carter Did Not Pay for 5 Flights," *The New York Times,* Sept. 1, 1977.

[72] Richard Reeves and Barry M. Hager, "The Good Old Boy Network," *The New Republic,* September 10, 1977, pp. 6-9; Jody Powell, "White House Response," Ibid., p. 9; Reeves and Hager, "A Brief Response to Jody Powell," Ibid., pp. 9-10.

[73] David M. Alpern with Richard Thomas, "Why Not the Best Accounts?", *Newsweek,* June 12, 1978, p. 44.

[74] Helen Dewar, "Carter Says It's Possible Ministers Got Campaign Cash," *The Washington Post,* August 9, 1976; Charles Mohr, "Carter Denies Knowing of 'Payments,'" *The New York Times,* August 9, 1976; "Carter Drive Funds Returned by Clergy," *The New York Times,* August 11, 1976; Andrew Mollison, "Campaign Audit Joy May Fade for Carter," *Miami News,* April 3, 1979; Peter Peckarsky, "Carter's Campaign Finances," *The Nation,* May 19, 1979.

[75] Andrew Mollison, "Last-Minute Spending By Carter Not Detailed," *Atlanta Journal,* December 8, 1976; Jerry Landauer, "Audit Is Still Awaited of Carter's Outlays in the '76 Campaign," *The Wall Street Journal,* June 1, 1978.

[76] George Lardner, Jr., " '76 Carter Campaign Unit Is Hit on Documentation," *The Washington Post,* December 26, 1977; Orlando B. Potter, FEC staff director, letter to Robert J. Lipshutz, November 16, 1977, and December 2, 1977.

[77] Joseph Albright, " 'Disclosure Problems' Gave Carter Close Call," *Atlanta Journal,* September 3, 1976.

[78] Martin Tolchin, "Carter Campaign Audit Likely to Be Published Soon," *The New York Times,* June 15, 1978.

[79] Grayson Mitchell, "Carter Election Group Fined for Illegal Use of Leftover Funds," *The Los Angeles Times,* October 14, 1978.

[80] "Carter Campaign Penalized Again for Funds Misuse," *The Washington Post,* October 14, 1978.

[81] "FEC Rules on Carter's 1976 Finances After Pondering Issue Two Years," *Campaign Practices Reports,* October 1, 1978, p. 4.

[82] "Carter's 1976 Election Campaign Fined Again for a Total $11,435," *Campaign Practices Reports,* February 19, 1979, p. 6.

[83] Jeff Gerth, "Loans Let Carter Increase Profits and Access to Cash, Records Show," *The New York Times,* February 11, 1979.

[84] Federal Election Commission, "Report of the Audit Division on the Committee for Jimmy Carter (Primary Election)," released April 2, 1979.

[85] Jo Thomas, "Carter Campaign Fund Audit Criticized," *The New York Times,* April 13, 1979.

[86] Jo Thomas, "Campaign Reporting for Carter Queried," *The New York Times,* April 29, 1979.

[87] Curran, a Republican, was appointed by Attorney General Griffin B. Bell as special counsel to investigate Carter family business financial records after Bell's handling of the investigation had been criticized, based on his close personal relationship with Carter.

[88] Federal Election Commission, "Report of the Audit Division on the 1976 Democratic Presidential Campaign Committee Inc.," released June 4, 1979.

[89] Fred Barbash, "FEC Audit Faults '76 Carter Campaign," *The Washington Post,* June 5, 1979; Barbash, "Unreported Carter Campaign Debt Termed Minor Bookkeeping Matter," *The Washington Post,* June 6, 1979.

[90] Joseph Albright, "Sudden List of Young Debts Interests Election Staff," *Atlanta Journal,* October 20, 1977.

[91] "FEC Fines Detroit Lawyer $10,000 for Illegal Carter Contributions," *Campaign Practices Reports,* July 10, 1978, p. 6.

[92] Suggested by John W. Ellwood and Robert J. Spitzer, "The Democratic National Telethons: Their Successes and Failures," *Journal of Politics* 41, no. 3 (August 1979).

[93] Alexander, *Financing the 1972 Election,* p. 307.

[94] Ellwood and Spitzer, "The Democratic National Telethons."

[95] Ibid.

[96] Ibid.

[97] Alexander, *Financing the 1972 Election,* p. 309.

[98] Jules Witcover, *Marathon: The Pursuit of the Presidency, 1972-1976* (New York: The Viking Press, 1977), p. 537.

[99] James M. Naughton, "Ford Cutting Off Campaign's Start," *The New York Times,* September 3, 1976.

[100] Witcover, *Marathon,* p. 546.

[101] R. W. Apple, Jr., "The Election Outcome: One Week Later, the Politicians Tell How it Happened," *The New York Times,* November 10, 1976.

[102] James M. Naughton, "Ford Says Remarks by Rival on Kelley are 'Contradictory,'" *The New York Times,* September 9, 1976.

[103] Witcover, *Marathon,* p. 554.

[104] Les Brown, "TV Covers Ford's News Session Only by Excerpts," *The New York Times,* October 21, 1976.

[105] Ibid.

[106] George Lardner, Jr. "Ford Flexed the Muscle of Incumbency," *The Washington Post,* October 31, 1976.

[107] Rowland Evans and Robert Novak, "Special Counsel For the Debates," *The Washington Post,* October 2, 1976; and Warren Weaver, Jr., "Ford's Campaign Group Provides Little Insight Into His Spending," *The New York Times,* October 18, 1976.

[108] Weaver, ibid.

[109] "Ford Making Unfair Use of White House Staff in Campaign, Democrats Complain to FEC," *Campaign Practices Reports,* October 18, 1976, p. 7.

[110] Weaver, "Ford's Campaign Group."

[111] "Ford Making Unfair Use. . .," pp. 7-8.

[112] Ibid, p. 8.

[113] Lardner, "Ford Flexed."

[114] Ibid.

[115] "RNC Role in Campaign Set by Rules," *First Monday,* September 1976, p. 7.

[116] "Final Report of Rule 29 Committee — Additional Recommendations and Related Commentary," sent to RNC members December 20, 1974, p. 7.

[117] "RNC Role in Campaign. . . ."

[118] "Byers Named Deputy to Finance Chief," *First Monday,* April 1976, p. 5.

[119] "RNC Waging Biggest Effort," *First Monday,* October 1976, p. 6.

[120] "Jeremiah Milbank's Remarks to the Republican National Committee — January 14, 1977," p. 3.

[121] "RNC Fund-Raising on Target for Ford, Congress Races," *First Monday,* September 1976, p. 11.

[122] Warren Weaver, Jr., "Parties Still Face Financing Trouble," *The New York Times,* September 12, 1976.

[123] "Reagan Joins Ford Campaign on Network TV," *First Monday,* October 1976, p. 8; Rowland Evans and Robert Novak, "Dole's Performance: An Asset to Mr. Ford," *The Washington Post,* September 22, 1976.

[124] Federal Election Commission, *FEC Disclosure Series, No. 4: National Party Political Committee Receipts and Expenditures, Democratic and Republican, 1976 Campaign* (Washington, D.C., April 1977).

[125] Jack Anderson and Les Whitten, "Ethnic Politics," *The Washington Post,* September 16, 1976.

[126] Jack Anderson and Les Whitten, "Campaign Violations Laid to GOP," *The Washington Post,* October 30, 1976.

[127] Paul G. Edwards, "Firm 'Made Mistake' on Political Items," *The Washington Post,* September 24, 1976.

[128] Federal Election Commission, *FEC Disclosure Series, No. 5: Index of Communication Costs by Corporations, Labor Organizations, Membership Organizations, Trade Associations, 1976 Campaign* (Washington, D.C., April 1977), p. 48.

[129] "Few Corporations Have Experienced Right to Convey Political Opinions to Shareholders and Executives," *The New York Times,* November 1, 1976.

[130] John Henry, "Biz New (Spending) Goal: Help Elect *Their* Politicos," *New York Daily News,* November 26, 1976.

[131] A. H. Raskin, "The Labor Scene: COPE's Impact on Election Outcome," *The New York Times,* December 20, 1976.

[132] "Few Corporations Have Experienced Right to Convey Political Opinions."

[133] David Ignatius, "Bashful Business — Despite Liberal Laws, Most Companies Shun 'Partisan' Politicking," *The Wall Street Journal,* October 27, 1976.

[134] Ibid.; Chamber of Commerce of the United States, *Get-Out-The-Vote for Private Enterprise — A New Action Program for National Chamber Members* (Washington, D.C., 1976).

[135] "Few Corporations Have Experienced Right to Convey Political Opinions."

[136] Ignatius, "Bashful Business."

[137] Malbin, "Labor, Business, and Money," p. 415.

[138] Weaver, "Parties Still Face Financing Trouble."

[139] Federal Election Commission, *FEC Disclosure Series, No. 3: Index of Independent Expenditures by Individuals and Receipts and Expenditures by Unauthorized Delegates, 1976 Campaign* (Washington, D.C., March 1977), pp. 108-112; Federal Election Commission, *Independent Expenditures by Individuals, Groups, and Political Committees — 1976 Election, January 1, 1975-October 24, 1976,* pp. 10-12.

[140] Andrew Mollison and Norman Guthartz, Cox Bureau news release, October 18, 1976.

[141] "FEC Clarifies Policy on Independent Expenditures," *Campaign Practices Reports,* October 4, 1976, p. 7.

[142] Mollison and Guthartz.

[143] "FEC Clarifies Policy on Independent Expenditures."

[144] Ibid., pp. 6-7.

[145] Mollison and Guthartz.

[146] Stephen Isaacs, "FEC Is Reviewing Six Ford Units Set Up by Two Californians," *The Washington Post,* September 25, 1976.

[147] "Of 247 Cases Investigated, FEC Has Taken 14 to Court," *Campaign Practices Reports,* January 24, 1977, p. 8.

[148] Bill Richards, "Carter is Sharply Criticized," *The Washington Post,* October 28, 1976.

[149] James M. Naughton, "Voting Surprise by Ford Forecast," *The New York Times,* August 29, 1976.

[150] Witcover, *Marathon.*

[151] Malcolm D. MacDougall, *We Almost Made It.* (New York: Crown Publishers Inc., 1977), p. 115.

[152] Philip H. Dougherty, "Beginning of Ford's Paid TV Spots," *The New York Times,* September 27, 1976.

[153] Joseph Lelyveld, "President's TV Commercials Portray Him as Father Figure Who Inspires Quiet Confidence," *The New York Times,* September 29, 1976.

[154] Joseph Lelyveld, "New Ads for Ford Show Man in Street Expressing Doubt About Carter," *The New York Times,* October 18, 1976.

[155] Ibid.

[156] Christopher Lydon, "Campaign Notes," *The New York Times,* October 25, 1976.

[157] R. W. Apple, Jr., "Ford Tactic: TV 'Documentary' Plus Chat With Sports Announcer," *The New York Times,* October 26, 1976.

[158] James M. Naughton, "Ford Sets TV-Radio Blitz," *The New York Times,* October 24, 1976; Lawrence M. O'Rourke, "A $4 Million Push to Remain in Office," *The Sunday Bulletin* (Philadelphia), October 24, 1976.

[159] "Urban League Critical of a Ford Ad," *The New York Times,* October 21, 1976.

[160] Warren Brown, "Ford Campaign Unit Agrees to Alter Ad Criticized by Black," *The Washington Post,* October 22, 1976.

[161] Lelyveld, "Ads for Ford Expressing Doubt About Carter"; Deirdre Carmody, "Ford and Carter Forces Dispute G.O.P. Ad Showing *Playboy* Cover," *The New York Times,* October 22, 1976.

[162] Weaver, "Parties Still Face Financing Trouble."

[163] James M. Naughton, "Ford to Aim at New York, Jersey and 8 Other Key Industrial States," *The New York Times,* September 23, 1976.

[164] Frank Lynn, "Liberal Party Will Endorse Carter; Conservatives Weigh Backing Ford," *The New York Times,* September 10, 1976; Frank Lynn, "Carter's Forces, in Effort to Recoup in New York, Stress City's Problems," *The New York Times,* October 19, 1976; Jon Nordheimer, "Fund Shortage Cools Interest in Race for President," *The New York Times,* October 25, 1976.

[165] Nordheimer, ibid.

[166] Lou Cannon, "As November 2 Countdown Begins, Ford Camp Plans Media Blitz," *The Washington Post,* October 22, 1976.

[167] R. W. Apple, Jr., "Republicans' Campaign in Texas Handicapped by Financing Curbs," *The New York Times,* October 14, 1976.

[168] Paul G. Edwards, "Carterites to Spend More in Virginia Campaign," *The Washington Post,* September 25, 1976.

[169] Lou Cannon, "Ford's Campaign Strategy: Stress Consistency, Record," *The Washington Post,* September 15, 1976; Witcover, *Marathon,* p. 539.

[170] Nicholas M. Horrock, "Possible Covert Union Gifts to Ford from '64 to '74 Called Target of Inquiry by Watergate Prosecutor," *The New York Times,* September 26, 1976.

[171] One commentator noted that the statute of limitations had lapsed on anything that had occurred during Ford's congressional campaign, since the law went back only three years on campaign violations. James R. Polk, "Watergate Shadow," *The New Republic,* October 9, 1976, pp. 11-12.

[172] Horrock, "Covert Union Gifts."

[173] Jesse Calhoun, president of the Maritime Engineers, sponsored a June 1976 fundraising dinner for Carter that raised $150,000. The maritime unions backed the Democratic nominee in the 1976 election.

[174] Carl Bernstein and Bob Woodward, "Watergate Prosecutor Clears Ford," *The Washington Post,* October 15, 1976.

[175] Lou Cannon, "President Denies Misuse of Any Campaign Funds," *The Washington Post,* October 10, 1976.

[176] "Ford's Toughest Week," *Time,* October 18, 1976, p. 12.

[177] "Text of Prosecutor's Statement on Probe," *The Washington Post,* October 15, 1976.

[178] Christopher Lydon, "U.S. Steel Reports It Entertained Ford," *The New York Times,* September 23, 1976.

[179] John W. Crewdson, "Ford Linked by Dean to '72 Fund Problem," *The New York Times,* September 23, 1976.

[180] "Ford's Toughest Week," *Time.*

[181] Rowland Evans and Robert Novak, "Probing Ford's Finances," *The Washington Post,* October 1, 1976.

[182] Ibid.

[183] Carole Shifrin, "Mrs. Dole Should Quit FTC or the Campaign, Moss Says," *The Washington Post,* September 26, 1976.

[184] Ibid.

[185] "Mrs. Dole's Campaigning Held Legal by Library of Congress," *The New York Times,* September 28, 1976.

[186] Clay Richards, UPI report, March 24, 1978.

[187] "Common Cause Announces National Program to Change Political Campaign," press release, November 5, 1975, p. 3.

[188] John W. Gardner, "Smoking Out the Candidates," October 1975, p. 1.

[189] John W. Gardner, "A Government That Works," December 1975, pp. 1-2.

[190] Ibid.

[191] *In Common*, VII (Winter, 1976), 2.

[192] "Common Cause Announces. . .," pp. 4-5.

[193] "Eleven Presidential Candidates Agree to Campaign Standards Proposed by Common Cause," press release, January 9, 1976, p. 1.

[194] *In Common*, VII (Winter, 1976), 41.

[195] Ibid.

[196] James J. Kilpatrick, "McCarthy vs. Common Cause," *New Brunswick Home News*, February 3, 1976.

[197] "Common Cause Calls on Presidential Candidates to List Budget Priorities," press release, January 15, 1975, p. 1.

[198] "Common Cause President Charges Democratic Candidates Fail to Meet Leadership Challenge," press release, April 22, 1976, p. 1.

[199] Ibid., p. 2.

[200] Ross K. Baker, " 'Naderism Is Running Amuck' With Its Rake," *The New York Times*, December 8, 1977.

[201] "Common Cause Releases Issue Profiles on Ford and Carter," press release, August 23, 1976, p. 2.

[202] "Common Cause Puts the New Congress on the Record," *In Common*, VIII (Winter, 1977), p. 7.

[203] Ibid.

[204] Ibid., p. 10.

[205] Ibid., p. 11.

[206] Ibid., p. 12.

[207] Ibid., p. 7.

[208] Andrew S. McFarland, "The Complexity of Democratic Practice Within Common Cause." Paper prepared for delivery at the 1976 annual meeting of the American Political Science Association, p. 26.

[209] Tom Wicker, "Mathias Sticks His Neck Out," *The New York Times*, November 28, 1975.

[210] David S. Broder, "Conservatives Put Off Bid on 3rd Party, *The Washington Post*, February 17, 1975.

[211] "The Third Party Movement: Is It Going Anywhere?" *First Monday*, March 1975, pp. 7-8.

[212] "Support Is Found for a Third Party: Conservatives Might Draw 25% of Vote, Poll Says," *The New York Times*, April 20, 1975.

[213] Daniel A. Mazmanian, "1976: A Third-Party Year?" *The Nation*, September 13, 1975, p. 204.

For a good description of recent legal challenges to state laws restricting ballot access for independent and minor-party candidates see John C. Armor and Philip L. Marcus, "The Bloodless Revolution of 1976," *American Bar Association Journal*, Volume 63, August 1977, pp. 1108-1112.

[214] Christopher Lydon, "Fund Raiser Quits Group of Rightists," *The New York Times*, October 6, 1975.

[215] Bill Peterson, "Mathias Joins Almost-Rans, Quits Independent Try," *The Washington Post*, March 3, 1976.

[216] When the American Independent Party gave rise to the American Party, several states permitted only one of the two to be listed on the ballot. Both parties were listed in seven states. Lester Maddox ultimately was listed as the American Party candidate (instead of Thomas Anderson) in six states. Maddox and other third-party candidates also were listed under different labels in some states. For Maddox, these unusual party affiliations included: Alabama Conservative Party, George Wallace Party (Connecticut), Conservative Party (Kansas), Constitution Party (Pennsylvania), and Concerned Citizens Party (Utah). "Minor-Party Presidential Candidates Get on the Ballot in 45 States and D.C.," *EA Reports*, October 27, 1976, p. 3.

[217] Federal Election Commission, *FEC Disclosure Series, No. 7: 1976 Presidential Campaign Receipts and Expenditures* (Washington, D.C., 1977), p. 28.

[218] Stephen Isaacs, "Newcomers' Hopes Are Scuttled at 3rd-Party Session," *The Washington Post,* August 29, 1976.

[219] Federal Election Commission, *FEC Disclosure Series, No. 7.*

[220] Ibid.

[221] "Campaign Gift Secrecy Sought by Leftist Party," *The Washington Post,* May 18, 1977; see FEC suits below, pp. 438-442.

[222] Federal Election Commission, *FEC Disclosure Series, No. 7.*

[223] William Chapman, "U.S. Labor Party, GOP Join Forces in 4 Vote Challenges,"*The Washington Post,* November 28, 1976. The National Caucus of Labor Committees (NCLC), a militant socialist organization, sought to ally with the Liberty Lobby, an ultraconservative group based in Washington. In late 1976, NCLC switched from loudly advocating revolution to arguing for the creation of an "industrial capitalist republic" under a "Whig" government, and it began to seek alliances with organizations on the American right. At one point, the FEC started to investigate NCLC's campaign contributors lists, based on an article that had appeared in *Spotlight,* the newspaper of Liberty Lobby, hinting at a Georgia-based drug-rock music promotion scheme to benefit the campaign of Jimmy Carter. The inquiry led the two groups to unite in criticism of the FEC for alleged Gestapo tactics against American political activity. In November 1976, NCLC officials sought political and financial support from the campaign of John B. Burcham, an ultraconservative Republican candidate who was defeated in Maryland's Fifth Congressional District. In particular, the NCLC asked for help with its lawsuits concerning election irregularities in Ohio, Wisconsin, Pennsylvania, and New York. Paul Valentine, "When Left Reaches Right," *The Washington Post,* August 16, 1977.

[217] Federal Election Commission, *FEC Disclosure Series, No. 7.*

[225] Ibid.

[226] Jim McClellan and David E. Anderson, "The Making of the Also-Rans," *The Progressive,* January 1977, pp. 28-29.

[227] Federal Election Commission, *FEC Disclosure Series, No. 7.*

[228] Rhodes Cook, "Third Parties: A Struggle for Attention," *Congressional Quarterly Weekly Report,* October 16, 1976, p. 2972. Also see Julian Weiss, "The Libertarian Party," *Practical Politics,* March/April 1978, pp. 32-33.

[229] Joseph Lelyveld, "Debates Facing Challenge by McCarthy and Maddox," *The New York Times,* September 3, 1976.

[230] "Socialist Party Wins Equal Time on NBC," *The New York Times,* September 30, 1976. Les Brown, "NBC Ordered to Sell Time to Labor Party," *The New York Times,* November 2, 1976.

[231] "Serene Gene," *Newsweek,* March 1, 1976, p. 34.

[232] Committee for a Constitutional Presidency press release, August 22, 1974.

[233] Joel Weisman, "McCarthy Declares for Presidency," *The Washington Post,* August 26, 1974.

[234] Joel Weisman, "McCarthy Launches Presidential Bid," *The Washington Post,* January 14, 1975.

[235] Weisman, "McCarthy Declares."

[236] Christopher Lydon, "McCarthy Running Again, Calls Issues 'Unfinished Business' of '68," *The New York Times,* January 18, 1975.

[237] Eugene J. McCarthy, "The Two-Party System: 'A Closed Circle,' " *The Washington Post,* October 31, 1976.

[238] Ibid.

[239] Eugene J. McCarthy, "Campaign Dollars and Sense," *Commonweal,* January 17, 1975.

[240] Quoted in "How New York Handled Challenges to McCarthy, Moynihan Listings," *Election Administration Reports,* November 10, 1976.

[241] Quoted in "McCarthy Loses Bid for a Role in Debate," *The New York Times,* October 23, 1976.

[242] Warren Weaver, Jr., "McCarthy Tells Whom He Would Choose for Cabinet," *The New York Times,* October 10, 1976.

[243] Ibid.
[244] "William Ford Off McCarthy Ticket," *The Washington Post*, February 13, 1976.
[245] 1976 Democratic Presidential Campaign Committee Inc., advertisement, *The New Republic*, November 6, 1976.
[246] Jules Witcover, "McCarthy Finds Solace In His Election Impact," *The Washington Post*, November 6, 1976.
[247] Walter Pincus, "McCarthy May Be in Costly Bind," *The Washington Post*, November 6, 1976.
[248] Eugene J. McCarthy, Fund-Raising Letter, January 1977.

8 Specialized Expenditures

Media

In 1976, $21.8 million was provided for each presidential candidate's general election campaign and another $3.2 million could be privately raised and spent by the national parties. Gerald Ford and Jimmy Carter each spent large sums on the media, and their campaigns were dominated by television. The large field of candidates seeking presidential nomination, and the increased number of state primaries, gave electronic broadcasting special prominence.

The candidates began to line up media consultants in late 1975. President Ford first enlisted Peter H. Dailey, a Los Angeles advertising executive and creator of the November Group, which had worked for the Committee to Reelect the President in 1972. Harry Treleaven, Jr., who had supervised Nixon's advertising campaign in 1968, became media consultant for Ronald Reagan. Senator Henry Jackson chose Lois, Holland, Gallaway Inc. of New York, a firm with experience promoting Democratic and Republican political candidates for House and Senate seats. George Wallace secured the services of Morgan Advertising Inc., an agency in Birmingham, Alabama. Jimmy Carter contracted with Gerald Rafshoon Advertising Inc. of Atlanta, the firm that had handled his gubernatorial campaign. Morris Udall hired Johnny Allen, a New York consultant, to plan a campaign in New Hampshire alone.

The Cost of Exposure

Inevitably, the candidate paid a substantial sum for the assistance of an advertising consultant to help him win the support of the voters. The services of a prominent political consultant may mean a monthly retainer of $10,000 to $15,000 for consultation, strategy, and research,

457

with additional fees of 15 percent for broadcast billings and production costs.[1]

In general, candidates seeking to use broadcasting effectively found the tab high, and inflation meant that their dollars bought less time than they had in 1972. While a network minute in 1972 had cost approximately $40,000, in 1976 the cost averaged about $90,000 and reached $120,000 for a minute on a prime-time show. Still, one analysis estimated that candidates in the seven presidential campaigns from 1948 through 1972 would have spent $300 million more on their campaigns if they had been unable to use the broadcast media. Per capita expenditure in states with low numbers of television homes far exceeded those in states where many people had television, the analysts noted. In other words, it was suggested that the availability of political advertising on radio and television reduced the amount of money necessary for a political campaign.[2] The FECA worked to reduce broadcast costs marginally by providing that licensees sell time to political candidates at the "lowest unit rate" offered to a most favored advertiser in a given time period.

With a premium on television exposure, one matter of vital concern to challengers was the advantage enjoyed by the incumbent president. The president traditionally has been granted prime time on the air free of charge by the major networks, and recent rulings by the FCC ensure that other candidates may not demand that a network supply time equal to that accorded a presidential address to the nation. During a 10-year period, three presidents sought simultaneous coverage on 45 occasions. Their requests were granted on 44 occasions, and members of Congress quickly noted that similar requests by other government officials, including congressional leadership, usually were denied by the networks. This observation naturally led to consideration of the networks' possible obligation to air different points of view of other speakers with a comparable claim to public attention — an issue of concern to congressional incumbents as well as to presidential challengers.[3]

The traditional access the networks afford to presidents extended on occasion to specifically local audiences. President Ford held interviews with Florida broadcasters in the White House Oval Office before that state's primary, thereby gaining television exposure before Florida viewers and prompting news stories both local and national. Interviews with other print and broadcast journalists were arranged in the White House before primaries in Illinois, Massachusetts, and New Hampshire. Many of the television stations in these states aired the interviews during prime time; the radio stations played the tapes at many times throughout the day. As with presidential news conferences, the equal time provisions of the Communications Act did not apply.

The campaign laws stipulated that any candidate who received federal matching funds could spend no more than $10.9 million to win the nomination. Broken down by state, some of the allowances were $551,071 in Wisconsin, $628,590 in Indiana, $505,351 in Tennessee, $1,072,671 in Michigan, $490,863 in Maryland, $280,343 in Oregon, $1,284,238 in Ohio, and $2,590,470 in California. By the standards of earlier elections, these figures were small, and as a result the candidates sought free exposure more aggressively than ever before. They were more concerned to participate in — and sometimes create — events that would receive news coverage. Hence Senator Jackson pumped gas at a Massachusetts filling station, hoping that the media would report his concern with rising fuel costs.

Even in the face of budgetary restrictions and the high cost of television, some candidates were reluctant or unwilling to accept free or program time. Their doubts that audience attention could be held for extended periods of political discussion seemed to be borne out by experience with the forums televised nationally under the auspices of the League of Women Voters. Five forums were planned and the first, held in February 1976, did not attract significant audiences in New York, Los Angeles, or Chicago markets. Not all of the candidates who had been invited to appear did so, and after the first forum four of the seven televised candidates withdrew from the series. Shriver, Udall, Bayh, and Harris indicated that they wanted to campaign in Massachusetts until the day of that state's primary, but spokesmen for the candidates made known that they might in any case have declined to appear again in the forums because the initial program had been so widely regarded as uninteresting.[4]

Despite the possibility that viewers subjected to a political program might switch channels, the Carter commercial strategy initially used five-minute spots. The advantage, in Gerald Rafshoon's eyes, was to make Carter appear to have more to say on television than did the other candidates — or at any rate those who were appearing in 30- and 60-second spots. In addition, it was felt that the longer period would effectively introduce Carter to voters who did not know of him. To counter a possible drop in audience before the end of the commercial, Rafshoon broke the five-minute period into 40- or 50-second segments during which Carter responded to different questions.

The five-minute spots proved difficult for broadcasting stations to accommodate. Insertion made it necessary to trim the length of regular nonnetwork programming or to aggregate time from commercials that were more lucrative. In addition, the primary period coincided with a rating period for the stations, and they too worried that the five-minute periods would reduce audiences and, as a result, depress advertising revenues. Encountering difficulties, Rafshoon noticed that the stations were selling two-minute blocks of time. Before launching his protest against resistance to five-minute commercials, he cut some of them to two minutes. For a time, the five-minute ads ran on independent stations and the two-minute segments on network affiliates.[5]

The Primary Campaigns

By April 1976 an overview was possible of the approaches and spending patterns of the seven major presidential candidates.[6] The media mix varied widely from state to state. In Massachusetts, Ford spent $23,474 on newspapers, or three times the amount he spent on radio and television. In North Carolina, Florida, and Wisconsin, he spent more on radio than on newspapers or television. Television was his most important medium in New Hampshire and Illinois. Most Ford television commercials were 30 seconds in length and documentary in style.

The Ford campaign was characterized by a number of changes in advertising strategy and consultants. In May the Ford campaign committee replaced Los Angeles consultant Peter Dailey with James J. Jordan, president of a prestigious New York agency. Jordan's commercials featured a "slice of life" approach to promoting Ford's candidacy that contrasted with the stately presidential image projected by Dailey's ads. The new ads almost immediately brought criticism from journalists who observed them. One writer described them as a complete reversal of the earlier Ford strategy and criticized the approach for attempting to sell the president in much the way that brand-name products are promoted on television.

Of all the candidates, Ronald Reagan was widely regarded as the most talented in broadcast delivery because of his acting career. His campaign made use of 30-minute programs and five-minute ads as well as 30- and 60-second spots.

In California, his home state, Reagan outspent Ford. The challenger's commercials showed him in a dignified setting speaking into the camera. In June, Reagan shifted funds from California to Ohio, increasing his budget for television from $50,000 to $100,000. The Ford campaign's chief expenditures in Ohio were for telephone banks. The president's committee budgeted $200,000 for the campaign there, with no paid television advertising and only $20,000 for radio. His 10 telephone banks were expected to complete 150,000 calls by June 7. Ford was said to be running close to the limit for primary spending in the Ohio campaign, and as a result he had to curtail spending until two days before the primary.[7]

Carter's media tactics drew press attention in June when he reserved for himself the largest political audience of the campaign to this point by buying time simultaneously on all three major networks. Some experts speculated that this might be the largest television audience ever assembled for a political broadcast.[8]

Gerald Rafshoon placed Carter's radio and television expenditures at $800,000 for the two weeks leading up to June 4 and approaching the conclusion of the primary season. Charlene Carl, vice-president and media director of the Rafshoon agency, estimated that between 4 and 5 percent of the primary ad budget was allotted to newspapers, 10 to 15 percent to radio, and the balance to television, with the media plan roughly the same for each state.[9]

Rafshoon adopted a cinema verité style of political advertising that sought to reflect and amplify the candidate without creating a "package" of the sort associated with Madison Avenue advertising. During the later weeks the advertising strategy shifted from two- and five-minute commercials to 30- and 60-second spots, as Carter's committee determined that the public had become better acquainted with the candidate. Carter's strategy also called for 60-second radio spots, and he outspent all Democratic candidates except Wallace on radio and television advertising.

Frank Church placed 30-minute and five-minute commercials on television in addition to 30- and 60-second radio and television spots, achieving saturation in Nebraska just before the primary there. Sixty percent of his media budget went to television, 30 percent to radio.

Henry Jackson's expenses favored television three to one over radio in Massachusetts and Florida. In New York and Pennsylvania his media budget went exclusively for television. Jackson's campaign concentrated on 30- and 60-second television spots in prime and fringe time, with many appearing during late shows. His commercials attempted to address the issues while at the same time projecting an image of the candidate's personality.

George Wallace's campaign strategy stressed appearances on television rather than at political rallies because of the candidate's physical handicaps. About 80 percent of his media spending consisted of expenditures for television. A typical state campaign began 15 days before a primary and made extensive use of 30-second television spots directed at heavily Democratic districts. Six days before the primary, 30-minute films would be added to the schedule, with as many as four appearing in one week. The films showed Wallace facing the viewer and discussing the issues, with no attempt made to conceal his wheelchair.[10]

Suspension of federal matching funds caused extreme disarray in the Udall campaign. In April 1976 he contracted for $80,000 worth of broadcast advertising in Pennsylvania and hoped to increase the figure to $100,000. This amount was about two-thirds of that spent on broadcast advertising in the state by Jimmy Carter. In Wisconsin, Udall spent $51,000 on television, $23,000 on radio, and about $26,000 on newspapers. In Massachusetts his media expenditures totaled $178,000 — 30 percent for television, 10 percent for radio, and 60 percent for newspaper advertising. In New York he spent $11,000 on radio and $38,000 on newspapers. His television campaign consisted almost exclusively of 30- and 60-second spots. Hardest hit, perhaps, by his inability to purchase greater quantities of air time, Udall criticized Congress for delaying passage of legislation that should have brought him $290,000 in federal matching funds.[11]

The Conventions

Journalists covering the Democratic National Convention in 1976 did not find much excitement to report, and network researchers produced unsurprising statistics regarding the television audiences. One out of four adult viewers was found to have watched as Carter accepted the presidential nomination, and although this was approximately the same number as had watched Richard Nixon accept the Republican nomination in 1972, both speeches were considered to have drawn fewer than half the usual number of viewers for addresses by a president during prime time. Researchers interpreted these results as reflecting audience attitudes toward the convention. Nielsen ratings indicated that more than 60 percent of those watching television during Carter's speech were tuned to independent stations airing other programs. NBC and CBS, the networks that offered full coverage of the convention live, did not express satisfaction with this approach; ABC professed greater satisfaction with its abbreviated coverage, yet the Nielsen ratings did not indicate that ABC's coverage attracted more viewers.[12]

The broadcasting industry itself blamed the poor audiences on the dullness of the convention, which it had sought to counteract with sophisticated electronic equipment and imaginative professionalism on the part of record numbers of journalists and technical crews. Radio and television coverage engaged approximately 3,700 newsmen, technicians, and other personnel, in contrast to the 3,000 individuals who attended the 1972 Florida convention in these capacities. The networks devoted more than 71 hours of air time to proceedings lasting four days, and the cost for all three networks to cover both the Democratic and Republican conventions was placed at $30 million, excluding dollars lost because regular programs were preempted. CBS won in the ratings when all three networks were covering the convention. National radio networks covered the convention using approaches that varied from gavel-to-gavel coverage (dispatched by Associated Press Radio to Washington for transmission to member stations) to live interviews and updates (sent by UPI Audio from its skybooth in Madison Square Garden to more than 300 member stations). The broadcasting industry billed the coverage as the "biggest ever" given to the Democratic convention.[13]

Network arrangements for the Republican convention in Kansas City were similar to those for the Democratic convention in New York. The network staffs had more space; still, they had difficulties, although different ones from those experienced in New York. The facilities in Kemper Arena required modification, whereas those in Madison Square Garden had required replacement in many cases.

Television coverage of the Republican convention was considered unsuccessful by some observers. One writer noted that although Ford's victory was closely contested, both its announcement and his selection of a running mate appeared anticlimactic after expressions of feeling for Ronald Reagan's defeat in his bid for nomination.

The Republican National Convention drew a television audience larger by 10 million people than that attracted to coverage of the Democratic convention, which had been watched by an estimated 100 million viewers. Both NBC and CBS gave complete live coverage to the Republicans for a total of about 25-3/4 hours; ABC continued its policy of abbreviated coverage of the conventions and provided about 16 hours of footage.[14]

The General Election Campaigns

After the conventions, attention focused on the campaign strategies of the two major candidates. Both Ford and Carter devised special advertising tactics for the period of the televised debates. Ford's consultants decided not to begin his television commercials until the first debate was three days past, although the Carter commercials were aired earlier. The decision of the Ford campaign reflected a desire to use the advertising to complement the impression left in viewers' minds by the debate itself. Rafshoon adopted a different policy, however, contending that it was better to reach the electorate "while it is fluid," that is, before the debates could shape public opinion.[15]

The policy of the Ford committee drew attention to the fact that the candidate's television advertising was planned late and that media consultants for the postnomination period had not been chosen until the day of Ford's nomination. The new consultants, John Deardourff and Douglas Bailey, were partners in a firm specializing in advertising for moderate Republicans. After surveying the Ford promotion during the primaries and caucuses, the new consultants concluded that an entirely new approach was desirable. They felt that the earlier commercials displayed Ford too much as an incarnation of the presidency and focused too little on the man's personal qualities. Accordingly, they announced that their plans would call for a fresh television campaign that would last five weeks — shorter by two weeks than the television campaign of Richard Nixon in 1972. The Ford campaign estimated that it would spend $6 million to $6.5 million on television time from mid-September until election day, with slightly more than half of that sum paid for network time. The new Ford strategy called for presenting the president as a man of inner serenity and accomplishment. Deardourff also indicated that Ford commercials would attack Carter, concentrating on his "inexperience" and "studied vagueness."

By late September the new Ford commercials were on the air with a theme song — "Feeling Good about America" — that would be heard in all of his television advertising until election day. The approach was cinema verité, with Ford shown delivering speeches or giving informal interviews. The Ford headquarters estimated that about 75 to 80 percent of the advertising budget would go for television, but noted that radio advertising would also be used extensively along with newspaper and farm journal advertising late in the campaign.[16]

At the end of July, Carter made it known that he projected his general election media advertising at $8.5 million. Rafshoon stressed that this advertising would focus on Carter's qualifications for the presidency rather than attack his opponents. In reporting the media budget, one journalist noted that it was less than half the $21.8 million allowed by federal law and less than the sums spent for advertising during some previous presidential campaigns. Two-thirds of the money was said to be directed toward television advertising, with half specifically allocated to network advertising. Carter's figure of $8.5 million for the postnomination period was more than double the $3.3 million he had spent in 38 states during the primaries and caucuses.[17]

In October 1976 one writer compared the political advertising on television being undertaken by the Ford and Carter campaigns.[18] He observed that the three major networks were carrying 10 to 15 ads a week, most of which were five-minute or 60-second spots appearing during prime time. The writer pointed to the similar images the candidates sought to project, then noted that whereas Carter's campaign had maintained a consistent theme and appeal from the beginning of the campaign, Ford's approach had changed in a variety of ways from the early days.

Commentators who noted similarities might have been echoing the opinions of the candidates' media directors themselves. John Deardourff argued that the question in the voters' minds was not the candidate's stand on national issues, but rather the candidate's character, experience, intellect, and decisiveness. Gerald Rafshoon said, "The issue is the candidate's character, leadership, and integrity." Speaking before the American Association of Advertising Agencies in New York in October 1976, the two consultants placed their candidates' advertising expenditures at approximately $10 million apiece.[19] According to Deardourff, Ford would spend about $7 million for television, $1.5 million for radio, $1.2 million for major newspapers, and $300,000 for ethnic and selected newspapers. Rafshoon analyzed Carter's expenditure, announcing that $7 million would go to television, $1 million to radio, $500,000 for the print media, and the balance for brochures and other forms of advertising.

The week of October 17, 1976, the president's network advertising schedule provided for a total of 64-1/2 minutes of paid network time. It consisted mainly of five-minute programs, with some 60-second and 30-second spots, approximately 10 minutes' worth appearing every day except Friday, when none appeared, and Saturday, when seven minutes of ads were shown. Most of the spots appeared on ABC (27-1/2 minutes), with CBS second (21 minutes), and NBC third (16 minutes).[20]

In mid-October the Ford campaign began to run TV spots that were critical of Carter. The ads showed street interviews with Georgians and other Americans critical of Carter's "lack of experience" and "fuzzy" position on the issues.

Shortly after these commercials began to appear, the Carter campaign employed Tony Schwartz to produce a new batch of ads for Carter. They differed from the commercials produced by Rafshoon in several respects: The candidate, in a dark suit and tie, faced the viewer squarely, and the tight framing seemed to one commentator to sharpen the focus of the ad. Presented in this fashion, Carter addressed issues such as inflation and taxes which, it was thought, would reflect poorly on the incumbent president. Noting the switch in television strategy, the commentator suggested that television had itself become the campaign, and that this phenomenon was attributable to the effects of the spending limits that reduced the amounts candidates might invest in organization, telephone facilities, billboards, buttons, and the like.[21]

A new and key part of Ford's late campaign television schedule proved to be 30-minute programs that were documentary in style. Each depicted the president campaigning and then talking with sports announcer Joe Garagiola, who asked various questions. These films were placed to coincide with Ford's visits to each of several major states. Nearly two-thirds of Ford's television budget was spent during the last two weeks of the campaign.[22]

Carter spent close to $9.8 million for broadcasting, or about $7.6 million on television and $1.1 million on radio, and the rest on production and incidentals. Only $350,000 of Carter's media expenditures went for print advertising.

Throughout the campaigns, considerable controversy centered on the difficulties candidates experienced in securing the types of air time they wanted. Equally controversial, however, was the use candidates made of the broadcast media. Many observers asked to what extent 30- and 60-second spots could be expected to inform the public, and still more expressed concern about the difficulties political programming presented to broadcasters and candidates alike. Some argued that broadcasters had too much control over political broadcasting and others thought that broadcasters had too little freedom. If commercial broadcasters seemed too reluctant to schedule public affairs programming, public broadcasters were hampered in doing so by funding difficulties and by the apparent preference of many candidates for paid time.

The Candidates, the Media, and the Law

The Communications Act of 1934 mandates equal time broadasting opportunities to all qualified candidates for a public office. While there was no initial obligation under the Act to provide any candidate with air time, if time is provided free or sold to one candidate for public office, equal opportunity, free or sold time must be made available to all candidates for that office. The Act further provided that stations could not censor material broadcasts. In 1959 Congress exempted from the equal time regulations all newscasts, news interviews, news documentaries, and on-the-spot coverage of such events as political conventions.

When the FECA was enacted in 1971, it included an amendment to the Communications Act of 1934 giving the FCC authority to revoke a station's license if it denied candidates for federal office reasonable access to the air. In addition, the FECA required broadcasters to sell time to candidates at the lowest unit rate offered to commercial advertisers during the 45-day period preceding primaries and the 60-day period preceding general elections.

Ford's News Conferences

Problems relating to equal time and reasonable access surfaced early in the campaigns. In July 1975 the Columbia Broadcasting System filed with the FCC a petition asking the agency to exempt presidential news conferences from the equal time provision. The CBS petition held that President Ford's announcement of his candidacy for the Republican nomination made him a legally qualified candidate, and the station expressed concern that broadcasts of Ford's news conferences might lead other candidates seeking the Republican nomination to request equal time.

In September 1975 Democratic National Committee Chairman Robert S. Strauss threatened to sue the FCC if it ruled in favor of exempting presidential press conferences and political debates from the equal time requirements. At issue here was the opportunity afforded the Democratic presidential candidate to compete with an incumbent Republican to whom broadcast time was immediately available upon request, free of charge.

Nevertheless, the FCC approved the exemption by a five-to-two vote. So controversial had the issue become, however, that the networks remained wary of claims from competing candidates, and two of the three major networks declined to broadcast President Ford's speech to the nation regarding tax proposals. ABC televised the address, saying that it was of vital interest to the nation; CBS and NBC saw the tax plan as the cornerstone of Ford's campaign, and NBC argued that it did not properly qualify as a news event exempt from equal time.[23]

The DNC was not alone in opposing the FCC exemption of news conferences. Speaking before the seven members of the FCC on November 12, 1975, Sen. John O. Pastore, D-R.I., accused them of usurping congressional authority and said, "What you're actually doing is destroying equal time."[24]

The Democratic National Committee, Rep. Shirley Chisholm, D-N.Y., and the National Organization for Women (NOW) appealed the FCC decision in the courts. Filing briefs in support of the FCC were CBS and the Aspen Institute Program for Communications and Society, which was joined in its brief by Common Cause. CBS was concerned that presidential news conferences be declared exempt; the Aspen Institute was concerned with exemption of political debates. Other supporters of the FCC decision included the National Association of Broadcasters, the Radio Television News Directors Association, ABC, and NBC. On April 12, 1976, a U.S. Court of Appeals upheld the agency's ruling by a two-to-one vote.[25]

These new exemptions from the equal time requirement proved to be the FCC's most controversial ruling in years. Spokesmen for the DNC and for Representative Chisholm and NOW voiced their conviction that the commission's ruling afforded too much freedom to broadcasters. They contended that Congress would have exempted presidential press conferences explicitly if such an exemption had been intended to be part of the Communications Act. Further, they noted that such press conferences are controlled by the candidate, that it is important to distinguish between a news event in which a candidate appears and an occasion when the candidate himself is the event. The FCC's ruling was thought to extend to the broadcasters' ultimate power to decide how much time a candidate will receive, to the exclusion of his opponent, and the protesting organizations also noted that the decision afforded major-party candidates a significant advantage over minor-party and fringe candidates.

Movies and Miscellany

In still another ruling, the FCC declared on November 20, 1975, that any identifiable appearance by a candidate on television qualified for the equal time rule. This statement meant that stations broadcasting old movies or other programs in which Ronald Reagan spoke or appeared would be liable for equal time claims from other candidates. Reagan anticipated the ruling, declaring that he would drop a radio comment program when he became a candidate to avoid claims for equal time from his opponents.

Other questions arose regarding matters on which the FCC was not asked to rule. One of these concerned cases in which someone made an independent expenditure for a candidate without his knowledge, undertaking to purchase and produce a political commercial without collaborating with the candidate or his committee. Would this commercial, if aired by a broadcaster, entitle the candidate's opponents to equal time? An FCC spokesman responded that the agency did not know, since it had not been asked to decide this question. One commentator conjectured that the issue was unlikely to arise frequently, since independent testimonials appear more often in print than through the broadcast media.[26] Moreover, broadcasters are not required to sell time to a noncandidate.

In March 1976 the FCC ruled on two different cases that arose during the primaries.[27] In one, the agency found that WGN-TV and WGN Radio in Chicago could not restrict the length of political commercials they would accept. The commission determined that the stations' policy was contrary to provisions of the FECA. The plaintiff in the case was President Ford's campaign committee. The station argued that candidates need at least five minutes of air time to state a position. The Ford committee, anxious not to lose viewers, wished to purchase 60- and 30-second spots. Its attitude found support with the National Black Media Coalition and the United Auto Workers, which opposed the station's policy on the ground that it discriminated against candidates who were not wealthy. The commissioners were split five-to-two on the issue.

The second case concerned station WCKT in Miami, which the commission ruled did not have to supply equal time to Ronald Reagan after broadcasting a series of interviews with President Ford in its news programs. In denying the claim of the Reagan committee, the commission indicated that news carried in regularly scheduled news programs is exempt from equal time provisions even if, as the Reagan committee argued, Ford discussed his and Reagan's candidacy for the Republican nomination during the broadcast.

Another battle over the equal time provision occurred when the Socialist Workers Party presidential candidate was refused time by NBC after Gus Hall, the Communist Party presidential candidate, had appeared on NBC and its New York City affiliate. NBC argued that the "Tomorrow" show, the program in question, was a bona fide news program exempt from the equal time requirement; the FCC disagreed, however, and directed the network to meet its obligations to Peter Camejo.[28] Lyndon H. LaRouche, the U.S. Labor Party presidential candidate, also won a contest with the network regarding equal time. The FCC ruled on November 1, 1976, that NBC must grant LaRouche the half hour that he had attempted to purchase.[29]

Buying Time

At the heart of some questions about reasonable access and equal time lay a conviction on the part of many informed individuals that the viewing public simply would not focus on presidential candidates for longer than the time required for a purchase spot. Many candidates accordingly felt that free time on the air, granted in programs a half-hour long or more, would cost them viewers who could more effectively be reached by a 30-second commercial inserted into a prime-time entertainment program.

When ABC's affiliate in Boston, WCVB-TV, invited all declared candidates in the New Hampshire and Massachusetts primaries to its studios for an hour of televised discussion, four candidates declined to appear. The station noted a decrease in viewers for the program. Yet the station indicated that it would not sell time for paid political commercials. Since candidates had been televised on a program not exempt from the equal time ruling, however, Ronald Reagan's committee attempted to place a political spot with the station, saying that Reagan preferred paid time. WCVB's lawyers determined that Reagan's position was legally sound, and the station reluctantly announced that it would sell time to candidates.[30]

Reagan also experienced difficulties in March 1976, when he approached the three major networks to buy time equal to that granted President Ford. The challenger criticized the networks' refusal to meet this request, and his press secretary explained that one network contended that to honor Reagan's request would require the network to honor requests from every candidate for president. The press reported Reagan's complaint, and NBC reversed its decision, agreeing to make a half-hour available to the candidate at 10:30 p.m. on Wednesday, March 31, 1976, at a cost of $100,000. The air time offered the candidate an important fund-raising opportunity at a moment when his campaign was deeply in debt and hard pressed for funds.[31]

Frank Church had similar difficulties when he sought to buy 30 minutes of prime time from all three major networks in April 1976. Since Reagan's 30 minutes had been televised by NBC, Church filed a petition with the FCC claiming violation of the reasonable access requirement. Church's campaign committee rejected NBC's argument that Church was not yet a candidate for the Democratic nomination. Henry Kimelman, national finance chairman for the Church committee, said Church was faced with a "Catch 22 situation. . . . He can't break out of the field without national news coverage. And he can't get national news coverage until he breaks out of the field." Senator Church's difficulties continued, and in May 1976, after he had requested a half-hour of prime time from station KGW-TV in Portland, Oregon, the FCC ruled five-to-two that the station could not refuse, as it had done, to sell him more than five minutes of prime time. The commission's decision seemed to many to reflect growing sympathy within the agency for presidential candidates to whom the networks refused to make prime time available.[32]

Access to Air Time

Probably the biggest single area of controversy was that surrounding the presidential debates between Gerald Ford and Jimmy Carter and sponsored by the League of Women Voters. The exclusion of other candidates for president was contested in court by several of them on various grounds described below. The FCC's rejection in October 1976 of equal time complaints from American Independent Party candidate Lester Maddox and independent candidate Eugene McCarthy was widely regarded as significant, however. The appeals court in Washington had earlier rejected a complaint from the Socialist Workers Party on grounds of violations of equal time regulation. In denying the Maddox and McCarthy complaints, the FCC rejected the idea that the suspension of the first debate owing to a technical failure 26 minutes in duration established that the league and the networks were collaborating. Actually, the studio audio system failed and even the live audience could not have heard it had the debate gone on. "No broadcaster is shown to have exercised control over the continuation or suspension of the debate," the commission concluded. On October 12, 1976, the Supreme Court declined to review the FCC's position regarding equal time, and only one of the nine justices indicated that he would have been willing to hear arguments in the case.[33]

In May 1977 the FCC ruled that a station was not obligated to sell a candidate the specific amount of time he requested. The decision appeared to some observers to reverse the ruling issued in the case of WGN radio and television stations in March 1976. In its new decision, the agency noted that the law conferred upon a political candidate the same standing as that of other advertisers only in the sense that the candidate must be charged the lowest commercial rate for air time. The FCC stressed that the law did not confer upon the candidate a right to access to all types of air time available to other advertisers. The FCC voted four-to-three in this case, and Commissioner Joseph R. Fogarty issued a separate statement declaring that Congress rather than the commission should determine whether nonfederal candidates should be given a specific right of access to broadcast facilities. Commissioner Benjamin L. Hooks objected to the ruling, arguing that it would create new difficulties for candidates seeking access to broadcast facilities. Also dissenting were Commissioners Robert E. Lee and Abbott Washburn, with Lee attempting to confine the vote to unanimous rejection of the complaint at hand. The complaint had been filed by Anthony Martin-Trigona, an unsuccessful candidate for mayor of Chicago.[34]

The ruling in this case led FCC Chairman Charles D. Ferris to declare that the commission must establish an explicit policy rather than relying on a continuing series of ad hoc decisions. Accordingly, the FCC began drafting regulations on several issues. Of specific concern was the time during a campaign when a station must provide a federal candidate with reasonable access to the air, whether licensed stations should be obligated to comply with candidates' requests for specific lengths of time, and whether public broadcasting stations and commercial stations should be subject to the same standards of reasonable access.[35]

In July 1978 the FCC announced a new policy to provide reasonable access to the air. The ruling stated that: Stations must give or sell "uses" of a station to legally qualified candidates for federal office in order to meet the reasonable access requirement; except in unusual circumstances, broadcasters must furnish candidates with prime program time and prime spot announcements to fulfill the obligation;

stations could not flatly prohibit federal candidates from applying for the types, lengths, and classes of time available to commercial advertisers; reasonable access must be provided at least during the 45 days before a primary and the 60 days before a general or special election; noncommercial stations were obliged to make available to candidates only lengths of program time that formed a normal component of a broadcast day; noncommercial broadcasters could not censor or reject any part of broadcast matter submitted by a candidate, even if the content indicated that the ad had been prepared for commercial television; and although commercial and noncommercial broadcasters might suggest the format for a candidate's appearance, the candidate was not obliged to accept their suggestions.[36]

In another ruling, the FCC clarified its definition of a legally qualified candidate entitled to equal opportunities and access to air time. In addition to publicly announcing his candidacy, being eligible to hold office, and qualifying for a place on the ballot or committing himself to seek election by the write-in method, the candidate must make a "substantial showing" of bona fide candidacy. Further, the commission ruled that persons qualifying for a party's nomination for president or vice president in 10 states must be regarded by broadcasters as qualified candidates, and it noted that no person would be considered a qualified candidate more than 90 days prior to a nominating convention.[37]

The Impact of the Media

One observer of the 1976 elections noted that the crowd around the political candidates stood three deep, with reporters covering the candidates, commentators examining media coverage, and sociologists studying the entire spectacle. The question prominent in many minds concerned the ways in which the media, and particularly television, both interpreted and served the contestants. How and to what degree did they influence the campaigns, public opinion, and the outcome of the vote?

The Unseeing Eye, written by Thomas E. Patterson and Robert D. McClure,[38] was one of the first book-length analyses of the role of the media in politics undertaken by political scientists since television assumed first rank among campaign advertising methods. Conducting interviews with voters during the 1972 general election campaign, the authors found that political commercials were more informative about election issues than were network news programs. They concluded that voters obtained little relevant information about the candidates and the issues from news programs.

In a subsequent report prepared under a grant from the Markle Foundation, Professor Patterson contended that many Americans found the 1976 presidential election frustrating and confusing, and that while the candidates contributed to this perception, much of the blame lay with the media's focus on the election primarily as a horse race or competition to be won or lost. This emphasis, Patterson maintained, acted to exclude debate over issues and national leadership.[39] He cited earlier studies indicating that the horse race aspects of elections have received increasing attention in recent decades and pointed to three innovations in election journalism as responsible for this trend: 1) increasingly scientific surveys undertaken by the media, with those taken in 1976 focusing on the candidates' standing among voters and the reasons for it, 2) an increase in "inside reports" on candidates' strategies and organization, and 3) extensive use of computer voting models whose sole function was to predict election outcomes in advance of the final tally.

At a convention of the American Psychological Association in September 1976, it was reported that studies of elections in Colorado, Wisconsin, and Michigan indicated that more than 60 percent of the individuals surveyed felt television commercials had helped them decide for whom to vote. Charles Atkin, the reporting psychologist, noted that political advertising was remembered more clearly by viewers than were other types of commercials. As many as 56 percent of the individuals he questioned were able to describe a political ad, or more than twice the number usually able to recall a commercial. He said viewers recalled candidates' positions rather than the imagery chosen by the media consultants, and he advised parties to give the public more substantive information.[40]

When the elections were past, one commentator remarked that profound changes were taking place in the nature of campaigns and the nature of their coverage. In part, he attributed these changes to the emergence of television as the dominant means for communication between candidate and voter. Nevertheless, this reporter argued, television cannot focus on the issues. It does not provide a forum for debate, but rather a medium for drama and political combat. He concluded that the weaknesses inherent in television as a vehicle for political candidates confer a greater obligation on print journalists, since the printed media have demonstrated a superior ability to tackle substantive issues effectively.[41]

The Journalist's Role

Much public attention was directed to evaluation of press coverage of the campaigns in 1976. Some observers charged the press with triviality in its criticism and general coverage of major candidates. In addition, there was discussion of the proper role and responsibility of newspaper publishers and reporters. Some debated the propriety of endorsements of presidential candidates, asking whether a paper should properly seek to guide the judgment of its readers. It was also noted that an undetermined number of weekly newspapers did not report that some candidates were running for political office unless the candidate paid for the article or took out paid political announcements, and critics held that this practice violated standards of journalistic ethics.[42]

In addition to these aspects of journalistic conduct, observers considered the extent to which the media could be relied upon simply to document a candidate's financial holdings and debts, permitting public evaluation of them without distorting the information; the degree to which presentation of the candidate by a newspaper or other publisher remained free from influence by that paper's other interests, financial and otherwise; and the extent to which publication itself necessarily conferred undue emphasis on forms of behavior to which a candidate might be considered entitled as a private citizen but not as a public official. Some individuals, including the publisher of *The Washington Post*, wondered whether investigative reporting had not gone too far.[43]

With criticism of news coverage came the difficulty of assigning the blame. If the media pictured the campaigns as a horse race and conferred undue attention on the candidates' slips of the tongue and similar mistakes, were the media or the candidates themselves to blame? Some commentators found the campaign depressing and banal. Jimmy Carter acknowledged the dearth of serious discussion in the press and pointed to the reporters on board his aircraft, complaining that they did not respond to questions of national interest. The journalists responded, in some cases claiming that Carter and other candidates had addressed serious issues very little and arguing that the candidates manipulated the press in the sense that the press simply covered events prepared by the candidates.[44]

Part of the general public shared Carter's expressed view that the media were at fault, and some scholars maintained that U.S. political campaigns are usually shallow. One observer suggested that intense coverage of the campaigns for the extended period of time during which they occur may act to raise expectations that cannot be fulfilled. Some surveys were more encouraging, however. In the last poll undertaken by CBS News and *The New York Times*, individuals were asked if the 1976 campaign was more interesting than the 1972 campaign. Sixty-seven percent answered affirmatively; another study, undertaken at the University of Michigan's Center for Political Studies, also indicated that public interest was higher in 1976 than in 1972.[45]

Proposals for Improvement

In May 1978 a report prepared by The American Assembly on Presidential Nominations and the Media recommended the following changes in journalistic practice:[46]

• Focusing more reports on comparisons of the candidates' positions on a single set of issues as distinguished from reports that simply describe the issue stance of a single candidate without the comparative dimension.

• Using journalists with specialized knowledge in specific subject matter areas to examine issue stances.

• Rotating reporters among the candidates' campaigns to furnish a fresh perspective and guard against reporters acquiring a vested interest in "their" candidate's success.

• Concentrating more resources on explorations of candidates' political and personal histories.

• Comparing candidates' most recent pronouncements with their previous statements.

In May 1978 the Campaign Study Group at Harvard University made a number of proposals for improving television's role in political campaigns. The proposals were based on a 132-page report, "A Study of Access to Television for Political Candidates," prepared by George White, a Harvard student.[47] The report found that candidates' use of television does not result in broad manipulation of the electorate, that television offers significant opportunities to challengers in particular, and that television constitutes the most efficient medium for communication between candidates for federal office and their potential constituencies. The Harvard report was critical of television election coverage; it noted that the quality of the coverage seemed to reflect news editors' belief that election campaigns lack interest or entertainment value for the public. In addition, the report suggested that television would play a larger role in the future education of voters because the political parties, traditionally active in this area, are waning in influence. To improve television access for candidates, the report recommended a system of tax incentives for public broadcasting licensees, public financing, under a voucher system, for paid time and an increase in the supply of prime-time spots.[48]

Technology. The importance of the media for campaigning politicians makes technological advance in communications a subject of compelling interest. Print, broadcasting, telecommunications, and cinema are no longer separate, noncompeting industries; further, new electronic developments are certain to alter human communication profoundly in ways that will certainly affect political messages and candidate spending.[49] Whether these innovations are communications satellites, cable packet switched computer networks, data and facsimile transmission via telephone circuits, or computer polling systems, it seems clear that they will make possible transmission of text or data anywhere at electronic speeds for costs similar to or less than those imposed by the international mails.

Technological developments in the media prompted many observers to speculate how advertisers, politicians, and others would communicate with the public in the years ahead. More flexibility is a possibility as is more precise targeting. One media specialist estimated that by the end of 1981 there would be between 20 million and 26 million cable subscribers, representing a 25 to 30 percent penetration of American homes by cable television, and that approximately 50 percent of all homes would have cable available to them at that time. Advertisers, the specialist conjectured, would be increasingly interested in this market, since 30 percent might be considered the critical figure in the emergence of electronic communications as a broad-based advertising medium. Noting that the 30 percent figure would also be important in enabling cable to become a major communications industry, the specialist then predicted that pay television would grow, as would use by broadcasters of domestic satellites and video discs. He concluded that in the future "[a]udiences will be reached differently and accumulate differently, and that means the messages we create and the schedules we execute will be different."[50] All of this undoubtedly will offer candidates many new benefits, but also will require new forms of regulation to ensure that the candidates and the public are fairly served.

Regulation. Regulation of the communications media is supervised in Congress by the House and Senate Commerce committees. Accuracy in Media (AIM), an organization with the stated objective of watching over the press, made known in winter 1977 that political action committees set up by large media organizations had filed reports with the Federal Election Commission indicating that they had channeled funds to members of both congressional committees. During the 1976 campaigns, the communications PACs were said to have contributed $20,000, television and radio PACS $50,000, and a cable television PAC $20,000, to incumbent congressmen.[51]

Other questions arose regarding possible conflicts of interest in the communications industry. The appointment of a former chairman of the Federal Communications Commission to trusteeship of the broadcasting group that distributed industry campaign contributions provoked comment from thoughtful observers. Richard E. Wiley, who had been FCC chairman from 1974 until September 1977, was elected in April 1978 to the board of trustees of the Television and Radio Political Action

Committee (affiliated with the National Association of Broadcasters). Furthermore, Wiley's law firm, Kirkland and Ellis, was asked by the association of broadcasters to advise it on possible antitrust violations suggested by the association's policy concerning toy advertisements on children's programs. Another former FCC commissioner, Robert Wells, was also a member of the PAC board.[52]

Dominance of Television

In sum, the impact of the media on the 1976 elections was a topic that received considerable attention from many students of American political life. There was little consensus regarding its precise nature, and analysts generally expressed awareness that more studies and more data were needed. The dominance of television was widely recognized, however, and in view of the discussion of its role by so many writers, the opinions of two unsuccessful candidates for president are noteworthy. One magazine asked George McGovern and Barry Goldwater about their views. McGovern commented that television had been essential to his nomination in 1972, but that the conditions under which he had been filmed during the 1972 general election campaign led him to suffer by comparison with Richard Nixon.

Goldwater and McGovern both agreed that television formed the nation's impression of a presidential candidate's personality and effectiveness, and they agreed as well that it presented an incumbent president with a tremendous advantage during an election campaign. When asked whether television adequately covered the issues, the two men noted that in their opinions the partial views television newscasts offered of rallies and other campaign events often seemed to give the viewer a misleading picture.

Goldwater in particular felt that television coverage had vastly changed the atmosphere of the national party conventions. The chief difference he noted was a greater seriousness in the proceedings. At the same time, he expressed a conviction that the conventions proceeded more smoothly as a result of the camera's presence. McGovern added that television, with its ability to shift from one commentator or camera to others on the convention floor, offered the viewer a more accurate sense of the progress of convention business than was available to a delegate on the floor. Although neither Goldwater nor McGovern directly answered a question regarding the quality of broadcast journalism as compared with that of the printed media, both seemed to feel that certain weaknesses in a candidate's composure were more likely to be accentuated by television. On balance, however, McGovern found certain print journalists guilty of conscious bias more frequently than broadcasters.[53]

The Presidential Debates [54]

The Federal Communications Act of 1934 stated that if a broadcaster allowed a political candidate to "use" his station, all other candidates for that office must have "equal time opportunities." In 1959 Congress passed an amendment to the 1934 Act that exempted from this rule all bona fide newscasts, news interviews, news documentaries, and on-the-spot coverage of news events.[55]

One year later, Congress suspended Section 315, the "equal time" section of the Act, but only for that year and only for the presidential campaigns. The three major television networks had sought repeal of Section 315, but Congress agreed only to a one-year suspension: Key members of Congress voiced the fear that repeal would give the networks undue influence on political campaigns in this country. Upon winning the Democratic presidential nomination, John F. Kennedy challenged Vice President Richard Nixon, the Republican Party's nominee, to a series of debates. After some hesitation, Nixon agreed, and four one-hour debates were held in September and October 1960.

John Kennedy did not live to debate his opponent in 1964, as he had promised following his inauguration. In 1964 Senate Democrats defeated a resolution suspending the equal time provision on the grounds that it would be unwise for incumbent President Lyndon B. Johnson to engage in televised debates. Interestingly, Barry Goldwater, Johnson's opponent, acknowledged the danger that an incumbent might reveal foreign policy secrets during debates.

In 1968 House and Senate Republicans prevented passage of a resolution suspending the equal time provision. Vice President Humphrey, who had avoided debates with Senators Robert Kennedy and Eugene McCarthy in the prenomination period, sought one with Richard Nixon in the general election. Nixon said that he would agree to the debates only if Governor George Wallace were included; Humphrey refused this condition and no debates took place. Nixon led in the polls and presumably thought debates might jeopardize that.

In 1972 the Senate repealed the equal time provision for the presidential election but the House killed the measure. President Nixon voiced his opposition to repeal of the provision unless it applied to congressional, as well as to presidential, candidates. Nixon refused to debate his Democratic opponent, George McGovern.

In sum, during the three presidential elections after 1960, the candidates who led in the polls (Lyndon Johnson in 1964 and Richard Nixon in 1968 and 1972) avoided debates with their opponents, and their party members in Congress prevented suspension of Section 315. In 1968 and 1972 the trailing major-party candidates sought debates. The favored candidate usually hid behind the equal time provision.

On September 25, 1975, the rules changed. The Aspen Institute Program on Communications and Society petitioned the Federal Communications Commission to exempt presidential debates from the equal time provision if the debates were: 1) covered live and completely and 2) sponsored by an organization other than the networks. The FCC ruled that political debates of this type were bona fide news events and thus exempt from the equal time law. The action reversed a 1962 ruling. In addition, the commission altered its position on candidates' news conferences. Reversing a 1964 decision, the FCC excluded these too from the equal time requirement.

League of Women Voters' Presidential Forums

In the spring of 1975, Marjorie and Charles Benton and Gene Pokorny developed a proposal for a series of "presidential forums" to be held during the primaries in the winter and spring of 1976. In July 1975 the William Benton Foundation made a grant of $50,000 to develop the idea. Jim Karayn, former head of National Public Affairs Center for Television, was named staff director, and discussion began with several major organizations involved in public television.[56] In November 1975, two months after the FCC's ruling, Karayn and Charles Benton suggested to the League of Women Voters of the United States that it sponsor a series of debates between the various presidential candidates during the primaries.

With a grant of $200,000 from the William Benton Foundation, the league's Presidential Forums were launched in the prenomination period. They were directed by Karayn, the league, and a steering committee that included prominent public officials and private citizens. The forums resembled town meetings and were held in public meeting places with live audiences of between 500 and 1,000 persons. Invitations to participate were extended to all presidential candidates who had qualified for public funding under the Federal Election Commission's rulings and were on the ballot in primaries grouped by regions. Since both President Ford and Ronald Reagan declined to participate, the forums turned out to be all-Democratic events. The president's advisers considered, and then rejected, a Ford-Reagan debate. The president argued that debates were useful only if the views of the candidates were not well known, as were his views and those of Reagan.

The league originally had arranged five forums, each dealing with a separate and important political topic. The final forum, scheduled for Los Angeles, was canceled because none of the candidates agreed to participate, an indication of the low priority most of them placed on the California primary. Carter's nomination seemed certain by then.

The forums were moderated by Elie Abel, dean of Columbia University's Graduate School of Journalism, and ran from 1-1/2 to 2-1/2 hours in length. Questions were posed by a regional panel of individuals knowledgeable about the topic under discussion. Queries from the audience were used, although they were screened beforehand. The forums were carried live and in their entirety by some stations in the Public Broadcasting System; National Public Radio also offered the forums to their stations.

The data available suggested that only a small proportion of the potential audience watched the programs. In New York City, for example, approximately 3.5 percent of the television audience watched the forum held in that city; about the same proportion of viewers tuned in to watch the debate in Miami. The viewer audience for the Boston program was too small to register on the Nielsen ratings. None of the commercial television networks carried any of the forums.[57]

Table 8-1
League of Women Voters Presidential Forums

Date	City	Topic	Participants
Feb. 23	Boston	High Employment, Low Inflation, and Cheap Energy: Can We Have Them All?	Bayh, Carter, Harris, Jackson, Shapp, Shriver, Udall
March 1	Miami	From Social Security to Welfare: What's the National Responsibility?	Carter, Church, Harris, Jackson, Udall
March 28	New York	Who Is Responsible for the Cities?	Carter, Church, Harris, Jackson, Udall
May 3	Chicago	Defense, Detente, and Trade: What Are Our Goals?	Church, Udall
May 24	Los Angeles	Growth and the Environment: How Much Can We Control?	(Canceled)

Each of the major Democratic presidential candidates, with the exception of George Wallace, participated in at least one debate (Table 8-1). Jimmy Carter participated in three of the four. Whether a candidate participated in a given debate seemed to be related to his expectations of success in the corresponding primary or primaries and the importance he attached to the debate's outcome.

It is hard to determine the impact of the forums on the outcome of the primaries or the convention. The league had had earlier experience in presenting candidates' night programs, and although the forums preceded serious plans for general election debates, their favorable reception enhanced the league's later proposal for debates between the two major presidential candidates after the conventions.

Arranging the Debates

In April 1976 Jim Karayn, Ruth Clusen, president of the league, and Peggy Lampl, executive director of the league, met with network representatives and learned that they did not plan to sponsor debates between the Democratic and Republican presidential candidates in the fall. As a result, on May 5 the League of Women Voters announced that its Education Fund would sponsor a series of four debates and that it had initiated a drive to collect 4,000,000 signatures on petitions urging the major-party presidential candidates to participate in a series of face-to-face debates.

The league's efforts were supported by many newspapers, many business and professional leaders, and much of the general public, to judge from the results of several public opinion polls. During the primary election period, league officials spoke with representatives of each of the major presidential contenders and sought promises that the candidates would agree to participate in a series of general election debates.

On Thursday, August 19, 1976, the league sent telegrams to both Gerald Ford and Jimmy Carter formally inviting them to debate. That evening, in his speech accepting the Republican nomination, the president declared: "I am ready, I am eager to go before the American people and debate the real issues, face to face, with Jimmy Carter." Carter soon accepted the president's challenge and stated that he had planned to issue a similar statement the day following the president's nomination speech.[58]

The 1976 debates were the first set of televised presidential debates in 16 years and only the second set in U.S. history. Lyndon Johnson and Richard Nixon could use Section 315 of the Federal Communications Act to avoid debating their opponents; Gerald Ford did not have this advantage. Johnson and Nixon were comforted by the fact that they had large leads over their opponents in nearly all the polls; Gerald Ford did not have that advantage.

Ford, the first U.S. president to enter the office as a result of a resignation by his predecessor, trailed in the polls by a wide margin. His party was associated in the public's mind with economic recession, and 1976 was a year of recession. Only one in five Americans called himself a Republican. Ford, who had entered the presidency with the nation's best wishes, had seen his support dwindle after his unexpected pardon of

Richard Nixon. From his perspective, challenging his opponent to a series of debates seemed a good idea. He may have agreed with one of his assistants who argued that the president had nowhere to go but up in the polls. Moreover, by issuing the challenge instead of merely responding to one from Jimmy Carter (as he would have done had he waited only 12 more hours) he gained some public support.

Jimmy Carter accepted, despite his massive lead in the polls. The Democratic nominee was not so well known as the president, and he was concerned about charges that he was not specific about the issues. While the president's camp viewed the debates as an opportunity to force Carter into clear and specific positions on a host of controversial issues, the Democratic nominee felt that the debates would show the contrast between the Ford record (numerous vetoes of social programs) and the president's rhetoric (an improved economy). Moreover, Carter like Ford confronted an electorate containing the largest percentage of independent and undecided voters in the nation's history. Both candidates had incentives to accept the League of Women Voters' offer of a series of televised debates.[59] In addition, the 1974 Amendments played a role in their decision, as will be noted shortly.

The league moved rapidly to set up the debates. On August 26, only one week after the president had issued his challenge, representatives from the Ford and Carter camps met to begin negotiations. On September 1 the two sides announced their acceptance of league sponsorship of the debates. In contrast to 1960, when more than a dozen meetings over a three-week period were held before agreement could be reached, in 1976 the two sides seemed eager to make arrangements for the confrontations. During the discussions, the Ford and Carter representatives compromised on the number of debates, their length, the dates and sites, and the topics to be covered in each.

Response of the Commercial Television Networks

Unlike the candidates, the three commercial television networks were unhappy with the proposed arrangements. After Ford and Carter had agreed to debate, NBC and CBS sought to have Congress suspend the equal time provision of the 1934 Communications Act as had been done in 1960. Senator John Pastore, chairman of the Communications Subcommittee of the Senate Commerce Committee and probably the most influential legislator in the area of communications, refused the networks' request on the grounds that the league's plans were well advanced. Pastore's views were echoed by Rep. Lionel Van Deerlin, D-Calif., his House counterpart. Thus the league's early development of a plan to hold the debates helped it avoid a potential source of trouble.

The networks complained that they would not be able to show audience reaction under the league's ground rules. The league's position reflected the candidates' desire to avoid shots panning the audience, since the audience's reactions could influence home viewers. The networks felt that this restricted their liberties and was a form of prior censorship. CBS threatened to boycott the debates, and in an October letter to *The New York Times*, Reuven Frank, former president of NBC News, criticized the league for allowing the candidates to control the debates. The league replied that the charges were false, noting that in 1960, when the networks supposedly were running the show, the candidates had been in a far more dominant position than they were in 1976. During the Kennedy-Nixon debates, for example, representatives from each of the two sides had been in the control rooms deciding which camera shots should be shown on the air. In the end, the networks (as well as foreign broadcasters and the U.S. Information Agency) acquiesced and agreed to broadcast the debates. Each network expected more than $2 million in unrecouped revenue loss from airing the debates. Since nearly all the advertising time for programs displaced by the debates had been sold, commercial time lost during the debates could not be made up later.[60]

Another contention of the networks was that the candidates had vetoed some of the panelists. The league retorted that each of the candidates had agreed to submit a list of 45 names — 15 print journalists, 15 television journalists, and 15 editorial writers or columnists — for each debate. These were added to names of other possible panelists selected by the league and including regional as well as national media personalities. The final choices were made by a committee of six persons that included, besides Ruth Clusen, Peggy Lampl, and Jim Karayn, Rita Houser, a prominent N.Y attorney, Charls E. Walker, former deputy secretary of Treasury, and Newton Minow, former chairman of the Federal Communications Commission.[61] The league stated that neither candidate exercised a veto over any panelist. Several CBS correspondents were invited to participate but declined because of disagreement with the ground rules.

The Legal Battles

Attempts by the television networks to alter the technical aspects of the debates were not the only efforts made to change them or to prevent them from being held. Other groups filed challenges relying on various legal arguments and appealed to several authorities including the FCC. Most were divided regarding the reasons for their suits, and in the end all of them lost.

The Federal Election Commission began to consider whether the funding for the program or the presentations themselves might constitute an illegal contribution during the general election. The league argued that the expenditure of funds for the debates was not a contribution as the term is used in the FECA because the debates 1) were not designed to advance the candidacy of either Ford or Carter, 2) would serve an educational and informational purpose, and 3) would advance the cause of free and robust speech. Furthermore, the bylaws of the league's Education Fund prohibited it from supporting candidates. In addition, the league's attorney contended that the term "contribution" in the FECA derived from the same term in the Federal Corrupt Practices Act. Under the latter act, the courts consistently had held that funds from labor unions and corporations were barred if they were given for the purpose of "active electioneering" on behalf of a candidate or party, but not if they were provided for activities intended solely to supply information.[62] [63]

The FEC in its August 30 ruling put the matter in a similar light. It ruled that[64]

> in the limited circumstances of presidential debate, the costs incident thereto which will be incurred by the (League of Women Voters Education) Fund are neither contributions nor expenditures under 2 U.S.C. 441a and 431 of the Federal Election Campaign Act of 1971, as amended.

The commission stated that it based its ruling on the league's history of nonpartisanship and educational activities and the fact that neither candidate was particularly favored by the debates. The commission went on to allow the league to receive tax deductible funds from individuals or corporate and labor political action committees, but it banned direct contributions from labor unions or corporations. The commission reasoned as follows:[65]

> The disbursements by the League's Education Fund are nonetheless 'in connection with' a Federal election and accordingly may not be made with funds from corporate or labor organization treasuries . . . or made by other persons forbidden to participate in the Federal election process by the Act.

The league was upset with the commission's ruling, feeling that it might harm future nonpartisan efforts to educate the electorate. As a result of the FEC's decision, the league was forced on September 11 to issue a public appeal for funds to finance the debates. The league decided against accepting money from political action committees, although it was permitted to do so, on the grounds that the PACs were established for campaign purposes and the debates were educational rather than political. The organization placed advertisements in a number of newspapers and conducted a direct-mail campaign. By the end of 1977 the league had spent approximately $325,000 in connection with the debates. It received $233,000 in contributions and paid more than $92,000 from reserves and the operating budget of the Education Fund treasury.

Long after the debates were held, the legal battles continued. On February 9, 1977, the league, the Education Fund, and the League of Women Voters of Los Angeles brought suit against the FEC in the U.S. District Court for the District of Columbia. The plaintiffs sought to have the court declare invalid that part of the commission's ruling that barred corporations and unions from contributing to the league to pay for the expenses of the debates.[66]

The league noted that the commission's ruling prevented it from accepting corporate and union offers of financial assistance made prior to the issuance of the Policy Statement and required the league to incur expenses that it otherwise would not have incurred in attempting to raise funds from other sources. In addition, the league as a corporation was precluded from lending financial support to the Education Fund to defray the costs of those debates. Furthermore, since many of the league's state and local affiliates are incorporated, they as well presumably were unable to provide financial assistance to the fund.

The commission's ruling not only prevented corporations and unions from contributing but forced several major incorporated foundations to rescind their promises to assist the league in paying the costs of the 1976 debates. The league argued in its suit that foundations, corporations, and unions would be unable to contribute if similar programs were held in the future.

The FEC asked the court to dismiss the league's complaint on April 12, 1977. The commission asked dismissal on the grounds the "court had no jurisdiction over this matter because the Commission's policy statement is not a final action ... but represents an attempt ... to give informal advice in an uncharted area of the law."[67]

After the suit and the FEC answer were filed, the FEC decided to reexamine its policy and called a hearing for comment. In testimony before the FEC in September 1977, the league argued that the ruling had a chilling effect on the organization's efforts to raise money to pay for the debates. As a result, the league fell short of its needs to pay the bills. League President Ruth Clusen stated that organizations would be reluctant to sponsor future debates unless the ruling was overturned.

A former staff attorney for the FEC, Benjamin M. Vandegrift, explained the ruling and said the FEC "simply had not had enough experience with the political industry to understand the scope of what we are doing. . . . Stories about corporate political contributions, both foreign and domestic, were everyday occurences. . . . It seemed better to err on the side of caution." [68]

Charles Benton testified that "Public financing imposes a new responsibility and mandate on candidates to make their views public. . . . Sooner or later you will have to tie together public financing and getting information . . . to the public." [69]

Considerable time during the hearing was spent discussing the role of minor and independent candidates in future TV debates. Nicholas Johnson, a former member of the FCC, noted that some Democratic voters might have been influenced had McCarthy been allowed to participate in the Ford-Carter debates. "Television is the ballgame in politics. . . . If minor parties are kept off television, they will be weak. If they are given access to it, they will be strong." [70]

A memorandum was submitted by the U.S. Chamber of Commerce commenting on the FEC policy and seeking to permit corporations to lend assistance in the future for nonpartisan activities that facilitate an informed and educated electorate.

In December 1977 the FEC approved a proposed regulation allowing corporations and labor unions to donate funds to certain nonprofit groups to pay for the costs of sponsoring candidate debates. The contributions would be restricted to those nonprofit organizations that are exempt from federal taxation, that have a history of neither supporing nor endorsing candidates or political parties, and that administer the debates. The definition clearly applies to the League of Women Voters.

The proposed regulation was considered by the league as a limited reversal by which the FEC probably intended to moot the league's suit. The league felt that the policy was still too restrictive, however, especially since it did not address the issue of minor parties or independent candidates. The proposed regulation was never submitted to Congress, but it was included in a series of proposed amendments to the FECA. The bill was adopted by the House Administration Committee in March 1978, but failed to pass both chambers of Congress. The league's suit, however, was dismissed as being a moot question.

A number of earlier challenges were filed to block or alter the televised debates after the announcement that the major-party candidates had agreed to them. On September 17, 1976, Judge Aubrey E. Robinson, Jr., of the U.S. District Court dismissed lawsuits brought by American Party presidential candidate Tom Anderson and independent presidential candidate Eugene McCarthy. The American Party's suit contended that the debates were merely panel discussions and thus not exempt from the equal time provision. In addition, the American Party argued that sponsorship by the League of Women Voters was the equivalent of an illegal contribution to, and expenditure on behalf of, the two major-party presidential candidates.

Five days later, the U.S. Court of Appeals for the District of Columbia upheld Judge Robinson. On September 24 the Federal Communications Commission refused to accept McCarthy's arguments that: 1) the league, in contradistinction to the FCC's 1975 ruling, was merely acting as an agent for the networks in arranging the debates and thus the programs were not exempt from the equal time provision as a bona fide news event, and 2) the debates were in violation of the fairness doctrine, since they would give the impression that McCarthy was not a bona fide candidate.

During this time, Lester Maddox, American Independent Party candidate for president, sought relief as well. He too was unsuccessful. On September 20 the FCC rebuffed his petition for inclusion in the debates. On the same day the FCC denied the request of the Socialist Workers Party that its presidential candidate, Peter Camejo, be included. Later, attorneys for McCarthy and Camejo made the argument that during the first debate the program was stopped when a mechanical failure caused a 26-minute delay, contending that in a true news event the program would have continued. They overlooked the fact that Karayn had attempted to continue the debate but was unable to do so since the public address system for the Walnut Street Theatre was connected to the television feed system. As a result, there were two separate systems in each of the subsequent debates so that Ford and Carter could continue speaking before the live audience if the mechanical difficulty recurred.

On October 12 the U.S. Supreme Court refused to review three petitions concerning the FCC's 1975 rulings. The plaintiffs included the Socialist Workers Party and those groups that had lost in April before the U.S. Court of Appeals in the District of Columbia. Each petition was opposed by the FCC, the league, the three networks, and the federal government. Finally, on October 22, Chief Justice Warren E. Burger denied McCarthy extraordinary relief and refused to enjoin the debates. In sum, the debates, though challenged, were upheld.

Financial Incentives to Debate

For the first time in American history no private contributions were permitted in the general presidential election campaigns, and the candidates were under rigid financial limitations. Each major-party candidate could spend, with party support, no more than $25 million. The innovation necessitated revisions in traditional campaign strategies. In particular, the media became an even more important tool. As Gerald Rafshoon of the Carter advertising team put it: "You can control your dollars better with media. A couple of hundred thousand in a state doesn't buy a whole lot of workers or a lot of headquarters." [71] Such a sum of money can, however, have a significant impact if it is used for media expenditures.

Both the Ford and Carter campaigns spent close to one-half of their allotted funds on media efforts. The new campaign law seemed to encourage such activities, and for Carter they were a natural outgrowth of previous political experience. Ever since he first ran for governor in 1966, the Democratic nominee had placed a heavy emphasis on television. His key media adviser, Rafshoon, was particularly attracted to five-minute television programs. During the campaign, he devoted a considerable part of the media budget to televising five-minute snippets of the Carter biography.

On the Republican side, Douglas Bailey and John Deardourff, codirectors of the Ford advertising campaign, signed on after the Republican National Convention. In contrast to the Democrats' continuity, the Ford team was hired at the last minute, seemingly an indication of little advance planning on the president's part. Concentration on winning the nomination perhaps made planning difficult.

The 1971 and 1974 federal legislation had another impact on the presidential campaigns. It accelerated a trend that had been developing over the past several elections — a centralization of broadcasting expenditures controlled by the national presidential organization. The 1972 Nixon campaign, for different reasons, exemplified this pattern and the 1976 Carter and Ford campaigns continued the tradition.[72] There were severe political and legal consequences if candidates failed to account for each dollar spent.

Comparing the 1960 and 1976 Debates

In general, the process of organizing and staging the debates was completed more easily and rapidly in 1976 than in 1960.[73] Perhaps the reasons lay in the personalities of the two candidates compared with their counterparts in 1960, or perhaps the evolution of television and the political sophistication of both the candidates and the public caused the 1976 discussion with the League of Women Voters to move so swiftly and smoothly.

Obviously the basis for the debates was a key difference in the two elections. In 1960 an amendment to the 1934 Federal Communications Act was required to enable Kennedy and Nixon to meet. The 1976 contests grew out of a ruling by the FCC. As a consequence, the Ford-Carter debates were sponsored by an outside organization, the League of

Women Voters Education Fund; in 1960 the networks had run the shows. While the 1960 contests had been held in television studios without any live audiences, the 1976 debates were held on a specially designed set that was moved to each of the four locations, none of which was a studio. Each of the 1976 programs was presented before a live audience.

Each of the Kennedy-Nixon debates ran for one hour. In 1976 the three presidential debates lasted for 90 minutes, and the vice presidential program was 15 minutes shorter. In general, the candidates in 1976 had more time to answer the questions than did their counterparts in 1960.

In 1960 the broadcast journalists who participated had been selected by the networks and the print journalists among them had been chosen by lot. In 1976 the League of Women Voters sought panelists from a broader selection pool, including regional as well as national correspondents.

The league's efforts reflected lessons learned from the 1960 debates. Moreover, in 1976 the Presidential Forums held in the spring gave experience in planning and handling such matters. The networks had no unified plan for the debates 16 years earlier; the league did. Despite the early preparations, the attendant publicity, and all the league's efforts, the proportion of households watching the first debate in 1976 was smaller than the percentage that had viewed the initial Kennedy-Nixon confrontation,[74] even though about 75 million to 95 million Americans viewed each program. According to Nielsen figures, the proportion of households watching declined from the first (53.5 percent) through the second (52.49 percent) and third (47.79 percent) presidential debates, with the smallest audience (35.5 percent of the households) tuning in for the Dole-Mondale contests. In all, 90 percent of households saw at least one debate and the average household in the United States saw 2.8 of the debates. The viewing figures for the debates were considerably higher than for the highest rated television shows.[75]

Responses to the Debates

Candidates. Both candidates considered the debates to be crucial to their campaigns. Both prepared for them, with Ford going through several full-scale mock rehearsals. Both thought the debates were good for the public. In an October press conference, the president remarked, "I think [the debates] have been very wholesome. I think they've been constructive."[76] Shortly after the election, Jimmy Carter echoed a similar sentiment, "The debates were good for the country. They were a good educational process and gave the people a good look at us and how we handled the issues." [77] Jim Karayn agreed: "The public won on this one as far as I'm concerned." [78]

Of course not everyone voiced the same sentiments. Some individuals contended that the debates had too much image, not enough focus on the issues. Obviously the debates were not truly debates in the sense that forensic specialists use the term. There was not a stated proposition on which the two candidates took opposing sides. They did, however, provide the public with an opportunity to see the two major candidates face to face answering the same questions sequentially. In most campaigns the public has no such advantage. Normally voters are exposed to messages from one or the other candidates, carefully controlled to present a point of view or to eliminate any possibility of a mistake. The League of Women Voters noted, "The debates . . . may have counterbalanced the effect of the candidates' own television presentations. . . . The debates presented the candidates in a neutral setting." [79] The debates provided the candidates with the largest possible audience and the president and his challenger used each of the debates as the basis for subsequent campaign remarks.

Commenting on the effect of the debates on Jimmy Carter's campaign, Patrick Caddell, Carter's pollster, stated that the debates helped the Georgian win by interrupting the presidential campaign at three key points. In each case Ford was closing in on Carter and the debates seemed to slow down or reverse the president's momentum.[80] Carter was even more explicit:

> There was a general feeling that I had lost the first debate because of what I subjectively analyzed as an overly deferential attitude toward Mr. Ford.
>
> I think the debates let the American people be kind of reassured that, "Well, at least, Jimmy Carter has some judgment about foreign affairs and defense and all." [81]
>
> I have a feeling that had it not been for the debates, I would have lost.[82]

No public statement indicated whether Ford thought the debates had helped or hurt his campaign. His staff believed they gave his campaign a lift by slowing the general campaign activity between the Republican presidential convention and the first debate, thus giving the Republican side a chance to organize its efforts following a close contest through the time of the convention.

Voters. Tens of millions of potential voters watched the debates and the league had some thoughts about the impact of the programs on those voters:

The effect of the debates on the election is far from simple. They are knitted into the whole campaign and it is difficult to unravel the different strands. Their impact was felt in the image they formed in the public's mind about the characters of the candidates, the hard substantive information they provided the voters on issues, the generation of public excitement in the debates as a "sporting event" with a winner and a loser, information and blunders made by the candidates becoming the fodder for further campaign stands and statements, and the fact that the debates took the place of other traditional campaign strategy.[83]

Several polls indicated that the public's interest in the campaign increased as it developed; the debates may have contributed, although the same phenomenon can be seen in presidential elections in which there were no debates. Some surveys showed an increase in the electorate's level of information about the campaign. Here the impact of the debates is probably more certain. Still, earlier studies suggest that the debates reinforced rather than converted many voters. Given the closeness of the election, it is possible that Carter's margin depended on his showing in the debates, as he himself claimed.

Two election-day polls give some food for thought. A CBS poll found that 10 percent of its sample agreed with the following statement: "I was impressed by (my candidate) in the debates." Twelve percent stated that they had decided upon a candidate during the debates. No data were provided on the distribution of Ford and Carter voters on this question.

The results of an NBC survey were different. One-third of its sample stated that they had made up their mind during the debates, while one-half said that the debates had had no impact on their vote. Three percent of the individuals interviewed stated that they had switched their choice as a result of the debate. Again, no data were provided on Ford and Carter voters separately.[84]

Whatever their impact, the debates were, in a sense, extra-legal. The debates gave the candidates immense exposure to the electorate not contemplated by the election law, and the contests could thus be considered an evasion of the expenditure limits. The debates were thought by many to have discriminated against minor-party and independent candidates.

The debates were sanctioned by key members of Congress, the Federal Communications Commission, the Federal Election Commission, a federal district judge, a federal court of appeals, and the U.S. Supreme Court. Nevertheless, they raised serious issues about the future of presidential elections in this country. If such programs were to become a permanent fixture on the American political landscape, then they would benefit the two major parties at the expense of other organized political entities. They would further enhance the role of television and the three commercial networks, as well as the League of Women Voters, if it remains as the sponsor. While Jimmy Carter has not committed himself to appearing in 1980, President Ford's actions as an incumbent will make it difficult for him to avoid doing so.

FECA Compliance

The presidential candidates, the political parties, the Federal Election Commission and independent professional associations undertook extraordinary efforts to ensure compliance with the campaign finance laws. Long memos explaining the new laws were circulated within the campaign organizations. The government, the campaigns, professional associations, and private firms published numerous booklets, manuals, and guides. The FEC established a toll-free "hot line" to answer questions on the new laws, and held a series of seminars in major cities across the country. Other groups held seminars and briefings. In sum, thousands of man hours and millions of dollars were spent to learn about compliance, and then to comply with the laws that were designed to regulate political finance.

Yet compliance activities undertaken during the presidential campaign could not be planned confidently in advance nor implemented efficiently. Many of the laws, rules, and regulations governing the fall campaign were still unsettled by the time of the nominating conventions, for several reasons: The FEC had been established in April 1975, it was slow in writing regulations, and Congress exercised its one-House veto twice; the *Buckley* case was decided on January 30, 1976, requiring the rewriting of some regulations and causing Congress to rewrite parts of the law in the 1976 Amendments enacted in May 1976; then the FEC again had to revise its regulations; Congress and the president delayed in reconstituting the FEC and then Congress delayed in consenting to proposed regulations before the 1976 elections, which were not finally made effective until April 1977. Moreover, scores of advisory opinions were being sought, and answers added to the needed knowledge necessary for compliance. The campaign organizations, therefore, could not fully plan ahead in this uncertain environment. The delays and changing policies created confusion concerning the conduct of the campaign, which resulted in even more need to seek information and clarifications, causing still more time and effort to be expended on behalf of compliance.

The accounting problems facing both major presidential candidates in the general election were significantly different from those encountered in the primaries. In the prenomination campaigns, each candidate had the traditional problems of cash flow (the timing of expenditures consistent with available funds to pay for them), compounded by the newly enacted contribution limits and by the need for timeliness and accuracy in making claims for certification of matching funds. Control over expenditures in each primary state was necessary to stay within the legislated spending limits, and required separate accounting. The 20 percent overage for fund-raising costs, and the later exemption of compliance costs, each also required separate accounting.

In the general election, public financing brought flat grants, which eliminated the cash-flow problem. The campaign committees had to focus both on the control and management of expenditures to make the most effective use of the public money available to them. In addition, the 1976 Amendments and FEC regulations belatedly allowed all compliance-related expenditures not only to be accounted for separately, but to be divorced from statutory limitations, and if necessary, to be paid from money raised separately to cover the cost.

The problems of compliance had become so substantial and costly that changes in the law finally were sought. Early in 1976 both the Ford and Carter organizations petitioned the FEC to exclude compliance costs from the expenditure restrictions. Both organizations argued that compliance should not be considered normal campaign costs subject to expenditure limitations. Indeed, both organizations realized that compliance-related costs could become so significant that, unless they were exempted, each candidate's election effort could be significantly constrained. The FEC, however, refused to allow an exemption on grounds it did not have the authority to do so. Thus, in parallel efforts, both Ford and Carter sought and achieved a legislated exemption of compliance costs included in the 1976 Amendments. This provision then caused candidates who were close to spending limits — Carter, Ford, and Reagan — to isolate compliance costs retroactively to January 1, 1975, and to recalculate their other expenditures. It had no effect on candidates not close to the spending limits.

The AICPA

The high cost of purchasing professional and technical assistance prompted the Carter campaign to seek ways to acquire and organize volunteer help. During the Democratic National Convention in July, Carter officials approached Theodore C. Barreaux, a vice-president of the American Institute of Certified Public Accountants (AICPA), and asked for the organization's assistance. The Carter people specifically wanted volunteer CPAs to assist state and major-city campaign officials in their compliance efforts. The AICPA was a logical group to turn to. The organization had, in 1976, published a manual[85] describing the campaign finance laws and advising candidates for federal office on ways to ensure conformity with the law. The AICPA was willing — indeed eager — to become involved in the presidential campaign's compliance efforts.

AICPA officials agreed to aid Carter and establish a national network of volunteers only if a similar effort was made for the Republican nominee.[86] Carter agreed and the Republicans accepted the AICPA's offer. The AICPA then began to recruit volunteers through the state societies of CPA, making the name of each volunteer available to the campaign organizations in each state.

The AICPA also offered assistance to the presidential candidates by conducting a two-day training seminar for all volunteer CPAs.[87] The seminar, which was held in Washington in late August, was a showcase for the nation's largest and most prestigious accounting firms. Representatives from these firms and others, as well as from the FEC, the General Accounting Office, and Congress, presented lectures and conducted panel discussions on various aspects of the law. The candidates themselves recognized the important role these volunteers would play in their campaign efforts. Each candidate made a gesture to the group; Carter addressed a luncheon gathering of more than 150 CPAs, and Ford invited the group to the White House for a staff briefing, although he was not present. The AICPA did not provide any assistance to House and Senate candidates who faced difficult, though different, compliance problems.

The Democrats implemented the program but the Republicans did in only a limited way. Following the seminar, the Carter campaign made extensive use of the volunteers. Each state coordinator had at least one volunteer working on a part-time but regular basis. Larger states used the services of two or three volunteers, and some additional ones were assigned in metropolitan areas. Some 23 volunteers were assigned to national Carter headquarters to cover accounting/compliance field operations for a specific area.[88] A national coordinator, Barry E. Wagman, was hired to work full time in Atlanta headquarters as liaison with the volunteers and also worked to ensure compliance; Wagman was an acountant experienced in political bookkeeping and was the author of *Campaign Treasurer's Handbook,* a Democratic Party publication.[89]

Furthermore, Carter and Ford officials continued to work closely with Barreaux and with Joseph Moraglio, the national coordinator for the AICPA in Washington. The AICPA conducted a continuing information program with practical advice for national and state operatives. Copies of FEC guides and information sheets were sent to cooperating accountants.

Legal Assistance

While the need for legal assistance in compliance efforts was equally obvious, the legal profession did not match the cooperation provided by the accountants. In early May 1976 representatives of the Carter campaign approached the American Bar Association to seek help in organizing and training volunteer lawyers. ABA officials were reluctant to provide any assistance to either of the campaigns, or to contribute to the process of finding and training volunteers.

The Carter organization pursued its own efforts to develop a network of volunteer lawyers similar to the volunteer accountants. Douglas Huron, a top Carter associate, worked closely with Philip Alston, an Atlanta attorney, to gather, through an informal chain of campaign officials and friends in each state, the names of more than 125 volunteer lawyers. Each volunteer agreed to assist Carter-Mondale state coordinators on a regular basis, beginning in early September 1976.

As was true with accountants, these volunteers needed to become thoroughly familiar with the varied aspects of the campaign finance laws and in early September, Huron and three assistants conducted two one-day training seminars for the volunteers. The seminars, one of which was held in Washington, the other in Denver, were similar in size and format to the accountants' seminar conducted by the AICPA. These seminars, however, were solely for the benefit of the Carter campaign.

The Ford campaign engaged a paid counsel and assistant counsel, and also had volunteer legal assistance from certain D.C. lawyers who were requested to prepare briefs or memos on special topics — such as communications or tax law — that the paid staff did not have time or the expertise to do themselves. The staff attorneys were involved in every high-level or relevant conference during the campaign, whether on strategy, organization, or finances — a situation different from other elections when counsel provided only limited and specific help. The FECA had an impact on every aspect of the campaign and hence its consequences had to be considered in most major actions.

Party Compliance Literature

The 1976 presidential campaigns produced a sizable collection of literature on a wide range of administrative and organizational aspects of presidential campaigning under FECA provisions. While each campaign planned in its own way to anticipate compliance problems, the FECA and several large accounting firms wrote and published manuals, reports, guides, memoranda, and other materials to aid compliance efforts.

The major political parties began soon after the 1974 Amendments were enacted to make their candidates for all federal offices familiar with the new laws. The Democrats hired an in-house counsel, Ralph Gerson, to supplement the volunteer help of its outside general counsel, Stuart Siegel. The Republican National Committee paid the law firm of its general counsel, William Cramer, for supplemental help performed by associates. As the presidential election approached, the parties revised and reissued their often extensive explanatory materials. For example, the RNC distributed a bulging three-ring binder containing a comprehensive assortment of compliance materials.[90] Included in the binder were RNC staff attorneys' interpretations of the scope and application of the laws, copies of FEC rulings and opinions and a collection of relevant laws and statutes.

The Democrats published a compilation of information concerning the election laws known as the Democratic Election Law Reporter.[91] The 56-page booklet discussed the major aspects of the law, attempting to explain in simple wording the sections of the law dealing with contributions, expenditures, fund raising, volunteer activities, the media, and the rest. The booklet also offered "advisory opinions" similar to those found in the RNC binder. Yet the authors of the booklet made it explicit that the material could not be relied upon as a "complete or definitive treatise on the election laws." [92] Even though each party put together thorough and exacting information on the law, the candidates and their committees had to rely in addition on personal and professional assistance of lawyers and accountants, which meant involving more of them in the campaigns than ever before.

During the presidential general election campaigns, each party continued to advise their candidates on the law while coordinating campaign activities where legal and practical. For example, Ralph Gerson, legal counsel to the DNC, Doug Huron, Carter's legal chief, and Robert J. Lipshutz, Carter campaign treasurer, distributed joint and separate memos on the finance laws during the initial phase of the campaign. They were concerned with making most effective use of the exemption from the FECA limitations of party voter registration drives and get-out-the-vote efforts. Gerson independently briefed the Democratic congressmen on the law and its relation to congressional races and the presidential campaign.[93]

Other Materials

The FEC, naturally, published the most comprehensive and detailed compliance materials. By late August 1976 the commission had produced five lengthy "campaign guides," a bookkeeping and reporting manual, several lengthy policy memos, and a 45-page chapter of proposed regulations in the *Federal Register*.[94] All this was in addition to a 120-page compilation of all relevant statutes and codes,[95] including broadcast, tax, and public employee provisions.

Some of the material went into extraordinary detail. The campaign guides discussed at length the definitions of key terms. The bookkeeping and reporting manual attempted to relate its proposed procedures with actual practices in campaigning, discussing, for example, methods of recording information in a file box, and of disbursing petty cash funds. It often made such mundane suggestions as, "Go to the bank every day."

FEC materials at times proved confusing. While the rules and regulations governing the presidential campaigns were distinct but similar to those governing senatorial and congressional races, the FEC combined in a single publication suggestions relating to each category of campaigning. Though a careful reading of the materials would eliminate any confusion, the frantic pace of campaign activities sometimes blurred the distinctions.

Private accounting/consulting firms contributed to the literature also. Arthur Andersen & Co., an accounting firm, published two manuals,[96] the first written soon after the FECA became effective in 1972, describing in extraordinary detail a financial manangement system for political campaigns. The manual contained both innovative and common-sensical suggestions for campaign organizations, containing models that were both general and specific. For example, it was suggested that the campaigns establish broad objectives that could be quantitatively measured through a budget. The publication also included dozens of possible forms or formats to be used to record information, and it specified the filing system to be created. Arthur Andersen & Co. also published a booklet describing audit criteria for federal campaigns. Price Waterhouse & Co. later marked out the area of political action committees and published a guide in August 1976.[97] These works are indicative of the efforts to educate practitioners and induce compliance.

Campaign Committee Operations

The campaign committees made the most useful contributions to the growing library of explanations and suggestions. Both the Ford and Carter committees circulated internal memoranda defining, improving, and at times, excusing administrative procedures. These materials put forth how each organization was to practically implement the requirements of the FECA. They therefore illustrate the results of the intense pressures toward professionalizing the campaigns as a result of the campaign finance laws.

The Carter campaign, for example, developed a comprehensive legal, financial and administrative manual that was distributed to the campaign staff.[98] The manual, like many policy guidelines circulated within private corporations, began with a memorandum from the chief executive officers — in this case, Carter and Mondale. The memorandum implored the staff to follow central instructions explicitly, made references to the harsh penalties associated with noncompliance, and reiterated the Democratic support for publicly financed elections. The manual then proceeded to address the most common expense-related activities in the campaign, indicating the responsible persons and procedures to be followed. For instance, Carter officials divided the campaign organization into "cost centers" representing state committees and functional areas of the campaign such as issues, media, press and nationalities. The manual instructed cost center directors on how to acquire office space and furniture in the field, hire and dismiss employees, pay a bill, rent a car, or receive a travel advance.

While one Carter manual presented the process for spending campaign funds, others made known the bookkeeping and reporting procedures the campaign would follow. As late as October 3, 1976, Carter officials were still circulating memos about assembling expense documentation and reporting requirements.[99] Earlier memos to field office coordinators and volunteer CPAs discussed the actions that needed to be taken to ensure compliance.[100] Several were written as questionnaires to be completed and sent to Atlanta for evaluation.[101] Others tried to explain the complex procedures in a lighthearted fashion. One Carter memorandum was entitled, "Everything you always wanted to know about bank drafts, leases, etc., but were afraid to ask."[102]

Carter compliance officials went so far as to establish an intricate "Technical Queries Flow Chart" at campaign headquarters.[103] The chart indicated which color form to use, whom to see and how to respond to the hundreds of questions coming in about the law. To get even more control over the process, Wagman and other campaign staffers supplemented these materials with personal visits to the field offices, which generated even more questionnaires, forms and instruction sheets. For example, Carter's accounting department developed a specialized "CPA Area Coordinator's Flow Chart."[104]

The campaign committees had to explain their procedures not only to their own staffs but also to the FEC, to whom dozens of letters were sent. On some compliance matters, the FEC was asked to approve the accounting compliance methods the committees were contemplating or actually using. For instance, one accounting problem followed candidate Carter around the country. Since Carter flew by chartered aircraft, he made seats available to the Secret Service and press that traveled with

him, as is customary in presidential campaigns. Both the Secret Service
and the press were to reimburse the committee for the airline service so
that the Democratic candidate would not be paying for their flights. The
FEC provided a method for calculating the cost of travel for proper
reimbursement. However, according to Carter's staff computation, the
two methods were inconsistent and yielded a net loss to the campaign of
$500,000. Carter officials sought to have this amount not charged against
their campaign accounts.[105]

Five weeks after the committee requested a ruling from the FEC,
the FEC informed them of their agreement with the Democratic nominee's accounting method.[106]

Though these mounds of paperwork, letters, and memos suggest
that strict compliance was the top priority the staffs often focused on
creating and expanding exceptions to the laws. One internal memorandum of the Carter campaign described the principle function of the legal
department and its team of volunteer lawyers as "assisting [campaign
organizations] in stretching your limited budgets as far as possible while
still staying well within the limits of the law."[107] Indeed, the time and
energy spent trying to stretch the laws was often equal to the efforts
made to comply with the law.

The FECA with FEC interpretation exempted from expenditure
control voter registration and party get-out-the-vote drives — including
the production of sample ballots or slate cards. The FEC saw these
activities as general voter education efforts and, so long as they were not
"clearly identified" with one candidate, they were not considered campaign expenditures. Campaign officials wanted to exploit these exceptions but the definition of "clearly identified" was not easily understood,
and the effectiveness of slate cards was often disputed. Though it
seemed that these activities offered a significant opportunity for positive
campaign efforts, few staffers envisioned how to use them continuously
and effectively. (The Democratic Whistlestop was one attempt.) Nevertheless, campaign memoranda describing compliance efforts invariably
discussed these exceptions in detail, encouraging their use but offering
few suggestions.

The FECA recognized that volunteers are essential to political
campaigns. The law thus allowed volunteers to contribute the value of
their own time to either campaign, but the regulations governing in-kind
contributions made this exception particularly confusing and therefore
time consuming for the campaign committees. The law rigorously defined the meaning of a person's "own time" in an effort to eliminate
campaign "volunteers" who might be on someone's payroll. If "volunteers" were paid, the value of their time would have to be considered as
a contribution to the campaign.

In the case of volunteer CPAs and lawyers working on compliance-related activities, it did not matter since those costs were exempt. But campaign officials could never be sure that their volunteers were adhering to the regulations; so to protect themselves Carter campaign officials, for example, required each volunteer, before working for the campaign, to sign a two-page statement[108] acknowledging the regulations and professing the volunteer's compliance with them. The procedure could have had a chilling effect, but Carter officials felt it was necessary.

Officials also were eager to avoid independent expenditures on behalf of the Carter campaign. One internal memorandum stated that "The dangers inherent in [these] expenditures are so great that it is the policy of the Carter-Mondale campaign to actively discourage them."[109] Carter staffers developed a form letter to be sent to any individual in the country known to be contemplating an independent expenditure. The "dangers inherent" in these expenditures involved possible charges that the expenditures were not "independent" but directly or indirectly coordinated by the campaign organization. This could result in the expenditure being charged against the candidate's limitation.

Though the official policy in most campaigns was to discourage independent expenditures, and in Carter's case the form letter reinforced this notion, some campaign officials are known to have tolerated minor expenditures involving some coordination of effort with the stern admonition to staff members of, "Don't tell me about it."

For the Democratic campaign, a great deal of attention was paid to exceptions in the law that allowed expenditures to be made on behalf of the candidate by other party elements. Indeed, Carter's legal counsel was able to persuade the FEC to extend the $1,000 expenditure allowance for state party committees to county, municipal, and congressional committees.[110] This substantially increased the amount of money available to be spent on the presidential campaign. The Huron decision, as it became known, proved to be a mixed blessing.

The Huron decision seemed a simple exception to the law. The FEC prohibited the pooling of the allowance by the committees to purchase, for example, media time. But the FEC did not make clear the reason for this critical restriction. Some observers saw no reason why the $1,000 could not "purchase" a portion of a larger expenditure nor why if each committee could spend the $1,000 on the same matchbooks or bumper stickers, why the committees should not be allowed to purchase the same TV time. Furthermore, this simple exception brought about another flurry of explanatory materials. The AICPA and the party legal staffs, as well as the accounting and legal staffs of each campaign, participated in this informational process.

Campaign field offices, already hurting from tight budgets, sought to spend any additional money available to them as soon as possible. The notion that there were thousands of dollars available to spend was in contrast to the planned and restricted budgets to which they were becoming accustomed. The restrictions and reporting requirements attached to the Huron decision made the effective use of the money an occasionally elusive and time consuming venture. Huron's legal success did provide an important outlet for party activities that otherwise would have been prohibited.

State regulations and taxing policies also affected nationwide campaigns or those in a series of state primaries. Although they were temporary organizations lacking standard operating procedures, they had to deal with mundane matters of unemployment compensation, Social Security, property taxes, OSHA, wages and hours regulations, and a great variety of government regulations. Payroll problems were so immense that the Ford prenomination campaign hired a bank to keep personnel records and prepare payrolls.

'Close-down' Operations

Perhaps it is indicative of the power of the campaign laws that in 1976, unlike any other year, officials of both campaigns were concerned with the financial dissolution of the campaign before the election date. Prior to November 2, the winning Carter organization had established a detailed set of procedures and plans to be followed and forms to be completed to close down all field offices.[111] Furthermore, Carter officials required all state campaign coordinators to travel to Atlanta four days after the election to be debriefed on the operation of the campaign.

Although the FEC would conduct an audit of their accounts, the Democrats hired Arthur Andersen & Co. to audit independently the campaign's finances, in part to prepare for the FEC audit to follow. The Ford campaign also hired Arthur Andersen & Co. for a preaudit. In addition, the Carter and Ford campaigns, as well as those of Senators Bayh and Jackson, and Sargent Shriver, had consulted with the Andersen company in setting up their bookkeeping and compliance accounts. Accounting systems were necessary to set up procedures for entering data to be transferred to disclosure reports later, but also to screen dubious contributions and to alert staffers as contributions approach or exceed their limits.

Campaign accountants worked for months at the cost of additional thousands of dollars to finally close the books on the presidential campaigns, and the actual costs had been underestimated; it took longer and cost more than expected.

Substantial amounts were budgeted by campaigns for compliance costs. One political accountant supports estimates of 5-10 percent of campaign budgets being allocated to accounting, computer and legal costs.[112] The presidential nomination campaign of Senator Lloyd Bentsen claimed about 10 percent of expenditures were compliance connected; the Ford and Carter compliance costs are noted elsewhere in this book.

Conclusion

The FECA made the 1976 presidential campaign unique. Its effect on the choice for president, on the advantages and disadvantages for Republicans and Democrats alike, still needs to be determined. The FECA as amended in 1974 and 1976 fundamentally altered the conduct of politics during the 1976 presidential campaigns. The campaign committees were forced to become better organized and more centralized, to a point where experts on the law became key operatives of the campaigns. Expertise in the law developed as candidates and political committees turned to lawyers, accountants, and computer specialists for advice on how to keep books and make reports that would comply with the law. The FECA was termed by some as the "Lawyers and Accountants Full Employment Act," and in the process of compliance a corps of well-informed advisers and operatives outside the government emerged.

A corollary development occurred in legal scholarship and litigation. For the first time, courses on the electoral process were taught in a few law schools and an increasing number of law review articles on various aspects of the new laws appeared.[113]

In addition, tax attorneys were drawn in more and more with reference to laws and IRS regulations relating to the gift tax, appreciated property, contributions to national conventions, and advertising in convention books. Public interest lawyers began to undertake a variety of court tests on disclosure and limitation aspects and on corporate and labor activity.

The new responsibilities thrust upon committee treasurers by the new law made it essential that persons accepting such positions be prepared to undergo thorough audits and be criminally liable for financial decisions that in earlier years would have gone unreported and unpublicized. More than one treasurer vowed never again to assume that role, possibly leaving such positions to paid professionals.

It is ironic that one of the impacts of legislation that, in part, was drafted to limit campaign spending was to increase costs in certain categories. But to meet the law sizable campaigns spent thousands of dollars for mechanization. Even photocopying costs were high when voluminous reports had to be duplicated for filing with the FEC as well as numerous secretaries of state; many national-level committees contributing to a large number of congressional candidates filed in all 50 states to be on the safe side. Presidential candidates for nomination seeking public funds were required to submit photocopies of all checks submitted for matching funds.[114]

It may be one of the ironies of Watergate that the legislation regulating political finance which it helped bring on, itself caused to be emulated in later campaigns the structure of the Committee to Reelect the President (CRP), in which so many of the 1972 aberrations were spawned. The requirements of the Amendments of 1974 and 1976 regarding the control of spending led to highly structured, tightly integrated political committees. The 1972 Nixon campaign served as a model for a centrally controlled committee designed to meet the new requirements, departing from traditional strategy and organization, in which the campaign apparatus was loose and decentralized.[115] Prior to 1972, presidential candidates dealt regularly with local and state party leaders, and with volunteer ad hoc supportive committees, on a coordinating but hardly controlling basis. As one analysis of the 1972 election noted, "for the first time in American politics, a completely centralized national political machine was created with direct lines of command from Washington that did not rely at all on local political parties or on local power centers for its operational efficiency."[116] Particularly since 1974, all spending on behalf of a presidential candidate must be cleared through the central committee to ensure that ceilings are not surpassed, reducing local spontaneity and flexibility.

Along with the centralization has come a professionalization of politics. In practice, campaigns are exceedingly difficult to run as efficiently as the provisions would try to impose; certain expenditures almost have to be made on an ad hoc basis, and this ability is now somewhat impaired. More important, the law restricts a candidate's ability to deal with new issues interjected into the campaign late in the race — if the spending ceiling has been reached, he will be unable to purchase advertising space or media time to state or modify his views, or to undertake a new campaign theme.

Footnotes

[1] Maurice Carroll, " 'Get Me Garth,' Cry the Very Neediest Politicians," *The New York Times*, October 10, 1977.

[2] Seymour Zucker, editor, "Economic Diary/Nov. 1-5, Why TV Cuts the Cost of Campaigning," *Business Week*, November 22, 1976, p. 12; Edwin Diamond, "The Election: How Will TV Cover the 'Strangest Campaign,' " *New York*, August 23, 1976, p. 47.

[3] U.S., Library of Congress, Congressional Research Service, *The Fairness Doctrine: A Campaign Perspective*, prepared by Bruce P. Moore (Washington, D.C.: Library of Congress, April 11, 1974).

[4] Christopher Lydon, "Carter Arouses Hostility Among McGovern's Aides," *The New York Times*, March 1, 1976. Wallace, Ford, and Reagan declined to appear on the first forum.

[5] Joseph Lelyveld, "The Selling of a Candidate: Carter's Image Is a Vision, or a Con, or a Little of Both. In Any Case, His Media Man Maintains, 'It's Jimmy,' " *The New York Times Magazine*, March 28, 1976, pp. 65-71.

[6] "Television Is Number-One Medium for Presidential Candidates' Advertising: Even the Money-Short Democrats Rely on It for Its Effectiveness and Awareness-Building Capabilities," *Broadcasting*, April 26, 1976, pp. 22-26. Also see "Top of the Week: TV Sales Still Soaring: TVB Nearly Doubles Its Predictions: Earlier Estimates for 12% Gain in 1976 Are Revised Up to 21%; Spot May Make It Over $2 Billion," *Broadcasting*, June 14, 1976, pp. 21-24.

[7] David S. Broder, "Ford, Reagan Scrambling for a Few Ohio Delegates," *The Washington Post*, June 6, 1976.

[8] "Carter Buying Simultaneous Time on Three Networks," *The New York Times*, June 5, 1976.

[9] Philip H. Dougherty, "Advertising: Atlanta Agency's Busiest Year," *The New York Times*, July 19, 1976.

[10] George Wallace purchased five minutes to talk on television the evening of Saturday, June 5, 1976, at a cost of $30,000. The aim of his appearance, it was announced, was to explain why his candidacy for the Democratic nomination was continuing and what its goals were. "Rockefeller Worried by Ford's Move to the Right," *The Washington Post*, May 28, 1976.

[11] Charles Mohr, "Udall Steps Up TV-Radio Effort: Pennsylvania Campaign to Spend $80,000, Less Than Carter Figure," *The New York Times*, April 23, 1976. It was perhaps ironic that Udall had been the author of both the 1971 and the 1974 campaign finance reform acts.

[12] Les Brown, "25% of Adults Saw Carter Speech on TV," *The New York Times*, July 17, 1976.

[13] "Top of the Week: Biggest News Coverage Ever for Democrats," *Broadcasting*, July 19, 1976, pp. 21-25.

[14] Joseph Lelyveld, "Climax of Ford Bid Anticlimax for TV," *The New York Times*, August 20, 1976; "The Republicans Drew Larger TV Audience,"*The New York Times*, August 22, 1976.

[15] Joseph Lelyveld, "Ford to Delay Ads on TV until After First Debate," *The New York Times*, September 14, 1976.

[16] Philip H. Dougherty, "Advertising: Beginning of Ford's Paid TV Spots," *The New York Times*, September 27, 1976.

[17] Helen Dewar, "Carter Sets $8.5-$10 Million Ad Budget," *The Washington Post*, July 31, 1976.

[18] L. Stuart Ditzen, "Carter, Ford Ad Pitches: Strikingly Similar, So Far," *Philadelphia Sunday Bulletin*, October 10, 1976.

[19] Deirdre Carmody, "Ad Aides See Presidential Candidates As Issues," *The New York Times*, October 15, 1976.

[20] President Ford Network TV Schedule, October 17-23, 1976, unpublished document, Campaign '76, Media Communications Inc.

[21] Sander Vanocur, "A Negative Note in the Battle of the Campaign Commercials," *The Washington Post*, October 21, 1976. For another discussion of the effect of the spending limits, see Donald Smith, "Tight Budget for Presidential Candidates," *Congressional Quarterly Weekly Report*, July 31, 1976, p. 2036.

[22] Lou Cannon, "As Nov. 2 Countdown Begins, Ford Camp Plans Media Blitz," *The Washington Post*, October 22, 1976; Warren Weaver, Jr., "TV Spending Record Is Set by Ford Group: Report Shows 3-Week Figure of $9.9 Million — Total Budget Increased to $12 Million," *The New York Times*, October 29, 1976.

[23] William Robbins, "CBS and NBC Bar Live Ford Speech," *The New York Times*, October 7, 1975; Les Brown, "Access to TV Time Is Creating Issue of Its Own for '76," *The New York Times*, October 8, 1975.

[24] "Pastore Assails the F.C.C. on Equal-Time Ruling," *The New York Times*, November 12, 1975.

[25] "Court Upholds F.C.C. on Equal-Time Ruling," *The New York Times*, April 13, 1976.

[26] Jay Sharbutt, "Twisting Question for FCC and the 'Equal Time' Rule," *Sunday News*, February 8, 1976.

[27] "How FCC Divided on Five-Minute Political Ruling: Though It Was 5-to-2 in Saying WGN Must Sell Shorter Spots, Majority Itself Disagreed Over Reasons for That Decision," *Broadcasting*, March 15, 1976, pp. 91-92; Les Brown, "F.C.C. Issues Two Rulings on Political Primaries," *The New York Times*, March 5, 1976.

[28] "Socialist Party Wins Equal Time on NBC," *The New York Times*, September 30, 1976.

[29] "FCC Says LaRouche Must Get NBC Time," *The Washington Post*, November 2, 1976.

[30] Joseph Lelyveld, "TV: Presidential Forums Are Offered in Boston," *The New York Times*, February 28, 1976.

[31] Lou Cannon and John Carmody, "Reagan Gets Half Hour For Speech on TV," *The Washington Post*, March 30, 1976.

[32] "FCC Maintains Church Rated Better Shake from KGW-TV on Time Request: It was a 5-to-2 Vote with FCC Unexpectedly Turning up with Majority; It May Represent a Feeling by the Commission More Favorable to Rejected Candidates," *Broadcasting*, May 24, 1976, p. 50.

[33] Lesley Oelsner, "Court Refuses to Review F.C.C. 'Equal Time' Ruling," *The New York Times*, October 13, 1976.

[34] "Political Candidates Set Back by F.C.C. on Broadcast Time," *The New York Times*, May 7, 1977.

[35] "FCC Drafting New Regulations on Candidates' Air-Time Rights," *Campaign Practices Reports*, April 3, 1978, pp. 7-8.

[36] "FCC Sets Policy to Ensure Reasonable Access for Candidates (BC Docket No. 78-102)," press release dated July 14, 1978, Federal Communications Commission, Washington, D.C.

[37] "FCC Revises Definition of Legally Qualified Political Candidate (BC Docket No. 78-103)," press release dated July 14, 1978, Federal Communications Commission, Washington, D.C.

[38] Thomas E. Patterson and Robert D. McClure, *The Unseeing Eye: The Myth of Televison Power in National Elections* (New York: G. P. Putnam Sons, 1976).

[39] Thomas E. Patterson, "The 1976 Horserace," *The Wilson Quarterly*, spring 1977.

[40] "American Imagery: Knock Off the Imagery," *Time*, September 20, 1976, p. 10.

[41] James McCartney, "The Triumph of Junk News," in "Reporting the 1976 Campaign," *Columbia Journalism Review*, January/February 1977, pp. 17-21.

[42] Deirdre Carmody, "Editors Differ on Ethics of Using Political Candidates' Paid Articles," *The New York Times*, September 27, 1976.

[43] Martin Arnold, "Dispute on Investigative Reporting Leads Press to Study Its Role," *The New York Times*, December 2, 1974.

[44] Joseph Lelyveld, "Has Campaign Cheated Voters? News Media Blame Candidates; Others Point to Media, But Electorate's Feeling Seems Deeper," *The New York Times*, November 1, 1976.

[45] Ibid.

[46] Report of The American Assembly 1977-1978, p. 6.

[47] George H. White, "A Study of Access to Television for Political Candidates," (Report to Campaign Finance Study Group, Institute of Politics, John F. Kennedy School of Government, Harvard University) May 1978.

[48] Ibid., pp. 101-110.

[49] MIT Research Program on Communications Policy, *Third Report: A Joint Program in the Center for Policy Alternatives, the Center for Advanced Engineering Study, The*

Center for International Studies, The Electronic Systems Laboratory (Cambridge, Mass.: Massachusetts Institute of Technology, July 1976).

[50] William J. Donnelly, "The Emerging Video Environment," *Young and Rubicam Issues 12,* n.d., pp. 1-8.

[51] "Congressional Cloakroom: The Press As a Special Interest Group," *Congress Today!* December 1977, p. 16.

[52] David Burnham, "Former Chairman of F.C.C. Agrees to Serve As a Trustee of the Political Arm of Broadcasters' Association," *The New York Times,* February 12, 1978.

[53] Michael Ryan, "View From the Losing Side: Senators McGovern and Goldwater, ABC's Newest Convention Commentators, Talk about TV's Influence on Politics," *TV Guide,* June 12, 1976, pp. 6-10.

[54] Published in different form, "The Making of the Debates," by Herbert E. Alexander and Joel Margolis in George Bishop and Robert Meadows (ed.), *The Presidential Debates: Media, Electoral and Policy Perspectives,* (New York: Praeger, 1978).

[55] Lesley Oelsner, "Court Refuses to Review FCC 'Equal Time' Ruling," *The New York Times,* October 13, 1976.

[56] Charles Benton, "How the Debates Came to Be," *Encyclopaedia Brittanica 1977 Book of the Year,* as quoted in U.S. *Congressional Record,* March 24, 1977 (daily edition), S4866.

[57] " 'Presidential Forum' Does Well in Rating," *The New York Times,* April 1, 1976.

[58] "Texts of Acceptance Speeches," Congressional Quarterly *Weekly Report,* August 21, 1976, p. 2314.

[59] League of Women Voters Education Fund, Effect of the Debates on the 1976 Campaign and Election, p. 6. (Draft Version)

[60] "From Primary to Post-Election, TV and Radio Were There," *Broadcasting,* January 3, 1977, p. 39.

[61] Just How Great Were Those 'Great Debates'?," *Broadcasting,* January 3, 1977, p. 62.

[62] See letters sent to the Federal Election Commission by Theodore Frank, counsel to the League of Women Voters Education Fund. August 25, 1976, and August 27, 1976.

[63] The Federal Election Campaign Act defines a contribution as "a gift, subscription, loan, advance, or deposit of money or anything of value" made for the purpose of: "Influencing the election of any person to Federal office . . .," 2 U.S.C. Sec. 301 (e).

[64] Federal Election Commission, Policy Statement on Presidential Debates. Undated.

[65] Ibid.

[66] *League of Women Voters, et. al. v. Federal Election Commission, et. al.,* Complaint for Declaratory Judgment and Injunction filed in the United States District Court for the District of Columbia, February 9, 1977, p. 9.

[67] Federal Election Commission, *Record,* June 1977, p. 4.

[68] "FEC Chided By Women Voters League For Upsetting TV Debate Payment," *Campaign Practices Reports,* September 19, 1977, p. 3.

[69] Ibid., pp. 3, 4.

[70] Ibid., p. 4.

[71] "Television, Medium of Choice and Necessity," *Broadcasting,* January 3, 1977, pp. 74, 75.

[72] Herbert E. Alexander, *Financing the 1972 Election* (Lexington, Massachusetts: D.C. Heath and Co., 1976), pp. 315-338.

[73] For information on the 1960 debates, see Sidney Kraus, ed., *The Great Debates: Background, Perspectives; Effects* (Bloomington, Indiana: Indiana University Press, 1962).

[74] "The First Debate: Up to Expectations of 90 Million People Who Watched It?" *Broadcasting,* October 4, 1976, p. 26.

[75] League of Women Voters Education Fund, Effect of the Debates on the 1972 Campaign and Election, pp. 1-2. (Draft Version)

[76] League of Women Voters Education Fund, The '76 Presidential Debates: A Summary Statement, November, 1976, p. 12. (Draft Version)

[77] Ibid.

[78] "Third and Fourth Debates Look to be Almost Routine for the Networks," *Broadcasting*, October 18, 1976, p. 26.

[79] League of Women Voters Education Fund, *The '76 Presidential Debates*, p. 12.

[80] Warren Weaver, Jr., "Timing of Three Debates Held Key to Victory," *The New York Times*, November 6, 1976.

[81] James T. Wooten, "Carter Says He Won Because of Exposure Gained in Three Debates," *The New York Times*, November 7, 1976.

[82] "From Primary to Post-Election, TV and Radio Were There," *Broadcasting*, January 3, 1977, p. 39.

[83] League of Women Voters Education Fund, *The '76 Presidential Debates*, p. 1.

[84] Herbert Gans, "Lessons 1976 Can Offer 1980," *Columbia Journalism Review*, January/February, 1977, p. 28.

[85] Federal Election Campaign Guide Task Force, *Compliance with Federal Election Campaign Requirements*, American Institute of Certified Public Accountants, New York, 1976. A second edition was published in 1978.

[86] AICPA news release, July 26, 1976.

[87] AICPA, "Presidential Campaign Advisors Conference," AICPA, N.Y., 1976.

[88] Barry Wagman to colleagues, Carter campaign memorandum, September 18, 1976.

[89] Barry E. Wagman, *The Democratic Party: Campaign Treasurer's Handbook*, (Beverly Hills: Oakdale Publishing Co., 1974).

[90] Republican National Committee, "Federal Election Law Manual," Republican National Committee, Washington, D.C., 1976.

[91] Democratic National Committee, *Democratic Election Law Reporter*, Democratic National Committee, Washington, D.C., 1976.

[92] Ibid., p. iii.

[93] Ralph Gerson, legal counsel, Democratic National Committee to Democratic members of Congress, Democratic National Committee memorandum, undated.

[94] See Federal Election Commission, "Campaign Guide for Federal Candidate," "Campaign Guide on Contributions and Expenditures," "Campaign Guide for the 1976 General Election," "Campaign Guide for Subordinate Party Committees," "Campaign Guide: The 1976 Amendments," and *Bookkeeping and Reporting Manual for Candidates and Political Committees*, Federal Election Commission, Washington, D.C., 1976.

[95] Federal Election Commission, *Federal Election Campaign Laws*, Washington, D.C., June, 1976.

[96] See Arthur Andersen & Co., *Financial Management System for Political Campaigns and Audit Criteria for Federal Political Campaigns*, Arthur Andersen & Co., Chicago, 1976.

[97] Price Waterhouse & Co., *Political Action Committees — A Guide to Organization, Accounting and Taxation*, Price Waterhouse & Co., New York, 1976.

[98] Robert Lipshutz, Doug Huron, Robert Andrews, and Richard Harden, "Carter/Mondale '76, Advance Guide — Legal/Financial Administrative Manual," Carter campaign memorandum, August 14, 1976.

[99] Barry Wagman to Robert Andrews et al., "Minimum Recordkeeping and Documentation Requirements for Expenditures," Carter campaign memorandum, October 3, 1976.

[100] See Doug Huron to staff, "Spending by Party Committees following FEC Ruling of August 26," Carter campaign memorandum, August 27, 1976; and Ralph Gerson to state chairpersons, "Important Developments on Federal Election Laws," Carter campaign memorandum, September 21, 1976.

[101] Carter/Mondale Campaign, "CPA Volunteers — Initial Field Office Contact Questionnaire," Carter campaign form, undated.

[102] _____, "Everything You Always Wanted to Know About Bank Drafts, Leases, etc. — But Were Afraid to Ask," Carter campaign memorandum, undated.

[103] _____, "Technical Queries Flow Chart," Carter campaign form, undated.

[104] _____, "CPA Area Coordinators Flow Chart," Carter/Mondale campaign form, undated.

[105] Robert Lipshutz to Vernon Thomson, August 20, 1976.

[106] N. Bradley Litchfield to Robert Lipshutz, September 27, 1976.

[107] Bob Lipshutz, treasurer; Morris Dees, general counsel; and Doug Huron, counsel; legal department to staff, "Federal Election Law and the Campaign," Carter campaign memorandum, undated.

[108] Ibid.

[109] Ibid., p. 4.

[110] Vernon Thomson to Doug Huron, August 26, 1976.

[111] Barry Wagman to Robert Andrews and Richard Harden, "Preliminary Plan for Financial Closeout of State Coordinators on November 6," Carter campaign memorandum, November 1, 1976.

[112] Barry E. Wagman, "Political Campaign Accounting — New Opportunities for the CPA," The Journal of Accountancy, March 1976, pp. 36-41; also see Warren Weaver, Jr., "Accountants are in Political Spotlight," The New York Times, August 8, 1975, "The Numbers Game," Forbes, May 1, 1976, pp. 20-21; Lawrence Minard and Brian Mcglynn, "The U.S.' Newest Glamour Job," Forbes, September 1, 1977, pp. 32-36.

[113] For a paper listing cases brought early regarding the 1971 FECA, see Elizabeth Yadlosky, "Constitutional Issues Raised With Respect to the Federal Election Campaign Act of 1971, P.L. 92-225," in Hearings before the Subcommittee on Communications of the Committee on Commerce, U.S. Senate, 93rd Cong., 1st sess., pp. 228-52. For one of the first publications of the subject, see Albert J. Rosenthal, Federal Regulation of Campaign Finance: Some Constitutional Questions, Milton Katz, ed. (Princeton: Citizens' Research Foundation, 1972). Exemplary among the many relevant law review articles was the entire issue of the Harvard Law Review devoted to "Developments in the Law — Elections," Harv. L. Rev., vol. 88 (1975).

[114] For guidelines and procedures for matching fund submissions to the FEC, see Appendix 2 in testimony of Commissioner Thomas E. Harris, in Public Financing of Congressional Elections, U.S. House, Committee on House Administration, 95th Cong. 1st Sess., pp. 318-328.

[115] Bruce F. Freed, "How to Sneak Around the New Campaign Reform Laws," Baltimore Sunday Sun, August 17, 1975.

[116] The Ripon Society and Clifford W. Brown, Jr., Jaws of Victory (Boston/Toronto: Little Brown and Co., 1977), p. 68.

9 Sources of Funds

By 1974 political fund-raisers were observing a tighter squeeze than in earlier election years and the shortage was evident all along the political spectrum; Democrats and Republicans alike reported lower receipts than usual from congressional dinners. The experience of the National Committee for an Effective Congress was representative. The organization had reported average contributions as high as $26 or $27 in good years; in 1974 it noted that the average contribution had dropped to $17. Blamed for the decline were political disorientation due to Watergate, the slump in the economy, the fact that contributions usually made by the Jewish community had been reduced by gifts to Israel following the 1973 war, and the absence of a prominent issue such as the Vietnam War.[1]

The fund-raising efforts of the 1976 presidential contenders were launched in this climate, and the new limits on contributions that became effective January 1, 1975, had a pronounced effect on campaigns. Contributions from individuals were restricted to $1,000 per candidate per election, with a total contribution limit per individual of $25,000 per year.[2] Political action committees were permitted to donate $5,000 per candidate per election, an allowance that encouraged a continuing and influential role for them in future elections.[3]

Individual Donations

In November 1974, even before the new laws took effect, most declared presidential hopefuls had imposed a ceiling on donations from individuals. Arizona Congressman Morris Udall and former North Carolina Governor Terry Sanford announced that they were abiding by the $1,000 limit before January 1975. Senators Henry Jackson of Washington, Walter Mondale of Minnesota, and Lloyd Bentsen of Texas announced that they had imposed a $3,000 limit on contributions, the limit contained in the Senate version of the reform measure. The $3,000 figure also was the maximum permitted an individual without payment of gift tax.

Sizable contributions within the allowed limits continued, and news sources reported the names of many campaign contributors. Morris Udall received contributions from fellow Democrats, including Rep. Jonathan B. Bingham of New York ($550), Rep. Don Edwards of California ($300), and House Majority Leader Tip O'Neill of Massachusetts ($100). Contributors of $3,000 to Jackson's campaign included John Shad of E. F. Hutton; Hank Greenspun, publisher of the Las Vegas *Sun;* and Lew Wasserman of MCA and his wife. Ronald Reagan found support from Conrad Hilton of Hilton Hotels ($250), the Coors brewing family, and certain law enforcement officers.[4]

Notables who contributed to Carter's campaign included former Secretary of State Dean Rusk and his wife ($800), Howard Stein of Dreyfus Corp. ($1,000), actor Burt Lancaster ($1,000), Donald J. Trump of the Trump Organization ($1,000), and Andrew Heiskell of Time Inc. ($500). President Ford secured donations from Happy and Nelson Rockefeller ($1,000 each), with smaller amounts coming from George Romney ($500), former Secretary of Defense Melvin Laird ($250), Richard Shinn of Metropolitan Life ($250), and Gene Autry ($250).

Questions were raised about the propriety of certain individual contributions. Thirty-six high government officials, including cabinet members, White House staff, ambassadors, and the vice-chairman of an independent agency, contributed $1,000 each to Ford's campaign in 1976. In all, Ford's primary campaign treasury received $65,527 from at least 106 federal employees who gave $100 or more. Many of these individuals had been selected by Ford for their posts, and some commentators called attention to statutes in the criminal code that prohibit federal servants from contributing money to political campaigns. When pressed for an interpretation, the Justice Department stated that the prohibition did not extend to contributions made voluntarily, but only to those made in response to coercion.

The contribution limits presented a challenge to those seeking sources of funds for financing campaigns. Veteran fund-raisers assert that it is far easier to find 10 contributors of $5,000 each than to find 1,000 contributors of $50, and the new legislation obliged finance managers to develop new fund-raising strategies. For example, one Los Angeles fund-raiser for Senator Jackson and others calls himself a "retail fund-raiser," seeking big money in small sums; he is developing new techniques including telephone/public address hook-ups, souvenir photos, and phone banks.[5] Traditional fund-raising dinners and events continue to form part of campaign activities, but they often seem to be a better source of special interest money than of individual contributions. An analysis of District of Columbia fund-raising events released by Common Cause in February 1978 indicated that the guests were largely Washington lobbyists and their interest groups. The degree of influence, if any, purchased at a fund-raiser for a congressional or presidential contender remains uncertain, but Fred Wertheimer, vice-president of Common Cause, noted that most of the money funded incumbents rather than challengers.[6]

Some summary information regarding the sources of funds for presidential and congressional candidates was released by the FEC in October 1976. FEC records indicate that the biggest contributions of special interest money were made by organized labor and the medical profession. Labor's political action committees spent $2,486,409 in the primary campaigns, or nearly half the $5,298,215 contributed by special interest groups to presidential and congressional candidates. The medical profession's committees spent $1,294,060 on selected candidates.[7]

Many contributors to President Ford's campaign were from oil companies, Michigan automobile corporations, and from eastern law firms. Many contributors to Carter's campaign came from Georgia, Georgetown, Manhattan, and Hollywood. While Ford contributed $1,000 to his own campaign, Carter gave his campaign $18,200 and received $1,000 from his mother. The law permits personal expenditures by candidates for president and vice president of as much as $50,000.[8]

Decline of the Wealthy Donor. Probably the single greatest change effected by the new campaign laws in the area of fund raising was the elimination of the prominent role previously played by the wealthy donor — the successful businessman or other individual whose political clout had been reflected in other years by the size of his campaign contributions. As campaigns progressed, much speculation centered on the effect and significance of this aspect of the new law. Many individuals who had poured hundreds of thousands of dollars into the campaigns of favored candidates in earlier years continued to contribute in 1976, but in the legally permissible amounts. Some were hostile to the new restrictions; others made little or no public comment about them. One commentator suggested that corporations should seize the occasion to promote the interests of the public and to reduce the tension between business and government. Another observer commented that the role formerly filled by donors such as Stewart Mott, the wealthy heir and longstanding contributor to political campaigns, had now been assumed by rock stars.[9]

One study examined these wealthy contributors as a group.[10] When questioned, 27 percent reported a family income over $100,000, 76 percent said they had finished college, and 16 percent had held public elective offices. One-half claimed to have written letters to the editor, and almost two-thirds had helped to found new organizations dealing with public problems. From these figures the writer argued that the campaign laws were unlikely to curtail the political influence wielded by wealthy donors; as a group, they were active politically in many other ways. It is improbable, the editorial concluded, that the FECA will significantly alter U.S. political life. Still, not all large contributors were happy; Stewart Mott described the FECA as "ridiculous" in the letter that accompanied his contributions to various members of Congress in October 1976 (see Appendix G).

Rise of the Fund-Raiser. As the 1976 campaigns progressed, it became evident that the $1,000 contribution limit was not only undercutting the importance of large contributors who had previously been prominent but was also correspondingly increasing the influence of fund-raisers, particularly those individuals capable of raising small sums of money from large numbers of contributors. The people thought best qualified to undertake this sort of fund raising included business executives, fund-raising professionals, and direct-mail specialists. Two direct-mail specialists played prominent roles in the Carter and Ford camps. Morris Dees, who had aided McGovern in 1972, worked for the former governor of Georgia in 1976. On the Republican side Robert Odell aided Ford. These professionals often were very successful.

A survey made by the FEC estimated that 57,000 individual contributions in amounts of $500 or more were made to federal campaigns. This figure does not include transfers of funds or PAC gifts, nor does it include an additional 1,318 individual contributions of $500 or more disclosed by a CRF survey of contributors to 1976 presidential candidates in their early campaign activity in 1974. Of the 57,000, some 16,400 were contributions of between $500 and $1,000 made to presidential candidates in the 1975-76 election cycle.[11] This leaves about 41,000 contributions of $500 or more given by individuals to 1976 congressional candidates, and to party and PAC committees. The FEC did not publish any 1976 contributor lists, breaking a tradition in presidential years since 1968.[12] The FEC has, however, made available in printout form only at FEC offices the $500-and-over donors to presidential candidates Brown, Carter, Ford, Udall, and Wallace, the work product of an abandoned attempt to compile such information on major candidates.

The FEC survey indicated approximately 31,000 individual contributors of $101-$499 to 1976 presidential candidates, but these were not computerized. For 1977-78, on the other hand, individual contributors of $101 and over to all federal candidates and to party and nonparty political committees are being placed in a computerized system on an ongoing monthly basis.

Appendix H is a compilation of numbers of individual contributions as derived from FEC data. It accounts for some $195.3 million contributed by individuals during 1975-76 to 1,068 committees. Information from smaller PACs would bring the total well in excess of $200 million. The compilation indicates much more money received in sums of $100 and less than in the categories in excess of $100. Numbers of contributions in the $499-and-under categories were not estimated, but some idea of their scope is indicated by the FEC-derived total of 975,493 individual contributions that were submitted for matching; the total dollars are incorporated in the presidential line of the Appendix, which appears on page 824.[13]

The CRF survey of individual contributors to 1976 presidential candidates in their 1974 campaign activity prior to the establishment of the FEC, indicating some 1,318 such contributions of $500 or more, is shown in Appendix I. It was compiled to show the contributions of $250 or less that would have been eligible for matching funds. The largest individual contributors are shown in Appendix J, including several who were still giving to erase Senator Muskie's 1972 debt. Appendix K indicates the largest family contributions in 1974, and Appendix L shows individuals giving to more than one candidate at that stage. As shown in Appendix G, Stewart Mott later gave to eight presidential candidates. The incompleteness of these data result from failure of the FEC or any private group to update such compilations to include 1975-76 contributions.

With the individual contribution limits in effect, contributions from political action committees assumed greater importance, but new attention also focused on modest donations from large numbers of blue-collar workers, small farmers, and middle-income groups, whom direct-mail specialists now sought out with renewed force.[14]

Help from Rock Stars. Campaign managers also were acutely aware of the value of volunteer workers and of the financial potential afforded by certain donations of time that were not restricted by the new campaign laws. One such source of funds proved to be benefit concerts by rock music groups and other entertainers. Although the new law restricted financial contributions from individuals, the services of entertainers were subject to no limitations. Presidential candidate Jerry Brown netted $75,000 from a benefit performance by Linda Ronstadt, the Eagles, and Jackson Browne; eligibility for matching funds became an issue between Brown's campaign and the FEC. Jimmy Carter's campaign received more than $200,000 from the efforts of the Allman Brothers and their manager. Carter also appeared with Black Oak Arkansas, the Marshall Tucker Band, and Johnny Cash. The Allman Brothers, Marshall Tucker, the Outlaws, and other southern rock stars helped raise about $100,000 of the first $800,000 in funds for the Carter campaign. As Brown and Carter sought out the big bands, Gerald Ford teamed up with Ella Fitzgerald and Sonny Bono, and Morris Udall was seen with Harry Belafonte. Richard Reeves has argued that the new rules of presidential politics require a candidate to be either independently wealthy or well known to garner the necessary seed money to start an effective campaign; in 1976 rock stars offered candidates who were not wealthy a means of raising seed money.[15]

Problems and Embarrassments. The constant search for money by political candidates even brought the Civil Aeronautics Board into the area of campaign finance in 1976. Since presidential candidates began chartering airplanes in the 1950s, it had become the practice for reporters accompanying the politicians to be charged amounts equaling or exceeding commercial rates for first-class travel. In some cases, the money received in payment for press tickets proved greater than the cost of chartering the aircraft, prompting charges that the press was subsidizing the campaign in such instances. In March 1976 the CAB ruled that campaigns could collect from media and government personnel the prorated share of the charter or the applicable first-class fare, but no more.[16]

In 1976 as in other election years, the winning presidential candidate was the target of criticism relating to various sources and efforts to obtain funds. In one instance, the Carter campaign was attacked because a loan was not reported at the proper time. In another case, 10 cosigners of a loan proved to be federal employees, and some observers speculated that pressure might have been brought to bear on them. A campaign official appointed by Carter as his top adviser on natural resources and the environment resigned, charging Carter's campaign with having distorted certain information to further its fund-raising efforts. A major contributor to Carter's campaign later appeared at the White House to argue against the gas deregulation bill, and news sources were quick to connect his campaign contribution and June 1977 visit with the fact that he was a gas pipeline executive.[17] The Carter campaign returned almost $40,000 to donors whose cumulative contributions exceeded the limit of $1,000.[18]

Another embarrassment for the president surfaced more than a year after the election. E. A. Gregory, a fund-raiser for the Democratic Party and a millionaire, had been a prominent contributor to candidates of both parties. He gave $2,000 to the "Save the President" campaign for Richard Nixon and $2,000 to George Wallace in 1974. In 1976 he and his wife gave $68,885 to politicians; they gave $20,667 in 1977. He was a friend of the Carter family, and as an important fund-raiser he was invited to a working lunch with the president in April 1978. Shortly before the lunch, however, Democratic Party Chairman John White informed Gregory that his presence would embarrass the president. Gregory and his wife had been indicted in April 1978 by an Alabama grand jury and were being investigated by the FBI and the Internal Revenue Service for questionable banking activities.[19]

Gregory had started buying banks in 1974. Shortly thereafter, federal and state examiners began investigations to determine whether he was using the banks to enrich himself and his political friends. Through Faith Investments Co. in Florida, it was charged, Gregory offered a wide range of services to banks and motels he owned, collecting large commissions. In addition, the examiners alleged that Gregory had overcharged the banks for expenses associated with his airplane. Cease-and-desist orders from state and federal authorities prompted Gregory to sell four banks. The fifth and last bank was placed in receivership by the Federal Deposit Insurance Corporation and the Alabama Banking Department in January 1978. Gregory filed suit for $10 million in damages, charging unlawful seizure. In addition, one of the banks he sold became insolvent, and the owner brought suit against Gregory alleging mismanagement of funds. The state grand jury indicted Gregory, his wife, and bank officials on charges that they received deposits after they knew of the bank's insolvency.

Gregory's critics found similarities between his situation and that of Bert Lance. Gregory himself noted that Armand Hammer had pleaded guilty in 1976 to charges of illegally concealing $54,000 in contributions to Nixon's campaign in 1972. Gregory also pointed out that Robert Sowa was a guest at a state dinner at the White House. Sowa, another Carter supporter, had pleaded guilty in 1977 to a felony charge of theft involving a car.

Large contributors reemerged in both Democratic and Republican party financing. The Democratic Party was helped out by the FEC, which agreed that long-term debts could be erased by contributions exceeding the present contribution limits, as noted elsewhere. President Carter held a White House luncheon that brought together individuals contributing as much as $100,000 each to retire old debts derived mainly from the 1968 presidential campaign.[20] The Republican Party, as noted elsewhere, similarly was helped out when large contributions for its headquarters purchase did not count against the $25,000-a-year individual maximum, and PACs and corporations could contribute directly.

Independent Expenditures

Independent expenditures represent a troublesome aspect of campaign finance regulation. On the one hand, to bar independent expenditures implies a limitation on an individual's or group's right of freedom of expression; on the other hand, such spending can render meaningless any attempt to place limits on campaign contributions and expenditures.

The 1974 Amendments established a $1,000 limit on personal or independent expenditures. In *Buckley v. Valeo,* the Supreme Court decided this ceiling was unconstitutional, but only if the spending was truly independent.[21] The ruling stated that if independent expenditures were not coordinated with the candidate or his campaign organization nor consented to by the candidate or his agent, there could be no upper limit. The 1976 Amendments wrote into law the Court's interpretation. Expenditures that did not meet this strict criterion could be limited to the $1,000 contribution limit.

During and subsequent to the 1976 campaign, the Federal Election Commission issued a series of rulings with respect to independent contributions and expenditures. A number of these rulings were in response to complaints involving specific campaign organizations. As expected, the subject proved very complex.

On February 10, 1976, the commission approved a policy statement concerning application of the Act to the presidential delegate selection process. It required the filing of reports by:[22]

1. An unauthorized delegate spending more than $100 for campaign communications that expressly advocate the election or defeat of a clearly identified candidate, not including costs for travel and subsistence. (An unauthorized delegate whose expenditures do not expressly advocate the election or defeat of a clearly identified candidate is not required to report.)
2. A person who contributes more than $100 in a calendar year to one or more unauthorized delegates.

In April 1976 FEC Counsel John Murphy warned the Wallace campaign that it could not close its field headquarters offices and then reopen them at the local coordinator's expense as an independent expenditure. The Wallace staff had planned to continue to use campaign materials from its national headquarters in these local offices and Murphy said that such actions could involve the inference that the local offices were operating with Wallace's cooperation or his consent.[23]

The following month the FEC issued a policy statement (which also was included in proposed regulations submitted to Congress) stating that groups making independent expenditures could not accept more than $5,000 a year from any individual contributor. Although the statement did not mention which groups the commission had in mind, the American Conservative Union (ACU) had been soliciting contributions up to $25,000 on behalf of Ronald Reagan's candidacy; $25,000 represented an individual's calendar year limit for contributions to federal candidates.

In June 1976 the FEC defined a candidate's agent as any person with express or implied oral or written authority to make or to authorize the making of expenditures on behalf of a candidate, or any person within the campaign organization who appears to have such authority.[24]

On September 30, 1976, the FEC issued another policy statement. It declared that contributions to political committees making independent expenditures were subject to the same limits as were contributions to candidates and candidate authorized committees. A $5,000-a-year contribution limit applied to contributions to committees making independent expenditures in support of more than one candidate. Contributions to political committees supporting only one candidate were limited to $1,000. Furthermore, the limits of $1,000 (or $5,000) per contribution were to apply to all contributions combined by a donor supporting a given candidate, including contributions to the candidate, to the candidate's authorized committees, and to unauthorized independent expenditure committees. The FEC noted that individuals still could make unlimited independent expenditures on their own in support of a candidate.[25]

This ruling was similar to one issued by the FEC during the spring but differed in one respect. Such donations no longer were considered contributions to the candidate but rather contributions to a political committee not authorized by the presidential candidate.[26] This change prevented the presidential nominees from being judged to have violated the ban on accepting contributions from private donors during the general election. In any case, the commission's ruling eliminated the large sums that independent committees traditionally have relied on for seed money.

Important contributors to previous presidential campaigns reacted in different ways to the limits on direct contributions and to the Supreme Court's ruling allowing unlimited independent expenditures. Lew Wasserman, head of MCA, said he did not know enough about politics to make intelligent decisions about spending funds to aid candidates he favored, and that he therefore was not going to make independent contributions. Others, however, were willing to make independent contributions.

In New Hampshire, Richard A. Viguerie, a prominent Virginia mail order fund-raiser for conservative candidates and causes, used $35,000 of his own money to have a four-page letter included in the Sunday preprimary edition of each of the state's 10 daily newspapers. The letter urged voters to write in John B. Connally's name in the Democratic primary. The effort, as noted elsewhere, had little impact on the outcome of the Granite State's primary.

In general, the campaign managers of the major candidates were wary of such expenditures. John Michels, the New Hampshire manager of Ford's campaign, said he knew of no independent expenditures on behalf of the president and added, "I prefer not to know." Morris Udall's coordinator in the state, David Evans, said he did not want any such expenditures on behalf of his candidate because they "would violate the spirit of the campaign reform that he's been fighting for."[27]

Reagan in Texas. Most independent expenditures were made on behalf of Republicans. The American Conservative Union (ACU), the biggest spender during the campaign, paid for radio commercials and newspaper advertisements in at least nine states to help nominate Ronald Reagan. In Texas the ACU spent $33,000, approximately one-fifth of Reagan's ad campaign in that state.

The individual who made the largest independent expenditure was Henry Grover, a former Texas Republican gubernatorial candidate. Grover spent $63,000 to help Reagan. In newspaper ads he paid for, Grover appealed to Wallace Democrats to cross over and vote for Reagan. He pointed out that Wallace was no longer effectively in the Democratic race and that voters could still choose a Democrat in November if they wanted to. Another major contributor to the Reagan cause was Joseph Coors, the brewery owner. Coors spent more than $20,000 for full-page advertisements in eight Florida newspapers and another $11,000 to influence the Texas primary. In the Lone Star state the money was used to broadcast a one-minute commercial that criticized Secretary of State Kissinger and his position on the Panama Canal. Although the Ford camp considered the commercial ineffective and unfair, Reagan won the primary.

The sizable independent effort made on behalf of Reagan in Texas prompted a complaint from the Ford camp. In April the President Ford Committee wrote to the Citizens for Reagan organization challenging the activities of the Texas Citizens for Reagan Committee and the Delegates for Reagan. The Ford campaign charged that, despite the explicit provisions of the FEC's proposed regulations, Delegates for Reagan, a Texas group, was not independent of the official Reagan effort in that state as claimed, but was actually tied to the official Reagan Texas campaign. The letter noted that more than 20 of the allegedly unauthorized delegate-candidates pledged to Reagan were members of the official Texas Citizens for Reagan Committee. In addition, the two groups apparently shared offices and facilities in several Texas cities and had engaged in joint fund-raising efforts. The president's supporters argued that the expenditures made by the so-called independent group should be charged to the Reagan totals, and that individuals who previously had given $1,000 to the Citizens for Reagan would be violating the law if they made additional contributions to such authorized delegates or to the group.[28]

The Reagan camp responded that the Ford committee's complaint was simply a political ploy. The Reagan forces said they had decided not to authorize delegate candidates financially. They noted, however, that the FEC had indicated its acceptance of a degree of political coordination by deleting from the delegate statement of February 10 a provision requiring campaign officials running as delegates to run as authorized delegates.[29]

Independent expenditures on Reagan's behalf were widespread and their "independence" was often questioned. In fact, in March 1977 the FEC began a full-scale investigation into the legality of more than $150,000 in expenditures by the ACU and the Conservative Victory Fund (CVF). Reports filed by these two committees and by Reagan's own committee indicated that several ACU staff members worked for and were paid by the Reagan committee at the same time that the ACU was engaged in a vigorous, supposedly independent public campaign supporting the Reagan candidacy.[30]

Officials from both the ACU and CVF claimed that their expenditures were not coordinated with the Reagan campaign and that those individuals with overlapping memberships were deliberately excluded from any participation in or knowledge of the expenditures. In a letter to the FEC, John R. Bolton, the attorney representing ACU and CVF, stated that as a matter of policy it was decided that all contributions to Citizens for Reagan would be made through CVF and that ACU would engage in an independent campaign effort. Moreover, the contributions made through CVF were to take the form of reimbursed expenses for persons who volunteered to work for Citizens for Reagan. The letter went on to say that no such reimbursements were made to any persons who had any decision-making role in ACU's independent effort.[31]

Apparently, the FEC could not prove otherwise. In December 1977 the commission voted to close its investigation. Neil Staebler, the one dissenter, took strong exception to the decision:[32]

> The record indicates that ACU personnel, by virtue of their active, widespread involvement in the Reagan campaign inevitably acquired from the candidate's agents material information about the campaign's plans, projects and needs; that the information was acquired at a time when the two organizations were working consciously toward the same goals; and that ACU expenditures paralleling and complementing [the Reagan committee's] efforts followed.

Staebler also commented on what he thought to be the larger implications of the decision:[33]

> There will always be temptation for an administrative body to avoid battles difficult to win and a general sentiment not to pursue a defeated candidate and his supporters. I fear the impression left [by the 5-1 vote] may be that if a committee is brazen enough and massive enough in its violations and sophisticated enough in its operations, the law will somehow not be applied.

Aid to Other Candidates. Ronald Reagan was not the only Republican candidate to receive substantial support from independent contributors. Gerald Ford was praised in advertisements placed in Ohio and Michigan newspapers and on radio commercials in Ohio that were paid for by the Friends of the First Family. The group, composed of Washington lobbyists and home-town associates of the president, spent $33,000 during the primaries.[34] Because both Ford and Reagan were short of funds during the late primaries, these expenditures undoubtedly helped their campaigns.

One effort to undertake independent expenditures in the California primary was aborted when the large network-owned television stations in Los Angeles and San Francisco refused to sell time to a wealthy person who wanted to buy spot announcements on behalf of Jimmy Carter. Since a campaign of independent expenditures would be most effective on television, and would be futile if not on major stations, the possibility was abandoned. Communications lawyers advised that litigation to force stations to sell time might be successful but would be lengthy, expensive, and would not be resolved in time to be effective before the primary date. Under the law and current practice, and with some exceptions, stations are required to sell time to candidates. But neither the law nor the fairness doctrine require selling time for controversial issues, and accordingly, stations can refuse to sell certain political advertising. The California licensees approached in this case did refuse and the individual did not pursue the course of litigation. On constitutional grounds, given the *Buckley* decision regarding independent expenditures, some lawyers believe a case can be made to compel sales of broadcast time if it can be shown that television is the most effective way to speak independently to large audiences.

In contrast to the primaries, relatively few independent expenditures were made during the general election. The reasons for the decline included the contributors' fear of publicity, the lack of a centralized effort, and belief that the election laws would be strictly enforced. Moreover, independent expenditures were not welcomed by the candidates. The Carter campaign strongly discouraged such activities during the general election in the belief that they involved political, financial, and legal risks.[35] In theory, if such expenditures were ever declared not independent, someone not connected with the central campaign might have determined how the candidate would spend part of his budget.

FEC Disclosure No. 3

On March 23, 1977, the FEC issued a disclosure report covering independent expenditures, unauthorized delegates, and their committees' receipts and expenditures for the period January 1, 1975, through February 28, 1977.[36] The index does not include independent expenditures made by nonparty-related political action committees or unauthorized single-candidate committees.

According to the FEC's data, individuals and groups spent a total of $454,128 in independent expenditures (Table 9-1). The largest individual expenditure, $63,000, was made by a Reagan ally in Texas, as noted above. The 15 largest spenders accounted for approximately two-thirds of all independent expenditures (Table 9-2).

Table 9-1
Summary Statistics of Independent Expenditures and Unauthorized Delegates, 1976 Election

Independent expenditures: (147)[a]		Delegates: (251)	
Total receipts	$ 4,201.00[b]	Total receipts	$ 33,934.00[b]
Total expenditures	454,128.00	Total expenditures	120,355.00
Average receipt	28.58	Average receipt	135.20
Average expenditure	3,089.31	Average expenditure	479.50
Largest independent expenditure	63,000.00		
(Henry C. Grover — Reagan)		Delegate Committees: (38)	
		Total committee receipts	$305,462.00[b]
Contributors: (61)		Total committee expenditures	295,613.00
Total amount contributed	$ 33,710.00	Average committee receipt	8,038.47
Average	552.62	Average committee expenditure	7,779.29
Largest contribution	3,136.00		
(Ellen C. Garwood — Reagan Delegate Committee)			

[a] Includes two groups of individuals that reported as a committee.
[b] Includes funds from outside contributors and some personal funds; however, many persons did not report personal funds as a receipt but only as an expenditure.

SOURCE: Federal Election Commission, *FEC Disclosure Series No. 3: Index of Independent Expenditures By Individuals and Receipts and Expenditures By Unauthorized Delegates — 1976 Campaign*, (Washington, D.C., 1977), p. 3.

Table 9-2
The Largest 'Independent Expenditures' Reported by Individuals in 1976

Person	Candidate	Amount
1. Henry C. Grover	Ronald Reagan	$63,000
2. Joseph Coors	Ronald Reagan	33,782
3. Milton Shapp	Jimmy Carter, Walter Mondale, William Green and "Democratic Congressional Candidates"	28,001
4. Edward Downe, Jr.	Jerry Litton	26,820
5. Stewart Mott	Unlisted	20,051
6. Raymond Donovan	James Buckley	18,836
7. Richard Kughn	Gerald Ford	18,625
8. Norton Simon	Gerald Ford	17,367
9. Howard Pack	Elmo Zumwalt	15,000
10. Russell Knott	Gerald Ford	14,347
11. Warren Manshell	Frank Church	11,998
12. Edward Downe, Jr.	Frank Church	11,998
13. Ted B. Brown	Gerald Ford	11,428
14. Fred Hearn	Gerald Ford	9,349
15. Walter Knott	Ronald Reagan	9,250

SOURCE: Federal Election Commission, "FEC Releases Index of Independent Expenditures," press release, March 23, 1977, p. 2.

Of the total spent, $373,993 (82 percent) could be identified as expenditures in support of or in opposition to 43 federal candidates in the 1976 election. Of this amount, $364,823 was spent in support of 43 candidates and $9,170 was spent against the two major-party presidential candidates.[37] Of the sums spent in behalf of federal candidates, 123 individuals and groups reported outlays of $267,686 (73 percent) for presidential candidates, $44,385 (13 percent) for senatorial candidates, and $52,752 (14 percent) for House candidates.[38]

In the presidential contest, more than four out of every five independent dollars were spent on the Republican side, with Reagan receiving slightly more assistance than Ford. More independent expenditures were made on behalf of Frank Church than any other Democratic candidate, but his total came to less than one-quarter of the independent expenditures of Reagan or Ford (Table 9-3).

The FEC report also disclosed that $415,968 was spent by unauthorized delegates and delegate committees. Of this amount, two-thirds ($277,167) could be identified with specific candidates, with 65 percent spent on Reagan's behalf and 19 percent for Lloyd Bentsen.[39]

Table 9-3
Independent Expenditures for 1976 Presidential Candidates

Candidate	Amount Spent	Percent of Total
Ronald Reagan	$115,957	43
Gerald Ford	108,214[a]	40
Frank Church	24,212	9
Jimmy Carter	17,091[b]	6
Morris Udall	675	1
Jerry Brown	630	1
Milton Shapp	448	—
George Wallace	445	—
Henry Jackson	14	—
Total	$267,686 [c]	

[a] Figure does *not* include a $650 expenditure made in opposition to Ford.
[b] Figure does *not* include a $8,520 expenditure made in opposition to Carter.
[c] Total does *not* include expenditures made in opposition to a candidate.

SOURCE: Federal Election Commission, "FEC Releases Index of Independent Expenditures," press release, March 23, 1977, p. 1.

1977-78 Independent Expenditures

On November 3, 1978, the FEC released a report on independent expenditures made on behalf of or against U.S. House and Senate candidates during the 1977-78 election cycle.[40] The report covered 18 Senate and 51 House candidates and was complete through October 10, 1978. During this period $104,901 was spent independently to influence federal elections. The top 10 candidates for or against whom the most money was spent along with the top 10 contributing political committees are listed in Table 9-4.

Sources of Funds Survey Data

Since 1952 two of the country's major public opinion research organizations have asked questions about political contributions of national samples of voters. In 1976 the Survey Research Center (SRC) found that 8.6 percent of the adult population had given money to a political party or made some other political contribution; the Gallup Poll found that 8 percent had done so. Applying these percentages to the adult population of the United States, the SRC results yield 12.6 million

Table 9-4
1977-78 Independent Expenditures[a]

Ten candidates for or against whom the most money was spent:

Candidate	Office/State	For	Against	Total
Lane Denton (D)	House Texas-11	$ —	$9,795	$9,795
Thomas S. Foley (D)	House Wash.-5	—	6,675	6,675
Ron Faucheux (D)	House La.-1	6,076	—	6,076
Donald M. Fraser (DFL)	Senate Minn.	183	5,765	5,948
Sam Nunn (D)	Senate Ga.	5,470	—	5,470
Abner J. Mikva (D)	House Ill.-10	—	4,825	4,825
Marvin Leath (D)	House Texas-11	4,454	—	4,454
Walter D. Huddleston (D)	Senate Ky.	—	3,682	3,682
Robert E. Short (DFL)	Senate Minn.	3,156	—	3,156
Bill Frenzel (R)	House Minn.-3	3,118	—	3,118

Ten political committees that have reported the greatest dollar amounts in independent expenditures:

Committee	For	Against	Total
American Medical PAC	$42,359	$ —	$42,359
National Conservative PAC	616	9,729	10,345
5th District Political Research Committee	—	6,675	6,675
Plaquemines Campaign Fund — Faucheux	6,076	—	6,076
NRA Political Victory Fund	—	4,825	4,825
Brown Committee for Marvin Leath	4,454	—	4,454
Minnesota Gun Owners' Political Victory Fund	—	4,072	4,072
Cook County Concerned Citizens	—	1,693	1,693
Conservative Caucus 2nd CD of South Dakota	1,505	—	1,505
Our United Republic PAC	1,178	—	1,178

[a] Figures are complete through October 10, 1978.

SOURCE: FEC Press Release, November 3, 1978.

individuals who said they made a contribution at some level to some campaign; the Gallup results yielded 11.7 million voters.

Broken down by party, 3.9 percent of the SRC respondents said they had contributed to Republicans, and 3.5 percent to Democrats. Another 0.6 percent gave to both Republicans and Democrats, 0.4 percent to other parties, and 0.3 percent did not know. Of the Gallup respondents, 3 percent said they had given to Republicans, 3 percent to Democrats, 1 percent to another party, and 1 percent responded Do Not Know or No Answer.

Table 9-5 shows the percentages of the adult population solicited for and making political contributions since 1952, as shown by both the

SRC and Gallup polls. These percentages translate into the approximate number of individuals making contributions, as follows:

3 million in 1952	12 million in 1944
8 million in 1956	8.7 million in 1968
10 million in 1960	11.7 million in 1972
	12.2 million in 1976

The percentage of adults making political contributions in 1976, as Table 9-5 shows, was lower than in any presidential election year since the polls began with the exception of the first year, 1952. This drop

Table 9-5
Percentage of National Adult Population Solicited and Making Political Contributions, 1952-76.

Year	Polling Organi- zation	Solicited by:			Contributed to:		
		Rep.	Dem.	Total[a]	Rep.	Dem.	Total[a]
1952	SRC				3	1	4
1956	Gallup	8	11	19	3	6	9
1956	SRC				5	5	10
1960	Gallup	9	8	15	4	4	9
1960	Gallup						12
1960	SRC				7	4	11
1964	Gallup				6	4	12
1964	SRC	8	4	15	6	4	11
1968	SRC	9	7	23[b]	4	4	9[c]
1972	SRC				4	5	10[d]
1974	SRC				3	3	8[e]
1976	Gallup				3	3	8[f]
1976	SRC				4	4	9[g]

[a]The total percentage may add to a total different from the total of Democrats and Republicans because of individuals solicited by or contributing to both major parties, other parties, nonparty groups, or combinations of these.
[b]Includes 4 percent who were solicited by both major parties and 1.4 percent who were solicited by Wallace's American Independent Party (AIP).
[c]Includes .7 percent who contributed to Wallace's AIP.
[d]Includes contributors to American Independent Party.
[e]Includes .7 percent who contributed to both parties, and .8 percent who contributed to minor parties.
[f]Includes 1 percent to another party and 1 percent Do Not Know or No Answer.
[g]Republican and Democratic figures are rounded. The total includes .6 percent who gave to both parties, .4 percent to other, and .3 percent Do Not Know.

SOURCE: Survey Research Center (SRC), University of Michigan; data direct from center or from Angus Campbell, Philip E. Converse, Warren E. Miller, Donald E. Stokes, *The American Voter* (New York: John Wiley and Sons, 1960), p. 91; Gallup data direct or from Roper Opinion Research Center, Williams College, and from American Institute of Public Opinion (Gallup Poll).

probably was due in part to the law prohibiting private contributions to the major-party nominees, which was in effect for the first time.

In spite of the low percentage, the total number of contributors was quite high in 1976. This size can be attributed to general increases in the population and to the inclusion of 18- to 21-year-olds in the population base.

For the first time, the SRC asked an additional question: "Now thinking about all of the presidential candidates who ran in the primaries across the country, did you contribute money for the campaigns of any candidate?" The results are shown in Table 9-6. The accuracy of the findings is questionable if the results are correlated with figures released by the FEC on the number of contributors to each of the

Table 9-6
Percentage Contributing to Presidential Primary Candidates

Candidate	Percentage of Population Contributing
Bayh	*
Brown	0.1
Carter	1.0
Church	0.1
Ford	1.1
Harris	*
Humphrey	*
Jackson	0.1
Kennedy	*
McCarthy	*
McCormack	*
Reagan	0.8
Sanford	*
Shapp	*
Shriver	*
Udall	*
Wallace	0.1
Democratic Party Candidates in General, or Don't Know which Democratic Candidate	0.4
Republican Party Candidates in General, or Don't Know which Republican Candidate	0.3
Other	0.2
Don't Know	0.3
No Answer	0.5
Total	4.9

*Less than 0.05 percent.

SOURCE: Survey Research Center, University of Michigan.

presidential candidates (see Table 9-7). The FEC shows, for instance, that Reagan had more than twice as many contributors as Ford, while the SRC poll shows Ford with a higher percentage. On the Democratic side, Udall had more contributors than Carter, and Wallace more than twice as many as either of them. The SRC data, however, indicated that Carter had more than 10 times as many contributors as Wallace, and more than 20 times as many as Udall. These discrepancies may indicate that prestigious answers were given by some respondents in favor of winning candidates. Also, some candidates did not submit all contributions eligible for matching to the FEC, so those figures are not fully accurate. The comparison thus raises interesting but unanswerable questions.

Table 9-7
Contributions Submitted to Federal Election Commission for Matching Funds Per Candidate

Candidate	Number of Contributions Submitted
Bayh	6,988
Bentsen	6,767
Brown	20,089
Carter	94,419
Church	18,812
Ford	114,661
Harris	56,021
Jackson	58,372
McCormack	14,161
Reagan	238,266
Sanford	1,960
Shapp	4,416
Shriver	2,745
Udall	97,764
Wallace	240,052
Total	975,493

SOURCE: Testimony of Thomas E. Harris before the Committee on Rules and Administration, United States Senate, *Federal Election Reform Proposals of 1977*, Appendix A, p. 426.

Checkoff

One source of campaign funds available for the first time in 1976 was money derived from the federal income tax checkoff. The Revenue Act of 1971 provided that any individual whose liability for any calendar year was one dollar or more could designate on his federal income tax form that one dollar of his tax money be paid to the Presidential Election Campaign Fund; couples filing joint returns could designate two dollars. The fund accumulated almost $96 million for the 1976 election, of which $72 million was used (Table 9-8).

Table 9-8
Federal Income Tax Checkoff

Tax Year	Approximate Percentages of Taxpayers Using Checkoff	Approximate Amount
1972 [a]	7.0	$12,900,000
1973	13.6	17,300,000
1974	24.2	31,900,000
1975	25.8	33,700,000
1976	27.0	36,600,000
1977	29.0	39,200,000
Total available for 1976 presidential election (approx.)		95,900,000
Total funds certified to candidates		72,000,000
Total remaining after 1976 election (approx.)		$23,900,000
Funds available as of December 31, 1977, for 1980 election [b] (approx.)		$60,500,000

[a] In its first year the tax checkoff form was separate from the 1040 form and was not readily available for many. In 1974 the tax checkoff form was included on the front page of the 1040 form. It also allowed taxpayers who had not checked off for 1972 to do so retroactively for that year. Only $4 million was checked off initially for 1972. Another $8.9 million was added retroactively, for a total of $12.9 million.
[b] Including 1976 surplus and 1976 income available in 1977.

SOURCE: Testimony of Thomas E. Harris before the Committee on Rules and Administration, United States Senate. *Federal Election Reform Proposals of 1977*, Appendix B, p. 430.

During its first tax year of operation (1972), the checkoff was provided on a form separate from the 1040 form and was not readily available for many taxpayers. Only $4 million was checked off initially in that year. For 1973 the checkoff was included on the front page of the 1040 form, and those taxpayers who had not checked off retroactively, a total of 7 percent of the taxpayers checked off $12.9 million for 1973.

The percentage of taxpayers using the checkoff rose to 13.6 in 1973 and 24.2 in 1974. It then remained relatively steady, with only slight changes to 25.8 in 1975, 27.0 in 1976, and 29.0 in 1977. However, throughout these years, those checking NO on the tax form have ranged persistently above 40 percent, reaching 46.2 percent in 1977. When added to those not checking either YES or NO, then some 75 percent fail to support public financing through the tax checkoff.

The Presidential Election Campaign Fund accumulated $95.9 million in the years 1972-75. Of this amount, $72.0 million was paid out in 1976: $24.3 million to presidential primary candidates, $4.1 million for the major-party conventions, and $43.6 million to the major-party presidential nominees. This left $23.9 million in the account, to which $36.6 million was added from the 1976 checkoff.

For the first time in 1976, the SRC recorded responses to its contribution question indicating that 7.6 percent claimed the checkoff as a means of making a contribution. This percentage is separate from the 8.6 percent who said they gave money. The percentage cannot be compared with the figure supplied by the IRS for the percentage of taxpayers who checked off in 1976, because the IRS percentage reflects individual taxpayers, a smaller universe than the national adult civilian population which comprises the poll universe.

Footnotes

[1] "Liberal Fund-Raisers: A Tighter Squeeze in 1974," *Congressional Quarterly Weekly Report*, June 15, 1974, pp. 1551-1555.

[2] It is not clear that the FEC had a procedure in 1976 for enforcing the annual limit, however.

[3] In 1974, 608 corporate, union, and trade association PACs were registered with the FEC. By September 30, 1977, the number had risen to 1,360. Donnie Radcliffe, " 'Buddy, Can You Spare $1,000?' The Chummy World of the Political Fund-raiser: Outreached Hands and the People Who Fill Them," *The Washington Post*, February 10, 1978.

[4] Aaron Latham, "The Capitol Letter: Funny Money," *New York*, April 26, 1976, pp. 8, 10.

[5] For a description of I. Hershey Gold, see Susan Littwin, "How the West's Best Fund-Raiser Gets His Hand in Your Pocket," *New West*, December 6, 1976.

[6] Donnie Radcliffe, "Buddy, Can You Spare $1,000?"; "Sixty-Three House Members Hold Washington, D.C. Fundraisers during First Nine Months of 1977, Common Cause Analysis Shows," Common Cause press release dated February 1, 1978.

[7] United Press International, "Top Givers Are Listed by the FEC," *The Washington Post*, October 24, 1976.

[8] Ibid.

[9] Edgar F. Bronfman, "Which Alley for 'Fat Cats' Now?" *The New York Times*, September 21, 1976; "The New King-Makers," editorial, *The Wall Street Journal*, June 23, 1976.

[10] An editorial, "The Same Faces," which appeared in *The Wall Street Journal* for October 21, 1977, discusses studies of large contributors made by Clifford Brown, Roman Hedges, and Lynda Powell at the State University of New York at Albany.

[11] Federal Election Commission, *FEC Disclosure Series, No. 7: 1976 Presidential Campaign Receipts and Expenditures* (Washington, D.C., May 1977), unnumbered tables on pp. 15 and 17.

[12] See Herbert E. Alexander and Caroline D. Jones, *CRF Listing of: Political Contributors of $500 or More in 1968* (Princeton: Citizens' Research Foundation, 1971); CRF Listing of: Political Contributors of $500 or More Voluntarily Disclosed by 1972 Presidential Candidates (Princeton, N.J.: Citizens' Research Foundation, 1972); and *CRF Listing of: Political Contributors and Lenders of $10,000 or More in 1972* (Princeton, N.J.: Citizens' Research Foundation, 1975). Government printouts included: Alphabetical Listing of 1972 Presidential Campaign Receipts, volumes I and II, Office of Federal Elections,

General Accounting Office (Washington, D.C.: U.S. Government Printing Office, November 1973); The Annual Statistical Report of Contributions and Expenditures Made During the 1972 Election Campaigns for the U.S. House of Representatives, parts I and II, by W. Pat Jennings, as Clerk of the House of Representatives and Supervisory Officer (Washington, D.C.: U.S. Government Printing Office, April/June 1974); The Annual Statistical Report of Receipts and Expenditures Made in Connection with Elections for the U.S. Senate in 1972, prepared under the direction of Francis R. Valeo, Secretary of the Senate, Supervisory Officer for Senate Elections (Washington, D.C.: U.S. Government Printing Office, October 1974).

[13] See Table 5-2, p. 210.

[14] Conservatives were particularly successful at tapping new segments of the population, and conservative direct mail combined with the proliferation of conservative political action committees to make the conservative movement by early 1977, in the words of one commentator, "awash in money and manpower." Lou Cannon, "Tapping the Little Guy: Conservatives Broaden Financial Base," The Washington Post, March 6, 1977.

[15] Maureen Orth, "Battle of the Bands," Newsweek, May 31, 1976, p. 44; Richard Reeves, "Pop Stars: The New Political Kingmakers," New York, February 16, 1976, pp. 31, 32.

[16] Carole Shifrin, "Ceiling is Set on Flight Fees in Campaign," The Washington Post, March 26, 1976.

[17] Andrew Mollison, "Loan," Cox Newspapers Washington Bureau news release dated September 16, 1976; Gladwin Hill, "Carter Adviser on Resources Quits, Citing Friction," The New York Times, November 20, 1976; Rowland Evans and Robert Novak, "Carter's Man on the North Slope," The Washington Post, June 29, 1977.

[18] "Carter Returning Up to $40,000," The New York Times, September 12, 1976.

[19] John F. Berry, "Why the White House Is Mean to Ed Gregory: Carter Contributor Barred from Luncheon After Legal Problems Develop," The Washington Post, April 19, 1978; Jack Nelson, "Carter Embarrassment Feared: Dilemma: Should Indicted Be Invited?" Los Angeles Times, April 15, 1978.

[20] Jeff Gerth, "A Secret White House Meeting: Carter's Fat Cats," New York, November 13, 1978, p. 15.

[21] Buckley v. Valeo, 424 U.S. 1 (1976).

[22] Federal Election Commission, FEC Disclosure Series No. 3: Index of Independent Expenditures by Individuals and Receipts and Expenditures by Unauthorized Delegates — 1976 Campaign (Washington, D.C., 1977), p. 2.

[23] "FEC Counsel Cautions Wallace on Use of Funds," Campaign Practices Reports, May 17, 1976, p. 10.

[24] "Unlimited Spending by Party Committees Independent of a Candidate is Barred by FEC," Campaign Practices Reports, June 28, 1976, p. 4.

[25] Federal Election Commission, "FEC Policy Statement on Independent Expenditures," press release, September 30, 1976, p. 1.

[26] "FEC Clarifies Policy on Independent Expenditures," Campaign Practices Reports, October 4, 1976, p. 7.

[27] Warren Weaver, Jr., "2 or 3 in New Hampshire Race Plan to Spend $218,000 Limit," The New York Times, February 14, 1976.

[28] Robert P. Visser and T. Timothy Ryan, counsel for President Ford Committee, letter to Loren Smith, counsel for Citizens for Reagan, April 14, 1976, pp. 3, 5.

[29] Loren A. Smith, counsel for Citizens for Reagan, letter to Robert P. Visser and T. Timothy Ryan, counsel for President Ford Committee, April 20, 1976, p. 2.

[30] "Staebler Hits FEC 'Credibility' After It Drops Reagan Case," Campaign Practices Reports, January 23, 1978, p. 1.

[31] Ibid., p. 2., citing John R. Bolton, Washington attorney representing the American Conservative Union and the Conservative Victory Fund, letter to Federal Election Commission, October 7, 1977.

[32] Ibid., p. 3.

[33] Ibid.

[34] Federal Election Commission, "FEC Releases Up-Dated Index of Independent Expenditures," press release, October 27, 1976.

[35] Despite this position, a number of unauthorized Carter-Mondale committees, run by seasoned Democratic professionals, sprang up in the campaign. These included Southern Farmers for Carter-Mondale, Illinois Consumers for Carter-Mondale, and Health Volunteers for Carter-Mondale.

[36] An independent expenditure "is an expenditure made to expressly advocate the election or defeat of a clearly identified candidate. This expenditure cannot be made 'in cooperation, consultation, or concert with, or at the request or suggestion of, any candidate or any authorized committee or agent of such candidate.' " An unauthorized delegate "is one that receives no financial or written support from the Presidential candidate. The expenditures of (such) Delegates do not count against any Presidential candidates' State or National spending limits." *FEC Disclosure Series No. 3,* p. 4.

[37] $8,250 was spent in opposition to Carter and $650 was spent in opposition to Ford. Ibid., pp. 3-4.

[38] Ibid.

[39] Ibid.

[40] Federal Election Commission, "FEC Releases Index of 1977-78 Independent Expenditures," press release, November 3, 1978.

10 Business and Labor in Politics

Corporate Involvement in Political Campaigns

The frequency and character of corporate involvement in the 1976 campaign were to a large extent a reaction to what had taken place following the 1972 elections, when 21 companies pleaded guilty to making illegal contributions of corporate funds to Nixon and other candidates. Fines assessed against these companies and in some cases their chief officers ran as high as $20,000. Fear of further accusations coupled with uncertainty about the new election laws led many corporations to maintain a low profile in the 1976 campaign. Considerable attention also was paid to corporate political involvement abroad.

The 21 companies that pleaded guilty and were fined in connection with the 1972 election were charged with contributing nearly $960,000 illegally, almost $850,000 of which had gone into the Nixon reelection campaign.[1] Nixon's Finance Committee to Reelect the President (FCRP) had conducted a systematic campaign of solicitation among corporate executives for contributions and help in obtaining further contributions from employees. The Corporate Group Solicitation Program (CGSP), which encouraged corporations to stimulate employee contributions, yielded $2,791,134 in legal contributions in support of Nixon from individuals associated with 1,893 corporations. An industry-by-industry program covering 60 industries and aimed at corporate employees from middle management and up yielded at least $7 million in contributions, according to Buckley M. Byers, director of the program. It concentrated on urging leading executives to make solicitations within their industry. The controversial, so-called "Responsiveness Program" produced an undetermined amount of support.[2] In suits filed by the Office of the

Special Prosecutor in the fall of 1973, it became clear that there had been a pattern of deliberate devious activity by certain corporations to contribute corporate funds and mask their origin by "laundering" them, in many cases by filtering them through foreign affiliates and allies. Among the 21 corporations that pleaded guilty and were fined were some of America's largest, including American Airlines, Braniff Airways, Carnation, Greyhound, Goodyear, Minnesota Mining and Manufacturing (3M), Gulf Oil, and Phillips Petroleum.[3]

To disguise or "launder" the use of corporate funds as campaign contributions, the companies most frequently resorted to channeling the money through foreign operations and distributing it in cash. American Airlines ran its $55,000 contribution through the Swiss bank account of a Lebanese agent and charged it off as a "special commission" in connection with the sale of "used aircraft to Middle East Airlines." Minnesota Mining and Manufacturing, which gave the Nixon fund $30,000, laundered its money through a Swiss attorney who submitted false billings for his services. Goodyear Tire & Rubber used an account maintained in a Swiss bank for rebates received from foreign manufacturers buying Goodyear supplies. Braniff Airways made a bogus payment to an agent in Panama to arrange its $40,000 illegal contribution to the Nixon campaign. The $100,000 Gulf Oil contribution to the Nixon campaign was arranged through a Gulf subsidiary in the Bahamas and charged to the firm's "miscellaneous expense account." Ashland Oil used an oil drilling subsidiary in Gabon on the west coast of Africa to launder its $100,000 contribution. American Ship Building Co. and its chairman, George M. Steinbrenner III, admitted arranging various contributions through illegal schemes, including giving fictitious bonuses to loyal employees, along with lists of committees to which they should make donations. The donations were in amounts smaller than the bonuses to cover taxes paid by the recipient. Both the company and its chairman were fined.

Illicit Funds

The revelations stemming from the Watergate scandals led to the discovery of longstanding secret political funds maintained by corporations and illegally financed with corporate funds. Among the companies with such funds were Minnesota Mining, Gulf Oil, and Firestone Tire & Rubber. In a detailed accounting in June 1978, to settle a civil suit filed by the Securities and Exchange Commission, Claude C. Wild, Jr., who was Gulf's Washington lobbyist from 1960 to 1973, said that he had available to dispense for political purposes "approximately $200,000 a year." Most of the money went to politicians from oil-producing states and the recipients included Lyndon B. Johnson when he was a senator and vice president, Jimmy Carter when he was governor of Georgia, and Judge Leander Perez, the political boss of Plaquemines Parish in Louisiana. Former Republican Sen. Hugh Scott of Pennsylvania received $10,000 a year from 1964 to 1973.

Following these revelations the corporate community found itself at the center of a whirlpool of investigative activity by the Senate Select Committee on Presidential Campaign Activities, by the Securities and Exchange Commission, by the Internal Revenue Service, and by stockholder groups. Self-examination became more commonplace as corporations instituted internal investigations on their own initiative or at the behest of the SEC, and attempts were made by many corporations to prevent future illegal political activity. The results of this self-investigation process and the stockholder suits were mixed. Some corporate officers were forced to resign or take early retirement, while others were allowed to continue in their positions. Some corporations sought to recover virtually all of the illegal contributions and related expenses from the officials responsible, while others reached settlements requiring repayment only of a small portion. The steps taken by corporations to prevent recurrence of illegal political contributions were varied as well.

Corporations became more convinced of the legitimacy and utility of the political action committee, although this took place too late for many to be effective in the 1976 campaign. Corporate leaders were unfamiliar with and uncertain about the new election law and feared accusations that they were making illegal contributions or exerting undue influence. The level of corporate PAC participation was low in part because business-related PACs rarely involved themselves in prenomination campaigns, which in the 1976 presidential elections were the only ones where private money was legal because of the advent of public funding for the general election campaigns.

Changes in the law had the effect of decreasing the likelihood of future illegal corporate political contributions. The Supreme Court decision in *Buckley v. Valeo,* which sanctioned parts of the FECA, minimized the probability of illegal contributions in several ways. First, the more stringent reporting requirements of the FECA made it relatively easy to investigate the sources of contributions and made large, anonymous contributions impossible. Second, cash contributions of more than $100 were prohibited. Third, the limitation on individual contributions also made arranging large gifts difficult, because so many donors would have to be involved. Fourth, as previously discussed, the availability of partial public financing for presidential primary campaigns and full public financing for presidential election campaigns tended to reduce the financial demands candidates might make on potential contributors.[4]

Investigations

Instances of questionable and illegal activity did continue to occur in the years following the Watergate disclosures and the advent of the FECA. The Office of Special Prosecutor had handled most of the early cases arising from Watergate, but the responsibility for conducting later investigations shifted to other agencies, including the newly formed Federal Election Commission. Some of the nation's largest corporations were investigated and in many cases they admitted to questionable or illegal political activities. Some of these matters resulted in legal action.

The Civil Aeronautics Board began an inquiry into airline accounting methods sparked by the accusations of the late William Gingery, CAB enforcement chief.[5] Gingery claimed in his suicide note that the agency was blocking a probe into illegal political contributions. The ensuing investigation revealed that American Airlines had an illegal fund aggregating $275,000, which it had been spending since 1964 on scores of federal and state candidates. Braniff Airways was found to have a revolving fund totaling as much as $927,000 that had been used for similar purposes. This secret political fund had been built up through the issuance and sale of at least 3,626 unreported flight tickets.[6] When a Senate subcommittee report was issued, it charged that the CAB had prematurely ended an investigation into possible illegal campaign contributions by 34 airlines.[7]

Southwestern Bell Telephone, a subsidiary of American Telephone & Telegraph (AT&T) was charged by two former employees with having maintained since 1966 a political slush fund generated by executive salary kickbacks totaling $100,000 a year. The company also was said to have used illegal practices to obtain rate increases, including falsifying data submitted to regulatory commissions, using lucrative contracts to place businessmen and politicians in economic bondage, and tapping the phones of city officials in communities where it desired rate increases. This set of charges touched off investigations by the Justice Department, the SEC, and other agencies.

Firestone admitted that it had operated a secret program for domestic political contributions from 1960 to 1973. The fund had held $1,161,495, of which Robert P. Beasley, chief financial officer, estimated that $330,000 had gone as political contributions from November 1970 through May 1973. Beasley received a four-year jail sentence and a fine of $14,000. Firestone sued Beasley for the recovery of $625,000 of this fund, which had not been contributed and could not be accounted for, and which Firestone claimed Beasley had converted to his personal use.

From 1961 through 1973, Gulf Oil Corp. spent more than $12 million on U.S. and foreign politicans to advance its interests. Corporate funds were laundered in a Bahamas subsidiary, and at least $5.4 million was given in American political campaigns. Hugh Scott, Senate minority leader, was implicated as a prime recipient and distributor of Gulf corporate funds.

Northrop Corp. admitted to the existence of a secret fund totaling at least $1.14 million from 1961 to 1973. Northrop claimed that it had created the fund after receiving numerous requests from politicians for contributions. The corporation and Thomas V. Jones, chairman and chief executive officer, pleaded guilty to felony charges brought by the Watergate special prosecutor's office and were fined $5,000 each. Jones resigned as chairman of the board but was later unanimously reelected. A furor also developed concerning 38 Pentagon officials who accepted entertainment at Northrop's hunting lodge. A defense contract audit agency reported that Northrop might have billed the government improperly for up to $6.1 million in questionable consultant fees, lobbyists' salaries, and expenses. The parties settled upon a repayment of $2.3 million. The SEC brought charges concerning violation of federal securities laws in illegal political contributions of corporate funds, and $30 million in payments to consultants which may have gone for other purposes. The IRS is investigating the corporation concerning possible fraud and improper deductions of political contributions.

In February 1976 Tenneco admitted to making $600,000 in political contributions in this country since 1966 and $12 million overseas from 1970 to 1975. The Okonite Co. was fined $500 by the FEC in June 1977 for placing newspaper advertisements thanking Rep. Robert A. Roe, D-N.J., for helping it to obtain a $13 million contract. The advertisements appeared four months before the 1976 general election. Another company, J. Ray McDermott, pleaded guilty in 1978 to charges by the FEC that it had made illegal contributions to federal candidates in 1974 and 1975. This was followed by a seven-count criminal action concerning racketeering, bribery, fraud, and illegal campaign contributions. McDermott was fined $1 million on these criminal charges.[8]

Questionable Corporate Payments

Probes of illegal corporate activity extended to inquiries into the influence of U.S. business on the governments and politics of foreign countries. Questions concerning the ethics of such activity were raised for the first time, and some attempt was made to arrive at a set of standards by which this behavior might be judged. These activities have been investigated by a variety of government agencies, congressional hearings have been held on the subject, several statutes have been enacted, and legislation has been proposed. Several individuals holding stock in affected companies brought suit against the corporations and implicated executives, while other shareholders introduced resolutions relating to these matters at annual meetings. Articles written by corporate heads and others concerning the need for a new corporate morality and improved business ethics began to appear in national publications.[9] Finally, some efforts were made at the international level to prevent questionable payments to foreign officials.

By 1975 the concern with illegal corporate political activity had spread from the Watergate special prosecutor's office to a host of agencies, and the focus had shifted from domestic activities to the multi-million-dollar efforts of major corporations to obtain contracts and political influence in other countries. It became clear that the amounts involved in these overseas activities were much larger than domestic contributions, and that the implications were grave. While a $100,000 contribution to an American campaign is significant, it pales in comparison with millions given in foreign contests. Contributions of this magnitude in Italy, Korea, and other countries where the cost of campaigns is much lower than in the United States can have enormous influence, conceivably deciding the outcome of elections and influencing the direction of public policies.

Among the agencies that became concerned with this problem were the Justice Department, the Securities and Exchange Commission, the Commerce Department, the Federal Trade Commission, the Internal Revenue Service, the Pentagon, the Senate Foreign Relations Subcommittee on Multinational Corporations, and a presidential task force. The IRS was concerned with the possibility that some of these overseas expenditures had been claimed illegally as business expenses. The Pentagon wanted accountings of certain government contracts, since many of the stories of bribery and corruption involved arms sales. The Senate subcommittee was primarily concerned with the political impact of U.S. corporate money in foreign countries.

Disclosures. The Securities and Exchange Commission elicited substantial information concerning corporate payments abroad as part of its independent probe into the subject. The SEC became involved on grounds that secret slush funds represented a threat to the integrity of the system of corporate accountability to investors. If a corporation was securing some portion of its business through bribery rather than through the quality of its products, the commission argued, the stockholders had a right to know. In July 1975 the SEC began to encourage corporations to "voluntarily" disclose any questionable or illegal payments, at the same time threatening court action against firms that had concealed such payments from their stockholders and suggesting that it would be more lenient on those who came forward than on those who did not. By May 12, 1976, the commission had uncovered or was investigating payments by 79 U.S. corporations.[10] By March 1977 more than 300 corporations had disclosed questionable foreign payments made between 1970 and 1976. The payments totaled more than $400 million, and included bribes, kickbacks, illegal political contributions, inflated commissions to consultants and sales agents to be split with government officials, and payoffs to low-level officials to facilitate performance of their normal duties.[11]

The Senate Foreign Relations Subcommittee on Multinational Corporations began its probe in May 1975 with a warning that bribery by U.S. corporations could have serious political repercussions in foreign countries. In August, Lockheed Aircraft Corp., the Pentagon's largest contractor, acknowledged payments of more than $22 million to foreign officials and political organizations to promote business. The repercussions prophesied by the subcommittee appeared when, in February 1976, it released documents disclosing payments of $12.6 million by Lockheed to Japanese interests. Right-wing leader Yoshio Kodama, a close associate of the ruling Liberal-Democratic Party, had been the recipient of $7 million, and the heated political scandal that ensued in Japan continued even after former Prime Minister Kakuei Tanaka was indicted on charges of accepting $1.7 million from Lockheed.[12]

Reasons Given. Corporations have given four basic reasons for their overseas political payments: avoiding harassment (which some corporate officials refer to as "defensive bribery") obtaining a competitive business advantage, influencing the political process to create a favorable political climate for the corporation, and supporting the political process, where payments are considered necessary to maintain the operation of democratic processes. This latter reason has been given by several corporations for contributions to both parties in Canadian elections. It has been noted that the donor corporation's expressed reason for these payments often may not be accepted without examining the circumstances in which they were made.[13]

Gulf Oil, which had earlier pleaded guilty to $125,000 in illegal 1972 campaign contributions, was found to have maintained a $10 million secret slush fund. Between 1960 and 1974, $5.4 million in cash from this fund (which was maintained through a Bahamas subsidiary) had gone into political campaigns.[14] Gulf also had made illegal gifts of $4 million to South Korea's governing Democratic Republican Party. Three million dollars were paid before the 1971 election in which President Park Chung Hee's party was kept in power by a thin majority. Bob R. Dorsey, Gulf's chairman, conceded to the Senate subcommittee that this sum might well have made the difference in keeping Park in power.[15]

Although the International Telephone and Telegraph Co. (ITT) initially denied it, the Senate subcommittee concluded that the conglomerate had channeled at least $350,000 to the opponent of Chile's Marxist President Salvador Allende in 1970, apparently in anticipation of his decision to nationalize the Chilean holdings of U.S. companies following his election. ITT had been coached by the CIA on how to channel funds safely to Allende's opponent and his National Party. In March 1976 ITT announced that questionable payments totaling $3.8 million had been made from 1971 to 1975 to improve or create favorable relations in foreign countries.[16]

The SEC's request in March 1976, for voluntary disclosure of any questionable political payments, brought a response from Firestone Tire & Rubber Co. that more than $390,000 in bribes and similar payments had been made in foreign countries by Firestone subsidiaries. Firestone did not identify the countries where these payments had been made. In one instance Firestone had contributed $32,000 — out of a total illegal gift of $175,000 by the tire industry — to a political party in an effort to raise the price at which tires could be sold to the government.

Northrop Corp. was found to have made payments totaling $30 million to 415 foreign agents between 1971 and 1973 that were not supported by records showing they had been made for the purposes claimed. Northrop also reached a settlement in April 1976 with the Department of Defense on charges that the corporation had billed the department for payments to cover several types of improper expenses. Northrop agreed to a settlement costing the corporation $2.3 million.

United Brands agreed in 1974 to pay a $2.5 million bribe to Gen. Oswaldo Lopez, then president of Honduras, to lower the export tax on bananas. The first payment of $1.25 million was made after the tax was reduced, but the second never was made because a hurricane devastated the banana crop and Lopez was ousted by the military when word of the first payment began to circulate. The corporation also had made payments of $750,000 in other countries.

Tenneco Inc. admitted to foreign payments totaling $12 million from January 1970 through September 1975. The company could not state with certainty that none of the payments was indirectly for the use or benefit of employees of foreign governments. The corporation had contractual commitments to pay another $12 million to consultants involved with purchases of raw materials in foreign countires.

United Technologies Corp. admitted to questionable transactions overseas involving almost $2 million from 1970 to 1975 paid to foreign sales representatives. Otis Elevator Co., which was acquired by United Technclogies, disclosed questionable overseas payments of $5 million to $6 million from 1971 to 1975.

Exxon, the world's largest corporation, disclosed improper and improperly recorded payments totaling $799,000 from 1963 through 1975.

In Italy, where corporate donations are legal, an Exxon subsidiary had made $27 million in authorized contributions of corporate funds to Italian political parties from 1963 through 1971, and an additional $19 million in unauthorized contributions.[17]

The confirmation of G. William Miller as chairman of the Federal Reserve Board was held up for six weeks as the Senate Banking Committee investigated his possible involvement in what appeared to be an overseas political payoff. Bell Helicopter, a subsidiary of Textron Inc., of which Miller was chairman, made a payment of $2.9 million to Air Taxi, an Iranian sales agent, for a $500 million helicopter sale to Iran. The now-deceased Gen. Mohammed Khatami, chief of the Iranian Air Force, was one of the founders and a secret owner of Air Taxi. The SEC was investigating the transaction. The question of interest to the Senate committee was whether Miller knew of Khatami's connection with the company. It could not be proved that Miller knew Khatami to be an owner of the company in the early 1970s, when the sale took place, although it was a matter of public record that he formerly had been one. On March 3, 1978, Miller's appointment as chairman of the Federal Reserve was confirmed.[18]

Stockholder Action. Not surprisingly, individuals who held stock in the companies accused of improprieties were appalled at the revelations, and acted by bringing suits charging individual corporate officers with responsibility for making illegal or questionable payments using corporate funds. None of the suits have gone to trial. If they do, the civil liability of the officers and directors will be determined by the corporate laws of the state where the company is incorporated; these standards vary. While there are few cases involving situations comparable to those posed by the illegal contribution/foreign bribe cases, the decisions reached in the relevant cases appear to support the conclusion that a corporate officer who uses company funds for clearly illegal purposes would be liable to the corporation for the amounts of those payments and for all damages suffered by the corporation as a consequence. Liability is less easily determined where no clear illegality was involved.[19]

As the case studies below will show, the increased popular concern with corporate ethics, as well as the response to specific allegations of illegal activity, prompted stockholders in major corporations to attempt to assert control over company political action through the use of shareholder resolutions. In almost all cases, corporations have recommended that shareholders vote against the resolutions, which they generally have done. In 1977, for example, shareholders in five corporations were asked to vote on seven resolutions concerning questionable payments the companies have made in countries outside the United

States. Three resolutions proposed the adoption of policies that would prohibit certain questionable payments; the other four asked the companies to report on their payments. Two resolutions sponsored by church groups affiliated with the Interfaith Center on Corporate Responsibility were submitted to Tenneco Inc. and United Brands Co. They asked the corporations to adopt policies prohibiting contributions of corporate assets to political candidates, political parties, or government officials to curry favor or to aid anyone to obtain or keep governmental power. Two additional resolutions, also sponsored by church groups affiliated with the Interfaith Center on Corporate Responsibility, asked ITT to report on its overseas political activities. One requested the corporation to describe all payments of $5,000 or more that were made by or on behalf of the corporation in the last 10 years to political parties or candidates overseas. The other resolution asked ITT for information about its political involvement, political contributions, and questionable payments in Chile. Church groups affiliated with the Interfaith Center submitted two resolutions to Gulf Oil Corp. concerning the company's business and political relationships with South Korea. One asked Gulf to report on aspects of its operations in that country, while the other requested the company to adopt a policy that would prohibit any political payments by the corporation in South Korea. Finally, a resolution sponsored by the Military Audit Project requested that Lockheed Aircraft Corp. establish a committee to investigate and report on the company's payments overseas.[20]

U.S. Campaigns. The reform efforts by stockholders have not been limited to overseas activity. Several stockholders have proposed resolutions at annual meetings concerning corporate involvement in political campaigns in the United States. In 1976 proponents of resolutions questioned more than two dozen corporations about their involvement in U.S. politics.

Four of the eight resolutions that received support exceeding 10 percent of the shares voted were directed at uncovering or curbing domestic political activity. In 1976 Edward C. Calvert and Evelyn Y. Davis sponsored resolutions concerning domestic politics. Calvert proposed a resolution to the Firestone Tire & Rubber Co., requiring that the audit committee of its board of directors consider engaging outside legal counsel and outside auditors to investigate, disclose to shareholders, and seek restitution for any illegal payments of company funds.[21] Davis submitted two types of resolutions to 17 corporations. One affirmed the corporations' political nonpartisanship,[22] the other requested disclosure of any political contributions ever made by the companies.[23]

The nonpartisanship resolutions were submitted to seven corporations: American Telephone & Telegraph Co. (where the same resolution was supported by 7.16 percent of the shares voted in 1976 and 6.61 percent in 1975); BankAmerica Corp. (6.05 percent in 1976); Bristol-Myers Co.; Chessie System (7.53 percent in 1976); Continental Corp.; Eastern Air Lines Inc.; and Washington Gas Light Co.[24]

Davis submitted the same resolution to several corporations each year since 1973, contending that it embodied sound principles deserving adoption. All but one of the corporations to which she submitted her motion opposed it. In 1975 the management of Continental Corp. recommended that shareholders vote in favor of the proposal. The other companies explained their opposition in several ways. Most of them stated that they do not engage in the practices that the resolution says are to be avoided. Some contended that adoption of the resolution would be inappropriate. Others contended that the resolution's affirmation of political nonpartisanship could restrict the corporation in presenting its positions on legislative and administrative decisions affecting its business interests. Finally, several claimed that the proposal could be construed as barring legal corporate political activity, including the formation of corporate political action committees or contributions to election campaigns in states where corporate contributions are allowed.[25]

Davis has submitted her disclosure resolution to 10 corporations — Baltimore Baseball Club Inc., Continental Oil Co., Fairchild Industries Inc., General Public Utilities Corp. (where the same resolution was supported by 18.82 percent of the shares voted in 1976 and 12.17 percent in 1975), Martin Marietta Corp. (7.07 percent in 1976), Merrill Lynch & Co. (6.53 percent in 1976), Potomac Electric Power Co. (13.04 percent in 1976), Southern Railway Co., Tenneco Inc., and Twentieth Century-Fox Film Corp. (20.51 percent in 1976). Davis has submitted similar motions since 1974 and in general these proposals have attracted less shareholder support than her nonpartisanship resolutions, but more support from institutional investors.[26]

Davis did not claim that any of the corporations to which she submitted the disclosure proposal had engaged in objectionable practices or made specific contributions that she felt were ill-advised. However, each of the corporations to which she submitted the disclosure resolution opposed it, most stating that they do not make contributions to political parties or candidates, and that any requirement that such contributions be reported in newspapers would therefore be unnecessary and wasteful of corporate funds. According to publicly available documents, only one of the 17 corporations to which Davis submitted her resolutions — American Telephone & Telegraph — had been involved in illegal or questionable political activities. Two wholly owned subsidiaries of AT&T — Southwestern Bell Telephone Co. and Southern Bell Telephone Co. — were under investigation by state and federal agencies as a result of charges by former employees of the subsidiaries that corporate funds were used for secret political contributions.[27] Two of the corporations — BankAmerica and Twentieth Century-Fox — regularly contribute to political and ballot measure campaigns at the state and local levels in California, where such contributions are not prohibited by law. In 1974 BankAmerica contributed more than $95,000 and Twentieth Century-Fox more than $34,000 to a wide variety of political candidates and committees in that state. Some of the corporations have affiliated political action committees that are registered with the FEC.

PACs in the 1976 Election

From April 7, 1972, through May 11, 1976, a series of major changes intended to reduce the influence of special interests were made in federal law. Ironically, they had the unintended effect of increasing the group gift component of election finance in the 1976 and 1978 congressional races as candidates relied to a greater extent than before on political action committees (PACs) for their campaign dollars. Two elements of the new legal environment were of special importance in this development.

The new contribution limits were one factor. While individuals were limited to maximum contributions of $1,000 per candidate per election, organizations qualifying as "multicandidate committees" were permitted to donate as much as $5,000, and an individual could contribute $5,000 to such a committee. PACs became an avenue through which smaller contributions could be aggregated into larger, more meaningful ones to give to candidates.

Another factor was the advent of public funding for the presidential election. Some interests such as labor unions, trade and professional associations, and corporations, finding this avenue closed for the general election, concentrated the efforts of their PACs on races for the House and Senate. Here, due to the lower cost of campaigns, their dollars would be proportionately more important, and a contribution of $5,000 would be of some significance.

These two factors contributed to a proliferation of PACs operating mainly to support candidates for Congress. In the 1972 election 520 multicandidate committees were not affiliated with any party, 176 were labor-related, 273 represented business, health, and agriculture, and 71 were classified as "ideological."[28] By 1976 there were 1,146 nonparty PACs. Some 303 labor committees expended $17.5 million to or on behalf of federal candidates,[29] and 450 corporate-related PACs similarly spent $5.8 million.[30] Labor outspent business by three to one, even though it had one-third fewer committees.

Table 10-1
Total Interest Group Contributions to 1976 Congressional Candidates

	1976 [a]	1974 [b]
Business/Professional/Agriculture		
Agriculture	$ 1,534,447	$ 361,040
Business	7,091,375	2,506,946
Health	2,694,910	1,936,487
Lawyers	241,280	—
	11,562,012	4,804,473
Labor	8,206,578	6,315,488
Miscellaneous	1,299,928	682,215
Ideological	1,503,394	723,410
Total interest committees	$22,571,912	$12,525,586

[a] This information is based on the campaign finance reports filed by registered interest groups for the period from January 1, 1975, to November 22, 1976.

[b] This information is based on the campaign finance reports filed by registered interest groups for the period from September 1, 1973, to December 31, 1974. While the eight-month period from January through August 1973 is not included in the 1974 figures, this constitutes a period of very limited giving by interest groups.

SOURCE: Common Cause, "Campaign Reports For 1976 Show Near Doubling Of Interest Group Contributions To Candidates For Congress," press release, February 15, 1977, Appendix A.

The PACs displayed a marked preference for congressional candidates and especially for incumbents. Common Cause figures indicate that $22.6 million flowed from these groups to congressional candidates, nearly doubling the 1974 figures of $12.5 million (Table 10-1). The most dramatic increase was among corporate, business, and trade association PACs, as their contributions to these candidates leaped from $2.5 million in 1974 to $7.1 million in 1976. While labor maintained its lead over business in absolute terms by donating $8.2 million directly to candidates, it showed only a 30 percent increase over 1972, in no way matching the startling increase by business groups.

While enough was contributed to provide an average of $25,000 for each of the more than 800 candidates for Congress, in fact more than 75 percent of the funds went to incumbents. Table 10-2 shows that incumbents were favored by a ratio of 3.14 to 1 by all PACs, with a high of 7.29 to 1 among agriculture groups. Business showed a greater preference for incumbents, at 4-1, than did labor, at 3-1. Generally, incumbents stand a greater chance of winning and therefore are often given preference.

Among incumbents, some fared considerably better than others. Minority Leader John J. Rhodes, R-Ariz., topped all members of the

Table 10-2
Incumbent/Challenger Ratio for 1976 Interest Group Giving

Agriculture	7.29-to-1
Business	4.01-to-1
Health	3.43-to-1
Lawyers	5.86-to-1
Business/professional	4.13-to-1
Labor	2.97-to-1
Miscellaneous	2.40-to-1
Ideological	.69-to-1
Total interest committees	3.14-to-1

SOURCE: Common Cause, "Report to the American People on the Financing of Congressional Election Campaigns," *Frontline,* April-May 1977, p. 8.

House of Representatives with PAC contributions of nearly $100,000. Other House members receiving especially large amounts from PACs were Mark W. Hannaford, D-Calif., John J. Duncan, R-Tenn., Jim Mattox, D-Texas, who was not an incumbent, and Samuel L. Devine, R-Ohio. In the Senate, Vance Hartke, D-Ind., was the greatest beneficiary, with $245,700 flowing from labor and corporate PACs into his unsuccessful campaign for a fourth term. Close behind in total contributions were Harrison A. Williams, Jr., D-N.J.; Robert Taft, Jr., R-Ohio, who was supported more heavily by business PACs than any other candidate; Lloyd Bentsen, D-Texas, and John V. Tunney, D-Calif., who received more from labor groups — $164,000 — than any other senator, although his proved to be a losing bid for reelection.[31]

House candidates generally were supported by either labor or business, but not both, Hannaford being a notable exception. Senate candidates, however, and especially incumbents, often received contributions from both. This may be a result of the greater size and diversity of senatorial constituencies. It may also reflect the fact that senators serve on more committees than do members of the House, and therefore are more likely to be influential in matters concerning both labor and business.

Political action committees generally showed a clear preference for House candidates. This may reflect the fact that House campaigns are much less expensive than most senatorial campaigns, and the opportunity for creating a sense of gratitude in the potential legislator is greater. The campaigns of House committee chairmen averaged $36,500 and PAC contributions accounted for 60 percent of their total spending. In the Senate, the average committee chairman's campaign cost $330,000, of which interest group contributions provided about 20 percent.[32]

Table 10-3
Largest Special Interest Group Contributors to Congressional Campaigns in 1974 and 1976

1976 Special-Interest Group Leaders	1974 Rank	1976 Contributions	1974 Contributions
American Medical Associations[a]	1	$1,790,879	$1,462,972
Dairy committees	unranked	1,362,159	—
AFL-CIO COPEs	2	996,910	1,178,638
Maritime-related unions	4	979,691	738,314
United Auto Workers	3	845,939	843,938
Coal, oil, and natural gas interests	unranked	809,508	—
National Education Associations	7	752,272	398,991
National Association of Realtors	11	605,973	260,870
Financial institutions	9	529,193	438,428
International Association of Machinists	5	519,157	470,353
United Steelworkers of America	8	463,033	361,225
American Dental Associations	unranked	409,835	—

[a] The American Medical Political Action Committee (AMPAC) asserts that it has no branches or subsidiary groups, and accordingly, claims the designation of "American Medical Associations" is incorrect.

SOURCE: Campaign Practices Reports, "Financing the 1976 Election: A Report on Special Interest Groups," Special Report 2 (Washington, D.C.: Plus Publications Inc., April 1977), p. 2.

The activity of labor groups was the most partisan. All but $250,000 of labor's general election assistance ($7.4 million) went to Democrats. Business and corporate donations favored Republicans at $3.8 million compared with $2.9 million for Democrats.[33] Business clearly placed greater weight on incumbency and less on party identification than did labor.

Committees associated with medical interests contributed $1.8 million to congressional candidates in 1976, up from $1.5 million in 1974 (Table 10-3). Others at or near the one-million-dollar mark in 1976 were dairy groups, which provided $1.4 million, AFL-CIO COPEs at $1 million, and committees of the maritime-related unions at $980,000.

With the advent in 1976 of public funding for the presidential campaigns, PACs as well as individuals were prohibited from contributing directly to nominated candidates for the presidency. The Democratic and Republican national committees, however, could have received funds from PACs as part of the $3.2 million they each were permitted to spend on behalf of their respective candidates. Neither of the national committees seriously pursued this assistance, and consequently few PACs were involved in the presidential general election

campaigns. The RNC raised only about $300,000 from political commit-
tees, and the DNC one-tenth of that during the fall.

There was limited PAC activity in the presidential primary campaigns, when direct contributions were permitted; something less than
$1 million was given to candidates seeking nomination. Business and
labor PACs provided $310,600 to Carter, most of it after he had become
the clear favorite to win the nomination, and Ford received $153,000
from business and professional PACs during the prenomination period.
In primary campaigns costing $12 million and $13 million respectively,
these were relatively small sums. However, dollar contributions do not
tell the whole story. Labor provided a great deal of support to the Carter
campaign in the form of internal partisan communication and volunteer
work supported by treasury funds for registration and get-out-the-vote
drives. The total value of this support is difficult to estimate, but one
observer placed it as high as $11 million.[34]

Labor Political Action Committees

Historically, political action committees have been a major arm of
labor support, and 1976 was no exception. FEC figures show that
$17,488,650 was contributed to or spent on behalf of federal candidates
by a total of 303 labor-related groups, with total receipts of about $18.6
million.[35] In addition to direct contributions to and expenditures on
behalf of candidates, the total includes spending to raise money for the
PACs, staff salaries and other operating costs, and other miscellaneous
PAC activities. As noted, only $8.6 million of the $17.5 million was
contributed directly to candidates. However, another $5.1 million was
given to committees organized by political parties, and most of this
probably found its way to candidates and their committees.[36]

Some of labor's 303 groups made a far better showing than others.
Forty-two committees, or 13.9 percent of the 303, expended 83.6 percent
of the total, with each spending more than $100,000 for a total of $16.9
million.[37] Political committees affiliated with the AFL-CIO were clearly
the backbone of labor support, spending $15.3 million. This represented
75.6 percent of organized labor's total expenditures. The 60 AFL-CIO
unions active in the election operated 230 of labor's 303 committees;
of these, 43 spent $2.4 million. Other heavy spenders were the National
Marine Engineers Beneficial Association (five committees, $1.4 million),
and the International Association of Machinists and Aerospace Workers
(25 committees, more than $1 million).

The 73 committees organized by independent unions accounted for
24.4 percent of labor's total expenditures. The 21 PACs operated by the
National Education Association led the independents by spending al-

most $2.5 million, the UAW's four PACs spent more than $1.3 million, and the 38 Teamster PACs expended about $887,000. (The heaviest spender among Teamster committees was the Alaska ALIVE Voluntary Committee, which spent $216,856.)[38]

Labor PAC support was heavily partisan, and favored incumbents to a lesser degree than did business, agriculture, and health groups. Figures compiled by the Republican National PAC indicate that Democrats received 96.5 percent of labor's spending in support of House and Senate candidates, Republicans only 3.5 percent. These same figures show that labor supported 67 Senate candidates in primary and general elections, of which 49 were Democrats receiving $3.5 million, and 18 were Republicans receiving $178,000. RNPAC reports that labor supported 485 House candidates, of which 395 Democrats received $6.3 million and 90 Republicans $174,000. Senate candidates were supported on a less-strictly partisan basis, which indicates that other factors such as incumbency, committee membership, and voting record on labor-related issues were involved to a greater extent.[39]

In Senate races 11 candidates, all Democrats, each received more than $100,000 from labor groups. John Tunney (California) led with $164,223 in his unsuccessful reelection bid; William Green (Pennsylvania) received $154,270; Harrison Williams (New Jersey), $149,225; Vance Hartke (Indiana), $143,650 (Hartke also received $102,050 from business groups and led all candidates in both houses of Congress in interest group contributions); Daniel Patrick Moynihan (New York), $132,944; Paul S. Sarbanes (Maryland), $122,000; Hubert H. Humphrey (Minnesota), $121,272; Howard M. Metzenbaum (Ohio), $111,720; Frank Moss (Utah), $107,675; James O'Hara (Michigan), $106,240; and Elmo Zumwalt (Virginia), $100,146. Five of these were incumbents: Tunney, Williams, Hartke, Humphrey, and Moss.

In House campaigns, the level of contributions was lower. Labor groups spent the most ($59,931) on Jim Mattox of Texas; other heavily supported candidates were Lloyd Meeds (Washington) at $56,000; Marty Russo (Illinois), $48,250; John H. Dent (Pennsylvania), $48,250; Thomas L. Ashley (Ohio), $45,772, Michael T. Blouin (Iowa), $41,890; Alvin Baldus (Wisconsin), $41,250; Floyd Fithian (Indiana), $40,300; Richard Vander Veen (Michigan), $39,910; and Mark Hannaford (California), $39,600. These 10 were Democrats and only Mattox was not an incumbent.[40]

Labor's success rate was good. The AFL-CIO COPE announced that 19 of the 28 senatorial candidates it supported won, and that 262 of 365 House candidates it backed were elected. There have been indications since the election, however, that labor is unhappy with some of the incumbents it backed. Some labor organizations were reported as having threatened to cut support for certain incumbents, but it was later denied that any "hit" list existed.[41]

Although labor's contributions and other spending were substantial and a very significant factor in the election, these dollar amounts do not tell the entire story. Two other kinds of support were a major part of labor's political efforts and are not entirely separable from a consideration of PAC activity: one is internal communications expenses of unions with their members, and the other is mobilization of union members for volunteer work.

Unions, corporations, and other organizations are allowed to spend treasury funds or dues on partisan communications with members, stockholders, executive and administrative personnel, and their families. They are required to report these costs on special forms to the FEC when they exceed $2,000 an election. Labor took this means, and business rarely did. Of the $2,146,899 reported by all organizations, 93.8 percent ($2,014,326) was spent by the 66 labor unions filing. Only four corporations filed reports totaling $31,045, or 1.4 percent. Six labor organizations reported spending more than $100,000 each. The AFL-CIO was the leader, with expenditures totaling $400,557; the UAW spent $323,067; the AFL-CIO Building and Construction Trades Department, $177,507; Communications Workers of America, $120,423; and AFL-CIO Pennsylvania, $101,056. The Retail Clerks Union was close at $97,097. Together these six groups spent $1,219,257 or 56.7 percent of all reported communications expenditures.

Most of this support was for clearly identified candidates. Sixty-one percent was in support of six presidential candidates, and almost all of that went to Jimmy Carter, who received 57.6 percent of the total, or $1,160,432. Ford received only $44,249 worth of such support, while $43,958 was spent opposing him. Forty-seven Senate candidates received 22.3 percent of the total, and 361 House candidates 16.6 percent.

In seeking to reach members and their families, direct mailings were the preferred method of communication, accounting for 87.1 percent of the total. Brochures, leaflets and flyers, phone banks, posters and banners, and miscellaneous items accounted for the remainder. In addition, union newsletters carried cover pictures of Carter, and issue after issue contained material praising Carter and criticizing Ford. Much of this was not reported to the FEC because it was part of regular publications reporting on union business, and would have required formulas allocating the portion supporting federal candidates.[42]

One observer feels that a conservative estimate of the total value of these communications would be $8.5 million, and that uncounted and unreported spending almost certainly pushed the figure to $11 million. While not all was directed to the presidential campaign, in a publicly funded campaign with a ceiling of $21.8 million, this parallel campaigning was a tremendous asset. Further, labor's efforts were closely coordinated with Carter's campaign strategy. In fact, it was noted that "By the time the campaign was over, it became difficult to distinguish labor's efforts from those of the Democratic National Committee (DNC) or Carter."[43]

Labor also provided a great deal of volunteer help for voter registration and get-out-the-vote drives, all of which worked to the benefit of the Democrats and Carter, and these amounts are not included in PAC totals. COPE and UAW say that they spent $3 million on these efforts. By comparison, the $2 million and $3 million spent on voter registration and identification by the DNC and RNC respectively were the largest efforts these organizations had ever mounted. It is reported that COPE sent out 80 million pieces of literature, registered 6 million new voters (with significant efforts in key states such as California, Ohio, and Texas), and utilized the services of 120,000 volunteers. On election day, COPE and its affiliated unions reportedly had 600 full-time organizers at work supervising thousands of volunteers including those making telephone calls, all part of a massive get-out-the-vote drive costing about $3 million.[44]

Nothing business did came close to matching labor's efforts along these lines. There were only scattered efforts. *The Wall Street Journal* reported that in 25 corporations with a history of political involvement only a few isolated low-key attempts were made to mobilize management-level employees through partisan communications. In September 1976 top officials of the RNC met with more than 100 corporate and trade association leaders in four cities asking them to become involved in marginal congressional contests where probusiness candidates were running, and requesting that corporate PACs stop contributing to incumbent Democrats. This appeal probably had little effect.[45]

Business Political Action Committees

Labor outspent business by a 3-1 ratio, and mounted a massive communications and volunteer effort that business could not come close to matching. Nevertheless, many labor leaders were unsettled by the tremendous growth of corporate PACs in the 1976 campaign.

Records of the FEC show that 450 corporate-related PACs were registered for the 1976 campaign, compared with 273 in 1972. These 450 committees reported receiving $6,782,322 and spending $5,803,415 during 1975 and 1976 (see Table 10-4). Most committees were small, with 86 percent reporting receipts and expenditures of less than $20,000. Only nine reported spending more than $100,000 and these spent $1,074,208, or 18.5 percent of all corporate PAC expenditures. (Labor, by way of contrast, had 42 committees in this category, and their spending of nearly $17 million was 83.6 percent of labor's PAC support.) Single committees making the largest contributions were affiliated with the Chicago and Northwestern Transportation Co. ($162,096), General Electric ($139,183), General Telephone of California ($124,911), Coca-Cola ($118,950), United Technologies ($116,350), Hughes Aircraft ($114,324), Union Oil of California ($100,847), Pacific Lighting Corp. ($97,048), and the combined committee of LTV and Vought corporations ($86,936). These rankings list only the single largest PAC for each company. Some had several. General Telephone with seven PACs spent $192,658, more than any other corporation, and General Electric's four PACs spent $172,392. There had been concern that corporations would spawn a multiplicity of PACs, but only 26 corporations had more than one, and these formed some 79 committees among them.[46]

Following the election, the Chamber of Commerce of the United States conducted a survey by questionnaire of all registered corporate PACs, aimed at ascertaining the nature and scope of their participation in the election. The 121 respondents reported soliciting an average of 2,352 individuals 1.3 times during 1976 and had a success rate of about 10 percent.

Table 10-4
Corporate Political Action Committees, Receipts and Expenditures 1975-76

Volume of Receipts and/or Expenditures	Number of Committees	Receipts	Percent of Total	Expenditures	Percent of Total
$100,000 and above	9	$1,112,684	16.41	$1,074,208	18.51
$90,000 - $99,999	2	192,869	2.84	163,100	2.81
$80,000 - $89,999	4	339,671	5.01	290,525	5.01
$70,000 - $79,999	4	265,107	3.91	253,095	4.36
$60,000 - $69,999	5	309,150	4.56	227,687	3.92
$50,000 - $59,999	6	292,206	4.31	286,515	4.94
$40,000 - $49,999	10	466,311	6.87	415,297	7.16
$30,000 - $39,999	18	643,224	9.48	519,862	8.96
$20,000 - $29,999	45	1,096,531	16.17	901,573	15.53
$10,000 - $19,999	89	1,234,568	18.20	1,025,614	17.67
Under $10,000	198	830,001	12.24	645,939	11.13
$0	60	0	0	0	0
Total	450	$6,782,322	100.00	$5,803,415	100.00

SOURCE: "Report Shows 390 Corporate PACs Gave $5.8 Million in 1976 Election," *CP Reports,* October 3, 1977, p. 9.

The percentage of persons contributing varied inversely with the number solicited, such that for group solicitations involving fewer than 200 people the success rate was 70 percent, and where more than 1,000 were solicited it fell to 5 percent. Only 2 percent had solicited lower-echelon employees twice a year, and about the same percentage solicited stockholders. Most appealed exclusively to executive and administrative personnel. Few established trustee plans or mailed partisan communications to stockholders. In a survey of trade associations, a similar pattern emerged. One-third solicited only the top management of firms allowing solicitation. Only 8 percent asked both management and stockholders for contributions, and 2 percent solicited stockholders only. The average was 5,256 persons solicited 1.7 times, and the average level of participation was 906 persons.[47]

Corporation PACs supported an average of 29 candidates. In deciding which to support, both corporate and trade association PACs reported placing the most emphasis on candidates' voting records on issues of concern to the industry. Other considerations in contribution decisions are shown in Table 10-5. Some corporate PACs placed considerable weight on whether the candidate represented a district where some of the company's operations were located. Incumbency was a factor for both corporations and associations, and neither said that party identification was important. Hence, considerable business support went to Democrats, since they controlled Congress. Many business

Table 10-5
Criteria Used by Corporate and Trade Association Political Action Committees in Determining Which Candidates to Support in 1976

(Criteria listed in order of importance)

Individual Companies	Trade Associations
1. Candidate's voting record on issues of concern to the industry of the PAC	1. Candidate's voting record on issues of concern to the industry of the PAC
2. Candidate's voting record on overall business issues	2. Congressional committee assignment (if incumbent)
3. Candidate's location in a congressional district that contains operations of the company	3. Candidate's overall record on business issues
4. Committee assignment (if incumbent)	4. Incumbent
5. Incumbent	5. Incumbent's seniority
6. Incumbent's seniority	6. Geographical location of the election contest

SOURCES: Chamber of Commerce of the United States, "Public Affairs Report," April 1977 and May 1977.

groups felt that unless they supported important Democrats, such as committee and subcommittee chairmen, they would not receive favorable treatment on Capitol Hill[48] and so business support was not so partisan as labor's and was dictated to a greater degree by incumbency, committee assignment, district location, and other nonideological factors.

Some corporations made innovative fund-raising efforts. Texaco solicited its 36,000 domestic employees and an unknown number abroad, raising more than $94,000 in one mailing. These funds were contributed in sums of less than $100, so those who participated did not have to be identified. The Budd Co. developed a discretionary plan involving about 30 percent of its high-level managers, in which monetary incentives were given for involvement in governmental affairs, including working in the election and soliciting funds. Dresser Industries solicited its stockholders, and while some told the corporation they disapproved of this action the predominant response of those who wrote was favorable. Sun Oil spent $190,000 on employee political councils, voter registration drives, candidate nights, and political seminars. About $100,000 was spent to solicit employee and stockholder contributions. Sun also produced a film featuring Lowell Thomas that urged employees to contribute to either SunPAC or SunEPA.[49] SunPAC contributed $46,000 to 90 candidates, of whom 78 were Republicans. In a strategy similar to labor's use of internal partisan communications on Carter's behalf, Robert Mosbacher, chairman of American Business Volunteers for Ford, wrote to the presidents of the 1,000 largest U.S. corporations asking them to mail appeals for Ford. Very few did.

There was criticism of business for not exploiting its full potential in fund raising. Only 44 of *Fortune* magazine's top 100 corporations established PACs. Although the FEC's SunPAC ruling (discussed below) opened the door for certain kinds of fund raising among employees, most companies solicited only top-level management personnel, and only a handful solicited stockholders. It is possible that business was cautious in the wake of prosecutions and unfavorable publicity concerning illegal corporate contributions in the 1972 election, particularly in the light of the series of legislative changes that had taken place. For example, after the adoption of the 1976 Amendments, most business PACs contributed less than $500 to each of the candidates they supported, although they could legally have given as much as $5,000. Fred Quigley, vice-president of Dow Chemical Co. and chairman of the National Association of Manufacturers' Public Affairs Committee, said in 1976 that many businessmen ". . . still don't understand the system. . . . They're afraid of a bad press. They're afraid that they will be accused of being illegal, or having undue influence. They're gun-shy." [50]

Clearly business PACs did not reach their potential in 1976. However, their rapid growth in the years before the election caused some consternation among labor organizations, and events since have tended to confirm predictions that business PACs will figure more prominently in the financing of future elections.

PACs Since the 1976 Election

The enactment of contribution limits and the institution of public funding for the presidential race were intended to reduce the influence of special interest groups; however, these provisions have had certain unintended consequences that have served to increase their influence. Limits on individual contributions have led to a relative increase in the importance of interest group donations. PACs sponsored by special interest groups have become more important, and the interest group component of campaign finance has increased while proportionally the individual component has decreased. Public funding of the presidential campaigns has led interest groups to place much financial weight on races for the House and Senate.

In all probability these trends will continue in the absence of new legislation raising the limits on individual contributions or lowering the ceiling on PAC donations. Evidence for this continuation is found in the years since the 1976 election. From the end of 1976 through September 1978 the number of active PACs increased from 1,146 to 1,828. The number of corporate PACs increased from 450 to 776 while the number of labor PACs decreased from 303 to 263. There were also, at the end of this period, 513 trade and membership association PACs as well as 276 PACs variously categorized as nonconnected organizations, cooperatives, and corporations without stock. During this period the PACs raised $67.8 million and spent $60.4 million, including $18.7 million spent as contributions to House and Senate candidates. Trade association and membership PACs led in direct contributions to federal candidates at $6.2 million. Labor PACs followed closely at $6 million and corporate PACs contributed $4.7 million. House candidates received 73 percent of the contributions or $13.7 million, with $5 million going to Senate candidates. Democrats received 63 percent and Republicans 37 percent of this support. As expected, labor gave 93 percent of its support to Democrats. Corporate PACs favored Republicans by 53 to 47 percent and trade association PACs split their support evenly between Democrats and Republicans.[51]

Evidence indicates that contributions by corporate and trade groups took a more partisan turn in the weeks just prior to the 1978 elections. Examining the financial activity of 10 major PACs, Congressional Quarterly's *Weekly Report* found that five business and trade association groups gave an average of 70 to 75 percent of their contributions to Republicans during September and the first three weeks of October 1978.[52]

The Growth of Corporate PACs

The growth of corporate PACs will continue to be significant. The two major political parties are making direct efforts at obtaining a share of corporate PAC money. By spring 1977 both the RNC and the DNC had hired staff to solicit PAC contributions, seeking in particular to channel funds into hotly contested congressional and gubernatorial elections. Both the RNC and DNC solicit corporate PACs, while only the Democrats approach labor PACs. The Republicans are particularly keen on increasing the role of corporate PACs in future elections. It appears that the political parties, and especially the Republicans, are eager to exploit an increased role for PACs established by corporations and trade associations.

Business fund raising often had consisted primarily of direct individual contributions to specific candidates. Hence there was less need for structured contribution procedures of the sort labor had been using for many years. However, individual contributions by businessmen fell into public disfavor after Watergate revelations of abuses such as the use of laundered corporate funds. Further, the law limited individual contributions, and a premium was placed on the ability to organize PACs. But business has not had the time to develop sophisticated solicitation approaches, while labor had taken years to build its efficient system of contribution and distribution. Further, business was not certain about what group contributions would be permitted under the new laws. The 1974 Amendments, the SunPAC ruling, the *Buckley* case, the 1976 Amendments, and the proliferation of FEC regulations came in rapid succession, and although not all the new developments were unfavorable to business, a spirit of caution prevailed. Many corporations did not establish PACs at all, and most that did waited until late in the campaign.

As late as September 1978, only 196 of *Fortune* magazine's top 500 companies had registered political action committees with the FEC. Seven of the top 25, 16 of the top 50 and 29 of the top 100 companies had no PACs. One Washington observer attributes the still relatively low number of corporate PACs at least in part to the following factors:[53]

A "holier-than-thou" attitude in which campaign financing is deemed too sleazy to be in character with the companies' emphasis on civic responsibility.

Continuing internal debate in some companies, between officers in the "ivory tower" of the corporate headquarters and lobbyists in the field, over the necessity for establishing a company-sponsored, political giving program. Lobbyists are pushing for PACs in most cases, because they are the ones who generally get the invitations to fundraising dinners, receptions, etc.

The growing number of trade association PACs provides companies with an outlet for contributions as well as a publicity shield. "The laundering factor here is a great attraction," he said, since the names of the company or its officials do not appear on the candidate's report.

Nevertheless, conditions have become more favorable for the rise of a corporate PAC movement and labor is worried about the possibility of a widespread, well-organized corporate PAC movement. A COPE newsletter of January 16, 1978, raised the specter of corporate PACs creating "a giant money funnel mostly to conservative candidates, perhaps accounting for $20-25 million." Labor is especially fearful of the growth of "ideological" PACs organized in support of right-wing causes, as they foresee an alliance between these groups and corporate PACs, "giving them a combined potential wallop in the $40-$50 million range." [54]

Some recent developments tend to suggest that business will present a more united front in the future. The Chamber of Commerce announced in October 1977 that its public affairs department had hired Harold R. Mayberry, Jr., as staff attorney "to insure that the National Chamber's positions are effectively presented to the Congress and the Federal Election Commission."[55] Business interests are forming tax-exempt legal foundations, along the lines of consumer groups, for the purpose of protecting their interest against regulatory agencies and consumer groups. Their activities are supported by individual contributions, corporations, and private charitable foundations.[56] Some of these groups have undertaken litigation in the area of election law.

Case Studies

The Chrysler Nonpartisan Political Support Committee was established in 1976. It has set up procedures for regular solicitations, collection of donations, and disbursement. Chrysler's Washington office identifies "plant city congressmen" and "members of committees on which we have some involvement and congressmen with whom we have dealings." The list is sent to a board of trustees which decides who to support. In 1977 Chrysler sent its single largest contribution, $1,000, to Sen. Donald W. Riegle, Jr., D-Mich., who needed money to pay off a campaign deficit. Riegle later declared his opposition to auto airbags as a safety device, although he was the first senator to advocate them. Riegle had met in his office with Chrysler executives and Joan Claybrook, head of the National Highway Traffic Safety Administration, to discuss the issue. Chrysler says that there was no connection between Riegle's decision and the contribution.[57]

General Motors and Ford more recently inaugurated PACs of their own. GM expected to raise $90,000 before the 1978 elections. It collected $57,296 in its first in-house solicitation, concentrating on executives and administrative employees, and sending a team with a slide show to all plant sites. The GM guidelines for contributing are "votes on issues of importance to the corporation and leadership in Congress and on committees in support of private enterprise." Ford is using a documentary film treating issues such as auto emissions affecting the industry. Showing the employees "how the industry was perceived" was said to have stimulated increased participation.[58]

American Telephone & Telegraph has established a PAC associated with several Bell company PACs. The Public Affairs Council and other organizations are holding regular seminars for company officials designed to show them how to establish PACs. The National Association of Manufacturers is circulating a handbook titled "Political Participation — Permissible Political Fund-Raising for Corporations" outlining the procedures for setting up a PAC and other fund-raising mechanisms. Its preface states: "We hope that you will use this manual in establishing a political fund program within your company and in that way provide much needed help to business-oriented candidates in the coming elections."[59] Some observers foresee corporate PACs coordinating their efforts more carefully, as labor unions have, and some feel that they may form a federation of business and/or trade association PACs.

It has been pointed out, however, that business may never be able to match the partisan unity of labor's political efforts because there is often a conflict between the narrow interests of a particular company and the broader issue-oriented interests of business as a whole. Labor does not often encounter this conflict.[60] It has been suggested that business might take advantage of internal communications in aid of candidates, and also might provide research phone banks and other services, along the lines of labor support. Others feel that massive corporate actions comparable to labor's would almost certainly provoke stockholder suits, even though they would not violate election laws.

In 1978, for the first time, corporate and other business-related PACs exceeded labor dollars. This reversal is expected to continue because there is so much potential if corporations not having PACs decide to establish them. There are limits to labor's capability because no growth is expected in the number of unions, currently about 300.[61]

Such corporate and business-related developments are not far in the future. Of course, rates of participation and amounts raised vary tremendously, some PACs producing few dollars, others relatively more. Results depend upon the degree of commitment of management, the extent of solicitation, the newness of the program, and the procedures used. But however much a single PAC raises, there is huge potential in the aggregate because most corporations have not yet established PACs. But they could pose awesome problems of imbalance in the political system.

Legislative History of Political Action Committees

The FECA's limitations on contributions by individuals tended to make political action committees more important in 1976 than ever before. However, this was by no means the first election in which they played a significant role. Business and labor long had used such committees in their efforts to assert themselves politically without running afoul of the laws against direct contributions by corporations and unions.

Since the Tillman Act of 1907, direct corporate contribution to federal campaigns has constituted a felony, punishable by a fine of $5,000 for the corporation and of $10,000 and a jail term for the individuals involved. Direct campaign contributions by labor unions were forbidden in 1943, for the duration of the war, under the Smith-Connally Act. The Taft-Hartley Act of 1947 made this prohibition permanent, and also barred all corporate and union contributions and expenditures in primaries and nominating conventions.

In this legal environment, the political action committee developed as an alternative to direct interest group contribution. Such committees were regulated by the Federal Corrupt Practices Act of 1925, which established disclosure requirements but did not overly restrict their activities. Labor unions were quick to make use of the PAC. In 1944 the first union-affiliated committee was established. These committees have continued to be the main avenue for labor's financial support of candidates for federal office. Union members are encouraged to make voluntary contributions, which the committees distribute.

There was a steady increase in the number of national-level labor committees and in their spending from 1956 to 1968, during which time disbursements increased from the $2.2 million spent by 17 committees in 1956 to the $7.1 million spent by 37 committees in 1968. The 1972 campaign was marked by serious division within labor. Even so, labor committees contributed $8.5 million during the year.

New restrictions on PAC activity were part of the Federal Election Campaign Act of 1971. An amendment offered by Idaho Republican

Rep. Orval H. Hansen to Section 610 allowed corporations and unions to use funds from their treasuries to 1) communicate with stockholders or members for partisan political purposes, 2) conduct nonpartisan registration and get-out-the-vote drives among their stockholders or members, and 3) establish and operate a "separate, segregated fund to be used for political purposes," consisting of voluntary contributions.

Section 611, however, banned both direct and indirect contributions by government contractors. Some representatives of the business community argued that the term "government contractors" could be broadly interpreted to include virtually all corporations. Such an interpretation would, it was contended, create a contradiction in the law. Paying the costs of administering corporate PACs was specifically authorized by Section 610, whereas under Section 611 such payments could be prohibited as indirect contributions. An attempt was made in 1972 to exempt corporations and unions entirely from the effects of Section 611. A bill with this purpose passed the House of Representatives in October despite strong opposition from Common Cause, and editorial opposition from *The New York Times* and *The Washington Post*. In the Senate, however, the efforts of Senators William Proxmire, D-Wis., George Aiken, R-Vt., and Robert T. Stafford, R-Vt., which included the threat of filibuster, stopped the bill for that year. In 1973, however, the Senate passed a bill that revised Section 611 to permit ·corporations and labor unions holding government contracts to establish and administer PACs and to solicit voluntary contributions to these "separate, segregated funds," as permitted under Section 610. This provision was adopted as one of the 1974 Amendments to the FECA.

While it might initially have been supposed that organized labor would oppose this change, the contrary was true. Labor was persuaded to support the amendment by the argument that a broad interpretation of the term "government contractors" would include unions holding federal manpower training contracts. The change proved to be a windfall for business and contributed to the growth of the corporate PAC movement.

The FECA, as amended in 1974, also allowed multicandidate committees to contribute up to $5,000 per election to each candidate, and set no limit on either the transfer of funds to other committees or on aggregate contributions.[62] Since contributions to candidates by individuals were limited to $1,000 with a $25,000 limit per calendar year on total contributions, and since PACs could contribute up to $5,000 per candidate per election, they became an important avenue where small contributions could be aggregated into larger, more meaningful ones, giving credit to the corporation, labor union, or trade or membership association conveying the donation.

The 1976 Amendments further tightened contribution limits and the definition of multicandidate committees. Transfers of funds from one committee to another were limited; transfers to national party committees were held to $15,000 a year, and to $5,000 a year for transfers to any other political committee. Individual contributions to committees were further restricted. As of 1974 an individual could contribute any amount to any federally related candidate or political committee, up to the total limit of $25,000 a year. In 1976 a $20,000-a-year limit was placed on contributions to national party committees, and a $5,000 limit on contributions to any other committee.

An estimated 520 PACs operated in 1972. They contributed $16.6 million to federal elections, and provided 26 percent of the total receipts of congressional candidates in that year. By the end of 1974 there were 608 nonparty PACs. During 1975, 189 new nonparty-related multicandidate committees registered and began to report.[63] By 1976 there were 1,146 and they provided $22.6 million to congressional candidates, showing a net increase over the last presidential year despite stricter contribution limits.

The SunPAC Ruling

As late as 1975 many corporations were reluctant to establish PACs. Adverse publicity concerning illegal corporate political contributions, both domestic and foreign, had been generated by investigations conducted by the Watergate special prosecutor's office, the Senate Watergate Committee, and the Securities and Exchange Commission. Uncertainty about the new election law made for even more reticence. Decisions by the Department of Justice and the Federal Election Commission, in a matter concerning the Sun Oil Corp., contributed to legitimizing corporate PAC activity and clarifying its permissible scope.

On July 9, 1975, Sun Oil requested an advisory opinion from the FEC regarding the configuration of a proposed political action committee (SunPAC) and a proposed "political giving program" of the sort commonly referred to as a trustee plan (SunEPA). SunPAC would be administered by the corporation, and would solicit voluntary contributions from employees as well as stockholders. It would then distribute these funds to candidates in accordance with its purposes, which were to promote the private enterprise system and the petroleum industry. SunEPA would encourage political contributions but allow the employee to designate the recipients of his or her contributions. Sun would be authorized to deduct from employees' paychecks amounts designated by the employee, or to make periodic collections. The funds would be deposited into individual accounts in a bank of Sun's choice. On a company-provided form, the employee would inform the bank when he wanted to contribute, to whom, and how much, and the bank would draw and transmit a check in that amount to the designated candidate. SunEPA was to be completely voluntary and confidential. Sun maintained that it would receive no report concerning individual account activity, and would only be informed quarterly of the total contributions to candidates, committees, and parties. All costs would be borne by Sun and not by employees participating.

The U.S. Chamber of Commerce and the National Association of Manufacturers filed statements with the commission urging that Sun be allowed to implement these programs. Unions were opposed to both plans, and saw solicitations of employees by management as an invasion of their territory.

The commission's legal staff initially proposed that Sun be restricted to soliciting only stockholders and not employees or the general public. The staff also recommended that Sun be barred from paying the expenses of SunEPA on the grounds that such payments were an illegal infusion of corporate funds into the political process.

Prosecution Declined. The commissioners delayed their decision until they received a statement from the Department of Justice on these issues. On November 3, 1975, the department said, in a letter from Richard L. Thornburgh, assistant attorney general, that it "would be disposed to decline prosecution" under Section 610 concerning SunPAC and SunEPA. Sun, Thornburgh said, had the right to use corporate funds to defray the administrative expenses of these two committees, with certain provisions: The company must not suggest which candidates should be supported under SunEPA; it must not apply pressure of any kind to induce participation in either program; and it must not artificially inflate employees' salaries as a way of contributing indirectly to certain candidates. Under these circumstances, the corporate funds spent on SunEPA would be nonpartisan expenditures under the Hansen amendment to Section 610, as they would not tend to favor one candidate over another. SunPAC was considered a voluntary segregated fund, and therefore a legal corporate expenditure under the same section. While that section referred only to corporate solicitation of stockholders and did not mention employees, the department felt that the logic used to justify allowing unions to spend their funds in support of voluntary associations of this sort — based on the employees' First Amendment rights to freedom of association and expression — was equally applicable to corporations.

Once the Justice Department indicated that it would not prosecute Sun if the committees that were established solicited employees, the FEC's decision was preempted. A ruling that the committees were illegal would not be enforced in any case. On November 18, 1975, the FEC issued an advisory opinion stating that SunPAC and SunEPA would be considered legal if established. With regard to SunPAC, the corporation was cautioned concerning the potential for coercion in soliciting employees. There were to be guidelines: No superior should solicit a subordinate, the solicitor must inform the employee of the political purpose of the fund for which the contribution was solicited, and the solicitor must inform the employee of his or her right to refuse to contribute without reprisal. SunEPA was to be considered legal so long as there were no efforts to direct contributions in any way.[64]

Split Vote. The commission's vote to approve these committees was four to two. Commissioner Neil Staebler voted with the three Republican members in opposition to the other two Democratic commissioners. These two, Robert Tiernan and Thomas Harris (former associate counsel of the AFL-CIO), contended that the majority ruling destroyed the balance of potential union and corporate influence. They pointed out that under this ruling unions presumably could communicate only with, and solicit only among, their own members while corporations could solicit among employees as well as stockholders. They followed the commission staff in favoring restrictions on corporate appeals to stockholders. The dissenters pointed to the construction and legislative history of the law in support of their position. With reference to internal communications, the statute clearly restricted corporations to their stockholders and unions to their members. Harris and Tiernan argued that the subsection which permitted solicitation of contributions to a PAC was meant to be read in conjunction with this restriction, as solicitation was patently impossible without communication. If the two subsections were not read together, they maintained, the statute became ambiguous. They rooted this interpretation in the legislative history of the Hansen amendment, claiming that certain of Representative Hansen's comments had emphasized a vision of separate spheres of union and corporate solicitation and other communication.

With regard to SunEPA, the dissenters maintained that the provisions of Section 610 which authorized expenditures of corporate and union funds in connection with federal elections were strictly limited to certain kinds of activities. Only three were specifically allowed — internal communications, nonpartisan voting registration and get-out-the-vote drives, and PAC activities. Trustee plans were not among these, and the dissenters therefore claimed that such activities were not permissible.

In fact, they contended it was much more likely that support of a trustee plan constituted expenditure of corporate funds in connection with a federal election, which is prohibited.

Corporate leaders applauded the advisory opinion and labor officials were outraged. Richard D. Godown, general counsel of NAM, said that the ruling "should go a long way toward balancing the scales and counteracting the considerable support that labor-oriented candidates have been receiving over the years." [65] Union leaders claimed that despite the guidelines corporate officials would inevitably put pressure on employees to contribute. One union leader at Sun maintained, "What Sun Oil wants is to buy legislation — and they want to do it by putting the arm on our membership." [66]

The SunPAC ruling lent legitimacy to corporate PACs and clarified the limits of their activity. Following the decision there was an increase in the number of corporate PACs, as well as evidence of concerted business effort.

Other FEC Decisions. SunPAC certainly had more to do with the recent rise of corporate PACs than any other decision; however other FEC rulings have contributed to paving the way for increased political participation by the business community.

In September 1975 the FEC unanimously voted to allow the Associated Milk Producers Inc. (AMPI) to spend unlimited amounts of money for nonpartisan registration and get-out-the-vote drives, even though the group planned to confine its efforts to districts favoring candidates backed by the dairy cooperative. The FEC said that C-TAPE (Committee for Thorough Agricultural Political Education), a subsidiary of AMPI, which handles its political activities, could spend as much as it wanted on such efforts so long as "no efforts [were] made to determine the candidate or party preference of individuals registered or turned out to vote." The group could not, however, conduct such drives in areas where it already had endorsed a candidate. [67]

In December 1975 the agency issued a ruling on campaign debts to corporations. If left unregulated, canceling or settling such debts could be indirect forms of corporate contributions. It decided that they could be canceled " 'in certain extenuating circumstances' when the corporation to whom the candidate owes money 'has treated the outstanding debt in a commercially reasonable manner' " by granting the extension of credit on normal terms and making serious efforts to recover it. The FEC went on to declare, however, that it would investigate instances of such practices on a case-by-case basis. [68]

In September 1976 the commission issued an Information Letter that allowed corporations to include voter registration pamphlets prepared by a group such as the League of Women Voters in the corporations' billings to their customers. In addition, federal contractors were allowed to contribute to the league for nonpartisan purposes. [69] In another case, the commission declared that bondholders were to be treated differently from stockholders; they were "not subject to unlimited solicitation by political action committees [nor] eligible to receive partisan political communications from the corporations." [70]

Other decisions have tended to draw limits to certain kinds of corporate political activity. Among these FEC rulings was a November 1975 advisory opinion stating that ADEPT (Agricultural and Dairy Education Political Trust Fund) could not evade the law's limits on campaign contributions by establishing a number of state committees, in addition to its national organization. The FEC concluded that the overall contribution limit would apply to state and local committees controlled by their parent national committee. However, autonomous state committees would not be affected by the ruling. [71]

In November 1976 the commission hinted that the double-envelope plan used by some corporations may be illegal. In these plans employee contributions are forwarded by the company to the designated candidate, and although the employee's name is not known to the company, the company's name is made known to the candidate. [72]

Since these early decisions, the FEC has issued numerous advisory opinions on the operation of PACs, fine-tuning the law as more PACs seek different ways of proceeding without violating the law.

A Note on Corporate PACs

Because unions have made such extensive use of PACs since the 1940s, it is often assumed that the growing corporate PAC movement represents a new development. This is not true. Corporate political activity relied to a large extent on individual contributions to candidates, and there was less reason for business to organize PACs on a large scale until the limits on individual direct contribution were enacted. However, corporate PACs had existed for many years prior to this development and they are worthy of note.

In 1958 Aerojet-General Corp. initiated a "Good Citizenship Program," providing for voluntary payroll deduction for contributions to recipients designated by the donors. In 1960 this program raised $59,641. Other companies active in the 1960 election were Ford Motor Co., which established a double-envelope system, Whirlpool, American Telephone & Telegraph, and Chase Manhattan Bank, [73] among others.

In 1964 Aerojet's program raised more than $136,000. Hughes Aircraft Co. inaugurated an Active Citizenship Campaign, which raised $86,053 through solicitation and voluntary payroll deduction; 26 percent of their employees contributed, and three parties and 99 candidates in 20 states received support. Thompson Ramo Wooldridge Inc. (TRW) conducted a Good Government Program that contributed $87,000 to candidates and parties.[74] Others operated as well, in this and in subsequent years,[75] as will be seen.

Communication Costs

On April 27, 1977, the Federal Election Commission released the fifth index in its *Disclosure Series*. This work is the direct result of the 1976 Amendments, which require corporations, labor and membership organizations, and trade associations to report to the FEC the cost of partisan communications to their respective stockholders, executive and administrative personnel, or members, and their families, when the costs exceed $2,000 per election.[76]

The index, 144 pages in length, includes summary graphs with descriptions, definitions of the various applicable terms, and a sample of the communication costs reports filed with the commission.[77] The bulk of the report consists of three indexes: 1) an alphabetical list of reporting organizations, with a list of all documents filed and the amounts of communications costs reported for each filing; 2) an alphabetical list of organizations that reported, with a cross index of candidates by office whose election or defeat was advocated by communication efforts; and 3) an alphabetical list of candidates, with a cross index of those organizations reporting communications supporting them and the total expenditures reported by each organization.[78]

The first index lists the following information for each reporting organization: for each report filed, the amount of receipts for primary and general elections; the amount of expenditures for primary and general elections; and the number of pages in the report. In addition, there are grand totals for each category. The second index lists the expenditures each reporting organization made for each federal candidate it supported. The data are not broken down by primary or general election campaign. In most cases this is not a problem since the organizations seemed to confine themselves largely to one or the other type of campaign (usually the general election). For those organizations that spent funds in both types of elections, the researcher cannot tell how the funds were divided among the various candidates. The third index, which constitutes the bulk of the report, presents the data by each federal candidate (there are separate sections for presidential, senatorial, and House candidates). For each candidate we are given the amount of expenditures made in his behalf by the various organizations that filed with the FEC. In addition, the total amount of money spent by such groups in his behalf is shown.

Of the 71 organizations that filed with the commission, 66 were labor organizations, four were corporations, and one was a membership organization. Labor organizations spent the overwhelming proportion

Table 10-6
Organizations Reporting the Largest Internal Communications Expenditures for the 1976 Election:

Organization	Amount Spent on Communications
1. AFL-CIO	$400,557
2. UAW (United Auto Workers)	323,067
3. Building and Construction Trades Department (AFL-CIO)	177,507
4. Communications Workers of America	120,423
5. National Rifle Association (Institute for Legislative Action)	101,528
6. Pennsylvania AFL-CIO	101,056
7. Retail Clerks International Union	97,097
8. Ohio AFL-CIO	69,448
9. Michigan State AFL-CIO	45,720
10. American Federation of State, County, and Municipal Employees, AFL-CIO	41,013

SOURCE: Federal Election Commission, "FEC Releases Indexes on Communication Costs and Party Finances," press release, April 27, 1977, p. 2.

(93.9 percent) of the reported funds. The one membership organization, the National Rifle Association's Institute for Legislative Action, spent more than three times as much as the four corporations — Cooper Industries Inc., Dresser Industries, Libbey-Owens-Ford Co., and PepsiCo Inc. — combined. The corporations accounted for a mere 1.4 percent of the reported funds. The AFL-CIO and the United Auto Workers combined accounted for one-third of all money spent for communications. The Pennsylvania State AFL-CIO, the Communications Workers of America, the Retail Clerks International Unions, and the Construction Trades Department of the AFL-CIO accounted for more than one-quarter of the funds so spent (see Table 10-6).

Of the communications expenditures reported, $2,012,435 was spent for clearly identified candidates. The largest percentage (61 percent) was spent in support of presidential candidates, and 57.6 percent of funds for presidential candidates ($1,160,432) was spent on behalf of Jimmy Carter. No funds were spent to oppose him. In contrast, nearly equal amounts of money were spent on behalf of ($44,249) and in opposition to ($43,758) Gerald Ford (see Table 10-7). Slightly more than one-fifth of all the funds were used in behalf of House candidates. Altogether 414 federal candidates were aided: six presidential, 47 senatorial, and 361 House. The overwhelming proportion of these communications addressed members of labor organizations, one membership association, and their families. Only 2 percent of reported costs were targeted at executive-administrative personnel, stockholders, and employees. Most of the communications took the form of direct mail (87.1 percent). Other methods included brochures, leaflets, and flyers (6.2 percent), phone banks (2.7 percent), posters and banners (2 percent), and miscellaneous methods such as distribution of peanuts, tie tacs, stickers, buttons, lapel pins, and emblems.[79]

Although the sums spent on internal communications by labor unions were quite extensive, the data do not tell the whole story. Only messages sent directly to their members and that focused on specific candidates were reported to the FEC. Admonitions to vote Democratic, for example, did not have to be reported, and direct advocacy of a specific candidate did not have to be reported if the basic purpose of the communication was not political or if the total cost did not exceed $2,000. Almost every labor newsletter mailed to members in September and October praised Carter or criticized Ford, and a picture of Carter usually was on the cover. Little of this communication was reported to the FEC, presumably because the material appeared in regular publications that report on union business.[80]

In sum, the 1976 Amendments changed the rules of campaign finance with respect to internal communications by various types of organizations, which responded in different fashions; in particular, labor unions made for greater use of these provisions than did corporations, trade associations, or membership organizations. The major beneficiary of these expenditures was Jimmy Carter.

It is instructive to compare the magnitude of the sums spent by labor unions with the expenditures of Richard Nixon's presidential campaign of 1972 — the richest presidential campaign in U.S. history. Labor's contribution to Carter's campaign in the form of expenditures on internal communications exceeded the sum received by Nixon in 1972 from any single source except that of Chicago insurance millionaire W. Clement Stone, who contributed $2.1 million. Nixon spent almost three times as much as Carter, however, and the sums spent by labor on internal communications were thus more important to Carter's campaign than Stone's contributions were to Nixon.[81]

The picture from the business side was far less encouraging. As one observer has noted: "Business groups were not much help to President Ford in the general election. Five organizations spent a total of $41,000 on internal communications to help him and that was about it."[82] Compared with the efforts made by labor, the activities by business to encourage political participation was much less vigorous or innovative. Most of the efforts made by business were similar to that of the Dresser Industries Inc., a Dallas, Texas, corporation, which sent a two-page letter to its stockholders on October 18, 1976, urging them to vote for

Table 10-7
Expenditures for Internal Communications with Union Members and
Corporate Stockholders and Administrative Employees, 1976

Labor for Carter	Amount Spent	Portion Spent for Carter
AFL-CIO	$ 400,557.90	$ 315,981.67
United Auto Workers	289,139.12	240,688.48
Building Construction Trades Department, AFL-CIO	177,508.85	41,974.58
Communications Workers of America	120,423.69	106,813.64
Pennsylvania AFL-CIO	101,056.24	9,430.93
Active Ballot Club-Retail Clerks International Association	97,097.98	69,889.97
Ohio AFL-CIO	69,448.00	38,326.00
Michigan AFL-CIO	45,720.79	—
Indiana AFL-CIO	42,034.16	4,045.98
American Federation of State, County, and Municipal Employees (AFSCME)	41,014.64	24,170.47
Maryland and D.C. AFL-CIO	34,972.33	3,281.39
New Jersey AFL-CIO	29,943.00	26,858.00
Texas AFL-CIO	25,196.20	12,946.16
Tennessee State Labor Council	23,622.42	9,462.61
United Steelworkers of America	23,696.61	15,678.99
Service Employees International	20,556.85	—
California Labor Federation, AFL-CIO	17,850.17	11,903.52
Colorado COPE	15,269.36	—
Buffalo AFL-CIO Council	14,683.35	6,412.94
International Association of Bridge, Structural, and Ornamental Iron Workers	13,494.05	13,494.05
Machinists Non-Partisan Political League	13,959.66	7,666.64
South Carolina Labor Council	13,466.28	6,342.97
International Ladies' Garment Workers' Union	12,571.75	5,342.64
Council 13, AFSCME, AFL-CIO	12,567.00	6,283.00
Los Angeles County Federation of Labor, AFL-CIO	12,187.50	3,046.87
Rhode Island AFL-CIO	10,307.37	7,124.00
Cleveland AFL-CIO	10,265.66	7,699.25
Others	187,877.66	63,446.18
Total	$1,901,703.40	$1,051,897.23

Organizations for Ford	Amount Spent	Portion Spent for Ford
National Rifle Association for Legislative Action	$ 101,328.37	$ 13,204.92
Libbey-Owens-Ford Co.	13,096.38	13,096.38
Dresser Industries Inc.	5,245.00	5,245.00
Cooper Industries Inc.	5,079.40	5,079.40
PepsiCo. Inc.	4,485.15	4,485.15
Total	$ 129,434.50	$ 41,110.85

SOURCE: Michael J. Malbin, "Labor Business and Money — A Post-Election Analysis,"
National Journal, March 19, 1977, p. 415.

Gerald Ford. The letter, signed by John V. James, chairman of the board, president and chief executive officer, said that Jimmy Carter and the Democrats favored increased government regulation, planning, and control of the economy while Ford and the Republicans "believe that government should seek to ensure an environment in which business can, with a minimum of interference, achieve its full productive and profitable potential." The letter said that Carter favored "new and expanded programs, which are likely to mean increased public spending and higher taxes." In contrast, "President Ford favor[ed] limits on both spending and taxes." The company enclosed a small pamphlet outlining the differences between the two candidates "on key issues affecting business."[83]

The FEC's data do not, of course, tell us what impact these internal communications had on the outcome of the 1976 presidential and congressional elections. While Jimmy Carter did not fare so well among union members as several previous Democratic presidential candidates, it is possible that without labor's efforts he would have done even more poorly. In any case it is clear that labor unions were far better able than any other type of organization to exploit the new provisions of the FECA relating to internal communications. It remains to be seen if these other entities, particularly business organizations, will be able or willing in future elections to improve their record in this area.

Directories of Political Action Committees

One measure of the increased interest in political action committees that became manifest during the 1976 campaign was the proliferation of directories and guides to these committees. These publications were most prevalent in the business sector and were further indications of an emergent business PAC movement.

The Chamber of Commerce of the United States published two directories. The first, entitled *A National Directory of Business Political Action Committees of Individual Companies,* was issued in January 1976 and covered all business PACs that had submitted reports to the FEC, GAO, Secretary of the Senate, or Clerk of the House of Representatives. It contained lists of corporate PACs active in 1974 that were affiliated with single companies, and of PACs active in 1975 that were affiliated with single financial institutions. The directory indicated whether the PAC contributed to House, Senate, or presidential campaigns, and provided the company name, committee chairman, and address. Updates of this directory appeared in March, May, July, and October of 1976, and in January 1977.

The chamber's second directory, *A National Directory of Business Political Action Committees of Associations/Groups,* was assembled from the same sources by the chamber's public affairs department. Name, address, and chairman of each PAC were supplied, and the directory also indicated whether each committee supported candidates for the House, Senate, or presidency. It contained lists of business PACs affiliated with national associations, unaffiliated business PACs, PACs affiliated with associations of financial institutions, and financial association PACs with no such affiliation. This directory appeared in July 1975, and was updated in March, June, August, and October of 1976, and in February 1977.

In March 1977 the chamber published a *Campaign Finance Report on Corporate Political Action Committees Active in 1976*. It included total money spent and cash on hand for each corporate PAC and the totals for all, as well as lists of corporate PACs that had spent more than $30,000 in 1976 and, of those, which had terminated between January 1976 and February 1977.

In 1974, before the SunPAC ruling, the chamber had issued a guide to assist executives and attorneys for corporations and professional associations in establishing PACs. *Political Action Committees*, by T. Neal Combs and Arthur L. Herold, described the organization of PACs, registration with federal agencies, solicitation and expenditure of funds, and legal provisions regarding disclosure. It contained brief discussions of federal tax requirements, campaign statutes, regulations, and court decisions. In a series of appendixes were samples of a PAC constitution or bylaws, a solicitation letter, receipts and accounting instructions.

On January 20, 1975, the chamber circulated a memorandum entitled "Federal Campaign Financing," which discussed the FECA's major provisions and its amendments with a view to encouraging corporate participation in the political process. A follow-up to this publication, "A Memorandum on the Federal Election Campaign Act Amendments of 1976 and A Summary of Key Provisions," appeared 28 months later.

The National Association of Manufacturers produced *Political Participation: Permissible Political Fund Raising for Corporations*, which appeared in April 1975, and was intended to assist NAM members in establishing and running company-sponsored political fundraising programs. It described the basic principles of a PAC, explained contribution limits, and treated in depth separate segregated funds, double-envelope plans, and trustee plans. Also included were legal analyses of the 1974 FECA Amendments and a set of sample forms. In January 1976 an updated version appeared that contained a detailed treatment of the SunPAC ruling, including the request for an advisory opinion, a letter from the attorney general's office explaining its disposition not to prosecute on the matter, and the FEC's decision itself.

In August 1976 Campaign Practices Reports, which publishes a biweekly newsletter on election regulation, issued a report entitled *Financing the 1976 Election: A Report on Special Interest Groups*, containing name, address, treasurer, and affiliated organization for 1,100 PACs registered with federal officials.[84] This report was updated in April 1977.[85]

In March 1978 the Business-Industry Political Action Committee (BIPAC) published *A Directory of Corporate and Trade Association Political Action Committees Registered with the Federal Election Commission*, and followed that up in July 1978 with a *Directory of Corporate and Trade and Professional Association Political Action Committees*. The latter is derived from sources other than the FEC and can be used for solicitation purposes.[86] It contains addresses and key officers of listed PACs.

In October 1978 BIPAC published an expanded, updated, directory of corporate and association PACs. One of the principal BIPAC publications is its *POLITIKIT,* acronym for Political Information Kit, a monthly document containing commentary and analysis on congressional races, information on Federal Election Commission advisory opinions and status reports on election law reform legislation.

Two other BIPAC publications are provided to supporters, a quarterly *Political Action Report* focusing on BIPAC election involvement and other races of interest to the business community and *POLITICS*, a bimonthly commenting on legislation affecting business and national political trends. Over the 1977-78 period, BIPAC conducted monthly briefings and congressional races and FEC developments for corporate and association executives, and about two dozen briefings and seminars in major cities throughout the country.

Another publication containing information obtained from sources other than the FEC or other federal, state, or local government agency is *Tyke's Register of Political Action Committees*, which contains the addresses and officers of corporate, association, labor union, ideological, and other PACs, as well as the congressional voting records and ratings of members of Congress.

Tyke Research Associates also began publishing in 1978 the *Political Action Report,* a monthly newsletter dealing mainly with PAC news.

In June 1978 the Federal Bar Association began publishing *The FBA Election Lawyer*, a monthly newsletter dealing with "the growing legal complexities" of election law, directed to "an enlarging segment of the membership which is becoming involved with the election laws."

Another sign of increasing organization in the corporate community for political purposes was the formation in Washington, D.C., of the National Association of Political Action Committees. NAPAC described itself as a "non-partisan and non-profit association of PAC executives that neither supports nor opposes any political candidate or party," and claimed to offer the business community an opportunity to promote rather than discourage involvement in politics.[87] It planned to conduct studies in campaign finance and to provide the corporate PAC executive with a voice in Washington before congressional committees and the FEC. Members — charged dues of $400 a year — were provided with *The Political Outlook,* a newsletter, and were to be kept informed concerning relevant events in Congress and the FEC, about political consultants, the activities of unions, and other matters. Through seminars and annual meetings, NAPAC hoped to expand the skills and understanding of PAC executives, and intended to assist in the establishment of new PACs and the improvement of those already established. Despite these many plans and goals, NAPAC failed to survive.

Case Studies of Corporate Political Activity

The elements of questionable and illegal corporate political activity at home and abroad, as discussed above, are exemplified in the following set of case studies. The corporations included in this section are Gulf, ITT, Firestone, Northrop, United Brands, AT&T, Tenneco, United Technologies, Okonite, and J. Ray McDermott. These corporations were not selected for examination because their misbehavior was necessarily more serious than that of other corporations, but because taken together they provide a fairly representative sample of the kinds of activities undertaken by American business in recent years to secure political influence. Okonite and McDermott are distinguished from the others in that their violations arose in the post-Watergate era, which labels them as companies that did not, apparently, learn from that experience. These latter cases differ as well because they were handled by the then newly formed Federal Election Commission.

These case studies also illustrate the responses of government agencies, stockholders, and the corporations themselves to what took place. Investigations, court actions, congressional and administrative hearings, and public disclosure led to action against individual corporations and their officers, and on a broader scale to efforts at reform of corporate practices in the area. Efforts along these lines included attempts by stockholders and concerned groups to secure voluntary compliance with stricter standards through such measures as resolutions and proposed codes of corporate ethics.

AT&T

Texas. Watergate is a gnat compared to the Bell System, wrote T. O. Gravitt, vice-president of the Texas subsidiary of the Southwestern

Bell Telephone Co., before killing himself on October 17, 1974. According to Gravitt, the company had maintained a political slush fund since 1966 that was generated by salary kickbacks totaling about $100,000 a year paid by Southwestern Bell executives. He also charged that the company falsified data submitted to regulatory commissions to justify rate increases, used lucrative contracts to place businessmen and politicians in economic bondage, and tapped the telephones of city officials in areas where it sought rate increases.[88] Southwestern denied all charges.

Two weeks after Gravitt's death, a friend and coworker, James H. Ashley, Southwestern's San Antonio manager and assistant vice-president in charge of rate making for 200 Texas cities, was fired by the company. Ashley supported Gravitt's charges, saying that Bell executives at the supervisory level were given $1,000 raises with the clear understanding each would give $50 a month to the political slush fund.[89] Ashley named H. D. Ames, a Southwestern vice-president, as the main conduit for political contributions.

Ashley's and Gravitt's families brought a $29 million libel and slander suit against Southwestern Bell, claiming that the company maintained a slush fund and caused irregularities in rate making and charging that the company had falsely accused the two men of stealing and taking kickbacks from suppliers after Ashley and Gravitt had complained about the company's Texas operations. Ashley, who had known Gravitt for many years, said the company had hounded his friend until he committed suicide.

In his suicide note, Gravitt listed 14 politicians whom he had flown in his private plane in efforts to create good will for the company. He charged that company executives had received raises of $1,000 beginning in 1966; the money remaining after taxes (approximately $600 for each executive) was placed in a political slush fund maintained by the company. He further stated that $25,000 of the $80,000-$100,000 raised each year went to a company lobbyist for payoffs, and that a midwestern governor received $10,000.

Ashley supported these charges and added that before 1966 the company executives had given $50 a month in cash to selected politicians, while after 1966 a political contact man had named individuals to whom money was to be sent by check.[90] He claimed that certain executives were required to participate in the program, and he produced canceled checks of $50 and $100 that he had written to various state and congressional politicians, as well as a list of candidates and amounts to be contributed. The list allegedly had been given to Gravitt by a company lobbyist.

Ashley explained to reporters that he had talked to Gravitt in 1970 about seeking to change the company's inflated claims for rate increases. He said that Gravitt had told him that the policy was set by senior AT&T and Southwestern officials, but he suggested that they work within the system to increase its integrity. Despite four years of effort, their plan failed.[91]

In the early 1970s a South Texas rate expert discredited a regional phone manager by exposing Southwestern's approach. The credibility and community standing of local division managers declined and fewer rate requests were successful. Some managers quit in protest and some careers were ruined.[92]

In early 1974 Gravitt and Ashley agreed to expose company practices, starting with the San Antonio offices and moving up the corporate ladder. Although Ashley at first received encouragement from his superiors, an assistant vice-president in St. Louis cautioned him. Ashley said that practically every security man in Southwestern Bell was then assigned to the case. Gravitt and Ashley were told that the other was under investigation and each was assured that he would not suffer if he cooperated with the investigation.[93]

Texas is the only state lacking a public utilities commission.[94] Some Texas cities served by Southwestern Bell lacked the ability to dispute the corporation's figures, and in others the company allegedly bribed the officials by sending business their way. If bribes failed, the company tapped telephones or found other means to manipulate public officials, according to the former executive. Several Texas politicians admitted that they had business dealings with Southwestern Bell.[95] While some said that the amount of money involved was extremely small, often no more than a few hundred dollars, it was found that large amounts of business were involved in a number of cases.

Charles Marshall, Gravitt's successor as head of Southwestern's Texas division, admitted that the company did business with politicans and said it would continue to do so, but he insisted that politicians would be insulted by the suggestion that they were influenced by the Bell System.[96]

Southwestern's response to the claims of Ashley and other executives concerning political contributions changed repeatedly. At first the company denied that contributions had been made. Later it admitted encouraging its employees to make contributions but claimed that the donations were personal rather than corporate.

In February 1975 Ward K. Wilkinson, chief Texas lobbyist for Southwestern Bell, disclosed that he had managed a political fund whose income from Bell executives in Texas averaged $14,500 a year. He said that he had given Sen. John G. Tower, R-Texas, $1,000 in cash on April 3, 1972, four days before the FECA went into effect. David Forbis, former Southwestern Bell general staff manager in Dallas, said that from 1966 to 1973 he had collected $50 a month from approximately 10 executives in that city and that he had given the money to Wilkinson in cash because, Forbis alleged, that was the way Wilkinson wanted it. The procedure changed in 1973 when a new Texas election law went into effect requiring the reporting of all contributions of $10 or more. Thereafter, all Bell contributions were made in the form of personal checks. Southwestern Bell admitted that executives in posts comparable to Forbis' had collected money in Houston and San Antonio for Wilkinson's fund. Some of these funds were given in local city council races and to help defeat Dallas referenda allowing police and firemen to engage in collective bargaining and instituting a commuter tax for suburbanites working in Dallas. Other moneys were given to support city council candidates endorsed by the Citizens' Charter Organization, a powerful conservative slate-making group in Dallas.

Many city councilmen in San Antonio, Austin, Fort Worth, and Dallas admitted receiving business contracts or campaign contributions from Bell officials but claimed that these did not affect their decisions regarding cases; most of the politicians said they considered the contributions to be personal rather than corporate gifts.[97]

North Carolina. The issue was not confined to Texas or to Southwestern Bell.[98] In January 1975 John J. Ryan, former vice-president of Southern Bell Telephone Co. and head of its North Carolina operations, told the *Charlotte Observer* that he had administered a secret political fund from 1964 through 1973. It was, he claimed, generated by salary kickbacks of $100 a month from between six and eight of his immediate subordinates. The money was given primarily to congressional and gubernatorial candidates favorable to Southern Bell. Each of the two Democratic and two Republican contenders in the 1972 North Carolina gubernatorial race received aid; the governor appoints the members of that state's public utilities commission responsible for setting the telephone rates. The money was given in Ryan's name.

Although Ryan claimed that he had never received a direct order from Southern Bell to make political contributions or collect the funds, he did say that he had been given a raise as early as April 1962 with instructions to use it as a political contribution. He added that after his transfer to North Carolina in 1964 subordinates in that division began to make payments to him without being asked. In January 1975 Southern Bell issued a statement denying that Ryan had ever been authorized to make clandestine political contributions on behalf of the company. It declared that he had been forced to resign in 1973 because company officials felt he was spending time on political and civic affairs at the expense of his managerial responsibilities. Southern admitted that it operated a voluntary contribution program for its top executives, but described the fund in terms very different from those Ryan had used. The company claimed that the program offered a savings account designed to encourage top managers to contribute voluntarily to the political process.[99]

By the end of the year an internal audit conducted by Southern had discovered approximately $142,000 in expense vouchers falsified between January 1971 and June 1973. Eleven Southern Bell executives were indicted in August 1976 under a North Carolina statute that covers malfeasance of corporate officers. The indictments were dropped after L. E. Rast, the president of Southern Bell, admitted that the company had authorized the falsification of the vouchers to finance political contributions. He stated that Southern Bell's directors were not aware of the illegalities. The Securities and Exchange Commission, the U.S. and state's attorneys in North Carolina, and the North Carolina Public Utilities Commission are continuing investigations of the company that were begun in 1975.[100]

On August 2, 1977, Southern Bell, Ryan, and Rast were indicted on conspiracy and fraud charges by a Mecklenburg County (N.C.) grand jury. The indictment charged both men with conspiring to falsify company books and with falsifying expense account vouchers in an attempt to defraud the company. Ryan was charged separately with 16 counts of embezzling company money. The indictment also named the company itself and three current vice-presidents. In February 1978 Southern Bell pleaded guilty to misapplication of corporate funds through false expense vouchers. Twenty-four similar counts against the company were dropped in return for the guilty plea. Recipients of the illegal funds had included Democratic North Carolina Gov. James B. Hunt, Jr., and Republican Sen. Jesse Helms, who claimed that they had believed the donations to be legal contributions from individuals.[101]

Company Audits. At its September 1975 annual meeting, AT&T announced the results of a year-long audit of its subsidiaries. It declared that it had found scattered instances of improper use of corporate funds for political contributions among six of its subsidiaries. Altogether, the report said, $9,520 had been improperly spent between 1971 and 1974 with no single contribution exceeding $500. The corporation stated that the funds had been returned to the six subsidiaries and that it had not discharged, suspended, transferred, or placed on probation any of the individuals involved. The monies had not been spent for political purposes but the report disclosed a few cases of improper use of corporate funds, mostly for the purchase of tickets to state or local fund-raising dinners.[102]

The report was less than completely open or detailed, however, since its figures excluded any possible violations found in the audits of

Southern or Southwestern Bell. AT&T Chairman John de Butts refused to comment on those audits on the grounds that the government investigations of the two subsidiaries were not yet complete. But such problems did not seem to faze most of the corporation's stockholders. When Evelyn Davis proposed that AT&T affirm its nonpartisanship and avoid any actions that might give the appearance of partisan favoritism, the overwhelming majority of the votes cast favored the company's position on the matter. AT&T opposed the resolution on the grounds that it would infringe upon the right of employees who wished to participate in the political process by channeling their support through a separate segregated fund as allowed by the 1974 Amendments. In addition, the board of directors charged that approval of the proposal could be construed as preventing the company from speaking out against or in favor of legislation or various government policies.[103]

In July 1977 de Butts announced that he had sent a letter to all Bell System presidents informing them that they were free to form political action committees if they so desired.

Federal, State Investigations. As might be expected, the charges made by Gravitt, Ashley, and Ryan led to numerous investigations of the operations of both Southwestern and Southern Bell. The fraud section of the U.S. Justice Department's Criminal Division is investigating to see whether the two companies violated the provisions of either the FECA or the Corrupt Practices Act by giving corporate contributions to political campaigns. The Securities and Exchange Commission is trying to discover if either company violated regulations that required publicly traded corporations to tell their stockholders of the purposes for which they have used corporate funds. The Federal National Wiretapping Commission and a federal grand jury in Texas are both investigating Ashley's and Gravitt's allegations concerning illegal wiretapping by Southwestern Bell, and several Texas police forces. The Federal Communications Commission has been asked by a competitor of Southwestern Bell, Roy M. Teel doing business as a Honotan Radiophone service,, to determine if the corporation illegally tapped phones, contributed to politicians, or violated required accounting practices.[104] The House Subcommittee on Communications and Power scheduled hearings on AT&T's request to increase interstate long distance rates and declared it would look into the allegations concerning Southern and Southwestern Bell. The Texas Senate's consumer affairs subcommittee received approval in January 1975 to spend more than $27,000 in its investigation of Southwestern, and there were renewed efforts in the Texas legislature to establish a statewide public utilities commission. As a result of the data Ashley and Gravitt made public, several Texas cities planned to review the rates they charged Southwestern Bell.[105]

Slander Suit. In August 1977, nearly three years after Ashley's and Gravitt's families had filed suits against Southwestern, the case went to trial before a state district court in San Antonio. Ashley testified that the company had started its investigation of Gravitt in 1974 because William Lindholm, then president of AT&T, wanted to fire Gravitt for his opposition to the allegedly inflated rate-fixing practices in Texas. The company responded that it had begun its probe of Gravitt and Ashley as a result of information it had concerning their receipt of kickbacks on printing contracts and submission of false vouchers. In addition, it charged Ashley with illicit sexual relations with female company employees and produced 13 women who testified to sexual advances made toward them by both former executives. Ashley admitted filing false expense statements.

On September 12 the jury ordered Southwestern Bell to pay $3 million to be split equally between the Ashley and Gravitt families. The jury concluded that both men had been slandered by the investigation into a printing company that did business with Southwestern Bell. The company announced that it planned to appeal the verdict. In November 1978 a Texas appeals court overturned the damage judgment.[106]

Firestone Tire & Rubber Co.

In March 1976 the Securities and Exchange Commission asked the Firestone Tire & Rubber Co. to disclose whether any company funds had been used to make domestic political contributions, whether improper payments had been made to officials of foreign governments, and whether the company had maintained any funds not reflected on its books. The corporation's board of directors ordered its audit committee to investigate all matters raised by the SEC inquiry. The committee submitted its final report to Firestone's board of directors and to the SEC in December 1976.

Beasley Role. The committee found that the corporation had operated a secret program for domestic political contributions that had begun prior to 1960 and had terminated in 1973. Robert P. Beasley, Firestone's chief financial officer and a member of the board of directors, administered the program from 1968 to 1973. The report noted that Beasley apparently had been the only Firestone officer fully aware of the program's scope.[107]

Beasley claimed that he assumed responsibility for the program in 1968 with the explicit approval of Raymond K. Firestone, then chairman and chief executive officer, and that he reported periodically on the overall scope of the program to Firestone and the two individuals who preceded him as president. Beasley said that Firestone and the two

Table 10-8
Sources and Uses of Funds Collected by Robert P. Beasley, Chief Financial Officer of the Firestone Tire & Rubber Co.

Sources of Funds		
Refunds received in connection with a foreign construction project	$235,700	
Insurance proceeds from a 1963 foreign fire loss	336,267	
Supplemental payment in 1971 in connection with sale of a foreign investment	169,602	
Cash received under the rebated salary program	351,841	
Funds received in six additional miscellaneous transactions	68,085	
		$1,161,495
Uses of Funds		
Amount estimated by Beasley to have been expended for domestic political contributions from Nov. 1, 1970, through May 1973	$330,000	
Amount refunded to the company by Beasley after initiation of the present investigation	206,101	
		$ 536,101
Remainder		$ 625,394

SOURCE: Investor Responsibility Research Center Inc., "Corporate Involvement in U.S. Political Campaigns: *The Firestone Tire & Rubber Co.,*" Analysis A, Supplement No. 1 (Jan. 13, 1977), A-16.

others played important roles in determining the recipients and the amounts of the contributions. These charges were denied by Raymond Firestone and Earl B. Hathaway, one of the two former presidents (the other is dead). According to Beasley, approximately $330,000 in Firestone funds were contributed to federal, state, and local campaigns between 1970 and 1973. Comparable contributions also were made during earlier years. The audit committee verified that contributions totaling $52,750 were made with corporate funds during the 1970-73 period but it did not identify any recipients.[108]

These donations were made from a secret cash fund generated through an elaborate salary rebate program at one of Firestone's foreign subsidiaries. Between September 1966 and April 1970 approximately $440,000 was raised through duplicate payments to employees of the subsidiary by the parent company and the subsidiary. The foreign currency fell steadily in dollar value between 1966 and 1972, and the audit committee estimates the dollar value of the items delivered to Beasley under the rebate program to have been approximately $351,000, a fund not recorded on the books of the parent company or the subsidiary. In addition, Beasley continued an established corporate practice by asking key current or retired Firestone executives to make political contributions and then reimbursing them. According to the financial officer, these contributions accounted for slightly less than half of all political contributions made with corporate funds between 1970 and 1973. The audit committee estimates that approximately $85,000 was raised during the 1970-73 period from reimbursed contributions by 21 executives. The contributions averaged between $1,000 and $2,000 a year.[109] These executives later were required to repay the corporation the amounts for which they had been reimbursed.

The Firestone audit committee discovered that Beasley had transferred at least $800,000 in corporate funds into at least 20 noncorporate bank accounts he controlled. Beasley refused to discuss these transactions, and the committee was unable to determine if these transfers involved any wrongdoing or were related to the political contribution program. Beasley refunded approximately $206,000 to the corporation. Although the committee could not determine exactly how much money had been contributed in the period from November 1, 1970, to May 31, 1973, it did provide an estimate of the amount of funds believed to have been appropriated by Beasley (Table 10-8).[110]

The audit's committee investigation uncovered a number of questionable foreign transactions involving total expenditures of more than $390,000 in bribes and similar payments by Firestone subsidiaries. These transactions included:[111]

1. A secret fund maintained by a foreign subsidiary that disbursed between $90,000 and $130,000 in illegal political contributions in the subsidiary's country between 1970 and 1976. The fund was created from confidential rebates paid to the subsidiary by its suppliers and was exhausted by mid-1976.

2. Another secret fund of a second foreign subsidiary was used to pay expenses not reflected on the company's books from 1970 through 1976. The money was used to pay $39,600 to the president of that nation's tire manufacturers' trade association. This was Firestone's share of a $400,000 payment by the tire industry to obtain government approval of a price increase; the increase was granted shortly after the delivery of the subsidiary's payment. The fund was terminated in 1976.

3. Payment to a tax consultant in a foreign country to negotiate a settlement of an assessment for additional income taxes.

4. Payment to a lawyer by a foreign subsidiary to expedite a tax refund.

5. An illegal contribution of $32,000 by a foreign subsidiary in 1974 to a political party in that country. The money represented

Firestone's share of a total contribution of $175,000 by the tire industry to obtain an increase in the price at which tires could be sold to the local government; the price increase was granted approximately three months after the payment by the subsidiary.

In June 1976 a federal court order enjoined the company, Firestone, and Beasley from violation of securities laws in connection with illegal political contributions. The SEC consent decree prohibited the use of corporate funds for illegal political purposes, the filing of false reports with the SEC, and the establishment of secret or unrecorded funds. The corporation, Beasley, and Firestone consented to this order, and Beasley and Firestone agreed to cooperate fully with the audit committee. Nevertheless, in August 1976 the SEC filed contempt charges in federal court against Beasley for his refusal to cooperate with the audit committee's investigation.[112]

Policy Statement. In reaction to these disclosures, the Internal Revenue Service undertook a special audit of Firestone. On September 21, 1976, the corporation's board of directors adopted a policy statement designed to govern conduct by company personnel worldwide. The policy statement prohibited use of the company's assets to support any political party in the United States or any candidate for local, state, or federal office; prohibited illegal political contributions in foreign countries and stipulated that legal political contributions in foreign countries be made only with the express approval of the chief executive officer; prohibited payments to employees of any government for the purpose of obtaining special benefits; prohibited the maintenance of secret funds; and prohibited false or incomplete entries in the company's accounting records.[113]

At the corporation's 1977 annual meeting, Edward C. Calvert proposed that the audit committee consider obtaining outside legal counsel and auditors to help prepare reports to be mailed to all stockholders to identify, disclose, and seek restitution for any illegal payments made from company funds, domestically or abroad. Firestone opposed adoption, arguing that it would serve no useful purpose. Its proxy statement claimed that the corporation already had "carefully considered and . . . taken appropriate action to reject or to effect substantially all of the recommendations contemplated by the proposal." John Floberg, Firestone's secretary-general counsel, indicated that the corporation had retained counsel to investigate accounting and recovery of any diverted funds. He noted that unless Beasley cooperated with the investigation it would be impossible to identify all the recipients of the domestic contributions. Moreover, he added that even if Beasley answered the corporation's questions recovery of the funds might be impossible because of the expiration of the statute of limitations. Floberg also said Firestone had decided that identification of the individuals and countries that had received questionable payments would not be in the best interests of the corporation and might provoke retaliation against the company or its employees.[114] According to Floberg, the company's main concern was ensuring that such payments were not made in the future rather than identifying previous illegal payments.

On February 28, 1977, Firestone filed suit against Beasley, charging that he had "fraudulently converted, transferred or diverted company funds to his personal use and benefit." Firestone's audit committee had failed in its attempts to account for more than $625,000 of the illlegal campaign funds. Beasley was indicted on October 25 for having stolen most of $1 million in corporate funds, which supposedly was being used for illegal campaign contributions. He pleaded not guilty to the 40-count indictment in a New York federal court on November 3.[115] On February 28, 1978, Beasley pleaded guilty to five of the 40 counts. In return for admission that he had, without Firestone's permission, used corporate funds for his personal expenses, the government agreed to move for dismissal of the remaining counts against him.[116] Federal Judge Milton Pollack sentenced Beasley to four years in prison and fined him $14,000 for the theft of corporate funds. The penalty carried the maximum fine; the maximum prison term would have been 30 years. In pronouncing sentence, Judge Pollack commented that it would be a "travesty of justice" if Beasley were not given an "appropriate punishment." Judge Pollack noted, however, that he had taken into account Beasley's advanced age and the possible effect of a lengthy prison term on Beasley's health. In addition to the fine, Beasley was instructed to reimburse the government for the expense of prosecution.[117]

Gulf Oil

The Gulf Oil Corp., one of the world's largest oil companies, has been wracked by disclosures of a major political slush fund it maintained. From 1961 through 1973, the company distributed more than $12 million to U.S. and foreign politicans to advance its interests.

Wild's Role. Claude C. Wild, Jr., played a key role in engineering Gulf's domestic political contributions. Hired by Gulf in 1959 as its legislative representative, he became vice-president of the corporation in 1968. Public knowledge of his involvement with Gulf's political contributions began with the campaign to reelect Nixon in 1972. In 1971 Wild gave Lee Nunn, an employee of the Committee to Reelect the President (CRP), $50,000 in cash. The following year he gave a similar amount, also in cash, to Maurice Stans, finance chairman of CRP, and he gave Sen. Henry M. Jackson, D-Wash., $10,000, and Rep. Wilbur D. Mills, D-Ark., $15,000. The Watergate special prosecutor's office eventually learned that these donations came from corporate funds and were therefore illegal. In November 1973 both Gulf and Wild pleaded guilty to a one-count violation of the U.S. code. Gulf was fined $5,000 and Wild $1,000.[118] Although Wild resigned from Gulf in 1974 as a result of these actions he subsequently was rehired on an emergency basis for more than half a year.[119]

The information disclosed at the 1973 trial led the Securities and Exchange Commission to examine Gulf in 1974 as part of its investigation of illegal corporate contributions.[120] On March 11, 1975, the SEC filed suit against Gulf and Wild, charging them with falsifying records filed with the commission to hide the existence of the secret fund used for corporate political contributions. The complaint alleged that the company had channeled more than $10 million in Gulf corporate funds to its subsidiary in the Bahamas and had redirected at least $5.4 million of this sum in cash to U.S. political campaigns. The remainder, it was claimed, had been distributed overseas by Gulf and others.[121]

In an agreement announced simultaneously with the filing of the suit, Gulf consented to a federal court order prohibiting further violations of SEC reporting and proxy regulations and use of corporate funds for illegal political contributions. The company also agreed to establish a special review committee approved by the SEC to investigate the use of Gulf corporate funds for political activity, and to report its findings to the SEC, the federal court, and Gulf's board of directors. After three extensions granted by Judge John Sirica, the committee submitted a 298-page report in December 1975.[122] It found that Gulf had begun to take a more active role in politics in the 1950s, when a secret fund was established by W. K. Whiteford, then chief executive officer, to build an organization around the country to increase Gulf's political influence. With the creation of the fund the Bahamas Exploration Co. Ltd. in Nassau, a wholly owned Gulf subsidiary, became a laundry for Gulf's political contributions.[123] Whiteford apparently had learned that other oil companies had similar arrangements.[124] Relatively few people in the corporation knew about Gulf's program, and Whiteford ordered that the fund be kept secret from the Mellon interests, which had founded Gulf, and from several company executives.

John J. McCloy and the other members of the review committee determined that from 1961 to 1973 Gulf spent a total of $12.3 million (a figure that included $2 million in contributions to Canada, Sweden, and Italy). According to the McCloy report and subsequent disclosures, domestic disbursements were made by William Viglia, comptroller of the Bahamian subsidiary, who withdrew approximately $25,000 in cash from the subsidiary's bank account about every two weeks. He would then deposit the money in a personal safe deposit box in another bank across the street and, when ordered, would fly to the United States with the requested funds. Most of the time he delivered the money to Wild in Washington and other cities, but there were occasions, he testified, when he gave it to at least three other company executives (William Henry, Joseph Bounds, and William Grummer) in Pittsburgh and other cities. From 1961 through 1973, when the fund was disbanded because of the Watergate scandal and Wild's illegal contribution to the Nixon campaign, Viglia and other couriers brought an estimated $5.4 million into the United States.

On the average, Wild received between $300,000 and $400,000 a year for political purposes. In addition to Wild, Frederick Myers, Thomas Kerester, Norval Carey (in Gulf's Washington office), and Arthur Harris (in Pittsburgh) testified that they had handed sealed envelopes to politicians either on Capitol Hill or elsewhere in the United States.

The money was given to scores of federal, state, and local politicians, almost always in cash.[125] Wild was known to have purchased numerous $100 tickets at cocktail parties given by or for political candidates and to have bought tables at $1,000 a person at both Republican and Democratic fund-raising dinners for Senate and House candidates. Many of the alleged recipients were national figures (Hubert Humphrey, Lyndon Johnson, Richard Nixon, Henry Jackson, Howard Baker, and Wilbur Mills). Although Wild appeared before the Senate Watergate Committee and briefly mentioned his congressional gifts, the committee did not question him on this matter (see Appendix L).

It is not entirely clear what Gulf thought its money was buying.[126] One participant in the program testified that no particular favors or benefits were expected after the company's lavish donations to the Nixon campaigns in 1968 and 1972, but on at least one occasion Gulf executives met with then Attorney General John N. Mitchell to discuss a Gulf acquisition. The company seemed convinced that its corporate rivals were all donating money in Washington and it should do likewise. Many politicians seemed to encourage Gulf in its actions. A messenger from the Nixon campaign headquarters reportedly told Wild in 1968 that it would be a good idea to contribute to the campaign if he wanted to be treated equally.[127]

Foreign Payments. The figures available indicate that Gulf's domestic political gifts were not so substantial as the sums spent abroad Gulf gave its largest contributions — more than $4 million — to the political party of President Park Chung Hee of South Korea.[128]

Before the Senate committee and the McCloy panel, Bob Rawls Dorsey, a corporate official, stated that in 1966 an official in the Park government had asked a Gulf executive in the Far East for a contribution of $1 million to the Democratic Republican Party, President Park's political organization, for the coming election.[129] The request was forwarded to Dorsey, who was then president. Dorsey considered that the request had been made in very strong terms — almost as if Park and his associates were saying that the company should contribute if it wished to survive in South Korea. He therefore authorized the payment from the company's Bahamian fund.

In 1970 President Park's party appeared to face a strong challenge in the national elections scheduled for early 1971. S. K. Kim, the finance officer of the Democratic Republican Party, called an official of Gulf's Korean subsidiary to his office in late 1970 and demanded a $10 million political contribution by the corporation. The Gulf official relayed the request to Dorsey, who was now Gulf's chairman. According to Dorsey, Kim exerted intense pressures on him. Ultimately, Dorsey succeeded in reducing the $10 million figure to $3 million, which he consented to give, believing that the contribution would be in the best interests of the company. President Park won the 1971 election, the last to be held in South Korea, by a margin of 51 to 49 percent. Gulf later determined that the contributions were illegal under South Korean law.[130]

The contributions were not the only illegal or questionable payments Gulf made in South Korea. The McCloy committee also discovered that Gulf had 1) given undetermined amounts to low-level Korean officials to facilitate Gulf's business with the Korean government, 2) paid an inflated price of $2 million for the purchase of a second 25 percent interest in an oil distribution company from a seller with close ties to the Park regime (of the total payment, $200,000 went to the Korean government), 3) made arrangements to sell and lease back tankers under terms that left Gulf with all commercial risks, but provided a guaranteed profit of several hundred thousand dollars a year to persons designated by the prime minister of Korea,[131] 4) paid more than $2 million in rebates to the Korean Ministry of Defense.

Gulf Oil became the largest foreign investor in South Korea. According to Dorsey, Gulf never received anything in return for the contributions except, perhaps, the right to continue its business in South Korea.[132]

In addition to the South Korean payments, the special review committee discovered that Gulf had made other foreign contributions, including: 1) payments of $627,000 over three years to publications owned by several political parties in Italy, 2) political contributions of $235,886 over a dozen years in Italy from a secret fund in that country, 3) expenditures of $107,925 to purchase a helicopter for President Rene Barrientos of Bolivia, possibly in violation of Bolivian law,[133] 4) political contributions of $6,000 in Sweden (such gifts are legal in Sweden), 5) political contributions of $1,390,982 over 14 years to political parties in Canada, where such contributions are legal, 6) a $50,000 contribution to a group circulating pro-Arab propaganda in the United States.

Undoubtedly Dorsey was informed about Gulf's foreign payments. In contrast, Dorsey told the McCloy committee that he did not know of the domestic fund or Wild's activities until July 1973, when he was informed that the Watergate special prosecution force had discovered an illegal Gulf contribution to the 1972 Nixon campaign. Dorsey said that when he learned of this donation, he immediately told all company employees to cooperate fully with the investigation.[134]

McCloy Report. When it came time to apportion the blame, McCloy and his fellow commissioners contended that there was plenty to be divided among key Gulf executives. Their report described Gulf's political contributions as "shot through with illegality." Although Gulf's clandestine actions generally disregarded federal statutes and some state statutes,[135] the report did note that a small percentage of the contributions were given legally through Gulf's Good Government Fund (see Appendix L).[136]

The report asserted that the illegal and questionable payments called into question the policy and management of the company in such matters. The special review committee concluded that the evidence it gathered was insufficient to show that Dorsey knew of Wild's illegal domestic political activities, but it suggested that Dorsey "perhaps chose to shut his eyes to what was going on," and it noted that he was in a position both to inquire and to put an end to the payments.[137]

The report also attacked E. D. Brockett, a former Gulf chairman; William Henry, president of Gulf Oil Real Estate Development Co. and an executive vice-president; Fred Deering, senior vice-president; Herbert Manning, a vice-president and corporation secretary; and Royce Savage, retired general counsel.[138] Both Henry and Deering had served as Gulf comptrollers in the 1960s and were in charge of disbursing corporate funds when the fund was in full operation. The panel said that the two men were responsibile for knowing where the money went and that they had failed to meet that responsibility. Manning came under fire for failing to inquire as diligently and as professionally as he should have into the source of the funds he received before paying out the substantial cash sums to support political campaigns, as he admitted he did when he was Gulf associate general counsel.[139] McCloy and his associates claimed that Savage was aware that Wild had corporate funds he probably was using for political contributions and payments.[140]

The report did not completely exonerate the recipients of the gifts, and the panel declared its difficulty in believing that many candidates did not identify Gulf's contributions as corporate funds. In conclusion, the committee noted that changes in the corporation's rules and procedures alone would not be sufficient to prevent a repetition of events, and that the legality of Gulf's conduct in the future would be determined by the tone and attitude of top management.[141]

Management Shake-up. Gulf's board of directors considered the McCloy report for two days in January 1976. After an apparently heated debate, the board led by the Mellon interests forced Dorsey, Deering, and Henry to resign and demoted Manning. The board chose Jerry McAfee, at the time head of Gulf's Canadian subsidiary, to replace Dorsey as chairman, chief executive, and a Gulf director. It was the most dramatic action taken by a large American corporation implicated in political funding scandals in recent years.[142]

Soon after assuming the chairmanship, McAfee sent a letter to all Gulf employees declaring Gulf's intention of following the highest ethical standards of business conduct and of respecting the law wherever the company operated. Continued employment at Gulf was conditioned on strict adherence to these principles. Gulf continued to modify its policies to bring them into line with the suggestions made by McCloy and his fellow commissioners. Even before the panel finished its report, the board of directors adopted more stringent auditing and reporting procedures. In addition, a number of senior corporate officials were required to submit to the director of internal auditing annual representation letters acknowledging compliance with company policy barring corporate political contributions. Illegal corporate political contributions were barred. Employees who knew of illegal activity on behalf of Gulf were required to notify the chairman or the general counsel.[143]

Gulf's policy changes did not satisfy everyone. At the company's annual meeting in 1976, a resolution was offered to amend Gulf's bylaws to prohibit any political contributions overseas by the corporation, but it was supported by only 2.97 percent of the shares voted. Three resolutions were introduced at the 1977 annual meeting. One, proposed by Mark Jaffe, asked Gulf to revise its certificate of incorporation to prohibit any illegal payments by the corporation in a foreign country. Gulf opposed the Jaffe motion, declaring its agreement with the sentiments expressed but arguing that the company had taken the action necessary to preclude illegal payments. The company also claimed that an amendment to the articles of incorporation would not be particularly effective. The best way, a company spokesman said, was to communicate clearly to Gulf employees that company policy forbids such payments and that violation of this policy would result in dismissal.[144]

The other two resolutions proposed at the 1977 annual meeting were submitted by the Sisters of Loretto, who are associated with the

Interfaith Center on Corporate Responsibility. One resolution asked Gulf to prepare a report on certain aspects of its operations in South Korea, including a list of all political contributions given in that country since 1966. The other asked Gulf to adopt a policy that would prohibit any political payments by the corporation in South Korea.[145]

Explaining its opposition to these two proposals, Gulf said it believed adoption of the resolutions might be interpreted as an expression of opposition to the government of South Korea. Since the company had adopted a policy of making no illegal political contributions — and corporate political contributions were illegal under existing South Korean law — adoption of the second Sisters of Loretto resolution would serve no useful purpose.[146] All three resolutions were defeated by the shareholders.

After the McCloy report became public, Gulf took action on behalf of the stockholders to recover as much of the illegal domestic contributions as possible. (It was one of only a few corporations that did so.) On March 4, 1976, Gulf Chairman Jerry McAfee sent a letter to all known recipients of the fund asking for return of the money. There was only a very limited response. Many of the elected officials who received the communication declared that they personally had never been given any contribution or had no recollection of such a donation. Others claimed that they were under the impression that the money came from Gulf employees and not from the corporation. A few who did return the funds attempted to portray their actions in the most favorable light possible. Rep. John Heinz, R-Pa., who was running for a Senate seat, and Sen. Bill Brock, R-Tenn., who was seeking reelection, announced publicly that they were returning the funds, although they continued to maintain that they had never knowingly taken any illegal corporate contributions. As of late September 1976, various recipients had returned $57,262 to Gulf, a mere fraction of the $5.4 million distributed by Wild and his associates.

Scott and Gulf. The politician who received perhaps the most attention from Gulf was Hugh Scott of Pennsylvania, the Senate minority leader. According to information collected by the McCloy commission and several government agencies, Scott's law firm (Obermayer, Rebmann, Maxwell, and Hippel) received an annual retainer of $25,000 from Gulf from 1959 to 1961. As a result of objections by Royce Savage, then Gulf's general counsel who claimed the firm did little work for the corporation, the retainer was first reduced to $12,500 in 1962 and then was discontinued. According to Savage, Scott went to Pittsburgh to protest this action.

Elimination of the retainer did not end Scott's ties with Gulf. Thomas Wright, a Pittsburgh attorney whose law firm did work for Gulf,

Table 10-9
Republican Senators Who Received Gulf Contributions from Hugh
Scott

Senator	State	Amount	Year
Strom Thurmond	South Carolina	$1,000	1968
Mark O. Hatfield	Oregon	$1,000	1972
William Scott	Virginia	$1,000	1972
J. Caleb Boggs	Delaware	$1,000	1972
Clifford P. Hansen	Wyoming	$100	1972
Norris Cotton [a]	New Hampshire	$100	1968
Jack Miller	Iowa	Couldn't remember amount or year	
Bob Packwood	Oregon	$900	1968
Robert P. Griffin	Michigan	$1,000	1971
Ted Stevens	Alaska	$2,500-$3,000	1970 and 1972
Charles H. Percy	Illinois	$1,000	1971

[a] Check from a third person forwarded by Scott.

testified that Claude Wild had told him in a meeting in August 1973
that beginning in either 1961 or 1962 the lobbyist had paid the Pennsylvania senator $10,000 a year — $5,000 in the spring and $5,000 in the
fall. Wright said Wild informed him that the payments were not campaign contributions but were used to defray Scott's personal and office
expenses. According to the McCloy committee, Scott had solicited a
personal cash gift from Wild as late as Christmas 1973. The report
declared that despite the publicity surrounding Watergate, Scott apparently did not understand why Wild could no longer pay him. A spokesman for Scott said that the funds received were given with the assurance
that they were employee contributions and not from corporate funds.
The money, the aide declared, was used for Scott's reelection campaigns
(particularly his 1970 contest) or was given to other Republican senators
(see Table 10-9). In a letter to Gulf dated November 28, 1975, Scott
declared: "As a political figure I have never knowingly received corporate contributions from Gulf Oil Co. through any of its representatives."[147] He contended that the funds he had received from Gulf went to
pay campaign expenses but he refused to discuss the case publicly or to
say which senatorial campaigns other than his own the money had
supported.[148]

At his January 1976 appearance before the Washington grand jury
investigating Gulf's political fund, Wild testified regarding his payments
to Scott during the years 1963-73. Although various government agencies
appeared to have relatively little success in learning more about the

case, a number of enterprising newspaper reporters had better luck. The *Philadelphia Evening Bulletin* reported in January 1976 that only seven Republican senators said they had received contributions from Scott. The names of several others subsequently were disclosed. Some of these individuals listed the contributions in their campaign filings.[149]

In mid-1976 the Hugh Scott Defense Fund was created by Scott aides and friends. Its goal was to raise money to pay for the senator's legal expenses in the Gulf case. The fund grew slowly; by the end of August it had received less than $1,000. At about this time, the Internal Revenue Service sent Scott a tax deficiency notice for 1973. Such a notice indicates that the recipient failed to pay tax on some of his income but did so without any willful intent to defraud the government.

In August 1976 Scott appeared before the Senate Ethics Committee and said he had received approximately $45,000 from Wild. He indicated that he had spent about $20,000 of the contribution on his own campaign in 1970 and had distributed the rest to about a dozen other candidates, particularly several incumbent Republican senators. Scott noted that this was a common practice for Senate minority and majority leaders. He apparently did not discuss the money he received from Wild before his election as minority leader in 1969. He again declared that he had never knowingly taken any corporate contributions.

On September 15, 1976, the Senate Ethics Committee voted 5-1 (Sen. Edward W. Brooke, R-Mass., was the only objector) not to take any action against Scott concerning alleged Gulf contributions on the grounds it lacked evidence of illegal actions. Perhaps the clearest indication of the committee's posture was its unwillingness to open a sealed financial statement submitted by Scott and its refusal to submit this statement to the IRS.[150]

Two days later Scott said he was pleased with the committee's action. Still, the issue has not been resolved. At the end of September, David Maxwell, one of the senator's law partners, and Elizabeth Dorsch and Patricia Mink, two Senate aides, testified before a federal grand jury in Washington at the request of Watergate Special Prosecutor Charles Ruff. Presumably their testimony dealt with the various contributions Scott had received from Gulf and Wild. The senator, who announced his retirement shortly after the scandal broke in late 1975, was under investigation by the IRS. The Watergate special prosecutor's office did not conclude its investigation of Scott when it closed its doors in June 1977, however.

Heinz. The Gulf contribution scandal also touched another Pennsylvania Republican, then-Representative Heinz. In 1975 Gulf lobbyist Arthur Harris told the federal grand jury that he had given a Heinz aide $2,000 in 1971 to help the newly elected congressman pay off a campaign debt of $11,000. At that time, federal law did not require the disclosure of the contribution, but Pennsylvania law did. Heinz responded by saying that the 1971 gift had not been reported because it was given after he had filed his campaign finance report.

In his January 1976 testimony, Wild told the grand jury that he personally had given $4,000 to Heinz in 1972. At first Heinz denied the charge; then he said that he personally had not received the funds; then he said that he had received the funds but they had come from a legally established fund created by Gulf employees. He finally admitted that he had not reported the funds, but declared that he did not feel legally culpable. Although the funds were given before April 7, 1972, the effective date of the FECA, the cash on hand and the expenditure had to be reported since the funds were spent after that day. Asked why the 1972 contribution was not reported to the Pennsylvania authorities, a Heinz aide replied that the federal statute "superseded" the state law.

The three-year statute of limitations expired and Heinz was not prosecuted. On March 4, 1976, he announced that he had agreed to refund out of his personal funds the $6,000 he had received. In 1976 Heinz succeeded Hugh Scott as a Pennsylvania senator. During both the primary and general elections, his opponents criticized him for accepting the Gulf money, but their criticism had no apparent effect on the outcome of the election.

Wild Testimony. Because he kept no records of his financial transactions and because most of the contributions were given in cash and in private, Wild was the key figure in the investigations of the various federal agenies. In his statements, Wild evidently sought to protect the recipients of Gulf's illegal contributions as well as himself. As he maneuvered, the special prosecutor and the SEC began to compete in their inquiries into Wild's testimony. The SEC was interested in a public accounting and it apparently wanted to grant Wild immunity from further prosecution. Under the November 1973 court settlement, Wild was supposed to disclose to the prosecutor's office full information regarding contributions to federal elections between 1968 and 1972.

Wild's delaying tactics hampered the special prosecutor's office; he confined his testimony to the legal activities of the previously unpublicized Gulf Good Government Fund,[151] and because of the press of business, the prosecutor's office did not fully investigate Gulf or Wild at that time. Since the 1974 Amendments shortened the span of the statute of limitations from five to three years, the prosecutor's office had to bring suit by June 1976 if the alleged lawbreakers were not to escape prosecution. (This change in the statute of limitations both limited the number of prosecutions and indictments in the Gulf case and played a key role in those cases that were brought to court.)

Gulf had signed the SEC consent decree in March 1975 but Wild decided to fight the case and, as a consequence, the SEC and the federal court took depositions from more than 20 politicians and numerous Gulf officials concerning the operation of the fund. As a result of these disclosures, the prosecutor's office discovered that Wild had omitted information from his earlier testimony. In September 1975 Wild's former assistants at the Gulf Washington office went before the grand jury for the first time and told how they had delivered envelopes with cash to various members of the House and Senate.[152] After many negotiating sessions, Wild was given a grant of limited immunity by Judge Sirica, and he testified before the grand jury in Washington concerning his gifts to Hugh Scott from 1963 to 1973 and other political contributions he made in 1973.

Although Wild allegedly named eight senators and representatives he had given money to in 1973, only one was prosecuted. On January 29, 1976, Rep. James Jones, an Oklahoma Democrat, pleaded guilty to a misdemeanor charge in federal court in Washington. Jones was charged with failing to report a 1972 contribution from Gulf. He was the first, and so far the only, incumbent politician convicted in connection with the probe of Gulf.

Apparently a Jones campaign worker had contacted Royce Savage, Gulf's former general counsel, in late 1972 asking for help to pay off the newly elected representative's campaign debt. Savage spoke to Wild, who agreed to the request and sent Savage an envelope containing between $1,000 and $2,000. Savage then gave this to Jones in the former's Tulsa law offices. According to the Watergate prosecutor's office, which brought the case, there was no evidence that Jones knew the money had come from corporate funds. On March 16, 1976, Jones, who could have been fined $1,000 and jailed for a year, was fined $200. He won reelection in November.

Prosecution. Although Wild's testimony helped convict Jones, the former lobbyist apparently did not cooperate fully with the Watergate prosecutor's office. As a consequence, the special prosecutor brought a two-count felony charge against Wild in March 1976. Wild was charged with 1) giving Sen. Sam Nunn a $2,500 contribution in 1972, (Nunn, a Georgia Democrat, was then a candidate for the Senate) and 2) contributing $5,000 in 1973 to the reelection campaign of Sen. Daniel K. Inouye, D-Hawaii.

For reasons to be explained, Wild was tried in July 1976 only on the Inouye contribution.[153] At the nonjury trial, Inouye's administrative assistant, Henry Giugni, said that he had received $5,000 from Wild in cash some time during the period March-April 1973. (Giugni admitted that when first questioned by the federal grand jury in September 1975 he had lied to protect Inouye.) Giugni said that he had given Inouye $1,200 in early 1973 to cover the senator's out-of-pocket campaign expenses and had used the rest of the money to pay various campaign-related expenses. He told the jury that he had not informed Inouye where he had gotten the money in 1973 and that the senator had never asked. Inouye said he assumed that the funds came from the campaign account and that he first learned of the true source of the money in September 1975, when Giugni informed him that he had lied to protect the legislator.

Wild's story was different. He said that he had promised the money to Giugni in December 1973 and had delivered the funds before February 7, 1973, when the Senate Watergate Committee, on which Inouye served, was established. The dates were important because, as previously noted, the 1974 Amendments provided for a three-year statute of limitations on prosecuting illegal campaign contributions and the special prosecutor's office had brought the suit against Wild on March 12, 1976. For Wild to be guilty of the charge, it would have to be found that he had given the funds on or after March 12, 1973.

On July 27, 1976, Wild was acquitted of the charges by U.S. District Court Judge Joseph Waddy on grounds that the prosecution had not proved the contribution had been made within three years of the indictment. The judge said he found Wild's testimony more credible than that of Giugni.

Giugni had repaid Gulf $5,000 from his own funds in April 1976. Since the money had been spent on campaign matters, Inouye said that Giugni could file for a refund from his campaign committee, which had a surplus of approximately $30,000. The senator indicated that he had removed his aide from all responsibilities concerning fund-raising matters after the grand jury proceedings, although he noted that there had been no fund raising since the 1974 campaign. In September 1976 the Senate Ethics Committee took the unusual step of calling on Inouye to fire Giugni. Customarily such matters are left to individual senators to decide. The committee indicated that the difference in this case lay in Giugni's admission of guilt — all the others (at least in the Senate) had maintained that they were innocent of any wrongdoing. Inouye refused to fire his aide, however, saying that he had been punished enough and deserved another chance.

The second felony charge brought against Wild in March 1976 concerned an allegation that Wild had given $2,500 to the Georgia senatorial campaign of Sam Nunn on or about September 27, 1972. Two days before the expiration of the statute of limitations on September 27, 1975, the special prosecutor agreed to Wild's request that the time limit be extended for that particular crime. Wild had switched attorneys during the negotiations, and he hoped that the waiver would give his new attorney time to familiarize himself with the case and that plea bargaining would spare him from prosecution. The new attorney argued that Wild and the special prosecutor's office had no power to waive the statute of limitations. In January 1977 the U.S. Circuit Court of Appeals in Washington upheld the indictment and the validity of the waiver in the first ruling of its kind.[154] The Supreme Court turned down Wild's appeal, thus requiring him to stand trial on the charges relating to Senator Nunn.

Other Action. A little-known Washington consultant also was discovered to have distributed illegal political contributions for Gulf and for Ashland Oil in the winter of 1971-72. Carl Arnold, formerly an official of the American Petroleum Institute, told how he obtained $15,000 from Wild and arranged for its delivery to Wilbur Mills' presidential campaign. At the request of Ashland Oil, Arnold redistributed $100,000 to Senate and House candidates during a six-month period. Others who received Gulf funds through Arnold included DNC Chairman Robert Strauss and Senator Hubert Humphrey. Arnold said he had never asked about the source of the money and did not know that it came from corporate funds. Mills did not find out about the contribution until months later, and he returned the money when the special prosecutor's office brought charges against Wild and Gulf.[155]

The case against Gulf, Wild, the recipients of the contributions, and others went on.[156] In April 1976 Special Prosecutor Ruff obtained court approval to give the IRS access to the grand jury testimony and the records of his investigation of Gulf. Ruff's aim was to see if any criminal tax laws had been violated by particular individuals, companies, or political committees.[157] These provisions of the tax code are subject to a six-year statute of limitation and the IRS therefore has been under somewhat less pressure to bring charges than was Ruff.

William Viglia pleaded guilty to making a false statement to a federal grand jury in 1974 and received a one-year jail sentence in August 1976. Viglia, who testified freely about bringing Gulf money into the United States, had lied about the amount he brought into the country after July 1972. In that month, the Bank Secrecy Act took effect, requiring any U.S. citizen to report the possession of cash in excess of $5,000 upon entering or leaving the country. Originally designed to curb traffic in drugs, the law was applied by the Treasury Department to corporate campaign violators at the suggestion of the House Monetary Affairs subcommittee. In its most spectacular application to date, the law resulted in a fine for Gulf of $229,500 — an estimated 90 percent of the unreported currency brought into the United States after July 1972.[158]

The disclosures by the SEC and McCloy's special review committee produced a spate of shareholder suits against Gulf and company officials.[159] In November 1976 a federal judge approved a proposed settlement of eight such suits, which had been consolidated into a single legal action. Under terms of the settlement, Dorsey forfeited $1.25 million in stock options and incentive compensation, and Manning forfeited incentive compensation. In addition, North River Insurance Co. paid Gulf $2 million under its liability and corporate reimbursement policies for Gulf's officers and directors (most of this sum paid lawyers' fees and expenses). Two retired Gulf officials forfeited Gulf stock worth a total of $250,000.

On March 7, 1978, a federal appeals court in Philadelphia upheld the settlement. The U.S. Third Circuit Court of Appeals also approved payment of $607,777 to attorneys for the plaintiff stockholders and upheld the dismissal of Price, Waterhouse & Co., accountants, as a defendant in the action.[160]

On May 11, 1978, a consent agreement regarding Wild's alleged federal securities violations settled the complaint that the SEC had filed against him three years earlier. Judge John Sirica enjoined Wild from violating securities laws in the future; Wild was not present in court, but his attorney stated that his client admitted to no violations in the agreement. Judge Sirica directed Wild to furnish a sworn statement to the SEC on his alleged activities.[161]

Wild's statement named more than 100 senators, many members of the House, 18 governors, state judges, and state and local politicians who received corporate contributions from Gulf. These politicians and elected officials included Lyndon Johnson and Jimmy Carter, who was given $1,000 during his 1970 race for governor of Georgia. Wild stated that most of the senatorial contributions ranged in size from $1,000 to $15,000 although he could not recall the precise amounts given to specific individuals. It could not be established that political recipients of the funds had been aware of their corporate source, and the statute of limitations had expired for many of the gifts. In addition, Wild's ledger did not record the amounts of contributions made after 1973, and corporate donations were legal in some states when the gifts were made.[162]

Despite these developments, it is unlikely that individuals other than Wild will be tried on allegations relating to Gulf's illegal political contributions. The bribery statute, although applicable, is difficult to apply without more detailed and verifiable information regarding the transactions. Response on Capitol Hill to the disclosures and the investigations has been confined almost exclusively to Senator Church's Subcommittee on Multinational Corporations. Perhaps most striking is the failure of the various investigators to determine the distribution of Gulf's funds. So far, less than one-third has been accounted for.

ITT

International Telephone and Telegraph has a record of political misdeeds, both domestic and foreign, involving the illegal contribution of large sums of money. The corporation was accused of certain domestic activities in 1972 that received a great deal of attention, and more recently there have been allegations concerning its influence upon foreign governments.

In May 1971 ITT pledged up to $400,000 to attract the 1972 Republican National Convention to San Diego, California. It was alleged that this pledge was made to encourage favorable treatment in an out-of-court settlement of three antitrust suits the Justice Department was bringing against ITT. The affair was intricate and led to the conviction of Attorney General Richard Kleindienst for making false and misleading statements under oath and to his resignation, to the perjury conviction (later overturned) of California Lt. Gov. Ed Reinecke, and to charges of cover-ups by the White House and the IRS.[163]

Chile. ITT is a corporate conglomerate whose interference in the internal political affairs of Chile and other developing countries has received considerable attention. In 1964 and in 1970 many U.S. corporations worried about the fate of their investments in Chile if Marxist Salvador Allende became president, and attempts were made in 1964 to channel funds to the campaign of Eduardo Frei, who was elected. In October 1970 the Chilean Congress elected Allende to succeed Frei as president and the Allende government nationalized the Chilean holdings of U.S. corporations, including ITT's investment of more than $150 million in the Chilean telephone company (Chiltelco), and imposed retroactive excess-profit assessments against them. As a result, some corporations received no compensation for the expropriation of their Chilean assets. These policies generated strong political opposition culminating in a military coup in September 1973 that ousted Allende and resulted in the death of the president and many of his supporters.[164]

In hearings before the Senate Subcommittee on Multinational Corporations in April 1973, CIA and ITT officials testified that ITT had offered to develop a large fund to support Allende's opponent in the 1970 general election, that ITT had offered $1 million to support a plan to block Allende's accession to the presidency after the general election, and that ITT and CIA officials had discussed proposals to create economic chaos in Chile after Allende had become president. However, all the witnesses testified that ITT had taken no action on these proposals.[165]

Harold S. Geneen, ITT's chairman, told the subcommittee that the corporation was concerned that its telephone subsidiary would be nationalized without compensation. While this did come to pass, Geneen swore that ITT did not encourage or participate in any way in any alleged plot to block the election of Allende either via a military coup or by other government or nongovernment officials. In addition, Geneen said that ITT had made no attempt to produce economic instability. A subcommittee report released in December 1974 gave a rather different version of events, concluding that ITT had funneled at least $350,000 to Allende's political opponent during the 1970 general elections in Chile and that a roughly equal amount had been contributed by other U.S. corporations. The committee charged that ITT representatives had met frequently with CIA representatives in Chile and in the United States, and that the CIA had advised ITT regarding ways in which ITT might safely channel funds to one of Allende's election opponents, rightist Jorge Allesandri, and to Allesandri's National Party.[166]

At the corporation's 1976 annual meeting, Geneen reported indications that about $350,000 of ITT funds had been sent to Chile in 1970 for the purpose of supporting the democratic, anticommunist cause there, but stated that no existing information suggested any support of irregular or violent action. Admitting that this information was inconsistent with his previous knowledge, he argued that such contributions were legal under both Chilean and U.S. statutes, were aimed only at preserving a major company investment, and were encouraged by U.S. authorities. In December 1976 several newspapers reported that a federal grand jury was investigating allegations that the CIA and ITT had conspired to fabricate and coordinate statements they had made during the 1973 Senate inquiry into their Chilean activities.[167]

In March 1976 the corporation announced the results of its review of potentially questionable payments made between 1971 and 1975. It reported that approximately $3.8 million in questionable foreign payments had been made over the five-year period to assist in developing or improving business opportunities or relationships. The report said that these payments had not been authorized by the corporation's senior directors or officers. The ITT report was quite limited; for instance, while the SEC disclosed that ITT subsidiaries had paid about $270,000 to Italian tax agents between 1969 and 1972 to facilitate negotiations over the amount of taxes owed, ITT refused to disclose specific details of any of its questionable transactions, arguing that to do so would be harmful to the corporation's and its stockholders' best interests.[168]

The ITT review also revealed that some of the corporation's domestic subsidiaries had spent approximately $4,300 between 1970 and 1975 to purchase tickets for fund-raising events in federal campaigns. The corporation noted that corporate contributions to federal election campaigns are illegal. "In addition, ITT reported that between 1971 and 1975 various subsidiaries had contributed an aggregate of approximately $60,000 to political parties or candidates in various jurisdictions where corporate political contributions were legal. It refused, however, to provide specific details about these contributions or even to say how much of the funds had been spent in the United States and how much in foreign nations." [169]

In February 1976 the Securities and Exchange Commission notified ITT that the commission was investigating questionable payments made by the corporation from 1968 through 1975, a time period that included three earlier years not covered in the company's own review of such payments. The SEC indicated in documents that it considered the corporation's review too limited in time span and in the methods it employed. In 1972 New Jersey state Sen. Anne Martindell filed a stockholder derivative action against ITT and some of its directors, charging that the defendants had caused ITT to expend corporate funds for political purposes, including an attempt to influence the course of political events in Chile in 1970, and that ITT had suffered losses as a result. Settlement was reached in 1975, and ITT agreed to reimburse Martindell for her legal expenses and to require its senior executives to affirm each year that they had not interfered in political processes.[170]

Policy Statement. Partially in response to these disclosures, ITT took a number of steps to prevent a recurrence of such difficulties. In February 1973 its board of directors adopted a resolution reaffirming the political nonpartisanship of the corporation and declaring that the corporation neither supported nor endorsed any political party or candidate. This policy was reiterated in a directive sent to employees in November 1973. The following year ITT amended its bylaws to include the policy of political nonpartisanship. The regulations now state that the corporation will not make any contributions or expenditures in behalf of any political candidate in the United States.[171]

In March 1976 ITT's board of directors adopted another policy statement that recognized responsibility of the corporation and its subsidiaries to conduct worldwide operations in a fashion consistent with the highest business, legal, and ethical considerations. The policy previously adopted and the bylaws concerning political nonpartisanship had been extended. The corporation now pledged itself to use no corporate assets either in the United States or abroad for any political purposes, even in countries where it was legal to do so. The statement went on to note that neither the corporation nor its subsidiaries would become involved in the internal political affairs of host countries, although the corporation reserved the right to express its opinion on issues that may have economic effect on the ITT system. The corporation further pledged not to engage in bribery, kickbacks, payoffs, or other corrupt business practices.[172]

The publicity concerning ITT's misdeeds produced a reaction from some stockholders. Several of them filed suits against the corporation and its directors concerning the questionable overseas payments. At the 1977 annual meeting the United Christian Missionary Society, the Nazareth Literary and Benevolent Institution, the Province of St. Joseph of the Capuchin Order, and the Congregation of the Passion introduced two resolutions. One asked the corporation to prepare a report on its political involvement, political contributions, and questionable payments in Chile from 1960 to 1975. The other resolution asked ITT to report on its political contributions abroad during the last 10 years.[173] Both resolutions were defeated, and ITT opposed them, saying that they were "moot, unnecessary and contrary to the best interests of the corporation and its stockholders." It went on to note that for the five-year period it had reviewed, the corporation's gross sales approximated $50 billion, while domestic and foreign political contributions amounted to only $64,300, of which $60,000 had been given in jurisdictions where such political contributions were legal.[174] ITT claimed that these contributions were minimal and were deviations from its general policy of political nonpartisanship.

Northrop

In 1961 Thomas V. Jones, chairman and chief executive officer of Northrop Corp., and James Allen, a vice-president, created a secret fund for political contributions. Allen later claimed that Northrop had received an increasing number of requests for political contributions just prior to 1961, and that after considering the risks involved in making political contributions and the possible disadvantages to the corporation if none were made, he and Jones had decided that the use of corporate funds was essential. Allen discussed ways of making political contributions with Stanley Simon, a New York management consultant, who volunteered a procedure that he claimed had been used successfully by many corporations for a number of years. Simon recommended that the corporation employ William Savy, a Paris-based consultant whom Simon described as smart, financially oriented, and discreet.[175]

Northrop took Simon's advice and retained Savy with the understanding that the latter would return portions of the fees Allen would pay him.[176] The amounts paid to Savy by Northrop between 1961 and 1968 ranged from $834 a month to $4,000 a month and increased in April 1969 to $5,000 a month, with additional payments of $10,000 a month starting in November 1969. Savy deposited these payments in bank accounts in Switzerland and Luxembourg and, at Allen's request, returned cash in $10,000 packets to Allen through Simon's office.[177]

Nixon Contribution. During the 13 years of the fund's existence (1961-73), Northrop paid Savy $1.14 million, of which $476,000 was returned to the corporation and used for political contributions. All but $58,000 of this money was spent in ways illegal under federal or state laws. In most cases, Jones or Allen wrote a personal check for each contribution and reimbursed himself out of the cash fund. The recipients of Northrop's contributions varied greatly in political orientation, and the contributions ranged in amounts from $25 for a ticket to a political dinner to a minimum of $150,000 contributed to President Nixon's campaign for reelection in 1972.[178]

The Nixon donation, which eventually became public knowledge, was given in two parts. The first was a contribution of $100,000 made by Jones after a visit from Herbert Kalmbach, the president's personal attorney, Maurice Stans, finance chairman of the Committee to Reelect the President, and Leonard Firestone, California finance chairman of CRP. Jones later said that he decided to give the $100,000 because he felt that continuation of Nixon's economic policies was important to the corporation. The second contribution of corporate funds came in August 1972 after Kalmbach requested an additional donation. Jones says he gave $50,000 in cash; Kalmbach claims the amount was $75,000.

By November 1972 the contributions were being questioned but Jones continued to deny that corporate funds were involved. In the weeks preceding the election the House Banking and Currency Committee announced its discovery that $30,000 received by the Finance Committee to Reelect the President (FCRP) had been contributed in cashier's checks "laundered" through a bank in Luxembourg. Kalmbach, who knew this money was part of the $100,000 Jones had given him, offered to have the FCRP return any or all of the money if it represented corporate funds. Jones asserted that the entire contribution had come from his personal funds and that no refund would be necessary.

To conceal the source of the $100,000 contribution, Jones in December 1972 asked Frank W. Lloyd and James D. Wilson, both Northrop officer-directors, and James Allen to create a series of back-dated documents to make it appear that they collectively had given $55,000 of the $100,000 contribution. Kalmbach told the Senate Watergate Committee in August 1973 that he had solicited money from Jones to help finance large payments being made to the Watergate burglars, although he had not mentioned this use to Jones. The $50,000 second contribution was disclosed and, as a result, several investigations were begun. The same month, Jones denied to the FBI, the General Accounting Office, and a federal grand jury that the second contribution had been drawn from corporate funds. Jones recanted his testimony before the grand jury, however, after Lloyd testified truthfully before a grand jury in March 1974.

On May 1, 1974, Northrop and Jones pleaded guilty in federal district court to felony charges brought by the Watergate prosecutor's office for contributions by a government contractor. Allen pleaded guilty to a misdemeanor charge for violation of federal election laws. Northrop and Jones were each fined $5,000; Allen was fined $1,000.[179] U.S. District Court Judge George L. Hart, Jr., levied the heaviest possible fine on Jones and the corporation, saying that his only reason for not sentencing Jones to jail was the fact that this was the first time a corporate executive had been convicted under this particular section of the Federal Corrupt Practices Act.

On May 30, 1974, Jay Springer, a holder of two shares of Northrop stock, filed a class action against Northrop, Jones and Allen in Los Angeles federal court. Springer was represented by attorneys from the Center for Law in the Public Interest. In November the two sides reached agreement on a settlement. Northrop promised to elect a new president within 18 months; to choose four new outside independent directors with the approval of federal Judge Warren Ferguson, Jr., in cooperation with the law firm; to make sure that in the future at least 60 percent of the board would be composed of independent outside directors; and to restructure the executive board to increase the influence of such directors. The corporation was also restrained from using any of its funds or facilities for political purposes for at least two years, and it was agreed that no funds or facilities would be used for these purposes at all without shareholder approval. Jones promised to repay the company an additional $50,000 (he already had repaid $122,000). Allen, who already had reimbursed the company for $15,000, agreed to repay $10,000 more. The reformers basically aimed to make the board of directors "less beholden to the chairman." [180]

Reforms. As a result of the various disclosures and criminal convictions, the executive committee of the corporation's board of directors undertook an investigation of the company's practices. Although the company had issued a statement at the time of Jones' conviction stating that he would stay on as president and chairman because of his achievements and because it believed the criminal action that led to the guilty plea was an aberration, the executive committee's report, submitted in July 1975, was far less supportive of Jones. It charged him with "a heavy share of the responsibility for the irregularities and improprieties" involving bribes and questionable relationships with consultants to advance sales abroad. The report said the directors were "not convinced that Mr. Jones has communicated fully and openly with the auditors, with the committee and with the board of directors itself or recognizes the seriousness of his involvement in matters addressed by the committee." [181] The committee recommended that Jones be replaced as chairman of the board but that he be retained as chief executive officer since there was no apparent successor. It also suggested that a new president be selected by June 1976 who would also be able to serve as the corporation's chief executive. Jones resigned as chairman of the board on July 17, 1975, and was succeeded by Richard W. Miller, chairman of the executive committee.

Seven months later, however, at its February 1976 meeting, the corporation's board of directors unanimously reelected Jones to be chairman of the board and chief executive officer. Pursuant to the settlement of the shareholder suit, the board elected Thomas O. Paine to be president and chief operating officer. Northrop explained its action by stating that in the interim Jones had helped to implement the reforms proposed in the executive committee's 1975 report and had acted in a fashion that "persuaded the directors that the security holders would be best served by his reinstatement as chairman of the board.[182]

Hunting Lodges. Illegal campaign contributions were not the only difficulties confronting the corporation. Northrop and several other defense contractors were also criticized for entertaining numerous military personnel, civilian Pentagon officials, members of Congress, and congressional aides at the corporation's hunting lodge in Maryland.[183]

On January 23, 1976, the Department of Defense announced that 38 Pentagon officials and officers including nine admirals and 17 Air Force generals had been reprimanded for accepting the firm's hospitality at the hunting lodge. Letters sent out on October 22, 1975, said that the officers had shown lack of judgment and that their actions had violated DOD rules barring Pentagon officials from accepting gratuities from defense contractors. The officials claimed that they had been invited by personal friends at Northrop. In response, Secretary of Defense James R. Schlesinger tartly commented at a news conference on the rapidity with which these old personal friendships seemed to have generated.[184] The secretary disagreed with the Defense Department's initial statement that no technical violation had occurred.[185] The letters of admonition were sent out after Schlesinger had made known his views; copies were not placed in the individual's personal records, however.

Schlesinger's position was supported by Senator Proxmire, vice-chairman of the Joint Committee on Defense Production, who criticized the Defense Department for not penalizing more severely those Pentagon officials who had partaken of Northrop's and other defense contractors' hospitality.[186] At hearings held by the Joint Committee in February 1976, the presidents of both Rockwell International and Northrop insisted that the trips to their corporations' hunting lodges were designed to promote "informal contacts with defense officials to improve communications and not to exert any improper influence." [187]

Northrop's difficulties extended into another area when Rep. Les Aspin, D-Wis., released a Defense Contract Audit Agency report completed in August 1975 which found that the corporation might have improperly billed the U.S. government for as much as $6.1 million in questionable consultant fees, lobbyists' salaries, and expenses.[188] The report's findings were disputed by Northrop but in February 1976 the Defense Department suspended some payments on Northrop contracts to allow time for a detailed audit of the company's records to determine if any government funds had been used improperly.[189] In April 1976 settlement was reached over the Defense Department's claims that Northrop had improperly billed the agency for certain payments to foreign agents and for lobbying, entertainment, and related expenses. Northrop agreed to withdrawal or repayment of some costs and to certain accounting adjustments in favor of the federal government. The total cost of the settlement to Northrop was approximately $2.3 million.[190]

Suits. In the meantime, another government agency had brought proceedings against Northrop. In April 1975 the SEC filed suit against Northrop, Jones, and Allen, charging them with violations of federal securities laws in connection with political contributions made with corporate funds, and with disbursement of $30 million to consultants between 1971 and 1973 without adequate records to prove that the payments had been made for the purposes claimed. As the suit was filed, Northrop and the individual defendants agreed to injunctions permanently barring them from making false entries in corporate records and from establishing secret funds.[191]

Word of Northrop's misdeeds reached the IRS, which was investigating the corporation to see if it or any of its officials should be charged with fraud in the preparation and submission of Northrop's tax returns. The corporation acknowledged that its domestic political contributions were improperly deducted as legitimate business expenses on its tax returns, but concluded that no further provision for expenses was required as a result of the IRS investigation.

The disclosures concerning Northrop's illegal activities also prompted a number of stockholder suits.[192] One stockholder, John M. McCrea, for several years pressed for company adoption of a resolution affirming political nonpartisanship and calling on the corporation's board of directors to seek restitution from the appropriate individuals of all corporate funds diverted as political contributions. At Northrop's annual meeting in 1976, McCrea's resolution received the support of 5.93 percent of the shares voted. It also was voted down in 1977.[193]

Cases Handled by the FEC

Many cases of illegal and questionable corporate political behavior were spawned by the special climate of the Watergate era. Most were related to the 1972 Nixon campaign and occurred in part as a result of the extensive solicitation of the corporate community by the Finance Committee to Reelect the President (FCRP). These cases were handled by the Watergate special prosecutor, the Department of Justice, and several other agencies, and involved violations of a variety of federal and state laws. The foregoing case studies are to a large extent part of this generation of cases; although not all the activities discussed concerned the 1972 Nixon campaign, they are part of a period in which illegal corporate political involvement was not closely policed, and was in some cases actively solicited by government officials at home and abroad.

In the years since a later generation of cases began to appear. These cases concerned business activities that took place after 1972 and hence involved corporations that had not learned the lessons of Watergate. They were brought under the FECA and were processed by the then-new Federal Election Commission, which was charged with handling civil violations of the act and thus shared election law enforcement with the Department of Justice, which handles criminal violations. The FEC, unlike the Watergate special prosecutor, is an ongoing organization that will continue to investigate and prosecute violations of federal election law, and it has a host of matters under review at all times. Many corporate matters have been closed without further action, some have been settled with conciliation agreements, and others have resulted in findings of probable cause and decisions to prosecute.

Two matters that went the conciliation route in June 1978 involved the Committee for Jimmy Carter and the National Bank of Georgia. Carter's campaign committee arranged for his use, during the campaign, of an airplane belonging to the National Bank of Georgia. The Bert Lance hearings disclosed that the bank had never billed the committee for the flights and therefore had not been paid until August 1977, while the matter was under review. The FEC found probable cause to believe that this constituted receipt of an in-kind campaign contribution by the bank. The committee agreed to pay a fine of $1,200, the approximate market value of the flights, and promised to avoid any similar violations in the future. The bank, which also had arranged for flights by DNC officials, agreed to a fine of $5,000 and made a similar promise.[194]

Two other cases presented here in detail illustrate the range of matters handled by the FEC in its first years of operation, from relatively minor, unintentional violations of the new and unsettled law to offenses of a much more serious nature. In the first of these, which was settled through conciliation, the Okonite Co. paid a small fine in a closely reasoned case decided on a narrow point of legal interpretation. In the second, which resulted in substantial civil and criminal sanctions, J. Ray McDermott Inc. was penalized for a variety of illegal activities, including making unlawful political contributions.

Okonite

In July 1976 the Okonite Co. placed advertisements in four New Jersey newspapers thanking Rep. Robert A. Roe, Democrat of the 8th Congressional District, for his help in securing a $13 million grant to fund the corporation's new employee stock option ownership trust. The funds were provided by the U.S. Economic Development Administration to the New Jersey Economic Development Authority and enabled the company to establish by June 30, 1976, the largest employee-owned company in the United States.

The advertisements appeared approximately five weeks after Roe's primary victory and less than four months prior to the general election. The congressman represents an area where two of the company's plants are located and he is chairman of the House Subcommittee on Economic Development. The ads, which cost $12,183.84, were financed by corporate funds.

Within a week, two complaints were filed with the FEC concerning the advertisements. Richard A. Zimmer, a member of New Jersey Common Cause, and Ellison Parker asked the agency to see if the ads violated federal statutes. In December 1976 FEC Counsel John G. Murphy, Jr., issued a report on the matter indicating that the company had not consulted Congressman Roe or his election committee prior to purchasing the advertisements. They were placed, claimed the company, to thank the congressman for his efforts in its behalf and to promote the company's business relations. Okonite admitted that it had not established a separate, segregated fund for political campaign purposes.

Murphy indicated that there were no direct court rulings on the issue at hand — "whether a corporate expenditure for a communication which does not contain words which directly call for the election of a clearly identified candidate but can be inferentially interpreted as doing so is 'in connection with' an election, and therefore within the ambit of" section 441b of the FECA. However, an examination of the statutory history and legislative intent of that section of the U.S. Code, Murphy claimed, led to the conclusion that Congress intended "to subject corporations to a different and more restrictive standard with respect to political activities than that applied to individuals." Murphy contended that:[195]

> The proximity of the general election and the content of the advertisements overshadow Okonite's purported informative purpose and give the advertisements a clear political message. The medium — general circulation newspapers which include Roe's district — and the timing of the advertisements — shortly after his primary victory — inevitably have the impact on voters of seeming to promote the merits of Roe as a candidate in the general election. . . . Although the advertisements do not expressly call for Roe's election, they unmistakably serve as a tribute to him.

Murphy therefore concluded that the company's expenditures were a violation of the FECA because they fell within the "ambit" of the law. On June 22, 1977, the FEC, by a 6-0 vote, approved a conciliation agreement prepared by its staff. Under this agreement, the company admitted that the costs of the ads "were in connection with a federal election, and therefore constitute an expenditure, within the meaning" [196] of the law. Okonite agreed to pay a civil penalty of $500 and did so.[197]

McDermott

On June 30, 1977, the FEC began an investigation into possible illegal political contributions by J. Ray McDermott Inc., the world's largest builder of offshore oil rigs. The results of the investigation indicated that Charles L. Graves, president of McDermott, had maintained a fund of corporate money to make substantial contributions to federal candidates during 1974 and 1975; this was one corporation that failed to learn from the Watergate convictions of other corporations. The evidence suggested that Graves had used the fund to reimburse various McDermott officers and employees who made contributions to candidates at his request. One of these employees was Ernest B. Gravois, an administrative aide.

In late 1977 the commission attempted unsuccessfully to enter into a voluntary conciliation agreement with McDermott. In December, after these efforts at an informal resolution failed, the FEC filed a civil suit against the corporation, Graves, and Gravois, requesting fines of $10,000 for each and a permanent injunction against any future activities of this nature.

On February 22, 1978, the U.S. attorney in New Orleans filed a seven-count criminal action against the corporation, charging it with racketeering, bribery, fraud, and making illegal campaign contributions. The latter charge was in essence the criminal counterpart of the FEC's civil action. McDermott pleaded guilty to all charges, and admitted that it had made illegal contributions of $2,000 to Rep. David Treen and $1,000 to Rep. W. Henson Moore, both Louisiana Republicans. The congressmen said that the contributions were made through individual employees, and that they had returned the money upon learning that it was from the corporation. McDermott was fined $1 million on all charges.[198]

On February 23 a federal grand jury granted immunity to current and former McDermott employees in an investigation of alleged foreign payoffs and domestic price-fixing. On the same day it was revealed that SEC investigators believed that Louisiana Gov. Edwin W. Edwards and Sen. J. Bennett Johnston also had received illegal contributions. They too returned the money after learning of its corporate origin.[199]

According to McDermott's internal audit committee, a pool of corporate funds totaling $300,000 called "the Wilson fund" was spent at the discretion of that former president of the company and may have gone for political purposes. Another fund of $12,000 called "the Graves fund" also existed. The committee estimated that it had uncovered nearly $1.1 million in illegal or questionable uses of corporate funds.[200]

Control of Questionable Payments

The continuing disclosures of illegal and questionable corporate political activity at home and abroad, which began with Watergate and continued through the 1976 campaign and beyond, led to demands for reform. Churches, stockholders, government agencies, congressional committees, and educational and political action groups took an interest in the reform issue. They approached the problem from a variety of perspectives and proposed a variety of remedial measures. Among these were recommendations for a universal corporate code of ethics, attempts to institute stricter enforcement of the criminal law and more stringent reporting and disclosure requirements, moves to pass legislation restricting corporate activity and, as the case studies have shown, efforts sponsored by individual stockholders and organized groups to induce corporations to adopt resolutions that would bind them to more restrictive standards of conduct. Some legislative changes did take place. The reform effort as a whole has had mixed results.

Corporate Reforms

Corporations themselves instituted certain reform measures voluntarily. Most of the corporations implicated in illegal activities have reviewed their tactics concerning political contributions and questionable payments in foreign countries and at home. These companies have adopted a variety of policies[201] that have been the subject of several surveys.

A survey conducted by the United Church Board for World Ministries in 1976 found 85 companies that said they had adopted policies prohibiting the use of corporate assets for any political purposes. Fifty-six companies indicated that they adopted policies prohibiting only those political uses of corporate assets that are in violation of the law.[202] These corporations generally took the position that under some circumstances it might be desirable to make contributions; for example, where state laws permit corporate contributions or where PACs make the contributions.

As for other types of payments, a 1976 Conference Board survey found that corporate opinion was divided on the subject of questionable payments abroad. Approximately half of the respondents argued that local moral standards should determine corporations' conduct, and about half suggested that moral standards appropriate to business in the United States should guide corporations. Those firms adopting the former approach usually felt that they would otherwise lose business to corporations that did not operate under the same constraints.

Their fears may have been overstated, however, according to a survey published by The Wall Street Journal, which polled 25 corporations that had admitted making large questionable payments abroad and that had adopted policies forbidding their employees from making any more such payments. Although several firms declined to comment, not one of the 25 corporations reported a significant loss to foreign business.[203]

Some commentators are more skeptical, contending that illegal payments are too widespread to be easily or quickly wiped out.

State, Federal Laws

The legal status of corporate political payments at home and abroad is determined under a variety of state and federal laws, and involves a host of administrative agencies with different jurisdictions. Some recent reform efforts have focused on these laws and the agencies that administer them as a starting point for controlling corporate political activity.

The Organization for Economic Cooperation and Development arranged for representatives of corporations in 24 countries to agree upon a code of conduct. The agreement, which was reached on June 21, 1976, evidenced a concern with preserving a broad field of permissible action for corporations. However, it did prohibit certain illicit activities; business should

> not render, and they should not be solicited or expected to render, any bribe or improper benefit, direct or indirect, to any public servant or holder of public office unless legally permissible, nor make contributions to candidates for public office or to political parties or other political organizations, and abstain from any improper involvement in local political activities.[204]

Questionable corporate payments abroad often give rise to legal consequences under the securities exchange laws, the Internal Revenue Code, and state corporate laws. Although these legal consequences do not explicitly bar payment of bribes or political contributions overseas, they do operate to discourage U.S. corporations from making such payments.[205] Further efforts are under way to pass legislation to bar American companies from engaging in such practices.

Corporations required by the Securities and Exchange Act of 1934 to file with the SEC — those companies with more than $1 million in assets and more than 500 stockholders — must submit full and accurate financial reports and file proxy statements including all material information about nominees for election as directors. Although U.S. securities laws do not expressly require that corporations report illegal or improper payments to the SEC, to shareholders, or to investors, the SEC nevertheless ruled, in March 1974, that failure to disclose corporate political contributions to the commission or to shareholders constituted a violation of securities laws. This ruling proved controversial, since it led to disclosures by hundreds of corporations of illegal or questionable payments abroad.[206]

Most of these disclosures were made under a voluntary program established by the SEC. In return for the release of such information, the agency promised not to prosecute the offending companies and allowed them to omit from public disclosure the names of recipients of payments and of countries where payments were made. The SEC applied three informal standards to determine which payments had to be disclosed. Companies were required to disclose payments that were large in magnitude or related to large or important transactions or payments that indicated lack of integrity on the part of management.

The SEC's voluntary disclosure program required corporations to take several additional steps. They had to authorize a detailed investigation by individuals not involved in the questionable activities; the committee that investigated was required to prepare a report for the full board of directors that would contain detailed information about each payment and would cover a period of not less than five years; the company was required to issue an appropriate policy statement or reaffirm an existing one. Finally, the SEC program demanded that the corporation communicate its policy to appropriate personnel, implement internal controls, check employees' compliance with auditing programs established by independent accountants, and file a final report with the SEC.[207]

In addition to the securities laws, corporations must obey the Internal Revenue Code, one section of which bars deductions for payments to support the political campaign of any candidate for public office. Moreover, no deduction may be claimed for any illegal bribe or kickback either in the United States or in foreign nations.

According to reports, the Internal Revenue Service is investigating the tax returns of virtually all corporations that have admitted they made political contributions or questionable payments in foreign countries, and of most other large multinational companies as well. Unless such payments are voluntarily disclosed, however, detection is difficult to achieve. Under the Internal Revenue Code, the IRS must prove that a payment was a bribe or kickback, and both the payer and the recipient of these payments have an interest in concealing the true nature of the payments.[208]

The Federal Trade Commission has been investigating whether U.S. laws concerning unfair competition were broken by companies making illegal overseas payments. In particular, the commission is attempting to determine whether these corporations had a competitive edge over businesses that did not engage in such practices.

The Justice Department's deputy chief of the Criminal Frauds Division headed a federal task force formed in 1976 to investigate allegations of corporate foreign payments. Representatives from the Justice Department, the SEC, and the IRS were included. The group focused on possible mail fraud, the securities laws, the Bank Secrecy Act, and statutes prohibiting the submission of false statements to government agencies. In spring 1977 the task force began presenting to grand juries in several cities criminal cases involving illegal foreign and domestic payments by U.S. corporations.

Ford Task Force

In response to the various reports and disclosures, President Ford on March 31, 1976, established the Cabinet Task Force on Questionable Corporate Payments Abroad and named Commerce Secretary Elliot Richardson as its chairman.[209] Ford assigned the task force the responsibility to review the actions of the federal government and to consider any additional steps to be taken. The task force concluded that the problem was serious and that additional initiatives were needed. The group contended that the ultimate legal solution would be an international treaty. Since the prospects for such action were uncertain, further efforts by the U.S. government were needed in the interim. The task force noted that either a disclosure approach or a criminal approach could be taken toward questionable payments.

The group opposed the criminal approach because the enforcement of a law making bribes and kickbacks a criminal offense would be difficult if not impossible. Successful prosecution of offenses typically would depend upon witnesses and information beyond the reach of the American judicial process. Instead, the group recommended disclosure as the best means of obtaining its objectives. While admitting that this method would entail additional paperwork for corporations, the task force claimed that disclosure offered several benefits: It would protect businessmen from extortion and other improper pressures, avoid the difficult problems of defining and proving bribery, and would offer a means to reassure the public of the essential accountability of multinational corporations.[210]

After meeting with the task force and reviewing its recommendations, the president announced a three-point program on June 14, 1976. First he called for additional legislation to require disclosure of payments that U.S.-controlled corporations made with the intent of influencing, directly or indirectly, the conduct of foreign government officials. Failure to comply with the legislation would lead to criminal and civil penalties. Second, the president announced his support for legislation then pending in Congress that would strengthen the provisions of the securities laws requiring corporations fully to inform their stockholders of their foreign payments and increasing the accountability of corporate executives. Finally, Ford called for increased efforts to achieve an international agreement. The president made it clear he opposed legislation that would impose criminal penalties on individuals who make illegal corporate payments in other nations because he felt such a provision would be unenforceable.[211]

Business Ethics

The issue not unexpectedly received attention from students of the business community. In April 1977 the American Assembly, a national educational body affiliated with Columbia University, held a conference of businessmen, legislators, and members of the academic and legal professions to discuss the question of corporate ethics. Their report expressed concern that corporate conduct conform to certain social standards, and their recommendations — in the areas of corporate governance, allied professions and associations, government, and overseas operations — included the proscription of bribery and kickbacks everywhere; corporate cooperation with institutions promoting international standards of conduct; and compliance with a set of universal principles to be applied in all facets of a corporation's activities. The conference further recommended that foreign subsidiaries of U.S. corporations not be prohibited from making contributions to foreign political parties as permitted by that country's laws.[212]

In 1978 the Foundation of the Southwestern Graduate School of banking, which is part of Southern Methodist University, reported the results of a survey of ethical policy statements of corporations.[213] Of 79 companies responding, only two said that they did not have a corporate code of ethics. The two — Crocker National Bank and Champion International — said that they believed there was no difference between corporate and personal ethics and no need for business codes of ethics because most people and corporations behaved properly.

Typical sections of business codes affecting politics prohibit slush funds and secret accounts and require clearance with the chief executive officer of the use of corporate funds for political purposes. (Although corporate funds may not be used in federal elections, 21 states permit their direct use in state and local elections; 23 states prohibit direct corporate contributions, eight ban labor, and six limit the amount of corporate, labor, or other group contributions. Those states that do not permit such groups to give directly do allow PAC activity on a voluntary basis.)

In commenting on the new corporate codes of ethics, Leonard Silk noted in *The New York Times* that:[214]

> The corporate reformation will be enduring only if statements of ethical standards are matched by the building of institutions and procedures within the corporation to insure that the standards are enforced. This will involve strengthening the independence and oversight powers of boards of directors and their audit committees. It will involve improving the flow of information to the board and up and down the organization. It will also require establishing oversight and review committees at different levels. Perhaps most important, it will mean supporting, encouraging and rewarding those individuals who express their own ethical values and who are willing to expose wrongdoing within the corporation, even when this is painful to the company's short-run financial interests.

Legislative Proposals. Two congressional panels also spent a great deal of time considering the matter. The Senate Foreign Relations Subcommittee on Multinational Corporations, chaired by Senator Church, held extensive hearings on illegal questionable overseas corporate payments. Executives from companies such as Gulf and ITT appeared before the subcommittee and told of their corporations' practices in foreign nations.

The Senate Banking, Housing, and Urban Affairs Committee, under the leadership of Senator Proxmire, focused its efforts on legislation to revise the nation's securities laws. In September 1976 the Senate overrode the objections of the Ford administration to pass a Proxmire bill that made it a crime for U.S. corporations to bribe foreign officials. The measure never cleared the House Interstate and Foreign Commerce Committee because of time pressures at the end of the 94th Congress. At the same time, neither house approved an administration-backed bill, first proposed by the SEC, that was designed to tighten corporate financial reporting by making it illegal to give false statements to auditors. The defeat resulted from the opposition of accountants who claimed their sources of information would disappear.

In May 1977 the Senate passed a measure similar to the one it had adopted in 1976. It barred corporations from making payments to foreign officials or politicians for the purpose of winning business contracts from other governments or to influence legislation or regulations of other governments. The bill did not bar "grease" payments to facilitate routine transactions. The SEC was given responsibility for enforcing the bribery ban. Another part of the bill amended the Securities Exchange Act to require firms to maintain books and records that accurately reflected their transactions and dispositions of assets.[215]

The version of the bill passed by the House imposed stiffer penalties on offenders than did the Senate version and was sent to a House-Senate conference. The conference resolved differences between the two bills, and the new law, entitled The Foreign Corrupt Practices Act, cleared Congress on December 7, 1977. It was signed by President Carter on December 18. Responsible company officials and shareholders could be fined as much as $10,000 and sentenced to jail terms of a maximum of five years, and companies would be prohibited from paying the fines of their convicted officials. The liability of an agent would be discounted if it was found that the firm itself was in violation. Small payments to expedite performance of routine duties by minor functionaries were not prohibited.

Surprisingly, business concerns did little lobbying on the measure. Some observers contended that business officials had avoided involvement because they did not believe that bribery was essential to success in foreign lands. Others, more skeptical but perhaps more knowledgeable, claimed that businessmen stood back because, in the wake of the Watergate scandal, it was politically unwise for them to oppose the legislation.[216]

Another factor may have been the change in administrations. When Jimmy Carter was sworn in, the atmosphere changed. Not only had the new president promised during his campaign to upgrade the level of government ethics, but his secretary of the Treasury, W. Michael Blumenthal, was a key leader in the business community's attempts to police itself.[217]

Two bills passed by Congress in 1976 also addressed illegal overseas corporate payments. The Tax Reform Act of 1976 requires all U.S. companies with foreign subsidiaries to report to the secretary of the Treasury all direct or indirect payments made to employees, officials, or agents of any other government. If the secretary determines that these arrangements are actually illegal bribes, the income produced does not qualify for any foreign tax benefits and is subject to immediate taxation in the United States.

The second law, the International Security Assistance and Arms Export Control Act of 1976, requires that a report be submitted to Congress within 60 days if the president determines that officials of a foreign country receiving security assistance have obtained illegal or otherwise improper payments from an American corporation in return for a contract to purchase defense articles or services, or have extorted money or other things of value in return for allowing a U.S. citizen or corporation to conduct business in that country. As a result, the State Department in September 1976 adopted new regulations requiring that political contributions and fees or commission payments on foreign military sales and some foreign commercial sales be reported.

Codes and Treaties. In June 1976, after more than a year of work, the Organization of Economic Cooperation and Development approved a voluntary code of standards for multinational corporations. The code declared that questionable corporate payments should not be expected or solicited by government officials. Many corporate officials and union leaders felt that statement did not go far enough, and they sought tougher language.

The United Nations Commission on Transnational Corporations met in Lima, Peru, in March 1976. At that time the United States proposed a treaty on corrupt practices. The proposal was forwarded to the U.N. Economic and Social Council and the U.S. government hoped the council would pass a resolution that would create a group of experts charged with writing the text of a proposed international treaty on corrupt practices.[218] Final U.N. action would require approval by the General Assembly.

By December 1977 some 370 U.S. corporations had reported having made a total of $745 million in questionable foreign payments. The SEC took legal action against a number of the companies, and more than 30 signed consent agreements to institute procedures that would inhibit wrongdoing in the future. Although the effectiveness of the new law making questionable overseas payments a criminal offense will not be apparent for several years, commentators have offered several observations on its relation to corporate practice. Some have concluded that most United States-based multinationals have reduced or eliminated foreign political payments other than "facilitating payments" of small sums.

The overall loss of business resulting from the new regulations and stricter climate is difficult to estimate. If many or most payments were made by managers of subsidiaries without the knowledge or authorization of top officials in the United States, a new American law may not prevent their recurrence. Some observers believe that an international treaty is required, and that it should call upon industrial nations to incorrorate within their domestic law the provisions of the new U.S. legislation. Others maintain that more effective than a treaty would be requirements that: 1) Audit committees composed of outside (nonmanagement) directors should enforce stern policies within U.S. corporations requiring obedience to the laws of the foreign countries within which they do business; 2) The State Department should protect U.S. companies against extortionate demands by foreign government officials; and 3) Foreign governments should adhere to codes of responsible behavior toward foreign investments.[219]

The Bellotti Decision

In April 1978 the Supreme Court issued a controversial decision that is expected to bring much new testing of the boundaries of permissible behavior, and much new litigation affecting the role of corporations and trade associations in politics.

The decision came in the Court's reversal of a ruling by the Massachusetts Supreme Judicial Court in a case involving five corporations (First National Bank of Boston, New England Merchants National Bank, the Gillette Co., Digital Equipment Corp., and Wyman-Gordon Co.). These companies had sought to spend money to influence voters on a referendum issue giving the state legislature the power to levy a graduated income tax on Massachusetts residents. Massachusetts law prohibited corporations from spending funds to influence the vote on questions that did not directly address material interests of the corporation. The plaintiffs in the case argued that they would be affected by the income tax since it would influence their ability to attract employees to work in offices in Massachusetts, but the Massachusetts court affirmed the ban on corporate involvement.

Majority Views

In *First National Bank of Boston v. Francis X. Bellotti,* the Court decided 5 to 4 that the Massachusetts law represented an unconstitutional limitation of free speech. The Court found no justification for a distinction between individual and corporate speakers and noted, "The inherent worth of the speech in terms of its capacity for informing the public does not depend upon the identity of its source, whether corporation, association, union or individual." [220]

The decision made several noteworthy distinctions. Massachusetts Assistant Attorney General Thomas R. Kiley had argued that the state law preserved the integrity of the initiative process by keeping it the people's process, protected the rights of corporate shareholders who might dissent from majority views, and guarded the political process from corporate influence. But the high Court held that these concerns were not jeopardized by corporate involvement in a referendum issue as they might be by corporate activity in a candidate election. In a footnote the Court insisted that its decision "implies no comparable right in the quite different context of participation in a political campaign for election to public office."

The ban on corporate contributions to political candidates was not reviewed, nor did the Court seek to determine the extent to which corporations share all of the rights constitutionally guaranteed to individuals. Criticizing the Massachusetts law, the majority asserted that there was no evidence of undue corporate influence on referendums; that the legislation failed to protect shareholders and that it made a questionable distinction in permitting corporation spending for lobbying efforts to influence the passage of enactments by the legislature; and that by excluding some types of organized groups, the legislation could be challenged on the ground that it offered unequal protection.

The majority opinion was written by Justice Lewis F. Powell, Jr.; Justices Potter Stewart, Henry A. Blackmun, John Paul Stevens, and Chief Justice Warren E. Burger concurred. Burger filed a separate concurring opinion. Justice William H. Rehnquist issued a dissent, and a second dissent by Justice Byron R. White was joined by Justices William J. Brennan, Jr., and Thurgood Marshall. Chief Justice Burger's concurrence focused on the relationship between "media conglomerates" using the corporate form and other corporate entities. He concluded: "In short, the First Amendment does not 'belong' to any definable category of persons or entities: it belongs to all who exercise its freedoms." [221]

Dissenting Views

The two dissenting views were distinctly different from each other. Justice White's opinion considered the Court to be judging the extent to which the state law balanced competing First Amendment interests fairly. The corporation operates to make a profit for its shareholders, he noted, and the shareholders' investment is made for purposes other than political or ideological statements. Corporate speech is therefore protected by the Constitution only insofar as it enriches the enterprise and, Justice White argued, "[i]deas which are not a product of individual choice are entitled to less First Amendment protection." In dissenting he also expressed concern regarding the implications the majority opinion might have for the prohibition of corporate contributions and expenditures set forth in the amended FECA.[222]

Justice Rehnquist's dissent stressed a distinction between the individual and the corporation, which he defined as an artificial being. He contended that its rights and existence are based on the discretion of a government entity and may be granted or implied. Justice Rehnquist stated, "[I]t cannot be readily concluded that the right of political expression is equally necessary to carry out functions of a corporation organized for commercial purposes." [223]

Potential Impact

The Court's decision in this case was viewed by some observers as significant in several areas. It invalidated state laws forbidding corporate expenditures on ballot and referendum issues in some 18 states, and some commentators anticipated that corporate participation in public debate would necessarily have greatest impact on the state level. Second, the decision could lead to judicial review of lobbying regulations predicated on a distinction between corporations and individuals where the First Amendment rights of speech, association, and right to petition the government are concerned. Third, tax laws construed as inhibiting a corporation's opportunities to exercise its First Amendment rights might be attacked. Specifically, the Internal Revenue Service has held that corporations may not deduct expenses associated with communications to shareholders on political issues; that trade associations' communications extending beyond the membership constitute grass-roots lobbying and carry adverse tax consequences; and that discussion of public issues in advertisements may also constitute grass-roots lobbying. Fourth, the decision could be broadly interpreted in conjunction with *Buckley v. Valeo* as permitting corporations to make independent expenditures to advocate the support or defeat of political candidates.

The distinction made in *Buckley* between contributions and independent expenditures is critically important here, and the question that could be raised would focus on whether the corporate expenditures might have a corrupting influence sufficient to warrant abridgement of

First Amendment rights. *Bellotti* and *Buckley* may be read as permitting limited corporate contributions to political candidates; expenditures that do not expressly advocate election or defeat and are not authorized by the candidate or his campaign committee are clearly allowed by this decision, in the view of one Washington attorney. Further, it has been noted that issues can play an important role in a candidate's campaign,[224] since candidates can identify with issue campaigns, or use code words that reinforce them.

Future decisions of the Supreme Court and the lower courts will further define the implications of the *Bellotti* ruling. Nevertheless, it immediately aroused considerable speculation regarding its probable effect on the political process.[225] While some observers consider that the ruling heralds profound changes, others disagree. They point out that the case's impact will be determined by how corporations choose to spend money and which responsibilities they incur through this exercise of First Amendment rights. Some writers believe that most publicly owned corporations are unlikely to make large expenditures on issues and candidates, although corporations involved in "public issue campaigns" might do so.

It is generally believed, however, that *Bellotti* will result in much new litigation as trade associations and corporations challenge regulations and various advisory opinions issued by the FEC and state election commissions. Whether or not the ruling eventually reverses earlier decisions regarding corporate political activity, it casts that activity in a new light. *Bellotti* is a landmark in another sense, however: It is most significant not for its conclusion that corporations have a right to freedom of speech, but rather for its delineation of citizens' right to hear from whatever source. This concept was formerly only implicit in the First Amendment and has never before been clearly enunciated.

Labor in Politics

Various labor unions and leaders took diverse positions as the field of presidential contenders began to take shape in 1975 and early 1976, but most shared an attitude of opposition to the Republican aspirants and varying degrees of support for several Democratic entrants, along with disappointment over the nonavailability of Hubert Humphrey.

In February 1975 George Meany announced that he and the AFL-CIO would take no part in the internal affairs of the political parties and no part in the selection of delegates to the Democratic National Convention. Most observers felt that the move would weaken labor's influence in the Democratic Party, and some even suspected that Meany was trying to leave himself open to support Nelson Rockefeller if the vice president should receive the Republican nomination.[226]

In fact, Meany's announcement turned out to be a purely personal statement and had little effect on union political activity. Individual unions within the federation as well as nonaffiliated unions were permitted, and even encouraged, to become politically involved. During the activities leading up to the caucuses in Iowa, the first state to select convention delegates, various unions in the state supported Jimmy Carter, Birch Bayh, Fred Harris, Morris Udall, Henry Jackson, and Sargent Shriver. In other cases, organized labor worked for Lloyd Bentsen, Milton Shapp, Jerry Brown, and Frank Church, as well as for uncommitted slates.

In general, the ultimate goal of union leaders was not the nomination of the particular candidate they were backing so much as the ensurance that union members would be represented in the delegations of all the candidates at the Democratic convention. Charles Gifford, the head of the United Auto Workers' political action committee in Iowa, said, "I'm not concerned about whom our people are for. I'm concerned about who those 47 Iowa delegtes are and what their political philosophy is. I want some of them to be our people, so when we get to New York we'll be in a position to bargain." [227]

This position was shared by labor leaders throughout the country, who hoped to send a labor caucus of at least 600 delegates to the Democratic convention. Because of the large number of candidates and the lack of an early front-runner, most unionists expected the Democratic convention to deadlock in the early ballots. In the resulting brokered convention, these leaders hoped, a unified caucus would then be in a position to play a major role, perhaps a dominant role, both in the selection of a nominee and in the drafting of a platform. [228]

On the Republican side, Ronald Reagan was considered anathema by unionists and Gerald Ford was held in little higher regard. Most labor leaders agreed with the assessment of AFL-CIO President Meany, made early in the campaign, that Ford was "completely without compassion" and concerned almost entirely with "keeping the corporations wealthy. . . . We've made up our minds about him." [229]

Whatever chance Ford might have had for some labor support was dispelled by two vetoes. These vetoes both constituted reversals of commitments that Ford allegedly had made to the two union groups that had most prominently backed Richard Nixon in 1972: the maritime unions and the building trades. In December 1974 Ford was considered by labor to have reneged on a pledge to the Seafarers International Union to sign a bill requiring 20 percent of all imported oil to be carried in U.S. flag tankers. A year later, he vetoed a bill that would have permitted a construction union involved in a dispute with one contractor at a building site to picket the entire site. The veto was claimed to have broken pledges the president had made to the unions, to the bill's sponsors, and to Secretary of Labor John T. Dunlop, who shortly thereafter resigned in protest. More importantly, the veto had the effect of virtually ensuring that labor would back the eventual Democratic nominee.

Support for Carter

Early in the primary season, Jimmy Carter had been one of many candidates receiving various degrees of labor support in various states. This support was rarely enthusiastic, however, and there was also an element of labor hostility toward Carter that was not expressed toward any of the other Democratic candidates except for Wallace. At the AFL-CIO's annual executive board meeting in February 1976, representatives of several affiliated unions distributed copies of a letter in which Carter appeared to support right-to-work laws. One AFL-CIO spokesman said, "He didn't have to run for governor in 1970 supporting right-to-work. It was already in the state constitution." [230] COPE Director Alexander Barkan was known to have resented Carter since he learned that Carter, at a 1974 governors' conference, had spoken disparagingly of "cigar-smoking labor dictators." [231]

Labor opposition to Carter came to a head, and was shown to be ineffective, in the primary campaign in heavily unionized Pennsylvania. James Mahoney, vice-president of the Pennsylvania AFL-CIO, Edward F. Toohey, president of the Philadelphia Council of the AFL-CIO, and other labor leaders claiming to represent 1.5 million workers joined with regular Democratic Party officials in an effort to stop Carter, by then the generally acknowledged front-runner, in the April 27 primary. The alliance supported Henry Jackson in the hope, if not of having Senator Jackson nominated, then at least of denying Carter a first-ballot victory and possibly of setting the stage for a Humphrey-draft at the convention. "One thing about the labor movement," said one Pennsylvania union leader, "we do have institutionalized machinery that on quick notice can be cranked into motion. . . . The labor movement won this state for Hubert in 1968 and we won the primary for him in 1972 and now we've got to beat Carter." [232]

The projected labor blitz for Jackson never really materialized. Very few unions in the state had organized their campaigns to the point even of having phone banks in operation or having adequate supplies of literature to distribute. Jimmy Carter won 64 delegates in Pennsylvania, to 22 for Udall and 19 for Jackson. The result not only forced Jackson out of the race, but also forced organized labor to confront the probability of Carter's nomination.

As Carter's nomination grew more likely, his support from labor continued to grow. On April 30 New Jersey AFL-CIO President Charles Marciante said, "There is no other group more intent on defeating President Ford in November than organized labor. If Mr. Carter can accomplish that, then we're all for it." [233] The United Auto Workers supported Carter in the May 18 Michigan primary.[234] George Meany agreed to meet with Carter in May, after having refused earlier requests for such a meeting.[235] And after Carter's June 8 victory in Ohio appeared to have locked up the nomination, virtually every unionist in the country let it be known that they would support Carter once the Democratic convention made his selection official. As one union official said of Carter at that time, "We're going to learn to love each other." [236]

Labor did indeed enter into a full-fledged marriage with the Carter campaign. The selection of Walter Mondale as the vice presidential nominee increased labor enthusiasm for the ticket. Within a week after the convention, the AFL-CIO Executive Council voted unanimously to back Carter, and labor provided all-out support during the general election campaign.

Impact on Congressional Races

A preview of labor's potential impact on the 1976 congressional campaigns occurred in a special election for a Senate seat from New Hampshire in September 1975. Under the 1974 Amendments, both candidates were held to an overall spending limit of $220,000 (such expenditure limits were later ruled unconstitutional in *Buckley v. Valeo*). John Durkin, the Democratic candidate and the winner of the New Hampshire election, received thousands of dollars' worth of support from organized labor that did not have to be counted against the spending ceiling. Union personnel working for Durkin telephoned every union household in New Hampshire several times, mailed literature, distributed absentee ballots and worked house-to-house in some working-class districts on the day of the election. Louis Wyman, the Republican candidate, had to pay for similar activities. Consequently, Durkin was able to afford $20,000 worth of television spots and $35,000 in radio advertising while spending only $191,000 overall. Wyman, who spent $218,000 overall, spent $22,000 on radio and nothing on television.

Many observers credited Durkin's victory to the labor campaign on his behalf and predicted similar campaigns in 1976. George Young, Wyman's campaign manager, said, "The new law brings a third entity into American politics. There used to be the Republicans and the Democrats. Now there's labor, which can materially affect the outcome of any race it chooses." [237]

Although the January 1976 *Buckley v. Valeo* decision freed congressional campaigns from expenditure limits, the contribution limits that were left intact continued to serve as de facto limits on the amounts that candidates could directly raise and spend. The potential for organized labor to play a significant role in congressional elections, through unlimited communications with union members and registration and get-out-the-vote drives, as well as through direct contributions by union PACs, therefore remained great.

Results

The labor movement claimed, with some justification, that it had provided Carter and Mondale's narrow margin of victory. COPE reported that Carter and Mondale had received 70 percent of the vote of union members. Furthermore, union members had registered in greater proportions than the population as a whole (80 percent to 70 percent), and a higher proportion of those registered actually voted (65 to 53 percent). COPE's estimation of its own contribution to the presidential ticket included 120,000 volunteers, 10 million phone calls, and 80 million pieces of literature distributed to union members.[238]

Congressional campaigns also brought generally favorable results to labor. COPE made endorsements in 28 Senate races; 19 of the candidates won. In the House, 262 of the 365 COPE-endorsed candidates won.[239] Of the 20 House candidates receiving the most financial assistance from labor, 17 were victorious. In Senate races, 13 of the 20 candidates receiving the highest labor contributions won. The losers, however, included three of the four most heavily labor-funded incumbents: Democrats William Green of Pennsyvania, John Tunney of California, and Vance Hartke of Indiana.[240]

Strengths and Weaknesses

Though COPE could claim much credit for the outcome of the 1976 election, it kept a watchful eye on the growing influence of corporate political action committees on national, state, and local elections. Prior to 1975 there were about 100 business-related PACs in existence. By 1978 there were more than 700 company PACs and about 400 trade and professional association PACs.

The crucial difference between business and union PACs involves the supportive services offered by unions. Unions feel that such services as registration, getting out the vote, education, and telephone banks are more important than direct monetary contributions. Accordingly, they spend at least as much if not more on services than on contributions, most of which come from international unions. In addition, unions include a voting membership that outnumbers that of corporate PACs.[241] Union political efforts extend beyond membership to include families of members. Counting family members, labor can claim three to four times the number of potential voters within any one union framework. In some cases, this might add up to as much as half of a state or district's voting population.[242]

On the other hand, union members are not required to support certain candidates. In *Abood v. Detroit Board of Education*[243] the Supreme Court held that a state may not, even indirectly, require as a condition of employment that an individual contribute to the support of an ideological cause he or she may oppose. At that time, Michigan law provided that unions and local government employers might agree to an agency-shop arrangement according to which every employee — even those not union members — must pay the union, as a condition of employment, union dues or a service fee equivalent in amount to union dues. The Court ruled that under such circumstances the use of funds contributed by dissenting employees for political purposes (unrelated to collective bargaining) impermissibly infringed upon their First Amendment right to adhere to their own beliefs.[244] In May 1978 the FEC approved a payroll deduction method to be used by the International Association of Machinists in soliciting contributions to its PAC.[245]

Though labor campaigns may have the edge over business at the grass-roots level, business still has the edge when it comes to financing. In 1976 labor unions outspent the relatively young business PACs. Unions spent $17,489,000 and business associations and companies spent $12,587,000 on that election; a slim margin considering the relatively short history of the business PACs.

Statistics show that most union political funds went to Democratic candidates in 1976. Although business has often been disappointed in the return from those it supported, labor is also worried over the increasing influence of business on traditional political factions. This led the AFL-CIO to adopt a resolution in late 1977 reminding candidates receiving labor PAC support to keep their campaign promises once elected.[246] On February 23, 1978, AFL-CIO spokesperson Al Zack pointed out that "the label 'Democrat' or 'Liberal' will no longer automatically identify supporters of labor." He added that labor's endorsements would be much more selective in the 1978 election.[247]

Another factor that was influential in 1976 and which grew to major proportions by 1978 was the rising tide of conservatism via "New Right" political groups. In contrast with the tendency of previous conservative or Republican groups to write off union members, some new groups focused their attention on organized labor. According to columnist Jack

Anderson, Rep. Philip M. Crane, R-Ill., led a group of young Republicans on a tour of labor strongholds, meeting secretly with local union officials. In late 1978 Crane, along with Rep. Mickey Edwards, R-Okla., designed a legislative package emphasizing issues that appeal to workers beset by high prices, factory closings, and stiff foreign competition. New Right strategists also were recruiting conservative candidates and conducting political workshops to tutor them on how to woo the labor vote for the November election.

The AFL-CIO has reacted to the conservative campaign by completing a $75,000 film entitled "The Right Wing Machine" to be shown in union halls across the country, and has published many newsletters with a similar theme, all designed to raise more political money from labor supporters as a means of counteracting the New Right activities.[248]

Cargo Preference

Consideration of a Carter administration cargo-preference bill, which would have required that a larger share of U.S. oil imports be carried on American ships than is currently the case, provided the setting for congressional and public debate on the role of labor in politics and on the ethics of private political contributions in general.

The cargo-preference bill was supported by the maritime industry and by the National Maritime Union, the Marine Engineers Beneficial Association, the Seafarers International Union, and other maritime-related unions. These unions, through their political action committees, had contributed $23,781 to Jimmy Carter's presidential primary campaign. Union officials and shipping executives making $1,000 contributions added at least $175,000 to the Carter campaign, according to CBS News.[249] According to Common Cause, the maritime union PACs also contributed $979,691 to 1976 congressional races, including $102,763 to members of the House Merchant Marine and Fisheries Committee, which was responsible for consideration of the cargo-preference bill (see Table 10-10). In addition, Rep. John M. Murphy, D-N.Y., chairman of the committee, held a fund-raising party on June 21, 1977, while his committee was holding hearings on the cargo-preference bill. Maritime industry officials and maritime union groups contributed $9,950 to Murphy at that time.[250]

'**Political Payoff.**' Because of these factors, debate on cargo preference concerned not only the merits of the legislation but also the motives of the bill's supporters, the relationship between campaign contributions and government decision-making, and the fine line distinguishing legitimate political contributing from seeking undue influence.

Table 10-10
1976 Campaign Contributions by Maritime Union Political Committees
to Members of the House Merchant Marine and Fisheries Committee

Members of the committee who voted for HR 1037: Total $82,263			
24 Democrats			
John M. Murphy, N.Y., chairman	$11,200	Norman E. D'Amours, N.H.	$ 800
John D. Dingell, Mich.	4,725	Jerry M. Patterson, Calif.	3,550
Paul G. Rogers, Fla.	0	Leo C. Zeferetti, N.Y.	18,138
Walter B. Jones, N.C.	1,000	James L. Oberstar, Minn.	2,500
Robert L. Leggett, Calif.	4,300	Barbara A. Mikulski, Md.	1,900
Mario Biaggi, N.Y.	6,800	David E. Bonior, Mich.	800
Glenn M. Anderson, Calif.	1,200	Daniel Akaka, Hawaii	300
E. "Kika" de la Garza, Texas	0		
Ralph H. Metcalfe, Ill.	3,500	7 Republicans	
John B. Breaux, La.	2,200	Philip E. Ruppe, Mich.	2,700
Fred B. Rooney, Pa.	1,000	Gene Snyder, Ky.	500
Bo Ginn, Ga.	0	David C. Treen, La.	0
David R. Bowen, Miss.	1,000	Joel Pritchard, Wash.	0
Joshua Eilberg, Pa.	1,500	Don Young, Alaska	1,500
Carroll Hubbard Jr., Ky.	1,300	David F. Emery, Maine	0
Don Bonker, Wash.	2,500	Paul S. Trible, Va.	0
Les AuCoin, Ore.	7,350		

Members of committee who voted against HR 1037: Total $1,000			
5 Republicans			
Robert K. Dornan, Calif.	$ 0	Edwin B. Forsythe, N.J.	$ 0
Paul N. McCloskey Jr., Calif.	500	Norman F. Lent, N.Y.	500
Thomas B. Evans, Del.	0		

Members of committee absent for vote on HR 1037: Total $19,500			
Thomas L. Ashley, D-Ohio	$18,000	Ron de Lugo, D-V.I.	not
Gerry E. Studds, D-Mass.	1,000		available
Robert E. Bauman, R-Md.	200	William J. Hughes, D-N.J.	300

Overall 1976 Campaign Contributions to Members of Committee From
Maritime Unions: Total $102,763

SOURCE: "Common Cause Releases Study of Maritime Interest Contributions to Members of House Merchant Marine and Fisheries Committee," Common Cause news release, August 18, 1977.

Republican National Chairman Bill Brock, Senate Minority Leader Howard Baker, and House Minority Leader John Rhodes all denounced the administration's support of the bill as "a blatant political payoff" to the maritime industry, while Common Cause Vice-President Fred Wertheimer said, "The maritime industry and the cargo-preference bill represent a textbook example for those who wonder how special interest campaign financing is used to influence government decisions." [251]

Further allegations of improprieties were fueled by revelations that Assistant Secretary of Commerce Robert J. Blackwell, the chief administration spokesman for the cargo-preference bill, had been offered a $100,000-a-year job by a group of shipping companies. In addition, Gerald Rafshoon, Carter's campaign advertising director, was commissioned by the maritime industry to undertake a million-dollar advertising and public relations campaign, and Patrick Caddell, Carter's pollster, received $5,000 from the industry for polling work.[252]

At one point, Republican Chairman Brock accused Representative Murphy of withholding a report by the General Accounting Office on the estimated cost of the projected cargo-preference policy and, linking the "suppression" of the report to Murphy's acceptance of maritime contributions at his recently held 1977 fund-raiser, said, "Murphy's activities are so blatant that it can be strongly argued they are criminal in nature since they come on the heels of what appears to be outright bribery."[253] Murphy dismissed Brock's accusation as "the ravings of an obvious lunatic."[254]

Legislative History. The bill that aroused all this controversy, HR 1037, was similar to 1974 legislation that had provided 30 percent preference and had cleared Congress before being vetoed by President Ford. The 1977 bill proposed a smaller total increase, raising the percentage of imported oil carried on American ships from the 1976 level of about 3.5 percent to 9.5 percent in 1982. It was hailed by Representative Murphy as "one of the landmark steps in the reconstitution of the U.S. flag fleet."[255]

The proposed legislation was introduced in July 1977 and soon came under fire from some members of Congress, the media, and the public. It first attracted widespread attention when White House documents released by Rep. Paul N. McCloskey, Jr., R-Calif., the bill's chief opponent, disclosed that Carter's top economic advisers had warned against the measure. Stuart E. Eizenstat, chief adviser on domestic policy, and Robert S. Strauss, special trade representative, had contended that the bill would decrease employment, reduce the gross national product, reverse U.S. policy favoring free competition, and violate U.S. treaties with more than 30 nations. Nevertheless, Assistant Commerce Secretary Blackwell insisted that administration support of the legislation was demanded by considerations of national defense and national security. Republican members of the House committee and of the Senate Commerce Committee sought to summon various administration witnesses, but Representative Murphy and Sen. Ernest F. Hollings, D-S.C., refused to permit such testimony.[256]

The bill's actual costs and benefits were much disputed. Republicans claimed that it would raise oil costs for consumers by $800 million a year. The administration estimated that the bill would cost $110 million to $180 million a year. An interim report from the GAO was at variance with the White House estimate, however, stating that the 9.5 percent share would raise U.S. oil prices $240 million a year.[257]

Despite the Republican charges and fiery editorials in the press, the bill was reported out of the House committee on August 2 by a 31-5 vote. Before the House approved the bill, 10 amendments were adopted, most of which had been proposed by the administration and offered in committee by Murphy.[258] The legislation provided 1) a guarantee that 4.5 percent of U.S. bulk oil imports would be carried in privately owned U.S. flag ships upon enactment of the bill, 2) an annual 1 percent increase in the amount promised to U.S. ships until the share reached 9.5 percent on October 1, 1982, 3) the restriction that guaranteed import percentages would be met only if enough oil tankers were available at reasonable rates as determined by the Commerce Department, 4) the stipulation that all carrier ships be built in the United States and fly the U.S. flag, 5) that vessels built or operated in the future with federal subsidies would be eliminated from the preference program, and that 6) the first 50,000 barrels a day of oil imported by a small independent refiner would be exempted.

Pro and Con. In reporting the bill, the House committee majority strongly contested objections raised to the bill. It asserted that the legislation would raise the price of gasoline less than .002 cents a gallon, that the bill would not greatly affect foreign policy, that the increased use of U.S. flag ships would strengthen national security, that employment in the maritime industry would increase, that greater use of U.S. vessels would reduce the likelihood of oil spills, that the bill would reduce the balance of payments deficit, and that the Treasury Department could collect some taxes currently being avoided by oil companies using foreign ships.[259]

The bill's critics not only pointed out the greater cost of transport on U.S. flag ships, but assailed the legislation as an uncertain means of eliminating unsafe tankers of any nationality. In addition, they complained that the use of foreign carriers did not, as the bill's supporters claimed, involve the risk of cutting off the country from oil imports. It was further pointed out that the tax-supported wages of the average U.S. seaman were $24,000 a year, while marine engineers received still higher supported wages. The size of the subsidy was attacked. The State and Treasury departments, it was noted, argued against cargo preference on the ground that it would encourage nations trading with the United States to protect their own weakest industries against competition from American exporters.[260]

On September 9, 1977, the GAO issued a final report containing a new and higher estimate of the cost of the cargo-preference bill. This report noted that the legislation could raise the nation's fuel bill by $550 million to $610 million annually — more than five times the estimate made by the administration in July. The report concluded that, in addition to increases in oil transportation fees, the American consumer would face an increase in the price of domestically produced oil.[261] At the request of Sen. Robert P. Griffin, R-Mich., the Federal Trade Commission also made a study. Examining the GAO's interim report, the FTC concurred with its original estimate of the bill's cost and told Griffin that a direct subsidy to the maritime industry would be more efficient than requiring oil companies to ship their imports in more costly U.S. ships.[262]

The maritime industry's promotional drive, prepared by Gerald Rafshoon Advertising, placed commercials on Washington television stations and bought advertising in newspapers in Washington and New York. One newspaper ad began: "America is sacrificing 200,000 jobs, a $75 million foreign trade balance, a strong merchant marine fleet, and the ecological safety of our shores. For what? For big oil companies and other multi-national corporations to build their oil tankers and cargo ships abroad." [263] At the same time, congressional lobbying for the bill was undertaken by the American Maritime Association, the Shipbuilders Council of America, the maritime unions, the AFL-CIO, the International Ladies' Garment Workers' Union, and the Communications Workers of America,[264] among others.

Despite angry Republican protests, the House Rules Committee voted on September 20 to send the cargo-preference legislation to the floor the following week. The Senate Commerce Committee announced that it would hold another day of hearings on the measure, and the date fixed — October 5 — indicated to observers that the Senate would not act on the bill in 1977. Then the House rescheduled debate on the bill from September 28 to October 5. The shift seemed to indicate the success of the opposition's efforts, and commentators noted the unusual alliance of Ralph Nader's Congress Watch, Chevron, Getty Oil, the Environmental Policy Center, the League of Women Voters, the American Farm Bureau, and others who fought the legislation.

Defeat. On October 5 the House again rescheduled a vote on the bill, and the leadership denied for a second time that opposition was responsible for the change in date. Finally, on October 19, the bill came to the floor. It passed on a voice vote, with its chief opponent, Paul McCloskey, remaining in his seat past the moment for demanding a roll-call vote. Belatedly, McCloskey requested a roll call, and the vote, tallied despite Murphy's protests, defeated the bill 257 to 165. The action killing the effort to build U.S. flag participation in the oil trade in 1977 was an example of reaction to unfavorable publicity generated by the effort to tie together campaign contributions with public policy results. The contributions issue had assumed more importance than the legislation itself, and in the end, as Stephan Lesher of Rafshoon Communications put it, "You had to vote against this bill to prove you were not a whore." [265]

Publicity surrounding the cargo-preference bill also gave rise to press reports of two Justice Department investigations of Murphy.[266] One investigation focused on his involvement with Korea (the House ethics committee was probing Murphy's closeness to Tongsun Park); the other inquiry dealt with Murphy's efforts to arrange financing in 1973-74 for the construction of an oil refinery in Nicaragua to be owned by a company controlled by General Anastasio Somoza Debayle, the dictator of Nicaragua and a West Point classmate of Murphy. It was alleged that Murphy also had attempted to arrange a source of Iranian crude oil for the Nicaraguan refinery, and several public interest groups, reviewing a number of Murphy's activities, charged that his conduct revealed a pattern of impropriety. Murphy denied both allegations, and no action was taken.

Footnotes

[1] Herbert E. Alexander, *Financing the 1972 Election* (Lexington, Mass.: Lexington Books, D.C. Heath and Co., 1976), p. 513.

[2] Ibid., pp. 470-72.

[3] A comprehensive treatment of these revelations and the prosecutions is presented in *Financing the 1972 Election*, pp. 513-557, and in Appendix X-1, pp. 708-710.

[4] Investor Responsibility Research Center Inc., "Corporate Involvement in U.S. Political Campaigns," Analysis A. (January 13, 1977), A-6, A-7.

[5] Leonard Curry, "The Multinational Corporation," *The Nation*, May 24, 1975, p. 619.

[6] Robert Lindsey, "Two Airlines Face New CAB Charges on Campaign Gifts," *The New York Times*, June 30, 1975.

[7] David Burham, "Senate Study Says CAB Broke Rules for Airlines," *The New York Times*, June 30, 1975.

[8] A fuller treatment of the matters involving AT&T, Firestone, Gulf Oil, Northrop, Tenneco, Okonite, and J. Ray McDermott, with citations, is presented below.

[9] For examples, see Murray L. Weidenbaum, "On the Causes of Business Corruption," *The New York Times*, May 4, 1975, and W. Michael Blumenthal, "Business Morality Has Not Deteriorated, Society Has Changed," *The New York Times*, January 9, 1977.

[10] *1976 Congressional Quarterly Almanac*, (Washington, D.C., Congressional Quarterly Inc., 1977), p. 244.

[11] Investor Responsibility Research Center Inc., "Questionable Corporate Payments Overseas," Analysis K (March 14, 1977), K-4.

[12] *1976 Congressional Quarterly Almanac*, p. 244.

[13] Investor Responsibility Research Center Inc., "Questionable Corporate Payments Overseas," K-5. According to a December 1976 report by *Business International*, based on confidential interviews with top executives of 55 multinational corporations: "The most important element by far in setting payment patterns is the attitude of the host country ... while the No. 2 determinant ... is the nature of the industry involved...."

Bribery on "a large scale is particularly common in the fields of drugs and health care, oil and gas, aerospace and chemicals ... as well as the construction, communications, automobile and shipping industries. . . ." Many of these industries are dependent for their sales on foreign government officials or purchasing agents. In addition, because sales are so large, bribes and kickbacks can be disguised in the purchase price. Ann Crittenden, "Business Bribes Abroad: A Deeply-Etched Pattern." *The New York Times*, December 20, 1976.

[14] Eileen Shanahan, "Gulf Oil Accused by SEC of Hiding $10 Million Fund," *The New York Times*, March 12, 1975.

[15] Richard D. Lyons, "Gulf Oil Admits it Illegally Gave $5-Million Abroad," *The New York Times*, May 17, 1975.

[16] A fuller treatment of the matters involving ITT, Firestone, Northrop, United Brands, Tenneco, and United Technologies, with citations, is presented below.

[17] Investor Responsibility Research Center Inc., "Corporate Political Contributions Overseas: Exxon Corp.," Analysis M, Supplement No. 7, (April 28, 1976), M-87-8.

[18] Judith Miller, "Senate Voice Vote Confirms Miller as Reserve Chief," *The New York Times*, May 4, 1978.

[19] Investor Responsibility, "Questionable Corporate Payments Overseas," K-5.

[20] Ibid., K-1.

[21] Ibid.

[22] Evelyn Y. Davis' nonpartisanship resolution read as follows: RESOLVED: That the stockholders of [name of corporation], assembled in annual meeting in person and by proxy, affirm the political nonpartisanship of the corporation. To this end, the following practices are to be avoided:

(a) Handing contribution cards of a single political party to an employee by a supervisor.

(b) Requesting an employee to send a political contribution to an individual in the corporation for subsequent delivery as part of a group of contributions to a political party of fund-raising committee.

(c) Requesting an employee to issue personal checks blank as to payee for subsequent forwarding to a political party, committee, or candidate.

(d) Using supervisory meetings to announce that contribution cards of one party are available and that anyone desiring cards of a different party will be supplied one on request to his supervisor.

(e) Placing a preponderance of contribution cards of one party at mail station locations;

Investor Responsibility Research Center Inc., "Corporate Involvement in U.S. Political Campaigns: Evelyn Y. Davis' Proposals to 17 Corporations," Analysis A, Supplement 2 (February 24, 1977).

[23] Evelyn Y. Davis' disclosure resolution:

RESOLVED: Within five days after approval by the shareholders of this proposal, the management shall publish in newspapers of general circulation in the cities of New York, Washington, D.C., Detroit, Chicago, San Francisco, Los Angeles, Dallas and Houston, and in *The Wall Street Journal* a detailed statement of each contribution made by the company, either directly or indirectly, within the immediately preceding fiscal year, in respect of a political campaign, political party, referendum of citizens' initiative, or attempts to influence legislation, specifying the date and amount of each such contribution, and the person or organization to whom the contribution was made. Subsequent to this initial disclosure, the management shall cause like data to be included in each succeeding report to shareholders; Investor Responsibility Research Center Inc., "Corporate Involvement in U.S. Political Campaigns: Evelyn Y. Davis' Proposals to 17 Corporations," Analysis A, Supplement 2 (February 24, 1977), A-29.

[24] Investor Responsibility Research Center Inc., "Corporate Involvement in U.S. Political Campaigns: Evelyn Y. Davis' Proposals to 17 Corporations," Analysis A, Supplement No. 2 (February 24, 1977), A-24.

[25] Ibid., A-26.

[26] Ibid., A-24, A-29.

[27] Ibid., A-30, A-32, A-34.

[28] Federal Election Commission press release, December 24, 1975.

[29] Federal Election Commission, *FEC Disclosure Series, No. 10: Labor-Related Political Committees Receipts and Expenditures — 1976 Campaign* (Washington, D.C., 1978) p. 1.

[30] Federal Election Commission, *FEC Disclosure Series, No. 8: Corporate-Related Political Committees Receipts and Expenditures — 1976 Campaign* (Washington, D.C., 1977) p. 3.

[31] Common Cause, "Campaign Reports for 1976 Show Near Doubling of Interest Group Contributions to Candidates for Congress," press release, February 15, 1977, Appendices C and D.

[32] Warren Weaver, Jr., "Special Interests Donated $325,000 to Campaigns of 15 House Leaders," *The New York Times,* February 5, 1977. If a PAC made the maximum contribution to the average senatorial candidate it would be equivalent to about 4 percent of his campaign budget; in the House such a donation would be equivalent to between 10 and 12 percent of the campaign budget.

[33] Common Cause, *1976 Federal Campaign Finances,* Vol. I, p. vii.

[34] Michael J. Malbin, "Labor, Business and Money — A Post-Election Analysis," *National Journal,* March 19, 1977, p. 412.

[35] FEC *Disclosure Series No. 10,* p. 1.

[36] FEC press release, February 6, 1978.

[37] FEC *Disclosure Series No.10,* p. 1.

[38] FEC *Disclosure Series No.10*

[39] Republican National Political Action Committee, *PAC Brief,* Vol. 1, No. 5, December, 1977.

[40] Common Cause, February 15, 1977, Appendices C and D.

[41] Lance Gay, "$20 Million Was Spent by Labor in '76 Election," *The Washington Star,* February 6, 1978.

[42] Malbin, "Labor; Business and Money," p. 414.

[43] Ibid., p. 413.

[44] Ibid., p. 414.

[45] *The Wall Street Journal,* October 27, 1976.

[46] FEC *Disclosure Series No. 10.* In contrast, labor's single largest committee, the AFL-CIO COPE Political Contributions Committee, spent almost $1.2 million, and the American Medical Association's AMPAC spent $1.8 million just in contributions to congressional candidates.

[47] Chamber of Commerce, *Political Action Information,* April 1977, p. 1.

[48] Altogether political committees provided nearly 60 percent of all funds raised by 15 House chairmen in 1976 ($325,000 of a total $548,000). Five individuals — Representatives Foley, Johnson, Rodino, Staggers, and Thompson — received more money from PACs than they spent on their entire campaigns. Weaver, February 5, 1977.

[49] The Sun Oil Company has two PACs. One is called SunPAC. The other, SunEPA, is an employee trust account plan that was held by the FEC to be lawful. FEC Advisory Opinion 1975-23 (see footnotes 64-67, below).

[50] David Ignatius, "Despite Liberal Laws, Most Companies Shun 'Partisan' Politicking," *The Wall Street Journal,* October, 1976.

[51] Federal Election Commission press release, November 2, 1978.

[52] Congressional Quarterly *Weekly Report,* "Election Results," November 11, 1978, p. 3261.

[53] *Campaign Practices Reports,* "Nation's Top 500 Companies Seem Reluctant to Launch Own Political Action Committees," October 30, 1978, p. 12.

[54] Memo from COPE, "The Radical New Right and Corporate PACs," January 16, 1978, p. 5.

[55] Chamber of Commerce of the United States, *Public Affairs Report,* October 1977, p. 1.

[56] Robert Lindsey, "Tax-Exempt Foundations Formed to Help Business Fight Regulation," *The New York Times,* February 12, 1978.

[57] Walter Pincus, "Investing in Politicians," *The Washington Post,* February 24, 1978.

[58] Ibid.

[59] National Association of Manufacturers, *Political Participation*, p. 1.

[60] Malbin, "Labor, Business and Money," p. 415.

[61] For an in-depth look at the role of PACs in the political process, see Edward M. Epstein, "The Emergence of Political Action Committees," in H. E. Alexander (ed.), *Sage Electoral Studies Yearbook*, Vol. 5 (1979).

[62] "Multi-candidate committees" are those meeting the following conditions:
   (1) has been registered under the Act for six months;
   (2) has received contributions from more than 50 persons;
   (3) has made contributions to five or more federal candidates.

[63] "Multi-candidate committees," FEC memo, December 24, 1975.

[64] FEC Advisory Opinion, Notice 1975-83, AO 1975-23.

[65] Michael C. Jensen, "Multiple Company Funds in Campaign Suggested," *The New York Times*, December 6, 1975.

[66] Tom Mathews, "Paying by the 'PAC,'" *Newsweek*, February 9, 1976, p. 18. Most large U.S. corporations have more stockholders than employees. Of course, in nearly all cases there are employees who are also stockholders in the corporations in which they work. For example, of Sun's 126,000 stockholders, 12,000 also are employees.

[67] "FEC Opinion Says Honorariums for Speeches May Fall Under 1974 Ceilings," *Campaign Practices Reports*, October 6, 1975, p.7.

[68] "Forgiveness of Debts Owed to Corporations," *Campaign Practices Reports*, December 15, 1975, pp.7-8.

[69] "Providing Voter Information to Corporate Customers," *Campaign Practices Reports*, September 27, 1976, p. 4.

[70] "Solicitation of Bondholders," *Campaign Practices Reports*, September 27, 1976, p. 4.

[71] "Limits Stand for Political Subunits," *Campaign Practices Reports*, November 17, 1975.

[72] "Double Envelope Plan," *Campaign Practices Reports*, November 15, 1976, p. 5.

[73] Herbert Alexander, *Financing the 1960 Election*, pp. 76-77.

[74] Herbert Alexander, *Financing the 1964 Election*, pp. 99, 105-6.

[75] Herbert Alexander, *Financing the 1968 Election*, pp. 201, 206-7.

[76] Federal Election Commission, "FEC Releases Index on Communications Costs and Party Finances," press release, April 27, 1977, pp. 1-2. The Amendments also declared that such communications were not contributions limited by law.

[77] The requirement that internal communications costs had to be reported to the commission if they exceeded the $2,000 figure "went into effect on May 11, 1976, and was supplemented by FEC regulations submitted to Congress on August 3, 1976. The first reports were due by December 2, 1976, and were to include expenditures from May 11, although some organizations reported expenditures during the first quarter of 1976. Thus the index includes expenditures reported for the period January 1, 1976, through November 22, 1976." Federal Election Commission, *FEC Disclosure Series No. 5: Index of Communications Costs by Corporations, Labor Organizations, Membership Organizations, Trade Associations, 1976 Campaign* (Washington, D.C., 1977), p. 1.

[78] Ibid.

[79] Ibid., pp. 6, 7.

[80] Malbin, "Labor, Business and Money," pp. 413-414.

[81] Ibid. In addition, it should be noted that labor unions spent far more on their registration and get-out-the-vote efforts than they did on internal communications.

[82] Ibid., p. 415.

[83] John V. James, Dresser Industries Inc. letter sent to stockholders, October 18, 1976.

[84] *Campaign Practices Reports*, "Financing the 1976 Election: A Report on Special Interest Groups, Special Report 1" (Washington, D.C.: Plus Publications Inc., August 1, 1976).

[85] *Campaign Practices Reports*, "Financing the 1976 Election: A Report on Special Interest Groups, Special Report 2" (Washington, D.C.: Plus Publications Inc., April 2, 1977).

[86] Federal law prohibits the use of information derived from FEC sources for solicita-

tion or commercial purposes. The reason is that disclosed data to inform the public is not considered available to build solicitation or "sucker" lists.

[87] National Association of Political Campaign Committees, "Why NAPAC?" (Washington, D.C.: NAPAC, n.d.). In at least one of its publications it lists itself as bipartisan rather than nonpartisan.

[88] Investor Responsibility Research Center Inc., "Corporate Involvement in U.S. Political Campaigns: Evelyn Y. Davis' Proposals to 17 Corporations," Analysis A, Supplement No. 2 (February 24, 1977), A-33. Also see Alexander, *Financing the 1972 Election*, pp. 478-479.

[89] "A Phone Executive Assails Bell System In His Suicide Note," *The New York Times*, November 19, 1974.

[90] Ashley also charged that Southwestern had canceled a bill for $25,000 that Waggoner Carr, former Texas attorney general, had run up in his unsuccessful race for U.S. Senate in 1966. Ashley claimed that the debt had been canceled by recording on the books that Carr had done legal work for the company. Carr responded by saying that he had done work for Southwestern and had been paid more than $5,000 in cash for his efforts.

Ashley also indicated that while working in St. Louis in 1970 (management practices at the corporation's various subsidiaries are fairly uniform and executives often serve in several Bell companies during their careers), he and 40 other Bell executives in Missouri had had to contribute $50 a month to political candidates named by Southwestern Bell. Corporate contributions are illegal under Missouri law.

[91] In March 1973 Gravitt had received a memorandum from J. M. Good, at that time a Southwestern vice-president, which said that the company's " 'approach in the Texas rate cases was out of step with the approach in Missouri and Kansas and that used by other Bell System companies . . . and that it would be extremely difficult to defend in court.' " Tom Curtis, "Charges Abound in Tangled Bell Case," *The Washington Post*, January 26, 1975.

[92] Ibid. Ashley charged that Southwestern Bell, which operates in five states including Texas and is the third most profitable of the 24 companies in the AT&T system, kept two sets of books covering its Texas operations. One showed the company's true financial position and the other was used to justify rate increases and to limit tax increases. (Utilities usually are allowed a profit of at least 6-7 percent on their investment and thus the higher investment figures, although falsified, could be used to justify higher rates.)

[93] Ibid. The company charged Ashley, who had been suspended three weeks prior to his dismissal, with incurring fictitious and fraudulent expenses (this charge also was lodged against Gravitt) and with forcing female Southwestern employees to have affairs with him. In a January 1975 interview, C. L. Todd, Southwestern vice-president, claimed Ashley had demanded $400,000 or else he threatened to reveal alleged corporate wrongdoing. Ashley admitted having occasional sexual liaisons with some of his coworkers but said it was a common practice in the Bell System. He denied submitting inacurate expense accounts or demanding "hush money."

[94] Telephone rates in Texas are set by each city separately, but there are few utility rate setting experts in the state and the company's operations were not investigated by state officials. Only in 1974 did several Texas cities begin to hire outside utility rate experts.

[95] Martin Waldron, "Southwestern Bell Investigation by S.E.C. Reported Under Way," *The New York Times*, January 21, 1975.

Martin Waldron, "Texas Studies Phone Rates Bell Has Charged Since World War II," *The New York Times*, February 11, 1975.

[96] Curtis, "Charges Abound. . . ."

[97] Disclosures concerning Southwestern's gifts were not confined to Texas. William R. Clark, a 10-year member and former chairman of the Missouri Public Utilities Commission, resigned rather than be ousted after he admitted he had been the guest of Southwestern on a three-day hunting trip in Texas in 1969. Two members of the Kansas Corporation Commission were attacked for having received toll-free phone credit cards from Southwestern and for being guests of the company in 1974 on an expense-paid trip.

[98] Tom Curtis, "Southwestern Bell Practices Urged as Subject of Hearings," *The Washington Post*, April 2, 1975.

[99] Nicholas M. Horrock, "U.S. Investigating 2 AT&T Concerns," *The New York Times*, February 9, 1975.

[100] Investor Responsibility. . . ., "Evelyn Y. Davis' Proposals. . .," A-33.

[101] "Southern Bell and 2 Executives Charged With Fraud, Conspiracy," *The New York Times*, August 3, 1977; "Guilty Plea Made by Southern Bell: Phone Company Admits Falsifying Expense Vouchers — 24 Similar Counts Are Dropped," *The New York Times*, February 14, 1978; "Illicit Bell Payments Listed in Testimony," *The New York Times*, February 16, 1978.

[102] Reginald Stuart, "A.T.&T. Reports Misuse of Funds," *The New York Times*, September 23, 1975.

[103] American Telephone & Telegraph Co., "Notice of 1975 Annual Meeting and Proxy Statement for Common Stockholders," p. 13. AT&T has long worked to develop an image of a public service organization where profits are secondary. Talk of political slush funds and illegal or unjustified rate increases, of course, would hurt this image. It must be borne in mind that AT&T, the world's largest privately owned corporation, is a profit-oriented entity with the annual rate increases granted by state, local, and federal commissions being crucial to its profitability.

[104] "One key issue before both state and Federal regulatory agencies that deal with A.T.&T. and its subsidiaries is whether the costs of [various] public relations or political contributions are charged against the costs of providing the telephone service or against the profits of the Bell companies. . . ." "When a Bell company is making an appeal for increased telephone rates, it must demonstrate its costs. Certain expenses, such as the [fishing trips Maryland Governor Marvin Mandel reported taking as a guest of Chesapeake and Potomac Telephone Company] are not to be charged against telephone service and passed on to the telephone user." Horrock, "U.S. Investigating. . .," *The New York Times*, February 9, 1975.

[105] In 1974 the Houston City Council increased Southwestern's local taxes by 25 percent. "Phone Company Verdict Reversed," *The New York Times*, February 17, 1978.

[106] "$3 Million Award is Overturned in a Suit Against Southwest Bell," *The New York Times*, November 30, 1978. The corporation faced a different kind of challenge from a lawsuit brought against it and all but one of its directors by two shareholders, Russell P. Miller and Margaret Jane Miller. The Millers brought a derivative action in the Eastern District Court of Pennsylvania charging the corporation with failure to collect an outstanding debt of approximately $1.5 million owed AT&T by the Democratic National Committee for communications services provided during the party's 1968 national convention. The plaintiffs alleged that the corporation had taken no action to recover the money at the time their suit was filed and this was a violation of the corporation's responsibility to exercise diligence, resulted in giving the Democratic National Committee a preference, and amounted to making a contribution to the DNC in violation of federal statutes. They sought an injunction requiring AT&T to collect the debt and to bar the corporation from providing further services to the DNC until it had paid off its debt.

The "district court dismissed the complaint for failure to state a claim upon which relief could be granted. . . . The court stated that collection procedures were properly within the discretion of the directors whose determination would not be overturned by the court in the absence of an allegation that the conduct of the directors was 'plainly illegal, unreasonable, or in breach of a fiduciary duty. . . .' " The Appeals Court for the Third Circuit on November 4, 1974, reversed the order of the District Court and remanded the case for further proceedings. But, the Appeals Court set a series of difficult standards for the Millers to meet if they hoped to win their suit. The jurists stated that in order to show that a contribution was given to the DNC, the plaintiffs must establish "that AT&T did in fact make a gift to the DNC of the value of the communications services provided to the 1968 Democratic convention. Such a gift could be shown, for example, by demonstrating that the services were provided with no intention to collect for them. . . ." "Plaintiffs must also establish that the contribution was in connection with a federal election. . . . Finally, plaintiffs must also convince the fact finder that the gift, whenever made, was made for the purpose of aiding one candidate or party in a federal election. Proof of non-collection of a debt owed by the DNC will be insufficient to establish the statutory violation upon which the defendants' breach of fiduciary duty is predicated. . . ." *Miller and Miller v. A.T.&T., et. al.,* 507 F 2d (1974), 761, 764-5.

[107] Investor Responsibility Research Center Inc., "Corporate Involvement in U.S. Political Campaigns: The Firestone Tire & Rubber Co.," Analysis A, Supplement No. 1, (January 13, 1977), A-13, A-14.

[108] Ibid.

[109] Ibid., A-15.

[110] Ibid., A-16.

[111] Ibid., A-16, A-17, A-18.

[112] Ibid., A-18.

[113] Ibid., A-18, A-19. In addition, the corporation has improved its internal auditing procedures and since "the termination of the domestic political contributions program in May 1973, new individuals have been appointed to fill the positions of chairman and chief executive officer, president, chief financial officer and chief accounting officer. According to the Audit Committee's report, 'None of the persons who presently occupies any of these key offices had any significant involvement in any of the transactions in this report.' "

[114] Ibid., A-12, A-20.

[115] "Firestone Tire is Suing to Recover $625,000 in Political Slush Fund," *The New York Times,* March 1, 1977; "Ex-Officer Indicted on Firestone Funds," *The New York Times,* October 26, 1977; "Firestone Official Pleads Not Guilty," *The New York Times,* November 4, 1977.

[116] Arnold H. Lubasch, "Ex-Firestone Officer Admits Fraud," *The New York Times,* March 1, 1978; Dow Jones News Service, "Former Official Pleads Guilty in Firestone Theft," *The Washington Post,* March 1, 1978.

[117] "Former Firestone Tire Officer Sentenced to 4 Years in Prison for Slush-Fund Theft," *The Wall Street Journal,* June 1, 1978.

[118] The $1,000 fine imposed on Wild was the maximum, although he could have received a jail sentence as well.

[119] In June 1976, the Project on Corporate Responsibility, one of the original plaintiffs against Gulf, charged Wild and Gulf with violating the court settlement. Part of the settlement had been that the corporation promised to rehire Wild only on an emergency basis and that Wild would repay Gulf $25,000 from his own personal funds, as a partial restitution of $56,750 in costs to Gulf that grew out of the illegal Nixon campaign contribution. In reality, the Project on Corporate Responsibility charged, Wild had borrowed the money from Gulf's Committee for Good Government Fund and been hired on an "emergency consultantship basis" for the period August 1974 through March 1975 at a rate of $75 an hour.

Wild apparently was rehired to lobby for Gulf on tax legislation then pending before Congress and earned more than $92,000. He used this money to repay the Committee for Good Government. The new suit claimed that this was fraud and sought nearly $650,000 in damages from Gulf and Wild.

[120] In "March 1974, the SEC ruled that failure to disclose corporate political contributions to the commission or to shareholders constitutes a violation of securities laws." The agency then developed a voluntary compliance program, under which more than 300 corporations have admitted making questionable or illegal payments. Investor Responsibility Research Center Inc., "Questionable Corporate Payments Overseas," Analysis K (March 14, 1977), K-8.

[121] Investor Responsibility Research Center Inc., "Questionable Corporate Payments Overseas: Gulf Oil Corp. (ban on payments)," Analysis K, Supplement No. 1 (March 29, 1977), K-16.

[122] Robert M. Smith, " 'Illegality' Cited in Gulf Payments," *The New York Times,* December 31, 1975. The company also at this time established a Washington office.

[123] When the Bahamas Exploration Company closed in 1972, as a result of an overall corporate cost-cutting program, Gulf established a similar operation with two other Bahamian subsidiaries, Midcarribean Investment Limited and Gulf Marine & Services Company, Ltd.

[124] Whiteford had learned that these other companies kept no records of the monies they gave to politicians and he ordered his subordinates to do likewise. However, at least one of them, William Viglia, disobeyed his chief and kept records on when and how much he carried into the United States. These aided the SEC in its investigation.

[125] On February 3, 1976, John Hill, Texas' attorney general, filed civil suits in state district court totaling $1.4 million against Gulf and the Phillips Petroleum Co. for allegedly making illegal political contributions to Texas politicians from 1960 through 1974. The suits, based on affidavits collected by the SEC, sought temporary and permanent injunctions against future corporate contributions by the two companies. The $1.05 million claim against Gulf was approximately three times the known amount of contributions Gulf made to Texas candidates during the 14-year period. Hill accused Gulf of operating " 'a systematic program of surreptitiously making campaign contributions for public officers in the state of Texas, all of which was patently illegal.' " "Gulf and Phillips Petroleum Cited in Suit," *The New York Times,* February 4, 1976.

[126] Wild said the only criterion he applied was that the money be spent to promote the general interest of Gulf and the oil industry.

[127] Allan J. Mayer, "Washington Money-Go-Round," *Newsweek,* December 8, 1975, p. 72.

[128] Investor Responsibility, ". . .Gulf Oil Corp. (ban on payments)," K-17.

[129] Investor Responsibility Research Center Inc., "Questionable Corporate Payments Overseas: Gulf Oil Corp. (business in Korea)," Analysis K, Supplement No. 2 (March 29, 1977), K-29.

[130] Ibid., K-30.

[131] Ibid., K-29.

[132] Ibid., K-29, K-30.

[133] A few days after the McCloy report became public, the Bolivian government issued a denial of the charges that its late president, General Barrientos, had received money and a helicopter from Gulf. Bolivian officials claimed that Gulf officials may have used the money for themselves but told their superiors they had given the funds to Barrientos.

[134] In May 1976, documents were filed in U.S. District Court in Pittsburgh which "tend to cast doubts on assertions by some Gulf Oil Corporation directors that they were kept in the dark about the extensive scope of the company's political slush fund." These documents contained memoranda and reports to the executive board from Cloyd R. Mellott, whose law firm had been hired by Gulf to investigate the political payments when the scandal first became public knowledge in August 1973. One of the Mellott reports, dated December 11, 1973, says that, in addition to the Nixon, Jackson, and Mills contributions in 1972, he had discovered other illegal payments going back possibly as early as 1960. A second report on February 12, 1974, included more information and said the payments totaled at least $4.8 million. The board's official minutes do not record any such remarks by Mellott. "Data Stir Doubts on Gulf Oil Fund," *The New York Times,* May 18, 1976.

[135] Smith, "Gulf Payments."

[136] "Gulf Leads Towards a Cleanup," *Time,* January 26, 1976, p. 59.

[137] According to the McCloy committee, the Good Government Fund collected $77,008.91, $71,177.34, and $74,718.33 in 1970, 1971, and 1972, respectively. The panel urged that if the fund was continued it should be completely restructured and run by a proper company committee.

[138] Royce Savage had been a federal judge and in the late 1950s he had dismissed a government charge of price fixing against 26 oil companies (including Gulf) on grounds of insufficient evidence. He joined Gulf as general counsel in November 1961 and remained with the company until 1971.

[139] Smith, "Gulf Payments."

[140] Ibid.

[141] Ibid.

[142] Most other corporations simply admonished the responsible officials and kept them on. The only comparable actions were those taken by American Airlines, American Ship Building Co., and Northrop Corp., but even here Gulf's severity stands out. George Spater, chairman of American, eventually quit; George Steinbrenner III moved from president and

chief executive to chairman at American Ship Building, and Thomas V. Jones lost his post as president of Northrop, but retained his titles as chairman of the board and chief executive officer.

[143] Investor Responsibility, "...Gulf Oil Corp. (ban on payments)," K-19, 20, 21.

[144] Ibid., K-16, K-17, K-22.

[145] Investor Responsibility, "...Gulf Oil Corp. (business in Korea)," K-24.

[146] Ibid., K-31.

[147] L. Stuart Ditzen, "Senator Scott Solicited Cash, Gulf Report Says," *Philadelphia Evening Bulletin,* December 31, 1975.

[148] There is some indication that after Gulf wrote him Senator Scott returned part, but not all, of the money he had received from Wild.

[149] Senators Percy, Griffin, Thurmond, and Hansen were questioned by the special prosecutor's office or the grand jury concerning the Gulf contributions they had received from Senator Scott.

[150] There was a feeling on the part of some that the Senate Ethics Committee, and perhaps the other investigatory bodies as well, wanted to allow Scott, who was a powerful legislator and an old man, to retire gracefully.

[151] Walter Pincus, "Recipients of $4 Million From Gulf Unidentified," *The Washington Post,* April 13, 1976.

[152] Ibid.

[153] Although some expected the names of other senators and representatives to be disclosed at the trial, only Inouye's name was mentioned.

[154] "Appeal on Gulf Payments Is Barred," *The New York Times,* May 17, 1977.

[155] Richard M. Cohen, " 'Johnny Appleseed' of Campaign Funds," *The Washington Post,* January 6, 1975.

[156] On July 13, 1976, the Washington, D.C., Court of Appeals disbarred Wild from practicing law for a year because of his illegal contributions to the Nixon re-election campaign in 1972. The court upheld the recommendation of the Washington, D.C., bar's disciplinary board and refused to accept Wild's motion that he receive a 30-day suspension, as had Richard Kleindienst, the former attorney general, who was involved in another Watergate-related issue.

[157] On July 16, 1976, a federal grand jury indicted Cyril Niederberger, a former IRS supervisor, who headed the team auditing Gulf's tax returns for 1963, 1964, and 1965. The indictment charged that Niederberger who, on March 28, 1974, had found that the corporation was not liable for taxes on money it had funneled into its political slush funds, and his family had been the guests of Gulf on five expense-paid trips. One of these had commenced the same day Niederberger had issued his ruling. On February 25, 1977, Niederberger was convicted on six of the 10 counts, two involving violations of the Internal Revenue Code and four involving violations of the U.S. Criminal Code. The following month Niederberger received a six-month jail sentence and a fine of $5,000, which he appealed. After the trial a Gulf spokesman declared that no evidence had been produced "that Mr. Niederberger was asked or gave Gulf any special treatment in his handling of Gulf's audits. IRS agents called to testify at the trial confirmed that none of Mr. Niederberger's actions or conclusions have been changed after review by superiors."

In additon to Niederberger, other members of the IRS Gulf audit team were penalized. Five were given dismissal notices and 27 others were given various administrative penalties. All of them had accepted gratuities from Gulf.

The government then went after the other side. On June 15, 1977, a federal grand jury returned a nine-count indictment against Fred Standefer, Gulf vice-president for tax administration, and Joseph Fitzgerald, manager of federal tax compliance. The two men were charged with bribing Niederberger by sending him and his wife between 1971 and 1974 on the five trips worth, according to the government's estimates, a total of $3,305.

"A Former I.R.S. Aide Convicted of Taking Gulf Oil's Trip Gifts," *The New York Times,* February 26, 1977.

[158] "U.S. Fines Gulf $229,500 for Gifts in Political Drives," *The New York Times,* November 12, 1977.

[159] Investor Responsibility, "...Gulf Oil Corp. (ban on payments)," K-19, K-20.

[160] Harmon Y. Gordon, "Accord Reached in Gulf Suits," *The Philadelphia Bulletin*, March 8, 1978.

[161] "Ex-Gulf Lobbyist Consents to Pact with U.S. on Political Payments," *The New York Times*, May 12, 1978.

[162] Judith Miller, "Gulf Lobbyist Describes Payments to Politicians," *The New York Times*, June 2, 1978.

[163] For a detailed treatment of the ITT affair, see Alexander, *Financing the 1972 Election*, pp. 263-268.

[164] Investor Responsibility Research Center Inc., "Questionable Corporate Payments Overseas: International Telephone and Telegraph Corp.," Analysis K, Supplement No. 5 (April 13, 1977), K-52.

[165] Ibid., K-52, K-53.

[166] Ibid., K-53.

[167] Ibid., K-55.

[168] Ibid., K-55, K-56.

[169] Ibid. According to Jack Anderson, ITT "gave away free plane rides, cutrate vacations, touring cars for congressional junketeers, legal business to the law firms of public officials and other forms of gravy, including a highly organized program of campaign contributions." Jack Anderson and Les Whitten, "ITT's Size, Political Activity Grow," *The Washington Post*, April 18, 1977.

[170] Ibid., K-56, K-57. "A federal court approved the proposed settlement in October 1975. However, before final judgment was entered, published reports charged that ITT had made political contributions in connection with the 1970 presidential election in Chile. In its proxy statement for the 1977 annual meeting, ITT notes that Ms. Martindell has completed an investigation of such published reports and states that 'the major terms of settlement have been agreed to substantially in accord with those previously approved by the court.' "

[171] Ibid., K-57.

[172] Ibid., K-57, K-58.

[173] Ibid., K-50.

[174] Ibid., K-59.

[175] Investor Responsibility Research Center Inc., "Corporate Involvement in U.S. Political Campaigns: Northrop Corp.," Analysis A, Supplement No. 3 (April 19, 1977), A-36.

[176] Allen claimed that "part of the Savy arrangement included a 'gentleman's agreement' that (in addition to his basic retainer fee) Savy could keep whatever portion of the fund sent to him he believed was appropriate as a 'fee' for his services in remitting the various payments to Allen. . . ." Henry Weinstein, "Northrop Admits to a Secret Fund," *The New York Times*, October 12, 1974.

[177] Investor Responsibility, ". . .Northrop Corp.," A-36-37.

[178] Ibid., A-37. One critic has claimed that the corporation did not spend its money very astutely since, with only one exception, none of the recipients sat on either the Senate or House Armed Services or Appropriations committees. The following individuals did receive funds from Northrop: Richard Nixon (1972 and 1968 presidential campaigns), Ronald Reagan (1970 gubernatorial campaign in California), Ed Reinecke (1970 campaign for lieutenant governor in California), Edmund G. Brown (1966 gubernatorial campaign in California), George Murphy (1970 senatorial campaign in California), Hubert Humphrey (1968 presidential campaign), Pierre Salinger (1964 senatorial campaign in California).

[179] Ibid., A-37, A-38.

[180] Ibid. Allen resigned from the board of directors in March 1974 and as executive vice-president and assistant to the president on December 31, 1974. Jones, Allen, Lloyd, and Wilson were not reimbursed for their legal and other expenses growing out of the various investigations but they were not required to pay the approximately $1,000,000 Northrop spent on audit and legal expenses.

[181] Ibid., A-39.

[182] Ibid., A-39-40.

[183] Rockwell International also entertained congressmen, congressional aides, and

Pentagon officials at its hunting lodge. In addition it hosted several congressmen as guests at the corporation's fishing lodge. In perhaps the most serious reaction to these trips, Secretary of Defense Donald Rumsfeld on March 16, 1976, severely reprimanded Malcom R. Currie, the department's research chief, for spending a Labor Day weekend with his daughter at a Bahamas retreat owned by Rockwell. Currie was forced to forfeit four weeks' pay, approximately $3,200, and to reimburse Rockwell for the weekend's expenses.

According to an audit by Northrop's auditing firm, Ernst & Ernst, between 1971 and 1973 the hunting lodge was visited 120 times by company personnel, 123 times by military personnel, 21 times by civilian Pentagon officials, 11 times by members of Congress, 85 times by congressional staffers, and 49 times by other individuals.

[184] John W. Finney, "Pentagon Admonishes 38 on Northrop Lodge Visits," *The New York Times,* January 24, 1976.

[185] Until 1975, Department of Defense regulations barred Pentagon officials from accepting gratuities from defense contractors unless they were offered on a personal basis. On November 21, 1975, this exemption was eliminated.

[186] In speeches made in February and March 1976, Senator Goldwater attacked the double standards of several members of Congress who criticized defense officials for accepting hospitality from defense contractors while they attended banquets and receptions hosted by various corporations, unions, and associations.

During 1976, six senators and 12 representatives admitted that they had accepted hospitality from at least one major defense contractor. Seventeen said they had gone to the hunting lodges between 1970 and 1975 and saw nothing improper with their behavior. Several of them noted that the companies had plants in their states or districts. Senator Proxmire and his committee never discussed these congressional trips.

In June 1975 *Newsday* reported that both Howard Cannon and Barry Goldwater, the chairman and ranking minority member of the Senate Armed Services Tactical Air Power Subcommittee, respectively, and their families had received free air travel on Northrop's private jets. According to the newspaper, the value of these trips came to $3,344. It went on to note that the two legislators had played crucial roles in helping Northrop secure a $77 million Air Force contract. Both Cannon and Goldwater said they saw nothing wrong in accepting such rides, noting that they had not solicited them and that the flights had not affected their decisions concerning the contract. The Ernst & Ernst audit showed that the corporation allowed public officials to ride on its private planes if the flights were already scheduled for company business.

[187] Pat Towell, "Pentagon Officials' Ties With Contractors Probed," Congressional Quarterly *Weekly Report,* April 3, 1976, p. 755.

[188] "Northrop Accused of Bilking Taxpayers," *The Philadelphia Bulletin,* October 16, 1975.

[189] The corporation had charged its $150,000 Nixon campaign gift to overhead on a U.S. Air Force contract; as part of its agreement with the Defense Department it agreed to repay this.

[190] Investor Responsibility, ". . .Northrop Corp.," A-40.

[191] Ibid., A-38, A-39. As part of its reaction to the convictions of Jones and the corporation, the company's board of directors ordered Northrop's auditing firm, Ernst & Ernst, to undertake a detailed audit of all company payments. As a result, the investigation spread from illegal political contributions in the United States to alleged attempts to influence arms contracts decisions in the Defense Department, Congress, and overseas. Much of the concern centered around the company's efforts to sell its F-5E fighter plane in other countries. "As a result of the [executive committee's July 1975] report's recommendations, Northrop adopted new procedures for assuring that laws are not broken by relationships between the company, its customers and government officials; and internal reforms to improve communications and strengthen financial controls throughout the company." Ibid., A-40.

[192] By one count, there have been nine official investigations of Northrop and as one analyst puts it, "perhaps no chief executive of a major American corporation has ever been as discredited in the public eye as Mr. Jones. . . . Other executives caught up in the scandals — Bob R. Dorsey of Gulf Oil, Daniel Haughton and A. Carl Kotchian of

Lockheed, Harry Heltzer of Minnesota Mining & Manufacturing — are gone from the scene. But Mr. Jones, who was connected to more types of alleged misdeeds than any of these men, is still in charge of Northrop." Apparently he has stayed on because of his reputation as an excellent manager, able to produce well-built planes without cost overruns. Robert Lindsey, "The New Adventures of Tom Jones," *The New York Times*, September 19, 1976.

[193] Investor Responsibility, ". . .Northrop Corp.,"A-35, A-36.

[194] Federal Election Commission, *In the Matter of Committee for Jimmy Carter*, June 21, 1978, *In the Matter of the National Bank of Georgia*, June 14, 1978, MUR 442 (77), conciliation agreements.

[195] Federal Election Commission, *In the Matter of The Okonite Company*, general counsel's report, December 17, 1976, MUR 200 (76), MUR 213 (76), p. 6.

[196] Federal Election Commission, *In the Matter of The Okonite Company*, conciliation agreement, June 22, 1977, MUR 213 (76), p. 3.

[197] "Corporation Fined for Funding Ad Praising Congressman in Campaign," *Campaign Practices Reports*, August 22, 1977, p. 3.

[198] "McDermott Pleads Guilty to Fraud, Fined $1 Million," *The New York Times*, February 23, 1978.

[199] "McDermott Staff Given Immunity," *The New York Times*, February 24, 1978.

[200] "Legal Woes Beset McDermott on Merger's Eve," *New York Times*, Feb. 27, 1978.

[201] Many corporations have adopted guidelines that attempt to spell out in some detail which "practices [are] to be avoided by the corporation and its employees" and what steps will be taken to monitor employee performance to ensure compliance with the company's policies. Although the guidelines vary, "the Conference Board reports that most corporations have included ten key elements in guidelines or policy statements they have issued to employees on questionable payments in foreign countries. . . ." But in the end, the individuals who administer such programs, particularly the corporations' chief executives, have the greatest responsibility for ensuring that American companies maintain high ethical and business standards. Investor Responsibility Research Center Inc. "Questionable Corporate Payments Overseas," Analysis K (March 24, 1977), K-3, K-13.

[202] Ibid., K-5.

[203] Ibid., K-6.

[204] "Excerpts From O.E.C.D. Text on Conduct Code," *The New York Times*, May 27, 1976.

[205] Investor Responsibility, "Questionable Corporate Payments Overseas," K-6.

[206] Ibid., K-7, K-8.

[207] Ibid., K-9.

[208] Another government agency that has become involved is the U.S. Customs Service. Under the Bank Secrecy Act it became illegal in 1972 for any individual or corporation to bring into or take out of the United States more than $5,000 in cash without declaring the full amount. As of June 1977, the Customs Service was investigating more than 100 multinational corporations suspected of violating the law. Among the companies involved are Northrop, Lockheed, and Exxon. Some cases were presented to federal grand juries.

The Customs Service has referred a case involving the Gulf Oil Corp. to the Treasury Department for civil action. Under the act, criminal violations of the statute carry a maximum fine of $500,000 and a five-year jail sentence, while civil violations can lead to penalties equal to the amount of money secretly transported into or out of the country.

[209] In addition to Richardson, the other members of the Task Force were: the secretaries of State, Treasury, and Defense; the attorney general; the special representative for trade negotiations; the director of the Office of Management and Budget; the assistant to the president for economic affairs; the assistant to the president for national security affairs; and the executive director of the Council on International Economic Policy.

[210] Elliot L. Richardson, letter to Senator William Proxmire, June 11, 1976, pp. 22-24.

[211] In August 1976 the administration introduced a bill that would have required corporations to report to the secretary of Commerce "any payments overseas in connection with 'an official action, or sale to or contract with a foreign government.' " The reports would not have been made public for at least a year, with either the secretary of State or

the attorney general having the right to request additional delays in release of the information.
There was a running battle between Secretary Richardson and the SEC over the proper way of handling the problem. The secretary claimed that the SEC's voluntary approach was not adequate. First, only 9,000 of the 30,000 companies doing business abroad reported to the SEC and thus many potential culprits would be missed if the agency handled the matter. Second, because the issue affected foreign relations, other departments should be consulted. (This was one reason for the administration's proposal to delay disclosure of the reports filed for at least one year.) Third, since the SEC's actions grew out of a ruling by the commissioners, a change in the agency's makeup, Richardson contended, could cause a change in the scope and nature of the disclosure program. With a federal statute, this was far less likely to occur. Pat Towell, "Overseas Corporate Bribes," *Congressional Quarterly Weekly Report*, September 18, 1976, p. 2576.

[212] The American Assembly, Columbia University, *The Ethics of Corporate Conduct*, Report of the Fifty-second American Assembly, April 14-17, 1977, Arden House, Harriman, New York.

[213] Working paper for the Southwest Assembly on Corporate Ethics and Governance, June 9-11, 1978, prepared by the Foundation of the Southwestern Graduate School of Banking, Southern Methodist University, Dallas, Texas.

[214] Leonard Silk, "Economic Scene: Ethical Guides for Companies," *The New York Times*, June 15, 1978.

[215] Pat Towell and Barry M. Hager, "Foreign Bribes: Stiff Penalties Proposed," *Congressional Quarterly Weekly Report*, May 14, 1977, p. 929.

[216] Michael C. Jensen, "Antibribery Law Has Some Teeth," *The New York Times*, December 25, 1977.

[217] In an article in the January 1977 issue of the *Advanced Management Journal*, Blumenthal had written:
"It seems to me that the root causes of the questionable and illegal corporate activities that have come to light recently are to be found in factors other than the profit motive or the structure of modern business. They can be traced to the sweeping changes that have taken place in our society and throughout the world and to the unwillingness of many in business to recognize or adjust to these changes. . . .
"Activities once considered as normal practices are now unacceptable. . . ."
Blumenthal, citing his own experience at the Bendix Corp., claimed that it was possible to operate a successful business and maintain high ethical standards at the same time. He called on business executives to take the lead in condemning improper conduct and urged them to establish "a national board or council that will monitor the behavior of corporations, provide a forum for resolving issues of morality, and write a code of ethics. . . ." W. Michael Blumenthal, *Advanced Management Journal* (January 1977), as excerpted in "Business Morality Has Not Deteriorated — Society Has Changed," *The New York Times*, January 9, 1977.

[218] Richardson, letter to Proxmire, p. 20.

[219] Neil H. Jacoby, Peter Nehemkis, Richard Eells, "Foreign Payoff Law: A Costly Error," *The New York Times*, January 22, 1978; William Proxmire, "The Foreign Payoff Law Is a Necessity," *The New York Times*, February 5, 1978.

[220] *First National Bank of Boston et al. v. Francis X. Bellotti*, U.S. Supreme Court No. 76-1172 (1978).

[221] Stanley T. Kaleczyc, *Special Litigation Report, The First National Bank of Boston et al. v. Bellotti, Supreme Court No. 76-1172* (Washington: National Chamber Litigation Center, 1978), p. 3.

[222] Ibid., pp. 4-5.

[223] Ibid.

[224] Ibid., pp. 6-8. "Supreme Court Ruling Means Victory for Some But Others See Potential for 'Deal of Mischief,'" *Campaign Practices Reports*, May 1, 1978, pp. 10-12.

[225] See for example, Benjamin M. Vandegrift, "Bellotti Decision Paves Way for Corporations to Participate In Varied Political Activities." *Legal Times of Washington*, June 26, 1978.

[226] R. W. Apple, Jr., "Meany and Labor's Role in '76," *The New York Times*, February 21, 1975.

[227] Apple, "Labor Playing Key Role in Iowa As Democrats Vie for Delegates," *The New York Times*, January 16, 1976.

[228] Harry Bernstein, "Labor Is Back in Politics," *The Nation*, March 13, 1976, pp. 306-307.

[229] Ibid.

[230] "Carter vs. Jackson: A New Problem for Labor," Congressional Quarterly *Weekly Report*, March 27, 1976, p. 681.

[231] "Labor's Best-Heeled Powerhouse," *Time*, March 1, 1976.

[232] Joseph R. Daughen, "Bloc Teams With Labor to Boost Humphrey," *The Philadelphia Bulletin*, April 11, 1976.

[233] Ronald Sullivan, "Jersey Labor Chief Hails Carter In First Hint of Shift by Unions," *The New York Times*, May 1, 1976.

[234] William K. Stevens, "Carter Backed by Auto Union Chief and Wins Praise of Henry Ford," *The New York Times*, May 8, 1976.

[235] Robert G. Kaiser, "Meany, Carter Will Meet," *The Washington Post*, May 13, 1976.

[236] Edward Cowan, "Labor Prepares To Back Carter," *The New York Times*, June 15, 1976.

[237] Warren Weaver, Jr., "Voting Law Gives Leverage to Labor," *The New York Times*, September 22, 1975.

The special election held September 16, 1975, in New Hampshire was a rerun of the November 4, 1974, general election. In the November election Wyman was the apparent winner by a two-vote margin. Durkin challenged the election results and the Senate refused to seat either candidate while the results were in dispute. After seven months of fruitless efforts to decide a winner, the Senate voted July 30, 1975, to declare the seat vacant effective August 8, 1975, which paved the way for the September special election won by Durkin.

[238] "COPE Election Report," *Memo from COPE*, November 22, 1976, p. 4.

[239] "COPE Box Score: Final," *Memo from COPE*, December 6, 1976, p. 3.

[240] U.S., Senate, "Labor's Political Expenditures to Congressional Candidates," 95th Cong., 1st sess. *Congressional Record*, May 12, 1977, p. S7497.

[241] William Kroger, "Business PAC's Are Coming of Age," *Nation's Business*, October 1978, pp. 38-41.

[242] "How Labor Has the Edge," *Nation's Business*, October 1978, p. 40.

[243] 431 U.S. 209 (1977).

[244] *First National Bank of Boston et al. v. Francis X. Bellotti*, Supreme Court Case No. 76-1172.

[245] *Campaign Practices Reports*, May 15, 1978, p. 7.

[246] Memo from COPE, January 2, 1978, p. 4.

[247] *Political Action Report*, May 1978, p. 7.

[248] Jack Anderson, "Republicans Battle for the Union Vote," *The Philadelphia Bulletin*, February 26, 1978.

[249] Common Cause, *1976 Federal Campaign Finances*, Vol. III, p. 530; Dan Rather, "Unions, Money and Politics," CBS News *60 Minutes*, October 3, 1976, p. 6.

[250] Common Cause, *1976 Federal Campaign Finances*, Vol. I, p. ix; Common Cause news release, "Common Cause Releases Study of Maritime Interest Contributions to Members of House Merchant Marine and Fisheries Committee," August 18, 1977.

[251] George Lardner, Jr., "GOP Leaders Assail Carter on Cargo-Preference Stand," *The Washington Post*, August 2, 1977; "Common Cause Releases Study...."

[252] George Lardner, Jr., "Carter Support of Cargo Plan Draws GOP 'Payoff' Charges," *The Washington Post*, July 29, 1977; Bill Brock, "Carter's Payoff Plan," *First Monday*, September 1977, p. 2.

[253] Judith Miller, "G.O.P. Chief Says Rep. Murphy Withheld Data on Oil Congress," *The New York Times*, August 28, 1977.

[254] Matthew L. Wald, "Murphy Denies Hiding Oil Report," *The New York Times*, August 30, 1977.

[255] "House Unit Backs Cargo Preference," *The New York Times*, August 3, 1977.

[256] Judith Miller, "Documents Suggest Politics Influenced Carter on Cargoes: Papers Released by McCloskey: White House Memos Cite Pledges to Maritime Unions and Industry on Backing for Oil Preference Bill," *The New York Times*, July 29, 1977; George Lardner, Jr., "Carter Support of Cargo Plan Draws GOP 'Payoff' Charges," *The Washington Post*, July 29, 1977; Judith Miller, "Republicans Attack Cargo Preference: Administration Support for Bill to Favor U.S. Ships Called Maritime Union 'Payoff,' " *The New York Times*, August 2, 1977; Associated Press, "House Panel Refuses to Subpoena Federal Officials on Cargo Bill," *The Washington Post*, August 3, 1977.

[257] Ann Cooper, "Shipping Boon: Republicans Charge Carter with Playing Politics on Cargo Preference Decision," Congressional Quarterly *Weekly Report*, August 6, 1977, p. 1635.

[258] For a description of amendments accepted and rejected, see Ibid., p. 1636.

[259] Ann Cooper, "Cost of Cargo Preference Bill Disputed," Congressional Quarterly *Weekly Report*, September 17, 1977, p. 1953.

[260] Alan Berlow, "Debate Delayed: Tactics by Lobbyists for Cargo Preference Bill Jeopardize House Passage," Congressional Quarterly *Weekly Report*, October 1, 1977, p. 2073.

[261] Judith Miller, "G.A.O. Says Cargo Bill May Raise Fuel Costs by Up to $610 Million: Figure Tops Estimates by Far: Controversial Bill Backed by Carter Would Mandate Percentage of Oil Imports to U.S. Ships," *The New York Times*, September 12, 1977.

[262] Ann Cooper, "Cost. . . ."

[263] *The New York Times*, September 16, 1977.

[264] Berlow, "Debate Delayed," p. 2072; George Lardner, Jr., "Cargo Preference For U.S. Tankers Scuttled by House," *The Washington Post*, October 20, 1977.

[265] "House Sinks Cargo Preference Bill," Congressional Quarterly *Weekly Report*, October 22, 1977, p. 2223.

[266] Martin Tolchin, "Murphy under Rising Scrutiny for Alleged Favors to Special Interests," *The New York Times*, November 27, 1977.

11 Reform

Carter's Election Proposals

On March 22, 1977, Vice President Walter F. Mondale, speaking for the Carter administration, announced the most comprehensive election reform package a president ever submitted to Congress. It consisted of five major elements: 1) "a legislative proposal for universal election day voter registration for federal elections with steps to encourge adoption of the same system in state and local elections," 2) support for a system of public financing for congressional campaigns, 3) suggested revisions in the "Presidential public campaign financing system to simplify . . . and to encourage greater grass roots participation in Presidential campaigns," 4) a recommendation that a constitutional amendment providing for the direct popular election of the president and vice president be approved, and 5) a liberalization "of the Hatch Act to permit federal civil servants with proper safeguards to exercise more fully the political rights of citizens in our democracy."

Both Carter and Mondale felt that the various elements in the package were interrelated. The basic goal was to make the political process more democratic, with the federal government leading the way. The vice president noted: "Adoption of these recommendations [will] help to curb the influence of special interests in elections to federal office. At the same time, it [will] help to increase the influence of the people by making it easier for all Americans to vote, and in the case of Presidential elections, by assuring that those votes are counted equally." [1]

The president's call for replacement of the electoral college with a direct election system was a surprise, since only a month before he had sidestepped the question.[2] According to press secretary Jody Powell, Carter apparently changed his mind after deciding that the new plan would not add greatly to the existing concentration of presidential campaigning in the more populous states.

Election Day Registration

Election day registration was the central element in the election package. Under the president's proposal, the Federal Election Commission would make grants to each state for each federal election.[3] The basic allotment would be equal to 20 cents times the number of voters in the most recent presidential election. If a state also adopted election day registration for state and local elections, it would receive a bonus of 20 cents times the number of voters in the election for which the grant had been made. If the state established an outreach program approved by the FEC to increase voter registration prior to election day, it would be eligible for a second bonus equal to the first. The White House estimated that the total package would cost approximately $50 million for the first two years.[4]

Only individuals qualified to vote under state law could register for federal elections, and the states might require an individual to prove his or her identity and residence with a proper identification or with an affidavit from an already registered voter. To curtail the possibility of fraudulent registration and voting, the proposed legislation made such actions federal felonies punishable by a fine of up to $10,000 and/or a prison sentence of up to five years. A second conviction would carry a maximum penalty of $25,000 and a 10-year jail sentence. To operate the program, a division of voter registration would be established within the FEC. This would be run by an administrator and an associate administrator affiliated with different parties.

Low Turnouts. Both the vice president and the president noted the general decline in voting in recent elections in this country and the fact that several states with election day registration had experienced increased turnout in 1976.[5]

Certain characteristics of American democracy have influenced voter turnout during the nation's history. Unlike nearly all other Western democracies, the United States places the major burden for registration on the individual, with consequent costs to candidate, party, or special interest group for getting people registered. In some democratic societies there is election day registration, in some there is no registration, and in some the government keeps voter rolls current. In some democracies voting is mandatory, with violators subject to court fines.

Because of the greater number of offices contested and the greater frequency of elections, the United States' turnout rate compares unfavorably with that of other industrial societies. While their turnout usually averages between 70 and 80 percent and, in some cases, reaches or exceeds 90 percent, figures in the United States are considerably lower. The recent peak for presidential elections occurred in 1960, when nearly 63 percent of the voting age population participated. Since then, the turnout every four years has declined, reaching a low of 53.3 percent in 1976. In that year, of the 147 million persons eligible to vote, only 99 million had registered and 82 million actually went to the polls in November.

Turnouts in presidential elections have not always been this low. From about 1840 to about 1900, between 70 percent and 80 percent of the eligible electorate (largely white adult males) cast ballots, but with the massive influx of immigrants at the turn of the century, registration laws were adopted to decrease fraud and, some observers believe, to decrease turnout. Whether the level of fraud declined is questionable, but there is no doubt that turnout fell off sharply. During the 1920s, in part because of the recently enacted 19th Amendment, fewer than half of the eligible electorate voted for president. The figures rose during the Roosevelt era, declined in 1948, and then rose until 1960.[6]

States' Experience. Five states — Maine, Minnesota, North Dakota, Oregon, and Wisconsin — have had election day voter registration,[7] and the system apparently has brought higher turnout, a Democratic advantage, and minimal fraud. North Dakota simplified its registration in 1951. In the remaining four states (all of which instituted election day registration in 1973 or 1975), Democrats gained seats in the state legislatures by 1977. The largest gain was that shown by Minnesota Democrats over a four-year period (11 seats in the state Senate, 26 in the House); the smallest gain was that shown by Oregon Democrats over a two-year period (two additional seats in the state Senate, the loss of one seat in the House).

Still, states involved are not representative of the nation as a whole. None is heavily industrial, none has large minority-group populations, and none had a history of fraud under earlier rules. Comparison of 1972 and 1976 turnout data shows that the five states had increases in turnout ranging from 0.6 to 4.1 percent, compared with a national decline of 1 percent. There were approximately 454,000 election day registrations in Minnesota and 215,000 in Wisconsin, and much controversy surrounds the interpretation of these increases relative to the new laws. Although many politicians disagree, the executive secretary of the Wisconsin election division contends that there was no correlation between the increased turnout and election day registration in his state, and that voters who registered on election day would have preregistered if necessary.[8]

In general, Democratic officials in the five states have supported election day registration. Republicans have been guarded in their disapproval. Lacking the votes to repeal or modify the programs in any of the states, they fear a public relations setback if they oppose easier registration on partisan grounds. They have therefore focused on such matters as the potential for fraud and the need for stronger safeguards.

Local administrative officials have been the most vocal opponents of election day registration in the five states. They have complained about long lines at the polling places, the complicated and often confusing bookkeeping required, and the increased cost of elections.[9]

While Jimmy Carter's victory in Wisconsin has been ascribed to heavy election day registration, the program's main impact has been on offices at the local level. In most cases, the Democrats have been the clear gainers, with the party's greatest advances coming in Minnesota. Although gains cannot be ascribed to election day registration, most commentators in the five states believe the new system has played a key role.

Background. President Carter's proposal grew out of a half-decade's struggle by Democrats to ease the burdens of registration. Since 1971 the party had focused on postcard registration, an idea that attracted little enthusiasm and, though it was backed by a majority of Democrats, had never cleared Congress. Republicans had argued that since voters would not have to register in person, the opportunities for fraud were tremendous. Presidents Nixon and Ford indicated that they would veto the bill if it ever cleared Congress. Although the Senate passed a postcard bill in 1973, a similar bill died in the House the following year. The measure was revived in 1975 and passed the House in August 1976,[10] after the Democrats had included a plank supporting the plan in their national platform and Carter had personally lobbied for it. The bill lacked a provision both Carter and congressional Democratic leaders wanted — a requirement that the Postal Service mail voter registration forms to every household in the country — and the legislation stalled in the Senate.

At a news conference on February 23, 1977, the president announced that Mondale would head an administrative study group considering electoral law revisions. Because the outlook for postcard registration in the 95th Congress did not look promising, the task force shifted its focus to election day registration. During the president's acceptance speech in New York, he had called for "universal voter registration," a phrase left undefined but different from the platform's call for postcard registration.[11]

Mondale also favored creation of a voter registration plan extending beyond the postcard bill. Consulting frequently with Minnesota officials who had experience in operating an election day registration system, and working with members of Congress and their aides, Mondale and his staff developed the administration's proposal.

GOP Reversal. It was not surprising that a Democratic president would endorse a proposal calling for election day registration, or that many Democratic congressmen would back it. The initial response by Republicans was unusual, however; Republican leaders at first responded cautiously, then House Minority Leader John Rhodes announced his enthusiastic support. This was an unexpected development and a gamble on the GOP's part, since most political observers expected the Democrats to benefit from the plan. Some Republicans claimed that, as the minority party, they had nothing to lose and that not all nonvoters were liberals.

Republican support soon evaporated, however. The reversal stemmed largely from a strong negative grass-roots reaction by state and local Republicans; the outcry was so great that John Rhodes reversed himself. In their new pose, the Republicans claimed that the proposal was an invitation to fraud, that the decline in turnout was not due to registration procedures, and that the bill would discourage rather than encourage citizen participation. No doubt the Republicans had reconsidered the probable impact of the bill, noting that Patrick Caddell had urged Jimmy Carter in a celebrated memo to push for eased voter registration to aid the Georgian's reelection campaign in 1980.[12]

Much of the Republican opposition grew out of partisan concerns (political researcher Kevin Phillips estimated that had the plan been in effect in 1976, Jimmy Carter would have carried nine additional states), but not all of the negative comment came from Republicans. The opposition consisted of an unusual alliance of organizations and individuals from both parties and both wings of the ideological spectrum.

Election Officials Wary. Perhaps the leading group of critics were state and local officials,[13] the individuals who would have to implement the bill's provisions if it were enacted. They were concerned about the potential for fraud, the likelihood that funds provided to pay for the increased costs would be insufficient, and the fact that they, and not the president or the members of Congress, would bear the responsibility if there were any problems such as long lines at the polling booths on election day. Some election officials did support the plan, but they were in the minority.

Democratic election officials in Philadelphia and Chicago, two cities noted for their election irregularities, testified against the proposal. John Hanly, chairman of the Chicago Board of Election Commissioners, voiced his strong disapproval. "Mandating registration at the

polling place on election day will set the cause of honest elections back
many years . . . what is good for Minnesota, Wisconsin or North Dakota
is not necessarily good for the rest of the country. . . . The proposal will
simply create chaos in our polling places."[14] Under the current system
in Chicago, registration closes 30 days prior to the election, thus enabling officials to conduct mail verification and door-to-door canvassing
of registered voters. Under the Carter plan, however, such checks would
be nonexistent. Other cities argued that there is no such thing as a good
identification card in the United States.[15] Instant registration might
well invalidate close elections throughout the country or raise questions
of legitimacy. Chicago apparently had made significant progress in
cutting back on fraudulent voting in recent years, and Hanly desired to
maintain that record. He was joined in this regard by the nonpartisan
civic group LEAP (Legal Elections in All Precincts), the Cook County
Republican Committee, and the Illinois affiliate of the Americans for
Democratic Action (ADA). The regular Democratic organization in Chicago also attacked the bill, although for different reasons; the machine
feared it might lose political control of the city.

Other Opposition. Critics contended that the administration's
data and analysis were faulty. While turnout was higher in states with
election day registration, it consistently had been well above the national average in these states even before the institution of election day
registration.[16] Election day registration, it was argued, would not necessarily produce growth in the electorate. The naysayers also noted that
a large part of Minnesota's increase in 1976 could be traced to the fact
that Hubert Humphrey, the state's most popular politician, was running
for reelection, and Walter Mondale, a native son, was the Democratic
candidate for vice president. In fact, in each of the four states that had a
candidate for president or vice president on the Democratic or the
Republican tickets (Michigan, Kansas, Georgia, and Minnesota) turnout was larger in 1976 than in 1972.

Critics also noted that a Gallup Poll taken in March 1977 showed
public opposition to the president's plan by a 55-40 percent margin.
Democrats as well as Republicans and independents lined up in opposition. The only groups supporting the idea were those under 30, eastern
voters, and residents of cities with populations of more than 1,000,000.
Even in these three cases, only small pluralities were in favor.[17] Similar
results could be seen in the 1974 Census Bureau postelection survey. The
bureau found that of the 31.9 percent of its respondents who said they
had not registered, only 3.8 percent gave as their reason "unable to
register." In the bureau's 1976 survey only 2 percent cited registration
barriers as their reason for not voting. In sum, claimed the critics, there
was no proof that turnout would increase dramatically.

In addition, the opponents noted that major barriers to registration and voting no longer existed. Since 1960 the states and the federal government have made substantial efforts to broaden the base of participation through the 1965 Voting Rights Act, the lowering of the voting age to 18, and the shortening of residency requirements and the simplifying of registration systems in many states. Despite these changes, though, turnout has continued to drop.

The New Republic asked: "What if election day registration doesn't work? What if we abandon preregistration and then discover the same tendency toward declining participation reappears? What next? Voting by telephone? Forcing people to vote?" The writer argued that the nation and politicians should have learned a lesson from the campaign finance law. "Universal registration masks the symptoms, but it doesn't treat the cause. It won't help cure the underlying attitudes of frustration and disbelief to temporarily hype the voting turnout statistics." [18] Ironically, some of the proponents, including both the president and vice president, contended that the decline in confidence in the American political system could be corrected in part through this means.

FEC, Justice Department Criticism. Surprisingly, the FEC also attacked parts of the bill. The commission's spokesman claimed the bill did not specify the scope of the agency's mandate and urged that civil as well as criminal penalties be included in the measure.

Another unexpected set of criticisms — and a more important one — came from within the Justice Department. When Deputy Attorney General Peter Flaherty testified in favor of the measure at the Senate Rules Committee's hearings, Senator Robert Griffin asked for a copy of an internal Justice Department memo that supposedly criticized the president's proposal. The memo had been drafted by Craig Donasto, head of the election unit of the public integrity section of the department's Criminal Division. It said that the bill involved "a dangerous relaxation of what precious few safeguards presently exist against abuse of the franchise." [19] Noting that increasing mobility made the detection of election day registration fraud more difficult, Donasto contended that the bill's provisions designed to counter vote fraud were inadequate. Identification cards can be forged; the Justice Department had the power to prosecute vote fraud under existing statutes but could not now enforce them (the department usually referred complaints to state officials). Finally, Donasto claimed that the FEC's staff was too small and ill equipped to handle the responsibilities being delegated to it by the bill. Donasto supported the existing system as enabling election officials to verify signatures and thus to limit and detect election fraud.[20]

In response to the memorandum, Attorney General Griffin B. Bell argued that there was a chance for fraud in all election systems but noted that most of the major election fraud cases handled by the Justice Department involved election officials rather than voters. Moreover, under the provisions of the pending legislation, federal funds would be provided to modernize election records, and this step, together with better training of election officials, might reduce the potential for fraud. Donasto's internal memo attained an importance perhaps as great as the Justice Department's official position, and probably heightened resistance to the bill.[21]

Counter Strategy. As critics attacked, the bill's proponents were not silent. They admitted that there might be some fraud under the administration's plan but maintained the changes made by the two congressional committees made fraud unlikely. They also pointed out that all electoral systems have fraud potential, and the question was relative rather than absolute. Moreover, argued the supporters, the prevention of fraud was not more important than certain other values, such as increasing the number of individuals who cast their ballots for public officials. Groups of disadvantaged persons in particular needed to be encouraged to participate in the U.S. political process.

The proponents did not hesitate to note that the individuals and groups attacking the bill were among the ones who had resisted all of the other recent attempts to expand the electorate and to ease the processes of voting and registration. They were, argued DNC Chairman Kenneth Curtis, conservatives and reactionaries who were opposed to letting the public's voice be heard.

House Committee Bill. In the light of such strong criticism, the House Administration Committee made important changes in the president's proposal. The committee required election day registrants to sign an affidavit, under penalty of perjury, attesting their citizenship and giving their name, address, residence, and date and place of birth. Under the original bill, the affidavit had been discretionary.

The committee increased from 20 cents to 35 cents per voter the amount of money to be paid to the states for installing the system, while decreasing from 20 cents to 10 cents per voter the bonus paid for extending the system to state and local elections. The position of associate administrator was abolished and the administrator, instead of being a presidential appointee, was to be selected by the FEC. As a partial check against fraud, states were required to conduct a post-election audit of at least 5 percent of the election day registrants. Individuals could vouch for no more than five persons on election day. In addition, the FEC was given the right to bring civil, as well as criminal, suits against alleged violators of the statute. At least 90 percent of the funds would have to be channeled to local election officials (the original bill said nothing about the distribution of funds between state and local officials). To overcome opposition from politicians and election officials in states where the legislature did not meet in 1978, the House committee bill provided that if a state legislature did not convene prior to the end of March 1978, the state could delay the program until 1980, a stipulation serving to exempt at least 16 states.[22]

Even with all these changes, the bill was reported on a straight party vote — Democrats in favor, Republicans opposed. Its troubles did not end then. On May 19 it was withdrawn from the calendar when House Administration Committee Chairman Frank Thompson found that the number of representatives supporting the bill was in doubt.[23] Thompson claimed he had the votes to pass the measure but was seeking additional support to undercut the possibility of a Senate filibuster. Withdrawal did not discourage the bill's opponents. The measure was delayed past June and then until July, while its backers sought additional support and sought to avoid its use as a vehicle to vent anger over the president's proposed cuts in water projects and possible vetoes of several appropriations bills.

Senate Committee Bill. On the Senate side, progress was no more swift. Although Majority Leader Robert Byrd sponsored the bill, he announced that it was not a major piece of legislation, implying that he would quickly withdraw it if Republicans and southern Democrats mounted a filibuster. The Senate Rules Committee in May reported the measure by a narrow 5-4 vote. Unlike the House committee bill, the Senate version required both the administrator and associate administrator to be confirmed by the Senate. An individual could vouch for either two persons or his family if it contained no more than four persons. The formula for distributing the funds also was altered. States would receive 25 cents per voter to implement the plan. If a state adopted an outreach plan, it would be given 11 cents times the voting age population.

Unsuccessful Efforts. When the plan ran into trouble, Vice President Mondale intervened. He persuaded the Justice Department to release the Donasto memorandum and got Claiborne Pell, D-R.I., a member of the Senate Rules Committee, to support the measure even though the Rhode Island secretary of state opposed it. Despite these efforts, opposition grew and in mid-June Mondale, Speaker O'Neill, House Majority Leader Wright, and Thompson announced an agreement on several changes in the bill in an attempt to gain additional backers for the plan. The new proposals included: 1) making the plan voluntary for the 1978 elections in all states and mandatory thereafter, 2) creating satellite voting stations where election day registrants could be enrolled, 3) requiring positive identification before an individual could be registered, 4) adding financial incentives to the bill to encourage states to adopt the plan in 1978 rather than in 1980, and 5) establishing a presidential commission, composed of state and local officials, to review the experience states had with the plan in 1978 and to report to Congress on any needed changes.

Even these concessions, however, were not enough, and in the face of continued opposition Democratic congressional leaders and White House officials on July 14 obtained the president's approval to make the entire program optional. The changes made in June failed to generate much additional support for the bill in either chamber and the measure was expected to face a filibuster in the Senate.

In addition to allowing the states to determine whether they would implement the program, the president agreed to two other amendments: 1) a proposal by Thompson to increase federal grants to implement election day registration for federal elections, but to delete funds for applying the system to state and local elections, and 2) an amendment by Rep. Don J. Pease, D-Ohio, requiring election day registrants to provide some positive form of identification or to sign an affidavit and be vouchered by a preregistered voter.[24] All efforts failed and no registration legislation was enacted before the 95th Congress adjourned.

Congressional Public Financing

Like the first of Carter's election reform proposals, the second was embattled, although 1977 appeared to be a propitious time for extending public funding to congressional campaigns. Congressman Frank Thompson, a long-time supporter, had replaced Wayne L. Hays, the leading congressional antagonist, as chairman of the House Administration Committee. Three key congressional leaders — Senate Majority Leader Byrd, Speaker O'Neill, and House Majority Leader Wright — all reversed their previous positions and endorsed the idea early in 1977. In recommending public funding of congressional campaigns, President Carter said the 1976 presidential election had shown that public financing was effective and had the support of the people. He urged Congress to adopt a similar system for congressional elections.

Carter Plan. According to the president, "public financing of candidates not only minimizes even the appearance of obligation to special interest contributors, but also provides an opportunity for qualified persons who lack funds to seek public office."[25] While saying that Congress was best suited to decide on a formula, he requested that any plan adopted be financed through the checkoff system on the personal income tax form, as is the presidential financing program. To prevent frivolous candidates from receiving government money, Carter said, candidates should be required to demonstrate substantial public support. He favored setting the limit on expenditures high enough to make possible an adequate presentation of candidates and their platforms to the people. He warned that candidates who accept public financing should not be placed at a serious disadvantage compared with candidates who do not accept public funds or who have access to very large private funds, and he suggested that the system should be applied as broadly as possible, ideally to include primaries as well as general elections. Recognizing the need for quick action, the president said he would accept a bill that confined the program to general elections in 1978.

While generally praising the FECA, the president recommended that Congress revise the statute in light of the experiences candidates had with it in the 1976 campaign. Carter suggested that: 1) presidential candidates be allowed to designate one committee in each state to raise and spend a limited amount of money (perhaps 2 cents for each eligible voter) for campaign activities within the state; 2) when congressional candidates mention in their advertising the presidential nominee of their party, the expenditure should not have to be reported by the presidential candidate; 3) presidential candidates be given an additional grant to cover the costs of complying with the FECA; 4) the FEC develop a common reporting and accounting system that all candidates could use, and 5) the law be clarified as it applies to financial aspects of the delegate selection process. Carter urged that contributions to delegates, or candidates for delegate, should be charged against a presidential candidate's limits only when delegates are pledged to the specific candidate. Expenses that delegates incurred in attending a national convention should not be considered as contributions or expenditures for the candidate supported.[26]

Other Proposals. Even before the president's March 22 message had been sent to the Congress, public funding bills were introduced in both houses. In the Senate, a bill providing public funds for senatorial primary and general elections was introduced by a bipartisan coalition led by Democratic Senators Dick Clark of Iowa, Alan Cranston of California, Edward Kennedy of Massachusetts, and Republicans Charles Mathias of Maryland and Richard Schweiker of Pennsylvania. In June the Senate Rules Committee reported a revised version of this bill,[27] with public financing of primary campaigns deleted to reduce costs and make the legislation more acceptable to the House. The bill also contained many amendments to the FECA.

The bill reached the Senate floor in late July and immediately encountered the opposition of a nearly united Republican Party, including some cosponsors, and southern Democrats. The opponents launched a filibuster to prevent the measure from coming to a vote and, after more than a week of debate and three unsuccessful cloture votes designed to put a time limit on further debate, the Democratic leadership conceded defeat and dropped the public funding provisions from the bill. It is believed that more support existed than was indicated by the cloture votes, and the Democratic leadership was criticized for abandoning further attempts when compromise with seven potential Republican supporters possibly could have salvaged public funding. Common Cause was critical of eight senators, seven of them Republicans, who went on record in favor of public funding and failed to vote, as Common Cause claimed they had pledged, for cloture to shut off debate and permit further consideration of the legislation.[28] The amendments to the FECA remained and were passed by a vote of 88 to 1.

House Opposition. The demise of the Senate committee bill in 1977 was but the latest episode in the movement for public funding of congressional elections. Both houses of Congress have considered the idea several times in recent years, and the Senate had twice approved bills embodying it only to see them thwarted by the House.

The issue of public funding was first considered by the Senate in July 1973. During debate on a comprehensive campaign reform bill, an amendment was introduced by Senator Edward Kennedy and Minority Leader Hugh Scott that would have provided Treasury funds to finance congressional general election campaigns, but not primaries. The amendment was tabled, but the 53-40 vote was closer than most observers had expected[29] and demonstrated the existence of a solid core group in the Senate sympathetic to the idea.

Public financing was passed by the Senate in November 1973. Using a parliamentary maneuver, proponents succeeded in mending an unrelated federal debt-ceiling bill to provide public funding of presidential primary and general election and congressional general election campaigns. After protests from the House, however, a compromise was reached that eliminated congressional races but retained public funding for the presidential elections. When this version was returned to the Senate, James B. Allen, D-Ala., led a filibuster to eliminate the public financing amendment.[30]

The issue was taken up again in 1974, when both houses considered amendments to the FECA. In April the Senate, by a vote of 53-32, passed a bill that included public financing of presidential and congressional races, covering both primary and general elections. The House version of the bill, however, provided funds only for the presidential elections, and when representatives of both houses met in conference committee, the House view prevailed.[31]

Another amendment package to the FECA was passed in 1976, but public funding of congressional races again was excluded, having failed by a tie vote in the Senate Rules Committee and by a 274-121 vote on the floor of the House.[32]

More than two months after the Senate's failure, the House turned to consideration of congressional public financing. Encouraged by the Democratic Study Group and Common Cause, some 155 Democratic members signed a letter asking Speaker O'Neill and House Administration Committee Chairman Frank Thompson for action. In late October the committee began to mark up a bill drafted by Thompson and his staff. Thompson aborted the effort after a combination of Republicans and Democrats adopted amendments considered certain to kill the legislation on the House floor. The crucial amendment would have extended public funding to primaries, raising costs and making the bill unpalatable to supporters of general election coverage only. Among those voting to include primaries were some nonsouthern Democrats who knew their actions would dash the bill's chances of passage. Another crippling amendment that was approved would have extended matching funds to all candidates, major party and minor party, who qualified by achieving a $10,000 threshold. This measure also was considered a barrier to passage. Unable to circumvent these obstacles, Thompson withdrew the bill for the 1977 session.[33]

Some cynics have suggested that the 1977 efforts may not have been sincere. It is pointed out that the Senate passed public financing in 1973 and 1974 knowing that Hays would defeat it in the House and in joint conference. In 1977 the outcome in the House was uncertain and was dependent upon the extent of Speaker O'Neill's influence, hence the Senate was afraid to take a chance on House acceptance and so defeated the bill. Then O'Neill encouraged Thompson to act, knowing the Senate would not try again in 1978. Thus both the Senate and House got credit for trying. While the outcome may have been in doubt in both cases, only the cynics are certain that the efforts were sure to fail.

The House did not consider revision of the presidential funding portions of the FECA, as the Senate had. All that remained of congressional efforts was the Senate-passed version of the FECA amendments. If it had been enacted, this new law would have had the effect of increasing participation by the political parties and by volunteers, and of easing the reporting burden on both candidates and political committees.

The provisions mainly complied with President Carter's proposals and they were small steps fine-tuning the FECA. The ideas were not controversial in the Senate, but the bill died when the House failed to act and the 95th Congress adjourned.

1978 Efforts. The first public-funding vote of 1978 came in March as a result of a House bill to reform the FECA. The bill, HR 11315, would have reduced the number of financial reports a candidate must file and eliminated random audits of candidates. These provisions were considered noncontroversial until the Democratic majority of the House Administration Committee added a series of amendments that would have provided for public funding of House elections and reduced the amounts that political parties and political action committees could contribute to candidates.

The public funding provisions, which applied only to general election campaigns for the House of Representatives, required candidates to decide whether to accept public funds within 10 days of qualifying for the ballot. A candidate who accepted the funds would be limited to spending no more than $125,000 plus $25,000 for fund raising on the campaign. The first $50,000 that he or she raised in contributions of $100 or less would be matched by funds from the income tax checkoff, provided that 80 percent of the contributions came from within the candidate's state. The candidate and his family could spend no more than $25,000 of their own money on the campaign. And if the candidate were running against an opponent who rejected public funding and raised more than $150,000, the candidate would be entitled to up to another $50,000 in matching funds.[34]

HR 11315 also reduced from $5,000 to $2,500 the amount that multicandidate committees could contribute to candidates. The most controversial aspects of the bill, however, concerned contributions to candidates by committees of the political parties. The national and congressional committees of a party would have been permitted to contribute a combined total of $5,000 per election year, and state and local committees another $5,000. In addition, the national party committee and state committee could each make $2,500 worth of expenditures on behalf of the candidate. Total party contributions to, and expenditures on behalf of, a candidate, therefore, were limited to $15,000 a year. Under the existing law, by contrast, a maximum of $50,000 worth of such activities was permitted.[35]

The House Administration Committee voted 16-9 to report the bill, with one southern Democrat joining the committee's eight Republicans in opposition. Democratic proponents of the bill argued that the low limits on political action committee and political party contributions were necessary to curb rising expenditures in congressional races. "The presidency can no longer be bought," said committee Chairman Frank Thompson, "but House and Senate races can." [36]

The Republicans, however, argued that the party spending limits were meant to cripple their party's election efforts. They pointed out

that national, congressional, state, and local Republican Party committees had raised $24.3 million in 1977 compared with $8 million for the
Democrats, and enjoyed a cash-on-hand advantage of $8.2 million to
$867,000. In 1976, 152 Republican and only 46 Democratic House can-
didates had received more than $10,000 in contributions from party
committees. Thus, the practical effect of limiting party spending to that
level would be primarily to curtail Republican campaign activities. Rep.
Guy Vander Jagt of Michigan, chairman of the Republican Congressional Campaign Committee, reflected the thinking of Republicans
when he called the bill "the sleaziest, most partisan attempt in the
history of the Congress to impose one-party rule on the United
States." [37] Even Fred Wertheimer, vice-president of Common Cause and
a leading lobbyist for public financing of congressional elections, denounced the bill as "a partisan grab." [38]

After the bill had been reported by his committee, Thompson
attempted to defuse some of the opposition by restoring party spending
to its existing levels. The bill nevertheless was killed when a procedural
motion to call it up was defeated 198 to 209, with Republicans voting 140
to 0 against the motion. Some observers blamed the defeat on the
atmosphere of bitter partisanship and mistrust remaining from the
party spending issue. Fred Wertheimer charged that "opponents of
congressional public financing could not have had better allies than
House Administration Chairman Frank Thompson and Majority Whip
John Brademas. Their legislative proposal to drastically cut political
party [spending] limits completely sabotaged this effort to enact
congressional public financing." Democratic leaders, however, said the
vote showed that public financing simply did not have enough congressional supporters to pass. "It was very clearly a public financing vote,"
said Thompson.[39]

A second attempt to pass a public financing bill in the House in
1978 began in May when four congressmen announced that they would
offer a public financing amendment to the annual authorization bill for
spending by the Federal Election Commission. This time, the amendment had bipartisan support from members having no connection with
the House Administration Committee. The four were Thomas B. Foley
of Washington, chairman of the House Democratic Caucus; Abner J.
Mikva of Illinois, chairman of the House Democratic Study Group; John
B. Anderson of Illinois, chairman of the House Republican Conference;
and Barber B. Conable, Jr., of New York, ranking Republican on the
Ways and Means Committee.

The amendment being offered was similar to the one considered in
March, with the exceptions that the effective date was pushed back
from 1978 to 1980, and the candidate spending limit raised to $150,000

plus $30,000 for fund raising. It was attached to a budget authorization for the FEC. The first test of the amendment's support was a vote to defeat a rule adopted by the House Rules Committee that would not allow the public financing amendment to be offered from the floor. Since, as the four sponsors noted in a letter to their colleagues, "there is no controversy surrounding the provisions" of the FEC authorization measure, that vote would be strictly a vote on public financing.[40]

This second effort failed although proponents were comforted by the closeness of the vote, 196 to 213, which was a clear up-or-down vote on public financing, not a procedural one, and the closest the House has ever come to enactment.[41] This encouraged Common Cause and others for the future. The usual recriminations were heard, among them criticisms of the White House role as ineffective, and some members of the House Administration Committee as being less than enthusiastic.

Brief History of Political Finance Legislation. Through the years, there have been few compensatory positive features to the generally negative character of laws regarding political finance. Historically, when the assessment of government employees was prohibited, no pattern of alternative statutory provisions followed to ease fund-raising problems or to reduce political costs; the gap or income loss was filled by corporate contributions. When corporate giving was prohibited, again no statutory alternatives were enacted; the gap was filled by contributions of wealthy individuals. When the wealthy were restricted in their giving (although there were many loopholes in these restrictions), again no legislation was enacted to help make available new sources of funds; the gap this time was filled by a miscellany of measures, such as fund-raising dinners and other devices currently in use. This last gap has never been adequately filled.

It was not until 1974 that the historical pattern began to be reversed; when strict limitations on contributions were imposed, reducing sources of money, the gap in lost revenue was filled by money from a new source, the government, at least for presidential elections. Whether Congress will follow this pattern for congressional campaigns remains a challenging question.

In federal campaigns, individuals are now prohibited from contributing more than $1,000, and political action committees from contributing more than $5,000, to a primary or general election campaign. In the 1976 congressional elections, when no public funding was provided and hence there could be no expenditure limits, some wealthy candidates spent large amounts of personal funds. The method of dealing with this inequity in the defeated Senate bill was to raise expenditure limits and provide additional matching funds for the opponents of candidates who exceed the personal or overall expenditure limits set by the bill.[42]

The contribution limits enacted by Congress in 1974, and upheld by the Supreme Court, were designed to reduce the influence of special interests in the electoral process. In this they were only partially successful. A Common Cause survey found that the aggregate amount of special interest contributions to congressional candidates increased substantially to $22.6 million in 1976, as compared with $12.5 million in 1974 and $8.5 million in 1972.[43] One reason for this is the dramatic increase in the number of political action committees, which have multiplied to a point where most trade and professional associations and many corporations, and nearly all labor unions, now sponsor them. Since these interests could no longer contribute to presidential candidates in the general election period where full funding was provided by the government, many turned their excess dollars to congressional races.[44] A strong possibility exists that with the continued growth in the number and size of political action committees, these numbers will increase in future years. In 1976 the $1,000 limit imposed on individual contributors had the effect of diminishing the individual gift component while increasing the group gift component as a percentage of total contributions in many congressional campaigns.

Partly as a result of the law, political fund-raising patterns are changing. To the extent that the wealthy donor is now limited, focus is shifting to fund-raisers who can organize and solicit interest groups. Thus, looking to the future, PACs and independent expenditures probably will become more important in the regulatory process. The successful candidate increasingly will be the one who can predicate his campaign upon organized interest groups whose memberships can be mobilized as small contributors to his campaign, in addition to whatever help the group's PAC may give.

The system of optional subsidies accompanied by both contribution and expenditure limitations pointed up the significance of the regulatory agency, the FEC, responsible for administering and enforcing the law. Some 30 to 50 members of the staff of the FEC were involved in the process of certifying matching funds for the 15 qualified presidential candidates in 1976. If 800 or more congressional candidates were to become eligible for public funds, the administrative burden on the FEC could become overwhelming unless some new procedures are devised, or flat grants made. The Senate bill provided for a combined flat grant and matching funds, a system designed to diminish the work load of the FEC while ensuring candidates with early public funds in states holding late primaries. In 1976 nine states had congressional primaries in August, 16 in September, and one in October. Without immediate flat grants upon nomination, candidates in these states would be under tremendous strain to raise the money to qualify for matching funds, to be certified by the FEC, and then to collect matching funds before the November election.

Tax Issues

One alternative to a subsidy and to an enlarged role for the FEC is a tax credit plan sponsored mainly by Republicans but with some Democratic and later Senate Finance Committee support. Under the law in 1978 a taxpayer who made political contributions to qualified political candidates or committees — whether national, state, or local — could itemize contributions as a deduction in determining taxable income. Alternatively, the taxpayer could claim a credit against tax liability for one-half the amount of his contributions. The maximum deduction was $100, or $200 in the case of a joint return. The maximum credit for one-half the amount of contributions was $25 on a single return, $50 on a joint return. The deduction and credit are alternatives and cannot be combined: The taxpayer must elect one or the other. In July 1977 the Senate Finance Committee struck the original provisions (pertaining to day care services) from a House-passed measure and substituted a change in the tax code's provisions concerning political contributions.[45]

The committee's report found a number of deficiencies in then-current law: 1) The maximum credit is too small and the credit rate too low. 2) Inclusion of the deduction option unfairly advantages upper income taxpayers because benefit is governed by the indivdiual's tax bracket. And 3) the taxpayer must wait until the filing of the next income tax return before receiving the tax benefit that results from the contribution. The committee's bill would: 1) quadruple the maximum credit for contributions to Senate races and increase the credit rate from 50 to 75 percent for the first $100 ($200 on a joint return), 2) eliminate the deduction for all political contributions, and 3) permit the taxpayer to apply for an immediate refund by treating the contribution generally as though it had been made in the preceding taxable year. The 50 percent credit rate for all other political contributions was maintained.

The bill's proponents contend that a 75 percent tax credit would give candidates and their supporters motivation to seek out millions of individuals who would be willing to make small contributions but who have not been asked to do so. It is argued that the tax credit with the quick refund would give these persons incentive to give. Supporters stress the versatility of tax credits, which they claim will achieve the same goals as direct public funding but with less government intervention. The tax incentive does not discriminate against independent candidates and finally, some claim, it could be implemented easily by the Internal Revenue Service without requiring expansion of the FEC.

Complexities. The bill's opponents recognize a host of difficulties. The Treasury Department is one of the strongest antagonists, claiming that the amendment is "hopelessly complex, difficult to administer, and almost totally unworkable as a device to broaden support." [46] The department also contends that enforcing the law with respect to tax incentives would be difficult. Some argue that the individuals who benefit from such a system would give anyway, and that tax incentives would not, despite the claims, increase the number of people making political contributions. [47]

Other objections are that the burden of payment for the tax credit plan falls largely on less affluent taxpayers who would not be likely to use it, that the tax credit would not ensure candidates of sufficient public assistance to provide a floor or minimum support for an effective campaign, and that it penalizes the candidate who receives smaller contributions. Finally, tax credit opponents point out that the tax credit system results in large revenue loss. For example, the Treasury Department reported that for 1975 political tax credits cost $37.6 million and tax deductions $61.4 million, whereas the $1 tax checkoff cost about $33 million. The tax checkoff involved about 26 percent of taxpayers whereas only 2.7 percent claimed tax incentives. [48]

The House passed a tax bill also eliminating the tax deduction and increasing the amount but not the percentage of the credit. The Senate finally accepted the House version in the Revenue Act of 1978, effective after December 31, 1978, raising the credit to $50, or $100 on a joint return. No provisions to increase the percentage credited, or to quicken the taxpayer's refund were enacted. [49]

Eliminating the deduction, although retaining the tax credit, was part of President Carter's 1978 tax reform package. The president said the deduction was inequitable, since it enables the wealthiest individuals . . . |to| contribute $200 at an after-tax cost to them of only $60" while "middle-income Americans incur a cost of $150 for the same contribution." [50]

IRS Rulings. In 1978 two IRS rulings attracted attention because of their probable effects on candidates and the voting public. The first of these regulations applied to nonprofit religious, charitable, and education groups exempt from federal income tax. The rule barred these organizations from polling candidates for public office and from publishing candidates' replies; the IRS argued that such actions represented intervention in politics rather than educational activities. The rule took effect on May 1, 1978, almost immediately arousing controversy as tax attorneys and spokesmen for some of the 159,000 affected nonprofit groups suggested that the IRS could be inhibiting the publication of basic data intended to inform the public. Further, it was noted that the rule might eventually be applied to tax exempt public television and radio stations, preventing them from airing some broadcasts relating to political opinion.

Michael Sanders, chairman of the exempt organizations committee of the American Bar Association's tax section, described the ruling as "outrageous"; Peggy Lampl, executive director of the League of Women Voters, found it potentially very damaging; and George E. Reed, general counsel of the U.S. Catholic Conference, called it "inconsistent with recent Supreme Court decisions which extend First Amendment protection even to commercial organizations engaged in political activity." The Rev. Dean M. Kelley, secretary for religious and civil liberties of the National Council of Churches, also was critical. "The limitations are primarily for the convenience of the holders of public offices," he noted, "who would rather be spared the rigors of the democratic process." [51]

As observers noted the possibility of a court challenge to the month-old rule, the IRS abruptly changed its position. On June 3, 1978, it announced that the political activities of tax-exempt organizations would again be reviewed, and that prohibitions would not be enforced before January 1, 1979. A second ruling with a more detailed explanation indicated that the agency sought to bar nonprofit organizations from focusing on a single issue or otherwise displaying bias. The change brought relief to organizations that had been critical of the rule, and the IRS was commended for its prompt action.[52]

The second troublesome ruling proposed by IRS aimed to tax the receipts of political organizations spending more than "an insubstantial amount" on activities unrelated to a political campaign.[53] Such activities included office-related expenses, and the ruling provoked further concern because the IRS did not define "insubstantial" and because the House and Senate had in 1977 passed rules prohibiting the receipt and use of private contributions to defray noncampaign expenses. Elected officials who knew that the FEC permitted expenditure of excess campaign contributions "for any lawful purpose" were thus particularly dismayed by the views of the IRS.

Incumbents and other observers looked to President Carter's tax reform package for a possible solution to the problem. Although the bill was still under scrutiny by the House Ways and Means Committee in May 1978, the Senate Finance Committee began preparing amendments to allow incumbent members of Congress to use campaign contributions to defray office expenses without jeopardizing their campaign committees' tax-exempt status or increasing the amount of their personal taxes. The committee recommended: 1) that the tax-exempt income of a political organization be considered by the IRS to include expenditures associated with ordinary and necessary business expenses, 2) that contributions received to defray such expenses should not be considered part of the member's income for the year in which they were received, 3) that such funds should not be regarded as income or a business deduction for the member if they were equal in amount to the expenses, and 4) that the funds should be viewed as income only if they exceeded the expenses incurred in a given year. The committee noted the need for a definition of an "ordinary and necessary business expense." [54]

Debate over these two IRS rulings was an indication of conflicting financial implications of tax law and election law. Incumbents and political action committees alike noted that the FEC and the IRS disagreed in a number of areas, including the definition of permissible political activities; voter registration programs, for example, were labeled "permissible" by the FEC and "non-political" by the IRS.

The Hatch Act

The last of the president's proposals concerned revision of the Hatch Act to allow most federal government employees to run for partisan political office, hold party posts, and work in partisan political campaigns. For nearly four decades, federal employees had been prevented from engaging in these activities.

In 1907 President Theodore Roosevelt issued the first civil service rule that barred federal government employees from taking an active part in political campaigns or from running for public office. This rule only applied to about 90,000 individuals, one-quarter of all federal employees, however, since most of the government work force was not under the civil service.

During the first two terms of Franklin Roosevelt's presidency, a host of New Deal agencies were created and most of the employees they hired were not under the civil service system. A Senate investigation discovered that some of these agencies had forced noncivil-service employees to aid the Democrats during the 1938 elections in return for continued employment. As a result, in 1939 the president called on Congress to protect those working on relief projects from political pressures. Congress went far beyond Roosevelt's suggestion. Sen. Carl Hatch, an anti-New Deal Democrat from New Mexico, pushed through a bill that barred all federal employees (about 950,000 at that time) from engaging in any political activities except voting and expressing opinions.[55]

In the next four decades, the number of federal employees tripled and there were numerous attempts to modify the system. The Hatch Act withstood three Supreme Court challenges. A number of changes were made, one allowing federal employees concentrated in communities such as metropolitan Washington a partial exemption from the law to permit participation in local nonpartisan political campaigns.[56] The large majority of federal employees lacked even these rights.

Over the years a number of federal employee unions have been established and have grown in size and power. Since their influence would increase significantly if the law were repealed, it is not surprising that they formed the main group seeking to revise or abolish the Hatch Act. In 1976 Congress passed a bill that would have given most federal employees the right to participate actively in all types of legal political activities. President Ford vetoed it, however, and Congress was unable to override the veto.

Congressional Action. In his March 22 message, President Carter urged passage of legislation to allow federal employees not in sensitive positions to engage in political activities. He recommended retention of the Hatch Act's provisions "for those employees who must retain both the appearance and substance of impartiality." The president suggested that the Civil Service Commission, acting on standards prescribed by Congress, should determine which positions should be treated as sensitive in all relevant government agencies. He went on to declare his support for "strong penalties for any federal employee who attempts to influence or coerce another federal employee into political activity, or who engages in political activity while on the job." [57]

The proposal was first considered by the House. On April 27, the House Post Office and Civil Service Committee by an 18-7 vote approved legislation largely in conformity with the president's recommendations. The vote was along party lines as only one Republican voted with the unanimous Democratic majority.

Opponents of the legislation were an odd bloc: Common Cause, right-to-work groups, the Civil Service League, the International Personnel Management Association, and the Republican National Committee. These critics argued that the Hatch Act had served the nation and federal employees well for nearly four decades and there was no need to repeal it, contending that if the act were repealed, the federal bureaucracy would be politicized with promotions and hirings made on the basis of political affiliation rather than merit. Grants and contracts would be given to one's political allies and denied to one's opponents. The spoils system would return. Moreover, federal employees, and especially federal employee unions, would form a potent political force able to influence federal elections and legislation.[58] The critics also contended that the penalties in the bill were too weak to protect either the employees from coercion or the public from possible illegal employee actions. Finally, the opponents attacked the claims of the supporters of the legislation: Federal employees were not in bondage. They could vote, make political contributions, express their own political opinions and, in some parts of the country, participate in nonpartisan local elections.

The supporters of the legislation — most congressional Democrats, the ACLU, the NAACP, and organized labor, especially federal employee unions such as the American Federation of Government Employees and the American Postal Workers Union — saw things in a different light. Arguing that the Hatch Act was an anachronism, they claimed that federal employees were deprived of rights that all other Americans could exercise freely and openly. Revision of the act would not lead to abuses, and its retention had not prevented them in the first place, as the Watergate scandals had shown.[59]

When the bill was considered in May, supporters of the legislation suffered a severe setback. After seven hours of debate the House adopted an amendment proposed by John M. Ashbrook, a conservative Ohio Republican, that barred federal employee unions from using dues, fees, or assessments for any political purpose. In effect this amendment repealed the exemption the FECA had granted unions, which allowed them to send internal political communications to their members and to engage in nonpartisan registration and get-out-the-vote drives. The amendment passed largely because of the lateness of the hour and a failure of the leadership.[60]

As soon as the Ashbrook amendment was adopted, House Democratic leaders pulled the bill off the floor. Labor lobbyists and Democratic spokesmen set about correcting the damage that had been done. On June 7 the bill was brought before the House again and this time the Democrats and their labor allies were well prepared. First they voted to nullify most of the Ashbrook amendment. The new language declared that no provision in the bill could declare illegal any union political activity previously considered legal. The House then passed the bill, known formally as the Federal Employees Political Activities Act of 1977, by a vote of 244-164. The tally was largely along party line: 222 of the 269 Democrats voted for it and 117 of the 139 Republicans stood in opposition.

This was the first of the president's election proposals to clear either chamber of Congress. Although a similar bill had cleared both houses in 1976 and President Carter supported the measure, there was no guarantee any bill would reach Carter's desk. Under the 1977 Senate committee reorganization, jurisdiction over civil service questions shifted from the defunct Post Office and Civil Service Committee to the Governmental Affairs Committee headed by Abraham Ribicoff. The Connecticut Democrat had opposed the 1976 bill and his committee had a heavy agenda of other measures to consider as well. Labor leaders, administration spokesmen, and Democratic House members hoped that the 80-vote margin in the House would persuade Ribicoff to schedule prompt hearings on the subject.

Partial Enactment. The Senate finally acted, a conference compromised differences, the bill passed both houses, and the president signed the legislation. Substantial changes in law were enacted, and new standards were set regarding political activity. Reprisals against federal employees who refuse to engage in political activity were prohibited, and any coercion to force political activity was barred.[61]

The heart of the president's message, the Universal Voter Registration Act, had met unexpectedly strong resistance. Despite the fact that both the president and Democratic congressional leaders had given it top priority, it ran into much difficulty. The administration's failure to develop bipartisan support for the bill combined with the opposition of many state and local election officials to prevent speedy congressional action. Even after the adminsitration had twice made major concessions, there was no guarantee that a bill would pass, and none did. Of all the president's proposals, only civil service reform was enacted. As shown, a tax-related provision also was enacted, affecting political financing, but it was not a part of the president's election reform proposals.

Disclosure at the State Level

Federal election law imposes the following requirements on state officials in connection with disclosure: maintenance of campaign finance reports filed by candidates for federal elections, preservation of these reports for 10 years in the case of presidential and senatorial candidates and five years in the case of candidates for the House, display of these reports for public inspection and copying, and compilation and maintenance of a list of all reports on each federal candidate.

The burdens these provisions imposed on the candidates and on federal and state officials led to proposals for simplifying them through amendments to the FECA. Late in 1976 the FEC staff considered various possibilities. These included small grants to state officials to defray administrative costs associated with disclosure, permission for the states to maintain campaign finance documents for five years on microfilm rather than in their original form, procedures for making the reports public after the five-year period, and prepackaged information on campaign finances for the state to supply to candidates seeking access to the ballot.[62]

To understand the difficulties state officials were having and to determine how best to help, the commission conducted a survey. Of 49 states responding, 31 indicated willingness to check the completeness of their federal filings against a computer printout of reports and statements to be issued periodically by the FEC. All responding states except two noted that they made reports available to the public either in their original form or in a photocopy of the original. The copying costs ranged from five cents a page (Arizona and Pennsylvania) to $1.50 a page (Alabama). The survey found that during a period of peak use — from 60 days before an election to 30 days afterward — nearly 3,000 persons viewed the documents each month at the state level, as compared with 800 persons a month at the Public Records office in Washington. Regarding disclosure requirements, responding states recommended that the federal government reimburse the states for the costs of implementation of the act, that the time period for retention of campaign reports be shortened, and that multicandidate committees file in each state only documents pertaining to elections held in that state.[63]

Bills Blocked

In summer 1977 the Senate passed a bill incorporating some of these suggestions. The legislation provided for maintenance of federal campaign reports and a study of voting equipment and standards, both of which would be subsidized with federal funds. The FEC would receive an appropriation of $250,000 for reimbursement of state offices that had applied to the governor and provided evidence to the commission that the amount claimed represented additional costs associated with disclosure. These provisions of the bill were passed by the Senate on August 3, 1977, after Republicans and southern Democrats had killed more important provisions for public financing of Senate general elections.[64]

On its own initiative, the FEC undertook in October 1977 to create a new job — coordinator of state disclosure — to aid state offices that maintain files on federal candidates. This coordinator would disseminate information to candidates and committees through state offices and would devise a procedure for comparison of reports filed with the FEC and reports filed by the same candidates with state offices. In addition, the coordinator would receive and maintain reports to be filed, preserve reports for the required period of time, make reports available for public inspection and copying by the end of the day on which they were received, and maintain a current list of all statements pertaining to each candidate.[65]

In March 1978 the House Administration Committee passed a bill reducing the period for retention of campaign reports by state officials to seven years for candidates for the Senate, five years for presidential candidates, and three years for House candidates. The House bill, unlike its Senate counterpart, did not authorize the use of federal funds to subsidize disclosure costs incurred by state officials. In addition to its provisions for simplifying reporting requirements and reducing the burden on candidates and political committees, the House measure advanced controversial changes in contribution limits. The House Rules Committee approved the proposed legislation on March 20 and authorized a floor amendment to provide limited public funding of House general election campaigns. On March 21, however, the House refused by a 198-209 vote to consider the bill, and its supporters blamed the provisions for public spending.[66] The 95th Congress adjourned with neither a Senate nor House bill enacted.

State Laws

In the meantime, one state simplified its own procedures for disclosure. The Illinois state board of elections approved a regulation permitting political committees in Illinois to file in that state reports identical with those required by the Federal Election Commission.[67]

The FEC issued an advisory opinion on May 11, 1978, affirming that some state election laws may not be superseded by the FECA. Although the commission ruled that federal candidates in the state of Washington were not obliged to include their party affiliation in political advertising, as required by state law, a commission spokesman noted, "It is clear that Federal law occupies the field with respect to reporting and disclosures of political contributions to and expenditures by Federal candidates and political committees, but does not affect state laws as to the manner of qualifying as a candidate or the dates and places of election." [68]

Footnotes

[1] Walter Mondale, White House statement concerning President Carter's election reform package, March 22, 1977, pp. 1-2.

[2] Numerous commentators had pointed out that a shift of a few thousand votes in Ohio and Hawaii would have produced a Ford victory.

[3] The proposal did not cover primaries because there was some question whether these were federal or state elections and because of the variety of primary systems in use. Some critics charged, however, that the true reason primaries were omitted was to win support from southern Democrats. In addition, the funds available as a result of the income tax checkoff plan would cover only general congressional elections.

[4] Stuart E. Eizensat, director of the Domestic Council, predicted that the states would be eager to apply the administration's proposed universal registration plan to their elections, as well as to those for president, senator, and representative, because of the generous federal aid offer. Warren Weaver, Jr., "States Held Likely To Adopt Vote Plan," *The New York Times,* March 24, 1977.

[5] Comparing the results of 1976 with those of 1972, we find that the five states with election day registration had an average increase in turnout of 2.8 percent (from 64.2 to

67.0 percent); all northern states and the District of Columbia that employed mail registration suffered a mean decline of 4.1 percent (from 57.8 to 53.7 percent), and the remaining 22 northern states had an average decline of 1.5 percent (from 60.1 to 58.6 percent).

[6] With the exception of the 1964 elections, nonvoters have exceeded the votes cast for either major-party candidate in presidential elections since 1928.

[7] In June 1977 the Ohio legislature also adopted an election day registration measure over the veto of Gov. James A. Rhodes.

[8] Rhodes Cook, "How Election Day Registration Has Worked Out So Far," Congressional Quarterly *Weekly Report*, May 14, 1977, p. 912.

[9] Ibid.

[10] Rhodes Cook, "Partisanship Growing on Voter Registration," Congressional Quarterly *Weekly Report*, May 14, 1977, p. 911.

[11] Ibid.

[12] According to a postelection Gallup Poll, if all eligible voters had turned out, Carter's margin over Ford would have grown from two to five points.

[13] At their annual conference in June, the International Association of Clerks, Recorders, Election Officials, and Treasurers unanimously adopted a resolution opposing an election day registration bill.

According to a poll conducted by the American Conservative Union in May, 29 state election commissioners or secretaries of state opposed the bill, 13 favored it and eight took no position.

[14] Rhodes Cook, "Is Carter's Election Package Dead?" Congressional Quarterly *Weekly Report*, May 28, 1977, p. 1035. During the debate on the proposal, Rep. Richard A. Tonry, a Louisiana Democrat, resigned from the House and was indicted and convicted of vote fraud.

[15] To demonstrate the ease with which an individual can obtain false identification, Reps. Robert K. Dornan of California and Steven D. Symms of Idaho, both conservative Republicans, used ads in the *Los Angeles Free Press* to locate firms producing mail order identifications. They requested seven false IDs and for their identities chose seven liberal Democrats on the House Administration Committee who supported Carter's plan, including Chairman Frank Thompson, Jr., D-N.J. Thompson, when he heard of their prank, was furious, claiming they had violated the law.

[16] Wisconsin has been above the national average in presidential elections since 1872, Minnesota and North Dakota since 1904, and Maine since 1952.

[17] The actual question read: "In order to vote in elections, each person must now be registered. It has been proposed that registration not be required in elections for national office if a person can produce proper identification, such as a driver's license, on Election Day. Would you oppose or favor this plan?" "A Majority in Poll Oppose Carter Plan To Register Voters," *The New York Times*, May 8, 1977.

[18] "Diminishing Democracy By Enlarging It," *The New Republic*, June 18, 1977, p. 6.

[19] Warren Weaver, Jr., "House Panel Approves Carter's Election Day Registration Proposal," *The New York Times*, May 6, 1977.

[20] Thomas Henderson, Jr., chief of the Justice Department's public integrity section, sent a telegram to all U.S. Attorneys saying: "We recognize that election-day registration may increase the opportunity for election fraud. . . ." "Bell Session Urged by Vote Plan Foes," *The Washington Post*, May 7, 1977. Many U.S. Attorneys concurred.

[21] Lou Cannon, "Election-Day Registration Narrowly Clears Senate Unit," *The Washington Post*, May 13, 1977. An unstated, but probably real, fear on the part of the opponents was their concern that the bill would produce a whole host of unintended and unexpected changes in the American electoral process. For instance, it might increase the power of labor unions and other groups that could mobilize large numbers of potential voters.

[22] The House committee also included a provision that exempted any new state laws under the election day provision from obtaining clearance from the Justice Department, a step the 1965 Voting Rights Act requires for all states and counties with past records of low voting by several minority groups. (The 1975 Amendments to the Voting Rights Act apply

to 10 states and parts of 23 others.) Attorney General Bell wrote the Senate Rules Committee stating his department's opposition to this provision, arguing that with such an exemption the outreach programs, for example, might be used to promote only white voting.

[23] Thompson had recently met defeat on the House floor with the common situs picketing bill, the first time he had ever lost a major piece of legislation, and apparently he had vowed not to go to the floor with this bill unless he was certain he had the votes.

[24] Rhodes Cook, "Weakened Voter Bill to Reach House Floor," Congressional Quarterly *Weekly Report*, July 23, 1977, p. 1494.

[25] Jimmy Carter, message to Congress, "Election Law Proposals," March 22, 1977, *1977 Congressional Quarterly Almanac* (Washington, D.C.: Congressional Quarterly Inc., 1978), p. 18-E.

[26] Ibid. According to Robert Lipschutz, Carter's counsel, the president's proposals would have increased by $4 million the limit that presidential candidates could spend. With the automatic cost of living adjustment, the total would have risen to $30 million. The president opposed an increase in contribution limits for either individual or political committees.

[27] U.S. Congress, Senate, 95th Cong., 1st Sess., *Public Financing of Senate General Elections Act and Federal Election Campaign Act Amendments of 1977*, Report 95-300, Report of the Committee on Rules and Administration, 1977.

[28] Common Cause, *Frontline*, "Public Financing Battle Moves to House," Vol. 3, No. 4, August-September 1977, pp. 1, 3-4.

[29] *1973 Congressional Quarterly Almanac* (Washington, D.C.: Congressional Quarterly Inc., 1974), p. 746.

[30] Ibid., pp. 752-755.

[31] Ibid., pp. 611-633.

[32] *Campaign Practices Reports*, March 8, 1976, p. 1; April 5, 1976, p. 2.

[33] Ibid., October 31, 1977, p. 1-3.

[34] Adam Clymer, "House Isn't Exactly Eager to Rearrange Funding," *The New York Times*, March 12, 1978.

[35] "A Comparison: Existing Law vs. HR 11315," Congressional Quarterly *Weekly Report*, March 18, 1978, p. 720.

[36] Rhodes Cook, "Bill Lowering Spending Levels Reported," Ibid., p. 718.

[37] Mary Russell, "Humphrey-Hawkins Held Hostage by House GOP," *The Washington Post*, March 9, 1978.

[38] David S. Broder, "House Democrats Unveil Amendments That Would Cut GOP Fund Advantage," *The Washington Post*, March 4, 1978.

[39] Mary Russell, "House Spurns Election Bill," *The Washington Post*, March 22, 1978.

[40] Ron Sarro, "Another House Try on Public Financing," *The Washington Star*, May 12, 1978; "Public Financing," Congressional Quarterly *Weekly Report*, May 13, 1978, p. 1191.

[41] "Backers Ponder Failure of Campaign Finance Bill," Congressional Quarterly *Weekly Report*, August 5, 1978, pp. 2029-2032.

[42] After the Senate deleted the public funding title from S 926, it voted to accept an amendment that restored a provision originally in that title. The amendment required that within 60 days of the election or within five days of qualification for inclusion on the general election ballot, whichever is later, a senatorial candidate must declare how much of his personal funds, in excess of $35,000, if any, he planned to spend in the general election. No penalty for spending beyond that limit was imposed, but presumably the supporters of the amendment believe the weight of public opinion will go against a candidate who admits that he plans heavy personal spending.

[43] Common Cause, "Campaign Reports for 1976 Show Near Doubling of Interest Group Contributions to Candidates for Congress," press release, February 15, 1977, p. 1.

[44] Stephen Gillers, "Opting for the Critics," *The New York Times*, January 25, 1977.

[45] U.S. Congress, Senate, 95th Cong., 1st Sess., *Increase in Credit for Contributions to Candidates for the U.S. Senate, Report*, 95-342, Report of the Committee on Finance, July 13, 1977. Also see "Panel Approves Bill to Increase Tax Credit for Contributions to Senate Candidates," *Campaign Practices Reports*, June 27, 1977, pp. 5-6.

After the Senate had defeated the public financing provisions in S 926, Bob Packwood, R-Ore., introduced an amendment to the remaining part of the bill, which contained the provisions included in HR 3340. Howard W. Cannon, D-Nev., made a point of order that the amendment violated Article I, section 7 of the U.S. Constitution in that it infringed on the prerogatives of the House of Representatives, which has sole authority to originate revenue measures. In response, Packwood contended that the Senate could pass tax legislation, so long as it did not send it to the House but instead kept it at the Senate majority leader's desk and waited for the other chamber to take action on another revenue bill. In fact, he claimed, the Senate had done so in the past. But by a vote of 53-43 the Senate upheld Cannon's point of order and thus did not act on the proposal.

[46] Testimony of Donald C. Lubick, Senate Finance Committee, *Hearings*, p. 5.

[47] Ibid., p. 6.

[48] For a criticism of tax incentives, see David Adamany, "The Failure of Tax Incentives for Political Giving," *Tax Notes*, July 3, 1978, pp. 3-5.

[49] "Congress Approves $18.7 Billion Tax Cut," Congressional Quarterly *Weekly Report*, October 21, 1978, p. 3032.

[50] "Key House Committee Votes To End Tax Deduction for Political Giving," *Campaign Practices Reports*, May 1, 1978.

[51] Ward Sinclair, "IRS Rule Alarms Tax-Exempt Groups," *The Washington Post*, May 27, 1978.

[52] Ward Sinclair, "IRS Cancels Rule Against Groups' Political Work," *The Washington Post*, June 3,1978; "Taxes & Acounting: Tax Exemption and Politics," editorial, *The New York Times*, June 6, 1978; "IRS Drops Threat to End Tax Exemptions for All Groups Doing 'Voter Education,' " *Campaign Practices Reports*, June 12, 1978, pp. 2-3.

[53] "Carter's Tax-Reform Bill May Be Boon to Incumbents Beset by IRS Jargon," *Campaign Practices Reports*, May 29, 1978, pp. 3-6.

[54] Ibid.

[55] The Hatch Act passed the Senate in 1939 without any public hearings, floor debate or a recorded vote. President Roosevelt signed the bill only reluctantly.

[56] About 11 percent of the federal employee work force was covered by this exemption.

[57] Jimmy Carter, message to Congress, "Election Law Proposals," *1977 Congressional Quarterly Almanac*, p. 81-E.

[58] Many Republicans expressed fear that if the Hatch Act were repealed federal employees would work on behalf of Democratic congressional candidates in 1978.

[59] According to polls released by the two sides, it appears that federal employees were divided on the issue; some wanted the Hatch Act retained, others wanted it modified or abolished.

[60] In a key vote, however, the House beat back an amendment by Joseph L. Fisher, D-Va., that would have allowed federal employees to run for part-time state and local offices but not for full-time or federal posts. Fisher represents a Virginia district in the Washington metropolitan area that contains many federal employees.

[61] "Congress Approves Civil Service Reforms," Congressional Quarterly *Weekly Report*, Oct. 14, 1978, pp. 2945-2951.

[62] "Washington Focus," *Election Administration Reports*, November 24, 1976, p. 1.

[63] "Survey of State Election Officers: Disclosure of Federal Election Campaign Reports in the States," *Federal Election Commission Record*, March 1978, p. 5.

[64] "States May Receive Funds for Maintaining Reports; Voting Machines Would Be Studied Under Senate Bill," *Election Administration Reports*, August 17, 1977, p. 4.

[65] "Election Commission Creates New Job — Coordinator of State Disclosure," *Election Administration Reports*, October 26, 1977, p. 8.

[66] "House Bill Would Reduce Time for Keeping Campaign Reports," *Election Administration Reports*, March 15, 1978, pp. 3-4; "House Refuses to Consider Bill to Ease Campaign Filing Time," *Election Administration Reports*, March 29, 1978, p. 4.

[67] "Illinois Accepts U.S. Filings Also as Valid State Reports," *Election Administration Reports*, April 26, 1978, p. 12.

[68] "Some State Election Laws Protected from Preemption by U.S. Campaign Act," *Election Administration Reports*, May 24, 1978, p. 1.

12 Aftermath

Carter Transition

Until 1964 the costs of the transition period for a president-elect between election day and the inauguration were financed by the political parties or from privately raised funds. In 1962 the President's Commission on Campaign Costs recommended a federal subsidy to cover certain of these costs, and the resulting Presidential Transition Act of 1963 became law. There was no change of party or president for the 1964-65 transition and less than $75,000 was used from appropriated funds to pay the salaries of Vice President-elect Hubert H. Humphrey's staff during the transition period. This enabled Humphrey to resign his Senate seat early so that his successor could be appointed.

In 1968 federal funds were available for the change involving both president and party. A total of $900,000 was appropriated for the transition period: $375,000 each for the incoming and outgoing presidents, and $75,000 each for the incoming and outgoing vice presidents. These funds proved to be inadequate. The Republicans spent $1 million in privately raised funds in addition to their half of the subsidy, bringing the total cost of the transition to about $1,500,000. Outgoing President Lyndon B. Johnson used other funds to cover his transition costs.[1]

After Richard M. Nixon left the White House in 1974, Gerald Ford requested $850,000 in government funds for his predecessor's transition to private life. Under the Former Presidents' Act, Nixon was entitled to a government pension for life of not less than $60,000 a year and annual office and staff maintenance expenses of not less than $96,000. The Ford request ran into sharp congressional and public opposition, and by the time the bill was signed in December the amount that Congress approved was down to $200,000 for the 1975 fiscal year, with $55,000 in pension for the last six months of fiscal 1975.[2]

The General Services Administration repeatedly asked Congress to increase the appropriation for transition funds since past appropriated

Table 12-1
1976-77 Transition Funds

Funds available	$2,000,000
Funds obligated	
Salaries and wages	$ 946,248
Personnel benefits	67,578
Travel and transportation	360,339
Telephone and telegraph	106,460
Office space	48,526
Rental of office equipment and furniture	45,175
Commercial services	52,229
Supplies and miscellaneous expenses	26,724
Postage	25,035
Printing	14,456
Services rendered by other government agencies	9,355
Total obligated	$1,702,125
Unobligated balance	$ 297,875 [a]

[a]This balance will be reduced by payments for the use of military aircraft and employment taxes not previously paid on employees' wages. The exact amounts had not been determined as of October 15, 1977.

SOURCE: U.S. Comptroller General, Audit of Ford-Carter Presidential Transition Expenditures, *Report*, to the House Committee on Government Operations, December 23, 1977.

funds had proved inadequate. The GSA was rebuffed until 1976, when Texas Congressman Jack Brooks, chairman of the House Government Operations Committee, introduced a bill to increase the transition authorization to $3 million.[3] By a 325-58 vote the House approved the measure, which was quickly passed by the Senate and signed into law by President Ford. Under the new provisions, an incoming administration was given $2 million while the outgoing administration was given $1 million.[4] These amounts proved to be adequate for the 1976-77 transition. A statement of expenditures prepared by the General Accounting Office in December 1977, shown in Table 12-1, indicated that an unobligated balance of approximately $297,875 remained of the original $2 million allotment to President-elect Carter for the period November 3, 1976, through January 20, 1977.[5]

Watson Heads Team

Candidate Jimmy Carter named Atlanta attorney Jack Watson to head his transition team on June 21, 1976. By August, Watson, assisted by Jules Sugarman, chief administrative officer for the city of Atlanta, had a staff of 15 working in Atlanta. Among others, Watson and Sugarman consulted with Clark Clifford, a longtime adviser to Democratic presidents and the main architect of John Kennedy's transition. Carter sought FEC permission to solicit private contributions to finance this preelection transition team. He also asked the FEC to exclude such funds from the $21.8 million general election limit. In July the FEC rejected this request on a 3-3 party vote. In the end, Carter financed the $150,000 effort out of his campaign budget.

During the presidential campaign, Watson attempted to insulate the transition team from political pressures. In late October he presented the Democratic nominee with budget options, a suggested calendar of activities for the first 30 days after the election, a list of candidates for posts in the new administration, and reorganization proposals for the White House and the executive branch.

In the original proposals submitted to Carter, Watson gave himself a major role in overseeing reorganization, congressional liaison, budget analysis, cabinet appointments, and recruitment of government officials.[6] Soon after the election, Hamilton Jordan convinced Carter that Watson lacked the political sensitivity for the personnel function. Jordan suggested that Watson be placed in charge of policy options during the transition period and that Jordan be given the personnel area. Carter agreed to Jordan's suggestions and Jordan emerged as the winner in what was perceived as political infighting.[7]

Three days after the election, President Ford met with his cabinet and urged its members to cooperate with the Carter transition team. At the same time, Ford stated he retained "total responsibility for running the government and making decisions until noon on January 20th."[8] Ford named John O. Marsh, Jr., a presidential assistant, as his transition representative. On the same day that the president met with his cabinet, Jack Watson met with the Ford transition group at the White House. The Carter group was given offices in the new Executive Office Building and in the Department of Health, Education, and Welfare. Small groups were assigned to meet and work with the head of each of the major federal departments and agencies.[9]

Three weeks after winning the election, Carter named 132 individuals to his transition team. Despite the early preparation, the group confronted many of the same problems its predecessors had faced. One month after the election, a *New York Times* reporter noted that "the Carter people are finding it more difficult to exercise power than to seek it — hard to keep peace among themselves, to satisfy their various constituencies, to maintain their sense of momentum, or to stick to the letter of campaign promises to set a new style and tone without falling into traditional ways of conducting the nations' business."[10]

Talent Search

One of the key tasks of the transition period was the selection of appointees to key posts. The initial list provided by Watson was supplemented by a more politically representative list by Jordan.[11] At the same time, Carter consulted key figures around the country by phone, and in meetings in Plains, Atlanta, and Washington. Carter asked Robert Strauss, outgoing chairman of the Democratic National Committee, to seek nominations from Democratic governors and other party leaders across the country. The newly elected vice president, Walter Mondale, joined in the selection process; still, it was clear that Carter had the final say on all key appointments.

Carter's talent search received much publicity as representatives of different interest groups and minorities sought appointment to top posts. Since the number of aspirants vastly exceeded the number of high-level positions, many were disappointed. A count taken in June 1977 indicated that of the first 300 top appointments 40 individuals were women, 32 were blacks, 10 were Hispanics, and one was Asian.[12]

Despite the efforts of the transition team and the president-elect's promises to bring in new people, many individuals chosen for key positions were familiar Washington faces drawn from the traditional hunting grounds of major corporations, prestigious commissions and foundations, and the personnel lists of past administrations.[13] The president-elect was criticized from all sides of the political spectrum for his selections. Some liberals noted that many foreign policy appointees had been involved in the Kennedy-Johnson Vietnam policy. The Coalition for a Democratic Majority, partly an AFL-CIO supported organization, submitted a long list for national security and foreign policy posts. The CDM, unhappy with the Carter nominees, charged that the nominees did not reflect the true divisions in the Democratic Party and felt that the liberals had won out.

Another view of the situation was offered by columnist Joseph Kraft. He argued that all sides had been given very little by the president and that the important constituencies of the party had received short shrift in the cabinet selection process: "The traditional groups — labor, farmers and producers — have been clobbered, and the new ones — blacks and women — held in check." [14] Kraft predicted that future clashes would take place in the halls of Congress where these groups had strong supporters.

Handling of Money

The transition team's handling of funds prompted the General Accounting Office in December 1977 to recommend stricter procedures.

The GAO found a number of irregularities: Fictitious travel vouchers were used to provide salary advances, thus circumventing delays connected with the use of military aircraft; and advance payments were made to employees. One of the salary and travel advances, amounting to $3,000, was owed by Hamilton Jordan, who ignored several attempts to collect the money before finally repaying it. While other advances were repaid and the government agency found no evidence of monetary damage to the United States, it did recommend that in the future expenditure of transition funds be approved in advance by the General Services Administration.

The GAO audit of presidential transition expenditures concluded with a number of recommendations for change. The Presidential Transition Act, it suggested, should apply only to the incoming administration; except for minor cash expenses, expenditure of transition funds should be approved in advance by the administrator of General Services; military aircraft should be available and the government should be reimbursed for its use. The GAO recommended that the Former Presidents Act provide services needed by the outgoing administration. These would include: funds for the president and vice president for a period of eight months and 10 days, to begin from the time they leave office; after this period, the former president alone would be eligible for additional funds. The president would be required to include in the proposed budget for the fiscal year in which his regular term of office expires sufficient funds to pay for transition services authorized by the Former Presidents Act. Again, except for minor cash expenditures, the administrator of General Services would approve expenditure of all transition funds.[15]

Inaugural Activities

An Inaugural Committee was established to plan various activities during the transition period. On November 26, 1976, the FEC ruled that corporations, unions, and government contractors could help pay the costs of inaugural activities.[16] The FEC placed no limits on the amount contributed and did not require the committee to release the names of contributors. Bardyl Tirana, cochairman of the committee, initially rejected the idea of contributions from unions and corporations but later agreed to accept such funds provided they did not exceed $5,000; individual contributors were limited to $1,000. The committee said it would release a list of contributors even though the law did not require it.

The committee was not very successful in its fund-raising efforts. On January 11, 1977, Carter aides asked more than 200 corporation executives to contribute approximately $350,000 to help pay for the inauguration. Until that point, the committee had raised only $70,000, far short of its goals. According to the Internal Revenue Service, corporation and union donations were considered tax-deductible.

Ambassadors

The practice of rewarding large contributors to political campaigns with ambassadorships has received much criticism as new administrations have assumed office, and no critic has been more vocal than the American Foreign Service Association, the trade union of diplomats. The AFSA contends that new administrations too frequently bypass senior Foreign Service officers of considerable experience to reward political donors who lack that experience.[17] Because Jimmy Carter declared during his campaign that he would take the selection of envoys out of the realm of politics, the AFSA and other observers paid particular attention to appointments during Carter's first 12 months in office. It is appropriate to consider these envoys here, although analysis of their campaign contributions is not practical since the Federal Election Commission has not compiled full lists of contributors and amounts donated for 1976, and limits on allowable contributions make their analysis less revealing than in previous election years.

Selection Process

In February 1977 the White House announced plans to replace about half of the 120 U.S. ambassadors around the world within six months by means of a highly unusual selection process. Carter's Advisory Board on Ambassadorial Appointments, a 20-member group, was asked to suggest and screen names of potential appointees. The plan originally called for the group to study a list of two to seven names for each ambassadorial post supplied by high State Department officials and to eliminate names of individuals deemed unqualified. The plan later was revised to require the group to study all names submitted by the State Department and to add individuals from lists compiled by the group's own members or other sources. A final list of those screened and found to be qualified would be submitted by the group to President Carter, who would then make the final selection.

This policy brought a wide variety of reactions from informed commentators, as did Carter's record in achieving his stated goal. One writer argued that the selection of ambassadors was properly a political process. He pointed out that campaign debts are not necessarily strictly financial, and that Carter would contend with pressure from a variety of special interest groups. When the selections were made, some charged that the appointees did not bear out Carter's campaign pledge and did not increase the percentage of career Foreign Service officers rewarded with top posts. Still another group disagreed, supporting Carter's choices and arguing that he had fulfilled his promise. Finally, some found the new ambassadors to be generally acceptable but undistinguished choices, and some complaints were heard that the shuffle of ambassadors following each election year involved a waste of dollars and of valuable job experience.[18]

The first 10 appointments were announced in April 1977. Former Sen. Mike Mansfield, D-Mont., was named ambassador to Japan; Democratic Gov. Patrick J. Lucey of Wisconsin was the envoy to Mexico; Kingman Brewster, president of Yale University, would be sent to Britain; and Robert F. Goheen, the former president of Princeton University, would go to India. Other appointments included Philip H. Alston, Jr., an Atlanta lawyer, to Australia; Anne Cox Chambers, chairman of Atlanta Newspapers, to Belgium; Wilbert J. LeMelle, a Ford Foundation executive, to Kenya and the Seychelles; Samuel W. Lewis, an assistant secretary of State under Kissinger, to Israel; William H. Sullivan, then ambassador to the Philippines, to Iran; and George S. Vest, a State Department official, to Pakistan.[19]

Some of the nominations were attacked.[20] Philip Alston was quoted as saying that he would consider resigning his private membership in clubs that excluded blacks and other minorities only if this membership offended Australians. This statement brought criticism, as did the fact of his early fund raising for Carter's campaign. Similar criticism was voiced against Anne Cox Chambers for her membership in the Atlanta Junior League, an organization that allegedly discriminated against blacks. It was noted that Chambers had given $18,000 to the DNC for Carter's campaign during its final days. She also gave $400 directly to the Carter nomination campaign, and her husband gave an additional $21,000 to the DNC.

The American Foreign Service Association openly opposed the appointments of Chambers and Alston, charging that both had been major contributors to Carter's past political campaigns and that neither was qualified for the post named. Fault was found with other nominees as well. John C. West, chosen to be ambassador to Saudi Arabia, was a former governor of South Carolina whose qualifications to be a diplomat were challenged by some observers. The appointment of Marvin L. Warner, an Ohio real estate developer, to Switzerland was also controversial. The Senate Foreign Relations Committee confirmed Warner despite testimony charging a political payoff: Warner reported that he and his family had contributed $66,000 to political campaigns since

January 1973, including $2,265 to the Carter campaign and $19,130 to the DNC. He also was an Ohio fund-raiser for Carter, arranging one breakfast netting $20,000.[21] Cleveland businessman Milton Wolfe was named ambassador to Austria; Wolfe was a former Jackson supporter who switched to Carter and was credited with helping to raise $80,000 in one evening from Cleveland contributors.

Reaction

Five of Carter's initial 17 noncareer choices drew opposition from the AFSA on grounds of inexperience. Then, too, various commentators questioned the criteria applied in the selection process. Some observers found that Carter's appointments to ambassadorial and other posts were not sufficiently political. These critics included the Democratic National Committee, which adopted a resolution opposing the new president's approach to patronage. A few observers questioned Carter's chances of reelection, pointing out that vast numbers of those who had worked for or supported his campaign had gone unrewarded and were unemployed.

Some argued that despite the attention given by the administration, the press, and the public to selection criteria and the value of nonpolitical appointments, little had really changed in the selection process.[22] When Carter assumed office, 74 percent of the embassies were headed by career Foreign Service diplomats and 26 percent by noncareer envoys; a State Department official estimated in June 1977 that the new administration would place 75 percent of embassies under the direction of career diplomats and 25 percent under the direction of noncareer ambassadors.[23] The AFSA maintained that no more than 10 percent of all ambassadors should be noncareer, and no more than 15 percent in any given geographical area. The figure had been highest during the presidencies of Roosevelt (44 percent) and Kennedy (42 percent). It was 32 percent under Nixon and 38 percent under Ford, and a reduction to 25 or 30 percent seemed to some an insignificant change.[24]

Conflict of Interest

During his campaign for the presidency, Jimmy Carter commented on his struggle against the "buddy system" in Washington, the tendency of administration appointees to deal with their friends outside the government and to find employment with those same individuals later on.[25] This "revolving-door" movement of personnel between federal regulatory agencies and regulated businesses would end, he implied in his speeches, if he were elected.

Carter was, of course, not the only one to criticize such patterns of employment. At the request of Democratic Reps. John E. Moss of California and Benjamin S. Rosenthal of New York, the General Accounting Office undertook an investigation of the financial reporting systems in 18 federal agencies. In its report, the GAO found that the statements filed by 12 percent of its sample of 7,193 officials disclosed holdings of an ethically questionable nature in light of the officials' duties; an additional 10 percent had not filed the required disclosure statements at all.[26]

Summarizing an earlier GAO study, Common Cause released data showing the prevalence of the revolving-door syndrome. Of the 42 regulatory commissioners who were appointed during fiscal years 1971-75, 52 percent came from the industries regulated by their agency or from their law firms. Of the 36 administrators who left government service during the same period, 48 percent went to work for regulated industries or their law firms. Actual or potential conflicts of interest were particularly apparent in agencies concerned with energy — the Federal Energy Administration, the Department of Interior, the Nuclear Regulatory Commission, and the Energy Research and Development Administration.[27] Senator William Proxmire noted a significant increase in revolving-door activity between the Pentagon and the defense industry. Analyzing movement from the Pentagon to the defense industry in 1975 and 1976, he cited a 68 percent increase among officers and a larger increase among civilians. The number of individuals who left the defense industry for work in the Pentagon had increased from 170 in 1975 to 374 in 1976.[28]

In July 1976, soon after he secured his party's nomination, Carter asked John L. Moore, Jr., an Atlanta attorney, to direct a study of conflict-of-interest regulations. Moore found an assortment of federal statutes, agency rules, and congressional committee practices relating to financial disclosure and restrictions on employment for those who leave government offices. The *Code of Federal Regulations* contained about 100 such provisions by 1976, including an executive order issued by President Johnson requiring publication of rules of conduct by each federal agency and department.[29] The Johnson order gave the Civil Service Commission the job of enforcing these regulations, but that agency did very little in this area until 1975.

Another potential check on conflicts of interest was the Senate confirmation process. Several of that chamber's committees had established informal rules concerning disclosure and/or divestiture of property owned by cabinet-level appointees. The Constitution contains several provisions regulating official conduct (e.g., members of Congress cannot accept government positions created during their terms of office), and there are many federal antibribery statutes, the first of which passed in the 1860s. Civil service regulations also were designed to prevent corruption and conflicts of interest.[30]

In general, however, the rules and statutes were ineffective: Reports of personal financial worth and holdings were kept confidential, the form and extent of disclosure were not specified in law, no procedure was set forth for handling of the reports by superiors, many officials never filed reports, no clear requirements concerned divestiture of conflicting financial interests, and the rules were rarely enforced.[31]

Carter's Program

Jimmy Carter announced his program on January 4, 1977.[32] The new regulations would apply to all cabinet-level appointees, several thousand other political nominees, and career bureaucrats in policy-making positions — between 22,000 and 77,000 government officials. These individuals would have to itemize their assets and liabilities, as well as those of their spouses, minor children, and other members of their immediate households, and to describe all items of value received since the start of 1975. The lists were to be filed at the time of appointment and annually thereafter until two years after departure from government service. In addition, the officials would have to divest themselves of investments that could involve conflicts of interest. Real estate, savings certificates, governmental securities, and diversified holdings such as mutual funds were exempted. The regulations also defined permissible benefits from previous private employers in matters such as severance, pensions, and stock options. The proposals extended to two years, from one year, the length of time that former federal employees were forbidden to handle matters they had been personally involved in while members of the administration. In addition, departing officials were not allowed to receive financial compensation for contracts with the agency in which they had served until a period of one year had elapsed.[33]

Since the new regulations were not yet part of statutory law nor an official executive order, each appointee was asked to sign a statement voluntarily placing himself under them. The appointee also agreed to serve the full term unless the president removed him beforehand — a provision whose constitutionality has been questioned.

On February 25, 1977, about two months after announcing the new regulations, the White House released the financial disclosure statements of 15 cabinet-level officials. The data showed that most of them lived in expensive homes, had significant stock or real estate holdings, and had incomes in excess of $75,000. The net worth of each individual was not released, however.[34] Instead, each appointee denoted his income range (e.g., $15,000-$49,999). The president's statement gave his actual worth ($611,892).[35]

On the same day that he announced his conflict-of-interest regulations for his appointees, the president-elect issued a statement describing how his own property would be handled during his term in office.[36] Carter created a trust agreement controlled by Charles Kirbo, an old and close confidant. The arrangement called for the trustee to weigh carefully the consequences of any sale or leasing arrangement for Carter's brother Billy, the manager and part-owner of the family warehouse business, and the president's son Chip, who might someday want to join the business.

Some months following announcement of Carter's trust agreement for his personal investments, the magazine *New York* charged that an undisclosed trust had been left to Carter by his father and that the president had managed this portfolio for some six months after taking office. The White House denied the allegations, saying that the president had resigned as executor of the estate on January 19 but that several additional months had been required to obtain the written consent of other potential beneficiaries.[37] The Securities and Exchange Commission also initiated an investigation to determine whether the National Bank of Georgia's loans to the Carter peanut warehouse had been diverted to Carter's presidential campaign.[38]

In some cases, conflicts of interest received publicity because individuals with special White House privileges appeared to use them on behalf of an employer or a personal cause. One example concerned a fund-raiser for Carter who gained access to the White House and pressed the case of a major defense contractor, Grumman Aerospace Corp., in a multibillion-dollar fight involving Navy and Marine Corps fighter and attack planes.[39]

The law firm of Robert Lipshutz, the White House counsel, attracted attention when *New York* reported that the firm's ambiguous involvement with the tax fraud case of convicted racketeer Wesley Merritt might figure in an IRS investigation of Merritt's sale and repurchase of properties reportedly worth more than $1 million. Critics asked whether it was proper for the president's legal affairs to be handled by a man involved with the doubtful transactions of a convicted criminal.[40]

In September 1977 an assistant secretary of Agriculture approached members of Congress and the Carter administration seeking special treatment for California's Imperial Valley in enforcement of a law governing federal water resources. Robert H. Meyer, assistant secretary for marketing, asked that federal projects provide water for irrigation to farmers living on their property and owning more than the 160-acre limit specified by statute. The statute had been intended to encourage family farming in the area, and Meyer's cause attracted publicity because he was known to own directly or to control through other members of his family more than 1,800 acres in the Imperial Valley. Meyer claimed that he made rigid distinctions between personal and official business in his discussions with government officials, but the White House ordered him to stop seeking preferential treatment and announced its continuing support for enforcement of the statute with the existing limitations.

Meyer's critics commented that any favors he received would entail obligations and chided the Department of Agriculture for its failure to guide Meyer in matters suggesting conflicts of interest.[41] On October 21 Meyer submitted his resignation rather than curb his lobbying efforts. The incoming administration had issued an executive order outlining more diligent enforcement of existing statutes, and submitted new legislation to Congress. The new regulations had been in effect only a short time when a highly publicized controversy arose concerning the appointment of Bert Lance as director of the Office of Management and Budget. The issues of ethical conduct and avoidance of conflicts of interest, figuring prominently in the public mind in the wake of the Watergate scandal, probably resulted in extraordinary attention by the media to the actions of Lance and a number of others.

Although the new regulations appeared broad in scope, especially as they prescribed conduct for public officials, close examination and the course of events both suggested a number of gaps, as critics were quick to point out.[42]

More embarrassing to the president than criticism, however, was early evidence that his proposals failed to address one area with conspicuous potential for conflicts of interest. Carter had focused on a federal employee's assets, but events quickly made it apparent that his debts also deserved attention. The debts of OMB Director Lance, one of Carter's closest associates, led to the first major scandal of the new administration.

The Lance Case

Starting as a teller, Thomas Bertram Lance had risen to be president of the Calhoun (Ga.) First National Bank. He had aided Carter in the 1970 gubernatorial campaign and had been chosen to head the state's Department of Transportation. In 1974, with the tacit support of Carter, Lance had sought, but failed to win, the Democratic nomination for governor.[43]

During his race for the governorship, Lance spent more than $235,000 of his own funds and took out loans totaling $350,000 from six

Georgia banks. It was later disclosed that the Calhoun First National Bank had permitted accounts maintained by Lance, his wife LaBelle, and the Lance for Governor Campaign Committee to be overdrawn. Although Lance had put up collateral to cover the costs of borrowing during his campaign, the overdrafts exceeded the collateral. In addition, nine of Lance's relatives and other bank officials had overdrafts totaling between $200,000 and $450,000 during the period September 1974-April 1975. An examiner from the Atlanta office of the Comptroller of the Currency discovered the overdrafts during a routine audit of the bank's finances.

Overdrafts. As a result of the audit, First National signed an agreement calling for monthly reviews of the bank's financial position and its management techniques by the comptroller's office. In addition, the bank halted its practice of not charging interest on overdrafts. Lance was required to pay the bank $6,881 in interest charges for overdrafts incurred after June 1974.

By honoring overdrafts in the campaign account without charging interest, the bank might have violated federal statutes barring national banks from making political contributions. Because of this possibility, the comptroller's office turned over its information to the Justice Department. The department's investigation dragged on for many months and was dropped after Carter named Lance as OMB director in December 1976. John Stokes, Jr., the U.S. Attorney in Atlanta who halted the probe, said that the investigation had revealed no illegalities and that the case should have been concluded months earlier. The agreement between Calhoun First National and the comptroller's office had been rescinded about two weeks before, at the bank's request, by Donald Tarleton, regional director of the comptroller's office in Atlanta. As a result of these events, Acting Comptroller Robert Bloom was able to write the Senate Governmental Affairs Committee at the time of Lance's confirmation hearing that his agency had found no violations of national banking laws by either Lance or the Calhoun bank.

After his 1974 campaign, Lance became president of the National Bank of Georgia (NBG). During the next two years he borrowed large sums of money from three out-of-state banks — Manufacturers Hanover Trust in New York, the United American Bank of Knoxville, and the First National Bank of Chicago[44] — to purchase shares of his new bank's stock.[45] NBG already had or soon opened a correspondence account in each of the lending banks, although it had similar accounts in other banks in New York and Chicago.

Critics charged that the correspondent accounts were really compensating balances and as such violated banking regulations. Moreover they claimed that Lance's borrowings were so large and had been made on terms so favorable to him that they enabled the lending institutions to exert considerable influence over one of the most powerful men in Washington. Lance and the banks involved said the personal loans were good business for both sides.[46]

Other questions were raised about the sizable deposits — $23 million — made by the Teamsters pension fund (the Central States, Southeast, and Southwest Areas Pension Trustees) in the National Bank of Georgia. Before these deposits were made, the bank's trust fund was quite small. The first deposit was made in February 1976, at a time when Jimmy Carter was beginning to attract national recognition, and critics later suggested that the Teamsters pension fund, under attack from several government agencies, was seeking future political support. Lance and his colleagues at the bank denied the charge.[47]

Stock Holdings. At his confirmation hearings before the Senate Governmental Affairs Committee, Lance revealed assets of nearly $8 million, liabilities in excess of $5.3 million, and a net worth of more than $2.6 million. He promised the committee that he would sell his stock in the NBG by the end of 1977 and would place most other holdings in a blind trust. In addition, Lance agreed not to involve himself in any banking legislation while head of OMB. In June, however, he signed a letter to the Senate Banking Committee urging it to reject a controversial proposal designed to encourge bank investments in older neighborhoods in urban areas. Chairman Proxmire, the only senator to vote against Lance's confirmation, attacked him for violating his agreement. In response, Lance said that one of his deputies had drafted the letter and that he thought of it as a housing, not a banking, issue. Lance soon assigned W. Bowman Cutter of OMB to banking matters.

It proved difficult for Lance to sell his stock in NBG before the end of the year. The bank omitted its second quarter dividend because of real estate and other losses of more than $4 million in the first half of 1977. Although Lance had bought the bank's stock for an average of more than $17, it was trading on the market for about half that value. Lance would lose approximately $1.6 million if he sold at the depressed price.[48] As a consequence, President Carter wrote in July to Senator Ribicoff, chairman of the Governmental Affairs Committee, asking that Lance be released from his year-end pledge and that the stock be transferred instead to a corporate trustee who would dispose of it as rapidly as possible. The president noted that the divestiture was not required either by law or by his administration's conflict-of-interest guidelines. He and Lance had decided upon divestiture simply to avoid the appearance of conflict. The problem was merely one of time, and no member of the administration should be unfairly punished for having agreed to serve in a government post.

After a brief hearing, the committee declared that Lance had done nothing improper in either his personal or his business affairs, and it appeared ready to agree to the president's request. When an Atlanta businessman seemed about to buy the stock, however, the committee delayed action.[49]

Comptroller's Investigation. In July, one day after he was sworn in as Comptroller of the Currency, John Heimann began an investigation of Lance's banking and personal finances. On August 18 he reported to the Senate Governmental Affairs Committee that he and his staff had not found Lance in violation of the national banking acts, but he did comment that the overdrafts Calhoun permitted constituted unsafe and unsound banking practices.[50] The report noted that the bank's policies regarding overdrafts had been corrected in 1976 but that Lance had not filed certain reports with the banks of which he was an officer; specifically, he had not informed his fellow directors at the two Georgia banks of 50 personal loans and 10 directorships. Regulations require filing such reports, and Heimann indicated that Lance would have been directed to file them even now, if he had still been an officer of these banks.[51]

No evidence was found to indicate that the Teamsters' deposits or Lance's personal loans had violated any federal banking statutes. Although a memorandum dated April 1975 seemed to suggest that the loan Manufacturers Hanover had made to Lance was tied to the correspondent account, all of the parties involved swore under oath that it was not. The report noted that constantly shifting bank relationships and patterns of personal borrowing raised unresolved questions of acceptable banking practices and it suggested that additional federal legislation might be necessary. In addition Comptroller Heimann asked Treasury Secretary Blumenthal to investigate whether the handling of the Lance affair in 1975 and 1976 by the comptroller's office had been complete and proper. To avoid any possible conflicts, the case was turned over to the Internal Revenue Service.

The president and Lance seized on the comptroller's findings as implying a clean bill of health for Lance. In fact, the report had been limited in scope and was confined solely to an investigation of potential violations of federal banking laws since January 1975. It did not deal with possible infractions of other federal statutes or state laws, nor did it address the question of Lance's personal ethics. Nevertheless, the president expressed his full confidence in Lance and indicated that the problem lay not with his appointee but rather with the laws regulating the conduct of bankers. Carter suggested that Congress consider tightening the laws regulating such activities. Lance declared that the report cleared him of any wrongdoing and he intended to remain in office.

Airplane Rides. The comptroller's investigation also discovered that Jimmy Carter had taken five trips in 1975 and 1976 on aircraft owned by the National Bank of Georgia and had not reimbursed the bank. White House spokesmen stated that the failure to pay was simply an oversight. Two of the trips were clearly related to Carter's campaign for the presidential nomination; another was partly political and partly personal. As for the remaining two flights, White House Counsel Lipshutz wrote the FEC asking the agency to determine how these travels should be classified. The president promised to reimburse the bank personally for the trips that were not related to his campaign, while his campaign organization would pay the remaining $1,793.70.

Under the FECA, national banks and corporations cannot legally provide cash or other gifts of value to presidential candidates and candidates may not knowingly accept such contributions. Noting this provision, John Stokes, the U.S. Attorney in Atlanta who investigated Lance's bank dealings, called for an investigation of the plane rides to determine if they were, in fact, contributions.

In late August the White House stated that the Carter campaign committee had not paid for five more trips the president had taken on corporate and state-owned planes in April 1975 during a campaign swing through North and South Carolina. Two of the flights had been paid for by R. R. Allen on a plane owned by D. R. Allen and Son Inc. of Fayetteville, North Carolina. R. R. Allen had contributed $1,000 to the Carter campaign, was a member of the finance committee for the Carter inauguration, and was on the executive board of the Democratic National Finance Council. Two flights had been paid for by the Diamond Supply Co., which is headed by Harvey Diamond of Charlotte, North Carolina. The fifth flight had been paid for by the state of South Carolina. The total cost for all five trips was approximately $1,000 and the Carter campaign committee announced repayment would be made.

On September 5, Senators Ribicoff and Percy, respectively the chairman and ranking minority member of the Senate Governmental Affairs Committee, met with President Carter. They claimed that they had received new and startling information and called on the president to ask Lance to resign. The president refused to do so.

Senate Hearings. The Senate committee began additional hearings. It was learned that Lance had met with Donald Tarleton, Atlanta regional administrator of the Comptroller of the Currency, on November 22, 1976, a few hours before Tarleton released the Calhoun bank from the year-old cease-and-desist agreement on the bank's overdraft policy. Tarleton acted despite advice from an attorney in his office that such agreements could be lifted only by the comptroller's office in Washington.

Stokes admitted that he had wanted to stay in his position until November 1977 so that he could receive increased pension benefits. Stokes said that he had closed the case on Lance one day after receiving a phone call about the case from Sidney Smith, Jr., Lance's attorney, and an old associate of Stokes. Stokes contended that the case should have been dropped several months earlier, and that his action had not been intended to curry favor with the new administration. Several of his assistants objected that the case had been closed too soon.

The Senate committee hearings showed that Smith had discussed with Robert Bloom, acting comptroller before Heimann's appointment, the wording of a press release concerning the comptroller's actions relating to the Calhoun bank. The proposed statement, couched in vague language favorable to the bank, was never released.

Bloom remarked that he had not told the Senate committee in January about Lance's banking difficulties because he assumed that Carter's aides already had given the information to the panel. Bloom claimed he had discussed the matter with these individuals before Lance was selected. He admitted that the letter he wrote to the committee on January 18, 1977, was misleading but said that it had not been intentionally so. Bloom blamed the committee for failing to ask him to discuss Lance's banking record.

In the comptroller's office in Washington, in its Atlanta regional office, and in the U.S. Attorney's office in Atlanta, the senior officials, Bloom, Tarleton, and Stokes, apparently had sought to protect their careers by avoiding conflicts with a key figure in the new administration, while their subordinates had objected and had sought more detailed inquiries.

During his appearance before the committee, Heimann disclosed that Lance, his wife, and their partnership (Lancelot & Co.) had borrowed $3.5 million during 1963-75 from the Fulton National, a Georgia bank with which the Calhoun First National had a correspondent relationship. Heimann also reported that Lance had borrowed $390,000 in 1975 from an Atlanta bank, Citizens and Southern, to pay his campaign debts.[52] It was discovered that NBG had opened a correspondent account with Citizens and Southern soon afterwards. Heimann concluded that the loans might not have been made without the correspondent accounts. He said that no prosecution was warranted, however.

Lance testified for three days before the Senate panel, trying to portray himself as having been unfairly accused by members of the committee as well as by the media. His opening statement was carefully constructed to avoid several key issues. With regard to the loans from corresponding banks, Lance noted that the comptroller's office had found no illegalities. As for the charge of poor management, Lance told

his critics to look at the record; under his stewardship, both the Calhoun
First National Bank and the National Bank of Georgia had increased
their assets significantly. He claimed that he had exerted no improper
influence with government officials. He had not tried to influence
Tarleton, Bloom, or Stokes, nor had any of his associates. When asked
about the 1974 campaign committee's overdrafts, he declared that he
had paid all the outstanding expenses and interest when the campaign
had ended, and that the bank had not violated the law. Despite the
contention of some committee members, Lance argued that he had been
forthright in his meetings with them in January, prior to the confirmation hearings. He said that he had discussed the matters that were now
being rehashed eight months later.

Banking Practices. One of the major questions surrounding the
investigation of Lance concerned the overdraft policies of the Calhoun
First National Bank. According to the comptroller's August report, the
bank paid $78,380 on behalf of Lance's campaign. The campaign
committee had not repaid these debts for two to five months, and service
charges had been levied on only $19,019. Although federal law does not
permit national banks to contribute to or pay the expenses of any
campaign, such banks are allowed to make loans to candidates in
accordance with banking laws and in the ordinary course of business.
Lance's critics claimed that the campaign committee's numerous
overdrafts throughout 1974 and the bank's failure to collect interest on
overdrafts before June 1974 amounted to political contributions from a
national bank, thus violating federal law.[53]

In his opening statement to the Senate Governmental Affairs
Committee, Lance responded that overdrafts were a means of extending
credit and were not illegal. He claimed that the Calhoun bank had had a
liberal overdraft policy for many years and that this had benefited both
the community and the bank. All depositors at the bank were permitted
overdrafts, he claimed. Nevertheless, Lance did not mention whether
such actions violated federal election and/or banking statutes. He focused on the bank's growth and on the fact that its overdrafts had cost it
only a small amount of money and none from any of his accounts.
Moreover, Lance argued, the bank had obeyed the cease-and-desist
order issued by the comptroller's office.

Bank Aircraft. In September the Justice Department's investigation of Lance's use of airplanes owned by the banks at which he had
worked became public. The department had responded to a request
from the comptroller's office; the SEC, the FEC, the IRS, and the
Federal Deposit Insurance Corporation (FDIC) also were looking into
the matter. Lance told the Senate committee that when he was presi-

dent of the Calhoun bank it had leased a Piper Seneca airplane from an operator in Calhoun. When he began campaigning for governor in 1973, he leased the plane from the bank and paid its rent on a monthly basis. The following year, Lancelot & Co. bought a Beechcraft Queen Air. Lance used this plane during the remainder of his campaign and paid all expenses connected with it.

In 1975 the National Bank of Georgia approached Lance about the possibility of his becoming the bank's president and chief operating officer. Its plans called for the development of a network of correspondent banking relationships, an agribusiness program, and an expanded international banking program, all of which required extensive travel. When Lance joined NBG the bank agreed to purchase a plane for his use. The bank initially leased the Beechcraft Queen Air from him and then bought it from him in July 1975.[54] This plane was sold in November 1976 and replaced with a Beechcraft King Air.

In its investigation of Lance, the comptroller's office found hundreds of trips involving NBG planes that did not appear to be business related. These included personal trips by Lance, trips to the Democratic National Convention in New York, and journeys to football games and the Mardi Gras. In addition, it appeared that the plane had been used to transport key members of the new Carter administration around Georgia.

These flights may have violated federal statutes. If the bank provided air travel to political parties or candidates for electoral purposes, it made an illegal campaign contribution; if corporate planes were used for personal trips by bank executives without knowledge of the stockholders and were deducted for tax purposes as a business expense, this use would constitute a violation of securities and tax laws.

Lance argued in his defense that use of the aircraft was essential to the task of creating a new image for the bank, and that this task by its nature made distinctions between personal use and business use impossible. Such distinctions, he asserted, ignore the ways in which new business must be developed.[55] The beleaguered OMB director noted that he had paid for several trips on the plane that were purely personal in nature. It was disclosed that a federal bank examiner in 1976 had found vouchers for flights valued at $44,000, of which only $8,000 worth could be adequately explained as business flights for Lance. In March 1977 Acting Comptroller Bloom had ordered the inquiry dropped on the grounds that Lance's use of the plane was *de minimus* — too little to warrant further inquiry.

Resignation and Indictment. Despite his spirited defense and support from some of the Democratic members on the Governmental

Affairs Committee, the pressure on Lance continued and on September 21 he resigned. Announcing the decision at a nationally televised news conference, President Carter defended Lance and stated his belief that the former OMB director had cleared his name; he had done no wrong. Claiming the decision was solely Lance's, the president contended that he had done a good job as OMB director and that the appointment had not been a mistake. He suggested that Lance needed time to go home and take care of his financial affairs.

Lance's difficulties did not end with his departure from Washington. He and three business associates were indicted May 23, 1979, by a federal grand jury in Atlanta for allegedly violating a series of federal banking laws. Lance was charged with 22 felony counts, including conspiracy, defrauding the government, making false entries in bank records, falsifying personal financial statements, and misapplying bank funds. The 71-page indictment said that the four men showed "reckless disregard" for the safety of the affected banks, while carrying out the conspiracy to obtain hundreds of loans totaling more than $20 million. The conspiracy allegedly began in 1970 and continued through Lance's nine months as OMB director.

Meanwhile, Lance's role in making loans to the Carter warehouse business was expected to come under close scrutiny from an investigation being conducted by a Justice Department special counsel, Paul J. Curran. Attorney General Bell early in 1979 named Curran, a Republican former U.S. Attorney, to probe allegations concerning almost $7 million in loans to the Carter warehouse — including the possible illegal diversion of loan money to Carter's 1976 campaign. On March 23, in response to Republican pressures, Bell upgraded Curran's powers to those of a Watergate-style special prosecutor, complete with the authority to seek indictments.[56]

Besides financial difficulties and a trial on the charges brought by the Justice Department, Lance also faced the prospect of continuing investigation by several other federal agencies, all perhaps more than usually eager to ground the allegations in fact. Both the Securities and Exchange Commission and the Federal Election Commission proceeded to investigate Lance's use of airplanes belonging to the National Bank of Georgia. The IRS attempted to determine whether Lance's overdrafts and his use of the aircraft should be regarded as taxable income.

The SEC investigation increasingly sought to determine the extent to which the former budget director might have misled the stockholders of the two Georgia banks or have otherwise failed to fulfill his legal obligations to them.

Effect on Carter. Two key questions raised during the Lance controversy were: How much did the president know and when did he know it? Lance said in his Senate testimony that he had met with Carter shortly after the election, on November 15, 1976, and had discussed his problems. Carter indicated that the meeting had focused solely on the campaign overdrafts. Lance met with Carter again in early December. Although he had learned from his attorney, Sidney Smith, about the criminal investigation, Lance claimed he did not tell Carter about it.

The president apparently did not read the FBI report on Lance before appointing him to head the OMB. Three of Carter's closest aides — Jody Powell, Hamilton Jordan, and Robert Lipshutz — had read it in January and had found nothing in it that was disturbing enough to tell Carter.

At his September 21, 1977, news conference, the president said he had been called from Atlanta on December 1 and told that the Justice Department inquiry concerning the Calhoun bank had been resolved by the Justice Department and the comptroller's office. The following day, press secretary Jody Powell said Carter "misspoke," and that the only matter discussed prior to the appointment was the question of campaign overdrafts. The discrepancy is important. If Carter's initial statement were correct, it would imply that he knew Lance was under criminal investigation prior to the formal announcement of the appointment and that Carter had been assured that the investigation would be dropped one day before Stokes actually closed the case. This would be evidence of an obstruction of justice.

Clearly, the president and his aides misjudged the damaging nature of the charges. The president lost valuable political capital as a result. His relationship with Congress was weakened, and his image as an honest, pure, and moral chief executive stained. Jimmy Carter became vulnerable to charges of cronyism, hasty judgment, and an unwillingness to concede mistakes.

Confirmation Process. While the president was criticized, so were confirmation hearings held by the Senate Governmental Affairs Committee. Although the committee considered potential conflicts raised by Lance's bank holdings, it failed to investigate his personal finances. In part the committee's failure could be ascribed to the circumstances: Lance was regarded as a confidant of the president, he was the first cabinet nominee to be considered, and the office for which he had been nominated was one traditionally viewed as closer to the president than were most other cabinet-level positions. Still, the committee's failure could be said to reflect on the confirmation process itself. Common Cause called Senate confirmation "a rubberstamp machine" and, in an analysis of 50 important appointments made by Carter, charged the system with three major flaws: 1) Senate failure to develop a full record on all nominees, 2) insufficient allowance of time for review and deliberations, and 3) lack of standards by which to judge nominations. Of the 14 Senate committees it surveyed, Common Cause found that none was doing a thorough job.[57]

In December 1977 it was announced that Lance had agreed to sell 60 percent of his stock in the National Bank of Georgia to a prominent Saudi Arabian businessman for $20 a share. The businessman was Ghaith R. Pharaon, a U.S.-educated contractor with interest in other American banks. His purchase of the NBG stock for $4 a share more than its current market value prompted speculation about the reasons for his purchase, especially because the bank had ceased to pay dividends during the past year. Although Lance reportedly insisted after his resignation that management of the bank or of an investment organization controlled by the buyer would be a condition of sale, the Saudi declined to specify plans for Lance's future. The transaction was estimated to provide Lance with about $2.4 million, enabling him to repay in early January 1978 his $443,466 debt to the United American Bank of Knoxville. Prior to repayment of this loan, the Georgian's debts had been placed as high as $5.9 million.[58] As these events received publicity, James T. McIntyre, Jr., was named to succeed Lance as OMB director, having served as deputy director during Lance's tenure. In January 1978 it was announced that Lance had taken a position as news commentator with an Atlanta television station. Since the position did not appear to be full time, speculation continued regarding other activities he might pursue.[59]

The White House turned its attention to other matters, but Lance continued to attract publicity. Unlike the scandals involving Sherman Adams in Eisenhower's administration and Howard Callaway in Ford's, Lance's alleged improprieties had occurred before his appointment to public office. Some commentators contended that his actions had been neither illegal nor immoral, and that in the post-Watergate era trivial matters were being exaggerated and distorted. An editor of *The Washington Monthly* found Lance's use of aircraft not extraordinary in the business world and suggested that the former OMB director had been judged by an unusually — and perhaps unfairly — strict standard.[60] Others argued that Carter had set impossibly high standards for himself and his appointees in general — standards that required unreasonable sacrifices and would discourage competent individuals from government posts. A columnist for *The Washington Post* charged that the judgmental character of press coverage had played a major role in shaping events.[61]

Weeks after his resignation, Bert Lance had still failed to respond adequately to inquiries from the Senate committee, and federal officials had found more to question as they unraveled his finances and those of the Calhoun bank.[62] Nevertheless, Lance apparently continued in an unofficial capacity to supply the administration with advice, and news reports disclosed that the White House had intervened when the State Department sought to recover Lance's diplomatic passport.[63] Throughout the weeks of controversy that had preceded his resignation, it had been clear that Lance's relationship with the president was special. His closeness to Carter both as a confidant and as a policy maker prompted speculation that the Saudi businessman might be buying connections in Washington by purchasing the NBG stock, and Pharaon was alleged to be acting on behalf of the deputy general manager of the National Commercial Bank of Saudi Arabia, said to have deposits approaching $3 billion and incentive to seek political connections through U.S. banks.[64] Both Lance and Pharaon denied that Lance's continuing friendship with Carter and ready access to the White House played any role in their business relationship.

SEC Suit. In February 1978 Lance's name was mentioned in connection with another bank. Financial General Bankshares, the second largest bank holding company in the Washington, D.C., area, accused Lance of violating federal and state securities laws by conspiring to purchase a controlling interest in its operations. The civil suit filed in U.S. District Court named Lance and others.[65]

On March 17 the Securities and Exchange Commission filed a complaint against Lance and 10 other individuals connected with the purchase of stock in Financial General Bankshares. The SEC civil suit was settled on March 18, when a federal court ordered Lance and his associates to clarify their relationship with Financial General. The settlement involved a consent agreement.

As the Financial General case received publicity, critics leveled a number of charges at Lance and noted in particular his continuing association with the president.[66] One commentator pointed out that Lance's activities in connection with Financial General had occurred after he had sworn to the Senate committee that he would not engage in banking activities once he had taken the oath of office. Observers also criticized the slowness of government agencies investigating Lance's banking activities in Georgia and pointed to conflicts of interest within the investigating teams. Finally, the president himself came under fire, particularly since Lance still carried a diplomatic passport, a White House pass, and the title of "special envoy to the president" — a designation that many found unfortunate in view of his continuing legal difficulties. As critical reports appeared in the press, Bert Lance surrendered his diplomatic passport; he announced no plans to give up the White House pass, however. Many observers noted that with or without the passport Lance clearly remained a valued friend of the president and someone whose influence was of considerable worth in the eyes of Arab investors and others.

On April 12, 1978, Lance addressed a meeting of the American Society of Newspaper Editors and charged a number of newspapers with careless and biased reporting of his career. The speech received widespread attention in the press, and *Time* magazine reported that White House aide Hamilton Jordan had met with Lance to ask him to place greater distance between himself and the president. Jordan denied that he had made this request, however, and Lance declared that several newspapers had erred in printing the accusations made by the SEC. Lance was quoted as saying, "There are more muckrakers around these days than muckmakers." [67]

On April 26, 1978, the Securities and Exchange Commission and the Comptroller of the Currency filed a 90-page civil complaint in U.S. District Court in Atlanta accusing Bert Lance of civil fraud and many violations of federal banking and securities laws. The offenses attributed to Lance by the suit covered a broad spectrum.[68] In addition to the charges brought by the federal grand jury in Atlanta and those specified in the SEC suit, the possibility emerged that civil suits might be lodged against Lance by bank stockholders or other individuals who could claim damage as a result of his actions. The various inquiries and legal proceedings against Lance promised to extend over a period of months, and a picture emerged gradually of the history of his banking activity.

Banking Legislation. As a result of publicity surrounding Lance's banking practices, the House Banking Committee began writing legislation that would prohibit many of the practices for which he had been criticized. Reform legislation adopted in the waning moments of the 95th Congress placed limits on amounts a bank officer or certain stockholders could lend to a campaign committee. The Financial Institutions Regulatory Act (HR 14279) imposed restrictions on national and state bank operations designed to guard against abuses of the type turned up by the investigations of Lance.

The reform law placed tight restrictions on the amount a bank executive or stockholder (holding 10 percent or more of the stock) may borrow, including any loans made to their campaign committees. Such "insiders" may not receive loans in excess of 10 percent of the capital accounts of the bank. The limit applies to loans to their affiliated companies and political or campaign committees as well as to personal loans. The board of directors must approve in advance all loans in excess of $25,000 to officers, directors, or 10 percent stockholders, including loans to their political or campaign committees. All "insider" loans, including those to directors who are not also officers or stockholders, must be nonpreferential — that is, the terms of such loans including rate and collateral must be substantially the same as those prevailing at the time the loan is granted for comparable transactions with other persons.[69]

The Mendelsohn Case

As controversy developed around Bert Lance, another Carter nominee found himself in difficulties. Robert H. Mendelsohn, a San Francisco city supervisor, was nominated to the post of assistant secretary of the Interior in February 1977. Mendelsohn had campaigned for various public offices in previous years, and in March he filed a statement saying that he owed $285,321 from past races, a figure he amended later to $150,000. Most of these debts stemmed from heavy spending in his unsuccessful 1974 race for state controller. Senate confirmation of Mendelsohn's nomination was delayed while he attempted to settle his debts.[70] In the meantime, Mendelsohn was paid $169 a day to work as a consultant in the Interior Department while continuing to serve on the Board of Supervisors in San Francisco.[71]

In March, Bruce Brugmann, owner-editor of *The San Francisco Bay Guardian*, began to attack the nomination, charging that Mendelsohn voted for special interests, especially developers and utilities, some of whom had been major contributors to his campaign.[72] At Brugmann's request and in accordance with state law, the California Fair Political Practices Commission (FPPC) began an investigation of Mendelsohn's campaign records.

Although the FPPC found no violations of the law by Mendelsohn, its evidence of fiscal irregularities included incorrect reporting by Mendelsohn's campaign of four loans amounting to $8,829. The campaign committee in May 1977 had reported these loans as forgiven when in fact they had not been, and Mendelsohn had confirmed the campaign workers' statement in his testimony before the Senate Committee on Energy and Natural Resources.

A second irregularity discovered by the FPPC attracted greater attention. In June 1977 an FPPC investigator noticed on a ledger sheet a change in the name shown as the source of a $15,000 loan and a $1,500 contribution. In investigating the altered entry, the FPPC determined that a total sum of $26,500 (including the original $16,500) had been contributed to Mendelsohn's campaign by Transcentury Properties Inc. When the funds were given, Mendelsohn was a member of the Regional Planning Commission, from which Transcentury was seeking approval for a massive housing development in the fishing village of Bodega Bay.[73] The investigating commission found that Transcentury's political contribution had been laundered through an intricate process involving

William F. Chamberlain (president of Transcentury), William F. Grader
(a fish wholesaler and Democratic Party activist), Wanda Zikich (owner
of a restaurant and motel complex near Bodega Bay and a member of a
California coastal commission), and Wanda Zikich's sister, Louise Drob.
Drob's name had been substituted for that of Grader on the ledger
entry.[74]

As inquiry into these irregularities continued, critics pointed out
that Mendelsohn's "budgetary sloppiness" reflected poorly on his ability
to oversee the budget of the Interior Department (one of his responsibilities as assistant secretary). On August 2, FPPC Chairman Daniel H.
Lowenstein issued an interim report on the commission's findings. This
report stated that evidence had been uncovered of serious violations
committed by the campaign committee in regard to the Drob transaction, but that the commission had not found evidence that
Mendelsohn knew Transcentury to be the true source of the contribution. The report noted in conclusion that it was intended neither to clear
nor to accuse Mendelsohn. As in the Lance affair, the report was cited
both by Mendelsohn in his own defense and by Brugmann in opposing
his confirmation. In September, Brugmann filed a lawsuit aimed at
making the FPPC release the evidence on which the interim report was
based, and he commented that Mendelsohn's difficulties were graver
than the charges against Bert Lance, since Mendelsohn's performance as
a public official was called into question.[75]

Nomination Withdrawn. In response to the allegations,
Mendelsohn indicated that he had not carefully reviewed the financial
statements filed by his campaign and that he had not known that Louise
Drob's contribution had originated elsewhere.[76] None of Mendelsohn's
campaign workers admitted to having made the alteration in the ledger,
and many individuals were said to have had access to it. Under California law the campaign treasurer rather than the candidate himself is
responsible for the accuracy of financial reports filed with the commission. Campaign treasurer Melvin M. Swig ascribed to Mendelsohn more
detailed knowledge of the campaign's finances than he himself pos-
sessed. Grader contended that while he had received $26,500 from
Transcentury, the $26,500 he had given to Mendelsohn's campaign
represented separate funds. Transcentury claimed that the money transferred to Grader had been payment for a legitimate option to purchase a
piece of property.[77]

The extent of Mendelsohn's knowledge continued to be questioned.
Asked about the affair in a news conference on October 13, President
Carter disclaimed any detailed knowledge but commented that if the
allegations were proven, the individuals responsible for confirming
Mendelsohn's nomination would not approve. On November 11, the

FPPC announced its intention to file a civil lawsuit against Mendelsohn, Grader, William F. Chamberlain, and campaign workers (including Melvin Swig). The suit charged Mendelsohn with widespread violations of campaign disclosure laws that centered on the laundered campaign funds. Although the commission did not conclude that Mendelsohn took part in a conspiracy to conceal the source of the funds, Lowenstein submitted a written dissent to the report stating that the evidence supported a conclusion that Mendelsohn knew the source of the money. The FPPC suit asked $80,684 in damages and charged Mendelsohn with failure to disclose properly the same amount in contributions made to his campaign for state controller in 1974. On the same day, Interior Secretary Cecil D. Andrus acceded to Mendelson's request that his nomination be withdrawn pending a court decision. Andrus added that he would recommend resubmission of Mendelsohn's name in spring 1978 following favorable action by the court.

Case Settled. The case was settled in April 1978, reportedly to the satisfaction of both the plaintiff and the defendants. A carefully phrased settlement dismissed the charges against Mendelsohn and his campaign committee "with prejudice." The campaign committee paid the commission $5,000; Mendelsohn paid nothing. The commission said the evidence did not support the conclusion that Mendelsohn knew the source of the illegal contribution. San Francisco District Attorney Joseph Freitas announced plans to seek criminal indictments against Chamberlain and Grader, however.

Secretary Andrus did not indicate whether he would resubmit Mendelsohn's name for Senate confirmation. California newspapers were critical of the state Fair Political Practices Commission. They charged that the case had been in litigation for one year at a cost to the taxpayer of $150,000, that Mendelsohn's claim to innocence had been affirmed by the court, and that the case apparently had accomplished nothing except damage to the career of a once-esteemed public servant.[78] Still, in June 1978 Mendelsohn was appointed to oversee urban, manpower, and youth programs in the Interior Department; in making the appointment, Andrus suggested that he might have named Mendelsohn a second time to the post of assistant secretary for policy, budget, and administration, but that a long and probably unsuccessful battle for Senate confirmation had seemed likely.[79] The new appointment did not require Senate confirmation.

The Costanza Case

In fall 1977 a third high-ranking official attracted publicity because of a campaign debt. The official, Margaret "Midge" Costanza, filled the

White House post of assistant to the president for public liaison. When she entered the White House on February 1977, Costanza had a $17,615 deficit lingering from her unsuccessful 1974 campaign for a congressional seat in New York State. On April 7, 1977, with White House approval, she held a $500-a-ticket fund-raising party featuring Vice President Mondale.[80] The party was a success and raised $3,000 more than Costanza's debt, all but $570 of which she owed to herself.[81] Costanza communicated with the FEC about the event, but she did not file until October the report that under the law should have been filed by July 10.[82]

In early October 1977 press attention to the affair brought criticism. Many felt that contributors might have been motivated by a desire to buy influence in the White House. Others criticized the White House for its decision not to screen donors, and some drew parallels with the situations of Bert Lance and Robert Mendelsohn. No rule existed prohibiting presidential aides from fund raising, yet some commentators believed that Costanza had not fulfilled the Carter administration's pledge to avoid "even the appearance of impropriety." Others, including House Republican Whip Robert H. Michel of Illinois, were more concerned about the failure of a senior aide to comply with the letter of the law and demanded Costanza's resignation because of her tardiness in filing reports with the FEC. Speaker of the House O'Neill called the criticism of Costanza "politically motivated" and "picayune."[83] At least one columnist demanded that the president and Congress take steps to avoid repetition of such fund-raising events.[84] In May 1978 Midge Costanza agreed to pay a $500 fine to the FEC. The commission had voted 5-1 to overrule the recommendation that Costanza be found innocent of having knowingly violated the law, and the case marked the first fine levied by the commission for late filing by a candidate for Congress or a staff member of the White House. FEC documents indicated that the fine had been reduced from $1,000; it was one of the largest fines imposed by the commission in its three-year history.[85]

Implications. The Lance, Mendelsohn, and Costanza affairs were inevitably embarrassing to the new administration because of its emphasis on ethical standards and stringent regulations to prevent conflicts of interest. All three cases indicated the need for consideration of an official's debts as well as his or her assets, and offered a further demonstration of the need for financial disclosure. In addition, the difficulties of Lance and Mendelsohn may be pondered as they reflect upon the confirmation process: Clearly it is desirable to discover possible conflicts before an official is nominated and to have full information available in advance of confirmation hearings. Common Cause has documented the need for fuller investigation;[86] it remains to be seen how

effectively legislation can prevent conflicts of interest and how responsive Congress will be to making it do so.[87]

DNC Aftermath

"The Republican Party," President Carter told Democratic fund-
raisers in 1977, "has always had plenty of money. The Democratic Party
has always been broke."[88] This historical pattern held true after the
1976 election when the Democrats, despite their electoral success, still
were not able to break into black ink.

At a meeting of the executive committee of the Democratic National Committee in February 1977, the party treasurer reported a
deficit of $3.5 million. This represented a substantial decrease from the
$9 million deficit that faced the party after the 1968 election, but
nevertheless a large debt remained.

The DNC hoped to raise $6.5 million in 1977. It fell short of that
goal, however, raising only $3.8 million in 1977 and $4.6 million in
1978.[89] A portion of the money raised for the DNC was used to retire old
debts. In April 1977 a court had ordered the DNC to pay American
Airlines $60,000 a month to meet debts incurred in 1972. Money also was
owed to telephone companies from the 1972 campaign.[90] Moreover, the
DNC decided that it had an obligation to pay back an illegal $50,000 gift
made by Ashland Oil between 1970 and 1972.[91] In its September 30,
1978, filing with the FEC, the DNC reported a $7,500 payment and a
remaining $42,500 debt to the oil company.

Outstanding debts from the 1976 election included $66,000 to
Amtrak for a whistle-stop train, $122,000 to pollster Pat Caddell, and
$440,000 to Gerald Rafshoon's ad agency,[92] as well as $200,000 in bank
loans taken out in December 1976 and January 1977 to cover the
transition and inauguration period.[93] By the end of 1978, net indebtedness had been reduced to $1.5 million.[94]

For the first several months of his presidency, President Carter had
asked the DNC to leave him out of all political activities until he could
get his administration's programs under way. The president even refused to sign his name to fund-raising letters. This self-imposed mora-
torium was maintained until June 1977, when Carter appeared at a
$1,000-a-plate dinner in New York City. The dinner was attended by
1,000 supporters, and netted more than $1 million for the party after
expenses. In attendance at the Democrats' first $1,000-a-plate fund-
raiser in eight years were, in addition to Carter, Vice President Mondale,
Senator Hubert Humphrey, some cabinet members, and New York's two
top Democrats, Gov. Hugh L. Carey and Mayor Abraham Beame.[95]

Somewhat less successful was a second $1,000-a-plate presidential dinner, held in Los Angeles in October. The DNC hoped to gross $1 million from the event, but actually raised only half that amount. The low turnout was partially due to hostility to Carter from American Jews concerned about his Middle East policy. In addition, some oil company executives failed to attend because the president had excoriated "special interests" in a recent speech on his energy bill. The California Democratic Party, which had to cancel a fund-raiser it had previously scheduled for the same week as that of the DNC, received 7-1/2 percent of the net proceeds.[96]

The most controversial aspect of DNC fund-raising was the formation of the Democratic National Finance Council. Patterned after the President's Club of the Kennedy and Johnson years, the idea of the council was formulated shortly after Carter's inauguration at a meeting between the president and Dallas mortgage banker Jess Hay. According to Hay, the overall strategy for a new fund-raising program was agreed to at this meeting.[97] The proposal called for the party to seek out contributions of all sizes but to emphasize larger donations, especially from owners of small businesses. The president felt that past fund-raising efforts had neglected this group and he said he was determined to change this pattern.[98]

The newly reconstituted Democratic National Finance Council, chaired by Hay, was to be responsible for raising the money. The council actually comprised three levels of donors under a formula devised by DNC Treasurer Joel McCleary. An executive committee of the council was created, composed of 100 members who agreed to contribute and/or solicit a total of $50,000 a year for four years. Finance Council members were individuals who agreed to contribute and/or solicit a total of $5,000 a year. The third level was the 1600 Club, comprised of individuals who agreed to contribute $1,000 a year. The program raised a gross total of $3,061,450 in 1977, while incurring $574,288 in expenses (See Table 12-2).

According to a prospectus given out at a meeting of the executive committee of the council, members were offered a chance "to assist the Administration in the evolution of its economic and governmental policies."[99] In addition, each member was encouraged to participate in the processes of the Democratic Party and all were offered an opportunity to express their views at informal seminars attended by key government officials.

Reaction to the new fund-raising plan was varied. One writer wondered whether "party fat cats" should have special access to officials and noted that many members of the executive committee were lobbyists, bankers, and real estate developers.[100] An editorial in *Business*

Table 12-2
Democratic National Committee and Affiliated Organizations, Combined Statement of Revenues and Expenses for Year Ended December 31, 1977

Revenues:
Contributions
Direct mail	$2,157,679	
Major contributors and fund-raising events	3,061,450	$5,219,129
Less fund-raising expenses		
Direct mail	—930,358	
Major contributors and fund-raising events	—574,288	1,504,646
		3,714,483
Old debt forgiveness		57,885
Other revenues		19,681
Total revenues		$3,792,049

Expenses:
General and Administrative
Payroll and related expenses	$1,601,150	
Rent	182,407	
Telephone and telegraph	144,909	
Travel	63,452	
Printing and office supplies	54,037	
Professional services	50,969	
Interest	44,530	
Old debt adjustments	94,481	
Postage	23,807	
Loss on disposition of assets	13,263	
Depreciation	12,535	
Other insurance and taxes	8,010	
Pension	6,500	
Repair and maintenance	5,784	2,305,834

Special Meetings and Projects
Campaign services	251,043	
White House	185,652	
General	95,442	
Field operations	80,712	
Transition	61,877	
Midterm conference	9,840	
Radio	—	
		684,566
Presidential election		15,633
Campaigns (1976 Nonpresidential)		—
Other expenses		52,359
Total expenses		$3,058,392
Revenues Over (Under) Expenses Before Provision for Income Taxes		733,657
Provision for Income Taxes		50
Revenues Over (Under) Expenses		$ 733,607

Week implied that the new givers were "suckers" who get nothing for their money but "free drinks, a look at the President, and some conversational gambits." [101] *Los Angeles Times* writer Robert Shogan wondered if the new plan of the Democrats could be interpreted as conflicting with the spirit of the federal campaign financing law, particularly the parts that prohibit any special consideration in return for a campaign gift. [102] Shogan also saw the possibility that party liberals would object to this new overture to the business community.

Administration officials defended the program. Party Treasurer McCleary was resentful of what he termed "the feeling that there is something dirty about giving money." [103] McCleary, reacting to charges that contributors were buying influence, responded that the Democrats were "putting together the cleanest, most above board, most antiseptic campaign that's ever been seen." Hope J. Boonshaft, then finance director of the council, referred to its members as political philanthropists. Both McCleary and Boonshaft admitted, however, that the members of the council would have "more impact than the guy who gives nothing." [104]

The Democratic National Finance Council was modeled on the President's Club, started in 1961 by President Kennedy[105] and originally intended as a means to formalize and institutionalize the seeking of large contributions, offering large donors status and contact with the president. The DNC also continued to raise money from small donors through direct-mail solicitation. This method raised $2,157,679 in 1977, at a cost of $930,358.

In July 1977 the DNC formulated a preliminary $2 million campaign budget for 1978. The plan envisaged $300,000 in direct contributions to Senate candidates, $700,000 for House candidates, and $40,000 for gubernatorial races. The largest of these contributions were to be "targeted" to Democratic candidates in close races who were given the best chance of winning. An additional $400,000 was to be furnished through in-kind services — polling, research, consultants — for Democratic hopefuls. The remainder was to be used for speakers, materials, and staff. The preliminary plan also called for extensive campaigning by President Carter and members of his family, Vice President Mondale, and several members of the cabinet. Requests for their time were to be coordinated by Frank Moore, the chief White House liaison with Congress. As DNC Chairman Kenneth M. Curtis noted, this role also would provide Moore with additional leverage that would "not hurt him" when seeking proadministration votes from incumbent congressmen up for reelection. [106]

Curtis described the upcoming 1978 campaign effort as the "largest" ever undertaken by the DNC. It did, however, lack one feature of the previous such campaign — the naming of a chairman of the midterm campaign committee. This position had been filled in 1974 by lame-duck Georgia Gov. Jimmy Carter, who used it to lay the groundwork for his own presidential campaign.

DNC expenses in 1977 included $40,000 a month budgeted for White House political expenses. This classification included presidential and vice presidential travel, polls by Patrick Caddell, and pens used by the president in signing legislation. It also covered the cost of sending Christmas cards from the president and First Lady to 150,000 Carter supporters.[107] In 1978 the DNC took out an $800,000 contract with Caddell's Cambridge Research Survey Co. for polling work.[108] This latter was criticized as excessive for White House and party polling when the DNC debt remained so large and 1978 candidates needed money; party officials claimed that congressional and other candidates in 1978 would benefit from the polls and could share in the results.

Another expense for the DNC was a $1,000 clothing allowance for Treasurer Joel McCleary. McCleary, who also received a $36,000 annual salary and was directly reimbursed for normal business expenses such as entertainment, hotel bills, and airline tickets, explained that it was necessary for him to dress properly so that he could "schmooze" with large contributors.[109]

The DNC was constantly aware of its poor financial situation, and tried to conserve its funds whenever possible. Members of the Winograd Commission on Party Rules, for example, were expected to pay for their own expenses when attending meetings. Only commissioners facing "severe hardship" were eligible to be reimbursed, and even then they were asked to cover part of the cost.[110]

Similarly, budget considerations played a major role in the debate on the 1978 midterm party conference. Party activists had proposed an increase in the size of the conference from 1,627 delegates to 2,513, claiming that the increase would make seats available for local party workers and would expand grass-roots participation. The DNC decided against the increase, largely because of the additional expense that would have been involved. Instead, it budgeted $400,000 to put on a "no frills" conference, and asked each state committee to contribute $125 per delegate to help defray costs.[111]

Money also played a paramount role in the resignation of DNC Chairman Curtis in December 1977. Curtis, a former governor of Maine and an early Carter supporter in 1976, had been elected chairman early in 1977 in what was considered a takeover of the party apparatus by the Carter forces. Less than a year later he resigned amidst rumors, denied both by Curtis and by the White House, that the president was dissatisfied with Curtis' work. At a news conference announcing this resignation, Curtis declared that the decision to resign had been his own, agreed with a questioner that the chairmanship of the DNC was "a lousy job," and asked rhetorically, "Did you ever try to meet the payroll every two weeks of a bankrupt organization, and try to keep 50 state chairmen happy?" [112]

Curtis' successor, John C. White, agreed that the party's debt should be its top priority. "This party can't always be in debt," he said. "We've got to get on the credit side of the ledger and build our credibility." [113]

Two fortuitous events occurred early in 1978 to make White's goal appear easier. First was a decision by President Carter to take a more active role in party fund raising. In 1977 he admitted to a meeting of the DNC that the party had not received "the support that was needed from the White House." He therefore agreed to speak at five $1,000-a-couple fund-raising dinners in 1978. He had addressed only two in 1977. But only four dinners actually were held in 1978, in Atlanta, Houston, and Washington, where proceeds of one of two dinners were earmarked for congressional candidates. [114] The fund-raising potential of Carter's action was somewhat clouded in view of the president's declining popularity and the effort by many congressional and state campaigners to distance themselves from Carter, feeling his presence would hurt rather than help their campaigns.

Perhaps even more important to the Democrats was a unanimous ruling by the Federal Election Commission in February 1978 that allowed the DNC to accept unlimited contributions to pay off old debts. The ruling exempted from the contribution limits set by the 1974 Amendments debts incurred before those amendments had been enacted. The Republicans had no such debts; by this time the Democrats still owed $2 million from the original $9 million in debts incurred from the expenses of the 1968 Democratic convention and from the party's assumption of debts taken over from the 1968 presidential campaigns of Robert F. Kennedy and Hubert H. Humphrey. Under the FEC ruling, individuals could make contributions of more than $20,000 to the DNC and more than $25,000 in total contributions during a year, and committees could contribute more than $15,000 to the DNC, as long as all contributions above these limits were earmarked to redeem old debt. [115]

During August and September 1978 several such contributions were made to the DNC, two of which provoked some controversy. On August 10, the same day they attended a private luncheon in the White House, Lew Wasserman and Richard O'Neil contributed $100,000 and $25,000, respectively, to the DNC. The question arose as to whether an old and rarely enforced law prohibiting the solicitation of contributions on federal property had been violated. On February 2, 1979, following a preliminary FBI investigation, the Justice Department released a report in which Attorney General Griffin Bell concluded that nothing illegal had transpired at the August 10 meeting and that no further investigation was warranted.[116]

The National Conservative Political Action Committee challenged the original FEC ruling in court, but the suit was dismissed on the grounds that NCPAC has no standing in court to file charges and had failed to exhaust the administrative remedies available to it before resorting to litigation.

White continued Curtis' policy of reducing the DNC staff as an economizing measure. Curtis cut the size of the staff from 110 to 80, White from 80 to 40. Most of the remaining personnel were assigned to the administrative/clerical and fund-raising areas. Only one employee at the DNC was involved with assisting local candidates (compared with at least 50 people performing similar work at the RNC).[117]

Joel McCleary resigned shortly afterwards. McCleary, who had been a fund-raiser for Carter's presidential campaign, had become party treasurer in January 1977. The reason for his resignation was reported to be displeasure over the cutbacks on his staff imposed by White.[118] Actually, McCleary left because fund raising was lagging and it was decided that new personnel were needed. Charles Manatt, former California Democratic chairman, who had considerable success as a fund-raiser in his home state, became chairman of the Finance Council and Evan Dobelle, former U.S. chief of protocol, became DNC treasurer at $50,000 a year. Dobelle's expressed goal was to reduce the pre-1975 debt by $1 million by the end of 1978. He suggested that the Democratic Party "cannot establish credibility as a party back in business until we make a major effort to pay off our debt." [119]

Several factors have had a negative impact on Democratic fund-raising, among them the domestic reaction to the Carter administration's Middle East policy. American Jews traditionally have played a major role in Democratic finances. One report estimated that at least a third of the major contributors to Jimmy Carter in 1976 were Jewish, as were more than half of the large donors to Morris Udall and perhaps two-thirds of those to Henry Jackson. In Carter's case, Jewish contributors played a particularly important role in California and New York, where Max Palevsky and Howard Samuels, respectively, were key early fund-raisers.[120]

Carter's Middle East policy, which included sales of combat planes to Egypt and Saudi Arabia, and was perceived as putting pressure on Israel to make territorial concessions, was seen by many Jews as a threat to the security of Israel. Relations between the Jewish community and the Carter administration deteriorated rapidly and reached a low point in March 1978 with the resignation of Mark Siegel as Carter's liaison with the Jewish community, an exchange of charges between Rabbi Alexander M. Schindler of the Conference of Presidents of Major American Jewish Organizations and national security adviser Zbigniew Brzezinski, and a tense U.S. visit by Israeli Prime Minister Menachem Begin that was marked by major disagreements with President Carter.

These developments gave rise to speculation that American Jews would express their disapproval of administration policy by withholding contributions from the Democratic Party. Harrison Dogole, chairman of the DNC's 1600 Club, feared that fund raising could become "very, very difficult" because "the Jewish community is turned off." [121] In fact, a $1,000-a-plate Democratic fund-raising dinner scheduled for May 22 in New York was postponed until December because of fears that it would be boycotted by Jewish contributors.[122]

At the same time, President Carter's popularity declined among other segments of the population as well. Some congressional and state campaigners in 1978 tried to distance themselves from Carter, feeling his presence would hurt rather than help their campaigns; others, especially during Carter's brief surge in popularity after the Camp David accords in September, were anxious to benefit from his intensive campaigning for congressional candidates in the weeks before the 1978 elections.[123] Vice President Mondale was also called on to do a great deal of campaigning for Democratic candidates.

RNC Aftermath

The Republican Party in 1976 lost its eight-year hold on the White House, declined by two seats in the House of Representatives to 143, and failed to increase its 38 Senate seats. In 1977 the Gallup Poll found that only 20 percent of the electorate considered itself Republican, the lowest figure in four decades. Commentators and political scientists speculated on imminent extinction of the Grand Old Party.

In spite of the setbacks, the Republicans did very well financially in the period following the 1976 election — incomparably better than the Democrats. The RNC had entered 1976 with $986,000 in cash, and closed out the year with $1,398,000. By the time of the meeting of the Republican National Committee in late April 1977, the party had more than $2.6 million in cash.

At that meeting, the RNC approved a budget of $7.4 million. This included $3 million for 1977 campaign operations that would concentrate on the development of municipal and state legislative candidates. "You can't rebuild the party from the top down," said Charles R. Black, Jr., newly appointed campaign director, in explaining the high priority given the races.

Table 12-3
Republican National Committee, Treasurer's Report for Year Ended
December 31, 1977

Cash balance — January 1, 1977	$ 1,405,500
Cash receipts:	
Direct mail	7,755,800
Major contributors	1,488,700
Telephone	511,400
Dinner	178,900
Promotionals	676,000
Miscellaneous	41,400
Total income from contributions	10,652,200
Miscellaneous refunds	2,106,500
Total cash receipts	12,758,700
Cash disbursements:	
1976 obligations	489,600
Affiliated committees	701,900
Fund raising	3,335,100
Candidate, state, local support	1,909,100
Party operations	5,176,500
Total cash disbursements	11,612,200
Cash balance — December 31, 1977	$ 2,552,000 [a]

[a] Includes $1,000,000 6.1% certificate of deposit.

The RNC budget included $700,000 for a new local election campaign division and $500,000 to help provide each state party with a trained political professional. In addition, $250,000 was earmarked for recruiting and assisting black candidates, for which the RNC hired the black-operated campaign firm of Wright, McNeill, and Associates, based in Columbus, Georgia, as consultants.

Overall, the party budgeted $375,000 for programs aimed at blacks. This was more than six times any such previous outlay, indicating the Republicans' desire to expand their base of support.[124]

Republican fund raising in 1977 included a $1,000-a-plate testimonial dinner to former President Ford in May. The proceeds of the dinner, which exceeded $1 million, were divided among the RNC, the National Republican Congressional Committee, the Republican Senatorial Campaign Committee, and the Republican Congressional Boosters Club.[125]

As shown in Table 12-3, the RNC received more than $10.6 million in contributions in 1977 — considerably more than its goal. Also shown are certain categories of expenditures.

The Republican National Sustaining Fund was organized in 1962. An annual sustaining membership costs $15 per contributor, with donors of up to $100 considered a part of the program. Other programs include: the Republican Campaigner Program for annual contributors of $100 to

$499, Republican Victory Associates for those contributing $500 to $999, and the Republican National Associates for annual contributors of $1,000 and above.

The years 1976 and 1977 were the two most successful for the Republican National Sustaining Fund. The following list shows the amounts raised by the fund since its formation in 1962:

1962	$ 700,000	1970	$3,040,000
1963	1,100,000	1971	4,369,000
1964	2,369,000	1972	5,282,000
1965	1,700,000	1973	3,964,000
1966	3,300,000	1974	4,759,482
1967	3,500,000	1975	5,971,877
1968	2,400,000	1976	10,112,078
1969	2,125,000	1977	7,755,800*

*Includes contributions of up to $499.

The success of the Republican fund-raising effort was marred somewhat by a dispute that arose between the RNC and conservative followers of Ronald Reagan over the funding of a campaign against ratification of the Panama Canal treaties.

After the RNC had voted to oppose ratification of the treaties in October 1977, a fund-raising letter was sent out over Reagan's signature. The letter read, in part: ". . .the Republican National Committee and the National Republican Congressional Committee have joined together to establish an Emergency Panama Canal fund and launch an unprecedented campaign to defeat the treaties and elect more Republicans to Congress who will defeat any giveaway schemes."

The RNC, NRCC, and Reagan's Citizens for the Republic each sent the letter to its own mailing list, and a total of $2 million was raised. The RNC raised $700,000 from the letter, before costs of $175,000.[126]

In December 1977 Reagan and Sen. Paul Laxalt of Nevada, chairman of CFTR's Steering Committee, requested $50,000 from the RNC to finance half the cost of a cross-country speaking tour by Republican congressmen to rally public opposition to the treaties. When the request was denied by RNC Chairman Bill Brock, Reagan withdrew permission for the RNC and the NRCC to use the letter. "My credibility is involved in this," he said. "After all, letters with my name on them have gone all across the country asking for money to help fight the treaties. Now we discover that money raised by the letters will not be used for that purpose. And worse than that, we discover that the national party has no plans to campaign against the treaties."[127]

Brock defended his denial of the funds on the grounds that the antitreaty "truth squad" was not an official party body and that the money should be used for the 1978 congressional elections. He pointed out that the Reagan letter had said contributions were needed to "defeat those who vote time and time again against a strong U.S. foreign policy." He said he would have no objection to financing a speaking tour if it was a "part of the Republican leadership program in Congress" and if it addressed "a whole range of issues, not just the treaty question." [128]

Laxalt announced that the antitreaty tour would go on as scheduled, financed by contributions from individuals and from organizations such as the Conservative Caucus, the American Conservative Union, the Committee for the Survival of a Free Congress, Citizens for the Republic, the Young Republicans, and the Council for National Defense.[129]

The effect of the incident was to put a serious strain on the relations between the Reagan wing and the party leadership. Reagan, in a letter to Brock, said the party could not use his name for fund raising again "until this issue has been resolved." And Laxalt, who was chairman of Reagan's 1976 presidential campaign, said the incident "reaffirms my feeling that if we are going to be effective as conservatives, it will have to be outside the RNC. It's obvious they're not sympathetic to our goals." [130]

Eventually, Brock attempted to defuse the issue. He sent letters explaining his position and offering refunds to all those who had sent contributions in response to the Reagan letter. By late February 1978 only 75 contributors had protested Brock's decision and fewer than 40 had requested refunds.[131]

The highlight of Republican fund raising in 1978 was a series of 14 $500- or $1,000-a-plate dinners held simultaneously across the country in April. Among the speakers were Gerald Ford in Los Angeles, Ronald Reagan in Chicago, Howard Baker in Houston, Robert Dole in Detroit, and Henry Kissinger in New York. The dinners grossed $3 million, which Peter Teeley, director of communications for the RNC, said was the party's best one-day effort in a nonpresidential year. Half of the net proceeds were to go to the state committees, and half to the RNC to be spent for congressional, legislative, and local Republican candidates in 1978.[132]

Republican Headquarters Purchase

In August 1977 the Republican National Committee announced a new fund-raising effort to purchase its headquarters at 310 First Street, Southeast, in Washington, seven years after the center's dedication as permanent party headquarters in 1971. Republicans were asked to contribute to the purchase of the building, which would be dedicated to President Dwight D. Eisenhower in commemoration of the 25th anniversary of his inauguration. The building was offered to the RNC by Capitol Hill Associates, a group of Republican investors who had it built originally for the price of $1.5 million, or $2.5 million less than its appraised value.

To make the purchase, the RNC altered its financial and organizational structure. A special committee was created to make the acquisition, and the RNC informed potential donors that the Committee to Preserve the National Republican Center was legally a distinct entity to which individuals, political action committees, and corporations could make gifts in any amount.[133]

Corporations and unions, which ordinarily are barred under the FECA from making political contributions out of corporate or union funds, were permitted legally to participate in this project by one section of the 1976 Amendments. The section exempts from the definition of campaign contributions money donated to a party specifically for use in purchasing or building an office facility not used to influence the election of a specific candidate. The amendment also exempts amounts contributed by individuals from the $25,000-a-year maximum allowable contribution by individuals to candidates or other party or nonparty committees.

Donors of $10,000 or more would be recognized with a plaque to be hung in the center's lobby. Donors of $1,000 would receive invitations to a fund-raising dinner featuring a "Salute to Ike." In addition, fund-raising drives would be mounted in each of the 50 states. Former Texas Gov. John B. Connally accepted the chairmanship of the committee and kicked off the fund-raising drive in January 1978.

By the end of March the committee already had raised $620,108, including some $224,000 in loans from the RNC, all of which were repaid by June. The committee also had received an additional $160,000 in pledges.[134]

Of the amount raised by the end of March, $140,850 was in the form of corporate contributions from 58 firms, the largest of which were: Atlantic Richfield Co., $25,000; Houston Natural Gas Corp., $12,000; Westinghouse Electric Corp., $10,000; Union Oil Co. of California, $10,000; and Getty Oil Co., $10,000. Substantial pledges came from Panax Corp. of East Lansing, Michigan (a newspaper publishing firm headed by John P. McGoff) and from members of the Rockefeller family.[135]

New Right

An increasingly active role has been played in recent years by a group of conservative political action committees known loosely as the

"New Right," which includes the National Conservative Political Action Committee, the Committee for the Survival of a Free Congress, the Gun Owners of America, and the Committee for Responsible Youth Politics. These organizations have differed from other conservative groups in that they all all been created since 1973, and they have shown disdain for the Republican Party as an instrument of conservatism. The most visible force uniting these and other conservative groups has been Richard A. Viguerie, whose direct-mail fund-raising apparatus has helped supply the financial power to make the New Right a viable force in American politics. Viguerie's activities are discussed in some detail below.

New Right groups are more interested in political philosophy than in party labels and consequently they supported conservative candidates from both parties in 1976. The National Conservative Political Action Committee contributed the largest amount to candidates, $406,514. The recipients included 118 Republicans, 16 Democrats, and three others running for the House of Representatives, as well as 12 Republicans and an independent running for the Senate. The NCPAC also made contributions to three candidates for the Senate and 19 for the House who were eliminated in primary elections.[136]

The Committee for the Survival of a Free Congress was the next most active New Right organization in 1976, making contributions of $314,019. In House campaigns it contributed to 94 Republicans, seven Democrats, one Libertarian, and an independent, as well as 24 potential candidates who lost in primaries. For the Senate it supported 12 Republicans, one Democrat, an independent, and four primary losers.[137]

The Gun Owners of America, another Viguerie-funded group, made contributions totaling $120,419. Recipients included four Republicans and a Democrat among Senate candidates, and 37 Republicans, two Democrats, and two independents running for the House. There were also two losers of Senate primaries and 11 of House primaries.[138]

The impact of New Right money in enabling congressional candidates to win elections appears to have been slight in 1976. Of the 47 candidates who received contributions of $3,000 or more from NCPAC, only 12 won their elections. The comparable figures for CSFC are seven out of 33; and for GOA, two out of 10.

New Right groups generally were more successful in 1977, when they were active in special elections for Congress, in state and local elections, and in the gubernatorial race in Virginia. In that state, Republican candidate John N. Dalton was supported by the National Conservative Political Action Committee, the Virginia Conservative Political Action Committee, and Independent Virginians for Responsible Government. All three organizations were funded by Viguerie's direct-mail company, and all three had John T. Dolan as chairman.[139]

In special House elections in 1977, seven major conservative groups contributed nearly $72,000 to John E. Cunningham in Washington, Robert T. Livingston in Louisiana, and Arlan Stangeland in Minnesota. All three conservative Republicans were victorious in traditionally Democratic districts, and all three credited the conservative organizations with having made their victories possible.[140]

Four groups associated with Viguerie were expected to contribute close to $2 million in 1978 to local, state, and congressional campaigns.[141] The NCPAC expected to raise "at least a million dollars" for campaigns, according to John Dolan. He said the organization would work with about 100 campaigns on a day-to-day basis and would contribute money and campaign services to approximately 200 others.

The Committee for the Survival of a Free Congress planned to contribute between $300,000 and $400,000 in salaries for precinct organization staff workers. Paul Weyrich, the committee's director, predicted the group would target 50 liberal House members for defeat and also would be involved in about half of the races for open seats.

H. L. "Bill" Richardson, chairman of the Gun Owners of America, said that in 1978 his group would exceed its 1976 spending total of $300,000 on state and federal campaigns. The GOA supports only challengers and open-seat contenders.

Another Viguerie-funded group, the Committee for Responsible Youth Politics, planned to contribute between $75,000 and $100,000 to House and Senate campaigns in 1978. The main task of CRYP was to train youth coordinators in campaigns according to the organization's director, Morton Blackwell.

Viguerie also planned to help raise funds directly for several conservative candidates, such as Republican Sen. Jesse Helms of North Carolina. By May 1978 Viguerie had raised $3.2 million for Helms. Campaign manager Tom Ellis, however, said that only $700,000 of this money reached the campaign, the rest going toward Viguerie's expenses and fees. Viguerie disputed this, saying the campaign had received $1.5 million.[142]

The most controversial aspect of the New Right's 1978 program was the funding of conservative challengers entering primaries against moderate Republican incumbents. In Illinois, support for fundamentalist minister Donald M. Lyon's campaign against John B. Anderson, an 18-year veteran and the third-ranking Republican in the House of Representatives, stirred dissension within the ranks of the New Right itself. The congressional sponsors of the Committee for the Survival of a Free Congress were reported to be evenly split on the matter. Rep. E. G. "Bud" Shuster, R-Pa., felt so strongly against supporting Lyon that he resigned from CSFC's advisory board, saying that opposition to Anderson would "impale the Republican Party on one more useless skewer." The NCPAC, on the other hand, supported Lyon's challenge. John Dolan, the executive director of NCPAC, said he felt that "John Anderson is wrong on too many issues ever to have a free ride again." [143]

New Right groups eventually contributed about $11,000 to Lyon's campaign, and more money was raised by a nationwide direct-mail solicitation sent out by Viguerie. As of a week before the primary, Lyon had reported total receipts of $140,000 and Anderson, $111,000. Anderson won the primary with 58 percent of the vote, however. His victory was attributed in large part to Democratic crossover votes. [144]

Other liberal Republicans who faced primary challengers financed by the New Right in 1978 were Senators Clifford P. Case of New Jersey, who was defeated by his New Right opponent, and Edward W. Brooke of Massachusetts, who survived the challenge but lost in November to his Democratic opponent.

Richard A. Viguerie

The primary key to the emergence of the New Right has been direct-mail fund raising by Richard Viguerie. [145] Viguerie had learned the direct-mail business in the early 1960s as executive secretary of the Young Americans for Freedom. In 1965 he founded his own company, RAVCO, which raised money for various conservative causes.

Viguerie's 1976 activities included directing an unauthorized write-in campaign for John Connally, raising funds via direct mail for George Wallace's campaign for the Democratic presidential nomination, seeking the vice presidential nomination of the American Independent Party for himself, and raising funds for a number of New Right organizations.

Viguerie's activities met with varying degrees of success. The Connally campaign was wholly unsuccessful. With no conservative Democrats entered in the New Hampshire primary and little time for fund raising, Viguerie invested $35,000 of his own money in a write-in campaign for the former secretary of the Treasury, who did not approve of the effort. The result was a total of 24 votes, making it perhaps the most expensive campaign ever in terms of cost-per-vote. [146]

Wallace Campaign. Viguerie was more successful in his fund-raising effort for George Wallace. He took over the Wallace effort in the summer of 1973, with the campaign $250,000 in debt. His direct-mail operation featured two aspects: a "prospecting" campaign to build a list of Wallace contributors, and a "house list" campaign to raise money from the proven contributors. The prospecting operation was completed in July 1975 with 400,000 names on what campaign finance chairman F. Alton Dauphin, Jr., called "our hard-core list" of "people we can go to rather regularly" for contributions. This operation ran at a deficit, with a net difference of $208,000 between the costs of renting lists, printing, mailing, and related costs, and the donations received from the new contributors.[147]

Use of the names gathered for the Wallace "house list," however, proved to be quite profitable, especially early in the campaign. By the end of January 1975 "house" mailings had raised $1.42 million with expenses of $382,000, for a net gain of more than $1 million.[148] By April of that year direct mail had enabled Wallace to become the first presidential candidate in either party to qualify for matching funds by raising $5,000 in each of 20 states in contributions of $250 or less.[149] By the time the Wallace campaign ended in June 1976, it had grossed $7 million from direct mail.[150] As of February of that year, Viguerie had been paid $2.6 million.[151]

After the collapse of the Wallace campaign, Viguerie and William Rusher, publisher of the *National Review,* developed the idea of taking over Wallace's old American Independent Party as a conservative vehicle. Viguerie spent $75,000 on his own campaign for the AIP vice presidential nomination, while hoping that his fund-raising ability would attract a reputable Republican conservative to lead the ticket. When the AIP chose Lester Maddox as its presidential candidate, however, Viguerie walked out of the party's convention.[152]

Other Mailings. Also in 1976, Viguerie raised funds for several political action committees supporting conservative congressional candidates. As of September 30 he had raised $1.3 million each for the Committee for the Survival of a Free Congress and the National Conservative Political Action Committee, and $1.6 million for the Gun Owners of America.[153] Viguerie's methods for these groups, as for the Wallace campaign, involved "prospecting" long lists of potential but unproven donors. The effort was expensive but succeeded in building a list of conservative contributors. The lists compiled for each group became the property of the group and of Viguerie, who also retained his lists from the Wallace campaign and from previous campaigns. By 1978 he had a list of more than five million contributors to conservative causes or candidates.[154]

Many of the New Right mailings were sent out over the signature of well-known conservative members of Congress, such as Senator Helms. This practice was put in jeopardy in 1978, when the Senate Select Committee on Ethics issued an advisory opinion stating that any senator who authorizes any group outside the Senate to use the words "United States Senate" or "official business" in its mailings would be engaging in "improper conduct" and face possible censure.[155]

Dispute Over Costs. The main criticism of Viguerie and his fund-raising has been the allegation that groups connected with him spend too much money on fund raising and pass on too little as contributions to candidates. In an article in the *National Observer*, James M. Perry charged that "The Right Wing Got Plucked" by the Committee for the Survival of a Free Congress, the National Conservative Political Action Committee, and the Gun Owners of America. In 1975 and through October 18, 1976, the three organizations had total expenditures of $6,384,214. Only $594,824, or 9.3 percent of the total, went as contributions to candidates. About $3 million went to Viguerie's direct-mail company. When asked if his contributors understood that most of the money would not be passed on to candidates, Paul Weyrich of the Committee for the Survival of a Free Congress replied, "No, I don't think they did." [156]

Viguerie and the groups with which he was involved defended their operations, arguing that they performed other valuable services for conservatives besides making campaign contributions, and that fund-raising costs would decrease in later elections. Weyrich said, "We spent money to recruit candidates, to train campaign managers, to analyze every vote cast in the House and the Senate, to publish newspapers and weekly reports, and none of this is reflected in the financial reports. People . . . should look at our total program." [157] Similarly, John Dolan of the NCPAC said, "It was meant to be this way. We didn't raise it for candidates, we planned most of it to go to research, lobbying, surveys, and other activities to build the conservative base." [158] As for the high fund-raising expenses, this was explained in terms of the high initial outlay needed to build a reliable mailing list. "The Gun Owners of America now have a list of 250,000 regular contributors," said Viguerie in 1976. "Next time, they'll raise twice as much money at half the fund-raising cost." [159] The other groups also were successful at developing proven lists that they hoped would enable them to raise money less expensively in the future.

Viguerie's fund-raising methods have provoked a great deal of controversy over the years. In 1974 *New York Post* correspondent Robert Walters reported that the "Fund to Defeat Jacob Javits" had raised almost $250,000. All of the money had gone to Viguerie and none to any campaign against Javits. [160]

In 1975 Christopher Lydon of *The New York Times* reported that the Wallace campaign was being fueled by generous credit arrangements with Viguerie. Viguerie allowed the campaign to delay paying for his fund-raising work until the money started coming in. The campaign's net indebtedness to Viguerie reached $266,000 as of August 1974, and $220,000 as of February 1975. To Viguerie's critics, these advances represented illegal corporate contributions or loans from Viguerie's company to the Wallace campaign. Viguerie and Charles S. Snider, national director of the Wallace campaign, contended that Viguerie was merely extending normal commercial credit to his client. There was always enough mail "out there working" and enough money "in the pipeline," they said, to cover past obligations.[161] The FEC eventually ruled that the Viguerie credit procedures were legal. But the expense of the Viguerie fund-raising operation prompted FEC Chairman Thomas B. Curtis to suggest that the FECA be amended to grant matching funds only on the net amount of campaign contributions after deducting fund-raising costs. "Are we really going to be matching gross when it costs 90 percent of that money to raise it?" he asked. "This law wasn't passed to make money for fund raisers." [162] This idea, however, was not adopted.

Although the New Right groups have benefited greatly from Viguerie's services, they have also had some problems. In 1976 allegations were made that the various New Right committees illegally coordinated their candidate contributions and transferred funds among the groups to circumvent the $5,000 contribution limit from any one committee. Harold Wolff of the National Committee for an Effective Congress, which supports liberal candidates, charged that contributions from the conservative groups occurred too close in time to be coincidental. As an example, Wolff pointed to Stan Burger's primary campaign for a Senate seat from Montana. After he already had been given the legal limit by several active conservative groups, Burger received another $5,000 from the Committee for Responsible Youth Politics, a group organized with help from Viguerie in 1973 but which had little visible fund-raising operation.[163] The NCEC filed a complaint with the FEC but the commission took no action.[164]

In 1977 Viguerie's company fraudulently used the names of members of Congress in fund-raising mailings for the Citizens Committee for the Right to Keep and Bear Arms and the Americans Against Union Control of Government. The mailings displayed the names of various congressmen in the return-address position of envelopes sent to the members' constituents and, in some cases, bore the designation "From:" before the member's name. In fact, the members had never given permission for the use of their names. Speaker of the House Tip O'Neill, Minority Leader John Rhodes, and a number of other congressmen complained about the misuse of their names to the attorney general, the Postal Service, and the organizations involved.[165]

The Citizens Committee for the Right to Keep and Bear Arms eventually signed a consent agreement with the Postal Service in which it agreed to return the 2,000 contributions it had received since the mailing had gone out, along with a statement saying the mailing "may have led you erroneously to believe that your congressional representative had sent the solicitation or had authorized or otherwise concurred in the use of his name on the solicitation." [166] The Americans Against Union Control of Government also were reported to have removed the congressmen's names from their envelopes after complaints were made.[167]

Competition for Funds. The growth of the New Right has also brought criticism from the Republican Party and from older conservative groups. As early as October 1975 Charles A. McManus, the founder of the conservative Americans for Constitutional Action, resigned from that organization in "total and complete frustration" over competition for conservative funds. The ACA had been in existence since 1959 and in 1974 had raised $450,000 for conservative candidates. But the emergence of New Right groups using Viguerie's direct-mail fund-raising methods were "splitting up the pot, and there aren't that many contributors." The ACA's fund raising by direct mail had declined by 75 percent less than $100,000 in 1975. This was too little, said McManus, to support the services that the organization traditionally had offered conservatives.[168] M. Stanton Evans, chairman of the American Conservative Union, also said of the New Right operations: "What I don't like is a saturation direct mail campaign that takes money away from donors and goes to pay huge fund-raising expenses." [169]

Similar complaints were made at a meeting of the Republican National Committee in September 1977. Montana Republican chairperson Florence S. Haegen said, "I resent [the New Right groups] tremendously. They are cutting into the money that rightfully belongs to our state, without sending money back to our states or accomplishing anything." RNC Chairman Bill Brock also attacked the New Right for drawing contributors away from the Republican Party, saying "Instead of joining political parties today, people join causes." [170] Other Republicans have attacked the New Right for promoting divisiveness within the party by encouraging primary challenges against incumbent Republicans. A group of eight Republican senators organized by Charles McC. Mathias, Jr., of Maryland charged in a letter to Brock that such activities were "not the kind of healthy competition we should encourage within the Republican Party. It is cannibalism." [171]

Direct Mail

Viguerie's effort for George Wallace was by no means the only incident of direct-mail fund raising in the 1976 campaign. Particularly because the elimination of big donors by the FECA dictated the necessity to collect large numbers of small contributions, almost all of the presidential candidates launched direct-mail campaigns, with varying degrees of success.

In 1975 Morris Dees offered free consultation on direct mail to all Democratic candidates except George Wallace. Dees had established a reputation as a direct-mail genius in 1972, when he raised $15 million for George McGovern at a cost of $4.5 million.[172] In February 1975 Henry Jackson accepted Dees' offer and a mailing was sent out to 400,000 names. The mailing was successful, especially with repeat solicitations of those who responded initially, but not overwhelmingly so. In general, direct mail has been found to be more effective for candidates at either end of the ideological spectrum than for centrists such as Jackson.

Late in 1975 Dees was enlisted as national finance chairman for Jimmy Carter's campaign. Again recognizing the limitations of direct mail for a centrist candidate, Dees did not make it the cornerstone of his fund-raising strategy for Carter. Instead, he used it to supplement other fund-raising techniques by sending monthly mailings to previous Carter donors. This selective approach was extremely profitable, raising $2.5 million at a cost of $163,000, exclusive of postage.

A number of other Democratic candidates also used direct-mail appeals, with varying degrees of success. One of Morris Udall's campaign managers called direct mail the "heart and soul" of the campaign's finances, and a member of Fred Harris' fund-raising staff said direct mail "kept us alive day to day." Birch Bayh, Terry Sanford, and Sargent Shriver also used direct-mail appeals, although with less success.

On the Republican side, direct mail was more effective for Gerald Ford, which was surprising since Ronald Reagan was more of an ideological candidate. Ford made extensive use of contributor lists provided by the Republican National Committee and the National Republican Congressional Committee. The RNC, trying to remain neutral in the contest, at first refused either candidate access to its lists, but later decided to rent the lists to both the Ford and Reagan campaigns. Response to the RNC and NRCC lists together accounted for $1.3 million of the $2,550,000 that Ford raised by direct mail. Reagan had some success with direct mail,[173] but found televised pitches to be more effective.

Congressional Codes of Ethics

Although the Constitution gives each house of Congress the power to punish its members for misconduct, this power rarely has been invoked. Only seven senators, 18 representatives, and one territorial delegate have ever been formally censured by their colleagues for misconduct; 15 senators and three representatives have been expelled.

Cases of other disciplinary actions have been equally rare, and one of the most important reasons has been the reluctance of most members to judge their colleagues. Many members have felt that only the electorate should be responsible for judging a colleague's behavior, except in cases where his actions are punishable by the courts. Loyalty toward Congress and among members, especially of the same party, also explains congressional reluctance. Finally, there is notable difficulty in defining conflict of interest and misuse of power. Before disciplinary action can be taken, institutional barriers must be overcome. Expulsion — the ultimate punishment — requires a two-thirds majority vote. Lesser penalties also are difficult. In most cases the House ethics committee has required a sworn complaint from a member of Congress before investigating, and in most instances House members have been reluctant to swear to charges against a colleague.[174]

Outsiders seeking to bring errant members to justice find their path strewn with numerous obstacles. The 1974 Amendments reduced from five to three years the statute of limitations on campaign law violations, a stricture that severely limited Justice Department investigations, especially in the Gulf and Ashland Oil cases, which stretched back some years. Voter apathy may have provided perhaps the most fundamental bar to congressional action on charges of misconduct, however; constituents often did not object when their representatives were charged with illegal actions or even convicted of crimes. Although members occasionally were defeated because of public scandal, the public seemed in general to react mildly to charges of impropriety, even if the charges were proven. As a result of the Korean lobbying investigations, for example, the House ethics committee in October 1978 recommended reprimands for California Democrats John J. McFall, Edward R. Roybal, and Charles H. Wilson. However, it cleared Democrat Edward J. Patten of New Jersey, who had been charged with making in his own name a political contribution that had originated with Korean Tongsun Park. While McFall was defeated in the 1978 election, the other members retained their seats.

It was not until the 1960s that both the House and the Senate, in response to several well-publicized scandals involving members and congressional aides, created committees to deal with the issue. Formed as a result of reaction to the behavior of Rep. Adam Clayton Powell, D-N.Y., the Committee on Standards of Official Conduct, as the House ethics committee is formally known, did little for the first nine years of its existence.[175]

In 1976 a shift began. A dramatic turnover in the composition of the House itself brought replacement of older members by younger, more reform-oriented congressmen.[176] In addition, the House Democratic

Caucus in January 1975 ousted Louisiana's F. Edward Hebert as chairman of the Armed Services Committee and replaced him with Melvin Price of Illinois. In replacing Hebert, Price gave up his chairmanship of the ethics committee. Of the five other Democrats on the ethics committee, only John J. Flynt, Jr., of Georgia was neither a committee chairman nor a deposed chairman. Flynt initially refused to lead the panel, but the House leadership was able to convince him to accept the post after three attempts.

During Flynt's first year as chairman, little action was taken. Then, in 1976, a report of a special House committee investigating the activities of the Central Intelligence Agency was leaked to the press. The full House voted to investigate the leak and gave Flynt and his committee the authority to do so. The committee next undertook an investigation of Rep. Robert L. F. Sikes, a Florida Democrat, who was charged with improper financial conduct. The committee approved a motion calling on the full House to reprimand Sikes for having benefited personally from a series of contracts involving the Army, Navy, and Air Force while serving as chairman of the Military Construction Subcommittee of the Appropriations Committee. This was the first such recommendation the ethics panel had ever made, and it was agreed to by the House of Representatives, 381-3.[177]

Later, as a result of formal complaints filed by many congressmen in June 1976, the committee voted to investigate allegations that Wayne Hays had kept his mistress on the public payroll. Despite Hays' efforts to block the committee's investigation, Chairman Flynt stood his ground. His action played an important role in forcing Hays to resign his House seat, as noted earlier.

House Commission on Administrative Review

The Hays case triggered efforts by members of the House to reform themselves. In June 1976 Speaker Carl Albert of Oklahoma created a three-man task force headed by Rep. David Obey, D-Wis., to study ways to improve accountability and to assure both propriety and the appearance of propriety in the administration of House funds. The task force reported back to the Democratic Caucus and recommended a number of changes in the House's administrative system to modernize its bookkeeping and housekeeping procedures and to prevent future scandals. The suggestions included denying the House Administration Committee the power to expand allowances, change their character, or create new categories without a vote on the House floor. In addition, the task force called for a complete overhaul of the existing system of allowances. A final recommendation was the creation of a 15-member commission to study and recommend changes in the House's personnel, administrative, and accounting procedures and members' perquisites.[178]

In July, after the House had approved the proposals, Speaker Albert appointed the Commission on Administrative Review, consisting of eight congressmen and seven private citizens, with Obey as chairman. The commission met for the first time in September 1976 and established a number of task forces to execute its mandate. Its first report, issued in December 1976, dealt with House scheduling. Noting the different attitudes toward scheduling held by majority leadership, committee and subcommittee chairmen, the minority leadership, and individual members, the report suggested a number of changes that would benefit all representatives.[179]

Financial Ethics. The scheduling changes the Obey commission suggested were not particularly controversial, but the same could not be said for its recommendations with respect to financial ethics. In early February 1977 the commission approved the strictest financial and ethical code yet proposed for House members. The proposals focused on financial disclosure, outside income, acceptance of gifts, unofficial office accounts, the franking privilege, and congressional travel. Commission members realized that the effectiveness of such proposals would be limited;[180] nevertheless, in their support the commission noted that many states in recent years had passed new or strengthened laws requiring financial disclosure, and it noted significant public support for strengthening public disclosure requirements.[181]

The objectives of financial disclosure, according to the commission, were to inform the public about the financial interest of government officials and thus increase confidence in government and deter potential conflicts of interest. The commission was guided in its deliberations by two basic principles: 1) Disclosure should be required only as it might reveal a potential conflict of interest. And 2) disclosure requirements should avoid excessively burdensome recordkeeping. It rejected the idea of requiring members to file either income tax returns or net worth statements, out of concern about possible invasion of privacy and the omission from these forms of some relevant information. The commission sought to require members of the House to disclose "categories of value," rather than specific dollar amounts.[182]

The most controversial topics in the report were outside income and unofficial office accounts. The commission noted the impossibility of compiling exact statistics on members' outside income because of the limitations in the current financial disclosure requirements. Nevertheless, it determined that 62 percent of all members had income in 1975 from honoraria and/or investments, and 53 members reported income from legal practice in excess of $1,000. Regarding unearned income, the commission asserted that potential conflicts of interest might best be deterred through disclosure and the discipline of the electoral process, but it viewed disclosure as insufficient regarding earned income. While some declared that the two types of income should be treated in an identical manner, the panel contended that more important than equity was the reasonable and effective handling of potential conflicts of interest in terms of both time and money. The commission noted that the public and the House members themselves viewed as particularly troublesome the possibility of conflicts of interest arising from a member's acceptance of sizable honoraria from an organization having an interest in his congressional work. The appearance of impropriety seemed as much of a consideration here as actual impropriety.[183]

In concludiing that disclosure of earned outside income was not sufficient, the panel did not feel that it was either necessary or desirable to bar totally all outside earned income, or to discourage representatives from making public appearances and contributing to public dialogue on important issues. Accordingly, the commission recommended that outside earned income not exceed 15 percent of a member's salary, that honoraria be restricted to $750 an appearance, and that expenses relating to honoraria be subject to strict regulations. Income from other sources such as family farms and businesses should be regarded as "return on equity" and should not be subject to the limitations on earned income. The recommendations were formulated to assure the public that members were not exploiting their positions of influence and were not being distracted from their public duties.[184]

Office Accounts. Another controversial area addressed was that of unofficial office accounts. These generally are established because official allowances are considered inadequate to meet all of the necessary expenses relating to the duties of a member of Congress, and because unofficial expenses provide an alternative source for supplementing office expenses without constraints imposed by the official accounting system. Since no limitations or disclosure requirements affected unofficial accounts, it was hard to determine their frequency or size. The commission nevertheless was able to obtain some data from the 31 accounts filed voluntarily with the Clerk of the House through December 1, 1976, from reports in the *Congressional Record* on 11 others, and from the results of a survey of 150 of the 372 members who returned to the 95th Congress. The survey disclosed that approximately 40 percent of these members maintained unofficial office accounts[185] ranging in size from $300 to $60,000, with a mean of $6,967 and a median of $5,000.

The commission recommended abolishing unofficial office accounts, including "newsletter funds." It suggested that the allowance for unofficial expenses outside the District of Columbia be designated "official expenses" without regard to location within the United States and that this allowance be increased by $5,000 to cover necessary expenses. It also maintained that private funds should be used only for politically related purposes, whereas official allowances should reflect the necessary cost of official expenses.[186]

Unofficial office accounts did not offer the only means by which members might apply private monies to official expenses, and the panel recommended a prohibition on the conversion of campaign funds to funds for personal use. Since not all members had unofficial accounts, some observers questioned the need to increase official allowances. In response, the commissioners noted that while 40 percent had such accounts, others paid official expenses with campaign or political funds. It affirmed its belief in the need for a distinction between political and official expenses, and argued that the increase was a step necessary for the elimination of private money from official business.[187] As noted earlier, incumbents' use of expense accounts for political purposes posed difficulties for the FEC in its regulatory capacity.

Gifts, Mail, Travel. The commission made other recommendations with respect to gifts, the franking privilege, and travel. Congressmen were subject to two limitations with respect to gifts. The Foreign Gifts and Decorations Act of 1966 prohibited federal officials from accepting any gift worth more than $50 from foreign governments or their representatives. In addition, a House rule declared that a member, officer, or employee of the House of Representatives could accept no gift of substantial value from any person, organization, or corporation having a direct interest in legislation before Congress. The commission proposed amending the House rule to make it more specific. The proposal suggested that gifts aggregating $100 or more in any calendar year be prohibited from any person, organization, or corporation having a direct interest in legislation before Congress. It defined "direct interest" to include (without being limited to) any person or organization who must file under the Federal Lobbying Act of 1946 or its successor statutes.[188]

Regarding the franking privilege, the commission deemed it inappropriate for franked mass mailings to be printed and prepared with private or political funds. It asserted that only mass mailings prepared and printed at public expense should be eligible for franking. The group's final recommendations centered on congressional travel. A public opinion survey had shown that the public strongly supported congressional travel, but favored tightened controls over such trips. Although lame-duck travel did not appear to be widespread, many felt it was inappropriate for members of Congress to travel at official expense when they no longer would participate in the legislative process. The commission therefore suggested that lame-duck travel be abolished.[189]

The commission was not completely united regarding the value of its recommendations. The three Republicans on the panel suggested additional proposals: regular audits for all congressional expenses, reform of the personnel system, better guarantees of the full availability to the public of required disclosures, and a requirement that Congress vote on all future salary increases.[190] The increase in official allowances was the proposal most strongly criticized by the minority, who expressed concern regarding the expenditure of an additional $2 million of taxpayers' money and charged that the increase served as a bribe for members forced to relinquish unofficial accounts.

Action on Proposals. Since the Commission on Administrative Review lacked legislative authority, its proposals were sent to three other House panels — the House Administration Committee, the Standards of Official Conduct Committee, and the Rules Committee. At each juncture, there was trouble. The House Administration Committee first rejected and then only reluctantly, under pressure from the Democratic leadership, accepted the proposal to increase House expense accounts by $5,000.

The leadership then demanded that the ethics committee approve its part of the package immediately. In response, the committee voted to drop the commission's provision exempting the reporting of gifts of less than $35 and those of personal hospitality; it substituted a proposal to require the reporting of all gifts no matter how small their value.[191]

The biggest fight occurred in the House Rules Committee. Obey and Tip O'Neill, who by then had succeeded Albert as Speaker, wanted the committee to approve a modified closed rule allowing a limited number of amendments on the floor rather than an open rule permitting unlimited amendments.[192] When the Democrats on the panel balked, the Speaker met with them privately to voice his strong feelings on the subject. In the end the committee approved a rule allowing the full House to approve or reject each of the major provisions of the package but to make only one substantive amendment. The amendment restricted outside earned income to $15,000 a year rather than to 15 percent of the annual congressional salary.[193]

The bill was called up on March 2 and the key fight centered on approval of the rule adopted by the House Rules Committee. The Republicans argued that it was a "gag" rule and that the Democrats did not trust the people or their elected representatives. The Democratic leadership finally prevailed, and the rule was adopted by a vote of 267-153, with only 15 Democrats defecting and only three Republicans supporting the rule.[194]

Once the rule was approved, the major battles concerned the limit on earned outside income and the proposal to raise the official allowance by $5,000. Otis G. Pike, a New York Democrat, argued in an emotional speech that the temptation of a member without adequate income was the largest single source of political corruption. In response, Jim Wright, the majority leader, argued: "[I]f our opportunities for substantial outside earnings are to some degree inhibited, let us reflect that serving in the Congress is not a part-time job but an all-consuming task worthy of our full time, our total talents and our undivided efforts." [195] By a vote of 79-344 the House defeated the motion to strike the section limiting earned outside income to 15 percent of congressional salaries.

The outcome of the fight on the increase in members' official allowances was much closer. Again, the commission's supporters prevailed, defeating a measure to eliminate this provision by a vote of 187-235. [196] After eight hours of heated debate, the bill passed 402 to 22.

Ethics Committee. On March 10, one day after the House had adopted a resolution creating the House Select Committee on Ethics (in addition to the existing Standards of Official Conduct Committee), Speaker O'Neill appointed 13 Democrats and six Republicans as members. Rep. Richardson Preyer, D-N.C., a former federal judge and a respected representative, was named chairman. The panel was to work with the Senate Ethics Committee to write laws incorporating appropriate portions of the separate House and Senate ethics rules. The Obey commission's recommendations for an ethics code were not considered sufficient because they had been adopted as a series of amendments to the House rules, and as such could be enforced only through internal bodies. Violators thus would be subject only to internal House punishment such as censure. Enactment into law would require Senate action and a presidential signature, and would subject violators to investigation by federal law enforcement agencies and to criminal penalties.

The House panel soon began issuing advisory opinions in a manner similar to those of the FEC. Most were prompted by requests from representatives for clarification of the newly enacted ethics code. Many congressmen felt that the public and the press were closely watching them to see whether the renewed interest in congressional ethics represented a temporary phenomenon or a permanent change in members' conduct.

By the committee's own admission, the most difficult issue during the first months of its existence was the question of trips for congressmen, their spouses, and congressional aides paid for by private companies and/or foreign foundations. The old House ethics code neglected this issue, while the new one limited gifts to members to $100 from any group or individual having a direct interest in legislation, or from foreign nationals or their agents. The panel concluded that it would be contrary to the public interest and the intent of the House rule to prohibit acceptance of necessary expenses associated with legitimate fact-finding. It did remind members and staff of the requirement that the member, officer, or employee certify to the committee that the fact-finding event related directly to official duties, and it emphasized that this "conditional exemption" applied only to necessary expenses directly associated with the fact-finding aspects of the trip.[197] The committee went on to note that such information would be made available to the public and would be published periodically in the *Congressional Record.* In addition, the ruling would be in effect only through the August 1977 recess, at which time the panel planned to reevaluate the question. By May 19, 1977, the committee had issued 11 advisory opinions. At that time a spokesman for the panel said that while the committee would consult informally with members and others needing advice on how to comply with the new ethics code, there were no plans to issue additional rulings.

Action on Senate Code

In early 1977 the Senate created a Special Committee on Official Conduct chaired by Gaylord Nelson. Nelson, like Obey, was a liberal Wisconsin Democrat, and the two were close personal friends; the Nelson panel used the work of the Obey commission as the basis for its own program. As a consequence, the Senate committee was able to report back to its parent body by mid-March. Although the Senate ethics code contained some provisions stricter than those of the House and some with no House equivalents, the two codes were in general quite similar.

As in the House, the Senate Democratic leadership — Majority Leader Robert Byrd and Majority Whip Alan Cranston — strongly supported the ethics program. Unlike the House, which completed action on its ethics code in one stormy day, Senate debate continued for two weeks, a result in part of the body's tradition of free and unlimited debate and of the greater ease with which amendments could be offered in the upper chamber.

The sharpest debate came on the issue of limiting earned outside income. Byrd claimed that senators were able to attract large honoraria precisely because they were senators.[198] His Republican counterpart, Howard H. Baker, Jr., disagreed, contending that legislators were in danger of becoming professional legislators wholly dependent on the federal Treasury. The strongest opponent of the 15 percent limit was Edmund S. Muskie. The Maine Democrat said that for many years he had made speeches because he felt it was the only ethical way to earn outside income. He claimed that the Senate was limiting outside earned income in a hasty reaction to the public criticism of the recent congressional pay raise. In contrast, Nelson argued for the importance of maintaining public confidence in public institutions. In the end, Byrd and Nelson prevailed and the amendment to remove the ceiling on earned outside income was defeated 62-35.

A different attack on the bill was launched by Lowell P. Weicker, Jr., Connecticut Republican, who contended that the proposed ethics plan simply blended arbitrary restrictions and incomplete regulations, and was not reform but a public relations gesture. Weicker proposed that the public should be given all the facts so that it, rather than the senators, might decide questions of propriety. He called for complete public disclosure of every financial detail through yearly publication of individual income-tax returns and itemized statements of net worth.[199] The majority of his colleagues disagreed and voted down his proposal 67-30.

Another approach was taken by Senator Baker, who favored the concept of the citizen-legislator. The Tennessee Republican proposed that the chamber meet only six months a year to write broad legislation, and that congressional salaries be reduced proportionately. The remainder of the year, he contended, should be spent at home working and getting to know one's constituents. Other senators attacked this idea as impractical. Richard S. Schweiker, R-Pa., argued that the laws were too complex and detailed to permit such treatment. In the end the amendment was killed.

Seeking to counteract negative publicity about its actions in January and February, which had blocked a roll call vote on the congressional pay raise, the Senate approved an amendment by Dewey F. Bartlett, R-Okla., that required both houses of Congress to take roll call votes on future pay increases for congressmen, federal judges, and top executive branch personnel. It defeated a second Bartlett amendment that would have repealed the pay raise.

Finally, on April 1, after two weeks of debate and action on 64 amendments, the Senate adopted the new code of ethics. One commentator noted that the 86-9 vote did not reflect the depth of feeling in the Senate against the new code. Nor did the action guarantee that the Senate would be more willing in the future to investigate allegations of misconduct by its own members. Many senators voting for the measure did so fearful of the political hazards of a negative vote.[200]

Senate Ethics Committee. To implement and enforce the new code, the Senate created a new panel, the Senate Ethics Committee, chaired by Adlai E. Stevenson III, D-Ill.[201] The committee and its chairman faced a rocky road. Two of its members — Harrison "Jack" Schmitt, R-N.M., and Lowell Weicker — voted against passage of the resolution. A third committee member, John G. Tower, R-Texas, missed the final vote but expressed strong opposition to the measure during floor debate.

Stevenson said that while the committee would look into allegations of wrongdoing on the part of senators, the rights of the accused would be protected as well. The Illinois Democrat had persuaded the Special Committee on Official Conduct to modify the enforcement mechanism of the code to allow the Ethics Committee greater flexibility in dealing with individual cases. He also persuaded the Nelson committee to allow the Ethics Committee the freedom to work out informal settlements of complaints.

The committee ran into trouble at its first meeting when it had to waive part of the new code. Several senators had been invited to travel to the People's Republic of China as guests of that government, but the ethics code barred senators from accepting gifts of more than $100 in aggregate value from any foreign national acting on behalf of a foreign organization or government. Majority Leader Byrd claimed that since the invitation came via the White House, the code did not apply. The incident might have been an omen.

Within two months of its creation, the panel concluded that the ethics code was impractical and needed revision. Much of this frustration stemmed from resentment at having to decide questions that seemed either trivial or best left to an individual senator's discretion. One such issue was the matter of the propriety of storing campaign material in office space; another concerned the acceptance by a Senate aide of a $150 ticket to play in a charity golf tournament.[202]

Some of the committee's rulings were more substantive, however. In summer 1977 the committee ruled, for example, that free copies could not be provided to a senator of a newsletter or other "research product subscription service" that would otherwise have market value.[203]

Committee Chairman Stevenson stated that he planned to recommend changes to make the code more intelligible and more enforceable. He favored simplifying the code's provisions to permit acceptance of all gifts of less than $100 and full disclosure for gifts above that figure. Stevenson admitted that if the Senate altered the code it might draw criticism, but said that he thought the change was nevertheless desirable.[204]

One loophole apparently was created inadvertently by an aide during drafting of the legislation. Stevenson's efforts to eliminate all "slush funds" had failed, and the Senate approved a policy of allowing expenses not reimbursed by Congress to be defrayed by money from a senator's campaign fund. The code as drafted permitted the use of funds from a political committee as defined in the FECA — a definition that included party senatorial as well as hundreds of other political commit-tees in addition to the senator's own campaign fund. Discovery of the loophole in November 1977 sparked partisan controversy, with Repub-licans arguing for retention of the loophole since it could be used to increase substantially financial aid to GOP senators in the 1978 election year.[205]

Code Relaxed. Continued resistance to the provisions restricting outside honoraria eventually brought changes in the Senate ethics code. Claiming that he had been left a beggar by the code, Daniel Patrick Moynihan, D-N.Y., convinced his colleagues that the use of campaign funds to pay office expenses should be allowed. On November 4 the Senate voted to relax the $25,000/year limit on honoraria. The amend-ment, sponsored by Moynihan and Robert Dole, R-Kan., permitted a member to select five charities from which a host organization could select one to receive the senator's honorarium without its counting toward his $25,000 limit, to return an honorarium without counting it toward the limit, and to count an honorarium toward the limit for the year in which it was received rather than the year in which it was earned.

The president signed the amendment into law on December 20, 1977. Nevertheless, Republicans Weicker, Paul Laxalt, Carl T. Curtis, Barry Goldwater, and S. I. Hayakawa filed a legal brief in U.S. District Court in February 1978 claiming that the limit on a senator's outside earned income violated his right to use his own funds in a political campaign, violated the First Amendment's guarantee of freedom of speech, and created a new requirement for membership in the Senate. They argued that the right of a candidate to spend unlimited personal funds on his own campaign — as established by *Buckley v. Valeo* — is meaningless if the incumbent candidates are prohibited from earning the funds. The ethics code contained no provision to separate one defective section, and the court's invalidation of one section would void the code. U.S. District Court Judge George Hart dismissed the suit on March 13, 1978, saying that it was not justiciable and that the limit was constitutional, since the case addressed a political issue rather than a legal one. He said that the rule on outside earned income did not require an additional qualification for holding a Senate seat but merely created a standard of ethical conduct.[206] The plaintiffs appealed to the Supreme Court, which refused to hear the case.

Pressures for New Codes

In formulating new codes of ethics, the House and the Senate did not respond simply to the presence of younger legislators. The events of

Watergate clearly played a role, as did scandals on Capitol Hill. Adam Clayton Powell, Wilbur Mills, Thomas Dodd, and Wayne Hays all had caused other members of Congress considerable discomfiture. While their actions were not unprecedented, they occurred in a period when the nation was especially concerned with ethical standards. Another event that contributed to creation of the new codes was the congressional pay raise that became effective in February 1977 without a formal roll call vote in either chamber.[207] While its supporters mustered cogent arguments justifying the 29 percent increase, many observers disagreed. Finally, the new codes may have reflected the emergence of new leadership aware of the need to restore confidence in government.

O'Neill, Byrd Roles. No doubt Speaker O'Neill exerted tremendous pressure on his Democratic colleagues in the House. Even before he had formally been chosen as Speaker, O'Neill told the freshman Democratic Caucus that the existing House ethics code was ineffective and that he would demand a tougher, more effective code. In January he made an unusual public appearance before the Obey commission, saying he favored the strongest code of ethics of any constitutional legislative body in America.[208] O'Neill also worked in private to persuade the Democrats on the ethics committee, the House Administration Committee, and the Rules Committee to support the Obey commission's recommendations. When the measure was debated on the House floor, he again spoke out, and passage of the revised House ethics code owed much to his efforts.

His Senate counterpart, Robert Byrd of West Virginia, played an effective though less public role in ensuring approval of the Senate's new ethics code. Byrd opened debate on the measure and helped defeat attempts to weaken the Nelson committee's proposal. Like the Speaker, Byrd stressed the need to restore public confidence in Congress. Although some alterations were made on the floor (largely to liken the Senate version to the House code), the plan emerged largely intact and stronger in some areas than the House measure. The Senate code included enforcement provisions and a section guaranteeing that senators would not discriminate against employees because of race, sex, national origin, or age. It also limited the extent to which senators and top Senate employees could engage in a profession. In addition, the General Accounting Office was instructed to undertake periodic audits of the reports filed with the Secretary of the Senate.

House, Senate Differences. Several other differences between the two codes reflected the contrasting composition of the two bodies. In both chambers the limit on earned outside income was the most hotly debated provision.[209] In the House, however, the rule on income from family businesses was tightened in response to objections from lawyer-congressmen that restrictions affected them more than they did those who had family companies. In contrast, the Senate eased provisions regarding outside earnings to stipulate that senators could earn income from family-owned businesses and farms if these activities did not require significant amounts of time while the Senate was in session.[210]

While the Senate barred lawyers and other professionals from working part time if they were associated with a firm or partnership (for example, they could practice law only on their own), the House allowed members to belong to law firms and to be listed on the firm's letterhead. Thus a representative and his law partners could capitalize on his name if the member engaged in little or no legal work. These differences reflect the fact that the House contains far more practicing lawyers than does the Senate, while the latter chamber has more members who own their own farms or business firms.

The disclosure requirements and the limit on outside earned income came under attack in the House again a year later. The Rules Committee voted to attach to three bills requiring financial disclosure by government officials a nongermane amendment permitting members to reconsider the limit imposed in 1977 on outside earned income. The portions of the bills that affected Congress immediately aroused controversy. In addition to requiring disclosure by top executive and judicial branch officials, the package was to put into statutory law the disclosure rules adopted as part of the congressional ethics codes. At this early stage, however, opponents of disclosure and the income limit thought that the House had gone too far. Since Speaker O'Neill had exerted much personal influence to pass the House code, the leadership feared that his prestige would be damaged if the House reversed itself on the issue.[211]

Later the House and Senate ethics codes were incorporated into law. In the House, the limit on outside earned income continued to prove controversial, and the Rules Committee agreed on August 15 to allow a vote to repeal the restriction. In addition to debate about the amounts of outside earned income permitted in both houses, there was disagreement regarding the effectiveness of the limit. Some legislators claimed that they could evade it by incorporating their businesses and drawing their income in dividends rather than salaries. Despite persistent opposition of some members, however, the House voted 97 to 290 on September 20, 1978, to reject the amendment repealing the provisions.[212]

Financial Disclosure

The House passed a broader disclosure measure by a 368-30 vote in September 1978. The bill required disclosure of personal and family finances by incumbent federal officeholders and their immediate families, and it reflected many disclosure provisions set forth in House rules when they were revised in March 1977. Still, it differed in certain major respects from its Senate counterpart, causing observers to anticipate a prolonged conference on the two measures. The chief differences between them were that the Senate bill (but not the House version) provided for: 1) the establishment of a procedure for the appointment of a special prosecutor to handle alleged violations; 2) establishment of criminal penalties in addition to civil penalties for violation of the disclosure provisions, including prison sentences of as much as a year; 3) the granting of power to the General Accounting Office to audit the incumbents' disclosure reports at intervals; and 4) the greater degree of detail required in reporting the worth of an official's holdings.

The House measure provided for filing of disclosure statements by candidates for Congress by November 1, or only six days before the 1978 election. The other major provisions included annual disclosure of personal finances by members of Congress by May 15, with nonincumbent candidates for Congress filing statements within 15 days of becoming a candidate. Disclosure was defined to mean: source, amount, and type of income, including honoraria from a single source valued at more than $100 in the aggregate (excluding government employment); source, estimated worth, and type of gifts received from a single source and valued at more than $100 (excluding gifts from relatives and items whose value was under $35); source and description of donated transportation, lodging, food, or entertainment received from any one source with an aggregate value of $250 or more (again excluding gifts worth less than $35); source and description of reimbursements totaling $250 or more in value.

Categories of value were to be designated for property held in a trade or business (or investment property or other income-producing property); total liabilities owed any creditor not a member of the individual's family when those liabilities exceeded $5,000 and were not loans related to household expenses; stocks, bonds, securities, and commodity futures exceeding $1,000 in value; and real property interests exceeding $1,000 in value. Authority to administer and enforce the provisions would reside with the House and Senate ethics committees, which would be able to issue advisory opinions, and the attorney general would be empowered to bring civil suits against offenders. The measure was extended to require annual disclosure from cabinet officials, government and legislative employees at a certain level or above, and federal judges and their assistants. In addition, it provided for the creation of an Office of Government Ethics within the Civil Service Commission.[213]

On October 6, 1978, House and Senate conferees approved a final version of the bill that included a mechanism for selecting a special prosecutor to probe allegations of wrongdoing by the president and other top officials of the executive branch. President Carter signed the bill into law on October 26. In its final form, the legislation incorporated the financial disclosure provisions of the House and Senate ethics codes; required disclosure by top-level officials in the executive and judicial branches according to the same standards applied to congressional legislators; required candidates for federal office to adhere to the same disclosure requirements made of incumbents; required disclosure of earned income, property holdings, debts, and other interests; required disclosure of some information about the finances of the officeholder's family; provided a maximum civil penalty of $5,000 for failure to comply (no criminal penalties were included in the legislation); required that the disclosed information be made available to the public; created the Office of Government Ethics; restricted the activities of federal employees leaving government for work in the private sector; and provided that the attorney general (and he alone) could appoint a special prosecutor to investigate allegations of criminal wrongdoing by government officials at a high level (the prosecutor's appointment would not extend beyond five years).[214]

Potential Impact

Clearly the new codes and legislation will have an impact on congressional operations and perhaps on the public image of Congress. The abolition of unofficial office accounts eliminated the last remaining channel through which representatives could accept unreported contributions from organizations and individuals and use the money for nearly any purpose. The provision limiting outside earned income put an important official seal on a trend toward full-time representation. The new codes also signaled the demise of the idea that a congressman's personal financial activities are nobody's business but his own — long a key argument against attempts to legislate financial disclosure. During floor debate not a single voice protested the concept of full financial disclosure by House members.[215]

Skepticism. Despite the general support for the new ethics codes among the public, newspaper editorial writers, public interest groups, and the members of Congress themselves, many objections were raised. Several individuals claimed that some of the provisions (for example, restrictions on earned outside income) were illegal or unconstitutional. Some felt the codes did not go far enough or were being implemented in a piecemeal fashion. Others worried whether the codes might produce unanticipated and negative consequences despite the good intentions. Voicing this sentiment, Sen. Bob Packwood, R-Ore., argued that if public financing of congressional elections was also approved, the combination of the restrictions on earned outside income and public financing of their elections would turn senators into full-time elected bureaucrats, publicly kept at taxpayer expense and eventually doomed to become "total political eunuchs." [216]

A more basic concern was enforcement. It remains to be seen if the Senate and House ethics committees will be any more diligent in the future than their predecessors have been in previous years,[217] and the effectiveness of the new standards remains to be tested.

Earlier, several commentators voiced their skepticism.[218] One noted with approval the limitation of the frank, abolition of the "slush fund," and limits on outside earned income and honoraria, but commented that the new codes leave ample room for personal gain and that few provisions have been made to date for enforcement — a poor augury for the codes, given the failure of Congress to police itself in the past.[219] Common Cause warned its membership of the need to watch legislators for signs of backsliding.[220] The organization noted that five provisions of the codes faced possible change or repeal: the limit on outside earned income, the limit on gifts to senators from lobbyists, the House requirement for disclosure of entertainment or travel contributed abroad as gifts, the Senate ban on using the frank to send bulk mail to occupants throughout the legislator's state, and the Senate ban on unofficial slush funds. In addition, Common Cause advocated a prohibition on the use of campaign funds for official activity, maintaining that privately raised funds should not finance public responsibilities.

House Reports. Despite the controversy they aroused, the codes did bring some changes. Members of Congress who were not planning to retire filed their first financial disclosure reports for the months October 1 to December 31, 1977, and the reports were released in May 1978. The congressmen were required to place their assets, liabilities, and income within certain financial categories. Although reports from members of both houses were eagerly scanned by observers, they did not immediately reveal any surprising information except, perhaps, that congressmen are a diverse group.

The reports indicated that many representatives held stocks and bonds; 153 had financial interests exceeding $100,000, excluding salaries and places of residence. Five of the respondents were clearly millionaires, although the broad categories made precise identification of all millionaires impossible. The wealthiest House members included S. William Green, R-N.Y., with securities worth more than $1 million; those heavily in debt included Charles C. Diggs, Jr., R-Mich., ($15,000) and George Hansen, R-Idaho, ($60,000); and those reporting almost no outside income included Majority Whip John Brademas, D-Ind., Phillip

Burton, D-Calif., and John J. Cavanaugh, D-Neb. A total of 22 congress-men reported no significant income beyond their salaries. The reports also indicated that many congressmen were still earning speaking fees from groups they served in their official capacities, and several members clearly had lucrative law practices.

The disclosures did not immediately reveal obvious conflicts of interest. *The New York Times* and CBS News undertook a computer study of the reports, tabulating the immediately identifiable holdings. The analysis showed that 1) 38.8 percent held mutual funds, municipal bonds, or the stocks or bonds of major corporations; 2) investments in banks were reported 31.4 percent of the House (23.4 percent of the members of the Banking, Finance, and Urban Affairs Committee); 3) 13.3 percent of respondents had investments in the top 60 defense contractors (8.3 percent of reporting members of the Armed Services Committee); 4) 10.1 percent of representatives had investments in oil and gas interests (5.3 percent of members of the Interior Committee); 5) 9.6 percent of House members received income from a law practice (18.8 percent of the Judiciary Committee); 6) 12.3 percent owned farms or ranches (32.6 percent of the Agriculture Committee); 7) 63.4 percent of Republican respondents owned real estate other than their residences. The analysis further indicated that members were cautious investors, and that the nature of their investments changed with the length of their tenure, with, for example, increasing numbers of senior members hold-ing investments in banks.

Party affiliation as well was manifested in the disclosures: Repub-licans led Democrats in every area of investment except banking (Demo-crats 32.1 percent, Republicans 29.9 percent). Republicans were more likely than Democrats to own pharmaceutical, insurance, and defense-related stocks as well as farms and ranches. Only 11 members reported gifts exceeding $100 in value, and only four of that number reported gifts of value greater than $1,000. The reports indicated that some members of the House Rules Committee who opposed the limit on earned outside income were individuals who stood to lose money if the limit took effect. James H. Quillen, R-Tenn., who had offered an amendment reopening the question of such a limit, sat on the board of directors of a bank and had several partnerships in addition to a successful insurance and real estate business. Claude Pepper, D-Fla., another opponent of the limit, reported receiving more than $100,000 from a law practice; of the other opponents, Democrats Morgan F. Murphy of Illinois had earned more than $120,000 as a lawyer and Shirley Chisholm of Brooklyn had re-ceived about $20,000 in speaking fees.[221]

Senate Reports. Computer analysis of the disclosure reports filed by senators showed that the typical senator had investments totaling about $500,000 but did not invest in enterprises related to his official duties nor hold other positions except, perhaps, that of board member of a college. Twenty-five of 96 reporting senators owned stock in the 60 largest defense contracting concerns, but only six had investments worth $50,000 or more. Only five of 24 members of the Appropriations Committee held such stock, although seven of 19 members of the Armed Services Committee did so. Sixteen of the 96 reporting senators had farm and ranch holdings, and three were members of the Agriculture Committee.

Senators most vocal in support of a measure or in opposition to it were not necessarily the individuals with large holdings in a business affected by the measure. The median Republican was discovered to have more assets than the median Democrat; the median committee chairman had still more, with assets just exceeding $1 million. Analysis further indicated that in the Senate, as in the House, a group of younger men reported no assets except their homes and deposits into a mandatory retirement plan. About 12 senators were identifiable as millionaires.[222]

The Brooke Case

The Senate ethics code was put to an early test as a result of publicity accorded in May 1978 to the financial affairs of two senators involved in divorce proceedings.

One case involved Edward W. Brooke, a Republican from Massachusetts and the only black in the Senate. Brooke had long been popular and, ironically, in May 1978 the cover of *First Monday* described him as a man of "integrity and independence in the U.S. Senate."

The Massachusetts senator's finances first drew public attention when *The Boston Globe* noted that a $49,000 loan mentioned in connection with his divorce had not been included on his Senate disclosure report. Court documents indicated that the money had been lent to Brooke by a friend who was a liquor distributor in Massachusetts. When questioned, however, Brooke said that the friend, Raymond A. Tye, had lent him only about $2,000 and that the balance of the money had come from a $100,000 insurance settlement of an auto accident in which his mother-in-law had been severely injured in 1962. The senator said that his mother-in-law had asked him to manage the money. Brooke offered conflicting reasons for his initial failure to reveal the true source of the funds. He first told reporters that he did not wish the existence of the money, which he described as a family fund created by his mother-in-law shortly before her death in 1977, to become publicly known, although his wife was aware of it; later he stated that his wife had not known of the money.[223]

Investigations. The divorce proceedings continued to draw publicity, and the Senate Ethics Committee met to consider whether Brooke
was in violation of any regulation. In June committee Chairman Stevenson noted that rules in force in 1974 (when Brooke received the money)
required disclosure, although disclosure rules taking effect in 1979 would
not require that money received from relatives be reported.[224]

Some observers speculated that Brooke might be charged with
perjury for testifying falsely regarding the source of the funds during the
divorce hearings. In Massachusetts, Middlesex County District Attorney
John Droney was ordered by the court to determine whether Brooke
should be prosecuted on such a charge, and the court postponed the
effective date of Brooke's divorce. In addition, it was charged that the
mother-in-law's transfer of $47,000 to Brooke had been accomplished in
order to make her eligible for Medicaid payments. The Massachusetts
Department of Welfare responded with its own investigation and eventually filed a claim as creditor in the mother-in-law's estate, and the
U.S. Attorney's office joined the inquiry.[225]

Repeated allegations of financial irregularities prompted investigation by the Internal Revenue Service, and news sources reported that
Brooke had claimed his two daughters as income tax exemptions during
years when he was not paying half of their support. In addition, questioning of Brooke revealed that he had mingled the funds from his
mother-in-law with his personal cash, using part of the money to pay for
his Watergate apartment. He had not yet complied with her request that
the family fund be distributed among certain members of the family.[226]
Continued inquiries led to a wide variety of alleged irregularities. It was
learned that Brooke had substantial real estate holdings, and seeming
contradictions in his statements led to questions as to how he had
managed to acquire these properties on a senator's salary.

More discrepancies emerged in Brooke's statements, and the
Massachusetts court offered Brooke's wife the opportunity to request a
new divorce hearing. She did so, leading observers to speculate about
the damage the acrimonious dispute would continue to do to Brooke's
career. A host of Democrats announced their candidacy for Brooke's
seat, and a contest that had been regarded as a safe bet for Brooke only a
few months earlier assumed considerable uncertainty, with observers
wondering whether the inquiries might be concluded by the time of the
September primary.[227]

Much attention aroused by Brooke's divorce consisted of speculation about actions the Senate Ethics Committee might take concerning
Brooke's alleged failure to report his debts and assets as required by law.
Meeting in closed session on May 31, the committee outlined the scope
of its inquiry and asked Brooke's wife and daughters to provide evidence

for their assertion that Brooke had improperly claimed the daughters as tax exemptions. Following a preliminary inquiry, the committee's second step would be an "initial review." If this uncovered evidence of wrongdoing, a wide range of actions was possible, from dismissal of allegations deemed unwarranted to referral of the violation to the Justice Department for prosecution. The Ethics Committee announced that it would retain special counsel for the case. Brooke conceded that he had not been truthful in his deposition about the loan from Raymond Tye. A Massachusetts court considered trying Brooke for perjury, but in August Suffolk County District Attorney Garrett H. Byrne decided not to press the charges.

In July, Brooke and his wife concluded their divorce proceedings and agreed on a property settlement. Publicity surrounding Brooke's financial affairs did not end, however, and it was reported in August that his late mother-in-law had fraudulently collected more than $72,000 in Medicaid payments. Brooke's daughter claimed that the Medicaid application had been filed at Brooke's direction. Brooke claimed, however, that he had not known of it. The Ethics Committee predicted that its investigation of Brooke's affairs would not be completed before mid-October — well after the September 19 Massachusetts primary.

Election Defeat. Brooke won the primary, but in September his wife filed a contempt of court petition charging him with not honoring the divorce settlement. As the general election approached, the Ethics Committee announced that its final report on the case would be delayed until after the November vote. Richard Wertheimer, the committee's special counsel, resigned, stating that Brooke's attorneys were withholding information from the committee and were altering documents already provided to investigators so that the evidence would support Brooke's position. Brooke's lawyers responded that all information had been supplied and that alterations had been made only for the sake of accuracy.

Following the resignation of the special counsel, however, Brooke requested that the Ethics Committee schedule a special hearing so that he might defend himself against Wertheimer's charges. The hearing was held on October 24, and on October 25 the committee stated that its evidence did not indicate Brooke personally was responsible for altering or withholding evidence from its investigators. The committee did not say whether Brooke's representatives had attempted to obstruct the inquiry.[228] The final committee report was not ready before the election, and Brooke lost his Senate seat. Interestingly, suggestions were made to put a lien on any surplus campaign funds to pay off or pay back any required monies.

In a report (S Rept 96-40) filed with the Senate March 21, 1979, the Ethics Committee said it found "credible evidence" of wrongdoing by Brooke, but that the violations were not serious enough to warrant further investigation or punishment of the former senator.

The Talmadge Case

In May 1978 Sen. Herman E. Talmadge, D-Ga., was engaged in divorce proceedings in his home state. Documents produced in the case disclosed that during the first seven years of the decade the senator had written only one check payable to cash. When questioned about this unusual finding, Talmadge responded that for many of the 22 years he had been in office he had used small gifts of cash from friends and supporters to pay for an assortment of personal expenses. The gifts ranged from $5 to $20, and the senator indicated that he had not reported them on his income tax returns because the IRS did not require such gifts to be reported.

Additional records indicated that Talmadge maintained a special bank account consisting of honorariums, Senate reimbursements, and campaign funds, which he used to pay "official expenses." [229] These allegations brought publicity, and Talmadge asked the Ethics Committee to advise him as to whether his practices complied with regulations. Common Cause called on the committee to make a full investigation and to publicize its report. A number of commentators remarked upon the oddity of a senator who accepted cash contributions to defray his personal expenses, and questioned the propriety of Talmadge's actions.[230]

Soon new information emerged about Talmadge's finances. In the course of its inquiry into Talmadge's campaign reports, the FEC noted that he had filed with the Senate a series of sworn statements indicating that he had spent no personal funds on his 1974 reelection campaign. On the day when he signed the statements, however, he was reimbursed $12,000 by his political committee for expenses he claimed in connection with the campaign. In addition, it was learned that he had reported no personal campaign expenditures for 1973. For those two years, a total of $27,000 had not been properly reported, and when asked to explain Talmadge's staff ascribed the omission to oversight and confusion as to how to report the funds on the forms provided. T. Rogers Wade, Talmadge's campaign manager and administrative assistant, said the reports would be corrected.[231]

Small Gifts. In June 1978 a third anomaly drew attention to Talmadge's financial affairs. News sources reported that for most of his 31 years in public life Talmadge had been given an annual birthday party. Guests were asked to pay $25 (men) or $15 (women), and the proceeds after expenses were given to Talmadge as a birthday present. Although Talmadge had reported these gifts to the Senate in 1973 and 1974, he did not do so in 1975 and 1976, and none of the gifts had been reported to the IRS.[232] Talmadge also apparently received other small gifts thrust into his hands and stuffed in his pockets at campaign rallies and elsewhere throughout the years. All gifts, if used for personal expenses, would require determination as to disclosure depending upon when given and their source. If the donating individual was the source, if the gift involved a relatively small amount of cash, and if a political campaign was not on, then IRS regulations and Senate rules might not have required disclosure. If the gifts were considered in the aggregate, however — unsolicited contributions received within one year or the proceeds from one birthday party, or for campaign purposes — the sums represented thousands of dollars and should have been reported.

On June 8, 1978, the Ethics Committee voted to conduct a full investigation into Talmadge's financial affairs. Chairman Adlai Stevenson indicated that the investigation would extend to allegations made by Talmadge's wife that the senator had misled the Senate by failing to include a $750,000 stock holding on his income tax return and on his disclosure statement to the comptroller general. The reported irregularities in Talmadge's financial affairs led the IRS to announce that it would audit Talmadge's income tax tax returns, but that it would wait to do so until the committee's investigation had been completed.

In July 1978 Talmadge filed with the Secretary of the Senate amended reports reflecting his personal spending during the 1974 campaign. These reports showed that Talmadge had spent $26,912 in personal funds on his campaign. He had been reimbursed by his campaign committee for these expenses, but he had not earlier disclosed his personal spending in 1973 as required by law, and sworn statements he had made indicated that in 1974 he had spent no money on his own behalf. The committee sought to determine why Talmadge had not reported personal spending on the 1974 campaign sooner, and Talmadge signed a waiver permitting the IRS to discuss his tax returns with committee investigators.[233] In addition, Talmadge's auditors, who had been called in to review his special office account, found that he had been reimbursed by the Senate during the years 1971-77 for about $35,000 in expenses that should not properly have been claimed for reimbursement; approximately $24,000 represented expenses that allegedly had never been incurred, and the remaining $11,000 apparently consisted of expenses not eligible for reimbursement.[234] These reports led the Justice Department to launch its own investigation of Talmadge's financial affairs.

Minchew Testimony. In August it was further disclosed that a former aide to Talmadge, Daniel Minchew, had withdrawn from the Senate approximately $13,000 using expense account vouchers to which Talmadge's name had improperly been signed. The money apparently went into a Washington bank account that was later revealed to belong to Talmadge. Talmadge's accountants and government auditors agreed that he owed the Senate $37,125 in improperly claimed expenses, and Talmadge repaid this amount, attributing the over-payment to errors on the part of his staff.[235]

Concern about the Washington bank account into which Senate funds had been deposited by Minchew led the Ethics Committee to subpoena bank records and to offer Minchew limited immunity in exchange for his testimony. The former aide claimed that the improperly obtained Senate funds were deposited into the bank account at Talmadge's request and were used by the Georgia senator and his family. In August news sources reported that the bank account had been used by Talmadge as a secret campaign account through which more than $25,000 — including undisclosed contributions — had been channeled into Talmadge's election effort during 1973 and 1974. Withdrawals from the account had been made with checks payable to cash and endorsed with an automatic device that reproduced Talmadge's signature. Minchew maintained that transactions invariably had been made according to Talmadge's instructions; Talmadge stated that he had not known of the account.[236] Minchew's limited immunity was delayed for 20 days by the Justice Department. The delay was interpreted to mean that Justice investigators sought time to document evidence against Minchew before his testimony supplied information that could not be used against him because of his immunity. Minchew was granted immunity in late September.

Investigation of bank records began to identify campaign contributions that had been placed in the secret account.[237] Investigators for both the Ethics Committee and the Justice Department were interested in determining the source of the gifts. In one case, a contribution of $5,000 from a Georgia businessman had been deposited in the account. Minchew estimated that $39,000 in illegally procured Senate funds and campaign contributions had passed through the account in 1973 and 1974.[238] Other contributions were also noted by news sources, and in several instances the contribution appeared related to efforts made by Talmadge on behalf of the donor's business interests.[239] Committee investigators concluded that the evidence of possible wrongdoing by Talmadge warranted a committee trial, which opened in May 1979.[240]

Because the cases of Brooke and Talmadge were the first to require action by the Senate Ethics Committee since passage of the new code, observers watched with particular interest to see how effective the committee's actions would be.[241]

Korean Lobbying Investigations

On October 14, 1978, the House concluded an investigation of Korean influence buying that had lasted for 18 months and had attracted considerable publicity. During the investigation, many individuals inside and outside Congress were implicated and a number of indictments were handed down. The House ethics committee had sought to determine how many congressmen were guilty of accepting contributions of cash from Korean nationals, and in the end it recommended its mildest form of punishment, a "reprimand," for three California Democrats: John J. McFall, Edward R. Roybal, and Charles H. Wilson. The action brought criticism of House procedures for enforcing standards of ethical conduct among its members, charges that gain in significance with consideration of some aspects of the complex scheme by which the Koreans sought to purchase support from American congressmen.[242]

Tongsun Park

Two years earlier, in October 1976, *The Washington Post* reported that a wealthy Korean businessman, Tongsun Park, had spent $500,000-$1,000,000 a year to influence U.S. policy toward South Korea while he lived in the United States during the 1970s. The newspaper claimed that Park and his associates had engaged in illegal activities, including bribery. After the first reports appeared, scores of legislators were implicated, other Koreans were named, and many government investigations were undertaken.

Tongsun Park came to the United States in the late 1950s and attended the Georgetown University School of Foreign Affairs, graduating in 1962. While in this country, Park became friends with Il Kwon Chung, then Korean ambassador to Washington and subsequently prime minister of South Korea. Chung introduced Park to a number of agents of the KCIA (Korean Central Intelligence Agency). Park tried to convince the agents that both he and the South Korean government could profit from his business ventures and his contacts. He would make money, and the KCIA and the South Koreans would be able to exert additional influence on American policymakers. In 1966 Tongsun Park founded the George Town Club in Washington's fashionable Georgetown area and the following year he allegedly received $3 million from the KCIA to finance it. With the money Park was able to turn the club into an exclusive meeting place for the powerful in Washington.

In 1970 the Nixon administration announced that it was withdrawing 20,000 of the 60,000 U.S. troops stationed in South Korea, a decision

strongly opposed by the Seoul regime. Earlier an important meeting had
been held in the Blue House, the presidential compound in Seoul.
Korean President Chung Hee Park, several of his closest aides, key
officials in the KCIA, and Tongsun Park allegedly attended. Tongsun
Park proposed that the South Korean government designate him the
sole agent for U.S. rice exports to South Korea. In turn, he would take
the commissions he received and spend them in a sophisticated lobbying
campaign to win additional support for the Park regime among important members of Congress and other Washington dignitaries. The government in Seoul apparently agreed to the proposal.

Congressional Targets. In the late 1960s Park gave some congressmen small cash gifts, but after his alliance with the regime in Seoul, his
political activities increased dramatically. Park cleverly matched his
interests with those of the congressmen he solicited. He focused on the
House of Representatives because its members were elected every two
years. Within the House, he sought out members of the Foreign Affairs
and Appropriations committees, legislators from rice growing areas,
those who had served in the armed forces during the Korean conflict,
and congressional leaders.

Rice exports to South Korea played a key role in Park's efforts. In
1969 he was a selling agent for the Rice Growers' Association of California, a farmers' cooperative in Representative McFall's district.[243]
McFall, a member of the Appropriations Committee and subsequently a
majority whip, became friendly with Park. In response to a request from
the rice growers in his area, he wrote to President Chung Hee Park
praising Tongsun Park. The latter subsequently gave McFall several
thousand dollars in cash. In 1972 Park and Representatives McFall and
Robert L. Leggett, another California Democrat, helped sell nearly all of
California's surplus rice crop to South Korea.

Park did not confine his contacts to the California delegation. In
1971 he went to Louisiana, another state producing a large rice crop, and
then, with Democratic Reps. Edwin W. Edwards and Otto E. Passman,
to Seoul to arrange the sale of surplus Louisiana rice to South Korea.
The three men obtained a $31 million loan for South Korea from the
Agency for International Development to finance the purchase of rice
from 1971 through 1973. This deal aided Edwards in his successful race
for governor of Louisiana in 1972.

Passman was chairman of the Foreign Operations Subcommittee of
the House Appropriations Committee and thus had some control over
foreign aid requests. He reportedly received gifts and cash, as well as
several expense-paid trips to South Korea. Allegedly, Passman and
Leggett tried to influence Agriculture Department decisions concerning
rice and other exports to South Korea. In 1975 Passman apparently used

his authority in an attempt to replace a shipping agency representing Egypt in the Food for Peace program with the Pan Mediterranean Shipping Corp., a company run by two of his friends — Tongsun Park and Grover Connell, head of Connell Rice and Sugar Co.

Edwards was a close friend of Park; the South Korean offered him a $10,000 contribution in 1971, when the congressman was seeking his state's governorship. Edwards turned down the offer because he mistakenly supposed such donations to be illegal. Park then gave Edwards' wife $10,000 as a gift for herself and her children. Edwards claimed that he did not learn about the gift until three years later, when the IRS investigated his income tax returns and required him to pay $5,000 in back taxes. Clyde Vidrine, a former Edwards aide, told a federal grand jury in 1977 that Park had given Edwards $20,000 in cash for his 1972 campaign. The governor denied the charges, saying Vidrine had a vendetta against him.

Two other former congressmen, Cornelius Gallagher, D-N.J., and Richard T. Hanna, D-Calif., also were investigated by the Justice Department for their ties to Park, who had accompanied both men on trips to Seoul while they were serving in the House. They allegedly told President Park that they would seek to stimulate support for Korea among their congressional friends. Tongsun Park helped Gallagher cash $16,000 in bonds in 1972. After the former congressman was released from a prison term of 17 months for tax evasion, he lived in Park's home. In 1975 the Korean lent him $250,000.

As noted, Park helped arrange sales of American rice through the Food for Peace program. By 1974 the situation had changed. There was a world food crisis and no shipments of rice to South Korea under the program were made. Instead, Park helped sell rice through commercial channels. In these matters, Park dealt largely with the Connell Rice and Sugar Co., the nation's largest rice exporter. In line with the agreement reached in Seoul in 1970, the South Korean agency responsible for all overseas rice purchases in March 1972 wrote Connell, as well as the other major exporting firms, stating that henceforth Tongsun Park would serve as its exclusive agent for rice exports from the United States. Connell forwarded a copy of a letter to the U.S. Agriculture Department, which told the parties involved that such an arrangement was illegal under guidelines for the Food for Peace program. Although the South Korean government formally withdrew Park as its exclusive agent, the Korean businessman continued to receive large commissions.

In 1971 Representative Hanna became a secret partner in Park's export-import business. During the next three years, this investment netted him between $60,000 and $70,000. The concern handled federally subsidized rice and other commodities.

William E. Minshall, an Ohio Republican who at one time was the ranking minority member of the House Defense Appropriations Subcommittee, also came under investigation by the Justice Department. He and Hanna were hosts at parties for fellow legislators at the George Town Club. Minshall and Park traveled to South Korea together in 1972. It was alleged that Park gave Hanna and Minshall $5,000 each in 1970.

In February 1976 Representatives Leggett and Joseph P. Addabbo, D-N.Y., admitted that they were being investigated by the Justice Department on charges of having accepted bribes from the South Korean government. Both vehemently denied the allegations.

Park seemingly had access to large sums of money on which he apparently paid no income taxes. Although his use of these funds may never be completely known, it appears that at least part of the money was spent to entertain legislators and other key government officials both in Washington and in Seoul. In addition, some of the money went into Park's numerous business ventures. The nearly destitute resident alien of the 1960s had become a prosperous member of the Washington social scene by the early 1970s. Park gave lavish parties at the George Town Club, many of which honored key congressmen such as Speaker Carl Albert, House Majority Leader Thomas P. O'Neill, and Majority Whip John McFall. Dozens of legislators attended these fetes, although most apparently did not know about Park's ties with the South Korean government.

Park's campaign contributions combined legal and illegal actions. Prior to January 1, 1975, foreign nationals could lawfully make political contributions. During this period Park apparently also made a number of illegal payments, however. In addition to bestowing gifts in the United States, the Koreans were very gracious hosts to visiting congressional delegations. Speaker Albert led one group to Seoul in 1971 and Majority Leader O'Neill led another in 1974. In 1975 Rep. John M. Murphy, D-N.Y., who received two campaign contributions from the Koreans, led a third group to commemorate the 25th anniversary of the outbreak of the Korean War. In 1975 and 1976 more than 60 congressmen visited Seoul, some several times. Some of their trips were paid for by the Korean Cultural and Freedom Foundation, a privately financed foundation with close ties to the Seoul regime. While in Korea, about a dozen legislators were given honorary degrees by several Korean universities. Nearly all congressional visitors were lavishly entertained and given antiques and jewelry.

After Tongsun Park's activities became known, the South Korean government in 1975 allegedly chose a replacement for him, Hancho C. Kim. Kim, a naturalized U.S. citizen, was a Maryland businessman and a trustee of American University. Kim had proposed to American University that it establish a vaguely defined international studies program with financial contributions from foundations and possibly from the Korean government. The actual purpose of the center, it has been said, was to allow scholars and others to enter the United States under cover and to make contact with administration officials, congressmen, congressional staffers, and academics. After considerable thought, the university rejected the proposal.

Another alleged Korean operative was Suzi Park Thomson. A naturalized U.S. citizen and a graduate of the University of South Carolina, Thomson spoke several Asian languages and worked on the staffs of a number of Democratic congressmen, including Speaker Albert. Suzi Thomson was known in Washington as a hostess who threw lavish parties for congressmen, lobbyists, and staff members. It is claimed that she introduced important Koreans to her congressional acquaintances in Washington and Seoul, and she accompanied several congressional delegations to South Korea. Hyung Wook Kim, a former KCIA chief, told the House Subcommittee on International Organizations that Thomson was a KCIA agent. She denied the charge and knowledge of any bribes. Many congressmen considered the activities of the Koreans to be perfectly acceptable, especially in light of South Korea's great dependence on the United States. Many legislators said that the Koreans never requested favors. John Brademas, D-Ind., and other congressmen pointed out that they were harsh critics of the Park regime. Clearly, however, some legislators did help Tongsun Park and the South Korean government. Several congressmen intervened with U.S. agencies and departments on Park's behalf, lobbied fellow congressmen, approached officials of other governments, gave Tongsun Park restricted information, aided him in his purchase of rice for South Korea, sought to counteract criticism of President Park's attacks on Korean dissidents, voted to increase economic and military aid for South Korea, helped Tongsun Park avoid Agriculture and Commerce department restrictions on his business activities, and wrote letters to President Park commending Tongsun Park's effectiveness on behalf of the Seoul government.

Executive Branch. Congressmen were not the only targets of the Korean effort. John Nidecker, a White House official who visited South Korea in May 1974, was given several expensive gifts that he turned over to the General Services Administration. Just before leaving Seoul, he was given $10,000 in cash by Chong Huy Park, head of President Park's security force. Nidecker turned the cash over to U.S. Ambassador Philip Habib. Shortly thereafter Chin Hwan Ro, a Korean national assemblyman, came to Washington and left expensive presents for about a dozen White House aides and their spouses. The gifts were returned to Ro. Ro also allegedly told the Nixon administration that the Koreans would supply $30,000 to any congressional candidate it designated. The administration turned down the offer.

Other Nixon administration officials were also involved. Former Attorney General Richard Kleindienst was retained by one of Park's companies for several months after he left the Justice Department. Melvin Laird, former secretary of Defense, was a member of the George Town Club and held a party there for President Ford and his wife Betty. Before becoming U.S. ambassador to India, William Saxbe was guest of honor at a party given by Park. William Timmons, former chief congressional liaison officer for the Nixon White House, received $60,000 for work he performed for Park shortly after Timmons left the government in 1975. It was rumored that the South Korean also had tried to establish a business deal with former Vice President Spiro Agnew.

House Action

As the reports of alleged Korean influence peddling grew, demands were made that the House ethics committee (formally known as the House Committee on Standards of Official Conduct) undertake an investigation. The committee responded in January 1977 by naming Philip Lacovara, a key member of the Watergate special prosecution team, as counsel to head its probe. On February 9, 1977, the House voted unanimously to authorize the committee to "conduct a full and complete inquiry to determine whether members of the House of Representatives, their immediate families, or their associates accepted anything of value, directly or indirectly, from the Government of the Republic of Korea or representatives thereof." [244] Although technically the resolution was not needed, its passage thwarted Common Cause and others who had called for the creation of a select committee to investigate the matter.

In March 1977 Lacovara submitted a memo to the committee urging the panel to hold congressmen to higher standards than those applied to private citizens. The committee adopted his suggestions and also voted to limit its investigation to gifts of $100 or more, unless they were part of a pattern of misconduct by members.

By this time, however, the committee was increasingly attacked for proceeding at a slow pace. Sides in the conflict were drawn up according to seniority. Junior members of the House elected after, during, or shortly before Watergate sought to purify the chamber. Senior representatives tended to seek to preserve the institution and its traditional modes of conduct. There was some partisan controversy as Republicans, seeing a potentially explosive campaign issue for 1978, charged that House Democrats were employing a double standard — one for Richard

Nixon and Watergate, another for colleagues of their own party who were implicated in the Korean scandal. Koreagate, as some Republicans called it, would help neutralize the public's memories of Watergate.

In June the panel voted to require (a) every member of the House to disclose details of his association with the South Koreans and (b) every member of the committee to acknowledge any gifts from Korean associates. The ethics committee sent a questionnaire to more than 700 current and former members of the House who had served since 1970. The survey asked whether the member, his family, or his staff had 1) visited South Korea, 2) been offered or accepted anything of a value greater than $100 from an agent or suspected agent of South Korea, or 3) attended a function or had business dealings with Tongsun Park, Hancho Kim, Suzi Park Thomson, Dong Jo Kim (formerly Korean ambassador to the United States), or Sang Keun Kim (a former Korean intelligence officer who defected in 1968).

The attacks on the committee continued, both from within and from without. On July 15, after committee Chairman Flynt publicly criticized him and ordered the GAO to audit his firm's legal fees, Lacovara resigned as counsel. On July 20 Leon Jaworski, who had served as Watergate special prosecutor, was chosen to replace Lacovara. The Houston attorney received a written agreement from Flynt and O'Neill that he could be removed only by a majority vote of the full House and an ironclad agreement that the committee would issue any subpoenas that he requested. Jaworski was to report to the panel any evidence of violations of the House rules or the criminal statutes and would recommend punishment in such cases. The final decisions were to be made by the full committee, however. In effect, Jaworski was given the powers that Lacovara had sought unsuccessfully.

In 1975 and 1976 the House International Relations (now Foreign Affairs) Subcommittee on International Organizations, chaired by Rep. Donald Fraser, D-Minn., held hearings on U.S.-South Korean relations. It discovered that KCIA agents had been harassing Koreans living in the United States who opposed the Park regime. In addition, the panel uncovered evidence of potentially illegal lobbying activities by some Korean agents. This information was forwarded to the Justice Department. When newspaper stories of alleged Korean bribe attempts appeared, the subcommittee decided to hold additional hearings. Its focus was not on the influence peddling per se but rather on the foreign policy implications of the lobbying campaign.

Senate Action

The House was not alone in looking into South Korean lobbying efforts. In June 1977 the Senate voted to authorize a special prosecutor to pursue the case. The amendment, proposed by Donald W. Riegle, Jr., D-Mich., gave the attorney general 90 days either to find the allegations unsubstantiated or to turn the matter over to a court-appointed prosecutor.

In July the Senate Ethics Committee asked CIA Director Stansfield Turner to brief its members in closed session on U.S. intelligence reports about possible involvement of senators in the affair. During the same month, Senators Adlai Stevenson and Harrison Schmitt, respectively chairman and ranking minority member of the Ethics Committee, announced that a preliminary investigation had turned up no improprieties on the part of any present or former senator. Stevenson subsequently examined Justice Department files, however, and reached different conclusions. He called for a full-scale investigation by the ethics panel.

Indictments

As a result of information provided by the State Department and the Fraser subcommittee, the Justice Department empaneled a grand jury in Washington in spring 1976 to probe the Korean affair. The department's investigation encountered a number of difficulties. After briefly cooperating with the department, Tongsun Park, a resident alien, fled first to London, where he was not extradited because the relevant treaty does not cover failure to register as a foreign agent. From London Park went to Seoul.

The grand jury's proceedings dragged on for more than a year amid outcries that the Justice Department was not acting quickly enough. Some called for the appointment of a special prosecutor to handle the matter. The president and Attorney General Griffin Bell rejected these demands. Bell pointed out that the case was complex and subtle, with legal and illegal activities interwoven.

In August 1977 the grand jury indicted Tongsun Park on charges of bribery and other offenses. The indictment was sealed in the hope that Park would return to London before it became public knowledge (the extradition treaty covers bribery). Information concerning the indictment was printed in U.S. newspapers while the South Korean businessman was in Seoul, however. On September 6 the Justice Department unsealed the indictment against Tongsun Park, charging him with 36 felony violations and naming former Representative Hanna and two former heads of the KCIA as unindicted coconspirators.[245] According to the indictment, Park was operating in the United States "with the knowledge and under the direction of the K.C.I.A."[246]

Hanna allegedly helped Park to become the sole agent for U.S. rice sales to South Korea. In return, Park was said to have given the

California Democrat more than $100,000 between 1967 and 1975. The charges against Hanna included providing pro-Korean statements to two congressmen who presented them to a congressional subcommittee investigating allegations of human rights violations in South Korea. Hanna also allegedly tried to influence congressmen to go to South Korea and to aid the Park regime. Twenty representatives and four senators were listed as having received funds from Park.

On September 8 the House narrowly defeated an amendment by Rep. Bruce F. Caputo, R-N.Y., a member of the ethics committee, that would have lowered the ceiling on a budget resolution by $108 million, the amount of money the United States had planned to spend on rice and other commodities for South Korea. O'Neill, who had succeeded Albert as Speaker, told his colleagues that if the Seoul government failed to cooperate with the House ethics probe it would harm its relations with the United States.

In the Senate, Adlai Stevenson announced that the Ethics Committee had named Victor Kramer, director of the Institute for Public Interest Representation at the Georgetown University Law Center, as special counsel to conduct a probe of potential abuses by senators or senatorial aides connected with Tongsun Park.

On September 27 a federal grand jury in Washington indicted Hancho C. Kim on two felony charges stemming from the alleged influence buying effort by the South Korean government. Kim was charged with making false declarations to the grand jury and with conspiracy to defraud the United States. The indictment claimed that he had received two packages of $300,000 in cash; the payments were said to have been made by Sang Keun Kim in September 1974 and again in mid-1975 for the purpose of supporting "Operation White Snow," evidently the code name of the South Korean project. The indictment relied heavily on the testimony of Sang Keun Kim, Hancho Kim, and Gen. Doo Wan Yang (also known as Sang Ho Lee), a former Washington KCIA station chief, were named unindicted coconspirators. The indictment stated that the South Korean embassy had provided cash to be used to influence members of Congress, thus formally implicating the Seoul regime in the scheme. A separate indictment handed up in Baltimore charged Kim and his wife with income tax evasion in 1974 and 1975.

Hearings

Jai Hyon Lee, a former Korean embassy official who sought political asylum in the United States in 1973, told the House ethics committee that in 1972 he had seen Dong Jo Kim, then the Korean ambassador to the United States, stuffing white envelopes with $100 bills. When Lee asked what he was doing, Kim reportedly answered that he was going to the Capitol to deliver the funds. A secretary in the office of Rep. Larry Winn, Jr., R-Kan., described how Kim had left an envelope with $100 bills on the congressman's desk and how she returned the money. Lee reported that the Korean effort had been undertaken because President Chung Hee Park feared losing U.S. military and economic aid. The wives of Reps. E. "Kika" de la Garza, D-Texas, and John T. Myers, R-Ind., reported that they were given money by a Korean woman, identified by Mrs. de la Garza as Mrs. Dong Jo Kim, on a trip to Seoul in August 1975. Both women told the panel that their husbands had returned the money. Sang Keun Kim told the committee that there were two Korean programs, one code named "Ice Mountain Snow," headed by Tongsun Park, and the other code named "White Snow" and directed by Hancho Kim. Both were aimed at winning support for the Park regime among American congressmen, administrators, journalists, and academics.

Hancho Kim was portrayed as a more active agent than had previously been supposed. According to Sang Keun Kim, Hancho Kim had boasted of controlling five Republican congressmen, whom he called the "advance guard." In addition, it was alleged that Hancho Kim had told Sang Keun Kim that he needed funds for two of President Ford's assistants. Sang Keun Kim told the panel that former Ambassador Pyong Choon Hahn had offered a congressman $20,000 and that President Park had known of the offer.[247] On the final day of testimony, Jai Shin Ryu, one of Tongsun Park's former aides, told how the latter had arranged an internship for him in 1971 in the offices of Rep. Frank Thompson Jr., D-N.J., and former Sen. Joseph Montoya, D-N.M.

South Korea Relations. From the moment the story broke, Tongsun Park and the South Korean government contended that no ties existed between them. Park claimed he was not an agent of the government — an important point, since as a government agent he would be in violation of the Foreign Agents Registration Act, which requires nearly all nondiplomatic personnel representing foreign governments to register with the Department of Justice.[248] Park contended that he had acted as a businessman to advance his own personal interests rather than to help the Seoul government. Despite public records to the contrary, he initially denied giving money, stating that his contacts with legislators and other officials had simply grown out of his many years of living in the area and his membership in high society.

As the scandal unfolded, the South Korean government recalled a number of its agents in the United States and apparently fired some involved officials. In April 1977 President Park told a group of congressmen that there would be no more lavish entertaining of visiting legislators at the expense of the government.

On October 14 a federal grand jury indicted Richard Hanna on 40 counts of felony. Hanna was charged with conspiring with Park and two former KCIA directors to manipulate the actions of the U.S. government and Congress, seeking about $100,000 in bribes, failing to register as an agent of a foreign government, and committing mail fraud. He was accused of urging other members of Congress to take action with regard to South Korean issues, advising Park as to how to influence congressmen, and communicating with Korean officials regarding efforts on behalf of Korea. The indictment also mentioned that on three occasions Hanna had obtained the assistance of Rep. Edward J. Patten, D-N.J., in promoting South Korean interests. Hyung Wook Kim and Hu Rak Lee, another former Korean CIA chief, were named unindicted coconspirators.

Park Testimony Sought. After Tongsun Park fled to Seoul, much effort on the part of U.S. investigators was required to secure his testimony and evenual return to the United States. As publicity continued, the House of Representatives refused to consider President Carter's request to transfer $800 million worth of weapons to South Korea. Officials in Seoul ordered Tongsun Park to stop talking with reporters. The House unanimously approved a resolution calling for Korean cooperation.

New information from Jai Shin Ryu further implicated former Representative Passman. Ryu claimed that Park had given $190,000 — the largest of his gifts — to Passman to obtain his support. Again, Park's testimony was needed to press charges. Tongsun Park's name emerged in a new connection as he was discovered to have contributed to a New Jersey county Democratic Party between 1971 and 1974, allegedly making the contributions through Edward Patten's office.

As U.S. negotiators continued their efforts to agree with Korean officials regarding questioning of Park, a measure introduced by the Korean opposition party proposing investigation of Korean officials was defeated in the South Korean parliament. On November 5 President Carter issued a statement accusing South Korea of impeding American justice through its continuing failure to facilitate inquiries in the United States. Under pressure from the House ethics committee, Korean embassy officials agreed to make embassy bank records available for investigators' use.

In November 1977 the Senate Ethics Committee sent questionnaires to all current senators and 50 former senators asking about visits to the Republic of Korea, acceptance of gifts valued in excess of $35 from representatives of the Korean government, and acceptance of gifts worth more than $35 from specific Korean individuals and organizations. Working with lists supplied by the Koreans, the committee investigated 30 incumbent and 15 former senators. The House committee, which had sent its questionnaire to representatives months before, reduced its list from 115 former and current members to about 50 by the time the Senate questionnaire was distributed.

Although no agreement was reached regarding interrogation of Tongsun Park, U.S. officials made some progress by the end of November. A federal Tax Court judge impounded a diary belonging to Park and requested by IRS agents for their investigation of taxes owed by the Korean businessman. The diary, dated 1972, included notations of payments made to at least one senator. Hancho Kim expressed interest in negotiating with House investigators and was questioned privately by the House ethics committee on November 26.

KCIA Plan. Then, in a more important breakthrough on November 29, the House Subcommittee on International Organizations disclosed a 1976 plan prepared by the KCIA, providing for manipulation of the Ford administration, Congress, news organizations, academicians, and the clergy. It included sweeping measures to establish an intelligence network in the White House, win the support of the Democratic Party's policy research committee in Congress, create public opinion favorable to South Korea, patronize the academic community, and win the allegiance of Korean residents in the United States. The scheme had been drafted after Vietnam fell to communist control, when American criticism of President Park's repression of human rights was intensifying. North Korea had adopted a diplomatic offensive at the time, and the South Korean plan included among its objectives the thwarting of North Korea's efforts to open contacts with the United States. The document was the most comprehensive and detailed yet disclosed, and its provisions for influencing Congress represented the most sophisticated section.

Park Questioned

In December 1977 agreement finally was reached between South Korean and U.S. officials regarding questioning of Tongsun Park. The accord provided that the Justice Department and Park sign a formal agreement in which Park would commit himself to truthful testimony and the Justice Department would drop all charges and grant him immunity in return. American and Korean officials would question Park, and he occasionally would be given polygraph tests. After the questioning, the Korean government would permit Park to travel in the United States to testify at trials resulting from the investigation — notably the trials of Hancho Kim and Richard Hanna.[249]

Tongsun Park signed the limited interrogation agreement on January 11, 1978. On January 14, his first day of questioning, he reviewed his relationships with congressmen, and reports reached the press of dozens of gifts. Park was said to have testified that he had disbursed $750,000 in gifts and political payments to U.S. officials and political campaigns between 1970 and 1975. On January 20 Leon Jaworski appealed to the House for a strong resolution calling for South Korea's unlimited cooperation with the investigation by the ethics committee. Jaworski suggested that the committee could complete its inquiry and determine who was guilty within 60 to 90 days if full disclosure were offered by Seoul.[250] He also indicated that committee investigators had evidence of wrongdoing by current members of Congress. A resolution insisting that South Korea provide the committee with testimony from Tongsun Park, Dong Jo Kim, and other officials was introduced in the House with the full bipartisan support. The South Korean government, aware of the most critical threat to U.S. aid to date, agreed to permit Park to appear at congressional hearings but refused to allow former Korean officials to be questioned.

New Names. The two inquiries and the publicity surrounding them continued to produce new names and to lead in new directions. Former President Ford acknowledged that he had been aware in 1975 of allegations of bribery by Korean officials; Henry Kissinger already had indicated his awareness of Korean lobbying in Washington in the early 1970s.[251] The end of Park's questioning by Justice Department officials in Korea coincided with the announcement that he had agreed to appear before both the House and Senate committees. It also was noted that he would be questioned a second time by Justice Department officials in Washington. Although Justice investigators acknowledged that many former and present legislative and executive officials had been mentioned in the course of Park's interrogation, Park himself admitted that he had recorded transactions that did not take place, possibly to give Korean officials the impression that he was spending greater amounts of money to influence Congress. In early February, former Representatives Passman and Minshall seemed likely to be indicted; Edwin Edwards, governor of Louisiana, and Cornelius Gallagher, former Democratic representative from New Jersey, also figured significantly in Park's testimony but seemed at that time unlikely to be indicted because the federal statute of limitations had expired.[252]

Park also told investigators that he had made contributions in recent years to former Senate members Montoya ($3,000) and Jack Miller, R-Iowa, ($3,000) as well as to Sens. Stuart Symington, D-Mo., ($500) and Harry F. Byrd, Ind-Va. ($500). Senator Hubert Humphrey of Minnesota also was named, but Park did not confirm that a contribution had actually been made.[253] In addition, Park's testimony was said to implicate 15 to 18 current members of Congress; according to Assistant Attorney General Benjamin Civiletti, about $1 million was given to U.S. officials, primarily congressmen, between 1968 and 1975.[254]

In February the House International Organizations Subcommittee announced plans to hold hearings on executive branch awareness of the Korean lobbying effort. This subcommittee approached the Justice Department for access to relevant secret U.S. intelligence reports, but Attorney General Bell denied the request because Rep. Edward J. Derwinski, R-Ill., earlier suspected of leaking information to the Korean government, was the ranking minority member of the committee.

Dong Jo Kim Role. As additional testimony was obtained from Tongsun Park, investigators increasingly perceived the need for information from Dong Jo Kim. Jaworski indicated his belief that Kim's testimony was needed to determine who had received the Korean funds and what had become of the money. The Seoul regime repeatedly blocked access to the former ambassador, citing diplomatic immunity; the U.S. investigators linked Korean cooperation with continued aid from the United States. Concerned observers — including some U.S. allies — noted that under the Vienna Convention, approved by the U.S. Senate in 1965, no former diplomat may be compelled to furnish evidence.[255] Nevertheless, on February 22 Senator Stevenson advised Seoul that without Korean cooperation he would block passage of the $500 million loan to Korea for nuclear reactors.

Tongsun Park returned to Washington, and he began testifying before the House ethics committee on February 28. The hearings did not proceed smoothly; participating House members found some sessions slow in producing new information, doubted the accuracy and completeness of Park's testimony, and termed him "evasive" in responding to some questions. The controversial Korean continued to deny any affiliation with the KCIA and claimed that his actions had been intended to serve only his personal interests as a rice dealer. His replies sometimes conflicted with documentary evidence and with his own earlier testimony. The congressmen who had received contributions from him were his friends, Park maintained. Establishment of his ties with the KCIA was important to investigators, since the Constitution prohibits members of Congress from accepting cash from foreign agents, while they were legally permitted to accept contributions from foreign businessmen until 1974.

Since Park's legal identity was uncertain in this regard, testimony from Dong Jo Kim became more important: Kim's identity as a foreign agent was beyond question, and evidence existed that Kim and his wife had made contributions to congressmen. Despite the concern of congressional investigators, the State Department opposed coercion of the Seoul regime. Some observers noted that interrogation of a diplomat would set a precedent, and more American than foreign emissaries had been accused of making political payoffs.[256]

As congressional interrogation proceeded, reports continued to reach the press of Park's testimony in Seoul. Some testimony from Park concerned his relations with Dong Jo Kim, who allegedly felt that Park's lobbying activities invaded an area where the ambassador had a monopoly.[257] Officials who monitored the lie detector tests administered to Park noted that he reacted nervously to some questions, particularly those concerning his relationship with the KCIA; other observers asserted that Park had simply failed the test on these questions.

Intelligence Reports. The House ethics committee concluded its interrogation of Park without substantial new revelations. The House International Organizations Subcommittee turned its attention to knowledge within the executive branch of Korean lobbying activities,[258] and news sources reported that former Secretary of State Henry Kissinger and former Attorney General John N. Mitchell had been asked to testify. The subcommittee focused on conspiracy by the Korean government to manipulate U.S. foreign policy and knowledge of the conspiracy by the Nixon administration. In mid-March, the subcommittee announced that it would release 500 pages of evidence, including information concerning discussions of the influence buying operation that had been conducted in the Blue House, the residence of the South Korean president.

The released documents contained varied information. Some evidence indicated that President Chung Hee Park personally had directed a covert lobbying campaign in the United States in the early 1970s; at this time, President Park apparently considered but rejected a plan to place Tongsun Park in charge of Washington operations. Instead, the South Korean president created a foreign policy review board to oversee the project. Representative Fraser noted that despite U.S. intelligence reports regarding this activity, the Nixon administration apparently did not attempt to halt the lobby. Although knowledge by the FBI of Korean activity was not documented, the State Department apparently exchanged memos with the Justice Department regarding Korean activity, including references to Tongsun Park and Bo Hi Pak. The Justice Department conducted a cursory inquiry into the affair. Nevertheless, a House subcommittee hearing indicated that the head of the State Department's Korean Desk evidently had believed Tongsun Park to be acting at KCIA direction; Donald Ranard, the State Department official, said he had determined from various sources that Park was somehow employed by the Seoul government.[259]

The House subcommittee released a summary of a memo issued on November 24, 1971, by J. Edgar Hoover, then head of the FBI. The top secret document had been prompted by a CIA report and was intended to inform John Mitchell, then attorney general, and Henry Kissinger, then White House national security adviser, that the Korean Blue House had funneled a $400,000 contribution to the Democratic Party in 1968 and a smaller six-figure sum to the Republican Party. Mitchell testified that he had never seen the memo, although it bore his initials. The document was one of three indicating that government officials had been aware of the Korean lobby;[260] the FBI agent who prepared the memo indicated that an investigation had not been undertaken because it would have compromised the source of the charges. The second document, dated November 24, 1971, reported payments by Tongsun Park to Richard Hanna; the third reported that Hanna had approached President Park for campaign contributions and had recommended that Tongsun Park be placed in charge of Korean lobbying in the United States.[261]

Henry Kissinger testified that reports of Korean bribery of congressmen did not reach him until 1975. He said he had told President Ford of these reports and added, "Indeed this whole investigation was started because I turned over to the attorney general a list of names we had." [262]

Hancho Kim, Hanna Convicted. As the investigation by the House subcommittee received increasing publicity, the trial of Hancho Kim began and that of former Representative Hanna concluded. Hanna pleaded guilty to receiving more than $200,000 as part of a conspiracy with the KCIA and Tongsun Park to defraud the United States. In return for his guilty plea, the U.S. government dropped 39 counts of alleged bribery, illegal gratuities, mail fraud, and failure to register as a foreign agent.[263] Hanna was the first sitting or former member of Congress to be convicted in the Korea probe, and he was sentenced on April 24, 1978, to between six and 30 months in prison. The maximum penalty would have been a five-year sentence and a $10,000 fine.

During proceedings against Hancho Kim — the first criminal trial to result from the probe — Sang Keun Kim testified that he had been advised of President Park's approval of a covert plan to lobby in the United States and that President Park had budgeted $1 million to influence Congress. Sang Keun Kim further testified that he had delivered $600,000 to Hancho Kim on September 12, 1974, and he produced a handwritten receipt that Hancho Kim denounced as a forgery. Sang Keun Kim said he had been under the impression that payments had been made with the money.

The U.S. government contended that Hancho Kim had replaced Tongsun Park as a KCIA agent and that Kim had received the money but had used it for personal purchases rather than to buy congressional influence. Kim denied receiving the money. The trial concluded in April 1978. Hancho Kim was convicted of accepting $600,000 in KCIA funds and lying about it to the federal grand jury probing the affair.[264] He was sentenced to six years in prison. As the sentence was handed down, the House ethics committee voted to begin a contempt action against him that could add one year to his prison term and result in a $1,000 fine.

Tongsun Park was interrogated by the Senate Ethics Committee after the hearings conducted by its counterpart in the House. Park described a total of about $21,500 in contributions paid to eight senators. Despite accumulating documentary evidence to the contrary, Park still denied that he had acted as an agent for the KCIA. Nevertheless, he mentioned that he had paid more than $1 million to officials in the legislative and executive branches of the Korean government.

Investigations Pressed

By late March 1978 the various inquiries being conducted into the Korean scandal were drawing the criticism of observers. Some charged that neither the congressional committees nor the Justice Department was displaying any urgency.[265] Adding to criticism of the House probes was the fate of a financial disclosure bill designed to provide a temporary special prosecutor for investigations involving the president, the vice president, and other important officials. In October 1977 a House Judiciary subcommittee approved a version that did not apply to Congress, and a proposal to extend the legislation to cover certain types of congressional inquiries was rejected. The proposal came from Elizabeth Holtzman, D-N.Y., who expressed her determination to present an amendment similar to the rejected proposal. Her attitude was considered by some individuals to be responsible for delay in bringing the bill before the full Judiciary Committee. Observers noted that the Senate had passed a similar measure in 1976, but that House action had been incomplete. Although related legislation that would have applied to the Korea probe had passed the Senate in July 1977, companion bills in the House did not reach the floor in 1977. While some observers noted that the Senate might attempt to force the House to act on these measures, to many the reluctance of the lower body seemed a further indication of its unwillingness to monitor its members' conduct.[266]

Passman Acquitted. On March 31, 1978, the Justice Department secured a fourth indictment. Otto E. Passman had been a member of Congress from 1947 to 1977 and had once been the powerful chairman of a House subcommittee on foreign aid. The indictment charged him with receiving $213,000 from Tongsun Park in payment for urging the South

Korean government to buy Louisiana rice through the Food for Peace program. When indicted, Passman was being treated for mental and physical exhaustion in a Louisiana hospital. Passman, who had denied receiving payments from Park, also was charged with having entered into a conspiracy with the Korean to advance Park's rice export trade.[267]

The indictment contained 26 pages of charges.[268] It alleged that Passman and Park had met in Hong Kong and Seoul in January 1972 to begin the conspiracy and in Washington at the Korean embassy with Ambassador Dong Jo Kim, Edwin W. Edwards (then governor-elect of Louisiana), and Gordon E. Dore, a leading rice miller from Louisiana. An attorney for Passman claimed he was too ill to come to court, and the district court judge postponed arraignment. On April 28 Passman was handed a second indictment by a federal grand jury that charged him with failing to report $143,000 of income related to the Korea scandal and received in 1972 and 1973.

In July a U.S. District Court judge ruled that Passman had to be tried in his home state of Louisiana on the charges in the two indictments (the charges had been consolidated to avoid the necessity of holding two trials). The decision was viewed by many observers as advantageous to Passman, who on April 1, 1979, after a trial at which Tongsun Park testified, was acquitted of all the charges against him.

Park's List. Following his 1978 testimony before the Senate Ethics Committee, Tongsun Park testified in a public hearing of the House ethics panel. Speaking in a casual manner that some observers found offensive, Park described $850,000 in payments he made over several years to members of Congress. Although documentary evidence indicated that Park worked in cooperation with the KCIA, he persisted in denying that he had been a foreign agent and repeatedly asserted that his actions had been intended to serve his personal interests. The larger part of his campaign contributions had, he said, been made to Otto Passman, Richard Hanna, and Cornelius Gallagher, who had all advanced his rice export business. He also listed a variety of other payments and favors, including birthday parties for Speaker O'Neill and a pair of hurricane lamps presented to O'Neill as a gift.[269]

Park's list of contributions included $3,500 in cash and checks given to Representative Patten from 1970 to 1976, payments that had been made in the form of contributions to the Middlesex County political party in New Jersey.

In all, Park named 31 current or former congressmen to whom he had made payments and two unsuccessful candidates who ran in 1974 for House seats.[270] In response, most of the congressmen named said that money from Park had been treated as campaign contributions and often had been given without their knowledge.

In April the House ethics committee released a document purport-
edly identified as a Korean intelligence report, asserting that Speaker
O'Neill had asked the Koreans for contributions to the campaigns of his
congressional supporters. The announcement caused a stir, but Tongsun
Park disclaimed knowledge of the report's source (it was found in his
house) and testified that O'Neill had made no such request.[271] Release of
the document brought criticism of the ethics committee from some
observers, who charged that the report had been held for three months
and released only tardily to avoid further investigation and publicity.[272]
O'Neill responded with indignation to the statement attributed to him.
In the course of testimony about the Speaker, however, Park did change
his testimony on a related matter: For the first time he asserted that
congressmen had approached him for funds.

Another witness added to the doubt in some minds as to the
veracity of Park's testimony. Testifying before the House ethics committee, Louisiana rice miller Gordon Dore swore that he never received
three payments that Park, also under oath, claimed to have made to him
in response to a request for a contribution to the campaign of Rep. John
B. Breaux, D-La.[273]

Weicker, Jaworski Resignations. Soon there were fresh signs of
public discontent with the progress of the investigations. Senator
Weicker of Connecticut resigned from the Ethics Committee's investigation, saying that Chairman Stevenson was making it impossible for an
effective inquiry to be conducted. Other commentators simply expressed
dissatisfaction with the pace of the investigations and the incompleteness of their findings.[274] Some pointed out that continuing financial aid
to Korea was undermining the power of the investigators to negotiate for
testimony from Dong Jo Kim. The House International Relations
Committee approved President Carter's request to transfer $800 million
in arms to South Korea over a five-year period of U.S. troop withdrawal,
and Senator Stevenson ceased objecting to American financing of $732
million to enable Korea to purchase nuclear reactors.

In May, however, Jaworski began to press for progress in the House
investigation. He called for a special ethics committee meeting to pass a
strong resolution that South Korea must make Dong Jo Kim available
for testimony. Jaworski's eagerness to press forward apparently related
to new and sensitive evidence regarding payments Kim had made to as
many as 10 House members. The evidence was said to consist of diplomatic messages in a Korean secret code that had been broken by the
National Security Agency.[275] In the wake of these reports, the International Relations Committee unanimously approved a resolution on May
24, 1978, to warn South Korea that the House would cut off economic
aid if South Korea failed to make Kim available to investigators.[276] In

Seoul, the resolution met with disapproval from both the ruling and opposition parties.

On May 30, 1978, the House voted 321 to 46 in support of the cautionary resolution. The Korean embassy quickly answered with a statement that the request was unacceptable. The investigations had now been under way for almost two years.

As negotiations with South Korea resumed, a fifth indictment stemming from the Korea probe was handed down. On May 26 a federal grand jury charged that Grover Connell, a rice trader, had concealed his illegal use of Tongsun Park as an agent for sales to the South Korean government under the Food for Peace program. Park was named an unindicted coconspirator, and the jury charged that he could not legally serve as a selling agent to Korea because of his ties with that government. Connell, president of the Connell Rice and Sugar Co., was nevertheless alleged to have paid Park $1.5 million in commissions placed in a Washington bank account in the name of Daiban Nongsan Co. Ltd. Connell's attorney, Richard Purcell, and Daiban Nongsan (a Korean agent) also were named unindicted coconspirators.[277]

On June 9, Leon Jaworski asked the ethics committee to determine whether four congressmen had violated House rules by accepting contributions from Tongsun Park. Those named were: McFall, Patten, Roybal, and Charles H. Wilson. In addition, Sen. John L. McClellan, D-Ark., was reported to have admitted before his death in 1977 that he had received an undisclosed campaign contribution from Tongsun Park. The House ethics committee voted secretly to proceed with disciplinary action against Patten, McFall, Roybal, and Wilson. The committee stated that these were the only four congressmen whose conduct warranted further proceedings, and it issued statements clearing nine other members and Speaker O'Neill, each of whom had acknowledged receipt of gifts or cash from Tongsun Park.[278] McFall was cited for having spent $4,000 from Park on expenses the committee considered related to the congressman's official duties. Roybal was said to have used $1,000 from Park for personal expenses and to have denied under oath that he had taken the money. Patten was considered in violation of New Jersey law, since he had contributed $500 to a county political organization using his own name rather than that of Park, the donor of the funds. Wilson had stated that he had received nothing of value from Park, although Park had testified that he gave Wilson $1,000 as a wedding gift.

In June the House voted to cut off $56 million in food aid to Korea. The vote coincided with a report from the Senate Intelligence Committee that U.S. intelligence agencies had known of the Korean lobby but that their information had been badly distributed. The agencies' knowledge apparently had included awareness of the Korean government's attempt to influence and intimidate the Korean community in the United States. The Senate committee's report said it found no evidence of a systematic coverup, but that the work of the U.S. intelligence agencies had been "unfocused, haphazard and without useful analysis," and it concluded that measures were necessary to prevent recurrence of such treatment.[279]

In June reports surfaced that congressional investigators were probing the circumstances surrounding a guilty plea filed in U.S. District Court in New York by Hyung Wook Kim. Kim had pleaded guilty to a charge of smuggling after he had been arrested at Kennedy Airport with $75,000 in cash.[280] On June 23 Dong Jo Kim resigned from his position as national security adviser to President Park.[281]

In late June the Senate Ethics Committee turned over to the Justice Department cases of possible perjury relating to cash payments Tongsun Park claimed to have made to three senators. Park had testified that he gave $5,000 in 1972 to John Morrison, a Humphrey aide; Morrison disclaimed knowledge of the donation. The second gift was $3,000 Park said he had given to aide Stan Browne for the campaign of Jack Miller; Browne claimed he had returned the funds. The third instance concerned Park's payment of $3,800 for a dinner for Birch Bayh, D-Ind., at the George Town Club.[282]

In early August, Leon Jaworski resigned as special counsel to the House ethics committee in protest over failure to secure testimony from Dong Jo Kim. The next day, the committee announced that it had accepted an offer by the Korean government that made possible interrogation of Kim by mail. Nevertheless, Kim's testimony remained unavailable.

Final Reports

Concluding its deliberations on the conduct of the four congressmen in October, the House committee cleared Patten's name. Key evidence in its decision was said to be a handwritten note on a letter explaining that Patten's $500 contribution to the New Jersey political organization had not originated with him. For McFall and Wilson, the committee recommended a reprimand by the House.

In Roybal's case, since his testimony under oath before the committee had been contradictory, censure was recommended. The reprimand punishment meant that the committee's findings against a congressman would be made part of the record; censure, on the other hand, would require Roybal to stand before the full House while a statement of his violations was read into the record.[283] Public response to the ethics committee's recommendations included protests from Hispanic groups that Roybal was being discriminated against on racial grounds. On October 14 the House voted on the ethics committee's recommendations, deciding in favor of a reprimand for Roybal as well as for McFall and Wilson.[284] The decision brought criticism and expressions of concern from many observers anxious that the House affirm its ability to monitor the actions of its members.[285]

International Organizations. In the wake of the House action, Fraser's International Organizations Subcommittee issued its final report on the Korean scheme. It found that the South Korean government had indeed sought to influence American officials, buy support from journalists and professors, obtain money from American companies and secure American military support; the report found that the Koreans' goals had been largely achieved, although not as a result of lobbying efforts.[286]

Ethics. In its final report, the House Committee on Standards of Official Conduct found that persons operating from the Republic of Korea embassy had, for limited periods of time, made payments to four current members of Congress and planned to pay two others, in an effort to seek votes for pro-Korea legislation. It concluded that Tongsun Park was closely related to the Korean government, and while Park paid out money principally to help himself receive rice commissions rather than to influence other policy matters, he did seek support on legislative matters of interest to the Korean government. The report stressed the role of former Representatives Cornelius Gallagher and Richard Hanna in helping Park, and noted the reprimands of Congressmen McFall, Roybal, and Wilson and the exoneration of Congressman Patten. It found "no impropriety" in campaign contributions to seven other House members or in two parties Park gave for Speaker O'Neill when O'Neill was majority leader.

The report further said it did not find in U.S. laws loopholes that permit undue foreign influence on Congress. It found that the South Korean government encouraged and participated in the sponsorship by private Korean organizations of trips to Korea by members of Congress, and it recommended that the House pass a rule forbidding members or employees to take overseas trips if paid for by foreigners unless the trip were exempted from the rule by the committee.[287]

Senate Staff Use in Campaigns

Although President Carter placed emphasis on the importance of ethical conduct by federal officials, the difficulty of legislating such conduct is apparent. After the 1976 election, attempts to unify and improve the various existing rules and codes coincided with new instances of questionable conduct of a sort not covered by the regulations, and observers increasingly recognized that practical legislation would be hard to draft.

One question raised was whether the Senate could eliminate the use of Senate staff or facilities in a senator's political campaign. Attempts at regulation encountered three types of difficulties. The first related to separation of activities financed by the Senate from activities undertaken by staff members or involving Senate facilities at little or no added cost to the Senate. A second concern bore on the sometimes blurred distinction between a senator's activities for campaign purposes and his legitimate duties as a representative of the people. Finally, Senate records and policy do not document officials' activities and schedules in such a way as to facilitate enforcement of rules of conduct, and some senators traditionally have been reluctant to monitor the actions of their colleagues.

Cannon Staff

The Senate's special committee formed to draft the new Code of Conduct in spring 1977 viewed the matter thus: "The line between public service and politics can blur at times, yet the public is entitled to know that those employed by the Senate, receiving government salaries, are doing the public's business and not working directly for the re-election of their employer." [288] Still, the rule proposed to restrict the political activities of Senate staffs was dropped from the final resolution, and the matter was referred to the Rules and Administration Committee.[289]

This Senate committee was chaired by Howard W. Cannon, D-Nev., whose staff during his 1976 reelection campaign was alleged to have engaged in some of the activities questioned by the reformers. An investigative review by journalist Edward Roeder of that campaign in 1975-76, when Cannon headed the Ethics Committee, indicated to Roeder a pattern of activities seemingly prohibited by rules that the Ethics Committee was charged with enforcing. According to the article, Senate aides had been responsible in large part for the planning, fund raising, and staffing of Cannon's campaign; these aides allegedly remained on Senate payrolls as full-time employees and used Senate offices and equipment for campaign purposes during office hours.

Cannon's campaign manager, Chet Sobsey, was paid $40,000 a year as the senator's administrative assistant. The article indicated that Sobsey ran the campaign from his Senate office and created the Howard Cannon Dinner Committee, a fund-raising effort that seems to have been conducted from Capitol Hill. Although most of the money came through the mail, Sobsey is alleged to have accepted payment in person in Cannon's office which, if substantiated, could be considered a felony since it is illegal to solicit or receive campaign contributions in a federal building. Other members of Cannon's staff alleged to have drawn Senate pay while working on the campaign included Sobsey's secretary Christine Poel and Cannon's personal secretary James Assuras. By July 1975, even before Cannon knew if he had an opponent, he had raised over $250,000, more than any other senator at the time. By the end of his campaign he had raised in excess of $420,000 — more than seven times the amount spent by his principal opponent.

The article also said that some of the activities in which Cannon's staff allegedly engaged may be unlawful according to federal civil or criminal statutes or violate existing Senate rules. Other activities seemed to fall into gray areas, however, or were not addressed by existing guidelines. As chairman of the Rules Committee, Cannon successfully backed a resolution to delete from the new Code of Conduct a prohibition on the solicitation of funds by Senate employees. The article stated that Cannon campaign documents filed with the FEC indicate honest if rather slipshod reporting.

Despite a mandate to formulate proposals by October 1, 1977, the Rules Committee postponed until 1978 any attempts to curtail improper political activities of Senate staff.[290] The delay in action was ascribed to the committee members' preoccupation with energy legislation, and has been further complicated by legal proceedings against Cannon. A suit charging Cannon with misuse of public funds during his 1976 campaign was filed in spring 1976 by Joel D. Joseph and Paul S. Kamenar, two former Federal Election Commission lawyers. Cannon denied the allegation as frivolous. The case was dismissed by the U.S. District Court and was appealed by the plaintiffs.

Proposed Changes

Senators J. Bennett Johnston, D-La., Carl T. Curtis, R-Neb., and Daniel K. Inouye, D-Hawaii, testified before the Rules Committee in September 1977. While they agreed with Cannon that no one is better able to judge the actions of a Senate employee than the senator himself, Inouye offered suggestions regarding activities that might be restricted or at least disclosed. They included:

● prohibiting Senate employees from serving in an official position in the member's campaign;

● making possible a reduction in an employee's official duties and salary in recognition of the difficulty of distinguishing in all cases between official duties and campaign activity;

● disclosing publicly the names of Senate staff engaged in campaign work, the percentage of time spent on this work, and the adjustment in Senate pay.[291]

Curtis endorsed the idea of prohibiting Senate staff from soliciting campaign contributions. Although Senate rules had banned such fundraising activity in the past, Cannon had been instrumental in changing the regulations to permit two members of each senator's staff to solicit and receive contributions, but not in the office. House staff members may engage in a member's reelection efforts as long as assigned congressional duties have been fulfilled.

Staff members most likely to be affected by rules distinguishing congressional duties from campaign work are high-level administrative assistants. A Capitol Hill News Service survey showed that 39 of 100 Senate and House administrative assistants reported direct knowledge of use of government facilities or congressional staffs to work on a member's reelection campaign. In a letter to Treasury Secretary W. Michael Blumenthal criticizing the use of taxpayers' money to support political campaigns, Common Cause President David Cohen pointed out that such staff activities violate the Appropriations Act. He urged that regulations be issued to prohibit the use of funds for such activities and that a reporting system be established to ensure compliance with the regulations.[292]

Meanwhile, existing rules governing staff campaign work are lenient and invite differing interpretations. In fact, rule interpretations often differ from campaign to campaign, and efforts toward compliance vary accordingly. For example, Tom E. Coker continued to receive his $44,000 annual pay as administrative assistant while serving as manager to the 1978 campaign of Sen. Maryon Allen, D-Ala. Coker said he did not attempt to hide his campaign activity, which he estimated to be 40 percent of his working day. On the other hand, Gerald W. Frank, who was adviser to Sen. Mark O. Hatfield, R-Ore., cut his staff salary from $40,000 to $10,000 when he began to manage Hatfield's reelection campaign. The cut reflected adherence to the minimum salary that a Senate employee can earn and still be designated to receive campaign contributions.[293]

In close races, it is not unusual to find a major shift of personnel from congressional work to the campaign. Because this offers an obvious target for an opponent, staff members in these contests almost always leave the government payroll. In one case, Mark W. Hannaford, D-Calif., who barely won in 1976, relied in 1978 on longtime administrative assistant and former campaign manager Bill Devine. However, neither Devine nor his main district representative, Dan Young, was on government payroll during the 1978 election,[294] which Hannaford lost. In Colorado, Democratic Sen. Floyd K. Haskell and his Republican opponent, Rep. William L. Armstrong, charged each other throughout the 1978 campaign with doubling congressional staff as campaign workers.

In this case, both campaigns were using staff who actually had left the government payroll.[295]

Franking

Members of Congress have had the statutory authority for nearly 200 years to use the U.S. mails for official business without charge, but the term "official business" was never precisely defined. Many lawsuits were filed between 1970 and 1973 alleging abuses of the franking privilege.

1973 Legislation

Litigation during the 1972 election campaigns sped passage in 1973 of the first law setting forth permissible uses of the frank. The new legislation dealt with two forms of the mailing privilege — the general use of a member's autographic or facsimile signature in place of a postage stamp and "postal patron" mailings (mass mailings addressed "occupant" that are sent out by a member).

The Postal Service maintains records of franked mail and it bills Congress each year for the cost of mail sent by members. Like its predecessor, the Post Office Department, the Postal Service does not inspect franked mail to determine the existence or extent of abuse, although the Post Office until 1968 issued rulings on specific abuses in response to official complaints made by private citizens. In cases of abuse, the Post Office sent the offending member a bill for postage for the improperly franked mail. In late 1968 the department ruled that it would discontinue this practice, however, since "Congress never intended that the Post Office should be a collection agency regulating Congress." [296]

Complaints. Since 1972 critics have charged with increasing frequency that congressional officeholders exploit the frank and that such abuses have multiplied as a result of the 1968 Post Office decision. The two major complaints have been that the franking privilege gives an incumbent an unfair advantage over his challenger during a political campaign and that use of the frank enables a member of Congress to campaign at taxpayers' expense.

Immediately before the 1972 political campaign two court decisions dealt with the franking privilege.[297] In 1972, however, 12 cases of alleged violations were brought before the courts, and two major rulings attracted attention. Rep. Frank Annunzio, D-Ill., was judged guilty of abusing the frank by mailing a questionnaire to residents of a district that he did not represent. Redistricting had placed Annunzio partly in the 11th District, and he had been representing the 7th District. His

opponent sought to prevent Annunzio from using the mails free of charge
to reach voters in the 11th District, charging that these mailings advanced Annunzio's candidacy without being official business. The other
1972 case involved Rep. Henry Helstoski, D-N.J., whose opponent
claimed that the frank was being used to mail some inappropriate
material. The court found Helstoski guilty. In both of these cases, the
decisions were appealed.

In a third case that never reached the court, Rep. Fletcher Thompson, R-Ga., was charged by his Democratic opponent, state Rep. Sam
Nunn, with abuse of the frank, and the success of Nunn's campaign for
the U.S. Senate eventually was attributed in part to his success in
impressing his criticism of Thompson upon voters.

Enactment. Some observers held that passage by Congress of legislation regarding the frank responded to many members' concern that the
courts would police congressional conduct if Congress did not undertake
to monitor its actions. Passage of the new legislation also was influenced
by statistics produced by the House Post Office and Civil Service
Committee. A committee report noted that franked mail had increased
since the Post Office dropped its surveillance: 178 million pieces of mail
had been franked in 1968; in 1969, the figure increased to 190 million
pieces; and the committee projected a further increase to 288 million
pieces for 1973 — at a cost of more than $23 million to the taxpayer.[298]

When the new legislation was drafted, many observers insisted that
it merely sanctioned established practice in the use of the frank. As
passed by the House in April 1973, the bill listed acceptable and
unacceptable uses of the frank and provided for the creation of a Select
Commission on Congressional Mailing Standards to advise members on
borderline cases and to decide disputes regarding accusations of
abuse.[299] Other provisions authorized mass mailings (including mailings
during the period before an election into areas added to a congressman's
district), allowed judicial review of the select commission's decisions in
legal matters but not in factual findings, restricted mailing of reprints
from the *Congressional Record* (reprints mailed were required to comply
with other stipulations of the law), and declared that the content of
material (rather than the source of funds used to pay for it) would
determine permissible use of the frank. If the select commission determined that a member was using the frank improperly, it would send its
findings to the House Committee on Standards of Official Conduct for
appropriate action.

Two groups actively opposed passage of the legislation. Jack Con-
way, then president of Common Cause, declared that the bill did not
clarify use of the frank but rather represented "an attempt to
legitimatize the use of the frank for political purposes and at the same

time to bar any effective challenge to congressional abuse of the frank." [300] A representative of the Fair Campaign Practices Committee argued that every qualified political candidate should have the privilege of mailing free of charge to every voter.

A major attempt to modify the House version of the bill was made by Rep. John F. Seiberling, D-Ohio, who proposed that franked mass mailings be prohibited for the 60-day period immediately preceding a general election. His amendment was defeated by a 21-68 standing vote. While Seiberling argued that Congress should "bend over backwards" to show that the bill was not intended to keep incumbents in office, Wayne L. Hays, D-Ohio, said, "I am not going to get uptight . . . about the advantage of incumbency; if we have any, I am glad of it, and I am going to use it." He added that incumbency also brought disadvantages. [301]

The Senate passed the bill in December 1973 with an important amendment similar to Seiberling's proposal. Although general address mailings are common in the House, the Senate does not allow postal-patron mailings by its members. Of particular concern to the Senate, then, was the failure of the House version of the bill to restrict postal-patron mailings immediately before an election, when a representative campaigning for a Senate seat might have an advantage over the incumbent senator. As passed by the Senate, the bill established a 31-day restriction on mass mailings before an election. The Senate version gave responsibility for Senate franking disputes to the Select Committee on Standards and Conduct, and it did not declare congressional findings of fact to be binding on federal courts. After Senate approval, the bill went into conference, where the restriction on mailings before an election was shortened from 31 to 28 days.

Common Cause Suit

As the legislation made its way through Congress, Common Cause filed suit against the postmaster general and the secretary of the Treasury to prevent what it termed abuses of the frank. The organization charged in October 1973 that the two executive agencies had acted unlawfully in failing to prevent unconstitutional and illegal use of the frank by members of Congress. In support of its case, Common Cause cited a study showing that nearly twice as much mail was sent by members of Congress during the three months preceding an election as during a comparable three-month period in nonelection years. The group also noted that the printing costs of newsletters (about 80 percent of all franked mail) were consistently met from campaign funds. It argued that the frank should enable members of Congress to communicate freely with their constituents in matters of official business, but that public interest demanded assurance that the frank did not become the basis for providing incumbents with an advantage over their challengers.[302]

Common Cause v. Bailar met with more than a little resistance from Congress, and it lingered in the courts. In June 1974 U.S. District Court Judge John H. Pratt refused a government motion to dismiss the case and called for a decision from a three-judge court. Common Cause lawyers then sought depositions on the use of the frank and the enforcement of the franking law. When the House and Senate did not supply the requested documents, lawyers for the group requested a court order requiring compliance. In July 1975 the U.S. District Court ruled that much of the material sought by counsel for Common Cause must be turned over by the defendants.

Alleged Abuses. The Common Cause suit aroused considerable publicity regarding alleged abuses. One charge concerned a mailing on which the White House and the Justice Department cooperated in 1973. The mailing had included copies of a speech by President Nixon on crime and drug abuse, which had been provided with a cover letter from Richard G. Kleindienst, then attorney general. In response to complaints from Rep. Patricia Schroeder, D-Colo., regarding this use of the frank, the Justice Department agreed to pay $10,240 in postage to the Postal Service. Another case attracting attention concerned Sen. Richard S. Schweiker, R-Pa., who sent consumer aid booklets with a cover page including his picture to Pennsylvania voters shortly before a 1974 primary in which he was uncontested. Schweiker's action aroused criticism because the 1973 franking law restricted mailings before an election. Sen. Jacob K. Javits, R-N.Y., was accused by Ramsey Clark, his Democratic opponent, of a violation in 1974, since a newsletter from the senator's office was received in Manhattan on October 15, fewer than 28 days before the election.

As inquiries were made into the more general topic of congressional political activity at taxpayers' expense, the focus of concern broadened from the frank and the content of material mailed under it to related questions such as the sources of funds that paid for mailing pieces and the special nature of mailing lists to which incumbent members of Congress (but not their challengers) had access. One commentator noted that more than 148,500,000 copies of newsletters including favorable comments about the sender were mailed annually from Capitol Hill. These newsletters were franked, and were written in most cases by staff members whose salaries were paid by taxpayers. Although paper and printing costs generally were not met from public funds, 31 Democrats and 15 Republicans were said to have used their government stationery allowance for this purpose. A few members refused to disclose the names of contributors to special funds for the production of newsletters.[303]

Questions were raised about special office equipment used by members of Congress for political as well as official activities, and in particular critics noted the sophisticated capabilities of computers that maintained, coded, and selected mailing lists for congressional use.[304] Several observers proposed suspension of franked mass mailings for a longer period before elections than had been stipulated by the 1973 law, and one source estimated that congressional officeholders had an advantage over their challengers that was worth $376,000.[305]

As members' perquisites generally came under fire, the House Administration Committee granted new benefits to representatives. These benefits, totaling more than $10 million a year, were enacted in May 1975. They included increases in the staff allowance for each member and payment of the printing costs of two newsletters to constituents each year — a measure said to free members from the need for private fund raising. In addition, members were authorized to spend up to $1,000 a month from their clerk-hire allowances to purchase computer services. It was estimated that Congress would send 322 million pieces of postage-free mail in fiscal 1976.[306]

In June 1975 new testimony in the Common Cause suit indicated that much of the mail sent by Congress at public expense related to the reelection campaigns of representatives and senators. Two direct-mail experts were said to have been put on the public payroll by Senate Republicans. An election manual prepared for Senate Democrats explains how newsletters may be used as an important part of a model political campaign. Sen. John G. Tower, R-Texas, was alleged to have mailed more than 800,000 letters at taxpayers' expense as part of his campaign and to have received in response offers of volunteer assistance and financial support. Senator Javits was said to have targeted a franked mailing to areas where he had less support from voters.

In response to these and other disclosures, Rep. Morris K. Udall, D-Ariz., who had supported the 1973 franking legislation, urged a 60-day cutoff of franked mailings before elections and noted the need for further changes in the law to curtail political abuse.[307] An analysis prepared by Americans for Democratic Action in August 1975 concluded that incumbents held a $488,505 advantage over their challengers for congressional seats. Benefits whose value was not calculated included research and writing services and the use of television and radio recording studios at special rates.[308]

In December 1975 Rep. Alphonzo Bell, R-Calif., brought suit against Democratic Sen. John V. Tunney for franking a newsletter that contained Tunney's name, the word "I," or "the senator" 64 times and was mailed to 1.3 million persons in California. Bell charged that the mailing had been improperly franked since its purpose was primarily political. Meanwhile, the Senate ethics committee changed the franking rules to restrict the number of references a senator might make to himself in a franked mailing on matters of public concern (a study undertaken four months later found most senators in compliance with the rule),[309] and the new Senate ethics code prohibited the use of campaign funds to produce franked mailings and required that all pieces to be franked be prepared in the Senate.

In February 1976, as subpoenas were issued in the Common Cause suit for mailing records of 100 senators, Rep. Ken Hechler, D-W.Va., started a drive to end the frank and to substitute a system for metering mail relating to official business and addressed to individual constituents.

Added Benefits. The House enacted a new benefits package in July 1976 that combined various allowances and was termed by critics "a giant slush fund which effectively removed spending limits on many items." [310] House expense allowances were made transferrable, enabling members to supplement depleted communications accounts with funds originally designated for travel or home office rental. In October 1976, shortly before the deadline for postal patron mailing before the election, congressional mail facilities were jammed with newsletters addressed to voters, and news sources noted Common Cause's estimate that the value of free mail was $70,000 a year for a House member and as much as $500,000 for a senator.

In 1977 the Senate continued to block court efforts to obtain documents for *Common Cause v. Bailar.* The House of Representatives had supplied most of the information requested by Common Cause after blocking the group's efforts to secure it for two years. The Senate claimed, however, that it was required to divulge only lists actually used in connection with a franked mailing. Senate counsel told the court that some material was simply not available. Two federal judges nevertheless declared that all information regarding computer mailing lists must be disclosed. Senate counsel Cornelius Kennedy gave the court a copy of a report prepared by an ad hoc committee on legislative immunity chaired by Sen. Lee Metcalf, D-Mont., and submitted to the Senate Democratic and Republican conferences. This 39-page report defended the frank as "an essential element in our representative democracy" that benefits the people and is "not an indulgence for the individual member of Congress." The report recommended no specific Senate response to the Common Cause suit but proposed changes in internal rules.[311]

The Senate continued to refuse to comply with the court order, and some observers speculated that the suit would have implications extending beyond proper use of the frank and other privileges to the question of congressional immunity. In court, however, Kennedy surprised his clients by agreeing to turn over the requested material. The resolution needed to obtain the documents was then blocked by Sen. James B. Allen, D-Ala., who secured approval to have the matter further studied by the Senate Rules Committee. He argued that Kennedy's commitment to the court was not a commitment agreed to by the Democratic conference or by any member of the ad hoc committee.

Proposed Limitations

On July 12, 1977, the House voted to write into law new limitations on the franking privilege, and some observers speculated that incentive had been provided by the fear that the franking privilege might otherwise be abolished. The proposed new legislation would prohibit: use of the frank for mailings sent less than 60 days before a primary or general election, mass mailings outside an officeholder's district, use of the frank to mail condolences or congratulations, and use of the frank to distribute material laudatory to the member unless praise was incidental to the mailing.

The bill also required postal-patron mail to be sent by the most economical means (currently third-class mail), limited the amount of postal-patron mail that a member could send each year, and required that a sample of the mailing be submitted in advance to the House Commission on Congressional Mailing Standards. Mass mailings were declared not to be eligible for franking unless all costs associated with them had been paid from public funds. Another provision of the legislation authorized the franking commission to issue regulations, to investigate violations of franking rules, and to investigate use of the frank by former members of Congress.

The 95th Congress adjourned in 1978 without enacting franking legislation. Bills that would have put into law the restrictions on franking contained in the House and Senate ethics codes of 1977, and that would have enabled more bulk mail to constituents, were threatened in the closing days by amendments loosening the restrictions, and failed to be enacted.[312]

Franked mail in 1976 included more than 400 million pieces at a cost of $60 million to the taxpayer.

Mailing Rates

On October 13, 1978, Congress passed a bill giving national and state committees of political parties the right to mail campaign material under reduced rates. Originally part of the House Administration Committee's proposed amendments to the FECA, the bill eventually was tacked on as a provision of the Overseas Voting Rights Act, which was designed to encourage more Americans living abroad to vote.[313]

The provision entitled "qualified political committees" to use the lower mail rate of 2.7 cents a letter rather than the regular bulk rate of 8.4 cents. This rate had been available to Common Cause, the National Right to Work Committee, labor unions, and other nonprofit issue-oriented groups. Mary Maginnis, a Congressional Budget Office analyst, estimated that the provision will cost taxpayers $2.5 million in 1979 (an off-election year) and $4.7 million in 1980 (a presidential election year) in subsidized mail rates for Democratic and Republican national and state campaign committees. Theoretically, the provision could provide subsidies to minor parties but not to nonparty or "candidate" committees.[314]

Although the bill had caused controversy earlier in the year, it passed unopposed as a provisional attachment to the noncontroversial Overseas Voting Rights Act.

The Financial Future

Americans seem increasingly ambivalent about the role of government in their lives. If the pendulum is swinging in favor of lowered budgets and lowered expectations, the gains of the 1970s with respect to election reform will be affected. We are on the receding side of election reform, which crested at the height of Watergate in 1974. A counter-reform may be developing. More than lip service is still being paid to reform; many politicians as well as others have been converted and are faithful to its precepts. Reformers are less strident now, however, and undoubtedly will lose some force by the processes of attrition and challenge. On the other hand, some reform measures, such as the FEC, are institutionalized and will not be repealed; they could be seriously hurt by weak appointments, poor staffing, and internal bickering.

The Federal Election Commission was launched to preside over new laws and new practices. In the course of issuing its regulations and advisory opinions, the commission has helped to define permissible practices, and thus sets the course of future political activity. The extent to which the commission is flexible or restrictive will set the legitimate bounds of the expansiveness or narrowness of future politics. Regulations can be stifling if a legalistic approach is taken, or they can be permissive without being lax, if a broader approach is adopted.

Citizen Participation

The broader approach to regulation must encompass an understanding of the voluntary and participative aspects of American electoral politics. Excessive regulation will only confirm the fears of those who already believe — erroneously — that money in politics is necessarily dirty and that every use of it has to be regulated and monitored. The goal should be to encourage citizen participation, including financial participation, in every way compatible with fairness and equity. It is very easy to turn people off from financial participation in politics, whether as donors or as solicitors or as treasurers of political committees. The diversity of the requests to the FEC for advisory opinions gives evidence of the heterogeneity of U.S. politics that is so worth preserving. In this context, flexibility and spontaneity are valuable, and the danger is in laws and regulations that rigidify the system.

One must assume that the major provisions for the regulation of politics are irreversible and that regulation will continue to be part of a design to recapture citizens' confidence in the electoral process. Lower levels of regulation are likely, however; not seeking to do as much, not over-regulating, but making small adjustments to keep politics fair and democratic without overburdening or stifling it. Refining and fine-tuning the law and regulations will go on indefinitely. The matter of extending public financing to cover Senate and House campaigns, in primary and general elections, will be controversial for years to come, and in the immediate future will be a major issue for Congress, the American people and, if it is enacted, the courts.

Reform is not neutral, but works to change institutions and processes, sometimes in unforeseen ways. The reform of our election laws — regulating elections that in turn help determine who will be elected to write other laws — has become a major issue since the revelations about 1972 campaign abuses. Election laws are used as instruments to achieve certain political goals. Laws that regulate relationships between candidates and political parties, and between citizens and politicians, and that affect the relative power of interest groups (including parties), are bound to influence the entire political process and change the ways in which citizens, candidates, parties, and other groups participate in elections.

The changes of the past several years are certain to have direct consequences for the two-party system, and to bring structural modifications in the institutions that participate in electoral activity.

The decline of political parties, the rise of single-issue groups, the increase in the number of political action committees and the raised volume of their dollars, all present problems for American democracy in a pluralistic society. Constitutional and practical concerns exist with respect to the possible dominance of money resources generated by certain groups, posing imbalances troublesome to our system of free elections.

Burgeoning Field of Study

Great changes have occurred in the study of political finance. Politics has become a big business and election reform a growth industry. There are now many government, academic, private, and popular publications on the subject, a steady flow of newsletters, documents, articles, studies, compilations, reports, books, all of which need to be distilled and integrated into a book such as this volume. Ethics have become a priority topic in each house of Congress, among candidates and political parties, in the corporate, media, and labor communities, and in the private sector generally.

The study of political finance now concerns not only election legislation, but regulation in the sunshine area with especial reference to lobbying and conflict of interest. Legislation and laws in the areas of broadcasting, communications, postal regulation, taxation, banking and corporate affairs, interstate commerce, all touch on aspects of the election and campaign processes. President Carter's 1977 message to Congress on election reform included proposals relating to voter registration, voter turnout, civil service reform, and the electoral college, all subjects falling within the purview of and affecting campaign and political finance. Congressional reform, too, is related in important ways to the campaign process, indeed to the winning and losing of elections.

Litigation as well as legislation helps to shape and modify public policy. Recourse to the courts has become a major course of action for enforcement matters, as well as a major means of challenging the laws and changing the regulations that government agencies have promulgated. Thus both the public and private sectors will continue to use the courts to seek to further their goals.

The prospect is for a continual burgeoning of this field of study, with more people employed in work resulting from the data explosion and law expansion inherent in comprehensive and detailed regulatory schemes, which include institutions such as the FEC constantly generating much more work.

The next presidential election year, 1980, will provide our second experience with federal public financing. By fall 1978 several candidates already had announced, getting early starts. Current law encourages lengthy campaigns because sufficient lead time is necessary to raise seed money and gear up to comply with the law.

Most of what happened in Watergate's aftermath has seemed to indicate that many of the fixed patterns to which American politics had grown accustomed were in a state of flux, and many are likely dead forever. Old institutions have been questioned, and new ones examined. Ways of collecting and spending campaign money seem immutably altered, and limited government funding a certainty, at least in presidential elections. The redistribution of sources of campaign finance was evident in 1976, not only in the first infusion of tax-checkoff dollars but in the new patterns that contribution limits triggered. The study of the 1980 and succeeding elections will help us understand better the processes, the impacts, the intended and unintended consequences of laws and practices that newly develop under changing circumstances.

Footnotes

[1] Herbert E. Alexander, *Financing the 1968 Election* (Lexington, Mass.: D.C. Heath and Co., 1971), p. 214.

[2] Herbert E. Alexander, *Financing the 1972 Election* (Lexington, Mass.: D.C. Heath and Co., 1976), p. 570.

[3] Bruce Howard, "$3 Million Sought for Transition Fund," *The Washington Post*, July 31, 1976.

[4] In April 1977 several news stories reported that the GSA was frustrated in its efforts to get a full accounting of some of the expenditures made by the Carter transition team. Particular emphasis was placed on a $250,000 checking account established by Carter aides who said the account was established to speed up payments and salaries because the GSA's system was cumbersome. At the same time, it was reported that Hamilton Jordan, a key White House aide, had so far failed to repay $3,000 he received in salary and travel advances from the transition staff, although he had promised to repay the money in six monthly installments.

[5] U.S., Comptroller General, Audit of Ford-Carter Presidential Transition Expenditures, *Report*, to the House Committee on Government Operations, December 23, 1977, p. 5.

[6] Of the 2.8 million federal employees only about 2,200 were exempt from civil service or similar regulations. Of these, 600 were presidential appointments, 650 were noncareer executives in policy-making positions and about 1,000 were Schedule C jobs.

[7] Hedrick Smith, "Strains in Carter Transition," *The New York Times*, December 10, 1976.

[8] Phillip Shabecoff, "Ford and Carter Expected to Meet This Month on Transfer of Power," *The New York Times*, November 6, 1976.

[9] OMB officials denied Carter transition aides the right to sit in on discussions on the proposed Ford fiscal year 1978 budget.

[10] Smith, "Strains in Carter Transition."

[11] Ibid.

[12] United Press International, "Carter Appointments: 13 Percent are Women, 11 Percent are Black," *The Washington Post*, June 19, 1977.

[13] James T. Wooten, "Many Carter Aides Picked From Often-Tapped Source," *The New York Times*, February 4, 1977.

[14] Joseph Kraft, "The Cabinet: Bad News for Pressure Groups," *The Washington Post*, December 30, 1976.

[15] "G.A.O., Citing Errors in Carter Transition, Urges More Curbs," *The New York Times*, December 29, 1977; U.S., Comptroller General, Audit of Ford-Carter Presidential Transition Expenditures, *Report*, to the House Committee on Government Operations, December 23, 1977, pp. 29-41.

[16] David Rosenbaum, "Donations Are Urged by Inaugural Panel," *The New York Times*, January 12, 1977.

[17] Political abuses of ambassadorships appeared to take various forms. In late November 1976, President Ford appointed Jack B. Olson, a Wisconsin businessman, to be ambassador to the Bahamas. Olson was a "recess" nomination (the Senate had refused to confirm him earlier), and his appointment drew criticism because he replaced Seymour Weiss, considered by many to be a popular and effective ambassador. Critics also noted

that Olson was certain to be replaced when Carter took office, and they argued that the appointment reflected Ford's desire to reward a major contributor to his campaign with a title of ambassador and a few months of leisure in the Caribbean.

Another alleged abuse concerned Vincent de Roulet, U.S. ambassador to Jamaica in 1971 and 1972. In 1976 news sources reported that de Roulet had solicited contributions to Jamaican political parties from the Aluminum Company of America (Alcoa). Robert D. Hershey, Jr., "U.S. Envoy Sought Gifts in Jamaica: Evidence Finds Ambassador Asked Alcoa for Money for Political Purposes," *The New York Times*, July 16, 1976. Rowland Evans and Robert Novak, "Lameduck Politics," *The Washington Post*, November 20, 1976.

[18] A sampling of public reactions may be found in the following sources: Clayton Fritchey, "A Chance to Stop the Embassy 'Auction,' " *The Washington Post*, August 7, 1976. C. L. Sulzberger, "Carter and the Diplomats," *The New York Times*, August 21, 1976. Chester E. Finn, Jr., "Ambassadorships 'Are Properly Political,' " *The Washington Post*, February 20, 1977. Jessica Cato, "The Ambassador Shuffle: Isn't There a Better Way?" *The Washington Post*, April 5, 1977. Lee Lescaze, "Carter Choices of Envoys Seem Inconsistent with Pledge," *The Washington Post*, May 25, 1977. Bernard Gwertzman, "Carter Ambassadors — Competence before Politics," *The New York Times*, June 19, 1977. Joseph Kraft, "Diplomatic Subtleties in Envoy Choices," *The Washington Post*, June 23, 1977. "The New Ambassadors," *Newsweek*, November 21, 1977, pp. 69-70. John M. Goshko, "Angry Foreign Service: Regulars Say Outsiders Get Key Posts," *The Washington Post*, January 1, 1978.

[19] Typical sworn statements of the political contributions made by Samuel Lewis and Robert F. Goheen and their families appear in the Senate *Congressional Record* of April 21, 1977, S6107; these are now required of appointees by the Senate Foreign Relations Committee before confirmation.

[20] "PostScript," *The Washington Post*, April 18, 1977. Associated Press, "Nominee Reconsidering Membership in 2 Clubs," *The Washington Post*, April 27, 1977. Reuter, "Group Criticizes Carter's Choices for Two Envoys," *The Washington Post*, April 28, 1977. Also see "Washington Notes" and "Carter's Patronage: Unspoiled Victors" in *The Baron Report*, No. 19, May 3, 1977, pp. 1 and 3.

[21] Don Oberdorfer, "Envoy Confirmation a Breeze for Lavish Democratic Donor," *The Washington Post*, June 7, 1977. "Why Not the Best?" *The Wall Street Journal*, June 10, 1977.

[22] Tad Szulc, "The Amateur Hour: Foreign Service posts still go to non-professionals," *The New Republic*, May 28, 1977, pp. 20-22.

[23] Bernard Gwertzman, "Carter Ambassadors — Competence before Politics," *The New York Times*, June 19, 1977.

[24] Tad Szulc, "The Amateur Hour," p. 22.

[25] Godfrey Sperling, Jr., "Carter Gets Tough on Conflicts of Interest," *Christian Science Monitor*, January 3, 1977.

[26] David Burnham, "G.A.O. Asks New Rules and Panel To Check on Conflicts of Interest," *The New York Times*, March 1, 1977.

[27] Common Cause, "Common Cause Study Shows Conflict of Interest Widespread Throughout Executive Branch Bureaucracy," press release, October 21, 1976, pp. 2-3.

[28] "Industry Hiring from Pentagon Up," *The Washington Post*, April 13, 1977.

[29] Elizabeth Wehr, "Precedents for Carter's Code of Ethics," *Congressional Quarterly Weekly Report*, January 8, 1977, p. 53.

[30] David Burnham, "Bar Panel in Capitol Told to Draft Guidelines on Conflict of Interest," *The New York Times*, December 6, 1976. During the winter of 1976-77, the District of Columbia and New York City Bar Associations began working on conflict of interest guidelines for attorneys who had left public service. Ibid. and Tom Goldstein, "Ethics Guidelines Set for Attorneys Leaving U.S. Jobs," *The New York Times*, December 5, 1976.

[31] The employees who violated the statutes and regulations were not totally at fault. A study conducted by Ralph Nader's Center for Law and Social Policy found that federal agencies usually provided scanty or no information on conflict-of-interest regulations. Jack Anderson and Les Whitten, "Conflict," *The Washington Post*, December 24, 1976.

[32] "Ethics Statements," Congressional Quarterly *Weekly Report*, January 8, 1977, pp. 56-57. Different facets of Carter's proposals also were enunciated in speeches and position papers issued during his campaign. For one example, see "Carter-Mondale on the Issues," address by Jimmy Carter to the American Bar Association, Atlanta, Georgia, August 11, 1976, p. 3.

[33] "Carter's Guidelines: New, Stringent Rules," Congressional Quarterly *Weekly Report*, January 8, 1977, p. 52.

[34] The cabinet-level appointees responded to the new regulations in different ways. Defense Secretary Harold Brown announced plans to sell those stocks he held in companies that were major defense contractors. OMB Director Bert Lance sold his stock in the National Bank of Georgia. Treasury Secretary Blumenthal placed his personal stocks in a blind trust. Blumenthal, who had signed an agreement with Bendix which guaranteed him $23,000 a year for life in consulting fees once he left the company, announced that he would not receive those payments during his tenure in office but the payments would resume once he had left government service.

[35] The statements revealed that Carter's cabinet members and other top aides already had taken some steps to avoid actual or potential conflicts of interest. Cecil D. Andrus, secretary of the Interior, sold stock he owned in four mining companies; Secretary of Agriculture Bob Bergland leased his 567-acre farm in Minnesota to his son-in-law; Bert Lance, director of the Office of Management and Budget, disclosed details of a trust agreement calling for eventual sale of his holdings in the National Bank of Georgia. In addition to the data's value in illuminating conflicts of interest either actual or potential, the information was considered to be of more than routine interest as gossip. Anthony Marro, "Carter's Top Aides Take Steps to Avoid Conflict of Interest," *The New York Times*, February 27, 1977; Alan B. Morrison, "Conflicts of Interest — Another Solution," *The Washington Post*, March 29, 1977.

[36] "Ethics Statements," Congressional Quarterly *Weekly Report*, January 8, 1977, p. 58.

[37] "Carter Denies Stock Role after Becoming President," *The New York Times*, October 5, 1977; Dan Dorfman, "Bottom Line: Carter's Blind Trust: Heaven Only Knows," *New York*, October 10, 1977, p. 12.

[38] "SEC Checks Campaign Funds: Carter Linked to Bank Probe," *The Evening Bulletin* (Philadelphia), Wednesday, October 12, 1977.

[39] Bernard Weinraub, "Carter Fund-Raiser Backs 2 Jet Fighters; Boston Consultant's Involvement in Navy Plane Issue Points Up Aerospace Competition," *The New York Times*, December 7, 1977.

[40] Dan Dorfman, "The Bottom Line: Another Scandal for Jimmy Carter? The Lipshutz Affair," *New York*, November 14, 1977, pp. 16, 18, 20.

[41] Seth S. King, "Bergland Sees Aide Who Sought Favors: He Discusses Actions by Assistant for U.S. Irrigation Rights — Accord Cited for a Nonofficial Role," *The New York Times*, September 29, 1977; "A Conflict of Interest," *The Washington Post*, September 30, 1977; Seth S. King, "Aide's Farm Action Barred by President," *The New York Times*, October 1, 1977

[42] Warren Weaver, Jr., "White House Studies Curb on Profits to Ex-Officials," *The New York Times*, May 16, 1977; Transcript of Carter news conference on foreign and domestic matters, *The New York Times*, May 27, 1977; Morton Mintz, "Carter Confidant Is Rules Subject To Conflict Curbs," *The Washington Post*, February 15, 1977; "Those Conflict-of-Interest Rules," *The Washington Post*, January 6, 1977; "The Too-High Price of Public Service: A businessman should not be forced to go through a humiliating ordeal when he responds to Washington's call," *Fortune*, December 1977, pp. 158-165; Anthony Marro, "Carter Issues Guide For Aides On Curbing Conflicts of Interest," *The New York Times*, January 5, 1977.

[43] For details on the Lance gubernatorial campaign, see Howell Raines, "Georgia: The Politics of Campaign Reform," in *Campaign Money: Reform and Reality in the States*, ed. by Herbert E. Alexander (N.Y.: Free Press, 1976), pp. 187-225. It should of course be noted that this account was published before Lance's nomination as director of the Office of Management and Budget.

[44] It was subsequently disclosed that Lance had arranged a meeting between Secretary of the Treasury Michael Blumenthal and Jake and C. H. Butcher, the owners of the Knoxville bank. The purpose of the meeting apparently was to help the Butchers push the Energy Expo '82, a world's fair scheduled to be held in Knoxville.

[45] Altogether Lance owned about 21 percent of the bank's stock and, together with two associates, controlled more than 60 percent.

[46] Both the Manufacturers Hanover and the First National Chicago loans were tied to the prime interest rate. In May 1977 Lance became the administration's key spokesman on interest rates, contending that they were too high.

[47] John Osborne, "White House Watch: Sticking Up For Bert," *The New Republic*, September 3, 1977, p. 10.

[48] Lance's liabilities forced him to pay large sums in interest payments, approximately $373,000 annually. Taking a government position reduced his annual income considerably. Since he received more than $150,000 a year in stock dividends from NBG, its failure to pay a dividend placed Lance in a difficult financial position.

[49] The businessman, David Smith, subsequently withdrew from negotiations.

[50] Comptroller of the Currency, Excerpts of the Report on T. Bertram Lance's Finances, in *The New York Times*, August 19, 1977.

[51] John G. Heimann, letter to Abraham Ribicoff, August 18, 1977, in *The New York Times*, August 19, 1977.

[52] Although Lance spent $1.2 million in his unsuccessful bid to win the Democratic nomination for governor, he managed to secure only $300,000 in contributions from individuals other than himself. There were plans to solicit individuals in 1977 to help pay off his campaign debts. The effort was suspended, however, after Lance discussed this with White House counsel Lipshutz.

[53] At a hearing conducted by his House Banking subcommittee, Chairman Fernand J. St Germain charged that the First National Bank of Calhoun had used its bank facilities to mail computerized campaign letters, donated supplies and letters to the Lance campaign, allowed the Lance family to run up huge campaign committee overdrafts, and transferred bank employees to Lance's election effort.

[54] Lance had bought the plane for $80,000 and sold it to NBG for $120,000, which was the average of two independent estimates.

[55] "Text of Statement by Lance and Excerpts From Testimony Before Senate Panel," *The New York Times*, September 16, 1977.

[56] John F. Berry and Ted Guys, "Bert Lance, 3 Associates Indicted," *The Washington Post*, May 24, 1979. "Bert Lance Indicted," Congressional Quarterly *Weekly Report*, May 26, 1979, p. 1021.

[57] "Senate Confirmation Process Is a 'Rubberstamp Machine,' New Common Cause Study Shows; Overhaul of Procedures Proposed," news release, Common Cause, November 13, 1977.

[58] Wayne King, "Lance, Saudi Term Georgia Bank Deal Strictly Business; Both Deny $20-a-Share Bid is Tied to Washington Links or Future Role in Arab Investments," *The New York Times*, December 28, 1977; Jim Hoagland, "Arab 'Wasta' Concept May Underlie Lance-Pharaon Deal," *The Washington Post*, January 1, 1978; "Around the Nation: Lance Repays $443,466 Lent by Knoxville Bank," *The New York Times*, January 7, 1978; "Bank Lance Headed Is Making Recovery," *The New York Times*, June 8, 1978.

[59] "Lance Accepts Atlanta TV Post," *The New York Times*, January 17, 1978.

[60] Nicholas Lemann, "Bert Lance, the Press, and Company Planes," *Washington Monthly*, November 1977, pp. 28-32.

[61] Lawrence B. Smith, "Lance: Did the Press Stack the Deck?" *The Washington Post*, October 4, 1977.

For an opposing view from a commentator who contributed to major publicity surrounding the affair, see William Safire, "Lancegate: Why Carter Stuck It Out," *The New York Times Magazine*, October 16, 1977, pp. 37-39, 108-116.

[62] Publicity given to Bert Lance's involvement with the bank has not been forgotten by regulatory authorities in the months since his resignation. In January 1978, the Federal Reserve Board, the Comptroller of the Currency, and the Federal Deposit Insurance Corporation announced their intention of using their "full legal authority" to halt illegal

political contributions and other questionable payments by banks. "Banks To Be Monitored on Political Payments," *The New York Times*, January 18, 1977.

[63] James T. Wooten, "Diplomatic Passport Is Retained by Lance: Decision Was Based on Possibility That Ex-Budget Chief Might Represent Carter Abroad," *The New York Times*, December 1, 1977. Lance's continuing influence with the president and others was evident in his role at a fund-raising dinner for the Democratic Party held in Atlanta on January 20, 1978. Lance served as master of ceremonies. "Lance, at Salute to Carter, Finds He Is Still the Life of the Party," *The New York Times*, January 21, 1978.

[64] William Safire, "Love Thy Enemies List," *The New York Times*, January 9, 1978.

[65] Judith Miller, "Lance Named in Suit by Financial General on 'Secret' Takeover: Hearing Is Set for March 16, Civil Case Alleges Conspiracy by Metzger and Others to Acquire Bank Holding Company," *The New York Times*, February 18, 1978.

[66] Charles R. Babcock, "Wallop Urges Special Prosecutor in Lance Case," *The Washington Post*, March 1, 1978; William Safire, " 'Bert — I'm Proud of You,' " *The New York Times*, March 20, 1978; "The President's Friend," editorial, *The New York Times*, March 22, 1978; "Bert Lance's Connections," *The Washington Post*, March 24, 1978; "Economy & Business: Another Loan for Lance: No Documents — But Passport X-000065 Is Gone," *Time*, April 3, 1978, p. 52; Art Harris and Ward Sinclair, "White House's Friendly Arm Still Rests on Lance Shoulder," *The Washington Post*, April 9, 1978.

[67] "Mr. Lance and the Press," editorial, *The Washington Post*, April 13, 1978; T. R. Reid, "Lance Assails Media for 'Erroneous . . . Biased Reporting,' " *The Washington Post*, April 13, 1978; Chalmers M. Roberts, "Muckraking History," *The Washington Post*, April 22, 1978; "National Affairs: Bert Lance: On the Attack," *Newsweek*, April 24, 1978, p. 42.

[68] Judith Miller, "S.E.C. Accuses Lance of Fraud as Banker; He Agrees to Curbs: 2 Banks Also Named: Comptroller Joins in Charge That Offenses Benefited Him and Family," *The New York Times*, April 27, 1978.

[69] *Campaign Practices Reports*, October 30, 1978, pp. 5-7.

[70] Mendelsohn continued to serve on the Board of Supervisors until September 8.

[71] After a fund-raising dinner in April 1977, Mendelsohn claimed that he had reduced his debt to $40,000. It was subsequently disclosed that the dinner had produced only $10,000 in cash, and that $100,000 had been secured in write-offs from individuals to whom Mendelsohn owed money. To avoid a possible conflict of interest, the solicitor's office of the Department of the Interior reviewed the payments made by guests at the dinner. Several contributions were returned.

[72] During his 1971 reelection campaign, Mendelsohn employed an intern who discovered an unreported contribution in the amount of $12,000 from Richard Miller, the San Francisco manager of the Pacific Gas and Electric Co. The intern reported his information to the *Guardian*. Mendelsohn explained that he had accepted the check from Miller as a friend, and said that it had not been logged because it had passed quickly to pay for advertising at the end of the campaign. After the *Guardian* disclosed that the interest-free loan had not been reported, Mendelsohn declared that he had discovered the omission and had filed an amended finance report. The *Guardian* reported on Mendelsohn as part of its coverage of the relationship between public officials and the Pacific Gas and Electric Co.

[73] Transcentury ultimately won approval after a four-year battle.

[74] The Mendelsohn campaign committee in 1974 reported the receipt of a $15,000 loan and a $1,500 contribution from Louise Drob, a telephone operator from San Pedro, California. In addition, the committee noted a $10,000 loan from "Ocean Traders," guaranteed by William F. Grader. On May 19, 1977, the committee filed a report stating that Drob and Grader had forgiven the loans. In sworn testimony on July 20 and 21, 1977, Grader asserted that he had arranged for part of the contribution to be given under another name to maximize his chances of being repaid, on the theory that a defeated candidate unable fully to repay his loans would reimburse one donor of the full amount less than two donors of smaller amounts.

State of California Fair Political Practices Commission, "Report to the United States Senate Committee on Energy and Natural Resources Regarding Campaign Statements Filed by Robert H. Mendelsohn and the Mendelsohn for Controller Committee and Related Matters," November 11, 1977, pp. 3-4, 37-38.

[75] Lou Cannon, "Interior Nominee's Case Parallels Lance Inquiry," *The Washington Post,* September 8, 1977.

[76] Several points were made in Mendelsohn's defense. Although Mendelsohn was criticized for work on a compromise by which Transcentury would receive much of the settlement it wanted from the Regional Planning Commission, Mendelsohn himself pointed out that the development firm already had begun its project when California voters passed a coastal control law in 1972. The FPPC agreed that Mendelsohn's actions on behalf of Transcentury could be characterized as reasonable and honest. It also noted that at his own request Mendelsohn had taken and passed a lie detector test, during which he was asked if he had at an earlier time known the source of the funds contributed under the name of Louise Drob. State of California Fair Political Practices Commission, pp. 154-156.

[77] The FPPC judged the option not to be a valid business transaction. It noted that Transcentury did not ordinarily purchase options on land, that the option was little used while it was in effect, and that the land in question was not suitable for the type of development normally undertaken by Transcentury. The amounts and timing of the checks also suggested to the commission that the business itself was less important than the transfer of funds, as did the fact that the basis for payment changed several times without affecting the amount. Ibid., pp. 149-151.

[78] Lou Cannon, "Former Nominee for Interior Post 'Wins' Court Fight," *The Washington Post,* April 20, 1978; "Of Mendelsohn and the FPPC," editorial, *San Francisco Chronicle,* April 20, 1978; "And They Call It 'Fair' Practices," opinion, *San Francisco Examiner,* April 21, 1978.

[79] Warren Brown, "Controversial Appointee Gets Interior Dept. Post," *The Washington Post,* June 6, 1978; Seth S. King, "Andrus Appoints an Aide 'Vindicated' in a Lawsuit over Gifts in Campaign," *The New York Times,* June 11, 1978.

[80] Mondale himself had campaign debts outstanding, and some prominent Minnesota corporate executives were helping to pay them off with contributions that the FEC considered legal, despite public funding of Mondale's campaign, because the debts had been incurred prior to Mondale's nomination. "Executives Aid Mondale In Paying Political Debts," *The Washington Post,* January 21, 1977.

[81] The Federal Election Commission informed Costanza that she could donate the surplus $3,000 to two charities, the American Cancer Society and a camp for handicapped children. Walter Pincus, "Costanza Can Give Funds to Charities," *The Washington Post,* January 6, 1978.

[82] Walter Pincus, "April Party Raised $21,025: Costanza Fails to File FEC Fund Report," *The Washington Post,* October 8, 1977.

[83] "GOP Whip Says Miss Costanza Should Resign Over Law Violation," *The New York Times,* October 27, 1977; "Criticism of Carter Aide Is Picayune, O'Neill Says," *The New York Times,* October 28, 1977.

[84] Alan B. Morrison, "The Costanza Extravaganza," *The Washington Post,* October 20, 1977; Hays Gorey, "That Woman in the West Wing," *The New York Times Magazine,* January 22, 1978, pp. 8-11, 17-24.

[85] Clay F. Richards, "Costanza," UPI news release dated May 10, 1978; "White House Aide fined $500 for late reporting," *Campaign Practices Reports,* May 15, 1978, p. 2.

[86] Common Cause, "The Senate Rubberstamp Machine: A Common Cause Study of the U.S. Senate's Confirmation Process." (Washington, D.C.: Common Cause, 1977).

[87] 380 congressmen respond to a Common Cause survey, one of whose questions was: "Will you vote for a rule that requires members of Congress to abstain from voting in committee on any matter that would provide a significant financial benefit to them?" 340 senators and representatives agreed to vote for such a role; 16 were opposed. "CC Put the New Congress on Record," *In Common: The Common Cause Report from Washington,* Winter 1977, Volume 8, Number 1, p. 10.

[88] Robert Shogan, "Democrats Try to Raise $20 Million," *Los Angeles Times,* July 24, 1977.

[89] Democratic National Committee, "Report of Receipts and Expenditures," FEC document for year ending 1978.

[90] Walter Pincus, "Democrats, $3.6 Million in Debt, Push Fund Drive," *The Washington Post,* April 29, 1977.

[91] Herbert E. Alexander, *Financing the 1972 Election,* p. 517.

[92] Robert H. Williams, "Postscript," *The Washington Post,* April 11, 1977.

[93] Pincus, "Democrats, $3.6 Million in Debt. . . ."

[94] DNC, "Report of Receipts and Expenditures" for 1978.

[95] William Claiborne, "For Carter, a Folksy Foray to Major Fund-Raiser," *The Washington Post,* June 24, 1977.

[96] "Dollars for Democrats," *The Baron Report,* October 25, 1977; Lou Cannon, "Democratic 'Outsiders,' in Western States Fault Carter Policies," *The Washington Post,* September 19, 1977.

[97] Shogan, "Democrats Try."

[98] Democratic National Finance Council, "A Statement of Purpose and Organizational Structure," 1977, p. 1.

[99] Shogan, "Democrats Try."

[100] John B. Oakes, "Democrats' Nest Egg," *The New York Times,* June 21, 1977.

[101] "Still a Sucker Game," *Business Week,* May 16, 1977, p. 202.

[102] Shogan, "Democrats Try."

[103] Ibid.

[104] Oakes, "Democrats' Nest Egg."

[105] For descriptions of the earlier President's Club, see Herbert E. Alexander, *Financing the 1964 Election* (Princeton, N.J.: Citizens' Research Foundation, 1966), pp. 78-80; ____ __, *Financing the 1968 Election* (Lexington, Mass.: D. C. Heath and Co., 1971), pp. 151-152; _____, *Financing the 1972 Election* (Lexington, Mass.: D.C. Heath and Co., 1976), pp. 3, 123, 488.

[106] Warren Weaver, Jr., "Carter Will Stump Country to Assist Democrats in '78," *The New York Times,* July 29, 1977; David S. Broder, "$2 Million Fund, Carter's Help Pledged Democratic Hopefuls," *The Washington Post,* July 29, 1977.

[107] "Dollars for Democrats;" Terence Smith, "It's Carter Folk vs. Regular Democrats," *The New York Times,* December 11, 1977.

[108] "Political Notes," *The Baron Report,* February 17, 1978.

[109] "Dollar Signs," *The Baron Report,* December 6, 1977.

[110] "Dollars for Democrats."

[111] "Democrats Support Canal Treaties," Congressional Quarterly *Weekly Report,* October 15, 1977, p. 2194.

[112] "Curtis Says Money Was Top Headache as DNC Chairman," *The Washington Post,* December 9, 1977.

[113] "Democratic Chief Says First Goal Is Funds for Debts and Campaign," *The New York Times,* January 4, 1978.

[114] Terence Smith, "Carter, Apologizing for Neglect, Makes Up With Party Committee," *The New York Times,* January 28, 1978.

[115] "Democrats Granted Election Law Waiver to Help Slash Debts," *The New York Times,* February 10, 1978.

[116] Charles R. Babcock and Edward Walsh, "Probe Finds Secret Oval Office Meeting Legal," *The Washington Post,* February 3, 1979.

[117] "Political Notes."

[118] "McCleary, Democrats' Treasurer, Resigns; Staff Had Been Cut," *The Washington Post,* February 24, 1978.

[119] Charles W. Hucker, "Political Party Finances: It's David vs. Goliath," Congressional Quarterly *Weekly Report,* June 24, 1978, p. 1607.

[120] Alan Baron, "The Politics of American Jews," *Politicks & Other Human Interests,* January 3, 1978, p. 9.

[121] Sandy Grady, "Jews and Jimmy — Jumpy as Jell-O," *The Evening Bulletin* (Philadelphia), March 9, 1978.

[122] Edward Walsh, "Siegel to Quit Carter's Staff in Mideast Dispute," *The Washington Post,* March 9, 1978.

[123] David S. Broder, "Politicians Clustering Around Carter Again," *The Washington Post,* September 23, 1978.

[124] Lou Cannon, "GOP Starts from Bottom in Preservation Struggle," *The Washington Post*, May 1, 1977.
[125] "Ford Renews Political Stance At Fund-Raising Dinner," *First Monday*, June 1977.
[126] "Citizens for the Republic," *Democratic Congressional Campaign Committee Report*, January 1978, pp. 3-4.
[127] "Reagan Protests Party Fund Drive," *The New York Times*, December 21, 1977.
[128] David S. Broder, "Brock Refusal to Fund Anti-Treaty Bid Angers Conservatives," *The Washington Post*, December 20, 1977.
[129] "Citizens for the Republic," p. 4.
[130] "Reagan Protests Party Fund Drive," Broder, "Politicians Clustering."
[131] Jack W. Germond and Jules Witcover, "Was Reagan Duped?" *The Washington Star*, February 21, 1978.
[132] Adam Clymer, "Ford Assails President on Defense and Urges Work on Neutron Bomb," *The New York Times*, April 7, 1978.
[133] Judith Hammerschmidt, "RNC to Buy Headquarters — in Memory of Ike," *First Monday*, August 1977, pp. 14-15.
[134] "Corporations Help Pay for GOP Headquarters," Congressional Quarterly *Weekly Report*, June 24, 1978, p. 1612.
[135] Ibid.
[136] Common Cause, *1976 Federal Campaign Finances*, Vol. I (Washington, D.C.: Common Cause, 1977).
[137] Ibid.
[138] Ibid,
[139] " 'New Right' Tactic — Swarm of Wasps," Memo from COPE, No. 22-77 (Nov. 7, 1977).
[140] "Right Active in '77 House Elections," Congressional Quarterly *Weekly Report*, December 24, 1977, p. 2652.
[141] Christopher Buchanan, "New Right: 'Many Times More Effective' Now," Congressional Quarterly *Weekly Report*, December 24, 1977, p. 2653.
[142] Phil Gailey, "Direct Mail King Defensive but Laughing," *The Washington Star*, May 9, 1978.
[143] David S. Broder, "Right Wing Makes a Progressive Republican Run Scared," *The Washington Post*, January 29, 1978.
[144] Broder, "Rep. Anderson, a GOP Leader, in Tough Place for Reelection," *The Washington Post*, March 16, 1978; "Illinois Primary: Anderson Survives Challenge," Congressional Quarterly *Weekly Report*, March 25, 1978, p. 749.
[145] For an account of Viguerie's operation and philosophy, see *Democratic Congressional Campaign Committee Report*, Vol. 1, No. 7 (Aug.-Sept. 1978).
[146] "Summary of 1976 New Hampshire Democratic Primary Write-In Effort for John Connally," FEC document.
[147] "Wallace Lists Costs," *The Washington Post*, September 11, 1975.
[148] Christopher Lydon, "Credit System Fuels Wallace Fund Drive," *The New York Times*, May 23, 1975.
[149] Lydon, "Washington Notes," *The New York Times*, April 14, 1975.
[150] Myra MacPherson, "A Final Irony for George Wallace," *The Washington Post*, June 10, 1976.
[151] "Wallace Mail Fund," *The Washington Post*, February 11, 1976.
[152] Gordon L. Weil, "Viguerie: The Man With the Golden List," *Politicks & Other Human Interests*, November 8, 1977, pp. 14-16.
[153] Alan Ehrenhalt, " 'New Right' Plans Move to Change Congress," Congressional Quarterly *Weekly Report*, October 23, 1976, p. 3029.
[154] Gailey, "Direct Mail King. . . ."
[155] " 'Official Business' Link With Outsiders Could Lead to Censure for U.S. Senators," *Campaign Practices Reports*, June 26, 1978.
[156] James M. Perry, "The Right Wing Got Plucked," *National Observer*, December 4, 1976.
[157] Ibid.

[158] William Claiborne, "Little in 'New Right' War Chest Finding Its Way to Candidates," *The Washington Post,* March 20, 1978.

[159] Perry, "Right Wing Got Plucked."

[160] Weil, "Man With the Golden List."

[161] Christopher Lydon, "Credit System Fuels Wallace Fund Drive," *The New York Times,* May 23, 1975.

[162] Ibid.

[163] Ehrenhalt, " 'New Right' Plans...," pp. 3029-30.

[164] Weil, "Man With the Golden List."

[165] "The Great Envelope Flap," *Democratic Congressional Campaign Committee Report,* December 1977, p. 4.

[166] "Lobby to Return Anti-Gun Control Guns," *The Washington Post,* January 16, 1978.

[167] Jack Anderson and Les Whitten, "False Advertising," *The Washington Post,* November 15, 1977

[168] Christopher Lydon, "Fund Raiser Quits Group of Rightists," *The New York Times,* October 6, 1975.

[169] Ehrenhalt, " 'New Right' Plans...," p. 3029.

[170] Andrew Mollison, "Nixon-Era GOP Chairmen Stepping Aside," *Atlanta Journal and Constitution,* October 2, 1977.

[171] Buchanan, "New Right...."

[172] Herbert E. Alexander, *Financing the 1972 Election.*

[173] See for example, Bruce W. Eberle, "Direct Response Fund Raising," *Practical Politics,* July-Aug. 1978.

[174] Congressional Quarterly, *Congressional Ethics* (Washington, D.C.: Congressional Quarterly Inc., 1977), pp. 4, 108.

[175] For background, see ibid., p. 114.

[176] On December 7, 1976, the House Democratic Caucus voted to accept a proposal made by Rep. Andrew Maguire of New Jersey to limit the tenure of Democrats serving on the House ethics committee to two terms beginning with the 95th Congress. The motion was favored by junior representatives who sought to increase the committee's rate of turnover and representativeness. In January 1977 four new members were appointed to the panel; these individuals tended to be younger and more aggressive than the representatives they replaced.

[177] After being reelected to a 19th term in November 1976, Sikes was stripped of his chairmanship of the House Military Construction Appropriations Subcommittee, by a 189-93 tally of the Democratic Caucus.

Many observers traced Sikes' loss of the chairmanship to his reprimand in 1976 for conflicts of interest and failure to disclose some financial assets. The reprimand and Sikes' loss of the chairmanship had been sought by Common Cause, which brought action from the ethics committee by submitting a sworn complaint for transmittal by a member. "Common Cause Submits Conflict of Interest Complaint Against Rep. Robert Sikes (D-Fla.) to House Ethics Committee; Scores Congressional Inaction," Common Cause press release, April 7, 1976. Common Cause also proposed a general change in caucus procedures to make all subcommittee chairmen answerable to the caucus and to enable the caucus to remove from chairmanship any member found guilty of criminal or ethical violations. Ann Cooper, "Inside Congress: Dozens of Rules Changes Set for Debate," Congressional Quarterly *Weekly Report,* p. 3192.

[178] Bruce F. Freed, "House Elects Thompson to Replace Hays: Controls on Perquisites Tightened," Congressional Quarterly *Weekly Report,* June 26, 1976, p. 1632.

[179] U.S. House of Representatives, Commission on Administrative Review, *Scheduling of Work of the House,* House Report 95-23, 94th Cong., 2nd Sess., 1976, pp. 10-21.

[180] To help them determine what recommendations to make, the Commission on Administrative Review ordered two surveys: one was a questionnaire filled out by 150 of the 372 returning House members of the 95th Congress, the other, conducted by Louis Harris, was a national survey of 1,510 voting-age adults. The results showed that the "public disapproves of Congress in general but wants to learn more about what it is doing, from news organizations and the members themselves, and is willing to pay for more first-

hand information with tax dollars. The members of the House of Representatives would rather spend their time making laws than providing services for their constituents, and they favor reform restricting outside income and the prevalent office 'slush funds' even more strongly than the voters do." Warren Weaver, Jr., "2 Polls Provide Support for Congressional Reforms," *The New York Times,* February 4, 1977. Interestingly, "those who knew most about Congress tended to rate it and its members higher than those who knew little. 'Familiarity does not breed contempt,' Harris said." Mary Russell, "Congress Rates 9th in Poll of Ethics," *The Washington Post,* February 4, 1977.

[181] U.S. Congress, House, Commission on Administrative Review, *Financial Ethics,* House *Report* 95-73, 95th Cong., 1st Sess., 1977, pp. 3, 4.

[182] Ibid., pp. 4, 5. While the commission took an approach similar to the Kastenmeier bill, there were some differences "because the government-wide approach of that bill requires disclosure of certain information that is not particularly relevant or appropriate to Members of Congress... (e.g., disclosure of patent rights)."

[183] Ibid., pp. 9-10.

[184] Ibid., p. 11.

[185] Ibid., p. 15. Unlike the House, Senate rules require each senator "to account for the receipt and distribution of all contributions over $50." Mary Russell, "House Members Still Wading in Unaccountable Slush Funds," *The Washington Post,* February 14, 1977. (For an analysis of disclosure reports for 1976 filed with the Clerk of the House and the Secretary of the Senate, see Thomas P. Southwick and David Loomis, "Financial Disclosure: New Rules Will Have Impact" Congressional Quarterly *Weekly Report,* July 23, 1977, pp. 1507-1517.)

[186] "The allowance to cover 'outside of the District of Columbia expenses' is currently $2,000. Except for trips between the Member's district and the Capital, and the district office rent, this allowance must cover *all* official expenditures incurred outside of Washington . . . the heaviest burden upon this account is travel within the district." See fn. 8. Ibid., pp. 17, 18.

[187] Prior to the passage of the Obey commission's recommendations, the House ethics code required separation of campaign funds from personal funds "unless specifically provided by law." This latter provision was added to the House rules in 1975 to refer to the FECA but technically it could be used to permit representatives to use campaign money for any legal purpose. One of the main culprits of this clause was Jim Wright, the House majority leader. The Senate had no equivalent provision; campaign funds in that chamber could be used only for political campaigning or for running Senate offices. Ibid., pp. 16, 18, 23.

[188] Ibid., p. 13. The Justice Department filed a civil suit related to the question of gifts on July 20, 1977. The department charged that the South African Foundation, acting as a front for the South Africa government, had arranged free trips and campaign contributions for two members of the House Agriculture Committee in order to "promote an understanding of South Africa." The House committee had jurisdiction over sugar import quotas in effect during the late 1960s and early 1970s, and the period of the questionable gifts was 1970-1974. The suit did not charge the House members with wrongdoing, and they claimed that they had not known the true source of the gifts at the time. "Suit Filed: Gifts to House Members Laid to South Africa Sugar Lobby," Congressional Quarterly *Weekly Report,* July 23, 1977, pp. 1492-1493.

[189] U.S. House of Representatives, Commission on Administrative Review, *Financial Ethics,* pp. 13-21.

[190] Ibid., p. 25.

[191] This provision was later stricken from the bill.

[192] Obey and O'Neill sought a modified closed rule from a fear that without it the proposal would be amended on the floor of the House to such an extent that the package would be killed.

[193] The House never actually voted on this amendment since no member ever called it up.

[194] Thomas P. Southwick, "House Adopts Tough Ethics Code," Congressional Quarterly *Weekly Report,* March 5, 1977, p. 388.

[195] Mary Russell, "House Ethics Code Is Nearing Passage," *The Washington Post,* March 3, 1977.

[196] Not everybody thought the House code was strict enough. The House Republican Task Force on Reform issued a report calling for several additional provisions, including: greater disclosure of instances of nepotism, a better accounting of the use of the frank, immediate elimination of unofficial office accounts and an independent and detailed audit of Member and committee expenditures.

[197] Richardson Preyer and Charles E. Wiggins, House Select Committee on Ethics, dear colleague letter, May 19, 1977, p. 1.

[198] Many, but not all the opponents of the limits on earned outside income had received substantial amounts from speeches in recent years. Data on honoraria have been available only since 1971. In the five-year period 1971-75, senators earned approximately $4,100,000 in honoraria. Senators can earn up to $25,000 in honoraria in 1977 and 1978. "Senate Unit Approves Earnings Limit, But Trouble Seen in House," *The Washington Post,* February 24, 1977.

[199] Lowell P. Weicker, Jr., "Full — *Full* — Disclosure," *The New York Times,* March 22, 1977.

[200] Thomas P. Southwick, "Senate Adopts New Code of Ethics," Congressional Quarterly *Weekly Report,* April 2, 1977, p. 591.

[201] The Senate Ethics Committee, like the House Select Committee on Ethics, was charged with drafting legislation to put into law the relevant portions of the new Senate ethics code.

[202] Thomas P. Southwick, "Senate Ethics Panel May Seek Code Changes," Congressional Quarterly *Weekly Report,* May 21, 1977, p. 973.

[203] "Getting Free 'Educational Materials' Ruled Violation of Senate Ethics Code," *Campaign Practices Reports,* July 25, 1977, p. 7.

[204] On June 13, 1977, the Senate changed its rules concerning solicitation of campaign funds. Under the new ethics code adopted in April each senator could designate two aides who could receive or distribute campaign funds, but none could solicit funds. Under the change approved in June, the two aides could also solicit funds. As the Senate Rules Committee noted, the prohibition on solicitation was inconsistent and unworkable, since solicitation was an integral part of the type of fund-raising activities the chamber had authorized in April.

[205] Paul Houston, "Efforts to Plug Loophole in Ethics Code Spark Battle," *Los Angeles Times,* November 10, 1977.

[206] Thomas P. Southwick, "Senators Seek Court Test of New Senate Ethics Code; Foreign Travel Rule Studied; Congressional Quarterly *Weekly Report,* July 16, 1977, p. 1445; "Senate Quietly Votes to Ease $25,000 Limit on Honoraria," *Campaign Practices Reports,* November 28, 1977, pp. 8-9; "Senators' Brief Hits Income Limit as Violating Right to Campaign Funds," *Campaign Practices Reports,* February 20, 1978, pp. 5-6; "Court Upholds Senate Rule Limiting Outside Earned Income," *Campaign Practices Reports,* March 6, 1978, pp. 1-2.

[207] Through various dilatory tactics, proponents of the increase were able to block votes on the raise and it automatically went into effect on February 20th. The annual salaries of congressmen went from $44,600 to $57,500. There was a major outcry about the increase and the way in which it was implemented among many members of Congress, the general public, and many newspaper editorialists.

[208] Richard L. Madden, "O'Neill Prods Panel on Ethics for House," *The New York Times,* January 14, 1977.

[209] See footnote 12, above.

[210] Other differences include the following: House rules limit gifts from foreign nationals to $100. The original Senate draft contained a similar provision but was altered at Senator Javits' request to a limit of $100 from foreign nationals with legislative interests. Finally, while both codes allow members to receive unlimited sums from book royalties, senators can get an advance from their publishers before the book is published, whereas representatives must wait for actual sales before collecting. Walter Pincus, "House, Senate Ethics Codes Reflect Interests of Members," *The Washington Post,* April 13, 1977.

[211] Ann Cooper, "House Income Limit Rule under Attack," Congressional Quarterly *Weekly Report*, April 15, 1978, pp. 867-868.

[212] Ann Cooper, "Inside Congress: House Retains Outside Income Limit," Congressional Quarterly *Weekly Report*, September 23, 1978, pp. 2529-2530.

[213] "House Backs Personal-Finance Disclosure for Officeholders, Candidates by Nov. 1," *Campaign Practices Reports*, October 2, 1978, pp. 1-3; Ann Cooper, "Inside Congress: Government-Wide Ethics Bill Passed by House," Congressional Quarterly *Weekly Report*, September 30, 1978, pp. 2610, 2696-2698.

[214] Ann Cooper, "Inside Congress: Carter Signs Government-Wide Ethics Bill," Congressional Quarterly *Weekly Report*, October 28, 1978, pp. 3121-3127. For the background of the special prosecutor provision, see Ann Cooper, "Inside Congress: Amendment Causes Concern: House May Vote on Bill to Deal with New Scandals in the Executive Branch," Congressional Quarterly *Weekly Report*, July 1, 1978, pp. 1667-1668. Also see: "Financial Disclosure," Congressional Quarterly *Weekly Report*, September 2, 1978, pp. 2311-2366.

[215] Southwick, "House Adopts...," pp. 387, 388.

[216] Walter Pincus, "Senators Weighing Restrictions on Outside Income," *The Washington Post*, March 17, 1977.

[217] The Senate defeated an amendment proposed by Senator Roth to create a three-member commission of private citizens to investigate allegations of misconduct by senators and Senate employees.

[218] " 'Ethics' on Capitol Hill," *The Progressive*, August 1977, pp. 8-10.

[219] Ibid., pp. 8-9.

[220] "Backsliding on Ethics," *In Common*, Fall 1977, pp. 3-11.

[221] Richard Lerner, "Financial Statements," UPI news release dated May 5, 1978; Mary Russell and George Lardner, Jr., "House Members' Holdings: They're Bullish on U.S." *The Washington Post*, May 5, 1978; Steven V. Roberts, "A Wide Range of Income for Congressmen," *The New York Times*, May 5, 1978; Wendell Rawls, Jr., "Financial Reports of 407 in House Show They Are Cautious Investors," *The New York Times*, May 8, 1978; Wendell Rawls, Jr., "House Income Limit Affects Committee: Some on Rules Panel Who Oppose Proposal Could Lose Large Sums If It Takes Effect," *The New York Times*, May 17, 1978; Wendell Rawls, Jr., "Members of House Disclose Data on Outside Income and Liabilities," *The New York Times*, May 5, 1978.

[222] Adam Clymer, "12 in the Senate Are Millionaires, Reports Under New Rules Show," *The New York Times*, May 20, 1978; _____, "The Net Worth of the Senate: Reports on Holdings Offer Few Surprises," *The New York Times*, May 22, 1978.

[223] "$49,000 Loan at Issue: Brooke: 'I Lied' on Finances," *The Washington Post*, May 27, 1978; "Brooke Admits to False Statement, Under Oath, About a $49,000 Loan," *The New York Times*, May 27, 1978; Michael Knight, "Brooke's Prospects in Election Assayed: Damage Expected from Disclosure on Loan — Group of Blacks Rallies behind Senator," *The New York Times*, May 29, 1978.

[224] Nicholas M. Horrock, "Senate Ethics Panel Opens Preliminary Inquiry into Brooke's Finances," *The New York Times*, June 2, 1978; Bill Richards, "Talmadge and Brooke: Two Senators Face Inquiry," *The Washington Post*, June 9, 1978.

[225] Michael Knight, "Brooke Faces 4 Official Inquiries, Adding to His Political Difficulties," *The New York Times*, June 4, 1978; Nicholas M. Horrock, "Senator Brooke Faces Problems on Money Dealings: More Legal and Ethical Questions Arising from Divorce," *The New York Times*, June 6, 1978.

[226] Nicholas M. Horrock, "Brooke Testimony on $49,000 Debt Raises New Points of Controversy: Under Oath, Senator Concedes He Misled Court Because He Feared for Political Career," *The New York Times*, June 8, 1978; Bill Richards and T. R. Reid, "Brooke Claimed Tax Exemptions for Married Kin," *The Washington Post*, June 18, 1978. Boston newspapers reported some additional alleged irregularities in Brooke's financial affairs. On June 14, *The Boston Herald American* charged that Brooke's Senate disclosure report failed to include his ownership of 2,000 shares of stock in the Earl Graves Publishing Co. of New York, his membership on the board of advisers of *Black Enterprise* magazine; in addition, his Senate disclosure report indicated that he had put up $125,000 of security on a loan used to purchase property in the French West Indies, whereas Brooke's latest

financial statement in the divorce case indicated that no security had been put up. "Brooke Accused of Failing to Report Stock Holdings," *The New York Times,* June 15, 1978.

[227] Stacy Jolna, "Judge Says Mrs. Brooke Can Get Divorce Retrial," *The Washington Post,* June 16, 1978; Joseph R. Daughen, "Brooke's Troubles Pile Up," *The Sunday Bulletin,* June 25, 1978; Michael Knight, "Prosecutor in Brooke Case Plans Investigation into Possible Perjury," *The New York Times,* June 17, 1978; Stacy Jolna, "Brooke's Seat Lures Another Mass. Hopeful," *The Washington Post,* June 23, 1978; Bill Richards and Stacy Jolna, "Brooke Assails Articles on His Financial Affairs," *The Washington Post,* June 21, 1978; Bill Peterson, "Smell of Blood Has 'Pack' on Sen. Brooke's Trail," *The Washington Post,* June 26, 1978; Michael Knight, "Brooke Divorce Heads for Trial; Move Could Harm His Campaign," *The New York Times,* June 28, 1978; David Mutch, "Brooke Loses Any Position as Shoo-in," *The Christian Science Monitor,* June 29, 1978.

[228] Ann Cooper, "Stormy Hearing: Brooke Didn't Hide Evidence, Senate Ethics Panel Says," Congressional Quarterly *Weekly Report,* October 28, 1978, pp. 3127-3128.

[229] *The Washington Star,* "Talmadge Says He Used 'Small Gifts' for Expenses," from *The New York Times,* May 22, 1978.

[230] "Alms for the Senator," editorial, *The Washington Star,* May 27, 1978; Mary McGrory, "Maybe Home Folks Just Won't Let Herman Talmadge Pay," *The Washington Star,* May 30, 1978; Edward T. Pound, "Hill Panel Asked to Probe Talmadge on Cash, Gifts," *The Washington Star,* May 27, 1978; "Talmadge's Generous Friends," *The Philadelphia Inquirer,* June 9, 1978.

[231] Edward T. Pound, "More on Talmadge's Money: Records Show 'Refund' Accepted Same Day He Said None Was Due," *The Washington Star,* June 2, 1978; "Around the Nation: Talmadge Aides to Amend Campaign Fund Report,"*The New York Times,* June 3, 1978; Fred Barbash, "Talmadge Neglected to Report $27,000 Campaign Spending," *The Washington Post,* June 3, 1978.

[232] "Friends and Aides of Talmadge Defend Birthday 'Gifts' of Cash," *The New York Times,* June 4, 1978; Bill Richards, "Talmadge Birthday Income Unreported," *The Washington Post,* June 4, 1978; Clyde H. Farnsworth, "Inquiry Incomplete on Gifts to Talmadge: Counsel to Senate Ethics Panel Says No Violations Found Yet in Birthday Donations, *The New York Times,* June 5, 1978.

[233] Edward T. Pound, "Talmadge Tells How He Spent Personal Funds for Campaign," *The Washington Star,* July 19, 1978.

[234] "$24,000 Questioned in Talmadge Audit: Aide Says Senator, Who Ordered Study, Will Repay Funds If He Was Overpaid by U.S.," *The New York Times,* July 24, 1978.

[235] Edward T. Pound, "Bank Data Subpoenaed in Talmadge Case," *The Washington Star,* August 22, 1978.

[236] Edward T. Pound, "Secret Campaign Fund for Talmadge **Bared**," *The Washington Star,* August 26, 1978; ———, "Funds in Account for Talmadge Changed to Cash," *The Washington Star,* August 27, 1978.

[237] Edward T. Pound, "Gift to Talmadge Went into Secret Bank Account," *The Washington Star,* September 21, 1978.

[238] Bill Richards, "Talmadge Probers Have Memo on $5,000," *The Washington Post,* October 6, 1978.

[239] For an example, see "Talmadge Given $1,000 Check by Ga. Executive, Report Says," *The Washington Post,* October 21, 1978.

[240] Ann Cooper, "Investigation Widens: Grand Jury, Senate Panel Probe Talmadge Funds Use," Congressional Quarterly *Weekly Report,* September 9, 1978, pp. 2437-2439; "Counsel: Talmadge Trial by Panel Urged," Congressional Quarterly *Weekly Report,* November 4, 1978, p. 3197.

[241] Colman McCarthy, "Ethics Code: Will the Senate Yawn?" editorial, *The Washington Post,* June 8, 1978; Steven V. Roberts, "Ethics Drive Encounters a Backlash in Congress," *The New York Times,* June 11, 1978; "The Senators' Finances," editorial, *The Washington Post,* June 7, 1978.

[242] Alan Berlow, "House Reprimands Roybal, Wilson, McFall as Korea Lobbying Probe Ends," Congressional Quarterly *Weekly Report,* October 21, 1978, pp. 3097-3098.

[243] Tongsun Park received at least $450,000 from the Rice Growers' Association.

[244] Barry M. Hager, "House Authorizes Probe of Korean Influence," Congressional Quarterly *Weekly Report*, February 12, 1977, p. 275.

[245] The charges included one count of conspiracy to defraud the United States, one count of bribery, one count of offering an illegal gratuity, one count of violating the Foreign Agents Registration Act by failing to register, one count of racketeering, two counts of illegal political contributions by a foreign agent, and 29 counts of mail fraud.

[246] Anthony Marro, "Indictment of Park Charges 36 Crimes," *The New York Times*, September 7, 1977.

[247] Richard Halloran, "Ex-Officer of Korean CIA Tells House Inquiry That Covert Lobby Was Aimed at 50 Prominent Americans," *The New York Times*, October 21, 1977.

[248] The Foreign Agents Registration Act of 1938 requires that "every person who becomes an agent of a foreign principal shall, within ten days thereafter, file with the Attorney General disclosing the existence of that ongoing relationship." The act exempts accredited diplomats and consular officials, individuals engaged in foreign trade or commerce for a foreign principal where there are no lobbying or political activities, charitable solicitation, academic and scientific activities, and lawyers engaged in legal representation of a foreign client before a U.S. court or execuive agency. "How Foreign Agents Registration Act Works," Congressional Quarterly *Weekly Report*, April 16, 1977, p. 701.

[249] Nicholas M. Horrock, "Seoul to Let Park Testify at Trials," *The New York Times*, December 31, 1977.

[250] Richard Halloran, "Jaworski Seeks a House Resolution Asking Korea to Cooperate in Inquiry," *The New York Times*, January 21, 1978.

[251] Richard Halloran, "Aide Says Ford Knew of Alleged Korean Bribery and Ordered Inquiry," *The New York Times*, January 24, 1978.

[252] William Chapman, "Park Testimony Likely to Yield 2 Indictments," *The New York Times*, February 4, 1978.

[253] Andrew H. Malcolm, "Tongsun Park Cites 5 Senators Including Humphrey," *The New York Times*, January 25, 1978.

[254] Richard Halloran, "Park Reportedly Links 15 in Congress to Cash Gifts," *The New York Times*, January 27, 1978.

[255] Rowland Evans and Robert Novak, "A Rising Allied Rumble Over Jaworski's Tactics," *The Washington Post*, February 13, 1978.

[256] Alan Berlow, "Tongsun Park Begins Long-Awaited Testimony," Congressional Quarterly *Weekly Report*, March 4, 1978, pp. 609-611.

[257] Nicholas M. Horrock, "Tongsun Park Says He Gave a Rice Miller $80,000," *The New York Times*, March 6, 1978; Charles R. Babcock, "Park Whets Hill Probers Appetite for Kim," *The Washington Post*, March 6, 1978.

[258] U.S., Congress, House, Subcommittee on International Organizations of the Committee on International Relations, Investigation of Korean-American Relations: Hearings, 95th Cong., 1st sess., 29 and 30 November 1977, Part 3; _____, 95th Cong., 2d sess., 15, 16, 21 and 22 March 1978, Supplement to Part 4.

[259] Charles R. Babcock, "President Park Said to Direct Lobbying," *The Washington Post*, March 16, 1978; T. R. Reid, "Park Is Described As Under Control of Seoul CIA," *The Washington Post*, March 17, 1978.

[260] Charles R. Babcock, "CIA Said Seoul Gave '68 Democrats $400,000: Hill Panel Probes Inaction on '71 Report," *The Washington Post*, March 22, 1978.

[261] Richard Halloran, "Nixon Aides Warned by Hoover on Korea: But Mitchell Denies Ever Seeing 2 About Payment to Congressman and Contribution to Democrats," *The New York Times*, March 22, 1978.

[262] Charles R. Babcock, "Kissinger Testifies He Notified Justice on Korean Scandal," *The Washington Post*, April 21, 1978.

[263] Richard Halloran, "Ex-Rep. Hanna Concedes Guilt in Korea Case, First to Be Convicted in Influence Buying," *The New York Times*, March 18, 1978.

[264] Timothy S. Robinson, "Korean Influence-Buying Scandal: Hancho Kim Convicted on Two Counts," *The Washington Post*, April 9, 1978; Richard Halloran, "Hancho Kim Is Guilty in Korean Bribe Plot: Businessman Is Also Convicted of Lying in Influence Inquiry," *The New York Times*, April 9, 1978.

[265] Richard Halloran, "The Korea Probe Clearly Is Sinking in the West," *The New York Times*, March 26, 1978.

[266] "Inside Congress: Special Prosecutor: Watergate-Inspired Bill May Force House to Vote on Korea Probe Issue," Congressional Quarterly *Weekly Report*, March 18, 1978, pp. 683-685; Tom Wicker, "A No-Priority Bill," *The New York Times*, March 28, 1978.

[267] Jack Anderson, "Korean Connection to Other Lands," *The Washington Post*, March 27, 1978.

[268] Timothy S. Robinson, "Passman Indicted in Korean Scandal: Allegedly Got $213,000 from Park," *The Washington Post*, April 1, 1978.

[269] Charles R. Babcock, "Mostly Cash: Park Tells of Giving about $850,000 to Members of Congress," *The Washington Post*, April 4, 1978.

[270] United Press International, "Congressional Recipients of Funds Named by Park on April 3, 1978 (House of Representatives Only)," *The New York Times*, April 4, 1978.

[271] Richard Halloran, "Tongsun Park Denies O'Neill Sought Funds: Speaker Terms Korean Document a 'Self-Serving Fabrication,'" *The New York Times*, April 5, 1978.

[271] William Safire, "The Tip and Tongsun Show," *The New York Times*, April 6, 1978.

[272] Richard Halloran, "Louisianan Contradicts Testimony of Tongsun Park," *The New York Times*, April 6, 1978.

[273] Daniel Schorr, "Korea Probe Wary of Looking Too Hard," *The Sunday Bulletin* (Philadelphia), May 7, 1978; "The Honor of the House," editorial, *The Washington Post*, May 12, 1978.

[275] Richard G. Zimmerman, "Korea's Secret Code Broken by U.S.," *The Washington Star*, May 24, 1978.

[276] Alan Berlow, "House Panel Warns Korea on Witness Holdout," Congressional Quarterly *Weekly Report*, May 27, 1978, p. 1300.

[277] "Rice Trader Indicted in Dealing with Park: Head of Jersey Concern Charged with Concealing Illegal Use of Korean as Sales Agent," *The New York Times*, May 27, 1978.

[278] "Korean Lobbying Probe: Ethics Panel Moves Against Four Members of House," Congressional Quarterly *Weekly Report*, July 15, 1978, p. 1833.

[279] Richard Halloran, "House Votes to Halt Food Aid for Korea in Influence Dispute: Protests Seoul's Refusal to Let Ex-Envoy Testify — Senate Unit Describes Covert Operations, *The New York Times*, June 23, 1978.

[280] Bill Richards, "Probers Studying Korean's Plea in Smuggling Case," *The Washington Post*, June 30, 1978.

[281] "Figure in U.S. Inquiry Resigns Korea Post: Official Sought by House Ethics Panel in Bribe Scandal Out as National Security Adviser," *The New York Times*, June 24, 1978; Charles R. Babcock, "Korean Adviser Quits, May Aid House Probers," *The Washington Post*, June 24, 1978.

[282] Charles R. Babcock, "Ethics Panel Finds Conflicts in Testimony on Korean Case," *The Washington Post*, June 20, 1978; Alan Berlow, "Korea Lobbying Probe: Senate Ethics Committee Details Evidence Against Bayh and Aide Berman," Congressional Quarterly *Weekly Report*, October 28, 1978, pp. 3136-3137.

[283] Alan Berlow, "Ethics Unit Recommends Censure for Roybal, Reprimand for Wilson," Congressional Quarterly *Weekly Report*, September 30, 1978, p. 2681.

[284] Alan Berlow, "House Reprimands Roybal, Wilson, McFall as Korea Lobbying Probe Ends," Congressional Quarterly *Weekly Report*, October 21, 1978, p. 3097.

[285] Joe Scott, "The Koreagate Report Card," *Los Angeles Herald Examiner*, October 22, 1978; Charles R. Babcock, "Finally, the House Settled for Knuckle-Rapping," *The Washington Post*, October 24, 1978.

[286] Alan Berlow, "House Unit Says Korea's Illicit U.S. Activities Went Beyond Lobbying," Congressional Quarterly *Weekly Report*, November 4, 1978, pp. 3198-3199.

[287] U.S. Congress, House, Committee on Standards of Official Conduct, "Korean Influence Investigation," House *Report* 95-1817, 95th Cong., 2nd sess., Dec. 22, 1978.

[288] "House, Senate Adopt New Codes of Ethics," *1977 Congressional Quarterly Almanac*, pp. 763-781.

[289] This account is drawn from Edward Roeder, "An Abuse of Power? Staff Use in Campaign Is Senate Dilemma," *The Washington Post*, August 28, 1977. Roeder's article

provides a fuller account of what he calls questionable activities in which Cannon's Senate staff may have engaged.

[290] U.S., Congress, House, *Report* of the Committee on Rules and Administration, 95th Cong., 1st sess., issued April 1, 1977. Report 95-500.

[291] "Rules Committee Postpones Until 1978 Action on Staffers' Election Work," *Campaign Practices Reports*, October 3, 1977, pp. 4-6.

[292] "CC Charges Misuse of Hill Staffers," *Frontline*, May-June 1978.

[293] "Campaigning by Staff Aides Is Still a Common Practice," Congressional Quarterly *Weekly Report*, October 28, 1978, p. 3116.

[294] Ibid., p. 3117.

[295] "Staff vs. Staff in Colorado Senate Race," Congressional Quarterly *Weekly Report*, October 28, 1978, p. 3117.

[296] "Congressional Mail: What Is Official Business?" Congressional Quarterly *Weekly Report*, April 28, 1973, pp. 1024-1026.

[297] In 1970 challenger John V. Tunney, later a Democratic senator from California, was awarded an injunction preventing the incumbent Sen. George Murphy, R-Calif., from using the frank to mail campaign material in California. Another decision denied an injunction against such use of the frank by Rep. Jacob Gilbert, D-N.Y., during a campaign in 1968. Ibid.

[298] Ibid., p. 1026.

[299] Frankable materials included: 1) mail to anyone involving matters of public concern, public service, or actions of Congress; 2) the "usual and customary" congressional newsletter or press release; 3) mail between a member's Washington office and his district; 4) letters of condolence or congratulations; 5) general mass mailings and other mail that consists of federal laws and regulations or federal publications containing general information; 6) nonpartisan election and registration information; 7) biographical material about a member or his family mailed as part of a federal publication or in response to a specific request; 8) mail including a picture of a member as part of a federal publication, in response to a specific request, or as part of a mass mailing providing that its size or repeated inclusion does not suggest the intent of advertising. Nonfrankable materials included: 1) purely personal or political mail that was laudatory or complimentary; 2) family greetings; 3) reports of nonofficial activities of a member and his family; 4) mail that specifically solicits a vote or political or financial support. "Franking privilege," Congressional Quarterly *Weekly Report*, April 14, 1973, pp. 876-881.

[300] "Congressional Mail: What is Official Business?" p. 1026.

[301] "Franking Privilege," *1973 Congressional Quarterly Almanac*, pp. 724-725.

[302] "Common Cause Sues to Prevent Abuse of the Congressional Frank," Common Cause news release dated October 5, 1973, pp. 1-5.

[303] Jack Anderson and Les Whitten, "Soviet Spies Make Quiet Gains Here," *The Washington Post*, January 17, 1975.

[304] The political advantage offered the congressman is reported in Ed Zuckerman, "Incumbents' Campaign Aid: The Computer," *The Washington Post*, February 27, 1978.

[305] Monty Hoyt, "Some Services Free, Others Provided at Low Cost: Valuable Extra Benefits for Congressmen," *The Christian Science Monitor*, January 30, 1975.

[306] "Congressional Mail: $46-Million," Congressional Quarterly *Weekly Report*, May 24, 1975, p. 1116.

[307] "Franked Mail Tie to Voting Shown: Testimony Finds the Volume Rises before Elections," *The New York Times*, June 2, 1975.

[308] United Press International, "Incumbent Has $488,000 Edge," *The Washington Post*, August 26, 1975.

[309] Spencer Rich, "Only a Few Senators Abuse Franking Rules," *The Washington Post*, April 16, 1976.

[310] The proposed changes would establish an allowance for mass mailings similar to ceilings on government funds spent by each member for telephone, travel, and other expenses; authorize the use of the Senate's computer to address mailings if the categories of names were eligible to be included in franked mailings; require members to file with the Secretary of the Senate a sample of each mass mailing, the number of pieces mailed, and a description of the addresses used; prohibit the use of Senate facilities for mailings

ineligible for franking; and prohibit the production of mailing labels, computer printouts, or computer tapes for use in facilities other than those operated by the Senate. The report also advocated elimination of the franking privilege for condolences and congratulations. U.S., Congress, Senate, Ad Hoc Committee on Legislative Immunity, *The Senator's Duty to Inform the People,* 95th Cong., 1st sess., 21 February 1977.

[311] "House Franking Restrictions Approved for Statutory Law," Congressional Quarterly *Weekly Report,* July 16, 1977, p. 1446. Martin Plissner, "Mail Abuse on Capitol Hill," *Politics & Other Human Interests,* November 8, 1977, pp. 20, 22.

[312] "Franking Bill Dies," Congressional Quarterly *Weekly Report,* October 28, 1978, p. 3121.

[313] "Congress Votes Lower Mail Rates for Political Campaign Material," *Campaign Practices Reports,* October 30, 1978, p. 5.

[314] Alan Berlow, "Unnoticed Rider on Voting Rights Bill Gives Bonanza to Campaign Committees," Congressional Quarterly *Weekly Report,* October 28, 1978, p. 3164.

APPENDIX
PART I

Appendix A

Federal Election Campaign Act of 1971

The Federal Election Campaign Act of 1971 (FECA) was the first comprehensive revision of federal campaign legislation since the Corrupt Practices Act of 1925. The act established detailed spending limits and disclosure procedures. PL 92-225 contained the following major provisions:

General

● Repealed the Federal Corrupt Practices Act of 1925.
● Defined "election" to mean any general, special, primary, or runoff election, nominating convention or caucus, delegate-selection primary, presidential preference primary, or constitutional convention.
● Broadened the definitions of "contribution" and "expenditure" as they pertain to political campaigns, but exempted a loan of money by a national or state bank made in accordance with applicable banking laws.
● Prohibited promises of employment or other political rewards or benefits by any candidate in exchange for political support, and prohibited contracts between candidates and any federal department or agency.
● Provided that the terms "contribution" and "expenditure" did not include communications, nonpartisan registration, and get-out-the-vote campaigns by a corporation aimed at its stockholders or by a labor organization aimed at its members.
● Provided that the terms "contribution" and "expenditure" did not include the establishment, administration, and solicitation of voluntary contributions to a separate segregated fund to be utilized for political purposes by a corporation or labor organization.

Contribution Limits

● Placed a ceiling on contributions by any candidate or his immediate family to his own campaign of $50,000 for president or vice president, $35,000 for senator, and $25,000 for representative.

Spending Limits

● Limited the total amount that could be spent by federal candidates for advertising time in communications media to 10 cents per eligible voter, or $50,000, whichever was greater. The limitation would apply to all candidates for president and vice president, senator and representative, and would be determined annually for the geographical area of each election by the Bureau of the Census.

● Included in the term "communications media" radio and television broadcasting stations, newspapers, magazines, billboards, and automatic telephone equipment. Of the total spending limit, up to 60 percent could be used for broadcast advertising time.

● Specified that candidates for presidential nomination, during the period prior to the nominating convention, could spend no more in primary or nonprimary states than the amount allowed under the 10-cent-per-voter communications spending limitation.

● Provided that broadcast and nonbroadcast spending limitations be increased in proportion to annual increases in the Consumer Price Index over the base year 1970.

Disclosure and Enforcement

● Required all political committees that anticipated receipts in excess of $1,000 during the calendar year to file a statement of organization with the appropriate federal supervisory officer, and to include such information as the names of all principal officers, the scope of the committee, the names of all candidates the committee supported, and other information as required by law.

● Stipulated that the appropriate federal supervisory officer to oversee election campaign practices, reporting, and disclosure was the Clerk of the House for House candidates, the Secretary of the Senate for Senate candidates, and the Comptroller General for presidential candidates.

● Required each political committee to report any individual expenditure of more than $100 and any expenditures of more than $100 in the aggregate during the calendar year.

● Required disclosure of all contributions to any committee or candidate in excess of $100, including a detailed report with the name and address of the contributor and the date the contribution was made.

● Required the supervisory officers to prepare an annual report for each committee registered with the commission and make such reports available for sale to the public.

● Required candidates and committees to file reports of contributions and expenditures on the 10th day of March, June, and September every year, on the 15th and fifth days preceding the date on which an election was held and on the 31st day of January. Any contribution of $5,000 or more was to be reported within 48 hours after its receipt.

• Required reporting of the names, addresses, and occupations of any lender and endorser of any loan in excess of $100 as well as the date and amount of such loans.

• Required any person who made any contribution in excess of $100, other than through a political committee or candidate, to report such contribution to the commission.

• Prohibited any contribution to a candidate or committee by one person in the name of another person.

• Authorized the office of the Comptroller General to serve as a national clearinghouse for information on the administration of election practices.

• Required that copies of reports filed by a candidate with the appropriate supervisory officer also be filed with the secretary of state for the state in which the election was held.

Miscellaneous

• Prohibited radio and television stations from charging political candidates more than the lowest unit cost for the same advertising time available to commercial advertisers. Lowest unit rate charges would apply only during the 45 days preceding a primary election and the 60 days preceding a general election.

• Required nonbroadcast media to charge candidates no more than the comparable amounts charged to commercial advertisers for the same class and amount of advertising space. The requirement would apply only during the 45 days preceding the date of a primary election and 60 days before the date of a general election.

• Provided that amounts spent by an agent of a candidate on behalf of his candidacy would be charged against the overall expenditure allocation. Fees paid to the agent for services performed also would be charged against the overall limitation.

• Stipulated that no broadcast station could make any charge for political advertising time on a station unless written consent to contract for such time had been given by the candidate, and unless the candidate certified that such charge would not exceed his spending limit.

Appendix B

Revenue Act of 1971

The Revenue Act of 1971, through tax incentives and a tax checkoff plan, provided the basis for public funding of presidential election campaigns. PL 92-178 contained the following major provisions:

Tax Incentives and Checkoff

● Allowed a tax credit of $12.50 ($25 for a married couple) or a deduction against income of $50 ($100 for a married couple) for political contributions to candidates for local, state, or federal office.
● Allowed taxpayers to contribute to a general fund for all eligible presidential and vice presidential candidates by authorizing $1 of their annual income tax payment to be placed in such a fund.

Presidential Election Campaign Fund

● Authorized to be distributed to the candidates of each major party (one which obtained 25 percent of votes cast in the previous presidential election) an amount equal to 15 cents multiplied by the number of U.S. residents age 18 or over.
● Established a formula for allocating public campaign funds to candidates of minor parties whose candidates received 5 percent or more but less than 25 percent of the previous presidential election vote.
● Authorized payments after the election to reimburse the campaign expenses of a new party whose candidate received enough votes to be eligible or to a minor party whose candidate increased its vote to the qualifying level.
● Prohibited major-party candidates who chose public financing of their campaign from accepting private campaign contributions unless their share of funds contributed through the income tax checkoff procedure fell short of the amounts to which they were entitled.
● Prohibited a major-party candidate who chose public financing and all campaign committees authorized by the candidate from spending more than the amount to which the candidate was entitled under the contributions formula.

• Provided that if the amounts in the fund were insufficient to make the payments to which each party was entitled, payments would be allocated according to the ratio of contributions in their accounts. No party would receive from the general fund more than the smallest amount needed by a major party to reach the maximum amount of contributions to which it was entitled.

• Provided that surpluses remaining in the fund after a campaign be returned to the Treasury after all parties had been paid the amounts to which they were entitled.

Enforcement

• Provided penalties of $5,000 or one year in prison, or both, for candidates or campaign committees that spent more on a campaign than the amounts they received from the campaign fund or who accepted private contributions when sufficient public funds were available.

• Provided penalties of $10,000 or five years in prison, or both, for candidates or campaign committees who used public campaign funds for unauthorized expenses, gave or accepted kickbacks or illegal payments involving public campaign funds, or who knowingly furnished false information to the Comptroller General.

NOTE: The Revenue Act of 1978, PL 95-600, raised the tax credit to $50 on a single tax return, $100 on a joint return, retaining the 50 percent of contribution provision as in the 1971 Act. The 1978 law eliminated the tax deduction for political contributions while increasing the tax credit.

Appendix C

Federal Election Campaign Act
Amendments of 1974

The 1974 Amendments set new contribution and spending limits, made provision for government funding of presidential prenomination campaigns and national nominating conventions, and created the bipartisan Federal Election Commission to administer election laws. PL 93-443 contained the following major provisions:

Federal Election Commission

• Created a six-member, full-time bipartisan Federal Election Commission to be responsible for administering election laws and the public financing program.
• Provided that the president, Speaker of the House, and president pro tem of the Senate would appoint to the commission two members, each of different parties, all subject to confirmation by Congress. Commission members could not be officials or employees of any branch of government.
• Made the Secretary of the Senate and Clerk of the House ex officio, nonvoting members of the FEC; provided that their offices would serve as custodian of reports for House and Senate candidates.
• Provided that commissioners would serve six-year, staggered terms and established a rotating one-year chairmanship.

Contribution Limits

• $1,000 per individual for each primary, runoff, or general election, and an aggregate contribution of $25,000 to all federal candidates annually.
• $5,000 per organization, political committee, and national and state party organization for each election, but no aggregate limit on the amount organizations could contribute in a campaign nor on the amount organizations could contribute to party organizations supporting federal candidates.

• $50,000 for president or vice president, $35,000 for Senate, and $25,000 for House races for candidates and their families to their own campaign.
• $1,000 for independent expenditures on behalf of a candidate.
• Barred cash contributions of over $100 and foreign contributions.

Spending Limits

• Presidential primaries — $10 million total per candidate for all primaries. In a state presidential primary, limited a candidate to spending no more than twice what a Senate candidate in that state would be allowed to spend *(see below)*.
• Presidential general election — $20 million per candidate.
• Presidential nominating conventions — $2 million each major political party, lesser amounts for minor parties.
• Senate primaries — $100,000 or eight cents per eligible voter, whichever was greater.
• Senate general elections — $150,000 or 12 cents per eligible voter, whichever was greater.
• House primaries — $70,000.
• House general elections — $70,000.
• National party spending — $10,000 per candidate in House general elections; $20,000 or two cents per eligible voter, whichever was greater, for each candidate in Senate general elections; and two cents per voter (approximately $2.9 million) in presidential general elections. The expenditure would be above the candidate's individual spending limit.
• Applied Senate spending limits to House candidates who represented a whole state.
• Repealed the media spending limitations in the Federal Election Campaign Act of 1971 (PL 92-225).
• Exempted expenditures of up to $500 for food and beverages, invitations, unreimbursed travel expenses by volunteers and spending on "slate cards" and sample ballots.
• Exempted fund-raising costs of up to 20 percent of the candidate spending limit. Thus the spending limit for House candidates would be effectively raised from $70,000 to $84,000 and for candidates in presidential primaries from $10 million to $12 million.
• Provided that spending limits be increased in proportion to annual increases in the Consumer Price Index.

Public Financing

• Presidential general elections — voluntary public financing. Major-party candidates automatically would qualify for full funding before the campaign. Minor-party and independent candidates would be eligible to receive a proportion of full funding based on past or current votes received. If a candidate opted for full public funding, no private contributions would be permitted.

● Presidential nominating conventions — optional public funding. Major parties automatically would qualify. Minor parties would be eligible for lesser amounts based on their proportion of votes received in a past election.

● Presidential primaries — matching public funds of up to $5 million per candidate after meeting fund-raising requirement of $100,000 raised in amounts of at least $5,000 in each of 20 states or more. Only the first $250 of individual private contributions would be matched. The matching funds were to be divided among the candidates as quickly as possible. In allocating the money, the order in which the candidates qualified would be taken into account. Only private gifts, raised after Jan. 1, 1975, would qualify for matching for the 1976 election. No federal payments would be made before January 1976.

● Provided that all federal money for public funding of campaigns would come from the Presidential Election Campaign Fund. Money received from the federal income tax dollar checkoff automatically would be appropriated to the fund.

Disclosure and Enforcement

● Required each candidate to establish one central campaign committee through which all contributions and expenditures on behalf of a candidate must be reported. Required designation of specific bank depositories of campaign funds.

● Required full reports of contributions and expenditures to be filed with the Federal Election Commission 10 days before and 30 days after every election, and within 10 days of the close of each quarter unless the committee received or expended less than $1,000 in that quarter. A year-end report was due in nonelection years.

● Required that contributions of $1,000 or more received within the last 15 days before election be reported to the commission within 48 hours.

● Prohibited contributions in the name of another.

● Treated loans as contributions. Required a cosigner or guarantor for each $1,000 of outstanding obligation.

● Required any organization that spent any money or committed any act for the purpose of influencing any election (such as the publication of voting records) to file reports as a political committee.

● Required every person who spent or contributed more than $100, other than to or through a candidate or political committee, to report.

● Permitted government contractors, unions, and corporations to maintain separate, segregated political funds.

● Provided that the commission would: receive campaign reports; make rules and regulations (subject to review by Congress within 30 days); maintain a cumulative index of reports filed and not filed; make special and regular reports to Congress and the president; and serve as an election information clearinghouse.

● Gave the commission power to render advisory opinions; conduct audits and investigations; subpoena witnesses and information; and go to court to seek civil injunctions.

● Provided that criminal cases would be referred by the commission to the Justice Department for prosecution.

● Increased existing fines to a maximum of $50,000.

● Provided that a candidate for federal office who failed to file reports could be prohibited from running again for the term of that office plus one year.

Miscellaneous

● Set January 1, 1975, as the effective date of the act (except for immediate preemption of state laws).

● Removed Hatch Act restrictions on voluntary activities by state and local employees in federal campaigns, if not otherwise prohibited by state law.

● Prohibited solicitation of funds by franked mail.

● Preempted state election laws for federal candidates.

● Permitted use of excess campaign funds to defray expenses of holding federal office or for other lawful purposes.

Appendix D

Federal Election Campaign Act
Amendments of 1976

The 1976 Amendments revised election laws following the Supreme Court decision in *Buckley v. Valeo.* The Amendments reopened the door to large contributions through "independent expenditures" and through corporate and union political action committees. PL 94-283 contained the following major provisions:

Federal Election Commission

● Reconstituted the Federal Election Commission as a six-member panel appointed by the president and confirmed by the Senate.

● Prohibited commission members from engaging in outside business activities; gave commissioners one year after joining the body to terminate outside business interests.

● Gave Congress the power to disapprove individual sections of any regulation proposed by the commission.

Contribution Limits

● Limited an individual to giving no more than $5,000 a year to a political action committee and $20,000 to the national committee of a political party (the 1974 law set a $1,000 per election limit on individual contributions to a candidate and an aggregate contribution limit for individuals of $25,000 a year.)

● Limited a multicandidate committee to giving no more than $15,000 a year to the national committee of a political party (the 1974 law set only a limit of $5,000 per election per candidate).

● Limited the Democratic and Republican senatorial campaign committees to giving up to $17,500 a year to a candidate (the 1974 law had set a $5,000 per election limit).

● Allowed campaign committees set up to back a single candidate to provide "occasional, isolated, and incidental support" to another candidate. (The 1974 law required a campaign committee to spend money only on behalf of the single candidate for which it was formed.)

● Restricted the proliferation of membership organization, corporate and union political action committees. All political action committees established by a company or an international union would be treated as a single committee for contribution purposes. The contributions of political action committees of a company or union would be limited to no more than $5,000 overall to the same candidate in any election.

Spending Limits

● Limited spending by presidential and vice presidential candidates to no more than $50,000 of their own, or their family's money, on their campaigns, if they accepted public financing.
● Exempted from the law's spending limits payments by candidates or the national committees of political parties for legal and accounting services required to comply with the campaign law, but required that such payments be reported.

Public Financing

● Required presidential candidates who received federal matching subsidies and who withdrew from the prenomination election campaign to give back leftover federal matching funds.
● Cut off federal campaign subsidies to a presidential candidate who won less than 10 percent of the vote in two consecutive presidential primaries in which he ran.
● Established a procedure under which an individual who became ineligible for matching payments could have eligibility restored by a finding of the commission.

Disclosure and Enforcement

● Gave the commission exclusive authority to prosecute civil violations of the campaign finance law and shifted to the commission jurisdiction over violations formerly covered only in the criminal code, thus strengthening its power to enforce the law.
● Required an affirmative vote of four members for the commission to issue regulations and advisory opinions and initiate civil actions and investigations.
● Required labor unions, corporations, and membership organizations to report expenditures of over $2,000 per election for communications to their stockholders or members advocating the election or defeat of a clearly identified candidate. The costs of communications to members or stockholders on issues would not have to be reported.

● Required that candidates and political committees keep records of contributions of $50 or more. (The 1974 law required records of contributions of $10 or more.)

● Permitted candidates and political committees to waive the requirement for filing quarterly campaign finance reports in a nonelection year if less than a total of $5,000 was raised or spent in that quarter. Annual reports would still have to be filed. (The exemption limit was $1,000 under the 1974 law.)

● Required that political committees and individuals making an independent political expenditure of more than $100 that advocated the defeat or election of a candidate file a report with the election commission. Required the committee and individual to state, under penalty of perjury, that the expenditure was not made in collusion with a candidate.

● Required that independent expenditures of $1,000 or more made within 15 days of an election be reported within 24 hours.

● Limited the commission to issuing advisory opinions only for specific fact situations. Advisory opinions could not be used to spell out commission policy. Advisory opinions were not to be considered as precedents unless an activity was "indistinguishable in all its material aspects" from an activity already covered by an advisory opinion.

● Permitted the commission to initiate investigations only after it received a properly verified complaint or had reason to believe, based on information it obtained in the normal course of its duties, that a violation had occurred or was about to occur. The commission was barred from relying on anonymous complaints to institute investigations.

● Required the commission to rely initially on conciliation to deal with alleged campaign law violations before going to court. The commission was allowed to refer alleged criminal violations to the Department of Justice for action. The attorney general was required to report back to the commission within 60 days an action taken on the apparent violation and subsequently every 30 days until the matter was disposed of.

● Provided for a one-year jail sentence and a fine of up to $25,000 or three times the amount of the contribution or expenditure involved in the violation, whichever was greater, if an individual was convicted of knowingly committing a campaign law violation that involved more than $1,000.

● Provided for civil penalties of fines of $5,000 or an amount equal to the contribution or expenditure involved in the violation, whichever was greater. For violations knowingly committed, the fine would be $10,000 or an amount equal to twice the amount involved in the violation, whichever was greater. The fines could be imposed by the courts or by the commission in conciliation agreements. (The 1974 law included penalties for civil violations of a $1,000 fine and/or a one-year prison sentence.)

Miscellaneous

● Restricted the fund-raising ability of corporate political action committees. Company committees could seek contributions only from stockholders and executive and administrative personnel and their families. Restricted union political action committees to soliciting contributions only from union members and their families. However, twice a year permitted union and corporate political action committees to seek campaign contributions only by mail from all employees they are not initially restricted to. Contributions would have to remain anonymous and would be received by an independent third party that would keep records but pass the money to the committees.

● Permitted trade association political action committees to solicit contributions from the stockholders and executive and administrative personnel and their families of member companies.

● Permitted union political action committees to use the same method to solicit campaign contributions that the political action committee of the company uses. The union committee would have to reimburse the company at cost for the expenses the company incurred for the political fund raising.

APPENDIX

PART II

Appendix E
1976 Democratic Presidential Campaign Committee Inc., General Election Broadcast Expenditure

State	Radio		TV		Total
Network	general	$ 42,695.00 ·	black	$ 12,000.00[a]	
			general	3,278,337.75	
				3,290,337.75	$3,333,032.75
Alabama	general	19,324.05	general	65,183.61	
	black	3,284.42			
		22,608.47			87,792.08
Arkansas	black	1,242.00	general	12,938.59	14,180.59
Arizona	Spanish	2,199.60	Spanish	466.42	2,666.02
California	black	9,559.10	general	560,673.05	
	general	148,661.56	Spanish	34,841.86	
	Spanish	27,173.19		595,514.91	
		185,393.85			780,908.76
Colorado	Spanish	2,073.00	general	28,148.00	
			Spanish	304.00	
				28,452.00	30,525.00
Connecticut	black	680.00	general	39,385.00	
	ethnic [b]	489.00			
		1,169.00			40,554.00
District of Columbia	black	6,258.00	general	77,850.00	
			Spanish	300.00	
				78,150,00	84,408.00
Florida	black	11,865.66	general	287,627.48	
	general	61,733.44	Spanish	4,691.74	
	Spanish	5,100.00		292,319.22	
		78,699.10			371,018.32
Georgia	general	768.25			
	black				
	victory [c]	1,101.00			
	victory [d]	2,890.72			
		4,759.97			4,759.97
Hawaii			general	9,928.88	9,928.88
Illinois	black	16,264.00	general	250,509.74	
	general	39,056.68	Spanish	3,280.00	
	ethnic	3,932.51		253,789.74	
	Spanish	7,841.42			
		67,094.61			320,884.35
Indiana	black	2,100.00	general	81,715.50	
	general	20,574.98			
	ethnic	261.00			
		22,935.98			104,651.48
Iowa			general	46,578.08	46,578.08
Kansas			general	9,775.00	9,775.00
Kentucky	black	662.00	general	27,218.00	
	general	21,309.00			
		21,971.00			49,189.00

State	Radio		TV		Total
Louisiana	black	$ 3,262.07	general	$ 62,896.73	
	general	22,628.27			
		25,890.34			88,787.07
Maine			general	15,804.00	15,804.00
Maryland	black	7,376.75	general	56,064.79	
	general	14,105.00			
		21,481.75			77,546.54
Massa-chusetts	black	1,200.00	general	84,700.00	
			Spanish	450.00	
				85,150.00	86,350.00
Michigan	black	11,425.01			
	general	41,683.22			
	ethnic	3,892.00			
	Spanish	2,200.59			
		59,200.82			59,200.82
Mississippi	black	2,516.70	general	19,134.27	
	general	10,894.74			
		13,411.44			32,545.71
Missouri	black	8,050.00	general	112,815.40	
	general	23,190.36			
		31,240.36			144,055.76
Montana			general	5,453.00	5,453.00
New Jersey	black	1,436.00			
	general	33,937.10			
	ethnic	28.23			
		35,401.33			35,401.33
New Mexico	Spanish	3,049.70	general	13,563.85	
			Spanish	1,853.00	
				15,416.85	18,466.55
New York	black	18,962.00	general	669,242,82	
	general	38,808.40	Spanish	17,395.00	
	ethnic	278.83		686,637.82	
	Spanish	11,854.00			
		69,903.12			756,541.05
North Carolina	black	3,836.19	general	77,122.44	
	general	27,351.48			
		31,187.67			$ 108,310.11
Ohio	black	10,263.00	general	355,694.44	
	general	58,223.36			
	ethnic	4,341.27			
	Spanish	1,510.94			
		74,338.57			430,033.01
Oklahoma			general	37,123.00	37,123.00
Oregon	general	5,138.00	general	36,342.12	41,480.12
Pennsyl-vania	black	9,763.00	general	405,104.00	
	general	45,834.58			
	Spanish	610.65			
		56,208.23			461,312.23

State	Radio		TV		Total
Rhode Island	general	9,534.35	general	15,235.00	24,769.35
South Carolina	black	2,946.13	general	47,095.50	
	general	14,720.53			
		17,666.66			64,762.16
South Dakota			general	5,321.90	5,321.90
Tennessee	black	3,682.43	general	93,123.47	
	general	21,813.69			
		25,496.12			118,619.59
Texas	black	16,533.60	general	383,297.80	
	general	39,495.87	Spanish	7,676.00	
	Spanish	12,330.14		390,973.80	
		68,359.61			459,333.41
Vermont			general	6,150.00	6,150.00
Virginia	black	4,649.55	general	59,175.00	96,337.99
	general	32,513.44			
		37,162.99			
Washington			general	28,242.00	28,242.00
West Virginia			general	24,285.00	24,285.00
Wisconsin	black	4,311.00	general	81,052.65	
	general	37,280.99			
	ethnic	165.00			
		41,756.99			41,756.99
GRAND TOTALS:[e]		$1,086,727.74		$7,553,165.88	$8,639,893.62

[a] The network cost classified as black is a "nonwired" network of 14 stations that carried football games between primarily black colleges.

[b] Ethnic as used in these electronic and print media breakdowns means East European, Italian, and Greek.

[c] These are advertisements targeted at blacks for the election night party held at the World Congress Center in downtown Atlanta.

[d] These are the general ads inviting people to the above-mentioned party.

[e] The following are the subtotals for the four target categories:

Radio

Black	$ 162,128.61
Spanish	75,943.23
Ethnic	13,387.84
Subtotal	251,459.68
General	835,268.06
Total	$1,086,727.74

Television

Black	12,000.00
Spanish	71,258.02
Ethnic	0
Subtotal	83,258.02
General	7,469,907.86
Total	$7,553,165.88

Appendix F

Escrow Agreement Made by Carter Campaign, United Air Lines, and First National Bank of Atlanta

THIS ESCROW AGREEMENT (the "Agreement"), made as of August 3, 1976 among the 1976 DEMOCRATIC PRESIDENTIAL CAMPAIGN COMMITTEE, INC. (the "Campaign"), UNITED AIR LINES, INC. ("United"), and the FIRST NATIONAL BANK OF AT-LANTA (the "Bank"),

WITNESSETH:

THE PARTIES do hereby agree for themselves, and for their respective successors and assigns as follows:

1. Campaign shall establish at the Bank for the benefit of United on or before August 27, 1976 an escrow checking account (the "Account"), with a minimum opening deposit of $225,000.00.

2. Funds may be paid out of the Account only to United, unless United consents otherwise in writing. All payments to United shall be by wire transfer from the Account to the Continental Illinois National Bank & Trust Co., for the account of United Air Lines, Inc. General Account, account no. 40-00609, attention of Don Danis. Payments shall be initiated by telephone call from the Campaign to the Bank, with written confirmation to follow. The only officers of the Campaign authorized to initiate payments from the Account are Robert Lipshutz, Richard Harden and Robert Andrews; and each acting singly has authority to give the Bank instructions for the Account.

3. Campaign shall initiate a payment from the Account to United on every Friday and every Monday during the term of this Agreement, unless the payment cannot be made because of a banking holiday. In the event of a banking holiday on a Friday, the Campaign shall initiate the payment on the preceding Thursday; and in the event of a banking holiday on a Monday, the Campaign shall initiate the payment on the following Tuesday. In the event that Campaign has not initiated a payment by 2:00 P.M. on each day required by this paragraph 3, then the Bank shall immediately notify United by telephone.

4. Campaign shall make a deposit to the Account on every Wednesday during the term of this Agreement, in an amount so that the Account's balance will not be less than the following:

If before September 3, 1976	$225,000.00
If before October 6, 1976 and after September 3, 1976	312,500.00
If before November 3, 1976 and after October 6, 1976	400,000.00
If on or after November 3, 1976	112,500.00

5. This Agreement shall terminate on November 30, 1976, unless sooner terminated by written notice from United. Upon termination of this Agreement, funds in the Account shall be paid upon the joint instructions of United and Campaign. In the event that United and Campaign fail to agree on instructions, then the Bank shall hold the funds subject to payment upon order of a court of competent jurisdiction.

IN WITNESS WHEREOF, the parties have executed this Agreement as of the date first above written.

1976 DEMOCRATIC PRESIDENTIAL CAMPAIGN COMMITTEE, INC.

By: _____

UNITED AIR LINES, INC.

By: _____

FIRST NATIONAL BANK OF ATLANTA

By: _____

Appendix G
Federal Political Gifts of Stewart R. Mott, 1976 [a]

President

Bayh	12/75	$ 250		McCarthy	12/75	$ 250 +$750 on 2/76 + 200 on 9/76
Brown	5/76	250				
Carter	12/75	250 +$750 on 3/76		Sanford	12/75	250
Church	12/75	250		Shriver	12/75	250
Harris	12/75	250		Udall	12/75	250 +$250 on 3/76
Total president						$ 4,200

Senate

Abzug	7/76	1,000 N.Y.		Mink	8/76	1,000 Hawaii
DeConcini	10/76	200 Ariz.		Moss	2/76	150 Utah + 500 on 10/76
Green	10/76	250 Pa.		Muskie	10/76	100 Maine
Hayden	12/75	1,000 Calif.		Riegle	12/75	1,000 Mich. + 600 on 9/76
Hayes	4/76	1,000 Ind.		Sarbanes	8/76	600 Md.
Humphrey	10/76	150 Minn.		Sasser	10/76	200 Tenn.
Kennedy	4/76	300 Mass.		Schaffer	8/76	1,000 Conn.
Maloney	8/76	300 Del.		Tunney	10/76	150 Calif.
Matsunaga	10/76	150 Hawaii		Tydings	12/75	1,000 Md.
Melcher	8/76	300 Mont.		Warner	8/76	1,000 Ariz.
Metzenbaum	8/76	600 Ohio				
Total Senate						12,550

House

Badillo	8/76	500 N.Y. 21		Mankiewicz	4/76	200 Md. 3
Baucus	8/76	100 Mont. 1		McCloskey	10/76	150 Calif. 12
Carr	8/76	500 Mich. 6		Meyer	10/76	100 N.Y. 23
Clancy	8/76	200 Ill. 6		Meyner	8/76	200 N.J. 13
Downey	8/76	500 N.Y. 2		Mezvinsky	10/76	100 Iowa 1
Drinan	10/76	150 Mass. 4		Mikva	10/76	150 Ill. 10
Fornos	4/76	200 Md. 4		Moffett	8/76	100 Conn. 6

Fullinwider	8/76	200 Ariz. 1		Pattison	8/76	100 N.Y. 29
Harkin	8/76	300 Iowa 5		Rapp	8/76	300 Iowa 3
Hechler	10/76	150 W.Va. 4		Schroeder	10/76	200 Colo. 1
Holtzman	6/76	200 N.Y. 16		Solarz	5/76	200 N.Y. 13
Keys	10/76	150 Kans. 2		Spellman	8/76	200 Md. 5
Kildee	7/76	500 Mich. 7		VanderVeen	10/76	150 Mich. 5
Koch	5/76	200 N.Y. 18		Weiss	8/76	100 N.Y. 20
Lowenstein	10/76	150 N.Y. 5		Wirth	8/76	200 Colo. 2
Maguire	8/76	100 N.J. 7		Wolpe	8/76	200 Mich. 3
Total House						6,750

Multicandidate Committees

Democratic Study Group	8/76	$ 500
National Committee for an Effective Congress (NCEC)	8/76	1,000
Total Multicandidate Committees		1,500

| Total Federal Political Gifts 1976 | $25,000 |

a As of October 27, 1976

Note: In December 1975 Mott gave $10,000 to NCEC and $6,000 to the Women's Campaign Fund — both for general operating activities, not included in the $25,000 ceiling.

Appendix H
1975-76 Contributions from Individuals [a]

Recipient	No. of Candidates, Committees Surveyed	Details in FEC Disclosure Series No.	Dollar Amount of Each Contribution		
			$0-$100	$101-$499 (No. of Contributions)	$500 and over (No. of Contributions)
Presidential	15	#7	$ 22,655,525	$ 7,307,710 (31,761)	$12,585,687 [b] (16,409)
Senate (General election names)	64	#6	11,088,150	5,228,970	10,592,867 (14,175)
House (General election names)	860	#9	23,680,016	7,537,932	7,270,785 (10,806)
Corporate PACs (Over $100,000)	9	#8	726,126	277,064	91,592 [c]
Labor PACs (Over $100,000)	42	#10	13,052,468	438,758	51,739 [c]
Membership, trade and other PACs (Over $100,000)	43	#11	17,182,255	2,039,404	1,611,855 [c]
National party-Democrat	18	#4	7,346,786	919,998	3,974,138 (3,069)

		#4			
National party- Republican	17	N/A	26,589,655	3,195,738	9,806,797 (8,912)
Totals	1,068		$122,320,980	$26,945,574	$45,985,460 (53,371)	$195,352,014

a Each study in the Disclosure Series states details on how contributions were totaled and which candidates or committees were covered.
b To this number can be added 1,318 contributions of $500 and over in the CRF survey of 1974 data.
c By subtracting total numbers of contributions shown from the 57,000 base, an estimated 3,629 additional contributions were made in sums of $500 and over to the corporate, labor, and other PACs.

SOURCE: Federal Election Commission Disclosure Series, and CRF Survey of 1974 Data for 1976 Presidential Elections.

Appendix I
1974 Individual Contributions to 1976 Presidential Candidates

	In Amounts Over $1,000 (No. given)	Per-cent	In Amounts $251-$1,000 (No. given)	Per-cent	In Amounts $250 Or Less	Per-cent	Total
Wallace	$ 15,500 (4)	1%	$ 26,045 (46)	1%	$1,689,430	98%	$1,730,975
Jackson	$791,617 (292)	70	$290,369 (373)	26	$ 44,159	4	$1,126,145
Bentsen	$362,616 (143)	56	$207,909 (276)	32	$ 73,568	12	$ 644,093
Percy	$ 19,500 (8)	18	$ 42,125 (80)	39	$ 47,563	43	$ 109,188
Mondale	$ 35,000 (13)	36	$ 42,200 (55)	43	$ 20,839	21	$ 98,039
Sanford	$ 3,000 (1)	5	$ 33,175 (55)	54	$ 25,116	41	$ 61,291
McCarthy	$ 36,500 (4)	76	$ 5,300 (7)	11	$ 6,308	13	$ 48,108
Carter	0		$ 16,700 (27)	44	$ 21,509	56	$ 38,209
Udall	0		$ 16,800 (22)	80	$ 4,176	20	$ 20,976
Harris	$ 2,849 (1)	100	0		0		$ 2,849

SOURCE: CRF Survey of 1974 Data for 1976 Presidential Elections.

Appendix J
Largest 1974 Individual Contributors for 1976 Presidential Elections

Contributor	Net Contributions	Recipient
1. William Clay Ford, Dearborn, Michigan (includes $9,000 loan outstanding to the committee)	$30,000	McCarthy
2. Arnold Picker, Golden Beach, Florida	$19,000 3,000 $22,000	Muskie Jackson
3. Mrs. R. L. Slaughter, Fort Worth, Texas	$ 9,500	Wallace
4. Edith Wasserman, Beverly Hills, California	$ 3,000 1,000 3,000 $ 7,000	Jackson Carter Bentsen
5. Lew Wasserman, Beverly Hills, California	$ 3,000 1,000 3,000 $ 7,000	Jackson Carter Bentsen
6. Donald A. Petrie, Washington, D.C. (includes a $6,859.14 loan converted to a contribution, and a $859.29 loan of which $770.27 was repaid)	$ 6.948.16	Muskie
7. Jimmy Carter, Atlanta, Georgia (contribution-in-kind)	$ 5,100	Carter
8. Neil H. Ellis, Manchester, Connecticut (previous loan converted to a contribution)	$ 5,000	Muskie
9. John Stephens, Santa Barbara, California	$ 3,000 2,000 $ 5,000	Jackson Bentsen
10. Joseph Robbie, Miami, Florida	$ 1,856.77 3,000 $ 4,856.77	Humphrey Jackson
11. Edward Crown, Chicago, Illinois	$ 3,500	Jackson
12. Walter T. Skallerup, Jr.	$ 5,000 loan —5,000 repaid 3,000 $ 3,000	Jackson
13. Jack Dahlstrom, Dallas, Texas	$ 3,125 —125 $ 3,000	Jackson returned
14. Mrs. Jack Dahlstrom, Dallas, Texas	$ 3,125 —125 $ 3,000	Jackson returned

SOURCE: CRF Survey of 1974 Data for 1976 Presidential Elections.

Appendix K
Large Contributions from Families

Family (No. of Contributors)		Amount	Recipient	
1. Bentsen family (12)	Texas	$30,000	Bentsen	
2. Picker family (2)	Florida	25,000	Muskie	$19,000
			Jackson	6,000
3. Paulucci family (5)	Minnesota	15,000	Mondale	
4. Wasserman family (2)	California	14,000	Carter	2,000
			Jackson	6,000
			Bentsen	6,000
5. Lentz family (4)	Texas	12,000	Jackson	
6. Cohen family (4)	Washington, D.C.	12,000	Jackson	
7. Rutherford family (3)	Texas	9,000	Bentsen	

SOURCE: CRF Survey of 1974 Data for 1976 Presidential Elections.

Appendix L
Individuals Giving in 1974 to More Than One 1976 Presidential Candidate

Name	Amount	Recipient	Date
Joseph B. Danzansky, Washington, D.C.	$ 500	Mondale Committee	2/28
	3,000	Jackson for President	12/27
	3,000	Bentsen Committee Fund	12/30
Cornelius G. Dutcher, La Jolla, Calif.	3,000	Jackson for President	11/5
	1,000	Udall 76 Committee	12/2
Herbert J. Frensley, Houston, Texas	500	George Wallace	3/19
	2,000	Bentsen Committee Fund	12/5
David Lloyd Kreeger, Washington, D.C.	500	Exploratory Committee	1/2
	3,000	Jackson for President	12/20
Walter H. Shorenstein, San Francisco, Calif.	3,000	Jackson Planning Committee	8/23
	1,000	Bentsen Committee Fund	9/12
R. Peter Straus, New York, N.Y.	500	Jackson for President	12/5
	500	Bentsen Committee Fund	12/18
Edith Wasserman, Beverly Hills, Calif.	1,000	Committee for Jimmy Carter	12/20
	3,000	Jackson for President	12/20
	3,000	Bentsen Committee Fund	12/30
Lew R. Wasserman Beverly Hills, Calif.	3,000	Jackson for President	12/20
	1,000	Committee for Jimmy Carter	12/20
	3,000	Bentsen Committee Fund	12/30
Judd A. Weinberg, Winnetka, Ill.	500	Exploratory Committee	6/14
	200	Jackson for President	9/20

SOURCE: CRF Survey of 1974 Data for 1976 Presidential Elections.

Appendix M
List of Recipients of Contributions from Gulf's Good Government Fund

Payee	Date	Amount	Check No.
Allott for Senate Committee	10/28/71	$ 2,000	142
Andrews, North Dakotans for D.C. Committee	2/22/72	1,000	143
Arends for Congress Committee	3/ 9/72	1,000	151
Baker, D.C. Friends for	3/28/72	2,500	170
Beall Dinner Committee	10/ 7/70	1,000	113
Beall for Senate Committee	8/ 5/70	2,000	103
Bentsen, Lloyd, Texas Dinner in Honor of	8/31/70	2,000	107
Better Ottumwa Club	10/26/70	1,000	120
Borden, Lew, Trustee	3/24/71	1,000	131
Brock, Citizens for	9/ 3/70	2,000	108
Brotzman Dinner Committee	3/ 8/72	1,000	148
Brown for Congress Committee	3/29/72	500	183
Burke, Committee to Keep in Congress	3/29/72	500	184
Burton for Senate Committee	10/ 9/70	2,000	115
Bush for Senate Committee	9/17/70	3,000	109
Byrd, Harry, D.C. Friends of	9/23/70	2,000	111
Byrd, Robert C., D.C. Reception for	10/26/70	2,000	118
California Democratic Congressional Committee	7/ 7/71	200	137
Cannon, Citizens for	10/26/70	2,000	123
Carter, Tim Lee, Campaign Committee	3/29/72	500	182
Cash (given to Dole for disbursement)	10/ 9/70	2,000	116
CBC Committee	3/ 9/72	1,500	149
Committee for Good Government	4/14/72	5,000	192
Committee for Good Government	5/24/72	12,254.49	193
Cramer, Citizens for Committee	10/ 8/70	2,000	114
Crane for Congress Committee	3/22/72	500	163
Curtis, Nebraska Boosters for	3/29/72	2,500	177
Dervinski, Citizens for	3/29/72	500	176
Ellender, Allen J., Friends of	3/30/72	2,500	185
Esch, Marvin, Support Committee	3/24/72	500	169
Fannin for Senate Committee	10/ 3/70	2,000	112
Findley for Congress Committee	3/23/72	500	161
Fong Testimonial Committee	7/20/70	1,000	102
Ford, Jerry, Committee to Re-elect	3/ 9/72	2,000	150
Frizzell for Governor	10/23/70	2,000	117
Goldwater, Friends of Committee	3/ 9/72	500	152
Goodling for Congress	3/29/72	500	178
Griffin Reception Committee (D.C.)	4/14/71	100	132
Hansen, Cliff, Loyal Supporters of	3/24/72	1,000	167
Hansen, Orval for Congress Committee	3/29/72	1,000	174
Harvey, Jim, Friends of Committee	3/22/72	500	160
Hawbaker for Congress Committee	4/ 5/72	500	191
Johnson, Albert, D.C. Friends of	3/24/72	500	168
Lloyd for Congress	3/28/72	1,000	171
Mailliard, Bill, Reception Committee	2/29/72	1,000	144
Maryland United Republican Finance Committee	2/17/71	200	127
Maryland United Republican Finance Committee	3/ 4/71	400	128
McClellan Arkansas D.C. Committee	3/20/72	2,500	158
McClure for Senate Committee	4/ 3/72	2,500	188

Payee	Date	Amount	Check No.
McCormack, Citizens for	3/29/72	500	166
Miller, D.C. Committee for	3/ 2/72	2,500	146
Minshall, Boosters for	10/28/70	500	126
Minshall, Boosters for Committee	3/14/72	1,000	154
Morris, Tom, D.C. Friends of	3/30/72	2,500	186
Murphy for Senate Campaign	8/ 6/70	2,000	105
Murphy, John, D.C. Friends of	3/ 1/72	1,000	145
Murphy, John M., D.C. Friends of	3/ 5/71	100	129
Myers for Congress	3/23/72	500	162
National Republican Congressional Committee	4/ 5/72	2,500	190
National Republican Senatorial Committee	10/27/70	1,000	124
Nelsen, Ancher, D.C. Friends of	3/22/72	500	159
Nineteenth Political Action Committee	3/28/72	500	172
O'Neill, Tip, Congressman, D.C. Friends of Committee	10/ 4/71	500	140
Pearson, Jim, Committee to Re-elect	3/28/72	2,500	165
Quie for Congress Voluntary Committee	3/29/72	500	179
Republican Dinner, Kick-off	3/15/71	1,000	130
Republican National Association	4/ 5/72	2,500	189
RN Associates	6/22/71	1,000	135
Robinson for Congress Committee	3/29/72	500	175
Roudebush, Hoosiers for	10/26/70	2,000	125
Schevie for Congress Committee	3/29/72	500	173
Senate-House Majority Dinner	3/ 3/72	5,000	147
Senate-House Majority Dinner	4/ 5/72	5,000	187
Shriver for Congress Committee	3/14/72	1,000	156
Skubitz for Congress Committee	3/14/72	1,000	155
Smith, Senator, Illinois Citizens Committee for	10/26/70	2,000	122
Sparkman Campaign Committee — D.C.	3/14/72	2,000	153
Stevens, District Committee for	4/21/71	100	133
Stevens, Ted, Friends of	6/12/70	2,000	101
Stevens, Ted, Friends of	3/20/72	2,500	157
Taft '71 Committee	7/21/71	100	138
Thompson, Congressman, D.C. Committee for	3/29/72	500	180
Tower, John, D.C. Friends of	9/14/71	200	139
Ullman, Al, Re-elect Committee	2/15/72	100	141
Vander Jagt for Congress Committee	3/29/72	500	181
Weicker, D.C. Committee for	9/21/70	1,000	110
Western Montana Congressional Club	3/28/72	500	164
Wold for Senate Committee	8/ 7/70	2,000	104

Note: Check numbers 106, 119, 121, 134, and 136, not listed above, were marked "Void" and never sent.

SOURCE: Special Review Committee of the Board of Directors of Gulf Oil Corp., *Report* (No place of publication, December 30, 1975), Appendix F.

Selected Bibliography

Books

Adamany, David. "Money, Politics, and Democracy: A Review Essay," *The American Political Science Review,* Vol. LXXI, No. 1, March 1977.
―――, and Agree, George E. *Political Money: A Strategy For Campaign Financing In America.* Baltimore: The Johns Hopkins University Press, 1975.
Agranoff, Robert. *The Management of Election Campaigns.* Boston: Holbrook Press Inc., 1976.
―――. *The New Style in Election Campaigns.* Boston: Holbrook Press Inc., 1976.
Alexander, Herbert E. *Financing the 1960 Election.* Princeton, N.J.: Citizens' Research Foundation, 1970.
―――. *Financing the 1964 Election.* Princeton, N.J.: Citizens' Research Foundation, 1968.
―――. *Financing the 1968 Election.* Lexington, Mass.: Lexington Books, D.C. Heath and Co., 1971.
―――. *Financing the 1972 Election.* Lexington, Mass.: Lexington Books, D.C. Heath and Co., 1976.
―――. *Money in Politics.* Washington, D.C.: Public Affairs Press, 1972.
―――. *Financing Politics: Money, Elections and Political Reform.* Washington, D.C.: Congressional Quarterly Press, 1976.
Barber, James David, ed. *Choosing the President.* Englewood Cliffs, N.J.: Prentice-Hall Inc., 1974.
―――. *Race for the Presidency: The Media and the Nominating Process.* Prentice-Hall Inc., Englewood Cliffs, N.J., 1978.
Beard, Edmund, and Horn, Stephen. *Congressional Ethics: A View From the House.* Washington, D.C.: The Brookings Institution, 1975.
Berg, Larry L.; Hahn, Harlan; and Schmidhauser, John R. *Corruption in the American Political System.* Morristown, N.J.: General Learning Press, 1976.

Bernstein, Carl, and Woodward, Bob. *All the President's Men.* New York: Simon and Schuster, 1974.

Bickel, Alexander M. *Reform and Continuity: The Electoral College, the Convention and the Party System.* New York: Harper & Row, Publishers, 1971.

Bolton, John R. *The Legislative Veto: Unseparating the Powers.* Studies in Legal Policy. Washington, D.C.: American Enterprise Institute for Public Policy Research, 1977.

Broder, David S. *The Party's Over: The Failure of Politics in America.* New York: Harper & Row, Publishers, 1972.

Caddy, Douglas. *The Hundred Million Dollar Payoff.* New Rochelle, N.Y.: Arlington House, Publishers, 1974.

Chester, Edward W. *Radio, Television and American Politics.* New York: Sheed and Ward, 1969.

Claude, Richard. *The Supreme Court and the Electoral Process.* Baltimore: The Johns Hopkins Press, 1970.

Crotty, William J. *Political Reform and the American Experiment.* New York: Thomas Y. Crowell Co., 1977.

Demaris, Ovid. *Dirty Business: The Corporate-Political Money-Power Game.* New York: Harper's Magazine Press, 1974.

DeVries, Walter, and Tarrance, Lance, Jr. *The Ticket-Splitter: A New Force in American Politics.* Grand Rapids, Mich.: William B. Eerdmans Publishing Co., 1972.

Domhoff, G. William. *Fat Cats and Democrats: The Role of the Big Rich in the Party of the Common Man.* Englewood Cliffs, N.J.: Prentice-Hall, 1972.

Dunn, Delmer. *Financing Presidential Campaigns.* Washington, D.C.: The Brookings Institution, 1972.

Heard, Alexander. *The Costs of Democracy.* Chapel Hill, N.C.: University of North Carolina Press, 1960.

Hess, Stephen. *The Presidential Campaign: The Leadership Selection Process After Watergate.* Washington, D.C.: The Brookings Institution, 1974.

Kirkpatrick, Jeane Jordan. *Dismantling the Parties: Reflections on Party Reform and Party Decomposition.* Washington, D.C.: American Enterprise Institute for Public Policy Research, 1978.

Kraus, Sidney. *The Great Debates: Background — Perspective — Effects.* Bloomington, Ind.: Indiana University Press, 1962.

McCarthy, Max. *Elections for Sale.* Boston: Houghton-Mifflin Co., 1972.

McGinniss, Joe. *The Selling of the President, 1968.* New York: Trident Press, 1969.

Minow, Newton N.; Martin, John Bartlow; and Mitchell, Lee M. *Presidential Television.* New York: Basic Books, 1973.

Moore, Jonathan, and Fraser, Janet, eds. *Campaign for President.* Cambridge, Mass.: Ballinger Publishing Co., 1977.

Nie, Norman H.; Verba, Sidney; and Petrocik, John R. *The Changing American Voter.* Cambridge: Harvard University Press, 1976.

Overacker, Louise. *Money in Elections.* New York: Macmillan, 1932.

Page, Benjamin I. *Choices and Echoes in Presidential Elections: Rational Man and Electoral Democracy.* Chicago: The University of Chicago Press, 1978.

Patterson, Thomas E., and McClure, Robert D. *The Unseeing Eye: The Myth of Television Power in National Politics.* New York: G. P. Putnam's Sons, 1976.

Peabody, Robert L.; Berry, Jeffrey M.; Frasure, William G.; and Goldman, Jerry. *To Enact A Law: Congress and Campaign Financing.* New York: Praeger Publishers, 1972.

Pollock, James K., Jr. *Party Campaign Funds.* New York: Alfred A. Knopf, 1962.

———. *Money and Politics Abroad.* New York: Alfred A. Knopf, 1932.

Rae, Douglas W. *The Political Consequences of Electoral Laws.* New Haven: Yale University Press, 1967.

Ranney, Austin. *Curing the Mischiefs of Faction: Party Reform in America.* Berkeley: University of California Press, 1975.

———. *Participation in American Presidential Nominations, 1976.* Studies in Political and Social Processes. Washington, D.C.: American Enterprise Institute for Public Policy Research, 1977.

Reeves, Richard. *Convention.* New York: Harcourt Brace Jovanovich, 1977.

Schram, Martin. *Running for President 1976: The Carter Campaign.* New York: Stein and Day, 1977.

Schwarz, Thomas, and Vandergrift, Benjamin M. *The Corporation in Politics 1978.* Corporate Law and Practice, Course Handbook Series, No. 267, Practising Law Institute, New York City, February-March, 1978.

Shannon, Jasper B. *Money and Politics.* New York: Random House, 1959.

Steinberg, Arnold. *Political Campaign Management: A Systems Approach.* Lexington, Mass.: Lexington Books, D.C. Heath and Co., 1976.

———. *The Political Campaign Handbook: Media, Scheduling, and Advance.* Lexington, Mass.: Lexington Books, D.C. Heath and Co., 1976.

Stroud, Kandy. *How Jimmy Won: The Victory Campaign From Plains to the White House.* New York: William Morrow and Co., 1977.

Thayer, George. *Who Shakes the Money Tree?: American Campaign Financing Practices from 1789 to the Present.* New York: Simon and Schuster, 1973.

White, Theodore H. *The Making of the President, 1960.* New York: Atheneum Publishers, 1961.

———. *The Making of the President, 1964.* New York: Atheneum Publishers, 1965.

———. *The Making of the President, 1968.* New York: Atheneum Publishers, 1969.

———. *The Making of the President, 1972.* New York: Atheneum Publishers, 1973.

Witcover, Jules. *Marathon: The Pursuit of the Presidency, 1972-1976.* New York: Viking Press, 1977.

Woodward, Bob, and Bernstein, Carl. *The Final Days.* New York: Simon and Schuster, 1976.

Reports and Articles

Adamany, David, "The Failure of Tax Incentives for Political Giving," *Tax Notes,* July 3, 1978.

——— and Agree, George. "Election Campaign Financing: The 1974 Reforms." *Political Science Quarterly,* Vol. 90, No. 2, summer 1975.

Alexander, Herbert E., ed. "Political Finance: Reform and Reality," *The Annals,* vol. 425, Philadelphia: The American Academy of Political and Social Science, May 1976.

The American Bar Association, Special Committee on Election Reform. *Symposium on Campaign Financing Regulation.* Tiburon, Calif., April 25-27, 1975.

Analysis of Federal and State Campaign Finance Law: Summaries. Prepared for the Federal Election Commission by American Law Division of the Congressional Research Service, Library of Congress, June 1975.

Bolton, John R., "Government Astride the Political Process (The Federal Election Commission)," *Regulation,* July/August 1978.

Clagett, Brice M., and Bolton, John R. *"Buckley v. Valeo,* Its Aftermath, and Its Prospects: The Constitutionality of Government Restraints on Political Campaign Financing," *Vanderbilt Law Review,* Vol. 29, No. 6, November 1976.

"Developments in the Law — Elections," *Harvard Law Review.* Vol. 88, no. 6, Cambridge, Mass.: Gannett House, April 1975.

Electing Congress: The Financial Dilemma. Report of the Twentieth Century Fund Task Force on Financing Congressional Campaigns. (Background paper by David L. Rosenbloom), New York, 1970.

Financing a Better Election System. A Statement on National Policy by the Research and Policy Committee of the Committee for Economic Development. New York: Committee for Economic Development, December 1968.

Financing Presidential Campaigns. Report of the President's Commission on Campaign Costs. Washington, D.C., April 1962.

Kirby, James C., Jr. *Congress and the Public Trust.* Report of the Association of the Bar of the City of New York Special Committee on Congressional Ethics. New York: Atheneum, 1970.

Malbin, Michael J. "Labor, Business and Money — A Post-Election Analysis," *National Journal,* March 19, 1977.

_____. "After Surviving Its First Election Year, FEC Is Wary of the Future," *National Journal,* March 26, 1977.

Moore, Jonathan, and Pierce, Albert C., eds. *Voters, Primaries and Parties.* Selections from a Conference on American Politics. Institute of Politics, John Fitzgerald Kennedy School of Government, Harvard University, 1976.

Murphy, John G., Jr. "The Federal Election Commission: A Rebuttal," *Regulation,* September/October 1978.

1972 Congressional Campaign Finances. Prepared by the Campaign Finance Monitoring Project, 3 vols. Washington, D.C.: Common Cause, 1974.

1972 Federal Campaign Finances: Interest Groups and Political Parties. Prepared by the Campaign Finance Monitoring Project, 10 vols., Washington, D.C.: Common Cause, 1974.

1974 Congressional Campaign Finances. Prepared by the Campaign Finance Monitoring Project, 5 vols., Washington, D.C.: Common Cause, 1976.

1976 Federal Campaign Finances. Prepared by the Campaign Finance Monitoring Project, 3 vols., Washington, D.C.: Common Cause, 1977.

Nomination and Election of the President and Vice President of the United States. Compiled by Thomas M. Durbin, Rita Ann Reimer, and Thomas B. Riby, Congressional Research Service, Library of Congress, for the United States Senate Library, under the direction of Francis R. Valeo, Secretary of the Senate. Washington, D.C.: U.S. Government Printing Office, 1976.

"The Political Money Tree," *In Common,* Vol. 7, No. 2, Washington, D.C.: Common Cause, spring 1976.

Rosenthal, Albert J. *Federal Regulation of Campaign Finance: Some Constitutional Questions.* Milton Katz, ed. Princeton, N.J.: Citizens' Research Foundation, 1972.

Schwarz, Thomas J. *Public Financing of Elections: A Constitutional Division of the Wealth.* Chicago: American Bar Association, Special Committee on Election Reform, 1975.

Tufte, Edward R., ed., "Symposium on Electoral Reform," *Policy Studies Journal,* Vol. 2, No. 4, Urbana, Ill.: Political Science Department and the Institute of Government and Public Affairs at the University of Illinois, summer 1974.

U.S. Congress, Senate. Select Committee on Presidential Campaign
Activities. *Final Report.* Pursuant to S Res 60, February 7, 1973.
Senate *Report* 93-981. 93rd Cong., 2d sess. Washington, D.C.: U.S.
Government Printing Office, 1974.

U.S. Congress, Senate. Select Committee on Presidential Campaign
Activities. *Election Reform: Basic References.* Pursuant to S Res
60. Committee Print, 93rd Cong. 1st sess. Washington, D.C.: U.S.
Government Printing Office, 1973.

Voters' Time. Report of the Twentieth Century Fund Commission on
Campaign Costs in the Electronic Era. New York, 1969.

Winter, Ralph K., Jr. *Watergate and the Law: Political Campaigns and
Presidential Power.* (Domestic Affairs Study No. 22.) Washington,
D.C.: American Enterprise Institute for Public Policy Research,
1974.

———, in association with John R. Bolton. *Campaign Financing and
Political Freedom.* (Domestic Affairs Study No. 19.) Washington,
D.C.: American Enterprise Institute for Public Policy Research,
1973.

Index

839

Largest interest group campaign contributors - 547
Findley for Congress Committee 830
Firestone, Leonard - 601
Firestone Tire & Rubber Co.
Case study of political activities - 579-583
Illicit political funds - 534, 536, 540
Stockholder reform efforts - 542
First National Bank of Atlanta - 820, 821
Fiske, David - 93
Fithian, Floyd (D Ind.) - 549
Flaherty, Peter - 651
Flynt, John J. Jr. (D Ga.) - 129, 724, 752
Fogarty, Joseph R. - 471
Foley, Thomas S. (D Wash.) - 524, 659
Fong Testimonial Committee 830
Ford, Gerald R.
Ambassadorial appointments - 682
Committee to Re-elect Jerry Ford - 830
Conventions. See Party Conventions
Corporate accountability task force - 611
Federal Election Campaign Act - 12, 16, 21, 36
Federal Election Commission (FEC)
Appointment of members - 35, 36, 143
FEC auditing delays - 95
Independent expenditures - 20, 120
Labor case (cartoon of Nixon, Ford) - 137
Matching funds - 209-211, 527
Presidential travel questions - 26, 27
Surplus federal funds - 96, 421
General Election
Details. See General Election Campaigns
Korean lobbying - 758, 761
Media consultants - 412, 463
Prenomination Campaign
Alleged violations - 125
Communications expenditures - 569
Compliance - 302
Costs - 308
Expenditures breakdown - 314
Fund raising - 304
Independent expenditures - 187, 408-410, 520, 522, 523
Labor opposition - 620, 622

Media costs - 460
Primary spending totals - 170-172
Presidential transition costs - 675, 676
Voter registration plan - 648
Ford, Henry II - 305, 383, 384
Ford Motor Co. - 126, 383, 565
Ford, William Clay - 435, 443, 827
Ford, William D. (D Mich.) - 141
Foreign Corrupt Practices Act (1977) - 614
Former Presidents Act - 679
Fornos, Werner - 822
Forsythe, Edwin B. (R N.J.) - 626
Franking privilege - 771-778
Fraser, Donald M. (D Minn.) - 524, 752, 760, 767
Freedom of Association
Minor parties disclosure exemption - 116
Freedom of Information Act (FOIA)
FEC confidentiality safeguards - 119
Freeman, Carl Floyd - 330
Frensley, Herbert J. 829
Frenzel, Bill (R Minn.) - 144, 524
Frey, Louis Jr. - 309
Frick, Henry Clay - 305
Friedersdorf, Max - 145
Frizzell for Governor 830
Fulbright, J. William - 443
Fullinwider, Patricia M. - 823
Fund Raising
Impact of new campaign laws - 45, 47
Personal-use funds - 131
Presidential candidates exemption - 83
Sources of Funds
Independent expenditures. See Independent Expenditures
Individual donations - 509-515
(See also) Individual candidates

G

Gabor, Patrick W. - 333
Gabusi, John - 290
Gallagher, Cornelius (D N.J.) - 748, 758, 767
Gambino, Angelo - 127
Garagiola, Joe - 414, 465
Gardner, John - 421
Garwood, Ellen C. - 521
Geneen, Harold S. - 598
General Accounting Office (GAO)
Ambassadorships and politics - 683

H

Habib, Philip - 750

Hafif, Herbert - 410

Hall, Gus
Communist Party candidates - 174, 175, 431
FCC equal time rulings - 434, 469
Receipts and expenditures - 332, 429

Hanna, Richard T. (D Calif.) - 748, 753, 756, 761

Hammer, Armand - 515

Hannaford, Mark W. (D Calif.) - 546, 549, 770

Hansen, Clifford P. (R Wyo.) - 590, 830

Hansen, George (R Idaho) - 128, 129, 738

Hansen, Orval H. (R Idaho) - 560, 563, 830

Harden, Richard - 369, 371, 379, 388, 389

Hardy, George - 255

Harkin, Tom (D Iowa) - 823

Harmon, John M. - 147

Harriman, Roland - 305

Harris, Arthur - 585, 591

Harris, Fred
Prenomination Campaign
Compliance - 254
Costs - 256
Expenditures, total votes cast - 211
FEC audits delay - 91, 99
Fund raising - 254-256
Individual contributions, 1974 - 822, 826
Matching funds cutoff - 32-34, 204
Presidential forums - 459
Primary expenditures - 169, 170
Primary matching funds - 210
Summary of matching funds activity - 209-211, 527
Total expenditures, matching funds - 209
Withdrawal - 205

Harris, Thomas E.
Audit program defense - 98
Congressional public financing - 86
Expiration of term - 147
FEC vice chairmanship - 73
Federal employee political activity - 400
Iowa committees sample advisory opinion - 68

NEA suit - 111
SunPAC ruling - 563
Unionizing the FEC - 141

Hart Research Associates - 43

Hartke, Vance (D Ind.) - 546, 549, 623

Harvard University Campaign Study Group
Television's role in political campaigns - 475

Harvey, Jim, Friends of Committee - 830

Haskell, Floyd K. (D Colo.) - 770

Hatch Act revision -, 344, 665

Hatfield, Mark O. (R Ore.) - 590, 770

Hawbaker for Congress Committee - 830

Hay, Jess - 704

Hayakawa, S. I. (R Calif.) - 195, 733

Hayden, Tom - 822

Hayes, Philip - 822

Hays, Wayne
Election reform opposition - 39
Elizabeth Ray affair - 41
Franking privileges - 773
Hansen case - 129, 130
House perquisites - 38, 39, 61
Presidential campaign expenditures - 330

Health Volunteers for Carter-Mondale - 363, 364

Health groups. See Membership Associations

Hearn, Fred - 522

Hebert, F. Edward (D La.) - 724

Hechler, Ken (D W.Va.) - 823

Heftel, Cecil (D Hawaii) - 128, 140

Hefner, Hugh - 227

Heimann, John
Lance case - 689, 691

Heinz, H. John III (R Pa.)
Gulf Oil funds investigation - 589, 591
Senate race personal spending - 194, 195

Heiskell, Andrew - 510

Helms, Jesse (R N.C.) - 426, 577, 716, 718

Helstoski, Henry (D N.J.) - 772

Hemple, Evylin 333

Henry, William - 587, 588

Hickel, Walter J. - 442

Hills, Carla A. - 306, 443

Hilton, Conrad - 510

Hoenig, Peggy - 333

Hollenbeck, Harold C. (R N.J.) - 127

O

X, Y, Z

About the Author

Herbert E. Alexander is professor of political science at the University of Southern California and is director of the Citizens' Research Foundation, an autonomous entity within the university. He received his B.S. from the University of North Carolina, his M.A. from the University of Connecticut, and his Ph.D. in political science from Yale University in 1958. He taught in the Department of Politics at Princeton University, 1956-58, and subsequently was a visiting lecturer at Princeton University, 1965-66, at the University of Pennsylvania, 1967-68, and at Yale University, 1977. During 1961-62 he was executive director of the President's Commission on Campaign Costs; during 1962-64 he was a consultant to the President of the United States; and during 1972-73 he served as a consultant to the Comptroller General of the United States and to the Office of Federal Elections in the General Accounting Office. In 1973-74 Alexander also undertook a consultancy with the U.S. Senate Select Committee on Presidential Campaign Activities. During 1974-75 he was a consultant with the New York State Board of Elections, the Illinois Board of Elections, and the Congressional Research Service of the Library of Congress. He was a consultant to the New Jersey Election Law Enforcement Commission from 1973 until 1978, when he moved from Princeton, New Jersey, to his current position in Los Angeles.

Alexander has written extensively on matters relating to money in politics. His books include *Financing Politics: Money, Elections and Political Reform*, *Money in Politics*, and predecessors of this volume on the financing of the 1960, 1964, 1968, and 1972 elections. In addition he has edited and written articles for numerous books and magazines. Alexander was special editor of the May 1976 election reform issue of *The Annals* of the American Academy of Political and Social Science and has edited and contributed to *Studies in Money and Politics*, Vol. I (1965), Vol. II (1970), and Vol. III (1974), published by the Citizens' Research Foundation. He also wrote "Trends in the Regulation of Political Finance," published by the Federal Election Commission in summaries entitled, *Analysis of Federal and State Campaign Finance Law*.